BUSINESS

FIFTH CANADIAN EDITION

RICKY W. GRIFFIN
TEXAS A&M UNIVERSITY

RONALD J. EBERT
UNIVERSITY OF MISSOURI-COLUMBIA

FREDERICK A. STARKE
UNIVERSITY OF MANITOBA

Toronto

To Ann, Eric, and Grant

National Library of Canada Cataloguing in Publication

Griffin, Ricky W
Business / Ricky W. Griffin, Ronald J. Ebert, Frederick A. Starke. — 5th Canadian ed.

Includes bibliographical references and indexes.
ISBN 0-13-121789-5

1. Industrial management. 2. Business enterprises. 3. Industrial management—Canada. 4. Business enterprises—Canada. I. Ebert, Ronald J. II. Starke, Frederick A., 1942– III. Title.

HD31.G75 2004 658 C2004-900610-X

ISBN 0-13-121789-5

Vice President, Editorial Director: Michael J. Young
Acquisitions Editor: James Bosma
Director of Marketing, Business and Economics: Bill Todd
Developmental Editor: Pamela Voves
Production Editor: Avivah Wargon
Copy Editor: Catharine Haggert
Production Coordinator: Andrea Falkenberg
Page Layout: Carol Anderson, Christine Velakis
Permissions Research: Marnie Lamb
Photo Research: Lisa Brant
Art Director: Julia Hall
Interior Design: David Cheung
Cover Design: David Cheung
Cover Image: Photonica

2 3 4 5 09 08 07 06 05

Printed and bound in the United States of America.

OVERVIEW

CONTENTS

PART THREE

Chapter 14: Understanding Accounting Issues 470

PART FOUR

Managing Marketing 509

Chapter 15: Understanding Marketing Processes and Consumer Behaviour 510

APPENDICES

PREFACE

This is the fifth Canadian edition of *Business.* As in previous editions, our intent is to excite and inform students about today's business world, and to support instructors with an interesting and attractive book that explains the basic ideas that beginning business students must learn. While always remembering the principle that guided the book's creation—**Doing the Basics Best**—*Business,* Fifth Canadian Edition, by Griffin, Ebert, and Starke continues its tradition of introducing cutting edge firsts with the most up-to-date issues shaping business today.

The fifth edition also maintains the strengths that made the first four editions so successful; once again, we have emphasized our fundamental objectives of being comprehensive, accurate, current, and readable. We believe that we have met all of these objectives, as this new edition of *Business* continues to offer significant coverage of both new ideas and traditional topics.

The Theme of Change

As we worked on the manuscript for this edition, we were struck by the truly stunning changes that have occurred in just the last few years. Some of these changes (for example, increased concern about terrorism) are essentially political in nature, but they impact business practice just as surely as new ideas in business processes and new products or services. The rules of the game are constantly changing and new forces are at work. For example, companies come together on short notice for collaborative projects and then, just as quickly, return to their original shapes as separate—and often competing—entities. Employees and companies share new ideas about the nature of work, when and where it takes place, how it is done, and who determines roles and activities in the workplace. Communication technologies are rapidly breaking down the barriers of physical distance, and tightly knit teams with members positioned around the world share information as effectively as groups that meet together in the same room.

In nearly every aspect of business today there are totally new ways of doing things. These new ways are replacing traditional business practices, usually with surprising speed and often with better competitive results. Along with new practices come a host of unique legal and ethical issues to challenge the creativity and judgment of business managers. Given these developments, we as authors and teachers felt that our goal had to be to communicate the theme of change by describing how real-world business firms cope with organizational change and conflict in the modern business world. Thus, we have tried to capture the flavour and convey the excitement of the "new economy" in all of its rapidly evolving practices.

As the main thoroughfare along the information superhighway, the internet has become a major new artery for ecommerce and ebusiness. Many aspiring start-up companies began operations in the late 1990s, only to quickly fall by the wayside as the economy turned down in 2001. What is the future of ecommerce and ebusiness? How will traditional companies—the so-called "bricks-and-mortar" businesses—compete in this brave new world? Or are ebusinesses going to have more problems as well?

Other Themes

In support of the overall theme of change, the organization and content of this fifth Canadian edition reflect five other trends that are important in today's businesses. These trends will likely accelerate as the twenty-first century unfolds.

- *The growth of international business*—Many business people see globalization of the economy as the dominant challenge of the twenty-first century. To keep students aware of this challenge, we've used many examples and cases that describe the experiences of global companies, and the experiences of Canadian companies in the global marketplace. As well, an entire chapter is devoted to international business (Chapter 4, Understanding International Business).
- *The role of ethics and social responsibility*—Business ethics and social responsibility are generating a sharply increased level of discussion and debate as a result of the debacles at Enron, WorldCom, and other companies where significant problems became evident. Because ethical and social issues are so pervasive in the business world, we present them early in the text so that students will have a frame of ethical reference throughout the book. We also devote an entire chapter to these topics (Chapter 5, Conducting Business Ethically and Responsibly).
- *The significance of small business*—Since many students will not work for major corporations, we have provided coverage of both large and small companies throughout the text. In various chapters, the implications of various ideas for small business are discussed. As well, a major section in Chapter 3 (Understanding Entrepreneurship, Small Business, and Business Ownership) is devoted to small business issues.
- *The importance of information and communication technology*—In our information-based society, the people and organizations that learn how to obtain and use information will be the ones that succeed. The explosive growth and change in these systems is recognized as we devote an entire chapter to the management of information (Chapter 13, Managing Information Systems and Communication Technology).
- *The quality imperative*—Quality and productivity became the key to competitive recovery for many companies in the global marketplace during the 1990s. These topics continue to be of special interest in the twenty-first century, and we devote a full chapter to their coverage (Chapter 12, Increasing Productivity and Quality).

Changes in the Fifth Canadian Edition

The fifth Canadian edition of *Business* incorporates many of the changes suggested by professors and students who used the previous four editions. It also includes changes suggested by reviewers. The following major changes have been made:

- A new chapter, "Understanding the Environments of Business," puts business operations in a contemporary context. The chapter explains the idea of an organization's boundary with its external environment, and how events in the external environment shape activities inside organizations. It also sets the stage for some of the most important topics covered in the rest of the book. The chapter is organized around a discussion of the major environments facing business firms: economic, technological, political-legal, socio-cultural, and business.

- Material in certain chapters has been reorganized for better student understanding. For example, Chapter 1 now explains the concepts of business and profit, describes the various economic systems that are used around the world for allocating scarce resources, and presents a brief history of Canadian business. Chapter 3 focuses on small business, entrepreneurship, and forms of business ownership. In combination with the new Chapter 2 (the environments of business), these changes give students a strong "big-picture" description of the contemporary business world.
- The text's 20 chapters have been reorganized and made more concise. The six major sections found in the previous edition have been reduced to five in this edition.
- A new feature, "Exercising Your Ethics," has been introduced. In each chapter, students are presented with a description of a situation that leads to an ethical dilemma. Students are then asked several questions that focus on how to approach and resolve these ethical challenges. This series of exercises is particularly important given the widespread concern about unethical business practices that have been so much in the news as of late.
- Another new feature, "On Location" Video Exercise, consists of nineteen custom videos that help students see how real-life businesses and the people who run them apply fundamental business principles on a daily basis. The format for each video is the same: (1) a moderator sets the scene; (2) the scene unfolds; (3) the moderator recaps core issues (and the video can be paused for additional in-class discussions); and (4) the video concludes with answers to the in-class discussion questions. The unique structure and format of these videos not only brings the concepts to life, but also provides an interactive environment to stimulate critical thinking and discussion in your course.
- Yet another new feature, "Crafting Your Business Plan," provides new chapter-ending exercises that apply text material to the task of developing a business plan, using Business Plan Pro software. The new version of this software allows users to create plans with greater ease and speed. Based on responses to a series of yes-no questions, the EasyPlan Wizard automatically selects the plan outline, reports, charts, and tables. This feature simplifies the plan-creation process and is unique to this software. In addition, Business Plan Pro provides numerous sample plans and step-by-step examples and instructions for making and assessing plans.
- All of the opening cases are either new or updated.
- Many new examples of business practice have been included in each of the chapters; some of these examples are brief and some are more detailed, but all of them help students to better understand important business issues.
- New cases are included at the end of each chapter.
- New CBC *Venture* video cases are included at the end of each major section of the text.
- Many examples of ebusinesses are given to demonstrate how technology is affecting business practice.
- A Media Companion CD-ROM accompanies and complements the text. In addition, an innovative, interactive CD, Mastering Business Essentials, is available as a supplement. For full descriptions of these new features, see page xxi.

Organization of the Text

The text is organized into five parts as follows:

Part One: Understanding the Contemporary Business World. This part introduces students to the basic ideas underlying business activity. **Chapter 1** describes how business activity is oriented towards satisfying consumer needs and making a profit. Several types of economic systems are described, and the Canadian mixed economic system is analyzed (including important interactions between business and government). The chapter concludes with a brief history of Canadian business. **Chapter 2** (new) introduces students to the important concept of organizational environments and describes several important facets of these environments. The discussion presents important information on *economics* (including economic growth, economic stability, and the global economy); *technology* (special attention is given to the importance of technology and research and development); *ethics* (describing not only what happened at companies like Enron, but why it happened); the *general business environment* (which includes a description of emerging areas of interest such as outsourcing and business process management); and *the aftermath of 9/11* (focusing on the effect of the uncertainty that was created by the attacks). **Chapter 3** presents information on small business, entrepreneurship, and several types of business ownership—sole proprietorships, partnerships, corporations, and co-operatives. **Chapter 4** describes the critical area of international business and free trade, and the importance of international business for Canada. **Chapter 5** discusses the impact of business ethics and social responsibility.

Part Two: Understanding the Business of Managing. The chapters in this part focus on the general management activities that are necessary in business firms and the most important resource in business firms: people. **Chapter 6** introduces the functions of management—planning, organizing, leading, and controlling—and the basic types of management skills that are required to carry out these functions. **Chapter 7** focuses on the planning and organizing functions of management and the strategic decisions that business managers must make. **Chapter 8** describes the activities that are required to recruit, hire, train, and compensate a company's human resources. **Chapter 9** presents information on Canadian labour unions and the way that unions affect management activity. **Chapter 10** deals with the managerial activities that are necessary to motivate and lead employees so they are both satisfied and productive.

Part Three: Managing Operations and Information. This part describes the managerial activities that are necessary to convert raw materials into the finished products and services that are needed by consumers. **Chapter 11** focuses on the production of goods and services, while **Chapter 12** deals with the crucial issues of productivity and quality. **Chapter 13** explains how managers use information to make business decisions, and how the dynamic and rapidly developing area of computers affects the practice of management. **Chapter 14** describes the accounting function and the financial statements that accountants develop for managers and investors.

Part Four: Managing Marketing. The chapters in this part explain the key activities that are carried out by marketing managers. **Chapter 15** introduces the "4 Ps of marketing"—product, place, promotion, and price. Other activities such as marketing research and the study of consumer behaviour help marketing managers carry out the marketing function effectively. **Chapter 16** explains new product development and the promotion of goods and services, and **Chapter 17** focuses on pricing and distributing goods and services.

Part Five: Managing Financial Issues. The chapters in this part introduce students to the key financial activities of business firms. **Chapter 18** explores the nature of money, the various financial intermediaries that exist in Canada, and the role of the Bank of Canada. **Chapter 19** looks at securities markets and the buying and selling of stocks, bonds, and other investments. **Chapter 20** explains why business firms need funds, and the way they go about acquiring these funds. The role of the financial manager is also described.

Major Features of the Text

The text contains the following features to stimulate student interest in, and understanding of, the material that is being presented about business.

Part Opener

At the beginning of each of the five parts of the book is a brief outline introducing the material that will be discussed in that part. By explaining the rationale for the structure of the part, these outlines give students a glimpse of the "big picture" as they head into a new area of the business world.

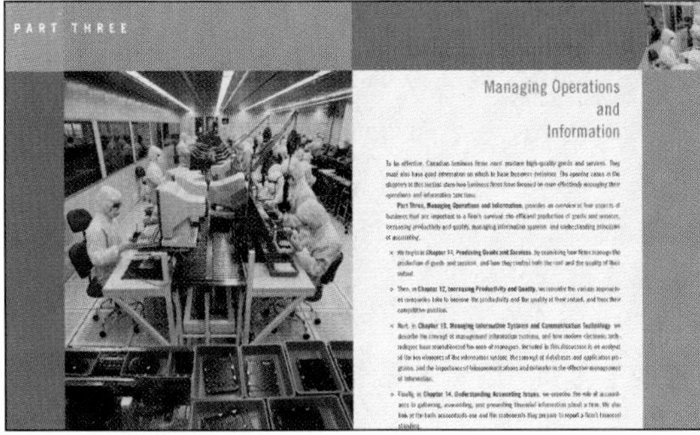

Chapter Materials

Each chapter contains several features that are designed to increase student interest in and understanding of the material being presented. These features are as follows:

Chapter Opener with Learning Objectives. A list of numbered learning objectives is presented at the beginning of each chapter. These objectives guide students in determining what is important in each chapter. In addition, these learning objectives are referenced in the margins opposite relevant content.

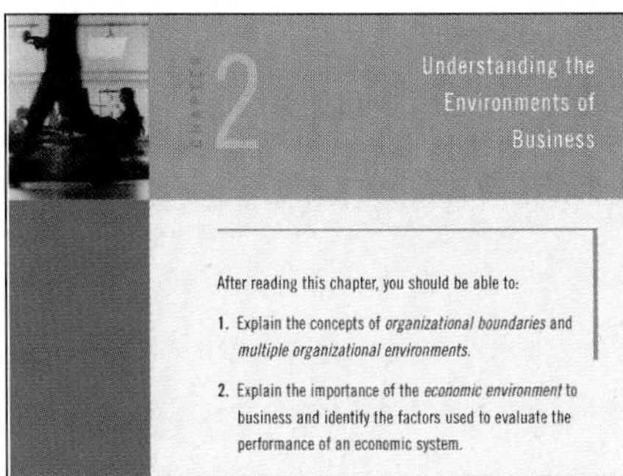

CHAPTER
2
Understanding the Environments of Business
After reading this chapter, you should be able to:
1. Explain the concepts of *organizational boundaries* and *multiple organizational environments*.
2. Explain the importance of the *economic environment* to business and identify the factors used to evaluate the performance of an economic system.

Opening Case. Each chapter begins with a description of a situation that is faced by a real Canadian or international company. The subject matter of this opening case is relevant to the material presented in that chapter, helping students bridge the gap between theory and practice.

Chapter 2 Understanding the Environments of Business 65

IT'S A WIRED WORLD

Replanning for Disruption Management

Remarkable, even violent, disruptions to business activities seem to have become the rule rather than the exception in recent years. Most memorable, of course, are the confusion, grief, and discontinuity in every walk of life wrought by the 9/11 terrorism attacks on the United States. But additional disruptions are arising more frequently than ever before from various sources. Financial fortunes are recast in a matter of mere minutes by sudden and steep changes on the stock market. Trusted suppliers, long relied upon for dependable goods or services, suddenly fail and shut down. Widespread product failures, such as fatally defective tires, leave companies facing consumer distrust. Products and business processes are suddenly revolutionized as new technologies require rapid redirection and changeovers to new ways of doing things. Business, of course, has always been threatened by disruption, but a number of factors make the threat today more frequent and severe. Moreover, when problems do arise, organizations are faced with the need for fast—nearly instantaneous—reaction if they want to minimize negative, even disastrous, consequences.

In response to the growing need to reduce adverse effects, a new technology called *disruption management (DM)* has emerged. DM is unlike traditional emergency-management procedures, which typically call for special organizations to respond to disaster by assisting victims in cleanup, treatment, and recovery on an as-needed basis. Instead of outside assistance, DM stresses internal self-reliance in planning for and preparing responses to disruptions in an organization's external environment. It calls for a firm to adapt its organizational structure, technology, and policies so that it will be better prepared to continue operations during and after major disruptions. In short, the firm becomes "disruption sensitive" in order to anticipate environmental disruptions and adapt rapidly when disaster strikes.

DM is a decision support system that's been under development for more than two years by researchers at the Technical University of Denmark's Department of Informatics and Mathematical Modelling. The core technology consists of computer-

es to various disruptions. Developers use mathematical models to represent cause-and-effect relationships among real-world variables. Then they test each model to evaluate its effectiveness in guiding management response to disruption. With the right model, managers can replan activities instantaneously in light of a disruption to ordinary activities. They can even make alternative plans in case of potential future problems.

DM replanning considers a complex set of variables, the ways they interact, and the consequences for the firm and its customers. The objective is to identify a recovery solution that minimizes negative effects—that is, minimizes costs and maximizes revenues—by considering two aspects of each replanning option: immediate (or short-term) consequences and strategic (long-term) effects.

Consider a hypothetical shutdown at Toronto's Pearson International Airport. An airline's least costly solution would be to cancel all incoming flights immediately. But although cancellation cuts the airline's operating costs, it is a terrible option for passengers who can't get where they're going. Replanning models consider alternatives to cancellation, such as rescheduling flights into neighbouring airports and providing ground transportation into Toronto. Of course, pilots and aircraft must also be rescheduled and diverted to new destinations. A DM model would quickly simulate the costs and benefits of these (and other) options in order to facilitate an effective decision.

In developing DM, researchers have experimented with various kinds of disruptions. A telecommunications system is disconnected, causing a communications blackout that deprives users of point-to-point connections. Airports are shut down due to weather conditions or terrorism, preventing scheduled flights from arriving or departing. Manufacturing firms are deprived of needed assembly components when suppliers are shut down by strike or flood. For every application, digital communications are the key to success in using DM. The simulator relies on information both from the organization's internal communications networks and from external sources (such as suppliers, customers, and news agencies) via the internet. Once replanning decisions have been made, directions can be sent instantaneously to facilities

Boxed Inserts. Each chapter contains three boxed inserts: "Business Today," "It's a Wired World," and "Exercising Your Ethics." The Business Today boxes describe activities in Canadian or international companies and show students how theoretical concepts are actually put into practice by business firms. The series entitled It's a Wired World describes the steps that businesses are taking to keep pace with competitors in the rapidly changing ebusiness environment. Each box describes the situation faced by a real firm, showing how challenges are being met by the introduction of technology. To bring ethics to the forefront, the Exercising Your Ethics features ask students to resolve an ethical situation. Each dilemma includes a description of the situation and concludes with questions that focus on how to approach and resolve these ethical challenges.

Examples. In addition to the boxed inserts, each chapter contains numerous examples of how businesses operate. These examples will further help students understand actual business practice in Canada and elsewhere.

BUSINESS TODAY

What Else Can Go Wrong?

SUMMARY OF LEARNING OBJECTIVES

Figures and Tables. The latest data available have been used to update tables and figures throughout the text. The "Top 10" tables provide information on the largest Canadian companies in various industries.

Weblinks. Internet addresses are supplied throughout the text for many of the corporations and organizations that are discussed.

End-of-Chapter Materials

Several important pedagogical features are found at the end of each chapter. These are designed to help students better understand the contents of the chapter.

SUMMARY OF LEARNING OBJECTIVES

1. **Define *small business* and discuss its importance to the Canadian economy.** A small business is independently owned and managed and does not dominate its market. Most Canadian businesses employ fewer than 100 people, and small firms employ most workers. The contribution of small business can be measured by its effects on three aspects of the economic system: (1) Job creation, (2) Innovation, and (3) Importance to big business.
2. **Explain *entrepreneurship* and describe some key characteristics of entrepreneurial personalities and activities.** Entrepreneurs assume the risk of business ownership with a primary goal of growth and expansion. Many small-business owners like to think of themselves as entrepreneurs, but a person may be a small-business owner only, an entrepreneur only, or both. The basic distinction between small-business ownership and entrepreneurship is aspiration—the entrepreneur's desire to start a business and make it grow. Most successful entrepreneurs are resourceful and concerned for customer relations. They have a strong desire to be their own boss and can handle ambiguity and surprises. Today's entrepreneur is often an open-minded leader who relies on networks, business plans, and consensus and is just as likely to be female as male.
3. **Describe the *business plan* and the *start-up decisions* made by small businesses.** Would-be entrepreneurs must decide how to get into business and know how to find financing. Entrepreneurs must assess their own skills as well as industry trends. The starting point for every new business is a business plan. A business plan defines strategies for production and marketing, legal elements and organization, and accounting and finance. It should answer three questions: (1) What are the entrepreneur's goals and objectives? (2) What strategies will be used to obtain them? (3) How will these strategies be implemented? After completing the business plan, the entrepreneur must decide whether to

Summary of Learning Objectives. Each chapter is concisely summarized to help students understand the main points that were presented in the chapter.

Key Terms. In each chapter, the key terms that students should know are highlighted and defined in the text, repeated in the margin, and listed at the end of the chapter (with page references).

Study Questions and Exercises. There are three types of questions here: review questions (straightforward questions of factual recall), analysis questions (which require students to think beyond simple factual recall and apply the concepts), and application exercises (which require students to visit local businesses or managers and gather additional information that will help them understand how business firms operate).

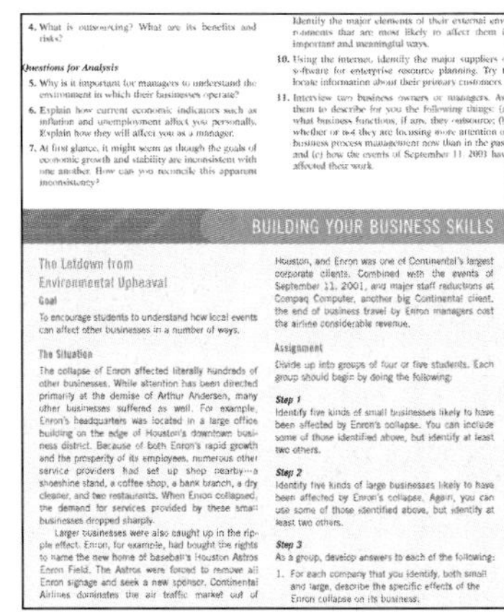

Building Your Business Skills. This feature is an in-depth exercise that allows students to examine some specific aspect of business in detail. The exercise may ask students to work individually or in a group to gather data about an interesting business issue and then develop a written report or a class presentation based on the information that was gathered.

Mastering Business Essentials Twelve interactive episodes are linked to the appropriate end-of-chapter material in the textbook (for a description of the CD-ROM, see p. xxi).

Crafting Your Business Plan. Chapter-ending exercises apply text material to the task of developing a business plan using Business Plan Pro software. The new version of this software allows users to create plans with greater ease and speed. For a full description, see page xv. The education version of the best-selling Business Plan Pro software can be packaged with the text for an extra charge in a value pack. Ask your Pearson sales representative for details!

Video Exercises Nineteen new, custom videos are linked to the end-of-chapter exercises to help students see how real-life businesses and the people who run them apply fundamental business principles on a daily basis. The format for each video is the same: (1) a moderator sets the scene; (2) concepts unfold; (3) the moderator recaps core issues as the video can be paused for additional in-class discussion; (4) the video concludes with answers to the in-class discussion questions. The unique structure and format of these videos not only brings the concepts to life, but also provides an interactive environment to stimulate critical thinking and discussion in your course.

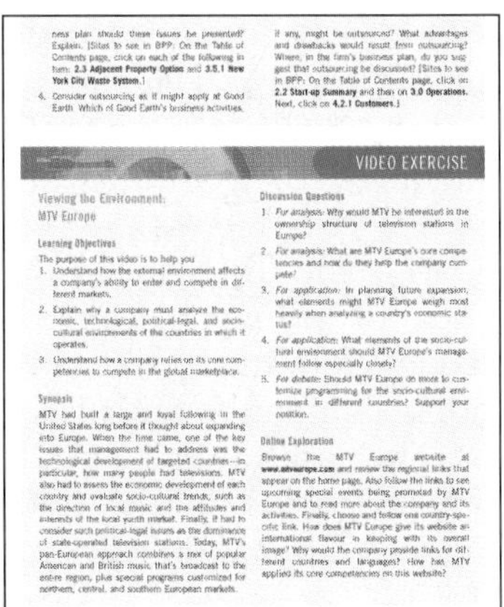

Exploring the Net. This feature gives students the opportunity to carry out interesting, business-related assignments by using the internet. By doing so, students gain important skills in locating and using information from Canadian and international websites.

Concluding Cases. Each chapter concludes with two case studies that focus on real Canadian or international companies. These cases are designed to help students see how the chapter material can be applied to a real company that is currently in the news. At the end of each case, several questions guide students in their analysis.

Video Case 1-2 CBC

Whistle-blowers

Questions for Discussion

End-of-Part Material

CBC Video Cases. At the end of each of the five major parts of the text, two recent CBC video cases are presented. The instructor can show the *Venture* episode in class and then either conduct a class discussion using the questions at the end of the written case as a guide or ask students to complete a written assignment that contains answers to the case questions. This approach to teaching adds a major new dynamic to classes because students will be able to relate text material to actual Canadian business situations. The cases are also available on the Companion Website for *Business*.

Supplementary Materials

For Instructors

Instructor's Resource CD-ROM with TestGen, Instructor's Resource Manual, and PowerPoint Presentations (ISBN 0-13-123810-8) *Pearson TestGen* is a special computerized test item file that enables instructors to view and edit the existing questions, add questions, generate tests, and print the tests in a variety of formats. Powerful search and sort functions make it easy to locate questions and arrange them in any order desired. TestGen also enables instructors to administer tests on a local area network, have the tests graded electronically, and have the results prepared in electronic or printed reports. The Pearson TestGen is compatible with IBM or Macintosh systems.

The *Instructor's Resource Manual* contains chapter outlines, teaching tips, and suggestions on how to use the text effectively. It includes material for classroom use, such as careers in business and additional cases (including the cases to accompany the "On Location" videos). The manual also provides answers to the end-of-chapter questions and cases (including Building Your Business Skills, Exploring the Net, and the CBC video cases).

PowerPoint Presentations, which are also available for downloading from the Companion Website, offer an average of about 40 PowerPoint slides per chapter, outlining the key points in the text. The slides include lecture notes that provide page references to the text, summaries, and suggestions for student activities or related questions from the text.

CBC Video Library (ISBN 0-13-121957-X). The CBC Video Library for *Business*, Fifth Canadian Edition, includes 10 segments from the CBC program *Venture* that accompany the video cases found at the end of each part in the text. These cases focus on Canadian companies and discuss business issues from a Canadian point of view. The cases are also available on the Companion Website, and answers are discussed in the Instructor's Resource Manual. (Please contact your Pearson Education sales representative for details.)

"On Location" Video Library (ISBN 0-13-127017-6). Nineteen new, custom videos are linked to the end-of-chapter exercises to help students see how real-life businesses and the people who run them apply fundamental business principles on a daily basis. For a full description of the format, see p. xix. These videos bring the concepts to life, and provide an interactive environment to stimulate critical thinking and discussion in your course. (Please contact your Pearson Education sales representative for details.)

Pearson Custom Publishing (www.prenhall.com/custombusiness). Pearson Custom Publishing can provide you and your students with texts, cases, and articles to enhance your course. Choose material from Darden, Ivey, Harvard Business School Publishing, NACRA, and Thunderbird to create your own custom casebook. Contact your Pearson sales representative for details.

Online Learning Solutions. Pearson Education Canada supports instructors interested in using online course management systems. We provide text-related content in WebCT, Blackboard, and Course Compass. To find out more about creating an online course using Pearson content in one of these platforms, contact your Pearson sales representative.

New! Instructor's ASSET. Pearson Education is proud to introduce Instructor's ASSET, the Academic Support and Service for Educational Technologies. ASSET is the first integrated Canadian service program committed to meeting the customization, training, and support needs for your course. Ask your Pearson sales representative for details!

Your Pearson Sales Representative. Your Pearson sales rep is always available to ensure you have everything you need to teach a winning course. Armed with experience, training, and product knowledge, your Pearson rep will support your assessment and adoption of any of the products, services, and technology outlined here to ensure our offerings are tailored to suit your individual needs and the needs of your students. Whether it's getting instructions on TestGen software or specific content files for your new online course, your Pearson sales representative is there to help. (Also available for your students. Ask your Pearson sales rep for details!)

For Students

Media Companion CD-ROM. Designed to complement the content of the text, the comprehensive Media Companion features a searchable electronic version of the text with hyperlinked URLs, the CBC videos and their cases, and a Glossary organized by chapter.

Learning Guide (ISBN 0-13-123818-3). This guide enables students to review the introductory business concepts presented in the text and understand their application. It provides summaries of the major sections within each chapter, as well as practice questions (multiple-choice, true/false, and essay) with answers.

Business PlanPro Software. Business PlanPro (BPP) provides students with a step-by-step approach to creating a comprehensive business plan. The software is designed to stimulate student thinking about the many tasks and decisions that go into planning and running a business. Preformatted report templates, charts, and tables do the mechanics so that students can focus on the thinking. Planners can also publish to a protected internet site, where readers can access all or part of posted plans. Available for a small extra charge in a value-package. Ask your Pearson sales representative for details!

Mastering Business Essentials CD-ROM. This innovative, cross-functional CD revolves around an ebusiness called CanGo. Twelve interactive episodes are linked to the appropriate end-of-chapter material in *Business*. The format for each episode includes: (1) unique video scenarios; (2) informative and stimulating interactive exercises with follow-up video clips; and (3) additional case and discussion questions. Available for a small extra charge in a value package. Ask your Pearson sales representative for details!

For Instructors and Students

Companion Website The Companion Website provides an online study guide that offers several exciting new features, including an audio glossary to help students with pronunciation of terms and "flash cards" to help students review key terms and concepts. The online study guide can also be downloaded for use on a PDA, enabling students to study on the go. The PowerPoint Presentations are available for downloading by both students and instructors. The Instructor's Resource Manual is also available for downloading in a protected area for instructors. Visit the site at **www.pearsoned.ca/griffin**.

Acknowledgments

We owe special thanks to Catharine Haggert, for her excellent copyediting; Karen Alliston, for her careful proofreading; Avivah Wargon, Production Editor, for her efficient management of this project; and Lisa Brant for her fine photo research. Thanks are also due to Michael J. Young, Publisher; James Bosma, Acquisitions Editor; Pamela Voves, Developmental Editor; Bill Todd, Director of Marketing, Business and Economics, and all the members of the Pearson Education Canada sales team.

In addition, we would like to acknowledge the contributions of Emmet Mellow, who researched the Weblinks, and Angela Davis of the University of Winnipeg, who prepared the new Exploring the Net exercises.

We appreciate the insights and suggestions of the following individuals who provided feedback on the fourth edition or reviewed the manuscript for the new edition: Ramon Baltazar, Dalhousie University; Tim Carroll, University of PEI; Angela Davis, The University of Winnipeg; Bob Fournier, Red Deer College; Ross Gowan, Fanshawe College; Robert Maher, University of New Brunswick; Lorna Martin Scriver, Seneca College; Valerie Miceli, Seneca College; Erica Morrill, Fanshawe College; Lisa Phillips, Douglas College; Susan Quinn, Mount Royal College; Jim Ridler, Queen's University; Barbara Smith, Niagara College; Frances Tuer, Brock University; and Michael Wade, Seneca College. Their comments were carefully considered and implemented wherever possible.

Frederick A. Starke
2004

A Great Way to Learn and Instruct Online

The Pearson Education Canada Companion Website is easy to navigate and is organized to correspond to the chapters in this textbook. Whether you are a student in the classroom or a distance learner you will discover helpful resources for in-depth study and research that empower you in your quest for greater knowledge and maximize your potential for success in the course.

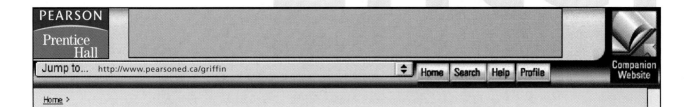

[www.pearsoned.ca/griffin]

PH Companion Website

Business, Fifth Canadian Edition, by Griffin, Ebert, and Starke

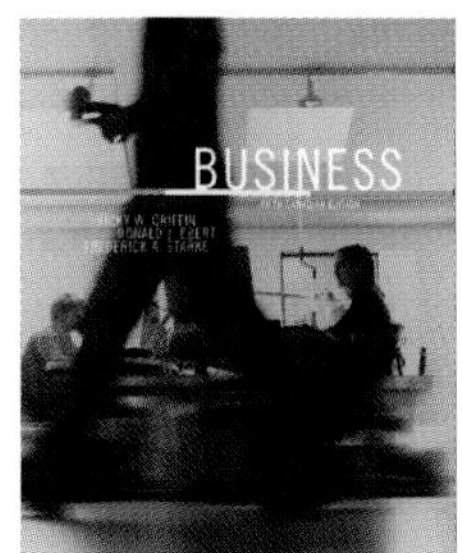

Student Resources

The modules in this section provide students with tools for learning course material. These modules include:

- Chapter Objectives
- Destinations
- Quizzes
- Internet Exercises
- PowerPoint Presentations
- Glossary
- CBC Videos and Cases
- "On Location" Videos and Exercises

In the quiz modules students can send answers to the grader and receive instant feedback on their progress through the Results Reporter. Coaching comments and references to the textbook may be available to ensure that students take advantage of all available resources to enhance their learning experience.

Instructor Resources

The modules in this section provide instructors with additional teaching tools. Downloadable PowerPoint Presentation and an Instructor's Manual are just some of the materials that may be available in this section. Where appropriate, this section will be password protected. To get a password, simply contact your Pearson Education Canada Representative or call Faculty Sales and Services at 1-800-850-5813.

PART ONE

Introducing the Contemporary Business World

In Chapters 1 to 5, you will read about five situations that may seem at first glance to have little in common: discovery of a large nickel deposit at Voisey's Bay, upheaval in the commercial airline business, family feuds in small business firms, the international activities of Bombardier Inc., and difficulties at the animation firm Cinar.

All of these situations, and many more that are described in this text, have a common thread: they all demonstrate the key elements of business as well as the excitement and complexity of business activity. Each case tells a part of the story of our contemporary business world.

Part One, Introducing the Contemporary Business World, provides a general overview of business today, including its economic roots, the environment in which it operates, the importance of entrepreneurship, the various forms of ownership of business firms, the globalization of business, and the ethical problems and opportunities facing business firms.

- We begin in **Chapter 1, Understanding the Canadian Business System**, by examining the role of business in the economy of Canada and other market economies. We also present a brief history of business in Canada.
- Then, in **Chapter 2, Understanding the Environments of Business**, we examine the external environments that influence business activity. These include the economic, technological, socio-cultural, legal-political, and general business environments.
- In **Chapter 3, Understanding Entrepreneurship, Small Business, and Business Ownership**, we examine the important concepts of entrepreneurship, small business, and the various forms of business ownership that have evolved to facilitate business activity.
- In **Chapter 4, Understanding International Business**, we look at why countries engage in international trade, how companies organize to operate internationally, the development of free trade agreements, and factors that help or hinder international trade.
- Finally, in **Chapter 5, Conducting Business Ethically and Responsibly**, we look at individual ethics and corporate social responsibility, and how these affect the firm's customers, employees, and investors. ◆

CHAPTER 1

Understanding the Canadian Business System

After reading this chapter, you should be able to:

1. Define the nature of Canadian *business* and identify its main goals.
2. Describe different types of global *economic systems* according to the means by which they control the *factors of production* through *input and output markets.*
3. Show how *demand* and *supply* affect resource distribution in Canada.
4. Identify the elements of *private enterprise* and explain the various *degrees of competition* in the Canadian economic system.
5. Trace the *history of business* in Canada.

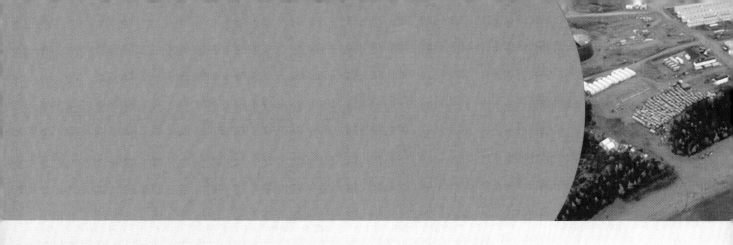

The Long Road to Voisey's Bay

On June 11, 2002, the government of Newfoundland and Inco Ltd. agreed on a deal to develop a mine at Voisey's Bay in Labrador. One month earlier, the Labrador Inuit Association and Labrador's Innu Nation had endorsed agreements with Inco regarding the nickel development project. Those agreements specified how the Aboriginal groups would benefit from revenue sharing, environmental protection, hiring quotas, and job training. The various agreements will create thousands of jobs in Newfoundland and Labrador, and will guarantee economic growth for Canada's poorest province.

The story of the development of Voisey's Bay is a classic story of Canadian business, and it demonstrates many of the key features of modern business activity. The story began in 1993, when two diamond prospectors stumbled upon one of the world's richest nickel finds in the rolling hills of northeast Labrador. In 1996, Inco decided to buy controlling interest in the site for $4.3 billion. Unfortunately, once Inco gained control of the deposit, things began to go wrong. Among other things, the price of nickel dropped, and so did Inco's stock price.

In 1997, Inco announced that it would have to delay development of the site because of a time-consuming and expensive environmental review process. The government of Newfoundland had also gotten into the act by insisting that Inco build a smelter in the province to smelt the ore it mined. The Innu Nation was demanding a 3 percent smelter royalty and a guarantee that the mine would operate for 25 years.

By 1999, though, things were looking up. Nickel prices (and Inco's stock price) had increased sharply, and Inco returned to the bargaining table with provincial politicians to try to work out an agreement. With its improved financial condition, Inco was now willing to talk about building the smelter in Newfoundland after all. But in February 2000, Inco announced the closing of its Newfoundland office because it had been unable to reach an agreement with the provincial government.

At the annual shareholders' meeting in April 2000, angry shareholders focused on the stalled Voisey's Bay project and the possibility of a strike by 3500 workers at Inco's Sudbury operations. Also present at the meeting was a group of Indonesian villagers who expressed concerns about growing social problems and unemployment difficulties near one of Inco's properties in their country.

In June 2001 negotiations with Newfoundland resumed, and by October 2001 the Newfoundland minister of mines and energy announced that most of the issues that were holding up development of Voisey's Bay had been resolved. Inco was more cautious, and said that it was facing an unexpected decline in its business because the terrorist attacks in New York had caused a slowdown in the world's economies.

At Inco's annual meeting in April 2002, CEO Scott Hand said he hoped to reach an agreement with Newfoundland by June 2002. Newfoundland Premier Roger Grimes seemed less optimistic in a CBC Radio broadcast. He said he didn't have the same level of confidence that a deal was close. The continuing point of contention was how much of the ore mined in Newfoundland would also be processed there. But finally agreement was reached. The Voisey's Bay mine will become operational in 2006, and the new smelter will be built in Argentia, Newfoundland, in 2011.

In March 2003, Inco announced that its current cost estimates for the first phase of the Voisey's Bay project were 14 percent higher than the original estimate for the program. After that announcement was made, the price of Inco's shares fell 2.3 percent in one day. The Inco story continues. ◆

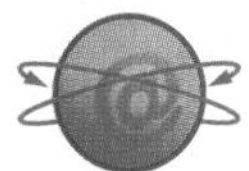

Inco
www.incoltd.com

THE CONCEPT OF BUSINESS AND PROFIT

The story of Inco's involvement with the nickel discovery at Voisey's Bay is a classic Canadian business story. What do you think of when you hear the word *business*? Does it conjure up images of huge corporations like Inco, General Motors Canada, and Wal-Mart? Smaller companies like your local supermarket? One-person operations like the hair stylist around the corner? Actually, each of these firms is a **business**—an organization that produces or sells goods or services in an effort to make a profit. **Profit** is what remains after a business's expenses have been subtracted from its revenues. Profits reward the owners of businesses for taking the risks involved in investing their time and money. In 2002, the most profitable companies in Canada were the Canadian Wheat Board ($4.2 billion profit), Caisse de dépôt et placement du Québec ($3.4 billion), and the Royal Bank of Canada ($2.7 billion).[1]

business
An organization that seeks to earn profits by providing goods and services.

profit
What remains (if anything) after a business's expenses are subtracted from its sales revenues.

1. Define the nature of Canadian *business* and identify its main goals.

In Canada's economic system, businesses exist to earn profits for owners who are free to set them up. But consumers also have freedom of choice. In choosing how to pursue profits, businesses must take into account what consumers want or need. No matter how efficient a business is, it won't survive if there is no demand for its goods or services. Neither a snow-blower shop in Victoria nor a beach-umbrella store in Rankin Inlet is likely to do very well.

But if enterprising business people can identify either unmet consumer needs or better ways of satisfying consumer needs, they can be successful. In other words, someone who can spot a promising opportunity and then develop a good plan for capitalizing on it can succeed. The opportunity always involves goods or services that consumers want or need—especially if no one else is supplying them or if existing businesses are doing so inefficiently or incompletely.

Businesses produce most of the goods and services we consume and employ the majority of working people. They create most new innovations and provide opportunities for other businesses, which serve as their suppliers. A healthy business climate also contributes directly to quality of life and standard of living. New forms of technology, service businesses, and international opportunities promise to keep production, consumption, and employment growing indefinitely. Business profits enhance the personal incomes of millions of owners and stockholders, and business taxes help to support governments at all levels. Many businesses support charities and provide community leadership.

In this chapter, we begin your introduction to Canadian business by looking at its role in our economy and society. Because a variety of economic systems are found around the world, we will first consider how the dominant ones operate. Once you have some understanding of different systems, you can better appreciate the workings of our own system. As you will see, the effect of economic forces on Canadian businesses and the effect of Canadian businesses on our economy produce dynamic and sometimes volatile results. We conclude the chapter by briefly tracing the history of Canadian business.

ECONOMIC SYSTEMS AROUND THE WORLD

A Canadian business is different in many ways from one in China. And both are different from businesses in Japan, France, or Peru. A major determinant of how organizations operate is the kind of economic system that characterizes the country in which they do business. An **economic system**

economic system
The way in which a nation allocates its resources among its citizens.

allocates a nation's resources among its citizens. Economic systems differ in terms of who owns and controls these resources, known as the "factors of production" (see Figure 1.1)

2. Describe different types of global *economic systems* according to the means by which they control the *factors of production* through *input and output markets.*

Factors of Production

The key difference between economic systems is the way in which they manage the **factors of production**—the basic resources that a country's businesses use to produce goods and services. Traditionally, economists have focused on four factors of production: *labour, capital, entrepreneurs,* and *natural resources*. In addition, information resources are now often included as well.[2]

factors of production

The resources used to produce goods and services: labour, capital, entrepreneurs, and natural resources.

Labour

The people who work for a company represent the first factor of production, **labour**. Sometimes called *human resources,* labour is the mental and physical capabilities of people. Carrying out the business of such a huge company as Imperial Oil, for example, requires a labour force with a wide variety of skills ranging from managers to geologists to truck drivers. Employees who are well trained and knowledgeable can be a real competitive advantage for a company.

labour

The mental and physical training and talents of people; sometimes called human resources.

Figure 1.1
Factors of production are the basic resources a business uses to create goods and services. The four basic factors used are natural resources, labour, capital, and entrepreneurs.

Capital

Obtaining and using labour and other resources requires **capital**—the financial resources needed to operate an enterprise. You need capital to start a new business and then to keep it running and growing. Time Warner needs millions of dollars in cash (and millions more in equipment and other assets) to run its operations. A major source of capital for small businesses is personal investment by owners. Investments can come from individual entrepreneurs, from partners who start businesses together, or from investors who buy stock. Revenue from the sale of products is a key and ongoing source of capital once a business has opened its doors.[3]

capital
The funds needed to operate an enterprise.

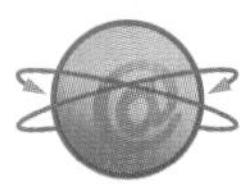

Time Warner
www.timewarner.com

Capital can also include the market value of corporate stock. When America Online (AOL) acquired Time Warner for $106 billion in 2001, the deal involved very little actual cash. Most of it was handled through transfers of stock. Bank lines of credit and the market value of liquid assets (those that can be quickly and easily sold for cash) are also forms of capital.

Entrepreneurs

entrepreneur
An individual who organizes and manages labour, capital, and natural resources to produce goods and services to earn a profit, but who also runs the risk of failure.

The people who accept the opportunities and risks involved in creating and operating businesses are **entrepreneurs**. Jimmy Pattison and Izzy Asper (who died in 2003) are well-known Canadian entrepreneurs. AOL was started by James Kimsey, who had the technical skills to understand how the internet works, the conceptual skills to see its huge future potential, and the risk-taking acumen to bet his own career and capital on the idea of AOL.

Natural Resources

natural resources
Items used in the production of goods and services in their natural state, including land, water, mineral deposits, and trees.

Land, water, mineral deposits, and trees are good examples of **natural resources**. Newer perspectives, however, tend to broaden the idea of "natural resources" to include all physical resources. For example, Imperial makes use of a wide variety of natural resources. It obviously has vast quantities of crude oil to process each year. But Imperial also needs the land where the oil is located, as well as land for its refineries and pipelines.

Information Resources

While the production of tangible goods once dominated most economic systems, today **information resources** play a major role. Businesses themselves rely heavily on market forecasts, the specialized expertise and knowledge of people, and various forms of economic data for much of their work. Much of what they do results in either the creation of new information or the repackaging of existing information for new users and different audiences. America Online, for example, does not produce tangible products. Instead, it provides numerous online services for its millions of subscribers in exchange for monthly access fees. AOL is in the information business.

information resources
Information such as market forecasts, economic data, and specialized knowledge of employees that is useful to a business and that helps it achieve its goals.

Types of Economic Systems

command economy
An economic system in which government controls all or most factors of production and makes all or most production decisions.

market economy
An economic system in which individuals control all or most factors of production and make all or most production decisions.

Different types of economic systems manage the factors of production in different ways. In some systems, ownership is private; in others, the government owns the factors of production. Economic systems also differ in the way that decisions are made about production and allocation. A **command economy**, for example, relies on a centralized government to control all or most factors of production and to make all or most production and allocation decisions. In **market economies**, individuals—producers and consumers—control production and allocation decisions through supply and demand. We will describe each of these economic types and then discuss the reality of the *mixed market economy*.

Command Economies

The two most basic forms of command economies are communism and socialism. As originally proposed by the nineteenth-century German economist Karl Marx, **communism** is a system in which the government owns and operates all sources of production. Marx envisioned a society in which individuals would ultimately contribute according to their abilities and receive economic benefits according to their needs. He also expected government ownership of production factors to be only temporary. Once society had matured, government would "wither away" and the workers would gain direct ownership.

communism
A type of command economy in which the government owns and operates all industries.

Most Eastern European countries and the former Soviet Union embraced communist systems until the 1980s. During the early 1990s, however, one country after another renounced communism as both an economic and a political system. Today, Cuba, North Korea, Vietnam, and the People's Republic of China are among the few nations with avowedly communist systems. Even in these countries, however, all levels of command economic systems are making room for features of the free-enterprise system.

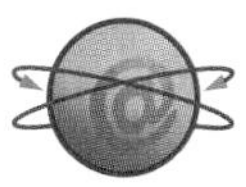

Karl Marx
www.marxists.org

In Cuba, for example, a variety of free-market activities are evident, even though they are technically illegal. Special shops that once were reserved for diplomats now sell goods to Cubans from all walks of life. These stores are surrounded by paid bicycle-parking lots, car washes, and stalls selling homegrown produce and homemade handicrafts. This street-corner commerce reflects a rapid growth in private enterprise as a solution to problems that Cuba's centralized economy has long been unable to solve.[4]

China is another country where dramatic changes are taking place. Prior to 1979, people who sold watches on street corners were sentenced to years of hard labour. But in 1999, China's constitution was amended to elevate private enterprise to a place alongside the state sector in China's official economic ideology. The private sector in China now generates more than one-third of the country's gross domestic product.[5]

In a less extensive command economic system called **socialism**, the government owns and operates only selected major industries. Smaller businesses such as clothing stores and restaurants may be privately owned. Although workers in socialist countries are usually allowed to choose their occupations or professions, a large proportion generally works for the government. Many government-operated enterprises are inefficient, since management positions are frequently filled based on political considerations rather than on ability. Extensive public welfare systems have also resulted in very high taxes. Because of these factors, socialism is generally declining in popularity.[6]

socialism
A kind of command economy in which the government owns and operates the main industries, while individuals own and operate less crucial industries.

Market Economies

A **market** is a mechanism for exchange between the buyers and sellers of a particular good or service. To understand how a *market economy* works, consider what happens when a customer goes to a fruit stand to buy apples. Let's say that while one vendor is selling apples for $1 per kilogram, another is charging $1.50. Both vendors are free to charge what they want, and customers are free to buy what they choose. If both vendors' apples are of the same quality, the customer will buy the cheaper ones. But if the $1.50 apples are fresher, the customer may buy them instead. In short, both buyers and sellers enjoy freedom of choice.

market
A mechanism for exchange between the buyers and sellers of a particular good or service.

The Wired World box discusses a much more complicated and technologically sophisticated market that has been created to bring buyers and sellers together through the internet. This market is an outgrowth of a trend in information technology called "business-to-business," or "B2B." Whereas most early commercial internet applications were directed toward consumers, B2B is a more recent development. Some experts think that it will be handling trillions of dollars annually in just a few years. As the term suggests, B2B involves electronic transactions between two or more businesses.

IT'S A WIRED WORLD

Jumping on the B2B Bandwagon

A new term—B2B—has become popular in strategic business thinking. B2B stands for business-to-business electronic commerce. It involves businesses joining together to create ecommerce companies that make them more efficient when they purchase the goods and services they need.

When people talk about ecommerce, they usually think of business-to-consumer (B2C) transactions such as buying books over the internet for personal use. These transactions are obviously important, but B2B transactions far exceed B2C transactions in dollar value. International Data Corp. Canada Ltd. (IDC) predicts that the value of B2B transactions in Canada will total $129 billion by 2004, while the value of B2C transactions will total only $19 billion. Dollar values in both of those categories are up sharply from the late 1990s. Worldwide, the numbers are even more staggering: B2B transactions are predicted to be about $2.2 trillion by 2004, while B2C transactions will total about $200 billion.

All of this B2B activity is good news for consumers, because businesses will become more efficient in their supply chain purchasing, which will allow them to reduce their costs. That, in turn, will allow them to reduce prices.

A good example of this trend is the recently announced partnership among some of the world's largest automobile manufacturers. It all started when various individual automakers began to create their own global purchasing websites. Ford Motor Co., for example, planned a site called Auto-Xchange. The company intended to post all of its global procurement needs on the site, and request that its suppliers post availability and prices for parts and equipment.

When it became apparent that other automakers were planning to do the same thing, major suppliers to the auto industry realized that they might soon be facing an unwieldy array of separate websites for each company—a situation that would potentially increase rather than reduce their own costs. Thus, a coalition of the largest suppliers approached Ford and General Motors with a novel proposal: Why not team up to create a single site that could be used by both automakers and their suppliers?

Ford and GM executives quickly saw the wisdom of this idea and then convinced DaimlerChrysler to join them. Now the three companies plan to establish a single website to serve as a marketplace for all interested automobile manufacturers, suppliers, and dealers—essentially, a global virtual market including all firms in the industry. Almost immediately, France's Renault and Japan's Nissan, which is controlled by Renault, indicated a desire to join; Toyota also indicated strong interest. The venture is now a stand-alone business called Covisint, and by 2002 it had offices in Michigan, Holland, and Japan. The impact on costs has already been profound. For example, it used to cost GM about $100 in ordering costs to buy parts or supplies in the traditional way—on paper, over the telephone, etc. Now, GM reports that it costs less than $10 under the new system. Clearly, then, the automakers will realize substantial cost savings. Suppliers, too, will benefit in various ways. Besides having more information about the immediate needs of different customers, they will be able to buy and sell among themselves.

Companies in other industries are also jumping on the B2B bandwagon:

- Thirty of the world's large commercial airlines, including Air Canada, have joined forces to purchase fuel, equipment, aircraft parts, and maintenance through an ecommerce site called Aeroxchange Ltd. In total, the airlines purchase about U.S.$50 billion on the site. Air Canada expects to save $11 million–$14 million on the items it buys through the exchange. The exchange also lowers transaction, processing, and inventory costs for the airlines.
- Companies in the oil and chemical industry launched an electronic procurement exchange that will spend more than U.S.$125 billion annually.
- A group of the world's largest defence contractors has launched a company that will facilitate annual purchases of about $71 billion. The company will link 37 000 businesses.
- Bell Canada, the Canadian Imperial Bank of Commerce, the Bank of Nova Scotia, and Mouvement Desjardins have formed an ecommerce joint venture to help themselves and businesses cut purchasing costs.

Ford
www.ford.ca

Input and Output Markets. Figure 1.2 provides a useful and more complete model for better understanding how the factors of production work in a pure market economy. According to this view, businesses and households interact in two different market relationships.[7] In the **input market**, firms buy resources from households, which are thus resource suppliers. In the **output market**, firms supply goods and services in response to demand on the part of households. (We will provide a more detailed discussion of supply and demand later in this chapter.)

input market
Firms buy resources that they need in the production of goods and services.

output market
Firms supply goods and services in response to demand on the part of consumers.

As you can see in Figure 1.2, the activities of these two markets create a circular flow. Ford Motor Co., for example, relies on various kinds of inputs. It buys labour directly from households, which may also supply capital from accumulated savings in the form of stock purchases. Consumer buying patterns provide information that help Ford decide which models to produce and which to discontinue. In turn, Ford uses these inputs in various ways and becomes a supplier to households when it designs and produces various kinds of automobiles, trucks, and sports utility vehicles and offers them for sale to consumers.

Capitalism. Individuals, meanwhile, are free to work for Ford or an alternative employer and to invest in Ford stock or alternative forms of saving or consumption. Similarly, Ford can create whatever vehicles it chooses and price them at whatever value it chooses. But consumers are then free to buy their next car from Ford or Toyota or BMW. This process contrasts markedly with that of a command economy, in which individuals may be told where they can and cannot work, companies are told what they can and cannot manufacture, and consumers may have little or no choice as to what they purchase or how much they pay for items. The political basis of market processes is called **capitalism**, which sanctions the private ownership of the factors of production and encourages entrepreneurship by offering profits as an incentive. The economic basis of market processes is the operation of demand and supply, which we discuss in the next section.

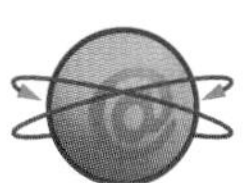

Capitalism
www.capitalism.org

capitalism
An economic system in which markets decide what, when, and for whom to produce.

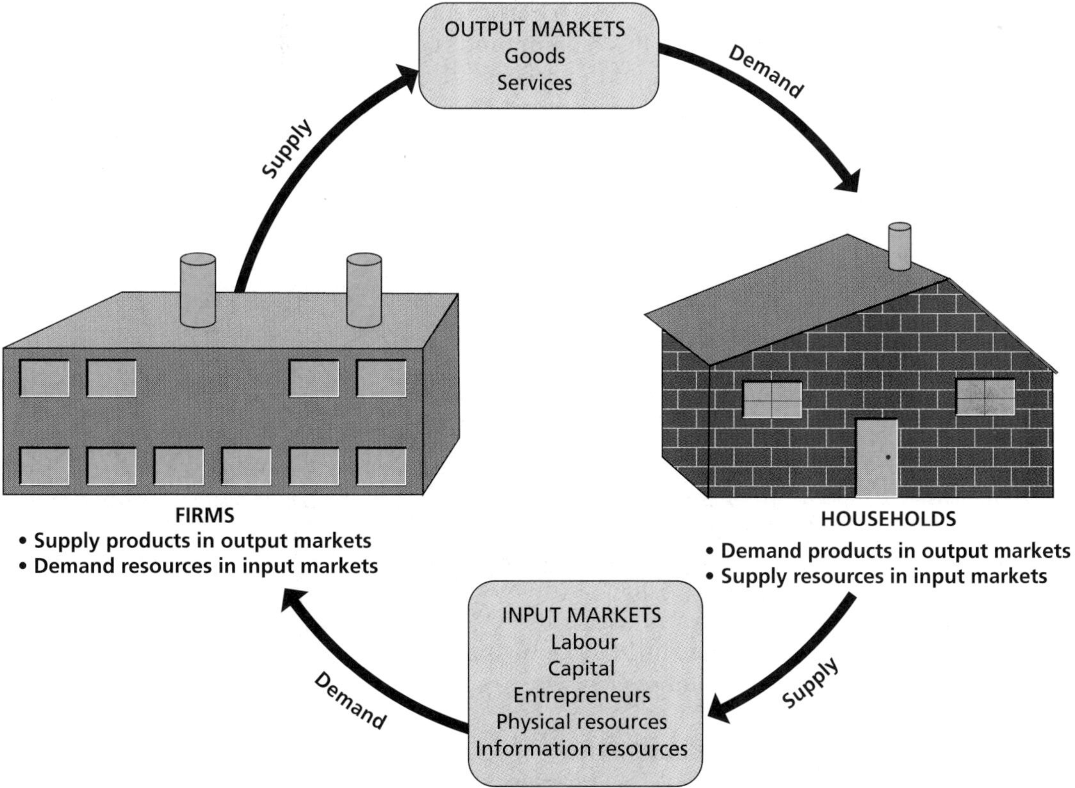

Figure 1.2
Circular flow in a market economy.

According to the model of circular flow in a market economy, this shopper plays a role in the output market. She demands goods that are supplied by a firm in the retailing business. Think of the employees who work for companies from which retailers buy their products as households that supply the input market with labour, time, and skills.

Mixed Market Economies

mixed market economy
An economic system with elements of both a command economy and a market economy; in practice, typical of most nations' economies.

privatization
The transfer of activities from the government to the public sector.

In their pure forms, command and market economies are often viewed as two extremes or opposites. In reality, however, most countries rely on some form of **mixed market economy**—a system featuring characteristics of both command and market economies. For example, most countries of the former Eastern bloc are now adopting market mechanisms through a process called **privatization**—the process of converting government enterprises into privately owned companies. In recent years this practice has also begun to spread to many other countries as well. For example, the postal system in most countries is government-owned and -managed, regardless of whether the country has a command or market economy. The Netherlands, however, recently began the process of privatizing its TNT Post Group N.V., already among the world's most efficient post office operations. Similarly, Canada has recently privatized its air traffic control system. In each case, the new enterprise reduced its payroll, boosted efficiency and productivity, and quickly became profitable.[8]

CANADA'S MIXED ECONOMIC SYSTEM

In Canada's mixed economic system, there are many important interactions between business and government. We first look at how government influences business, and then examine the way that business influences government.

How Government Influences Business

Government plays several different roles in the Canadian economy, and each of these roles influences business activity in some way. The roles government plays follow.

Government as Customer

Government buys thousands of different products and services from business firms, including office supplies, office buildings, computers, battleships, helicopters, highways, water treatment plants, and management and engineering consulting services. The government is also the largest purchaser of advertising in Canada. Many businesses depend on government purchasing, if not for their survival at least for a certain level of prosperity. Government expenditures on goods and services amount to billions of dollars each year.

Government as Competitor

Government also competes with business through Crown corporations, which are accountable to a minister of parliament for their conduct. Crown corporations exist at both the provincial and federal level, and account for a significant and wide variety of economic activity in Canada (see Table 1.1).

Government as Regulator

Federal and provincial governments in Canada regulate many aspects of business activity. Government regulates business through many administrative boards, tribunals, or commissions. At the federal level, examples include the Canadian Radio-television and Telecommunications Commission (CRTC) (which issues and renews broadcast licences), the Canadian Transport Commission (CTC) (which makes decisions about route and rate applications for commercial air and railway companies), and the Canadian Wheat Board (which regulates the prices of wheat). Provincial boards and commissions also regulate business through their decisions.

As the Business Today box demonstrates, sometimes business people feel that government is unfair in the way it performs its role as regulator. There is also controversy about how effective privatization is in the area of liquor sales.

There are several important reasons for regulating business activity. These include protecting competition, protecting consumers, achieving social goals, and protecting the environment.

Protecting Competition. One of the reasons that government regulates business is to ensure that healthy competition exists among business firms, because competition is crucial to a market economy. Without restrictions, a large company with vast resources could cut its prices and drive smaller firms out of the market. In 1999, five international drug companies were fined $88.4 million for price fixing in the food additives and vitamins market. In 2000, both WestJet Airlines and CanJet Airlines filed complaints with the Competition Bureau, claiming that Air Canada was engaging in predatory pricing on routes that the two airlines were flying.[9]

Table 1.1 The Top 10 Crown Corporations in Canada

	Company	Annual Revenue (in billions)
1.	Hydro-Quebec	$ 13.0
2.	B.C. Hydro	6.3
3.	Canada Post Corp.	5.9
4.	Ontario Power Generation	5.7
5.	Ontario Lottery and Gaming Corp.	5.4
6.	Canadian Wheat Board	4.2
7.	Hydro One Inc.	4.0
8.	Caisse de dépôt et placement du Québec	3.5
9.	Alberta Gaming and Liquor Commission	2.9
10.	Liquor Control Board of Ontario	2.9

BUSINESS TODAY

Controversy in the Liquor Business

In recent years, two controversies have arisen in the area of government regulation of business activity. Interestingly, both of these controversies revolve around the sale of liquor. The first has to do with government competition with private sector liquor firms. The second has to do with the effect of privatization of liquor sales.

Government Competition with Private Businesses

In some provinces, government liquor stores compete with private sector liquor stores. Consider the case of Magnotta Winery Corp., the third-largest vintner in Ontario. The company achieved that status despite the fact that its products were shut out of the 600 provincially owned and operated liquor stores of the Liquor Control Board of Ontario (LCBO). Magnotta battled to succeed in an environment in which its competitor was also its regulator.

When Gabe Magnotta started his wine business in 1989, he says the LCBO assured him he would be allowed sell wine in provincial stores. However, when he tried to ship his first batch of wine, the stores told him there was no room for it on their shelves. So, he started selling his wine at his own on-site store at the vineyard. Since he was not part of the LCBO system, he was free to set his own prices. He decided to charge $3.95 for a 750-mL bottle, undercutting the LCBO's price of $5.15. Soon he was selling 10 000 cases per month. But the LCBO then invoked a rule known as "non-discriminatory reference price" (NDRP), which prohibited Magnotta from selling his products for less than the cheapest wine carried in an LCBO store. The LCBO argued that the rule was designed to discourage the sale of really inexpensive wine, which some people feel promotes irresponsible drinking behaviour.

In 1997, the LCBO introduced a promotion in which customers could buy a bottle of wine for $4.58 as long as they bought a minimum of 12 bottles. When Magnotta heard about this, he reduced the price of his wine to $4.58 per bottle. The LCBO promptly told him he couldn't do that because the LCBO had set a reduced price only for wine sold by the LCBO. This led one commentator to conclude that the LCBO was exempting itself from its own policy. Magnotta spent over $500 000 in legal fees fighting the LCBO, but finally won a victory of sorts. In July 2000, the province of Ontario stripped its government-owned liquor stores of their regulatory status to make competition fairer.

The same sort of dispute was evident in Manitoba, where 6 privately owned wine stores sell over half the wine sold in Winnipeg, while 22 Manitoba Liquor Control Commission (MLCC) stores sell the rest. A Probe Research poll showed that 90 percent of Winnipeggers didn't want the province to phase out private wine stores. More than half of those polled said that private wine stores forced the MLCC stores to improve their service. The private wine sellers in Manitoba were saying the same thing as Gabe Magnotta was saying: the MLCC is in a conflict of interest because it has the power to regulate its competitors.

Privatization of Liquor Sales

For many years in Canada, provincial governments held a monopoly on the sale of liquor. Alberta was typical; there were 202 stores in the province, and they were neat, orderly, and boring. Then, in 1993, the province unexpectedly announced that it was getting out of the liquor business and would allow private sector operators to begin selling liquor. It was doing so because it said it would save $65 million annually in salaries and operating costs. Within a year, 500 privately owned liquor stores had opened up.

In 2003, a policy research group at the University of Alberta issued a report that analyzed the province of Alberta's 10-year experience with privatized liquor stores. The report reached the following conclusions:

- liquor prices had increased by about one-third since 1993 (12 percent more than inflation for the period)
- the province had lost $511 million in revenue since liquor stores were privatized
- the number of liquor stores had more than tripled since privatization

The report concluded that the benefits of privatization were modest at best. The Klein government dismissed the findings of the report as simply opinions. It noted that the private liquor stores were paying business taxes, and that lots of jobs had been created.

A 2003 report by the B.C. branch of the Consumers Association of Canada (CAC) compared liquor prices in British Columbia (where the government has a monopoly on liquor sales) with prices in Alberta. It found that B.C. prices were competitive with, or lower, than prices in Alberta. The study also concluded that if British Columbia privatized its liquor sales consumers would pay 10–20 percent more. The B.C. government had, in fact, been looking at the possibility of closing 224 government liquor stores and replacing them with privately owned stores. But the provincial government put the plan on hold so they could do more analysis of the situation. Not surprisingly, the Government and Service Employees union expressed concerns about what privatization would do to its members' jobs. Nova Scotia also granted four permits for private liquor stores in the Halifax area, but the government apparently doesn't have any big move toward privatization in mind.

Competition policy tries to eliminate restrictive trade practices and thereby stimulate maximum production, distribution, and employment. The guidelines for Canada's competition policy are contained in The Competition Act (see Table 1.2).

Protecting consumers. The federal government has initiated many programs that protect consumers. Consumer and Corporate Affairs Canada administers many of these. Important legislation includes the **Hazardous Products Act** (which requires poisonous, flammable, explosive, or corrosive products to be appropriately labelled), the **Tobacco Act** (which prohibits cigarette advertising on billboards and in stores), the **Weights and Measures Act** (which sets standards of accuracy for weighing and measuring devices), the **Textile Labelling Act** (which regulates the labelling, sale, importation, and advertising of consumer textile articles), and the **Food and Drug Act** (which prohibits the sale of food that contains any poisonous or harmful substances). Consumers are also protected by municipal bylaws such as the "no-smoking" bylaws that are so controversial in some Canadian cities.

Achieving Social Goals. Social goals promote the well-being of our society. Social goals include universal access to health care, safe workplaces,

Hazardous Products Act

Regulates banned products and products that can be sold but must be labelled hazardous.

Tobacco Act

Prohibits cigarette advertising on billboards in retail stores, and assigns financial penalties to violators.

Weights and Measures Act

Sets standards of accuracy for weighing and measuring devices.

Textile Labelling Act

Regulates the labelling, sale, importation, and advertising of consumer textile articles.

Food and Drug Act

Prohibits the sale of food unfit for human consumption and regulates food advertising.

Table 1.2 The Competition Act

Section 32	Prohibits conspiracies and combinations formed for the purpose of unduly lessening competition in the production, transportation, or storage of goods. Persons convicted may be imprisoned for up to five years or fined up to $1 million or both.
Section 33	Prohibits mergers and monopolies that substantially lessen competition. Individuals who assist in the formation of such a monopoly or merger may be imprisoned for up to two years.
Section 34	Prohibits illegal trade practices. A company may not, for example, cut prices in one region of Canada while selling at a higher price everywhere else if this substantially lessens competition. A company may not sell at "unreasonably low prices" if this substantially lessens competition. (This section does not prohibit credit unions from returning surpluses to their members.)
Section 35	Prohibits giving allowances and rebates to buyers to cover their advertising expenses, unless these allowances are made available proportionally to other purchasers who are in competition with the buyer given the rebate.
Section 36	Prohibits misleading advertising including (1) false statements about the performance of a product, (2) misleading guarantees, (3) pyramid selling, (4) charging the higher price when two prices are marked on an item, and (5) referral selling.
Section 37	Prohibits bait-and-switch selling. No person can advertise a product at a bargain price if there is no supply of the product available to the consumer. (This tactic baits prospects into the store, where salespeople switch them to higher-priced goods.) This section also controls the use of contests to sell goods, and prohibits the sale of goods at a price higher than the advertised one.
Section 38	Prohibits resale price maintenance. No person who produces or supplies a product can attempt to influence upward, or discourage reduction of, the price of the good in question. It is also illegal for the producer to refuse to supply a product to a reseller simply because the producer believes the reseller will cut the price.

employment insurance, and decent pensions. All of these goals require the interaction of business firms and government.

Canada Water Act
Controls water quality in fresh and marine waters of Canada.

Fisheries Act
Regulates the discharge of harmful substances into water.

Environmental Contaminants Act
Establishes regulations for airborne substances that are a danger to human health or to the environment.

deregulation
A reduction in the number of laws affecting business activity.

Protecting the Environment. Key government legislation designed to protect the environment includes the **Canada Water Act** (which controls water quality in fresh and marine waters), the **Fisheries Act** (which controls the discharge of any harmful substance into water), and the **Environmental Contaminants Act** (which establishes regulations for airborne substances that are a danger to human health or the environment).

In spite of all these regulations, there has been a move toward **deregulation**—a reduction in the number of laws affecting business activity. Deregulation is evident in many industries, including airlines, pipelines, banking, trucking, and communications. Deregulation has caused serious problems in the electricity market (see Concluding Case 1-2 on p. 35). The province of Ontario has capped electricity rates until 2006 because open-market pricing had caused soaring electricity prices for consumers.[10]

Government as Taxation Agent

revenue taxes
Taxes whose main purpose is to fund government services and programs.

progressive revenue taxes
Taxes levied at a higher rate on higher-income taxpayers and at a lower rate on lower-income taxpayers.

regressive revenue taxes
Taxes that cause poorer people to pay a higher percentage of income than richer people pay.

restrictive taxes
Taxes levied to control certain activities that legislators believe should be controlled.

Taxes are imposed and collected by federal, provincial, and local governments. **Revenue taxes** (e.g., income taxes) are levied by governments primarily to provide revenue to fund various services and programs. **Progressive revenue taxes** are levied at a higher rate on higher-income taxpayers and at a lower rate on lower-income taxpayers. **Regressive revenue taxes** (e.g., sales tax) are levied at the same rate regardless of a person's income. They cause poorer people to pay a higher percentage of their income for these taxes than rich people pay. **Restrictive taxes** (e.g., taxes on alcohol, tobacco, and gasoline) are levied partially for the revenue they provide, but also because legislative bodies believe that the products in question should be controlled.

Government as Provider of Incentives

Federal, provincial, and municipal governments offer incentive programs that help stimulate economic development. In Quebec, for example, Hyundai Motors received $6.4 million to build a production facility and an additional $682 000 to train workers. Both Toyota and Hyundai have received millions of dollars in incentives from government in the form of training incentives, interest-free loans, and the suspension of customs duties.[11]

Governments also offer incentives through the many services they provide to business firms through government organizations. These include the Export Development Corporation (which assists Canadian exporters by offering export insurance against nonpayment by foreign buyers and long-term loans to foreign buyers of Canadian products), Energy, Mines and Resources Canada (which provides geological maps of Canada's potential mineral-producing areas), and Statistics Canada (which provides data and analysis on almost every aspect of Canadian society).

There are many other government incentive programs, including municipal tax rebates for companies that locate in certain areas, design assistance programs, and remission of tariffs on certain advanced technology production equipment. Government incentive programs may or may not have the desired effect of stimulating the economy. They may also cause difficulties with our trading partners (see the Opening Case in Chapter 4 for an example).

Government as Provider of Essential Services

The federal, provincial, and municipal governments facilitate business activity through the wide variety of services they supply. The federal government provides highways, the postal service, the minting of money, the armed forces, and statistical data on which to base business decisions. It also tries to maintain stability through fiscal and monetary policy. Provincial and municipal governments provide streets, sewage and sanitation systems, police and fire departments, utilities, hospitals, and education. All of these activities create the kind of stability that encourages business activity.

How Business Influences Government

While government activity influences what businesses do, businesses also influence the government through lobbyists, trade associations, and advertising (see Figure 1.3). A **lobbyist** is a person hired by a company or industry to represent its interests with government officials. The Canadian Association of Consulting Engineers, for example, regularly lobbies the federal and provincial governments to make use of the skills possessed by private sector consulting engineers on projects like city water systems. Some business lobbyists have training in the particular industry, public relations experience, or a legal background. A few have served as legislators or government regulators.

lobbyist
A person hired by a company or an industry to represent its interests with government officials.

The Lobbyists Registration Act came into effect in 1989. Lobbyists must register with the Registrar of Lobbyists so that it is clear which individuals are being paid for their lobbying activity. For many lobbying efforts, there are opposing points of view. The Canadian Cancer Society and the Tobacco Institute present very different points of view on cigarette smoking and cigarette advertising.

Employees and owners of small businesses that cannot afford lobbyists often join **trade associations**. Trade associations may act as an industry lobby to influence legislation. They also conduct training programs relevant to the particular industry, and they arrange trade shows at which members display their products or services to potential customers. Most publish newsletters featuring articles on new products, new companies, changes in ownership, and changes in laws affecting the industry.

trade association
An organization dedicated to promoting the interests and assisting the members of a particular industry.

Corporations can influence legislation indirectly by influencing voters. A company can, for example, launch an advertising campaign designed to get people to write their MPs, MPPs, or MLAs demanding passage—or rejection—of a particular bill that is before parliament or the provincial legislature.

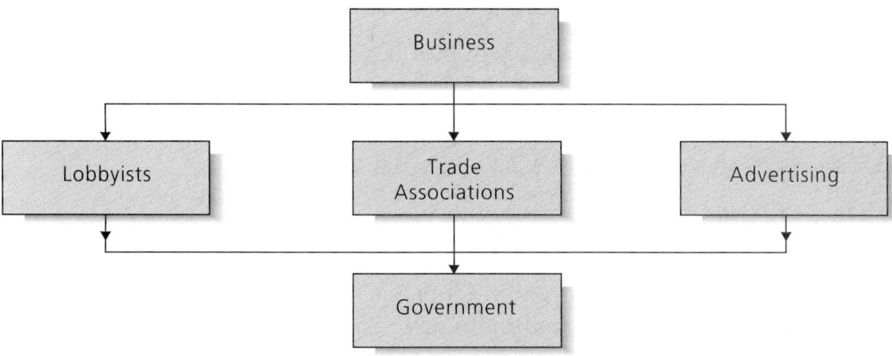

Figure 1.3
Business influences the government in a variety of ways.

THE CANADIAN MARKET ECONOMY

3. Show how *demand* and *supply* affect resource distribution in Canada.

Understanding the complex nature of the Canadian economic system is essential to understanding Canadian businesses. In the next few pages, we will examine the workings of our market economy in more detail. Specifically, we look at markets, demand, supply, the business cycle, private enterprise, and degrees of competition.

Demand and Supply in a Market Economy

A market economy consists of many different markets. We have already described input and output markets, but we need to remember that the inputs used by business and the products created by business have their own markets. In each of these markets, businesses decide what inputs to buy, what to make and in what quantities, and what prices to charge. Likewise, customers decide what to buy and how much they want to pay. Literally billions of such exchanges take place every day between businesses and individuals; between businesses; and among individuals, businesses, and governments. Moreover, exchanges conducted in one area often affect exchanges elsewhere.

Since 2000, for example, several factors have influenced computer purchases. In the late 1990s, for instance, many companies increased computer budgets in anticipation of Y2K problems but then cut them once the scare was over. Some companies began to reallocate outlays for technology, spending less on desktop computers and more on back-office equipment for ebusiness.

In addition, some firms simply started to slow down their upgrade cycles because brand-new computers were not sufficiently superior to those they had purchased just a few years earlier. Rather than upgrade every two or three years, as they had in the 1990s, many firms now upgrade every three or four years. As demand dropped, firms like Dell and IBM cut prices to keep sales from slumping too far, and lower prices mean lower profits per unit. At the same time, however, demand in other parts of the world, notably in China and India, has continued to rise, though not enough to offset declines in North America. Finally, lower profit expectations induced investors to pay less for the stocks of some computer firms, causing those prices to fall as well.[12]

The Laws of Demand and Supply

demand
The willingness and ability of buyers to purchase a product or service.

supply
The willingness and ability of producers to offer a good or service for sale.

law of demand
The principle that buyers will purchase (demand) more of a product as price drops.

law of supply
The principle that producers will offer (supply) more of a product as price rises.

On all economic levels, decisions about what to buy and what to sell are determined primarily by the forces of demand and supply.[13] **Demand** is the willingness and ability of buyers to purchase a product (a good or a service). **Supply** is the willingness and ability of producers to offer a good or service for sale. Generally speaking, demand and supply follow basic "laws":

- The **law of demand**: Buyers will purchase (demand) more of a product as its price drops and less of a product as its price increases.
- The **law of supply**: Producers will offer (supply) more of a product for sale as its price rises and less as its price drops.

The Demand and Supply Schedule

To appreciate these laws in action, consider the market for pizza in your town. If everyone in town is willing to pay $25 for a pizza (a high price), the town's only pizzeria will produce a large supply. If everyone is willing to pay only $5 (a low price), however, the restaurant will make fewer pizzas. Through careful analysis, we can determine how many pizzas will be sold at different prices. These results, called a **demand and supply schedule**, are obtained from marketing research and other systematic studies of the market. Properly applied, they help managers better understand the relationships among different levels of demand and supply at different price levels.

demand and supply schedule
Assessment of the relationships between different levels of demand and supply at different price levels.

Demand and Supply Curves

The demand and supply schedule, for example, can be used to construct demand and supply curves for pizza in your town. A **demand curve** shows how many products—in this case, pizzas—will be demanded (bought) at different prices. A **supply curve** shows how many pizzas will be supplied (cooked) at different prices.

Figure 1.4 shows hypothetical demand and supply curves for pizzas. As you can see, demand increases as price decreases; supply increases as price increases. When the demand and supply curves are plotted on the same graph, the point at which they intersect is the **market price** or **equilibrium price**—the price at which the quantity of goods demanded and the quantity of goods supplied are equal. Note in Figure 1.4 that the equilibrium price for pizzas in our example is $10. At this point, the quantity of pizzas demanded and the quantity of pizzas supplied are the same: 1000 pizzas per week.

demand curve
Graph showing how many units of a product will be demanded (bought) at different prices.

supply curve
Graph showing how many units of a product will be supplied (offered for sale) at different prices.

market price (or equilibrium price)
Profit-maximizing price at which the quantity of goods demanded and the quantity of goods supplied are equal.

Surpluses and Shortages

But what if the restaurant chooses to make some other number of pizzas? For example, what would happen if the owner tried to increase profits by making more pizzas to sell? Or what if the owner wanted to reduce overhead, cut back on store hours, and reduce the number of pizzas offered for sale? In either case, the result would be an inefficient use of resources—and perhaps lower profits. For example, if the restaurant supplies 1200 pizzas and tries to sell them for $10 each, 200 pizzas will not be purchased. The demand schedule clearly shows that only 1000 pizzas will be demanded at this price. The pizza maker will have a **surplus**—a situation in which the quantity supplied exceeds the quantity demanded. The restaurant will thus lose the money it spent making those extra 200 pizzas.

Conversely, if the pizzeria supplies only 800 pizzas, a **shortage** will result: the quantity demanded will be greater than the quantity supplied. The pizzeria will "lose" the extra money that it could have made by producing

surplus
Situation in which quantity supplied exceeds quantity demanded.

shortage
Situation in which quantity demanded exceeds quantity supplied.

Economically speaking, surfing's up, but demand for surfware is riding an even higher crest. Surfware covers a lot of products—from wet suits to bikinis to boardshorts—and the demand comes from free spending though notoriously fickle teenagers. Suppliers have to work hard not merely to meet demand, but to figure out what's going to be hot from one week to the next. "I hang out at high schools and shopping malls," admits one designer. "I try to be a sponge and see what they want."

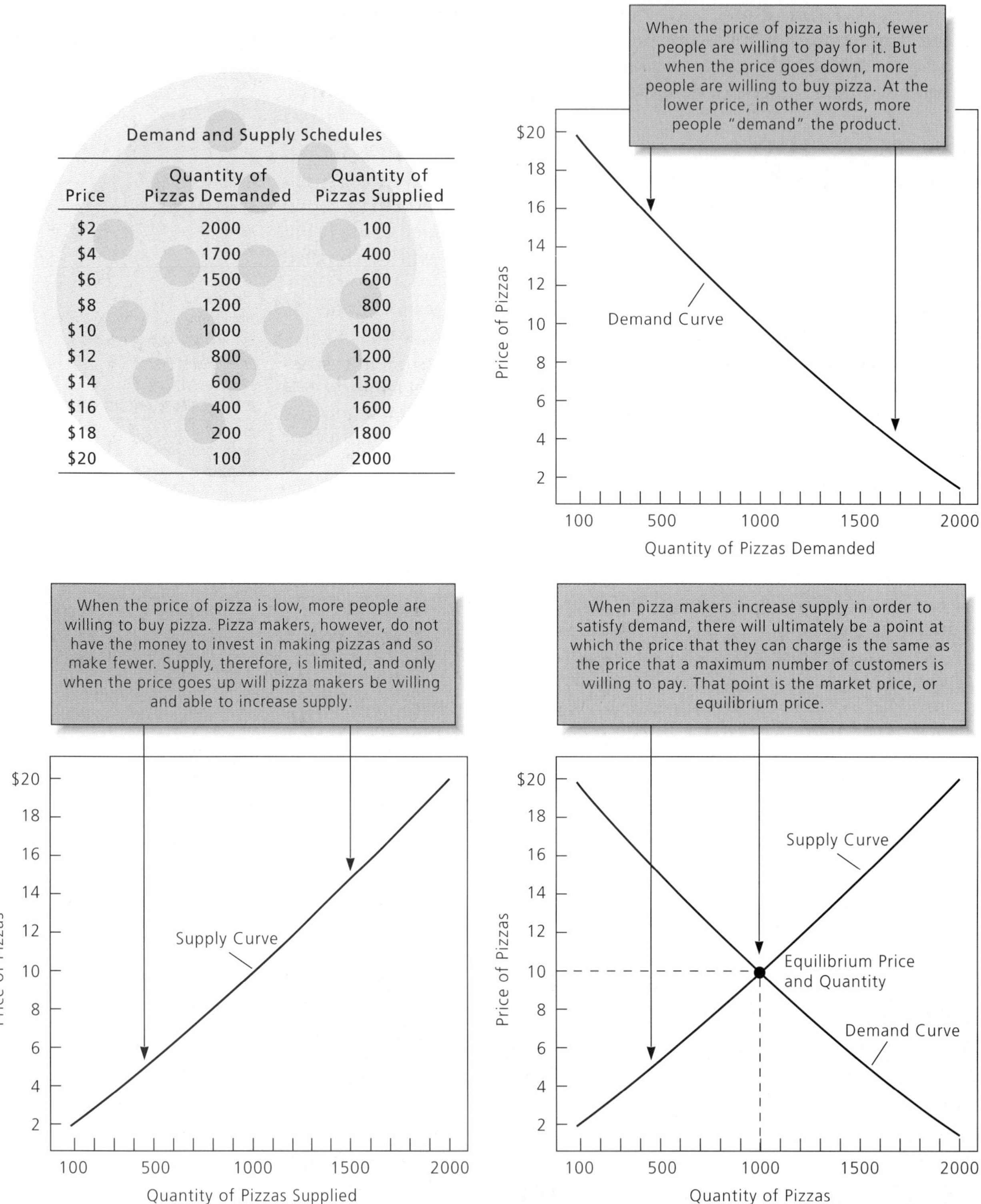

Figure 1.4
Demand and supply.

200 more pizzas. Even though consumers may pay more for pizzas because of the shortage, the restaurant will still earn lower profits than it would have if it had made 1000 pizzas. In addition, it will risk angering customers who cannot buy pizzas. To optimize profits, therefore, all businesses must constantly seek the right combination of the price charged and the quantity supplied. This "right combination" is found at the equilibrium point.

This simple example, of course, involves only one company, one product, and a few buyers. The Canadian economy is far more complex. Thousands of companies sell hundreds of thousands of products to millions of buyers every day. In the end, however, the result is much the same: companies try to supply the quantity and selection of goods that will earn them the largest profits.

A practical illustration of the issues of supply and demand is contained in the Exercising Your Ethics box.

Private Enterprise and Competition in a Market Economy

Market economies rely on a **private enterprise** system—one that allows individuals to pursue their own interests with minimal government restriction. In turn, private enterprise requires the presence of four elements: private property rights, freedom of choice, profits, and competition.

private enterprise
An economic system characterized by private property rights, freedom of choice, profits, and competition.

4. Identify the elements of *private enterprise* and explain the various *degrees of competition* in the Canadian economic system.

- *Private property.* Ownership of the resources used to create wealth is in the hands of individuals.[14]
- *Freedom of choice.* You can sell your labour to any employer you choose. You can also choose which products to buy, and producers can usually choose whom to hire and what to produce.
- *Profits.* The lure of profits (and freedom) leads some people to abandon the security of working for someone else and to assume the risks of entrepreneurship. Anticipated profits also influence individuals' choices of which goods or services to produce.

EXERCISING YOUR ETHICS

Prescribing a Dose of Competitive Medicine

The Purpose of the Assignment

Demand and supply are key elements of the Canadian economic system. So, too, is competition. This exercise will challenge you to better understand the ethical dimensions of a system that relies on demand, supply, and competition.

The Situation

You are a business person in a small town, where you run one of two local pharmacies. The population and economic base are fairly stable. Each pharmacy controls about 50 percent of the market. Each is reasonably profitable, generating solid if unspectacular revenues.

The Dilemma

The owner of the other pharmacy has just approached you. He has indicated an interest either in buying your pharmacy or in selling his to you. He argues that neither of you can substantially increase your profits and complains that if one pharmacy raises its prices, customers will simply go to the other one. He tells you outright that if you sell to him, he plans to raise prices by 10 percent. He believes that the local market will have to accept the increase for two reasons: (1) The town is too small to attract national competitors, and (2) local customers aren't likely to go elsewhere to shop because the nearest town with a pharmacy is 60 kilometres away.

Questions for Discussion

1. What are the roles of supply, demand, and competition in this scenario?
2. What are the underlying ethical issues?
3. What would you do if you were actually faced with this situation?

competition
The vying among businesses in a particular market or industry to best satisfy consumer demands and earn profits.

- *Competition.* If profits motivate individuals to start businesses, competition motivates them to operate those businesses efficiently. **Competition** occurs when two or more businesses vie for the same resources or customers. To gain an advantage over competitors, a business must produce its goods or services efficiently and be able to sell at a reasonable profit. To achieve these goals, it must convince customers that its products are either better or less expensive than those of its competitors. Competition, therefore, forces all businesses to make products better or cheaper. A company that produces inferior, expensive products is likely to fail. We discuss competition more fully in the next section.

Degrees of Competition

Even in a free enterprise system, not all industries are equally competitive. Economists have identified four degrees of competition in a private enterprise system: *perfect competition, monopolistic competition, oligopoly*, and *monopoly*. Table 1.3 summarizes the features of these four degrees.

perfect competition
A market or industry characterized by a very large number of small firms producing an identical product so that none of the firms has any ability to influence price.

Perfect Competition. For **perfect competition** to exist, two conditions must prevail: (1) all firms in an industry must be small and (2) the number of firms in the industry must be large. Under these conditions, no single firm is powerful enough to influence the price of its product. Prices are therefore determined by such market forces as supply and demand. In addition, these two conditions also reflect four principles:

1. The products of each firm are so similar that buyers view them as identical to those of other firms.
2. Both buyers and sellers know the prices that others are paying and receiving in the marketplace.
3. Because each firm is small, it is easy for firms to enter or leave the market.
4. Going prices are set exclusively by supply and demand and accepted by both sellers and buyers.

Canadian agriculture is a good example of perfect competition. The wheat produced on one farm is the same as that from another. Both producers and

Table 1.3 Degrees of Competition

Characteristic	Perfect Competition	Monopolistic Competition	Oligopoly	Monopoly
Example	Local farmer	Stationery store	Steel industry	Public utility
Number of competitors	Many	Many, but fewer than in pure competition	Few	None
Ease of entry into industry	Relatively easy	Fairly easy	Difficult	Regulated by government
Similarity of goods or services offered by competing firms	Identical	Similar	Can be similar or different	No directly competing goods or services
Level of control over price by individual firms	None	Some	Some	Considerable

buyers are aware of prevailing market prices. It is relatively easy to start producing wheat and relatively easy to stop when it's no longer profitable.

Monopolistic Competition. Fewer sellers are involved in **monopolistic competition** than in perfect competition, but because there are still many buyers, sellers try to make products at least *seem* to differ from those of competitors. Differentiating strategies include brand names (Tide and Cheer), design or styling (Polo and Tommy Hilfiger jeans), and advertising (Coke and Pepsi). For example, in an effort to attract health-conscious consumers, the Kraft Foods division of Philip Morris promotes such differentiated products as low-fat Cool Whip, low-calorie Jell-O, and sugar-free Kool-Aid.

monopolistic competition
A market or industry characterized by a large number of firms supplying products that are similar but distinctive enough from one another to give firms some ability to influence price.

Monopolistically competitive businesses may be large or small, but they can still enter or leave the market easily. For example, many small clothing stores compete successfully with large apparel retailers such as Liz Claiborne and Limited Brands. bebe Stores is a good case in point. The small clothing chain controls its own manufacturing facilities and can respond just as quickly as firms like Gap Inc. to changes in fashion tastes.[15] Many single-store clothing businesses in college towns compete by developing their own T-shirt and cap designs with copyrighted slogans and logos.

Product differentiation also gives sellers some control over prices. For instance, even though Sears shirts may have similar styling and other features, Ralph Lauren Polo shirts can be priced with little regard for lower Sears prices. But there are limits. Although Polo might be able to sell shirts for, say, \$20 more than a comparable Sears shirt, it could not sell as many shirts if they were priced at \$200 more.

Oligopoly. When an industry has only a handful of sellers, an **oligopoly** exists. As a general rule, these sellers are quite large. It is difficult for new competitors to enter the industry because large capital investment is needed. Thus oligopolistic industries like the automobile, airline, and steel industries tend to stay that way.[16] For example, only two companies make large commercial aircraft: Boeing (a U.S. company) and Airbus (a European consortium). Furthermore, as the trend toward globalization continues, most experts believe that, as one forecaster puts it, "global oligopolies are as inevitable as the sunrise."[17]

oligopoly
A market or industry characterized by a small number of very large firms that have the power to influence the price of their product and/or resources.

Oligopolists have more control over their strategies than monopolistically competitive firms, but the actions of one firm can significantly affect the sales of every other firm in the industry. For example, when one firm cuts prices or offers incentives to increase sales, the others usually protect sales by doing the same. Likewise, when one firm raises prices, others generally follow suit. Therefore, the prices of comparable products are usually similar. When an airline announces new fare discounts, others adopt the same strategy almost immediately. Just as quickly, when discounts end for one airline, they usually end for everyone else.

Monopoly. When an industry or market has only one producer, a **monopoly** exists. Being the only supplier gives a firm complete control over the price of its product. Its only constraint is how much consumer demand will fall as its price rises. Until 1992, the long-distance telephone business was a monopoly in Canada, and cable TV, which has had a local monopoly for years, will lose it when telephone companies and satellite broadcasters are allowed into the cable business.[18]

monopoly
A market or industry with only one producer, who can set the price of its product and/or resources.

In Canada, laws such as the Competition Act forbid many monopolies. In addition, the prices charged by "natural monopolies" are closely watched by provincial utilities boards. **Natural monopolies** are industries in which one company can most efficiently supply all the product or service that is needed. For example, like most utilities, your provincial electric company is a natural monopoly because it can supply all the power (product) needed in

natural monopoly
A market or industry in which having only one producer is most efficient because it can meet all of consumers' demand for the product.

Consumers often buy products under conditions of monopolistic competition. For example, there are few differences between different brands of toothpaste, cold tablets, detergents, canned goods, and soft drinks.

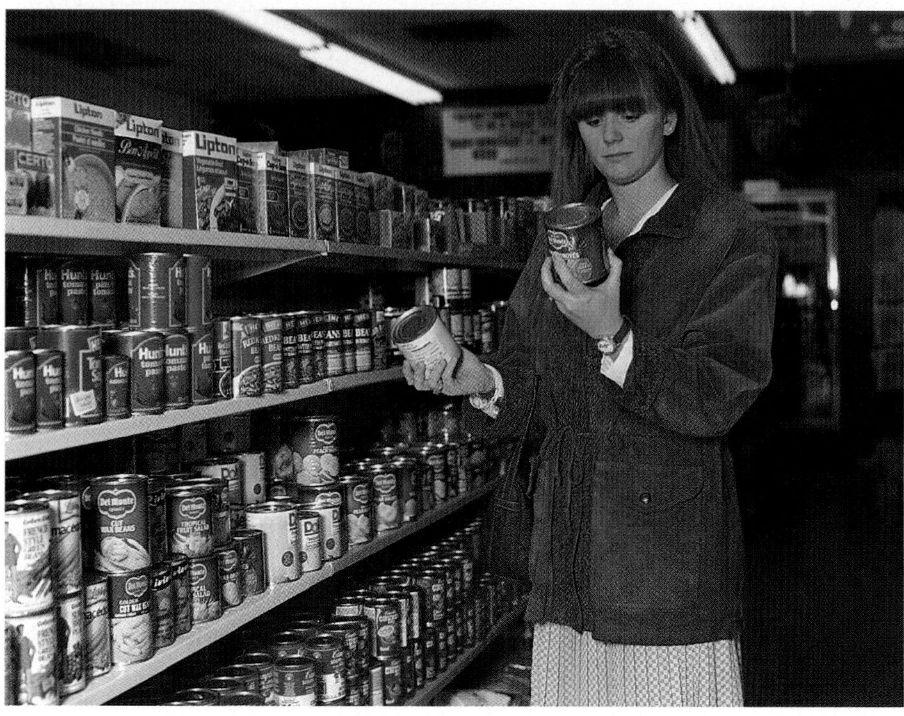

an area. Duplicate facilities—such as two nuclear power plants, two sets of power lines, and so forth—would be wasteful.

A BRIEF HISTORY OF BUSINESS IN CANADA

5. Trace the *history of business* in Canada.

Canadian business has not always had a variety of complex structures. Indeed, a look at the history of business in Canada shows a steady development from sole proprietorships to the complex corporate structures of today. In this section, we will trace the broad outlines of the development of business in Canada. Table 1.4 highlights some of the specific events in Canadian business history.[19]

The Early Years

Business activity and profit from commercial fishing were the motivation for the first European involvement in Canada. In the late 1400s, ships financed by English entrepreneurs came to the coast of Newfoundland to fish for profit. By the late 1500s, the Newfoundland coast was being visited by hundreds of fishing vessels each year.

Beginning in the 1500s, French and British adventurers began trading with the native peoples. Items such as cooking utensils and knives were exchanged for beaver and other furs. One trading syndicate made over 1000 percent profit on beaver skins sold to a Paris furrier. Trading was aggressive and, over time, the price of furs rose as more and more Europeans bid for them. Originally the fur trade was restricted to eastern Canada, but by the late 1600s, coureurs de bois were travelling far to the west in search of new sources of furs.

European settlers who arrived in Canada in the sixteenth and seventeenth centuries initially had to farm or starve. Gradually, however, they began to produce more than they needed for their own survival. The gov-

Table 1.4 Some Important Dates in Canadian Business History

Year	Event
1490	English fishermen active off the coast of Newfoundland
1534	Account of first trading with native peoples written by Jacques Cartier
1669	*Nonsuch* returns to London with a cargo of furs from Hudson Bay area
1670	Hudson's Bay Company founded
1730–40	Hat-making industry arises in Quebec and is stifled by French home officials
1737	Compagnie des forges du St. Maurice formed to produce iron
1779	North West Company forms
1785	Molson brewery opens
1805	First Canadian paper mill built at St. Andrew's, Quebec
1809	First steamboat (the *Accommodation*) put into service on the St. Lawrence River by John Molson
1817	Bank of Montreal chartered
1821	Hudson's Bay Company and North West Company merge
1830–50	Era of canal building
1836	First railroad train pulled by a steam engine
1850–60	First era of railroad building
1855	John Redpath opens first Canadian sugar refinery in Montreal
1856	Railroad trains begin running between Toronto and Montreal
1857–58	First oil well in Canada drilled near Sarnia, Ontario
1861	Toronto Stock Exchange opens
1869	Eaton's opens for business in Toronto
1879	National Policy implemented; raised tariffs on foreign goods to protect and encourage Canadian manufacturers
1880–90	First western land boom
1885	Last spike driven to complete the Canadian Pacific Railroad
1896	First large pulp and paper mill in Canada opened at Sault Ste. Marie, Ontario
1897–99	Klondike gold rush
1907	First issue of *The Financial Post*
1917–22	Creation of Canadian National Railways
1920	First ship-plate steel mill in Canada opens in Sydney, Nova Scotia
1926	U.S. replaces Great Britain as Canada's largest trading partner
1927	Armand Bombardier sells first "auto-neige" (forerunner of the snowmobile)
1927	Canadian Tire begins operations in Toronto
1929	Great stock market crash
1929–33	Great Depression
1930	Canadian Airways Limited formed
1932	Canadian Radio Broadcasting Corporation formed. (It became the CBC in 1936.)
1935	Bank of Canada begins operations
1937	Canadian Breweries Limited is formed
1940	C.D. Howe appointed as Minister of Munitions and Supply
1945	Argus Corporation Limited formed
1947–51	Early computer built at the University of Toronto
1947	Leduc Number 1 oil well drilled in Alberta
1949	A.V. Roe (Avro) makes Canada's first commercial jetliner
1964	Volvo of Sweden begins assembling cars in Nova Scotia
1965	Auto Pact signed with the U.S.
1969	Canada becomes world's largest potash producer
1980–86	Dome, Canadair, and Massey-Ferguson receive financial assistance from the federal government
1989	Free trade agreement with U.S. comes into effect
1993	North American Free Trade Agreement comes into effect

ernments of the countries from which the settlers came (notably England and France) were strong supporters of the mercantilist philosophy. Under mercantilism, colonists were expected to export raw materials like beaver pelts and lumber at low prices to the mother country. These raw materials were then used to produce finished goods such as fur coats, which were sold at high prices to settlers in Canada. Attempts to develop industry in Canada were thwarted by England and France, who enjoyed large profits from mercantilism. As a result, Canadian manufacturing was slow to develop.

Industrial Revolution
A major change in goods production that began in England in the mid-eighteenth century and was characterized by a shift to the factory system, mass production, and specialization of labour.

The Factory System and the Industrial Revolution

British manufacturing took a great leap forward around 1750 with the coming of the **Industrial Revolution**. This revolution was made possible by advances in technology and by the development of the **factory system**. Instead of hundreds of workers turning out items one at a time in their cottages, the factory system brought together in one place all of the materials

factory system
A process in which all the machinery, materials, and workers required to produce a good in large quantities are brought together in one place.

mass production
The manufacture of products of uniform quality in large quantities.

specialization
The breaking down of complex operations into simple tasks that are easily learned and performed.

and workers required to produce items in large quantities, along with newly created machines capable of **mass production**.

Mass production offered savings in several areas. It avoided unnecessary duplication of equipment. It allowed firms to purchase raw materials at better prices by buying large lots. And most important, it encouraged **specialization** of labour. No longer did production require highly skilled craftspeople who could do all the different tasks required to make an item. A series of semiskilled workers, each trained to perform only one task and supported by specialized machines and tools, greatly increased output.

In spite of British laws against the export of technology and manufacturing in North America, Canadian manufacturing existed almost from the beginning of European settlement. Modest manufacturing operations were evident in sawmills, breweries, gristmills for grinding grain, tanneries, woollen mills, shoemakers' shops, and tailors' shops. These operations were so successful that by 1800, exports of manufactured goods were more important than exports of fur.

With the advent of steam power in the early 1800s, manufacturing activity began to increase rapidly. By 1850, more than 30 factories—employing more than 2000 people—lined the Lachine Canal in Montreal alone. Exports of timber to England in 1850 were 70 times greater than what they had been in 1800. The demand for reliable transportation was the impetus for canal building in the mid-1800s and then the railroad-building boom in the mid- and late 1800s.

The Entrepreneurial Era

One of the most significant features of the last half of the nineteenth century was the emergence of entrepreneurs willing to take risks in the hope of earning huge profits. Adam Smith in his book *The Wealth of Nations* argued that the government should not interfere in the economy, but should let businesses function without regulation or restriction. The Canadian government often adopted this laissez-faire attitude. As a result, some individuals became immensely wealthy through their aggressive business dealings. Some railway, bank, and insurance executives made over $25 000 per year in the late 1800s, and their purchasing power was immense. Entrepreneurs such as Joseph Flavelle, Henry Pellatt, and John MacDonald lived in ostentatious mansions or castles.

The size and economic power of some firms meant that other businesses had difficulty competing against them. At the same time, some business executives decided that it was more profitable to collude than to compete. They decided among themselves to fix prices and divide up markets. Hurt by these actions, Canadian consumers called for more regulation of business. In 1889, the first anti-combines legislation was passed in Canada, and legislation regulating business has increased ever since.

The Production Era

The concepts of specialization and mass production that originated in the Industrial Revolution were more fully refined as Canada entered the twentieth century. The Scientific Management Movement focused management's attention on production. Increased efficiency via the "one best way" to accomplish tasks became the major management goal.

production era
The period during the early twentieth century when businesses focused almost exclusively on improving productivity and manufacturing methods.

Henry Ford's introduction of the moving assembly line in the U.S. in 1913 ushered in the **production era**. During the production era, less attention was paid to selling and marketing than to technical efficiency when producing goods. By using fixed workstations, increasing task specializa-

In the eighteenth century, the home crafts industry provided our young nation with clothing and foodstuffs. During the nineteenth century, machinery such as the cotton gin changed the way the world worked. Today, automation continues to alter our work lives and the types of products that are available to us.

tion, and moving the work to the worker, the assembly line increased productivity and lowered prices, making all kinds of products affordable for the average person.

During the production era, large businesses began selling stock—making shareholders the owners—and relying on professional managers. The growth of corporations and improved production output resulting from assembly lines came at the expense of worker freedom. The dominance of big firms made it harder for individuals to go into business for themselves. Company towns run by the railroads, mining corporations, and forest products firms gave individuals little freedom of choice over whom to work for and what to buy. To restore some balance within the overall system, both government and labour had to develop and grow. Thus, this period saw the rise of labour unions and collective bargaining. We will look at this development in more detail in Chapter 10. The Great Depression of the 1930s and the Second World War caused the federal government to intervene in the economic system on a previously unimaginable scale.

Today, business, government, and labour are frequently referred to by economists and politicians as the three *countervailing powers* in our society. All are big. All are strong. Yet, none totally dominates the others.

The Sales and Marketing Eras

By the 1930s, business's focus on production had resulted in spectacular increases in the amount of goods and services for sale. As a result, buyers had more choices and producers faced greater competition in selling their wares. Thus began the so-called **sales era**. According to the ideas of this time, a business's profits and success depended on hiring the right salespeople, advertising heavily, and making sure products were readily available. Business firms were essentially production- and sales-oriented, and they produced what they thought customers wanted, or simply what the company was good at producing. This approach is still used by firms that find themselves with surplus goods that they want to sell (e.g., used-car dealerships).

sales era
The period during the 1930s and 1940s when businesses focused on sales forces, advertising, and keeping products readily available.

Following the Second World War, pent-up demand for consumer goods kept the economy rolling. While brief recessions did occur periodically, the 1950s and 1960s were prosperous times. Production increased, technology advanced, and the standard of living rose. During the **marketing era**, business adopted a new philosophy of how to do business—use market research to determine what customers want, and then make it for them. Firms like Procter & Gamble and Molson were very effective during the marketing era, and continue to be profitable today. Each offers an array of products within a particular field (toothpaste or beer, for example), and gives customers a chance to pick what best suits their needs.

marketing era
The period during the 1950s and 1960s when businesses began to identify and meet consumer wants in order to make a profit.

The Finance Era

In the 1980s, emphasis shifted to finance. In the **finance era** there was a sharp increase in mergers and in the buying and selling of business enterprises. Some people now call it the "decade of greed." As we will see in the next chapter, during the finance era there were many hostile takeovers and a great deal of financial manipulation of corporate assets by so-called corporate raiders. Critics charged that these raiders were simply enriching themselves and weren't creating anything of tangible value by their activity. They also charged that raiders were distracting business managers from their main goals of running the business. The raiders responded that they were making organizations more efficient by streamlining, merging, and reorganizing them.

finance era
The period during the 1980s when there were many mergers and much buying and selling of business enterprises.

The Global Era

The last few years have seen the continuation of technological advances in production, computer technology, information systems, and communication capabilities. They have also seen the emergence of a truly global economy. Canadians drive cars made in Japan, wear sweaters made in Italy, drink beer brewed in Mexico, and listen to stereos made in Taiwan. But we're not alone in this. People around the world buy products and services from foreign companies.

While it is true that many Canadian businesses have been hurt by foreign imports, numerous others have profited by exploring new foreign markets themselves. And domestic competition has forced many businesses to work harder than ever to cut costs, increase efficiency, and improve product and service quality. We will explore a variety of important trends, opportunities, and challenges of the global era throughout this book.

The Internet Era

The turn of the century has been accompanied by what many experts are calling the internet era of business. Internet usage in North America grew from about 100 users per 1000 people in 1995 to over 450 users per 1000 people in 2000. Projections call for this figure to grow to nearly 750 users per 1000 people by 2005. The growth rate in Western Europe, however, is expected to be even faster and, by 2005, will also become significant in the Asia-Pacific region.

How does the growth of the internet affect business? In at least three different ways:

1. The internet will give a dramatic boost to trade in all sectors of the economy, especially services. If the internet makes it easier for all trade to grow, this is particularly true for trade in services on an international scale.
2. The internet will level the playing field, at least to some extent, between larger and smaller enterprises, regardless of what products or services they sell. In the past, a substantial investment was typically needed to enter some industries and to enter foreign markets. Now, however, a small business based in central Alberta, southern Italy, eastern Malaysia, or northern Brazil can set up a website and compete quite effectively with much larger businesses located around the world.
3. The internet holds considerable potential as an effective and efficient networking mechanism among businesses. Business-to-business (B2B) networks can link firms with all of their suppliers, business customers, and strategic partners in ways that make it faster and easier for them to do business together.

SUMMARY OF LEARNING OBJECTIVES

1. **Define the nature of Canadian *business* and identify its main goals.** *Businesses* are organizations that produce or sell goods or services to make a profit. *Profits* are the difference between a business' revenues and expenses. The prospect of earning profits encourages individuals and organizations to open and expand businesses. The benefits of business activities also extend to wages paid to workers and to taxes that support government functions.

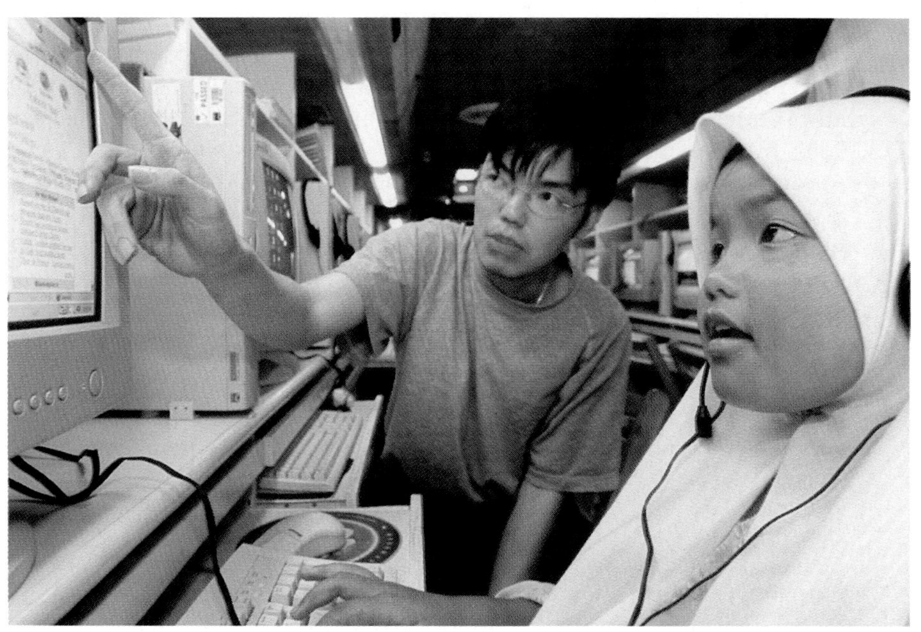

The Mobile Internet Unit is a sort of digital bookmobile for students at the poorest, most remote schools in Malaysia. Developed in conjunction with the United Nations, the program introduces students to PCs and provides teachers to help them learn how to navigate the internet and send email. The program also donates PCs, modems, and internet account numbers so that students can practise and teachers can build computer skills into their curricula.

2. **Describe different types of global *economic systems* according to the means by which they control the *factors of production* through *input and output markets*.** An *economic system* is a nation's system for allocating its resources among its citizens. Economic systems differ in terms of who owns or controls the basic *factors of production*: labour, capital, entrepreneurs, physical resources, and, more recently, information resources. In *command economies*, the government controls all or most of these factors. In *market economies*, which are based on the principles of capitalism, individuals and businesses control the factors of production and exchange them through *input and output markets*. Most countries today have *mixed market economies* that are dominated by one of these systems but include elements of the other. The process of *privatization* is an important means by which many of the world's planned economies are moving toward mixed market systems.
3. **Show how *demand* and *supply* affect resource distribution in Canada.** The Canadian economy is strongly influenced by markets, demand, and supply. *Demand* is the willingness and ability of buyers to purchase a good or service. *Supply* is the willingness and ability of producers to offer goods or services for sale. Demand and supply work together to set a *market* or *equilibrium price*—the price at which the quantity of goods demanded and the quantity of goods supplied are equal.
4. **Identify the elements of private enterprise and explain the various degrees of competition in the Canadian economic system.** The Canadian economy is founded on the principles of *private enterprise: private property rights, freedom of choice, profits*, and *competition*. Degrees of competition vary because not all industries are equally competitive. Under conditions of *perfect competition*, numerous small firms compete in a market governed entirely by demand and supply. An *oligopoly* involves a handful of sellers only. A *monopoly* involves only one seller.
5. **Trace the history of business in Canada.** Modern business structures reflect a pattern of development over centuries. Throughout much of the colonial period, sole proprietors supplied raw materials to English manufacturers. The rise of the factory system during the Industrial Revolution brought with it mass production and specialization of labour. During the entrepreneurial era in the nineteenth century, large corporations—and monopolies—emerged. During the production era of the early twentieth century, companies grew by emphasizing output and production. During the sales and marketing eras of the 1950s and 1960s, business began focusing on sales staff, advertising, and the need to produce what consumers wanted. The 1980s saw the emergence of a global economy. Many Canadian companies have profited from exporting their goods to foreign markets. The most recent development is the use of the internet to boost business. It should level the playing field between large and small companies.

KEY TERMS

business, 6
Canada Water Act, 16
capital, 8
capitalism, 11
command economy, 8
communism, 9
competition, 22
demand and supply schedule, 19
demand curve, 19
demand, 18
deregulation, 16
economic system, 6
entrepreneur, 8
Environmental Contaminants Act, 16
factors of production, 7
factory system, 25
finance era, 28
Fisheries Act, 16
Food and Drug Act, 15

QUESTIONS AND EXERCISES

Questions for Review

1. What are the factors of production? Is one factor more important than the others? If so, which one? Why?

2. What are input and output markets? How are they related?

3. What is a demand curve? A supply curve? What is the term for the point at which they intersect?

4. Explain the differences between the four degrees of competition and give an example of each one. (Do not use the examples given in the text.)

Questions for Analysis

5. In recent years, many countries have moved from planned economies to market economies. Why do you think this has occurred? Can you envision a situation that would cause a resurgence of planned economies?

6. Cite an instance in which a surplus of a product led to decreased prices. Cite an instance in which a shortage led to increased prices. What eventually happened in each case? Why?

7. In your opinion, what industries in Canada should be regulated by the government? Why?

Application Exercises

8. Choose a locally owned business. Interview the owner to find out how it uses the factors of production and have him or her describe its means of acquiring them.

9. Visit a local shopping mall or shopping area. List each store that you see and determine what degree of competition it faces in its immediate environment. For example, if there is only one store in the mall that sells shoes, that store represents a monopoly. Note those businesses with direct competitors (two jewellery stores) and show how they compete with one another.

10. Go to the library or log onto the internet and research 10 different industries. Classify each according to degree of competition.

BUILDING YOUR BUSINESS SKILLS

Analyzing the Price of Doing Ebusiness

Goal

To encourage students to understand how the competitive environment affects a product's price.

Situation

Assume that you own a local business that provides internet access to individuals and businesses in your community. Yours is one of four such businesses in the local market. Each of the four companies charges the same price: $12 per month for unlimited dial-up service. Your business also provides users with email service; two of your competitors also offer email service. One of these same two competitors, plus the third, also provides the individual user with a free, basic personal webpage. One competitor just dropped its price to $10 per month, and the other two have announced their intentions to follow suit. Your break-even price is $7 per customer. You are concerned about getting into a price war that may destroy your business.

Method

Divide into groups of four or five people. Each group is to develop a general strategy for handling competitors' price changes. In your discussion, take the following factors into account:

- how the demand for your product is affected by price changes
- the number of competitors selling the same or a similar product
- the methods—other than price—you can use to attract new customers and/or retain current customers

Analysis

Develop specific pricing strategies based on each of the following situations:

- Within a month after dropping the price to $10, one of your competitors raises its price back to $12.
- Two of your competitors drop their prices further—to $8 per month. As a result, your business falls off by 25 percent.
- One of your competitors that has provided customers with a free webpage has indicated that it will start charging an extra $2 per month for this optional service.
- Two of your competitors have announced that they will charge individual users $8 per month, but will charge businesses a higher price (not yet announced).
- All four providers (including you) are charging $8 per month. One goes out of business, and you know that another is in poor financial health.

Follow-Up Questions

1. Discuss the role that various inducements other than price might play in affecting demand and supply in the market for internet service.
2. Is it always in a company's best interest to feature the lowest prices?
3. Eventually, what form of competition is likely to characterize the market for internet service?

MASTERING BUSINESS ESSENTIALS

Episode 2 Episode 2 reminds us that although we live in a world of limited resources, our wants and needs remain unlimited. It thus encourages students to think about such phenomena as scarcity and such principles as opportunity costs. *This episode focuses on the chapter discussion of factors of production by raising issues about the use and availability of resources among modern organizations.*

CRAFTING YOUR BUSINESS PLAN

Making Scents of Competition

The Purpose of the Assignment

1. To acquaint you with the process of navigating the Business PlanPro (BPP) software package.
2. To stimulate your thinking about how two chapter topics—forms of competition and factors of production—can be integrated as components in the BPP planning environment.

Assignment

After reading Chapter 1 in the textbook, open the BPP software and look around for information about types of competition and factors of production as they apply to a sample firm: Fantastic Florals Inc. To find Fantastic Florals, do the following:

Open the Business PlanPro. If it asks if you want to "create a new business plan" or "open an existing plan," select "create a new business plan" (even though you're not going to create a plan at this time). You will then be taken to the Business PlanPro EasyPlan Wizard. Click on the option entitled **Research It**. You will then be presented a new list of options, including Sample Plan Browser. After clicking on the **Sample Plan Browser**, go down the alphabetical list of sample plans and double-click on **Import—Artificial Flowers**, which is the location for Fantastic Florals Inc. The screen you are looking at is the introduction page for Fantastic Florals' business plan. Next, scroll down until you reach the **Table of Contents** for the company's business plan.

Now respond to the following items:

1. The Table of Contents page contains an outline of the company's business plan. After scanning the outline, click on **1.0 Executive Summary**. Explore the information on the screen to see what an Executive Summary looks like in BPP. As you will see, the length of the Executive Summary will vary for different companies' plans, with some containing longer summaries.
2. After returning to the Table of Contents page, scroll down the outline to review the categories within the business plan. Then click on some of the lines that you think might contain information about two of the chapter topics—forms of competition and factors of production. For example, **3.2 Competitive Comparison** may be one of the likely places to find information on forms of competition. As you explore, see how many of this company's factors of production (labour, capital, entrepreneurs, physical resources, information resources) you can find. Try to identify at least one example of each factor in Fantastic Florals' business plan.
3. After finishing with one sample company, you can get to other companies in various industries by returning to the **Sample Plan Browser**, entering the selection box containing the list of sample plans, and double-clicking on the plan for another firm of your choice. Choose at least one other plan, open it, and scan its contents.

When you are finished, you can close the Sample Plan Browser page by going to the top of the screen and clicking on **File** (on the bar menu). Then select **Exit**. You can then exit from the BPP program by going to the top of the screen and clicking on **File** (on the bar menu) and selecting **Exit**.

VIDEO EXERCISE

Helping Businesses Do Business

Learning Objectives

The purpose of this video is to help you:

1. Understand world economic systems and their effect on competition.
2. Identify the factors of production.
3. Discuss ways in which supply and demand affect a product's price.

Synopsis

The U.S. Department of Commerce (DOC) seeks to support U.S. economic stability and help U.S.-based companies do business in other countries. In contrast to the planned economy of the People's Republic of China, the United States features a market economy in which firms are free to set their own missions and transact business with any other company or individual. They do, however, face some constraints. U.S. firms must comply with governmental regulations that set such standards as minimum safety requirements. When doing business in other countries, they must consider tariffs and other restrictions that govern imports to those markets. In addition, supply and demand affects a company's ability to set prices and generate profits.

Discussion Question

1. *For analysis:* If a U.S. company must pay more for factors of production such as human resources, what is the likely effect on its competitiveness in world markets?

Online Exploration

Visit the U.S. Department of Commerce website **(www.doc.gov)** and follow various links from the home page to examine some of the agency's resources for businesses. Also follow the link to the DOC's history. What assistance can a U.S. business expect from this agency? How have the agency's offerings evolved over the years to meet the changing needs and demands of business?

EXPLORING THE NET

"Easy as Dell"

In the first part of this chapter, we defined a business as an organization that provides goods and services to earn profits. What's the difference between a good and a service? To fit our definition, must a business offer both goods and services? Or do some businesses offer just goods and some just services?

Let's look further into these questions by exploring the website of a successful company—Dell Computer Corp., at **www.dell.com**. The home page shows that the site is divided into six major areas:

Servers, Storage & Networking

Notebooks & Desktops

Printers

Handhelds

Software & Peripherals

Services & Training

Click on **Notebooks & Desktops**.

1. What general product categories are promoted on this page?

Now click on **Desktops**.

2. What general product categories are promoted on this page? Are these products primarily goods or services?
3. What is the first service that Dell offers on this page?

Now go back to the home page at **www.dell.com**. Click on **Services & Training**.

4. How does Dell classify its service products?

On the Services & Training page, scroll up the menu and click on **Case Studies**. Now look under the heading Deployment. Scroll down the list and click on **Solvay**.

5. What did Dell do for Solvay?

Concluding Case 1-1 CJ

The Perils of Palladium

In 2002, Ford Motor Company took a $1 billion write-off on the value of the palladium it had stockpiled for use in its automobile catalytic converters. Ford originally stockpiled this raw material because it thought it would need increasing amounts of palladium, and because it was concerned that palladium was going to be high-priced and hard to get.

Most people have never heard of palladium, a greyish metal produced primarily in Russia and South Africa. In the mid-1990s, when automakers adopted tighter pollution emission standards, they switched from platinum to palladium because palladium does a better job of cleaning auto emissions, and because at that time palladium was much cheaper than platinum (platinum then cost about $400 per ounce, palladium only $200). Ford was particularly aggressive in using palladium because it wanted to convey the image to consumers that it was very environmentally responsible.

The automobile manufacturers knew that switching to palladium would cause demand to exceed world production, which was then about 5 million ounces per year. They also knew that this increased demand would cause the price of palladium to rise, but they were not prepared for the price rise that actually occurred when Russian exports of palladium suddenly ceased in 1997. The official explanation was a bureaucratic problem, and when supplies resumed, the price dropped again to about $200 per ounce.

In 1998, the same thing happened, but this time the price went up to over $400 per ounce. When supplies resumed, the price dropped back to only $300 per ounce. Now the auto manufacturers were becoming very concerned. Even though only small amounts of palladium are used in catalytic converters, price increases of this magnitude meant that the price of the average car would have to increase $100 to cover the cost of palladium. Some automakers set up teams of experts to figure out how to use less palladium and still meet the tighter pollution standards. By 2000, when the price of palladium had risen to over $1000 per ounce, automakers took the unprecedented step of stipulating the maximum amount of palladium that would be allowed in engineers' car designs.

At Ford, the purchase of palladium was left to the same purchasing agents who bought less exotic raw materials such as steel and copper. These purchasing agents apparently didn't take the same kinds of precautions that sophisticated buyers normally take when buying raw materials that fluctuate wildly in price. During this same time period, Ford's engineers were having success in figuring out ways to reduce the amount of palladium they needed. In fact, they predicted that they could cut the use of palladium in half by using new technology. So, Ford's purchasing agents were buying lots of palladium at high prices (fearing the price would go even higher) while Ford's engineers were figuring out ways to reduce the company's need for the metal.

By 2001, the price of palladium had again dropped to about $400 dollars per ounce. This happened because demand dropped (other automakers had also discovered ways to get by with less palladium) and supplies increased (because the extremely high prices of palladium in 1999–2000 had caused more producers to get into the business of supplying the market).

Unfortunately, Ford was stuck with a large supply of the metal that it had purchased at high prices.

Questions for Discussion

1. What is profit? How does the price of palladium relate to the profits of automakers?
2. Define supply and demand. What factors have influenced the supply of, and demand for, palladium?
3. Did automakers respond to increases in the price of palladium in the way predicted by economic theory? Explain.
4. Could Ford managers have done anything to avoid being stuck with a large amount of palladium? Explain. ◆

Concluding Case 1-2

Megawatt Laundering and Other Bright Ideas

The final chapters haven't been written yet, but the Enron saga is already world famous. Enron is the largest U.S. company ever to fail (also managing to bring down its auditor, Arthur Andersen, in the process). Enron is no doubt destined to figure in dozens of case studies on such themes as fraudulent financial practices, corrupt corporate strategy, and lawless leadership. The Enron story also throws light on some of the basics of the capitalistic free-enterprise system—namely, supply, demand, and freedom of choice. As we will see, Enron managers exploited the relationships between supply and demand to an almost unprecedented degree in their quest for riches beyond legitimate profit.

The Enron story opens in California. Like most states, California had long regulated public utility companies. A state agency dictated how much energy was produced and the prices at which it was sold. In the process, the profits of utility companies were indirectly controlled as well. Regulation also meant that supply and demand were closely aligned. Utilities produced just as much energy as customers needed. After all, there was no reason to produce more than they could sell, and the state wouldn't let them produce any less. State rules also required each customer to buy energy from a single local provider authorized to conduct business in a specified geographic area.

But in the late 1990s, California adopted a new hands-off policy regarding supply and demand in the utilities business. This shift in thinking resulted from a massive lobbying effort by major utilities interests, as representatives from Enron and other big energy companies persuaded the state to loosen its grip on the production and delivery of electricity. They argued that increased competition among producers and suppliers would make them deliver energy more efficiently while allowing consumers to choose their own providers.

Under the new system, responsibility for matching supply and demand fell to an Independent System Operator (ISO). This intermediary agent (or wholesaler) bought electricity from unregulated providers such as Enron, Dynegy, and Calpine and then sold it to local energy retailers such as Pacific Gas & Electric. The ISO paid providers to sell excess electricity out of state if supplies grew too large. Consumers, meanwhile, could choose to buy electricity from different retailers, making decisions based on price, service, and so forth.

The integrity of the system required the big companies involved to operate with a sense of social responsibility and fair play. Says David Freeman, top energy adviser to California governor Gray Davis, "It never occurred to us in our innocence that something so vital to society would be treated like a casino. We thought that somehow the [invisible] hand of Adam Smith would be benign."

Another flaw in the system was the fact that the state hadn't really created a free market for electricity. It had merely laid down a new and more bewildering array of rules and regulations. In some cases, regulations actually masked incentives for companies to misuse the system. With or without such incentives, however, Enron—and other energy providers—seized every opportunity they could to exploit the system by ducking through highly profitable loopholes.

Two of Enron's most notorious plans were code-named Death Star and Ricochet. With Death Star, Enron took advantage of the payouts through which the state managed its power grid. Essentially, California paid as much as $750 per megawatt hour to persuade providers not to ship power on overburdened power lines, especially those running north to south. To create the illusion of congestion on these lines, Enron began overbooking shipments and scheduling power transmissions that it had no intention of making. In each case, it then collected money from the state for changing plans that it never meant to carry out.

Ricochet was a scheme known as "megawatt laundering." To protect consumers from price gouging by unregulated suppliers, California had set price caps for electrical power. Those caps, however, applied only to electricity that was bought and transmitted within the state. Enron began buying electricity in California, which it then transmitted across state lines over a regional power grid. It then turned around and transmitted the same electricity back to California. Naturally, it looked as if it were coming from out of state. Because California price caps didn't apply, Enron was free to sell the rerouted power at much higher prices.

The energy situation in California became dire in late 2000. Weakened by complicated market patterns and the schemes of Enron and other energy providers, the state's ISO could no longer monitor everything, and control of the process was essentially abandoned. An early cold spell in Oregon and Washington forced those states to keep all their surplus energy, thus reducing the supply of power available for sale to California. Meanwhile, Enron and other suppliers had managed to manufacture their own power shortage in California by sending much of their electricity to other markets with higher prices. Blackouts became more common because the electricity supply could not meet consumer demand.

In response, California lifted its price caps, raising the price of a megawatt hour from $43.80 at the beginning of 2000 to $292.10 at the beginning of 2001. Although the supply of power increased immediately, consumer electric bills shot up by 67 percent, causing a statewide uproar. Price caps were reinstated in June 2001, but only as a temporary measure. Shortly thereafter, Enron began to collapse like a house of cards, and California seems to have been spared future shenanigans. Critics of current measures, however, worry that if price caps are permanently lifted, other companies can step in and do the same sort of things that Enron did.

Adam Smith, who wrote *The Wealth of Nations* in 1776, argued that a society's interests are best served by allowing individuals to pursue their own interests without governmental regulation. Although Smith lived in simpler times, it's amazing how well his theories of free enterprise hold up today. But in our complex business world, it is also clear that in the process of amassing profits, businesses which focus exclusively on profits can do a great deal of harm. Enron is today's standard for abuse of the free-enterprise system, but other examples will no doubt emerge in years to come. On the other hand, we shouldn't forget that there are literally thousands of businesses that routinely rely on supply and demand and freedom of choice while applying ethical and socially responsible principles, appropriate corporate strategies, and effective leadership in their pursuit of legitimate goals.

Questions for Discussion

1. What were the basic factors of production used by Enron?
2. Describe the concepts of input and output markets as they apply to Enron's operations.
3. Explain how the concepts of demand and supply affected both Enron's successes and failures.
4. Does the Enron case increase or decrease your confidence in a capitalistic system based on private enterprise?
5. What degree of competition exists in a regulated utility environment? What kind of competition did California attempt to create? ◆

CHAPTER 2

Understanding the Environments of Business

After reading this chapter, you should be able to:

1. Explain the concepts of *organizational boundaries* and *multiple organizational environments*.
2. Explain the importance of the *economic environment* to business and identify the factors used to evaluate the performance of an economic system.
3. Discuss the current economic picture in Canada and summarize expert predictions about its future.
4. Describe the *technological environment* and its role in business.
5. Describe the *political-legal environment* and its role in business.
6. Describe the *socio-cultural environment* and its role in business.
7. Identify emerging challenges and opportunities in the *business environment*.

Upheaval in the Airline Industry

Pity the poor commercial airline business. During the last few years, it has been hit with one problem after another. Four specific problems have recently interacted to cause major difficulties: (1) intense competition from low-cost, new start-up airlines, (2) fallout from the 9/11 terrorist attacks, (3) declining demand for air travel because of fears about SARS, and (4) declining demand for air travel as a result of the war in Iraq.

Competition from No-Frills Airlines

In both Canada and the United States, the airlines that used to dominate the industry (United, American, and Air Canada) are in big trouble because of competition from newly started, no-frills airlines like JetBlue, WestJet, and Jetsgo. These start-ups use a completely different business model than their larger and older counterparts. They charge extremely low air fares, fly mostly short-haul trips to selected cities, achieve faster turnaround time between flights, and have a much lower cost structure than their bigger counterparts. These no-frills airlines have become so successful that they may just drive some of the big airlines out of business. The big airlines are trying to compete, but their higher cost structures make that difficult. It appears that the big companies have no alternative but to drastically change the way they do business. This will cause wrenching changes at the big airlines as they try to avoid bankruptcy.

In 2003, something occurred that would have seemed unthinkable just a few years ago—a judge in the Ontario Superior Court declared Air Canada insolvent and gave it protection from its creditors. Air Canada was being harassed on all sides. Labour unions, for example, demanded that their job security be protected. The Canadian Union of Public Employees complained that they were given an ultimatum to accept wage cuts and other concessions, and that Air Canada had basically "put a gun to their head." NAV CANADA demanded that Air Canada pay about $4 million per week for airport services it receives. NAV CANADA said that the money from Air Canada—its biggest customer—was critical to its ability to continue providing navigation services at Canadian airports. Other creditors also wanted to make sure they didn't lose out.

Fallout from the 9/11 Terrorist Attacks

Although the attacks on the World Trade Center occurred in 2001, there has been a lingering impact on the commercial airline business. The vivid images that were continuously repeated on television screens caused a deep-seated concern about the safety of air travel, which, in turn, caused demand for airline seats to drop. Demand has still not returned to pre-9/11 levels. Many businesses have cut their travel budgets, partly as a result of the terrorist attacks, and partly because of a desire to cut their own costs in order to cope with intense competition in their own industries.

The SARS Outbreak

In 2003, a new strain of pneumonia was identified. Severe Acute Respiratory Syndrome (SARS) was first seen in Asia, but a cluster of cases also appeared in Toronto. The SARS outbreak caused major problems for the airlines because people were fearful that they were more likely to contract the disease in the confined air of commercial airlines. As a result, demand for seats—particularly on flights to Asia—dropped dramatically. Since airlines make higher profit margins on international flights, this was particularly bad for the airlines. The epidemic also caused economic growth to stall in Hong Kong, China, and other Asian countries. That, in turn, reduced the demand for air travel even further. The World Health Organization recommended that people not travel to Hong Kong or China unless it was absolutely necessary. A recommendation like this made by such a prominent organization further depressed demand for air travel.

The Toronto outbreak was serious enough that it led to predictions of reduced economic growth for Canada. Tourists avoided Toronto, and this caused significant losses for hotels, restaurants, and other businesses. The perception developed that Canada was not a safe place to visit, and businesses all across Canada were affected. For example, the owner of Anne's Ocean View Haven in Stratford, PEI, said that her business was down 80 percent. In Toronto, Cullingford Coaches' fleet of 17 buses was idle because the tourists the company usually shuttles around simply weren't coming. And in Halifax, a Norwegian cruise ship that had reserved 12 buses to take passengers to Peggy's Cove found that it only needed 7 because passengers were concerned about SARS. All of this negative publicity further reduced the demand for airline seats. The SARS outbreak did create opportunities for some businesses, however. Manufacturers of face masks, for example, experienced skyrocketing demand, and retailers had difficulty keeping the masks in stock. 3M Canada's corporate communication manager said that the company has been besieged by phone calls asking for masks.

The War in Iraq

Some airline industry observers predicted that the war in Iraq would reduce the demand for international air travel, and that it would take six months to a year for demand to return to pre-war levels. The International Air Transport Association predicted that passenger numbers would drop by 15 to 20 percent because of the war. The war may also hasten the changes that are occurring in the airline industry. Joseph D'Cruz, a professor at the University of Toronto, said that war would speed the decline of the major airlines that use the now questionable hub-and-spoke system to organize their flights. More flexible operations—like those used by Southwest Airlines and WestJet—are going to be required in the future for airlines to be successful. ◆

ORGANIZATIONAL BOUNDARIES AND ENVIRONMENTS

The opening case clearly shows how the external environment of Air Canada has affected its operations. Air Canada is not unique; all businesses, regardless of their size, location, or mission, operate within a larger external environment. This **external environment** consists of everything outside an organization's boundaries that might affect it. The external environment plays a major role in determining the success or failure of any organization. Managers must therefore have a complete and accurate understanding of the environment facing their company, and then strive to operate and compete within it. While no single firm can control the environment, managers should not simply react to changes; they should also be proactive and at least try to influence their environment.

external environment
Everything outside an organization's boundaries that might affect it.

To better explain the environment of business, we begin by discussing *organizational boundaries*, and then we introduce the concept of *multiple organizational environments*.

Organizational Boundaries

An **organizational boundary** separates the organization from its environment. Boundaries were once relatively easy to identify, but they are becoming increasingly complicated and hard to pin down. Consider the simple case of a small neighbourhood grocery that includes a retail customer area, a storage room, and an owner/manager's office. In many ways, the store's boundary coincides with its physical structure. When you walk through the door, you're crossing the boundary into the business, and when you go back onto the sidewalk, you cross the boundary back into the environment.

organizational boundary
That which separates the organization from its environment.

But even this simple example isn't as simple as it seems. During the course of the business day, distributors of soft drinks, beer, snack foods, ice, and bread products may enter the store, inventory the products that they distribute, and automatically refill coolers and shelves just as if they were employees. Although these distributors are normally considered part of the environment rather than the organization, during the time that they're inside the store, they are essentially part of the business. Assuming that they're store employees, customers may ask them questions as they restock shelves. The bread distributor may even offer someone a fresh loaf instead of the one that he or she has taken from the shelf.

1. Explain the concepts of *organizational boundaries* and *multiple organizational environments.*

Now consider the case of a large domestic business (such as GM Canada) that is owned by an even larger international corporation (U.S.-based General Motors). The domestic business has a complex network of relationships with other businesses. GM Canada, for example, deals with companies that supply tires, glass, steel, and engines. But GM Canada also functions within the boundaries of its international parent, which has its own network of business relationships, some overlapping and some distinct from GM Canada's network.

We can also examine similar complexities from the customer's perspective. McDonald's, for example, has a contract with Coca-Cola, stipulating that it will sell only Coke soft-drink products. McDonald's also has partnerships with Wal-Mart and Disney that allow it to open stores inside those firms' facilities. So when you buy a Coca-Cola soft drink from a McDonald's restaurant located inside a Wal-Mart store or Disney theme park, you are essentially affecting, and being affected by, multiple businesses. As you can see, the boundaries of any specific business are becoming increasingly difficult to define and more complicated to manage.

McDonald's
www.mcdonalds.ca

Multiple Organizational Environments

Although we tend to speak of "the external environment" as if it were a single entity, organizations actually have multiple environments. Some of them are relatively general. Prevailing economic conditions, for instance, will affect the performance of almost every business. But other dimensions are much more precise. Our neighbourhood grocery will be influenced not only by an increase in unemployment in the area, but also by the pricing and other marketing policies of its nearest competitor.

Figure 2.1 shows the major dimensions and elements of the external environment as it affects most businesses. As you can see, these include economic conditions, technology, political-legal considerations, social issues, the global environment, issues of ethical and social responsibility, the business environment itself, and numerous other emerging challenges and opportunities. Because this book provides detailed coverage of global and ethical issues in Chapters 4 and 5, respectively, we will introduce them here only as they relate directly to the other areas in this chapter.

THE ECONOMIC ENVIRONMENT

The **economic environment** refers to the conditions of the economic system in which an organization operates.[1] For example, McDonald's Canadian operations are (as of this writing) functioning in an economic environment characterized by moderate growth, moderate unemployment, and low inflation. Moderate unemployment means that most people can afford to eat out, but it also means that McDonald's must pay higher wages

economic environment
Conditions of the economic system in which an organization operates.

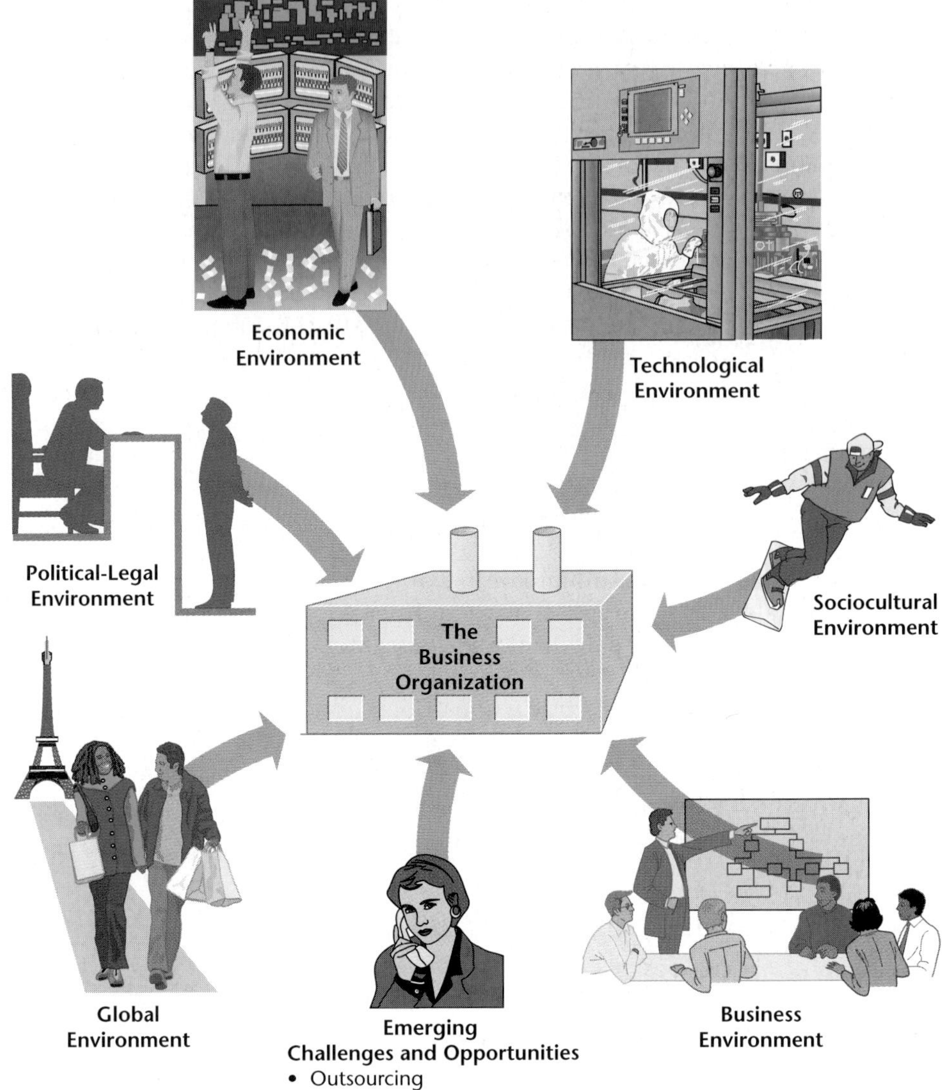

Figure 2.1
Dimensions of the external environment.

2. Explain the importance of the *economic environment* to business and identify the factors used to evaluate the performance of an economic system.

to attract employees. Low inflation means that McDonald's pays relatively constant prices for its supplies, but it also means that McDonald's can't really increase the prices it charges consumers.

Given the importance of the economic environment, we will closely examine the three key goals of the Canadian economic system: *economic growth, economic stability*, and *full employment*. We begin by focusing on the tools we use to measure economic growth, including *aggregate output, standard of living, gross domestic product*, and *productivity*. We then discuss the main threats to economic stability—namely, *inflation* and *unemployment*. We conclude this section by discussing government attempts to manage the Canadian economy in the interest of meeting national economic goals.

Economic Growth

At one time, about half the population of Canada was involved in producing food. Today, less than 2.5 percent of the population works in agriculture. Agricultural efficiency has improved because we devised better ways of producing products and invented better technology for getting the job done. We can therefore say that agricultural production has grown because we have been able to increase total output in the agricultural sector.

Aggregate Output and the Standard of Living

We can apply the same concepts to a nation's economic system, but the computations are much more complex. A fundamental question, then, is how we know whether or not an economic system is growing. Experts call the pattern of short-term ups and downs in an economy the **business cycle.** It has four recognizable phases: peak, recession, trough, and recovery (see Figure 2.2). Periods of expansion and contraction can vary from several months to several years. During the latter half of the 1990s, the Canadian economy was continuously expanding, leading some people to believe that the business cycle was a thing of the past. This belief was particularly evident among people who invested in high-tech stocks. They learned a hard lesson when tech stocks crashed in 2000.

business cycle
Pattern of short-term ups and downs (expansions and contractions) in an economy.

The main measure of growth in the business cycle is **aggregate output**: the total quantity of goods and services produced by an economic system during a given period.[2] To put it simply, an increase in aggregate output is growth (or economic growth).[3] When output grows more quickly than the population, two things usually follow: Output per capita—the quantity of goods and services per person—goes up and the system provides relatively more of the goods and services that people want.[4] And when these two things occur, people living in an economic system benefit from a higher **standard of living**, which refers to the total quantity and quality of goods and services that they can purchase with the currency used in their economic system.

aggregate output
Total quantity of goods and services produced by an economic system during a given period.

standard of living
Total quantity and quality of goods and services that a country's citizens can purchase with the currency used in their economic system.

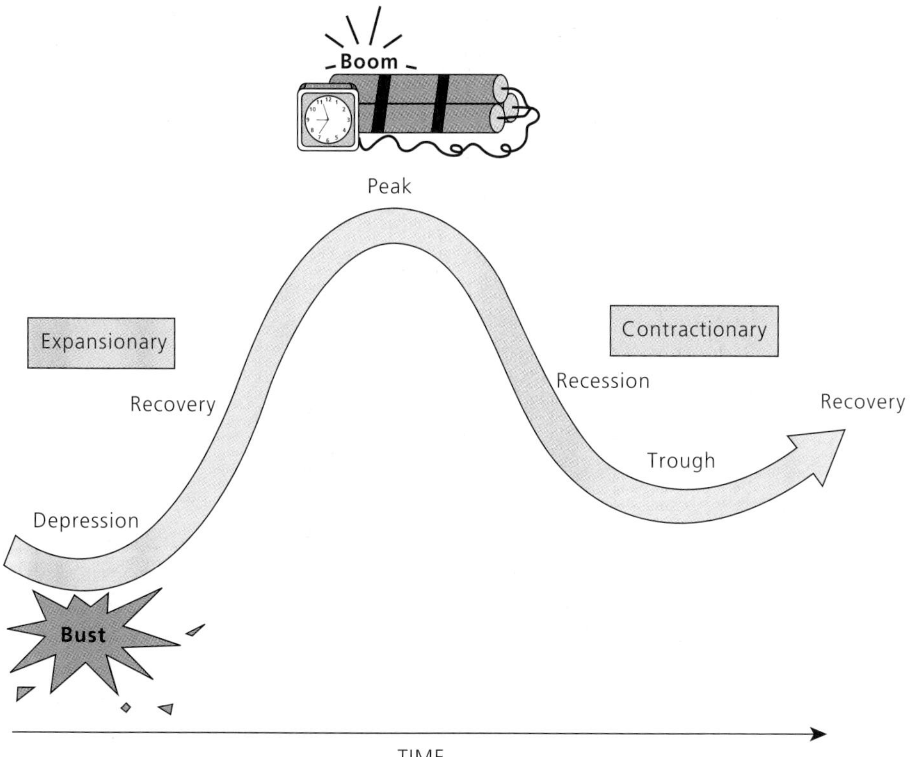

Figure 2.2
The business cycle.

Among other things, then, growth makes possible higher standards of living. Thus, to know how much your standard of living is improving, you need to know how much your nation's economic system is growing.

Gross Domestic Product

gross domestic product (GDP)
Total value of all goods and services produced within a given period by a national economy through domestic factors of production.

gross national product (GNP)
Total value of all goods and services produced by a national economy within a given period regardless of where the factors of production are located.

The term **gross domestic product (GDP)** refers to the total value of all goods and services produced within a given period by a national economy through domestic factors of production. If GDP is going up, the nation is experiencing economic growth. Canada's GDP in 2002 was approximately $1 trillion.[5]

Sometimes, economists also use the term **gross national product (GNP)**, which refers to the total value of all goods and services produced by a national economy within a given period regardless of where the factors of production are located. Thus, the profits earned by a Canadian company abroad are included in GNP, but not in GDP. Conversely, profits earned by foreign firms in Canada are included in GDP. Consider the example of a Canadian-owned manufacturing plant in Brazil. The profits earned by the factory are included in Canadian GNP—but not in GDP—because its output is not produced domestically (that is, in Canada). Conversely, those profits are included in Brazil's GDP—but not GNP—because they are produced domestically (that is, in Brazil). Calculations like these quickly become complex because of different factors of production. The labour, for example, will be mostly Brazilian but the capital mostly Canadian. Thus, wages paid to Brazilian workers are part of Brazil's GNP even though profits are not.

GDP and GNP are useful measures of economic growth because they allow us to track an economy's performance over time. An organization called Redefining Progress has proposed a more realistic measure to assess economic activity—the Genuine Progress Indicator (GPI). GPI treats activities that harm the environment or our quality of life as costs and gives them negative values. For example, the Exxon Valdez oil spill in 1986 increased GDP because the activities required to clean up the mess were included in measurements of economic growth. But the oil spill was not a good thing. The new GPI measure shows that while GDP has been increasing for many years, GPI has been falling since the 1970s.[6]

Real Growth Rates. GDP and GNP usually differ slightly, but GDP is the preferred method of calculating national income and output. The *real growth rate of GDP*—the growth rate of GDP *adjusted for inflation and changes in the value of the country's currency*—is what counts. Remember that *growth depends on output increasing at a faster rate than population*. If the growth rate of GDP exceeds the rate of population growth, then our standard of living should be improving.

GDP per Capita. *GDP per capita* means GDP per person. We get this figure by dividing total GDP by the total population of a country. As a measure of economic well-being of the average person, GDP per capita is a better measure than GDP.

Real GDP. "Real GDP" means that GDP has been adjusted. To understand why adjustments are necessary, assume that pizza is the only product in an economy. Assume that in 2001, a pizza cost $10, and in 2002 it cost $11. In both years, exactly 1000 pizzas were produced. In 2001, the GDP was $10 000 ($10 × 1000); in 2002, the GDP was $11 000 ($11 × 1000). Has the economy grown? No. Since 1000 pizzas were produced in both years, aggregate output remained the same. The point is that we should not be misled into believing that an economy is doing better than it is. If it is not adjusted, GDP for 2002 is **nominal GDP**, that is, GDP measured in current dollars or with all components valued at current prices.[7]

nominal GDP
GDP measured in current dollars or with all components valued at current prices.

Purchasing Power Parity. In our example, current prices would be 2002 prices. On the other hand, we calculate **real GDP** when we calculate GDP to account for *changes in currency values and price changes*. When we make this adjustment, we account for both GDP and **purchasing power parity**—the principle that exchange rates are set so that the prices of similar products in different countries are about the same. Purchasing power parity gives us a much better idea of *what people can actually buy with the financial resources allocated to them by their respective economic systems*. In other words, it gives us a better sense of standards of living across the globe.

real GDP
GDP calculated to account for changes in currency values and price changes.

purchasing power parity
Principle that exchange rates are set so that the prices of similar products in different countries are about the same.

Productivity

A major factor in the growth of an economic system is **productivity**, which is a measure of economic growth that compares how much a system produces with the resources needed to produce it. Let's say, for instance, that it takes 1 Canadian worker and 1 Canadian dollar to make 10 soccer balls in an 8-hour workday. Let's also say that it takes 1.2 Saudi workers and the equivalent of $1.2 (in riyals, the currency of Saudi Arabia) to make 10 soccer balls in the same 8-hour workday. We can say, then, that the Canadian soccer-ball industry is more *productive* than the Saudi soccer-ball industry. The two factors of production in this extremely simple case are labour and capital.

productivity
Measure of economic growth that compares how much a system produces with the resources needed to produce it.

Now let's look at productivity from a different perspective. If more products are being produced with fewer factors of production, what happens to the prices of these products? They go down. As a consumer, therefore, you would need less of your currency to purchase the same quantity of these products. In short, your standard of living—at least with regard to these products—has improved. If your entire economic system increases its productivity, then your overall standard of living improves. In fact, *standard of living improves only through increases in productivity*.[8] Real growth in GDP reflects growth in productivity.

There are several factors that can help or hinder the growth of an economic system, but we'll focus on just two of them: *balance of trade* and the *national debt*.

Balance of Trade. The **balance of trade** is the economic value of all the products that a country *exports* minus the economic value of its *imported* products. The principle here is quite simple:

balance of trade
The total of a country's exports (sales to other countries) minus its imports (purchases from other countries).

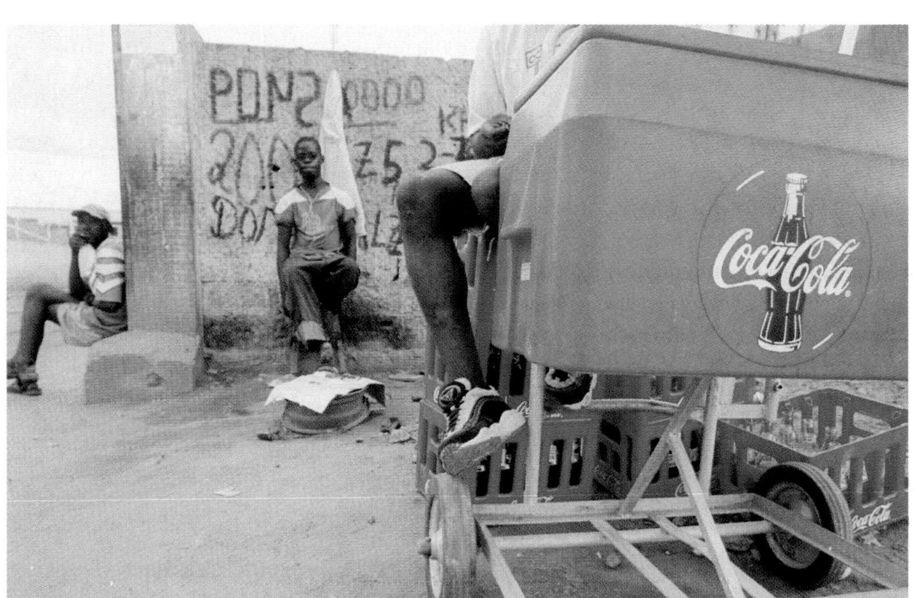

The GDP of Angola is $11.6 billion. Adjusted to calculate purchasing power parity, GDP per capita is U.S.$1000. Angolans can buy a 12-ounce bottle of Coke for 8 new kwanza (the country's currency), or about 40 cents. Thus, although the country is extremely poor, Coke is not prohibitively expensive. Working from about 8 a.m. to 7 p.m., street vendors like this one in the capital city of Luanda can sell five cases and take home $8 per day. If he works six days a week, he makes more than enough to pay the rent.

- A *positive* balance of trade results when a country exports (sells to other countries) more than it imports (buys from other countries). A positive balance of trade helps economic growth.
- A *negative* balance of trade results when a country imports more than it exports. A negative balance of trade inhibits economic growth.

A negative balance of trade is commonly called a *trade deficit*. Canada usually has a positive balance of trade. It is therefore a *creditor nation* rather than a *debtor nation*. In 2002, for example, Canada received $54 billion more for exports than it spent on imports.[9] By contrast, the United States usually has a negative balance of trade. In 2001, for example, it spent $360 billion more on imports than it received for exports. It is therefore a debtor nation rather than a creditor nation.

How does a trade deficit affect economic growth? The deficit exists because the amount of money spent on foreign products has not been paid in full. In effect, therefore, it is borrowed money, and borrowed money costs more money in the form of interest. The money that flows out of the country to pay off the deficit can't be used to invest in productive enterprises, either at home or overseas.

National Debt. A country's national debt is the amount of money that the government owes its creditors. Like a business, the government takes in revenues (primarily in the form of taxes) and has expenses (military spending, social programs, and so forth). For many years, the government of Canada incurred annual **budget deficits**; that is, the government spent more money each year than it took in. These accumulated annual deficits have created a huge **national debt**—the amount of money that Canada owes its creditors.

budget deficit
The result of the government spending more in one year than it takes in during that year.

national debt
The total amount of money that Canada owes its creditors.

Until the mid-1990s, annual budget deficits and the total national debt were increasing at an alarming rate. From Confederation (1867) to 1981, the *total* accumulated debt was only $85.7 billion, but in the period 1981–94, *annual deficits* were in the $20 to $40 billion range. Since 1994, however, things have changed dramatically. Annual deficits declined rapidly between 1994 and 1996, and in 1997 the first budget surplus in many years occurred. Canada is the only highly industrialized country in the world that continues to have a budget surplus. In 2002, government revenues were $199 billion and expenditures were $183.5 billion.[10]

How does the national debt affect economic growth? While taxes are the most obvious way the government raises money, it also sells *bonds*—securities through which it promises to pay buyers certain amounts of money by specified future dates. The government sells bonds to individuals, households, banks, insurance companies, industrial corporations, nonprofit organizations, and government agencies, both at home and overseas.[11] These bonds are attractive investments because they are extremely safe: The Canadian government is not going to *default* on them (that is, fail to make payments when due). Even so, they must also offer a decent return on the buyer's investment, and they do this by paying interest at a competitive rate. By selling bonds, therefore, the Canadian government competes with every other potential borrower—individuals, households, businesses, and other organizations—for the available supply of loanable money. The more money the government borrows, the less money is available for the private borrowing and investment that increases productivity.

Economic Stability

Combining the material from Chapter 1 with the preceding discussion, we have now learned a great deal about economic systems and the ways in which they allocate resources among their citizens. We know that households, for example, receive capital in return for labour. We know that when households enter consumer markets to purchase goods and services, their decisions (and those of the firms trying to sell them goods and services) are influenced by the laws of demand and supply. We know that the laws of demand and supply result in equilibrium prices when the quantity of goods demanded and the quantity of goods supplied are equal. We know that households enjoy higher standards of living when there is balanced growth in the quantity of goods demanded and the quantity of goods supplied. We know that we can measure growth and productivity in terms of gross domestic product and standard of living in terms of the purchasing power parity of a system's currency: Living standards are stable when purchasing power parity remains stable.[12]

We may thus conclude that a chief goal of an economic system is **stability**: a condition in which the amount of money available in an economic system and the quantity of goods and services produced in it are growing at about the same rate. Now we can focus on certain factors that threaten stability—namely, *inflation, deflation*, and *unemployment*.

stability

Condition in an economic system in which the amount of money available and the quantity of goods and services produced are growing at about the same rate.

Inflation

Inflation occurs when there are widespread price increases throughout an economic system. How does it threaten stability? Inflation occurs when the amount of money injected into an economy outstrips the increase in actual output. When this happens, people will have more money to spend, but there will still be the same quantity of products available for them to buy. As they compete with one another to buy available products, prices go up. Before long, high prices will erase the increase in the amount of money injected into the economy. Purchasing power, therefore, declines.

inflation

Occurrence of widespread price increases throughout an economic system.

Obviously, then, inflation can also hurt you as a consumer because your primary concern when deciding whether to purchase a product is often price. In other words, you will probably decide to make a purchase if the value of the product justifies the price that you'll have to pay. Now look at Table 2.1, which reduces a hypothetical purchase decision to three bare essentials:

1. Your household income over a three-year period
2. The price of a hamburger over a three-year period
3. The rates of increase for both over a three-year period

In which year did the cost of a hamburger go up? At first glance, you might say in both YR2 and YR3 (to $4 in YR2 and to $7.50 in YR3). In YR2, your income kept pace: Although a hamburger cost twice as much, you had twice as much money to spend. In effect, the price to you was actually the same. In YR3, however, your income increased by 250 percent while the price of a hamburger increased by 275 percent. In YR3, therefore, you got hit by inflation (how hard, of course, depends on your fondness for hamburgers). This ratio—the comparison of your increased income to the increased price of a hamburger—is all that counts if you want to consider inflation when you're making a buying decision. Inflation, therefore, can be harmful to you as a consumer because *inflation decreases the purchasing power of your money*.

Measuring Inflation: The CPI. Remember that inflation means widespread price increases throughout an economic system. It stands to reason, therefore, that we can measure inflation by measuring price increases. To do this, we can turn to such price indexes as the **consumer price index (CPI)**, which measures changes in the cost of a "basket" of goods and serv-

consumer price index (CPI)

Measure of the prices of typical products purchased by consumers living in urban areas.

Table 2.1 When Did the Cost of a Hamburger Go Up?

YR1 Income	YR2 Income	YR2 % Increase Over YR1 Base	YR3 Income	YR3 % Increase Over YR1 Base
$5,000	$10,000	100	$17,500	250
YR1 Hamburger Price	**YR2 Hamburger Price**	**YR2 % Increase Over YR1 Base**	**YR3 Hamburger Price**	**YR3 % Increase Over YR1 Base**
$2	$4	100	$7.50	275

ices that a typical family buys. Figure 2.3 shows how inflation has varied over the last 20 years in Canada.

Deflation

During the last several decades, the Canadian government has been preoccupied with fighting inflation. When inflation gets too high, the Bank of Canada increases interest rates. This causes consumers to buy less, which "cools off" the economy. When **deflation** (generally falling prices) occurs, the Bank of Canada reduces interest rates in an attempt to increase consumer demand. Prices may fall because industrial productivity is increasing and cost savings can be passed on to consumers (this is good), or because consumers have high levels of debt and are therefore unwilling to buy very much (this is bad).

deflation
A period of generally falling prices.

Consumer Price Index (CPI)
www.bankofcanada.ca/en/cpi.htm

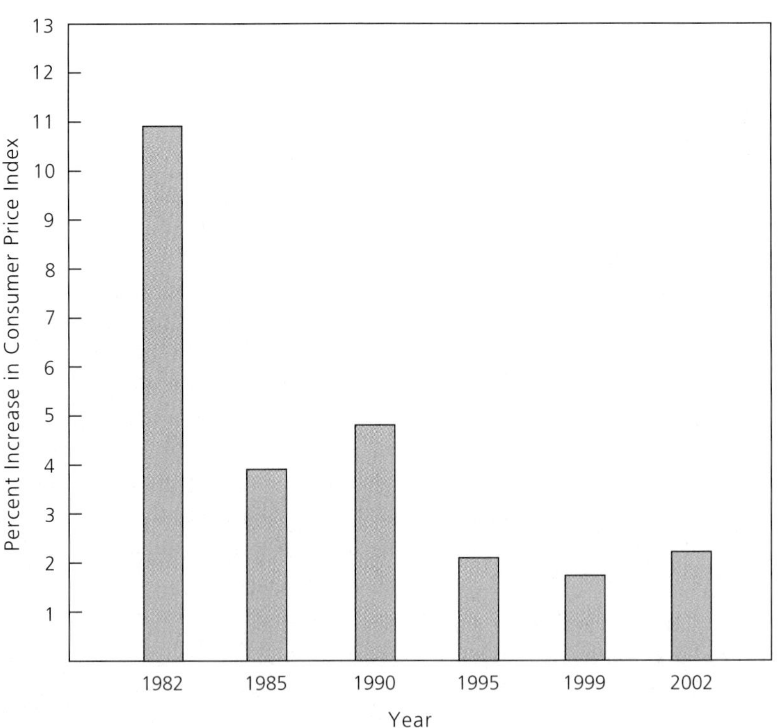

Figure 2.3
In the last few years the rate of price increases in Canada has dropped.

If deflation occurs at the same time that interest rates are very low, the Bank of Canada has very little room to lower interest rates further in an attempt to stimulate the economy. This is currently the situation in Japan, where prices have been falling for several years, even though interest rates are nearly zero. Deflationary tendencies are also developing in Germany.[13] That means that two of three largest economies in the world are experiencing deflation. Since interest rates in North America are so low at present, it is possible that deflation might become a threat to the economic stability of Canada.

Unemployment

Unemployment is the level of joblessness among people actively seeking work. When unemployment is low, there is a shortage of labour available for businesses. As these businesses compete with one another for the available supply of labour, they raise the wages that they are willing to pay. Then, because higher labour costs eat into profit margins, businesses raise the prices of their products. Thus, although consumers have more money to inject into the economy, this increase is soon erased by higher prices. Purchasing power declines.

unemployment
Level of joblessness among people actively seeking work in an economic system.

If wage rates get too high, businesses will respond by hiring fewer workers and unemployment will go up. Businesses could, of course, raise prices to counter increased labour costs, but if they charge higher prices, they won't be able to sell as much of their products. Because of reduced sales, they will cut back on hiring and, once again, unemployment will go up. What if the government tries to correct this situation by injecting more money into the economic system—say, by cutting taxes or spending more money? Prices in general may go up because of increased consumer demand. Again, purchasing power declines and, indeed, inflation may set in.[14]

Cyclical Unemployment. Unemployment is sometimes a symptom of a system-wide disorder in the economy. During a downturn in the business cycle, people in numerous sectors may lose their jobs at the same time. As a result, overall income and spending may drop. Feeling the pinch of reduced revenues, businesses may cut spending on the factors of production—including labour. Yet more people will be put out of work and unemployment will only increase further. Unemployment that results from this vicious cycle is called *cyclical unemployment*.[15]

In examining the relationship between unemployment and economic stability, we are reminded that as prices increase, consumer demand for goods and services goes down. We are also reminded that when demand for products goes down, producers cut back on hiring and, not surprisingly, eventually start producing less. Aggregate output then decreases. When we go through a period during which aggregate output declines, we have a **recession**. During a recession, producers need fewer employees—less labour—to produce products. Unemployment, therefore, goes up.

How do we know whether or not we're in a recession? We must start by measuring aggregate output. Recall that this is the function of real GDP, which we find by making necessary adjustments to the total value of all goods and services produced within a given period by a national economy through domestic factors of production. A **recession**, therefore, is more precisely defined as a period during which aggregate output, as measured by real GDP, declines (usually defined as two consecutive quarters). A prolonged and deep recession is a **depression**.[16]

recession
Period during which aggregate output, as measured by real GDP, declines.

depression
Particularly severe and long-lasting recession.

Full Employment

Full employment means that everyone who wants to work has an opportunity to do so. In reality, full employment is impossible. There will always be people looking for work. These people generally fall into one of four categories. Some people are out of work temporarily while looking for a new job, a situation known as *frictional unemployment*. A skilled engineer who has just quit her job but who will find a new job soon is in this category. Other people are out of work because of the seasonal nature of their jobs, a situation known as *seasonal unemployment*. Farm workers and construction workers, for example, may not work much in the winter. Sometimes people are out of work because of reduced economic activity, a situation known as *cyclical unemployment*. Finally, some people are unemployed because they lack the skills needed to perform available jobs, a situation known as *structural unemployment*. A steelworker laid off in a town that is looking for computer programmers falls into this category.

The Exercising Your Ethics box describes a typical dilemma that business firms face regarding the issue of unemployment.

Because of the many reasons for unemployment, the rate of unemployment has varied greatly over the years, as Figure 2.4 shows (see p. 52). And because full employment is essentially impossible, our real goal is to minimize unemployment. High unemployment wastes talent and is a drain on resources that must be allocated to unemployment-associated welfare programs. Higher welfare costs, in turn, result in higher taxes for everyone.

Managing the Canadian Economy

fiscal policies
Policies by means of which governments collect and spend revenues.

The government acts to manage the Canadian economic system through two sets of policies: fiscal and monetary. It manages the collection and spending of its revenues through **fiscal policies**. Tax increases can function as fiscal policies, not only to increase revenues but to manage the economy as well. When there is evidence that the growth rate of the economy is decreasing, tax cuts will normally stimulate renewed economic growth. When the government of Canada cuts taxes that people have to pay, government action is being taken to bring stability to the economic system.

Accountancy, dentistry, and medical technology may not have been the professions of choice during the dot-com boom years of the late 1990s, but they offered steady employment during the recession that followed.

EXERCISING YOUR ETHICS

Assessing the Ethics of Trade-Offs

The Purpose of the Assignment

Managers must often make choices among options that are presented by environmental circumstances. This exercise will help you better appreciate the nature and complexity of the kinds of trade-offs that often result.

The Situation

You are owner and manager of a medium-sized non-unionized manufacturing company located in a town of about 15 000 people. The nearest major city is about 200 kilometres away. With about 500 workers, you are one of the five largest employers in town. A regional recession has caused two of the other largest employers to close down (one went out of business and the other relocated to another area). A new foreign competitor has set up shop in the area, but local unemployment has still risen sharply. All in all, the regional economic climate and the new competitor are hurting your business. Your sales have dropped 20 percent this year, and you forecast another drop next year before things begin to turn around.

The Dilemma

You face two unpleasant choices.

Choice 1: You can tell your employees that you need them to take cuts in pay and benefits. You know that because of the local unemployment rate, you can easily replace anyone who refuses. Unfortunately, you may need your employees to take another cut next year if your forecasts hold true. At the same time, you do have reason to believe that when the economy rebounds (in about two years, according to your forecasts), you can begin restoring pay cuts. Here are the advantages of this choice: You can probably (1) preserve all 500 jobs, (2) maintain your own income, (3) restore pay cuts in the future, and (4) keep the business open indefinitely. And the disadvantages: Pay cuts will (1) pose economic hardships for your employees and (2) create hard feelings and undercut morale.

Choice 2: You can maintain the status quo as far as your employees are concerned, but in that case, you'll be facing two problems: (1) You'll have to cut your own salary. While you can certainly afford to live on less income, doing so would be a blow to your personal finances. (2) If economic conditions get worse and/or last longer than forecast, you may have to close down altogether. The firm has a cash surplus, but because you'll have to dip into these funds to maintain stable wages, they'll soon run out. The advantages of this option: You can (1) avoid economic hardship for your workers and (2) maintain good employee relations. The downside: You will reduce your own standard of living and may eventually cost everyone his or her job.

Questions for Discussion

1. What are the basic ethical issues in this situation?
2. Can you identify any other options?
3. Of the two options posed in the situation as presented, which would you choose? Why?

Monetary policies focus on controlling the size of the nation's money supply. Working primarily through the Bank of Canada (the nation's central bank), the government can influence the ability and willingness of banks throughout the country to lend money. It can also influence the supply of money by prompting interest rates to go up or down. The power of the Bank of Canada to make changes in the supply of money is the centrepiece of the Canadian government's monetary policy. The principle is fairly simple:

monetary policies
Policies by means of which the government controls the size of the nation's money supply.

- Higher interest rates make money more expensive to borrow and thereby reduce spending by both those who produce goods and services and by those who buy those goods and services. When the Bank of Canada restricts the money supply, we say that it is practising a *tight monetary policy*.
- Lower interest rates make money less expensive to borrow and thereby increase spending by both those who produce goods and services and by the consumers who buy those goods and services. When the Bank of

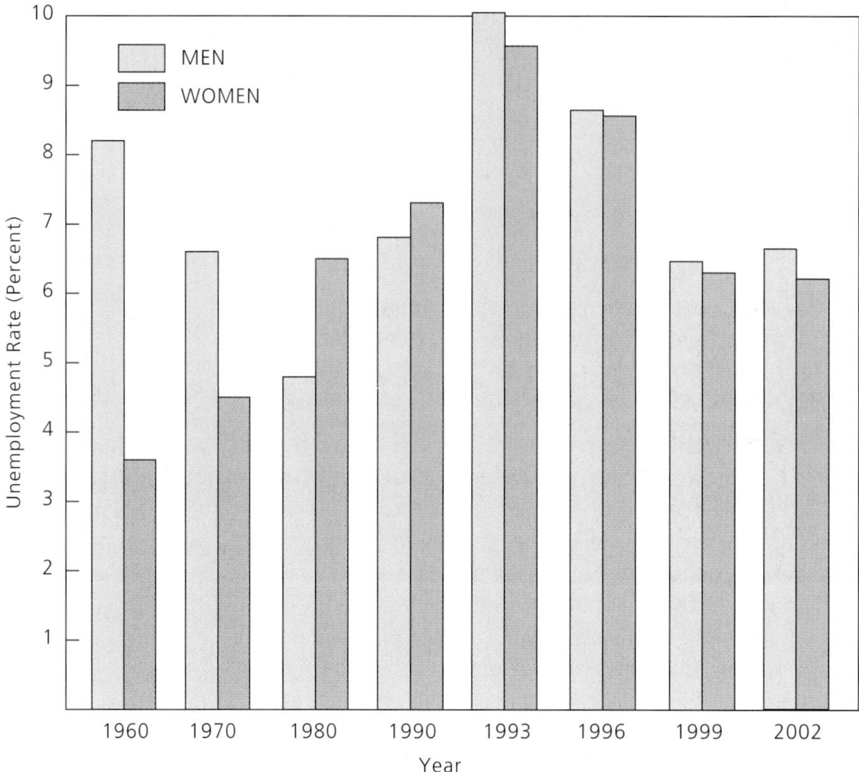

Figure 2.4
Historical unemployment rate.
During the period 1950–93, there was a steady upward trend in unemployment rates, but the rate began to decline again during the last half of the 1990s.

Canada loosens the money supply—and thus stimulates the economy—we say that it is practising an *easy monetary policy*. In both Canada and the United States, the interest rate was cut several times in late 2001 to help the economy recover from the terrorist attacks in the United States on September 11. But in Canada, we experienced a recovery during 2002, so the Bank of Canada had actually been raising interest rates to head off the possibility of inflation. By mid-2003, however, the Bank of Canada decided to hold interest rates steady to protect the economic recovery.

In short, the Bank of Canada can influence the aggregate market for products by influencing the supply of money. Taken together, fiscal policy and monetary policy make up **stabilization policy**: government economic policy whose goal is to smooth out fluctuations in output and unemployment and to stabilize prices.

stabilization policy
Government policy, embracing both fiscal and monetary policies, whose goal is to smooth out fluctuations in output and unemployment and to stabilize prices.

THE GLOBAL ECONOMY IN THE TWENTY-FIRST CENTURY

3. Discuss the current economic picture in Canada and summarize expert predictions about its future.

The decade of the 1990s was a sustained period of expansion and growth that increased business profits, boosted individual wealth, and fuelled optimism. In 2001 and 2002, however, economic growth slowed sharply. Business profits started to taper off, stocks declined in value, and optimism waned. But experts themselves disagreed as to whether the slowdown was temporary or represented a major shift in the Canadian (and world) economy that might last for years.[17]

Three Major Forces

What does the economic future hold? Most experts see three major forces driving the economy for at least the next decade:

1. The information revolution will continue to enhance productivity across all sectors of the economy, most notably in such information-dependent industries as finance, media, and wholesale and retail trade.[18]
2. New technological breakthroughs in areas such as biotechnology will create entirely new industries.
3. Increasing globalization will create much larger markets while also fostering tougher competition among global businesses; as a result, companies will need to focus even more on innovation and cost cutting.[19]

Figures 2.5 through 2.7 clearly illustrate the significance of these forces. Figure 2.5 highlights the increased use of the internet per 1000 people for the world and for North America, Western Europe, and the Asia Pacific region for 1995 and 2000, and provides an estimate for 2005. The trends are clear: More and more people are using the internet, and although North America still leads the way, Western Europe is catching up. The Asia Pacific region is growing rapidly as well.

Figure 2.6 amplifies these trends by isolating information-technology spending as a proportion of gross domestic product for numerous countries. The United States leads the way, but Sweden, Britain, and Canada are close behind.[20]

Finally, Figure 2.7 underscores the fact that world exports are growing. Exports grew rapidly from the late 1980s through 1997 but then flattened and subsequently declined for two years. This downward trend was primarily attributable to the currency crisis and resultant economic downturn in Asia. Between 1999 and 2000, however, exports again began increasing and are projected to continue to rise.[21] Taken together, then, these data clearly reinforce the significance of information, technology, and globalization as the economic forces to be reckoned with in the twenty-first century.

Projected Trends and Patterns

As a result of these forces, economists also predict certain trends and patterns in economic indicators and competitive dynamics for the rest of this decade. Projected trends and patterns include the following:

- Some experts foresee the current economic slowdown ending quickly, while others predict that the economy will remain stalled for several years.
- Inflationary surges are unlikely, but budget deficits are once again beginning to be a problem in most countries (but so far not in Canada).
- Countries that encourage free trade, innovation, and open financial systems will bounce back first and will prosper in the long term.
- The most successful businesses will be those that are able most effectively to master new technologies and keep abreast of their competitors.[22]

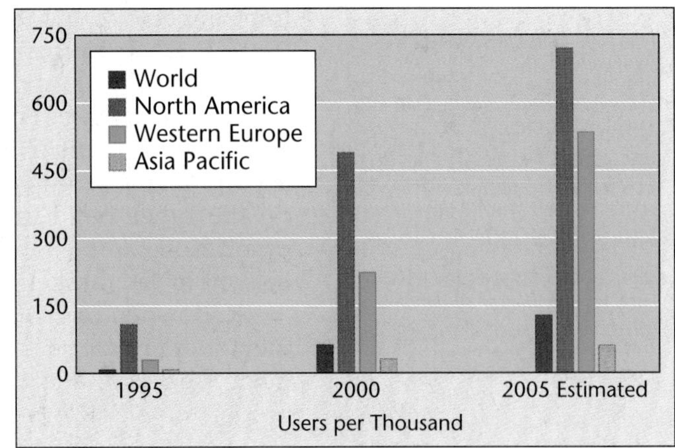

Figure 2.5
Internet users per 1000 people.

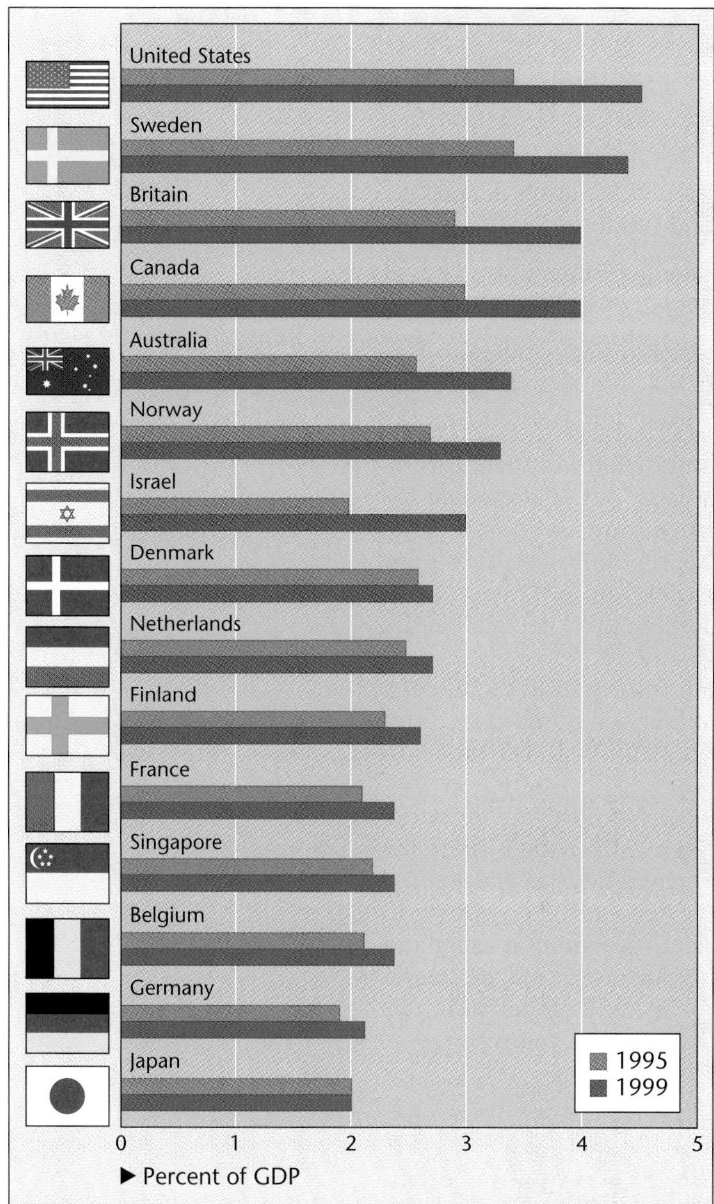

Figure 2.6
Information-technology spending

All things considered, there is cautious optimism about both the Canadian economy and the global economy. The solid economic foundation built in the 1990s should serve as a platform for new growth and expansion in the future. Businesses and entrepreneurs will continue to enjoy opportunities for growth and expansion, and managers who are astute enough to navigate economic currents will achieve considerable prosperity.

THE TECHNOLOGICAL ENVIRONMENT

Technology has a variety of meanings, but as applied to the environment of business, it generally includes all the ways firms create value for their constituents. Technology includes human knowledge, work methods, physical equipment, electronics and telecommunications, and various processing systems that are used to perform business activities. Although technology is applied within the organization, the forms and availability of that technology come from the general environment. Boeing, for example, uses computer-assisted manufacturing and design techniques developed by external vendors to simulate the four miles of hydraulic tubing that run through a 777 aircraft. The advantages include decreased warehouse needs, higher quality tube fittings, and overall lower costs.

Technological improvements and innovation in general are important contributors to the economic development of a country. The innovation process includes **research and development (R&D)**, which provides new ideas for products, services, and processes. (See Chapter 16 for a discussion of the importance of R&D in the marketing of products.) There are two types of R&D. **Basic (or pure) R&D** involves improving knowledge in an area without a primary focus on whether any discoveries that might occur are immediately marketable. For example, chemists in a laboratory might examine how certain chemical compounds behave. The knowledge gained from this activity might or might not result in a marketable product. **Applied R&D**, on the other hand, means focusing specifically on how a technological innovation can be put to use in the making of a product or service that can be sold in the marketplace.

technology
All the ways firms create value for their constituents.

research and development (R&D)
Those activities that are necessary to provide new products, services, and processes.

basic (or pure) R&D
Improving knowledge in an area without a primary focus on whether any discoveries that might occur are immediately marketable.

applied R&D
Focusing specifically on how a technological innovation can be put to use in the making of a product or service that can be sold in the marketplace.

R&D spending in Canada in 2002 totalled about $12 billion.[23] The Canadian private sector accounts for about 56 percent of R&D, the government 9 percent, and universities 33 percent.[24] In the private sector, a large proportion of R&D is carried out by just a few large firms, and just 0.4 percent of firms accounted for more than half the R&D performed.[25] A large proportion of GDP is carried out in just a few industries as well—communi-

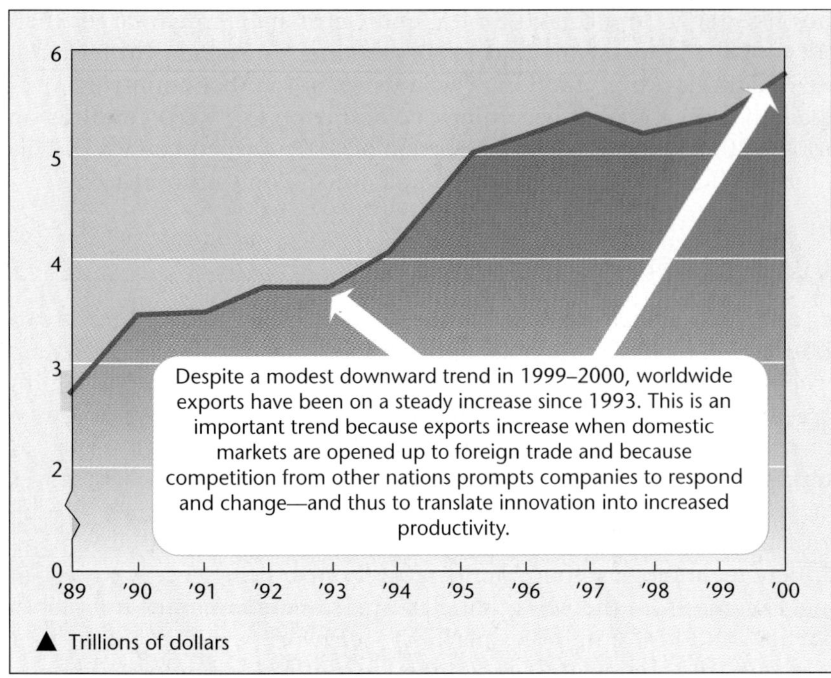

6
5
4
3
2
0
'89 '90 '91 '92 '93 '94 '95 '96 '97 '98 '99 '00
▲ Trillions of dollars
Despite a modest downward trend in 1999–2000, worldwide exports have been on a steady increase since 1993. This is an important trend because exports increase when domestic markets are opened up to foreign trade and because competition from other nations prompts companies to respond and change—and thus to translate innovation into increased productivity.

Figure 2.7
The export resurgence.

cations equipment, aerospace products, semiconductor and other electronic components, pharmaceuticals, computer system design, and wholesale trade.[26] Ontario accounted for 58 percent of all R&D activities in Canada.[27]

4. Describe the *technological environment* and its role in business.

As a proportion of GDP, Canada's level of R&D lags behind that of other countries (see Figure 2.8). When we take into account that the GDP of

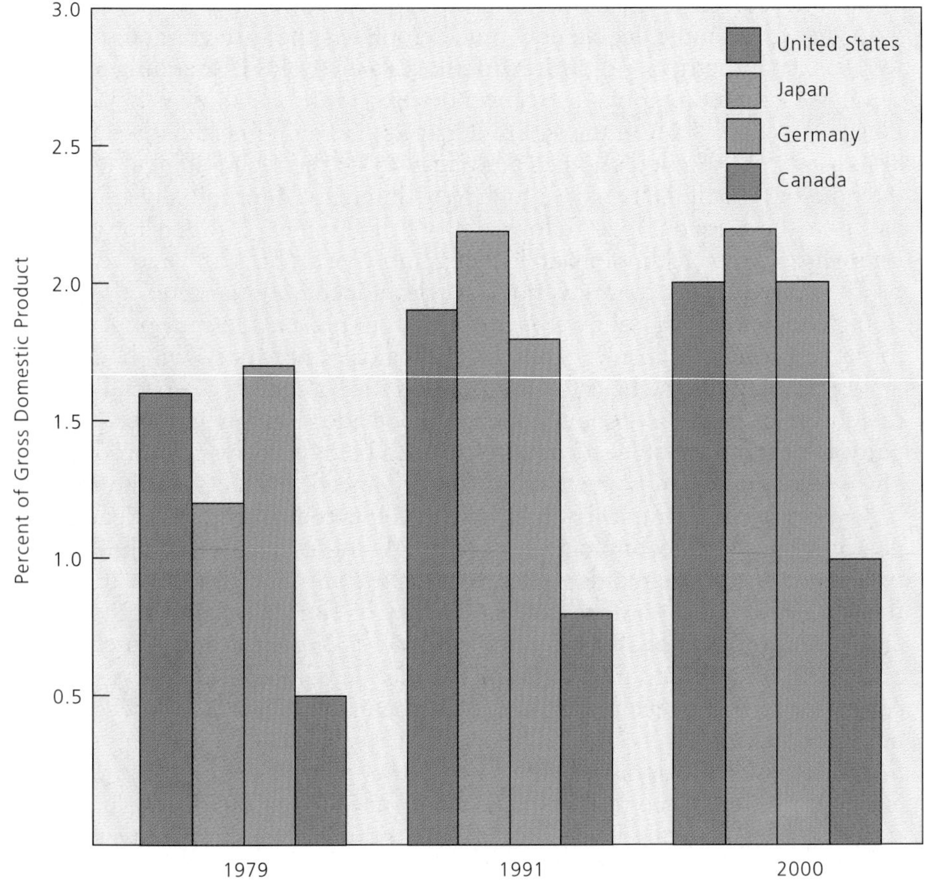

Figure 2.8
R&D expenditures as a proportion of GDP.

countries like Japan, the United States, and Germany is much larger than the GDP of Canada, it means that R&D spending in Canada (in terms of absolute dollars) is a tiny fraction of what is spent in other countries.

Canada has set a goal of becoming one of the top five R&D countries in the world by 2010 in terms of the proportion of GDP we spend on R&D. This goal will be difficult to achieve since Canada ranked only 15th in 1999.[28]

Product and Service Technologies

Product and service technologies are the technologies employed for creating products—both physical goods and services—for customers. Although many people associate technology with manufacturing, it is also a significant force in the service sector. Just as an automobile is built as it follows a predetermined pathway along an assembly line, a hamburger at McDonald's is cooked, assembled, and wrapped and bagged as it moves along a predefined path. The rapid advancement of the internet into all areas of business is also a reflection of the technological environment. Indeed, new technologies continue to revolutionize nearly every aspect of business, ranging from the ways that customers and companies interact to where, when, and how employees perform their work.

Companies must constantly be on the lookout for technological breakthroughs that might make their products or services obsolete and thereby threaten their survival. Many of these breakthroughs do not come from direct competitors or even from the industry the company is part of. Microsoft, for example, originally didn't pay much attention to internet technology because it was busy competing with companies like WordPerfect in the word processing and operating software market. When Netscape entered the market with a browser program that threatened to make operating systems unnecessary, Microsoft had to spend a lot of time and money developing its own Internet Explorer browser.[29]

R&D intensity

R&D spending as a percentage of a company's sales revenue.

Companies must decide how much emphasis they are going to place on R&D as a competitive tool. **R&D intensity** refers to R&D spending as a percentage of the company's sales revenue. Research has shown that companies with a high R&D intensity are better able to gain market share in global markets.[30] If a company has a strategy to be the technological leader in its industry, it will likely have a high R&D intensity. Alternatively, if its strategy is to be a technology follower, it will likely have a much lower R&D intensity. Being a technological leader is more risky, but can yield very large profits if technological innovations are developed and marketed effectively. Being a technological follower is less risky, but presents fewer opportunities for large profits because very few technological innovations will be evident.

Technology is the basis of competition for some firms, especially when the company's goal is to be the technology leader in their industry. A company, for example, might focus its efforts on being the low-cost producer or always having the most technologically advanced products on the market. But because of the rapid pace of new developments, keeping a leadership position based on technology is increasingly difficult. Another challenge is meeting constant demands to decrease *cycle time*—the time that it takes a firm to accomplish some recurring activity or function from beginning to end. **Technology transfer** refers to the process of getting a new technology out of the lab and into the marketplace where it can generate profits for the company. Efficient technology transfer means an increased likelihood of business success.

technology transfer

The process of getting a new technology out of the lab and into the marketplace.

Businesses are more competitive if they can systematically decrease cycle times. Many companies, therefore, now focus on decreasing cycle times in areas ranging from developing products to making deliveries and

collecting credit payments. Twenty years ago, it took a carmaker about five years from the decision to launch a new product until it was available in dealer showrooms. Now most companies can complete the cycle in less than two years. The speedier process allows them to respond more quickly to changing economic conditions, consumer preferences, and new competitive products while recouping their product-development costs more quickly.

Some firms compete directly on how quickly they can get things done for consumers. In the early days of personal computers, for instance, getting a made-to-order system took six to eight weeks. Today, firms like Dell can usually ship exactly what the customer wants in a matter of days.

Intel exemplifies the challenge and the risks of adopting a strategic dependence on technological leadership. In 1964, before co-founding Intel with Bob Noyce in 1968, Gordon Moore made a prediction about microprocessors (the processing components of microcomputers) that eventually became known as Moore's Law: He said that the amount of information stored on a given amount of silicon would double every 18 months. In effect, this rate would entail a twofold increase in processing power every 18 months—a seemingly impossible pace. Intel, however, has adopted Moore's Law as a performance requirement for each new generation of processor since 1970, up through the Pentium 4.

Intel spent $7.5 billion in 2001 for research and development, and is aggressively searching for ways to cram twice as many transistors into a space that already holds millions. Such a task will require a revolution in technology that, as yet, Intel hasn't found. Without a technological breakthrough, Moore's Law—and Intel's technological leadership position—may not be sustainable. The financial stakes, of course, are high. If Intel can't meet industry-wide goals, it faces threats from new competitors, such as Advanced Micro Devices (AMD), whose microprocessor market share recently grew from 13 percent to 18 percent in just one year.

Process Technologies

Process technologies are used to improve a firm's performance of internal operations (such as accounting, managing information flows, creating activity reports, and so forth). They also help create better relationships with external constituents, such as suppliers and customers. One recent process technology innovation that is worthy of special attention is **enterprise resource planning (ERP)**. ERP is a large-scale information system for organizing and managing a firm's processes across product lines, departments, and geographic locations. Company-wide processes—such as materials management, production planning, order management, and financial reporting—can all be managed by ERP. Figure 2.9 shows some of the areas in which ERP can be applied, including some of the common processes performed in each area.[31]

enterprise resource planning (ERP)
Large-scale information system for organizing and managing a firm's processes across product lines, departments, and geographic locations.

In developing the ERP system, the firm starts by identifying the processes that need critical attention, such as supplier relationships, materials flows, or customer order fulfillment. The resulting system would thus integrate the sales process with production planning and then both of these operations into the financial accounting system. Let's say that a customer in Rome orders a product to be manufactured in Ireland. The ERP-integrated seller can schedule the order shipment via air cargo to Rome, where it can be picked up by a truck at the airport and delivered to the customer's warehouse by a specified date. All of these activities are synchronized in one massive database.

The ERP also stores updated real-time information on activities, reports recent and upcoming transactions, and posts electronic notices that

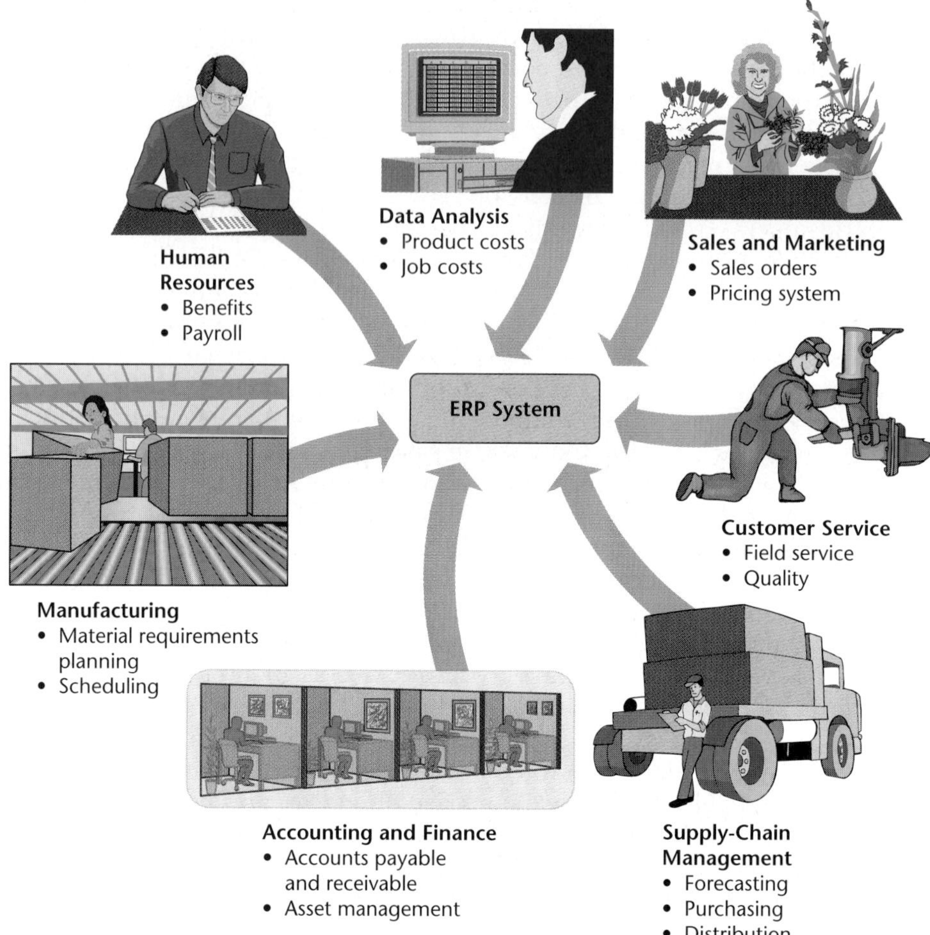

Figure 2.9
ERP applications.

certain action is required if certain schedules are to be met. It coordinates internal operations with activities by outside suppliers and notifies customers of current order status and upcoming deliveries and billings. It can integrate financial flows among the firm, its suppliers, customers, and banks and generate up-to-the-minute financial reports at a moment's notice (reduced from the traditional one-month time span).

THE POLITICAL-LEGAL ENVIRONMENT

political-legal environment
Conditions reflecting the relationship between business and government, usually in the form of government regulation.

5. Describe the *political-legal environment* and its role in business.

Royal Bank
www.royalbank.com

The **political-legal environment** reflects the relationship between business and government, usually in the form of government regulation of business. It is important for several reasons. First, the legal system defines in part what an organization can and can't do. Although Canada is a free market economy, it still has major regulation of business activity, as we saw in Chapter 1.

Pro- or anti-business sentiment can further influence business activity. During periods of pro-business sentiment, firms find it easier to compete and have fewer concerns about antitrust issues. On the other hand, during a period of anti-business sentiment, firms may find their competitive activities more restricted. There may, for example, be fewer opportunities for mergers and acquisitions because of antitrust concerns. When the Royal Bank wanted to merge with the Bank of Montreal, the Canadian government blocked the merger on the grounds that it would reduce competition and harm consumers. Nestlé has considered buying Hershey for some time, but the Swiss-owned company worries that the acquisition would be

This local McDonald's in Istanbul, Turkey, was bombed in September 2001. As one of the most recognized brands in the world, and with restaurants in more than 120 countries, McDonald's is often the target of people who see the company as an icon of American imperialism. McDonald's tries to be sensitive to local cultures, even encouraging foreign franchisers to run outlets. "We're a confederation of very local companies," says a McDonald's spokesperson.

blocked because the two firms, if combined, would dominate the U.S. confectionery market at a level unacceptable to the U.S. government.

Political stability is also an important consideration, especially for international firms. No business wants to set up shop in another country unless trade relationships with that country are relatively well defined and stable. Thus, Canadian firms are more likely to do business with England, Mexico, and the United States than with Haiti and Afghanistan. Similar issues also pertain to assessments of local and provincial governments. A new mayor or provincial leader can affect many organizations, especially small firms that do business in a single location and are thus susceptible to zoning restrictions, property and school taxes, and the like.

Relations between sovereign governments can also affect business activity. When Canada refused to send troops to support the U.S.-led invasion of Iraq, relations between the United States and Canada were very cool for a time. A survey revealed that nearly half the Americans polled said they would consider switching away from Canadian goods in favour of goods from other countries because of Canada's lack of support of the war. This would obviously have a negative effect on Canadian exports if U.S. consumers acted on these opinions.[32]

THE SOCIO-CULTURAL ENVIRONMENT

The **socio-cultural environment** includes the customs, values, attitudes, and demographic characteristics of the society in which an organization functions. Socio-cultural processes determine the goods and services as well as the standards of business conduct that a society is likely to value and accept.

socio-cultural environment
Conditions including the customs, values, attitudes, and demographic characteristics of the society in which an organization functions.

6. Describe the *socio-cultural environment* and its role in business.

Customer Preferences and Tastes

Customer preferences and tastes vary both across and within national boundaries. In some countries, consumers are willing and able to pay premium prices for designer clothes with labels such as Armani or Calvin

Klein. But the same clothes have virtually no market in other countries. Product usage also varies between nations. In China, bicycles are primarily seen as a mode of transportation, but in Canada, they are marketed primarily for recreational purposes.

Similarly, consumer preferences can also vary widely within the same country. Customs and product preferences in Quebec, for example, differ from those in other parts of Canada. In the United States, pre-packaged chili is more popular in the southwest states than in the northeast. McDonald's is just one company that is affected by socio-cultural factors. In response to concerns about nutrition and health, McDonald's has added salads to its menus and experimented with other low-fat foods. It was the first fast-food chain to provide customers with information about the ingredients in its products, and it attracted media attention in late 2002 when it announced that it would reduce the fat content in its popular French fries.

Consumer preferences and tastes also change over time. Preferences for colour, style, taste, and so forth change from season to season. In some years, brightly coloured clothes sell best, while in other years people want more subdued colours. Soft drinks usually sell better during the hot summer months than in the cold winter months. Drinking whiskey, vodka, and gin and smoking cigarettes are less common today than they were just a few years ago. These and many other related issues regarding businesses and their customers are explored more fully in Part 3 of this book, which deals with the principles of marketing products.

Finally, socio-cultural factors influence the way workers in a society feel about their jobs and organizations. In some cultures, work carries meaningful social significance, with certain employers and job titles being highly desired by workers. But in other cultures, because work is simply a means to an end, people are concerned only with pay and job security. McDonald's has occasionally struggled with its operations in the Middle East because many people there are not interested in working in food-service operations.

Ethical Compliance and Responsible Business Behaviour

An especially critical element of the socio-cultural environment is the practice of ethical conduct and social responsibility. While we cover these areas in detail in Chapter 5, they are sufficiently important to justify a preview of current issues here. The central issue today revolves around the fact that rapid changes in business relationships, organizational structures, and financial flows pose difficulties in keeping accurate track of a company's financial position. The public—current and potential investors—often gets blurred pictures of a firm's competitive health. The stakeholders of business firms—employees, stockholders, consumers, unions, creditors, and government—are entitled to a fair accounting so they can make enlightened personal and business decisions. Keeping up with today's increasingly fast-paced business activities is putting a strain on the accounting profession's traditional methods for auditing, financial reporting, and time-honoured standards for professional ethics.

The Enron scandal in the United States, for example, involved extended enterprises using fast-moving financial transactions among layers of subsidiary firms, some domestic and many offshore, with large-scale borrowing from some of the world's largest financial institutions. The flood of electronic transactions that drove financial flows through a vast network of quickly formed and rapidly dissolved partnerships among energy brokers and buyers was so complex that Enron's accounting reports failed completely to reflect the firm's disastrous financial and managerial condition. In a blatant display of social irresponsibility, Enron's public reports concealed many of its partnerships (and obligations) with other companies, thus hiding its true operating condition.

These activities were not limited to U.S. companies. In a report released on July 28, 2003, court-appointed examiner Neal Batson charged that the Canadian Imperial Bank of Commerce, one of Enron's lenders, knew that Enron was concealing billions of dollars in debts. The report further charged that CIBC helped Enron executives manipulate their financial statements. CIBC immediately denied that it was involved in such activity.[33] The report also showed that the Toronto-Dominion Bank contributed more than $1 billion in financing to Enron.[34]

Furthermore, Arthur Andersen LLP, the accounting firm that audited Enron's finances, did not catch its client's distorted reports. Auditors are supposed to provide an objective and independent assessment of the accuracy of financial information reported by corporations to key stakeholders, such as investors and governmental agencies. Indeed, publicly traded corporations are legally required to use an external auditor for just this purpose. Andersen, like other major accounting firms, had expanded from auditing into more lucrative non-accounting areas such as management consulting. Reports suggest that Andersen's desire for future high-revenue consulting services with Enron may have motivated the auditors to turn a blind eye to questionable practices that eventually turned up during audits of Enron's finances.

Arthur Andersen was one of the premier accounting firms, but its unethical and illegal practices—including obstruction of justice for shredding and doctoring documents related to Enron audits—destroyed the public's trust. After 89 years in business, Andersen notified the U.S. Securities and Exchange Commission in September 2002 that it was giving up its licences to audit public companies. None of the firm's 1200 corporate clients remain, nearly all of its 28 000 employees are gone, and the last of the firm's office supplies have been donated to charity.[35]

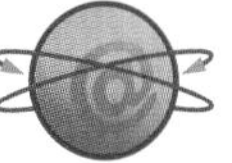

U.S. Securities and Exchange Commission
www.sec.gov

Andersen's downfall can be attributed, at least in part, to its expansion into new lines of business and the accompanying client relationships that created conflicts of interest. Potential conflicts of interest pose serious ethical questions for surviving accounting firms, the accounting profession,

Don't blame these workers for dismantling Arthur Andersen. The international accounting firm did a nice job of self-destructing. Andersen was the auditor behind some of the biggest corporate scandals in history. Enron and WorldCom were among the firm's high-profile clients. The U.S. government prosecuted Andersen for obstruction of justice.

and their clients. Accountants have identified many of the reasons for these new complications. These include corporate globalization and collaboration, the growth in outsourcing, fragmented employee-employer relationships, and the electronic mobility of capital.

Appropriate standards of business conduct also vary across cultures. In Canada, accepting bribes in return for political favours is unethical. In other countries, however, payments to local politicians are expected in return for favourable responses to such common business transactions as zoning and operating permits. The shape of the market, the ethics of political influence, and the attitudes of its workforce are only a few of the many ways in which culture can affect an organization. We examine these issues in more detail in Chapter 6.

THE BUSINESS ENVIRONMENT

7. Identify emerging challenges and opportunities in the *business environment.*

Business today is faster paced, more complex, and more demanding than ever before. The 2002 KPMG/Ipsos-Reid poll of 314 business leaders found that the three most serious issues facing Canadian businesses are (1) globalization/international competitiveness, (2) taxation, and (3) productivity. But these three are only a portion of the issues in the business environment.

The hunt for new goods and services has been accelerated by product life cycles measured in weeks or months rather than years. Individual consumers and business customers want high-quality goods and services—often customized, and with lower prices and immediate delivery. Sales offices, service providers, and production facilities are shifting geographically as new markets and resources emerge in other countries. Employees want flexible working hours and opportunities to work at home. Stockholder expectations also add pressure for productivity increases, growth in market share, and larger profits. At the same time, however, a more vocal public demands more honesty, fair competition, and respect for the environment.

The Industry Environment

Each business firm operates in a specific industry, and each industry has different characteristics. The intensity of the competition in an industry has a big influence on how a company operates. To be effective, managers must understand the company's competitive situation, and then develop a competitive strategy to exploit opportunities in the industry.

One of the best known examples of an effective competitive strategy is Wal-Mart's satellite-based distribution system (discussed in Chapter 17). WestJet has a unique management system that helps it minimize aircraft turnaround time and thus keep its costs lower than its competitors. Managers try hard to find a competitive strategy for their firm, because doing so will slow down or stop new competitors from entering the industry.

One of the most popular tools to analyze competitive situations in an industry is Michael Porter's five forces model.[36] The model (see Figure 2.10) helps managers analyze five important sources of competitive pressure, and then decide what their competitive strategy should be. We briefly discuss each of the elements of the model in the following paragraphs.

Rivalry Among Existing Competitors

The amount of rivalry between companies varies across industries. Rivalry can be seen in activities like intense price competition, elaborate advertising

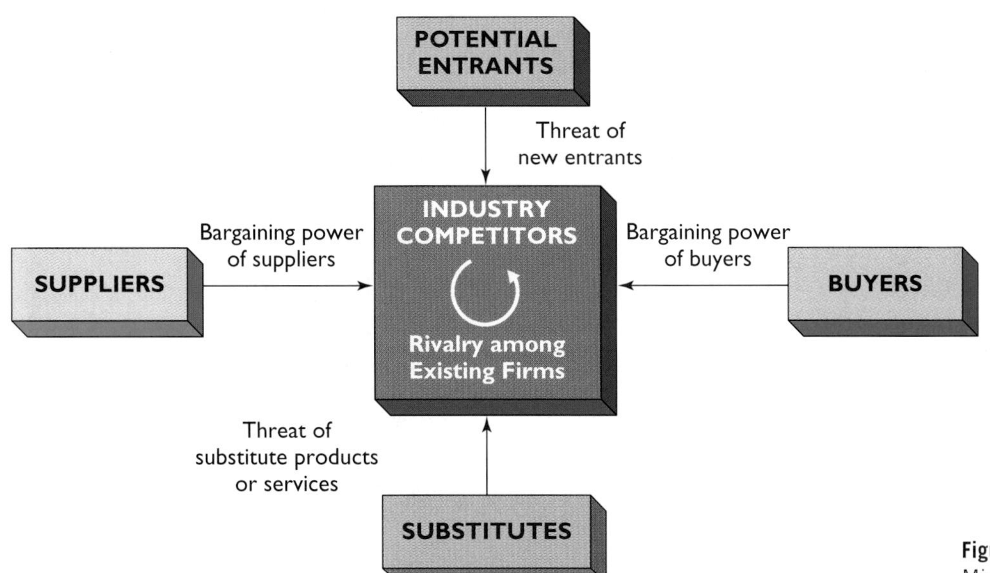

Figure 2.10
Michael Porter's five forces model.

campaigns, and an increased emphasis on customer service. For many years, the rivalry among Chartered Accountants, Certified General Accountants, and Certified Management Accountants in Canada was low-key, but it has recently become much more intense. These firms are responding by merging to attain more market power, cutting costs, making pricing deals with clients, and trying to find ways to differentiate themselves from their competitors.

Threat of Potential Entrants

When new competitors enter an industry, they may cause big changes. For example, when Microsoft introduced Encarta, it caused the sale of hard-copy encyclopedias by companies like Encyclopaedia Britannica to drop sharply. If it is easy for new competitors to enter a market, competition will likely be intense and the industry will not be very attractive. Some industries (for example, automobile manufacturing) are very capital-intensive and are therefore difficult to enter, but others (for example, home cleaning or lawn care services) are relatively easy to enter.

Suppliers

The amount of bargaining power suppliers have in relation to buyers helps determine how competitive an industry is. When there are only a few suppliers in an industry, they tend to have great bargaining power. The power of suppliers is influenced by the number of substitute products that are available (i.e., products that perform the same or similar functions). When there are few substitute products, suppliers obviously have more power.

Buyers

When there are only a few buyers and many suppliers, the buyers have a great deal of bargaining power. Retail powerhouse Wal-Mart, for example, is often cited as a buyer that puts tremendous pressure on its suppliers to reduce their prices. Wal-Mart can do this because it buys so much from these suppliers.

Substitutes

If there are many substitute products available, the industry is more competitive. For example, various synthetic fibres can be used as substitutes for cotton.

Managers use Porter's ideas to help them decide the level of competitive intensity in an industry. A good example is the emergence of the internet in the sale of airline tickets. By making it easier for consumers to compare prices, the internet has increased the competitive intensity of the airline industry (and many other industries, for that matter). In the airline industry, the internet increased the bargaining power of ticket buyers.

Redrawing Corporate Boundaries

Successful companies are responding to challenges like increasing competition in new, often unprecedented ways. To stay competitive, they are redrawing traditional organizational boundaries. Today, firms join together with other companies, even with competitors, to develop new goods and services. Some of these relationships are permanent, but others are temporary alliances formed on short notice so that, working together, partners can produce and deliver products with shorter lead times than either firm could manage alone.

core competency
Skills and resources with which an organization competes best and creates the most value for owners.

The most successful firms are getting leaner by focusing on their **core competencies**—the skills and resources with which they compete best and create the most value for owners. They outsource non-core business processes, paying suppliers and distributors to perform them and thereby increasing their reliance on suppliers. These new business models call for unprecedented coordination—not only among internal activities, but also among customers, suppliers, and strategic partners—and they often involve globally dispersed processes and supply chains. The key to coordinating all these elements is new networking and communications technologies. Interestingly, the same technologies can be instrumental in meeting a firm's social-responsibility requirements as well as improving its operations. The Wired World box highlights another new method, called *disruption management*, by which some organizations are responding to crises in their environments.

Emerging Challenges and Opportunities in the Business Environment

There are numerous emerging challenges and opportunities in today's business environment. In this section, we'll discuss some of the most publicized steps that companies have taken to respond to challenges and opportunities in the business environment. These developments (which are sometimes controversial) include *outsourcing, viral marketing,* and *business process management*.

Outsourcing

outsourcing
Strategy of paying suppliers and distributors to perform certain business processes or to provide needed materials or services.

Outsourcing is the strategy of paying suppliers and distributors to perform certain business processes or to provide needed materials or services. It is an increasingly popular strategy because it helps firms focus on their core activities and avoid getting sidetracked onto secondary activities.[37] The Bank of Montreal (BMO), for example, outsourced its human resource processing services to Exult Inc. Over 100 people who used to work for BMO now work for Exult. They manage payroll and benefits administration, employee records, HR call centre services, and other functions that used to be performed in-house at BMO. The new arrangement will mean a 20 percent reduction in HR costs for BMO. It will also free up BMO managers to concentrate on more "value-added" work.[38]

IT'S A WIRED WORLD

Replanning for Disruption Management

Remarkable, even violent, disruptions to business activities seem to have become the rule rather than the exception in recent years. Most memorable, of course, are the confusion, grief, and discontinuity in every walk of life wrought by the 9/11 terrorism attacks on the United States. But additional disruptions are arising more frequently than ever before from various sources. Financial fortunes are recast in a matter of mere minutes by sudden and steep changes on the stock market. Trusted suppliers, long relied upon for dependable goods or services, suddenly fail and shut down. Widespread product failures, such as fatally defective tires, leave companies facing consumer distrust. Products and business processes are suddenly revolutionized as new technologies require rapid redirection and changeovers to new ways of doing things. Business, of course, has always been threatened by disruption, but a number of factors make the threat today more frequent and severe. Moreover, when problems do arise, organizations are faced with the need for fast—nearly instantaneous—reaction if they want to minimize negative, even disastrous, consequences.

In response to the growing need to reduce adverse effects, a new technology called *disruption management (DM)* has emerged. DM is unlike traditional emergency-management procedures, which typically call for special organizations to respond to disaster by assisting victims in cleanup, treatment, and recovery on an as-needed basis. Instead of outside assistance, DM stresses internal self-reliance in planning for and preparing responses to disruptions in an organization's external environment. It calls for a firm to adapt its organizational structure, technology, and policies so that it will be better prepared to continue operations during and after major disruptions. In short, the firm becomes "disruption sensitive" in order to anticipate environmental disruptions and adapt rapidly when disaster strikes.

DM is a decision support system that's been under development for more than two years by researchers at the Technical University of Denmark's Department of Informatics and Mathematical Modelling. The core technology consists of computer-based models to simulate different possible responses to various disruptions. Developers use mathematical models to represent cause-and-effect relationships among real-world variables. Then they test each model to evaluate its effectiveness in guiding management response to disruption. With the right model, managers can replan activities instantaneously in light of a disruption to ordinary activities. They can even make alternative plans in case of potential future problems.

DM replanning considers a complex set of variables, the ways they interact, and the consequences for the firm and its customers. The objective is to identify a recovery solution that minimizes negative effects—that is, minimizes costs and maximizes revenues—by considering two aspects of each replanning option: immediate (or short-term) consequences and strategic (long-term) effects.

Consider a hypothetical shutdown at Toronto's Pearson International Airport. An airline's least costly solution would be to cancel all incoming flights immediately. But although cancellation cuts the airline's operating costs, it is a terrible option for passengers who can't get where they're going. Replanning models consider alternatives to cancellation, such as rescheduling flights into neighbouring airports and providing ground transportation into Toronto. Of course, pilots and aircraft must also be rescheduled and diverted to new destinations. A DM model would quickly simulate the costs and benefits of these (and other) options in order to facilitate an effective decision.

In developing DM, researchers have experimented with various kinds of disruptions. A telecommunications system is disconnected, causing a communications blackout that deprives users of point-to-point connections. Airports are shut down due to weather conditions or terrorism, preventing scheduled flights from arriving or departing. Manufacturing firms are deprived of needed assembly components when suppliers are shut down by strike or flood. For every application, digital communications are the key to success in using DM. The simulator relies on information both from the organization's internal communications networks and from external sources (such as suppliers, customers, and news agencies) via the internet. Once replanning decisions have been made, directions can be sent instantaneously to facilities and customers throughout the firm.

The cafeteria in a museum may be important to employees and some customers, but running it is not the museum's main line of business and expertise. The museum's managers need to focus on exhibits that will interest the general public, not on food-service operations. That's why museums usually outsource cafeteria operations to food-service management companies whose main line of business is to run cafeterias. The result is more attention to museum exhibits and better food service for customers. Firms today outsource numerous activities, including payroll, employee training, and research and development.

vertical integration
Strategy of owning the means by which an organization produces goods or services.

Outsourcing Versus Vertical Integration. Many firms used to practise **vertical integration**, that is, they owned businesses ranging from raw-material suppliers to retail outlets. But vertical integration is no longer as popular as it once was. Although owning a supplier ensures a steady supply of incoming materials, ownership also means learning to manage the supplier's business—which is usually quite different from the owner's. Too often, the owner ends up devoting too many resources to the supply business and too few to its own core competencies.

Consider a company that cuts and packages paper for photocopiers and computer printers. It can reduce the risk of paper shortages by buying a mill that makes paper from wood pulp. But in reducing the risk of paper shortages, the company increases the risk of losing focus on its main line of business—cutting and packaging paper. Moreover, in trading one risk for another, managers with no expertise in running a paper mill will find themselves competing against firms that are. Facing keen competition in both industries, they may well end up by failing to compete in either.

A basic rule of thumb is that the advantages of vertical integration are the disadvantages of outsourcing, and vice versa. In many cases, however, outsourcing often saves time and money, increases effectiveness in a firm's core business, and results in more value for customers and owners.[39] "Vertical integration," observes one expert, "makes sense only when a company can't be sure of getting the supplies or distribution channels it needs—as in the former Soviet Union.... If you have functioning markets, you don't need it."

Disadvantages of Outsourcing. Not everyone, however, agrees. A Dun & Bradstreet study found that one-quarter of all outsourcing relationships fail within two years, and one-half within five. In addition, many executives told researchers that suppliers too often don't understand what they are supposed to do, that they charge too much, and that they provide poor service. Moreover, when disruptions occur in the supply chain, the costs to both parties can be high. For one thing, replacing failed outsourced operations can be very expensive, especially if the firm wants to return to the outsourced activity. Another risk in outsourcing is loss of control over both operations and information.

Viral Marketing

viral marketing
Strategy of using the internet and word-of-mouth marketing to spread product information.

Combining technology with marketing methods usually results in new ways to attract customers. **Viral marketing**, so called because it uses word of mouth that spreads information like a virus from customer to customer, relies on the vast reaches of the internet to replace face-to-face communications. Messages about new cars, sports events, and numerous other goods and services flow via the internet among potential customers who pass the information on to others. Using various formats—games, contests, chat rooms, and bulletin boards—marketers encourage potential customers to try out products and tell other people about them.[40]

Viral marketing can lead to consumer awareness faster and with wider reach than traditional media messages—and at a lower cost. It works for two reasons. First, people rely on the internet for information that they used to get from newspapers, magazines, and television. Equally important, however, is the interactive element: The customer becomes a participant in the process of spreading the word by forwarding information to other internet users.

Business Process Management

Every company performs numerous processes that provide the goods or services, whether for customers or for other departments within the firm. Human resource departments perform interviewing and hiring processes; payroll departments perform the employee-payment process; the purchasing department performs the process of ordering materials; accounting performs the financial reporting process; marketing performs the process of taking orders from customers. A **process**, in short, is any activity that adds value to some input, transforming it into an output for a customer (whether external or internal).[41]

process

Any activity that adds value to some input, transforming it into an output for a customer (whether external or internal).

In today's business environment, many firms are moving away from the department-oriented organization—one that is organized around departments grouped according to processes or functions. Firms are moving toward process-oriented team structures that cut across old departmental boundaries. This approach is called **business process management**. Often, they begin by asking, "What must we do well to stay in business and win new orders?" Next, they identify the major processes that must be performed well to satisfy these general goals. Then they organize resources and skills around those essential processes. By organizing according to processes rather than functional departments, they gain a number of benefits. Decision making is faster and more customer-oriented, materials and operations are coordinated, and products get to customers more rapidly.[42]

business process management

Approach by which firms move away from department-oriented organization and toward process-oriented team structures that cut across old departmental boundaries.

The Aftermath of 9/11

It seems almost trite to say that the terrorist attacks on September 11, 2001, changed everything. But the tragic events of that day continue to affect not only the United States, but other nations as well. The months following the terrorist attacks witnessed a worldwide decline in stock markets, major problems with commercial aviation, a significant drop in personal wealth, widespread corporate corruption, and much uncertainty about the world's economy. As of mid-2003, much of this uncertainty remained.

Businesses around the world now face major changes. In Canada and the United States, the federal governments have, for the last 20 years or so, maintained a fairly low profile in business-related matters. Our economy has been characterized by an emphasis on free markets, deregulation, and private enterprise. But September 11 may change all that. As well, the scandals in corporate governance that dominated the news in 2002 will probably mean more market controls and more calls for regulation.

A more specific effect that businesses themselves are already addressing involves workplace security. Gated entrances, restricted access to sensitive areas, and the requirement that visitors sign in and wear badges are long-time practices at many firms. But the events of September 11 have further heightened security concerns in many firms. Some are conducting more extensive background checks when hiring new employees. Others have not only beefed up security, both for physical work sites and information networks, but also developed elaborate crisis plans.

Actions taken by the U.S. government to cope with terrorism have had an impact on Canadian business firms. At border crossings into the United States, for example, increased security has meant long lines as people and goods await entry. This is very disruptive for Canadian firms that export

Increased security measures in the United States have meant long waiting lines at U.S. border crossings and closer scrutiny of Canadian travellers to the United States. These tighter levels of security have caused Canadian firms that do business in the United States to think carefully about who they send to the United States and what expenses (particularly in time) that they will incur.

into the United States. The U.S. government has also begun restricting border crossings for individuals who come from certain countries. Some of those individuals are Canadian citizens working for Canadian firms, but they are no longer allowed to enter the United States.

The external environments that we have described in this chapter—economic, technological, political-legal, socio-cultural, and business—have a profound effect on business firms. From time to time, other factors that do not neatly fit into one of these categories also can have a big impact on business firms. The unusually cold winter of 2002–2003, for example, drove up heating and transportation costs for both business and consumers, but it also helped the tourism business because many people either went skiing or travelled south for a winter vacation. The Business Today box describes two other environmental factors that influenced Canadian businesses in 2003.

BUSINESS TODAY

What Else Can Go Wrong?

During 2003, two highly publicized medical emergencies arose in Canada—the SARS outbreak, and a case of "mad cow" disease. These two emergencies affected a variety of Canadian business firms.

SARS

A contagious disease called Severe Acute Respiratory Syndrome (SARS) popped up in scores of people in Toronto during the spring of 2003. The disease was also a big problem in China. Because it was fatal in about 15 percent of the cases, efforts were immediately made to quarantine those who had the disease so they wouldn't spread it to others. In addition to the serious health threat it posed, SARS had a negative effect on many different business firms in both Canada and the Far East:

- The outbreak caused a noticeable slowdown of business activity in China and Hong Kong and a decline in travel to and from the Far East; companies like Air Canada experienced sharp declines in demand for air travel to Hong Kong, Singapore, Beijing, and Taiwan
- A slowdown in the Asian economy was expected to also cause a decrease in tourism in Canada, as well as a decline in the number of Asian students coming to Canada to study
- Employment dropped sharply in the Toronto area in industries that were most affected by SARS (health sector, hotel and restaurant business)
- Cullingford Coaches, which shuttles tourists around Ontario, saw its business decline dramatically as tourists cancelled bookings they had made before the SARS outbreak

- The SARS outbreak caused major problems for Manulife Financial agents who sold life insurance in Hong Kong and other parts of China (the agents were reluctant to meet clients face-to-face for fear of contracting the disease)
- When Hewlett-Packard Canada learned that one of its employees had broken quarantine and come to work, managers immediately contacted 102 employees and 95 visitors and told them to quarantine themselves for 10 days
- Anne Olson, the owner of Anne's Ocean View Haven in Prince Edward Island, saw her summer bookings drop by 80 percent as a result of a combination of SARS, the Iraq war, and a slowdown in the U.S. economy

These examples show how a crisis like SARS can have an impact far beyond the obvious medical problems. But when problem situations like this occur, opportunities may also arise. The SARS outbreak, for example, created some unexpected opportunities for business firms.

- RW Packaging, which makes disinfectant products, experienced increased demand for its products because of SARS
- Sales Dynamic Inc. introduced a clip-on holder for small bottles of hand sanitizer that showed the company's name; the sale of alcohol-based sanitizers increased as a result of the fear of SARS
- HerbaMedicine.com promoted its Cureal herbal tea as a way to reduce susceptibility to infections like SARS
- Hardware merchant Andrew Rotblott could not keep face masks in stock because the medical community snapped them all up

Mad Cow Disease

In April 2003, a cow on an Alberta ranch was found to be suffering from bovine spongiform encephalopathy (BSE, or "mad cow disease"). In Britain during the 1990s, thousands of cows were infected with the disease, and in 1996, the British government announced that there was a possible link between BSE and Creutzfeldt-Jakob disease, a fatal brain condition in humans. Customers' concerns about the safety of beef sold in fast-food outlets and in restaurants in Britain caused companies like McDonald's and Burger King to announce that they would no longer sell products made with British beef.

When the disease was discovered in Canada in 2003, there was an immediate uproar. The United States slapped a ban on the importation of Canadian beef, and this caused a major Canadian export industry to go into a tailspin. The Canadian government provided $469 million in aid for the beef industry, but most of that money went to two large meat-packing plants (owned by American companies). After the discovery of BSE was announced, the price of slaughter cattle dropped 45 percent. This meant that cattle ranchers who were raising calves received far less for their products than formerly.

BSE also caused major disruptions in the trucking business. With no beef to haul to the United States, truckers were forced to sit idle. In June 2003, a group of truckers gathered in Lethbridge, Alberta, before driving down to the U.S. border to publicize the problems of the Canadian beef industry. Before Canadian beef could begin moving south into the United States again, both the United States and Japan would have to be convinced that the Alberta case was just an isolated one, and that there was no "mad cow" outbreak in Canada.

SUMMARY OF LEARNING OBJECTIVES

1. **Explain the concepts of *organizational boundaries* and *multiple organizational environments*.** All businesses operate within a larger *external environment*. An *organizational boundary* is that which separates the organization from its environment. Boundaries were once relatively easy to identify; they are becoming harder to pin down. Organizations have multiple environments. Some environments are relatively general, such as prevailing economic conditions. Others are much more precise, such as the pricing policies of competitors. A full picture of a company's organizational environments would include the following elements: economic conditions, technology, political-legal considerations, social issues, the global environment, issues of ethical and social responsibility, the business environment itself, and numerous other emerging challenges and opportunities.

2. **Explain the importance of the *economic environment* to business and identify the factors used to evaluate the performance of an economic system.** The *economic environment* is the economic system in which business firms operate. The health of this environment affects business firms. The three key goals of the Canadian system are economic growth, economic stability, and full employment. *Economic growth* is influenced by the pattern of short-term ups and downs in an economy known as the *business cycle*. The main measure of *growth* in this cycle is *aggregate output*. An increase in aggregate output is growth. *Gross domestic product (GDP)* is the total value of all goods and services produced within a given period by a national economy through domestic factors of production. If GDP is going up, so is aggregate output; if aggregate output is going up, we have economic growth.

   Economic stability means that the amount of money available in an economic system and the quantity of goods and services produced in it are growing at about the same rate. There are three threats to stability: inflation, deflation, and unemployment.

   Unemployment is the level of joblessness among people actively seeking work. If people in different sectors lose their jobs at the same time, overall income and spending drop and businesses cut spending further—including spending on labour. Unemployment goes up further. This kind of unemployment is called *cyclical unemployment*. Meanwhile, producers also start producing less because they can't sell as much. Aggregate output then decreases and we have a *recession*. A prolonged and deep recession is a *depression*.

   The government manages the economy through *fiscal policies* and *monetary policies*. Through the Bank of Canada, the Canadian government can influence the ability and willingness of banks to lend money. It can also influence the supply of money by prompting interest rates to go up or down.

3. **Discuss the current economic picture in Canada and summarize expert predictions about its future.** Most experts see three major forces driving the economy for the next decade: (1) the information revolution will continue to enhance productivity, (2) new technological breakthroughs will create new industries, and (3) increasing globalization will create larger markets while also fostering tougher global competition. As a result of these forces, economists also predict certain economic trends: (1) we'll avoid inflationary surges and large budget deficits, (2) countries that encourage free trade and open financial systems will prosper, and (3) successful businesses will be the ones that master new technologies.

4. **Describe the *technological environment* and its role in business.** *Technology* refers to all the ways by which firms create value for their constituents, including human knowledge, work methods, physical equipment, electronics and telecommunications, and various processing systems. There are two general categories of business-related technologies: *product and service technologies* and *business process technologies*. Product and service technologies create products—both physical goods and services—for customers. Business process technologies are used to improve a firm's performance of internal operations (such as accounting) and to help to create better relationships with external constituents, such as suppliers and customers. *Enterprise resource planning (ERP)* is a large-scale information system for organizing and managing a firm's processes across product lines, departments, and geographic locations.

5. **Describe the *political-legal environment* and its role in business.** The *political-legal environment* reflects the relationship between business and government, usually in the form of government regulation. The legal system defines in part what an organization can and can't do. Various government agencies regulate important areas such as advertising practices, safety and health considerations, and acceptable standards of business conduct. Pro- or anti-business sentiment in government can further influence business activity. During periods of pro-business sentiment, firms find it easier to compete and have fewer concerns about antitrust issues. During periods of anti-business sentiment, firms may find their competitive activities more restricted.

6. **Describe the socio-cultural environment and its role in business.** *The socio-cultural environment* includes the customs, values, and demographic characteristics of the society in which an organization functions. Socio-cultural processes determine the goods and services as well as the standards of business conduct that a society values and accepts. Appropriate standards of conduct also vary across cultures. The shape of the market, the ethics of political influence, and the attitudes of its workforce are only a few of the many ways in which culture can affect an organization.

7. **Identify emerging challenges and opportunities in the *business environment*.** Successful companies are responding to challenges in new ways. They are focusing on their core competencies. The innovative ways in which companies respond to emerging challenges and opportunities include *outsourcing, viral marketing,* and *business process management*. Outsourcing is the strategy of paying suppliers and distributors to perform certain business processes or to provide needed materials or services. Viral marketing relies on the internet to replace face-to-face communications. Many firms are moving away from the department-oriented organization and toward process-oriented team structures that cut across old departmental boundaries—an approach called business process management.

KEY TERMS

QUESTIONS AND EXERCISES

Questions for Review

1. What is GDP? Real GDP? What does each measure?
2. Why is inflation both good and bad? How does the government try to control it?
3. What is technology? How does it affect organizations?
4. What is outsourcing? What are its benefits and risks?

Questions for Analysis

5. Why is it important for managers to understand the environment in which their businesses operate?
6. Explain how current economic indicators such as inflation and unemployment affect you personally. Explain how they will affect you as a manager.
7. At first glance, it might seem as though the goals of economic growth and stability are inconsistent with one another. How can you reconcile this apparent inconsistency?
8. What is the current climate regarding the regulation of business? How might it affect you if you were a manager today?

Application Exercises

9. Select two businesses with which you are familiar. Identify the major elements of their external environments that are most likely to affect them in important and meaningful ways.
10. Using the internet, identify the major suppliers of software for enterprise resource planning. Try to locate information about their primary customers.
11. Interview two business owners or managers. Ask them to describe for you the following things: (a) what business functions, if any, they outsource; (b) whether or not they are focusing more attention on business process management now than in the past; and (c) how the events of September 11, 2001 have affected their work.

BUILDING YOUR BUSINESS SKILLS

The Letdown from Environmental Upheaval

Goal

To encourage students to understand how local events can affect other businesses in a number of ways.

The Situation

The collapse of Enron affected literally hundreds of other businesses. While attention has been directed primarily at the demise of Arthur Andersen, many other businesses suffered as well. For example, Enron's headquarters was located in a large office building on the edge of Houston's downtown business district. Because of both Enron's rapid growth and the prosperity of its employees, numerous other service providers had set up shop nearby—a shoeshine stand, a coffee shop, a bank branch, a dry cleaner, and two restaurants. When Enron collapsed, the demand for services provided by these small businesses dropped sharply.

Larger businesses were also caught up in the ripple effect. Enron, for example, had bought the rights to name the new home of baseball's Houston Astros Enron Field. The Astros were forced to remove all Enron signage and seek a new sponsor. Continental Airlines dominates the air traffic market out of Houston, and Enron was one of Continental's largest corporate clients. Combined with the events of September 11, 2001, and major staff reductions at Compaq Computer, another big Continental client, the end of business travel by Enron managers cost the airline considerable revenue.

Assignment

Divide up into groups of four or five students. Each group should begin by doing the following:

Step 1

Identify five kinds of small businesses likely to have been affected by Enron's collapse. You can include some of those identified above, but identify at least two others.

Step 2

Identify five kinds of large businesses likely to have been affected by Enron's collapse. Again, you can use some of those identified above, but identify at least two others.

Step 3

As a group, develop answers to each of the following:

1. For each company that you identify, both small and large, describe the specific effects of the Enron collapse on its business.

2. Describe the most logical organizational response of each company to these effects.
3. What kinds of plans, if any, should each organization develop in the event of similar future events?
4. Identify businesses that might have benefited economically from the collapse of Enron.

Alternative Assignment

Select a different high-profile environmental upheaval, such as the U.S. duties that were placed on Canadian softwood lumber being shipped to the United States, and substitute it for Enron. Then proceed with Steps 1–3 above.

Follow-Up Questions

1. What does this exercise demonstrate about the pitfalls of relying too heavily on one business?
2. Could any of these businesses have been better prepared for the Enron collapse?
3. Managers must be on the alert for environmental changes that might negatively affect their business. Is it possible for a manager to spend too much time trying to anticipate future events? Why or why not?

CRAFTING YOUR BUSINESS PLAN

Waste Not, Want Not

The Purpose of the Assignment

1. To determine where, in the framework of the Business PlanPro (BPP) software package, external environment issues for a business might appropriately be presented in developing a sample business plan.
2. To familiarize students with some of the planning issues faced by a firm as it considers how it fits into and interacts with the external environment.

Assignment

After reading Chapter 2 in the textbook, open the BPP software and search for information about the types of external environment considerations that would be of concern to a sample firm: Good Earth Resources Inc. To find Good Earth Resources, do the following:

Open the Business PlanPro. If it asks if you want to "create a new business plan" or "open an existing plan," select "create a new business plan" (even though you are not going to create a plan at this time). You will then be taken to the Business PlanPro EasyPlan Wizard. Click on the option entitled **Research It**. You will then be presented with a new list of options, including Sample Plan Browser. After clicking on the **Sample Plan Browser**, go down the alphabetical list of sample plans and double-click on **Recycling-Energy Conversion**, which is the location of Good Earth Resources Inc. The screen you are looking at is the introduction page for the Good Earth business plan. Next, scroll down until you reach the **Table of Contents** for the company's business plan. Read section **1.0 Executive Summary** to gain an understanding of Good Earth's business concept.

Now respond to the following items:

1. Consider today's economic environment as it relates to Good Earth's business plan. Is the present economic climate suitable for starting such a business? Discuss why or why not. [Sites to see in BPP (for this item): On the Table of Contents page, click on each of the following in turn: **1.1 Objectives, 2.2 Start-up Summary, 2.0 Company Summary, 3.2 Competitive Comparison, 4.1 Market Trends,** and **7.1 Important Assumptions**.]
2. Consider the technological environment for Good Earth's line of business. What role, if any, does technology play in Good Earth's business plan? Do you find any evidence that this industry might benefit from new technologies? Explain. [Sites to see in BPP: From the Table of Contents page, click on each of the following in turn: **1.1 Objectives, 1.3 Keys to Success, 2.0 Company Summary, 3.0 Operations,** and **3.4 Technology**.]
3. Do you believe that today's political and legal environments would be receptive to Good Earth's business concept? Where in Good Earth's busi-

ness plan should these issues be presented? Explain. [Sites to see in BPP: On the Table of Contents page, click on each of the following in turn: **2.3 Adjacent Property Option** and **3.5.1 New York City Waste System**.]

4. Consider outsourcing as it might apply at Good Earth. Which of Good Earth's business activities, if any, might be outsourced? What advantages and drawbacks would result from outsourcing? Where, in the firm's business plan, do you suggest that outsourcing be discussed? [Sites to see in BPP: On the Table of Contents page, click on **2.2 Start-up Summary** and then on **3.0 Operations.** Next, click on **4.2.1 Customers**.]

VIDEO EXERCISE

Viewing the Environment: MTV Europe

Learning Objectives

The purpose of this video is to help you

1. Understand how the external environment affects a company's ability to enter and compete in different markets.
2. Explain why a company must analyze the economic, technological, political-legal, and socio-cultural environments of the countries in which it operates.
3. Understand how a company relies on its core competencies to compete in the global marketplace.

Synopsis

MTV had built a large and loyal following in the United States long before it thought about expanding into Europe. When the time came, one of the key issues that management had to address was the technological development of targeted countries—in particular, how many people had televisions. MTV also had to assess the economic development of each country and evaluate socio-cultural trends, such as the direction of local music and the attitudes and interests of the local youth market. Finally, it had to consider such political-legal issues as the dominance of state-operated television stations. Today, MTV's pan-European approach combines a mix of popular American and British music that's broadcast to the entire region, plus special programs customized for northern, central, and southern European markets.

Discussion Questions

1. *For analysis:* Why would MTV be interested in the ownership structure of television stations in Europe?
2. *For analysis:* What are MTV Europe's core competencies and how do they help the company compete?
3. *For application:* In planning future expansion, what elements might MTV Europe weigh most heavily when analyzing a country's economic status?
4. *For application:* What elements of the socio-cultural environment should MTV Europe's management follow especially closely?
5. *For debate:* Should MTV Europe do more to customize programming for the socio-cultural environment in different countries? Support your position.

Online Exploration

Browse the MTV Europe website at **www.mtveurope.com** and review the regional links that appear on the home page. Also follow the links to see upcoming special events being promoted by MTV Europe and to read more about the company and its activities. Finally, choose and follow one country-specific link. How does MTV Europe give its website an international flavour in keeping with its overall image? Why would the company provide links for different countries and languages? How has MTV applied its core competencies on this website?

EXPLORING THE NET

"The Cisco Connection"

This chapter introduced the many environments of business, including the economic and technological, in which firms must operate. We've seen that these external environments—and the ability of managers to understand and respond to them—can play a major role in a firm's success or failure.

Cisco Systems Inc., the worldwide leader in networking for the internet, both operates in and contributes to the technological environment of business. We can begin to understand Cisco's complex relationship to the technological environment by exploring its website at **www.cisco.com**. Scroll down to the bottom of the home page and click on **About Cisco**. You'll find menus for several different kinds of information, including:

Corporate information
Executive thought leadership
Corporate programs

Scroll down to **Executive thought leadership**, and from the menu, click on the biography of CEO **John Chambers**. On the left side of the page, select **Vision**:

1. In what ways does Chambers think the internet will change the way we live?
2. How has technology already changed the way Cisco operates?

Use your Back button to return to **About Cisco Systems**. Select **Corporate Fact Sheet**:

3. In how many different international markets does Cisco operate?

Concluding Case 2-1

Making the Grade

It seems almost laughable these days to talk about businesses that are admired. Whether it is simply poor performance like Air Canada, or illegal behaviour like that at RT Capital, Enron, Arthur Andersen, and WorldCom, business seems to have lost a lot of respect lately. We might conclude that the term *admirable* no longer applies to the institution of business. But there is another side to the story, and it doesn't get enough attention. That story concerns the large number of corporations that perform well and do good things for the constituents in their external environment. And they do it without a lot of fanfare.

Who are these companies? Each year since 1994, KPMG/Ipsos-Reid has published a list of the most respected corporations in Canada. A random sample of 314 CEOs was asked to assess Canadian corporations on eight performance categories, including long-term investment value, innovation and product/service development, financial performance, corporate social responsibility, corporate governance, and customer service. The winner for 2002 was the Royal Bank of Canada (by a wide margin). The next four companies (in order) were Bombardier, BCE, Magna International, and Loblaw.

The same sort of survey is conducted each year in the U.S. by *Fortune* magazine. Evaluations are based on data collected from 10 000 executives, directors, and securities analysts. Eight criteria are used in the *Fortune* survey, many of which are the same as the Canadian survey. General Electric tops the list in the United States, followed (in order) by Southwest Airlines, Wal-Mart, Microsoft, and Berkshire Hathaway. GE has an enviable record among its peers. For one thing, it's known as a major training ground for corporate executives. Rubbermaid made the top 10 under CEO Stanley Gault, a former GE executive. Under recently retired CEO Jack Welch, GE managed to achieve smooth and steady earnings growth quarter after quarter. It's also America's number-one wealth creator, and current CEO Jeff Immelt has already announced that one of his goals is to be on top of the *Fortune* list again next year.

Fortune has also begun to compile a list of the most admired global companies. The top 23 businesses are American firms. The top 10 non-U.S. companies include Nokia, Toyota, Sony, Nestlé, Honda, BP, Singapore Airlines, L'Oréal, Royal Dutch/Shell, and Canon.

A review of these lists—and the criteria that are used to generate them—provides some reassuring testimony on the vitality and values of many businesses. It also shows the manner in which they conduct their operations, and gives us some insights into how companies must perform to gain the kind of stellar reputation necessary to get on the list.

These criteria all have one underlying theme: They reflect in one way or another the extent to which an organization and its managers effectively meet or exceed the needs and expectations of their external constituents. For example, hiring and developing the brightest and most motivated people from the labour market results in high levels of employee talent. Likewise, respecting the needs of shareholders and other investors affects several criteria, including financial soundness, use of corporate assets, and long-term investment value. Says one expert, "We admire companies that cater to their constituents."

Questions for Discussion

1. What is your opinion of the value of the rankings like these?
2. Do you think the criteria that are used are appropriate? Can you suggest others?
3. Is the ranking something that investors should rely on in buying stock?
4. If you were a top manager and wanted your firm to move up in the rankings, how would you proceed? ◆

Concluding Case 2-2

Maybe Malthus Was Wrong

Most people have heard of Thomas Malthus, who became famous by proposing that all species have a tendency to reproduce to the point where their food supply runs out. The application of this idea to human population was simple: the world's population would tend to increase until the food supply was no longer sufficient to support everyone. Starvation would then result. But is this correct? Recent population trends are very startling, and call into question the predictions of Malthus.

The fertility rate—the average number of lifetime births per woman—declined in many industrialized European countries in the mid-twentieth century, and has stayed low ever since. In fact, it has stayed below the "replacement rate"—the rate needed to ensure that the population maintains itself. That rate is 2.1 births per woman. Some of the implications of Europe's declining fertility rate are profound. In Russia, for example, the current population of 150 million people will drop to 105 million by 2050 if current trends continue.

While the fertility rate is low in industrialized Europe, in developing countries it has always been high. And, until recently, it was assumed that it would always be high. This would lead, it was feared, to eventual overpopulation of the world and Malthusian famine on a large scale. But something unexpected is happening. Fertility rates in most developing countries, including India, Mexico, and Iran, are declining.

In 2000, the United Nations population division predicted that the fertility rate in developing countries in 2050 would be 2.1 children per woman. But in 2002, it revised its prediction downward to 1.85 children per woman. If this latest prediction turns out to be accurate, the world's population should stabilize at about 9 billion people by 2050. This is a significant change from predictions that were made in 1992, when it was thought that world population would reach 12 billion people by 2050. There are several interesting implications of a stabilizing world population:

- In the future, a smaller proportion of the population in most countries will be children, and a larger proportion will be very old people
- More and more women will be involved in the worldwide workforce because they are having fewer children, and they are having them later in life
- The population of Japan will start declining in 2006, so businesses there will have to find ways to increase productivity to cope with the decline in the working population
- Mexico's fertility rate has dropped precipitously in the last 25 years (from 7.0 to 2.1), and that means that for the first time in its history Mexico has the opportunity to develop a significant middle class of consumers; but this development may also make it difficult for Mexico to compete with other emerging markets for foreign investment
- Countries where the fertility rate has dropped sharply will benefit from a so-called demographic bonus: labour costs decline because a greater proportion of the population works when there are fewer children; Thailand and China are just two countries that have benefited this way, and India will soon start benefiting

Some countries are so concerned about the decline in fertility rates that they have begun offering incentives to convince women to have more babies. In Australia, for example, couples that have a baby can put off a house loan payment for three months. In Singapore, parents are paid a bonus in cash if they have one more child. But these initiatives have had virtually no effect. It seems that the combination of high literacy rates, increasing prosperity, and improvements in women's rights are an irresistible force in reducing fertility rates.

Questions for Discussion

1. Consider each of the issues discussed in the chapter with regard to the economic environment. What will be the impact of declining fertility rates on each of these issues? Be specific.
2. What will be the impact of declining fertility rates on the technological, political-legal, and socio-cultural environments? Be specific.
3. If the fertility rate continues to decline worldwide, what are the implications for individual business firms? Be specific. ◆

CHAPTER 3

Understanding Entrepreneurship, Small Business, and Business Ownership

After reading this chapter, you should be able to:

1. Define *small business* and discuss its importance to the Canadian economy.
2. Explain *entrepreneurship* and describe some key characteristics of entrepreneurial personalities and activities.
3. Describe the *business plan* and the *start-up decisions* made by small businesses.
4. Identify the main reasons for success and failure in small businesses.
5. Explain *sole proprietorships* and *partnerships* and discuss the advantages and disadvantages of each.
6. Describe *corporations*, and discuss their advantages and disadvantages.
7. Explain the basic issues involved in creating and managing a corporation and identify recent trends in business ownership.

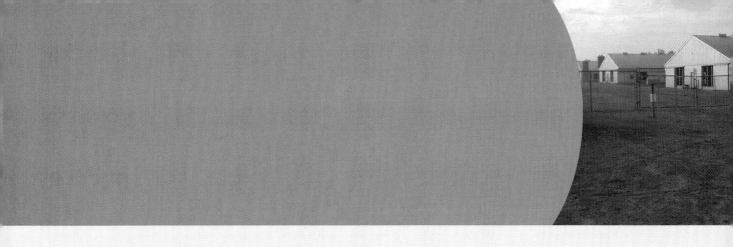

Family Feuds

Many family businesses are operating in Canada. In addition to the usual challenges facing business firms, these family businesses have to cope with the often emotional interactions between family members. This can complicate the running of the business. The two examples discussed below—the Mitchell family and the Cuddy family—illustrate the kinds of problems that can arise. While they may appear amusing and petty to outsiders, these conflicts can affect the very survival of the family business.

The Mitchell Family

Mitchell's Gourmet Foods Inc. is a Saskatchewan-based family business. The feud started in the late 1980s when Fred Mitchell, the CEO at the time, claimed that his mother and brother Charles were trying to wrest control of the business from him. Both sides in the dispute then sued each other. An accommodation of sorts was reached in 1997 when the disputing parties agreed to divide up the assets of the company. Fred (and his wife LuAn) kept Mitchell's and Charles (and his wife Camille) kept a beef plant the company owned.

When Fred Mitchell died in 1998, LuAn took over as company chairwoman. She persuaded Schneider Corp. to make an investment in Mitchell's, which she later claimed saved the company from bankruptcy. LuAn's claims are supported by the United Food and Commercial Workers union, which says that she was instrumental in keeping the plant operating. LuAn has recently been portraying herself as an entrepreneur, and she is writing a book entitled *LuAn: Dare to Be Successful.*

Charles and his wife Camille aren't quite ready to give her so much credit. In late 2002, about the same time that LuAn was to be married in a high-profile wedding, they placed an advertisement in *The Globe and Mail* praising Fred and other family members for being instrumental in the success of Mitchell's. Camille, who is considering suing LuAn for defamation, said the ad was placed to correct misinformation that had been distributed by LuAn. Sources familiar with the feud say the advertisement was designed to challenge LuAn's claim that she was the person who was instrumental in saving the company. It also embarrassed LuAn on her wedding day.

All of this squabbling seems pointless now, given that the disputing parties no longer have any ownership stake in the business. LuAn sold her remaining stake in Mitchell's to Schneider Corp. in 2002, and Charles and Camille sold the beef plant they were given in the 1997 deal.

The Cuddy Family

Cuddy International Corp. is the largest turkey breeding and hatching company in Canada. It also holds the lucrative contract to supply chicken products to McDonald's. The company's founder, Mac Cuddy, is known as "the turkey king of Canada." Cuddy is a brilliant entrepreneur who created a great company, but then couldn't manage it, partly because he couldn't get along with his five sons and one daughter. Gordon Pitts, the author of *In the Blood*, a book about family businesses, says that the Cuddy case is a classic example of everything that can go wrong in a family business—a control-oriented founding father, no succession plan, and untrained children who have worked only in the business.

All of Mac's sons have worked in the family business at one time or another, but Mac was doubtful about their ability to manage the company. Three of his sons—Peter, Bruce, and Brian—made several attempts to take control of the business, but they failed. Eventually, Mac fired Peter and Brian and demoted Bruce (who then quit the business and became a competitor of his father). Squabbles of various sorts have been evident, like the time Peter sued the company, claiming that he had not been given financial information that he was entitled to. He was then sued by the company for making allegedly defamatory remarks at a press conference.

All of these events have had a negative effect on the company. Five CEOs came and went during the mid- and late-1990s, and annual company sales have declined from about $500 million to just $350 million.

One possible way to avoid these feuds is to appoint someone as CEO who is not a member of the family. This is unusual, but Dare Foods Ltd. did it in 2003 when Fred Jaques was appointed CEO. He is the first non-family member to hold that position since the company was founded in 1892. The company is the second largest cookie maker in Canada (behind Kraft), and makes Dare Cookies, Breton Crackers, and Canada's Girl Guide Cookies. ◆

WHAT IS A "SMALL" BUSINESS?

1. Define *small business* and discuss its importance to the Canadian economy.

The term *small business* is not easy to define. Locally owned and operated restaurants, hair salons, service stations, and accounting firms are obviously small businesses, while giant corporations such as Canadian National Railways and Noranda are obviously big businesses. Between these two extremes fall thousands of companies that cannot be easily categorized.

Two common measures of small business are sales revenues and the number of employees. The Canadian government's Small Business Office, in conjunction with Statistics Canada, defines a small business as having less than $2 million in annual sales. Various government agencies also use numbers of employees to define small business. However, this number differs widely among government agencies: the federal Ministry of State for Small Business stipulates 50 or fewer, the Business Development Bank of Canada says 75 or fewer, and Statistics Canada uses numbers ranging from 100 to 1500 for manufacturing industries, and 50 for service industries.

small business
An independently owned and managed business that does not dominate its market.

Because it is sometimes hard to define in strictly numerical terms, we define a **small business** as one that is independently owned and operated and is not dominant in its field of operations. It possesses most of the following characteristics:

- Management of the firm is independent. Usually the managers are also the owners.
- An individual or a small group supplies the capital and holds the ownership.
- The area of operations is usually local, and the workers and owners live in the same community (the markets the firms serves, however, are not always local).
- The enterprise is smaller than others in the industry. This measure can be in terms of sales volume, number of employees, or other criteria. It is free of legal or financial ties to large business enterprises.
- The enterprise qualifies for the small business income tax rate under the Canada Income Tax Act.

Small businesses can be found in every industry and are particularly prominent in the retail trade. In terms of numbers, small business is the dominant type of business in Canada. Of the approximately 2.2 million businesses in Canada, 58 percent consist of self-employed individuals, while 41 percent employ fewer than 50 persons. Less than 1 percent of all businesses have between 50 and 499 employees, and less than 0.1 percent employ more than 500.[1]

A common type of small business in Canada is the convenience store. It attracts customers from its immediate area through its long hours of operation and the product lines it carries.

The Importance of Small Business in the Canadian Economy

On the basis of numbers alone, small business is a strong presence in the Canadian economy. The contribution of small business can also be measured in terms of its effects on key aspects of our economic system, including *job creation, innovation,* and *importance to big business.*

Job Creation

Relative job growth among businesses of different sizes is hard to determine. For one thing, when a successful small business starts adding employees at a rapid clip, it may quickly cease being small. Dell Computer had just one employee in 1984 (Michael Dell, the founder). But the payroll grew to 100 employees in 1986, to 2000 in 1992, and to 4000 in 2001. While it is difficult to say exactly when Dell Computer changed from "small" to "large," some of the jobs it created should be counted in the small business sector and some in the large.

Dell Computer
www.dell.ca

Small businesses—especially in certain industries—are an important source of new (and often well-paid) jobs. Jobs, of course, are created by companies of all sizes, all of which hire and lay off workers. Although small firms often hire at a faster rate, they are also likely to cut jobs at a far higher rate when they encounter difficulties. They are the first to hire in times of economic recovery, but big firms are the last to lay off workers during downturns.

Innovation

History has shown that major innovations are as likely to come from small businesses (or individuals) as from big businesses. This is partly the result of the high degree of autonomy and freedom small business people have. Small firms and individuals, for example, invented the personal computer, the stainless-steel razor blade, the transistor radio, the photocopying machine, the jet engine, and the self-developing photograph. They also gave us the helicopter, power steering, automatic transmissions, air conditioning, cellophane, and the ballpoint pen.

Not surprisingly, history is repeating itself infinitely more rapidly in the age of computers and high-tech communication. For example, much of today's most innovative software is being written at new start-up companies such as Trilogy Software Inc. Trilogy's products help optimize and streamline complicated sales and marketing processes for big-business customers such as IBM. Yahoo! and Netscape brought the internet into the average Canadian living room, and online companies such as Chapters are using it to redefine our shopping habits. Each of these firms started out as a small business.

Remember that innovations are not always new *products*. Michael Dell didn't invent the PC, but he developed an innovative way to build it (buy finished components and then assemble them) and an innovative way to sell it (directly to consumers, first by telephone and now via the internet).

Importance to Big Business

Most of the products made by big businesses are sold to consumers by small ones. For example, the local hardware store sells paint made by a large paint company, but the hardware store is independently operated. Moreover, small businesses provide big ones with many of their services and raw materials. Microsoft, for instance, relies on hundreds of small firms for most of its routine code-writing functions.

The value of small business to Canada's economy has been recognized by the federal and provincial governments with the establishment of small business departments and lending institutions catering to these enterprises. Government agencies sponsor awards to recognize entrepreneurs or enterprises that have performed in an outstanding manner. An example of one such award is the Canada Awards for Business Excellence. Begun in 1984 by the federal government, these awards were created to acknowledge exceptional business achievements, ones that contribute to Canada's competitiveness in national and international business. The awards are given each year to honour extraordinary performance in various categories of business activity, including entrepreneurship and small business.

Popular Areas of Small-Business Enterprise

The degree of small business varies across different industries. As shown in Figure 3.1, small business firms are dominant in the construction and retailing industries, but not as dominant in manufacturing. About 6 of every 10 Canadians employed in the private sector works in a firm with fewer than 500 employees.

Each industry differs in its needs for employees, money, materials, and machines, but as a general rule, the more resources required, the harder it is to start a business and the less likely an industry is dominated by small firms. Remember, too, that *small* is a relative term. The criteria (number of employees and total annual sales) differ from industry to industry and are often meaningful only when compared with truly large businesses.

Services

Small-business services range from marriage counselling to computer software, from management consulting to professional dog walking. Partly because they require few resources, service providers are the fastest-growing segment of small business. A retailer, for example, sells products made by other firms directly to consumers. Usually, people who start small retail businesses favour specialty shops—say, big men's clothing or gourmet coffees—that let them focus limited resources on narrow market segments.

Construction

About 10 percent of businesses with fewer than 20 employees are involved in construction. Because many construction jobs are small local projects,

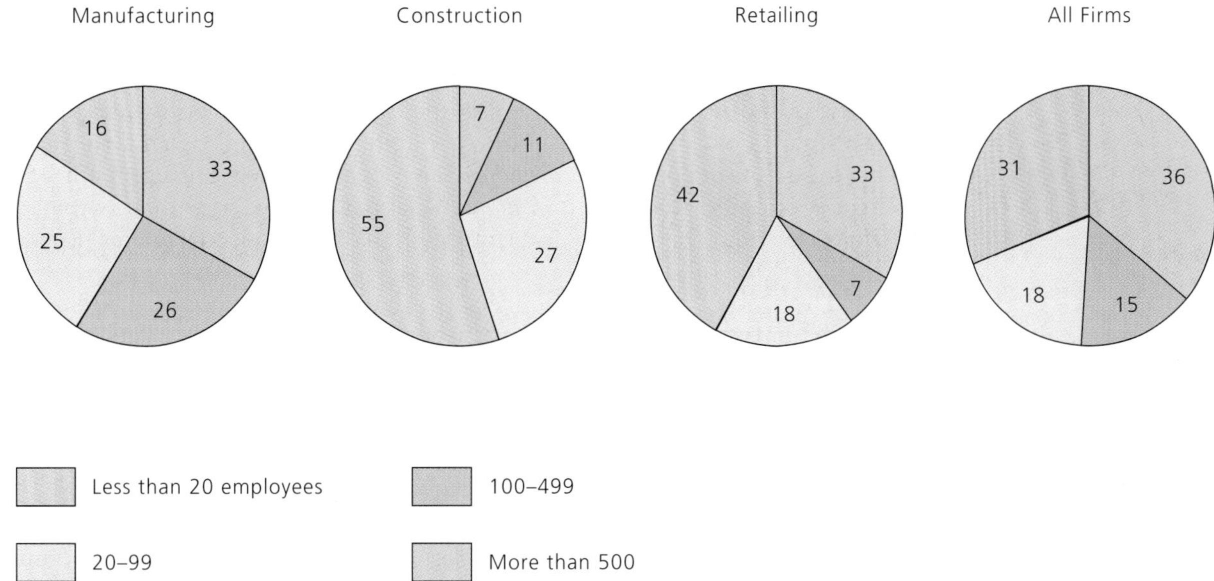

Figure 3.1
Employment distribution by enterprise size.

local firms are often ideal contractors. Financial and insurance firms also account for about 10 percent of all firms with fewer than 20 employees. Most of these businesses are affiliates of or agents for larger national firms.

Wholesaling

Small-business owners often do well in wholesaling; about 8 percent of businesses with fewer than 20 employees are wholesalers. Wholesalers buy products from manufacturers or other producers and sell them to retailers. They usually purchase goods in bulk and store them in quantities at locations convenient for retailers. For a given volume of business, therefore, they need fewer employees than manufacturers, retailers, or service providers.

Transportation and Manufacturing

Some small firms—about 5 percent of all companies with fewer than 20 employees—do well in transportation and related businesses. These include taxi and limousine companies, charter airplane services, and tour operators. More than any other industry, manufacturing lends itself to big business, but this doesn't mean that there are no small businesses that do well in manufacturing; about 5 percent of firms with fewer than 20 employees are involved in manufacturing. Indeed, small manufacturers sometimes outperform big ones in such innovation-driven industries as electronics, toys, and computer software.

ENTREPRENEURSHIP

We noted earlier that Dell Computer started as a one-person operation and grew into a giant corporation. Dell's growth was spurred by the imagination and skill of Michael Dell, the *entrepreneur* who founded the company. Although the concepts of *entrepreneurship* and *small business* are closely related, there are often subtle differences between them.

Distinctions Between Entrepreneurship and Small Business

entrepreneur
A business person who accepts both the risks and the opportunities involved in creating and operating a new business venture.

Entrepreneurs are people who assume the risk of business ownership with a primary goal of making money through growth and expansion of their business.[2] As reported in *Canadian Business*, the 2002 Entrepreneur of the Year was David Robson, the CEO of Veritas DGC Inc., a company that provides seismic surveys to international oil and gas companies that are searching for oil.

2. Explain *entrepreneurship* and describe some key characteristics of entrepreneurial personalities and activities.

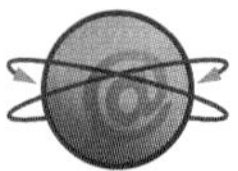

Global Entrepreneurship Monitor (GEM)
www.gemconsortium.org

The amount of economic freedom that exists in a country affects how much entrepreneurial activity there is. Each year, the Heritage Foundation publishes an index of economic freedom, which assesses the extent to which entrepreneurs have freedom to pursue new business opportunities. In 2003, Canada ranked eighteenth out of 156 countries. Hong Kong ranked first, and North Korea ranked last.[3] A study by the Global Entrepreneurship Monitor (GEM) rated Canada as sixth out of 21 countries for entrepreneurial activity. Brazil ranked first. The GEM research program is an annual assessment of the national level of entrepreneurial activity. About 1 in 16 Canadians tried to start a new business in 2000.[4] Canada also ranks highly as a good place to do business generally. In 2003, the *Economist* magazine ranked Canada as the best country in the world in which to do business.[5]

Many small business owners characterize themselves as entrepreneurs, but a lot of them don't really aspire to expand their business the way the true entrepreneur does. Thus, a person may be a small business person only, an entrepreneur only, or both. Consider an individual who starts a small pizza parlour with no plans other than to earn enough money from the restaurant to lead a comfortable lifestyle. That individual is clearly a small business person. With no plans to grow and expand, however, the person is not really an entrepreneur. In contrast, an entrepreneur may start with one pizza parlour and turn it into a national chain. Although this individual may have started with a small business, the growth of the firm resulted from the entrepreneur's desire to expand the business. Thus, the small business owner usually has no plans for dramatic growth, seeking only a secure and comfortable income, while the entrepreneur is motivated to grow, expand, and build—that is, to take risks.

More and more women are starting and successfully operating their own small businesses. They now account for half of all new businesses that are formed.

Entrepreneurial Characteristics

Many successful entrepreneurs share characteristics that set them apart from most other business owners—for example, resourcefulness and a concern for good, often personal, customer relations. Most of them also have a strong desire to be their own bosses. Many express a need to "gain control over my life" or "build for the family" and believe that building successful businesses will help them do it. They can also deal with uncertainty and risk.

Yesterday's entrepreneur was often stereotyped as "the boss"—self-reliant, male, and able to make quick, firm decisions. Today's entrepreneur is seen more often as an open-minded leader who relies on networks, business plans, and consensus. Although today's entrepreneur may be male, she is just as likely to be female. Past and present entrepreneurs also have different views on such topics as how to succeed, how to automate business, and when to rely on experience in the trade or basic business acumen.[6]

The typical entrepreneur is about 42 years old, as compared with the typical employee, who is about 34 years old. An increasing number of women are becoming entrepreneurs. A Royal Bank of Canada study estimates that one-quarter to one-third of all businesses worldwide are owned by women, and that women now account for half the increase in new businesses each year. Women are more conservative than men in running a small business, and their failure rate is lower than that of men.[7] About half of all new businesses are now started by women. Laura Polley is typical of women entrepreneurs in Canada. She started Independent Film Financing Inc., a company that raises money to produce feature films, after her former employer, Paragon Entertainment Corp., ran into trouble. Her company has already been involved in the production of major films like *The Whole Nine Yards* (Bruce Willis and Matthew Perry) and *Angel Eyes* (Jennifer Lopez).[8]

Dozens of studies have identified common traits among entrepreneurs. A researcher at the University of Western Ontario compiled a list of many of the characteristics identified by these studies, including assertiveness, challenge-seeking nature, charisma, ability to cope, creativity, improvisational skills, openness to opportunity, risk taking, self-confidence, tenacity, venturesomeness, and orientation toward achievement and action.[9]

STARTING AND OPERATING A SMALL BUSINESS

The internet has changed the rules for starting and operating a small business. Setting up is easier and faster than ever before, there are more potential opportunities than at any time in history, and the ability to gather and assess information is at an all-time high. Today, for example, many one-person retailers do most of their business—both buying and selling—on internet auction sites such as eBay.

Even so, would-be entrepreneurs must make the right start-up decisions. They must decide how to get into business—should they buy an existing business or build from the ground up? They must know when to seek expert advice and where to find sources of financing. If, for example, a new firm needs financial backing from investors or a line of credit from vendors or distributors, the entrepreneur should have in place a comprehensive, well-crafted business plan.

Crafting a Business Plan

The starting point for every new business is a **business plan** in which the entrepreneur summarizes business strategy for the new venture and shows how it will be implemented.[10] The contents of such a plan are shown in Table 3.1. The real benefit of a business plan is the act of preparing it; the would-be entrepreneur must develop the business idea on paper and firm up his or her thinking about how to launch it before investing time and money in it.

business plan
Document in which the entrepreneur summarizes her or his business strategy for the proposed new venture and how that strategy will be implemented.

3. Describe the *business plan* and the *start-up decisions* made by small businesses.

Setting Goals and Objectives

A business plan describes the match between the entrepreneur's abilities and experiences and the requirements for producing and/or marketing a

Table 3.1 A Business Plan

The contents of a business plan vary depending upon the information required by the financial institutions or government agencies. Some entrepreneurs develop plans as a personal guide to check on where they are or want to be. The following are the components that might be included in such a plan:

Cover Page
Contains the enterprise's name, address, telephone numbers, and key contacts.

Table of Contents

Executive Summary
A brief statement, usually about one page long, summarizing the plan's contents.

Background/History of the Enterprise
A concise outline of when and how the enterprise got started, the goods or services it sells, and its major suppliers and customers.

Management
Background information on the entrepreneur and other employees, especially other managers (if there are any).

Marketing Assessment
Descriptions of the products or a service profile, the results of any market research, a market description and analysis, an identification of competition, and an account of the marketing strategy.

Production Assessment
A brief description of the production process, the technological process employed, quality requirements, location and physical plant, and details of machinery and equipment.

Financial Assessment
A review of the capital structure and the money needed to finance the business. Usually includes a projected balance sheet, profit and loss statement, and a cash flow forecast. Lenders may also require details of loan collateral and a repayment proposal.

Research and Development (R&D)
For many enterprises, R&D is important and a statement of what is planned would be included. There may also be an assessment of the risks anticipated with any new products or ventures.

Basic Data
Data on the enterprise's bankers, accountants, lawyers, shareholders (if any), and details of incorporation (if applicable).

Appendices
The following might be attached to a plan: detailed management biographies, product literature, evaluation of assets, detailed financial statements and cash flow forecast, and a list of major contracts.

particular product. It also defines strategies for production and marketing, legal elements and organization, and accounting and finance. In particular, a business plan should answer three questions: (1) What are the entrepreneur's goals and objectives? (2) What strategies will be used to obtain them? (3) How will these strategies be implemented? (We discuss goals and objectives in Chapter 6.)

Sales Forecasting

Business plans should also account for the sequential nature of strategic decision making in new ventures. Entrepreneurs, for example, can't forecast sales revenues without first researching markets. Simply asserting that the new venture will sell 100 000 units per month is not credible. Instead, the entrepreneur must demonstrate an understanding of the current market, of the strengths and weaknesses of existing firms, and of the means by which the new venture will compete. In fact, the *sales forecast* is among the most important elements in the business plan. Without it, no one can estimate the required size of a plant, store, or office or decide how much inventory to carry and how many employees to hire.

Financial Planning

Financial planning refers to the entrepreneur's plan for turning all other activities into dollars. It generally includes a cash budget, an income statement, balance sheets, and a break-even chart. It also includes keeping track of cash flow (inflows and outflows of cash). Most important is the *cash budget*, which shows how much money you need *before* you open for business and how much you need to *keep the business going* before it starts earning a profit.[11]

Starting the Small Business

An old Chinese proverb says that a journey of 1000 miles begins with a single step. This is also true of a new business. The first step, of course, is the individual's commitment to becoming a business owner. In preparing a business plan, the entrepreneur must choose the industry and market in which he or she plans to compete. This choice means assessing not only industry conditions and trends but also one's own abilities and interests. Like big-business managers, small-business owners must understand the nature of the enterprises in which they are engaged.

Most people become involved in a small business in one of three ways: they buy an existing business (this includes taking over a family business), they start their own firm from scratch, or they buy a franchise.

Buying an Existing Business

An entrepreneur must decide whether to buy an existing business or start from scratch. About one-third of all new businesses that were started in the past decade were bought from someone else. Many experts recommend buying an existing business because the odds of success are better. An existing business has already proven its ability to attract customers. It has also established relationships with lenders, suppliers, and other stakeholders. Moreover, an existing track record gives potential buyers a much clearer picture of what to expect than any estimate of a new business's prospects.[12]

But an entrepreneur who buys someone else's business may not be able to avoid certain problems. For example, there may be uncertainty about the exact financial shape the business is in, the business may have a poor reputation, the location may be poor, or it may be difficult to determine an appropriate purchase price.

Taking Over a Family Business. A special case of buying an existing business involves family businesses. Taking over a family business poses both challenges and opportunities. On the positive side, a family business can provide otherwise unobtainable financial and management resources because of the personal sacrifices of family members. Family businesses often have a valuable reputation or goodwill that can result in important community and business relationships. As well, employee loyalty is often high, and an interested, unified family management and shareholders group may emerge.

On the other hand, major problems can arise in family businesses, as we saw in the opening case. There may be disagreement over which family member assumes control. If the parent sells his or her interest in the business, the price to be paid may be an issue. The expectation of other family members may also be problematic; some family members may feel that they have a right to a job, promotion, and impressive title simply because they are part of the family. Choosing an appropriate successor and ensuring that he or she receives adequate training, and disagreements among family members about the future of the business, are two other problem areas. Sometimes the interests of the family and those of the enterprise conflict. As a result, family enterprises often fail to respond to changing market conditions.

Starting from Scratch

Some people seek the satisfaction that comes from planting an idea, nurturing it, and making it grow into a strong and sturdy business. There are also practical reasons to start a business from scratch. A new business does not suffer the ill effects of a prior owner's errors. The start-up owner is also free to choose lenders, equipment, inventories, locations, suppliers, and workers, unbound by a predecessor's commitments and policies. About two-thirds of all new businesses started in the past decade were started from scratch. Many of the ecommerce businesses that were started in the 1990s are already out of business, but the ones that remain seem to be doing pretty well (see the Wired World box).

The risks of starting a business from scratch are greater than those of buying an existing firm. New-business founders can only make projections about their prospects. Success or failure depends on identifying a genuine opportunity, such as a product for which many customers will pay well but which is currently unavailable. To find openings, entrepreneurs must study markets and answer the following questions:

Who are my customers?
Where are they?
At what price will they buy my product?
In what quantities will they buy?
Who are my competitors?
How will my product differ from those of my competitors?

IT'S A WIRED WORLD

What Doth It Profit a Dot-Com?

As we all know, dot-coms don't make money and they're all doomed to failure. The phrase "profitable internet company" is a contradiction in terms. But is internet business really *that* bad? During the short-lived glory days of dot-coms, venture capitalists were virtually throwing money at them, and some experts predicted that they would soon take over and make over the business world. But big shakeouts in 2000 and 2001 sent most of the upstarts packing.

A closer look reveals, however, that the survivors are holding up pretty well. In fact, many are starting to show nice profits. In the travel sector, Expedia, Hotels.com, and Priceline are making money. No fewer than 10 public finance dot-com companies are now profitable, with firms such as E*Trade™ performing quite well.

Although hurt by a recent ad slump, some media and advertising businesses are in the black, and several etailers, including Amazon.com and Ticketmaster USA, are doing well. In other sectors, successful dot-coms include auctioneer eBay, Intuit and McAfee (software), WebEx Communications (infrastructure), and Razorfish and Inforte (consulting).

But just because some firms seem to have turned the corner doesn't mean that there will be another spurt in internet start-ups. In fact, just the opposite may be true, because entrepreneurs have come to realize that ecommerce is much more than putting up a website. As in most other areas of the business world, firms with strong business plans and well-considered strategies are most likely to survive.

Finding answers to these questions is a difficult task even for large, well-established firms. But where can the small business owner get the necessary information? Other sources of assistance are discussed later in this chapter, but we briefly describe three of the most accessible here:

- The best way to gain knowledge about a market is to work in it before going into business in it. For example, if you once worked in a bookstore and now plan to open one of your own, you probably already have some ideas about the kinds of books people buy.
- A quick scan of the local Yellow Pages or an internet search will reveal many potential competitors, as will advertisements in trade journals. Personal visits to these establishments and their websites can give you insights into their strengths and weaknesses.
- Studying magazines, books, and websites aimed specifically at small businesses can also be of help, as can hiring professionals to survey the market for you.

Many new businesses start as **microenterprises**—enterprises operated from the home part-time while the entrepreneur continues to work as a regular employee of another organization. Sometimes such a business is operated in partnership with others. The obvious advantage of beginning as a microenterprise is that the entrepreneur can test his or her idea before quitting regular employment. Canadians are using this approach increasingly.

microenterprise
An enterprise that the owner operates part-time from the home while continuing regular employment elsewhere.

Buying a Franchise

If you drive or walk around any Canadian town, you will notice retail outlets with names like McDonald's, Pizza Pizza, Swiss Chalet, Yogen Früz, 7-Eleven, RE/MAX, Comfort Inn, Blockbuster Video, Sylvan Learning Centre, and Super Lube. What do all these businesses have in common? They are all franchises, operating under licences issued by parent companies to local entrepreneurs who own and manage them.

Franchising became very visible in the 1950s with fast-food franchisers like McDonald's, but it actually started in the early 1800s. In 1898, General Motors began franchising retail dealerships, and similar systems were created by Rexall (pharmacies) in 1902, and by Howard Johnson (restaurants and motels) in 1926. Franchising continues to increase in importance in the twenty-first century. Depending on how it is defined, franchising now accounts for 43 percent of retail sales in Canada.[13] There are thousands of franchise establishments in Canada, and they generate approximately $30 billion in annual sales revenue.

A **franchise** is an arrangement that gives franchisees (buyers) the right to sell the product of the franchiser (the seller). A **franchising agreement** outlines the duties and responsibilities of each party. For example, it stipulates the amount and type of payment that franchisees must make to the franchiser. Franchisees usually make an initial payment for the right to operate a local outlet of the franchise; they also make royalty payments to the franchiser ranging from 2 to 30 percent of the franchisee's annual revenues or profits. The franchisee also pays an advertising fee so that the franchiser can advertise in the franchisee's local area. Franchise fees vary widely, from as little as $30 000 for a Fantastic Sams's hair salon to $1 million for a Burger King franchise. A professional sports franchise may cost hundreds of millions of dollars.

franchise
An arrangement that gives franchisees (buyers) the right to sell the product of the franchiser (the seller).

franchising agreement
Stipulates the duties and responsibilities of the franchisee and the franchiser.

The Advantages and Disadvantages of Franchising. Both franchisers and franchisees benefit from the franchising way of doing business (see Table 3.2 on p. 91). However, franchising is not without problems, particu-

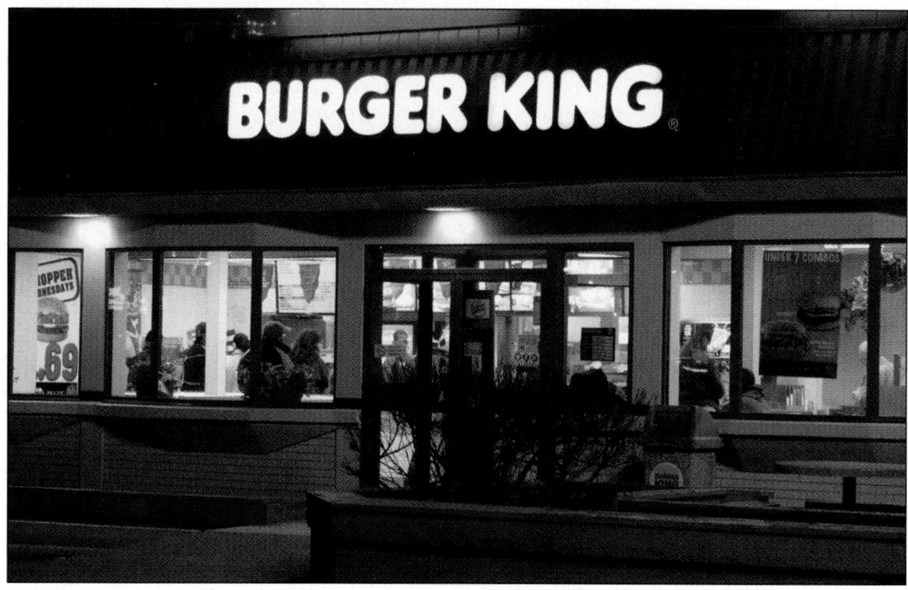

Franchising is very popular in Canada. It offers individuals who want to run their own business an opportunity to establish themselves quickly in a local market.

larly from the franchisee's perspective. Over the years, certain problems have been noted with some frequency:

- franchisers may impose policy changes without consulting with their franchisees
- the local market may be saturated with too many outlets of one franchise; this reduces the profits that each franchisee is able to make
- the franchisee has little room to develop a unique identity in the local community because the head office of the franchise stipulates how the business must be run and how the product must be made
- franchise agreements can be difficult to terminate, or the franchiser can terminate them even if the franchisee wants to continue

Is Franchising for You? Do you think you would be happy being a franchisee? The answer depends on a number of factors, including your willingness to work hard, your ability to find a good franchise to buy, and the financial resources you possess. If you are thinking seriously of going into franchising, you should consider several areas of costs that you will incur:

- the franchise sales price
- expenses that will be incurred before the business opens
- training expenses
- operational expenses for the first six months
- personal financial needs for the first six months
- emergency needs

Financing the Small Enterprise

The amount of capital needed to start a small business prevents some people from becoming entrepreneurs. However, many different sources of funding are available (see the list in Table 3.3 on p. 92). Some sources are more likely than others to provide money. Lenders may or may not lend money to entrepreneurs, depending on whether the enterprise is just beginning or is ongoing.

Table 3.2 The Benefits of Franchising

For the Franchiser	For the Franchisee
• the franchiser can attain rapid growth for the chain by signing up many franchisees in many different locations • franchisees share in the cost of advertising • the franchiser benefits from the investment money provided by franchisees • advertising money is spent more efficiently (the franchiser teams up with local franchisees to advertise only in the local area) • the franchiser benefits because franchisees are motivated to work hard for themselves; the more revenue the franchisee generates, the more money the franchiser makes • the franchiser is freed from all details of a local operation, which are handled by the franchisee	• franchisees own a small business that has access to big business management skills • the franchisee does not have to build up a business from scratch • franchisee failure rates are lower than when starting one's own business • a well-advertised brand name comes with the franchise and the franchisee's outlet is recognizable because it looks like all other outlets in the chain • the franchiser may send the franchisee to a training program run by the franchiser (e.g., the Canadian Institute of Hamburgerology run by McDonald's) • the franchiser may visit the franchisee and provide expert advice on how to run the business • economies in buying allow franchisees to get lower prices for the raw materials they must purchase • financial assistance is provided by the franchiser in the form of loans; the franchiser may also help the franchisee obtain loans from local sources • franchisees are their own bosses and get to keep most of the profit they make

Funds for Starting a Business

The most likely sources of financing are the personal funds of individuals, in particular, the entrepreneurs themselves. Some government agencies may provide assistance funds for start-up and so may chartered banks if they think that the proposed business has promise.

Funds for an Ongoing Business

After the enterprise has operated for some time, other financial services are more likely to be used, if a good financial reputation has been established. Sources include trade credit (that is, the delayed payment terms offered by suppliers), chartered banks, trust companies, and venture capitalists. Another source of funds is profits from the business.

SUCCESS AND FAILURE IN SMALL BUSINESS

4. Identify the main reasons for success and failure in small businesses.

Numerous statistics on the survival rate of small businesses have been compiled. The following data are representative:

- About 13 to 15 percent of all business enterprises disappear each year.
- One-half of new businesses fail in the first three years. After that the failure rate levels off.
- After 10 years, only 25 percent of businesses are still in existence.
- The average lifespan of small enterprises is 7.25 years.
- Female entrepreneurs have a survival rate about twice as high as that of males.[14]

Table 3.3 Principal Sources of Funds for Small Business Enterprises

Debt Sources

These are funds borrowed by the enterprise. They may come from:

- The entrepreneur, who may lend money to the enterprise
- Private lenders, that is, individuals or corporations
- Financial institutions such as banks, credit unions, trust companies, and finance companies. Such borrowing may be by the enterprise but guaranteed by the entrepreneur or secured against other non-business assets of the entrepreneur.
- Trade credit, that is, the delayed payment terms offered by suppliers
- Government agencies, for example, the Business Development Bank of Canada
- The selling of bonds or debentures (usually only done when the enterprise is larger)

Equity Sources

This money is invested in the enterprise and represents an ownership interest. It comes from:

- The entrepreneur's personal funds
- Partners, either individuals or corporations
- Family and friends
- Venture capitalists
- Governments
- The selling of shares to the public (usually only done when the enterprise is larger)
- Employees who may participate in a stock purchase plan or simply invest in the enterprise

Retained Earnings

Profits, that is, funds generated from the operation of the business, can be either paid to the owners in dividends or reinvested in the enterprise. If retained or reinvested, profits are a source of funds.

The low survival rate need not be viewed as a serious problem, since failures are natural in a competitive economic system. In some cases, enterprises are poorly managed and are replaced by more efficient and innovative ones. In recent years, more enterprises have started than have failed, indicating the resiliency of small business and entrepreneurs.

Reasons for Success

Four factors are typically cited to explain the success of small business owners:

1. *Hard work, drive, and dedication.* Small business owners must be committed to succeeding and be willing to put in the time and effort to make it happen. Long hours and few vacations generally characterize the first few years of new business ownership.
2. *Market demand for the product or service.* If the area around a college has only one pizza parlour, a new pizzeria is more likely to succeed than if there are already 10 in operation. Careful analysis of market conditions can help small business people assess the reception of their products in the marketplace.

3. *Managerial competence.* Successful small business people have a solid understanding of how to manage a business firm. They may acquire competence through training (by taking courses in small business management at a local college), experience (by learning the ropes in another business), or by using the expertise of others.
4. *Luck.* Luck also plays a role in the success of some firms. For example, after one entrepreneur started an environmental clean-up firm, he struggled to keep his business afloat. Then the government committed a large sum of money for toxic waste clean-up. He was able to get several large contracts, and his business is now thriving.

Reasons for Failure

Small businesses collapse for a number of reasons (see Table 3.4). Entrepreneurs may have no control over some of these factors (for example, weather, fraud, accidents), but they can influence most items on the list. This is the main reason entrepreneurs should learn as much as possible about management.

FORMS OF BUSINESS ORGANIZATIONS

All business owners must decide which form of legal organization—a sole proprietorship, a partnership, a corporation, or a co-operative—best suits them and their business. Few decisions are more critical, since the choice

Table 3.4 Causes of Small Business Failure

Poor management skills

- poor delegation and organizational ability
- lack of depth in management team
- entrepreneurial incompetence, such as a poor understanding of finances and business markets
- lack of experience

Inadequate marketing capabilities

- difficulty in marketing product
- market too small, nonexistent, or declines
- too much competition
- problems with distribution systems

Inadequate financial capabilities

- weak skills in accounting and finance
- lack of budgetary control
- inadequate costing systems
- incorrect valuation of assets
- unable to obtain financial backing

Inadequate production capabilities

- poorly designed production systems
- old and inefficient production facilities and equipment
- inadequate control over quality
- problems with inventory control

Personal reasons

- lost interest in business
- accident, illness
- death
- family problems

Disasters

- fire
- weather
- strikes
- fraud by entrepreneur or others

Other

- mishandling of large project
- excessive standard of living
- lack of time to devote to business
- difficulties with associates or partners
- government policies change

affects a host of managerial and financial issues, including income taxes and the owners' liability. In choosing a legal form of organization, the parties concerned must consider their likes, dislikes, and dispositions, their immediate and long-range needs, and the advantages and disadvantages of each form.

Sole Proprietorships

sole proprietorship
Business owned and usually operated by one person who is responsible for all of its debts.

5. Explain *sole proprietorships* and *partnerships* and discuss the advantages and disadvantages of each.

As the very first legal form of business organization, **sole proprietorships** date back to ancient times. This is still the most numerous form of business in Canada. Despite their numbers, however, they account for only a small proportion of total business revenues in this country.

Because most sole proprietorships are small, often employing only one person, you might assume that all are small businesses. However, sole proprietorships may be as large as a steel mill or as small as a lemonade stand. Some of Canada's largest companies started out as sole proprietorships. One of Canada's biggest sole proprietorships is the Jim Pattison Group, with annual sales of $5.5 billion and 26 000 employees.[15] Figure 3.2 summarizes the basic advantages and disadvantages of the sole proprietorship form of ownership.

Jim Pattison Group
www.jimpattison.com

Advantages

Freedom is the most striking feature of sole proprietorships. Because they alone own their businesses, sole proprietors need answer to no one but themselves. They can also maintain a high level of privacy, since they are not required to report information about their operations to anyone. Sole proprietorships are also easy to form and dissolve. Rock concerts or athletic events may be organized as sole proprietorships by individuals who then dissolve the business entity when the events are over. Low start-up costs are yet another attractive feature of sole proprietorships. Legal fees are likely to be low, since sole proprietorships need only register the business with the provincial government to ensure that no other business bears the same name. Some proprietorships do need to take out licences, however. For example, restaurants and pet shops need special licences.

Sole proprietorships also offer tax benefits for new businesses likely to suffer losses before profits begin to flow. Tax laws permit sole proprietors

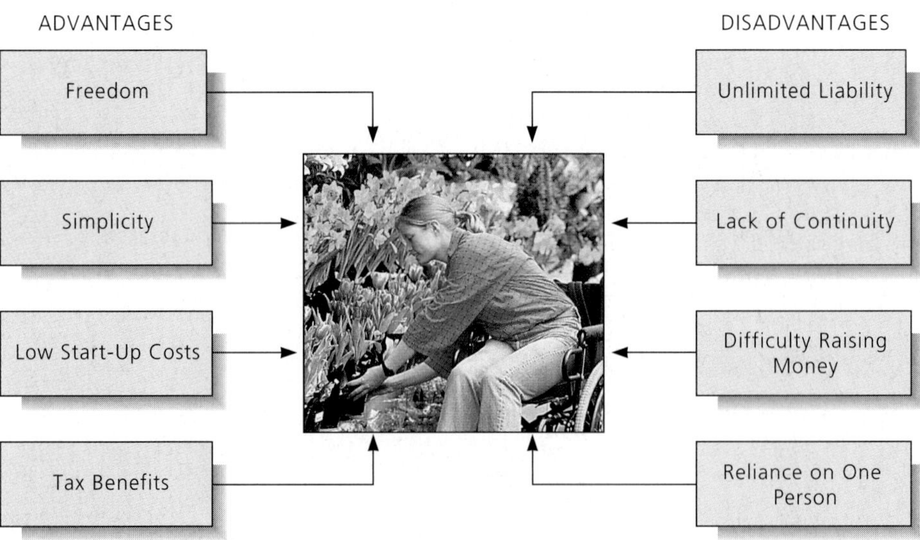

Figure 3.2
The sole proprietorship is a popular form of business ownership. There are both advantages and disadvantages with this form of ownership.

to treat the sales revenues and operating expenses of the business as part of their personal finances. Thus, a proprietor can cut taxes by deducting any operating losses from income earned from sources other than the business. Since most businesses lose money at the beginning, this tax situation is very helpful to entrepreneurs starting up.

Disadvantages

One major drawback of sole proprietorships is their **unlimited liability**. A sole proprietor is personally liable for all debts incurred by the business. Bills must be paid out of the sole proprietor's own pocket if the business fails to generate enough cash. Otherwise, creditors can step in and claim the proprietor's personal possessions, including a home, furniture, and automobile. Actually, the law does protect some of the proprietor's assets, but many can be claimed.

unlimited liability
A person who invests in a business is liable for all debts incurred by the business; personal possessions can be taken to pay debts.

Another disadvantage is lack of continuity. A sole proprietorship legally dissolves when the owner dies. The business can, of course, be reorganized soon after the owner's death if a successor has been trained to take over the business. Otherwise, executors or heirs must *liquidate* (sell the assets of) the business. Finally, a sole proprietorship is dependent upon the resources of a single individual. If the proprietor has unlimited resources and is a successful manager, this characteristic is not really a problem. Sole proprietors often find it hard to borrow money not only to start up, but also to expand. Banks often reject such applications, fearing that they will not be able to recover the loan if the sole proprietor becomes disabled.

Partnerships

A **partnership** is established when two or more individuals agree to combine their financial, managerial, and technical abilities for the purpose of operating a company for profit. **General partners** are actively involved in managing the firm and they have unlimited liability. **Limited partners** generally don't participate actively in the business, and their liability is limited to the amount they invested in the partnership (see Table 3.5). Partnerships are often an extension of a business that began as a sole proprietorship. The original owner may want to expand, or the business may have grown too big for a single person to handle. Figure 3.3 summarizes the advantages and disadvantages of the partnership form of organization.

partnership
A business with two or more owners who share in the operation of the firm and in financial responsibility for the firm's debts.

general partner
A partner who is actively involved in managing the firm and has unlimited liability.

limited partner
A partner who generally does not participate actively in the business, and whose liability is limited to the amount invested in the partnership.

Advantages

The most striking feature of general partnerships is their ability to grow by adding talent and money. Partnerships also have a somewhat easier time borrowing funds than do sole proprietorships. Banks and other lending institutions prefer to make loans to enterprises that are not dependent on a single individual.

Like a sole proprietorship, a partnership is simple to organize, with few legal requirements. Even so, all partnerships must begin with an agreement of some kind. It may be written, oral, or even unspoken. Wise partners, however, insist on a written agreement to avoid trouble later. This agreement should answer such questions as:

Who invested what sums of money in the partnership?
Who will receive what share of the partnership's profits?
Who does what and who reports to whom?
How may the partnership be dissolved? In that event, how would leftover assets be distributed among the partners?

Table 3.5 Types of Partnerships and Partners

Types of Partnerships	
General partnership	All partners have unlimited liability for the firm's debts.
Limited partnership	This partnership has at least one general partner and one or more limited partners. The latter's liability is limited to their financial investment in the firm.
Types of Partners	
General partner	Actively involved in managing the firm and has unlimited liability.
Secret partner	Actively participates in managing the firm and has unlimited liability. A secret partner's identity is not disclosed to the public.
Dormant partner	Does not actively participate in managing the firm. A dormant partner's identity is not disclosed to the public. Has unlimited liability.
Ostensible partner	Not an actual partner but his or her name is identified with the firm. Usually an ostensible partner is a well-known personality. Promotional benefits accrue from using his or her name for which the person is usually paid a fee. Has unlimited liability.
Limited partner	Liability is limited to the amount invested in the partnership.

How would surviving partners be protected from claims by surviving heirs if a partner dies?
How will disagreements be resolved?

The partnership agreement is strictly a private document. No laws require partners to file an agreement with some government agency. Nor are partnerships regarded as legal entities. In the eyes of the law, a partnership is nothing more than two or more persons working together. The partnership's lack of legal standing means that the partners are taxed as individuals.

Disadvantages

As with sole proprietorships, unlimited liability is the greatest drawback of general partnerships. By law, each partner may be held personally liable for

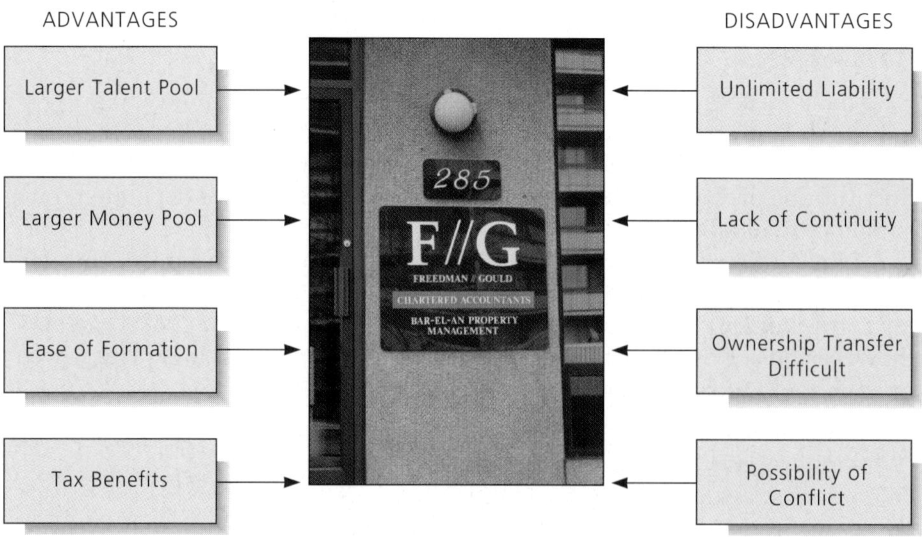

Figure 3.3
Partnerships are common in professional organizations like CA firms.

all debts incurred in the name of the partnership. And if any partner incurs a debt, even if the other partners know nothing about it, they are all liable if the offending partner cannot pay up. Another problem with partnerships is lack of continuity. When one partner dies or pulls out, a partnership may dissolve legally, even if the other partners agree to stay.

A related drawback is the difficulty of transferring ownership. No partner may sell out without the other partners' consent. Thus, the life of a partnership may depend on the ability of retiring partners to find someone compatible with the other partners to buy them out. Finally, a partnership provides little or no guidance in resolving conflict between the partners. For example, suppose one partner wants to expand the business rapidly and the other wants it to grow slowly. If under the partnership agreement the two are equal, it may be difficult for them to decide what to do.

A practical illustration of the kinds of problems that can arise in partnerships is described in the Exercising Your Ethics box.

EXERCISING YOUR ETHICS

Breaking Up Is Hard to Do

The Situation

Connie and Mark began a 25-year friendship after finishing college and discovering their mutual interest in owning a business. Established as a general partnership, their home-furnishings centre is a successful business sustained for 20 years by a share-and-share-alike relationship. Start-up cash, daily responsibilities, and profits have all been shared equally. The partners both work four days each week except when busy seasons require both of them to be in the store. Shared goals and compatible personalities have led to a solid give-and-take relationship that helps them overcome business problems while maintaining a happy interpersonal relationship.

The division of work is a natural match and successful combination because of the partners' different but complementary interests. Mark buys the merchandise and maintains up-to-date contacts with suppliers; he also handles personnel matters (hiring and training employees). Connie manages the inventory, buys shipping supplies, keeps the books, and manages the finances. Mark does more selling, with Connie helping out only during busy seasons. Both partners share in decisions about advertising and promotions.

The Dilemma

Things began changing two years ago, when Connie became less interested in the business and got more involved in other activities. While Mark's enthusiasm remained high, Connie's time was increasingly consumed by travel, recreation, and community-service activities. At first, she reduced her work commitment from four to three days a week. Then she indicated that she wanted to cut back further, to just two days. "In that case," Mark replied, "we'll have to make some changes."

Mark insisted that profit sharing be adjusted to reflect his larger role in running the business. He proposed that Connie's monthly salary be cut in half (from $4000 to $2000). Connie agreed. He recommended that the $2000 savings be shifted to his salary because of his increased workload, but this time Connie balked, arguing that Mark's current $4000 salary already compensated him for his contributions. She proposed to split the difference, with Mark getting a $1000 increase and the other $1000 going into the firm's cash account. Mark said no and insisted on a full $2000 raise. To avoid a complete falling out, Connie finally gave in, even though she thought it unfair for Mark's salary to jump from $4000 per month to $6000. At that point, she made a promise to herself: "To even things out, I'll find a way to get $2000 worth of inventory for personal use each month."

Questions for Discussion

1. Identify the ethical issues, if any, regarding Mark's and Connie's respective positions on Mark's proposed $2000 salary increase.
2. What kind of salary adjustments do you think would be fair in this situation? Explain why.
3. There is, of course, another way for Mark and Connie to solve their differences: Because the terms of participation have changed, it might make sense to dissolve the existing partnership. What do you recommend in this regard?

Corporations

corporation

A business considered by law to be a legal entity separate from its owners with many of the legal rights and privileges of a person; a form of business organization in which the liability of the owners is limited to their investment in the firm.

6. Describe *corporations*, and discuss their advantages and disadvantages.

When you think of corporations you probably think of giant businesses such as Air Canada, Imperial Oil, or Nortel Networks. The 10 largest corporations in Canada are listed in Table 3.6. The very word **corporation** suggests bigness and power. Yet, the tiny corner newsstand has as much right to incorporate as does a giant oil refiner. And the newsstand and oil refiner have the same basic characteristics that all corporations share: legal status as a separate entity, property rights and obligations, and an indefinite lifespan. In 2002, changes to the Ontario Business Corporations Act made it legal for professionals like chartered accountants and lawyers to incorporate. Professionals can also incorporate in British Columbia and Alberta.[16]

A corporation has been defined as "an artificial being, invisible, intangible, and existing only in contemplation of the law."[17] As such, corporations may sue and be sued, buy, hold, and sell property, make and sell products to consumers, and commit crimes and be tried and punished for them. Corporations can be found in both the private and the public sector in Canada, although our emphasis in this text is on the private sector. We discussed Crown (government) corporations in Chapter 1.

Public Versus Private Corporations

public corporation

A business whose stock is widely held and available for sale to the general public.

private corporation

A business whose stock is held by a small group of individuals and is not usually available for sale to the general public.

A **public corporation** is one whose shares of stock are widely held and available for sale to the general public. Anyone who has the funds to pay for them can buy shares of companies such as Brascan, George Weston, or Canadian Pacific. The stock of a **private corporation**, on the other hand, is held by only a few people and is not generally available for sale. The controlling group may be a family, employees, or the management group. Para Paints of Canada and Bata Shoes are private corporations.

initial public offering (IPO)

Selling shares of stock in a company for the first time to the general investing public.

Most new corporations start out as private corporations, because few investors will buy an unknown stock. As the corporation grows and develops a record of success, it may issue shares to the public as a way of raising additional money. This is called its **initial public offering (IPO)**. Going public may not be easy. The Quebec weekly business magazine *Les Affaires* reported on seven companies that had decided to go public. Three of them gave up halfway through the process, another three reduced the size of their IPO, and one was successful with its original plan.[18] Just as companies can "go public," they can also "go private," that is, a public corporation can be converted to a private corporation.

Table 3.6 The Top 10 Corporations in Canada

	Company	Annual Revenues (in billions of $)
1.	General Motors of Canada	37.0
2.	George Weston Ltd.	27.4
3.	Bombardier Inc.	23.6
4.	Ford Motor Co. of Canada	23.2
5.	Royal Bank of Canada	23.2
6.	Sun Life Financial Services of Canada	23.1
7.	Onex Corp.	22.6
8.	Magna International Inc.	20.3
9.	BCE Inc.	19.7
10.	DaimlerChrysler Canada Inc.	19.3

Formation of the Corporation

7. Explain the basic issues involved in creating and managing a ccr-poration and identify recent trends in business ownership.

The two most widely used methods to form a corporation are federal incorporation under the Canada Business Corporations Act and provincial incorporation under any of the provincial corporations acts. The former is used if the company is going to operate in more than one province; the latter is used if the founders intend to carry on business in only one province. Except for banks and certain insurance and loan companies, any company can be federally incorporated under the Canada Business Corporations Act. To do so, articles of incorporation must be drawn up. These articles include such information as the name of the corporation, the type and number of shares to be issued, the number of directors the corporation will have, and the location of the company's operations.

All corporations must attach the word "Limited" (Ltd./Ltée), "Incorporated" (Inc.), or "Corporation" (Corp.) to the company name to indicate clearly to customers and suppliers that the owners have limited liability for corporate debts. The same sorts of rules apply in other countries. British firms, for example, use PLC for "public limited company" and German companies use AG for "Aktiengesellschaft" (corporation).

Provincial incorporation takes one of two forms. In certain provinces (British Columbia, Alberta, Saskatchewan, Manitoba, Ontario, Newfoundland, Nova Scotia, and the three territories), the registration system or its equivalent is used. Under this system, individuals wishing to form a corporation are required to file a memorandum of association. This document contains the same type of information as required under the Canada Business Corporations Act. In the remaining provinces, the equivalent incorporation document is called the letters patent. In Quebec, a corporation may be formed either by issuing a letters patent or by drawing up articles of incorporation. The specific procedures and information required vary from province to province. The basic difference between these incorporation systems is that the registration system forms corporations by authority of parliament, while the letters patent system forms corporations by royal prerogative.

Corporate Governance

Corporate governance, which is specified for each firm in its bylaws, involves three distinct bodies. **Stockholders** (or **shareholders**) are the real owners of a corporation—investors who buy shares of ownership in the form of stock. The *board of directors* is a group of people elected by stockholders to oversee the management of the corporation. Corporate *officers* are top managers hired by the board to run the corporation on a day-to-day basis.

corporate governance
The relationship between shareholders, the board of directors, and other top managers in the corporation.

stockholders (or shareholders)
Those who own shares of stock in a company.

Stock Ownership and Stockholders' Rights. Corporations sell shares in the business (that is, **stock**) to investors, who then become stockholders, or shareholders. Stockholders are the owners of a corporation. As noted earlier, in a closely held corporation, only a small number of people own the stock. In a publicly held corporation, on the other hand, large numbers of people own the stock.

stock
A share of ownership in a corporation.

Profits may be distributed among stockholders in the form of dividends, although corporations are not required to pay dividends. Instead, they often reinvest any profits in the business. If a dividend is declared, **preferred stock** pays fixed dividends, much like the interest paid on savings accounts. Preferred stockholders are so called because they have preference, or priority, over common stockholders when dividends are distributed and, if a business liquidates, when the value of assets is distributed. Preferred stockholders do not vote.

preferred stock
Shares whose owners have first claim on the corporation's assets and profits but who usually have no voting rights in the firm.

common stock
Shares whose owners usually have last claim on the corporation's assets (after creditors and owners of preferred stock) but who have voting rights in the firm.

In contrast, common stock holders have the last claim to any assets if the company folds. Dividends on **common stock**, like those on preferred stock, are paid on a per share basis (if a dividend is declared). Thus, a shareholder with 10 shares receives 10 times the dividend paid a shareholder with one share. *Class A* common shares always have voting rights, but *Class B* common shares usually do not. Shareholder rights advocates argue that Class B common shares prevent democracy from working in companies because controlling shareholders hold most of the Class A stock and sell non-voting Class B stock to the general public. When investors cannot attend a shareholders' meeting, they can grant authority to vote the shares to someone who will attend. This procedure, called voting by *proxy*, is the way almost all individual investors vote.

board of directors
A group of individuals elected by a firm's shareholders and charged with overseeing, and taking legal responsibility for, the firm's actions.

The Board of Directors. The governing body of a corporation is its **board of directors**. The directors choose the president and other officers of the business and delegate the power to run the day-to-day activities of the business to those officers. The directors set policy on paying dividends, on financing major spending, and on executive salaries and benefits. Large corporations tend to have large boards with as many as 20 or 30 directors. Smaller corporations, on the other hand, tend to have no more than five directors. Usually, these are people with personal or professional ties to the corporation, such as family members, lawyers, and accountants.

inside directors
Members of a corporation's board of directors who are also full-time employees of the corporation.

outside directors
Members of a corporation's board of directors who are not also employees of the corporation on a day-to-day basis.

Many boards have outside as well as inside directors. **Inside directors** are employees of the company and have primary responsibility for the corporation. That is, they are also top managers, such as the president and executive vice-president. **Outside directors** are not employees of the corporation in the normal course of its business. Attorneys, accountants, university officials, and executives from other firms are commonly used as outside directors. The basic responsibility of both inside and outside directors is the same, however—to ensure that the corporation is run in a way that is in the best interests of the shareholders.

In recent years, *shareholder activism* has forced board members to take their responsibilities more seriously. Shareholders have, for example, shown an increased willingness to vote out board members if they feel they are doing a poor job. The Business Today box describes some important developments regarding boards of directors.

Corporations hold annual meetings with their shareholders. At such meetings, managers summarize what the corporation accomplished during the last year, announce plans for the coming year, and answer questions from individual shareholders. Shareholders also elect new members to the board of directors.

BUSINESS TODAY

Board Games

The financial scandals of the past few years have caused people to question how corporations are run. One of the areas that has attracted a lot of attention is the role of the board of directors. In times past, many boards were groups of "old boys" that simply rubber stamped decisions made by company executives. But times are changing fast. In 2002, tough new standards regulating boards of directors were introduced in the United States. Many of Canada's largest corporations do not meet these standards. In fact, many don't meet existing Canadian regulations.

The key issue is the independence of board members. Many investors feel that board members are not independent enough to make objective decisions. The problem is that directors see themselves as being chosen by management (often the CEO), so they feel a responsibility to management, but not to the shareholders. As a result, board members often give managers only a "slap on the wrist" when they do something wrong. Board members may also be reluctant to reduce management salaries when the firm is doing poorly. And when takeover bids come along, board members often reject them, even if the takeover would benefit the shareholders. They do this so they can maintain their own power and position. These problems are reduced when a majority of the members of a board are truly independent from the company.

One illustration of this issue occurred in 2003, when Gerald Schwartz, CEO of Onex Corporation, named his wife to sit on the board of directors of Onex. Institutional shareholders and corporate governance experts said such a move is contrary to the efforts of most public companies to increase the independence of their directors. One securities lawyer asked how a board member could evaluate a CEO's performance if the CEO is her husband.

The independence of board members is not the only important criterion. Other indications of good board governance characteristics include (1) independent compensation committees, (2) board members owning shares of stock in the company, (3) fair treatment of shareholders, (4) modest use of stock options, and (5) full disclosure of information to investors.

Some illustrative questions that can be asked regarding corporation governance are listed below. The more questions that can be answered "Yes," the better the state of corporate governance.

- Are the majority of the board's members independent of the company (i.e., they are not part of the company's management, they don't work for another company that does business with the company, and they do not come from a parent company that controls the company)?
- Are the majority of the compensation committee's members independent (the compensation committee determines executive pay)?
- Are the majority of the nominating committee's members independent (the nominating committee recommends new board members)?
- Does the company have a system for formally evaluating the performance of its board of directors?
- Do the directors and the CEO own stock in the company?
- Do directors have to stand for re-election every year?
- Does the company have a written statement of its corporate governance practices?
- Does the company have only voting common shares, and no non-voting shares?

These (and numerous other) issues were systematically examined in a 2002 *Globe and Mail* survey of Canadian board practices at 270 companies. Four key criteria—board composition, shareholding and compensation issues, shareholder rights issues, and disclosure issues—were used to develop a scoring system to rate boards of directors.

The five best Canadian companies were (in order): Manulife Financial, TransAlta Corp., TransCanada PipeLines Ltd., Canada Life Financial Corp., and Finning International Inc. All these companies scored more than 90 points out of a possible 100. The five worst companies were Alliance Atlantis Communications Inc., Bema Gold Corp., Rand A Technologies Corp., Great-West Lifeco Inc., and Crystallex International Corp. All these companies scored less than 40 out of 100 possible points.

Not surprisingly, companies that scored near the top embraced the rating system. Those scoring near the bottom offered the view that a "one size fits all" scoring system was inappropriate. One thing everyone can probably agree on is this: The challenges facing Canadian companies mean that the board of directors is more important than ever. In an era of intense global competition, active strategic leadership that can be provided by the board is absolutely essential.

Annual Meetings. Corporations hold annual meetings with their shareholders. At such meetings, managers summarize what the corporation accomplished during the last year, announce plans for the coming year, and answer questions from individual shareholders. Shareholders also elect new members to the board of directors.

chief executive officer (CEO)
The person responsible for the firm's overall performance.

Officers. Although board members oversee the corporation's operation, most of them do not participate in day-to-day management. Rather, they hire a team of top managers to run the firm. As we have already seen, this team, made up of officers, is usually headed by the firm's **chief executive officer**, or **CEO**, who is responsible for the firm's overall performance. Other officers typically include a president, who is responsible for internal management, and vice-presidents, who oversee various functional areas such as marketing or operations. Some officers may also be elected to serve on the board, and in some cases a single individual plays multiple roles. For example, one person might serve as board chairperson, CEO, and president. In other cases, a different person fills each slot.

Advantages of the Corporation

limited liability
Investor liability is limited to their personal investments in the corporation; courts cannot touch the personal assets of investors in the event that the corporation goes bankrupt.

The biggest advantage of the corporate structure is **limited liability**, which means that the liability of investors is limited to their personal investments in the corporation. In the event of failure, the bankruptcy courts may seize a corporation's assets and sell them to pay debts, but the courts cannot touch the personal possessions of investors. Another advantage of a corporation is continuity. Because it has a legal life independent of its founders, a corporation can continue to exist and grow long after the founders have retired or died. In theory, a corporation can go on forever.

Most corporations also benefit from professional management. In a sole proprietorship, a single person typically owns and manages the business. In most corporations, on the other hand, professional managers run the company but do not necessarily own any part of it. Finally, corporations have a relatively easy time raising money. By selling more stock, they can expand the number of investors. In addition, the legal protections afforded corporations and the continuity of such organizations tend to make bankers more willing to grant loans.

Disadvantages of the Corporation

tender offer
An offer to buy shares made by a prospective buyer directly to a corporation's shareholders.

Ease of transferring ownership, which is one of the corporation's chief attractions, can also complicate the life of its managers. Using a legal process called a **tender offer**—an offer to buy shares made by a prospective buyer directly to a corporation's shareholders—a corporation can be taken over even if the managers are opposed. Because a tender offer may benefit shareholders, it may create conflict between shareholders (the owners of the corporation) and managers (who are employees of the corporation). Forming a corporation also costs more than forming either a sole proprietorship or a partnership. The main reason is that someone who wants to incorporate must meet all the legal requirements of the province in which it incorporates. Corporations also need legal help in meeting government regulations because they are far more heavily regulated than are proprietorships or general partnerships.

double taxation
A corporation must pay taxes on its profits, and the shareholders must pay personal income taxes on the dividends they receive.

Some people say that **double taxation** is another problem with the corporate form of ownership. By this they mean that a corporation must pay income taxes on its profits, and then shareholders must also pay personal income taxes on the dividends they receive from the corporation. Since dividends paid by the corporation are not tax deductible to the corporation, this amounts to double taxation. Others point out that shareholders get a "dividend tax credit" which largely offsets the effect of double taxation. The advantages and disadvantages of the corporate form of ownership are summarized in Figure 3.4. Table 3.7 compares the various forms of business ownership, using different characteristics.

Co-operatives

A **co-operative** is an organization that is formed to benefit its owners in the form of reduced prices and/or the distribution of surpluses at year-end. The process works like this: suppose some farmers believe they can get cheaper fertilizer prices if they form their own company and purchase in large volumes. They might then form a co-operative, which can be either federally or provincially chartered. Prices are generally lower to buyers and, at the end of the fiscal year, any surpluses are distributed to members on the basis of how much they purchased. If Farmer Jones bought 5 percent of all co-op sales, he would receive 5 percent of the surplus.

co-operative
An organization that is formed to benefit its owners in the form of reduced prices and/or the distribution of surpluses at year-end.

Voting rights are different from those in a corporation. In the co-operative, each member is entitled to one vote, regardless of how many shares he or she holds. This system prevents voting and financial control of the business by a few wealthy individuals.

Types of Co-operatives

There are hundreds of different co-operatives, but they generally function in one of six main areas of business:

- Consumer co-operatives—These organizations sell goods to both members and the general public (e.g., co-op gasoline stations, agricultural implement dealers).
- Financial co-operatives—These organizations operate much like banks, accepting deposits from members, giving loans, and providing chequing services (e.g., credit unions).
- Insurance co-operatives—These organizations provide many types of insurance coverage, such as life, fire, and liability (for example, the Co-operative Hail Insurance Company of Manitoba).

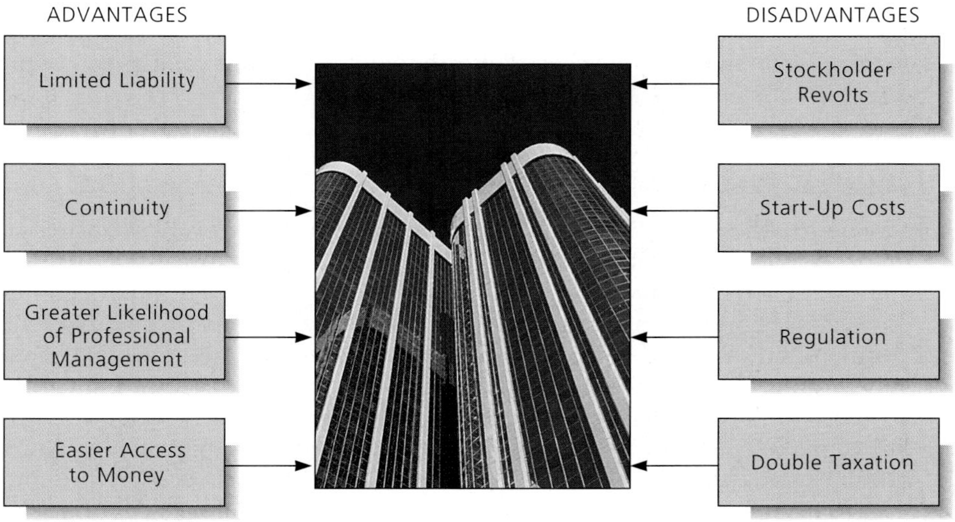

Figure 3.4
Corporations dominate the Canadian business system. Like sole proprietorships and partnerships, the corporate form of ownership has several advantages and disadvantages.

Table 3.7 A Comparison of Three Forms of Business Ownership

Characteristic	Sole Proprietorship	Partnership	Corporation
Protection against liability for bad debts	low	low	high
Ease of formation	high	high	medium
Permanence	low	low	high
Ease of ownership transfer	low	low	high
Ease of raising money	low	medium	high
Freedom from regulation	high	high	low
Tax advantages	high	high	low

- Marketing co-operatives—These organizations sell the produce of their farm members and purchase inputs for the production process (e.g., seed and fertilizer). Some, like Federated Co-operatives, also purchase and market finished products.
- Service co-operatives—These organizations provide members with services, such as recreation.
- Housing co-operatives—These organizations provide housing for members, who purchase a share in the co-operative, which holds the title to the housing complex.

In terms of numbers, co-operatives are the least important form of ownership. However, they are of significance to society and to their members; they may provide services that are not readily available or that cost more than the members would otherwise be willing to pay.

TRENDS IN BUSINESS OWNERSHIP

Several trends in business ownership have become evident in recent years. Significant among these are *acquisitions and mergers, divestitures and spin-offs, employee-owned corporations, strategic alliances,* and *subsidiary/parent corporations*.

Acquisitions and Mergers

acquisition
The purchase of a company by another, larger firm, which absorbs the smaller company into its operations.

merger
The union of two companies to form a single new business.

horizontal merger
A merger of two firms that have previously been direct competitors in the same industry.

In an **acquisition**, one firm simply buys another firm. For example, America Online bought Time Warner and Air Canada bought Canadian Airlines International. The transaction is similar to buying a car that then becomes your property. In contrast, a **merger** is a consolidation of two firms, and the arrangement is more collaborative. For example, Canadian National Railways merged with the Illinois Central Railroad, Rogers Communication merged with Groupe Videotron Ltd., and Toronto-Dominion Bank merged with Canada Trust. When the companies are in the same industry, as when Arthur Andersen Canada merged with Deloitte & Touche or Agricore and United Grain Growers merged to form Agricore United, it is called a **horizontal merger**. When one of the companies in the merger is a supplier or customer to the other, it is called a **vertical merger**. Finally, when the companies are in unrelated businesses, it is called a **conglomerate merger**.

A merger or acquisition can take place in one of several different ways. In a **friendly takeover**, the acquired company welcomes the acquisition, perhaps because it needs cash or sees other benefits in joining the acquiring firm. But in a **hostile takeover**, the acquiring company buys enough of the other company's stock to take control even though the other company is opposed to the takeover.

A *poison pill* is a defence that management adopts to make a firm less attractive to an actual or potential hostile suitor in a takeover attempt. The objective is to make the "pill" so distasteful that a potential acquirer will not want to swallow it. BCE Inc., for example, adopted a poison pill that allowed its shareholders to buy BCE stock at a 50 percent discount if another company announced its intention to acquire 20 percent or more of BCE's shares.[19]

vertical merger
A merger of two firms that have previously had a buyer–seller relationship.

conglomerate merger
A merger of two firms in completely unrelated businesses.

friendly takeover
An acquisition in which the management of the acquired company welcomes the firm's buyout by another company.

hostile takeover
An acquisition in which the management of the acquired company fights the firm's buyout by another company.

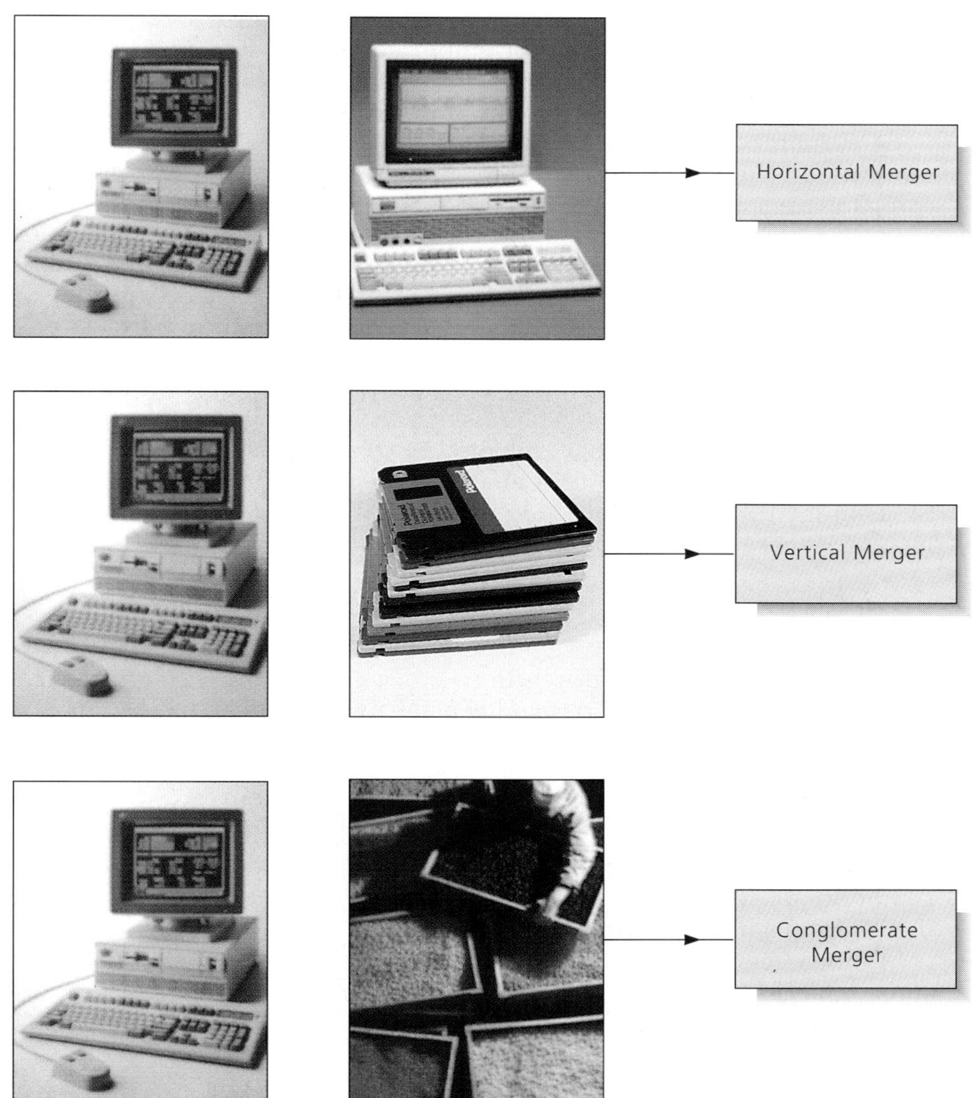

There are several types of mergers. The three most common types are horizontal, vertical, and conglomerate.

Divestitures and Spinoffs

divestiture
Occurs when a company sells part of its existing business operations to another company.

A **divestiture** occurs when a company decides to sell part of its existing business operations to another corporation. For example, Unilever—the maker of Close-Up toothpaste, Dove soap, Vaseline lotion, and Q-tips—at one time owned several specialty chemical businesses that made ingredients for its consumer products. The company decided that it had to focus more on the consumer products themselves, so it sold the chemical businesses to ICI, a European chemical company.

spinoff
Strategy of setting up one or more corporate units as new, independent corporations.

In other cases, a company might set up one or more corporate units as new, independent businesses because a business unit might be more valuable as a separate company. This is known as a **spinoff**. For example, PepsiCo spun off Pizza Hut, KFC, and Taco Bell into a new, separate corporation called Tricon Global Restaurants. Canadian Pacific spun off Canadian Pacific Railways, CP Ships, PanCanadian Petroleum, and Fording Coal.

Employee-Owned Corporations

Corporations are sometimes owned by the employees who work for them. While the individuals who founded them own many smaller corporations, there is a growing trend today for employees to buy significant stakes of larger corporations. The current pattern is for this ownership to take the form of **employee stock ownership plans**, or **ESOPs**.

employee stock ownership plan (ESOP)
An arrangement whereby a corporation buys its own stock with loaned funds and holds it in trust for its employees. Employees "earn" the stock based on some condition such as seniority. Employees control the stock's voting rights immediately, even though they may not take physical possession of the stock until specified conditions are met.

A corporation might decide to set up an ESOP to stimulate employee motivation or to fight a hostile takeover attempt. Here's how it works: The company first secures a loan, which it then uses to buy shares of its stock on the open market. A portion of the future profits made by the corporation is used to pay off the loan. The stock, meanwhile, is controlled by a bank or other trustee. Employees gradually gain ownership of the stock, usually on the basis of seniority. But even though they might not have physical possession of the stock for a while, they control its voting rights immediately.

A survey of 471 Canadian and U.S. companies conducted by Western Compensation & Benefits Consultants of Vancouver found that three-quarters of the companies that have adopted ESOPs have experienced improvement in both sales and profits. Canadian companies such as Celestica and St. Laurent Paperboard Inc. have found that ESOPs give employees an increased sense of belonging in the company.[20]

Strategic Alliances

strategic alliance
An enterprise in which two or more persons or companies temporarily join forces to undertake a particular project.

A **strategic alliance**, or joint venture, involves two or more enterprises cooperating in the research, development, manufacture, or marketing of a product. For example, GM and Suzuki formed a strategic alliance at the Ingersoll, Ontario, plant where Trackers and Grand Vitaras are made. Northern Empire, Stornoway, and Hunter Exploration Group formed a three-way joint venture to explore for diamonds on Melville Island in the Arctic Ocean.[21] Inco Ltd. and LionOre Mining International formed a joint venture to do research on processing technologies for the recovery of base metals from sulphide ores.[22]

Companies form strategic alliances for two main reasons: (1) to help spread the risk of a project, and (2) to get something of value (like technological expertise) from their strategic partner.

Subsidiary and Parent Corporations

Sometimes corporations own other corporations. A **subsidiary corporation** is one that is owned by another corporation. The corporation that owns the subsidiary is called the **parent corporation**. For example, Unilever is the parent corporation of Lever Brothers, Lipton, and Chesebrough Ponds.

subsidiary corporation
One that is owned by another corporation.

parent corporation
A corporation that owns a subsidiary.

SUMMARY OF LEARNING OBJECTIVES

1. **Define *small business* and discuss its importance to the Canadian economy.** A small business is independently owned and managed and does not dominate its market. Most Canadian businesses employ fewer than 100 people, and small firms employ most workers. The contribution of small business can be measured by its effects on three aspects of the economic system: (1) Job creation, (2) Innovation, and (3) Importance to big business.

2. **Explain *entrepreneurship* and describe some key characteristics of entrepreneurial personalities and activities.** Entrepreneurs assume the risk of business ownership with a primary goal of growth and expansion. Many small-business owners like to think of themselves as entrepreneurs, but a person may be a small-business owner only, an entrepreneur only, or both. The basic distinction between small-business ownership and entrepreneurship is aspiration—the entrepreneur's desire to start a business and make it grow. Most successful entrepreneurs are resourceful and concerned for customer relations. They have a strong desire to be their own boss and can handle ambiguity and surprises. Today's entrepreneur is often an open-minded leader who relies on networks, business plans, and consensus and is just as likely to be female as male.

3. **Describe the *business plan* and the *start-up decisions* made by small businesses.** Would-be entrepreneurs must decide how to get into business and know how to find financing. Entrepreneurs must assess their own skills as well as industry trends. The starting point for every new business is a business plan. A business plan defines strategies for production and marketing, legal elements and organization, and accounting and finance. It should answer three questions: (1) What are the entrepreneur's goals and objectives? (2) What strategies will be used to obtain them? (3) How will these strategies be implemented? After completing the business plan, the entrepreneur must decide whether to buy an existing business, to start from scratch, or to buy a franchise.

4. **Identify the main reasons for success and failure in small businesses.** Four basic factors explain most small-business success: (1) hard work, drive, and dedication; (2) market demand for the products or services being provided; (3) managerial competence; (4) luck. Four factors contribute to small-business failure: (1) managerial incompetence or inexperience; (2) neglect; (3) weak control systems; (4) insufficient capital.

5. **Explain *sole proprietorships* and *partnerships* and discuss the advantages and disadvantages of each.** The sole proprietorship is owned and usually operated by one person. The ease of setting up a sole proprietorship makes it appealing to self-starters, as do the low start-up

costs. There are tax benefits for new businesses that are likely to suffer losses in early stages: Because sole proprietors may treat revenues and expenses as part of their personal finances, they can cut their taxes by deducting business losses from income earned elsewhere. A major drawback is unlimited liability. A sole proprietor is personally liable for all debts incurred by the business. Another disadvantage is lack of continuity: A sole proprietorship dissolves when the owner dies. Finally, a sole proprietorship depends on the resources of a single individual.

The general partnership is a sole proprietorship multiplied by the number of partner-owners. The biggest advantage is its ability to grow by adding new talent and money. Because banks prefer to make loans to enterprises that are not dependent on single individuals, it's easier for partnerships to borrow money. They can also invite new partners to join by investing. Although they must meet only a few legal requirements, all partnerships must have a partnership agreement. Partners are taxed as individuals, and unlimited liability is a drawback. Each partner may be liable for all partnership debts. Partnerships may lack continuity, and transferring ownership may be hard. No partner may sell out without the consent of the others.

6. **Describe *corporations*, and discuss their advantages and disadvantages.** All corporations share certain characteristics: legal status as separate entities, property rights and obligations, and indefinite lifespans. They may sue and be sued; buy, hold, and sell property; make and sell products; commit crimes and be tried and punished for them. The biggest advantage of incorporation is limited liability: Investor liability is limited to one's personal investments in the corporation. If it fails, the courts may sell a corporation's assets but cannot touch the personal possessions of investors. Another advantage is continuity. With a legal life independent of founders and owners, a corporation can continue forever. Shares can be sold or passed on to heirs, and most corporations benefit from the continuity of professional management. Finally, corporations have advantages in raising money. By selling stock, they expand the number of investors and the amount of available funds. Legal protections tend to make lenders more willing to grant loans.

   One disadvantage goes hand in hand with ease of transferring ownership. An offer to buy shares can be made by a prospective buyer directly to a corporation's shareholders. Thus, a corporation can be taken over against the will of its managers (but it may benefit shareholders). Another disadvantage is start-up cost. Corporations are heavily regulated and must meet complex legal requirements in the provinces in which they're chartered. A potential drawback to incorporation is double taxation. A corporation pays income taxes on company profits, and its stockholders pay taxes on income returned by their investments. Thus, corporate profits are taxed twice—at the corporate and at ownership levels (but the dividend tax credit given to owners may offset the effects of double taxation).

7. **Explain the basic issues involved in creating and managing a corporation and identify recent trends in business ownership.** The corporate entity is managed by people who understand the principles of corporate governance—the roles of shareholders, directors, and other managers in corporate decision making. Corporations sell shares, called stock, to investors who then become stockholders (or shareholders) and the real owners. Profits are distributed among stockholders in the form of dividends, and managers serve at their discretion. Preferred

stock offers holders fixed dividends. Preferred stockholders have preference, or priority, over common stockholders when dividends are distributed and, if a business fails, when the value of assets is distributed. Common stock usually pays dividends only if the corporation makes a profit, and holders have the last claims to any assets. Dividends on both types of stock are paid on a per-share basis. While preferred stockholders have no voting rights, common stockholders always have one vote per share.

The governing body of a corporation is its board of directors. Boards communicate with stockholders and other stakeholders through such channels as the annual report—a summary of the company's financial health. They set policy on dividends, major spending, and executive compensation. They are legally responsible for corporate actions and are increasingly being held liable for them. Most board members do not participate in day-to-day management but rather hire a team of managers. This team, called officers, is usually headed by a chief executive officer, or CEO, who is responsible for overall performance. Other officers typically include a president, who is responsible for internal management, and vice presidents, who oversee various functional areas such as marketing and operations.

An acquisition occurs when one firm buys another outright. A merger occurs when two firms combine to create a new company. A divestiture occurs when a corporation sells a part of its existing business operations or sets it up as a new and independent corporation. When a firm sells part of itself to raise capital, the strategy is known as a spin-off. The employee stock ownership plan (ESOP) allows employees to own a significant share of the corporation through trusts established on their behalf. In a strategic alliance, two or more organizations collaborate on a project for mutual gain.

KEY TERMS

QUESTIONS AND EXERCISES

Questions for Review

1. Why are small businesses important to the Canadian economy?
2. What is the basic difference between a small business owner and an entrepreneur?
3. From the standpoint of the franchisee, what are the primary advantages and disadvantages of most franchise arrangements?
4. Which industries are easiest for start-ups to enter? Which are hardest? Why?

Questions for Analysis

5. Why might a closely held corporation choose to remain private? Why might it choose to be publicly traded?

6. If you were going to open a small business, what type would it be? Why?

7. Would you prefer to buy an existing business or start from scratch? Why?

8. Do you think you would be a successful entrepreneur? Why or why not?

Application Exercises

9. Interview the owner-manager of a sole proprietorship or a general partnership. What characteristics of that business form led the owner to choose it? Does he or she ever contemplate changing the form of the business?

10. Identify two or three of the fastest growing businesses in Canada during the last year. What role has entrepreneurship played in the growth of these firms?

BUILDING YOUR BUSINESS SKILLS

Working the Internet

Goal

To encourage students to define opportunities and problems for small companies doing business on the internet.

Situation

Suppose you and two partners own a gift basket store, specializing in special-occasion baskets for individual and corporate clients. Your business is doing well in your community, but you believe there may be opportunity for growth through a virtual storefront on the internet.

Method

Step 1

Join with two other students and assume the role of business partners. Start by researching internet businesses. Look at books and articles at the library and contact the following websites for help:

Canada Business Service Centres: **www.cbsc.org**

Small Business Administration (United States): **www.sba.gov**

IBM Small Business Center: **www.businesscenter.ibm.com**

Apple Small Business Home Page: **www.apple.com/business/**

These sites may lead you to other sites, so keep an open mind.

Step 2

Based on your research, determine the importance of the following small business issues:

- an analysis of changing company finances as a result of expansion to the internet
- an analysis of your new competitive marketplace (the world) and how it affects your current marketing approach, which focuses on your local community
- identification of sources of management advice as the expansion proceeds
- the role of technology consultants in launching and maintaining the website
- customer service policies in your virtual environment

Follow-Up Questions

1. Do you think your business would be successful on the internet? Why or why not?
2. Based on your analysis, how will internet expansion affect your current business practices? What specific changes are you likely to make?
3. Do you think that operating a virtual storefront will be harder or easier than doing business in your local community? Explain your answer.

CRAFTING YOUR BUSINESS PLAN

Fitting into the Entrepreneurial Mould

The Purpose of the Assignment

1. To familiarize students with the ways in which entrepreneurship and small business considerations enter into the business planning framework of the Business PlanPro (BPP) software package.
2. To encourage students to think about how to apply their textbook information on entrepreneurship to the preparation of a small business plan using the BPP planning environment.

Assignment

After reading Chapter 3 in the textbook, open the BPP software and look around for information about the types of small business and entrepreneurship considerations that would be of concern to a sample firm: Corporate Fitness. To find Corporate Fitness, do the following:

Open the Business PlanPro. If it asks if you want to "create a new business plan" or "open an existing plan," select "create a new business plan" (even though you are not going to create a plan at this time). You will then be taken to the Business PlanPro EasyPlan Wizard. Click on the option entitled **Research It**. You will then be presented with a new list of options, including Sample Plan Browser. After clicking on the **Sample Plan Browser**, go down the alphabetical list of sample plans and double-click on **Health Fitness Program**, which is the location for **Corporate Fitness**. The screen you are looking at is the introductory page for the Corporate Fitness business plan. Next, scroll down from this page until you reach the **Table of Contents** for the company's business plan.

Now respond to the following items:

1. In the Table of Contents page, click on **1.0 Executive Summary** to familiarize yourself with an overview of this firm. Which industry category for small business—construction, wholesaling, services, transportation, or manufacturing—best describes the Corporate Fitness line of business?
2. The textbook identifies several characteristics of successful entrepreneurs. Judging by its business plan, do you think the management team of Corporate Fitness has an entrepreneurial orientation? Explain why or why not. [Sites to see in BPP for this item: On the Table of Contents page, click on each of the following in turn: **6.0 Management Summary, 6.2 Management Team,** and **6.3 Management Team Gaps.**]
3. The textbook identifies several sources of advice and assistance for starting and running small businesses. Judging from its business plan, do you think that Corporate Fitness is planning to seek advice from any of those sources in getting started? Do you think it is a good idea to discuss the planned uses of such sources in the business plan? Explain why or why not. [Sites to see in BPP: From the Table of Contents page, explore the Corporate Fitness business plan using your judgment as to where you would expect to find information on start-up advice.]
4. What sources of advice and assistance do you recommend for getting Corporate Fitness off to a sound start? In which areas of the business and for which of its business activities will it benefit the most from outside advice and assistance? Where in its business plan do you recommend reporting its planned use of such assistance?

VIDEO EXERCISE

Doing Business Privately: Amy's Ice Creams

Learning Objectives

The purpose of this video is to help you:

1. Distinguish among types of corporations.
2. Consider the advantages and disadvantages of incorporation.
3. Understand the role that shareholders play in a privately held corporation.

Synopsis

Amy's Ice Creams, based in Austin, Texas, is a privately held corporation formed in 1984 by Amy Miller and owned by Miller and a small group of family members and friends (**www.amysicecreams.com**). At the outset, one of the most important decisions Miller faced was choosing an appropriate legal ownership structure for the new business.

Fuelled by the founder's dedication to creating happy ice cream memories for customers, Amy's has continued to evolve and grow. The company now operates nine stores and rings up close to $3.5 million in annual sales. Applying for a job is an adventure in creativity, and Miller welcomes employees' suggestions for new flavours and new promotions.

Discussion Questions

1. *For analysis:* How does Amy's Ice Creams differ from a publicly held corporation?
2. *For analysis:* What are some of the particular advantages of corporate ownership for a firm such as Amy's Ice Creams?
3. *For application:* How well do you think Amy's is working to ensure its continued survival and success? Looking ahead to future growth, what marketing, financial, or other suggestions would you make?
4. *For application:* What are some of the issues that Amy Miller may have to confront because her 22 investors are family members and friends?
5. *For debate:* Should Amy's Ice Creams become a publicly held corporation? Support your chosen position.

Online Exploration

Find out what's required to incorporate a business in your province. You might begin by searching the CCH Business Owner's Toolkit site at **www.toolkit.cch.com**. If you were going to start a small business, would you choose incorporation or a different form of legal organization? List the pros and cons that incorporation presents for the type of business that you would consider.

EXPLORING THE NET

Help for the Small-Business Person

A valuable information source for small-business persons is the Online Small Business Workshop. You can reach the website at the following address: **www.cbsc.org/osbw/.**

1. Review the outline of a business plan in the text. Within the website, where would you find the information to help you complete a business plan? For example, where in the website would you find information or tools to assist you in completing the market assessment section of a business plan?
2. Write down a type of business you'd like to start. In the "Financing Your Business" section of the website, investigate small business loan opportunities for your new business. List the loans you qualify for because of the nature of your proposed business, your geographic region, or other criteria.
3. Review the possible ups and downs of starting your own small business as described in the "Planning Fundamentals" section. Assess your own weaknesses in possible areas that are controllable (e.g., a weather disaster is beyond your control). What resources could help you overcome these shortcomings?
4. Evaluate the usefulness of the "Sample Business Plan."

Concluding Case 3-1

The Big Cheese

People familiar with the business landscape in Vermont point with justifiable pride to Ben Cohen and Jerry Greenfield, founders of Ben and Jerry's Homemade Holdings Inc., as the state's foremost entrepreneurs. But the ice cream boys are getting some competition these days from another pair of entrepreneurs who are making a popular line of cheese products the cream of local business.

The story starts in 1919, when 94 Vermont dairy farmers banded together to create a co-operative to make and market cheese. The initial membership fee was $5.00 per cow and a cord of wood to fuel the boiler. Cabot Creamery (**www.cabotcheese.com**) is now a multimillion-dollar dairy-products company with a membership of 1500 farm families. Its cheeses have won numerous awards, including Best Cheddar in the World at the World Cheese Championship in Green Bay, Wisconsin.

Cabot has always built its brand on quality. Whereas many companies use enzymes to speed up the cheesemaking process, Cabot uses only natural methods. Naturally processing high-quality cheese means that a 640-pound block of cheddar might have to sit in a warehouse for a year before it gets its rich, full-bodied flavour. At any time, therefore, Cabot might have 25 million pounds of cheese in the warehouse. And because costs are pegged to the price of milk when the cheese is first manufactured, profit margins are hard to predict. Managers have to forecast both the price of milk and the demand for cheese as much as a year in advance. Furthermore, the price of milk fluctuates just as much as the price of crude oil. "There's a pretty good temptation to play around with enzymes," admits Cabot CEO Richard Stammer. "If you can put out an extra-sharp cheddar in 5 months instead of 12, you're less likely to get stung by a spread in the price of milk."

In the early 1990s, Cabot was in danger of going under. Even with revenues of $35 million a year, annual profits were less than $1 million. Members were getting restless, and there was talk of abandoning Cabot and launching a new co-operative. But because a new venture would have been a big risk, members decided on another approach: In 1992, Cabot agreed to be taken over by Agri-Mark Inc., a dairy co-op based in Methuen, Massachusetts. Agri-Mark (**www.agrimark.net**) was the fourteenth largest dairy co-op in the United States and wanted to expand. Given the obvious fit between a dairy co-op and a cheese maker, the move seemed like a good one.

After Agri-Mark took control of Cabot in 1992, parent-company president Paul Johnston decided to install a new CEO. He didn't have to look far. His choice was Richard Stammer, Agri-Mark's chief economist. While Johnston was working his way up the ladder at an Agri-Mark milk-producing plant, Stammer had been an economics professor at Rutgers, where he had developed a strong understanding of the dynamics of prices in agricultural markets.

Johnston and Stammer couldn't have been more different, but they worked well together. Johnston is a demanding boss known for his bluntness and, occasionally, lack of tact. Stammer is reserved, polite, and gracious. But the two executives have managed to set aside their differences and focus on a common goal: running an efficient business that earns profits for its owners.

Among the first things they did was improve forecasting methods. The process is never perfect, but Cabot now does a much better job of predicting demand and prices for milk and cheese. They also set about to make Cabot a national brand by concentrating more heavily on product marketing. So far, the plan seems to be paying off: Profits have topped $8 million on annual revenues of $175 million.

Questions for Discussion

1. Why do you think Cabot is organized as a co-operative?
2. What elements of business ownership are illustrated in this case?
3. What role has entrepreneurship played in the history and success of Cabot?
4. Under what circumstances might it make sense for Cabot to reorganize as a corporation?
5. What issues of taxation and legal liability might be especially pertinent for Cabot and Agri-Mark? ◆

Concluding Case 3-2

Employees Are Stockholders at WestJet

WestJet Airlines started operations on February 29, 1996. Its strategy is to sell tickets at bargain prices, offer good customer service, keep costs down by running a low-cost operation, and fly short-haul trips to carefully chosen markets. In just a few short years, WestJet's fleet has grown to 21 jets and sales revenues have grown to over $330 million annually. WestJet's share price on the Toronto Stock Exchange has increased 240 percent since its initial public offering (IPO) in 1999. WestJet's performance has made its founders rich, but they aren't the only ones who are benefiting.

WestJet's employees have been actively involved in buying up shares of the company's stock. For every dollar an employee invests, the company matches that amount. This means that employees are essentially able to buy shares of stock in WestJet at half the normal market price. Therefore, it isn't surprising that 83 percent of employees own shares in the company. The employees who bought in before the IPO now have an impressive portfolio. Some flight attendants now own more than $400 000 in stock, and some WestJet pilots are millionaires.

WestJet CEO Clive Beddoe has encouraged a corporate culture that aligns the interests of the employees with those of the company. He recognizes that in the commercial airline business employees are spread out all over the country as they work in various airports and on the airplanes. He knows that he has to encourage people to manage themselves. WestJet therefore gives a lot of latitude to workers to perform their jobs. This strategy means fewer layers of supervisors and a much higher level of productivity per worker. The strategy seems to be working: WestJet operates with fewer than 60 people per aircraft, while rival Air Canada uses more than 140 per aircraft.

Beddoe isn't so naive as to assume that workers will automatically take ownership of their job. He realizes the value of incentives, so WestJet has instituted a profit-sharing plan that encourages employees to be interested in maximizing profits. The plan works as follows: If WestJet's profit margin is, say, 10 percent, then 10 percent of net income is given to employees (prorated by salary). If the profit margin is 15 percent, employees get 15 percent, and so on up to a maximum of 20 percent. On November 17, 2000, cheques totalling more than $8 million were handed out to employees. WestJet pays salaries that are slightly lower than the industry average, but when the profit sharing is added in, employees are better off than others in the industry.

WestJet receives more than 3000 résumés a week from people who want to join the company. Most of these people do not currently work in the airline industry. Beddoe views that positively, saying that it's important to hire people who have new ideas and a new vision. WestJet is particularly interested in applicants who are enthusiastic and have a sense of humour, because Beddoe thinks that everyone should have fun while working.

An employee association called the Pro-Active Communication Team (PACT) is active at WestJet. It includes all employees in the company, and has chapters representing the various employee groups, such as pilots and flight attendants. Each of these groups has representatives who sit on a council. PACT helps management keep in touch with rank-and-file workers and address any concerns they may have. PACT provides workers many of the same services a union would, but without the adversarial environment that a union can create. PACT may make it very difficult for a union to get into WestJet because of the way PACT is organized. If an employee group (such as flight attendants) wants to leave PACT, it must receive approval from 75 percent of the members. That is not very likely to happen.

Questions for Discussion

1. Is WestJet a private corporation or a public corporation? Explain how the offering of an IPO affects whether a corporation is public or private.
2. How have WestJet employees benefited from owning shares in the company? Why would employees who bought stock before the IPO have benefited more than others who bought shares later?
3. What rights do WestJet employees have as stockholders? To what extent will these rights influence their day-to-day behaviour on the job?
4. What is an ESOP? Does WestJet have an ESOP, or doesn't it? Explain.
5. Consider the following statement: "When a company forms an employee association like PACT, it is just trying to get employees to do what management wants, but under the guise of consulting with employees. Management and workers have basically conflicting goals, and these conflicting goals can't be removed simply by forming an employee association." Do you agree or disagree with this statement? Explain. ◆

CHAPTER 4

Understanding International Business

After reading this chapter, you should be able to:

1. Explain how *free trade agreements* assist world trade.
2. Describe the rise of international business and identify the *major world marketplaces*.
3. Explain how different forms of *competitive advantage, import-export balances, exchange rates,* and *foreign competition* determine the ways in which countries and businesses respond to the international environment.
4. Discuss the factors involved in deciding to do business internationally and in selecting the appropriate *levels of international involvement* and *international organizational structure*.
5. Describe some of the ways in which *social, cultural, economic, legal,* and *political differences* act as barriers to international trade.

Bombardier Encounters Turbulence in International Airspace

In December 2002, Paul Tellier became CEO of Montreal-based Bombardier Inc., a diversified Canadian company that specializes in transportation equipment, recreational products, aerospace products, financial, and real estate services. The company was founded in 1942 to manufacture a classic Canadian product—tracked vehicles for transportation across snow-covered terrain. Many of the Bombardier snowmobiles that were manufactured decades ago can still be seen in remote areas of Canada. One such half-track sits on the windswept shores of Yathkyed Lake in the Northwest Territories, hundreds of kilometres from any town. It is a mute reminder of the important role Bombardier played in opening up Canada's remote North.

While Bombardier's headquarters are in Montreal, Bombardier employees also work in the United States, Mexico, Europe, and the Middle East. More than 90 percent of company revenues come from outside Canada. Bombardier is on a mission of expansion to accelerate growth in foreign markets. Bombardier's mandate is to:

- search for and identify new business opportunities in countries other than those in North America and Europe
- act as an intermediary with government authorities and business communities in foreign locations
- explore opportunities for acquisitions and strategic alliances

Tellier was hired to revive the sagging fortunes of Bombardier, which has recently fallen on hard times. The problems have been caused in part by several high-profile world events, most notably the September 11, 2001, World Trade Center disaster. As we saw in the Opening Case in Chapter 2, the 9/11 terrorist attack caused major problems for commercial airlines. Their business has declined, so they have reduced their purchases of airplanes. Since a big chunk of Bombardier's business is selling planes to these commercial aviation companies, Bombardier is now having problems of its own. Since September 2001, over 8000 employees have been laid off as Bombardier has tried to cope with a difficult environment.

Everyone knows by now that the commercial airline business is in the throes of massive change. Companies like WestJet and Southwest Airlines have revolutionized the airline business and have become serious competitors to the major airlines like Northwest and Air Canada. The fact is that the old "business model" no longer works in the aviation business. How will this affect Bombardier? No one is sure.

The corporate jet market is even more uncertain because it goes up and down with the economy. Bombardier delivered 203 corporate jets in 2001, but only 162 in 2002. The numbers are expected to drop even further for 2003. With intense international competition, and with companies buying less, this business looks questionable. Although Bombardier has historically done well in the business jet market, the competition is fierce. In the mid-1990s, Bombardier held two-thirds of the market for regional jets, but then Brazilian rival Embraer captured 45 percent of that market. Bombardier complained to the World Trade Organization that the Brazilian government was unfairly subsidizing Embraer by giving it large sums of money. But the Canadian government was also giving loans to Bombardier's customers.

Events that occur in other companies (and over which Bombardier has no control) have also caused problems for Bombardier. For example, when United Airlines filed for bankruptcy in the United States, 29 percent of Bombardier's order backlog was put at risk. The rail business also has problems of excess capacity. This means that Bombardier will likely be forced to consolidate some of its operations. The problem is that to successfully get orders in certain countries, it is necessary to have a manufacturing presence there. That works against consolidation.

All of these problems have caused Bombardier's stock price to plummet. In April 2003, Bombardier's stock was trading at less than $3.00 per share. This was far below its price of $15.00 per share a year earlier. With its stock price so low, investors are less interested in buying into the company. The company may therefore have difficulty raising the money it needs to continue operations. Investor confidence has to be restored to keep the company from going the way of Nortel.

Some investors are also concerned that Bombardier has a "cozy" relationship with the Canadian government, and that too much of its business is done with taxpayers' dollars. Through the Export Development Corporation, the Canadian government loans money to Bombardier's customers so they can purchase the planes and trains the company manufactures. But what happens if the government decides to stop handing out this money? Critics also say that Bombardier needs to be more open in its accounting methods so potential investors have good information on which to base their stock purchase decisions.

Paul Tellier has a lot of work to do. Four months after joining the company, he announced a four-point plan to turn the company around. It included (1) an equity offering to raise $800 million, (2) asset spinoffs that will raise $1.5 billion, (3) reducing dividends to conserve cash, and (4) focusing on aerospace businesses and selling off other assets to raise cash. ◆

THE RISE OF INTERNATIONAL BUSINESS

globalization
The integration of markets globally.

imports
Products that are made or grown abroad and sold in Canada.

exports
Products made or grown in Canada that are sold abroad.

Bombardier is just one of many Canadian companies that are involved in international business activities. The total volume of world trade today is immense—around $8 trillion each year. As more and more firms engage in international business, the world economy is fast becoming a single interdependent system—a process called **globalization**. Even so, we often take for granted the diversity of goods and services available today as a result of international trade. Your television set, your shoes, and even the roast lamb on your dinner table may all be **imports**—that is, products made or grown abroad but sold in Canada. At the same time, the success of many Canadian firms depends in large part on **exports**—products made or grown domestically and shipped for sale abroad.

The Contemporary Global Economy

International business is nothing new. Trade between nations can actually be traced back as far as 2000 BCE, when North African tribes took dates and clothing to Assyria and Babylonia in the Middle East and traded them for olive oil and spices. Christopher Columbus's voyages of discovery were motivated by the search for new trade routes. Still, there is a tendency for people to forget that international business has been around for a long time. An understanding of historical forces can significantly improve our understanding of the contemporary global economy—how it works, why it works, and what trends will likely shape its future.[1]

MIT professor Paul Krugman argues that what we now regard as an extremely active "global economy" is not as big a change as you might imagine. He points out that imports now represent only a slightly higher proportion of GDP than they did 100 years ago, and that capital mobility (the movement of money from country to country) is about the same as it was in 1914. At that time, moreover, England's trade surplus—4 percent of GDP—was the same as the surplus enjoyed by Japan during the peak decade of the 1980s.

On the other hand, it is also true that international trade is becoming increasingly central to the fortunes of most nations of the world, as well as to their largest businesses. Whereas in the past many nations followed strict policies to protect domestic business, today more and more countries are aggressively encouraging international trade. They are more freely opening their borders to foreign businesses, offering incentives for their own domestic businesses to expand internationally, and making it easier for foreign firms to partner with local firms through various alliances. Similarly, as more and more industries and markets become global, firms that compete in them are also becoming global.

Several forces have combined to spark and sustain globalization. For one thing, governments and businesses have simply become more aware of the benefits of globalization to their countries and shareholders. For another, new technologies make international travel, communication, and commerce increasingly easier, faster, and cheaper than ever before. Overseas phone calls and seaborne shipping costs per tonne have both declined over the last several decades. Likewise, transatlantic travel once required several days aboard a ship. Today, travellers can easily fly between major cities in North America and Europe in less than a day. Finally, there are competitive pressures: sometimes, a firm simply must enter foreign markets just to keep up with its competitors.

Trade Agreements

Various free trade agreements have sparked international trade. Indeed, virtually every nation has formal trade treaties with other nations. Among the most significant agreements are the General Agreement on Tariffs and Trade, the World Trade Organization, the North American Free Trade Agreement, and the European Union.

1. Explain how *free trade agreements* assist world trade.

General Agreement on Tariffs and Trade

The General Agreement on Tariffs and Trade (GATT), which was often humorously referred to as the General Agreement to Talk and Talk, was signed after World War II. Its purpose was to reduce or eliminate trade barriers, such as tariffs and quotas. It did so by encouraging nations to protect domestic industries within agreed-upon limits and to engage in multilateral negotiations. While 92 countries signed GATT, not all complied with its

General Agreement on Tariffs and Trade (GATT)
International trade agreement to encourage the multilateral reduction or elimination of trade barriers.

Fisherman Ratish Karthikeyan can sometimes double the revenue from a day's take by phoning around to compare prices at markets within reach of his boat. India is a thriving export market for cellular phones. About half of India's 600 000 rural communities aren't even wired for fixed-line phone service. The number of mobile-phone users in India should jump from 3 million to 30 million in the next few years.

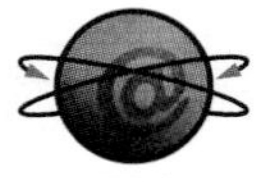

GATT Guide
www.ciesin.org./TG/PI/TRADE/gatt.html

rules. The United States was one of the worst offenders. A revision of GATT went into effect in 1994, but many issues remained unresolved—for example, the opening of foreign markets to most financial services.

World Trade Organization

World Trade Organization (WTO)
Organization through which member nations negotiate trading agreements and resolve disputes about trade policies and practices.

On January 1, 1995, the **World Trade Organization (WTO)** came into existence as the successor to GATT. The 140 member countries are required to open markets to international trade, and the WTO is empowered to pursue three goals:

1. Promote trade by encouraging members to adopt fair trade practices.
2. Reduce trade barriers by promoting multilateral negotiations.
3. Establish fair procedures for resolving disputes among members.

The WTO is overseeing a one-third reduction in import duties on thousands of products that are traded between countries. Canada, the United States, and the European Union are founding members of the WTO.[2] Unlike GATT, the WTO's decisions are binding, and many people feared that it would make sweeping decisions and boss countries around. But the WTO is off to a slow start. It has not been very successful in toppling global barriers to trade in three critical areas—world financial services, telecommunications, and maritime markets—because political leaders from various countries are fearful of the consequences of freer trade.[3] But the WTO did rule in 1999 that Canada had to scrap the Auto Pact because it was essentially an export subsidy program, which is prohibited.[4] It also ruled in 2003 that the United States acted illegally when it placed import duties on steel from the European Union, but exempted Canadian steel from the import duties (because of NAFTA).[5]

One of the most controversial issues confronting the WTO is agricultural subsidies. Governments in industrialized countries often pay subsidies to their own farmers to grow certain crops, but these subsidies distort international markets for agricultural commodities and hurt growers in poor countries, particularly in Africa.

On several occasions when the WTO has held talks on trade liberalization, protestors have disrupted the meetings. WTO meetings in Seattle, Prague, and Montreal were disrupted by protestors who resent the power of the WTO and who are concerned about what world trade is doing to both the environment and the developing countries that are not sharing in its benefits.[6] Protestors included labour unions (who regard Third World imports as unfair), environmentalists (who are concerned about business activity harming the environment), social activists (who are concerned about poor working conditions in developing countries), and farmers (who are concerned about the effect of free trade on grain prices).

The European Union (EU)

European Union (EU)
Agreement among major Western European nations to eliminate or make uniform most trade barriers affecting group members.

Originally called the Common Market, the **European Union (EU)** includes the principal Western European nations, which have eliminated most quotas and set uniform tariff levels on products imported and exported within their group. In 1992, virtually all internal trade barriers went down, making the EU the largest free marketplace in the world. We discuss the EU more fully later in the chapter.

North American Free Trade Agreement

North American Free Trade Agreement (NAFTA)
Agreement to gradually eliminate tariffs and other trade barriers among the United States, Canada, and Mexico.

The **North American Free Trade Agreement (NAFTA)** came into effect in 1994. It removes tariffs and other trade barriers among Canada, the United

States, and Mexico (see Figure 4.1). An earlier agreement, the Canada–U.S. Free Trade Agreement (FTA), took effect in 1989. Its goal was to achieve freer trade between Canada and the United States. Surveys conducted prior to the introduction of the FTA showed that the majority of Canadians were opposed to free trade. They feared that (1) jobs would be lost to other countries, (2) Canada would be flooded with products manufactured in lower-wage countries such as Mexico, (3) Canada would lose the right to control its own environmental standards, (4) the United States might take our natural resources, and (5) Canadian cultural sovereignty would be lost.

Supporters of free trade, by contrast, argued that (1) access to U.S. markets would be guaranteed by free trade, which was therefore crucial to protecting Canadian employment, (2) Canadian exports would increase because of free trade, (3) the environment was not covered in free trade agreements, (4) there was nothing in the free trade agreements that threatened Canada's control over its energy resources, and (5) the free trade agreement was about trade and tariffs, not cultural sovereignty.

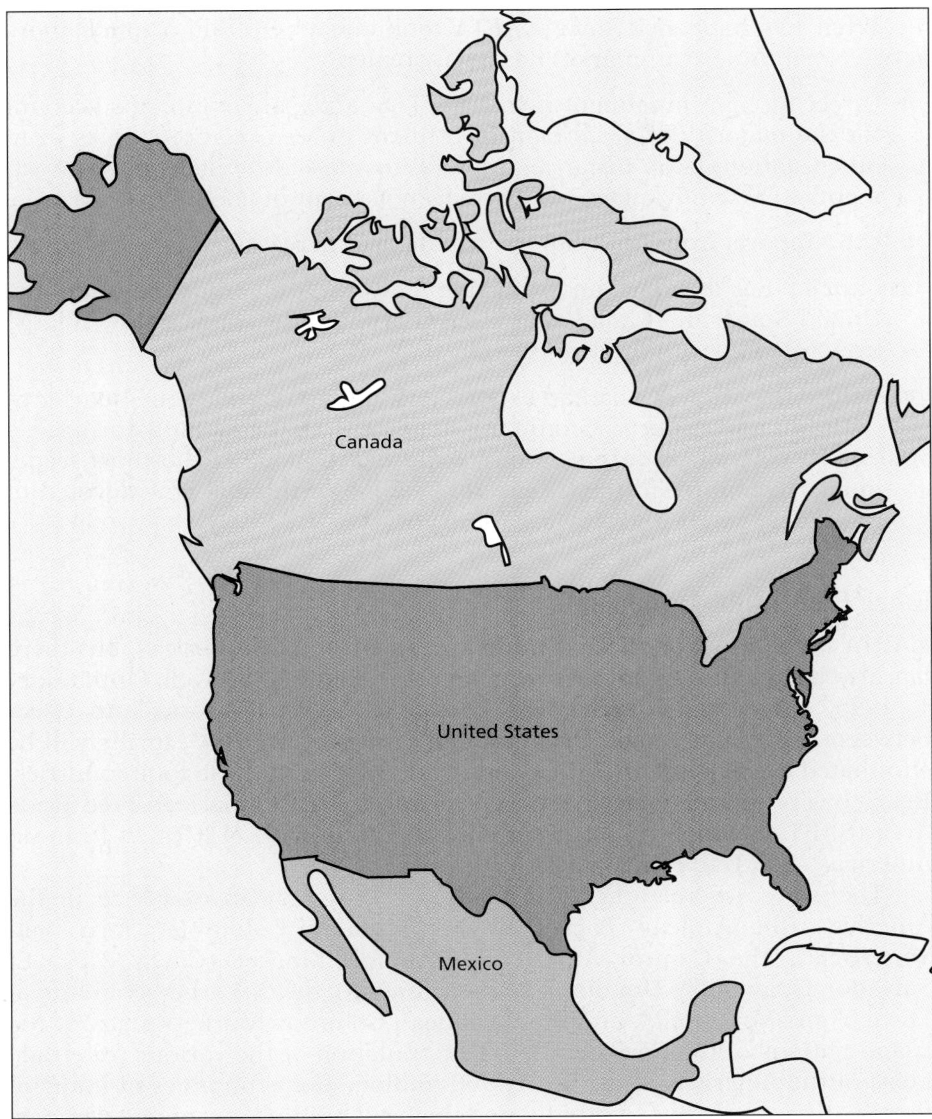

Figure 4.1
The North American marketplace.

The Palliser Furniture showroom in Winnipeg, Manitoba. In the 1990s, employment at Palliser surged due to the company's success in exporting its products to U.S. markets. More recently, competition from manufacturers in China has caused difficulties for Palliser.

What has happened since NAFTA took effect? Overall, a much more active North American market has been created.

- Direct foreign investment increased. U.S. and Canadian firms account for the majority of all foreign investment in Mexico. Companies from other nations—for instance, Japan's Toyota—also made new investments to take advantage of the freer movement of goods.
- U.S. imports from (and exports to) Mexico increased.
- Canada has become an exporting powerhouse. Trade between the United States and Canada has risen sharply, and Canada enjoys a large trade surplus with the United States.
- Before free trade, Canadian exports accounted for about one-quarter of GDP, but now exports account for 40 percent. In the manufacturing sector, 60 percent of output is now exported. Canada is the most trade-intensive country in the G7 group. One job in three is now devoted to producing goods and services for export.[7]

Other Free Trade Agreements

NAFTA is the most publicized trade agreement in the Americas, but there has also been a flurry of activity among other countries as well. On January 1, 1995, a free trade agreement known as Mercosur went into effect between Argentina, Brazil, Uruguay, and Paraguay. By 2005, tariffs will be eliminated on 80 percent of the goods traded between those four countries. Brazil has proposed enlarging Mercosur into a South American Free Trade Area (SAFTA), which might eventually negotiate with NAFTA to form an Americas Free Trade Area (AFTA).

There are several other free trade areas already in existence in the Americas: the Andean Pact (Bolivia, Ecuador, Colombia, Peru, and Venezuela), the Central American Common Market (Costa Rica, El Salvador, Guatemala, Honduras, and Nicaragua), the G-3 group (Columbia, Mexico, and Venezuela), and the Caribbean Common Market (many of the island nations of the Caribbean).[8] The population of the various free trade areas of the Americas totals nearly 900 million. The economies of many of these nations are growing rapidly, and they will become increasingly important to Canada during the next decade.

Free trade agreements are not restricted to the Americas. A high level of activity is evident around the world as groups of nations band together to form regional trade associations for their own benefit. Some examples:

- the ASEAN Free Trade Area (Brunei, Indonesia, Malaysia, the Philippines, Singapore, Thailand, and Vietnam)
- the Asia-Pacific Economic Cooperation (many nations of the Pacific Rim, as well as the United States, Canada, and Mexico)
- the Economic Community of Central African States (many nations in equatorial Africa)
- the Gulf Cooperation Council (Bahrain, Kuwait, Oman, Qatar, Saudi Arabia, and United Arab Emirates).

In the remainder of this section, we examine some key factors that have shaped—and are shaping—today's global business environment. First, we identify and describe the *major world marketplaces*. Then we discuss some important factors that determine the ways in which both nations and their businesses respond to the international environment: the roles of different forms of *competitive advantage, import-export balances,* and *exchange rates*.

The Major World Marketplaces

2. Describe the rise of international business and identify the *major world marketplaces.*

The contemporary world economy revolves around three major marketplaces: North America, Europe, and Asia-Pacific. These three geographic regions are home to most of the world's largest economies, biggest multinational corporations, most influential financial markets, and highest-income consumers.

The World Bank, an agency of the United Nations, uses **per capita income**—the average income per person—as a measure to divide countries into one of three groups:[9]

per capita income
The average income per person of a country.

- *High-income countries* are those with per capita income greater than U.S.$9386. These include Canada, the United States, most countries in Europe, Australia, New Zealand, Japan, South Korea, Kuwait, the United Arab Emirates, Israel, Singapore, and Taiwan. Hong Kong, while technically no longer an independent nation, also falls into this category.
- *Middle-income countries* are those with per capita income of less than U.S.$9386 but more than U.S.$765. Some of the countries in this group are the Czech Republic, Greece, Hungary, Poland, most countries comprising the former Soviet Bloc, Turkey, Mexico, Argentina, and Uruguay. Some of these nations, most notably Poland, are undergoing successful industrialization and economic development and are expected to move into the high-income category very soon.
- *Low-income countries*, also called developing countries, are those with per capita income of less than U.S.$765. Some of these, such as China and India, have huge populations and are seen as potentially attractive markets for international business. Due to low literacy rates, weak infrastructures, unstable governments, and related problems, other countries in this group are less attractive to international business. For example, the East African nation of Somalia, plagued by drought, civil war, and starvation, plays virtually no role in the world economy.

This boy's home country, the arid landlocked nation of Burkina Faso, is a "low-income" country. That's why he's working on a cocoa plantation in the Ivory Coast, one of the continent's more prosperous nations, for about 50 cents (U.S.) a day. Even at that rate, he's far from the bottom rung on Africa's economic ladder. As for the cocoa farmer who pays him, he's finally been able to buy a tractor after farming 48 acres for 33 years. The cocoa is sold to local buyers and then to exporters who sell it to companies like Nestlé and Hershey.

North America

The United States dominates the North American business region. It is the single largest marketplace and enjoys the most stable economy in the world. Canada also plays a major role in the international economy. Moreover, the United States and Canada are each other's largest trading partner. Many U.S. firms, such as General Motors and Procter & Gamble, have maintained successful Canadian operations for years, and many Canadian firms, such as Bombardier, Nortel Networks, and Alcan Aluminum, are also major international competitors.

Mexico has also become a major manufacturing centre, especially along the southern U.S. border, where cheap labour and low transportation costs have encouraged many firms, from the United States and other countries, to build manufacturing plants. The auto industry has been especially active. For example, DaimlerChrysler, General Motors, Volkswagen, Nissan, and Ford have large assembly plants in this region. Moreover, several of their major suppliers have also built facilities in the area. From 1993 to 2001, exports of automobiles and automobile parts from Mexico increased from $7.2 billion to a stunning $23.6 billion, and the auto industry in Mexico now employs over 400 000 workers.[10]

Europe

Europe has often been regarded as two regions—Western Europe and Eastern Europe. Western Europe, dominated by Germany, the United Kingdom, France, and Italy, has long been a mature but fragmented marketplace. But the transformation of the European Union (EU) in 1992 into a unified marketplace has further increased the region's importance (see Figure 4.2). Major international firms such as Unilever, Renault, Royal Dutch/Shell, Michelin, Siemens, and Nestlé are all headquartered in Western Europe.

Ecommerce and technology have also become increasingly important in this region.[11] There has been a surge in internet start-ups in southeast England, the Netherlands, and the Scandinavian countries, and Ireland is now the world's number-two exporter of software (after the United States).[12] Strasbourg, France, is a major centre for biotech start-ups. Barcelona, Spain, has many flourishing software and internet companies,

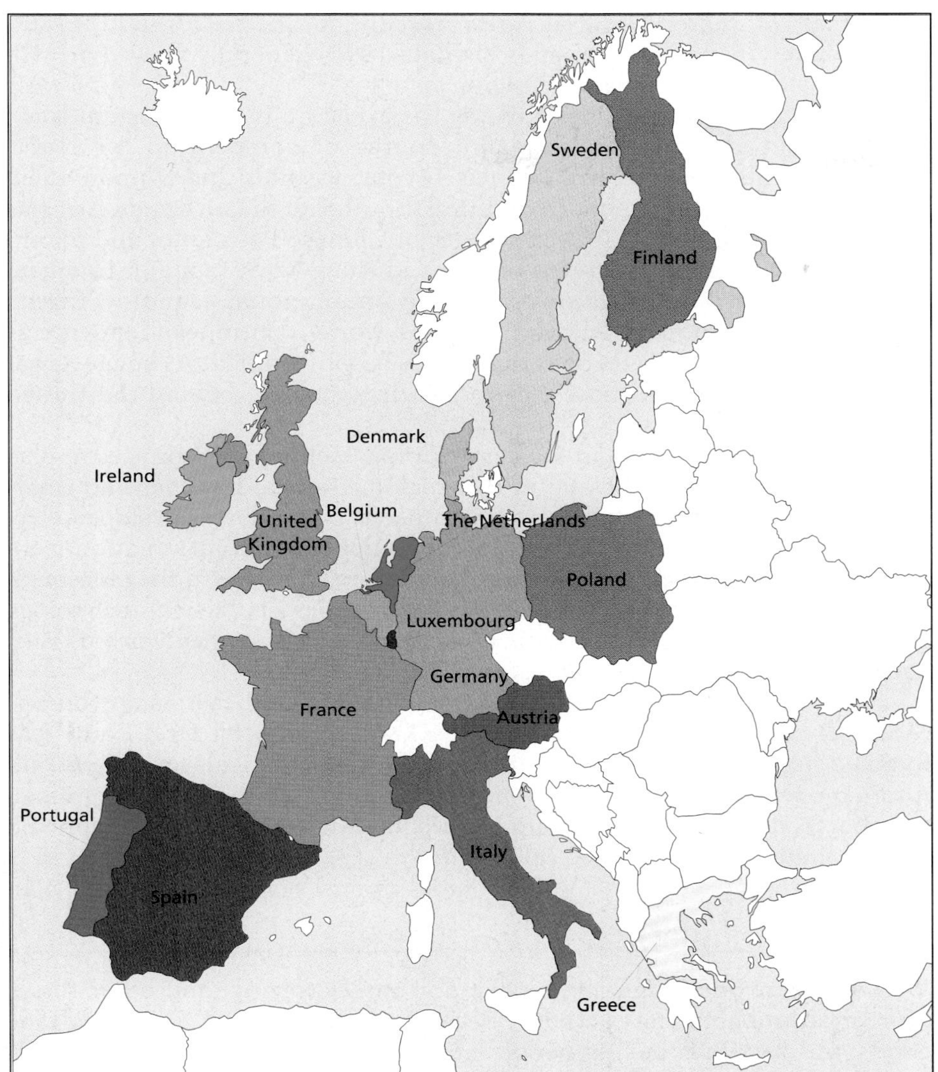

Figure 4.2
Europe and the nations of the European Union.

and the Frankfurt region of Germany is dotted with both software and biotech start-ups.[13]

Eastern Europe, once primarily communist, has also gained in importance, both as a marketplace and as a producer. For example, such multinational corporations as Daewoo, Nestlé, General Motors, and ABB Asea Brown Boveri have all set up operations in Poland. Similarly, Ford, General Motors, Suzuki, and Volkswagen have all built new factories in Hungary. On the other hand, government instability has hampered economic development in Russia, Bulgaria, Albania, Romania, and other countries in this region.

Asia-Pacific

Asia-Pacific consists of Japan, China, Thailand, Malaysia, Singapore, Indonesia, South Korea, Taiwan, the Philippines, Australia, and New Zealand. Some experts still identify Hong Kong as a separate part of the region, although the former city-state is now actually part of China. Vietnam is sometimes included as part of the region. Fuelled by strong entries in the automobile, electronics, and banking industries, the economies of these countries grew rapidly in the 1970s and 1980s. Unfortunately, a currency crisis in the late 1990s generally slowed growth in virtually every country of the region.

The currency crisis aside, however, Asia-Pacific is an important force in the world economy and a major source of competition for North American firms. Led by firms such as Toyota, Toshiba, and Nippon Steel, Japan dominates the region. In addition, South Korea (with such firms as Samsung and Hyundai), Taiwan (owner of Chinese Petroleum and manufacturing home of many foreign firms), and Hong Kong (a major financial centre) are also successful players in the international economy. China, the most densely populated country in the world, continues to emerge as an important market in its own right. In fact, most indicators suggest that the Chinese economy is now the world's third largest, behind the United States and Japan.

As in North America and Western Europe, technology promises to play an increasingly important role in this region. In Asia, however, the emergence of technology firms has been hampered by a poorly developed electronic infrastructure, slower adoption of computers and information technology, a higher percentage of lower-income consumers, and the aforementioned currency crisis. Thus, while the future looks promising, technology companies in this region are facing several obstacles as they work to keep pace with competitors based elsewhere.[14]

ASEAN Free Trade Area
www.aseansec.org

Figure 4.3 shows a map of the Association of Southeast Asian Nations (ASEAN) countries of Asia-Pacific. ASEAN (pronounced OZZIE-on) was founded in 1967 as an organization for economic, political, social, and cultural co-operation. In 1995, Vietnam became the group's first communist member. Today, the ASEAN group has a population of over 500 million and a GNP of approximately $800 billion.[15]

3. Explain how different forms of *competitive advantage, import–export balances, exchange rates,* and *foreign competition* determine the ways in which countries and businesses respond to the international environment.

Forms of Competitive Advantage

Why are there such high levels of importing, exporting, and other forms of international business activity? Because no country can produce all the goods and services that its people need. Thus, countries tend to export products that they can produce better or less expensively than other countries, using the proceeds to import products that they cannot produce as effectively.

Of course, this principle does not fully explain why various nations export and import what they do. Such decisions hinge partly on the kind of advantages a particular country may enjoy regarding its abilities to create and/or sell various products and resources.[16] Traditionally, economists focused on *absolute* and *comparative advantage* to explain international trade. But because this approach focuses narrowly on such factors as natural resources and labour costs, a perspective has emerged that focuses on a more complex view of *national competitive advantage*.

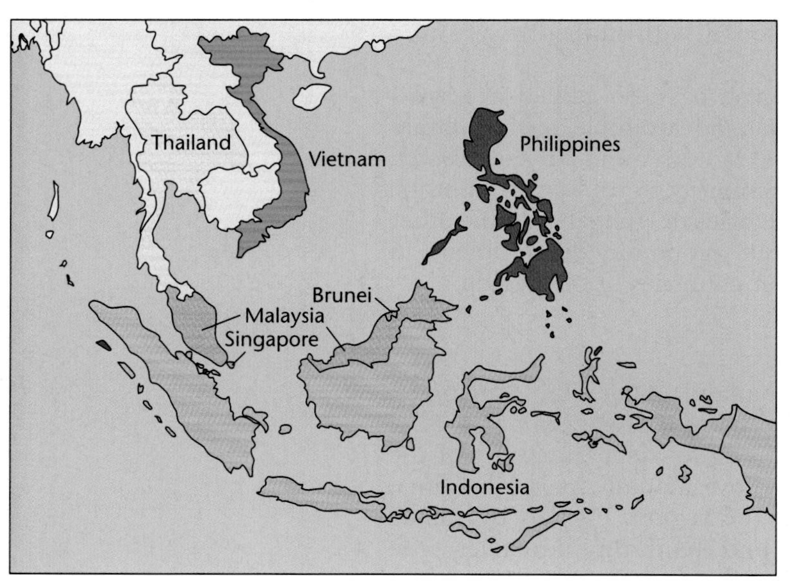

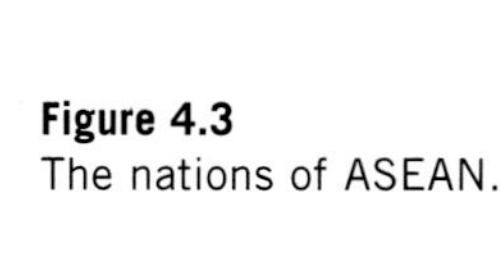

Figure 4.3
The nations of ASEAN.

Absolute Advantage

An **absolute advantage** exists when a country can produce something more cheaply and/or of higher quality than any other country. Saudi oil, Brazilian coffee beans, and Canadian timber approximate absolute advantage, but examples of true absolute advantage are rare. In reality, "absolute" advantages are always relative. For example, most experts say that the vineyards of France produce the finest wines in the world. But the burgeoning wine business in California and Ontario attests to the fact that producers there can also produce very good values in wine—wines that are perhaps almost as good as French wines and that also are available in more varieties and at lower prices.

absolute advantage
A nation's ability to produce something more cheaply or better than any other country.

Comparative Advantage

A country has a **comparative advantage** in goods that it can produce more efficiently or better than other goods. For example, if businesses in a given country can make computers more efficiently than they can make automobiles, that nation's firms have a comparative advantage in computer manufacture. Canada has a comparative advantage in farming (because of fertile land and a temperate climate), while South Korea has a comparative advantage in electronics manufacturing (because of efficient operations and cheap labour). As a result, Canadian firms export grain to South Korea and import VCRs and stereos from South Korea.

comparative advantage
A nation's ability to produce some products more cheaply or better than it can others.

National Competitive Advantage

In recent years, a theory of national competitive advantage has become a more widely accepted model of why nations engage in international trade.[17] Basically, **national competitive advantage** derives from four conditions:

1. *Factor conditions* are the factors of production that we identified in Chapter 1.
2. *Demand conditions* reflect a large domestic consumer base that promotes strong demand for innovative products.
3. *Related and supporting industries* include strong local or regional suppliers and/or industrial customers.

national competitive advantage
A country will be inclined to engage in international trade when factor conditions, demand conditions, related and supporting industries, and strategies/structures/rivalries are favourable.

For thousands of years, the Indonesian islands held an absolute advantage in the kinds of spices—cinnamon, pepper, nutmeg, cloves—being sold in this market in the country's capital city of Jakarta. The local market is still worth U.S.$1.5 billion per year, and although Indonesia no longer enjoys an absolute advantage, the cultivation of exotic natural resources still accounts for about 40 percent of the nation's jobs.

4. *Strategies, structures, and rivalries* refer to firms and industries that stress cost reduction, product quality, higher productivity, and innovative new products.

Figure 4.4 shows why these four attributes are referred to as a national diamond. The interaction of the four elements determines the environment in which a nation's firms compete.

When all of these conditions exist, a nation will naturally be inclined to engage in international business. Japan, for instance, has strong domestic demand for automobiles. Its automobile producers have well-oiled supplier networks, and domestic firms have competed intensely with each other for decades. This set of circumstances explains why Japanese automobile companies such as Toyota, Honda, Nissan, and Mazda are generally successful in foreign markets.

Import–Export Balances

Although international trade involves many advantages, trading with other nations can pose problems if a country's imports and exports do not strike an acceptable balance. In deciding whether an overall balance exists, economists use two measures: *balance of trade* and *balance of payments*.

balance of trade
The difference in value between a country's total exports and its total imports.

trade deficit
Occurs when a country imports more than it exports.

trade surplus
Occurs when a country exports more than it imports.

Balance of Trade

A nation's **balance of trade** is the total economic value of all products it exports minus the total economic value of all products it imports. Canada has enjoyed a favourable balance of merchandise trade since 1980 (see Figure 4.5). The United States is by far the largest trading partner Canada has, and our trade balance is favourable only because we export so much more to the United States than we import from them. Canada's trade balance with almost all of its other trading partners is unfavourable (see Table 4.1).

A study by the World Trade Organization (WTO) found that Canada's economic dependence on the United States is growing, and that this trend leaves Canada vulnerable. The United States accounts for about 85 percent of Canada's merchandise exports and two-thirds of its imports. What's worse, only 50 companies operating in Canada account for nearly half of all merchandise exports, and these companies are often U.S.-owned. Although Canada is an exporting powerhouse, our exports are too focused on the United States. Canada has too many of its eggs in one basket.[18]

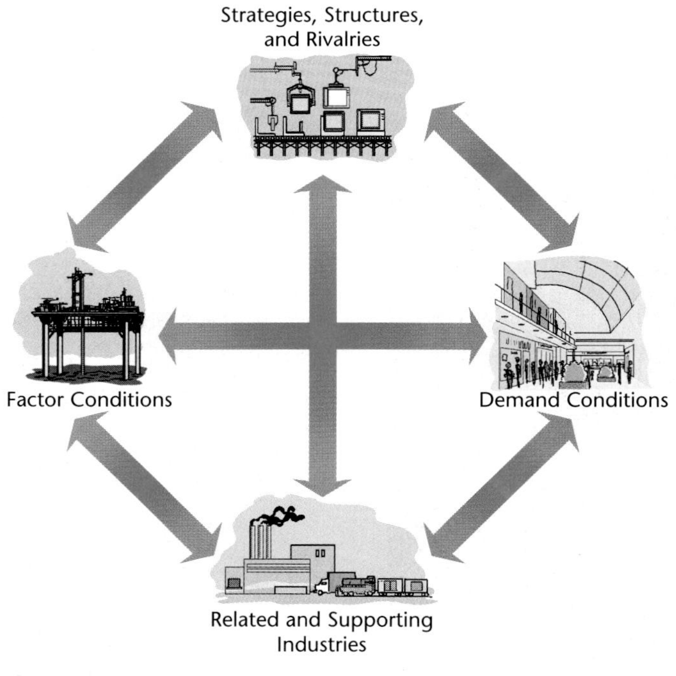

Figure 4.4
Attributes of national competitive advantage.

Trade Deficits and Surpluses. When a country's imports exceed its exports—that is, when it has a negative balance of trade—it suffers a **trade deficit**. In short, more money is flowing out of the country than flowing in. A positive balance of trade occurs when a country's exports exceed its imports and it enjoys a **trade surplus**: more money is flowing into the country than flowing out of it. Trade deficits and surpluses are influenced by an array of factors, such as the absolute, comparative, or national competitive advantages enjoyed by the relevant trading partners, the general economic conditions prevailing in various countries, and the effect of trade agreements. For example, higher domestic costs, greater

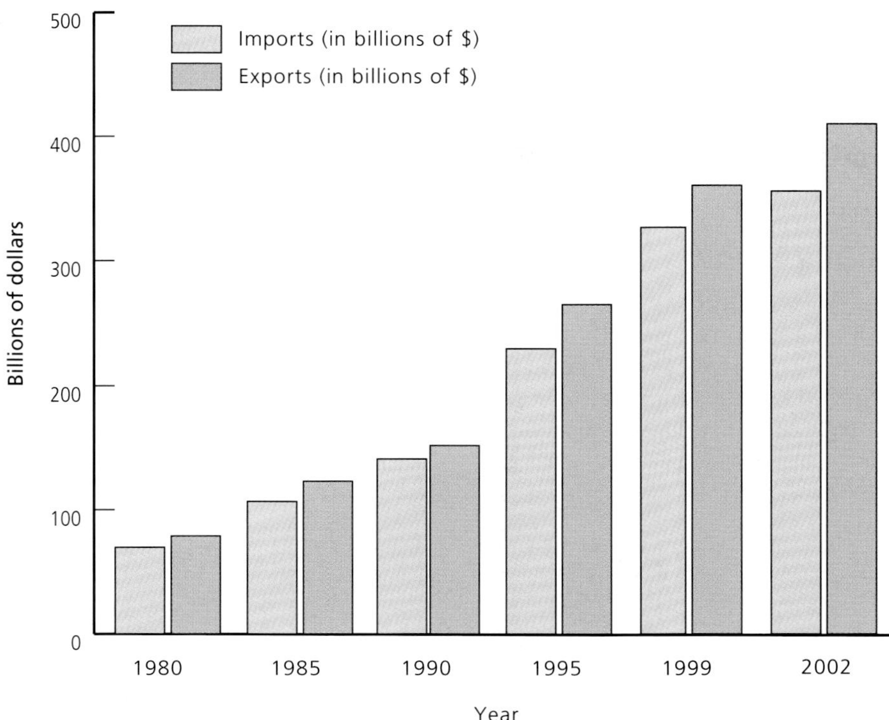

Figure 4.5
Canadian imports and exports of merchandise.

international competition, and continuing economic problems of some of its regional trading partners have slowed Japan's exports from the tremendous growth it enjoyed several years ago. But rising prosperity in both China and India have resulted in strong increases in both exports from and imports to those countries.

Balance of Payments. The **balance of payments** refers to the flow of money in to or out of a country. The money a nation pays for imports and receives for exports—that is, its balance of trade—comprises much of its balance of payments. Other financial exchanges are also factors. For example, money spent by tourists, money spent on foreign-aid programs, and money spent and received in the buying and selling of currency on international money markets all affect the balance of payments.

balance of payments
The difference between money flowing in to and out of a country as a result of trade and other transactions.

An unfavourable balance means that more money is flowing out than in. For Canada to have a favourable balance of payments for a given year, the total of our exports, foreign tourist spending in this country, foreign investments here, and earnings from overseas investments must be greater than the total of our imports, Canadian tourist spending overseas, our for-

Table 4.1 Canadian Exports to, and Imports from, Selected Countries, 2002

Country	Exports To (billions)	Imports From (billions)
United States	$348.3	$254.6
European Union	21.2	36.1
Japan	9.7	11.7
United Kingdom	6.2	10.3
All others	31.3	53.5

eign aid grants, our military spending abroad, the investments made by Canadian firms abroad, and the earnings of foreigners from their investments in Canada. (See Figure 4.6.) Canada has had an unfavourable balance of payments for many years, but it is getting smaller. In 2002, $75 billion more money flowed out of Canada than flowed in. In 1999, the figure was $142 billion.[19]

Exchange Rates

exchange rate
The ratio of one currency to another.

The balance of imports and exports between two countries is affected by the rate of exchange between their currencies. An **exchange rate** is the rate at which the currency of one nation can be exchanged for that of another.[20] In August 2003, the exchange rate between Canadian dollars and British pounds was 1 to 2.26. This means that it costs $2.26 in Canadian dollars to "buy" one

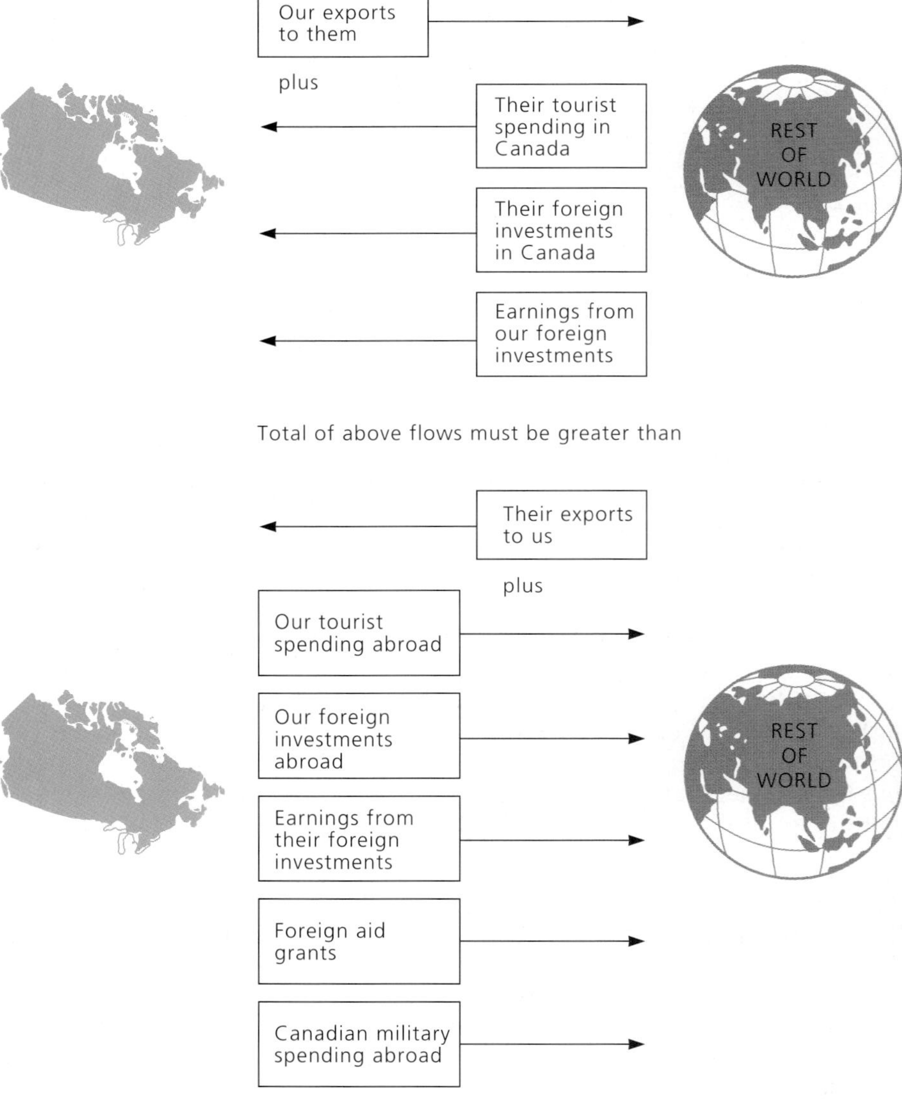

Figure 4.6
Requirements for Canada to have a favourable balance of payments. (The arrows indicate the direction of the flow.)

British pound; alternatively, it costs only .44 of a British pound to "buy" one Canadian dollar. This exchange rate means that .44 of a British pound and one Canadian dollar should have exactly the same purchasing power.

At the end of the Second World War, the major nations of the world agreed to establish fixed exchange rates. Under *fixed exchange rates*, the value of any country's currency relative to that of another country remains constant. Today, however, *floating exchange rates* are the norm, and the value of one country's currency relative to that of another country varies with market conditions. For example, when many English citizens want to spend pounds to buy Canadian dollars (or goods), the value of the dollar relative to the pound increases, or becomes "stronger"; *demand* for the Canadian dollar is high. In other words, a currency is said to be "strong" when demand for it is high. It is also "strong" when there is high demand for the goods manufactured at the expense of that currency. Thus, the value of the dollar rises with the demand for Canadian goods. In reality, exchange rates typically fluctuate by very small amounts on a daily basis. More significant variations usually occur over greater spans of time.

Fluctuation in exchange rates can have an important impact on the balance of trade. Suppose, for example, that you wanted to buy some English tea for 10 British pounds per box. At an exchange rate of 2.26 Canadian dollars to the British pound, a box will cost you \$22.60 (10 pounds × 2.26 = 22.60). But what if the pound is weaker? At an exchange rate of, say, 1.5 dollars to the pound, the same box of tea would cost you only \$15.00 (10 pounds × 1.5 = \$15.00).

Changes in the exchange rate, of course, would affect more than just the price of tea. If the Canadian dollar becomes stronger in relation to the British pound, the prices of all Canadian-made products would rise in England and the prices of all English-made products would fall in Canada. As a result, the English would buy fewer Canadian-made products, and Canadians would be prompted to spend more on English-made products. The result could conceivably be a Canadian trade deficit with England. The recent increase in the value of the Canadian dollar has Canadian exporters very concerned (see the Opening Case for Chapter 18 on p. 639).

One of the most significant developments in foreign exchange has been the introduction of the **euro**—a common currency among most of the members of the European Union (Denmark, Sweden, and the United Kingdom do not participate). The euro was officially introduced in 2002 and will, for a while, circulate along with currencies of the participating nations. But those currencies will be phased out, and they are to be replaced by the euro as the only accepted currency. The EU anticipates that the euro will become as important as the dollar and the yen in international commerce. Though of course subject to fluctuation, the euro has risen in value against the U.S. dollar and was worth about U.S.\$1.20 in late 2003.

euro
A common currency shared among most of the members of the European Union (excluding Denmark, Sweden, and the United Kingdom).

Exchange Rates and Competition

Companies that conduct international operations must watch exchange-rate fluctuations closely because these changes affect overseas demand for their products and can be a major factor in international competition. In general, when the value of a country's domestic currency rises—becomes "stronger"—companies based there find it harder to export products to foreign markets and easier for foreign companies to enter local markets. It also makes it more cost-efficient for domestic companies to move production operations to lower-cost sites in foreign countries. When the value of a country's currency declines—becomes "weaker"—just the opposite patterns occur. Thus, as the value of a country's currency falls, its balance of trade should improve because domestic companies should experience a boost in exports. There should also be a corresponding decrease in the incentives for foreign companies to ship products into the domestic market.

A good case in point is the recent fluctuation of the Canadian dollar relative to the U.S. dollar. In 1990, the Canadian dollar was worth about 91 cents U.S.; as a result, Canadian consumers frequently drove south of the border to shop for bargains in the United States. But during the 1990s, the Canadian dollar weakened dramatically, and by 2002 had dropped to only 63 cents U.S. At that price, it was cheaper for U.S. consumers to drive across the border to shop in Canada. Table 4.2 illustrates the effects of this trend. For example, the same hamburger that cost U.S.$2.39 in Niagara Falls, New York, sold for only U.S.$2.18 just across the border in Ontario. Likewise, a caffe latte in Seattle cost U.S.$2.70 but in Vancouver only U.S.$2.29. As one Vancouver store owner puts it, "There has been an exact switch. Five years ago, we would go down to Seattle to get good deals. Now the Americans come here for shopping."[21] More recently, the value of the Canadian dollar has again risen, and in late 2003 was worth 77 cents U.S.

Because the U.S. dollar is so strong compared with other currencies, some economists are recommending something called "dollarization." This means having countries outside the United States adopt the U.S. dollar as their currency. Ecuador and Panama have already done this, and half the money circulating in Peru is in U.S. dollars. Since the value of Canada's currency is still well below that of the U.S. dollar, some Canadians have proposed that Canada also adopt the U.S. dollar.[22] But others say that adopting the U.S. dollar will reduce Canadian policy flexibility and will mean a loss in our sovereignty.[23]

INTERNATIONAL BUSINESS MANAGEMENT

4. Discuss the factors involved in deciding to do business internationally and in selecting the appropriate *levels of international involvement* and *international organizational structure*.

Wherever a firm is located, its success depends largely on how well it is managed. International business is so challenging because the basic functions of management—planning, organizing, directing, and controlling—are much more difficult to carry out when a business operates in several markets scattered around the globe. (We discuss these functions of management in detail in Chapter 6.)

Managing, of course, means making decisions. In this section, we examine the three most basic decisions that a company's management must make when faced with the prospect of globalization. The first decision is whether to "go international" at all. Once that decision has been made,

Table 4.2 Canadian Versus U.S. Prices

	Niagara Falls NY	Niagara Falls ON
Saturday stay at Days Inn, with Jacuzzi	$260.00	$165.00
Whopper with cheese at Burger King	$2.39	$2.18
	Seattle	**Vancouver**
Lauryn Hill CD	$17.99	$12.60
Nintendo 64 game system	$130.00	$119.00
Grande latte at Starbucks	$2.70	$2.29
Levi's 501 jeans at Original Levi's Store	$50.00	$45.00

managers must decide on the company's level of international involvement and on the organizational structure that will best meet its global needs.

"Going International"

The world economy is becoming globalized, and more and more firms are conducting international operations. As Figure 4.7 shows, several factors enter into the decision to go international. One overriding factor is the business climate of other nations. Even experienced firms have encountered cultural, legal, and economic roadblocks. (These problems are discussed in more detail later in this chapter.) In considering international expansion, a company should also consider at least two other questions: Is there a demand for its products abroad? If so, must those products be adapted for international consumption?

Gauging International Demand

Products that are seen as vital in one country may be useless in another. Snowmobiles, for example, are not only popular for transportation and recreation in Canada and the northern United States, but actually revolutionized reindeer herding in Lapland. But there would be no demand at all for this product in Central America. Although this is an extreme example, the point is quite basic to the decision to go international: namely, that foreign demand for a company's product may be greater than, the same as, or weaker than domestic demand.

Adapting to Customer Needs

If there is international demand for its product, a firm must consider whether and how to adapt that product to meet the special demands and

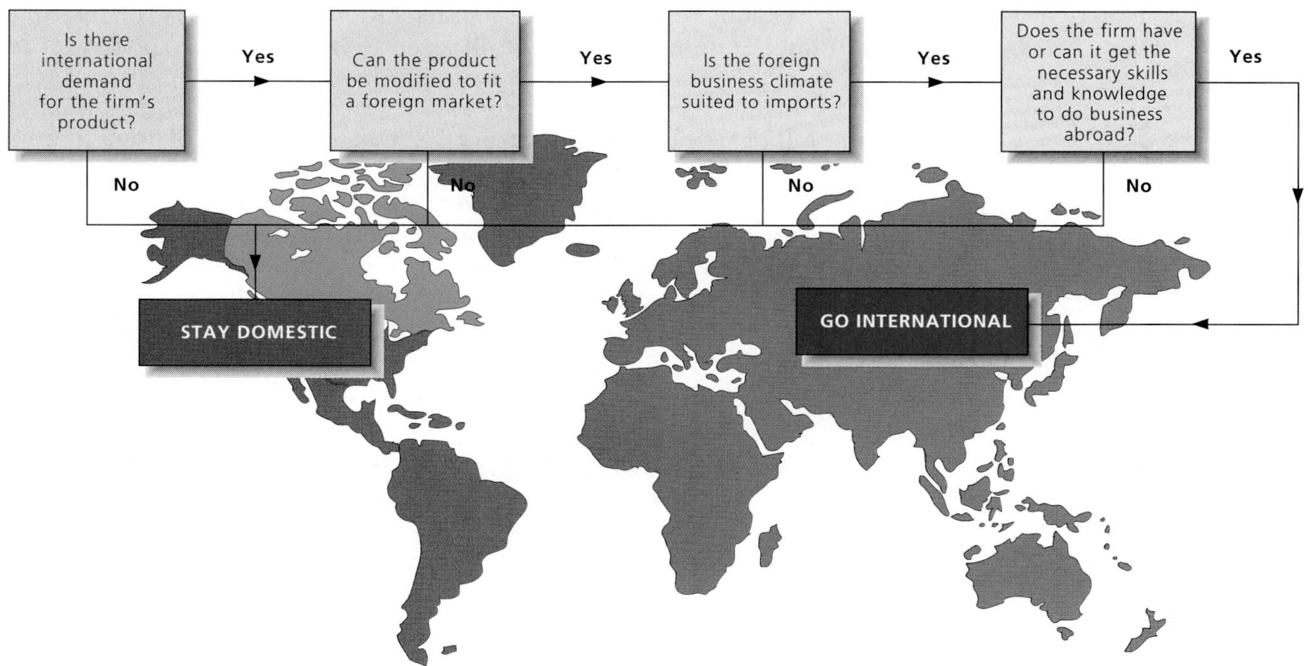

Figure 4.7
The decision to go international.

expectations of foreign customers. Movies, for example, have to be dubbed into foreign languages. Likewise, McDonald's restaurants sell wine in France, beer in Germany, and meatless sandwiches in India to accommodate local tastes and preferences. Ford products must have their steering wheels mounted on the right if they are to be sold in England and Japan. When Toyota launches upscale cars at home, it retains the Toyota nameplate; but those same cars are sold under the Lexus nameplate in Canada because the firm has concluded that Canadian consumers there will not pay a premium price for a "Toyota."

Levels of Involvement in International Business

After a firm decides to go international, it must decide on the level of its international involvement. Several different levels of involvement are possible. At the most basic level, a firm may act as an *exporter* or *importer*, organize as an *international firm*, or operate as a *multinational firm*. Most of the world's largest industrial firms are multinationals.

Exporters and Importers

exporter
A firm that makes products in one country and then distributes and sells them in others.

importer
A firm that buys products in foreign markets and then imports them for resale in its home country.

An **exporter** is a firm that makes products in one country and then distributes and sells them in others. An **importer** buys products in foreign markets and then imports them for resale in its home country. Exporters and importers tend to conduct most of their business in their home nations. Both enterprises entail the lowest level of involvement in international operations and are excellent ways to learn the fine points of global business.

Almost 40 percent of all goods and services produced in Canada are exported. Canada ranks first among the G8 countries in the proportion of its production that is exported.[24] McCain Foods, for example, is a formidable presence in Europe. It holds 75 percent of the "oven fries" market in Germany, and dominates the frozen French fry market in France and England.[25] MacMillan-Bloedel and Abitibi-Price sell newsprint and other forest products around the world. Small firms also export products and services. Seagull Pewter & Silversmiths Ltd., Magic Pantry Foods, and Lovat Tunnel Equipment Inc. have all recently won Canada Export Awards. Sabian Cymbals sells 90 percent of its products to 80 different countries outside Canada. Electrovert Ltd. does 95 percent of its business outside Canada. Other companies that export a high proportion of their output include Repap B.C. Inc. (95 percent), Pratt & Whitney Canada (86 percent), Noranda Inc. (86 percent), and General Motors of Canada (85 percent). These companies have little in common with firms that concentrate on the Canadian market and then unload what is left somewhere else.[26]

The Wired World box shows how the internet and other advances in technology have made it easier for small firms to compete in global markets.

International Firms

international firm
A company that conducts a significant portion of its business abroad and maintains manufacturing facilities overseas.

As firms gain experience and success as exporters and importers, they may move to the next level of involvement. An **international firm** conducts a significant portion of its business abroad. International firms also maintain manufacturing facilities overseas. Wal-Mart, for instance, is an international firm. Most of the retailer's stores are still in the United States, but the company is rapidly expanding into Canada and other markets.

Although an international firm may be large and influential in the global economy, it remains basically a domestic firm with international operations: its central concern is its own domestic market. Despite its obvious presence (and impact) in Canada, Wal-Mart still earns 90 percent of its revenues from U.S. sales.

IT'S A WIRED WORLD

Rolling in the Worldwide Dough

Is any business more confined to a local market than a bakery? Breads and pastries get stale quickly, and even the largest operations, such as those that make buns for McDonald's, only move products over short distances. But a baker in Paris has refused to accept geographic limitations and is now selling his famous bread in global markets.

When Lionel Poilane took over the family business about 30 years ago, he was determined to return bread making to its roots. As a result of studying the craft of bread making, Polaine built clay ovens based on sixteenth-century plans and technology. Then he trained his bread makers in ancient techniques and soon began selling old-style dark bread known for a thick, chewy, fire-tinged flavour. It quickly became a favourite in Parisian bistros, and demand soared.

To help meet demand, Poilane built two more bakeries in Paris, and today he sells 15 000 loaves of bread a day—about 2.5 percent of all the bread sold in Paris. Polaine has opened a bakery in London, but his efforts to expand to Japan were stymied because local ordinances prohibited wood-burning ovens, and Polaine refused to compromise. During this negotiation process, however, he realized that he didn't really want to build new bakeries all over the world. "I'm not eager to have a business card that says 'Paris, London, New York' on it," he explains.

Instead, he turned to modern technology to expand his old-fashioned business. The key was the big FedEx hub at Roissy-Charles-de-Gaulle Airport near Polaine's largest Paris bakery. After launching a website with minimal marketing support, Polaine started taking international orders. New orders are packaged as the bread cools and then picked up by FedEx. At about four pounds, the basic loaf travels well, and a quick warm-up in the customer's oven gives it the same taste as it had when it came out of Polaine's. Today, a loaf of bread baked in Paris in the morning can easily be reheated for tomorrow night's dinner in more than 20 countries.

Multinational Firms

Most **multinational firms** do not ordinarily think of themselves as having domestic and international divisions. Instead, planning and decision making are geared to international markets.[27] The locations of headquarters are almost irrelevant. Royal Dutch/Shell, Nestlé, IBM, and Ford are well-known multinationals.

multinational firm
Controls assets, factories, mines, sales offices, and affiliates in two or more foreign countries.

The economic importance of multinational firms should not be underestimated. Consider, for example, the economic impact of the 500 largest multinational corporations. In 2001, these 500 firms generated $14 trillion in revenues and $306 billion in owner profits. They owned $38.9 trillion in assets, and they employed almost 48 million people, bought supplies, materials, parts, equipment, and materials from thousands of other firms, and paid billions of dollars in taxes. Moreover, their products affected the lives of hundreds of millions of consumers, competitors, investors, and even protestors.[28]

International Organizational Structures

Different levels of involvement in international business require different kinds of organizational structure. For example, a structure that would help coordinate an exporter's activities would be inadequate for the activities of a multinational firm. In this section, we briefly consider the spectrum of international organizational strategies, including *independent agents, licensing arrangements, branch offices, strategic alliances,* and *direct investment*.

Independent Agents

independent agent
A foreign individual, or organization, who agrees to represent an exporter's interests in foreign markets.

An **independent agent** is a foreign individual or organization that agrees to represent an exporter's interests in foreign markets. Independent agents often act as sales representatives: They sell the exporter's products, collect payment, and ensure that customers are satisfied. Independent agents often represent several firms at once and usually do not specialize in a particular product or market. Levi Strauss uses agents to market clothing products in many small countries in Africa, Asia, and South America.

Licensing Arrangements

licensing arrangement
An arrangement by an owner of a process or product to allow another business to produce, distribute, or market it for a fee or royalty.

Canadian companies seeking more substantial involvement in international business may opt for **licensing arrangements**. Firms give individuals or companies in a foreign country the exclusive right to manufacture or market their products in that market. In return, the exporter typically receives a fee plus ongoing payments called royalties.[29] Royalties are usually calculated as a percentage of the licence holder's sales. For example, Can-Eng Manufacturing, Canada's largest supplier of industrial furnaces, exports its furnaces under licensing arrangements with Japan, Brazil, Germany, Korea, Taiwan, and Mexico.

Franchising is a special form of licensing that is also growing in popularity.[30] McDonald's and Pizza Hut franchise around the world. Similarly, Accor SA, a French hotel chain, franchises its Ibis, Sofitel, and Novotel hotels. Allied Domecq PLC, a British firm, owns and franchises Baskin-Robbins and Dunkin' Donuts stores in dozens of countries.

Branch Offices

branch office
A location that an exporting firm establishes in a foreign country in order to sell its products more effectively.

Instead of developing relationships with foreign companies or independent agents, a firm may simply send some of its own managers to overseas **branch offices**, where it has more direct control than it does over agents or licence holders. Branch offices also give a company a more visible public presence in foreign countries. Potential customers tend to feel more secure when a business has branch offices in their country.

When a business operates branches, plants, or subsidiaries in several countries, it may assign to one plant or subsidiary the responsibility for researching, developing, manufacturing, and marketing one product or line of products. This is known as *world product mandating*. At Nortel Networks, for example, the company's Belleville, Ontario, plant was chosen as the one to produce a new business telephone system designed for the world market. The plant won out in a competition with two other Nortel plants, one in Calgary and one in Santa Clara, California.

Strategic Alliances

strategic alliance
An enterprise in which two or more persons or companies temporarily join forces to undertake a particular project.

In a **strategic alliance**, a company finds a partner in the country in which it would like to conduct business. Each party agrees to invest resources and capital in a new business or else to co-operate in some way for mutual benefit. This new business—the alliance—is then owned by the partners, who divide its profits. Such alliances are sometimes called joint ventures.[31] As we saw earlier, however, the term *strategic alliance* has arisen because of the increasingly important role that such partnerships play in the larger organizational strategies of many major companies.

The number of strategic alliances among major companies has increased significantly over the last decade and is likely to grow even more. In many countries, including Mexico, India, and China, laws make alliances virtually the only way to do international business within their borders. Mexico, for example, requires all foreign firms investing there to have local partners. Similarly, Disney's new theme park currently under construction near Hong Kong is a joint venture with local partners.

In addition to easing the way into new markets, alliances give firms greater control over their foreign activities than independent agents and licensing arrangements. (At the same time, of course, all partners in an alliance retain some say in its decisions.) Perhaps most important, alliances allow firms to benefit from the knowledge and expertise of their foreign partners. Microsoft, for example, relies heavily on strategic alliances as it expands into new international markets. This approach has successfully enabled the firm to learn the intricacies of doing business in China and India, two emerging markets that are difficult to crack.

Foreign Direct Investment

The term **foreign direct investment (FDI)** means buying or establishing tangible assets in another country.[32] Dell Computer, for example, is building a new assembly plant in Europe, and Volkswagen is building a new factory in Brazil.

foreign direct investment (FDI)
Buying or establishing tangible assets in another country.

As we've seen, many Canadian firms export goods and services to foreign countries; they also set up manufacturing operations in other countries. But a debate has been going on for many years in Canada about how FDI here affects Canadians. The Foreign Investment Review Agency (FIRA), which was established in 1973, was designed to ensure that FDI benefited Canadians. After FIRA was established, the proportion of various industries controlled by foreign firms declined from a high of 38 percent in the early 1970s to a low of 25.7 percent in 1988 (just before NAFTA took effect).

In 1985, FIRA's title was changed to **Investment Canada**, and its mandate was changed to focus on attracting foreign investment to Canada. Since the late 1980s, foreign ownership of Canadian industry has again been on the rise, and in the late 1990s it reached 31.5 percent. But foreign ownership may in fact be higher than it appears, since many firms that seem to be Canadian are actually multinational companies. For example, before it was bought by Paris-based Vivendi, Seagram had been run from New York City, and Nortel Networks runs all of its business divisions from Dallas, Texas. Table 4.3 lists the top 10 foreign-owned companies in Canada.

Investment Canada
Replaced FIRA in 1985; designed primarily to attract and facilitate foreign investment in Canada.

Over 200 major Canadian companies trade their stock on the New York Stock Exchange, and more than half of the trading in many of those companies' stock takes place in the United States.[33] A *Globe and Mail* study in 1998 showed that in just one 12-month period, 10 companies with a total market value of $39 billion disappeared from the Toronto Stock Exchange (TSE) because they were purchased by foreign firms. These firms accounted for 6 percent of the value of the S&P/TSX index.[34]

Canadian business leaders are beginning to sound the warning that Canadian firms are vulnerable to takeovers by foreign companies.[35] This concern is a bit ironic, since business leaders have generally been the ones most in favour of free trade.

BARRIERS TO INTERNATIONAL TRADE

Whether a business is selling to just a few foreign markets or is a true multinational, a number of differences between countries will affect its international operations. Success in foreign markets will largely depend on the way the business responds to social, economic, legal, and political barriers to international trade.

5. Describe some of the ways in which *social, cultural, economic, legal,* and *political differences* act as barriers to international trade.

Table 4.3 The Top 10 Foreign-Controlled Companies in Canada

	Company	Annual Canadian Revenues (in billions of $)
1.	General Motors of Canada	37.0
2.	Ford Motor Co. of Canada	23.2
3.	DaimlerChrysler Canada	19.3
4.	Imperial Oil	16.8
5.	Honda Canada	12.3
6.	Costco Wholesale Canada	7.3
7.	Shell Canada	7.2
8.	Sears Canada	6.5
9.	Canada Safeway	5.4
10.	IBM Canada	5.3

Note: Wal-Mart is the largest company in the world, but it has no Canadian subsidiary.

Social and Cultural Differences

Any firm involved in international business needs to understand something about the society and culture of the countries in which it plans to operate. Unless a firm understands these cultural differences—either by itself or by acquiring a partner that does—it will probably not be successful in its international business activities.

Some differences are relatively obvious. Language barriers can cause inappropriate naming of products. In addition, the physical stature of people in different countries can make a difference. For example, the Japanese and French are slimmer and shorter on average than Canadians, an important consideration for firms that intend to sell clothes in these markets.

In addition to such obvious differences, a wide range of subtle value differences can have an important impact on international business. For example, many Europeans shop daily. To Canadians used to weekly trips to the supermarket, the European pattern may seem like a waste of time. But for Europeans, shopping is not just "buying food." It is also meeting friends, exchanging political views, gossiping, and socializing.

Even more subtle behavioural differences that can influence business activity exist. For example, crossing your legs in a business meeting in Saudi Arabia is inappropriate, because showing the sole of your foot is viewed as an insult to the other people in the room. In Portugal, it is considered rude to discuss business during dinner, and in Taiwan, tapping your fingers on the table is a sign of appreciation for a meal. Knowledge of local dos and don'ts is important in international business activity.

Economic Differences

Although cultural differences are often subtle, economic differences can be fairly pronounced. In dealing with economies like those of France and Sweden, for example, firms must be aware of when—and to what extent—the government is involved in a given industry. The French government, for example, is heavily involved in all aspects of airplane design and manufacturing.

Similarly, a foreign firm doing business in a command economy must understand the unfamiliar relationship of government to business, including a host of idiosyncratic practices. General Motors, which entered a $100 million joint venture to build pickup trucks in China, found itself faced with an economic system that favoured state-owned companies over foreign investors. So, while its Chinese suppliers passed on inflation-based price increases for steel and energy, GM could not in turn pass increases on to Chinese consumers. With subsidized state-owned automakers charging considerably less per truck, GM had no choice but to hold its own prices—and lose money on each sale.

Despite such problems, however, not all companies have had entirely negative experiences. For example, when Motorola opened a factory in China to manufacture paging devices, it planned to export most of the pagers because it forecasted limited internal demand. In a pleasant surprise, Motorola was forced to reassess the Chinese market after repeatedly selling out its weekly output of 10 000 units. This experience helped convince Motorola to build a $120 million plant in the northern port city of Tianjin to manufacture pagers, simple integrated circuits, and cellular phones. As part of the largest manufacturing venture in China, it involved Chinese technicians in the production process. Chinese designers and engineers also played key roles in creating an operation that integrates manufacturing, sales, research, and development.

Legal and Political Differences

Closely linked to the structure of the economic systems in different countries are the legal and political issues that confront businesses as they try to expand internationally. These issues include *tariffs and quotas, local-content laws,* and *business-practice laws*. An awareness of differences in these areas can be crucial to a business's success.

Quotas, Tariffs, and Subsidies

Even free-market economies often use some form of quota and/or tariff that affects the prices and quantities of foreign-made products in those nations. A **quota** restricts the total number of certain products that can be imported into a country. It indirectly raises the prices of those imports by reducing

quota
A restriction by one nation on the total number of products of a certain type that can be imported from another nation.

On the first Muslim holy day after American warplanes went into Afghanistan, this crowd in Karachi, Pakistan, set fire to a locally owned KFC outlet. The immediate problem was a political one: Pakistanis objected to their government's support of the U.S. assault on the Muslim government of neighbouring Afghanistan. A deeper problem, however, reflects social and cultural conflict. Muslim societies resent the invasion of "Western" influences that are at odds with their traditional social life. The KFC symbol is a conspicuous example of these "foreign" influences.

embargo
A government order forbidding exportation and/or importation of a particular product.

tariff
A tax levied on imported products.

their supply. The ultimate form of quota is an **embargo**: a government order forbidding exportation and/or importation of a particular product—or even all products—of a particular country. For example, many countries control bacteria and disease by banning certain plants and agricultural products.

A **tariff** is a tax charged on imported products. Tariffs directly affect the prices of products, effectively raising the price of imports to consumers who must pay not only for the products but also for the tariff. Tariffs may take either of two forms. A *revenue tariff* is imposed strictly to raise money for the government. But most tariffs in effect today are *protectionist tariffs* meant to discourage the import of a particular product.

Governments impose quotas and tariffs for a wide variety of reasons. For example, the U.S. government restricts the number of Japanese automobiles that can be imported into that country. Italy imposes high tariffs on imported electronic goods. Consequently, Sony Walkmans cost almost $150, and CD players are prohibitively expensive there. Canada also imposes tariffs on many imported goods. The Business Today box describes an important dispute over duties on softwood lumber that Canada exports to the United States.

subsidy
A government payment to help domestic business compete with foreign firms.

A **subsidy** is a government payment to help a domestic business compete with foreign firms. Many European governments subsidize farmers to help them compete with U.S. grain imports. The U.S. government pays large subsidies to its cotton farmers, guaranteeing them a price of about 70

BUSINESS TODAY

The United States Puts the Lumber to Canada

Canada and the United States have a long history of arguing about Canadian exports of softwood lumber to the United States, and Canadian lumber has been subject to various tariffs and duties over the last 100 years. This dispute reached a new low in March 2002, when the U.S. Commerce Department imposed a 29 percent duty on softwood lumber exported from Canada to the United States. In August 2001, the Commerce Department had imposed temporary countervailing duties, and in November 2001 added anti-dumping duties ranging from 6 percent to 20 percent.

The final decision by the United States came after months of negotiations between the two countries failed to yield an agreement. After the Commerce Department announcement, Ottawa immediately appealed the decision under the provisions of both the North American Free Trade Agreement (NAFTA) and the World Trade Organization (WTO). In both 2002 and 2003, the WTO ruled against the United States on various points in the appeal. These rulings will make it harder for the United States to justify the duties against Canadian lumber, but the process of resolving the dispute will likely take many months. In early 2003, Canadian and U.S. negotiators met again to try to hammer out an agreement. The basic idea is to have Canada put a temporary tax on lumber exports until the provinces can overhaul the way they sell timber to private Canadian companies.

There is some support in the United States for the Canadian position. A coalition of U.S. lumber consumers has panned the duties, saying they will raise the price of an average home by $1500, and that would not be good for the industry or for people who buy homes. The U.S. Commerce Department defended the duty and said that it took the action because Canadian provinces were selling trees very cheaply to Canadian lumber companies, and this allowed the Canadian companies to sell lumber at unreasonably low prices in the United States. This, in turn, harmed U.S. lumber companies that had difficulty competing.

Back in 1996, Canada agreed to limit exports to the United States for a 5-year period as part of a deal to head off some long-standing problems. The expiry of that deal in 2001 was what set off the current round of negotiations. In an earlier phase of the negotiations, it looked like a temporary deal might be made which would impose export duties of up to 25 percent on Canadian softwood exported to the United States. The plan was to have the deal remain in place until Canadian provinces began charging more realistic prices for trees that they sold to private Canadian lumber companies.

At the time of the decision, the U.S. housing industry was booming, and higher priced Canadian lumber would depress that market. Eighty-four percent of Canadian lumber is exported to the United States, and Canada supplies nearly one-third of the lumber for the entire U.S. home building market.

The duty on Canadian lumber was vigorously supported by a U.S. organization called The Coalition for Fair Lumber Imports, which represents the U.S. lumber industry. Canadian negotiators said that the Coalition was more interested in destroying the Canadian lumber industry than it was in reaching a deal on lumber duties. In commenting on the U.S. decision, Prime Minister Chrétien noted with some unhappiness that the United States wants some of our natural resources (like oil and gas), but not others (our lumber). He said that under the principle of free trade they couldn't pick and choose.

British Columbia, which accounts for half of Canada's lumber exports to the United States, was the hardest hit by the new duties. Only hours after the decision was announced, Doman Industries Ltd. announced that it would close two sawmills in British Columbia. In 2001 and 2002, the B.C. lumber business laid off thousands of workers and several sawmills were closed. For the Canadian lumber industry as a whole, the duties could total as much as $3 billion, and up to 30 000 jobs could be lost. For towns like Campbell River, British Columbia, and The Pas, Manitoba, the effect could be overwhelming because a large amount of the economic activity of those towns depends on forestry.

In the wake of the U.S. decision, the Truck Loggers Association in British Columbia asked the Canadian government to give financial assistance to Canadian lumber companies. The money would be used to help them defray the cost of pursuing appeals with the WTO and NAFTA. But the Canadian government was reluctant to give financial assistance, because critics in the United States would claim that further subsidies were being given to the lumber industry.

In July 2003, Canada and the United States tentatively agreed on a proposal that would end the dispute. Canada would have to agree to limit its exports to the United States to 16.8 billion board feet (down from the 19 billion board feet Canada formerly exported). In August 2003, a NAFTA panel ruled that U.S. duties on Canadian lumber must be cut drastically.

cents per pound, even though the market price for cotton is only about 40 cents a pound.[36] In 2002, the World Trade Organization ruled that Brazil could impose $248 million in sanctions against Canada because the Canadian government gave illegal cut-rate loans (subsidies) to Air Wisconsin to buy jets from Montreal-based Bombardier. The WTO also ruled that Brazil had given illegal cut-rate loans to some customers of Embraer SA, the Brazilian jet maker.[37]

When the government of a country pays subsidies to one of its domestic industries, it can have a negative effect on other producers in other countries. The European Union, for example, pays subsidies to encourage sugar cultivation in unlikely places like Sweden and Finland. This has created a surplus of sugar on the world market, reducing prices and contributing to poverty-level income for sugar producers in some developing countries in the tropics.[38]

Protectionism—the practice of protecting domestic business at the expense of free market competition—has both advocates and critics. Supporters argue that tariffs and quotas protect domestic firms and jobs. In particular, they protect new industries until they are truly able to compete internationally. Some claim that, since other nations have such measures, so must we. Still others justify protectionism in the name of national security. They argue that a nation must be able to produce goods needed for its survival in the event of war and that advanced technology should not be sold to potential enemies.

protectionism
Protecting domestic business at the expense of free market competition.

But opponents of protectionism are equally vocal. They note that protectionism reduces competition and drives up prices to consumers. They cite it as a cause of friction between nations. They maintain that, while jobs in some industries would be lost if protectionism ceased, jobs in other industries would expand if all countries abolished tariffs and quotas.

Protectionism sometimes takes on almost comic proportions. Neither European countries nor the United States grow bananas, but both European and U.S. firms buy and sell bananas in foreign markets. Problems arose when the EU put a quota on bananas imported from Latin America—a market dominated by two U.S. firms, Chiquita and Dole—to help firms based in current and former European colonies in the Caribbean. To retaliate, the United States imposed a 100 percent tariff on certain luxury products imported from Europe, including Louis Vuitton handbags, Scottish cashmere sweaters, and Parma ham.[39]

Local-Content Laws

A country can affect how a foreign firm does business there by enacting local-content laws. **Local-content laws** require that products sold in a particular country be at least partly made in that country. These laws typically mean that firms seeking to do business in a country must either invest directly in that country or have a joint-venture partner from that country. In this way, some of the profits from doing business in a foreign country are shared with the people who live there.

local-content laws
Laws requiring that products sold in a particular country be at least partly made in that country.

Many countries have local-content laws. In a fairly extreme case, Venezuela forbids the import of any product if a like product is made in Venezuela. Even when an item is not made in Venezuela, many companies choose to begin making their product in Venezuela both to drive out competitors and to prevent being forced out by local firms.

Local-content laws may even exist within a country; when they do, they act just like trade barriers. In Canada, for example, a low bid on a bridge in British Columbia was rejected because the company that made the bid was from Alberta. The job was given to a B.C. company. A New Brunswick window manufacturer lost a contract in Nova Scotia despite having made the lowest bid; the job went to a Nova Scotia company. Recognizing that these interprovincial barriers are not helping Canada's international competitiveness, the federal government has committed itself to removing such barriers.

The Agreement on Internal Trade (AIT) requires all 10 Canadian provinces to remove barriers to agricultural trade. But when Quebec—which has a strong dairy lobby—prohibited margarine coloured to look like butter, it was in violation of the agreement.[40] In 2002, Unilever Canada Ltd. challenged the legality of the ban on coloured margarine in court.[41] In another case, Prince Edward Island ignored a dispute panel ruling that stated P.E.I.'s milk import restrictions also violated the AIT.[42] If provincial governments do not honour their obligations, the AIT will become meaningless.

business practice law
Law or regulation governing business practices in given countries.

A Quebec customs official seizing illegal butter-coloured margarine. The dairy industry in Quebec has been successful in maintaining the legislation that makes it illegal to make margarine the same colour as butter.

Business Practice Laws

Many businesses entering new markets encounter problems in complying with stringent regulations and bureaucratic obstacles. Such practices are affected by the **business practice laws** that host countries use to govern business practices within their jurisdictions.

As part of its entry strategy in Germany, Wal-Mart has had to buy existing retailers rather than open brand-new stores. Why? Because the German government is not currently issuing new licences to sell food products. Wal-Mart also had to stop refunding price differences on items sold for less by other stores because the practice is illegal in Germany. Finally, Wal-Mart must comply with business-hour restrictions: Stores can't open before 7 a.m., must close by 8 p.m. on weeknights and 4 p.m. on Saturday, and must remain closed on Sunday.

Sometimes, what is legal (and even accepted) business practice in one country is illegal in another. The most prominent example is paying bribes to government officials to get business. Transparency International (TI), an organization devoted to stamping out global corruption, says that Canadian business firms operating abroad are least likely to pay bribes to win business. As well, Canada is a country that has little tolerance for corruption at home. But as more Canadian companies do business abroad, they are finding themselves competing against companies that are not so reluctant to pay bribes in order to get business. As a result, Canadian companies are losing business to these companies.[43]

TI says that bribery is most devastating and common in developing countries because government officials in those countries are poorly paid. TI publishes a "Corruption Perceptions Index" that ranks countries based on the amount of corruption that is perceived to exist, based on ratings by business people, academics, and risk analysts. The least corrupt countries are Finland, Denmark, New Zealand, Singapore, and Canada. The most corrupt are Angola, Paraguay, Madagascar, Nigeria, and Bangladesh.[44] In an attempt to create fairer competition among multinational companies, ministers from 29 member countries of the Organization for Economic Cooperation and Development (OECD) agreed in 1997 to criminalize bribery of foreign public officials.[45]

The Exercising Your Ethics box gives a practical illustration of the problems of bribery in international business.

Cartels and Dumping. A **cartel** is an association of producers whose purpose is to control the supply and price of a commodity. The most famous cartel is the Organization of Petroleum Exporting Countries (OPEC). It has given oil-producing countries considerable power in the last 25 years. In 1994, the major aluminum producing countries, including Canada, worked out a deal to curb world aluminum production in an attempt to raise prices.[46] The diamond and shipping cartels have also been successful in keeping the prices they charge artificially high.[47] In 2000, the world's coffee-producing countries formed an OPEC-style cartel to control the price of coffee. They immediately raised coffee prices by 37 percent, which increased the price of a cup of coffee by about 15 cents. Surprisingly, most coffee buyers were sympathetic to the cartel, since coffee prices had been at their lowest level in seven years and coffee farmers in developing countries were struggling.[48]

cartel
Any association of producers whose purpose is to control supply of and prices for a given product.

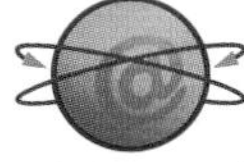

Organization of Petroleum Exporting Countries (OPEC)
www.opec.org

Many countries forbid **dumping**—selling a product abroad for less than the comparable price charged at home. Antidumping legislation typically views dumping as occurring if products are being sold at prices less than fair value, or if the result unfairly harms domestic industry. In 2000, the Canada Customs and Revenue Agency determined that refrigerators, dishwashers, and dryers produced by Whirlpool and Frigidaire in the United States were being "dumped" in Canada.[49]

dumping
Selling a product for less abroad than in the producing nation; illegal in Canada.

EXERCISING YOUR ETHICS

Paying Heed to Foreign Practices

The Purpose of the Assignment

Managers conducting business in other countries must often contend with differences in legal systems, customs, values, attitudes, and business practices. This exercise will help you better understand how such differences can affect the success of managers and companies trying to conduct business in foreign markets.

The Situation

Assume that you're an up-and-coming manager in a regional Canadian distribution company. Firms in your industry are just beginning to enter foreign markets, and you've been assigned to head up your company's new operations in a Latin American country. Because two of your competitors are also trying to enter this same market, your boss wants you to move as quickly as possible. You also sense that your success in this assignment will likely determine your future with the company.

You have just completed meetings with local government officials, and you're pessimistic about your ability to get things moving quickly. You've learned, for example, that it will take 10 months to get a building permit for a needed facility. Moreover, once the building is up, it will take another six months to get utilities. Finally, the phone company says that it may take up to two years to install the phone-lines that you need for high-speed internet access.

The Dilemma

Various officials have indicated that time frames could be considerably shortened if you were willing to pay special "expediting" fees. You realize, of course, that these "fees" are bribes, and you're well aware that the practice of paying such "fees" is both unethical and illegal in Canada. In this foreign country, however, it's not illegal and not even considered unethical. Moreover, if you don't pay and one of your competitors does, you'll be at a major competitive disadvantage. In any case, your boss isn't likely to understand the long lead times necessary to get the operation running. Fortunately, you have access to a source of funds that you could spend without the knowledge of anyone in the home office.

Questions for Discussion

1. What are the key ethical issues in this situation?
2. What do you think most managers would do in this situation?
3. What would you do?

SUMMARY OF LEARNING OBJECTIVES

1. **Explain how *free trade agreements* assist world trade.** Several *trade agreements* have attempted to eliminate restrictions on free trade internationally. The *General Agreement on Tariffs and Trade* (GATT) was instituted to eliminate tariffs and other trade barriers among participating nations. The *European Union* (EU) has eliminated virtually all trade barriers among the 12 principal Western European nations. The *North American Free Trade Agreement* (NAFTA) eliminates many of the barriers to free trade that exist among the United States, Canada, and Mexico.

2. **Describe the rise of international business and identify the *major world marketplaces*.** More and more business firms are engaged in international business. The term *globalization* refers to the process by which the world economy is fast becoming a single interdependent entity. The global economy is characterized by a rapid growth in the exchange of information and trade in services. The three major marketplaces for international business are *North America* (the United States, Canada, and Mexico), *Western Europe* (which is dominated by Germany, the United Kingdom, France, and Italy), and *Asia-Pacific*

(where the dominant country, Japan, is surrounded by such rapidly advancing nations as South Korea, Taiwan, Hong Kong, and China).

3. **Explain how different forms of *competitive advantage, import-export balances, exchange rates,* and *foreign competition* determine the ways in which countries and businesses respond to the international environment.** With an absolute advantage, a country engages in international trade because it can produce a good or service more efficiently than any other nation. But more often countries trade because they enjoy comparative advantages, that is, they can produce some items more efficiently than they can produce other items. A country that exports more than it imports has a favourable balance of trade, while a country that imports more than it exports has an unfavourable balance of trade. If the exchange rate decreases (the value of the Canadian dollar falls), our exports become less expensive for other countries so they will buy more of what we produce. The reverse happens if the value of the Canadian dollar increases. Changes in the exchange rate therefore have a strong impact on our international competitiveness.

4. **Discuss the factors involved in deciding to do business internationally and in selecting the appropriate *levels of international involvement* and *international organizational structure*.** In deciding whether to do business internationally, a firm must determine whether a market for its product exists abroad, and if so, whether the firm has the skills and knowledge to manage such a business. It must also assess the business climates of other nations to ensure that they are conducive to international operations. A firm must also decide on its level of international involvement. It can choose to be an *exporter* or *importer*, to organize as an *international firm*, or to operate as a *multinational firm*. The choice will influence the organizational structure of its international operations, specifically, its use of *independent agents, licensing arrangements, branch offices, strategic alliances,* and *direct investment*.

5. **Describe some of the ways in which *social, cultural, economic, legal,* and *political differences* act as barriers to international trade.** *Social* and *cultural differences* that can serve as barriers to trade include language, social values, and traditional buying patterns. Differences in economic systems may force businesses to establish close relationships with foreign governments before they are permitted to do business abroad. *Quotas, tariffs, subsidies,* and *local-content laws* offer protection to local industries. Differences in *business practice laws* can make standard business practices in one nation illegal in another.

KEY TERMS

QUESTIONS AND EXERCISES

Questions for Review

1. Explain the difference between a nation's balance of trade and balance of payments.
2. What are the three possible levels of involvement in international business? Give examples of each.
3. What are the advantages and disadvantages of multinational corporations?
4. How does the economic system of a country affect foreign firms interested in doing business there?

Questions for Analysis

5. Make a list of all the major items in your bedroom. Identify the country in which each item was made. Give possible reasons why that nation might have a comparative advantage in producing this good.
6. Do you support protectionist tariffs for Canada? If so, in what instances and for what reasons? If not, why not?
7. Is NAFTA good for Canada? Give supporting reasons for your answer.
8. Do you think that a firm that is operating internationally is better advised to adopt a single standard of ethical conduct or to adapt to local conditions? Under what kinds of conditions might each approach be preferable?

Application Exercises

9. Interview the manager of a local firm that does at least some business internationally. Identify reasons why the company decided to "go international," as well as the level of the firm's international involvement and the organizational structure it uses for its international operations.
10. Select a product familiar to you. Using library references, learn something about the culture of India and identify the problems that might arise in trying to market this product to India's citizens.

BUILDING YOUR BUSINESS SKILLS

Putting Yourself in Your Place

Goal

To encourage students to apply global business strategies to a small-business situation.

Background

Some people might say that Yolanda Lang is a bit too confident. Others might say that she needs confidence—and more—to succeed in the business she's chosen. But one thing is certain: Lang is determined to grow INDE, her handbag design company, into a global enterprise. At only 28 years of age, she has time on her side—if she makes the right business moves now.

These days, Lang spends most of her time in Milan, Italy. Backed by $50 000 of her parents' personal savings, she is trying to compete with Gucci, Fendi, and other high-end handbag makers. Her target market is women willing to spend $200 on a purse. Ironically, Lang was forced to set up shop in Italy because of the snobbishness of these customers, who buy high-end bags only if they're European-made. "Strangely enough," she muses, "I need to be in Europe to sell in North America."

To succeed, she must first find ways to keep production costs down—a tough task for a woman in a male-dominated business culture. Her fluent Italian is an advantage, but she's often forced to turn down inappropriate dinner invitations. She also has to figure out how to get her 22-bag collection into stores worldwide. Retailers are showing her bags in Italy and Japan, but she's had little luck in the United States. "I intend to be a global company," says Lang. The question is how to succeed first as a small business.

Method

Step 1

Join together with three or four other students to discuss the steps that Lang has taken so far to break into the U.S. retail market. These steps include:

- buying a mailing list of 5000 shoppers from high-end department store Neiman Marcus and selling directly to these customers
- linking with a manufacturer's representative to sell her line in major U.S. cities while she herself concentrates on Europe

Step 2

Based on what you learned in this chapter, suggest other strategies that might help Lang grow her business. Working with group members, consider whether the following options would help or hurt Lang's business. Explain why a strategy is likely to work or likely to fail.

- Lang could relocate to the United States and sell abroad through an independent agent
- Lang could relocate to the United States and set up a branch office in Italy
- Lang could find a partner in Italy and form a strategic alliance that would allow her to build her business on both continents

Step 3

Working alone, create a written marketing plan for INDE. What steps would you recommend that Lang take to reach her goal of becoming a global company? Compare your written response with those of other group members.

Follow-Up Questions

1. What are the most promising steps that Lang can take to grow her business? What are the least promising?
2. Lang thinks that her trouble breaking into the U.S. retail market stems from the fact that her company is unknown. How would this circumstance affect the strategies suggested in Steps 1 and 2?
3. When Lang deals with Italian manufacturers, she is a young, attractive woman in a man's world. Often, she must convince men that her purpose is business and nothing else. How should Lang handle personal invitations that get in the way of business? How can she say no while still maintaining business relationships? Why is it often difficult for women to do business in male-dominated cultures?
4. The American consulate has given Lang little business help because her products are made in Italy. Do you think the consulate's treatment of an American business person is fair or unfair? Explain your answer.
5. Do you think Lang's relocation to Italy will pay off? Why or why not?
6. With Lang's goals of creating a global company, can INDE continue to be a one-person operation?

MASTERING BUSINESS ESSENTIALS

Episode 9 stresses the importance of developing a marketing strategy that identifies and makes the best use of a company's competitive advantage. A firm must not only develop one or more capabilities that are superior to those of competitors, but it must also turn its advantage into an effective marketing strategy and growth plan. *This episode illustrates and enhances the concept of national competitive advantage.*

Episode 10 reminds us that there are international variations in the consumer buying process. *This episode shows how personal, psychological, social, and cultural influences on consumer behaviour differ across borders.*

CRAFTING YOUR BUSINESS PLAN

Considering the World

The Purpose of the Assignment

1. To familiarize students with issues faced by a firm that has decided to go global.
2. To determine where, in the framework of the BPP business plan, global issues might appropriately be presented.

Assignment

After reading Chapter 4 in the textbook, open the BPP software and examine the information dealing with the types of global business considerations that would be of concern to the sample firm of Acme Consulting.

Now respond to the following items:

1. What products does Acme plan to offer and in which international markets will they be competing? [Sites to see in BPP (for this assignment): In

the **Plan Outline screen**, click on **1.0 Executive Summary**; then click on **1.2 Mission** and then **4.0 Market Analysis Summary** and **4.1 Market Segmentation**. Next, while still in the Plan Outline screen, click on **2.0 Company Summary**. Finally, in the Plan Outline screen, click on **5.2 Strategic Alliances**.]

2. In Acme's business plan, see if you can find any discussion of the international organizational structures used by Acme's competitors. Do you think this information is adequate or inadequate? [Sites to see in BPP for this item: In the **Plan Outline screen**, click on **4.3.2 Distribution Service** and **4.3.4 Main Competitors**.]
3. What is the planned organization structure for Acme's international activities? Would you categorize Acme's relationship to its Paris partner as that of a branch office or that of a strategic alliance? [Sites to see in BPP for this item: In the **Plan Outline screen**, click on **6.1 Organization Structure** and then on **6.2 Management Team**.]
4. Chapter 4 states that going international requires "necessary skills and knowledge." Does Acme's business plan indicate that the company possesses the skills and knowledge to succeed internationally? [Sites to see in BPP for this item: In the **Plan Outline screen**, click on **6.0 Management Summary** and then on **6.2 Management Team**. Next, in the **Plan Outline screen**, click on **3.1 Service Description**, and then click on **3.2 Competitive Comparison**.]

VIDEO EXERCISE

Globalizing the Long Arm of the Law

Learning Objectives

The purpose of this video is to help you

1. Understand how and why a company adapts to the needs of foreign customers.
2. Identify the levels of international involvement that are available to companies.
3. Discuss some of the legal and ethical obstacles to a company's international operations.

Synopsis

Scotland Yard and the RCMP are only two of the many worldwide organizations that use security technology from Printrak (**www.printrakinternational.com**). Originally a computerized fingerprint-management system, Printrak, a Motorola company, has added a number of security and criminal-information products as it's expanded from its California headquarters to serve international customers. In addition to studying each country's legal, political, economic, and cultural characteristics, general manager Darren Reilly and his management team analyze local demand and customer needs. Rather than invest in local plants and equipment, Printrak works through local sales agents to ensure that its products are presented in a culturally savvy way in each market. Despite country-by-country differences in business customs and ethics, the decisions and actions of Printrak employees are guided by parent company Motorola's code of conduct.

Discussion Questions

1. *For analysis:* What are some of the barriers that affect Printrak's ability to do business in foreign markets?
2. *For analysis:* From Printrak's perspective, what are the advantages and disadvantages of hiring and training local sales agents in each foreign market?
3. *For application:* In addition to establishing users committees, what else should Printrak do to track changing customer needs?
4. *For application:* How would you suggest that Printrak build on its relations with "beachhead customers" to expand in particular regions?
5. *For debate:* Printrak employees and managers must comply with Motorola's global ethics policy. Should local sales agents be allowed to take any action they deem necessary to make local sales, regardless of Motorola policy? Support your chosen position.

Online Exploration

Browse Printrak's home page (**www.printrakinternational.com**), find out where the company has customers, and read some of the news releases about international operations. Also look at the resource links that Printrak has posted for customers and site visitors. Why would Printrak publicize its customer list in this way? Why would it post a glossary of security-related terms and acronyms? Finally, do you think the company should translate some or all of its website to accommodate foreign customers? Explain your response.

EXPLORING THE NET

The Best-Known Brand Name in the World

In this chapter, we looked at the major world marketplaces and saw just a sampling of the ways in which the needs and wants of customers can differ from region to region. How does a truly global company deal with the complexities of a global market? One good example is Cola-Cola Co., whose website, at www.coca-cola.com, offers an interesting glimpse into the consumer markets of nearly 200 different countries.

You'll probably notice that the home page is designed to serve several purposes and cover a wide range of topics, including:

Consumer Information
Online Shopping for Coca-Cola Merchandise
Product Promotions
Information about Employment Opportunities
Public Relations Information
Company Information

Start at the top of the home page by clicking on **Coca-Cola Worldwide**:

Scan the list of countries. Are there any that surprise you? Now click in turn on the sites for Denmark, Malaysia, and Turkey.

1. What do they all have in common?

Now return to the home page and click on **The Coca-Cola Company**:

2. When was Cola-Cola founded, and how many different beverages did it produce?

Click on **Brands**. Examine the complete list of Coca-Cola's beverage brands:

3. How does this list demonstrate a possible competitive advantage for Coca-Cola?

Return to **Brands** and click on **Brand Fact Sheets.** Select **Cappy**:

4. What is this drink like, and where is it popular?

Now try clicking on **Tian Yu Di**:

5. What can you find out about this beverage?

Concluding Case 4-1

Toyota's International Push

Toyota is a giant Japanese car company with a stellar reputation for quality, but today it's also a firm with an apparent identity crisis. Although it's among the world's largest—and most profitable—companies, Toyota seems to be changing its mind about the character of its operations and, indeed, its perception of itself as a global manufacturer.

Toyota was founded in 1930 and first entered the U.S. market in 1957, where, despite a few early missteps, it has enjoyed almost unqualified success. By 1970, Toyota was the world's fourth-largest automaker, and today, it's in third place. Profits in 2001 were $5.5 billion on revenues of $108 billion. The firm employs 215 000 workers worldwide and operates 56 manufacturing facilities in 25 countries. It opened its tenth U.S. assembly plant in Alabama in 2003.

Since it first ventured into foreign markets, however, Toyota has steadfastly remained a Japanese company. It's long been the market leader at home, and new product design has always been handled by Japanese designers from a centralized development centre. Company policy has always been to fill top spots in foreign affiliates with senior Japanese executives, and managers at foreign operations have always had to get key decisions reviewed by corporate headquarters in aptly named Toyota City.

In the early 1990s, Toyota also had a clear strategy for growth based on competitive advantages and economic forecasts. The firm intended to grow steadily in its domestic market, make modest gains in the United States, expand significantly in Europe, and make significant gains in Southeast Asia. Formidable domestic competition dampened prospects in the United States, but the Japanese market was booming, and Toyota fully expected to be able to extend its market dominance into neighbouring countries. Europe, too, was targeted as an area with growth opportunities.

But even the best plans and forecasts sometimes go awry. Over the course of the 1990s, Toyota's market situation began to change on all fronts. The home market stalled along with the rest of the Japanese economy, and Toyota also began to lose its youngest domestic consumers to Honda and a resurgent Nissan. In addition, a currency crisis in Southeast Asia, coupled with competition from youth-oriented upstarts such as Kia and Hyundai, undermined Toyota's plans in South Korea, Indonesia, and China. Toyota also stalled in Europe, where it faced an economic downturn and renewed competition from Volkswagen and Renault.

Ironically, however, it's in the U.S. market that things have turned out better than Toyota had hoped. In 2001, Toyota sold more vehicles in the United States (1.74 million) than in Japan (1.71 million). Its U.S. factories and dealerships also employ 123 000 Americans—more than Coca-Cola, Microsoft, and Oracle combined. More and more of the firm's top U.S. executives are local hires who have either climbed the ladder or been lured away from domestic firms like Ford and General Motors. Toyota's recent U.S. successes, such as the Tundra pickup and Sequoia sport utility vehicle (SUV), have had significant input from U.S. design teams.

Most of these successes come from changes in Toyota's American operations. "Thirty years ago," says James Press, the COO of Toyota Motor Sales USA, "we were more dependent on Japan, [but now] there's not much Japanese influence on a day-to-day basis." In fact, the influence of U.S. operations is beginning to be felt in Japan, where CEO Fujio Cho has advised his managers that "We must Americanize."

Although Toyota has enjoyed increasing success in the United States, it is not sure how to take the fullest advantage of this situation. In fact, the growing importance of U.S. operations has created some tension between corporate and subsidiary operations. Some top managers at home, for example, don't want Toyota to lose too much of its Japanese heritage. They also remain committed to the practices responsible for the firm's long-term success—consensus-style decision making, merciless cost cutting, and fanatical devotion to quality and customer satisfaction.

To help ensure that these qualities and practices aren't sacrificed, the company recently opened a new training centre in Toyota City. Called the Toyota Institute, the centre offers management-development courses patterned after M.B.A. courses but largely taught by senior company executives. Of course, compromises are necessary even here. When academic instructors are needed, they'll come from the University of Pennsylvania's Wharton School of Business.

As it moves forward on the international front, Toyota is flexible when it comes to accommodating national identity to global aspirations. One positive result of this stance is a willingness to learn from its foreign subsidiaries. Officials in Japan, for example, long resisted making a full-size pickup truck with a V8 engine because they saw such a vehicle as useful only for commercial purposes. So when U.S. executives invited their Japanese counterparts to a Dallas Cowboys football game in Texas, they had an ulterior motive. As they walked through the parking lot before the game, the visitors were overwhelmed by row upon row of full-size pickups with chrome logos touting horsepower and towing capacity. Shortly thereafter, Japanese headquarters okayed the new Tundra pickup truck that has become a top seller almost overnight.

Toyota has been doing well in the United States, but it still faces a few problems down the road. Perhaps the biggest potential concern is the aging of its customer base. The average age of an American Toyota buyer is 45, highest among any Japanese carmaker. To help counter this threat to future market share, the company has begun introducing new models specifically targeted at younger buyers. It also plans to launch an entirely new brand called Scion. Although the new line is aimed at younger buyers, Toyota's marketing strategy is patterned on the strategy by which it has successfully marketed its Lexus luxury line—distancing the new line from the parent brand and sidestepping consumer preconceptions.

Questions for Discussion

1. What are Toyota's primary advantages and disadvantages in its current competitive environment?
2. What are Toyota's biggest challenges in trying to maintain harmony between Japanese and U.S. operations?
3. How important is it for a company to maintain a national identity?
4. What are your own personal impressions of Toyota products? ◆

Concluding Case 4-2 CC

The Story of McDonald's Canada in Russia

Starting a business in another country can be a huge challenge, as George Cohon, senior chairman of McDonald's Restaurants of Canada Ltd., discovered when he decided to introduce the famous fast-food to Russia. In a country known for its communist ideology, the introduction of a restaurant that symbolized Western capitalism was viewed with considerable suspicion.

Negotiations began in 1976 and took 12 years to complete. The first McDonald's outlet finally opened in Moscow in 1990. However, there were several key problems that had to be solved along the way:

- Local processors could not meet McDonald's exacting standards for milk and beef, so the company had to build a huge complex to process the food that serves as the inputs for its restaurants; at the beginning, about one-half of the food items had to be imported.
- Getting inputs to the right place at the right time was a major problem in a country that had one of the worst-run agricultural sectors in the world; at one point, McDonald's workers actually had to go out and harvest potatoes.
- The idea of private enterprise was ridiculed in Russia (one critic said, "The trouble with Russia is that no one ever had a paper route").
- Russian workers had to learn to be consumer-oriented and to be polite to customers; in the beginning, Western managers were brought in to provide training and direction to Russian workers.

McDonald's had to face other uncertainties as well. For example, it was not clear whether Western-style food would appeal to Russians, or whether they would have enough money to purchase McDonald's hamburgers, fries, and shakes. A Big Mac is priced at $2.80, which doesn't sound like much unless you understand that the average monthly wage of Russian workers is only $200. This is equivalent to asking Canadians to pay about $35 for a Big Mac. In spite of this, demand was high from the start, and McDonald's Canada is now making profits in Russia.

The restaurant in Moscow's Pushkin Square, for example, was an instant success. It now serves about 40 000 customers per day, making it the busiest McDonald's in the world. The restaurant on the Old Arbat is the second busiest, serving about 20 000 people per day. The three biggest restaurants in Moscow serve as much food as 30 average-sized McDonald's restaurants in North America. Cohon has since expanded operations to other Russian cities, and in 1999 there were 49 McDonald's restaurants operating in Russia.

Most of the problems that were initially encountered have now been solved. In the early days, about 80 percent of the managers were from the West. However, with the right coaching the Russian staff gained skills and management expertise. Now only a handful of Western managers remain. In addition, almost all of McDonald's ingredients are provided by 150 local businesses.

Although there are still problems with high taxes and excessive government red tape, this is a Canadian success story. It proves that opportunities exist in the global economy for Canadians who are willing to take calculated risks, who are persistent, and who are willing to adapt to local cultures and circumstances.

Questions for Discussion

1. How does the activity of McDonald's in Russia affect Canada's balance of trade? How does it affect Canada's balance of payments?
2. In deciding to "go international," how did McDonald's answer each of the basic questions shown in Figure 4.7 (see page 133)?
3. What level of involvement has McDonald's Canada decided on as it pursues business in Russia?
4. What skills must an expatriate manager possess to work effectively with local managers and employees?
5. Explain how the various barriers to trade (social/cultural, economic, legal/political) affected McDonald's Canada as it tried to establish itself in Russia. ◆

CHAPTER 5

Conducting Business Ethically and Responsibly

After reading this chapter, you should be able to:

1. Explain how individuals develop their personal *codes of ethics* and why ethics are important in the workplace.
2. Distinguish *social responsibility* from *ethics*, identify *organizational stakeholders*, and characterize social consciousness today.
3. Show how the concept of social responsibility applies both to environmental issues and to a firm's relationships with customers, employees, and investors.
4. Identify four general *approaches to social responsibility* and describe the four steps a firm must take to implement a *social responsibility program.*
5. Explain how issues of social responsibility and ethics affect small businesses.

Back on Track at Cinar Corp.?

At the annual meeting of Cinar Corp. on April 9, 2003, newly appointed CEO Stuart Snyder told shareholders that the company is finally moving forward again after years of financial scandal, and is once again going to start producing children's television shows.

The story of Cinar, which produced children's shows like *Arthur, Caillou, The Adventures of Paddington Bear,* and *Wimzie's House,* is a long and tortured one. The key drivers in the company were Micheline Charest and Ronald Weinberg, who tirelessly promoted their company to the media and to financial markets. But in March 2000, they both resigned as co-chief executives of the company amid several allegations that: (1) over $100 million had been invested without proper approval from Cinar's board of directors; (2) Cinar had fraudulently obtained Canadian tax credits by putting the names of Canadians on television scripts actually written by Americans; and (3) Cinar had breached securities rules with its financial statements and other disclosure documents. All of this upheaval caused the company's stock to drop sharply in value, and Cinar was eventually delisted from both NASDAQ and the Toronto Stock Exchange. Although they are no longer executives or board members at Cinar, the two continue to hold 63 percent of the voting stock of the company.

No charges were laid in the tax fraud area, but in 2002 Charest and Weinberg were eventually fined $1 million each by the Quebec Securities Commission (QSC). They were also required to resign from the board of directors, and were banned from holding directorships or voting for directors of publicly held companies in Canada.

It was originally thought that the QSC ruling would prevent Charest and Weinberg from influencing who would be appointed to Cinar's board of directors. But the QSC settlement allowed them to appoint a trustee who could nominate or vote for directors, and at Cinar's annual shareholders meeting in April 2002, trustee Robert Despres used his new-found voting clout to install directors he wanted instead of the company's proposed slate. Despres claimed that he did not represent former co-CEOs Charest and Weinberg, and was simply interested in getting a board of directors in place that would move the company forward and increase shareholder value.

The chair of Cinar's board at that meeting was Lawrence Yelin. He and CEO Barrie Usher were under fire from various people because they were unsuccessful in their attempts to sell Cinar in 2001. Yelin said that it was well known that Charest and Weinberg wanted to replace the entire existing board at Cinar. Charest and Weinberg also had several disagreements with Usher about the strategy that Cinar should pursue. Despres admitted that Charest and Weinberg had suggested some names for the new board.

By the summer of 2003, Despres was under fire from Charest and Weinberg, who asked the Quebec Superior court to remove Despres from his position as trustee of the couple's 64 percent stake in Cinar. The suit charged that Despres was occupying his position just for prestige and money, and wasn't really trying to help the company, and that he had refused orders to sell the company.

When problems originally arose at Cinar, Richard Finlay, chairman of the Centre for Corporate and Public Governance, offered the view that Cinar's top management and board structure were rather peculiar and likely contributed to Cinar's difficulties. The husband–wife team of Charest and Weinberg functioned as co-CEOs, one acting as president and the other chairing the board to which both reported. The corporate governance guidelines of the Toronto Stock Exchange call for a non-executive and independent director as chairperson of the board. ◆

ethics
Individual standards or moral values regarding what is right and wrong or good and bad.

ethical behaviour
Behaviour that conforms to individual beliefs and social norms about what is right and good.

unethical behaviour
Behaviour that individual beliefs and social norms define as wrong and bad.

business ethics
Ethical or unethical behaviours by a manager or employee of an organization.

1. Explain how individuals develop their personal codes of ethics and why ethics are important in the workplace.

ETHICS IN THE WORKPLACE

The problems at Cinar illustrate just some of the complexities of the modern business world. They also demonstrate the controversy that often arises when the issue of ethics is discussed. **Ethics** are beliefs about what is right and wrong or good and bad. An individual's personal values and morals and the social context in which they occur determine whether a particular behaviour is perceived as ethical or unethical. **Ethical behaviour** is behaviour that conforms to individual beliefs and social norms about what is right and good. **Unethical behaviour** is behaviour that individual beliefs and social norms define as wrong and bad. **Business ethics** is a term often used to refer to ethical or unethical behaviours by a manager or employee of an organization.

Individual Ethics

Because ethics are based on both individual beliefs and social concepts, they vary from person to person, from situation to situation, and from culture to culture. Social standards are broad enough to support differences in beliefs. Without violating general standards, therefore, people may develop personal codes of ethics reflecting a wide range of attitudes and beliefs.

Thus ethical and unethical behaviour is determined partly by the individual and partly by culture. For instance, virtually everyone would agree that if you see someone drop a $20 bill in a store, it would be ethical to return it to the owner. But there'll be less agreement if you find $20 and don't know who dropped it. Should you turn it in to the lost-and-found department? Or, since the rightful owner isn't likely to claim it, can you just keep it?

Societies generally adopt formal laws that reflect prevailing ethical standards or social norms. For example, because most people regard theft as unethical, we have laws against such behaviour and ways of punishing those who steal. We try to make unambiguous laws, but interpreting and applying them can still lead to ethical ambiguities. Real-world situations can often be interpreted in different ways, and it isn't always easy to apply statutory standards to real-life behaviour. Samuel Waksal, former CEO of ImClone, was convicted of insider trading for tipping off certain investors, allegedly including Martha Stewart and members of his own family, about the impending fall of ImClone stock. But what about the behaviour of Stewart? She says that she'd already ordered her broker to sell the stock if it slipped below $60. Whether she had or hadn't, she's widely suspected of questionable behaviour, and the stock of her own company, Martha Stewart Living Omnimedia, has dropped 60 percent since this incident became public. Meanwhile, Waksal's daughter, who also sold her ImClone stock after getting information from her father, has so far been treated as an "innocent tippee"—someone who got inside information but didn't think that's what it was at the time.[1] Unfortunately, the epidemic of recent scandals ranging from Enron and Arthur Andersen to Tyco and WorldCom only serves to show how willing people can be to take advantage of potentially ambiguous situations. The Business Today box examines this difficult situation in more detail.

ImClone
www.imclone.com

Individual Values and Codes

How should we deal with business behaviour that we regard as unethical—especially when it's legally ambiguous? No doubt we have to start with the individuals in a business—its managers, employees, agents, and other legal representatives. Each of these people's personal code of ethics is determined by a combination of factors. We start to form ethical standards as children in response to our perceptions of the behaviour of parents and

BUSINESS TODAY

Whatever Happened to Ethics?

Over the years, there have been some classic high-profile cases where business executives were found guilty of either unethical or illegal behaviour. But the cases were always small in number. Until now. During the last few years, it seems we have been inundated with such cases. Consider the following:

- the Ontario Securities Commission alleged that executives at ATI Technologies had engaged in illegal insider trading, and had sold shares they owned before a quarterly profit warning was given to the general public
- senior executives at Livent Inc. were charged with falsifying financial statements and bilking investors and creditors out of $500 million
- the CEO of ImClone was found guilty of insider trading and sentenced to seven years in prison
- employees at Arthur Andersen shredded documents to foil investigators looking into the Enron debacle
- the CEO of Tyco International has been charged with tax evasion and making secret deals

These are just a few of the cases. Many other executives have been charged with, or convicted of, behaviours like making undisclosed loans to shareholders, obstructing justice, overstating sales revenues, and misleading clients.

What is going on? Has the ethical level of business executives suddenly declined? Perhaps. But a more likely reason is that the stock market "bubble" of the late 1990s magnified some already existing human weaknesses, including greed and a tendency to "skate on the edge." Human greed didn't increase in the 1990s, but the opportunities to satisfy it did.

Another reason is the failure of checks and balances that were supposed to prevent this kind of behaviour. Professionals such as accountants, lawyers, audit committees, government regulators, the press, and securities analysts are supposed to make sure that executives do not do things that are detrimental to shareholders. However, there seems to have been a decline in professionalism during the last few decades to the point where these groups may actually facilitate bad executive behaviour. Arthur Andersen's role in Enron is an example.

A third reason is stock options. These give executives the right to purchase shares of their company's stock at a certain price. If the option price is less than the market price of the company's stock, this benefits the executives because they can purchase stock below the market price. Originally, it was thought that stock options would align the interests of shareholders and executives by motivating executives to manage the company in a way that would increase the market price of the company's stock. But, in fact, options motivated executives to do things like overstating revenues so that the stock price would increase and they could cash in their options for a big profit. Once the overstatement was discovered, the stock price would drop sharply and shareholders would be left holding the bag.

The best explanation of unethical executive behaviour in the 1990s is probably a combination of these three reasons. But now what? Were the excesses of the 1990s caused by just a "few bad apples," or is the system broken? The view that there are just a "few bad apples" is supported by some statistics. For example, in the United States (where much of the high-profile bad behaviour has occurred), the Securities and Exchange Commission (SEC) investigated 570 companies in 2001. That sounds like a lot, but it's only slightly higher than the number investigated in 1994. Another statistic: more than 150 companies restated their earnings in 2001, but that was only one company in 100. Statistics such as these lead some to believe that the system needs only a minor fix-up.

The other view is that there really has been a decline in the general level of ethical behaviour, and that the headline cases are just symptomatic of a very big problem. If we accept this view, it follows that the current legislation is inadequate to deal with the problem, and the only solution is to develop tough new legislation that will control the tendency of executives to behave in an unethical and illegal fashion.

other adults. Soon, we enter school, where peers influence us, and as we grow into adulthood, experience shapes our lives and contributes to our ethical beliefs and our behaviour. We also develop values and morals that contribute to ethical standards. If you put financial gain at the top of your priority list, you may develop a code of ethics that supports the pursuit of material comfort. If you set family and friends as a priority, you'll no doubt adopt different standards.

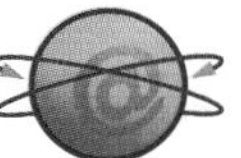

Ontario Securities Commission
www.osc.gov.on.ca

Managerial Ethics

managerial ethics
Standards of behaviour that guide individual managers in their work.

Managerial ethics are the standards of behaviour that guide individual managers in their work.[2] Although your ethics can affect your work in any number of ways, it's helpful to classify them in terms of three broad categories.

Behaviour Toward Employees

This category covers such matters as hiring and firing, wages and working conditions, and privacy and respect. Ethical and legal guidelines suggest that hiring and firing decisions should be based solely on ability to perform a job. A manager who discriminates against any ethnic minority in hiring exhibits both unethical and illegal behaviour. But what about the manager who hires a friend or relative when someone else might be more qualified? Such decisions may not be illegal; but they may be objectionable on ethical grounds.

Wages and working conditions, though regulated by law, are also areas for controversy. Consider a manager who pays a worker less than he deserves because the manager knows that the employee can't afford to quit or risk his job by complaining. While some people will see the behaviour as unethical, others will see it as smart business. Cases such as these are hard enough to judge, but consider the behaviour of Enron management toward company employees. It encouraged employees to invest retirement funds in company stock and then, when financial problems began to surface, refused to permit them to sell the stock (even though top officials of the company were allowed to sell their stock). Ultimately, the firm's demise cost thousands of jobs.

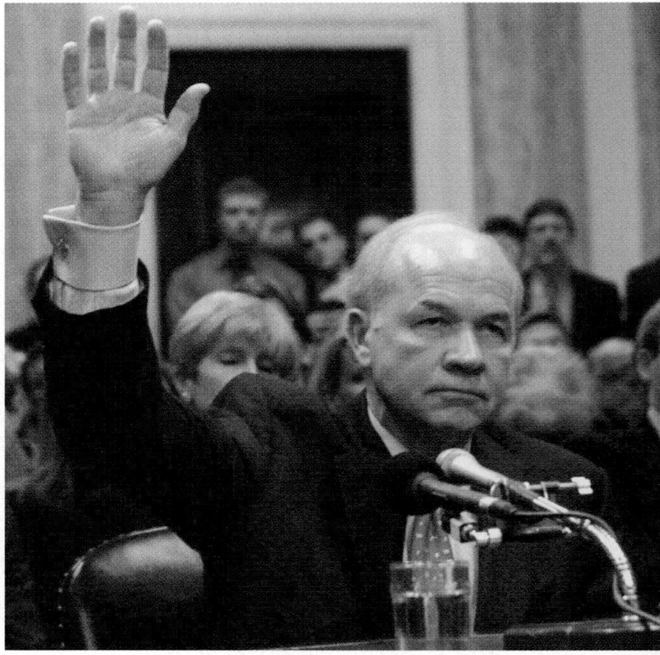

Former employees protest their treatment by Enron (left), which laid off thousands of workers when it encountered financial difficulties. Employees were also barred from selling any company stock in their retirement accounts. As the value of the company's stock plummeted, many lost 70–90 percent of their retirement assets. Former Enron Chairman Kenneth Lay (right) told the U.S. Congress that he felt "a profound sadness about what has happened to...current and former employees." While employees were barred from selling their stock Lay reportedly sold his Enron stock for over U.S.$100 million.

Behaviour Toward the Organization

Ethical issues also arise from employee behaviour toward employers, especially in such areas as conflict of interest, confidentiality, and honesty. A conflict of interest occurs when an activity may benefit the individual to the detriment of his or her employer. Most companies have policies that forbid buyers from accepting gifts from suppliers. Businesses in highly competitive industries—software and fashion apparel, for example—have safeguards against designers selling company secrets to competitors. Relatively common problems in the general area of honesty include such behaviour as stealing supplies, padding expense accounts, and using a business phone to make personal long-distance calls. Most employees are honest, but most organizations are nevertheless vigilant. Again, Enron is a good example of employees' unethical behaviour toward an organization. Top managers not only misused corporate assets, but they often committed the company to risky ventures to further personal interests.

Behaviour Toward Other Economic Agents

Ethics also comes into play in the relationship between the firm and its employees with so-called primary agents of interest—mainly customers, competitors, stockholders, suppliers, dealers, and unions. In dealing with such agents, there is room for ethical ambiguity in just about every activity—advertising, financial disclosure, ordering and purchasing, bargaining and negotiation, and other business relationships.

For example, businesses in the pharmaceuticals industry are under criticism because of the rising prices of drugs. They argue that high prices cover the costs of research and development programs to develop new drugs. The solution to such problems seems obvious: find the right balance between reasonable pricing and price gouging (responding to increased demand with overly steep price increases). But like so many questions involving ethics, there are significant differences of opinion about the proper balance.[3]

Another recent area of concern is financial reporting, especially by high-tech firms like WorldCom. Many companies have been very aggressive in presenting their financial positions in a positive light, and have overstated earnings projections to entice more investment.[4] Certainly, Samuel Waksal's aggressive promotion of ImClone stock fits into this category. And again, there's Enron.

- Senior officials continued to mislead investors into thinking that the firm was solvent long after they knew that it was in serious trouble.
- The company violated numerous regulations during the California energy crisis, causing thousands of consumers hardships and inconvenience.
- Many of its partnerships with other firms violated terms of full disclosure and honesty, resulting in losses for other firms and their employees.

Another problem is global variations in business practices. In many countries, bribes are a normal part of doing business. Canadian law, however, forbids bribes, even if rivals from other countries are paying them. One power-generating company recently lost a $320 million contract in the Middle East because it refused to pay bribes like the Japanese firm that won the bid.

Critics say that far too little attention has been paid to ethical failures in business. Government, educational institutions, professional organizations, and businesses themselves have all failed to make it a priority to improve the state of ethics in business.

Assessing Ethical Behaviour

By definition, what distinguishes ethical behaviour from unethical behaviour is often subjective and subject to differences of opinion.[5] So, how does one go about deciding whether a particular action or decision is ethical? A three-step model can be used for applying ethical judgments to situations that may arise during the course of business activities:

1. Gather the relevant factual information.
2. Determine the most appropriate moral values.
3. Make an ethical judgment based on the rightness or wrongness of the proposed activity or policy.

Unfortunately, the process does not always work as smoothly as the three steps suggest. What if the facts are not clear-cut? What if there are no agreed-upon moral values? Nevertheless, a judgment and a decision must be made. Experts point out that, otherwise, trust is impossible; and trust, they add, is indispensable to any business transaction.

To assess more fully the ethics of a particular behaviour, we need a more refined process. Let's consider a common dilemma faced by managers involving their expense accounts. Companies routinely provide managers with accounts to cover work-related expenses when they are travelling on company business and/or entertaining clients for business purposes. Common examples of such expenses include hotel bills, meals, rental cars or taxis, and so forth. Employees, of course, are expected to claim only those expenses that are accurate and work-related. For example, if a manager takes a client to dinner while travelling on business and spends $100, submitting a receipt for that dinner to be reimbursed for $100 is clearly accurate and appropriate. Suppose, however, that the manager then has a $100 dinner the next night in that same city with a good friend for purely social purposes. Submitting that receipt for full reimbursement would be unethical. A few managers, however, will rationalize that it is acceptable to submit a receipt for dinner with a friend. They will argue, perhaps, that they are underpaid and are simply increasing the income due to them.

Other principles that come into play in a case like this include various ethical norms. Consider four such norms and the issues that they entail:

Utility: Does a particular act optimize what is best for those who are affected by it?
Rights: Does it respect the rights of the individuals involved?
Justice: Is it consistent with what we regard to be fair?
Caring: Is it consistent with people's responsibilities to each other?

Figure 5.1 incorporates the consideration of these ethical norms.

Now, let's return to the case of the inflated expense account. While the utility norm would acknowledge that the manager benefits from padding an expense account, others, such as co-workers and owners, do not. Likewise, most experts would agree that it does not respect the rights of others. Moreover, it is clearly unfair and compromises the manager's responsibilities to others. This particular act, then, appears to be clearly unethical.

Figure 5.1, however, also provides mechanisms for considering unique circumstances—those that apply only in certain limited situations. Suppose, for example, that the manager loses the receipt for the legitimate dinner but retains the receipt for the social dinner. Some people will argue that it is acceptable to submit the illegitimate receipt because the manager is only doing so to be reimbursed for what he or she is entitled to. Others, however, will continue to argue that submitting the other receipt is wrong under any circumstances. We won't pretend to arbitrate the case. For our

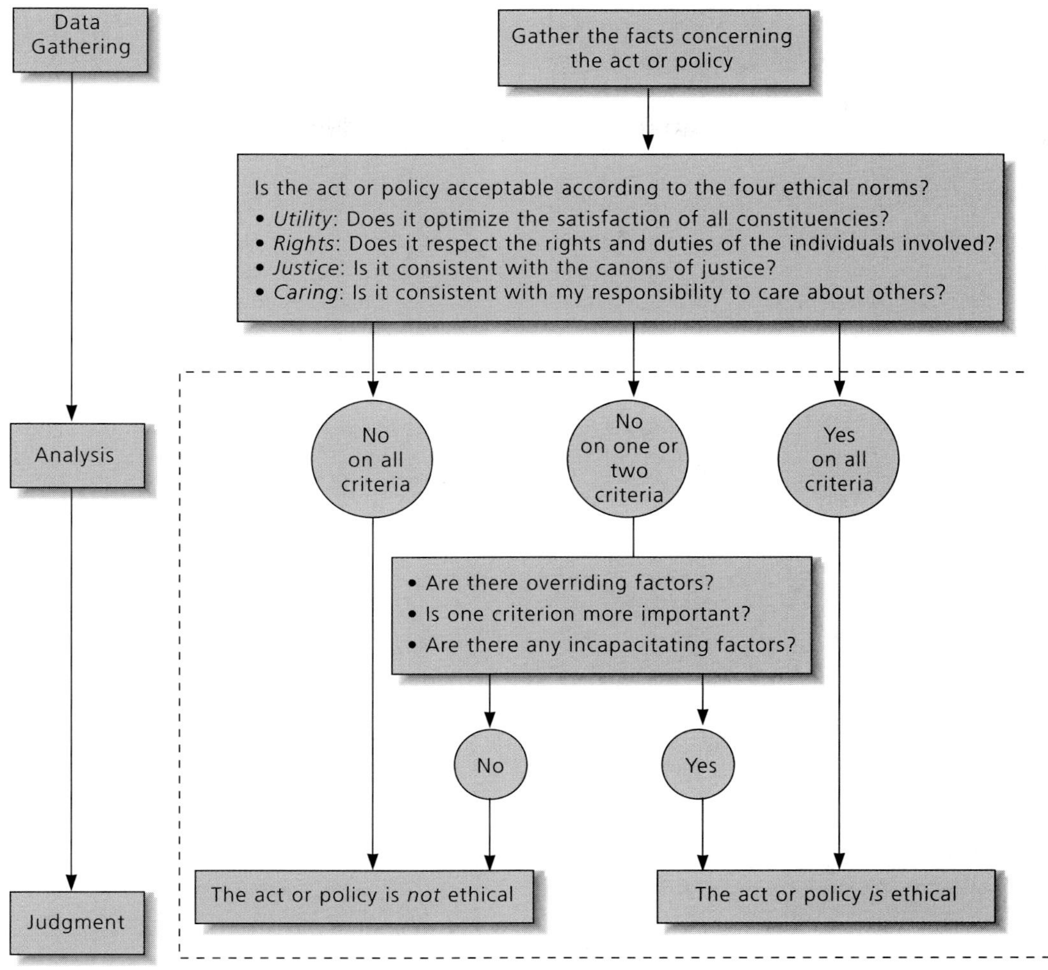

Figure 5.1
Expanded model of ethical judgments.

purposes, we will simply make the following point: Changes in the situation can make issues more or less clear-cut.

When judging how ethical a certain behaviour is, one of the simplest "tests" to use is the so-called "newspaper test." This means asking yourself this question: If you were to make a decision on an ethical issue and then read about it on the front page of tomorrow's paper, how would you feel? If you would feel embarrassed, you are very likely violating ethical standards and shouldn't make the decision.

Company Practices and Business Ethics

Organizations try to promote ethical behaviour and discourage unethical behaviour. As unethical and even illegal behaviour by both managers and employees plagues more and more companies, many firms have taken additional steps to encourage ethical behaviour in the workplace. Many, for example, establish codes of conduct and develop clear ethical positions on how the firm and its employees will conduct its business. An increasingly controversial area regarding business ethics and company practices involves the privacy of email and other communications that take place inside an organization. The Wired World box discusses these issues more fully.

IT'S A WIRED WORLD

Online Griping and Other Issues in High-Tech Ethics

Technological developments are creating all sorts of brand-new ethical problems—cloning, satellite reconnaissance, and bioengineered foods, to name just a few. For every innovation that promises convenience or safety, there seems to be a related ethical issue. The internet and email, for example, are certainly convenient and efficient, but they present business people with a variety of ethics-related problems.

In one set of age-old concerns, electronic communications merely substitute for traditional forms of communication, such as mail or the telephone. By the same token, however, they make it possible to run all the classic swindles, such as Ponzi or pyramid schemes, with greater efficiency than ever before. Federal law enforcement personnel routinely surf the web looking for illegal or unethical practices, often finding hundreds of questionable sites in a typical sting. Employers are also using email to test employee loyalty, as in the case of the manager who sent false emails to his workers, pretending to be a recruiter from a competing firm. Any employees who responded were skipped for promotion.

Sophisticated software is another source of potential abuse. Email management software can be legally used to monitor employee email. Critics complain, however, that if monitoring is secret or used inappropriately, employees' privacy rights can be infringed. And, in fact, 46 percent of employers monitor employee email—most of them without employees' knowledge. There's a good reason for the policy, says William Caple, Executive VP of OTG Software, a maker of email management systems: "To help protect their businesses from potential liability or security threats, companies need a...monitoring system."

Employees have been known to post opinions about employers on online message boards. For some managers, such as Agency.com CEO Kyle Shannon, the messages can be wake-up calls. When Shannon's company was slammed on Vault.com, Shannon discovered that his employees felt ill-prepared, stressed, and uninformed. He hired a VP of People Management to alleviate the problem. "In this new information environment," he warns, "you've got to assume everyone knows everything. So being straight with employees is important. Don't spin anything. Don't try to hide anything."

Agency.com
www.agency.com

Perhaps the single most effective step a company can take is to demonstrate top management support of high ethical standards. This policy contributes to a corporate culture that values ethical standards and announces that the firm is as concerned with good citizenship as with profits. When United Technologies (UT), a Connecticut-based industrial conglomerate, published its 21-page code of ethics, it also named a VP for business practices to see that UT conducted business ethically and responsibly.[6] With a detailed code of ethics and a senior official to enforce it, the firm sends a signal that it expects ethical conduct from its employees.

Another example involves the operations of Coca-Cola in Europe. First, some Belgian schoolchildren suffered minor illnesses after drinking Coke made from a bad batch of carbon dioxide. Then Coke cans shipped from the company's plant in Dunkirk, France, were found to have some fungicide on their bottoms. Neither problem was serious, but the two events combined to create a public relations problem. Coke CEO Douglas Ivester flew directly to Brussels and made a straightforward public apology: "My apologies to the consumers of Belgium." The furor died down almost immediately, primarily due to the top manager's quick, forthright response.[7]

In addition to demonstrating an attitude of honesty and openness, firms can take specific and concrete steps to formalize their commitment to ethical business practices. Two of the most common approaches to formalizing commitment are adopting written codes and instituting ethics programs.

Adopting Written Codes

Many companies have adopted written codes of ethics that formally acknowledge their intent to do business in an ethical manner. Figure 5.2 shows the code of ethics adopted by Great-West Life Assurance.

Figure 5.3 illustrates the role that corporate ethics and values should play in corporate policy. You can use it to see how a good ethics statement might be structured. Basically, the figure suggests that although strategies and practices can change frequently and objectives can change occasionally, an organization's core principles and values should remain steadfast. Hewlett-Packard, for example, has had the same written code of ethics, called The HP Way, since 1957. Its essential elements are as follows:

- We have trust and respect for individuals.
- We focus on a high level of achievement and contribution.
- We conduct our business with uncompromising integrity.
- We achieve our common objectives through teamwork.
- We encourage flexibility and innovation.

Two-thirds of Canada's largest corporations have codes of ethics (90 percent of large U.S. firms do). More and more regulatory and professional associations in Canada are recommending that corporations adopt codes of ethics. The Canada Deposit Insurance Corp., for example, requires that all deposit-taking institutions have a code of conduct that is periodically reviewed and ratified by the board of directors. The Canadian Competition Bureau, the Canadian Institute of Chartered Accountants, and the Ontario Human Rights Commission are all pushing for the adoption of codes of ethics by corporations.[8] Many Canadian and U.S. firms are adding a position called "Ethics Director" or "Ethics Officer."

Canadian Competition Bureau
cb-bc.gc.ca/epic/internet/incb-bc.nsf/vwGeneratedInterE/home

1. Great-West Life's management recognizes that, to prosper, the company must serve its clients, staff members and sales representatives, shareholders, and the community at large, with integrity and according to the highest standards of conduct.
2. We will maintain an environment of trust in, and respect for, the dignity of the individual. We will strive to select superior people. We will build and maintain a dynamic organization through an open and participative style of management. We will give staff members and sales personnel every opportunity to make the most of their abilities and reward them according to their contribution to meeting our objectives.
3. We will distribute our products and services in the best interests of our clients through distribution systems that are contemporary, innovative, and socially responsible.
4. Our investment program will carefully balance the quality, terms, and rate of return on our investments. We will strive to achieve a consistently superior rate of return to meet our overall financial objectives and obligations to our clients.
5. We will find new and better ways to serve our clients by offering products and services that are both contemporary and innovative to satisfy their changing needs and desires. We will maintain their goodwill by meeting our commitments to them both in spirit and letter with particular emphasis upon the financial management and security of their funds.
6. We will work to increase the long-term value of shareholders' investment to maintain our reputation as a sound and growing financial institution.

Figure 5.2
Guiding principles—the Great-West Life Assurance Company.

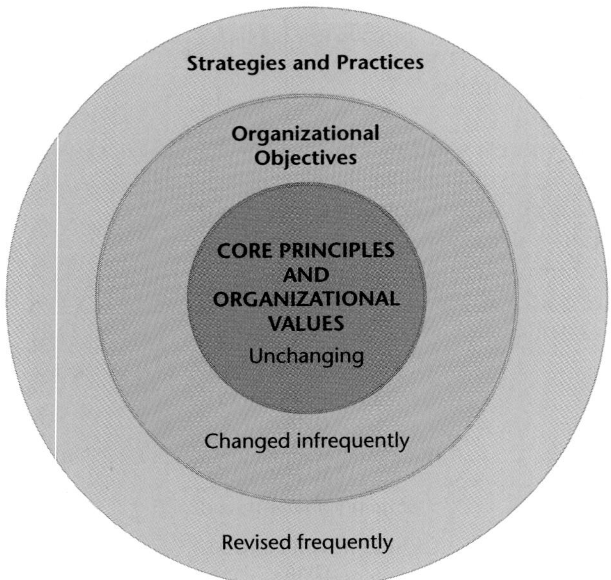

Figure 5.3
Core principles and organizational values.

Instituting Ethics Programs

Many examples suggest that ethical responses can be learned through experience. For instance, in a classic case several years ago, a corporate saboteur poisoned Tylenol capsules, resulting in the deaths of several consumers. Without waiting for instructions or a company directive, employees at Johnson & Johnson, maker of Tylenol, knew that they should get to retailers' shelves and pull the product as quickly as possible. In retrospect, they reported simply knowing that this was what the company would want to do.

But can business ethics be taught, either in the workplace or in schools? Not surprisingly, business schools have become important players in the debate about ethics education. Even though business schools must address the issue of ethics in the workplace, the practical reality is that companies must take the chief responsibility for educating employees. In fact, more and more firms are doing so. Imperial Oil, for example, conducts workshops for employees that emphasize ethical concerns. The purpose of these workshops is to help employees put Imperial's ethics statement into practice.

SOCIAL RESPONSIBILITY

social responsibility
A business's collective code of ethical behaviour toward the environment, its customers, its employees, and its investors.

organizational stakeholders
Groups, individuals, and organizations that are directly affected by the practices of an organization and that therefore have a stake in its performance.

Ethics affect individual behaviour in the workplace. **Social responsibility**, however, refers to the way in which a business tries to balance its commitments to certain groups and individuals in its social environment. **Organizational stakeholders** are those groups, individuals, and organizations that are directly affected by the practices of an organization and that therefore have a stake in its performance.[9]

The Stakeholder Model of Responsibility

2. Distinguish social responsibility from ethics, identify organizational stakeholders, and characterize social consciousness today.

Most companies that strive to be responsible to their stakeholders concentrate on five main groups: customers, employees, investors, suppliers, and the local communities in which they do business (see Figure 5.4). They may then select other stakeholders that are particularly relevant or important to the organization and try to address their needs and expectations as well.

Contemporary Social Consciousness

Canadian society and Canadian business have changed dramatically in the last two centuries. Not surprisingly, so have views about social responsibility. The late nineteenth century was characterized by the entrepreneurial spirit and the laissez-faire philosophy. During this era of labour strife and predatory business practices, both individual citizens and the government first became concerned about unbridled business activity. This concern was translated into laws regulating basic business practices.

During the Great Depression of the 1930s, many people blamed the failure of businesses and banks and the widespread loss of jobs on a general climate of business greed and lack of restraint. Out of the economic turmoil emerged new laws that described an increased expectation that business should protect and enhance the general welfare of society.

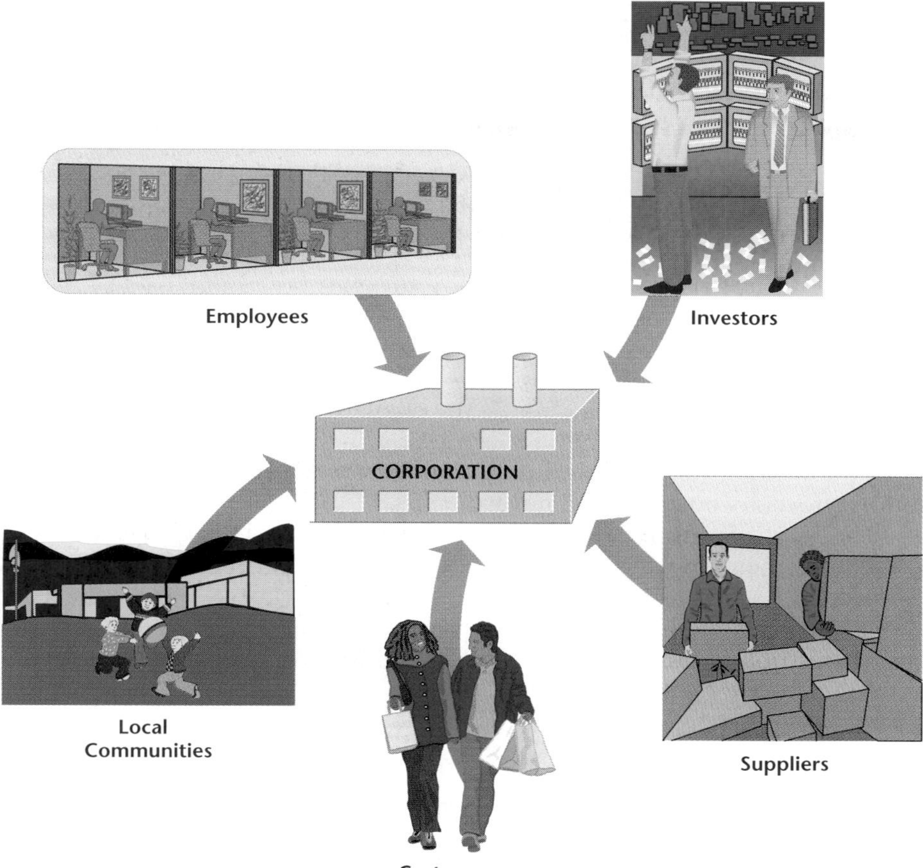

Figure 5.4
Major corporate stakeholders.

During the social unrest of the 1960s and 1970s, business was often characterized as a negative social force. Eventually, increased activism prompted increased government regulation in a variety of areas. Health warnings, for example, were placed on cigarettes, and stricter environmental protection laws were enacted.

Social consciousness and views toward social responsibility continue to evolve in the twenty-first century. Today's attitudes seem to be moving toward an enlightened view stressing the need for a greater social role for business. An increased awareness of the global economy and heightened campaigning on the part of environmentalists and other activists have combined to make many businesses more sensitive to their social responsibilities.

For example, retailers such as Sears have policies against selling handguns and other weapons, and toy retailer Toys "R" Us refuses to sell toy guns that look too realistic. Firms in numerous other industries have also integrated socially conscious thinking into their production plans and marketing efforts. The production of environmentally safe products, for example, has become a potential boom area, as many companies introduce products designed to be "environmentally friendly."

Electrolux, a Swedish appliance maker, has developed a line of water-efficient washing machines, a solar-powered lawnmower, and, for Brazil, the first refrigerators that are free of ozone-depleting refrigerants. Herman Miller, a Michigan-based office-furniture business, uses recycled materials and focuses on products that are simple in design, durable, and recyclable. Ford has set up an independent brand called Think to develop and market low-pollution and electric-powered vehicles.[10]

Electrolux
www.electrolux.com

3. Show how the concept of social responsibility applies both to environmental issues and to a firm's relationships with customers, employees, and investors.

AREAS OF SOCIAL RESPONSIBILITY

In defining its sense of social responsibility, most firms must confront four areas of concern: responsibilities toward the environment, customers, employees, and investors.

Responsibility Toward the Environment

One critical area of social responsibility involves how the business relates to its physical environment. In the following sections, we focus on the nature of the problems in these areas and on some of the current efforts to address them.[11] Controlling pollution—the injection of harmful substances into the environment—is a significant challenge for contemporary business. Although noise pollution is attracting increased concern, air pollution, water pollution, and land pollution are the subjects of most anti-pollution efforts by business and governments.[12]

Kyoto Protocol
unfccc.int/resource/convkp.html

The Kyoto Summit in 1997 was an attempt by various governments to reach agreement on ways to reduce the threat of pollution. In 2002, Canada committed itself to the provisions of the Kyoto Protocol, but controversy immediately erupted. Opponents charged that the government was seriously underestimating the cost to taxpayers and to businesses.[13]

Air Pollution

Air pollution results when a combination of factors converge to lower air quality. Large amounts of chemicals such as the carbon monoxide emitted by automobiles contribute to air pollution. Smoke and other chemicals emitted by manufacturing plants also help to create air pollution.

Legislation has gone a long way toward controlling air pollution. Under new laws, many companies have had to install special devices to limit the pollutants they expel into the atmosphere. Such clean-up efforts are not without costs, however. The bill to private companies for air pollution control devices runs into billions of dollars.

Figure 5.5 tells a troubling story. The chart shows atmospheric carbon dioxide (CO2) levels for the period between 1750 and 2000, and it offers three possible scenarios for future levels under different sets of conditions. The three projections—lowest, middle, highest—were developed by the Intergovernmental Panel on Climate Change, which calculated likely changes in the atmosphere during this century if no efforts were made to reduce so-called greenhouse emissions—waste gases that trap heat in the atmosphere. The criteria for estimating changes are population, economic growth, energy supplies, and technologies: The less pressure exerted by these conditions, the less the increase in CO2 levels. Energy supplies are measured in exajoules—roughly the annual energy consumption of a large metropolitan area like New York or London.

Under the lowest, or best-case, scenario, by 2100 the population would only grow to 6.4 billion people, economic growth would be no more than 1.2 to 2.0 percent a year, and energy supplies would require only 8000 exajoules of conventional oil. However, under the highest, or worst-case, scenario, the population would increase to 11.3 billion people, annual economic growth would be between 3.0 and 3.5 percent, and energy supplies would require as much as 18 400 exajoules of conventional oil.

The resulting changes in climate would be relatively mild, and we would not experience dramatic changes in the weather. We would, however, increase the likelihood of having troublesome weather around the globe: droughts, hurricanes, and so forth. The charges levelled against greenhouse

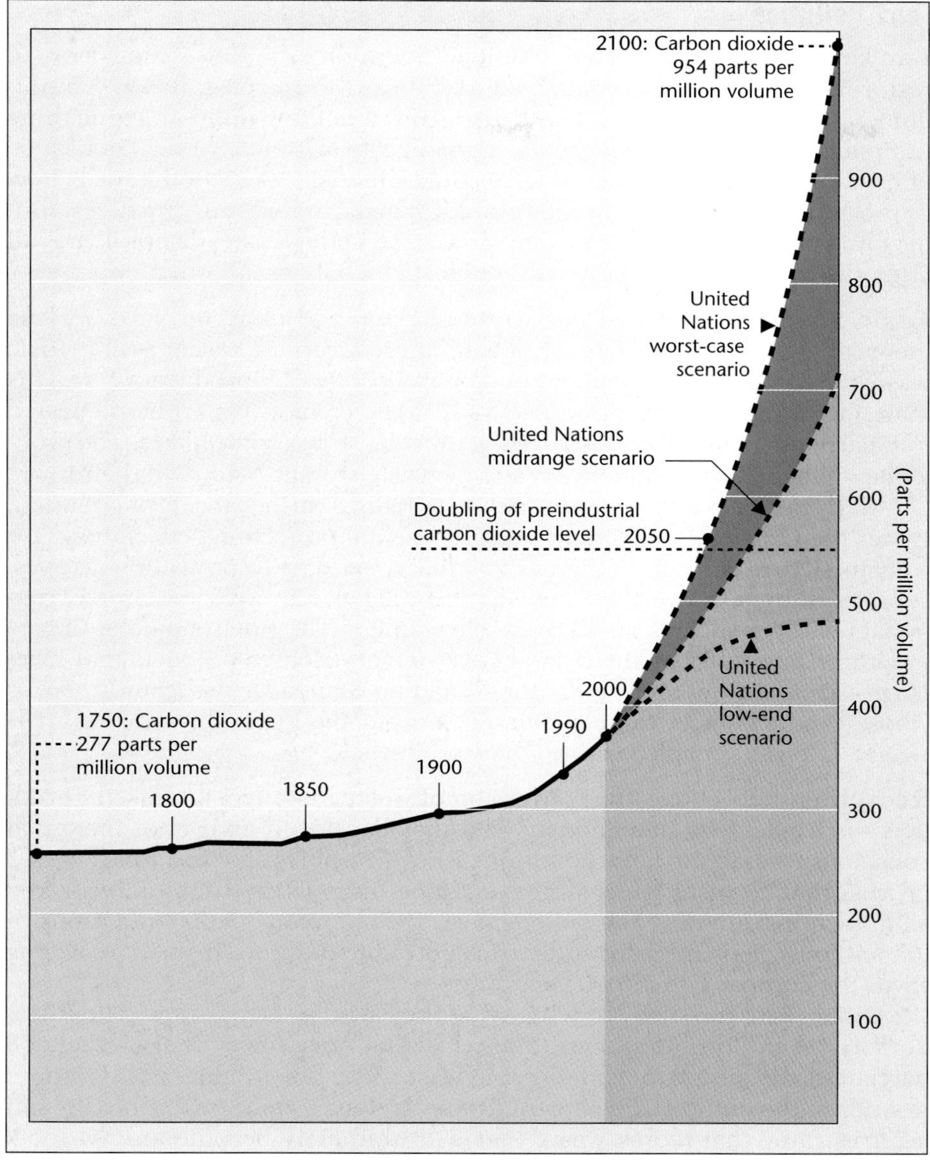

Figure 5.5
CO_2 emissions, past and future.

emissions are disputed, but as one researcher puts it, "The only way to prove them for sure is hang around 10, 20, or 30 more years, when the evidence would be overwhelming. But in the meantime, we're conducting a global experiment. And we're all in the test tube."[14]

Water Pollution

For years, businesses and municipalities dumped their waste into rivers, streams, and lakes with little regard for the effects. Thanks to new legislation and increased awareness on the part of businesses, water quality is improving in many areas. Millar Western Pulp Ltd. built Canada's first zero-discharge pulp mill at Meadow Lake, Saskatchewan. There is no discharge pipe to the river, no dioxin-forming chlorine, and next to no residue. Dow Chemical built a plant at Fort Saskatchewan that will not dump any pollutants into the nearby river.[15] However, water pollution problems remain. In 2000, seven people died in Walkerton, Ontario, after the town's water supply was contaminated with E. coli bacteria.

Land Pollution

Two key issues are associated with land pollution. The first issue is how to restore the quality of land damaged and abused in the past. In 1998, 5 million cubic litres of toxic waste escaped from a holding pond at a zinc mine in Spain that was operated by the Canadian firm Boliden Ltd. Thousands of hectares of agricultural land were contaminated.[16] A second issue is how to prevent such problems in the future. Changes in foresting practices, limits on types of mining, and new forms of solid waste disposal are all attempts to address this issue, although such changes are often opposed.

Toxic Waste Disposal. Toxic waste disposal and clean-up have become increasingly important areas of debate and concern in recent years. Toxic wastes are dangerous chemical and/or radioactive by-products of various manufacturing processes. Because toxic waste cannot usually be processed into harmless material or destroyed, it must be stored somewhere. The problem is—where? Few people want a toxic waste storage facility in their town.

Many business firms are now acting to reduce various forms of pollution. Under the Canadian and Ontario environmental protection acts, liability for a business firm can run as high as $2 million per day. To protect themselves, companies must prove that they showed diligence in avoiding an environmental disaster such as an oil or gasoline spill.[17] The Environmental Choice program, sponsored by the federal government, licenses products that meet environmental standards set by the Canadian Standards Association. Firms whose products meet these standards can put the logo—three doves intertwined to form a maple leaf—on their products.[18]

Recycling. Recycling—the conversion of waste materials into useful products—is a relatively new industry that has developed as part of increased consciousness about land pollution. RBW Graphics, for example, uses a process that cleanses paper fibres and other impurities from ink recovered from printing presses. The system saves the company 35 000 kilograms of ink annually. This ink used to be transported to a dump. Instead, recycling saves the company $175 000 each year.[19]

Other firms are also reducing what they send to city dumps. The Royal York Hotel in Toronto, for example, installed machinery that extracts 70 percent of the moisture from organic waste. The hotel reduced the amount it sends to the dump by 50 percent. Ramada Renaissance in Toronto bought a refrigerator that stores waste that will ultimately become animal food. The hotel has reduced the waste it sends to the dump by 75 percent.[20] Bell

Toxic waste disposal and clean-up have become increasingly important areas of debate and concern in recent years.

Canada has reduced the amount of garbage it generates each day from 800 kilograms to 22 kilograms at its Etobicoke, Ontario, location.[21]

Recycling is not without controversy. Consider the problem of wooden pallets—those splintery wooden platforms used to store and transport consumer goods. Pallets are popular because they provide an efficient method for stacking and moving large quantities of smaller items. Boxes of canned goods, batteries, hair dryers, cans of paint, bags of fertilizer, and bundles of roofing shingles can all be stacked on pallets and wrapped with plastic or other binding material. Pallets of merchandise can be easily and efficiently forklifted from factories to trucks, from trucks to warehouses, from warehouses to different trucks, and, finally, to Wal-Mart, Home Depot, and Safeway storerooms.

Pallets are eminently recyclable, but the cost of new ones is still generally lower than the cost of returning and/or redistributing used ones. As a result, many companies just toss used pallets aside and collect more. Some entrepreneurs have tried to sell them for firewood, but because the wood is thin and tends to be quite dry, it burns both too quickly and too hot for most applications. Because pallets are heavy and prone to dangerous splintering, they are also hard to handle without a forklift. Thus, many landfills refuse to take them, and others assess surcharges for recycling them. They eventually biodegrade after several decades. Ironically, some environmentalists argue that abandoned pallets actually serve a useful purpose: in urban areas, they often become refuges for animals such as raccoons, rats, and abandoned pets.[22]

Concern for the environment has influenced the actions of many Canadian firms as they do business abroad. In many cases, there is opposition to a project by the local people because they fear that some sort of pollution will result. For example, Calgary-based TVI Pacific Inc.'s planned open-pit mine and cyanide processing plan in the Philippines has led to violent clashes between the company and the Subanon people. Critics of Inco Ltd.'s proposed Goro mine in New Caledonia claim that it will damage the second-largest barrier reef system in the world. And a group of villagers in Thailand are objecting to a potash mine that is being proposed by Asia Pacific Potash Corp., arguing that the project will increase salt levels in the soil and damage their ability to grow rice.[23]

Responsibility Toward Customers

Social responsibility toward customers generally falls into one of two categories: providing quality products and pricing those products fairly. As with the environment, firms differ in their level of concern about responsibility to customers. Yet unlike environmental problems, customer problems do not require expensive technological solutions. Most such problems can be avoided if companies obey the laws regarding consumer rights, avoid illegal pricing practices, and behave ethically when advertising their products.

Rights of Consumers

Much of the current interest in business responsibility toward customers can be traced to the rise of consumerism. **Consumerism** is a form of social activism dedicated to protecting the rights of consumers in their dealings with businesses.

consumerism

A social movement that seeks to protect and expand the rights of consumers in their dealings with businesses.

Consumers have the following rights:

1. The right to safe products. For example, when you buy a new paint sprayer, it must be safe to use for spraying paint. It must come with instructions on how to use it, and it must have been properly tested by its manufacturer. Dow Corning Corp. halted production of silicone

breast implants after questions were raised about the product's safety. When the British government announced a possible link between "mad cow disease" and Creutzfeld-Jakob disease, McDonald's and Burger King suspended the sale of all British beef products. More recently, Canadian beef was banned from the United States when one case of mad cow disease was found in Alberta.

2. The right to be informed about all relevant aspects of a product. Food products must list their ingredients. Clothing must be labelled with information about its proper care. And banks must tell you exactly how much interest you are paying on a loan. Cereal companies have come under fire recently for some of the claims they have made about the oat bran content of their cereals, as well as its likely effects.
3. The right to be heard. Many companies today have complaints offices. Retailers like Kmart offer a money-back guarantee if consumers aren't satisfied. Procter & Gamble puts a toll-free number on many of its products that consumers can call if they have questions or complaints. When companies refuse to respond to consumer complaints, consumer protection agencies such as the Better Business Bureau and consumer interest groups such as the Airline Passengers Association may intervene.
4. The right to choose what they buy. Central to this right is free and open competition among companies. In times past, "gentlemen's agreements" were often used to avoid competition or to divide up a market so that firms did not have to truly compete against each other. Such practices are illegal today and any attempts by business to block competition can result in fines or other penalties.
5. The right to be educated about purchases. All prescription drugs now come with detailed information regarding dosage, possible side effects, and potential interactions with other medications.
6. The right to courteous service. This right is hard to legislate, but as consumers become increasingly knowledgeable, they're more willing to complain about bad service. Consumer hotlines can also be used to voice service-related issues.

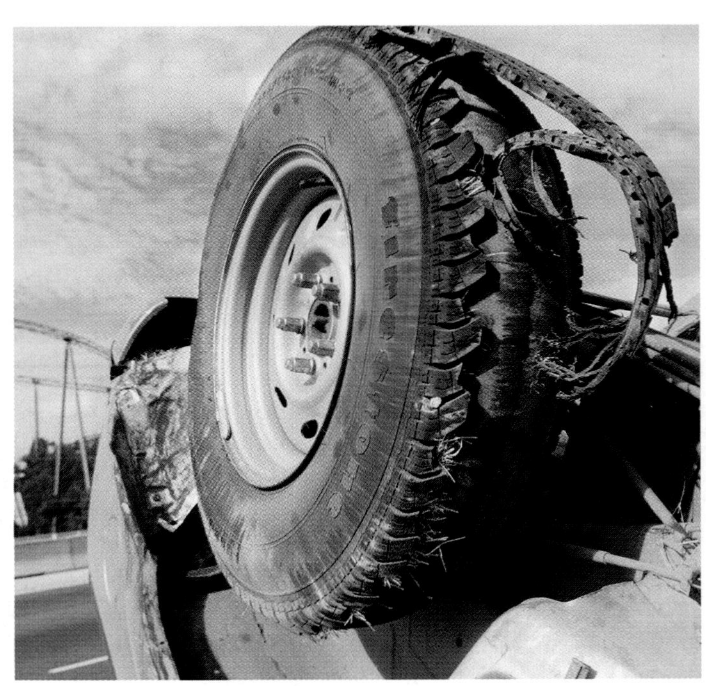

In August 2000, Bridgestone/Firestone Inc. announced a consumer-protection recall of 6.5 million light truck tires that blew or lost tread and that may have contributed to dozens of fatal accidents. The cost to the tire manufacturer was U.S.$450 million. The cost to Ford Motor Co., which had installed and issued warranties for most of those 6.5 million tires on its SUVs, ran to U.S.$500 million. The next year, following further consumer-protection measures, Ford took an after-tax charge of U.S.$2.1 billion to replace another 13 million Firestone tires.

The problems with the diet pill called Pondimin illustrate what can happen to a firm that violates one or more of these consumer rights. Throughout the early 1990s, American Home Products aggressively marketed the drug, which contained fenfluramine. Doctors wrote millions of prescriptions for Pondimin and other medications containing fenfluramine. In 1997, however, a link was discovered between the pills and heart-valve disease. A class-action lawsuit followed, and the firm eventually agreed to pay $3.75 billion to individuals who had used the drug.[24]

Unfair Pricing

Interfering with competition can also mean illegal pricing practices. **Collusion** among companies—getting together to "fix" prices—is against the law. Polar Plastic Ltd. of Montreal pled guilty to conspiring to fix prices of disposable cups, glasses, and cutlery in the U.S. market. Although secret meetings and phone conversations took place between executives of competing companies as they tried to fix prices, the conspiracy was not successful.[25]

collusion
An illegal agreement among companies in an industry to "fix" prices for their products.

The U.S. Justice Department charged three international pharmaceutical firms with illegally controlling worldwide supplies and prices of vitamins. France's Aventis Pharma, then called Rhone Poulenc, co-operated with the investigation, helped break the case several months earlier than expected, and was not fined. Switzerland's F. Hoffmann-LaRoche was fined U.S.$500 million, and one of its senior executives was sentenced to four months in a U.S. prison. Germany's BASF was fined U.S.$225 million.[26]

Under some circumstances, firms can also come under attack for price gouging—responding to increased demand with overly steep (and often unwarranted) price increases. For example, when DaimlerChrysler launched its PT Cruiser in 2000, demand for the vehicles was so strong that some dealers sold them only to customers willing to pay thousands of dollars over sticker prices. Some Ford dealers adopted a similar practice when the new Thunderbird was launched in 2002.

Ethics in Advertising

In recent years, increased attention has been given to ethics in advertising and product information. Because of controversies surrounding the potential misinterpretation of words and phrases such as "light," "reduced calo-

Until about 1993, London-based Sotheby's and New-York-based Christie's competed for 90 percent of the world's art auctions. Then, however, Sotheby CEO Alfred Taubman and Christie CEO Sir Anthony Tenant secretly agreed to charge the same rates for all sales. Within a few years, they had collected an extra half billion dollars in commissions paid by dealers. The U.S. Justice Department began investigating in 1999, and in 2002 the two auction houses agreed to pay a U.S.$537 million settlement with former customers. Taubman is looking at three years in prison.

rie," "diet," and "low fat," food producers are now required to use a standardized format for listing ingredients on product packages. Similarly, controversy arose over a commercial aired during the 2000 Super Bowl game. The ad featured Christopher Reeve, a quadriplegic actor, apparently standing up from his wheelchair and walking to a podium. In reality, the images were computer altered and were intended to convey a message of hope and optimism for a foundation supporting spinal cord research. However, many viewers were confused by the ads, and the day after the game, dozens of quadriplegics called their doctors and hospitals to inquire about the procedure that had evidently cured the actor. The ad was quickly pulled after widespread media criticism.

Benetton
www.benetton.com

Another issue concerns advertising that some consumers consider to be morally objectionable. Benetton, for example, aired a series of commercials featuring inmates on death row. The ads, dubbed "We, on Death Row," prompted such an emotional outcry that Sears dropped the Benetton USA clothing line.[27] Other ads receiving criticism include Victoria's Secret models in skimpy underwear and campaigns by tobacco and alcohol companies that are accused of targeting young people.

Responsibility Toward Employees

Organizations also need to employ fair and equitable practices with their employees. Later, in Chapter 8, we describe the human-resource management activities essential to a smoothly functioning business. These same activities—recruiting, hiring, training, promoting, and compensating—are also the basis for social responsibility toward employees. A company that provides its employees with equal opportunities for rewards and advancement without regard to race, sex, or other irrelevant factors is meeting its social responsibilities. Firms that ignore their responsibility to employees leave themselves open to lawsuits. They also miss the chance to hire better and more highly motivated employees.

Legal and Social Commitments

Some progressive companies go well beyond these legal requirements, hiring and training the so-called hard-core unemployed (people with little education and training and a history of unemployment) and those who have disabilities. The Bank of Montreal, for example, sponsors a community college skills upgrading course for individuals with hearing impairments. The Royal Bank provides managers with discrimination awareness training. Rogers Cablesystems Ltd. provides individuals with mobility restrictions with telephone and customer-service job opportunities.[28] Bell Canada employs more than 1000 people with disabilities (2 percent of its permanent workforce). But, in Canada, over 50 percent of those with physical disabilities are still unemployed.[29]

In addition to their responsibility to employees as resources of the company, firms have a social responsibility to their employees as people. Firms that accept this responsibility ensure that the workplace is safe, both physically and emotionally. They would no more tolerate an abusive manager or one who sexually harasses employees than they would a gas leak.

Business firms also have a responsibility to respect the privacy of their employees. While nearly everyone agrees that companies have the right to exercise some level of control over their employees, there is great controversy about exactly how much is acceptable in areas such as drug testing and computer monitoring. When Canadian National Railways instituted drug testing for train, brake, and yard employees, 12 percent failed. Trucking companies have found that nearly one-third of truckers who have been involved in an accident are on drugs.[30]

Employees are often unaware that they are being monitored by managers who are using new computer technology. Computer software firms even sell programs called "Spy" and "Peek" to facilitate monitoring. This type of monitoring increases employee stress levels because they don't know exactly when the boss is watching them. A lawsuit was brought against Nortel Networks by employees who charged that the firm installed telephone bugs and hidden microphones in one of its plants.[31]

The safety of workers is an important consideration for all organizations. The required use of hardhats, for example, is designed to protect workers from head injuries.

Whistle-blowers. Respecting employees as people also means respecting their behaviour as ethically responsible individuals. Suppose, for instance, an employee discovers that a business has been engaging in practices that are illegal, unethical, or socially irresponsible. Ideally, this employee should be able to report the problem to higher-level management, confident that managers will stop the questionable practices. Enron's Sherron Watkins reported concerns about the company's accounting practices well before the company's problems were made public, warning top management that Enron would "implode in a wave of accounting scandals." CEO Kenneth Lay commissioned a legal review of the firm's finances but told his investigators not to "second-guess" decisions by Enron's auditor, accounting firm Arthur Andersen.[32]

Too often, people who try to act ethically on the job find themselves in trouble with their employers. If no one in the organization will take action, the employee might elect to drop the matter. Occasionally, however, the individual will inform a regulatory agency or perhaps the media. At this point, he or she becomes a **whistle-blower**—an employee who discovers and tries to put an end to a company's unethical, illegal, or socially irresponsible actions by publicizing them.[33] The 1999 Al Pacino–Russell Crowe movie *The Insider* told the true story of a tobacco-industry whistle-blower named Jeffrey Wigand.

whistle-blower
An individual who calls attention to an unethical, illegal, and/or socially irresponsible practice on the part of a business or other organization.

Unfortunately, whistle-blowers are often demoted—and even fired—when they take their accusations public. Jeffrey Wigand was fired. "I went from making $300 000 a year," he reports, "plus stock options, plus, plus, plus—to making $30 000. Yes, there is a price I've paid."[34] Even if they retain their jobs, they may still be treated as outsiders and suffer resentment or hostility from co-workers. Many co-workers see whistle-blowers as people who simply can't be trusted. One recent study suggests that about half of all whistle-blowers eventually get fired, and about half of those who get fired subsequently lose their homes and/or families.[35] New federal legislation to protect whistle-blowers was introduced in Canada in 2003.

When Phillip Adams worked in the computer industry, he discovered a flaw in the chip-making process that, under certain circumstances, could lead to data being randomly deleted or altered. He reported the flaw to manufacturers, but several years later, he found that one company, Toshiba, had ignored the problem and continued to make flawed chips for 12 years. He went on to report the problem and became actively involved in a class-action lawsuit based heavily on his research. Toshiba eventually agreed to a U.S.$2.1 billion settlement. Adams's share was kept confidential, but he did receive a substantial reward for his efforts.[36] Unfortunately, the prospect of large cash rewards has also generated a spate of false or questionable accusations.

Responsibility Toward Investors

It may sound odd to say that a firm can be irresponsible toward investors, since they are the owners of the company. But if the managers of a firm abuse its financial resources, the ultimate losers are the owners, since they do not receive the earnings, dividends, or capital appreciation due them.

Improper Financial Management

Occasionally, organizations are guilty of financial mismanagement. In other cases, executives have been "guilty" of paying themselves outlandish salaries, spending huge amounts of company money for their own personal comfort, and similar practices. Creditors can do nothing. Even shareholders have few viable options. Trying to force a management changeover is not only difficult, it can drive down the price of the stock, a penalty shareholders are usually unwilling to assign themselves.

Cheque Kiting

cheque kiting
The illegal practice of writing cheques against money that has not yet arrived at the bank on which the cheque has been written, relying on that money arriving before the cheque clears.

Other practices are specifically illegal. **Cheque kiting**, for instance, involves writing a cheque against money that has not yet arrived at the bank on which it is drawn. In a typical scheme, managers deposit customer cheques totalling, say, $1 million into the company account. Knowing that the bank will not collect all of the total deposit for several days, they proceed to write cheques against the total amount deposited, knowing that their account is so important to the bank that the cheques will be covered until the full deposits have been collected.

Insider Trading

insider trading
The use of confidential information to gain from the purchase or sale of stock.

Another area of illegal and socially irresponsible behaviour by firms toward investors is the practice of **insider trading**. Insider trading occurs when someone uses confidential information to gain from the purchase or sale of stocks. In July 2000, an Ontario court found Glen Harper, president of Golden Rule Resources Ltd., guilty of insider trading. He had sold $4 million worth of shares in his company after he found out that its supposedly huge gold find in Ghana was in doubt. When Harper sold his shares, the price of Golden Rule's stock was trading at about $13 per share. After the bad news became public, the stock fell to $2.50 per share, and eventually to 10 cents a share. Harper was sentenced to one year in prison and fined $3.95 million.[37]

The most celebrated recent case is that of Martha Stewart, who sold some of her stock in ImClone just before it dropped sharply in price. Did the CEO of ImClone warn Stewart that her stock was going to drop in value? Was prior knowledge the basis of her decision to sell? If the answer is yes, both could be guilty of insider trading. But if Stewart didn't know about the impending news and the timing of her stock sale was purely coincidental, then she did nothing wrong.

Misrepresentation of Finances

Certain behaviours regarding financial representation are also illegal. In maintaining and reporting its financial status, every corporation must conform to generally accepted accounting principles (GAAP) (see Chapter 14). Sometimes, however, unethical managers project profits far in excess of what they actually expect to earn; others go so far as to hide losses and/or expenses in order to boost paper profits. When the truth comes out, however, the damage is often substantial.

Various issues involving the misrepresentation of finances were central in the Enron case. One review, for example, called Enron's accounting practices "creative and aggressive." It seems that CFO Andrew Fastow had set up a complex network of partnerships that were often used to hide losses. Enron, for instance, could report all the earnings from a partnership as its own while transferring all or most of the costs and losses to the partnership. Inflated profits would then support increased stock prices.[38]

IMPLEMENTING SOCIAL RESPONSIBILITY PROGRAMS

Thus far, we have discussed social responsibility as if a consensus exists on how firms should behave in most situations. In fact, dramatic differences of opinion exist as to the appropriateness of social responsibility as a business goal. As you might expect, some people oppose any business activity that cuts into profits to investors. Others argue that responsibility must take precedence over profits.

Even people who share a common attitude toward social responsibility by businesses may have different reasons for their beliefs. Some opponents of such activity fear that if businesses become too active in social concerns, they will gain too much control over how those concerns are addressed. They point to the influence many businesses have been able to exert on the government agencies that are supposed to regulate their industries. Other critics of business-sponsored social programs argue that companies lack the expertise needed. They believe that technical experts, not businesses, should decide how best to clean up a polluted river, for example.

Supporters of social responsibility believe that corporations are citizens just like individuals and therefore need to help improve our lives. Others point to the vast resources controlled by businesses and note that since businesses often create many of the problems social programs are designed to alleviate, they should use their resources to help. Still others argue that social responsibility is wise because it pays off for the firm.

The late Max Clarkson, formerly a top-level business executive and director of the Centre for Corporate Social Performance and Ethics at the University of Toronto, said that business firms that had a strong consciousness about ethics and social responsibility outperform firms that do not. After designing and applying a social responsibility rating system for companies, he found that companies that had the highest marks on questions of ethics and social responsibility also had the highest financial performance.[39]

Approaches to Social Responsibility

4. Identify four general approaches to social responsibility and describe the four steps a firm must take to implement a social responsibility program.

Given these differences of opinion, it is little wonder that corporations have adopted a variety of approaches to social responsibility. As Figure 5.6 illustrates, the four stances an organization can take concerning its obligations to society fall along a continuum ranging from the lowest to the highest degree of socially responsible practices.

Obstructionist Stance

obstructionist stance
A company does as little as possible to solve social or environmental problems.

The few organizations that take what might be called an **obstructionist stance** to social responsibility usually do as little as possible to solve

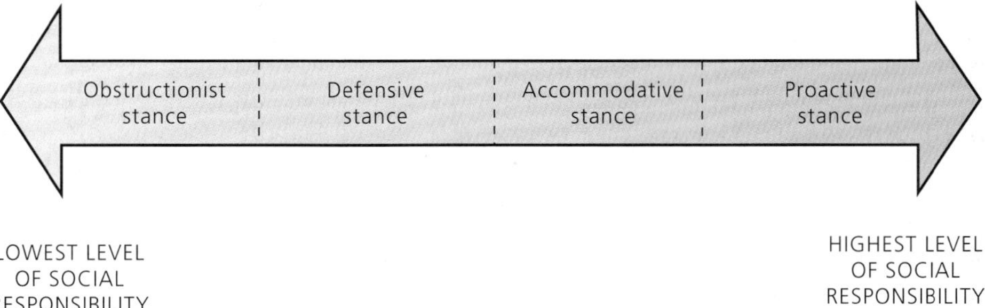

Figure 5.6
Spectrum of approaches to corporate social responsibility.

social or environmental problems. When they cross the ethical or legal line that separates acceptable from unacceptable practices, their typical response is to deny or cover up their actions. Firms that adopt this position have little regard for ethical conduct and will generally go to great lengths to hide wrongdoing.

Defensive Stance

defensive stance
An organization does only what is legally required and nothing more.

One step removed from the obstructionist stance is the **defensive stance**, whereby the organization will do everything that is required of it legally but nothing more. This approach is most consistent with arguments against corporate social responsibility. Managers who take a defensive stance insist that their job is to generate profits. Such a firm, for example, would install pollution-control equipment dictated by law, but would not install higher-quality equipment even though it might further limit pollution.

Tobacco companies generally take this position in their marketing efforts. In Canada and the United States, they are legally required to include warnings to smokers on their products and to limit advertising to prescribed media. Domestically, they follow these rules to the letter of the law but use more aggressive marketing methods in countries that have no such rules. In many Asian and African countries, for example, cigarettes are heavily promoted, contain higher levels of tar and nicotine than those sold in Canada and the United States, and carry few or no health warning labels. Firms that take this position are also unlikely to cover up wrongdoing, will generally admit to mistakes, and will take appropriate corrective actions.

Accommodative Stance

accommodative stance
A company meets all of its legal and ethical requirements, and in some cases even goes beyond what is required.

A firm that adopts an **accommodative stance** meets its legal and ethical requirements, but will also go further in certain cases. Such firms voluntarily agree to participate in social programs, but solicitors must convince them that these programs are worthy of their support. Many organizations respond to requests for donations to community hockey teams, Girl Guides, youth soccer programs, and so forth. The point, however, is that someone has to knock on the door and ask; accommodative organizations do not necessarily or proactively seek avenues for contributing.

Proactive Stance

proactive stance
An organization actively seeks opportunities to be socially responsible.

The highest degree of social responsibility a firm can exhibit is the **proactive stance**. Firms that adopt this approach take to heart the arguments in favour of social responsibility. They view themselves as citizens in a society and proactively seek opportunities to contribute. The most common—and direct—way to implement this stance is by setting up a foundation through which to provide direct financial support for various social programs.

The Exercising Your Ethics box gives you an opportunity to think more deeply about the pros and cons of the various stances toward social responsibility.

These stances are not sharply distinct; they merely label stages along a continuum of social responsibility. Organizations do not always fit neatly into one category or another. The Ronald McDonald House program has been widely applauded, for example, but McDonald's has also come under fire for allegedly misleading consumers about the nutritional value of its food products. Likewise, while UPS has sincere motives for helping Olympic athletes, the company will also benefit by featuring their photos on its envelopes and otherwise promoting its own benevolence.

Corporate Charitable Donations. Donating money to different "causes" is one way that business firms try to show that they are socially responsible. Many groups that used to receive government funding (but no longer do because of government spending cuts) are increasingly seeking corporate support for their activities. More and more corporations are being asked to donate money to educational institutions, welfare agencies, service clubs, arts and culture groups, and athletic organizations.

A Decima Research survey found that 80 percent of Canadians think that businesses should give some of their profits to social causes.[40] An Environics survey of people in 23 different countries found that two-thirds of them thought that business was not doing enough if it simply abided by the law and provided employment. Instead, these people think that companies should also contribute to the broader goals of society.[41] A third survey, conducted by the Centre for Philanthropy, found that Canadian corporations contributed less than 2 percent of all charitable revenue. Canadians think that this number is closer to 20 percent, and that it should be 30 percent.[42]

EXERCISING YOUR ETHICS

Taking a Stance

The Situation

A perpetual debate revolves around the roles and activities of business owners in contributing to the greater social good. Promoting the so-called proactive stance, some people argue that businesses should be socially responsible by seeking opportunities to benefit the society in which they are permitted to conduct their affairs. Others maintain a defensive stance, saying that because businesses exist to make profits for owners, they have no further obligation to society.

The Dilemma

Pair up with one of your classmates. Using a coin toss, each of you should be assigned to one side of this debate. You and your partner should then enter into a dialogue to formulate the three most convincing arguments possible to support each side. Then select the single strongest argument in support of each position. Each team of two partners should then present to the class its strongest arguments for and against social responsibility on the part of business.

Questions for Discussion

1. Which side of the debate is easier to defend? Why?
2. What is your personal opinion about the appropriate stance that a business should take regarding social responsibility?
3. To what extent is the concept of social responsibility relevant to non-business organizations such as universities, government units, health-care organizations, and so forth?

Top corporate givers in 2001 included CIBC ($40 million), RBC Financial ($34.3 million), BMO Financial ($21.7 million), Scotiabank ($20 million), and TD Bank ($19.2 million). As a percent of profit, these amounts ranged from 0.9 percent to 2.4 percent.[43] Although the typical corporation gives less than half of 1 percent of its pre-tax profits to charity, many corporations have demonstrated a willingness to give money and products when disasters strike. When seven people died in Walkerton, Ontario, as a result of drinking contaminated water, companies such as Petro-Canada, Shoppers Drug Mart, Sobeys, and Zellers contributed products such as bleach and bottled water. Companies generally receive favourable publicity when they make contributions like these.

Most large business firms in Canada have clear procedures for dealing with requests from charities and community organizations. The company first determines how much money it will give each year, usually stated as a percentage of profit. It then decides which specific organizations will receive the money and the amount each will receive. The board of directors makes these decisions after it receives a recommendation from a committee that has been set up to consider charitable requests. Companies are increasingly taking a community-based approach to giving; they try to determine how they can achieve value for the community (and the company) with their donations.

Managing Social Responsibility Programs

Making a company truly socially responsible in the full sense of the proactive stance takes an organized and managed program. In particular, managers must take four steps to foster social responsibility, as shown in Figure 5.7.

1. Social responsibility must start at the top and be considered as a factor in strategic planning. Without the support of top management, no program can succeed. Thus, top management must embrace a strong stand on social responsibility and develop a policy statement outlining that commitment.

2. A committee of top managers must develop a plan detailing the level of management support. Some companies set aside percentages of profits for social programs. Levi Strauss, for example, earmarks 2.4 percent of pre-tax earnings for worthy projects. Managers must also set specific priorities. For instance, should the firm train the hard-core unemployed or support the arts?

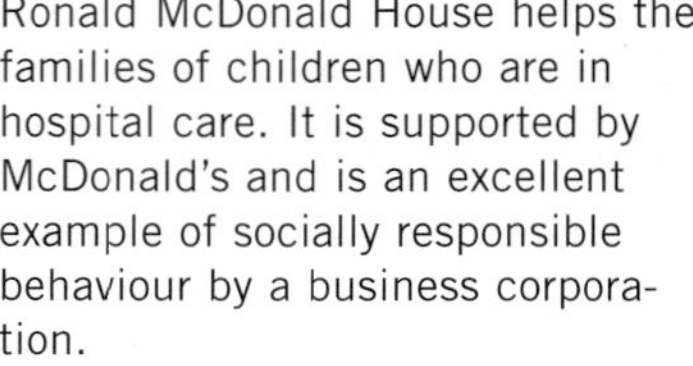

Ronald McDonald House helps the families of children who are in hospital care. It is supported by McDonald's and is an excellent example of socially responsible behaviour by a business corporation.

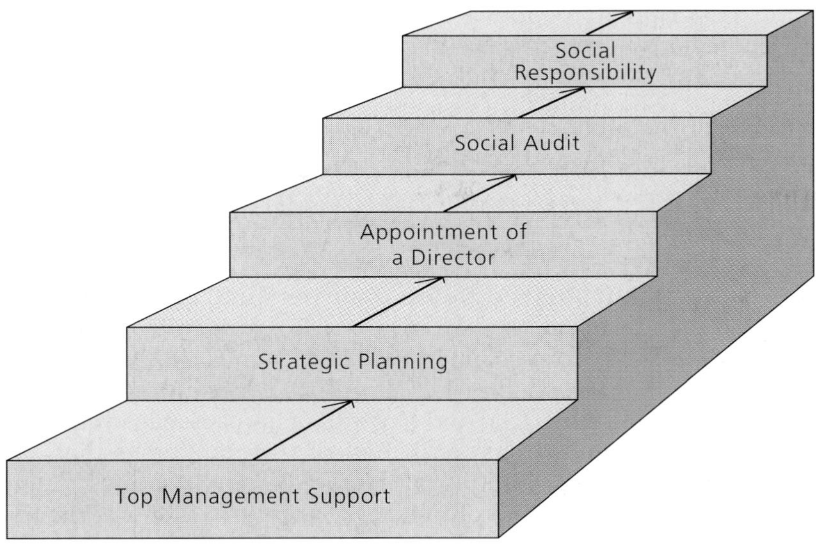

Figure 5.7
Establishing a social responsibility program involves four basic steps.

3. One executive must be put in charge of the firm's agenda. Whether the role is created as a separate job or added to an existing one, the selected individual must monitor the program and ensure that its implementation is consistent with the firm's policy statement and strategic plan.
4. The organization must conduct occasional social audits. **Social audits** are systematic analyses of its success in using funds earmarked for its social responsibility goals.[44] Consider the case of a company whose strategic plan calls for spending $100 000 to train 200 hard-core unemployed people and to place 180 of them in jobs. If at the end of a year, the firm has spent $98 000, trained 210 people, and filled 175 jobs, a social audit will confirm the program's success. But if the program has cost $150 000, trained only 90 people, and placed only 10 of them, the audit will reveal the program's failure. Such failure should prompt a rethinking of the program's implementation and its priorities.

social audit
A systematic analysis of how a firm is using funds earmarked for social-responsibility goals and how effective these expenditures have been.

Social Responsibility and the Small Business

5. Explain how issues of social responsibility and ethics affect small businesses.

Although many of the examples in this chapter illustrate responses to social responsibility and ethical issues by big business, small businesses face many of the same questions. As the owner of a garden supply store, how would you respond to a building inspector's suggestion that a cash payment would expedite your application for a building permit? As the manager of a nightclub, would you call the police, refuse service, or sell liquor to a customer whose ID card looks forged? Or as the owner of a small laboratory, would you actually call the board of health to make sure that it has licensed the company you want to contract with to dispose of the lab's medical waste? Is the small manufacturing firm justified in overcharging a customer by 5 percent whose purchasing agent is lax? Who will really be harmed if a small firm pads its income statement to help get a much-needed bank loan?

Can a small business afford a social agenda? Should it sponsor hockey teams, make donations to the United Way, and buy light bulbs from the Lion's Club? Is joining the Chamber of Commerce and supporting the

Better Business Bureau too much or just good business? Clearly, ethics and social responsibility are decisions faced by all managers in all organizations, regardless of rank or size. One key to business success is to decide in advance how to respond to these issues.

SUMMARY OF LEARNING OBJECTIVES

1. **Explain how individuals develop their personal *codes of ethics* and why ethics are important in the workplace.** Individual codes of ethics are derived from social standards of right and wrong. Ethical behaviour is behaviour that conforms to generally accepted social norms concerning beneficial and harmful actions. Because ethics affect the behaviour of individuals on behalf of the companies that employ them, many firms are adopting formal statements of ethics. Unethical behaviour can result in loss of business, fines, and even imprisonment.

2. **Distinguish *social responsibility* from *ethics*, identify *organizational stakeholders*, and characterize social consciousness today.** Social responsibility refers to the way a firm attempts to balance its commitments to organizational stakeholders. One way to understand social responsibility is to view it in terms of stakeholders—those groups, individuals, and organizations that are directly affected by the practices of an organization and that therefore have a stake in its performance. Until the second half of the nineteenth century, businesses often paid little attention to stakeholders. Since then, however, both public pressure and government regulation, especially as a result of the Great Depression of the 1930s and the social activism of the 1960s and 1970s, have forced businesses to consider public welfare, at least to some degree. A trend toward increased social consciousness, including a heightened sense of environmental activism, has recently emerged.

3. **Show how the concept of social responsibility applies both to environmental issues and to a firm's relationships with customers, employees, and investors.** Social responsibility toward the environment requires firms to minimize pollution of air, water, and land. Social responsibility toward customers requires firms to provide products of acceptable quality, to price products fairly, and to respect consumers' rights. Social responsibility toward employees requires firms to respect workers both as resources and as people who are more productive when their needs are met. Social responsibility toward investors requires firms to manage their resources and to represent their financial status honestly.

4. **Identify four *general approaches to social responsibility* and describe the four steps a firm must take to implement a *social responsibility program*.** An obstructionist stance on social responsibility is taken by a firm that does as little as possible to address social or environmental problems and that may deny or attempt to cover up problems that may occur. The defensive stance emphasizes compliance with legal minimum requirements. Companies adopting the accommodative stance go beyond minimum activities, if asked. The proactive stance commits a company to actively seek to contribute to social projects. Implementing a social responsibility program entails four steps: (1) drafting a policy statement with the support of top management, (2) developing a detailed plan, (3) appointing a director to implement the plan, and (4) conducting social audits to monitor results.

5. **Explain how issues of social responsibility and ethics affect small businesses.** Managers and employees of small businesses face many of the same ethical questions as their counterparts at larger firms. Small businesses face the same issues of social responsibility and the same need to decide on an approach to social responsibility. The differences are primarily differences of scale.

KEY TERMS

accommodative stance, 176
business ethics, 156
cheque kiting, 174
collusion, 171
consumerism, 169
defensive stance, 176
ethical behaviour, 156
ethics, 156
insider trading, 174
managerial ethics, 158
obstructionist stance, 175
organizational stakeholders, 164
proactive stance, 176
social audit, 179
social responsibility, 164
unethical behaviour, 156
whistle-blower, 173

QUESTIONS AND EXERCISES

Questions for Review

1. What basic factors should be considered in any ethical decision?
2. Who are an organization's stakeholders? Who are the major stakeholders with whom most businesses must be concerned?
3. What are the major areas of social responsibility with which businesses should be concerned?
4. What are the four basic approaches to social responsibility?
5. In what ways do you think your personal code of ethics might clash with the operations of some companies? How might you try to resolve these differences?

Questions for Analysis

6. What kind of wrongdoing would most likely prompt you to be a whistle-blower? What kind of wrongdoing would be least likely? Why?
7. In your opinion, which area of social responsibility is most important? Why? Are there areas other than those noted in the chapter that you consider important?
8. Identify some specific ethical or social responsibility issues that might be faced by small-business managers and employees in each of the following areas: environment, customers, employees, and investors.

Application Exercises

9. Develop a list of the major stakeholders of your college or university. As a class, discuss the ways in which you think the school prioritizes these stakeholders. Do you agree or disagree with this prioritization?
10. Using newspapers, magazines, and other business references, identify and describe at least three companies that take a defensive stance to social responsibility, three that take an accommodative stance, and three that take a proactive stance.

BUILDING YOUR BUSINESS SKILLS

To Lie or Not to Lie: That Is the Question

Goal

To encourage students to apply general concepts of business ethics to specific situations.

Background

Workplace lying, it seems, has become business as usual. According to one survey, one-quarter of working adults said that they had been asked to do something illegal or unethical on the job. Four in 10 did what they were told. Another survey of more than 2000 secretaries showed that many employees face ethical dilemmas in their day-to-day work.

Method

Step 1

Working with four other students, discuss ways in which you would respond to the following ethical dilemmas. When there is a difference of opinion among group members, try to determine the specific factors that influence different responses.

Would you lie about your supervisor's whereabouts to someone on the phone?

Would you lie about who was responsible for a business decision that cost your company thousands of dollars to protect your own or your supervisor's job?

Would you inflate sales and revenue data on official company accounting statements to increase stock value?

Would you say that you witnessed a signature when you did not if you were acting in the role of a notary?

Would you keep silent if you knew that the official minutes of a corporate meeting had been changed?

Would you destroy or remove information that could hurt your company if it fell into the wrong hands?

Step 2

Research the commitment to business ethics at Johnson & Johnson (**www.jnj.com/our_company/our_credo/index.htm**) and Texas Instruments (**www.ti.com/corp/docs/ethics/home.htm**) by visiting their respective websites. As a group, discuss ways in which these statements are likely to affect the specific behaviours mentioned in Step 1.

Step 3

Working with group members, draft a corporate code of ethics that would discourage the specific behaviours mentioned in Step 1. Limit your code to a single typewritten page, but make it sufficiently broad to cover different ethical dilemmas.

Follow-Up Questions

1. What personal, social, and cultural factors do you think contribute to lying in the workplace?
2. Do you agree or disagree with the following statement? "The term *business ethics* is an oxymoron." Support your answer with examples from your own work experience or that of a family member.
3. If you were your company's director of human resources, how would you make your code of ethics a "living document"?
4. If you were faced with any of the ethical dilemmas described in Step 1, how would you handle them? How far would you go to maintain your personal ethical standards?

MASTERING BUSINESS ESSENTIALS

Episode 3 raises the issue of corporate social responsibility when CanGo management debates the potential effects of violent online games. As team members try to balance the firm's image and needs against the demands of its market, they discuss its social responsibility toward the environment and toward key stakeholders, including customers, employees, and investors. *This episode presents some key problems encountered by managers who want to coordinate company policy and strategy with personal values.*

Episode 8 shows what kind of dilemmas can arise in a workplace where different people have different ethical values. *This episode provides a practical illustration of the textbook discussion on the purpose and value of written codes of ethics.*

CRAFTING YOUR BUSINESS PLAN

Going in the Ethical Direction

The Purpose of the Assignment

1. To familiarize students with some of the ethical and social responsibility considerations faced by a sample firm in developing its business plan, in the planning framework of the Business PlanPro (BPP) software package.
2. To show where ethical and social responsibility considerations can be found in various sections of the BPP planning environment.

Assignment

After reading Chapter 5 in the textbook, open the BPP software, and look around for information about the types of ethical considerations and social responsibility factors that would be of concern to the sample firm: Southeast Health Plans Inc. To find Southeast Health Plans, do the following:

Open the Business PlanPro. If it asks if you want to "create a new business plan" or "open an existing plan," select "create a new business plan" (even though you are not going to create a plan at this time). You will then be taken to the Business PlanPro EasyPlan Wizard. On the screen, go to the option entitled **Research It**, and click on that option. You will then be presented with a new list of options, including Sample Plan Browser. After clicking on the **Sample Plan Browser**, go down the alphabetical list of sample plans and double-click on **Plan Administration—Health**, which is the location for Southeast Health Plans Inc.

The screen you are looking at is the introduction page for Southeast's business plan. On this page, scroll down until you reach the **Table of Contents** for the company's business plan.

Now respond to the following questions:

1. Do you think a company in Southeast's line of business should have a code of ethics? Call up Southeast's Table of Contents page. In which sections of the company's business plan would you expect to find its code of ethics? Go into those sections, and identify information pertaining to the firm's code of ethics. What did you find?
2. The textbook states that a firm's social responsibility includes providing quality products for its customers. Explore Southeast's business plan and describe its position on providing quality products. [Sites to see in BPP for this item: On the Table of Contents page, click on **1.0 Executive Summary**. Then click on and read each of the following in turn: **1.1 Objectives, 1.2 Mission**, and **1.3 Keys to Success**.]
3. Another dimension of social responsibility is pricing products fairly. Search through Southeast's plan for information about its policies for pricing services. Does Southeast's planned gross margin reflect "fair pricing"? Why or why not? [Sites to see in BPP: From the Table of Contents page, click on **3.1 Competitive Comparison** and then on **3.3 Fulfillment**. After returning to the Table of Contents page, click on **5.1.1 Pricing Strategy** and then **1.0 Executive Summary**.]

VIDEO EXERCISE

Doing the Right Thing: American Red Cross

Learning Objectives

The purpose of this video is to help you:

1. Identify some of the social responsibility and ethics challenges faced by a non-profit organization.
2. Discuss the purpose of an organizational code of ethics.
3. Understand the potential conflicts that can emerge between an organization and its stakeholders.

Synopsis

Founded in 1881 by Clara Barton, the American Red Cross is a non-profit organization dedicated to helping victims of war, natural disasters, and other catastrophes. The organization's 1000 chapters are governed by volunteer boards of directors who oversee local activities and enforce ethical standards in line with community norms and the Red Cross's own code of ethics. Over the years, the Red Cross has been guided in its use of donations by honouring donor intent. This policy helped the organization deal with a major ethical challenge after the terrorist attacks of September 11, 2001. The Red Cross received more than $1 billion in donations and initially diverted some money to ancillary operations, such as creating a strategic blood reserve. After donors objected, however, the organization reversed its decision and—honouring donor intent—used the contributions to directly benefit people affected by the tragedy.

Discussion Questions

1. *For analysis*: What are the social responsibility implications of a decision like the one the Red Cross made when it decided to divert some donations that were intended for 9/11 victims?
2. *For analysis*: What kinds of ethical conflicts might arise because the American Red Cross relies so heavily on volunteers?
3. *For application*: What can the American Red Cross do to ensure that local chapters are properly applying its code of ethics?
4. *For application*: How might a non-profit such as the American Red Cross gain a better understanding of its stakeholders' needs and preferences?
5. *For debate*: Should the American Red Cross have reversed its initial decision to divert some of the money donated for September 11 relief efforts to pressing but ancillary operations? Support your chosen position.

Online Exploration

Visit the American Red Cross site (**www.redcross.org**) and scan the headlines referring to the organization's response to recent disasters. Also look at the educational information available through links to news stories, feature articles, and other material. Next, carefully examine the variety of links addressing the needs and involvement of different stakeholder groups. What kinds of stakeholders does the American Red Cross expect to visit its website? Why are these stakeholders important to the organization? Do you think the organization should post its code of ethics prominently on this site? Explain your answer.

EXPLORING THE NET

Incentives for Corporate Social Responsibility?

One of the areas of social responsibility outlined in this chapter is the organization's responsibility toward the environment. *The Globe and Mail* and the Globe Foundation of Canada recognize Canadian business leaders through their annual presentation of the Globe Awards for Environmental Excellence (**www.theglobeawards.ca**). Each year one winner in each of these five categories is selected to receive this prestigious award.

Award for Excellence in Brownfield Redevelopment
The Corporate Award for Technology Innovation and/or Application
The Industry Association Award for Environmental Performance
The Corporate Competitiveness Award
The Capital Markets Award for Sustainable Investment and Banking

1. Examine the categories of awards listed. Thinking about the four business approaches to social responsibility, visit some of the past award recipients' websites. Which approach is each organization using?
2. Based on the information presented on the firm's website vs. the criteria for each award, would you have given such an award to these organizations?

Concluding Case 5-1

The Rules of Tipping

ImClone was a darling of biotech. But alleged improprieties caused the firm to crash and burn, and its CEO has been convicted of insider trading and sentenced to seven years in prison. The scandal rubbed off on popular lifestyle maven Martha Stewart, who was charged with obstruction of justice and making false statements. If convicted, she could receive up to 30 years in prison. Much of the problem, as it turns out, hinges on who said what, when, and to whom.

Dr. Samuel Waksal spent much of his career as a respected immunologist. But in 1984, he decided to leave the research field and launch a biotech business called ImClone. Its mission was to explore new treatment options for serious illnesses such as cancer. Shortly after launching the company, Waksal hired his brother Harlan, also a physician, to help run it. For the next several years, they struggled to keep the enterprise afloat, dividing their time between seeking investment money and trying to develop drugs that would make them rich.

It seemed that they'd found just the ticket in the early 1990s, when a professional acquaintance, research scientist John Mendelsohn, indicated that he'd made a discovery that might eventually be a major breakthrough in the fight against cancer. Based on Mendelsohn's preliminary tests, Erbitux, as the new drug was called, seemed to show significant potential for treating certain forms of cancer. With additional funding, Mendelsohn was confident that he could get federal approval to market the drug. The Waksals convinced Mendelsohn to license Erbitux to ImClone.

For the next few years, as the drug was being further developed and refined, Samuel Waksal devoted much of his time to building enthusiasm for Erbitux. After all, a medical breakthrough on the cancer front would have incredible market value. Waksal's marketing efforts paid off. Investors seemed to be lining up at his door, and ImClone became the talk of New York. Mick Jagger came to Waksal's Christmas party, and the Doobie Brothers entertained at the ImClone party at a major cancer-research meeting. Waksal himself partied with Martha Stewart and dated her daughter.

As Erbitux drew closer to becoming a reality, enthusiasm continued to mount. The American Society of Clinical Oncologists predicted that Erbitux would be for the twenty-first century what polio and smallpox vaccines were for the twentieth. Waksal, meanwhile, began dropping hints that the testing process at the Food and Drug Administration (FDA) was going well and that he anticipated full approval just as soon as FDA evaluations were complete.

In the fall of 2001, Bristol-Myers Squibb announced plans to invest $2 billion in ImClone. In return, the giant drug maker would get a 20 percent stake in ImClone and a share of the U.S. rights to Erbitux. Fuelled in part by the Bristol-Myers investment and in part by Waksal's promotional campaign, ImClone stock, already performing impressively, took off, reaching a high of $75.45 a share in early December 2001. But then a giant shoe dropped.

In early December 2001, rumours began to circulate among key Bristol-Myers and ImClone officials that the Erbitux approval was in trouble. Allegedly, Samuel and Harlan Waksal launched furious lobbying efforts with personal contacts at the FDA in order to get the decision delayed or deferred. On December 6, Harlan sold $50 million of his ImClone stock. On December 26, Samuel learned that the FDA had made up its mind: It had denied the Erbitux application and refused to approve commercial production.

That night and early the next morning, Waksal reportedly relayed this information to certain family members and close friends. On December 27, family members sold more than $9 million in ImClone stock. Waksal tried to unload $5 million in ImClone stock but was refused by his broker, who had already put a hold on all ImClone transactions. On the same day, good friend Martha Stewart sold 3928 shares of ImClone. Responding to suggestions that she had acted on the basis of inside information, Stewart stated, "In placing my trade I had no improper information. My transaction was entirely lawful. After directing my broker to sell, I called Dr. Waksal's office to inquire about ImClone. I did not reach Dr. Waksal and he did not return my call."

The official FDA announcement came on December 28. On December 31, the first day of trading after the announcement, the volume of ImClone trading increased 179 percent as its value dropped 15 percent. Throughout the spring of 2002, ImClone stock continued to plummet, and by June 2002, it stood at a measly $7.83 a share. The ImClone board persuaded Samuel Waksal to resign because the Securities and Exchange Commission (SEC) investigation into his actions was hurting the firm's performance.

On June 12, 2002, the FBI arrested Samuel Waksal, charging him with insider trading and obstruction of justice. Although no other formal charges were filed, investigators continued to look into Harlan Waksal's stock sale of December 6 and Stewart's sale of December 27. Things remained quiet for several weeks, but so far, only one shoe had dropped.

Just when things couldn't seem to get any worse for Samuel Waksal and ImClone, they did. In early August 2002, several new charges were filed against Waksal, including perjury and bank fraud. At the heart of these new charges was an allegation that he had deceived two major financial institutions, Bank of America and Refco Capital Markets. Authorities claim that in late 1999, Waksal had in his possession a warrant allowing him to buy 350 000 shares of ImClone for $5.50 a share. He used that warrant as collateral in obtaining loans from each lender, neither of which knew that it was being used to get a loan from the other one. In 2000, Waksal cashed in the warrant, rendering it worthless as collateral for either loan.

Later that year, Bank of America requested confirmation from Waksal that he still held the warrant. According to indictments handed down in August 2002, Waksal forged the signature of ImClone's general counsel on a letter dated November 10, 2000, verifying that the warrant was still valid as collateral. This news, of course, only fuelled suspicions about Waksal's other activities. He now faces additional charges, and family members and friends are under growing scrutiny. Two major lenders are looking at major losses from worthless loans. ImClone stock value has plummeted, and Bristol-Myers's investment in the company will almost certainly have to be written off as well. As for all other investors, the best they can do is hope that there are no more shoes to be dropped.

Questions for Discussion

1. What are the major legal issues in this case? What are the major ethical issues?
2. Aside from personal greed, what factors might lead a drug company like ImClone to aggressively promote potential new products before they have been approved?
3. Some observers argue that the FDA should be more open in sharing news of pending product reviews with the public. What are the pros and cons of such an argument?
4. Distinguish between ethical issues and social responsibility issues as they apply to the ImClone case. ◆

Concluding Case 5-2

Nortel Changes Its Corporate Giving Policy

Like many companies, Nortel Networks used to make contributions to a variety of charitable organizations. It also used to match employee contributions to the United Way. But its new corporate giving strategy means no more matching contributions to the United Way and a more focused giving strategy for the contributions it does make. In the future, Nortel will focus on education efforts that have a direct relationship to its business objectives and bottom line.

CEO John Roth is the force behind the new policy. He believes that it makes sense for companies to fund programs that benefit them. Roth has some allies in this thinking; they argue that profit generated by a company is the property of shareholders, not corporate managers, and that shareholders should decide where it goes. Not surprisingly, Nortel's new policy has alarmed some charitable organizations, most obviously the United Way.

Nortel's new policy was developed because of concerns about the effectiveness of its traditional giving patterns. Like most major corporations in Canada, Nortel was bombarded with requests to sponsor events such as art exhibits, ballet companies, the United Way, and hospital fundraisers. But the traditional corporate citizenship model of scattering contributions among many different good causes may not be effective, so Nortel will now concentrate on three areas of giving: business fundamentals, science and technology education, and community support.

Specifically, Nortel will fund scholarships and research initiatives that link back to the company's corporate objectives. For example, $18 million will be given to establish an Institute in Advanced Information Technology at Waterloo University, and $14 million will be given to fund 7000 students in engineering and computer science. These programs benefit Nortel both directly and indirectly.

Nortel recognizes that its new approach is a departure from the traditional social responsibility model that has been evident in corporate philanthropy in Canada for many years. The company says it is "reinventing corporate citizenship for a connected world." Nortel will continue to encourage its employees to donate time and money on a voluntary basis, but the company will pursue its new strategy as well. It argues that its new approach makes sense because education benefits everyone by providing access to rewarding careers, decent wages, and opportunities for growth. It also increases the talent pool and helps industry by providing educated students.

Questions for Discussion

1. In general, what are the arguments for and against corporate philanthropy?
2. What are the arguments for and against Nortel's new policy?
3. "Corporate profits are the property of shareholders and should not be given to charity." Do you agree or disagree? Explain. ◆

Video Case 1-1 CBC

Softwood Lumber

Rick Delman is the reluctant president of Doman Industries, B.C.'s largest logging company. When his father became ill, Rick was named president of the company. He feels the pressure to keep his father's dream alive, but the dream is troubled because Doman Industries is struggling to survive. One big problem is duties on softwood lumber that have been imposed by the U.S. in the ongoing softwood lumber dispute with Canada. These duties cost Doman \$3–\$5 million a month. A truck with a \$25 000 load of lumber has to pay \$7000 in duties when it crosses the border into the U.S.

The Saltair lumber mill is one of eight that are fed by 2 million acres of timberland. The mill ships finished lumber to Japan, Europe, and the U.S. These days, workers are very concerned about the security of their jobs. Pressure is high. Across Canada, more than 15 000 workers have been laid off. Half of Doman's employees are out of work, and panic is starting to set in.

Employees are wondering if the company is going under. The workweek is down to three and a half days, and three mills are already shut down. Markets in Japan declined some time ago and haven't recovered. Union leaders are worried that workers will show up for work one day and find the gate locked.

At the Saltair mill, workers tell Rick that they know he's working hard to try to keep the company going. Rick is planning a trip to Japan to look for possible sales there. He also likes to visit the mills and talk to workers. But he knows he's one step ahead of his creditors, and that his company is surviving one day at a time. He's encouraged by the World Trade Organization's decision declaring the U.S. duties to be illegal. He hopes to get refunds on duties he has already paid, and he's asking for loans from the Canadian government to tide him over.

Rick meets with his treasurer to look over the books. A big debt (\$1 billion) forces the company to pay \$365 000 in interest *every day*. Doman Industries is effectively owned by its creditors, but it's restructuring in an effort to survive. The problem has arisen because over the last 10 years Doman has made several ill-timed purchases; the company also failed to adapt to changing market conditions. Investors are scared by all the uncertainty.

Some people think the U.S. wants to shut down Canadian lumber companies so that it can get access to their logs, but U.S. companies dismiss this charge. It's clear, though, that U.S. companies don't like the fact that Canadian companies have captured one-third of the U.S. lumber market. U.S. companies want more raw logs so that they can create more jobs in U.S. lumber mills. American companies are also buying up Canadian companies. U.S.-based Weyerhauser, for example, bought Macmillan-Bloedel.

Some people are asking whether the Canadian softwood lumber business is profitable enough to merit saving.

Questions for Discussion

1. What are the basic provisions of the North American Free Trade Agreement? Why have Canadian companies been forced to pay duties when shipping lumber to the U.S. even though NAFTA exists?
2. What is the difference between absolute and comparative advantage? How are these concepts relevant to the softwood lumber industry?
3. What are the various levels of involvement that are possible in international business? What level does Canadian softwood lumber represent?
4. What are the barriers to international trade? Which barrier(s) are relevant in this case? Explain.

Source: CBC *Venture*, "Doman Industries," September 22, 2002.

Video Case 1-2 CBC

Whistle-blowers

In 2002, *Time* magazine named three female whistle-blowers as Persons of the Year for reporting wrongdoing at the companies they worked for. Two of these women were accountants (one from Enron and one from WorldCom). Because of the publicity given to whistle-blowers, many people see the activity as a noble pursuit. But it's not very glamorous when you look behind the scenes.

Just ask Joanna Galtieri, who went to the media and blew the whistle on the foreign affairs department of the Canadian government. She claimed that the activities of the department were not cost-effective, and she cited the example of a Canadian diplomat who was stationed in Japan. He was supposed to be housed in a Canadian-owned residence there that was sitting vacant. But he asked for $350 000 to rent another apartment because he didn't like the residence. Galtieri says foreign affairs refused to deal with her concerns about irresponsible spending of taxpayers' money. She also claimed that her employer ostracized her in the workplace. She suffered an emotional breakdown and her physical health also deteriorated. Now she visits high schools and talks to young people about the issue of whistle-blowing.

Mike Hilson is an Ontario accountant who blew the whistle on shoddy accounting practices at Philip Services, the Hamilton waste disposal company. He knew the company was stockpiling waste but not recording the cost it would take to get rid of it. Hilson raised the issue with his boss several times, but nothing happened. The last time he raised the issue he was fired. A few months later, he noticed that Philip Services was applying to open another landfill site near his parents' home. He was concerned because he thought it likely that the company was going to go bankrupt. If that happened, there would be no money to clean up the landfill. So, he sent a letter to Ontario's minister of the environment expressing his concerns. Soon after, he was sued for libel by Philip Services for $30 million. The company also interrogated several other people who had seen Hilson's letter to the minister. Hilson eventually triumphed over Philip Services, however; they withdrew their lawsuit and were required to pay his legal bills. The company later went bankrupt and now faces several class action suits.

Writer Mark Wexler interviewed 200 whistle-blowers and found that they were generally disillusioned with their experience. Wexler says that whistle-blowers think that if they speak out someone will do something about the problems they identify. Yet they often aren't listened to, he says, because the public is skeptical about their claims. Wexler notes that reality is complex, and sometimes whistle-blowers make overblown claims about wrongdoing at their companies.

When confronted with a whistle-blower's claim, companies may embark on an aggressive campaign to discredit the whistle-blower. This can include attacking his or her character. If this is successful, the whistle-blower will appear to have no credibility and less weight will be given to the charges that are being made.

Some people feel that strong laws are needed to protect whistle-blowers. Countries that are taking that approach include the U.S., South Korea, Israel, Britain, Australia, and Russia. The Liberal government of Canada promised such legislation years ago, but nothing has ever been done. When political parties are in opposition, they're all for whistle-blowing legislation, but when they get in power, they seem to lose interest.

Questions for Discussion

1. What is whistle-blowing? What are the arguments in favour of it? Are there any arguments against it?
2. Why do companies react negatively when they hear a whistle-blower's claim?
3. Suppose a law was passed that was designed to protect whistle-blowers, and one provision of the law allowed for penalties like prison time for any company personnel who threatened a whistle-blower. What do you think would happen?
4. *"It is impossible to protect whistle-blowers because the company can always claim it has done nothing wrong. By the time any proof is provided, the case will be forgotten and the whistle-blower will likely have been fired. Therefore, whistle-blowers shouldn't bother."* Do you agree or disagree? Explain your reasoning.

Source: CBC *Venture*, "Whistle-blowers," May 1, 2003.

PART TWO

The Business of Managing

Corporate strategy, organization structure, gender equity, labour–management relations, and leadership are five issues you will read about in the opening cases of Chapters 6 to 10. These and many other issues must be dealt with if companies hope to grow and prosper. Managers in all business firms—indeed, in any kind of organization—must carry out the basic management functions of planning, organizing, leading, and controlling. These important functions are the focus of this section of the text.

Part Two, The Business of Managing, provides an overview of business management today. It includes a look at the importance of managers in business firms, how businesses are structured to achieve their goals, the management of the firm's human resources, labour–management relations, and the importance of motivating and leading employees.

- We begin in **Chapter 6, Managing the Business Enterprise**, by describing how managers set goals and choose corporate strategies. The basic functions of management—planning, organizing, leading, and controlling—are examined, as are the different types and levels of managers that are found in business firms, and the corporate culture that is created in each firm.
- In **Chapter 7, Organizing the Business Enterprise**, we look at the basic organizational structures that companies have adopted, and the different kinds of authority that managers can have. The impact of the informal organization is also analyzed.
- In **Chapter 8, Managing Human Resources**, we explore the activities that are necessary to effectively manage employees, including assessing employee needs, training, promoting, and compensating employees.
- In **Chapter 9, Understanding Labour–Management Relations**, we look at the development of the union movement in Canada, why and how workers organize, and how government legislation has affected workers' rights to organize into unions.
- Finally, in **Chapter 10, Motivating and Leading Employees**, we examine the reasons why firms should establish good relationships with their employees, and how managers' attempts to maintain productivity can affect their relations with employees.

CHAPTER 6

Managing the Business Enterprise

After reading this chapter, you should be able to:

1. Explain the importance of setting *goals* and formulating *strategies* as the starting points of effective management.
2. Describe the four activities that constitute the *management process*.
3. Identify *types of managers* by level and area.
4. Describe the five basic *management skills*.
5. Describe the development and explain the importance of *corporate culture*.

What to Do After Seagram?

In May 2003, Edgar Bronfman, Jr., and his father Edgar Bronfman, Sr., both resigned from the board of Paris-based Vivendi Universal. They had been given positions on the board when Vivendi purchased Seagram, the legendary Canadian liquor company, in 2000. After their resignation, the Bronfmans announced that they wanted to buy back Vivendi's entertainment business, which includes Universal Studios and Polygram. This is just the latest chapter in a long and complicated story of a famous Canadian family.

The Seagram Company was started in the 1920s by Sam Bronfman, who sold liquor by mail order. His son, Edgar Bronfman, Sr., became CEO in 1957, and for the next 40 years the company focused on the production of wine and distilled spirits. In the process, it became a household name in Canada. In the mid-1990s, the company (now led by third-generation family member Edgar Bronfman, Jr.) made some dramatic strategic moves that turned the company away from its traditional products and moved it toward the high-risk entertainment business. For example, Edgar Jr. bought MCA Inc. (now Universal) for $5.7 billion and Polygram NV for $10.6 billion. These moves caused some people to recall Sam Bronfman's concern that third-generation family members often dissipate the family fortune. Edgar Jr. was keenly aware of the criticism that was being directed his way, and he was determined not to fulfill his grandfather's prophecy.

In mid-2000, he sold Seagram to Vivendi SA, a French conglomerate, for approximately $33 billion in stock. The CEO of Vivendi was Jean-Marie Messier, who had a grandiose vision that his company would become a French media and telecom powerhouse that was capable of competing head-to-head with U.S. media giants. Messier concluded that Vivendi (which started as a water utility) needed to acquire a Hollywood studio to provide things like movies and music to fulfill his vision. The only company that had what Messier wanted, and was priced low enough, was Seagram, so Messier bought it.

As part of the deal, Edgar Jr. was appointed a vice-chairman of the merged companies, with responsibilities for music and internet activities. From a financial perspective the deal looked good because Seagram was paid the equivalent of approximately $75 for each of its shares, even though the shares were trading at less than $50 on the stock exchange. The Seagram family fortune actually increased as a result of the deal, and it seemed that Edgar Jr. had avoided his grandfather's concern that the third generation would fritter away the family fortune.

But the deal soon started looking bad for Seagram. Critics had been saying all along that Messier's acquisition strategy was misguided and unworkable, and time proved the critics right. By the end of 2001, Vivendi was in deep financial trouble, and its stock price had declined to $50 per share (from a high of more than $130 per share in early 2000). In 2002, Messier was ousted from Vivendi after board members became convinced that the company was headed for disaster.

By this time, the Seagram fortune had declined markedly because the family had taken Vivendi stock instead of cash when Vivendi originally purchased Seagram. When the merger with Vivendi was first announced, the Seagram family fortune was worth nearly U.S.$7 billion, but by 2003, the value of Seagram's investment in Vivendi was less than U.S.$1 billion. People started thinking that Sam Bronfman was right after all.

The latest rumours about Edgar Bronfman, Jr. include speculation that he wants to get back into the entertainment business to repair his image among his family members and to avoid fulfilling his grandfather's prediction. But he also seems to have a genuine interest in being actively involved in the day-to-day management of an entertainment company. ◆

WHO ARE MANAGERS?

All corporations depend on effective management. Regardless of the type of business they work in, managers like Edgar Bronfman perform many of the same functions, are responsible for many of the same tasks, and have many of the same responsibilities. The work of all managers involves developing strategic and tactical plans. They must also analyze their competitive environments and plan, organize, direct, and control day-to-day operations.

Although our focus is on managers in *business* settings, remember that the principles of management apply to all kinds of organizations. Managers work in charities, churches, social organizations, educational institutions, and government agencies. The prime minister of Canada, the president of the University of Toronto, the executive director of the United Way, the dean of your business school, and the chief administrator of your local hospital are all managers. Remember, too, that managers bring to small organizations much the same kinds of skills—the ability to make decisions and respond to a variety of challenges—that they bring to large ones. Regardless of the nature and size of an organization, managers are among its most important resources.

SETTING GOALS AND FORMULATING STRATEGY

goals
Objectives that a business hopes and plans to achieve.

1. Explain the importance of setting *goals* and formulating *strategies* as the starting points of effective management.

The starting point in effective management is setting **goals**, objectives that a business hopes (and plans) to achieve. Every business needs goals, and we begin by discussing the basic aspects of organizational goal setting. However, deciding what it *intends* to do is only step one for an organization. A company's managers must also make decisions about *actions* that will and will not achieve its goals. From this perspective, *strategy* is the broad program that underlies those decisions; the basic steps in formulating strategy are discussed later in the chapter.

Setting Goals

Goals are performance targets, the means by which organizations and their managers measure success or failure at every level. In this section, we identify the main purposes for which organizations establish goals, classify the basic levels of business goals, and describe the process by which goals are commonly set.

The Purposes of Goal Setting

An organization functions systematically because it sets goals and plans accordingly. Indeed, an organization functions as such because it commits its resources on all levels to achieving its goals. Specifically, we can identify four main purposes in organizational goal setting:

1. *Goal setting provides direction, guidance, and motivation for all managers.* If managers know precisely where the company is headed, there is less potential for error in the different units of the company. Starbucks, for example, has a goal of increasing capital spending by 15 percent, with all additional expenditures devoted to opening new stores. This goal clearly informs everyone in the firm that expansion into new territories is a high priority for the firm.
2. *Goal setting helps firms allocate resources.* Areas that are expected to grow will get first priority. The company allocates more resources to

new projects with large sales potential than it allocates to mature products with established but stagnant sales potential. Thus, Starbucks is primarily emphasizing new store expansion, while its ecommerce initiatives are currently given a lower priority. "Our management team," says CEO Howard Schultz, "is 100 percent focused on growing our core business without distraction...from any other initiative."

3. *Goal setting helps to define corporate culture.* General Electric's goal, for instance, is to push each of its divisions to number one or number two in its industry. The result is a competitive, often stressful, environment and a culture that rewards success and has little tolerance for failure. At the same time, however, GE's appliance business, television network (NBC), aircraft engine unit, and financial services business are each among the very best in their respective industries.

GE
www.ge.com

4. *Goal setting helps managers assess performance.* If a company sets a goal to increase sales by 10 percent in a given year, managers in units who attain or exceed the goal can be rewarded. Units failing to reach the goal will also be compensated accordingly. GE has a long-standing reputation for stringently evaluating managerial performance, richly rewarding those who excel—and getting rid of those who do not. Each year, the lower 10 percent of GE's managerial force are informed that either they make dramatic improvements in performance or consider alternative directions for their careers.

Kinds of Goals

Naturally, goals differ from company to company, depending on the firm's purpose and mission. Every enterprise, of course, has a *purpose*—a reason for being. Businesses seek profit, universities work to discover and transmit new knowledge, and government agencies exist to provide service to the public. Most enterprises also have a **mission statement**—a statement of how it will achieve its purpose. Bell Canada's mission, for example, is to be a world leader in helping communicate and manage information. DaimlerChrysler's mission statement emphasizes "delighted customers." Atco Ltd.'s mission is to provide products and services to the energy and resource industries, and to invest principally in energy-related assets in North America. The mission of Investor's Group is to satisfy clients who are in need of general and comprehensive financial planning. Mission statements should also include some statement about the company's core values and its commitment to ethical behaviour.

mission statement
An organization's statement of how it will achieve its purpose in the environment in which it conducts its business.

Two business firms can have the same purpose—for example, to sell watches at a profit—yet they have very different missions. Timex sells low-cost, reliable watches in outlets ranging from department stores to corner drugstores. Rolex, on the other hand, sells high-quality, high-priced fashion watches through selected jewellery stores.

Regardless of a company's purpose and mission, every firm needs long-term, intermediate, and short-term goals:

- **Long-term goals** relate to extended periods of time—typically five years or more into the future. MasterCard, for example, might set a long-term goal of doubling the number of participating merchants during the next 10 years. Similarly, Kodak might adopt a long-term goal to increase its share of the 35-mm film market by 10 percent during the next eight years.

long-term goals
Goals set for extended periods of time, typically five years or more into the future.

- **Intermediate goals** are set for a period of one to five years into the future. Companies usually have intermediate goals in several areas. For example, the marketing department's goal might be to increase sales by

intermediate goals
Goals set for a period of one to five years.

3 percent in two years. The production department might want to decrease expenses by 6 percent in four years. Human resources might seek to cut turnover by 10 percent in two years. Finance might aim for a 3 percent increase in return on investment in three years.

short-term goals
Goals set for the very near future, typically less than one year.

- Like intermediate goals, **short-term goals**—which are set for one year or less—are developed for several different areas. Increasing sales by 2 percent this year, cutting costs by 1 percent next quarter, and reducing turnover by 4 percent over the next six months are all short-term goals.

Formulating Strategy

Planning is concerned with the nuts and bolts of setting goals, choosing tactics, and establishing schedules. In contrast, strategy tends to have a wider scope. It is by definition a "broad program" that describes an organization's intentions. A business strategy outlines how it intends to meet its goals, and includes the organization's responsiveness to new challenges and new needs. **Strategy formulation** involves three basic steps, as shown in Figure 6.1.

strategy formulation
Creation of a broad program for defining and meeting an organization's goals.

Setting Strategic Goals

strategic goals
Long-term goals derived directly from a firm's mission statement.

Strategic goals are long-term goals derived directly from the firm's mission statement. Ferdinand Piech, CEO of Volkswagen, has clear strategic goals for the European automaker. When Piech took over in 1993, Volkswagen was only marginally profitable, and regarded as an also-ran in the industry. Over the next few years, however, Piech totally revamped the firm and now it is making big profits. Volkswagen is now a much more formidable force in the global automobile industry. It currently competes with Toyota for the number-three spot in the industry (behind only General Motors and Ford), but Piech is clearly not finished. "For the moment," he reports, "we are happy with the bronze medal. But we want to step up the stairway."[1]

SWOT
Identification and analysis of organizational strengths and weaknesses and environmental opportunities and threats as part of strategy formulation.

SWOT Analysis. After strategic goals have been established, organizations usually go through a process called a **SWOT** analysis as they continue to formulate their strategy. This process involves assessing organizational *S*trengths and *W*eaknesses (the *S* and the *W*) and environmental *O*pportunities and *T*hreats (the *O* and the *T*). Note that strengths and weaknesses are internal to the company, while opportunities and threats are external. In formulating strategy, companies attempt to capitalize on organizational strengths and take advantage of environmental opportunities. During this same process, they seek ways to overcome organizational weaknesses and cope with environmental threats.[2]

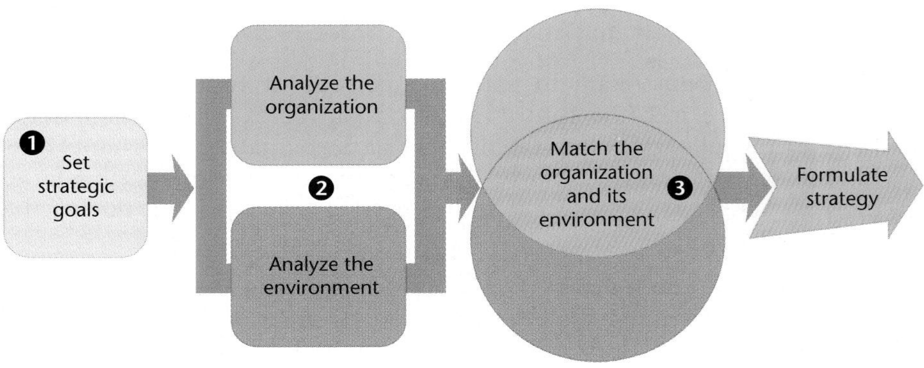

Figure 6.1
Strategy formulation.

Analyzing the Organization and Its Environment

The term **environmental analysis** means scanning the environment for threats and opportunities. Changing consumer tastes and hostile takeover offers are *threats*, as are new government regulations. Even more important threats come from new products and new competitors. *Opportunities*, meanwhile, are areas in which the firm can potentially expand, grow, or take advantage of existing strengths.

environmental analysis
The process of scanning the environment for threats and opportunities.

Consider, for example, the case of British entrepreneur Richard Branson and his company, Virgin Group Ltd. Branson started the firm in 1968, when he was 17, naming it in acknowledgment of his own lack of experience in the business world. Over the years, he has built Virgin into one of the world's best-known brands, comprising a conglomeration of over 200 entertainment, media, and travel companies worldwide. Among the best known of his enterprises are Virgin Atlantic (an international airline), Virgin Megastores (retailing), and V2 Music (record labels). Branson sees potential threats from other competitors such as British Airways and KLM for Virgin Atlantic, Tower Records for retailing, and the EMI Group for recorded music.

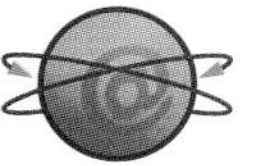

Virgin Group Ltd.
www.virgin.com

But he also sees significant opportunities because of his firm's strong brand name (especially in Europe). Indeed, one of his most recent ventures is a new ecommerce firm. The business is called Virgin Mobile and operates like a cellular telephone company. But in addition to providing conventional cellular service, the Virgin telephone permits the user to press a red button to go directly to a Virgin operator who can sell products, make airline and hotel reservations, and provide numerous other services. A companion website complements the cellular service and its related programs. Virgin Mobile is signing up new customers at a rate of 100 000 per month.[3]

In addition to performing environmental analysis, which is analysis of *external* factors, managers must examine *internal* factors. The purpose of **organizational analysis** is to better understand a company's strengths and weaknesses. Strengths might include surplus cash, a dedicated workforce, an ample supply of managerial talent, technical expertise, or weak competition. The absence of any of these strengths could represent an important weakness.

organizational analysis
The process of analyzing a firm's strengths and weaknesses.

Branson, for example, started up Virgin Mobile in part because he saw so many of his current operations as old-line, traditional businesses that might be at future risk from new forms of business and competition. One strength he has employed has been the widespread name recognition that his businesses enjoy. Another strength relates to finances. Branson sold 49 percent of Virgin Atlantic to Singapore Airlines for almost $1 billion in cash, retaining ownership control but raising all of the funds he needed to launch his new venture. On the other hand, he also admits that neither he nor most of his senior managers have much experience in or knowledge about ecommerce, which may be a significant weakness.

Matching the Organization and Its Environment

The final step in strategy formulation is matching environmental threats and opportunities with corporate strengths and weaknesses. The matching process is the heart of strategy formulation: More than any other facet of strategy, matching companies with their environments lays the foundation for successfully planning and conducting business.

Over the long term, this process may also determine whether a firm typically takes risks or behaves more conservatively. Either strategy can be successful. Blue Bell, for example, is one of the most profitable ice-cream makers in the world, even though it sells its products in only about a dozen U.S. states. Based in Brenham, Texas, Blue Bell controls more than 50 percent of the market in each state where it does business. The firm has resisted the temptation to expand too quickly. Its success is based on product freshness and frequent deliveries—strengths that may suffer if the company grows too large.

A Hierarchy of Plans

Plans can be viewed on three levels: strategic, tactical, and operational. Managerial responsibilities are defined at each level. The levels constitute a hierarchy because implementing plans is practical only when there is a logical flow from one level to the next.

strategic plans
Plans that reflect decisions about resource allocations, company priorities, and steps needed to meet strategic goals.

tactical plans
Generally, short-range plans concerned with implementing specific aspects of a company's strategic plans.

operational plans
Plans setting short-term targets for daily, weekly, or monthly performance.

- **Strategic plans** reflect decisions about resource allocations, company priorities, and the steps needed to meet strategic goals. They are usually set by the board of directors and top management. General Electric's decision that viable products must be number one or number two within their respective categories is a matter of strategic planning.
- **Tactical plans** are shorter-range plans concerned with implementing specific aspects of the company's strategic plans. They typically involve upper and middle management. Coca-Cola's decision to increase sales in Europe by building European bottling facilities is an example of tactical planning.
- Developed by middle and lower-level managers, **operational plans** set short-term targets for daily, weekly, or monthly performance. McDonald's, for example, establishes operational plans when it explains precisely how Big Macs are to be cooked, warmed, and served.

Levels of Strategies

corporate-level strategy
Identifies the various businesses that a company will be in, and how these businesses will relate to each other.

business-level (competitive) strategy
Identifies the ways a business will compete in its chosen line of products or services.

functional strategies
Identify the basic courses of action that each department in the firm will pursue so that it contributes to the attainment of the business's overall goals.

There are three levels of strategy in a business firm (see Figure 6.2). A **corporate-level strategy** identifies the various businesses that a company will be in, and how these businesses will relate to each other. A **business-level (competitive) strategy** identifies the ways a business will compete in its chosen line of products or services. **Functional strategies** identify the basic courses of action that each department in the firm will pursue so that it contributes to the attainment of the business's overall goals. Each of these strategies is discussed below.

Corporate-Level Strategies

There are several different corporate-level strategies that a company might pursue, including concentration, growth, integration, diversification, and investment reduction.

concentration strategy
Involves focusing the company on one product or product line.

market penetration
Boosting sales of present products by more aggressive selling in the firm's current markets.

geographic expansion
Expanding operations in new geographic areas or countries.

product development
Developing improved products for current markets.

Concentration. A **concentration strategy** involves focusing the company on one product or product line. Organizations that have successfully pursued a concentration strategy include McDonald's and Canadian National Railway. The main advantage of a concentration strategy is that the company can focus its strengths on the one business it knows well. The main disadvantage is the risk inherent in putting all of one's eggs in one basket.

Growth. Companies have several growth strategies available to them, including **market penetration** (boosting sales of present products by more aggressive selling in the firm's current markets), **geographic expansion** (expanding operations in new geographic areas or countries), and **product development** (developing improved products for current markets). These three strategies focus on *internal* activities that will result in growth.

Integration. There are two basic integration strategies. **Horizontal integration** means acquiring control of competitors in the same or similar markets with the same or similar products. For example, Hudson's Bay Company purchased Kmart and Zellers. **Vertical integration** means owning or controlling the inputs to the firm's processes and/or the channels through which the products or services are distributed. Thus, major oil companies like Shell not only drill and produce their own oil, but refine the oil into different products and then sell those products through company-controlled outlets across Canada. Another example of vertical integration is Irving Forest Products' purchase of Royale Tissue from Procter & Gamble. Horizontal and vertical integration focus on *external* activities that will result in growth.

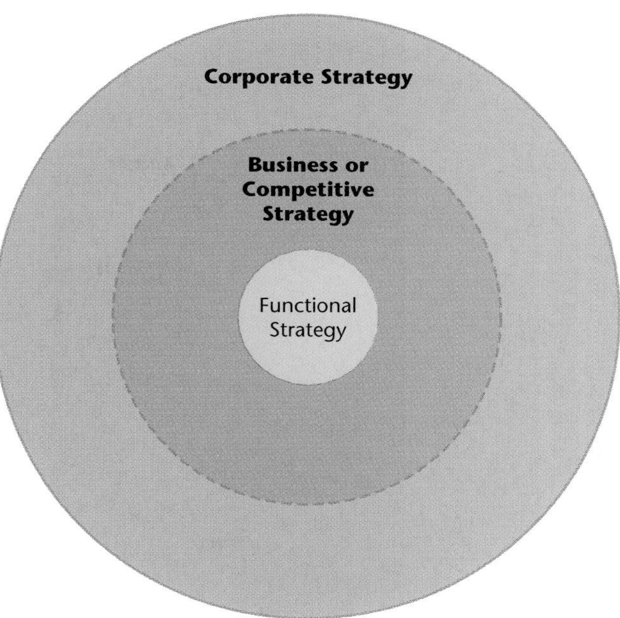

Figure 6.2
Hierarchy of strategy.

Diversification. Diversification means expanding into related or unrelated products or market segments. Diversification helps the firm avoid the problem of having all of its eggs in one basket by spreading risk among several products or markets. *Related diversification* means adding new, but related, products or services to an existing business. For example, CN diversified into trucking, an activity that is clearly related to railway operations. Maple Leaf Gardens Ltd., which already owned the Toronto Maple Leafs, also acquired the Toronto Raptors basketball team. *Conglomerate diversification* means diversifying into products or markets that are not related to the firm's present businesses. For example, Brascan Ltd. owns companies in the mining, real estate, electric power generation, and financial services businesses. Conglomerate diversification is not nearly as popular as it was a few years ago.

horizontal integration
Acquiring control of competitors in the same or similar markets with the same or similar products.

vertical integration
Owning or controlling the inputs to the firm's processes and/or the channels through which the products or services are distributed.

diversification
Expanding into related or unrelated products or market segments.

Investment Reduction. Investment reduction means reducing the company's investment in one or more of its lines of business. One investment-reduction strategy is *retrenchment*, which means the reduction of activity or operations. *Divestment* is another investment-reduction strategy; it involves selling or liquidating one or more of a firm's businesses. For example, BCE sold its Yellow Pages and White Pages for $4 billion.

investment reduction
Reducing the company's investment in one or more of its lines of business.

Business-Level (Competitive) Strategies

Whatever corporate-level strategy a firm decides on, it must also have a competitive strategy. A competitive strategy is a plan to establish a profitable and sustainable competitive position against the forces that determine industry competition.[4] Michael Porter identifies three competitive strategies: cost leadership, differentiation, and focus.

Cost Leadership. Cost leadership means becoming the low cost leader in an industry. Wal-Mart is an industry cost leader. Its distribution costs are minimized through a satellite-based warehousing system, its store-location costs are minimized by placing stores on low-cost land, and the stores themselves are very plain.

cost leadership
Becoming the low cost leader in an industry.

Differentiation. In a **differentiation** strategy, a firm seeks to be unique in its industry along some dimension that is valued by buyers. For example, Caterpillar Tractor emphasizes durability, Volvo stresses safety, Apple Computer stresses user-friendly products, and Mercedes-Benz emphasizes quality.

differentiation
A firm seeks to be unique in its industry along some dimension that is valued by buyers.

focus strategy
Selecting a market segment and serving the customers in that market niche better than competitors.

Focus. A **focus strategy** means selecting a market segment and serving the customers in that market niche better than competitors. Before it was acquired by Nexfor, Fraser Inc. focused on producing high-quality, durable, lightweight paper that is used in bibles. While it still has a good reputation in the production of bible paper, Nexfor Fraser Papers now is more diversified and produces papers for a variety of uses, including dog food bags and doughnut boxes.

Functional Strategies

Each business's choice of competitive strategy (cost leadership, differentiation, or focus) is translated into supporting functional strategies for each of its departments to pursue. A functional strategy is the basic course of action that each department follows so that the business accomplishes its overall goals. To implement its cost-leadership strategy, for example, Wal-Mart's distribution department pursued a functional strategy of satellite-based warehousing that ultimately drove distribution costs down to a minimum.

CONTINGENCY PLANNING AND CRISIS MANAGEMENT

Disney
www.disney.go.com

Because business environments are often difficult to predict, and because the unexpected can create major problems, most managers recognize that even the best-laid plans sometimes become impractical. For instance, when Walt Disney Co. announced plans to launch a cruise line replete with familiar Disney characters and themes, managers also began aggressively developing and marketing packages linking three- and four-day cruises with visits to Disney World in Florida. The first sailing was scheduled for early 1998, and the company began to book reservations a year in advance. However, the shipyard constructing Disney's first ship (the *Disney Magic*) notified the company in October 1997 that it was behind schedule and that the ship would be delivered several weeks late. When similar problems befall other cruise lines, they can offer to rebook passengers on alternative itineraries. But because Disney had no other ship, it had no choice but to refund the money it had collected as prebooking deposits for its first 15 cruises.

The 20 000 displaced customers were offered substantial discounts if they rebooked on a later cruise. Many of them, however, could not rearrange their schedules and requested full refunds. Moreover, quite a few blamed Disney, and a few expressed outrage at what they perceived to be poor planning by the entertainment giant. Fortunately, *Disney Magic* was eventually launched and has now become both very popular and very profitable.[5]

Because managers know that such things can happen, they often develop alternative plans in case things go awry. Two common methods of dealing with the unknown and unforeseen are *contingency planning* and *crisis management*.

Contingency Planning

contingency planning
Identifying aspects of a business or its environment that might entail changes in strategy.

Contingency planning takes into account the need to find solutions for specific aspects of a problem. By its very nature, a contingency plan is a hedge against changes that might occur. **Contingency planning**, then, is planning for change: it attempts to identify in advance important aspects of a business or its market that might change. It also identifies the ways in which a company will respond to changes. Today, many companies use computer programs for contingency planning.

Suppose, for example, that a company develops a plan to create a new business. It expects sales to increase at an annual rate of 10 percent for the next five years and develops a marketing strategy for maintaining that level. But suppose that sales have increased by only 5 percent by the end of the first year. Does the company abandon the business, invest more in advertising, or wait to see what happens in the second year? Any of these alternatives is possible. However, things will go more smoothly if managers have decided in advance what to do in the event of lower sales. Contingency planning can help them do exactly that.

Disney learned from its mistake with its first ship, and when the second ship (the *Disney Wonder*) was launched a year later, managers did several things differently. First, they allowed for an extra two weeks between when the ship was supposed to be ready for sailing and its first scheduled cruise. They also held open a few cabins on *Disney Magic* as a backup for any especially disgruntled customers who might need to be accommodated due to unexpected delays launching *Disney Wonder*.

Crisis Management

A crisis is an unexpected emergency requiring immediate organizational response. **Crisis management** involves an organization's methods for dealing with emergencies. The tragic events of September 11, 2001, clearly served to underscore the importance of crisis management. In addition to the loss of human life, virtually every business in the United States experienced direct or indirect financial costs. Because all U.S. airlines were shut down for several days and air traffic was slow to return, they lost billions of dollars. Other businesses were also affected. Tourist destinations like Disney World and resort hotels lost customers. Because fewer people travelled in the months after September 11, profits also declined at restaurants, car rental agencies, and gasoline retailers. Broadway shows in New York sold fewer tickets, and shaken consumers across the country delayed major purchases and withdrew funds from their banks. Shipping companies like FedEx and UPS found it necessary to subject cargo to more intense (and costly) security screenings. And many people simply stayed home for a few days after that tragic day, resulting in lost work time and a drop in productivity.

crisis management
An organization's methods for dealing with emergencies.

The SARS outbreak in Toronto in 2003 is another example of a crisis. When the World Health Organization put Toronto on a list of areas that travellers should avoid, problems arose for all kinds of businesses in the

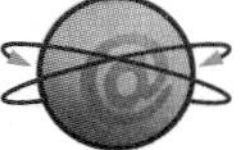

World Health Organization
www.who.int/en

Commercial airlines have contingency plans to deal with problems like major snowstorms. These contingency plans involve making sure that planes are not stranded at airports that are experiencing snow delays.

Toronto area. Beyond the tragedy of illness and loss of life, several major conferences that were scheduled to be held in Toronto were cancelled, and the hospitality industry suffered considerable losses.

2. Describe the four activities that constitute the *management process*.

To prepare for emergencies, many organizations maintain crisis plans. These plans, designed to enable employees to cope when disasters do occur, typically outline who will be in charge in different kinds of circumstances, how the organization will respond, and so forth. In addition, they typically lay out plans for assembling and deploying crisis-management teams.

THE MANAGEMENT PROCESS

management
The process of planning, organizing, leading, and controlling a business's financial, physical, human, and information resources in order to achieve its goals.

Management is the process of planning, organizing, leading, and controlling an enterprise's financial, physical, human, and information resources to achieve the organization's goals of supplying various products and services. Thus, the CEO of Walt Disney Productions is a manager because he regularly carries out these four functions as films are being made. Actors such as Julia Roberts or Tom Cruise, while they may be the stars of the movies, are

BUSINESS TODAY

What Do Managers Actually Do?

Henry Mintzberg of McGill University conducted a detailed study of the work of five chief executive officers and found the following:

1. Managers work at an unrelenting pace.
2. Managerial activities are characterized by brevity, variety, and fragmentation.
3. Managers have a preference for "live" action, and emphasize work activities that are current, specific, and well-defined.
4. Managers are attracted to the verbal media.

Mintzberg believes that a manager's job can be described as 10 roles (in three categories) that must be performed. The manager's formal authority and status give rise to three *interpersonal roles*: (1) *figurehead* (duties of a ceremonial nature, such as attending a subordinate's wedding); (2) *leader* (being responsible for the work of the unit); and (3) *liaison* (making contact outside the vertical chain of command). These interpersonal roles give rise to three *informational roles*: (1) *monitor* (scanning the environment for relevant information); (2) *disseminator* (passing information to subordinates); and (3) *spokesperson* (sending information to people outside the unit).

The interpersonal and informational roles allow the manager to carry out four *decision-making roles*: (1) *entrepreneur* (improving the performance of the unit); (2) *disturbance handler* (responding to high-pressure disturbances, such as a strike at a supplier); (3) *resource allocator* (deciding who will get what in the unit); and (4) *negotiator* (working out agreements on a wide variety of issues, such as the amount of authority an individual will be given).

Insight into what managers actually do can also be gained by looking at the so-called *functions* of management (planning, organizing, leading, and controlling). Consider the work of Marina Pyo, who is a Publisher, School Division, at Pearson Education Canada, a publisher of textbooks for elementary and secondary schools, colleges, and universities. Her job is to manage the activities that are necessary to develop resources in math and science for the Canadian elementary school market. Her work is at times intense, fragmented, rewarding, frustrating, and fast-paced. In short, she is a typical manager.

Pyo carries out the *planning* function when she drafts a plan for a new book. She is *organizing* when she develops a new organization chart to facilitate goal achievement. She is *leading* when she meets with a subordinate to discuss that person's career plans. And she is *controlling* when she checks sales prospects for a book before ordering a reprint.

Some of Pyo's activities do not easily fit into this "functions of management" model. For example, it is not clear which function she is performing when she negotiates the size of a reprint run with the manager of the sales division, or when she talks briefly with the president of her division about recent events in Pyo's area of responsibility.

not managers because they don't carry out the four functions of management. The Business Today box explains the dynamic nature of managerial jobs.

The planning, organizing, leading, and controlling aspects of a manager's job are interrelated. While these activities generally follow one another in a logical sequence, sometimes they are performed simultaneously or in a different sequence altogether. In fact, a manager is likely to be engaged in all these activities during the course of a business day.

Planning

Determining what the organization needs to do and how best to get it done requires planning. **Planning** has three main components. As we have seen, it begins when managers determine the firm's goals. Next, they develop a comprehensive strategy for achieving those goals. After a strategy is developed, they design tactical and operational plans for implementing the strategy.

planning
That portion of a manager's job concerned with determining what the business needs to do and the best way to achieve it.

When Yahoo! was created, for example, the company's top managers set a strategic goal of becoming a top firm in the then-emerging market for internet search engines. But then came the hard part—figuring out how to do it. They started by assessing the ways in which people actually use the web. They also studied ways in which they would probably use it in the future, analyzed the successful strategies of other growing firms, and assessed the ways in which big companies were using the internet. They concluded that people wanted an easy-to-understand web interface. They also wanted to be able to satisfy a wide array of needs, preferences, and priorities by going to as few sites as possible to find what they were looking for.

One key component of Yahoo!'s strategy, therefore, was to foster partnerships and relationships with other companies so that potential web surfers could draw upon several sources through a single portal—which would, of course, be Yahoo! Thus, the goal of partnering emerged as one set of tactical plans for moving forward.

Yahoo! managers then began fashioning alliances with such diverse partners as Reuters, Standard & Poor's, and the Associated Press (for news coverage), RE/MAX (for real estate information), and a wide array of information providers specializing in sports, weather, entertainment, shopping, travel, and so forth. The creation of individual partnership agreements with each of these companies represents a form of operational planning.

organizing
That portion of a manager's job concerned with mobilizing the necessary resources to complete a particular task.

Organizing

The portion of a manager's job that is concerned with mobilizing the necessary resources to complete a particular task is known as **organizing** (we examine this topic further in Chapter 7). The importance of the organizing function of management can be seen by considering what happened at Hewlett-Packard, which lost some of its lustre a few years ago. One of the major reasons for its slide could be traced back to what had once been a major strength. Specifically, HP had long prided itself on being little more than a corporate confedera-

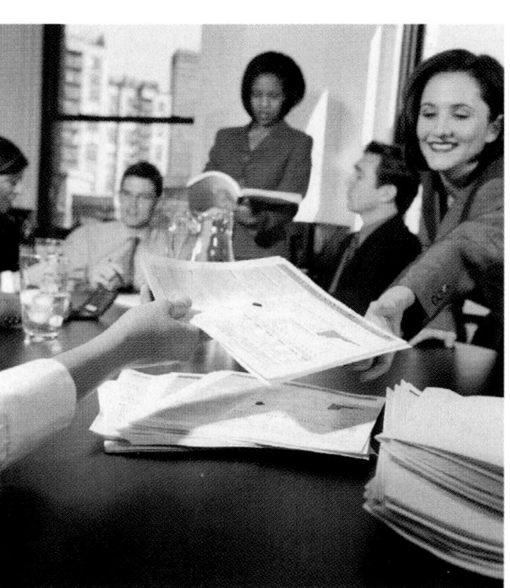

Managers usually work together to set goals and determine corporate strategy. These activities take a great deal of time but are critical to the success of any organization.

tion of individual businesses. Sometimes these businesses even ended up competing against themselves. This approach had been beneficial for much of the firm's history: it was easier for each business to make its own decisions quickly and efficiently, and the competition kept each unit on its toes. By 1998, however, problems started to become apparent, and no one could quite figure out what was going on.

Enter Ann Livermore, then head of the firm's software and services business. Livermore realized that it was the structure that had served so well in the past that was now holding the firm back. Specifically, to regain its competitive edge HP needed an integrated, organization-wide internet strategy. Unfortunately, the company's highly decentralized organization made that impossible. Livermore led the charge to create one organization to drive a single internet plan. "I felt we could be the most powerful company in the industry," she says, "if we could get our hardware, software, and services aligned." In fact, a reorganized HP has bounced back and is quickly regaining its competitive strength.[6]

Leading

leading
That portion of a manager's job concerned with guiding and motivating employees to meet the firm's objectives.

The activities involving interactions between managers and their subordinates to meet the firm's objectives are known as **leading** (or directing). By definition, managers have the power to give orders and demand results. Leading, however, goes beyond merely giving orders. Leaders attempt to guide and motivate employees to work in the best interests of the organization. At discount airline WestJet, for example, CEO Clive Beddoe has been very successful in motivating employees to go above and beyond normal work practices to ensure the company's (and their own) financial success. We discuss leadership more fully in Chapter 10.

Controlling

controlling
That portion of a manager's job concerned with monitoring the firm's performance and, if necessary, acting to bring it in line with the firm's goals.

Controlling is the process of monitoring a firm's performance to make sure that the firm is meeting its goals. All CEOs must pay close attention to costs and performance. Indeed, skilful controlling, like innovative directing, is one reason that Gordon Bethune, CEO of Continental Airlines, has been so successful. The firm focuses relentlessly on indicators of performance that can be constantly measured and adjusted. Everything from on-time arrivals to baggage-handling errors to the number of empty seats on an airplane to surveys of employee and customer satisfaction are regularly and routinely monitored. If on-time arrivals start to slip, Bethune focuses on the problem and gets it fixed. If a manager's subordinates provide less than glowing reviews, that manager loses part of his or her bonus. As a result, no single element of the firm's performance can slip too far before it's noticed and fixed.

As manager of the Toronto Blue Jays, Carlos Tosca has the job of motivating and leading a group of highly talented individuals to play effectively as a team.

Figure 6.3 illustrates the control process that begins when management establishes standards, often for financial performance. If, for example, a company wants to increase sales by 20 percent over the next 10 years, then an appropriate standard might be an increase of about 2 percent a year. Managers then measure actual performance against standards. If the two amounts agree, the organization continues along its present course. If they vary significantly, however, one or the other needs adjustment. If sales have increased 2.1 percent by the end of the first year, things are probably fine. If sales have dropped 1 percent, some revision in plans may be needed. Perhaps the original goal should be lowered or more money should be spent on advertising.

Control can also show where performance is running better than expected and, thus, can serve as a basis for providing rewards or reducing costs. For example, when Ford recently introduced the new Explorer SportsTrac (an SUV with a pickup bed), initial sales were so strong that the firm was able to delay a major advertising campaign for three months because it was selling all the vehicles it could make anyway.

TYPES OF MANAGERS

3. Identify *types of managers* by level and area.

Although all managers plan, organize, lead, and control, not all managers have the same degree of responsibility for each activity. Moreover, managers differ in the specific application of these activities. Thus we can divide managers by their *level* of responsibility or by their *area* of responsibility.

Levels of Management

The three basic levels of management are top, middle, and first-line management. In most firms there are more middle managers than top managers and more first-line managers than middle managers. Moreover, as the cat-

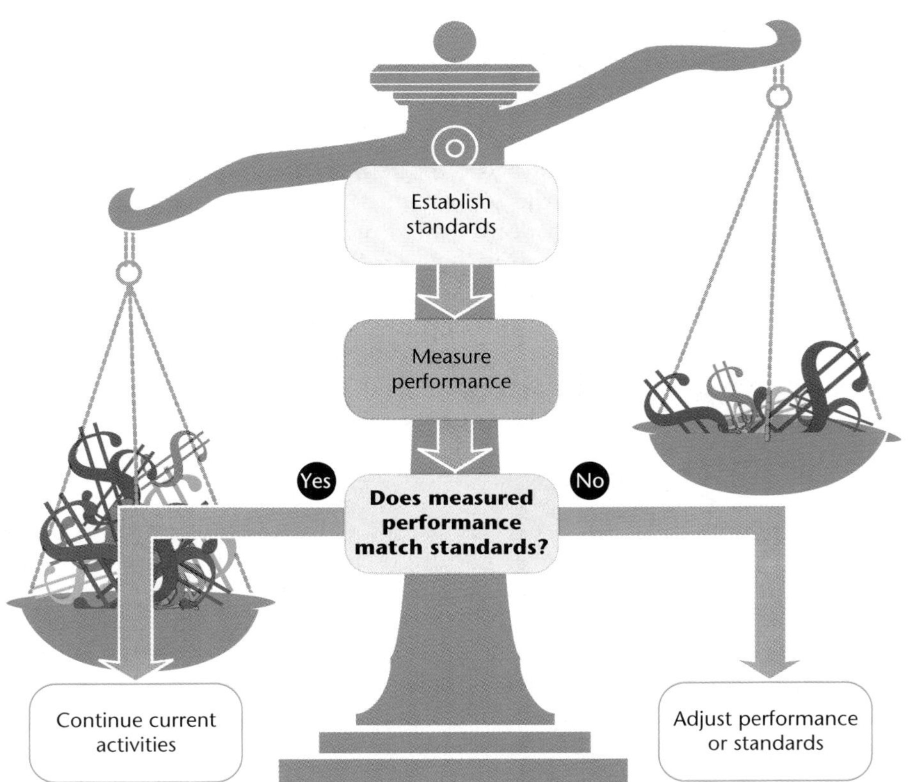

Figure 6.3
The control process.

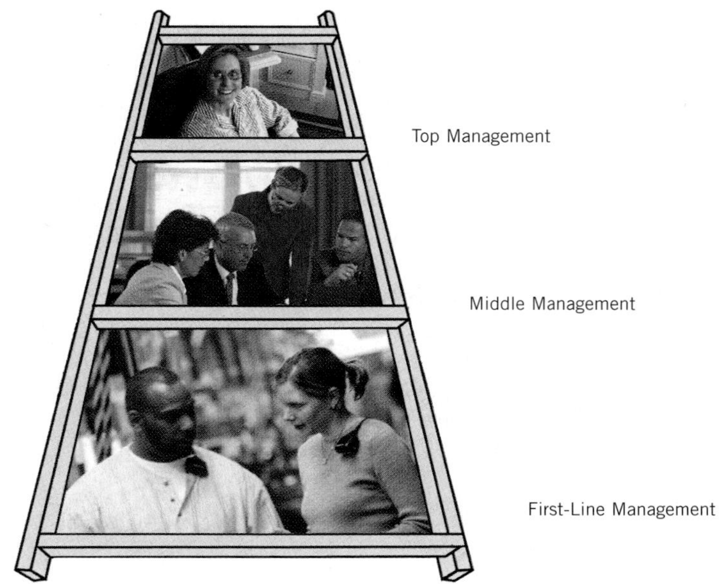

Organizations have three basic levels of management.

egories imply, the power of managers and the complexity of their duties increase as we move up the pyramid.

Top Managers

top managers
Those managers responsible for a firm's overall performance and effectiveness and for developing long-range plans for the company.

The fairly small number of executives who guide the fortunes of most companies are **top managers**. Common titles for top managers include President, Vice-President, Treasurer, Chief Executive Officer (CEO), and Chief Financial Officer (CFO). Top managers are responsible to the board of directors and shareholders of the firm for its overall performance and effectiveness. They set general policies, formulate strategies, oversee all significant decisions, and represent the company in its dealings with other businesses and government.[7]

Middle Managers

middle managers
Those managers responsible for implementing the decisions made by top managers.

Although below the ranks of the top executives, **middle managers** occupy positions of considerable autonomy and importance. Titles such as Plant Manager, Operations Manager, and Division Manager are typical of middle-management jobs. In general, middle managers are responsible for implementing the strategies, policies, and decisions of the top managers. For example, if top management decides to bring out a new product in 12 months or to cut costs by 5 percent, middle management will have to decide to increase the pace of new product development or to reduce the plant's workforce.

First-Line Managers

first-line managers
Those managers responsible for supervising the work of employees.

Those who hold titles such as Supervisor, Office Manager, and Group Leader are **first-line managers**. Although they spend most of their time working with and supervising the employees who report to them, first-line managers' activities are not limited to that arena. At a building site, for example, the Project Manager not only ensures that workers are carrying out construction as specified by the architect, but also interacts extensively with materials suppliers, community officials, and middle and top managers at the home office. The manager of an Old Navy store and the flight-services manager for a specific Air Canada flight would also be considered first-line managers.

Areas of Management

Within any large company, the top, middle, and first-line managers work in a variety of areas, including marketing, finance, operations, human resources, and information.

Marketing Managers

Marketing includes the development, pricing, promotion, and distribution of a product or service. *Marketing managers* are responsible for getting products and services to buyers. Marketing is especially important for firms dealing in consumer products, such as Procter & Gamble, Coca-Cola, and Roots. These firms often have large numbers of marketing managers at various levels. For example, a large firm will probably have a vice-president for marketing (top manager), regional marketing managers (middle managers), and several district sales managers (first-line managers). A marketing person often rises to the top of this type of corporation. In contrast, firms that produce industrial products such as machinery and janitorial supplies tend to put less emphasis on marketing and to have fewer marketing managers. However, these firms do not ignore marketing altogether. In recent years, law firms and universities have also come to recognize the value and importance of marketing. We look at marketing in detail in Chapters 15 to 17.

Financial Managers

Management of a firm's finances, including its investments and accounting functions, is extremely important to its survival. Nearly every company has *financial managers* to plan and oversee its financial resources. Levels of financial management may include a vice-president for finance (top), division controller (middle), and accounting supervisor (first-line). For large financial institutions, effective financial management is the company's reason for being. No organization, however, can afford to ignore the need for management in this area. Chapters 18 to 20 cover financial management in detail.

Operations Managers

A firm's operations are the systems by which it creates goods and services. *Operations managers* are responsible for production control, inventory control, and quality control, among other duties. Manufacturing companies like Steelcase, Bristol Aerospace, and Sony need operations managers at many levels. Such firms typically have a vice-president for operations (top), plant managers (middle), and foremen or supervisors (first-line). In recent years, sound operations management practices have also become increasingly important to service organizations, hospitals, universities, and the government. Operations management is the subject of Chapters 11 and 12.

Human Resource Managers

Every enterprise uses human resources. Most companies have *human resource managers* to provide assistance to other managers when they are hiring employees, training them, evaluating their performances, and determining their compensation level. In many companies, human resource managers are involved in negotiations with labour unions. Large firms may have several human resource departments, each dealing with specialized activities. Imperial Oil, for example, has separate departments to deal with recruiting and hiring, wage and salary levels, and labour relations. Smaller firms may have a single department, while very small organizations may have a single person responsible for all human resource activities. Chapters 8 to 10 address issues involved in human resource management.

Information Managers

A new type of managerial position appearing in many organizations is that of *information manager*. These managers are responsible for designing and implementing various systems to gather, process, and disseminate information. Dramatic increases in both the amount of information available to managers and the ability to manage it have led to the emergence of this important function. While relatively few in number now, the ranks of information managers are increasing at all levels. Federal Express, for example, has a Chief Information Officer. Middle managers engaged in information management help design information systems for divisions or plants. Computer systems managers within smaller businesses or operations are first-line managers. Information management is discussed in Chapter 13.

Other Managers

Some firms have more specialized managers. Chemical companies such as CIL have research and development managers, for example, whereas companies such as Petro-Canada and Apple have public relations managers. The range of possibilities is endless; the areas of management are limited only by the needs and imagination of the firm.

BASIC MANAGEMENT SKILLS

4. Describe the five basic *management skills.*

While the range of managerial positions is almost limitless, the success that people enjoy in those positions is often limited by their skills and abilities. Effective managers must possess several skills: *technical, human relations, conceptual, decision-making,* and *time management skills*.

Technical Skills

technical skills
Skills associated with performing specialized tasks within a firm.

Skills associated with performing specialized tasks within a company are called **technical skills**. A secretary's ability to type, an animator's ability to draw a cartoon, and an accountant's ability to audit a company's records are all technical skills. People develop their technical skills through education and experience. The secretary, for example, probably took a keyboarding course and has had many hours of practice both on and off the job. The animator may have had training in an art school and probably learned a great deal from experienced animators on the job. The accountant earned a university degree and, possibly, professional certification.

As Figure 6.4 shows, technical skills are especially important for first-line managers. Most first-line managers spend considerable time helping employees solve work-related problems, monitoring their performance, and training them in more efficient work procedures. Such managers need a basic understanding of the jobs they supervise.

As a manager moves up the corporate ladder, however, technical skills become less and less important. Top managers, for example, often need only a cursory familiarity with the mechanics of basic tasks performed within the company. Michael Eisner, for example, freely admits that he can't draw Mickey Mouse or build a ride for Disney World.

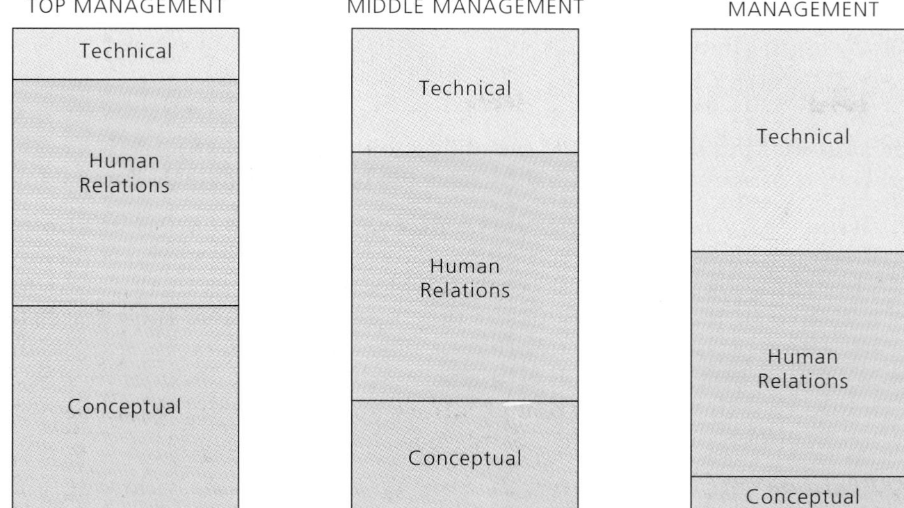

Figure 6.4
Different levels in an organization require different combinations of managerial skills.

Human Relations Skills

A few years ago, Hyatt Hotels checked 379 corporate employees into the chain's 98 hotels. They were not, however, treated as guests. Rather, they were asked to make beds, carry luggage, and perform the other tasks necessary to make a big hotel function. Top management at Hyatt believes that learning more about the work of lower-level employees will allow executives to understand them better as human beings (and as co-workers).

The Hyatt experiment was designed to test and improve the **human relations skills** of upper-level managers—that is, skills in understanding and getting along with other people. A manager with poor human relations skills may have trouble getting along with subordinates, cause valuable employees to quit or transfer, and contribute to poor morale.

human relations skills
Skills in understanding and getting along with people.

While human relations skills are important at all levels, they are probably most important for middle managers, who must often act as bridges between top managers, first-line managers, and managers from other areas of the organization. Managers should possess good communication skills. Many managers have found that being able to understand others—and to get them to understand—can go far toward maintaining good relations in an organization.

Conceptual Skills

Conceptual skills refer to a person's ability to think in the abstract, to diagnose and analyze different situations, and to see beyond the present situation. Conceptual skills help managers recognize new market opportunities (and threats). They can also help managers analyze the probable outcomes of their decisions. The need for conceptual skills differs at various management levels: top managers depend most on conceptual skills, first-line managers least. Although the purposes and everyday needs of various jobs differ, conceptual skills are needed in almost any job-related activity.

conceptual skills
Abilities to think in the abstract, diagnose and analyze different situations, and see beyond the present situation.

In many ways, conceptual skills may be the most important ingredient in the success of executives in ecommerce businesses. For example, the ability to foresee how a particular business application will be affected by or can be translated to the internet is clearly conceptual in nature. The Wired World box discusses this idea in more detail.

Decision-Making Skills

decision-making skills
Skills in defining problems and selecting the best courses of action.

Decision-making skills include the ability to define problems and select the best course of action. Figure 6.5 illustrates the basic steps in decision making.

1. ***Define the problem, gather facts, and identify alternative solutions.*** Vivendi Universal is a large French entertainment and media company. The firm's top managers recently decided that they needed a stronger presence in the United States if they were to continue their quest to become a global media powerhouse. Thus, they defined their problem as how to best enter the U.S. media market. They subsequently determined that there were two alternatives: starting a new media business from scratch or buying an existing one.
2. ***Evaluate each alternative and select the best one.*** Managers at Vivendi realized that it would take many years and a huge cash investment to launch a new media enterprise from scratch. They also recognized that because there was ongoing consolidation in the U.S. media industry, buying an existing firm might be relatively easy. Further analysis identified Houghton Mifflin, one of the last remaining independent publishers, as an attractive acquisition target.

IT'S A WIRED WORLD

Always in Touch

Once a novelty, cellular telephones are ubiquitous today. If you walk through any large airport or business centre, you'll see dozens of people sitting in chairs, leaning against walls, or strolling around while conducting business on their cellphones. Other popular communication technologies include personal digital assistants (PDAs) and extra-small "subnotebook" laptop computers. Some devices incorporate all three functions: phone communication, computing, and internet connectivity. You can get accessories (portable printers, folding keyboards), and if you don't want to learn an array of new technologies, internet service providers can make voice mail, email, and business information available over the World Wide Web through your conventional computer.

New technologies have made many managers considerably more productive than before. It's easier to supervise workers in remote locations, to stay in touch with clients and customers, and to share information with the home office when they're on the road. At the same time, however, the same devices pose certain problems for many busy executives. Because they're always available, they have less downtime and less opportunity to disconnect from their work. Without the opportunity to step back from immediate demands at work, managers sometimes find it difficult to see the broader picture or to bring fresh energy to problems.

In the past, managers had free time when they were travelling to and from work or when they were away from their offices at lunch. Now, many are readily accessible during these times. Thus what might have once been a nice hour-long break for lunch in the middle of the day may turn into a work session conducted over the phone at the corner deli. Even vacations are falling victim to the technology—parents vacationing at Disney World with their children can duck into the resort's internet café for a few minutes to take online messages from the office.

Fortunately, astute managers who want to regain some control over this aspect of their life actually have more control than you might expect. Let's face it—all they have to do is turn everything off. Even so, with the onslaught of more ways to stay connected, it's getting harder for stressed managers to find a few minutes' respite from the ongoing demands of the executive's life.

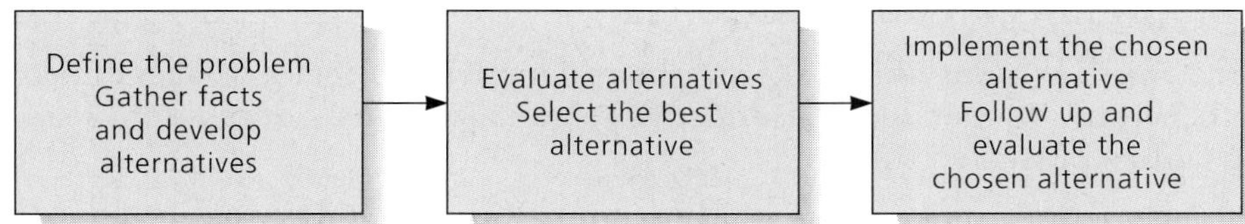

Figure 6.5
The decision-making process.

3. ***Implement the chosen alternative, periodically following up and evaluating the effectiveness of that choice.*** Vivendi executives quietly began negotiating with senior managers at Houghton Mifflin in mid-2001. Within a matter of weeks, the two firms had reached an agreement: Vivendi Universal would acquire 100 percent of Houghton Mifflin, thus providing the French company with exactly what it had been seeking—a viable entry into U.S. markets.[8] Unfortunately, Vivendi subsequently fell on hard times, and on August 14, 2002, it announced that it would attempt to sell Houghton Mifflin to raise much-needed cash.

As this example demonstrates, decision making can be a complicated activity for managers. The Exercising Your Ethics box presents another decision-making opportunity for a manager.

EXERCISING YOUR ETHICS

Making Room for Alternative Actions

The Situation

Assume that you are the manager of a large hotel adjacent to a medical centre in a major city. The medical centre itself consists of 10 major hospitals and research institutes. Two of the hospitals are affiliated with large universities and two with churches. Three are public and three are private. The centre has an international reputation and attracts patients from around the world.

Because so many patients and their families travel great distances to visit the medical centre and often stay for days or weeks, there are also eight large hotels in the area, including three new ones. The hotel that you manage is one of the older ones and, frankly, is looking a bit shabby. Corporate headquarters has told you that the hotel will either be closed or undergo a major remodelling in about two years. In the meantime, you are expected to wring every last cent of profit out of the hotel.

The Dilemma

A storm has just struck the area and brought with it major flooding and power outages. Three of the medical centre hospitals have been shut down indefinitely, as have six of the nearby hotels. Fortunately, your hotel sustained only minor damage and is fully functional. You have just called a meeting with your two assistant managers to discuss what actions, if any, you should take.

One assistant manager has urged you to cut room rates immediately for humanitarian reasons. This manager also wants you to open the hotel kitchens 24 hours a day to prepare free food for rescue workers and meals to donate to the hospitals, whose own food service operations have been disrupted. The other assistant manager, meanwhile, has urged just the opposite approach: raise room rates by at least 20 percent and sell food to rescue workers and hospitals at a premium price. Of course, you can also choose to follow the advice of neither and continue doing business as usual.

Questions for Discussion

1. What are the ethical issues in this situation?
2. What do you think most managers would do in this situation?
3. What would you do?
4. Once you have made your decision, how would you implement it, given the short time frame that is available?
5. How would you measure the success of your decision?

Time Management Skills

time management skills
Skills associated with the productive use of time.

Time management skills refer to the productive use that managers make of their time. To manage time effectively, managers must address four leading causes of wasted time:

Paperwork. Some managers spend too much time deciding what to do with letters and reports. Most documents of this sort are routine and can be handled quickly. Managers must learn to recognize those documents that require more attention.

The telephone. Experts estimate that managers are interrupted by the telephone every five minutes. To manage time more effectively, they suggest having a secretary screen all calls and setting aside a certain block of time each day to return the important ones.

Meetings. Many managers spend as much as four hours per day in meetings. To help keep this time productive, the person handling the meeting should specify a clear agenda, start on time, keep everyone focused on the agenda, and end on time.

Email. Increasingly, of course, more and more managers are also relying heavily on email and other forms of electronic communication. Like memos and telephone calls, many email messages are not particularly important; some are even trivial. As a result, time is wasted when managers have to sort through a variety of electronic folders, in-baskets, and archives. As the average number of electronic messages grows, the potential time wasted also increases.

Management Skills for the Twenty-First Century

Managers face some major challenges in the twenty-first century. We will touch on two of the most significant challenges: *global management* and *technology*.

Global Management Skills

Tomorrow's managers must equip themselves with the special tools, techniques, and skills necessary to compete in a global environment. They will need to understand foreign markets, cultural differences, and the motives and practices of foreign rivals.

On a more practical level, businesses will need managers who are capable of understanding international operations. In the past, most Canadian businesses hired local managers to run their operations in the various countries in which they operated. More recently, however, the trend has been to transfer Canadian managers to foreign locations. This practice helps firms better transfer their corporate cultures to foreign operations. In addition, foreign assignments help managers become better prepared for international competition as they advance within the organization.[9]

Management and Technology Skills

Another significant issue facing tomorrow's manager is technology, especially as it relates to communication. Managers have always had to deal with information. In today's world, however, the amount of information has reached staggering proportions. New forms of technology have added to a manager's ability to process information while simultaneously making it even more important to organize and interpret an ever-increasing amount of input.

Technology has also begun to change the way the interaction of managers shapes corporate structures. Computer networking, for example, exists because it is no longer too expensive to put a computer on virtually every desk

MTV needed someone to run its operation in China who understood both conservative Chinese television regulators and China's young urban elite. The company chose Li Yifei, a former UN intern, public relations consultant, and tai chi champion. Li has already brought the Chinese equivalent of the MTV awards to state-owned television, and the show had 150 million viewers.

in the company. In turn, this elaborate network controls the flow of the firm's lifeblood—information. Information no longer flows strictly up and down through hierarchies. It now flows to everyone at once. As a result, decisions are made more quickly—and more people are directly involved. With email, teleconferencing, and other forms of communication, neither time nor distance—nor such corporate "boundaries" as departments and divisions—can prevent people from working more closely together. More than ever, bureaucracies are breaking down, while planning, decision making, and other activities are beginning to benefit from group building and teamwork.

MANAGEMENT AND THE CORPORATE CULTURE

Every organization—big or small, more successful or less successful—has an unmistakable "feel" to it. Just as every individual has a unique personality, every company has a unique identity, called **corporate culture**: the shared experiences, stories, beliefs, norms, and ethical stance that characterize an organization. This culture helps define the work and business climate that exists in an organization.

corporate culture
The shared experiences, stories, beliefs, and norms that characterize a firm.

5. Describe the development and explain the importance of *corporate culture.*

A strong corporate culture serves several purposes. First, it directs employees' efforts and helps everyone work toward the same goals. Some cultures, for example, stress financial success to the extreme, while others focus more on quality of life. Second, corporate culture helps newcomers learn accepted behaviours. If financial success is the key to a culture, newcomers quickly learn that they are expected to work long, hard hours and that the "winner" is the one who brings in the most revenue. But if quality of life is more fundamental, newcomers learn that it's more acceptable to spend less time at work and that balancing work and non-work is encouraged. The following examples illustrate how culture differs across firms:

- Magna International, a large Canadian producer of auto parts, is a firm with a strong culture. Its founder, Frank Stronach, is well known for his views about employees, working conditions, daycare centres, unions, the free enterprise system, and profit distribution.[10]

- Four Seasons Hotels and Resorts has a different, but equally strong, culture. Managers are judged by deeds, not words, and act as role models; employees take their cues from the managers.[11]
- At Toyota's Cambridge, Ontario, plant the corporate culture stresses values, principles, and trust. The culture is one of continuous improvement.[12]
- At WestJet Airlines the corporate culture emphasizes profit maximization. Most of the employees own shares in the company, and all of them get to keep some of the profits. This is a powerful incentive for them to work productively.[13]
- Mainframe Entertainment of Vancouver has one of the lowest turnover rates in the animation business. Its culture emphasizes giving young artists and designers opportunities to acquire new skills and develop leadership potential—opportunities not available in the bigger Los Angeles studios.

Forces Shaping Corporate Culture

A number of forces shape corporate cultures. First, the values held by top management help set the tone of the organization and influence its business goals and strategies. Frank Stronach (Magna International), Timothy Eaton (Eaton's), Max Ward (Wardair), Larry Clark (Spar Aerospace), and Jean de Grandpre (BCE) are just a few of the leaders who have had a profound impact on the culture of their respective organizations. Even a large, long-time firm like Ford still bears the traces of founder Henry Ford.

The firm's history also helps shape its culture. The championship banners that line the arena where the Montreal Canadiens play signify that they are winners. Maintaining a corporate culture draws on many dimensions of business life. Shared experiences resulting from norms sustain culture. Thus, working long hours on a special project becomes a shared experience for many employees. They remember it, talk about it among themselves, and wear it as a badge of their contribution to the company.

Stories and legends are also important. Walt Disney has been dead for many years now, but his spirit lives on in the businesses he left behind. Quotations from Disney are affixed to portraits of him throughout the company's studios. And Disney's emphasis on family is still visible in corporate benefits such as paying for spouses to accompany employees on extended business trips. In fact, employees are often called "the Disney family."

Finally, strong behavioural norms help define and sustain corporate cultures. For example, a strong part of the culture at Hewlett-Packard Canada is that everyone wears a name tag and that everyone is called by his or her first name. And at Sony Corporation every employee wears a corporate smock.

Mainframe Entertainment of Vancouver has one of the lowest turnover rates in the animation business. Its culture emphasizes giving young artists and designers opportunities to acquire new skills and develop leadership potential—opportunities not available in the bigger Los Angeles studios.

Communicating the Culture and Managing Change

Corporate culture influences management philosophy, style, and behaviour. Managers, therefore, must carefully consider the kind of culture they want for their organization, then work to nourish that culture by communicating with everyone who works there. Wal-Mart, for example, is acutely conscious of the need to spread the message of its culture as it opens new stores in new areas. One of the company's methods is to regularly assign veteran managers to lead employees in new territories. At Continental Airlines, Gordon Bethune delivers weekly messages to all employees to update them on what's going on in the firm; the employees can either listen to it on a closed-circuit broadcast or else call an 800 telephone number and hear a recorded version at their own convenience.

Communicating the Culture

To use its culture to a firm's advantage, managers must accomplish several tasks, all of which hinge on effective communication. First, managers themselves must have a clear understanding of the culture. Second, they must transmit the culture to others in the organization. Communication is thus one aim in training and orienting newcomers. A clear and meaningful statement of the organization's mission is also a valuable communication tool. Finally, managers can maintain the culture by rewarding and promoting those who understand it and work toward maintaining it.

Managing Change

Not surprisingly, organizations must sometimes change their cultures. Ontario Hydro, for example, had an "engineering" culture for many years. This meant that everything was planned and analyzed down to the last detail before any action was taken. But Ontario Hydro's culture is changing toward a more consumer-oriented, risk-taking culture as it tries to cope with large debt and changes in its markets. The RCMP is also much different now than it was in the days when military tradition dominated the organization. It completed a "visioning process" that resulted in a new mission statement, a new set of core values, and a commitment to the communities in which it works.[14]

Individual managers can have a big impact on a company's culture. James Bonini was only 33 years old when he was named manager of DaimlerChrysler's van plant in Windsor, Ontario. He quickly concluded that he was going to have to change the culture at the plant, which was characterized by quality problems, managers who acted like drill sergeants, and workers who were demoralized. Bonini took several actions, including dealing with the disappointed individuals who thought they should have gotten his job, spending a lot of time on the production floor, boosting the sale of vans by ensuring that the plant was responsive to special customer orders, and giving workers much more authority to make production decisions.[15]

When cultural change is required, the process usually goes through three stages:

1. At the highest level, analysis of the company's environment highlights extensive change as the most effective response to its problems. Conflict and resistance typically characterize this period.

2. Top management begins to formulate a vision of a new company. Whatever that vision is, it must include renewed focus on the activities of competitors and the needs of customers.

3. The firm sets up new systems for appraising and compensating employees that enforce its new values. The purpose is to give the new culture solid shape from within the firm.

Procter & Gamble is in the midst of a major overhaul designed to remake its corporate culture into one more suited to today's competitive global business environment. Because its brands have been dominant for such a long time, managers at P&G have been criticized for having tunnel vision—focusing only on the ways they've done things in the past and then trying to repeat them. Procter & Gamble's popular Tide laundry detergent, for example, has been through more than 60 formula upgrades since it was first introduced. A new top-management team, however, is working to shake things up by advocating new approaches, new ways of thinking, and new models of product development.[16]

SUMMARY OF LEARNING OBJECTIVES

1. **Explain the importance of setting *goals* and formulating *strategies* as the starting points of effective management.** *Goals*—the performance targets of an organization—can be *long-term, intermediate,* and *short-term*. They provide direction for managers, they help managers decide how to allocate limited resources, they define the corporate culture, and they help managers assess performance. *Strategies*—the methods that a company uses to meet its stated goals—involve three major activities: setting strategic goals, analyzing the organization and its environment, and matching the organization and its environment. These strategies are translated into *strategic, tactical,* and *operational plans*. To deal with crises or major environmental changes, companies develop *contingency plans* and plans for *crisis management*.
2. **Describe the four activities that constitute the *management process*.** *Management* is the process of planning, organizing, leading, and controlling an organization's financial, physical, human, and information resources to achieve the organization's goals. *Planning* means determining what the company needs to do and how best to get it done. *Organizing* means determining how best to arrange a business's resources and the necessary jobs into an overall structure. *Leading* means guiding and motivating employees to meet the firm's objectives. *Controlling* means monitoring the firm's performance to ensure that it is meeting its goals.
3. **Identify *types of managers* by level and area.** Managers can be differentiated in two ways: by level and by area. By level, *top managers* set policies, formulate strategies, and approve decisions. *Middle managers* implement policies, strategies, and decisions. *First-line managers* usually work with and supervise employees. Management areas include marketing, financial, operations, human resource, and information. Managers at all levels may be found in every area of a company.
4. **Describe the five basic *management skills*.** Most managers agree that five basic management skills are necessary for success. *Technical skills* are associated with performing specialized tasks ranging from typing to auditing. *Human relations* skills are associated with understanding and getting along with other people. *Conceptual skills* are the abilities to think in the abstract, to diagnose and analyze different situations, and to see beyond present circumstances. *Decision-making skills* allow managers to define problems and to select the best course of action. *Time management* skills refer to managers' ability to make productive use of the time available to them.
5. **Describe the development and explain the importance of *corporate culture*.** *Corporate culture* is the shared experiences, stories, beliefs, and norms that characterize an organization. A strong, well-defined culture

can help a business reach its goals and can influence management styles. Culture is determined by several factors, including top management, the organization's history, stories and legends, and behavioural norms. If carefully communicated and flexible enough to accommodate change, corporate culture can be managed for the betterment of the organization.

KEY TERMS

QUESTIONS AND EXERCISES

Questions for Review

1. What are the four main purposes of setting goals in an organization?

2. Identify and explain the three basic steps in strategy formulation.

3. Relate the five basic management skills to the four activities in the management process. For example, which skills are most important in leading?

4. What is corporate culture? How is it formed? How is it sustained?

Questions for Analysis

5. Select any group of which you are a member (your company, your family, or a club or organization, for example). Explain how planning, organizing, directing, and controlling are practised in that group.

6. Identify managers by level and area at your school, college, or university.

7. In what kind of company would the technical skills of top managers be more important than human relations or conceptual skills? Are there organizations in which conceptual skills are not important?

8. What differences might you expect to find in the corporate cultures of a 100-year-old manufacturing firm based in Winnipeg and a 2-year-old ecommerce firm in Ottawa?

Application Exercises

9. Interview a manager at any level of a local company. Identify that manager's job according to level and area. Show how planning, organizing, directing, and controlling are part of this person's job. Inquire about the manager's education and work experience. Which management skills are most important for this manager's job?

10. Compare and contrast the corporate cultures of two companies that do business in most communities. Be sure to choose two companies in the same industry—for example, a Bay department store and a Wal-Mart discount store.

BUILDING YOUR BUSINESS SKILLS

Speaking with Power

Goal

To encourage students to appreciate effective speaking as a critical human relations skill.

Background

A manager's ability to understand and get along with supervisors, peers, and subordinates is a critical human relations skill. At the heart of this skill, says Harvard University professor of education Sarah McGinty, is the ability to speak with power and control. McGinty defines "powerful speech" in terms of the following characteristics:

- the ability to speak at length and in complete sentences
- the ability to set a conversational agenda
- the ability to deter interruption
- the ability to argue openly and to express strong opinions about ideas, not people
- the ability to make statements that offer solutions rather than pose questions
- the ability to express humour

Taken together, says McGinty, "all this creates a sense of confidence in listeners."

Method

Step 1
Working alone, compare your own personal speaking style with McGinty's description of powerful speech by taping yourself as you speak during a meeting with classmates or during a phone conversation. (Tape both sides of the conversation only if the person to whom you are speaking gives permission.) Listen for the following problems:

- unfinished sentences
- an absence of solutions
- too many disclaimers ("I'm not sure I have enough information to say this, but...")
- the habit of seeking support from others instead of making definitive statements of personal conviction (saying, "I recommend consolidating the medical and fitness functions," instead of, "As Emily stated in her report, I recommend consolidating the medical and fitness functions")
- language fillers (saying, "you know," "like," and "um" when you are unsure of your facts or uneasy about expressing your opinion)

Step 2
Join with three or four other classmates to evaluate each other's speaking styles. Finally,

- Have a 10-minute group discussion on the importance of human relations skills in business.
- Listen to other group members, and take notes on the "power" content of what you hear.
- Offer constructive criticism by focusing on what speakers say rather than on personal characteristics (say, "Bob, you sympathized with Paul's position, but I still don't know what you think," instead of, "Bob, you sounded like a weakling").

Follow-Up Questions

1. How do you think the power content of speech affects a manager's ability to communicate? Evaluate some of the ways in which effects may differ among supervisors, peers, and subordinates.
2. How do you evaluate yourself and group members in terms of powerful and powerless speech? List the strengths and weaknesses of the group.
3. Do you agree or disagree with McGinty that business success depends on gaining insight into your own language habits? Explain your answer.
4. In our age of computers and email, why do you think personal presentation continues to be important in management?
5. McGinty believes that power language differs from company to company and that it is linked to the corporate culture. Do you agree, or do you believe that people express themselves in similar ways no matter where they are?

MASTERING BUSINESS ESSENTIALS

Episode 12 stresses the consequences of CanGo's failure to recognize goal setting and strategy formulation as the starting points of effective management. *This episode demonstrates why evaluating plans is a necessary part of the process of improving operations.*

CRAFTING YOUR BUSINESS PLAN

Furnishing Yourself with Management Skills

The Purpose of the Assignment

1. To familiarize students with management-related issues that a sample firm may address in developing its business plan, in the planning framework of the Business PlanPro (BPP) software package.
2. To demonstrate how three chapter topics—business goals, business strategies, and management skills—can be integrated as components in the BPP planning environment.

Assignment

After reading Chapter 6 in the textbook, open the BPP software and search for information about business goals, business strategies, and management skills as they apply to a sample firm: Willamette Furniture. To find Willamette Furniture, do the following:

Open the Business PlanPro. If it asks if you want to "create a new business plan" or "open an existing plan," select "create a new business plan" (even though you are not going to create a plan at this time). You will then be taken to the Business PlanPro EasyPlan Wizard. On the screen, click on the option entitled **Research It**. You will then be presented with a new list of options, including Sample Plan Browser. After clicking on **Sample Plan Browser**, go down the alphabetical list of sample plans and double-click on **Furniture Mfr.—Office**, which is the location for Willamette Furniture. The screen you are looking at is the introduction page for Willamette's business plan. Scroll down this page until you reach the **Table of Contents** for the company's business plan.

Now respond to the following items:

1. Evaluate Willamette Furniture's business objectives. Are they clearly stated? Are they measurable? [Sites to see in BPP (for this item): On the Table of Contents page, click on **1.1 Objectives**.]
2. Evaluate Willamette's mission and strategy statements. Do they clearly state how Willamette Furniture intends to achieve its purposes? [Sites to see in BPP: On the Table of Contents page, click on **1.0 Executive Summary.** Then click on **1.2 Mission**. Next, click on each of the following in turn: **5.0 Strategy and Implementation Summary** and **5.1 Strategy Pyramids**.]
3. In what areas of the business does each of Willamette's top managers work? [Sites to see in BPP: From the Table of Contents page, click on **6.0 Management Summary**. Now click on each of the following: **6.1 Organization Structure** and **6.2 Management Team**.]
4. What management skills areas are lacking in Willamette furniture's management team? Would you classify the missing skills as technical, human resources, conceptual, or decision-making skills? [Sites to see in BPP: On the Table of Contents page, click on **6.3 Management Team Gaps**.]

VIDEO EXERCISE

Imaginative Management: Creative Age Publications

Learning Objectives

The purpose of this video is to help you:

1. Understand how and why managers set organizational goals.
2. Identify the basic skills that managers need to be effective.
3. Discuss ways in which corporate culture can affect an organization.

Synopsis

Creative Age Publications uses creativity in managing its beauty-industry publications. With offices or franchised operations in Europe, Japan, Russia, and other areas of the world, the company has expanded rapidly—thanks to sound management practices. In fact, one of the company's goals is to avoid overtaxing its management team by growing more slowly in the future. The CEO is working toward delegating most or all decisions to her management team, and as Creative Age managers move up through the ranks, they hone both their technical skills and their skill in working with others. "Having heart" is a major part of the company's culture—an important element that, in the CEO's opinion, many companies lack.

Discussion Questions

1. *For analysis*: How does global growth affect Creative Age's emphasis on the management skill of interacting well with other people?
2. *For analysis*: How does moving managers up through the ranks help them develop conceptual skills?
3. *For application*: How would you suggest that the CEO spread the Creative Age culture throughout its global offices?
4. *For application*: How might the CEO manage growth through the process of controlling?
5. *For debate*: Do you agree with the CEO's policy of allowing managers and employees to work on any company magazine they choose? Support your position.

Online Exploration

Visit the Creative Age website at **www.creativeage.com** and follow the link to *Day Spa* magazine. Scan the magazine's home page and then click on **About Us** to read more about the magazine and its parent company. Why would Creative Age call attention to each magazine's goals and market rather than focusing on the parent company? How might Creative Age use a corporate website to communicate with other people and organizations that affect its ability to achieve its goals?

EXPLORING THE NET

Do You Yahoo?

This chapter has described some of the challenges of managing a business and highlighted the kinds of skills and strategies that help managers meet those challenges. Goal setting and planning are critical elements at every stage of the business life cycle, as are organizing, directing, and controlling performance.

Let's see how a highly successful internet firm, Yahoo!, handles the management process by exploring the portion of its website dedicated to company information (**http://docs.yahoo.com/info/**). Yahoo! was the first online navigational guide to the web and is now the leader in traffic, advertising, and household and business reach. It's also the most recognized and valuable internet brand in the world, reaching over 237 million users in 25 countries and 13 languages. You'll notice that Yahoo!'s information home page contains several categories:

Employment Opportunities
Press Room
Yahoo Speakers Bureau
Investor Relations
Advertising Opportunities
Business Opportunities
Privacy Center and Others

Start at the home page (don't confuse this page with the home page for Yahoo!'s popular search engine) and select **Press Room** and then **Company History**:

1. How old is Yahoo!, and how was it started?
2. Who were among the earliest hires at the fast-growing firm, and what do you think they brought to Yahoo! that founders Filo and Yang found attractive?

Return to the **Press Room** page and select **Management Team**:

3. Who is the current chief executive officer, and what does he or she do?

Return to the **Press Room** page and select **FAQ**:

4. How many different types of businesses and services does Yahoo! provide?

Return once more to the **Press Room** page, click on **The World of Yahoo!**, and scroll down to **World Yahoo's!**:

5. Take a quick look at several of Yahoo!'s international sites (choose any that interest you). What do you notice about the similarities among these sites? What do these similarities suggest about the nature of Yahoo!'s corporate strategy?

Concluding Case 6-1 CC

Yellow Delivers the Goods

Since its founding in 1923, Yellow Corporation has been a leader in the transportation industry, using trucks to haul goods between points in Canada, the United States, and Mexico. For decades, Yellow achieved success by concentrating virtually all of its attention on increasing efficiency at every turn. Yellow has long been a master at ensuring that trucks are full before they leave a warehouse, and it has also developed precisely timed delivery schedules.

Ironically, Yellow eventually fell victim to its own success. As operational efficiency increased, customer service received less and less attention, and before long, newer and more responsive companies were luring away the firm's customers. Compounding this problem was the fact that the customers most likely to seek a more service-oriented transportation provider were also the ones willing to pay premium prices for the extra service. As a result, Yellow's financial performance began to decline, slowly at first, but then more dramatically. Naturally, the decline in revenue led to even worse across-the-board service.

To help turn Yellow around, the board of directors offered Bill Zollars the position of chief executive officer (CEO) in 1996. Already a highly respected manager, Zollars was intrigued by the opportunity to revitalize the carrier. "We were a defensive company—a follower, not a leader," recalls James Welch, president and chief operating officer. "We were yearning for leadership. This company was ready for change."

Zollars quickly learned that organizational change at Yellow would have to be profound. Over a period of decades, people throughout the company had come to accept mediocrity and were often willing to do only the minimal amount necessary to get their jobs done. Zollars knew that he had to alter the attitudes, behaviour, and performance of 30 000 employees. He began by improving communication. The CEO spent 18 months travelling to several hundred locations, and at each site, he talked face-to-face with customers and with employees at all levels. He asked for opinions and consistently provided his own message—namely, that enhanced customer service was to become the firm's new calling card.

Zollars's plan consisted of more than promises and motivational speeches. Whereas previous leaders often glossed over problems and refused to divulge information about the firm's performance, Zollars openly acknowledged the company's defect rate—the percentage of shipments that were late, wrong, or damaged. Employees were stunned to find that the rate was a whopping 40 percent, but that knowledge was necessary to enhance motivation and set a benchmark for improvement. Zollars also instituted the company's first ongoing program for surveying customer satisfaction, and the results were reported openly throughout the company. Zollars made a real effort to listen to employees, gave them authority to make decisions, and developed an enviable reputation for honesty and commitment. "If people doing the work don't believe what's coming from the leadership," says Zollars, "it doesn't get implemented. Period."

Of course, leadership alone is seldom enough to turn around a major company. Technology has also played a big role in Yellow's recent success. For instance, the firm implemented a variety of automated systems to improve customer service and satisfaction. These systems use the internet to provide up-to-the-minute information about the progress of shipments, maintain a customer database that enables faster scheduling, and develop the trailer-loading timetables and routes that ensure on-time delivery. Ultimately, the real technology success story at Yellow isn't merely the innovative and efficient use of technology, but rather the savvy application of those systems in support of employees and customers.

Beyond leadership and technology, however, perhaps the most challenging and yet the most important change at Yellow was the revision of the company's mission, transforming it from the delivery of freight to a strong and consistent focus on customer service. For instance, when the firm's employees saw their primary goal as the efficient movement of cargo, the firm focused on one set of processes. Today, thanks to the efforts of Zollars and other managers, employees realize that supporting the customer by meeting his or her delivery needs is the paramount task. This shift in perspective now enables the firm to provide better service, to develop innovative new products and services, to improve performance, and ultimately, to compete successfully in an increasingly tough industry. As Bill Zollars says in the firm's 2000 Annual Report, "...[O]ur business really isn't about moving freight. It's about earning the trust of the consumers of our services."

Questions for Discussion

1. Describe the role of goals and strategy at Yellow.
2. What kind of crisis or contingency plans does a firm like Yellow need?
3. Identify examples to illustrate each of the various parts of the management process at Yellow.
4. Identify and briefly describe management titles that Yellow most likely has that reflect both the different levels and the different areas of management.
5. Discuss how Bill Zollars has used various management skills in his turnaround of Yellow. ◆

Concluding Case 6-2

Strategic Decision Making at BCE

In April 2002, Jean Monty, the CEO of BCE Inc., unexpectedly announced that he was stepping down from his position. Michael Sabia, the new CEO, was immediately faced with a very difficult strategic decision, namely what kind of company BCE would be. Would it be a telephone company, a telecommunications company, a media company, or a New Economy company? This strategic decision was necessary because BCE had been acquiring companies in many different businesses, but several of them were not performing well. A CIBC World Markets research note said that BCE's strategy appeared to be in disarray.

To see why Sabia had a difficult strategic decision to make, consider the makeup of BCE in 2002. BCE had been pursuing a strategy that is often characterized by industry observers as "commerce, content, and connectivity." The commerce part of the equation included BCE Emergis (electronic commerce in the health and financial services industries) and CGI Group Inc. (information technology consulting). The content part of the equation was represented by Bell Globemedia, which includes CTV (television stations), ROBTv (business reporting), *The Globe and Mail* (a national newspaper), and Sympatico-Lycos (internet portals). The connectivity part of the equation included Bell Canada (telephones), Bell ExpressVu (satellite broadcasting), Teleglobe (international voice and data network), and Bell Canada International (telecom services in emerging markets).

The economic performance of these diverse holdings has varied widely. Bell Canada is the most successful and will continue to provide steady cash flow to the company. CGI Group is also doing well. But there are problems in each of the other areas. BCE Emergis, for example, has had difficulty reaching revenue projections because new customers simply haven't materialized. In spite of that, Sabia says that BCE is very committed to making Emergis a success. The same sorts of problems exist with Teleglobe and BCI. Bell Globemedia is also losing money, partly because of a slump in advertising.

Former CEO Jean Monty's strategy was to take money earned in the reliable Bell Canada part of the business and use it to acquire other New Economy businesses, some of which would likely grow very fast and make a lot of money for BCE. Monty's leadership style was active and decisive. He would analyze a situation, then take action. For example, in 2000 he decided to sell BCE's stake in Nortel Networks, which BCE had owned since 1957. His timing was perfect. BCE received a huge windfall when it sold its shares for $90 a share (by mid-2002, Nortel was trading for less than $1 a share).

But decisive action does not guarantee success. In 2000, BCE bought a 77 percent stake in Teleglobe for $7.4 billion as part of its "convergence" strategy to bring together various media in one organization. By 2002, however, Teleglobe was essentially worthless because of a glut in the market, and even though BCE considered Teleglobe a "core holding," it was cut loose. Teleglobe became known as "Monty's folly" in investment circles. Soon after being dropped by BCE, Teleglobe sought bankruptcy protection.

Monty saw BCE as a growth company, not a stodgy utility, and took the lead in getting BCE into wireless, high-speed internet and electronic commerce. His actions were a continuation of a long series of diversification decisions. Between 1980 and 2000, for example, BCE invested in TransCanada Pipelines (oil and gas), Quebecor (media and printing), Montreal Trustco (financial services), and BCE Developments (real estate). These ventures were generally unsuccessful, and some of them generated large losses ($440 million in the case of BCE Developments).

Given all that had happened in the past, Michael Sabia had some major strategic decisions to make. Diversification had not seemed to have worked very well for BCE, and some industry analysts were now saying that Sabia should forget diversification and focus on the telephone utility business. If he did that, BCE might be able to both dominate the market and generate a lot of profit.

Observers didn't have long to wait for Sabia's decision. In July 2002, BCE announced that it planned to repurchase 20 percent of Bell Canada from SBC Communications (which it had sold to SBC in 1999 for $5.1 billion). Michael Sabia said that BCE would concentrate on Bell, while other holdings would be reviewed to determine how they help the phone utility. The company would concentrate on cutting costs, reducing staff, and strengthening operations.

Questions for Discussion

1. Briefly describe the various corporate-level strategies that a company can pursue. What strategy has BCE been pursuing until recently? What strategy is it pursuing now? Why did it change its strategy?
2. What are the main steps in the decision-making process? How do they apply in this case?
3. Describe the skills of management. What skills are particularly important to a person like Michael Sabia? Defend your answer.
4. What is corporate culture? How might the corporate culture have changed at BCE over the last decade? Explain your reasoning. ◆

CHAPTER 7

Organizing the Business Enterprise

After reading this chapter, you should be able to:

1. Discuss the elements that influence a firm's *organizational structure*.
2. Describe *specialization* and *departmentalization* as the building blocks of organizational structure.
3. Distinguish between *responsibility* and *authority* and explain the differences in decision making in *centralized* and *decentralized organizations*.
4. Explain the differences between *functional, divisional, project,* and *international organization structures*, and describe the most popular forms of organizational design.
5. Describe the *informal organization* and discuss *intrapreneuring*.

Frantic Films Gets Organized

Frantic Films is a Winnipeg-based special effects film production company. Founded in 1997, the company has grown rapidly and now has 55 employees. In 2001 it was named one of Canada's Hottest 50 Start-Ups by *Profit Magazine*, and it ranked fourth on the *Manitoba Business* list of the province's 50 fastest growing companies in 2002. Frantic Films is a private corporation that is owned and managed by three principal shareholders—Jamie Brown (Chief Executive Officer), Chris Bond (Creative Director), and Ken Zorniak (Chief Operating Officer). Brown notes that the three principal shareholders work together on all major issues.

The company is organized into three divisions (see Figure 7.1). The TV Commercials division produces television commercials for local Winnipeg companies, and does special effects for commercials produced by companies located across North America. The writers, producers, designers, compositors, animators, and editors have created award-winning spots for local, national, and international companies as diverse as the Royal Winnipeg Ballet, the Disney Channel, and Procter & Gamble Canada.

The Live Action division produces and owns programs that have been broadcast around the world. The division first develops the ideas for special-interest programs, then promotes the idea to broadcasters and financiers. If there is a strong interest, a budget is provided and the division produces the program. Frantic has produced programs like *Pioneer Quest* (one of the highest rated documentary series ever broadcast on a Canadian specialty channel), *Quest for the Bay* (the highest rated series to air on History Television in 2002), and *Klondike: The Quest for Gold* (which recently sold in the United States, Latin America, and the United Kingdom).

The Visual Effects division produces special effects for TV and movies. Using special effects software packages such as Maya, Houdini, Digital Fusion, and 3Dstudio Max, the division has established a reputation as one of the top visual effects providers in North America. Its recent output includes special effects for *X-Men 2, The Core*, and *Swordfish*. The division uses a matrix organization structure. A project team, made up of specialists in areas like 3D animation, 2D animation, compositing, and hardware/software support, is put together. When the project is completed, the team disbands and its members are assigned to other projects. These teams are typically given specific goals that must be achieved, and then the team members use their technical expertise to decide how they can best achieve the goal.

Each of the three divisions operates independently, but the company is still small enough that individuals

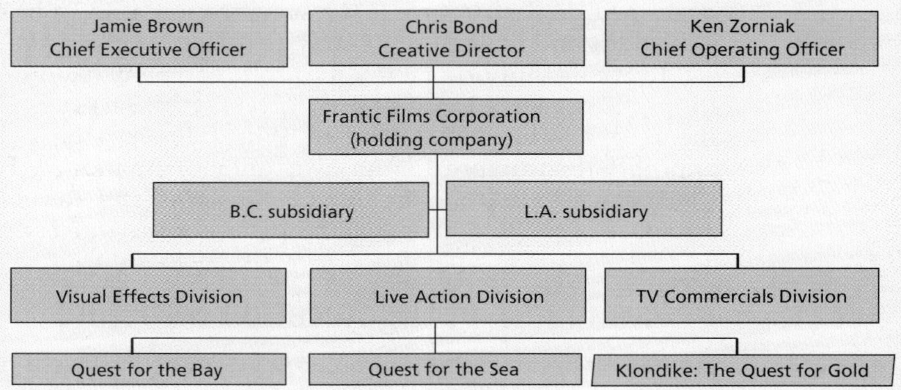

Figure 7.1
Organization chart for Frantic Films.

from one division regularly get involved in decisions in other divisions. For example, since the company does not have a marketing vice-president, marketing decisions are often made jointly by Brown, Bond, and Zorniak for each of the divisions. This means that Frantic Films does not have a "pure" functional or divisional structure.

Because Bond and Zorniak aren't experts in the activities of the Live Action division, Brown makes most of the key decisions there. But he frequently checks with them to make sure that everyone is "on side." Brown says that the three individuals are learning to increasingly trust each other's expertise when decisions are made, but that they still check with each other frequently about who is making what decisions. They have also adopted a policy that there must be unanimity on any new hires in any division.

To date, the authority structure of the company has been quite centralized because the principal shareholders have both the expertise to make decisions and the motivation to do so. But Brown thinks it is important to increase the involvement of lower-level workers in decisions, so he is trying to delegate more authority to them. He is also encouraging employees to make recommendations on various issues to top management. Brown recognizes that giving employees more discretion can sometimes lead to less-than-optimal decisions, but he also wants to give people more experience in making decisions that affect the company.

Brown observes that at this point in its history, the organization structure of Frantic Films is quite fluid. Everyone knows who the top managers are, who is skilled in what areas, and who is responsible for what. Beyond that, in this rapidly growing company there are many on-the-spot adjustments and decisions that must be made as the three managers work toward achieving the goals they have set for the company. ◆

WHAT IS ORGANIZATIONAL STRUCTURE?

1. Discuss the elements that influence a firm's *organizational structure.*

What do we mean by the term *organizational structure*? In many ways, a business is like an automobile. All automobiles have an engine, four wheels, fenders and other structural components, an interior compartment for passengers, and various operating systems including those for fuel, braking, and climate control. Each component has a distinct purpose but must also work in harmony with the others. Automobiles made by competing firms all have the same basic components, although the way they look and fit together may vary.

Similarly, all businesses have common structural and operating components, each of which has a specific purpose. Each component must fulfill its own purpose while simultaneously fitting in with the others. And, just like automobiles made by different companies, how these components look and fit together varies from company to company. Thus, **organizational structure** is the specification of the jobs to be done within a business and how those jobs relate to one another.

organizational structure
The specification of the jobs to be done within a business and how those jobs relate to one another.

Every institution—be it a for-profit company like Frantic Films, a not-for-profit organization like the University of Saskatchewan, or a government agency like the Canadian Wheat Board—must develop the most appropriate structure for its own unique situation. What works for Air Canada will not work for Canada Customs and Revenue. Likewise, the structure of the Red Cross will not work for the University of Toronto.

Determinants of Organization Structure

How is an organization's structure determined? Does it happen by chance or is there some logic that managers use to create structure? Does it develop by some combination of circumstance and strategy? Ideally, managers carefully assess a variety of important factors as they plan for and then create a structure that will allow their organization to function efficiently.

Many elements work together to determine an organization's structure. Chief among these are the organization's *purpose, mission,* and *strategy*. A dynamic and rapidly growing enterprise, for example, achieved that position because of its purpose and successful strategies for achieving it. Such a firm will need a structure that contributes to flexibility and growth. A stable organization with only modest growth will function best with a different structure.

Size, technology, and changes in environmental circumstances also affect structure. A large manufacturer operating in a strongly competitive environment requires a different structure than a local barbershop or video store. Moreover, even after a structure has been created, it is rarely free from tinkering—or even outright re-creation. Indeed, most organizations change their structures on an almost continuing basis.

Since it was first incorporated in 1903, for example, Ford Motor Co. has undergone literally dozens of major structural changes, hundreds of moderate changes, and thousands of minor changes. In the last decade alone, Ford has initiated several major structural changes. In 1994, the firm announced a major restructuring plan called *Ford 2000*, which was intended to integrate all of Ford's vast international operations into a single, unified structure by 2000. By 1998, however, midway through implementation of the plan, top Ford executives announced major modifications, indicating that (1) additional changes would be made, (2) some previously planned changes would not be made, and (3) some recently realigned operations would be changed again. In 1999, managers announced another sweeping set of changes intended to eliminate corporate bureaucracy, speed decision making, and improve communication and working relationships among people at different levels of the organization.[1] In 2001, still more changes were announced that were intended to boost the firm's flagging bottom line and stem a decline in product quality.[2]

The Chain of Command

Most businesses prepare **organization charts** that illustrate the company's structure and show employees where they fit into the firm's operations. Figure 7.2 shows the organization chart for a hypothetical company. Each box represents a job within the company. The solid lines that connect the boxes define the chain of command, or the reporting relationships within the company. Thus, each plant manager reports directly to the vice-president for production who, in turn, reports to the president. When the **chain of command** is not clear, many different kinds of problems can result.

organization chart
A physical depiction of the company's structure showing employee titles and their relationship to one another.

chain of command
Reporting relationships within a business; the flow of decision-making power in a firm.

THE BUILDING BLOCKS OF ORGANIZATIONAL STRUCTURE

2. Describe *specialization* and *departmentalization* as the building blocks of organizational structure.

The first step in developing the structure of any business, large or small, is twofold:

- *Specialization*: determining who will do what
- *Departmentalization*: determining how people performing certain tasks can best be grouped together

These two tasks are the basic building blocks of all business organization.

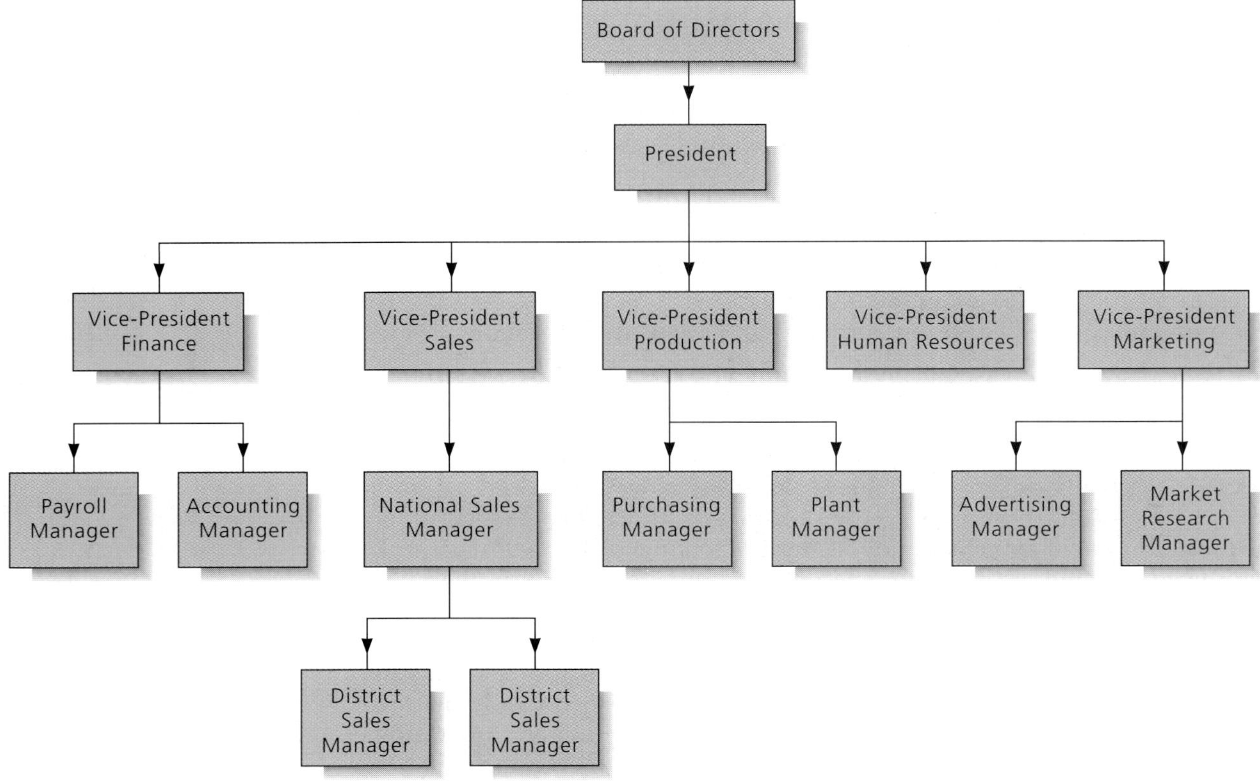

Figure 7.2
An organization chart shows key positions in the organization and interrelationships among them. An actual organization chart would, of course, be far more complex and include individuals at many more levels. Indeed, because of their size, larger firms cannot easily draw a diagram with everyone on it.

Specialization

job specialization
The process of identifying the specific jobs that need to be done and designating the people who will perform them.

The process of identifying the specific jobs that need to be done and designating the people who will perform them leads to **job specialization**. In a sense, all organizations have only one major "job"—for example, making a profit by manufacturing and selling men's and boys' shirts. But this job, of course, is broken into smaller components. In turn, each component is assigned to an individual. Consider the manufacture of men's shirts. Because several steps are required to produce a shirt, each job is broken down into its component parts—that is, into a set of tasks to be completed by a series of individuals or machines. One person, for example, cuts material for the shirt body, another cuts material for the sleeves, and a third cuts material for the collar. Components are then shipped to a sewing room, where a fourth person assembles the shirt. In the final stage, a fifth person sews on the buttons.[3]

Specialization and Growth

Mrs. Fields Cookies
www.mrsfields.com

In a very small organization, the owner may perform every job. As the firm grows, however, so does the need to specialize jobs so that others can perform them. To see how specialization can evolve in an organization, consider the case of Mrs. Fields Cookies. When Debbi Fields opened her first store, she did everything herself: bought the equipment, negotiated the lease, baked the cookies, operated the store, and kept the records. As the business grew, however, Fields found that her job was becoming too much for one person. She first hired a bookkeeper to handle her financial records.

She then hired an in-store manager and a cookie baker. She herself concentrated on advertising and promotions. Her second store required another set of employees—another manager, another baker, and some salespeople. While Fields focused her attention on other expansion opportunities, she turned promotions over to a professional advertising director. Thus the job that she once did all by herself was increasingly broken down into components and assigned to different individuals.

Job specialization is a natural part of organizational growth. It is neither a new idea nor limited to factory work. In the ancient art of winemaking, for example, a high degree of specialization has existed for centuries. The activities necessary to make wine—picking and crushing grapes, fermenting the juice, aging and clarifying the wine, and selling it through specialized intermediaries—are performed by individuals who can draw on the knowledge and experience of their predecessors.

Job specialization has certain advantages: individual jobs can be performed more efficiently, the jobs are easier to learn, and it is easier to replace people who leave the organization. On the other hand, if job specialization is carried too far and jobs become too narrowly defined, people get bored, derive less satisfaction from their jobs, and often lose sight of how their contributions fit into the overall organization.

Departmentalization

After jobs are specialized, they must be grouped into logical units. This process is called **departmentalization**. Departmentalized companies benefit from the division of activities. Control and coordination are narrowed and made easier, and top managers can see more easily how various units are performing. Departmentalization allows the firm to treat a department as a **profit centre**—a separate unit responsible for its own costs and profits. Thus, by assessing profits from sales in a particular area—for example, men's clothing—Sears can decide whether to expand or curtail promotions in that area.

departmentalization
The process of grouping jobs into logical units.

profit centre
A separate company unit responsible for its own costs and profits.

Managers do not group jobs randomly. They group them logically, according to some common thread or purpose. In general, departmentalization may occur along *customer, product, process, geographic,* or *functional* lines (or any combination of these).

Whether they're produced manually or digitally, the drawings that comprise a full-length cartoon such as *Ice Age* are the result of highly coordinated job specialization. Blue Sky Studios of White Plains, New York, made *Ice Age*. It used its own CGI (computer-generated imagery) software. Blue Sky reorganized as an assembly line operation in which about 170 artists who were used to multitasking on commercials and special effects jobs had to perform specialized tasks on a rigidly coordinated production schedule.

Customer Departmentalization

customer departmentalization
Departmentalization according to the types of customers likely to buy a given product.

Stores like HMV are divided into departments—a classical music department, an R&B department, a pop department, and so on. Each department targets a specific customer category (people who want to buy different genres of music). **Customer departmentalization** makes shopping easier by providing identifiable store segments. Thus, a customer shopping for Shania Twain's latest CD can bypass World Music and head straight for Country. Stores can also group products in locations designated for deliveries, special sales, and other service-oriented purposes. In general, when it is departmentalized the store is more efficient and customers get better service—in part because salespeople tend to specialize and gain expertise in their departments.[4]

Product Departmentalization

product departmentalization
Departmentalization according to the products being created or sold.

Both manufacturers and service providers often opt for **product departmentalization**—dividing an organization according to the specific product or service being created. A bank, for example, may handle consumer loans in one department and commercial loans in another. On a larger scale, 3M Corp., which makes both consumer and industrial products, operates different divisions for Post-it brand tape flags, Scotch-Brite scrub sponges, and the Sarns 9000 perfusion system for open-heart surgery.

Process Departmentalization

process departmentalization
Departmentalization according to the production process used to create a good or service.

Other manufacturers favour **process departmentalization**, in which the organization is divided according to production processes. This principle, for example, is logical for the pickle maker Vlasic, which has separate departments to transform cucumbers into fresh-packed pickles, pickles cured in brine, and relishes. Cucumbers destined to become fresh-packed pickles must be packed into jars immediately, covered with a solution of water and vinegar, and prepared for sale. Those slated for brined pickles must be aged in brine solution before packing. Relish cucumbers must be minced and combined with a host of other ingredients. Each process requires different equipment and worker skills.

Many department stores are departmentalized by product. Concentrating different products in different areas of the store makes shopping easier for customers.

Geographic Departmentalization

Some firms may be divided according to the area of the country—or even the world—they serve. This is known as **geographic departmentalization**. The Personal Services division of Montreal Trust, for example, is organized around four regions—Atlantic, Quebec, Central, and BC/Western. Levi Strauss has one division for the United States, one for Europe, and one for the Asia Pacific region.

geographic departmentalization
Departmentalization according to the area of the country or world supplied.

Functional Departmentalization

Many service and manufacturing companies develop departments according to a group's functions or activities—a form of organization known as **functional departmentalization**. Such firms typically have production, marketing and sales, human resource, and accounting and finance departments. Departments may be further subdivided. For example, the marketing department might be divided geographically or into separate staffs for market research and advertising.

functional departmentalization
Departmentalization according to functions or activities.

Because different forms of departmentalization have different advantages, larger companies tend to adopt different types of departmentalization for various levels. For example, the company illustrated in Figure 7.3 uses functional departmentalization at the top level. At the middle level, production is divided along geographic lines. At a lower level, departmentalization is based on product groups.

ESTABLISHING THE DECISION-MAKING HIERARCHY

After jobs have been appropriately specialized and grouped into manageable departments, the next step in organizing is to establish the decision-making hierarchy. That is, managers must explicitly define *reporting relationships* among positions so that everyone will know who has responsibil-

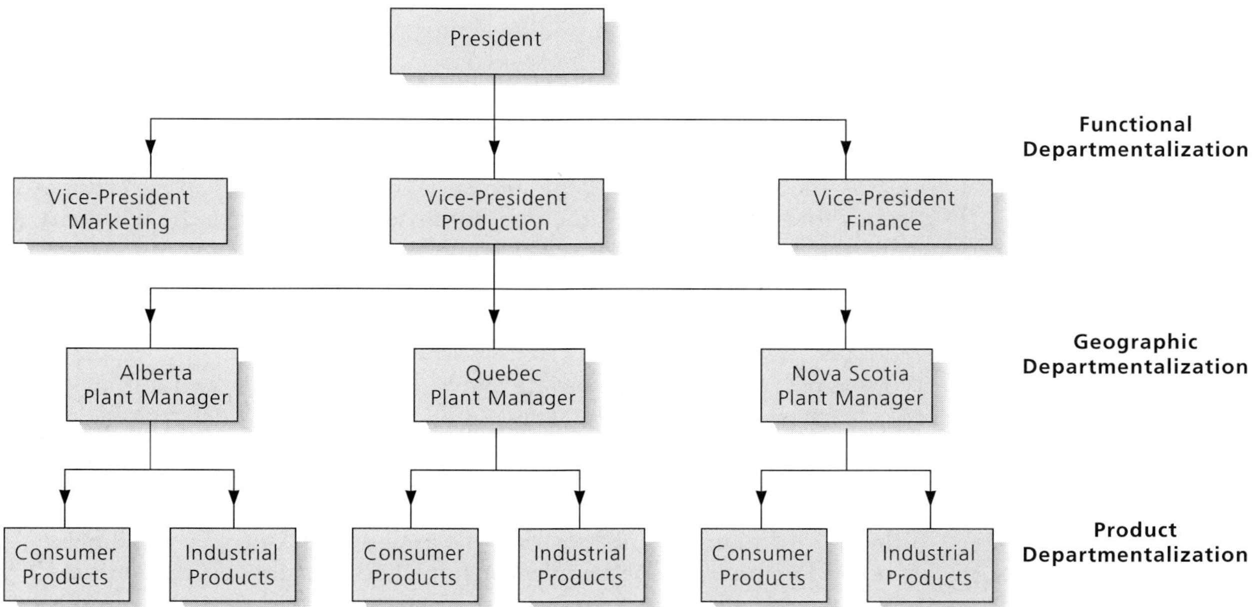

Figure 7.3
Most organizations use multiple bases of departmentalization. This organization, for example, is using functional, geographic, and product departmentalization.

ity for various decisions and operations. The goal is to figure out how to structure and stabilize the organizational framework so that everyone works together to achieve common goals.

A major question that must be asked about any organization is this: *Who makes which decisions?* The answer almost never focuses on an individual or even on a small group. The more accurate answer usually refers to the decision-making hierarchy. The development of this hierarchy generally results from a three-step process:

1. *Assigning tasks*: determining who can make decisions and specifying how they should be made
2. *Performing tasks*: implementing decisions that have been made
3. *Distributing authority*: determining whether the organization is to be centralized or decentralized

For example, when Jack Greenberg took over as CEO of McDonald's, he immediately implemented several changes in the firm's decision-making hierarchy. McDonald's has always been highly centralized, but Greenberg restructured both the company's decision-making process and its operations so that more decisions are made at the regional level. He also purchased a stake in three new restaurant chains with an eye on expansion: Donatos Pizza, Chipotle Mexican Grill, and Aroma, a British coffee chain. Greenberg then installed four new managers, one to head up international operations and the others to oversee the three new restaurant partner groups. Why the changes? "Maybe it was arrogance," said Greenberg. "For 40 years, all we did was open restaurants. That's not enough anymore."[5]

Assigning Tasks

responsibility
The duty to perform an assigned task.

authority
The power to make the decisions necessary to complete a task.

3. Distinguish between *responsibility* and *authority* and explain the differences in decision making in *centralized* and *decentralized organizations.*

The question of who is supposed to do what and who is entitled to do what in an organization is complex. In any company with more than one person, individuals must work out agreements about responsibilities and authority. **Responsibility** is the duty to perform an assigned task. **Authority** is the power to make the decisions necessary to complete the task.

For example, imagine a mid-level buyer for The Bay who encounters an unexpected opportunity to make a large purchase at an extremely good price. Let's assume that an immediate decision is absolutely necessary—but that this decision is one that this buyer has no authority to make without confirmation from above. The company's policies on delegation and authority are inconsistent, since the buyer is responsible for purchasing the clothes that will be sold in the upcoming season but lacks the authority to make the needed purchases.

Performing Tasks

delegation
Assignment of a task, a responsibility, or authority by a manager to a subordinate.

accountability
Liability of subordinates for accomplishing tasks assigned by managers.

Trouble occurs when appropriate levels of responsibility and authority are not clearly spelled out in the working relationships between managers and subordinates. Here, the issues become delegation and accountability. **Delegation** begins when a manager assigns a task to a subordinate. **Accountability** falls to the subordinate, who must then complete the task. If the subordinate does not perform the assigned task properly and promptly, he or she may be reprimanded or punished, possibly even dismissed.

Fear of Delegating

Subordinates sometimes cannot complete a task because their managers have not also delegated the necessary authority. Such employees face a dilemma: they cannot do what the boss demands, but that boss will probably still hold them accountable. Successful managers surround themselves with a team of strong subordinates and then delegate sufficient authority to those subordinates to get the job done.

Experts pinpoint certain indicators that managers are having trouble delegating effectively:

- the feeling that employees can never do anything as well as they can
- the fear that something will go wrong if someone else takes over a job
- the lack of time for long-range planning because they are bogged down in day-to-day operations
- the sense of being in the dark about industry trends and competitive products because of the time they devote to day-to-day operations

To overcome these tendencies, small business owners must admit that they can never go back to running all aspects of the business and that they can, in fact, prosper—with the help of their employees—if they learn to let go. But this problem isn't always confined to small businesses. Some managers in big companies also don't delegate as much or as well as they should. There are several reasons for this problem:

- the fear that subordinates don't really know how to do the job
- the fear that a subordinate might "show the manager up" in front of others by doing a superb job
- the desire to keep as much control as possible over how things are done
- a simple lack of ability as to how to effectively delegate to others

The remedies in these instances are a bit different. First, managers should recognize that they cannot do everything themselves. Second, if subordinates cannot do a job, they should be trained so that they can assume more responsibility in the future. Third, managers should recognize that if a subordinate performs well, it reflects favourably on that employee's manager. Finally, a manager who simply does not know how to delegate might need specialized training in how to divide up and assign tasks to others.

Distributing Authority

Delegation involves a specific relationship between managers and subordinates. Most businesses must also make decisions about general patterns of authority throughout the company. This pattern may be largely *centralized* or *decentralized* (or, usually, somewhere in between).

Centralized Organizations

In a **centralized organization**, top management retains the right to make most decisions that need to be made. Upper management must approve most lower-level decisions before they can be implemented.[6] McDonald's practises centralization as a way to maintain standardization. All restaurants must follow precise steps in buying products and making and packaging burgers and other menu items. Most advertising is handled at the corporate level, and a regional manager must approve any local advertising. Restaurants even have to follow prescribed schedules for facilities' maintenance and upgrades like floor polishing and parking lot cleaning.[7]

centralized organization
Top managers retain most decision-making rights for themselves.

Although Exxon-Mobil owns large reserves of natural gas, like this field in the former Soviet republic of Turkmenistan, it does not have much experience in the volatile market of natural gas, which is becoming increasingly valuable as an alternative to coal and oil. ExxonMobil is a highly centralized company, and experts are skeptical about its ability to decentralize authority to make the quick decisions that are needed in this market.

Decentralized Organizations

decentralized organization
Lower- and middle-level managers are allowed to make significant decisions.

As a company gets larger, more decisions must be made, and the company usually adopts a more decentralized pattern. In a **decentralized organization**, much decision-making authority is delegated to levels of management at various points below the top. The purpose of decentralization is to make a company more responsive to its environment by breaking the company into more manageable units, ranging from product lines to independent businesses. Reducing top-heavy bureaucracies is also a common goal. Jack Welch, former CEO of General Electric, is a long-time proponent of decentralized management. As he put it, "If you don't let managers make their own decisions, you're never going to be anything more than a one-person business." This logic also explains why cereal maker Kellogg Co. has been decentralizing. Top managers realize that to keep pace with today's eat-on-the-run lifestyles, lower level managers need more autonomy to make decisions and rush new products to market.[8]

At General Electric's Bromont, Quebec, plant, every effort has been made to involve employees in a wide range of decision making.[9] Traditional jobs like supervisor and foreman do not exist at the plant, and all hiring is done by committees made up of workers. Some workers spend only 65 percent of their time on production work; the other 35 percent is spent on training, planning, and in meetings. At Hymac Ltée., a Laval, Quebec, producer of pulp processing machinery, managers encourage employees to meet with customers to determine how Hymac can serve them more effectively.[10] Decentralization can cause some difficulties, as the Business Today box illustrates.

Tall and Flat Organizations

flat organizational structure
An organization with relatively few layers of management.

tall organizational structure
An organization with many layers of management.

Related to the concept of centralized or decentralized authority is the concept of tall or flat organizational structures. With relatively fewer layers of management, decentralized firms tend to have a **flat organizational structure** such as the one shown in Figure 7.4. In contrast, companies with centralized authority systems typically require multiple layers of management and thus have a **tall organizational structure**. The Canadian Forces is an example of such an organization. Because information, whether upward or downward bound, must pass through so many organizational layers, tall structures are prone to delays in information flow.

BUSINESS TODAY

Centralization and Decentralization at Home Depot

Home Depot was founded in the early 1980s by Bernie Marcus and Arthur Blank. The founders encouraged store managers to think for themselves and to do what was best for their store. Authority was decentralized. Marcus and Blank said that they hired people who were actually more suited for self-employment or for running their own business. Many of those people became store managers because they liked the freedom they were given to run their store as they saw fit.

Marcus and Blank even praised employees who behaved in outlandish ways. One classic example was a store manager who refunded a customer's money for a set of car tires, even though the store didn't even sell that product. The tires were then displayed in the store to remind managers that the customer was always right.

Marcus and Blank are no longer with the company, and the new CEO—Robert Nardelli—is moving the company toward a much more centralized structure. He emphasizes operating efficiencies, expense controls, and head office directives to store managers. He feels that operations were sometimes too loosely controlled under the founders (even Bernie Marcus agrees with that). Nardelli says he loves the entrepreneurial spirit, but that it has to be compliant more often.

The move to centralization can be seen most clearly in the purchasing area. Formerly, Home Depot had nine regional purchasing offices, and each one of them could buy a different array of products. At that time, Arthur Blank felt that this boosted sales because the people doing the purchasing in the various regions understood what was needed for their region. However, there were two problems with this approach. First, it reduced Home Depot's clout with suppliers because each region purchased much smaller quantities than a national purchasing office would have. Second, it was difficult to develop nationwide store displays because stores in different regions carried different products.

Nardelli resolved these problems by centralizing purchasing out of Atlanta, Georgia. The change has meant that Home Depot gets better terms from suppliers, which, in turn, increases Home Depot's margins.

Not surprisingly, when Nardelli embarked on his move toward centralization, there was resistance from employees who didn't like the change. Nardelli acknowledges that change often creates fear in employees, but he says that headquarters must know what is going on in the retail stores if the company hopes to be successful.

Nardelli also had to cope with employees who fondly remember the retired founders of the company. A number of managers left when Nardelli became CEO, and he asked some others to leave as well. Consultant Robert Oxley, who used to train Home Depot employees, says that things have changed and the "excitement" is gone from Home Depot.

To date, Nardelli's actions seem to be viewed as positive by industry observers, but the price of Home Depot stock has fallen more than 50 percent since he took over. The drop in the stock price has reduced employee morale because many employees received bonuses in the form of stock options. These options are now worth much less than they were before. Employees are also unhappy about Nardelli's $13.8 million compensation for 2002.

As organizations grow in size, it is both normal and necessary that they become at least somewhat taller. For instance, a small firm with only an owner-manager and a few employees is likely to have two layers—the owner-manager and the employees who report to that person. But as the firm grows, more layers will be needed. Born Information Services, for instance, is a small consulting firm created and run by Rick Born. At first, all employees reported to him. But when his firm grew to more than 20 people, he knew he needed help in supervising and coordinating projects. As a result, he added a layer of management consisting of what he called "staff managers" to serve as project coordinators. This move freed him up to seek new business clients.[11] Like other managers, however, Born must ensure that he has only the number of layers his firm needs. Too few layers can create chaos and inefficiency, while too many layers can create rigidity and bureaucracy.

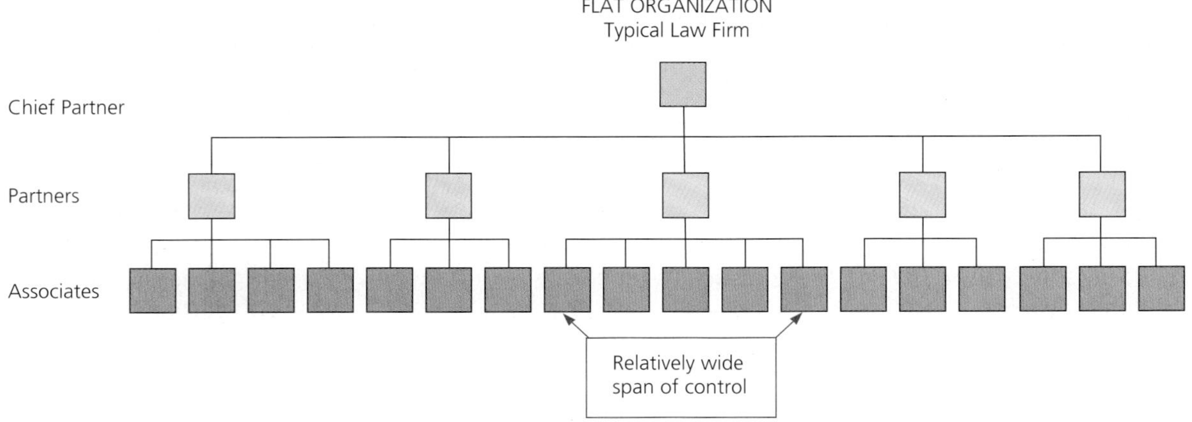

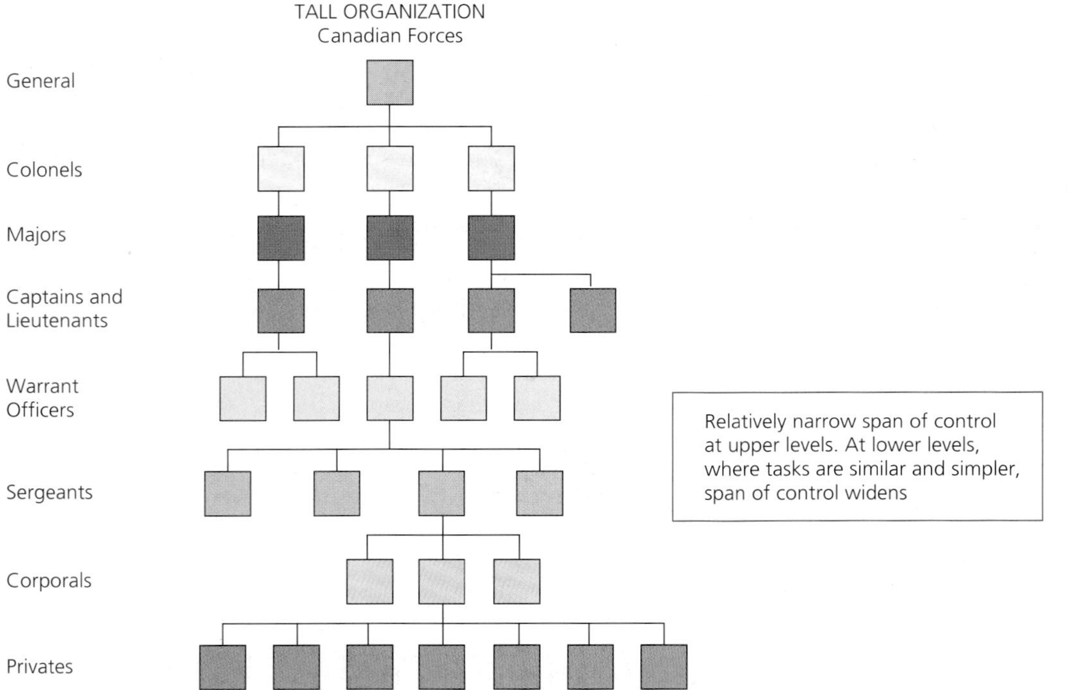

Figure 7.4
Organizational structure and span of control.

Span of Control

As you can see from Figure 7.4, the distribution of authority in an organization also affects the number of people who work for any individual manager. In a flat organizational structure, the number of people managed by one supervisor—the manager's **span of control**—is usually wide. In tall organizations, span of control tends to be relatively narrow. Span of control, however, depends on many factors. Employees' abilities and the supervisor's managerial skills help determine whether span of control is wide or narrow, as do the similarity and simplicity of those tasks performed under the manager's supervision and the extent to which they are interrelated.[12]

span of control
The number of people managed by one manager.

If lower level managers are given more decision-making authority, their supervisors will have less work to do because some of the decisions they previously made will be transferred to their subordinates. By the same token, these managers may then be able to oversee and coordinate the work of more subordinates, resulting in an increased span of control. At McDonald's, the creation of regional offices freed up time for the CEO, Jack Greenberg. In turn, reorganization allowed him to then create four new executive positions, one to oversee international expansion and the others to work with new restaurant partners.

Similarly, when several employees perform either the same simple task or a group of interrelated tasks, a wide span of control is possible and often desirable. For instance, because all the jobs are routine, one supervisor may well control an entire assembly line. Moreover, each task depends on another. If one station stops, everyone stops. Having one supervisor ensures that all stations receive equal attention and function equally well.

In contrast, when jobs are more diversified or prone to change, a narrow span of control is preferable. At Case Corp., farm tractors are made to order in five to six weeks. Farmers can select from among a wide array of options, including engines, tires, power trains, and even a CD player. A wide assortment of machines and processes is used to construct each tractor. Although workers are highly skilled operators of their assigned machines, each machine is different. In this kind of set-up, the complexities of each machine and the advanced skills needed by each operator mean that one supervisor can oversee only a small number of employees.[13]

Three Forms of Authority

In an organization, it must be clear who will have authority over whom. As individuals are delegated responsibility and authority in a firm, a complex web of interactions develops. These interactions may take one of three forms of authority: *line, staff,* or *committee and team*. In reality, like departmentalization, all three forms may be found in a given company, especially a large one.

Line Authority

Line authority is authority that flows up and down the chain of command (refer back to Figure 7.2 on page 228). Most companies rely heavily on **line departments**—departments directly linked to the production and sales of specific products. For example, Clark Equipment Corp. has a division that produces forklifts and small earthmovers. In this division, line departments include purchasing, materials handling, fabrication, painting, and assembly (all of which are directly linked to production) along with sales and distribution (both of which are directly linked to sales).

line authority

An organizational structure in which authority flows in a direct chain of command from the top of the company to the bottom.

line department

A department directly linked to the production and sales of a specific product.

Each line department is essential to an organization's success. Line employees are the "doers" and producers in a company. If any line department fails to complete its task, the company cannot sell and deliver finished goods. Thus, the authority delegated to line departments is important. A bad decision by the manager in one department can hold up production for an entire plant. For example, say that the painting department manager at Clark Equipment changes a paint application on a batch of forklifts, which then show signs of peeling paint. The batch will have to be repainted (and perhaps partially reassembled) before the machines can be shipped.

Staff Authority

Most companies also rely on **staff authority**. Staff authority is based on special expertise and usually involves counselling and advising line managers. Common **staff members** include specialists in areas such as law, accounting, and human resource management. A corporate attorney, for

staff authority

Authority that is based on expertise and that usually involves advising line managers.

staff members

Advisers and counsellors who aid line departments in making decisions but do not have the authority to make final decisions.

example, may be asked to advise the marketing department as it prepares a new contract with the firm's advertising agency. Legal staff, however, do not actually make decisions that affect how the marketing department does its job. Staff members, therefore, aid line departments in making decisions but do not have the authority to make final decisions.

Suppose, for example, that the fabrication department at Clark Equipment has an employee with a drinking problem. The manager of the department could consult a human resource staff expert for advice on handling the situation. The staff expert might suggest that the worker stay on the job but enter a counselling program. But if the line manager decides that the job is too dangerous to be handled by a person whose judgment is often impaired by alcohol, that decision will most likely prevail.

Typically, the separation between line authority and staff responsibility is clearly delineated. As Figure 7.5 shows, this separation is usually shown in organization charts by solid lines (line authority) and dotted lines (staff responsibility). It may help to understand this separation by remembering that while staff members generally provide services to management, line managers are directly involved in producing the firm's products.

Committee and Team Authority

committee and team authority
Authority granted to committees or work teams involved in a firm's daily operations.

Recently, more and more organizations have started to use **committee and team authority**—authority granted to committees or work teams that play central roles in the firm's daily operations. A committee, for example, may consist of top managers from several major areas. If the work of the committee is especially important, and if the committee will be working together for an extended time, the organization may even grant it special authority as a decision-making body that goes beyond the individual authority possessed by each of its members.

At the operating level, many firms today are also using *work teams*—groups of operating employees empowered to plan and organize their own work and to perform that work with a minimum of supervision. As with permanent committees, the organization will usually find it beneficial to grant special authority to work teams so that they may function more effectively.[14]

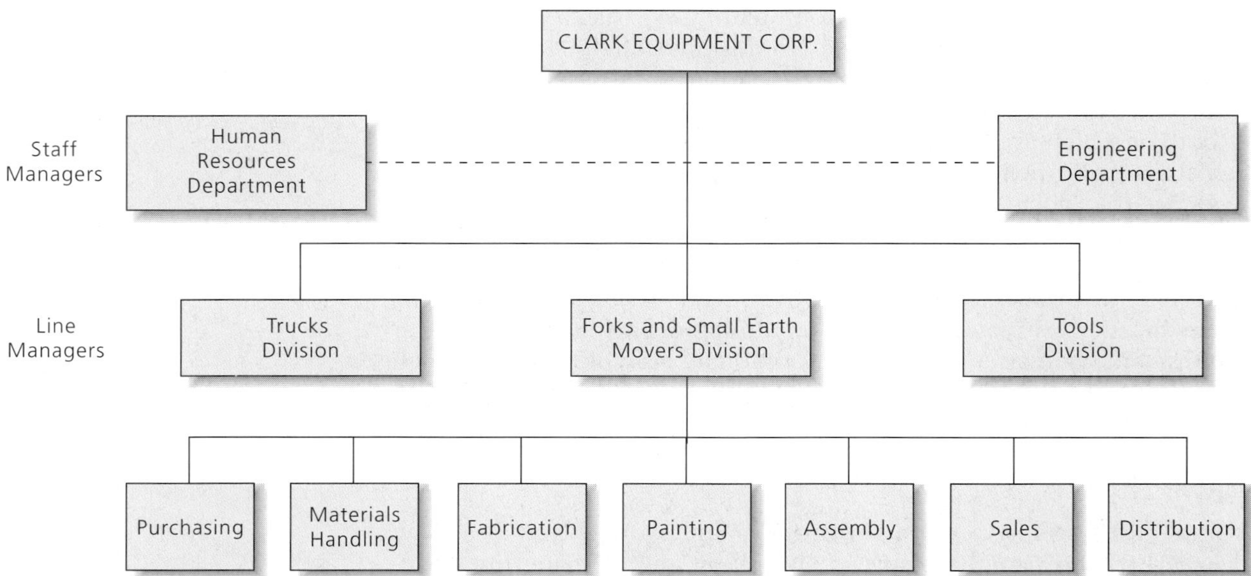

Figure 7.5
Line and staff organization: Clark Equipment Corp.

BASIC ORGANIZATIONAL STRUCTURES

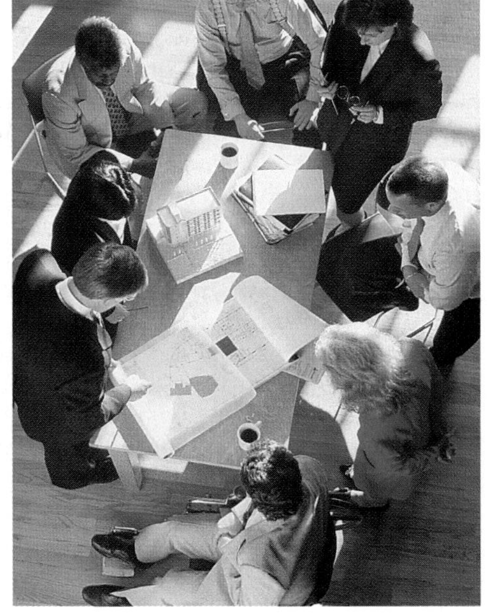

Business firms are increasingly using work teams and allowing groups of employees to plan and organize their own work with a minimum of supervision. This contributes to employee empowerment.

A glance at the organization charts of many organizations reveals what appears to be an infinite variety of structures. However, closer examination shows that it is possible to identify four basic forms: functional, divisional, project, and international. These structures are described below.

4. Explain the differences between *functional, divisional, project,* and *international organization structures,* and describe the most popular forms of organizational design.

The Functional Structure

The **functional structure** is the oldest and most commonly used. In the functional organization, the various units in the organization are formed based on the functions that must be carried out to reach organizational goals. The functional structure makes use of departmentalization by function. An example of a functional structure is shown in Figure 7.2 (see page 228). The advantages and disadvantages of the functional structure are summarized in Table 7.1.

functional structure
Various units are included in a group based on functions that need to be performed for the organization to reach its goals.

The Divisional Structure

The functional structure's disadvantages can make it inappropriate for some companies. Many companies have found that the **divisional structure** is more suited to their needs. The divisional structure divides the organization into several divisions, each of which operates as a semi-autonomous unit and profit centre. Divisions in organizations can be based on products, customers, or geography. In 2002, for example, Bell Canada created three divisions based on which customers were being served: consumers, small- and medium-sized businesses, and large corporations. This new structure replaces the former divisional structure that was geographically based.[15]

divisional structure
Divides the organization into divisions, each of which operates as a semi-autonomous unit.

Table 7.1 Advantages and Disadvantages of a Functional Structure

Advantages	Disadvantages
1. Focuses attention on the key activities that must be performed.	1. Conflicts may arise among the functional areas.
2. Expertise develops within each function.	2. No single function is responsible for overall organizational performance.
3. Employees have clearly defined career paths.	3. Employees in each functional area have a narrow view of the organization.
4. The structure is simple and easy to understand.	4. Decision making is slowed because functional areas must get approval from top management for a variety of decisions.
5. Eliminates duplication of activities.	5. Coordinating highly specialized functions may be difficult.

H.J. Heinz
www.heinz.com

H.J. Heinz, one of the world's largest food-processing companies, is divisionalized along seven product lines: food service (selling small packaged products such as mustard and relish to restaurants), infant foods, condiments (Heinz ketchup, steak sauce, and tomato sauce), Star-Kist tuna, pet foods, frozen foods, and miscellaneous products, including both new lines being test-marketed and soups, beans, and pasta products. Because of its divisional structure, Heinz can evaluate the performance of each division independently. Until recently, for example, Heinz also had a division for its Weight Watchers business. But because this business was performing poorly, the company sold the Weight Watchers classroom program and folded its line of frozen foods into its existing frozen-foods division.[16] Because divisions are relatively autonomous, a firm can take such action with minimal disruption to its remaining business operations.

Like Heinz, other divisionalized companies are free to buy, sell, create, and disband divisions without disrupting the rest of their operations. Divisions can maintain healthy competition among themselves by sponsoring separate advertising campaigns, fostering different corporate identities, and so forth. They can also share certain corporate-level resources (such as market research data). Of course, if too much control is delegated to divisional managers, corporate managers may lose touch with daily operations. Competition between divisions has also been known to become disruptive, and efforts of one division may be duplicated by those of another.

The advantages and disadvantages of the divisional structure are summarized in Table 7.2.

Project Organization

A typical line or line-staff organization is characterized by unchanging vertical authority relationships. It has such a set-up because the organization produces a product or service in a repetitive and predictable way. Procter & Gamble, for example, produces millions of tubes of Crest toothpaste each year using standardized production methods. The company has done this for years and intends to do so indefinitely.

But some organizations find themselves faced with new product opportunities or with projects that have a definite starting and end point. These organizations often use a project structure to deal with the uncertainty encountered in new situations. **Project organization** involves forming a team of specialists from different functional areas of the organization to work on a specific project.[17] A project structure may be temporary or permanent; if it is temporary, the project team disbands once the project is completed and team members return to their regular functional area or are assigned to a new project.

project organization
An organization that uses teams of specialists to complete specific projects.

Table 7.2 Advantages and Disadvantages of a Divisional Structure

Advantages	Disadvantages
1. Accommodates change and expansion.	1. Activities may be duplicated across divisions.
2. Increases accountability.	2. A lack of communication among divisions may occur.
3. Develops expertise in the various divisions.	3. Adding diverse divisions may blur the focus of the organization.
4. Encourages training for top management.	4. Company politics may affect the allocation of resources.

Project organization is used extensively by Canadian firms, for example, in the construction of hydroelectric generating stations like those developed by Hydro-Québec on La Grande River and by Manitoba Hydro on the Nelson River. Once the generating station is complete, it becomes part of the traditional structure of the utility. Project organization is also used at Genstar Shipyards Ltd. in Vancouver. Each ship that is built is treated as a project and supervised by a project manager; the project manager for a given ship is responsible for ensuring that the ship is completed on time and within budget.[18] Project organization has also proven useful for coordinating the many elements needed to extract oil from the tar sands. Project management is also used in other kinds of tasks, including construction, military weapons, aerospace, and health care delivery.[19]

Manitoba Hydro
www.hydro.mb.ca

A **matrix organization** is a variation of project structure in which the project manager and the regular line managers share authority. Ford, for example, used a matrix organization to design the Ford Thunderbird that was launched in 2001. A design team composed of people from engineering, marketing, operations, and finance was created to design the new car. During the time the team was working on the Thunderbird project, the engineering, marketing, operations, and finance experts reported primarily to the project manager, but the line managers of the departments they came from also had some say about what work they did. After the team's work was done, team members moved back to their permanent functional jobs.

matrix organization
A project structure in which the project manager and the regular line managers share authority until the project is concluded.

In other companies, the matrix organization is a semi-permanent fixture. Figure 7.6 shows how Martha Stewart Living Omnimedia Inc. has created a permanent matrix organization for its burgeoning lifestyle business. The company is organized broadly into media and merchandising groups, each of which has specific product and product groups. Layered on top of this structure are teams of lifestyle experts organized into groups such as cooking, crafts, weddings, and so forth. Although each group targets spe-

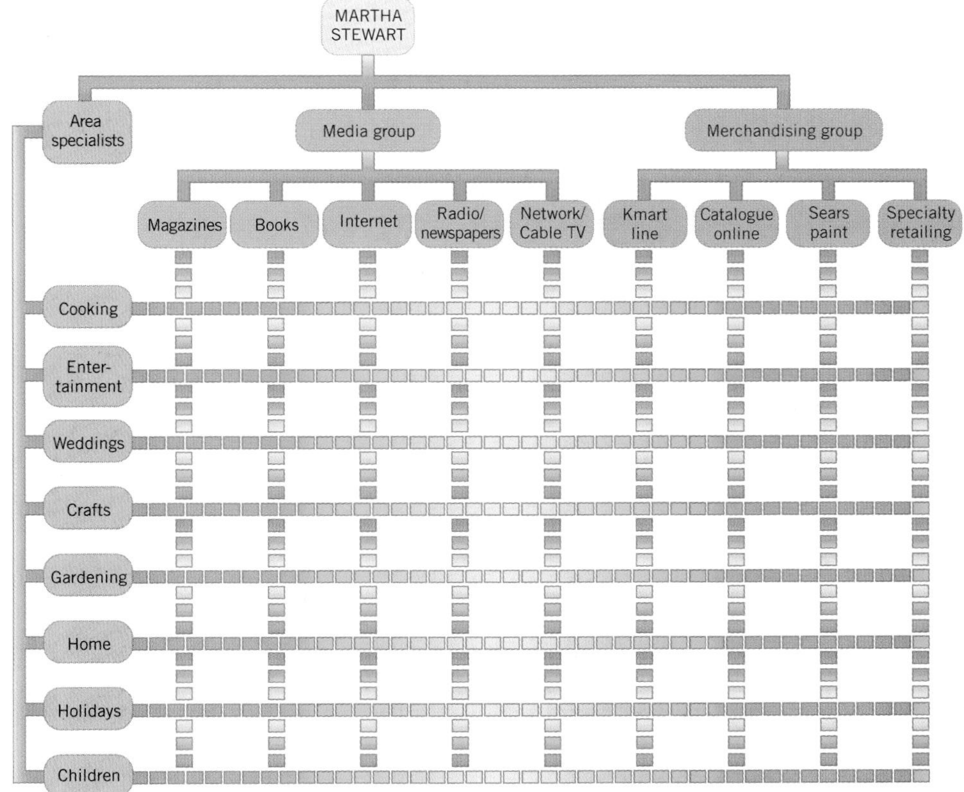

Figure 7.6
Matrix organization at Martha Stewart.

cific customer needs, they all work across all product groups. A wedding expert, for example, might contribute to an article on wedding planning for a Martha Stewart magazine, contribute a story idea for a Martha Stewart cable television program, and supply content for a Martha Stewart website. This same individual might also help select fabrics suitable for wedding gowns that are to be retailed.[20]

International Organization

international organizational structure

An organizational structure that is designed to help a company succeed in international markets. International departments, international divisions, or an integrated global organization are all variations of the international organizational structure.

As we saw in Chapter 4, many businesses today manufacture, purchase, and sell in the world market. Thus, several different **international organizational structures** have emerged. Moreover, as competition on a global scale becomes more complex, companies often find that they must experiment with the ways in which they respond.

For example, when Wal-Mart opened its first store outside the United States in 1992, it set up a special projects team to handle the logistics. As more stores were opened abroad in the mid-1990s, the firm created a small international department to handle overseas expansion. By 1999, however, international sales and expansion had become such a major part of Wal-Mart's operations that the firm created a separate international division headed up by a senior vice-president. And by 2002, international operations had become so important to Wal-Mart that the international division was further divided into geographic areas where the firm does business, such as Mexico and Europe.

Wal-Mart typifies the form of organization outlined in Figure 7.7. Other firms have also developed a wide range of approaches to international organization structure. The French food giant Danone Group, for instance, has three major product groups: dairy products (Danone yogourt), bottled water (Evian), and cookies (Pim's). Danone's structure does not differentiate internationally, but rather integrates global operations within each product group.[21]

Finally, some companies adopt a truly global structure in which they acquire resources (including capital), produce goods and services, engage in research and development, and sell products in whatever local market is appropriate, without any consideration of national boundaries. Until a few

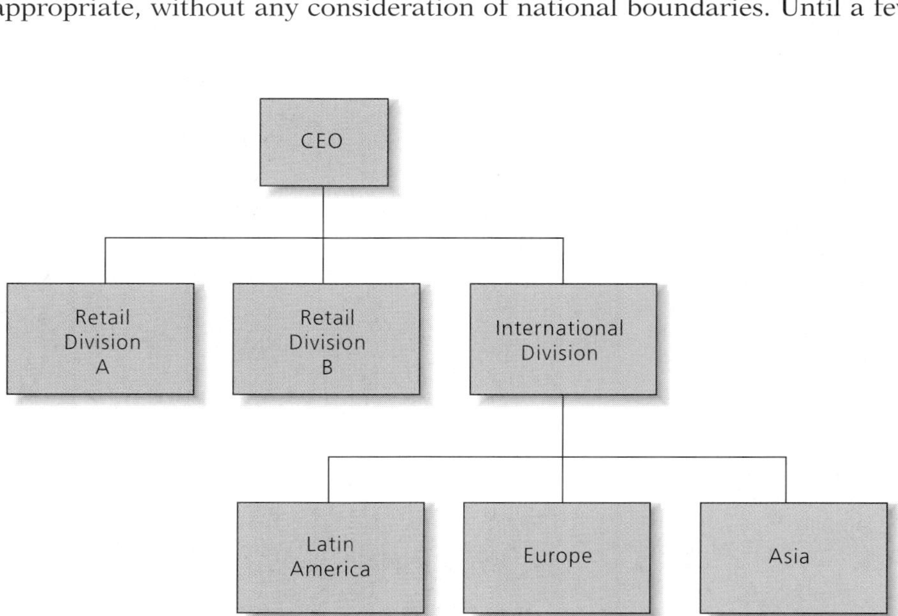

Figure 7.7
International division structure.

years ago, for example, General Electric kept its international business operations as separate divisions. Now, however, the company functions as one integrated global organization. GE businesses around the world connect and interact with each other constantly, and managers freely move back and forth among them. This integration is also reflected in the top management team: the head of its audit team is French, the head of quality control is Dutch, and a German runs one of GE's core business groups.[22]

Organizational Design for the Twenty-First Century

As the world grows increasingly complex and fast paced, organizations continue to seek new forms of organization that permit them to compete effectively. Among the most popular of these new forms are the *boundaryless organization*, the *team organization*, the *virtual organization*, and the *learning organization*.

Boundaryless Organization

The *boundaryless organization* is one in which traditional boundaries and structures are minimized or eliminated altogether. For example, General Electric's fluid organization structure, in which people, ideas, and information flow freely between businesses and business groups, approximates this concept. Similarly, as firms partner with their suppliers in more efficient ways, external boundaries disappear. Some of Wal-Mart's key suppliers are tied directly into the retailer's vaunted information system. As a result, when Wal-Mart distribution centres start running low on, say, Wrangler blue jeans, the manufacturer receives the information as soon as the retailer. Wrangler proceeds to manufacture new inventory and restock the distribution centre without Wal-Mart having to place a new order.

Team Organization

Team organization relies almost exclusively on project-type teams, with little or no underlying functional hierarchy. People "float" from project to project as dictated by their skills and the demands of those projects. At

As the term suggests, the boundaryless organization has erased certain boundaries. GE Power Systems, which sells electricity-generating turbines, uses the internet to eliminate a boundary that once separated its traditional functions from those of its customers. Using the web to connect with GE's turbine optimizer, any operator of a GE turbine can compare its performance with other turbines of the same model. GE will also calculate the long-term savings of a given improvement—another task that, in the pre-ebusiness era, would have been performed by the buyer-operator.

IT'S A WIRED WORLD

The Technology of Personal Contact

Some observers worry that recent advances in communications signal the end of face-to-face dialogue, human interaction, collaboration, and teamwork. Surprisingly, however, many companies are finding that technology actually enhances and extends traditional interactions. "There's an opportunity for a whole new level of business-performance improvements in the collaborative redesign of processes, using the internet," according to James A. Champy, chairman of consulting at Perot Systems.

Lockheed Martin uses a system of 90 web software tools to coordinate its $200 billion project for building the next generation of stealth fighter aircraft for the U.S. government. The manufacturer brings together 40 000 users, 80 subcontractors, and 187 locations around the world. Lockheed uses the web to exchange documents and designs and to monitor project progress. "We're getting the best people, applying the best designs, from wherever we need them," says Mark Peden, Lockheed information systems vice-president.

At General Motors, web collaboration helps engineers and parts suppliers collaborate on product design. Complex designs might involve 14 worldwide sites in addition to the dozens of partner firms that design components and subsystems. Saving time allows the engineers to complete three or four alternative designs, instead of just one, and often still finish weeks sooner than anticipated.

Prospective students at Yale University use an internet-based system to investigate the school, complete an application, and apply for financial aid. Admissions staff around the country share information about applicants, with online discussion and comments posted to documents. Yet admissions director James Stevens notifies every accepted applicant with a phone call. "[They'll] hear from me personally. It is very important to us for people to understand how personal the experience is here."

The Children's Hospital at Montefiore has integrated a facility-wide patient-information system. Patients and family members use smart cards for customized access to information about illness and treatment, for video games or movies on demand, and for internet access. "It's about the patient's ability to control [the] environment," says software designer Jeb Weisman. The intent, says chief designer David Rockwell, is "to provide information, insight, and a sense of wonder and delight." Patients and their families thus become participants in their own treatment.

The technology is helpful, but of course it doesn't manage itself. Paul R. Gudonis, chairman and CEO of Genuity Inc., says that while managers have made a good start in encouraging teams to use technology, "they've now found that it's going to take more effort off-line to integrate off-line and online processes to get the kind of changed behaviour and benefits that they're looking for." Jon Katzenbach, consultant and author of *The Discipline of Teams*, reminds managers about the enduring value of hands-on management and face-to-face meetings. "Without meaningful personal interaction and doing 'real' work together," he warns, "it's hard to build understanding and accountability."

Cypress Semiconductor, units or groups that become large are simply split into smaller units. Not surprisingly, the organization is composed entirely of small units. This strategy allows each unit to change direction, explore new ideas, and try new methods without having to deal with a rigid bureaucratic superstructure. Although few large organizations have actually reached this level of adaptability, Apple Computer and Xerox are among those moving toward it.

Virtual Organization

Closely related to the team organization is the virtual organization. A *virtual organization* has little or no formal structure. Typically, it has only a handful of permanent employees, a very small staff, and a modest administrative facility. As the needs of the organization change, its managers bring in temporary workers, lease facilities, and outsource basic support services to meet the demands of each unique situation. As the situation changes, the temporary workforce changes in parallel, with some people leaving the organization and others entering it. Facilities and subcontracted services also change. In other words, the virtual organization exists only in response to its own needs.

Global Research Consortium (GRC) is a virtual organization that offers research and consulting services to firms doing business in Asia. As clients request various services, GRC's staff of three permanent employees subcontracts the work to an appropriate set of several dozen independent consultants and/or researchers with whom it has relationships. At any given time, therefore, GRC may have several projects underway and 20 or 30 people working on various projects. As the projects change, so too does the composition of the organization. Figure 7.8 illustrates a hypothetical virtual organization.

Learning Organization

The so-called *learning organization* works to integrate continuous improvement with continuous employee learning and development. Specifically, a learning organization works to facilitate the lifelong learning and personal development of all of its employees while continually transforming itself to respond to changing demands and needs.

While managers might approach the concept of a learning organization from a variety of perspectives, the most frequent goals are improved quality, continuous improvement, and performance measurement. The idea is that the most consistent and logical strategy for achieving continuous improvement is constantly upgrading employee talent, skill, and knowledge. For example, if each employee in an organization learns one new thing each day and can translate that knowledge into work-related practice, continuous improvement will logically follow. Indeed, organizations that wholeheartedly embrace this approach believe that only through constant employee learning can continuous improvement really occur.

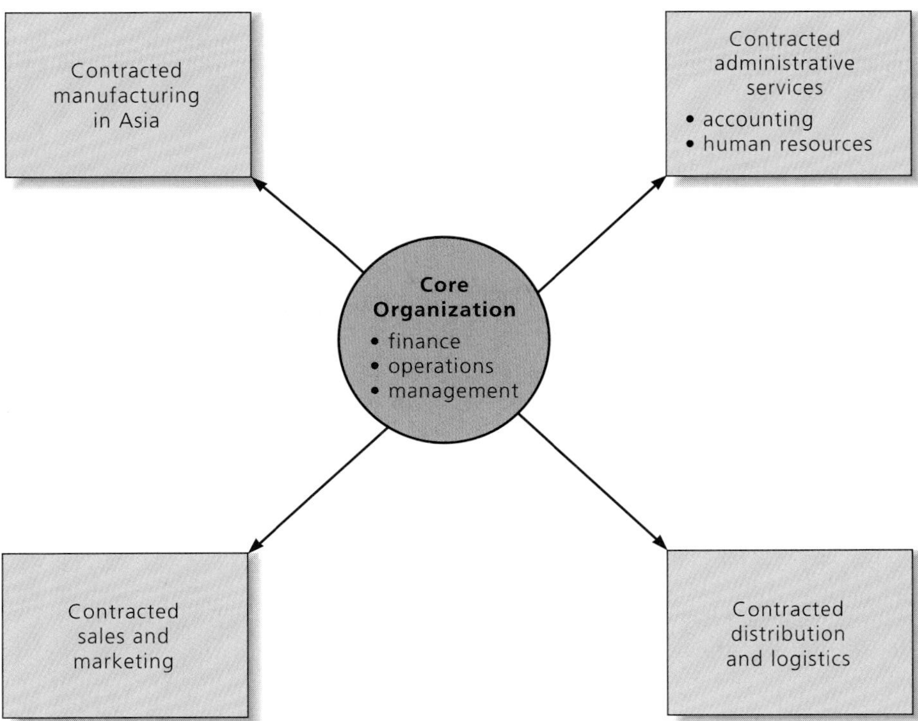

Figure 7.8
A virtual organization.

In recent years, many different organizations have implemented this approach on various levels. Shell Oil Co., for example, recently purchased an executive conference centre called the Shell Learning Center. The facility boasts state-of-the-art classrooms and instructional technology, lodging facilities, a restaurant, and recreational amenities, such as a golf course, swimming pool, and tennis courts. Line managers at the firm rotate through the centre and serve as teaching faculty. Teaching assignments last anywhere from a few days to several months. At the same time, all Shell employees routinely attend training programs, seminars, and related activities, all the while gathering the latest information they need to contribute more effectively to the firm. Recent seminar topics have included time management, balancing work and family demands, and international trade theory.

THE INFORMAL ORGANIZATION

5. Describe the *informal organization* and discuss *intrapreneuring*.

Much of our discussion so far has focused on the organization's *formal* structure—its "official" arrangement of jobs and job relationships. In reality, however, all organizations also have another dimension—an informal organization within which people do their jobs in different ways and interact with other people in ways that do not follow formal lines of communication. The Exercising Your Ethics box presents an interesting situation that illustrates the informal organization.

Formal Versus Informal Organizational Systems

The formal organization of a business is the part that can be seen and represented in chart form. The structure of a company, however, is by no means limited to the organization chart and the formal assignment of authority. Frequently, the **informal organization**—everyday social interactions among employees that transcend formal jobs and job interrelationships—effectively alters a company's formal structure. Indeed, this level of organization is sometimes just as powerful, if not more powerful, than the formal structure.

informal organization
A network of personal interactions and relationships among employees unrelated to the firm's formal authority structure.

EXERCISING YOUR ETHICS

Minding Your Own Business

The Situation

Assume that you have recently gone to work for a large high-tech company. You have discovered an interesting arrangement in which one of your co-workers is engaging. Specifically, he blocks his schedule for the hour between 11:00 a.m. and 12:00 noon each day and does not take a lunch break. During this one-hour interval, he is actually running his own real estate business.

The Dilemma

You recently asked him how he manages to pull this off. "Well," he responded, "the boss and I never talked about it, but she knows what's going on. They know they can't replace me, and I always get my work done. I don't use any company resources. So, what's the harm?" Interestingly, you also have a business opportunity that could be pursued in the same way.

Questions for Discussion

1. What are the ethical issues in this situation?
2. What do you think most people would do in this situation?
3. What would you do in this situation?

On the negative side, the informal organization can reinforce office politics that put the interests of individuals ahead of those of the firm. Likewise, a great deal of harm can be caused by distorted or inaccurate information communicated without management input or review. For example, if the informal organization is generating false information about impending layoffs, valuable employees may act quickly (and unnecessarily) to seek other employment. Among the more important elements of the informal organization are *informal groups* and the *organizational grapevine*.

Informal Groups

Informal groups are simply groups of people who decide to interact among themselves. They may be people who work together in a formal sense or who simply get together for lunch, during breaks, or after work. They may talk about business, the boss, or non-work-related topics such as families, movies, or sports. For example, at the New York Metropolitan Opera, musicians and singers play poker during the intermissions. Most pots are in the $30 to $40 range. Luciano Pavarotti, the famed tenor, once played and lost big.

The impact of informal groups on the organization may be positive (if they work together to support the organization), negative (if they work together in ways that run counter to the organization's interests), or neutral (if what they do is unrelated to the organization).

Organizational Grapevine

The **grapevine** is an informal communication network that can run through an entire organization.[23] Grapevines are found in all organizations except the very smallest, but they do not always follow the same patterns as formal channels of authority and communication, nor do they necessarily coincide with them. The internet is a worldwide grapevine. When people gather around the water cooler or on the golf course to exchange gossip and pass on information, they have names and faces. But with the internet, you may not know whom you are talking to and how reliable the person is who is providing the information.[24]

grapevine
An informal communications network that carries gossip and other information throughout an organization.

Because the grapevine typically passes information orally, messages often become distorted in the process. But most office gossip has at least some kernel of truth to it. Those passing on news may deliberately alter it, either to advance their own goals or to submarine someone else's chances. Listening to and passing on information damaging to someone's reputation can backfire, harming your credibility and making you a target for similar gossip.

In general, the more detailed the information, the less likely it is to be true. Likewise, beware the hush-hush "don't quote me on this" rumour. (Cynics claim that the better the news, the less likely it is to be true, too.) The higher the source, the greater the likelihood that the grapevine has the real story. Don't reject information from "lower" sources, however. Many an executive assistant can provide valuable insights into a corporation's plans.

Attempts to eliminate the grapevine are fruitless, but managers do have some control over it. By maintaining open channels of communication and responding vigorously to inaccurate information, they can minimize the damage the grapevine can do. In fact, the grapevine can actually be an asset. By getting to know the key people in the grapevine, for example, the manager can partially control the information they receive and use the grapevine to determine employee reactions to new ideas (e.g., a change in human resource policies or benefit packages). The manager can also receive valuable information from the grapevine and use it to improve decision making.

Wise managers will tune in to the grapevine's message because it is often a corporate early warning system. Ignoring this valuable source of information can cause managers to be the last to know that they are about to get a

The grapevine is a powerful communications network in most organizations. These workers may be talking about any number of things—an upcoming deadline on an important project, tonight's football game, the stock market, rumours about an impending takeover, gossip about forthcoming promotions, or the weather.

new boss, or that they have a potentially fatal image problem. The grapevine is not infallible, however. In addition to miscommunication and attempts by some people to manipulate it for their own ends, it may carry rumours with absolutely no basis in fact. Such rumours are most common when there is a complete lack of information. Apparently, human nature abhors such a vacuum and fills it. Baseless rumours can be very hard to kill, however.

Intrapreneuring

Sometimes organizations actually take steps to encourage the informal organization. They do so for a variety of reasons, two of which we have already discussed. First, most experienced managers recognize that the informal organization exists whether they want it or not. Second, many managers know how to use the informal organization to reinforce the formal organization. Perhaps more important, however, the energy of the informal organization can be harnessed to improve productivity.

intrapreneuring
The process of creating and maintaining the innovation and flexibility of a small-business environment within the confines of a large organization.

Many firms, including Compaq Computer, Rubbermaid, 3M, and Xerox, are supporting a process called **intrapreneuring**: creating and maintaining the innovation and flexibility of a small-business environment within the confines of a large, bureaucratic structure. The concept is basically sound. Historically, most innovations have come from individuals in small businesses (see Chapter 3). As businesses increase in size, however, innovation and creativity tend to become casualties in the battle for higher sales and profits. In some large companies, new ideas are even discouraged, and champions of innovation have been stalled in mid-career.

Compaq, which is now part of Hewlett-Packard, is an excellent example of how intrapreneuring works to counteract this trend. The firm has one major division called the New Business Group. When a manager or engineer has an idea for a new product or product application, he or she takes it to the New Business Group and "sells" it. The managers in the group are then encouraged to help the innovator develop the idea for field testing. If the product takes off and does well, it is then spun off into its own business group or division. If it doesn't do as well as hoped, it may be maintained as part of the New Business Group or phased out.

SUMMARY OF LEARNING OBJECTIVES

1. **Discuss the elements that influence a firm's *organizational structure*.** Every business needs structure to operate. *Organizational structure* varies according to a firm's mission, purpose, and strategy. Size, technology, and changes in environmental circumstances also influence structure. In general, while all organizations have the same basic elements, each develops the structure that contributes to the most efficient operations.

2. **Describe *specialization* and *departmentalization* as the building blocks of organizational structure.** The building blocks of organizational structure are *job specialization* and *departmentalization*. As a firm grows, it usually has a greater need for people to perform specialized tasks (specialization). It also has a greater need to group types of work into logical units (departmentalization). Common forms of departmentalization are *customer, product, process, geographic,* and *functional*. Large businesses often use more than one form of departmentalization.

3. **Distinguish between *responsibility* and *authority* and explain the differences in decision making in *centralized* and *decentralized organizations*.** *Responsibility* is the duty to perform a task; *authority* is the power to make the decisions necessary to complete tasks. *Delegation* begins when a manager assigns a task to a subordinate; *accountability* means that the subordinate must complete the task. *Span of control* refers to the number of people who work for any individual manager. The more people supervised by a manager, the wider his or her span of control. Wide spans are usually desirable when employees perform simple or unrelated tasks. When jobs are diversified or prone to change, a narrower span is generally preferable.

   In a *centralized organization*, only a few individuals in top management have real decision-making authority. In a *decentralized organization*, much authority is delegated to lower-level management. Where both *line* and *line-and-staff systems* are involved, *line departments* generally have authority to make decisions while *staff departments* have a responsibility to advise. A relatively new concept, *committee and team authority*, empowers committees or work teams involved in a firm's daily operations.

4. **Explain the differences between *functional, divisional, project,* and *international organization structures*, and describe the most popular new forms of organizational design.** In a *functional organization*, authority is usually distributed among such basic functions as marketing and finance. In a *divisional organization*, the various divisions of a larger company, which may be related or unrelated, operate in a relatively autonomous fashion. In *project organization*, in which individuals report to more than one manager, a company creates teams to address specific problems or to conduct specific projects. A company that has divisions in many countries may require an additional level of *international organization* to coordinate those operations. Four of the most popular new forms of organizational design are (a) boundaryless organizations (traditional boundaries and structures are minimized or eliminated), (b) team organizations (relies on project-type teams, with little or no functional hierarchy), (c) virtual organizations (has little formal struc-

ture and only a handful of permanent employees, a small staff, and a modest administrative facility), and (d) learning organizations (work to facilitate employees' lifelong learning and personal development while transforming the organization to meet changing demands and needs).

5. **Define the *informal organization* and discuss *intrapreneuring*.** The *informal organization* consists of the everyday social interactions among employees that transcend formal jobs and job interrelationships. To foster innovation and flexibility, some large companies encourage *intrapreneuring*—creating and maintaining the innovation and flexibility of a small business environment within the confines of a large bureaucratic structure.

KEY TERMS

accountability, 232
authority, 232
centralized organization, 233
chain of command, 227
committee and team authority, 238
customer departmentalization, 230
decentralized organization, 234
delegation, 232
departmentalization, 229
divisional structure, 239
flat organizational structure, 234
functional departmentalization, 231
functional structure, 239
geographic departmentalization, 231
grapevine, 247
informal organization, 246
international organizational structures, 242
intrapreneuring, 248
job specialization, 228
line authority, 237
line department, 237
matrix organization, 241
organization chart, 227
organizational structure, 226
process departmentalization, 230
product departmentalization, 230
profit centre, 229
project organization, 240
responsibility, 232
span of control, 236
staff authority, 237
staff members, 237
tall organizational structure, 234

QUESTIONS AND EXERCISES

Questions for Review

1. What is an organization chart? What purpose does it serve?
2. Explain the significance of size as it relates to organizational structure. Describe the changes that are likely to occur as an organization grows.
3. What is the difference between responsibility and authority?
4. Why do some managers have difficulties in delegating authority? Why does this problem tend to plague smaller businesses?
5. Why is a company's informal organization important?

Questions for Analysis

6. Draw up an organization chart for your college or university.
7. Describe a hypothetical organizational structure for a small printing firm. Describe changes that might be necessary as the business grows.
8. Compare and contrast the matrix and divisional approaches to organizational structure. How would you feel personally about working in a matrix organization in which you were assigned simultaneously to multiple units or groups?

Application Exercises

9. Interview the manager of a local service business—a fast-food restaurant. What types of tasks does this manager typically delegate? Is the appropriate authority also delegated in each case?
10. Using books, magazines, or personal interviews, identify a person who has succeeded as an intrapreneur. In what ways did the structure of the intrapreneur's company help this individual succeed? In what ways did the structure pose problems?

BUILDING YOUR BUSINESS SKILLS

Getting with the Program

Goal

To encourage students to understand the relationship between organizational structure and a company's ability to attract and keep valued employees.

Situation

You are the founder of a small but growing high-technology company that develops new computer software. With your current workload and new contracts in the pipeline, your business is thriving except for one problem: You cannot find computer programmers for product development. Worse yet, current staff members are being lured away by other high-tech firms. After suffering a particularly discouraging personnel raid in which competitors captured three of your most valued employees, you schedule a meeting with your director of human resources to plan organizational changes designed to encourage worker loyalty. You already pay top dollar, but the continuing exodus tells you that programmers are looking for something more.

Method

Working with three or four classmates, identify some ways in which specific organizational changes might improve the working environment and encourage employee loyalty. As you analyze the following factors, ask yourself the obvious question: If I were a programmer, what organizational changes would encourage me to stay?

Level of job specialization. With many programmers describing their jobs as tedious because of the focus on detail in a narrow work area, what changes, if any, would you make in job specialization? Right now, for instance, few of your programmers have any say in product design.

Decision-making hierarchy. What decision-making authority would encourage people to stay? Is expanding employee authority likely to work better in a centralized or decentralized organization?

Team authority. Can team empowerment make a difference? Taking the point of view of the worker, describe the ideal team.

Intrapreneuring. What can your company do to encourage and reward innovation?

Follow-Up Questions

1. With the average computer programmer earning nearly $70 000, and with all competitive firms paying top dollar, why might organizational issues be critical in determining employee loyalty?
2. If you were a programmer, what organizational factors would make a difference to you? Why?
3. As the company founder, how willing would you be to make major organizational changes in light of the shortage of qualified programmers?

MASTERING BUSINESS ESSENTIALS

Episode 7 describes the formation of a work team given responsibility for making an extremely important presentation. It shows why organizations sometimes find it beneficial to delegate responsibility and authority for special projects to committees or teams. *This episode illustrates the issues that arise when managers must be flexible within an existing organizational structure.*

CRAFTING YOUR BUSINESS PLAN

Doctoring the Organization

The Purpose of the Assignment

1. To provide an example that illustrates ways in which organizational options can be presented in a business plan, in the framework of the Business PlanPro (BPP) software package.
2. To demonstrate how three chapter topics—organization structure, departmentalization, and authority and responsibility—can be integrated as components in the BPP planning environment.

Assignment

After reading Chapter 7 in the textbook, open the BPP software and look for information about organizational structure, departmentalization, and authority and responsibility as they apply to a sample firm, Medquip Inc. To find Medquip Inc., do the following:

Open the Business PlanPro. If it asks if you want to "create a new business plan" or "open an existing plan," select "create a new business plan" (even though you are not going to create a plan at this time). You will then be taken to the Business PlanPro EasyPlan Wizard. On the screen, click on the option entitled **Research It**. You will then be presented with a new list of options, including Sample Plan Browser. After clicking on the **Sample Plan Browser**, go down the alphabetical list of sample plans and double-click on **Medical Equipment Development—Instruments**, which is the location for Medquip Inc. The screen you are looking at is the introduction page for Medquip's business plan. Next, scroll down until you reach the **Table of Contents** for the Medquip business plan.

Now respond to the following questions:

1. Construct an organization chart for Medquip Inc. [Sites to see in BPP for this item: On the Table of Contents page, click on each of the following in turn: **6.0 Management Summary, 6.1 Organizational Structure, 6.2 Management Team,** and **6.4 Personnel Plan**, including **Table: Personnel**.]
2. Explain how Medquip's organizational structure is set up to take advantage of its competitor's weakness in product innovation. [Sites to see in BPP: On the Table of Contents page, click on **4.2.4 Main Competitors**.]
3. Which type of departmentalization—customer, product, functional, or process—does Medquip use? Give examples from Medquip's business plan to support your answer.
4. For each job position at Medquip, how clearly are authority and responsibility delineated in the business plan?

VIDEO EXERCISE

Juicing Up the Organization: Nantucket Nectars

Learning Objectives

The purpose of this video is to help you:

1. Recognize how growth affects an organization's structure.
2. Discuss the reasons why businesses departmentalize.
3. Understand how flat organizations operate.

Synopsis

Tom Scott and Tom First founded Nantucket Nectars in 1989 when they had an idea for a peach drink. In the early days, the two ran the entire operation from their boat. Now, Nantucket Nectars has more than 130 employees split between headquarters in Cambridge, Massachusetts, and several field offices. As a result, management has developed a more formal structure, and the company relies on cross-functional teams to handle special projects, such as the implementation of new accounting software. This and other strategies have helped Nantucket Nectars successfully manage rapid growth.

Discussion Questions

1. *For analysis:* What type of organization is in place at Nantucket Nectars?
2. *For analysis:* How would you describe the top-level span of management at Nantucket Nectars?

3. *For application:* Nantucket Nectars may need to change its organizational structure as it expands into new products and new markets. Under what circumstances might some form of divisional organization be appropriate?
4. *For application:* Assume that Nantucket Nectars is purchasing a well-established beverage company with a tall structure stressing top-down control. What are some of the problems that management might face in integrating the acquired firm into the existing organizational structure of Nantucket Nectars?
5. *For debate:* Assume that someone who is newly promoted into a management position at Nantucket Nectars cannot adjust to the idea of delegating work to lower level employees. Should this new manager be demoted? Support your chosen position.

Online Exploration

Visit the Nantucket Nectars site at **www.juiceguys.com** and follow the links about the company and its products. Then use Hoover's Online at **www.hoovers.com** to search for the latest news about the company, which is formally known as Nantucket Allserve. Has a larger company acquired it, or has it acquired one or more smaller firms? What are the implications for the chain of command and decision-making and organizational structure of Nantucket Nectars?

EXPLORING THE NET

Organizing AOL

In this chapter, we've introduced some of the many ways in which businesses are organized and shown how specialization and departmentalization affect organizational structure. We've also seen that its organization plays a large part in establishing a firm's procedures for decision making.

Although few companies disclose the details of their business processes, we can usually find some information about basic structure on their websites. AOL is one example. Let's explore AOL's corporate website at **www.corp.aol.com**. You probably know that AOL is the world leader in interactive and ecommerce services, web brands, and internet technologies. Its goal is to build a global medium as central to people's lives as the telephone or television. Founded in 1985, AOL also operates some of the most popular services on the web, including MapQuest, AOL Instant Messenger, and AOL Moviefone, and is now a part of the world's largest communications company, Time Warner. AOL's home page divides its coverage of the company into the following categories:

Who We Are
Press Releases
Careers
Member Benefits
Help 24/7

We'll start at the home page (don't confuse this page with the home page for AOL's internet service). First click on **AOL Time Warner** at the top of the page and then select **Companies**.

1. Where does AOL appear to fit into the structure of its parent company, Time Warner?
2. Look carefully at the way Time Warner is organized. Based on this webpage, what can you infer about the company's organizational structure?

Now return to the AOL corporate home page (you must return to the **Companies** page first, choose **America Online**, and then select **Company Website**). Click on **Who We Are** and go to the **Who's Who** page:

3. What kind of organizational structure do you think is revealed by this list of AOL executives?
4. Find the Chief Marketing Officer and click on his or her name. What can you deduce about this manager's levels of responsibility and authority and span of control?

Return to **Who's Who** and compare the list of executives with the positions listed under **Who We Are, AOL Brands, Products and Services**:

5. How do you think executive areas of responsibility might differ in these two groups?

Concluding Case 7-1

A Supersonic Project Gets Off the Ground

Lockheed Martin (**www.lockheedmartin.com**) has been a major defence contractor for a long time. But while it's had its share of government contracts, it has all too often played second fiddle to competitors such as Boeing and Northrop Grumman. All that changed on October 21, 2001, a truly red-letter day for Lockheed and for Tom Burbage, aeronautics engineer, executive vice president, and head of the firm's Joint Strike Fighter program.

On that day, the Department of Defense chose Lockheed over rivals Boeing and McDonnell Douglas to develop and manufacture its new Joint Strike Fighter (JSF) jet. Lockheed immediately received $19 billion to begin design, and the 6000-aircraft, 40-year contract should ultimately be worth as much as $200 billion. The contract made Lockheed the leading maker of fighter jets and main supplier of jet aircraft for the U.S. Air Force, Navy, and Marines, as well as for the Royal Air Force and Royal Navy of England.

How did a firm that has long been regarded as an industry also-ran come to win this highly lucrative defence contract? It might have something to do with the attitude expressed by Air Force acquisition chief Darleen Druyun: "This competition," explained Druyun, "is not about an airplane. It's about a management team." All three contract bidders boasted the excellent technical skills needed to manufacture an acceptable product. But the Pentagon was looking for management experience needed to coordinate an immensely costly and complex project.

Perhaps the key to Lockheed's victory was naming Burbage to head the program. Burbage, in turn, credits his time as a Navy test pilot with teaching him leadership and management skills. As a team commander on board an aircraft carrier he was known for flying top performing sailors to Italy for a weekend jaunt. His crew set numerous performance records.

"...You can build a high-performing team in some pretty austere environments," says Burbage. "But first, you've got to take care of your people. And second, you've got to understand the difference between the carrot and the stick—and in my view, the former is a lot more useful than the latter. In the end, I stopped trying to motivate people. I learned that if you recognize and reward them, people will motivate themselves."

One problem that Burbage encountered almost immediately was a rift in Lockheed ranks. Two large and powerful divisions were competing for control of the project. "Lockheed wasn't known for pulling teams together," says a high-ranking manager at one of Lockheed's project partners. From the outset Burbage had to work tirelessly to get different units of his own company to adopt the idea of teamwork.

Meanwhile, another manager at Lockheed, Harry Blot, seeing that Lockheed lacked some of the skills needed to complete the project, recommended that the firm partner with rivals BAE Systems and Northrop Grumman. At first, competitors were concerned. "Lockheed and Northrop have battled each other for 60 years," says Northrop Manager Martin McLaughlin. "At the time, I couldn't believe it: We're supposed to partner with these guys?" Representatives from the three firms met, and according to Taylor, "We expected the discussions to revolve around how to divide the work. But as it turned out, Lockheed was more interested in how we'd build a relationship." In fact, Lockheed put its money where its corporate mouth was by making the unheard-of decision to grant Northrop and BAE 30 percent financial and strategic shares in the program—effectively promoting them from subcontractors to equal partners.

Throughout the project development process, Lockheed maintained a sharp focus on the needs of its customers, including the armed forces of the United States and United Kingdom. The U.S. Navy would be the biggest buyer, but the Marines were more assertive and had the most political and military influence. When the Marines demanded that the JFS jet be able to make vertical landings on smaller ships, Lockheed made that one of its top priorities. Designing a vertical-lift system for such a large jet had never been done, and when it hit a snag, engineers worked around the clock for weeks to solve the problem.

Burbage's team also anticipated and planned strategies for addressing future problems. Managers from the three partner firms worked together to create an extensive list of lessons learned about building modern aircraft. In a technique that Burbage dubbed the "premortem," they compared the list with their 10-year schedule to identify high-risk points. Solutions for these high-risk points are already being worked out, years before they will be implemented. Preplanning gives the team confidence in meeting its deadlines, which are critical to the JSF program. "If you can't control your schedule," explains Burbage, "the implication is that you can't control costs. And if you can't control costs, you won't keep the [military] services interested in funding your program."

Lockheed is on track to reach its goal of a flying prototype by 2005. This accomplishment, while meaningful, is even more extraordinary in light of the challenges that had to be overcome to reach it. Loren Thompson, a defence analyst at the Lexington Institute, explains it best: "The Lockheed guys were like the patient who undergoes heart surgery while running for his life. They had to fix themselves in the midst of the biggest battle they'd ever been in."

Questions for Discussion

1. Describe the basic structural components at Lockheed Martin that are most relevant to the JSF project.
2. What role does specialization play at Lockheed Martin?
3. What kinds of authority are reflected in this case?
4. What kind of organizational structure does Lockheed Martin seem to have?
5. What role did the informal organization play in Lockheed's successful bid for the contract? ◆

Concluding Case 7-2

Jersak Holdings

Vaclav Jersak was born in Prague, Czechoslovakia, in 1930. His family had long been active in the retail trade in that city. The Jersak family was very close, but the 1930s and 1940s were a time of great turbulence in central Europe. In 1938, Hitler's troops invaded Czechoslovakia and five years of war followed. After the war, Czechoslovakia came under the influence of the Soviet Union, and capitalistic ventures that had been such an integral part of the Jersak family were severely restricted. By the early 1960s, there were some hints of a return to a more capitalistic economy. To Jersak's dismay, these were snuffed out by the Soviet Union's invasion of Czechoslovakia in 1968.

The invasion was the last straw for Jersak, who had felt for some years that the environment for private business activity was very poor. At age 38, he decided to leave Czechoslovakia for a better life in Canada. He arrived in Toronto in December 1968, determined to apply his entrepreneurial talents in a more promising business environment. Jersak quickly discovered the freedom that entrepreneurs had in Canada. He started a small gas station, and over the next three years he opened several more. In 1971, he purchased a franchise of a major fast-food outlet, and by 1977 he owned four fast-food restaurants. His entrepreneurial instincts led him into a wide variety of business operations after that. From 1977 to 1991, he expanded his activity into the manufacture of auto parts, microcomputers, textiles, and office furniture. He purchased five franchises of a retail auto parts store, two automobile dealerships, and a carpet business that sells to both residential and commercial users. A mining company, a soft drink bottling plant, and a five-store chain of shoe stores are also part of Jersak Holdings Ltd.

As each new business venture was added, Jersak hired a person to manage the operating company. He also added individuals with expertise in accounting, finance, marketing, and production in his head office. Currently, Jersak Holdings Ltd. contains 17 operating companies, each headed by a manager (see Figure 7.9).

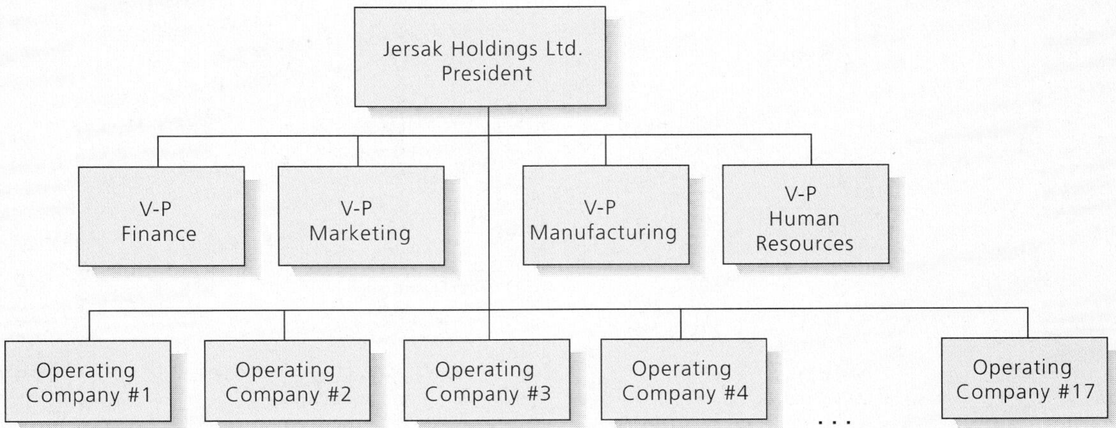

Figure 7.9
Organization of Jersak Holdings Ltd.

Employment ranges from five to ten people in each company. In 2003, sales totalled $37 million and profits were $4.7 million.

Head office staff make most of the strategic decisions in the firm. Jersak and the other top executives have frequent informal meetings to discuss matters of importance to the firm. Discussions usually continue until a consensus is reached on a course of action. The operating managers are expected to put into practice the strategic plans that are made at head office.

Vaclav Jersak is now 73. As he looks back on the last 35 years, he feels a great sense of satisfaction that he has accomplished so much. He has been thinking that the top management group operates smoothly because the people have worked together for many years. But he feels that areas of authority should be more clearly defined so that when changes occur in top management because of retirements, the new people will know exactly what they are responsible for.

Some of Jersak's business acquaintances are of the view that he should delegate considerably more authority to the managers of the operating companies. In effect, they recommend that he turn these operating managers into presidents of their own firms, each of them being responsible for making a profit in their particular enterprise. His acquaintances point out that giving the managers of the operating companies this level of responsibility will motivate them to achieve much more than they are now. Also, it should motivate the employees in these firms because they will have more discretion as well. Jersak sees some real benefits in this approach, but worries that the current managers of the operating companies haven't had much experience in making important decisions. He also fears that head office will lose control of the operating companies. Jersak feels that it is important for head office staff to know some of the details of each operating company. Without this knowledge, he feels that the head office staff will be unable to make good decisions regarding the operating companies.

Other friends of Jersak argue that the time has come to centralize control at head office because the firm has gotten so large and is so diverse. Only in this way, they argue, will top management be able to effectively control all the activities of Jersak Holdings Ltd.

Jersak is uncertain about what to do, but he feels he must do something to ensure that his life's work will not disappear when he retires next year.

Questions for Discussion

1. Discuss the advantages and disadvantages of centralization and decentralization as they relate to Jersak Holdings Ltd.
2. Which basic approach—centralization or decentralization—should Jersak Holdings Ltd. adopt? Defend your answer.
3. What problems are evident in the current organizational structure of Jersak Holdings Ltd.? Design a new organization chart for the company that will solve these problems. ◆

CHAPTER 8 Managing Human Resources

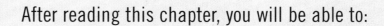

After reading this chapter, you will be able to:

1. Define *human resource management*, discuss its strategic significance, and explain how managers plan for human resources.
2. Identify the issues involved in *staffing* a company, including *internal* and *external recruiting* and *selection*.
3. Discuss different ways in which organizations go about developing the capabilities of employees and managers.
4. Explain ways in which organizations evaluate employee performance.
5. Discuss the importance of *wages and salaries, incentives*, and *benefit programs* in attracting and keeping skilled workers.
6. Describe some of the key legal issues involved in hiring, compensating, and managing workers.
7. Discuss *workforce diversity*, the management of knowledge workers, and the use of c*ontingent and temporary workers* as important changes in the contemporary workplace.

Progress, but Not Parity

In 2003, Catalyst Canada released a study analyzing how well women were represented in the top ranks of Canada's 500 largest companies. These are positions like Chief Executive Officer (CEO), Chief Financial Officer (CFO), and Chief Operating Officer (COO). The study found that while women continue to make progress, they have not yet achieved anything approaching parity with men. Some of the study's highlights are as follows:

- women hold 14 percent of the corporate officer positions in Canadian companies (up from 12 percent in 1999)
- at least one corporate officer is female in 62.2 percent of the companies (up from 56.4 percent in 1999)
- women hold 6.7 percent of the "clout" titles (CEO, CFO, or COO). This is up from 3.4 percent in 1999. These include Belinda Stronach (CEO, Magna International), Irene Rosenfeld (President, Kraft Canada), Heather Reisman (CEO, Indigo Books), and Michelle Carinici (CEO, Atlantic Lottery)
- 30 of the 88 women with "clout" titles are found in the financial services sector
- Canadian companies have fewer women in top jobs than U.S. companies do (85.6 percent of Fortune 500 companies have at least one female corporate officer, while only 62.2 percent of Canadian companies do)
- women in Canadian companies hold 35.2 percent of the "line" management jobs, while in the United States they hold only 29.6 percent of such jobs

Both male and female top managers in Canadian companies recognize that it's going to take quite a while to achieve parity. Tony Comper, chairman and CEO of the Bank of Montreal, notes that the bank has increased the proportion of women in the executive pool to 34 percent (up from only 9 percent in 1991). The goal is to achieve parity by 2007. But he says it's frustrating that progress has not been faster. He likens the process to a marathon, not a sprint. Elisabetta Bigsby, a senior vice-president at Royal Bank of Canada, says that she used to think achieving parity would be resolved during her generation, but she now realizes that it's going to take until the next generation to do so.

During the 1990s, much was written about how the "glass ceiling," the invisible barrier that prevented women from moving into the very top jobs in business firms, was starting to break down. Some dramatic changes did occur in the automobile industry, which had been dominated by men since its inception. For example, Maureen Kempston-Darkes was appointed CEO and president of General Motors of Canada, Bobbie Gaunt became CEO of Ford Motor of Canada, and Cynthia Trudell became president of Saturn Corp., a subsidiary of GM.

The trend toward more women in the very top jobs is clearly going to continue because women are increasingly holding jobs just below the top level. Getting to these positions is obviously very important if women are going to occupy more of the very top jobs. A survey of 461 female executives found that four strategies were important for women who had top-level career aspirations and who wanted to break through the glass ceiling:

- consistently exceed performance expectations
- develop a style with which male managers are comfortable
- seek difficult or high-visibility work assignments
- have an influential mentor

The same survey found disagreements between males and females about why so few women were represented in the top ranks of business firms. Male CEOs, for example, thought that women didn't advance to the very top ranks of management because they lacked general management experience, and because women had not been "in the pipeline" long enough. Women, on the other hand, felt that the key barriers to their success were male stereotyping of women, the exclusion of women from informal networks, and an inhospitable corporate culture.

A third survey, of 350 top-ranking Canadian women, was conducted by Pollara Inc. It found that women are still encountering resistance from the "old boys" in companies. Male attitudes like a lack of comfort when dealing with professional women were cited as a major problem by 69 percent of the respondents. Balancing work and home was also rated as a significant problem. Sixty-five percent of the respondents felt that they worked in an environment that made it easier for men to succeed than women. ◆

THE FOUNDATIONS OF HUMAN RESOURCE MANAGEMENT

human resource management (HRM)
Set of organizational activities directed at attracting, developing, and maintaining an effective workforce.

1. Define *human resource management*, discuss its strategic significance, and explain how managers plan for human resources.

Human resource management (HRM) is the set of organizational activities directed at attracting, developing, and maintaining an effective workforce. Human resource management takes place within a complex and ever-changing environmental context and is increasingly being recognized for its strategic importance.[1]

The Strategic Importance of HRM

Human resources are critical for effective organizational functioning. HRM (or *personnel*, as it is sometimes called) was once relegated to second-class status in many organizations, but its importance has grown dramatically in the last two decades. This new importance stems from increased legal complexities, the recognition that human resources are a valuable means for improving productivity, and the awareness today of the costs associated with poor human resource management.

Indeed, managers now realize that the effectiveness of their HR function has a substantial impact on a firm's bottom-line performance. Poor human resource planning can result in spurts of hiring followed by layoffs—costly in terms of unemployment compensation payments, training expenses, and morale. Haphazard compensation systems do not attract, keep, and motivate good employees, and outmoded recruitment practices can expose the firm to expensive and embarrassing legal action. Consequently, the chief human resource executive of most large businesses is a vice-president directly accountable to the CEO, and many firms are developing strategic HR plans that are integrated with other strategic planning activities.

Human Resource Planning

The starting point in attracting qualified human resources is planning. In turn, HR planning involves *job analysis* and *forecasting* the demand for and supply of labour (see Figure 8.1).

Job Analysis

job analysis
A detailed study of the specific duties in a particular job and the human qualities required for that job.

job description
The objectives, responsibilities, and key tasks of a job; the conditions under which it will be done; its relationship to other positions; and the skills needed to perform it.

job specification
The specific skills, education, and experience needed to perform a job.

Job analysis is a systematic analysis of jobs within an organization. A job analysis is made up of two parts:

- the **job description** lists the duties of a job, its working conditions, and the tools, materials, and equipment used to perform it
- the **job specification** lists the skills, abilities, and other credentials needed to do the job

Job analysis information is used in many HR activities. For instance, knowing about job content and job requirements is necessary to develop appropriate selection methods and job-relevant performance appraisal systems and to set equitable compensation rates.

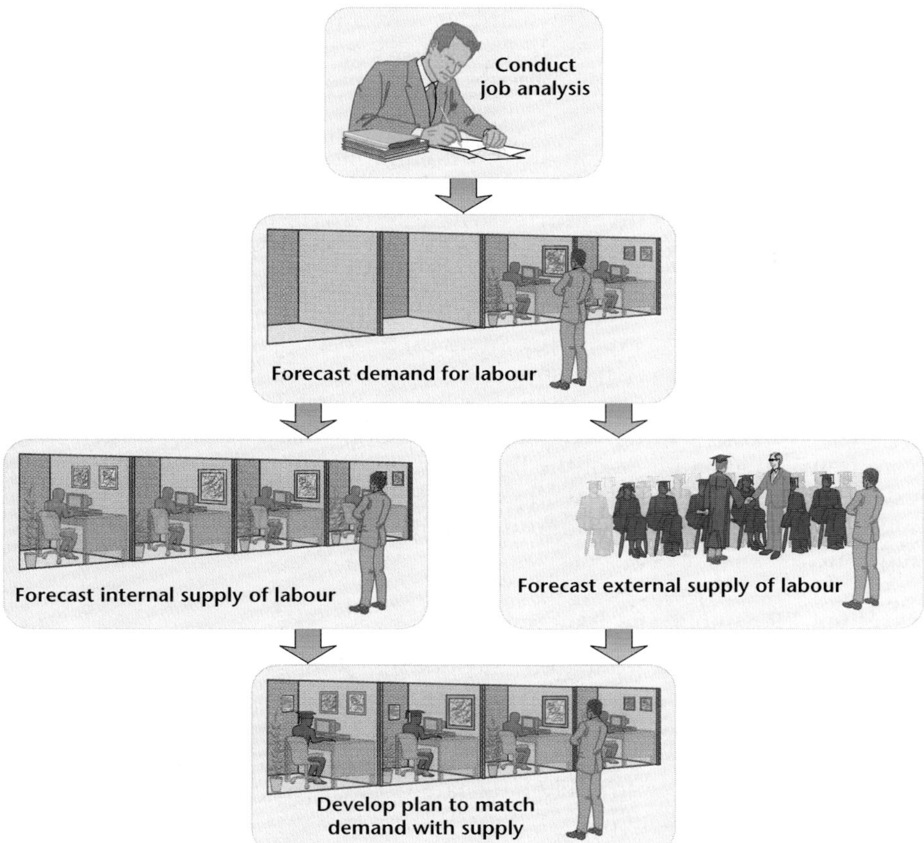

Figure 8.1
Planning for human resources.

Forecasting HR Demand and Supply

After managers fully understand the jobs to be performed within an organization, they can start planning for the organization's future HR needs. The manager starts by assessing trends in past HR usage, future organizational plans, and general economic trends. A good sales forecast is often the foundation, especially for smaller organizations. Historical ratios can then be used to predict demand for types of employees, such as operating employees and sales representatives. Large organizations, of course, use much more complicated models to predict HR needs.

Forecasting the supply of labour involves two tasks:

- forecasting *internal supply*—the number and type of employees who will be in the firm at some future date
- forecasting *external supply*—the number and type of people who will be available for hiring from the labour market at large

The simplest approach merely adjusts present staffing levels for anticipated turnover and promotions. Large organizations use extremely sophisticated models to keep track of the present and future distributions of professionals and managers. This allows the company to spot areas where there will eventually be too many qualified professionals competing for too few promotions or, conversely, too few good people available to fill important positions.

replacement chart
An HR technique that lists each important managerial position, who occupies it, how long he or she will probably stay in it before moving on, and who (by name) is now qualified or soon will be qualified to move into it.

Replacement Charts. At higher levels of the organization, managers make plans for specific people and positions. The technique most commonly used is the **replacement chart**, which lists each important managerial position, who occupies it, how long he or she will probably stay in it before moving on, and who (by name) is now qualified or soon will be qualified to move into it. This technique allows ample time to plan developmental experiences for people identified as potential successors to critical managerial jobs.

employee information systems (skills inventories)
Computerized systems that contain information on each employee's education, skills, work experience, and career aspirations.

Skills Inventories. To facilitate both planning and identifying people for transfer or promotion, some organizations also have **employee information systems**, or **skills inventories**. These systems are usually computerized and contain information on each employee's education, skills, work experience, and career aspirations. Such a system can quickly locate every employee who is qualified to fill a position requiring, say, a degree in chemical engineering, three years of experience in an oil refinery, and fluency in French.

Forecasting the external supply of labour is a different problem altogether. How does a manager, for example, predict how many electrical engineers will be seeking work in Ontario or British Columbia three years from now? To get an idea of the future availability of labour, planners must rely on information from outside sources, such as government reports and figures supplied by colleges and universities on the number of students in major fields.

Matching HR Supply and Demand

After comparing future demand and internal supply, managers can make plans to manage predicted shortfalls or overstaffing. If a shortfall is predicted, new employees can be hired, present employees can be retrained and transferred into understaffed areas, individuals approaching retirement can be convinced to stay on, or labour-saving or productivity-enhancing systems can be installed.

If the organization needs to hire, the external labour-supply forecast helps managers plan how to recruit according to whether the type of person needed is readily available or scarce in the labour market. The use of temporary workers also helps managers in staffing by giving them extra flexibility. If overstaffing is expected to be a problem, the main options are transferring the extra employees, not replacing individuals who quit, encouraging early retirement, and laying people off.

STAFFING THE ORGANIZATION

2. Identify the issues involved in *staffing* a company, including *internal* and *external recruiting* and *selection*.

Once managers have decided what positions they need to fill, they must find and hire individuals who meet the job requirements. A study by the Canadian Federation of Independent Business found that the top three characteristics employers are looking for when they hire people are a good work ethic, reliability, and willingness to stay on the job.[2] Staffing of the corporation is one of the most complex and important aspects of good human resource management. The top 10 employers by number of employees in Canada are listed in Table 8.1.

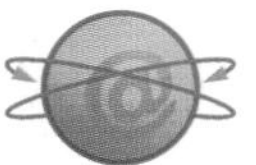

Canadian Federation of Independent Business
www.cfib.ca

In this section, we will describe both the process of acquiring staff from outside the company (*external staffing*) and the process of promoting staff from within (*internal staffing*). Both external and internal staffing, however, start with effective recruiting.

Recruiting Human Resources

recruiting
The phase in the staffing of a company in which the firm seeks to develop a pool of interested, qualified applicants for a position.

Once an organization has an idea of its future HR needs, the next phase is usually recruiting new employees. **Recruiting** is the process of attracting qualified persons to apply for the jobs that are open. Where do recruits

Table 8.1 The Top 10 Employers in Canada

	Company	Number of Employees
1.	George Weston Ltd.	139 000
2.	Onex Corp.	98 000
3.	Laidlaw Inc.	91 000
4.	McDonald's of Canada	77 000
5.	Bombardier Inc.	75 000
6.	Magna International Inc.	73 000
7.	Hudson's Bay Co.	71 445
8.	BCE Inc.	66 266
9.	Canada Post Corp.	65 767
10.	Royal Bank of Canada	59 549

come from? Some recruits are found internally; others come from outside the organization.

Internal Recruiting

Internal recruiting means considering present employees as candidates for openings. Promotion from within can help build morale and keep high-quality employees from leaving. In unionized firms, the procedures for notifying employees of internal job-change opportunities are usually spelled out in the union contract. For higher-level positions, a skills inventory system may be used to identify internal candidates or managers may be asked to recommend individuals who should be considered.

internal recruiting
Considering present employees as candidates for job openings.

External Recruiting

External recruiting involves attracting people outside the organization to apply for jobs. External recruiting methods include advertising, campus interviews, employment agencies or executive search firms, union hiring halls, referrals by present employees, and hiring "walk-ins" or "gate-hires" (people who show up without being solicited). Of course, a manager must select the most appropriate method for each job. Private employment agencies can be a good source of clerical and technical employees, and executive search firms specialize in locating top-management talent. Newspaper ads are often used because they reach a wide audience and thus allow minorities "equal opportunity" to learn about and apply for job openings.

external recruiting
Attracting people outside the organization to apply for jobs.

The old-fashioned *job fair* has survived in spite of internet career postings and the proliferation of employment agencies and headhunters. At a job fair, candidates browse through the positions available and employers can see a sample of the skills candidates have. While job postings on the internet are impersonal, at job fairs candidates and recruiters can talk to each other face-to-face. Job fairs are also cheaper than posting jobs with an employment agency or headhunter. When IBM Canada held a job fair at its Markham, Ontario, office, nearly 5000 people came hoping to snap up one of the 500 jobs that were available.[3]

IBM Canada
www.ibm.com/ca/en

Selecting Human Resources

Once the recruiting process has attracted a pool of applicants, the next step is to select someone to hire. The intent of the selection process is to gather information from applicants that will predict their job success and then to hire the candidates likely to be most successful. Of course, the organization

At job fairs, students and recruiters can talk face-to-face about jobs that are available. Here, recruiters from a financial management firm talk to students about the opportunities at their company.

can only gather information about factors that are predictive of future performance. The process of determining the predictive value of information is called **validation**.

validation
The process of determining the predictive value of information.

To reduce the element of uncertainty, managers use a variety of selection techniques, the most common of which are shown in Figure 8.2. Each organization develops its own mix of selection techniques and may use them in almost any order.

Application Forms

The first step in selection is usually asking the candidate to fill out an application form. An application form is an efficient method of gathering information about the applicant's previous work history, educational back-

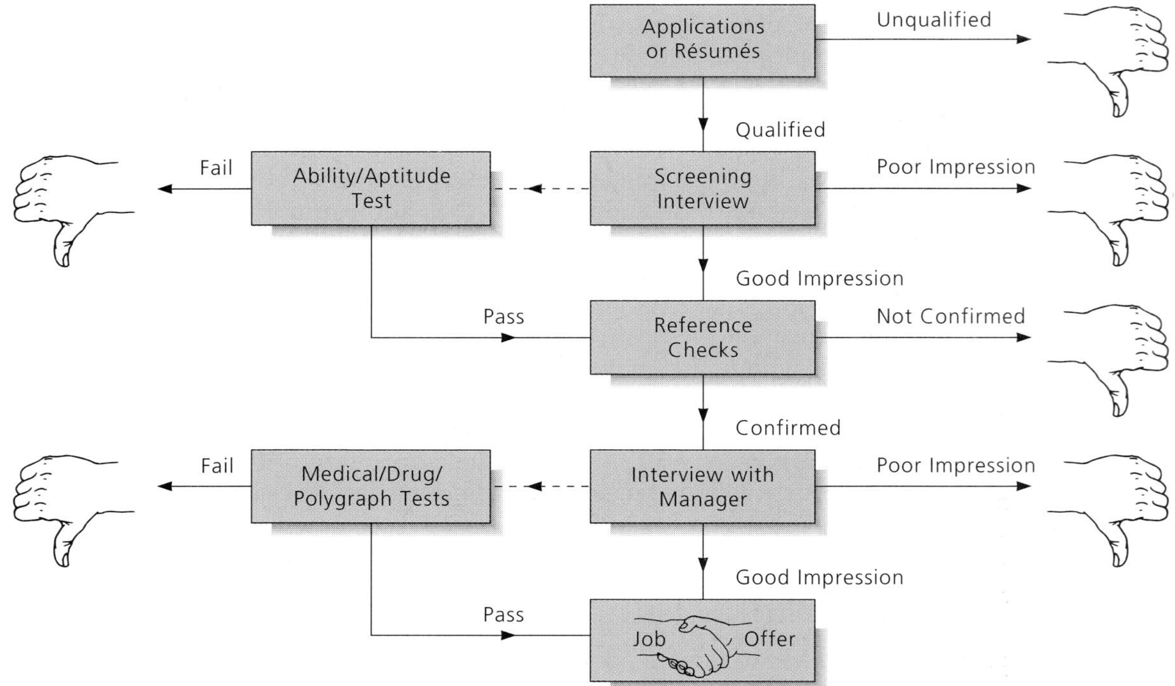

Figure 8.2
General steps in the selection process.

ground, and other job-related demographic data. It should not contain questions about areas unrelated to the job, such as gender, religion, or national origin. Application-form data are generally used informally to decide whether a candidate merits further evaluation, and interviewers use application forms to familiarize themselves with candidates before interviewing them.

Tests

Tests of ability, skill, aptitude, or knowledge that is relevant to a particular job are usually the best predictors of job success, although tests of general intelligence or personality are occasionally useful as well. In addition to being validated, tests should be administered and scored consistently. All candidates should be given the same directions, allowed the same amount of time, and offered the same testing environment (e.g., temperature, lighting, distractions).

For some positions, ability or aptitude tests may be part of the initial screening process. When Toyota hired workers for its Cambridge, Ontario, plant, applicants were put through a series of tests to determine their math, verbal, and communication skills and their ability to work on a team. Even though most of the workers had never worked for an automobile firm before, they are now producing the highest-rated car in North America.

An **assessment centre** is a series of exercises in which candidates perform realistic management tasks under the watchful eye of expert appraisers. A typical assessment centre might be set up in a large conference room and go on for two or three days. During this time, potential managers might take selection tests, engage in management simulations, make individual presentations, and conduct group discussions. Assessors check to see how each participant reacts to stress or to criticism by colleagues. A relatively new type of test that evolved from assessment centres is **video assessment**. Here, potential hires are shown videos of realistic work situations and then asked to choose a course of action to deal with the situation. Video assessment is fast, reliable, cheap, and versatile.

Regardless of the type of test that is used, it must be job-related (that is, it must not serve as a basis for discriminating against anyone for reasons unrelated to the job) and it must be a valid predictor of performance (that is, it must provide evidence that people who score well on it are more likely to perform well in the job than are people who score poorly on it).

assessment centre
A series of exercises in which management candidates perform realistic management tasks while being observed by appraisers.

video assessment
Involves showing potential hires videos of realistic work situations and asking them to choose a course of action to deal with the situation.

Interviews

The interview is a popular selection device, but it is sometimes a poor predictor of job success because biases inherent in the way people perceive and judge others on first meeting affect subsequent evaluations. Interview validity can be improved by training interviewers to be aware of potential biases and by increasing the structure of the interview. In a structured interview, questions are written in advance and all interviewers follow the same question list with each candidate. Such structure introduces consistency into the interview procedure and allows the organization to validate the content of the questions. For interviewing managerial or professional candidates, a somewhat less structured approach can be used. Although question areas and information-gathering objectives are still planned in advance, specific questions vary with the candidates' backgrounds.

Other Techniques

Organizations also use other selection techniques that vary with the circumstances. A manufacturer afraid of injuries to workers on the job might require new employees to have a physical examination. This gives the com-

An in-depth interview with a prospective employee is often part of the recruiting process, particularly for managerial jobs.

pany some information about whether the employees are physically fit to do the work and what (if any) pre-existing injuries they might have.

Polygraph (lie detector) tests are largely illegal now, and drug tests are also coming under fire. In 1998, for example, the Ontario Divisional Court decided that Imperial Oil Ltd.'s drug policy (which included pre-employment drug testing that made offers of work conditional on a negative result) was unlawful because Imperial failed to prove that a positive drug test would indicate a failure to perform essential duties. Imperial's policy also required random drug and alcohol testing, but that was also judged to be discriminatory because the company could not prove that such testing was necessary to deter alcohol or drug impairment on the job.[4] The Toronto Dominion Bank wanted to give drug tests to all new employees because it wanted to have the public's trust. However, a federal court ruled that the bank's policy was discriminatory and that it wasn't related closely enough to job performance.[5]

DEVELOPING HUMAN RESOURCES

3. Discuss different ways in which organizations go about developing the capabilities of employees and managers.

Regardless of how effective a selection system is, most employees need additional training if they are to grow and develop in their jobs. This process begins with *orientation* and then proceeds to the *assessment of training and development needs* (including the performance of a *needs analysis*) and the selection of the best *training techniques and methods*.

New Employee Orientation

orientation
The initial acquainting of new employees with the company's policies and programs, personnel with whom they will interact, and the nature of the job.

An important part of an organization's training and development program is new employee orientation. **Orientation** is the process of introducing new employees to the company's policies and programs, personnel with whom they will interact, and the nature of the job so that they can more quickly become effective contributors. Poor orientation can result in disenchantment, dissatisfaction, anxiety, turnover, and other employee problems. But effective orientation can play a key role in job satisfaction, performance, and retention. An effective orientation program will help newcomers feel like part of a team, introduce them quickly to co-workers, supervisors, and other new employees, and in a variety of other ways ease the transition from outsider to insider.

Some organizations also find it appropriate to include as a part of their orientation a general overview of and introduction to the business itself. This introduction may include such things as information about the firm's history, its evolution, its successes, and perhaps even some of its failures. Organizations with strong corporate cultures are especially likely to include such information because it is quick and efficient in helping to provide information about the firm's culture to new hires. This makes it easier for them to understand the culture and to know how to function within it.

Training and Development

Beyond orientation for new employees, most organizations also find it effective to continue training and development on a regular basis. In other words, employees must be continually trained and developed to enhance and otherwise improve the quality of the contributions they make to the organization.

The starting point in assessing training and development needs is conducting a *needs analysis*—determining the organization's true needs and the training programs necessary to meet them. This analysis generally focuses on two things: the organization's job-related needs and the capabilities of the current workforce. The organization's needs are determined by the nature of the work that the organization needs to be done. That is, what knowledge, skills, and abilities does the organization need to compete? What skills must its workforce possess to perform the organization's work effectively?

Depending on both the content of the program and the instructors selected to present it, a number of techniques and methods can be used for the actual delivery of information. We examine some of the more popular techniques and methods in this section.

Work-Based Programs

One major family of techniques and methods consists of various **work-based programs** that tie training and development activities directly to task performance. The most common method of work-based training is **on-the-job training**. The employee is placed in the actual work situation and is shown how to perform a task by a supervisor or an experienced employee. Much on-the-job training is informal, as when one employee shows another how to operate the photocopy machine.

work-based programs
A technique that ties training and development activities directly to task performance.

on-the-job training
Those development programs in which employees gain new skills while performing them at work.

Another work-based program is **vestibule training**, which involves a work simulation in which the job is performed under conditions closely simulating the actual work environment. Commercial airline pilots, for example, regularly undergo training and assessment in a flight simulator. Likewise, machine operators in a factory might be trained on simulated equipment that is comparable to that which they would use in the actual job setting.

vestibule training
A work simulation in which the job is performed under conditions closely simulating the actual work environment.

Another method of work-based training program is **systematic job rotations and transfers**. This method is most likely to be used for lower level managers or for operating employees being groomed for promotions to supervisory management positions. As the term suggests, the employee is systematically rotated or transferred from one job to another. The employee thus learns a wider array of tasks, acquires more abilities, and develops a more comprehensive view of the work of an organization or a particular sub-unit.

systematic job rotations and transfers
A technique in which an employee is systematically rotated or transferred from one job to another.

Instructional-Based Programs

instructional-based programs
Training workers through the use of classroom-based programs such as the lecture approach.

lecture or discussion approach
An instructional-based program in which a trainer presents material in a descriptive fashion to those attending a trainee program.

A second family of techniques and methods involves **instructional-based programs**. The most commonly used of these programs is the **lecture or discussion approach**. In these situations, a trainer presents material in a descriptive fashion to those attending a trainee program. Just as a professor lectures students on a particular subject matter, an organizational trainer "lectures" trainees. Depending on the situation and the size of the training class, the instructor may opt for a pure lecture method or may include discussion with trainees. Sometimes lectures are on video or audio tapes so that various individuals in the organization can receive the same training at different times and/or at different locations.

off-the-job training
Those development programs in which employees learn new skills at a location away from the normal work site.

Off-the-job training is performed at a location away from the work site. It may be at a classroom within the same facility or at a different location altogether. For example, refresher courses are offered to managers of McDonald's 600 Canadian restaurants at the Canadian Institute of Hamburgerology; in addition, training videotapes are shown to restaurant workers.[6] Coffee College is a two-week cram course run by Second Cup Ltd., Canada's largest retailer of specialty coffee. During their stay at Coffee College, franchisees and managers learn how to hire workers, keep the books, detect employee theft, and boost Christmas sales.[7]

Another instructional-based program is computer-assisted instruction. A trainee sits at a personal computer and operates software that has been specifically developed to teach certain material. The actual training materials are stored on the computer's hard drive, a CD-ROM, or a website. One major advantage of this method is that it allows self-paced learning and immediate feedback.

Training Technology

In recent years, the technology used for training has changed dramatically. Until just a few years ago, virtually all training involved paper and pencil, individual instruction, and mechanical reproduction of tasks. More recently, however, new technology has reshaped the way many companies deliver training. As we already noted, for example, computer-assisted instruction has become more popular. Obviously, computer-assisted instruction was impossible before the advent of computers, but it has only been within the last few years with the widespread adoption of personal computers that computer-assisted instruction has become widely used.

Video Teleconferencing. Video teleconferencing is also used increasingly as a training tool. Companies find that when trainers in centralized locations deliver material live by satellite hookup to remote sites, training can be delivered just as effectively as transporting people to common training sites while saving travel costs. In the early days of video teleconferencing, communication tended to be one way: both the trainer and trainees simply saw the material as it was presented on a monitor. Now, however, there is considerably more interaction. Trainees usually have the ability to interact verbally or electronically.

Interactive Video. Yet another new training tool is interactive video, which is essentially a combination of standard video and computer-based instruction. The material is presented via video technology on a monitor from a central serving mechanism, a videodisk, CD-ROM, or website. The trainee interacts with the system through a mouse or keyboard. Feedback can be provided when inadequate responses or improper answers are given, and the trainee can also skip over material that has already been learned.

Videoconferencing has become an important part of the training function in organizations because significant interaction is possible between the trainer and trainees.

Team Building and Group-Based Training

Also increasingly popular in recent years are various team-building and group-based methods of training. As more and more organizations are using teams as a basis for doing their jobs, it should not be surprising that many of the same companies are developing training programs specifically designed to facilitate intragroup co-operation among team members.

One popular method involves various outdoor training exercises. Some programs, for example, involve a group going through a physical obstacle course that requires climbing, crawling, and other physical activities. Outward Bound and several other independent companies specialize in offering these kinds of programs, and their clients include such firms as General Foods, Xerox, and Burger King. Participants, of course, must see the relevance of such programs if they are to be successful. Firms don't want employees returning from team-building programs to report merely that the experience "was childlike and fun and fairly inoffensive."[8]

Outward Bound
www.outwardbound.com

EVALUATING EMPLOYEE PERFORMANCE

Another important part of human resource management is **performance appraisal**: the specific and formal evaluation of an employee to determine the degree to which he or she is performing effectively. Appraisals are important because they provide a benchmark to assess the extent to which recruiting and selection processes are adequate. In other words, performance appraisals help managers assess the extent to which they are recruiting and selecting the best employees. They also contribute to effective training, development, and compensation. The Wired World box provides information about technological advances and how they facilitate the performance appraisal process.

performance appraisal
A formal program for evaluating how well an employee is performing the job; helps managers to determine how effective they are in recruiting and selecting employees.

4. Explain ways in which organizations evaluate employee performance.

The Performance Appraisal Process

Several questions must be answered as part of the performance appraisal process. These questions generally relate to who conducts the performance appraisal and provides feedback to the individual whose performance is being evaluated.

IT'S A WIRED WORLD

From the Smushy to the Scientific

Advances in technology permit companies to gather, analyze, report, and apply information in ways that would have been impossible a decade ago. One area that has long cried out for better use of information is worker performance measurement. "[W]hat was once a smushy, subjective effort by finger-in-the-wind managers is hitting new levels of scientific precision," reports *Business Week*.

Consider the technology revolution in performance measurement at household goods retailer Pier 1 Imports. In the past, because daily sales reports could be calculated only at the end of the day, employees didn't know how well they were doing until it was too late to do anything about it. Now, Pier 1 uses technology to tabulate sales continuously. In cities where Pier 1 has multiple stores, the same technology pits one store against the others by allowing employees to see not only their own results, but also results from other stores. Employees check performance regularly, and use improvement goals to increase their bonuses.

At British Airways, software monitors employees to ensure that coffee breaks and personal phone calls don't get charged to the company. Progress toward corporate goals, such as ticket sales and complaint resolutions, is also tracked. Workers have instant access to performance scores and can see the impact of incentive compensation on their daily pay. Other firms, however, are using even more intrusive technologies, such as entry card data (to determine what time workers arrive and leave) and security cameras (sometimes without notification to the employees) that are placed in cubicles, hallways, and even restrooms. Software also allows managers to receive reports of every website accessed and can even record workers' every keystroke on company PCs. Many workers see the benefits of accurate and objective performance measurement, but some, not surprisingly, claim that technology is invading their privacy. As technology continues to progress, the debate is sure to continue.

Conducting the Performance Appraisal

British Airways
www.britishairways.com

The individual's supervisor is the person most likely to conduct a performance appraisal. Supervisors usually have both the most knowledge of the job requirements and the most opportunity to observe employees performing their jobs. In addition, the supervisor is usually responsible for the performance of his or her subordinates. Thus, the supervisor is both responsible for employees' high performance and accountable for their inadequate performance.

Sources of Information. One possible source of information in the performance appraisal process is the subordinates of the individual being appraised. Subordinates are an especially important source of information when the performance of their own managers is being evaluated. Their input is perhaps most useful when the performance appraisal focuses on the manager's leadership potential. Another source of information is self-evaluation. In many professional and managerial situations, individuals occasionally may be asked to evaluate their own performance. A final source of information is customers. Restaurants such as Red Lobster, for example, place feedback forms in the envelopes in which customers receive their bills. These types of forms typically ask customers to rate their servers, the cook, and so forth on various characteristics.

Managers must recognize that each source of information is subject to various weaknesses and shortcomings. As a result, many organizations find it effective to rely on a variety of different information sources in the conduct of appraisals. They may, for example, gather information not merely from supervisors or peers, but from both. Indeed, some organizations gather information from every source described in this section. This comprehensive approach is called **360-degree feedback**.

360-degree feedback
Gathering information from a manager's subordinates, peers, and superiors when assessing the manager's performance.

Providing Performance Feedback

After the performance appraisal, the next major activity is providing feedback, coaching, and counselling. Many managers do a poor job in this area, in part because they don't understand how to do it properly and in part because they don't enjoy it. Almost by definition, performance appraisal in many organizations tends to focus on negatives. As a result, managers may have a tendency to avoid giving feedback because they know that an employee who receives negative feedback may be angry, hurt, discouraged, or argumentative. But clearly, if employees are not told about their shortcomings, they will have no concrete reason to try to improve and receive no guidance as to how to improve. It is critical, therefore, that managers follow up on appraisals by providing feedback.

Methods for Appraising Performance

Because of the nature of many jobs today, especially managerial work, most methods for appraising performance rely on judgments and ratings. A great deal of effort has therefore been expended trying to make relatively subjective evaluations as meaningful and useful as they can be. While some of the methods are based on relative rankings, others are based on ratings. In this section, we examine a few of the more popular methods, which we have categorized as either *ranking* or *rating methods*.

Ranking Methods

The **simple ranking method** requires a manager to rank-order from top to bottom or from best to worst each member of a particular work group or department. The individual ranked first is the top performer, the individual ranked second is the second-best performer, and so forth. The basis for the ranking is generally global or overall performance. Another ranking method, the **forced distribution method**, involves grouping employees into predefined frequencies of performance ratings. Those frequencies are determined in advance and are imposed on the rater. A decision might be made, for instance, that 10 percent of the employees in a work group will be grouped as "outstanding," 20 percent as "very good," 40 percent as "average," 20 percent as "below average," and the remaining 10 percent as "poor." The forced distribution method is familiar to many students because it is the principle used by professors who grade on a so-called "bell curve" or "normal curve."

simple ranking method
A method of performance appraisal that requires a manager to rank-order from top to bottom or from best to worst each member of a particular work group or department.

forced distribution method
A method of performance appraisal that involves grouping employees into predefined frequencies of performance ratings.

Rating Methods

One of the most popular and widely used methods is the **graphic rating scale**, which consists simply of a statement or question about some aspect of an individual's job performance. Following the statement or question is a series of answers or possible responses from which the rater must select the one that fits best. For example, one common set of responses to a graphic rating scale with five possible alternatives is *strongly agree, agree, neither agree nor disagree, disagree,* and *strongly disagree.* These responses, or "descriptors," are usually arrayed along a bar, line, or similar visual representation marked with numbers or letters corresponding to each descriptor. Figure 8.3 shows a sample graphic rating scale.

graphic rating scale
A statement or question about some aspect of an individual's job performance for which the rater must select the response that fits best.

Graphic rating scales are appealing because they are relatively easy to develop. A manager simply "brainstorms" or otherwise develops a list of statements or questions that are presumably related to relevant indicators of performance. Moreover, a wide array of performance dimensions can be tapped with various rating scales on the same form. As we noted, a number

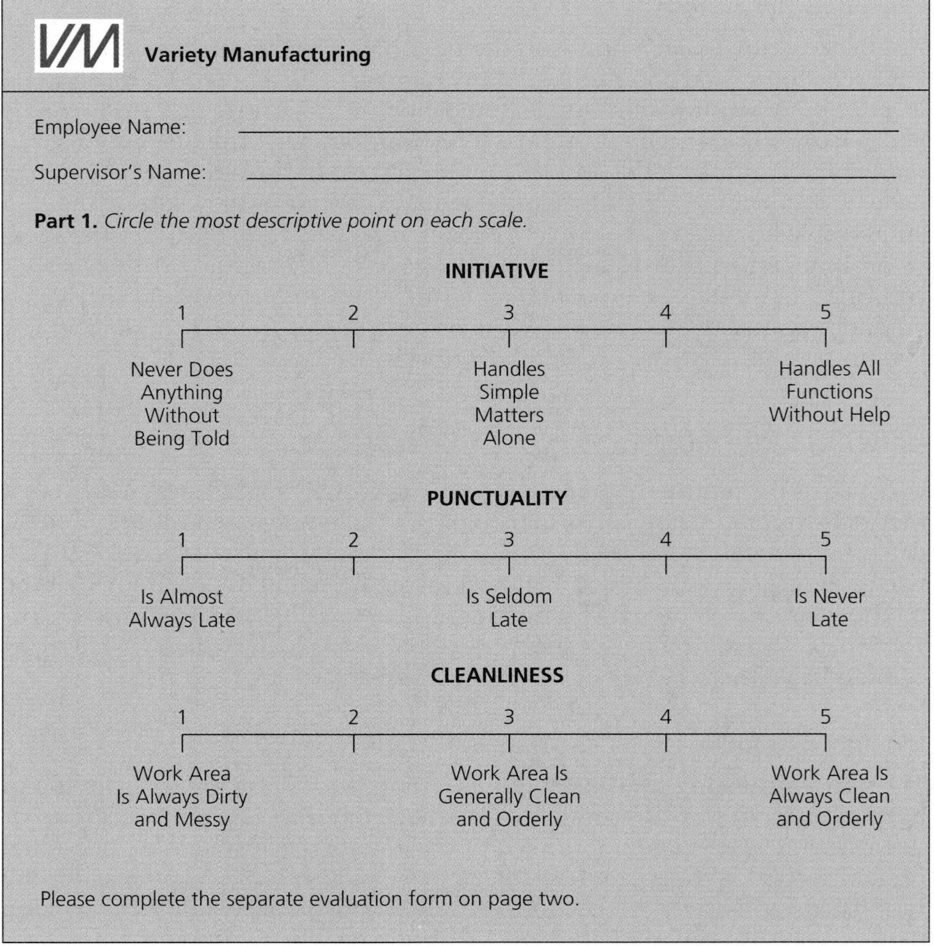
VM Variety Manufacturing

Employee Name: ____________________

Supervisor's Name: ____________________

Part 1. *Circle the most descriptive point on each scale.*

INITIATIVE

1	2	3	4	5
Never Does Anything Without Being Told		Handles Simple Matters Alone		Handles All Functions Without Help

PUNCTUALITY

1	2	3	4	5
Is Almost Always Late		Is Seldom Late		Is Never Late

CLEANLINESS

1	2	3	4	5
Work Area Is Always Dirty and Messy		Work Area Is Generally Clean and Orderly		Work Area Is Always Clean and Orderly

Please complete the separate evaluation form on page two.

Figure 8.3
Performance rating scale.

or a letter accompanies each descriptor on the rating form. Most rating scales have ranges of one to five or one to seven. To develop a performance measure, the manager simply adds up the "points" for a particular employee's responses to obtain an overall index of performance.

critical incident method
A technique of performance appraisal in which raters recall examples of especially good or poor performance by an employee and then describe what the employee did (or did not do) that led to success or failure.

Somewhat different is the **critical incident method**. A critical incident is simply an example of especially good or poor performance on the part of the employee. Organizations that rely on this method often require raters to recall such instances and then describe what the employee did (or did not do) that led to success or failure. This technique not only provides information for feedback but also defines performance in fairly clear, behavioural terms. In other cases, managers keep logs or diaries in which they record examples of critical incidents.

5. Discuss the importance of *wages and salaries, incentives,* and *benefit programs* in attracting and keeping skilled workers.

PROVIDING COMPENSATION AND BENEFITS

compensation
What a firm offers its employees in return for their labour.

Employees do not work for free—they expect to be compensated for the time, talent, and effort they devote to their jobs and to helping the organization achieve its goals. In this section, we explore basic compensation, incentives and performance-based rewards, and employee benefits and services. **Compensation** is the set of rewards that organizations provide to individuals in return for their willingness to perform various jobs and tasks within the organization. As we shall see, compensation includes a number of different elements, including base salary, incentives, bonuses, benefits, and other rewards. Compensation should never be a random decision, but rather the result of a careful and systematic strategic process.

The compensation received by CEOs can be extremely large, especially when bonuses are included. The most highly paid managers in the 2002 Globe and Mail Survey of Compensation were Frank Stronach of Magna International (who earned \$58 000 000), Richard Currie of George Weston Ltd. (who earned \$48 000 000), and Galen Weston of George Weston Ltd. (who earned \$31 000 000).[9] High executive compensation has generated considerable debate (see the Opening Case in Chapter 10 for more information on this issue).

Determining Basic Compensation

Basic compensation means the base level of wages or salary paid to an employee. **Wages** generally refer to hourly compensation paid to operating employees. Most of the jobs that are paid on an hourly wage basis are lower-level and/or operating-level jobs. Rather than expressing compensation on an hourly basis, the organization may instead describe compensation on an annual or monthly basis. Many college and university graduates, for example, compare job offers on the basis of annual **salary**, such as \$36 000 versus \$38 000 a year.

wages
Dollars paid based on the number of hours worked.

salary
Dollars paid at regular intervals in return for doing a job, regardless of the amount of time or output involved.

Pay Surveys in Compensation

One common source of information that many organizations use to determine base compensation is **pay surveys**—surveys of compensation paid to employees by other employers in a particular geographic area, an industry, or an occupational group. Pay surveys provide the information that an organization needs to avoid an imbalance between its own pay scale and those of comparable organizations. Some pay surveys are conducted by professional associations. For example, the Canadian Federation of Business School Deans publishes an annual summary of salaries for professors teaching in business schools in Canadian universities.

pay survey
A survey of compensation paid to employees by other employers in a particular geographic area, an industry, or an occupational group.

In general, a pay survey simply asks other organizations what they pay people to perform various jobs. Most organizations participate in such surveys because they will have access to the resulting data. There is, for example, a consortium of eight large electronic companies in the United States that routinely survey one another to determine what each pays new engineers and other professional employees who are hired directly out of college or university. The companies alternate the responsibility for conducting surveys from year to year, with the responsible organization sharing its results with the other members.

Job Evaluation

Another means of determining basic compensation is *job evaluation*, which should not be confused with job analysis. Recall that managers use job analysis to understand the requirements and nature of a job and its performance so that appropriate individuals can be recruited and selected. **Job evaluation** is a method for determining the relative value or worth of a job to the organization so that individuals who perform it can be appropriately compensated. In other words, it is mostly concerned with establishing internal pay equity. A number of well-established job evaluation techniques and methods have been established.

job evaluation
A method for determining the relative value or worth of a job to the organization so that individuals who perform it can be appropriately compensated.

Establishing a Pay Structure

A third method for determining basic compensation is establishing a *pay structure*. Compensation for different jobs is based on the organization's assessment of the relative value to the organization of each job class. Thus, there should be a logical rank ordering of compensation levels from the most valuable to the least valuable jobs throughout the organization. The organization, of course, may also find it necessary to group certain jobs together; thus, two or more jobs that are valued relatively equally will be compensated at approximately the same level. In addition, the organization decides on minimum and maximum pay ranges for each job or job class. Managers might use performance, *seniority* (a system that gives priority in promotions to employees with greater length of service), or a combination of the two to determine how much a person can be paid for doing a particular job.

The internet allows job seekers and current employees to more easily get a sense of what their true market value is. If they can document the claim that their value is higher than what their current employer now pays or is offering, they may be in a position to demand higher salaries. One manager who met with a subordinate to discuss her raise was surprised when she produced data from five different websites to support her request for a bigger raise than he had intended to offer.

Performance-Based Compensation

Besides basic compensation, many organizations also offer performance-based rewards. The reason is obvious: When rewards are associated with higher levels of performance, employees will presumably be motivated to work harder in order to reap those awards.

Merit Pay Plans

merit pay
Pay awarded to employees according to the relative value of their contributions.

merit pay plans
Compensation plans that formally base at least some meaningful portion of compensation on merit.

Merit pay refers to pay awarded to employees according to the relative value of their contributions. Employees who make greater contributions receive higher pay than those who make lesser contributions. **Merit pay plans**, then, are compensation plans that base at least some meaningful portion of compensation on merit. The most general form of a merit pay plan is the raise—an annual salary increase granted to an employee because of his or her relative merit. In such plans, merit is usually determined or defined according to individual performance and overall contribution to the organization. The Business Today box analyzes some controversial questions about merit pay.

skill-based pay
Pay awarded to employees not for any specific level of performance, but for the acquisition of job-related skills.

knowledge-based pay
Pay awarded to employees for learning.

Skill- and Knowledge-Based Pay Systems. Although these systems are usually not strictly viewed as merit systems, it is worth noting how **skill-based pay** or **knowledge-based pay** systems focus employee attention on different areas but still rely on similar motivational processes. Instead of rewarding employees for increased performance, such systems reward them for the acquisition of more skills or knowledge. Skill-based pay systems reward employees for the acquisition of job-related skills. Knowledge-based pay systems reward employees for learning, because presumably, as they acquire more and more skills and knowledge, employees become more valuable to the organization.

Incentive Compensation Systems

piece-rate incentive plan
A compensation system in which an organization pays an employee a certain amount of money for every unit produced.

Incentive compensation systems are among the oldest forms of performance-based rewards. Indeed, some companies were using individual piece-rate incentive plans over 100 years ago. Under a **piece-rate incentive plan**, the organization pays an employee a certain amount of money for every

BUSINESS TODAY

What About Merit Pay and Rewards?

The idea that employees should be rewarded according to the relative value of their contribution to the company seems to make good sense. Many managers do, in fact, view merit pay and rewards as important tools in attracting and retaining high-performing employees. But workers don't necessarily agree with this view. At Hudson's Bay Co., for example, 800 workers went on strike in 2002 because they didn't want management to introduce a merit system. The strike ended when management agreed to retain the straight wage system. Many union leaders object to merit pay, saying that it causes dissension in the workplace.

One reason that many workers don't like the concept of merit pay is that managers usually decide to give it on the basis of annual or semi-annual performance appraisals. While workers don't necessarily object to the basic idea of performance appraisals, they may be done so poorly that workers don't understand why they received (or didn't receive) merit pay. Another reason is that merit pay may be perceived to be given on the basis of some highly subjective criterion, such as who the boss favours, or who is best at self-promotion. Employees who are not on the boss's list of favourites, or who don't effectively promote their performance, can easily conclude that they should have received merit pay but didn't. Unhappiness then results. If merit pay systems are to work, performance appraisals must be frequent, perceived to be fair, objective, and based on clearly defined goals that are to be achieved by all workers.

Merit pay is a private agreement between the employer and the employee, while other types of rewards—cash bonuses, prizes, and employee-of-the-month awards—are much more public. Employee reactions to these reward schemes vary widely. Employee-of-the-month awards, for example, have certain positive attributes (public recognition of employees who have done good work, increased status for winners of the award, and increased employee motivation). But there are also problems with these awards (lack of co-operation between workers as they compete for the award, negative feelings on the part of those who didn't win, perceived favouritism in the choice of winners, and lack of interest in the award on the part of some employees).

Alfie Kohn, an outspoken critic of rewards, sees four basic problems. First, rewards are actually a form of punishment and control. Those who don't get the rewards feel punished, and those who do get them feel controlled by someone else. Second, co-operation and working together are necessary to achieve organizational goals. But when a boss gives or withholds a reward, subordinates may spend too much time trying to do what pleases the boss and not enough time doing the task properly. Third, the focus on outcomes such as productivity ignores the factors that inhibit or facilitate productivity. Without an understanding of these causes, it is difficult to improve performance. Finally, rewards cause employees to focus on those things that are necessary to get the reward. They may get so involved in trying to figure that out that they do not have the time or interest to look for new ways of doing things.

unit produced. An employee might, for example, be paid $1 for every 12 units of a product successfully completed. But such simplistic systems fail to account for such factors as minimum wage levels and rely on two questionable assumptions: (1) that performance is totally under an individual's control, and (2) that the individual employee does a single task continuously during the course of his or her work time. Today, therefore, incentive compensation systems tend to be much more sophisticated.

Incentive Pay Plans. Generally speaking, **individual incentive plans** reward individual performance on a real-time basis. That is, rather than increasing a person's base salary at the end of the year, an employer gives an individual a salary increase or some other financial reward for outstanding performance immediately or shortly after the performance occurred. For example, many baseball players have clauses in their contracts that pay them bonuses for hitting more than .300 over a season.

individual incentive plans
A compensation system in which an employer gives an individual a salary increase or some other financial reward for outstanding performance immediately or shortly after the performance occurred.

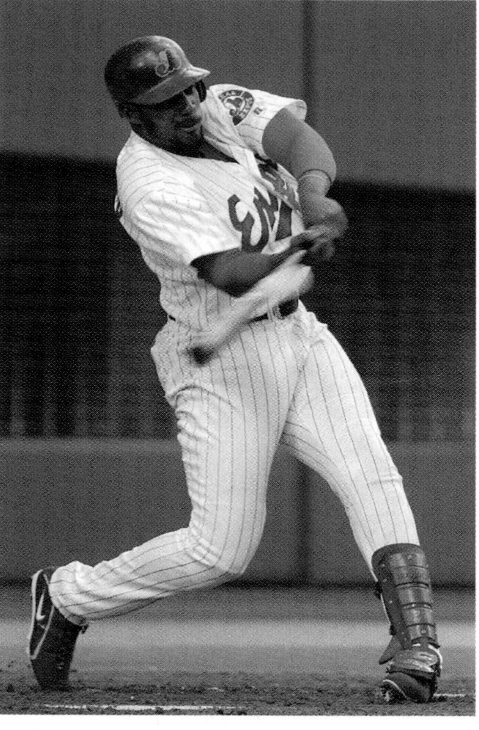

Individual incentive plans have been a big part of professional sports for many years. Players like Vladimir Guerrero of the Montreal Expos receive multi-million dollar annual compensation for outstanding individual performance.

sales commission

Paying salespeople based on the number of units they sell or the dollar value of sales they generate for the company.

Individual incentive systems are most common where performance can be assessed objectively (for example, by the number of units of output) rather than subjectively by a superior. Perhaps the most common form of individual incentive is the **sales commission** paid to people engaged in sales work. Salespeople "on commission" are paid based on the number of units they sell or the dollar value of sales they generate for the company.

Other Forms of Incentives. Occasionally organizations use other forms of incentives. For example, a non-monetary incentive, such as additional time off or a special perk, might be useful. At some companies, recognition is given to employees in the form of special points that are awarded on the recommendation of a supervisor. Recipients can convert their points into money or they can use them to buy merchandise or trips from a special online catalogue.[10]

Team and Group Incentive Systems

The merit compensation and incentive compensation systems described in the preceding sections deal primarily with reward plans for individuals. There are also performance-based reward programs for teams and groups. Given today's increasing trend toward team- and group-based methods of work, such programs are growing in importance.

gain sharing program

An incentive program in which employees receive a bonus if the firm's costs are reduced because of greater worker efficiency and/or productivity.

Gain Sharing. Many organizations use **gain sharing programs**, which are designed to share with employees the cost savings from productivity improvements. Palliser Furniture Ltd., for example, introduced a gain-sharing plan that rewards employees for increasing production. Any profit resulting from production above a certain level is split 50–50 between the company and the employees.[11] The underlying assumption is that employees and the employer have the same goals and should therefore share in incremental economic gains. In general, organizations start by measuring team- or group-level productivity. The team or work group itself is then charged with lowering costs and otherwise improving productivity through any measures that members develop and their manager approves. Any resulting cost savings or productivity gains are then quantified and translated into dollar values. According to a predetermined formula, these dollar savings are then allocated to both employer and employees.

Palliser Furniture
www.palliser.com

Performance Increases. Some companies use incentives at the team or group level. Just like individual incentives, some team or group incentives tie rewards directly to performance increases. Like individual incentives, team or group incentives are also paid as they are earned rather than added to base salaries.

Profit Sharing. Other team- or group-level incentives go beyond the contributions of a specific work group. These are generally organization-wide incentives. One long-standing type of incentive program is called a **profit-sharing plan**. At the end of the year, some portion of the company's profits is paid into a profit-sharing pool that is then distributed to all employees. In 2000, Dofasco's profit-sharing plan gave each worker $7906 beyond his or her regular pay. Dofasco annually contributes 14 percent of its pre-tax profits to the profit-sharing plan.[12] Ipsco Steel of Regina introduced a profit-sharing plan that gives all workers an identical year-end bonus. In one recent year, over $9 million was distributed to employees.[13]

profit-sharing plan
An incentive program in which employees receive a bonus depending on the firm's profits.

Benefits

In addition to financial compensation, most organizations provide employees with an array of other indirect compensation in the form of benefits. **Benefits** generally refer to various rewards, incentives, and other things of value that an organization gives employees in addition to wages, salaries, and other forms of direct financial compensation. Because these benefits have tangible value, they represent a meaningful form of compensation even though they are not generally expressed in financial terms.

benefits
What a firm offers its workers other than wages and salaries in return for their labour.

Canada's universal health care system is a real advantage to doing business in Canada because business firms do not have to pay to provide this coverage. Rather, its cost is supported largely from general tax revenues. A study of the cost of employee benefits as a percentage of wages and salaries in nine industrialized countries found that Canada's percentage (25 percent) was the lowest, and Germany's was the highest (70 percent). The other seven countries (the United States, United Kingdom, Japan, Netherlands, Austria, Italy, France) were somewhere between these two extremes.[14]

Mandated Protection Plans

Protection plans protect employees when their income is threatened or reduced by illness, disability, death, unemployment, or retirement. A number of these plans are required by law, but others are optional. One mandated benefit is **employment insurance**, which provides a basic subsistence payment to employees who are between jobs. It is intended for people who have stopped working for one organization but who are assumed to be actively seeking employment with another. Both employers and employees pay premiums to an employment insurance fund.

protection plan
A plan that protects employees when their income is threatened or reduced by illness, disability, death, unemployment, or retirement.

employment insurance
A protection plan that provides a basic subsistence payment to employees who are between jobs.

Also mandated are Canada Pension Plan payments. The original purpose of this program was to provide some limited income to retired individuals to supplement personal savings, private pensions, part-time work, and so forth. It is funded through employee and employer taxes that are withheld from payroll.

Workers' compensation is mandated insurance that covers individuals who suffer a job-related illness or accident. Employers bear the cost of workers' compensation insurance. The exact premium is related to each employer's past experience with job-related accidents and illnesses. For example, a steel company might pay $20 per $100 of wages, while an accounting firm might pay only 10 cents per $100 of wages.

workers' compensation
Mandated insurance that covers individuals who suffer a job-related illness or accident.

Optional Protection Plans

Another major category of employee benefits consists of various optional protection plans. These plans provide protection in many of the same areas as those discussed above, except that organizations can choose whether to provide them. Perhaps the most common optional protection plan is insurance coverage. Health insurance is probably the most important type of coverage. In recent years, it has been expanded by many organizations to include such things as special programs for prescription drugs, vision care products, mental health services, and dental care. Other kinds of coverage include life insurance, long-term disability insurance, and company pension plans.

Company pension plans can cause problems for employers. The decline of the stock market in recent years has led to underfunding of many pension plans (that is, the money in the pension plan is not sufficient to pay all the people who have claims on it). A 2003 study by three benefits consulting firms found that pension plans are collectively facing a $225 billion shortfall. To solve this problem, more contributions will have to be made to the plans (either by companies or their employees), or employees will receive lower benefits when they retire.[15]

Paid Time Off

Paid vacations are usually for periods of one, two, or more weeks during which an employee can take time off from work and continue to be paid. Most organizations vary the amount of paid vacation with an individual's seniority. Another common paid time off plan is *sick leave*. This benefit is provided when an individual is sick or otherwise physically unable to perform his or her job. Most organizations allow an individual to accumulate sick time according to a schedule, such as one sick day per month.

Sometimes an organization will allow an employee to take off a small number of days simply for "personal business." This benefit is usually called *personal leave*. Occasions might include funerals, religious observances, weddings, birthdays, or simply personal holidays. Finally, organizations are usually required by law to allow employees to miss work if they are called for jury duty.

Other Types of Benefits

wellness program
A program that concentrates on preventing illness in employees rather than simply paying their expenses when they become sick.

In addition to protection plans and paid time off, many organizations offer a growing number of other benefit programs. **Wellness programs**, for example, concentrate on preventing illness in employees rather than simply paying their expenses when they become sick. In some organizations, these programs are simple and involve little more than organized jogging or walking during lunch breaks. More elaborate programs include smoking cessation, blood pressure and cholesterol screening, and stress management. Some organizations maintain full-fledged health clubs on site and provide counselling and programs for fitness and weight loss.

Childcare benefits are also becoming extremely popular. In fact, any organization that wants to be considered "family-friendly" must have some type of childcare benefits, and being a "family-friendly" company is increasingly becoming a competitive advantage. These plans might include scheduling help, referrals to various types of services, or reimbursement accounts for childcare expenses. In many cases, they actually include company-paid daycare. Eldercare is also going to become increasingly common as the population ages and workers care for their elderly parents.

Cafeteria-Style Benefit Plans

cafeteria-style benefit plans
A flexible approach to providing benefits in which employees are allocated a certain sum to cover benefits and can "spend" this allocation on the specific benefits they prefer.

Most benefit programs are designed for all employees in an organization. Although the exact benefits may vary according to the employee's level in the organization, within those levels plans are generally "one size fits all." In contrast, **cafeteria-style benefit plans** allow employees to choose the benefits they really want. Under these plans, the organization typically establishes a budget, indicating how much it is willing to spend, per employee, on benefits. Employees are then presented with a list of possible benefits and the cost of each. They are free to put the benefits together in any combination they wish. Employees at Toyota's Cambridge, Ontario, plant are given the opportunity once each year to restructure their benefit packages. For example, they can give more weight to dental coverage if they have young children, or to life insurance or disability coverage, depending on their circumstances.[16]

THE LEGAL CONTEXT OF HRM

6. Describe some of the key legal issues involved in hiring, compensating, and managing workers.

As much or more than any area of business, HRM is heavily influenced by federal law, provincial law, and judicial review. In this section, we summarize some of the most important and far-reaching areas of HR regulation. These include *equal employment opportunity, comparable worth, sexual harassment, employee safety and health,* and *retirement*.

Equal Employment Opportunity

The opening case described some of the imbalances that exist between men and women in managerial positions. The basic goal of all **equal employment opportunity regulations** is to protect people from unfair or inappropriate discrimination in the workplace. Let's begin by noting that discrimination in itself is not illegal. Whenever one person is given a pay raise and another is not, or when one person is hired and another is not, the organization has made a decision to distinguish one person from another. As long as the basis for this discrimination is purely job-related (made, for instance, on the basis of performance or qualifications) and is applied objectively and consistently, the action is legal and appropriate. Problems arise when distinctions among people are not job-related. In such cases, the resulting discrimination is illegal.

equal employment opportunity regulations
Regulations to protect people from unfair or inappropriate discrimination in the workplace.

Anti-Discrimination Laws

When recruiting, firms must be careful not to violate anti-discrimination laws. The key federal anti-discrimination legislation is the **Canadian Human Rights Act** of 1977. The goal of this act is to ensure that any individual who wishes to obtain a job has an equal opportunity to compete for it. The act applies to all federal agencies, federal Crown corporations, any employee of the federal government, and business firms that do business interprovincially. Thus, it applies to such firms as the Bank of Montreal, Air Canada, Telecom Canada, Canadian National Railways, and many other public and private sector organizations that operate across Canada. Even with such wide application, the act affects only about 10 percent of Canadian workers; the rest are covered under provincial human rights acts.

Canadian Human Rights Act
Ensures that any individual who wishes to obtain a job has an equal opportunity to apply for it.

Canadian Human Rights Act of 1977
laws.justice.gc.ca/en/H-6/index.html

The Canadian Human Rights Act prohibits a wide variety of practices in recruiting, selecting, promoting, and dismissing personnel. The act specifically prohibits discrimination on the basis of age, race and colour, national and ethnic origin, physical handicap, religion, gender, marital status, or prison record (if pardoned). Some exceptions to these blanket prohibitions are permitted. Discrimination cannot be charged if a blind person is refused a position as a train engineer, bus driver, or crane operator. Likewise, a firm cannot be charged with discrimination if it does not hire a deaf person as a telephone operator or as an audio engineer.

These situations are clear-cut, but many others are not. For example, is it discriminatory to refuse women employment in a job that routinely requires carrying objects with a mass of more than 50 kilograms? Difficulties in determining whether discrimination has occurred are sometimes dealt with by using the concept of **bona fide occupational requirement**. An employer may choose one person over another based on overriding characteristics of the job in question. If a fitness centre wants to hire only women to supervise its women's locker room and sauna, it can do so without being discriminatory because it established a bona fide occupational requirement.

bona fide occupational requirement
When an employer may choose one applicant over another based on overriding characteristics of the job.

The Canadian Human Rights Commission carries out enforcement of the federal act. The commission can either respond to complaints from individuals who believe they have been discriminated against, or launch an investigation on its own if it has reason to believe that discrimination has occurred. During an investigation, data are gathered about the alleged discriminatory behaviour and, if the claim of discrimination is substantiated, the offending organization or individual may be ordered to compensate the victim.

Each province has also enacted human rights legislation to regulate organizations and businesses operating in that province. These provincial regulations are similar in spirit to the federal legislation, with many minor variations from province to province. All provinces prohibit discrimination on the basis of race, national or ethnic origin, colour, religion, sex, and marital status, but some do not address such issues as physical handicaps, criminal record, or age. Provincial human rights commissions enforce provincial legislation.

The **Employment Equity Act of 1986** addresses the issue of discrimination in employment by designating four groups as employment disadvantaged—women, visible minorities, aboriginal people, and people with disabilities. Companies covered by the act are required to publish statistics on their employment of people in these four groups.

Employment Equity Act of 1986
Federal legislation that designates four groups as employment disadvantaged—women, visible minorities, aboriginal people, and people with disabilities.

The Bank of Montreal recently became the first company outside the United States to win a prestigious award for promoting women's careers. The Bank of Montreal has introduced initiatives such as flexible working hours, a mentoring program, a national career information network, and a gender awareness workshop series.[17]

Companies are increasingly making provisions for disabled employees. At Rogers Cablevision, a division of Rogers Communications Inc., a large workplace area was completely redesigned to accommodate workers who were either visually disabled or in wheelchairs. Special equipment was also installed—a large-print computer for workers with partial sight, and a device that allows blind workers to read printed materials.[18]

Comparable Worth

In spite of recent advances, the average woman still earns only about three-quarters of what the average man earns; the average single woman, however, earns 99 percent of what single men earn. The most recent gains by women have occurred because men lost four of every five jobs that disappeared during the 1990s. Most top jobs in the public and private sector continue to be held by men.[19]

Comparable worth is a legal concept that aims at paying equal wages for jobs that are of comparable value to the employer. This might mean comparing dissimilar jobs, such as those of nurses and mechanics or secretaries and electricians. Proponents of comparable worth say that all the jobs in a company must be evaluated and then rated in terms of basic dimensions such as the level of skill they require. All jobs could then be compared based on a common index. People in different jobs that rate the same on this index would be paid the same. Experts hope that this will help to reduce the gap between men's and women's pay.

comparable worth
A legal idea that aims to pay equal wages for work of equal value.

Critics of comparable worth object on the grounds that it ignores the supply and demand aspects of labour. They say, for example, that legislation forcing a company to pay people more than the open market price for their labour (which may happen in jobs where there is a surplus of workers) is another example of unreasonable government interference in business activities. They also say that implementing comparable worth will cost business firms too much money. A study prepared for the Ontario Ministry of Labour estimated that it would cost approximately $10 billion for the public and private sectors in Ontario to establish equitable payment for jobs of equal value. Yet the cost defence cannot be easily used. In one case, the Quebec Human Rights Commission ruled that 24 female office employees of the Quebec North Shore Paper Company were performing work of equal value to that done by male production workers. The company was required to increase the secretaries' salaries by $701 annually and give them over $1000 in back pay.[20]

In 1999, the Canadian Human Rights Tribunal ruled that the federal government must pay a total of more than $3 billion to thousands of civil servants because it discriminated against workers in female-dominated job classifications. About 85 percent of these workers were women.

There is one very interesting fact in this debate about comparable worth: Male earning power has been declining for decades. Young males who are now entering the labour market, regardless of their education, will likely earn dramatically less than their predecessors did. Young, female university graduates, on the other hand, have recently earned more than their predecessors.[21]

Sexual Harassment

Within the job context, **sexual harassment** refers to requests for sexual favours, unwelcome sexual advances, or verbal or physical conduct of a sexual nature that creates an intimidating or hostile environment for a given employee. The Canadian Human Rights Act takes precedence over any policies that a company might have developed on its own to deal with sexual harassment problems.

sexual harassment
Requests for sexual favours, unwelcome sexual advances, or verbal or physical conduct of a sexual nature that creates an intimidating or hostile environment for a given employee.

Quid pro quo harassment is the most blatant form of sexual harassment. It occurs when the harasser offers to exchange something of value for sexual favours. A male supervisor, for example, might tell or suggest to a female subordinate that he will recommend her for promotion or give her a raise in exchange for sexual favours. The creation of a **hostile work environment** is a subtler form of sexual harassment. A group of male employees who continually make off-colour jokes and lewd comments and perhaps decorate the work environment with questionable photographs may create a hostile work environment for a female colleague. Regardless of the pattern, the same bottom-line rules apply: Sexual harassment is illegal, and the organization is responsible for controlling it.

quid pro quo harassment
Form of sexual harassment in which sexual favours are requested in return for job-related benefits.

hostile work environment
Form of sexual harassment deriving from off-colour jokes, lewd comments, and so forth.

If a manager is found guilty of sexual harassment, the company is also liable because the manager is an agent of the company. In fact, even if one employee makes another employee feel uncomfortable, the instigator may be guilty of sexual harassment. To deal effectively with the potential for sexual harassment, managers should:

- develop clear and enforceable policies dealing with sexual harassment
- inform all employees about the existence of these policies
- train employees to recognize and refrain from sexual harassment
- take complaints about sexual harassment seriously

- establish a procedure for dealing with harassment complaints
- take action against those who are involved in sexual harassment

Employee Safety and Health

Employee safety and health programs help to reduce absenteeism and turnover, raise productivity, and boost morale by making jobs safer and more healthful. Government regulations about employee safety are becoming stricter. Ontario, which loses more than 7 million working days yearly because of on-the-job injuries, has passed amendments to the Ontario Occupational Health and Safety Act. Officers and directors of companies are held personally responsible for workplace health and safety and are punishable by jail terms and fines for permitting unsafe working conditions.[22]

repetitive strain injuries (RSIs)
Injuries that occur when workers perform the same functions over and over again.

Some industrial work—logging, construction, fishing, and mining—can put workers at risk of injury in obvious ways. But other types of work—such as typing or lifting—can also cause painful injuries. **Repetitive strain injuries (RSIs)** occur when workers perform the same functions over and over again. These injuries disable more than 200 000 Canadians each year and account for nearly half of all work-related time loss claims.

In Canada, each province has developed its own workplace health and safety regulations. The purpose of these laws is to ensure that employees do not have to work in dangerous conditions. These laws are the direct result of undesirable conditions that existed in many Canadian businesses at the close of the nineteenth century. While much improvement is evident, Canada still has some problems with workplace health and safety. In one study of six Western industrialized nations, Canada had the worst safety record in mining and construction and the second-worst record in manufacturing and railways.

The Ontario Occupational Health and Safety Act illustrates current legislation in Canada. It requires all employers to ensure that equipment and safety devices are used properly. Employers must also show workers the proper way to operate machinery. At the job site, supervisors are charged with the responsibility of ensuring that workers use equipment properly. The act also requires workers to behave appropriately on the job. Employees have the right to refuse to work on a job if they believe it is unsafe; a legal procedure exists for resolving any disputes in this area.

In most provinces, the Ministry of Labour appoints inspectors to enforce health and safety regulations. If the inspector finds a sufficient hazard, he or she has the authority to clear the workplace. Inspectors can usually arrive at a firm unannounced to conduct an inspection.

Retirement

Some employees are ready for retirement earlier than others. But because many retirement plans are based on an employee's age, some workers who should retire earlier stay on the job while others, who are still useful workers, leave before they would like to. This mishandling of valuable resources—skilled employees—is short-sighted. A compromise is to grant year-to-year extensions to productive employees who want to continue working past the traditional retirement age.

Canadian courts have typically upheld 65 as the mandatory retirement age, but there have been many complaints from older workers who want to continue working past this age. As a result, the Ontario Human Rights Commission has launched a review of age discrimination and mandatory retirement. The commission is also studying downsizing practices that may push older workers into early retirement.[23] The commission is going ahead with the study even though Canadians generally are retiring earlier than they used to. In the period 1976–1980, for example, the median retirement age in Canada was 64.9 years, but in the period 1991–1995 that figure dropped to 62.3 years.[24] Two other interesting facts: Workers over age 65 are nearly four times as likely to die from work-related causes than younger workers, and older workers have double the health care costs that workers in their forties do.[25]

NEW CHALLENGES IN THE CHANGING WORKPLACE

7. Discuss *workforce diversity*, the management of *knowledge workers*, and the use of *contingent and temporary workers* as important changes in the contemporary workplace.

As we have seen throughout this chapter, HR managers face several ongoing challenges in their efforts to keep their organizations staffed with effective workers. To complicate matters, new challenges arise as the economic and social environments of business change. We conclude this chapter with a discussion of several of the most important HRM issues facing business today: *managing workforce diversity, managing knowledge workers,* and *managing contingent and temporary workers*.

Managing Workforce Diversity

One extremely important set of human resource challenges centres on **workforce diversity**—the range of workers' attitudes, values, beliefs, and behaviours that differ by gender, race, age, ethnicity, physical ability, and other relevant characteristics. In the past, organizations tended to work toward homogenizing their workforces, getting everyone to think and behave in similar ways. Partly as a result of affirmative action efforts, however, many organizations are now creating more diverse workforces by embracing more women, ethnic minorities, and foreign-born employees than ever before.

workforce diversity
The range of workers' attitudes, values, beliefs, and behaviours that differ by gender, race, age, ethnicity, physical ability, and other relevant characteristics.

Today, organizations are recognizing not only that they should treat everyone equitably, but also that they should acknowledge the individuality of each person they employ. They are also recognizing that diversity can be a competitive advantage. For example, by hiring the best people available from every group rather than hiring from just one or a few groups, a firm can develop a higher-quality workforce. Similarly, a diverse workforce can bring a wider array of information to bear on problems and can provide insights on marketing products to a wider range of consumers. Says the head of workforce diversity at IBM: "We think it is important for our customers to look inside and see people like them. If they can't...the prospect of them becoming or staying our customers declines."

Managing Knowledge Workers

Traditionally, employees added value to organizations because of what they did or because of their experience. In the "information age," however, many employees add value because of what they know.[26]

The Nature of Knowledge Work

These employees are usually called **knowledge workers**, and the skill with which they are managed is a major factor in determining which firms will be successful in the future. Knowledge workers, including computer scientists, engineers, and physical scientists, provide special challenges for the HR manager. They tend to work for high-tech firms and are usually experts

knowledge workers
Workers who are experts in specific fields like computer technology and engineering, and who add value because of what they know, rather than how long they have worked or the job they do.

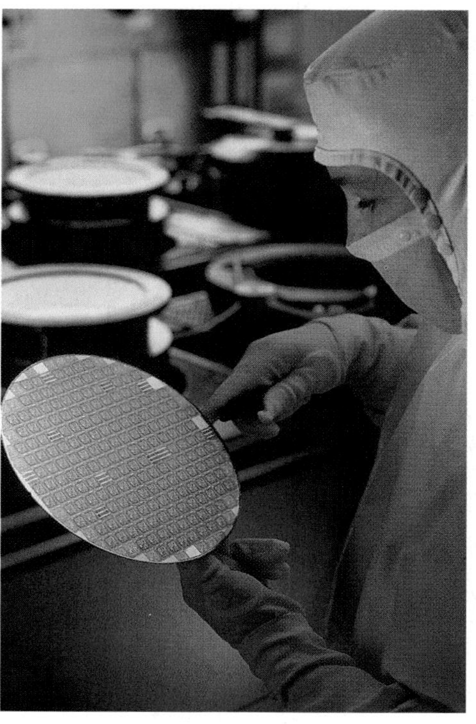

Every year the toy industry sells about 10 million scientific toys, such as chemistry sets. It also sells about 30 million electronic toys. More and more science-minded students—like this Power PC chip builder at Intel Corp.—are opting for computer-industry jobs instead of jobs in the traditional hard sciences, such as chemistry. Many experts predict that the current lure of quick financial gain will result in a future shortage of science teachers and researchers.

in some abstract knowledge base. They often prefer to work independently and tend to identify more strongly with their professions than with any organization—even to the extent of defining performance in terms recognized by other members of their professions.

As the importance of information-driven jobs grows, the need for knowledge workers continues to grow as well. But these employees require extensive and highly specialized training, and not every organization is willing to make the human capital investments necessary to take advantage of these jobs. In fact, even after knowledge workers are on the job, training updates are critical to prevent their skills from becoming obsolete. It has been suggested, for example, that the "half-life" of a technical education in engineering is about three years. The failure to update such skills will not only result in the loss of competitive advantage but also increase the likelihood that the knowledge worker will move to another firm that is more committed to updating his or her knowledge.

Knowledge Worker Management and Labour Markets

In recent years, the demand for knowledge workers has been growing at a dramatic rate. As a result, organizations that need these workers must introduce regular market adjustments (upward) to pay them enough to keep them. This is especially critical in areas in which demand is growing, as even entry-level salaries for these employees are skyrocketing. Once an employee accepts a job with a firm, the employer faces yet another dilemma. Once hired, workers are subject to the company's internal labour market, which is not likely to be growing as quickly as the external market for knowledge workers as a whole. Consequently, the longer an employee remains with a firm, the further behind the market his or her pay falls—unless, of course, it is regularly adjusted upward.

Not surprisingly, the growing demand for these workers has inspired some fairly extreme measures for attracting them in the first place.[27] High starting salaries and sign-on bonuses are common. British Petroleum Exploration was recently paying starting petroleum engineers with undersea platform-drilling knowledge—not experience, just knowledge—salaries in the six figures, plus sign-on bonuses of over U.S.$50 000 and immediate profit sharing. Even with these incentives, HR managers complain that they cannot retain specialists because young engineers soon leave to accept sign-on bonuses from competitors. Laments one HR executive: "We wind up six months after we hire an engineer having to fight off offers for that same engineer for more money."[28]

Managing Contingent and Temporary Workers

A final contemporary HR issue involves the use of contingent and/or temporary workers. Indeed, recent years have seen an explosion in the use of such workers by organizations.

Trends in Contingent and Temporary Employment

A contingent worker is a person who works for an organization on something other than a permanent or full-time basis. Categories of contingent workers include independent contractors (freelancers), on-call workers, temporary employees (usually hired through outside agencies), and contract and leased employees. Another category is part-time workers. The financial services giant Citigroup, for example, makes extensive use of part-time sales agents to pursue new clients.

Managing Contingent and Temporary Workers

Given the widespread use of contingent and temporary workers, HR managers must understand how to use such employees most effectively. That is, they need to understand how to manage contingent and temporary workers. One key is careful planning. Even though one of the presumed benefits of using contingent workers is flexibility, it still is important to integrate such workers in a coordinated fashion. Rather than having to call in workers sporadically and with no prior notice, organizations try to bring in specified numbers of workers for well-defined periods of time. The ability to do so comes from careful planning.

A second key is understanding contingent workers and acknowledging both their advantages and their disadvantages. That is, the organization must recognize what it can and cannot achieve by using contingent and temporary workers. Expecting too much from contingent workers, for example, is a mistake that managers should avoid.

Third, managers must carefully assess the real cost of using contingent workers. Many firms adopt this course of action to save labour costs. The organization should be able to document precisely its labour-cost savings. How much would it be paying people in wages and benefits if they were on permanent staff? How does this cost compare with the amount spent on contingent workers? This difference, however, could be misleading.

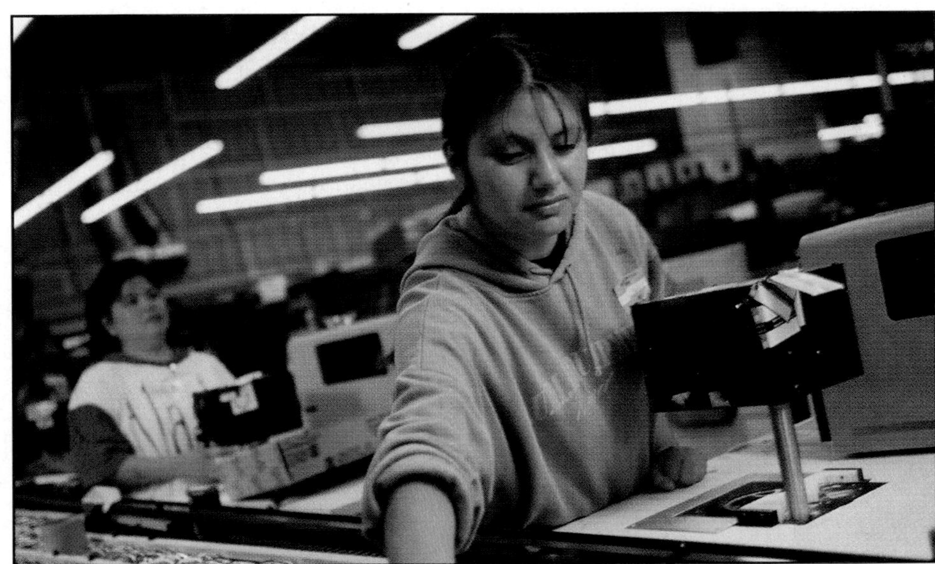

This young woman is one of 1500 temporary workers at Sola Optical. Sola keeps at least 100 temps working at all times, because it gives human resource managers both scheduling flexibility and the opportunity to try potential permanent employees.

Contingent workers might be less effective performers than permanent and full-time employees. Comparing employees on a direct-cost basis, therefore, is not necessarily valid. Organizations must learn to adjust the direct differences in labour costs to account for differences in productivity and performance. Ethical issues regarding contingent workers are addressed in the Exercising Your Ethics box.

Finally, managers must fully understand their own strategies and decide in advance how they intend to manage temporary workers, specifically focusing on how to integrate them into the organization. On a very simplistic level, for example, an organization with a large contingent workforce must make some decisions about the treatment of contingent workers relative to the treatment of permanent, full-time workers. Should contingent workers be invited to the company holiday party? Should they have the same access to such employee benefits as counselling services and childcare? Managers must understand that they need to develop a strategy for integrating contingent workers according to some sound logic and then follow that strategy consistently over time.[29]

SUMMARY OF LEARNING OBJECTIVES

1. **Define *human resource management*, discuss its strategic significance, and explain how managers plan for human resources.** *Human resource management,* or *HRM,* is the set of organizational activities directed at attracting, developing, and maintaining an effective workforce. HRM plays a key strategic role in organizational per-

EXERCISING YOUR ETHICS

Taking Advantage of Contingent Workers

The Situation

You are a store manager in a large retail organization. Your job is full-time, and you receive good benefits from the company. However, many people in your store (cashiers, shelf-stockers, greeters, etc.) work only part-time for the company. You know that many of them want to work full-time but the company does not allow it. One of the reasons is that part-time workers are not eligible for benefits and this reduces the company's human resources expenses. Top management has emphasized on several occasions that it is imperative that costs be controlled so your store can remain competitive, and reducing human resource costs is one obvious way to do that.

The Dilemma

You have become increasingly concerned that the human resource management policies of your organization leave something to be desired. In the past few months, several workers have expressed their deep concerns to you that they are having extreme financial difficulty because they are not given enough hours of work each week. You know these workers, and they are hard-working, reliable people. You have great sympathy for them, particularly the ones who have families. You also know, however, that competition from competitors like Wal-Mart is intense, and that keeping costs low is absolutely imperative if your firm hopes to compete. You know that if the prices you charge are not competitive, customers will shop elsewhere. If that happens, there won't be any jobs for anybody, full-time or otherwise.

Questions for Discussion

1. What are the ethical issues in this situation?
2. What do you think most managers would do in this situation?
3. What would you do? Defend your answer.

formance. Planning for human resource needs entails several steps. Conducting a *job analysis* enables managers to create detailed, accurate job descriptions and specifications. After analysis is complete, managers must forecast demand and supply for both the numbers and types of workers they will need. Then they consider steps to match supply with demand.

2. **Identify the issues involved in *staffing* a company, including *internal* and *external recruiting* and *selection.*** *Recruiting* is the process of attracting qualified persons to apply for jobs that an organization has open. *Internal recruiting* involves considering present employees for new jobs. This approach helps build morale and rewards an organization's best employees. *External recruiting* means attracting people from outside the organization to apply for openings. When organizations are actually selecting people for jobs, they generally use such selection techniques as *application forms, tests, interviews,* and other techniques. Regardless of what selection techniques are used, they must be valid predictors of an individual's expected performance in the job.
3. **Discuss different ways in which organizations go about developing the capabilities of employees and managers.** If a company is to get the most out of its workers, it must develop both those workers and their skills. Nearly all employees undergo some initial *orientation* process that introduces them to the company and to their new jobs. Many employees are given the opportunity to acquire new skills through various *work-based* and/or *instructional-based programs*.
4. **Explain ways in which organizations evaluate employee performance.** *Performance appraisals* help managers decide who needs training and who should be promoted. Appraisals also tell employees how well they are meeting expectations. Although a variety of alternatives are available for appraising performance, employee supervisors are most commonly used. No matter who does the evaluation, however, feedback to the employee is very important. Managers can select from a variety of ranking and rating methods for use in performance appraisal.
5. **Discuss the importance of *wages and salaries, incentives,* and *benefit programs* in attracting and keeping skilled workers.** *Wages and salaries, incentives,* and *benefit packages* may all be parts of a company's compensation program. By paying its workers as well as or better than competitors, a business can attract and keep qualified personnel. *Incentive programs* can also motivate people to work more productively. *Indirect compensation* also plays a major role in effective and well-designed compensation systems.
6. **Describe some of the key legal issues involved in hiring, compensating, and managing workers.** In hiring, compensating, and managing workers, managers must obey a variety of federal and provincial laws. *Equal employment opportunity* and *equal pay* laws forbid discrimination other than action based on legitimate job requirements. The concept of *comparable worth* states that equal wages should be paid for jobs that are of comparable value to the employer. Firms are also required to provide employees with safe working environments, as set down by the guidelines of provincial occupational health and safety acts. *Sexual harassment* is another key contemporary legal issue in business.
7. **Discuss *workforce diversity,* the management of *knowledge workers,* and the use of *contingent and temporary workers* as important changes in the contemporary workplace.** *Workforce diversity* refers to

the range of workers' attitudes, values, beliefs, and behaviours that differ by gender, race, ethnicity, age, and physical ability. Today, many businesses are working to create workforces that reflect the growing diversity of the population as it enters the labour pool. Although many firms see the diverse workforce as a competitive advantage, not all are equally successful in or eager about implementing diversity programs.

Many firms today also face challenges in managing *knowledge workers*. The recent boom in high-tech companies has led to rapidly increasing salaries and high turnover among the workers who are best prepared to work in those companies. *Contingent workers* are temporary and part-time employees hired to supplement an organization's permanent workforce. Their numbers have grown significantly since the early 1980s and are expected to rise further. The practice of hiring contingent workers is gaining in popularity because it gives managers more flexibility and because temps are usually not covered by employers' benefit programs.

KEY TERMS

QUESTIONS AND EXERCISES

Questions for Review

1. What are the advantages and disadvantages of internal and external recruiting? Under what circumstances is each more appropriate?
2. Why is the formal training of workers so important to most employers? Why don't employers simply let people learn about their jobs as they perform them?
3. What different forms of compensation do firms typically use to attract and keep productive workers?
4. What are some of the most significant laws affecting human resource management?

Questions for Analysis

5. What are your views on drug testing in the workplace? What would you do if your employer asked you to submit to a drug test?
6. Have you or anyone you know ever suffered discrimination in a hiring decision? Did you or the person you know do anything about it?

7. What training do you think you are most likely to need when you finish school and start your career?
8. How much will benefit considerations affect your choice of an employer after graduation?

Application Exercises

9. Interview an HR manager at a local company. Focus on a position for which the firm is currently recruiting applicants and identify the steps in the selection process.
10. Identify some journals in your library that might be useful to an HR manager. What topics have been covered in recent features and cover stories?

BUILDING YOUR BUSINESS SKILLS

Getting Online for a Job

Goal

To introduce students to career-search resources available on the internet.

Situation

If companies are on one side of the external staffing process, people looking for work are on the other. Companies need qualified candidates to fill job openings and candidates need jobs that are right for them. The challenge, of course, is to make successful matches. Increasingly, this matchmaking is being conducted on the internet. Companies are posting jobs in cyberspace, and job seekers are posting résumés in response. The number of job postings has grown dramatically in recent years. On a typical Sunday, you might find as many as 50 000 postings on the Monster Board, a leading job site. With so many companies looking for qualified candidates online, it makes good business sense to learn how to use the system.

Method

Using internet career resources means locating job databases and preparing and posting a résumé. (You will therefore need access to the internet to complete this exercise.)

Step 1

Team up with three classmates to investigate and analyze specific job databases. In each case, write a short report describing the database (which you and other group members may use during an actual job search). Summarize the site and its features as well as its advantages, disadvantages, and costs. Start with the following sites and add others you may find on your own:

The Monster Board, **www.monster.com**
Careerbuilder.com, **www.careermosaic.com**
College Grad Job Hunter, **www.collegegrad.com**

Step 2

Investigate the job opportunities listed on the home pages of various companies. Consider trying the following companies:

Air Canada, **www.aircanada.ca**
Dofasco, **www.dofasco.ca**
Royal Bank, **www.royalbank.com**
IBM, **www.can.ibm.com**
Wal-Mart, **www.walmartstores.com**
McDonald's, **www.mcdonalds.com**
Bombardier, **www.bombardier.com**

Write a summary of the specific career-related information you find on each site.

Step 3

Working with group members, research strategies for composing effective cyber résumés. The following websites provide some helpful information on formats and personal and job-related information that should be included in your résumé. They also offer hints on the art of creating a scannable résumé:

JobSource, **www.jobsource.com**
Career Magazine, **www.careermag.com**

Two books by Joyce Lain Kennedy, *Electronic Job Search Revolution* and *Electronic Résumé Revolution*, also contain valuable information.

Step 4

Working as a group, create an effective electronic résumé for a fictitious college or university graduate looking for a first job. Pay attention to format, language, style, and the effective communication of background and goals.

Step 5

Working as a group, learn how to post your résumé online. (Do not submit the résumé you created for this exercise, which is, after all, fictitious.) The databases provided will guide you in this process.

Follow-Up Questions

1. Why is it necessary to learn how to conduct an electronic job search? Do you think it will be more or less necessary in the years ahead?
2. Why do you think more computer-related jobs than non-technical jobs are posted online? Do you think this situation will change?
3. Why is it a waste of time to stylize your résumé with different fonts, point sizes, and centred headings?
4. What is the advantage of emailing your résumé directly to a company rather than applying for the same job through an online databank?

CRAFTING YOUR BUSINESS PLAN

Maintaining Healthy Human Resources

The Purpose of the Assignment

1. To familiarize students with the HR issues faced by a sample firm as it develops its business plan.
2. To demonstrate how four chapter topics—legal and ethical issues in managing people, hiring and training employees, financial incentives programs, and external versus internal staffing—can be integrated as components in the BPP planning environment.

Assignment

After reading Chapter 8 in the textbook, open the PPB software and look for information about HRM as it applies to a sample firm: Southeast Health Plan Inc. To find this plan, do the following:

Open Business PlanPro. If it asks if you want to "create a new business plan" or "open an existing plan," select "create a new business plan" (even though you are not going to create a plan at this time). You will then be taken to the Business PlanPro EasyPlan Wizard. On the screen, click on the option entitled **Research It**. You will then be presented with a new list of options, including Sample Plan Browser. After clicking on the **Sample Plan Browser**, go down the alphabetical list of sample plans and double-click on **Plan Administration—Health**, which is the location for Southeast Health Plan Inc. The screen you are looking at is the introduction page for Southeast's business plan. Next, scroll down until you reach the **Table of Contents** for Southeast's business plan.

Now respond to the following items:

1. Explore Southeast's business plan, paying special attention to the management team, the types of employees the company has, and the clients that will be buying its products. In doing so, identify legal and ethical issues you expect Southeast to experience in managing its people. [Sites to see in BPP for this item: On the **Table of Contents** page click on each of **1.0 Executive Summary, 1.1 Objectives,** and **1.2 Mission**. After returning to the **Table of Contents** screen, examine each of the following: **Table: Startup** (located beneath **2.2 Startup Summary**), **3.3 Fulfillment, 3.4 Future Services, 6.2 Management Team,** and **6.5 Other Management Considerations**.]
2. Judging from the company's growth expectations, the contents of its business expectations, and the contents of its business plan, describe Southeast's plans for hiring and training its sales staff. [Sites to see in BPP: On the **Table of Contents** page, click on **1.0 Objectives**. Then click on each of the following: **1.2 Mission** and **1.3 Keys to Success**.]
3. Considering Southeast's growth projections, what type of incentives program would you recommend for its sales staff? Individual merit pay? Individual bonuses? Company-wide profit sharing? Explain the reasons for your recommendations. [Sites to see in BPP: On the **Table of Contents** screen, click on each of the following in turn: **4.0 Market Analysis Summary**, **Table: Sales Forecast** (located beneath **5.2.1 Sales Forecast**).] From there, click on **5.1.1 Pricing Strategy.**]
4. Judging from the contents of its business plan, do you think Southeast intends to rely on external or internal staffing for future management personnel? In what ways might the choice between external and internal options affect Southeast's performance? [Sites to see in BPP: On the **Table of Contents** page, click on each of the following: **6.0 Management Summary, 6.2 Management Team,** and **Table: Personnel** (located beneath **6.4 Personnel Plan**).]

VIDEO EXERCISE

Managing the Human Side of Business: Park Place Entertainment

Learning Objectives

The purpose of this video is to help you

1. Recognize the ways in which human resource management contributes to organizational performance.
2. Understand how and why HR managers make plans and decisions about staffing.
3. Identify some of the ways in which HR managers handle evaluation and development.

Synopsis

Park Place Entertainment owns and operates resorts and casinos around the world. Its human resource department is responsible for hiring, training, and managing a diverse group of more than 52 000 employees. Because its customers come from many countries and speak many languages, the company seeks employees from diverse backgrounds and varies the recruitment process for different properties in different areas. HR managers have created specific job descriptions for each position, instituted programs for employee and management development, and established incentive programs to reward good performance. Park Place's 360-degree evaluation method allows supervisors to get performance feedback from the employees they supervise.

Discussion Questions

1. *For analysis:* What are the advantages and disadvantages of centralizing the recruiting process at a company such as Park Place Entertainment?
2. *For analysis:* Why did Park Place begin the restructuring of its HR department by standardizing training for supervisors?
3. *For application:* What steps might Park Place HR managers take to reduce employee turnover at particular resorts?
4. *For application:* How might Park Place encourage employees to refer friends as candidates for open positions?
5. *For debate:* Rather than hiring employees when business booms and then laying them off when it slumps, should Park Place temporarily rehire retired employees during peak periods? Support your chosen position.

Online Exploration

Visit the Park Place Entertainment website at **www.ballys.com** and browse the home page to find the names and locations of the company's resorts and casinos. Then follow the corporate information link to find information on career opportunities and company benefits. What kinds of jobs are featured on the website? Why does Park Place arrange jobs by region? How does the firm make it convenient for applicants to submit résumés online? Why would Park Place put so much emphasis on internet recruiting?

EXPLORING THE NET

Doing It Right at Canadian Tire

In this chapter we have examined the human resource functions involved in staffing an organization. Such functions include: recruiting, staff selection, wages/salaries, incentives and benefits. Many companies can manage all of these functions, but how many can manage them well? The Canadian Tire Company has proved that it can, as it has made The Report on Business's "Top 50 Best Employers in Canada" listing. Canadian Tire's career opportunities website can be found at **www2.canadiantire.ca/CTCwebsite/welcome.html.**

1. Based on the Canadian Tire website, how many employees does Canadian Tire have?
2. What is the Canadian Tire Way? How does it relate to Canadian Tire's employees?
3. In exploring the **Rewards Along the Way** section of the Canadian Tire website, identify some of the benefits of working for Canadian Tire.
4. Of the items listed in **Rewards Along the Way**, which would aid in motivating Canadian Tire employees? Why? Which of these items would motivate you?
5. How does Canadian Tire use its website as a staffing tool?

Concluding Case 8-1

From Hard Bargains to Hard Times

During the economic boom times of just a few years ago, workers had the advantage in the employment equation. A general labour shortage combined with an acute shortage of knowledge and other skilled workers to make the labour market a seller's market. Top university and college graduates had multiple offers, and skilled technical workers could take their pick of jobs. Moreover, businesses began rolling out new benefits, perquisites, and incentives to attract and retain the best and the brightest.

Some companies offered employees unlimited sick days, on-site childcare, flexible work schedules, and free beverages. Others offered concierges, laundry pickup and delivery, and even on-site pet care. Some companies offered cash or new cars as signing bonuses. But as the economy slowed in 2001 and into 2002, the advantage shifted to employers. Throughout the 1990s, as it turns out, companies had relied on technological advances ranging from robotics to the internet to reduce costs in areas as diverse as advertising, production, and purchasing. When the economy turned sour, they realized that they had cut as many costs as possible from most areas of their operations, and not surprisingly, many turned to their labour forces for the next round of cuts. Many firms have reduced or stopped hiring, and the hardest hit have even started layoffs. Many of the dot-coms, among the most aggressive employers in terms of new and innovative benefits, have disappeared altogether.

The reduction in employee benefits stems in part from the realization that workers have fewer options, either in finding or leaving jobs. One of the first areas hit was perquisites, or "perks." These are not trivial issues. "There is a huge dent in morale when you take anything away from employees, no matter how minuscule it may look," says workplace consultant Sharon Jordan-Evans.

Next in line have been more traditional benefits. Many firms have either reduced contributions to benefits programs or eliminated them altogether. Ford Motors and Lucent Technologies are just two of the many organizations that now pay less for health insurance or retirement plans. Bonuses, sick leave, and vacation time are also being squeezed. As a last resort, some firms are even asking workers to accept pay cuts. Pay at Agilent Technology has dropped 10 percent, and Disney has cut some pay rates by 30 percent.

Firms that have frozen hiring or reduced benefits and perquisites have found that current economic conditions give them more flexibility than they had just a few years ago. While these actions may lower costs and protect profits in the short term, firms that follow this path may face problems when the economy rebounds. In particular, they may find that they've tarnished their reputations as employers and find it more difficult to attract workers when they need them again.

The immediate repercussions may include low morale, reduced productivity, or worse. And the effects can be long-lasting. Says one executive whose company instituted pay cuts, "People are lying low, but when the economy improves, they'll be out of here." Workers complain that they shouldn't bear a disproportionate share of the cost cutting burden. Workers are particularly upset when CEO compensation rises while profits are falling.

The good news for struggling firms is that there are still effective incentives. The most powerful, and least expensive, perk can be time off. Experts suggest, for example, that up to 20 percent of workers would be willing to work fewer hours for lower pay. Siemens, a German electronics firm, is offering workers a year-long "time-out," with reduced pay and a guaranteed job when they return. "It's a possibility for us not to lose good workers despite bad times," says Siemens' spokesperson Axel Heim. Firms are also finding that technology workers and professionals, who need to stay on the leading edge of their fields, want more training and increased job responsibilities. Many people, warns Patti Wilson, founder of a high-tech career-management firm, "will jump jobs to learn more or stay if they feel that they're being challenged."

Questions for Discussion

1. What are the basic human resource issues reflected in labour force reductions and other HR cutbacks?
2. What benefits seem to be the most valuable to employees, and what benefits seem trivial and/or extravagant?
3. Aside from laying off workers, what other costs might be cut in managing an organization's labour force?
4. What other incentives besides benefits might a company be able to offer its best workers to retain them?
5. How might current employment trends affect unionization? Why? ◆

Concluding Case 8-2

What About Contracting?

Years ago, when people thought about a career, they usually thought of going to work full-time for a company and, if they liked it, staying at that company for many years. Even if a person didn't stay at one firm, the idea still was that the person would work full-time for a company for at least a few years.

But times are changing. A growing number of workers are becoming contract workers, or freelancers—individuals who contract with a company for a set period of time, usually until a specific project is completed. After the project is completed, the contract worker moves on to another project in the firm, or to another firm. Statistics Canada estimates that 30 percent of working adults are doing contract work.

Why is contracting work becoming so common? As the economic situation has become more uncertain, more and more companies are using contract workers so they don't have to make long-term financial commitments. Playdium Corp., which operates virtual reality entertainment centres, uses contract employees for a variety of purposes: to fill in for regular employees who call in sick, to replace those who are on maternity leave, and to meet changes in seasonal demand for its products. Most contractors work three or four months.

Competitive pressures are also forcing firms to reduce their costs and increase their productivity. The current buzzword is "flexibility" and this can often be achieved by hiring contract workers to solve specific company problems. This allows a firm to maintain a minimum number of full-time workers and then supplement them with contractors. Recent advances in information technology have also facilitated contract work, since workers do not necessarily have to be at the workplace to do their work.

But companies also hire contractors to save money (contract workers may cost companies 10 percent less than permanent staff). For one thing, they don't have to pay Canada Pension Plan or Employment Insurance premiums. But pressures are building to change this. In 1994, the province of Saskatchewan became the first in Canada to require companies to pay contract and part-time workers at least some benefits.

Ray Sherwood is the Chief Financial Officer (CFO) for Winnipeg-based Frantic Films, a firm that produces historical television series and special effects for movies. As CFO, he closely watches cash flows, generates financial projections, and generally ensures that the company achieves its short- and long-term financial goals. Sherwood is a contract worker who started with Frantic Films on May 1, 2002. He receives payment for his services, but he receives no other fringe benefits. His contract is reviewed each year. Frantic Films requires about 70–80 percent of his time. Sherwood also presents seminars on accounting and finance topics to managers in both public- and private-sector companies on a contract basis.

After graduating with a B. Comm. degree, Sherwood worked in the banking industry for a few years, but he has been a contract worker since then. That has included working as a financial officer for Credo Entertainment and VZS Films, as well as sessional lecturer work at the University of Manitoba, the University of Winnipeg, and Red River College.

Sherwood is very happy about being a contract worker. He says that he is an entrepreneurial, risk-taking sort of person and he likes the flexibility and independence that contract work offers him. He also says that contractors who "put all their eggs in one basket" and only work for one company can be exposed to higher risk than those who have client diversification. The variety of experiences he has with multiple companies is very interesting.

He recognizes that as a contract worker he does not get certain benefits (e.g., a pension), and he may be forgoing promotions that he might get if he were an employee, but he feels that the benefits of contract work clearly outweigh the costs. He points out that in today's uncertain economic environment there is really very little job security even for regular employees, so he feels that he is not giving up much to be a contract worker. In the long term, he wants to continue working with Frantic Films through his consulting company and to provide financial expertise to other clients on a contract basis.

Why are people willing to work on a contract basis if they don't get the benefits that full-time workers get? Some do contract work simply because they can't get full-time work with one company, but others, like Ray Sherwood, do it by choice. Accomplished contract workers can control their own destiny, make above-average incomes, and have a strong sense of flexibility and freedom. Contractors also bring new ideas into companies.

While companies often contract out the work of technical or professional employees, the management of other functions may also be contracted out. Some years ago the Halifax District School Board contracted out the management of custodial services for the district's 42 schools to ServiceMaster Canada Ltd. And Manpower Temporary Services managed a packaging department for a pharmaceutical firm that sometimes numbers as many as 130 people, and sometimes as few as 70, depending on demand. A Manpower manager is on site at the pharmaceutical firm; she recruits the temporary workers, does some of the necessary training, conducts performance appraisals of temporary workers, and handles the payroll.

With the massive layoffs that have been evident in recent years, workers are beginning to realize that large firms do not necessarily provide job security. Rather, security comes from having confidence in your own knowledge and skills, and marketing yourself in innovative ways. There are both positive and negative aspects to the idea of non-standard work. From the worker's perspective, those with marketable skills will find that non-standard work will result in high pay and satisfying work. For those without marketable skills, non-standard work will likely mean part-time work in low-paying service jobs. Those individuals who lack either the ability or interest to capitalize on non-standard work will find that there is much uncertainty in their careers.

From the organization's perspective, a conclusion about the value of non-standard work means weighing the value of long-term employee loyalty and commitment against the benefits of the increased flexibility that is possible with contract workers.

Questions for Discussion

1. What kind of people are most likely to want contract work?
2. What are the pros and cons of contract work from the individual's perspective? From the organization's perspective?
3. Is it unethical to hire contract workers in order to avoid paying them company benefits? ◆

CHAPTER 9

Understanding Labour–Management Relations

After reading this chapter, you will be able to:

1. Explain why workers unionize.
2. Trace the evolution of and discuss trends in *unionism* in Canada.
3. Describe the *major laws governing labour–management relations*.
4. Describe the union *certification* and *decertification processes*.
5. Identify the steps in the *collective bargaining process*.

Management and Unions Sing the Blues at Air Canada

Most Canadians are well aware of the troubles that faced Air Canada during 2002 and 2003. In early 2003, Air Canada was losing $5 million each day. Clearly, something had to be done, and it had to be done quickly. Because the demand for air travel was not likely to increase, the reduction of costs was seen as crucial. To achieve this reduction, Air Canada did two things. First, it reduced capacity. For example, it suspended service between Toronto and certain U.S. cities (New Orleans, Kansas City, and St. Louis), and suspended flights until 2004 on several other routes (including Calgary to Chicago, Montreal to Atlanta, and Vancouver to Nagoya, Japan). But these actions were not nearly enough to achieve the total cost reduction goal, so Air Canada took a second action: laying off large numbers of people. Not surprisingly, the unions fiercely objected. In the first few months of 2003, negotiations with Air Canada's various unions failed to convince them of the magnitude of the problem Air Canada was facing.

On April 1, 2003, Justice James Farley of the Ontario Superior Court declared Air Canada insolvent and placed it under the protection of the Companies Creditors Arrangement Act (CCAA). By doing this, he shielded Air Canada (for a specified time period) from actions by creditors as the company tried to work out a survival plan. Air Canada was by far the largest airline ever to seek bankruptcy protection under the CCAA. No Canadian airline had ever successfully reorganized as Air Canada tried to do, but everyone assumed that Air Canada would be successful, simply because it was so big that it just couldn't be allowed to fail. As part of the CCAA arrangement, Air Canada was to have a reorganization plan in place by the end of July 2003.

Air Canada CEO Robert Milton blamed the unions for the mess the company found itself in, and claimed the unions did not take seriously his warnings that major reductions in labour costs were necessary for Air Canada to survive. Milton also said that everyone recognized that the world of commercial air travel had changed, but that union leadership had not been able to comprehend it. Union leaders responded by saying that Milton "put a gun to their heads" by telling them to surrender their contract rights or the company would be put in bankruptcy protection.

After Justice Farley's initial ruling, Air Canada and the unions resumed negotiations in an attempt to reach some sort of agreement. And indeed, by the end of May 2003, deals had been reached with several unions. For example, an agreement was struck between Jazz (an Air Canada subsidiary) and three of its unions that would reduce labour costs by up to 48 percent and cut costs by over $58 million annually. There were no reductions in wages or pensions, but 200 jobs were cut. Those agreements will increase productivity by 60 percent.

Air Canada also reached agreement with the machinists union and with the CAW (which represents ticket agents). The agreements called for the preservation of pensions, but included job cuts totalling 2300 jobs (this is in addition to 2700 cuts in maintenance and baggage handling). These were major concessions by the unions, who apparently recognized that the alternative was the unemployment line for everyone.

In May 2003, approximately 1000 Air Canada mechanics in Montreal, Vancouver, and Calgary were abruptly told to take their paid holiday and overtime between the end of May and September. Union representatives said they were stunned. This unit also did maintenance work for other airlines, so everyone thought their jobs were pretty secure. But some of that work was for U.S.-based United Airlines, also in bankruptcy protection.

The Air Canada case is particularly important for labour unions. If Air Canada is successful in re-negotiating collective agreements while it is in bankruptcy protection, other companies that are having difficulties may get the same idea. Until now, that simply has not happened in Canada. A lawyer representing the Canadian Auto Workers (CAW) union argued that Justice Farley's decision gave Air Canada far too much scope to escape

Air Canada
www.aircanada.com

from collective agreements that had already been negotiated. Other observers noted that Air Canada had already refused to pay bonuses and wage increases that were included in collective agreements. Air Canada has said it will try to get out of the labour contracts completely if the unions don't go along with its cost-cutting strategy. Everyone recognizes that if Air Canada doesn't survive this crisis, the whole issue will be irrelevant because no one will have a job.

In the United States, a judge can cancel a labour contract, but not in Canada. In January 2003, Justice Pierre Dalphond of the Quebec Court of Appeals ruled that a collective agreement at Jeffrey Mine Inc. could not be set aside. That decision was one reason why Air Canada filed its bankruptcy motion in Ontario, even though Air Canada is based in Quebec. ◆

WHY DO WORKERS UNIONIZE?

1. Explain why workers unionize.

Over 2000 years ago, the Greek poet Homer wrote, "There is a strength in the union even of very sorry men." There were no labour unions in Homer's time, but his comment is a particularly effective expression of the rationale for unions. A **labour union** is a group of individuals working together to achieve shared job-related goals, such as higher pay, shorter working hours, more job security, greater benefits, or better working conditions.[1] **Labour relations** describes the process of dealing with employees who are represented by a union. The opening case describes some of the complexities in labour relations at Air Canada.

labour union
A group of individuals who work together to achieve shared job-related goals.

labour relations
The process of dealing with employees who are represented by a union.

Labour unions grew in popularity in Canada in the nineteenth and early twentieth centuries. The labour movement was born with the Industrial Revolution, which also gave birth to a factory-based production system that carried with it enormous economic benefits. Job specialization and mass production allowed businesses to create ever-greater quantities of goods at ever-lower costs.

But there was also a dark side to this era. Workers became more dependent on their factory jobs. Eager for greater profits, some owners treated their workers like other raw materials: as resources to be deployed with little or no regard for the individual worker's well-being. Many businesses forced employees to work long hours; 60-hour weeks were common, and some workers were routinely forced to work 12 to 16 hours per day. With no minimum-wage laws or other controls, pay was also minimal and safety standards were virtually nonexistent. Workers enjoyed no job security and received few benefits. Many companies, especially textile mills, employed large numbers of children at poverty wages. If people complained, nothing prevented employers from firing and replacing them at will.

Unions appeared and ultimately prospered because they constituted a solution to the worker's most serious problem: They forced management to listen to the complaints of all their workers rather than to just the few who were brave (or foolish) enough to speak out. The power of unions, then, comes from collective action. **Collective bargaining** is the process by which union leaders and managers negotiate common terms and conditions of employment for the workers represented by unions. Although collective bargaining does not often occur in small businesses, many mid-size and larger businesses must engage in the process, which we will discuss in more detail later in this chapter.

collective bargaining
The process through which union leaders and management personnel negotiate common terms and conditions of employment for those workers represented by the union.

THE DEVELOPMENT OF CANADIAN LABOUR UNIONS

2. Trace the evolution of and discuss trends in *unionism* in Canada.

The earliest evidence of labour unions in Canada comes from the maritime provinces early in the nineteenth century. Generally, these unions were composed of individuals with a specific craft (e.g., printers, shoemakers, barrel makers). Most of these unions were small and had only limited success. However, they laid the foundation for the rapid increase in union activity that occurred during the late nineteenth and early twentieth centuries.

A succession of labour organizations sprang up and just as quickly faded away during the years 1840–1870. In 1873, the first national labour organization was formed—the Canadian Labour Union. By 1886, the Knights of Labour (a U.S.-based union) had over 10 000 members in Canada. The Canadian labour movement began to mature with the formation of the Trades and Labour Congress (TLC) in 1886. The TLC's purpose was to unite all labour organizations and to work for the passage of laws that would ensure the well-being of the working class.

The growth of labour unions began in earnest early in the twentieth century as the concept of organized labour gradually came to be accepted. Various disputes arose that resulted in numerous splits in labour's ranks. For example, there was concern that U.S.-based unions would have a detrimental effect on Canadian unions. The Canadian Federation of Labour was formed in 1908 to promote national (Canadian) unions over U.S. unions. These and other disputes (such as how communists in the movement should be handled) often led to the creation of rival union organizations that competed for membership. By 1956, these disputes had been largely resolved, and the two largest congresses of affiliated unions—the Trades and Labour Congress and the Canadian Congress of Labour—merged to form the Canadian Labour Congress. This amalgamation brought approximately 80 percent of all unionized workers into one organization. Table 9.1 highlights some of the important events in Canadian labour history.

Canadian Labour Congress
www.clc-ctc.ca

The Canadian Labour Congress (CLC), which was formed in 1956, brought the majority of unionized workers in Canada into one organization.

Table 9.1 Some Important Dates in Canadian Labour History

Year	Event
1827	First union formed: boot and shoemakers in Quebec City
1840–70	Many new unions formed; influenced by U.S. and British unions
1871	Formation of Toronto Trades Assembly, composed of five craft unions; went out of existence a few years later
1873	Canadian Labour Union formed; objective was to unite unions across Canada
1879	First coal miners union in North America formed in Nova Scotia
1881	The U.S.-based Knights of Labor enter Canada
1883	Canadian Labour Congress formed; lasted until 1886
1886	Canadian Trades and Labour Congress formed; later became known as the Trades and Labour Congress of Canada (TLC)
1902	Knights of Labor expelled from TLC
1902	Expelled unions form the National Trades and Labour Congress (became the Canadian Federation of Labour [CFL] in 1908); purpose was to promote national unions instead of international ones
1902–20	Rapid growth of union membership in both major unions (TLC and CFL)
1919	One Big Union formed; organized in opposition to the TLC
1919	Winnipeg General Strike
1921	Canadian Brotherhood of Railway Employees (CBRE) expelled from TLC
1921	Confédération des Travailleurs Catholiques du Canada (CTCC) organized by the Roman Catholic clergy in Quebec; goal was to keep French-Canadian workers from being unduly influenced by English-speaking and American trade unions
1927	All-Canadian Congress of Labour (ACCL) formed; objective was to achieve independence of the Canadian labour movement from foreign control; made up of One Big Union, the CFL, and the CBRE
1939	TLC expels industrial unions; Canadian Congress of Industrial Organization (CIO) Committee formed
1940	ACCL and the Canadian CIO Committee unite to form the Canadian Congress of Labour (CCL)
1956	TLC and CCL merge to form the Canadian Labour Congress; remnants of One Big Union join new organization
1960	CTCC drops association with Roman Catholic Church and chooses a new name—Confédération des Syndicats Nationaux (CSN); in English, the Confederation of National Trade Unions (CNTU)
1960–69	Rapid growth of CNTU in Quebec
1971	Centre for Democratic Unions formed as a result of secession from the CNTU by dissident members
1981	International building trades unions suspended from CLC
1982	Founding convention of Canadian Federation of Labour (CFL)
1985	Formation of United Auto Workers of Canada; formerly part of international UAW
1989	Merger of Canadian Union of Postal Workers (CUPW) and Letter Carriers Union of Canada
1992	First-ever strike of NHL players
1994	Major league baseball players strike; no World Series played; NHL players also locked out; only half of hockey season played
1997	Strike of primary and secondary school teachers in Ontario
1999	Quebec nurses strike

UNIONISM TODAY

While understanding the historical context of labour unions is important, so too is appreciating the role of unionism today, especially trends in union membership, union–management relations, and bargaining perspectives.

Trends in Union Membership

During the last 40 years, unions have experienced difficulties in attracting new members. As a result, although millions of workers still belong to labour unions, union membership *as a proportion of the total workforce* has stagnated, and only a minority of workers belong to unions. As shown in Figure 9.1, union membership as a proportion of the total workforce has

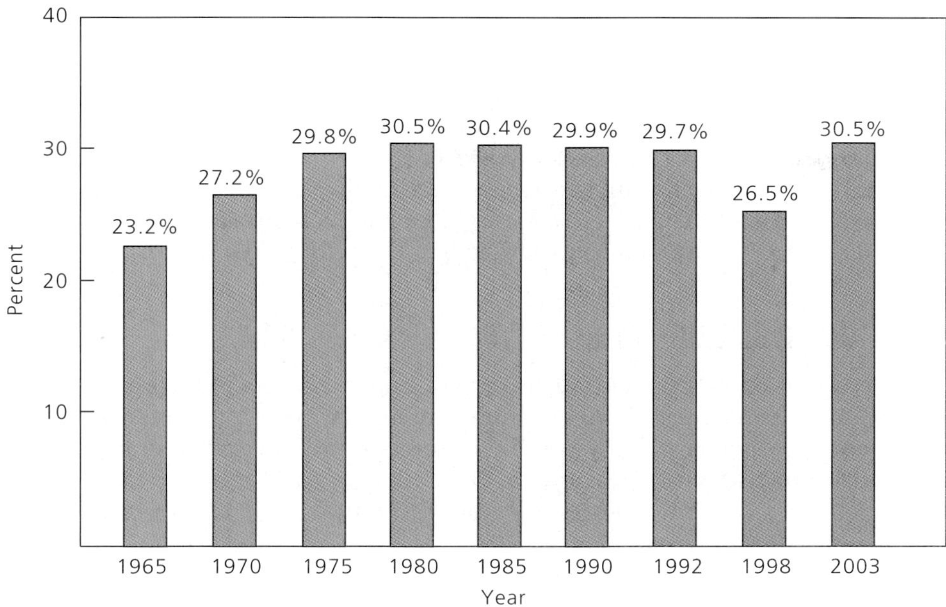

Figure 9.1
Union members as a proportion of the total workforce.

ranged from 23.2 percent in 1965 to 30.5 percent in 1980 and 2003. Thus, less than one-third of the Canadian labour force is unionized.

The highest rates of unionization are found in Newfoundland (37.7 percent) and Quebec (37.5 percent). The lowest rates are found in Alberta (23.0 percent) and New Brunswick (26.4 percent). The public sector is quite heavily unionized (72.7 percent), but the private sector is not (18.1 percent).[2] In some occupations—for example, teaching and nursing—over 80 percent of workers are unionized. In other occupations—for example, management and food and beverage workers—less than 10 percent of the workers belong to unions.[3] The union movement is more successful in Canada than it is in the U.S., where only 13 percent of the workforce is unionized.

Over the years, unions have experienced ups and downs in terms of their success at becoming certified at new locations. Many years ago, unions routinely won certification votes. But in recent years, they have encountered increasing opposition from management of companies that are trying to survive in a fiercely competitive global environment. Two factors help explain the difficulties that unions have faced in recent years.

Composition of the Workforce

Traditionally, union members have been predominantly white males in blue-collar jobs. But today's workforce is increasingly composed of women and ethnic minorities. Because these groups have much weaker traditions of union affiliation, their members are less likely to join unions when they enter the workforce. In a related trend, the workforce is increasingly employed in the service sector, which traditionally has been less heavily unionized.

Anti-Unionization Activities

A second reason for declining union membership is more aggressive anti-unionization activity on the part of employers. Although federal and provincial labour legislation restricts what management of a company can do to keep out a union, companies are free to pursue certain strategies to minimize unionization. As we saw in Chapter 8, many companies have tried to create a much more employee-friendly work environment and are increasingly treating workers with more respect and dignity. One goal of this approach is to minimize the attractiveness of labour unions for employees.

Many Japanese manufacturers who have set up shop in North America have avoided unionization efforts by the United Auto Workers (UAW) by providing job security, higher wages, and a work environment in which employees are allowed to participate and be actively involved in plant management. The Toyota plant in Cambridge, Ontario, is just one example.

Trends in Union–Management Relations

The gradual decline in unionization in Canada has been accompanied by some significant trends in union–management relations. In some sectors of the economy, perhaps most notably in the automobile and steel industries, labour unions remain quite strong. In these areas, unions have large memberships and considerable power in negotiating with management. The CAW, for example, is still a strong union.

In most sectors, however, unions are clearly in a weakened position. As a result, many have taken much more conciliatory stances in their relations with management. This situation contrasts sharply with the more adversarial relationship that once dominated labour relations in this country. Increasingly, for instance, unions recognize that they don't have as much power as they once held and that it is in their own best interests, as well as in the best interests of the workers they represent, to work with instead of against management. Ironically, then, union–management relations in many ways are better today than they have been in years. Admittedly, the improvement is attributable in large part to the weakened power of unions. Even so, most experts agree that improved union–management relations have benefited both sides.

Trends in Bargaining Perspectives

Given the trends described in the two previous sections, we should not be surprised to find changes in bargaining perspectives as well. In the past, for example, most union–management bargaining situations were characterized by union demands for dramatic increases in wages and salaries. A secondary issue was usually increased benefits for members. Now, however, unions often bargain for different benefits, such as job security. Of particular interest in this area is the trend toward relocating jobs to take advantage of lower labour costs in other countries. Unions, of course, want to restrict job movement, whereas companies want to save money by moving facilities—and jobs—to other countries.

As a result of organizational downsizing and a decade of low inflation in Canada, many unions today find themselves able to achieve only modest wage increases for their members. A common goal of union strategy is therefore to preserve what has already been won. Unions have also tried to place greater emphasis on improved job security, but with limited success. A trend that has become especially important in recent years is toward improved pension programs for employees.

The Future of Unions

Despite declining membership and loss of power, labour unions remain a significant factor in Canadian business. The labour organizations in the Canadian Labour Congress and independent major unions such as the

International Brotherhood of Teamsters and the Canadian Union of Public Employees can disrupt the economy by refusing to work. The votes of their members are still sought by politicians at all levels. In addition, the concessions they have won for their members—better pay, shorter working hours, and safer working conditions—now cover many non-unionized workers as well.

The big question is this: Will unions be able to cope with the many challenges that are currently facing them, or will their power continue to dwindle? The challenges facing unions are many, including:

- the decline of the so-called "smokestack industries," where union power has traditionally been very strong
- employment growth in service industries, where union power has traditionally not been strong
- deregulation, which has led to mergers and layoffs and to the emergence of new, non-unionized companies
- free trade and the globalization of business, which has raised the very real possibility of many jobs being moved to areas of the world with lower labour costs
- technological change, which allows telecommuting and increases the difficulty of organizing workers

Unions are increasingly aware that they must co-operate with employers if both companies and unions are to survive and prosper. The goal is to create effective partnerships in which managers and workers share the same goals: profitability, growth, and effectiveness, with equitable rewards for everyone. The recently improved situation between the Canadian Auto Workers and General Motors of Canada is illustrative. During the 1990s, there was often bitter antagonism between the union and company management. In 1996, 26 000 CAW workers went on strike and shut down all of GM's Canadian operations. GM also experienced strikes at its Dayton, Ohio, and Flint, Michigan, plants in the late 1990s. The damage done by those strikes apparently convinced both workers and management that they had to begin working together if GM hoped to become as efficient as its competitors. The union and the company have therefore spent a lot of time exchanging information about the business challenges each of them is facing.

United Auto Workers
www.uaw.org

Some experts think that a new wave of unionism may be about to sweep across Canada. This movement may be fuelled by young people (including college and university graduates) who fear they will be stuck in low-wage jobs and who hope unions can help them avoid that fate. Other changes are also occurring, including the increased number of women as union members. In 1967, women accounted for less than 20 percent of union membership in Canada, but now they represent nearly half of all union workers. These unionized women are highly concentrated in the public sector, which provides jobs for only 19 percent of the workforce but accounts for 43 percent of all union members.[4]

THE LEGAL ENVIRONMENT FOR UNIONS IN CANADA

3. Describe the *major laws governing labour–management relations.*

Political and legal barriers to collective bargaining existed until well into the twentieth century. Courts held that some unions were conspirators in restraint of trade. Employers viewed their employees' efforts to unionize as attempts to deprive the employers of their private property. The employment contract, employers contended, was between the individual worker and the employer—not between the employer and employees as a group. The balance of bargaining power was very much in favour of the employer.

The employer–employee relationship became much less direct as firms grew in size. Managers were themselves employees. Hired managers dealt with other employees. Communication among owners, managers, and workers became more formalized. Big business had more power than workers. Because of mounting public concern, laws were passed to place the worker on a more even footing with the employer.

In 1900, government concern about labour disputes resulted in the passage of the Conciliation Act. The act was designed to help settle labour disputes through voluntary conciliation and was a first step in creating an environment more favourable to labour. A more comprehensive law, the 1907 **Industrial Disputes Investigation Act**, provided for compulsory investigation of labour disputes by a government-appointed board before a strike was allowed. However, this act was later found to violate a fundamental provision of the BNA Act (see below).

Industrial Disputes Investigation Act (1907)
Provided for compulsory investigation of labour disputes by a government-appointed board before a strike was allowed.

The current positive environment for labour did not come into being until 1943 when **Privy Council Order 1003** was issued. This order recognized the right of employees to bargain collectively, prohibited unfair labour practices on the part of management, established a labour board to certify bargaining authority, and prohibited strikes and lockouts except in the course of negotiating collective agreements. Approximately 45 years of dealings among labour, management, and government were required before the labour movement achieved its fundamental goal of the right to bargain collectively.

Privy Council Order 1003 (1943)
Recognized the right of employees to bargain collectively.

The **Constitution Act** (originally the BNA Act), passed in 1867, has also affected labour legislation. This act allocated certain activities to the federal government (e.g., labour legislation for companies operating interprovincially) and others to individual provinces (labour relations regulations in general). Thus, labour legislation emanates from both the federal and provincial governments but is basically a provincial matter. That is why certain groups of similar employees might be allowed to go on strike in one province but not in another.

Constitution Act (1867)
Divided authority over labour regulations between the federal and provincial governments.

Federal Legislation—The Canada Labour Code

The **Canada Labour Code** is a comprehensive piece of legislation that applies to the labour practices of firms operating under the legislative authority of parliament. The code is composed of four major sections.

Canada Labour Code
Legislation that applies to the labour practices of firms operating under the legislative authority of parliament.

Fair Employment Practices

This section prohibits an employer from either refusing employment on the basis of a person's race or religion or using an employment agency that discriminates against people on the basis of their race or religion. These prohibitions apply to trade unions as well, but not to non-profit, charitable, and philanthropic organizations. Any individual who believes that a violation has occurred may make a complaint in writing to Labour Canada. The allegation will then be investigated and if necessary, an Industrial Inquiry Commission will be appointed to make a recommendation in the case. (Since 1982, fair employment practices have been covered by the Canadian Human Rights Act; they are also covered by the Canadian Charter of Rights and Freedoms.)

Standard Hours, Wages, Vacations, and Holidays

This section deals with a wide variety of mechanical issues such as standard hours of work (8-hour days and 40-hour weeks), maximum hours of work per week (48), overtime pay (at least one and a half times the regular pay), minimum wages, equal wages for men and women doing the same jobs, vacations, general holidays, and maternity leave. The specific provisions are changed frequently to take into account changes in the economic and social structure of Canada, but their basic goal is to ensure consistent treatment of employees in these areas.

Safety of Employees

This section requires that every person running a federal work project do so in a way that will not endanger the health or safety of any employee. It also requires that safety procedures and techniques be implemented to reduce the risk of employment injury. This section requires employees to exercise care to ensure their own safety; however, even if it can be shown that the employee did not exercise proper care, compensation must still be paid. This section also makes provisions for a safety officer whose overall duty is to ensure that the provisions of the code are being fulfilled. The safety officer has the right to enter any federal project "at any reasonable time."

Canada Industrial Relations Regulations

The final major section of the Canada Labour Code deals with all matters related to collective bargaining. It is subdivided into seven divisions:

- Division I—gives employees the right to join a trade union and gives employers the right to join an employers association.
- Division II—establishes the Canada Labour Relations Board whose role is to make decisions on a number of important issues (e.g., certification of trade unions).
- Division III—stipulates the procedures required to acquire or terminate bargaining rights.
- Division IV—establishes the rules and regulations that must be adhered to during bargaining; also presents guidelines for the content and interpretation of collective agreements.
- Division V—states the requirement that the Minister of Labour must appoint a conciliation officer if the parties in the dispute cannot reach a collective agreement.
- Division VI—stipulates the conditions under which strikes and lockouts are permitted.
- Division VII—a general conclusion giving methods that might be used to promote industrial peace.

Provincial Labour Legislation

Each province has enacted legislation to deal with the personnel practices covered in the Canada Labour Code. These laws vary across provinces and are frequently revised; however, their basic approach and substance is the same as in the Canada Labour Code. Certain provinces may exceed the minimum code requirements on some issues (e.g., minimum wage). Each province also has a labour relations act. To give an indication of what these acts cover, the Ontario Labour Relations Act is briefly described below.

Ontario Labour Relations Board
www.gov.on.ca/lab/olrb/eng/homeeng.htm

The Ontario Labour Relations Act

The Ontario Labour Relations Act is a comprehensive document dealing with the conduct of labour relations in that province. Some illustrative provisions of the Ontario law are noted below.

- A trade union may apply at any time to the Ontario Labour Relations Board (OLRB) for certification as the sole bargaining agent for employees in a company.
- The OLRB has the right to call for a certification vote. If more than 50 percent of those voting are in favour of the trade union, the board certifies the union as the bargaining agent.
- Following certification, the union gives the employer written notification of its desire to bargain, with the goal being the signing of a collective agreement. The parties are required to begin bargaining within 15 days of the written notice.
- On request by either party, the Minister of Labour appoints a conciliation officer to confer with the parties and to help achieve a collective agreement. On joint request, the Minister of Labour can appoint a mediator.
- The parties may jointly agree to submit unresolved differences to voluntary binding arbitration. The decision of the arbitrator is final.
- Employers are required to deduct union dues from the union members and remit these dues directly to the union.
- Every agreement must include a mechanism for settling grievances—differences between the parties arising from interpretation, application, or administration of the collective agreement.
- If a person objects to belonging to a labour union because of religious beliefs, he or she is allowed to make a contribution equal to the amount of the union dues to a charitable organization.
- If a trade union is not able to negotiate a collective agreement with management within one year of being certified, any of the employees in the union can apply to the OLRB for decertification of the union.
- No employer can interfere with the formation of a union. The employer is, however, free to express an opinion about the matter.
- No employer shall refuse to employ an individual because he or she is a member of a trade union.

The basic provisions of the Ontario Labour Relations Act are found in one form or another in the labour relations acts of all provinces, but the details and procedures vary from province to province. It is obvious that administering labour relations activity is complex and time-consuming. Company management, the union, and the government all expend much time and energy in an attempt to ensure reasonable relations between management and labour.

UNION ORGANIZING STRATEGY

A union might try to organize workers when a firm is trying to break into a new geographical area, when some workers in a firm are members and it wants to cover other workers, or when it is attempting to outdo a rival union. In some cases, a union might try to organize workers for purposes other than helping a group of employees to help themselves.

Management often becomes aware of a union organizing effort through gossip from the company grapevine. In 1999, management at Honda of Canada's Alliston, Ontario, plant and at Toyota Canada's Cambridge, Ontario, plant learned that the CAW had launched organizing drives at their plants. The CAW distributed leaflets at plant gates and contacted groups of workers inside the plant as part of its organizing drive.[5]

When management discovers that an organizing drive is underway, it may try to counteract it. However, management must know what it can legally do to discourage the union. In Quebec, McDonald's has been the target of union organizing drives at several of its restaurants. In 1998, the McDonald's restaurant in St. Hubert closed when it appeared that the teamsters union might be successful in getting certified as the bargaining agent for the employees. Critics immediately called for a government investigation into the possibility of unfair labour practices on the part of the company.[6] The Exercising Your Ethics box illustrates some of the actions management may take as it tries to thwart union organizing.

Certifying a Union: An Example

4. Describe the union *certification* and *decertification processes.*

Suppose that a union is trying to organize employees of a Manitoba company. If it can show that at least 50 percent of the employees are members of the union, it can apply to the Manitoba Labour Board (MLB) for certification as the bargaining agent for the employees.

EXERCISING YOUR ETHICS

Operating Tactically

The Situation

Assume that you work as a manager for a medium-size non-union company that is facing a serious union organizing campaign. Your boss, who is determined to keep the union out, has just given you a list of things to do to thwart the efforts of the organizers. For example, he has suggested each of the following tactics:

- Whenever you learn about a scheduled union meeting, you should schedule a "worker appreciation" event at the same time. He wants you to offer free pizza and barbecue and to give cash prizes (that winners have to be present to receive).
- He wants you to look at the most recent performance evaluations of the key union organizers and to terminate the one with the lowest overall evaluation.
- He wants you to make an announcement that the firm is seriously considering such new benefits as on-site childcare, flexible work schedules, telecommuting options, and exercise facilities. Although you know that the firm is indeed looking into these benefits, you also know that, ultimately, your boss will provide far less lavish benefits than he wants you to imply.

The Dilemma

When you questioned the ethics—and even the legality—of these tactics, your boss responded by saying, "Look, all's fair in love and war, and this is war." He went on to explain that he was seriously concerned that a union victory might actually shut down the company's domestic operations altogether, forcing it to move all of its production capacities to lower-cost foreign plants. He concluded by saying that he was really looking out for the employees, even if he had to play hardball to help them. You easily see through his hypocrisy, but you also realize that there is some potential truth in his warning: If the union wins, jobs may actually be lost.

Questions for Discussion

1. What are the ethical issues in this situation?
2. What are the basic arguments for and against extreme measures to fight unionization efforts?
3. What do you think most managers would do in this situation? What would you do?

Manitoba Labour Board
www.gov.mb.ca/labour/labbrd

bargaining unit
Individuals grouped together for purposes of collective bargaining.

certification vote
A vote supervised by a government representative to determine whether a union will be certified.

craft unions
Unions organized by trades; usually composed of skilled workers.

A problem may arise regarding the right of different types of workers to join or not join the union. For example, supervisors may or may not be included in a bargaining unit along with non-management workers. The **bargaining unit** includes those individuals deemed appropriate by the province. The MLB has final authority in determining the appropriateness of the bargaining unit. Professional and non-professional employees are generally not included in the same bargaining unit unless a majority of the professional employees wish to be included.

Once the MLB has determined that the unit is appropriate, it may order a **certification vote**. If a majority of those voting are in favour of the union, it is certified as the sole bargaining agent for the unit. The Wired World box describes how unions are using the internet to achieve their goals.

Types of Unions

The two basic types of union are craft and industrial unions. **Craft unions** are organized by crafts or trades—plumbers, barbers, airline pilots, etc. Craft unions restrict membership to workers with specific skills. In many cases, members of craft unions work for several different employers during the course of a year. For example, many construction workers are hired by their employers at union hiring halls. When the particular job for which they are hired is finished, these workers return to the hall to be hired by another employer.

Craft unions have a lot of power over the supply of skilled workers because they have apprenticeship programs. A person who wants to become a member of a plumbers' union, for example, must go through a training program. He or she starts out as an apprentice. After the training, the apprentice is qualified as a journeyman plumber.

industrial unions
Unions organized by industry; usually composed of semiskilled and unskilled workers.

local union
The basic unit of union organization.

Industrial unions are organized according to industries, for example, steel, auto, and clothing. Industrial unions include semiskilled and unskilled workers. They were originally started because industrial workers were not eligible to join craft unions. Industrial union members typically work for a particular employer for a much longer period of time than do craft union members. An industrial union has a lot of say regarding pay and human resource practices within unionized firms.

The outcome of this certification vote will determine whether these workers will be represented by a union.

The **local union** (or local) is the basic unit of union organization. A local of a craft union is made up of artisans in the same craft in a relatively small geographical area. A local of an industrial union is made up of workers in a given industry or plant in a relatively small geographical area. Thus, plumbers in a local labour market may be members of the local plumbers' union. Truck drivers and warehouse workers in that same area may be members of a teamsters' local.

The functions of locals vary, depending not only on governance arrangements but also on bargaining patterns in particular industries. Some local unions bargain directly with management regarding wages, hours,

IT'S A WIRED WORLD

The Web as a Bargaining Tool

It's no secret that the internet now plays a key role in the plans and operations of many businesses. A bit less obvious, though certainly no less important, is the approach that organized labour is taking to the internet. There are at least three different areas in which labour is taking advantage of the internet to promote various agendas.

First, just like many if not most businesses, many unions have websites. National and international unions post some of these sites; local unions post others. Websites provide information for members, promote the union's current agenda, and contain links to other relevant sites. Some of the more aggressive union websites go so far as to provide warnings and directives to management as to what it can and cannot do during ongoing organizing and/or collective bargaining periods—even pointing out that the website itself is a union organizing location and thus off-limits to managers.

The internet is also important to unions as a source of information and means of research. A critical part of effective collective bargaining—for both sides—is having the right information. Both sides, for example, need to know such statistics as employment rates, cost-of-living changes and projections, and so forth. They also need to know what contract terms have been negotiated in similar industries and settings. The internet makes this information more accessible.

The internet also makes it easier for a union to learn more about a company, especially when it is a privately held corporation. A long-time union practice has been to obtain employment for what is called a "salt"—essentially, an employee planted for espionage purposes. These individuals try to find out whatever they can about the lifestyles and wealth of business owners. Learning, for instance, that a business owner has expensive hobbies, travels in lavish style, and maintains a fleet of expensive cars makes it easier for the union to argue for higher wages. The internet makes it easier to locate this same information more quickly and more easily.

Finally, the internet is used more and more frequently as a recruiting tool during organizing campaigns. Whereas organizers once had little choice but to hang out in company parking lots or neighbourhood bars to strike up conversations with a business's employees, they can now do most of their work electronically. Today, for example, they can put up websites at the start of a campaign. All they have to do is recruit a few people and then wait for the recruits to pass along the web address to co-workers. Interested parties can visit the site, review what the union says it can and will do, and post emails with questions and comments. One day soon, certification elections may even be conducted online.

and other terms and conditions of employment. Many local unions are also active in disciplining members for violations of contract standards and in pressing management to consider worker complaints.

A **national union** has members across Canada. These members belong to locals affiliated with the national union. There are many national unions in Canada, including the Canadian Union of Public Employees, the National Railway Union, and the Canadian Airline Pilots Union. About two-thirds of unionized Canadian workers belong to national unions.

national union
A union with members across Canada.

An **international union** is a union with members in more than one country. One example is the United Steelworkers of America, made up of locals in the United States and Canada. About 30 percent of unionized workers in Canada belong to international unions.

international union
A union with members in more than one country.

An **independent local union** is one that is not formally affiliated with any labour organization. It conducts negotiations with management at a local level, and the collective agreement is binding at that location only. The University of Manitoba Faculty Association is an independent local union. Less than 5 percent of unionized workers in Canada belong to independent local unions. Table 9.2 lists the 10 largest unions in Canada.

independent local union
One not formally affiliated with any labour organization.

Union Structure

Just as each organization has its own unique structure, so too does each union create a structure that best serves its own needs. As Figure 9.2 shows, however, there is a general structure that characterizes most national and international unions. A major function of unions is to provide service and support to both members and local affiliates. Most of these services are carried out by the types of specialized departments shown in Figure 9.2.

Officers and Functions

shop steward
A regular employee who acts as a liaison between union members and supervisors.

business agent (business representative)
In a large union, the business agent plays the same role as a shop steward.

Each department or unit represented at the local level elects a **shop steward**—a regular employee who acts as a liaison between union members and supervisors. For example, if a worker has a grievance, he or she takes it to the steward, who tries to resolve the problem with the supervisor. If the local is very large, the union might hire a full-time **business agent** (or **business representative**) to play the same role.

Within a given union, the main governing bodies are the national union (or international union when members come from more than one country) and its officers. Among their other duties, national and international unions charter local affiliates and establish general standards of conduct and procedures for local operations. For example, they set dues assessments, arrange for the election of local officers, sanction strikes, and provide guidance in the collective bargaining process. Many national unions also engage in a variety of political activities, such as lobbying. They may also help coordinate organizing efforts and establish education programs.

Given the magnitude of their efforts, it is little wonder that unions often take on many of the same characteristics as the companies for which their members work. For example, almost all large unions have full-time administrators, formal organizational structures, goals and strategic plans, and so forth.

Union Security

The growing security consciousness of Canadian workers is reflected in union goals. The seniority provision in most contracts spells out the workers' rights when layoffs, transfers, and promotions occur. Employees are ranked by length of service. Those with longer service receive better treatment. Much conflict exists regarding seniority. For example, women and

Table 9.2 The Top 10 Unions in Canada (By Membership)

Union	2003 Membership
1. Canadian Union of Public Employees	521 600
2. National Union of Public and General Employees	325 000
3. Canadian Auto Workers	263 000
4. United Food and Commercial Workers	220 000
5. United Steelworkers of America	180 000
6. Communications, Energy, and Paperworkers Union of Canada	150 000
7. Public Service Alliance of Canada	150 000
8. International Brotherhood of Teamsters	110 000
9. Fédération de la santé et des services sociaux	103 600
10. Fédération des syndicates de l'enseignement	81 200

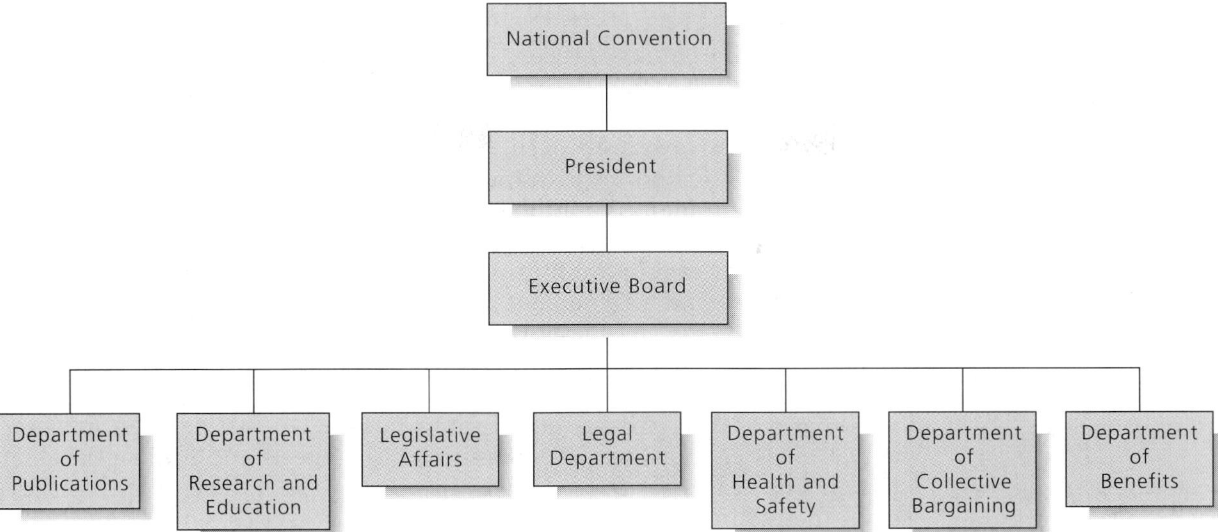

Figure 9.2
Organization of a large national union.

members of minority groups typically have less seniority and are the first to be laid off and the last to move up to higher jobs. These workers tend to oppose the tradition of seniority.

Union security refers to the means of ensuring the union's continued existence and the maintenance of its membership so that it can continue to meet the criteria for certification. There is always a danger—particularly in bad economic times—that the membership may drop below the required absolute majority. The union may then lose its certification.

union security
The maintenance of a union's membership so that it can continue to meet the criteria for certification.

The greatest union security is found in the closed shop. In a **closed shop**, an employer can hire only union members. For example, a plumbing or electrical contractor who hires workers through a union hiring hall can hire only union members.

closed shop
An employer can hire only union members.

In a **union shop**, an employer may hire non-union workers even if the employer's current employees are unionized. New workers, however, must join the union within a stipulated period of time (usually 30 days).

union shop
An employer can hire non-unionized workers, but they must join the union within a certain period.

In an **agency shop**, all employees for whom the union bargains must pay dues, but they need not join the union. This compromise between the union shop and the open shop is called the Rand Formula after the judge who proposed it. In the Quebec Labour Code, the Rand formula applies to all unions certified under this code.

agency shop
All employees for whom the union bargains must pay dues, but they are not required to join the union.

In an **open shop**, an employer may hire union and/or non-union labour. Employees need not join or pay dues to a union in an open shop.

open shop
An employer may hire union or non-union workers.

COLLECTIVE BARGAINING

5. Identify the steps in the *collective bargaining process.*

Too often, people associate collective bargaining with the signing of a contract between a union and a company or industry. In fact, collective bargaining is an ongoing process involving not only the drafting but also the administering of the terms of a labour contract.

Reaching Agreement on the Contract's Terms

The collective bargaining process begins with the recognition of the union as the exclusive negotiator for its members. The bargaining cycle begins when union leaders meet with management representatives to agree on a new contract. By law, both parties must sit down at the bargaining table and negotiate "in good faith." When each side has presented its demands, sessions focus on identifying the *bargaining zone*. This process is shown in Figure 9.3. For example, although an employer may initially offer no pay raise, it may expect to grant a raise of up to 6 percent. Likewise, the union may initially *demand* a 10 percent pay raise while *expecting* to accept a raise as low as 4 percent. The bargaining zone, then, is a raise between 4 and 6 percent. Ideally, some compromise is reached between these levels and the new agreement is submitted for a ratification vote by union membership.

Sometimes, this process goes quite smoothly. At other times, however, the two sides cannot—or will not—agree. The speed and ease with which such an impasse is resolved depend in part on the nature of the contract issues, the willingness of each side to use certain tactics, and the prospects for mediation or arbitration.

Contract Issues

The labour contract itself can address an array of different issues. Most of these issues concern demands that unions make on behalf of their members. In this section we will survey the categories of issues that are typically most important to union negotiators: *compensation, benefits,* and *job security*. Although few issues covered in a labour contract are company sponsored, we will also describe the kinds of management rights that are negotiated in most bargaining agreements.

First, note that bargaining items generally fall into two categories:

- *Mandatory items* are matters over which both parties must negotiate if either wants to. This category includes wages, working hours, and benefits.

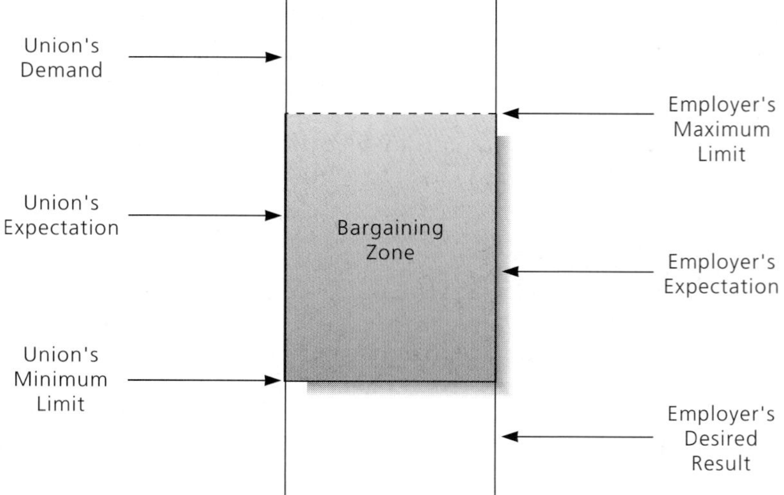

Figure 9.3
The bargaining zone.

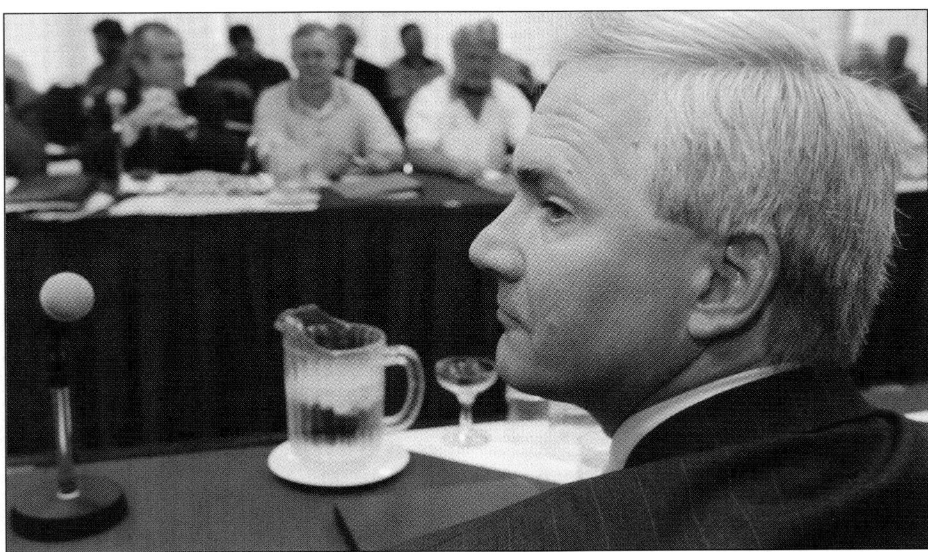

Representatives of labour and management negotiate in an attempt to reach an agreement on a labour contract. Here, members of the Canadian Auto Workers and managers representing Ford Canada are preparing to negotiate the terms of a collective agreement.

- *Permissive items* may be negotiated if both parties agree. For example, a union demand for veto power over the promotion of managerial personnel would be a permissive bargaining item.

Neither party may bring illegal items to the table. For example, a management demand for a non-strike clause would be an illegal item.

Compensation

The most common issue is compensation. One aspect of compensation is current wages. Obviously, unions generally want their employees to earn higher wages and try to convince management to raise hourly wages for all or some employees. Of equal concern to unions is future compensation: wage rates to be paid during subsequent years of the contract. One common tool for securing wage increases is a **cost-of-living adjustment (COLA)**. Most COLA clauses tie future raises to the *consumer price index (CPI)*, a government statistic that reflects changes in consumer purchasing power. The premise is that as the CPI increases by a specified amount during a given period of time, wages will automatically increase.

cost-of-living adjustment (COLA)
A contract clause specifying that wages will increase automatically with the rate of inflation.

Wage reopener clauses may also be included. Such a clause allows wage rates to be renegotiated at preset times during the life of the contract. For example, a union might be uncomfortable with a long-term contract based solely on COLA wage increases. A long-term agreement might be more acceptable, however, if management agrees to renegotiate wages every two years.

wage reopener clause
A contract clause that allows wage rates to be renegotiated at preset times during the life of the contract.

Benefits

Employee benefits are also an important component of most labour contracts. Unions typically want employers to pay all or most of the costs of insurance for employees. Other benefits commonly addressed during negotiations include retirement benefits and working conditions.

Job Security

Job security is an increasingly important agenda item in bargaining sessions today. In some cases, demands for job security entail the promise that a company will not move to another location. In others, the contract may dictate that if the workforce is reduced, seniority will be used to determine which employees lose their jobs.

Other Union Issues

Other possible issues might include such things as working hours, overtime policies, rest period arrangements, differential pay plans for shift employees, the use of temporary workers, grievance procedures, and allowable union activities (dues collection, union bulletin boards, and so forth).

Management Rights

Management wants as much control as possible over hiring policies, work assignments, and so forth. Unions, meanwhile, often try to limit management rights by specifying hiring, assignment, and other policies. At one DaimlerChrysler plant, for example, the contract stipulates that three workers are needed to change fuses in robots: a machinist to open the robot, an electrician to change the fuse, and a supervisor to oversee the process. As in this example, contracts often bar workers in one job category from performing work that falls within the domain of another. Unions try to secure jobs by defining as many different categories as possible (the DaimlerChrysler plant has over 100). Of course, management resists this practice, which limits flexibility and makes it difficult to reassign workers.

When Bargaining Fails

An impasse occurs when, after a series of bargaining sessions, management and labour fail to agree on a new contract or a contract to replace an agreement that is about to expire. Although it is generally agreed that both parties suffer when an impasse is reached and action is taken, each side can employ several tactics to support its cause until the impasse is resolved.

Union Tactics

Unions can take a variety of actions when their demands are not met. Chief among these are strikes, picketing, boycotts, and work slowdowns.

strike

A tactic of labour unions in which members temporarily walk off the job and refuse to work to win concessions from management.

The Strike. A **strike** occurs when employees temporarily walk off the job and refuse to work. In 2003, Inco workers were on strike for nearly three months.[7] Strikes triggered by impasses over mandatory bargaining items are called *economic strikes*, even if they occur over non-economic issues such as working hours. Most strikes in Canada are economic strikes. The strike by Inco workers in 2003, by major league baseball players in 1994, by Canada Safeway workers in 1997, by Quebec nurses in 1999, and by British Columbia forestry workers in 2000 were largely over economic issues.

During a strike, workers are not paid and the business is usually unable to produce its normal range of products and services. During this time, the union may try to convince the general public that the company is being unfair. When Canada Safeway workers went on strike in Alberta in 1997, they were very successful at convincing the general public not to shop at Safeway. So many people refused to cross the union's picket lines that sales at some Safeway stores fell by as much as 70 percent.[8]

After a strike is over, employees may exhibit low morale, anger, increased absenteeism, and decreased productivity. In these situations, care must be taken to improve communications between management and workers.[9]

Strikes may occur in response to an employer's unfair labour practices. A firm that refuses to recognize a duly certified union may find itself with a striking workforce and having to explain its refusal to the provincial labour relations board. Such strikes are rare, however.

Workers who belong to the United Steelworkers of America walk the picket line during a strike at Inco in Sudbury, Ont.

Not all strikes are legal. The Ontario primary and secondary school teachers strike in 1997 against the province of Ontario was illegal because the teachers had not gone through the necessary steps prior to going out on strike. The teachers voluntarily returned to work after striking for only two weeks. Nurses in Quebec and Saskatchewan also carried out illegal strikes in 1999. *Sympathy strikes* (also called secondary strikes), where one union strikes in sympathy with strikes initiated by another labour organization, may violate the sympathetic union's contract. Wildcat strikes, strikes unauthorized by the union that occur during the life of a contract, deprive strikers of their status as employees and thus of the protection of labour laws.

Unions are more reluctant to use the strike weapon than they used to be. There are several reasons for this: more and more workers are in profit-sharing plans and therefore receive a portion of company profits, workers' own shares of the company's stock and their personal payoffs are tied to the success of the company, union membership continues to decline, strikes are bad publicity and hurt union efforts to recruit new union members, and technology and globalization mean that companies can easily displace highly paid but low-skilled workers.[10]

Picketing. As part of or instead of a strike, unions faced with an impasse may picket their employer. **Picketing** involves having workers march at the entrance to the company with signs explaining their reasons for striking.

picketing
A tactic of labour unions in which members march at the entrance to the company with signs explaining their reasons for striking.

Boycotts. A **boycott** occurs when union members agree not to buy the product of the firm that employs them. Workers may also urge other consumers to shun their firm's product.

boycott
A tactic of labour unions in disputes with management in which members refuse to buy the products of the company and encourage other consumers to do the same.

Work Slowdowns. In a **work slowdown**, workers perform their jobs at a much slower pace than normal. A variation is the "sickout," during which large numbers of workers call in sick.

work slowdown
Instead of striking, workers perform their jobs at a much slower pace than normal.

Management Tactics

Management can also respond forcefully to an impasse. These tactics include lockouts, strikebreakers, plant closures, contracting out, forming employers' associations, and decertification.

lockout

A tactic of management in which the firm physically denies employees access to the workplace to pressure workers to agree to the company's latest contract offer.

Lockouts. To some extent, **lockouts** are the flip side of the strike coin. Lockouts occur when employers physically deny employees access to the workplace. Lockouts are illegal if they are used as offensive weapons to give the firm an economic advantage in the bargaining process. They might be used, for example, if management wants to avoid a build up of perishable inventory or in similar circumstances. The lockout is not widely used, but almost half of the 1998–1999 NBA season was lost when team owners locked out their players over contract issues.[11]

strikebreaker

An individual hired by a firm to replace a worker on strike; a tactic of management in disputes with labour unions.

Strikebreakers. Firms faced with a strike can hire temporary or permanent replacements (**strikebreakers**) for the absent employees. When players in the National Football League went out on strike during the 1987 season, the team owners hired free agents and went right on playing. In 1992, National Hockey League owners planned to use minor league hockey players if they could not reach an agreement with striking NHL players.

Plant Closures. In extreme cases, management may simply close down a plant if they cannot reach agreement with the union. In 1997, Maple Leaf closed its Edmonton hog processing plant when the workers went on strike. This cost 850 workers their jobs. A less obvious tactic is to simply not build manufacturing plants in Canada and thereby avoid union problems. Ipsco Steel of Regina, for example, is not expanding its operations in Canada because it feels that Canada's labour laws are too restrictive. The company is constructing new steel mills in U.S. states where workers can opt out of a union.[12]

Contracting Out. Some firms contract out work as a way to blunt their unions' effects. Instead of doing all the assembly work they used to do themselves, many firms now *contract out* work to non-union contractors. This lessens the impact the unions can have and results in fewer union workers.

employers' association

A group of companies that get together to plan strategies and exchange information about how to manage their relations with unions.

Employers' Associations. Employers' associations are groups of companies that get together to plan strategies and exchange information about how to manage their relations with unions. They are especially important in industries that have many small firms and one large union that represents all workers. Member firms sometimes contribute to a strike insurance fund. Such a fund could be used to help members whose workers have struck. They are similar in purpose to the strike funds built up by unions.

decertification

The process by which employees terminate their union's right to represent them.

The same law that grants employees the right to unionize also allows them to decertify. **Decertification** is the process by which employees legally terminate their union's right to represent them. A labour dispute over job security and safety that arose at Goldcorp Inc.'s gold mine near Red Lake, Ontario, led to a strike involving 100 workers. The strike was settled when workers agreed to decertify their union in return for severance pay that was four times the rate mandated by Ontario law.[13] The first union ever at a McDonald's outlet was certified in 1998 in British Columbia, but decertified by its members in 1999.

Decertification campaigns do not differ much from certification campaigns (those leading up to the initial election). The union organizes membership meetings, house-to-house visits, and other tactics to win the election. The employer uses meetings, letters, and improved working conditions to try to obtain a decertification vote. The Business Today box reports on a series of events at Wal-Mart that culminated in decertification of a union.

BUSINESS TODAY

Certification and Decertification at Wal-Mart

In 2003, the Labour Relations Board of British Columbia found Wal-Mart guilty of unfair labour practices, namely, that it undermined a union organizing drive at the Wal-Mart store in Quesnel, B.C. Local 1518 of the United Food and Commercial Workers (UFCW) was the union that successfully brought the charge against Wal-Mart. As part of their decision, the Labour Relations Board of British Columbia required Wal-Mart management to schedule an employee meeting and read aloud the board's decision to the assembled employees. Wal-Mart was also required to give the union 30 minutes to talk to employees about the benefits of joining a union. Michael Fraser, the national director of UFCW, said that Wal-Mart went to great lengths to prevent its employees from exercising their legal rights. He also said Wal-Mart interfered with workers' rights to decide whether or not to join a union in an atmosphere that was free from intimidation.

This incident is just the latest in a series of union–management confrontations at the world's largest company. Until the mid-1990s, Wal-Mart had never had a union in any of its stores in the United States, Canada, Puerto Rico, Argentina, Brazil, or Mexico. It had been able to resist unions partly by promoting its family-like culture. The company argued that forcing employees to work under a collective agreement would reduce their motivation and damage the company's successful formula for keeping consumers happy. The company had also resisted unionization in more direct ways. For example, when it purchased 122 Woolco stores in Canada, it pointedly did not buy the 9 stores that were unionized.

Union pressure on Wal-Mart began in earnest in the mid-1990s. Consider what happened at the Windsor, Ontario, Wal-Mart store. In 1996, management first began hearing rumours that employees at the store were being approached about joining a union. Wal-Mart employees are supposed to be one big, happy family, but the prospect of a union caused squabbling among employees at the store. One anti-union employee gave a speech exhorting other employees not to join the union, but when pro-union employees asked for the opportunity to respond, they were denied the right to do so.

Four days before the certification vote was to be held, the Windsor store manager told at least one employee that unionization would mean a lot of changes at the store, and that employees might lose certain benefits they currently had. When the certification vote was held, the union lost by a margin of 151–43. In spite of this, the Ontario Labour Relations Board (OLRB) certified the union as the bargaining agent for employees at the Windsor store, ruling that Wal-Mart had used intimidation tactics to try to prevent unionization.

The first collective agreement was approved by workers in a 109–39 vote. However, a group of 80 employees then signed a petition claiming that they did not vote in favour of the contract. A few months later, a majority of workers at the store filed an application with the OLRB to have the union decertified, claiming that there were irregularities in voting on the first collective agreement. The decertification application also claimed that the union had only minority support at the store. In April 2000, the union was decertified and the Canadian Auto Workers decided to abandon its efforts to represent workers.

The story of unionization at Wal-Mart is far from over. In mid-2003, the UFCW confirmed that it was trying to organize Wal-Mart stores in Winnipeg.

Mediation and Arbitration

Rather than using weapons on one another, labour and management can agree to call in a third party to help resolve the dispute. In **mediation**, the neutral third party (a mediator) can only advise—not impose—a settlement on the parties. In **voluntary arbitration**, the neutral third party (an arbitrator) dictates a settlement between two sides that have agreed to submit to outside judgment.

mediation
A method of settling a contract dispute in which a neutral third party is asked to hear arguments from both the union and management and offer a suggested resolution.

voluntary arbitration
A method of settling a contract dispute in which the union and management ask a neutral third party to hear their arguments and issue a binding resolution.

compulsory arbitration

A method of settling a contract dispute in which the union and management are forced to explain their positions to a neutral third party who issues a binding resolution.

In some cases, arbitration is legally required to settle bargaining disputes. Such **compulsory arbitration** is used to settle disputes between government and public employees such as firefighters and police officers.

Administering a Labour Agreement

Once a labour agreement has been reached, its details are written down in the form of a contract that is legally enforceable in the courts. Labour contracts almost always have precise agreements as to how the agreement will be enforced. In some cases, of course, enforcement is quite clear. If the two sides agree that the company will increase wages by 2 percent per year over the next three years according to a prescribed schedule, then there is little opportunity for disagreement because wage increases can be mathematically calculated and union members will see its effects in their paycheques. However, other provisions may be much more prone to misinterpretation and different perceptions.

Suppose, for example, that a labour contract specifies the process for allocating overtime assignments. Such strategies are often complex, and the employer may have to take into account a variety of factors, such as seniority, previous overtime allocations, the hours or days in which the overtime work is needed, and so forth. Now suppose that a factory supervisor is trying to follow the labour contract and offers overtime to a certain employee. This employee, however, indicates that before he or she can accept the overtime, it may be necessary to check with the individual's spouse or partner about other obligations and commitments. The supervisor may feel the pressure of a deadline and instead award the overtime opportunity to someone else. If the first employee objects to this course of action, he or she may file a complaint with the union.

When such differences of opinion arise, the union member takes the complaint to the shop steward. The shop steward may advise the employee that the supervisor handled things properly, but there are other appeal mechanisms, and the employee, even if refuted by the shop steward, still has channels for appeal.

Of course, if the shop steward agrees with the employee, prescribed methods for pursuing the complaint are followed. The prescribed methods might include talking with the supervisor to hear the other side of the story and then providing for lines of appeal further up the hierarchy of both the union and the company. In some cases, mediation or arbitration may be tried, as may other efforts to resolve the dispute. The overtime, for example, may be reassigned to the employee to whom it was first offered. Or the overtime may remain with the second employee while the first employee is also paid.

grievance

A complaint on the part of a union member that management is violating the terms of the contract in some way.

A **grievance** is a complaint by a worker that a manager is violating the contract. Figure 9.4 traces a typical grievance procedure. The union generally promises not to strike over disputes about contract interpretation. In return, unions get the right to file grievances in a formal procedure that culminates in binding arbitration. Most grievance arbitrations take place over disputes regarding the discipline or discharge of employees, but safety issues are a cause for arbitration in some industries.

SUMMARY OF LEARNING OBJECTIVES

1. **Explain why workers unionize.** The Industrial Revolution and the emergence of a factory-based production system made many workers dependent on continuing factory employment. The treatment of labour

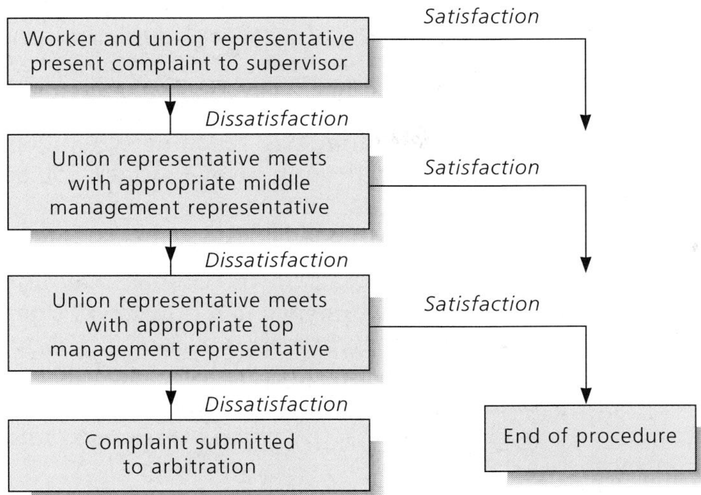

Figure 9.4
A typical grievance procedure.

as a raw material led to such abuses as minimal pay, long workdays and workweeks, unsafe working conditions, and even child labour. Individuals had little recourse in rectifying problems. By organizing into labour unions, however, workers are able to act collectively to improve work conditions. Most importantly, acting as a group, they can engage in *collective bargaining* for higher wages, greater benefits, or better working conditions.

2. **Trace the evolution of and discuss trends in *unionism* in Canada.** The first unions were formed in the early nineteenth century in the maritime provinces. Many labour organizations sprang up and then faded away during the nineteenth century. In the twentieth century, unions began to develop in earnest. In 1943, Privy Council Order 1003 gave unions the right to bargain collectively with employers.

   Since the mid-1970s, labour unions in Canada have experienced increasing difficulties in attracting new members. While millions of workers still belong to labour unions, union membership as a percentage of the total workforce has begun to decline. Increasingly, unions recognize that they do not have as much power as they once held and that it is in their own best interests, as well as the best interests of the workers they represent, to work with management instead of against it. Bargaining perspectives have also altered in recent years.

3. **Describe the *major laws governing labour–management relations*.** Privy Council Order 1003 gave unions the right to collectively bargain in Canada. The Constitution Act of 1867 allows the federal government to pass labour legislation (such as the Canada Labour Code) for companies that operate interprovincially, and allows the provincial governments to pass legislation (such as the Ontario Labour Relations Act) for companies that operate in only one province.

4. **Describe the union *certification* and *decertification processes*.** If a union can show that a certain percentage (usually 50 percent) of employees of a company are members of the union, it can apply to a provincial labour relations board for certification as the sole bargaining agent for the employees. A certification vote is then held. If a majority

of the employees is in favour of the union, it is certified. To decertify a union, employees must vote to do so.

5. **Identify the steps in the *collective bargaining process*.** Once certified, the union engages in collective bargaining with the organization. The initial step in collective bargaining is reaching agreement on a *labour contract*. Contract demands usually involve wages, job security, or management rights.

   Both labour and management have several tactics that can be used against the other if negotiations break down. Unions may attempt a *strike* or a *boycott* of the firm or may engage in a *slowdown*. Companies may hire replacement workers (*strikebreakers*) or *lock out* all workers. In extreme cases, mediation or arbitration may be used to settle disputes. Once a contract has been agreed on, union and management representatives continue to interact to settle worker *grievances* and interpret the contract.

KEY TERMS

agency shop, 311
bargaining unit, 308
boycott, 315
business agent (business representative), 310
Canada Labour Code, 304
certification vote, 308
closed shop, 311
collective bargaining, 298
compulsory arbitration, 318
Constitution Act (1867), 304
cost-of-living adjustment (COLA), 313
craft unions, 308
decertification, 316
employers' association, 316
grievance, 318
independent local union, 309
Industrial Disputes Investigation Act (1907), 304
industrial unions, 308
international union, 309
labour relations, 298
labour union, 298
local union, 308
lockout, 316
mediation, 317
national union, 309
open shop, 311
picketing, 315
Privy Council Order 1003 (1943), 304
shop steward, 310
strike, 314
strikebreaker, 316
union security, 311
union shop, 311
voluntary arbitration, 317
wage reopener clause, 313
work slowdown, 315

QUESTIONS AND EXERCISES

Questions for Review

1. Why do workers in some companies unionize while workers in other companies do not?

2. Why did it take so many years for the union movement to mature in Canada? Describe some of the key events along the way.

3. The proportion of the Canadian workforce that is unionized has been constant for more than 15 years. Why hasn't the proportion increased or decreased?

4. Describe the kinds of employment issues that the Canada Labour Code deals with.

5. How are craft and industrial unions different? How are international, national, and local unions different?

Questions for Analysis

6. Workers at the Canadian plants of Ford, General Motors, and DaimlerChrysler are represented by the Canadian Auto Workers. Why are automobile workers at Toyota's Cambridge, Ontario, plant—who are doing exactly the same kind of work—not unionized?

7. Suppose that you are a manager in a non-unionized company. You have just heard a rumour that some of your workers are discussing forming a union. What would you do? Be specific.

8. What are the implications for management of a closed shop, a union shop, and an agency shop?

Application Exercises

9. Interview the managers of two local companies, one unionized and one non-unionized. Compare the wage and salary levels, benefits, and working conditions of workers at the two firms.

10. With your instructor playing the role of management and a student playing the role of a union organizer, role play the processes involved in trying to form a union.

BUILDING YOUR BUSINESS SKILLS

A Little Collective Bargaining

Goal

To encourage students to understand why some companies unionize and others do not.

Situation

You've been working for the same non-union company for five years. Although there are problems in the company, you like your job and have confidence in your ability to get ahead. Recently, you've heard rumblings that a large group of workers want to call for a union election. You're not sure how you feel about this because none of your friends or family members are union members.

Method

Step 1

Come together with three other "co-workers" who have the same questions as you do. Each person should target four companies to learn their union status. Avoid small businesses; choose large corporations such as Canadian National Railways, General Motors, and Wal-Mart. As you investigate, answer the following questions:

- Is the company unionized?
- Is every worker in the company unionized or only selected groups of workers? Describe the groups.
- If a company is unionized, what is the union's history in that company?
- If a company is unionized, what are the main labour–management issues?
- If a company is unionized, how would you describe the current status of labour–management relations? For example, is it cordial or strained?
- If a company is not unionized, what factors are responsible for its non-union status?

To learn the answers to these questions, contact the company, read corporate annual reports, search the company's website, contact union representatives, or do research on a computerized database.

Step 2

Go to the website of CUPE (**www.cupe.ca**) to learn more about the current status of the union movement. Then, with your co-workers, write a short report about the advantages of union membership.

Step 3

Research the disadvantages of unionization. A key issue to address is whether unions make it harder for companies to compete in the global marketplace.

Follow-Up Questions

1. Based on everything you have learned, are you sympathetic to the union movement? Would you want to be a union member?
2. Are the union members you spoke with satisfied or dissatisfied with their union's efforts to achieve better working conditions, higher wages, and improved benefits?
3. What is the union's role when layoffs occur?
4. Based on what you have learned, do you think the union movement in Canada will stagnate or thrive in the years ahead?

CRAFTING YOUR BUSINESS PLAN

Taking the Occasion to Deal with Labour

The Purpose of the Assignment

1. To acquaint students with the labour and management relations issues faced by a sample start-up firm as it develops its business plan in the framework of the Business PlanPro (BPP) software package.
2. To stimulate students' thinking about the application of the textbook's concepts and methods on labour and management relations to the preparation of a business plan in the BPP planning environment.

Assignment

After reading Chapter 8 in the textbook, open the BPP software and search for information about labour and management relations as it applies to a sample firm: Occasions, The Event Planning Specialists. To find Occasions, do the following:

Open Business PlanPro. If it asks if you want to "create a new business plan" or "open an existing plan," select "create a new business plan" (even though you are not going to create a plan at this time). You will then be taken to the Business PlanPro EasyPlan Wizard. On the screen, click on the option entitled **Research It**. You will then be presented with a new list of options, including Sample Plan Browser. After clicking on the **Sample Plan Browser**, go down the alphabetical list of sample plans and double-click on **Event Planning—Personal**, which is the location for Occasions, The Event Planning Specialists. The screen you are looking at is the introduction page for the Occasions business plan. Next, scroll down until you reach the **Table of Contents** for Occasion's business plan.

Now respond to the following items:

1. Explore the business plan for this company, paying special attention to its product line and the types of clients who will be buying its products. Do you suspect that there will be union members among the employees of some Occasions customers? [Sites to see in BPP for this item: On the **Table of Contents** page, click on each of the following in turn: **1.0 Executive Summary**, **1.1 Objectives**, and **1.2 Mission**. After returning to the **Table of Contents** page, examine each of the following: **Table 2.2: Startup** (beneath **2.2 Startup Summary**), **3.0 Products and Services**, **3.1 Competitive Comparison**, and **4.1 Market Segmentation**.]
2. Considering Occasion's growth projections, do you foresee increasing likelihood for unionization of its employees? Why or why not? What should Occasions do to accommodate clients' unions? [Sites to see in BPP: In the **Table of Contents** page, click on **1.1 Objectives**. Also look at both **2.0 Company Summary** and **6.1 Organization Structure**.]
3. Explain why some experience with labour laws and union–management contract issues would be valuable for Occasions' salespeople in their dealings with clients. [Sites to see in BPP for this item: In the **Table of Contents** page, click on each of the following in turn: **1.0 Executive Summary**, **3.0 Products and Services**, and **4.1 Market Segmentation**. After returning to the **Table of Contents** page, examine each of the following: **4.2 Target Market Segment Strategy** and **4.3 Industry Analysis**. After returning once again to the **Table of Contents** page, click on **1.3 Keys to Success**.]

EXPLORING THE NET

The Ontario Labour Relations Board

As highlighted in this chapter, in addition to the Canada Labour Code each province also has its own separate Labour Relations Act. A Labour Relations Board in each province is charged with the task of upholding this legislation. Let's examine the Ontario Labour Relations Board's website at **http://www.gov.on.ca/lab/olrb/eng/homeeng.htm**.

1. What is the Ontario Labour Relations Board (OLRB) and what responsibilities does this particular board have?
2. What is meant by the term *mediation*? What steps are followed by the OLRB in such a situation?
3. How does adjudication differ from mediation? What is the role of the OLRB in this type of situation?
4. Normally an OLRB decision is binding. Are there any conditions when an OLRB decision may be reconsidered?
5. In addition to the Ontario Labour Relations Act, which other legislation does the OLRB deal with? Specifically what type of concerns should be brought to the OLRB?

Concluding Case 9-1

What's the Future of Labour–Management Relations?

For most of the twentieth century, relations between labour unions and management were very adversarial. Strikes were common, and much hostility was evident when new collective agreements were being negotiated. In the 1990s, however, it appeared that union–management relations might just be moving toward more co-operation rather than conflict. One high-visibility case that is consistent with this argument is the agreement reached in 1999 between General Motors Canada and the Canadian Auto Workers (CAW) union.

On October 19, 1999, the negotiating team for General Motors of Canada walked into the Royal York Hotel's Tudor Room and received a standing ovation from the CAW members who were assembled there. The GM managers then applauded the workers. GM's first offer met the pattern of wages and benefits that the CAW had already negotiated with DaimlerChrysler Canada and Ford Motor of Canada. A cost of living allowance was also given, as were generous improvements in pensions. GM also settled hundreds of outstanding grievances at the Oshawa and St. Catharines plants. CAW president Buzz Hargrove said that the atmosphere during negotiations was positive. The turnaround came on the heels of a serious dispute between the CAW and GM of Canada in 1996, when 26 000 CAW workers went on strike and shut down all of GM's Canadian operations. GM also experienced strikes at its Dayton, Ohio, and Flint, Michigan, plants in the late 1990s. Those strikes apparently convinced both workers and management that they had to begin working together if GM hoped to compete with its rivals.

The improvements in union–management relations were achieved because each side recognized that it had problems it had to resolve. GM, for example, had more capacity than market share, and industry analysts said it would have to close manufacturing plants to bring its output in line with its market share. GM was also experiencing increased foreign competition from companies such as Honda and Toyota. The union's problem was the decline in the number of unionized autoworkers (caused by auto makers' downsizing).

Does this development at GM Canada represent a real change in union–management relations, or are the goals of unions and management so fundamentally different that co-operation is not possible? Unions understandably want the best deal possible for their members, but management is always concerned that agreeing to workers' demands will threaten the financial viability of the company. The increasing intensity of international competition means that a company's managers are under tremendous pressure to keep prices low. To achieve this goal, they may feel compelled to take drastic actions such as laying off workers (many of whom are unionized). In the short period between April and June 2003, for example, the following items were in the business news:

- Imperial Tobacco Canada Ltd. announced that it was closing a cigarette making plant in Montreal and laying off 44 percent of its workforce; 430 unionized employees lost their jobs
- Canadian Pacific Railway Ltd. announced that it was cutting 520 jobs because of declining grain shipments; the announcement came at the same time that 200 unionized rail traffic controllers went on strike demanding higher wages
- Dominion Tanners declared bankruptcy and laid off 47 unionized workers
- DaimlerChrysler cancelled its plan for a new assembly plant in Windsor, blaming poor auto markets for the cancellation; the plant would have created 2500 jobs
- Bombardier Inc. warned that it might have to lay off 1000 unionized employees if they did not agree to major concessions in the areas of health benefit payments and work flexibility; the concessions are necessary to cut costs so that Bombardier can be competitive
- Air Canada told its unions that it needed to cut salaries by 10 percent because its revenues had dropped sharply, partly because of the SARS outbreak; two of Air Canada's biggest unions also accepted major layoffs as part of a plan to save Air Canada from bankruptcy
- members of several different unions at Air Canada's Jazz subsidiary agreed to pay cuts as a way to cut costs for the airline

Actions like these certainly don't facilitate trust and co-operation between labour and management. While it has always been the case that management can decide to lay off unionized workers, the magnitude of such layoffs has increased dramatically in the last few years. What does this do to the relationship between labour and management? Will negotiations become more hostile as labour unions try to protect their members? Or will negotiations become more focused on ways that labour and management can work together to meet threats from outside the company?

Another idea that suggests co-operation between labour and management is the idea of teams, which has significant implications for labour–management co-operation. In a traditional assembly line operation, an individual worker performs only one specified task. In contrast, the team concept breaks down job distinctions. All members of a team are "cross-trained" to perform every necessary function to produce a good or service. Teams also solve minor problems as they arise. Individuals who show the most leadership within the team—not necessarily those with the most seniority—are promoted. The team idea suggests that co-operation, not conflict, is necessary.

But reservations are evident here as well. Managers are concerned about the issue of power since they are accustomed to giving orders and having them carried out. The need to share power and ask for suggestions—which is central to the team concept—conflicts with the traditional practice of issuing commands, so it is difficult for many managers to accept. First-line managers are particularly likely to resist such changes since fewer such managers are needed under the team concept.

Labour unions also have concerns about the team concept. Although some unions support the team concept when management is willing to link it to guarantees of job security, others see it as just another union-busting attempt by industry. Some individual workers object to the team concept because it transfers responsibility but not authority to them. They also feel it makes them work harder. To get Canadian workers to "buy into" working harder for their employers, companies are going to have to consider worker demands for greater input into management. There is also a debate about the benefits of the job rotation aspect of the team concept. Some workers like the chance to change assignments because it reduces job boredom and makes the day go by faster, but others argue that doing six monotonous jobs is no more fulfilling than doing one.

Questions for Discussion

1. Can labour and management really be a team, or do their conflicting goals make that impossible?
2. What are the differences between the new team concept and the old assembly-line concept? What problems might a company encounter when it tries to implement the team concept?
3. Is the team concept simply a gimmick to allow management to get more work out of workers or to "bust" unions? Even if it is a gimmick, might there be advantages for workers?
4. "Unions are going to have less and less power in the future because global competition will force all companies to reduce costs. Management will simply lay off large numbers of union workers to achieve cost-cutting goals." Do you agree or disagree? Why? ◆

Concluding Case 9-2

A Close Call at Canada Post

In June 2003, the 45 000 members of the Canadian Union of Postal Workers (CUPW) voted 92 percent in favour of going on strike if their contract demands were not met by Canada Post. The key issues in the impasse were work safety, workload, retirement, subcontracting, and salaries. On July 12, CUPW announced that its members would go on strike on July 18 if no agreement was reached. But on July 19, a new strike deadline of July 21 was set because negotiators felt that they were getting closer to reaching an agreement. Over the next couple of days the deadline was extended twice more. An agreement was finally reached on July 27, so a strike did not actually occur. The new agreement gave CUPW members a 12.5 percent wage increase over four years and full job security.

Union president Deborah Bourque said that the atmosphere in the latest round of negotiations was much more positive than it was in 1997, when the union and management were unable to agree and a strike occurred. She noted that Canada Post is no longer trying to break the union, nor is it trying to privatize. During the 1997 negotiations, Canada Post wanted to introduce technological improvements in the way work was done to reduce the number of employees it needed. CUPW vigorously opposed the idea from the start. Bargaining dragged on for many months without much progress. A mediator was then appointed in the hope that he could get the disputing parties to reach an agreement and avert a strike. But after a few days of talks, the mediator concluded that the two sides were not willing to bargain seriously, and he gave up. CUPW then went on strike, and its members began walking the picket line.

Tensions were high, and during the strike CUPW workers delayed some commercial airline flights by preventing cargo and food from reaching the planes. They also snarled traffic in some locations, and picketed the Reform party's official Ottawa residence to show their displeasure with the Reform party's view that the postal service was "essential," and CUPW should not be allowed to go on strike.

About two weeks after the strike started, the Liberal Minister of Labour, Lawrence MacAuley, introduced back-to-work legislation that forced the postal workers to return to work. CUPW immediately condemned the legislation, and promised large-scale civil disobedience if the workers were forced back to work. Darrell Tingley, then the CUPW president, claimed that the Canadian Direct Marketing Association was putting pressure on the government to get the postal workers back on the job. Back-to-work legislation levied fines of $1000 per day against workers who defied the order. Union leaders could be fined up to $50 000 per day, and CUPW could face fines of up to $500 000 if it defied the back-to-work order. MacAuley said he felt compelled to introduce the legislation since so many Canadians were suffering during the labour dispute. Many businesses and charities, for example, were being hurt by the strike since they could not carry on their usual activities without mail service. While MacAuley scolded both Canada Post and CUPW for failing to reach a new agreement, the Reform party criticized the Liberal government for not having acted sooner.

On December 4, 1997, the defiant postal workers grudgingly returned to work. Tingley suggested that postal workers disrupt normal Canada Post activities by purposely misdirecting business mail, and by sending mail through the system without stamps. Canada Post president Georges Clermont said that it was unbelievable that the postal workers would listen to advice like this, because it would mean hurting Canada Post's customers—the very people who are responsible for the workers having jobs in the first place. Clermont said the workers who followed Tingley's suggestions would be disciplined. But Tingley said that Canada Post could expect a campaign of workplace defiance for the remainder of the three-year agreement.

All of this unpleasant history was on the minds of the negotiators in 2003 as they tried to reach an agreement. While they were negotiating, there was speculation in Canada's newspapers about the impact of another strike. Some observers feel that Canada Post is becoming less important in mail delivery because consumers are increasingly using electronic bill payment, and because there is steadily increasing competition from private-sector delivery firms like UPS and FedEx. In fact, the volume of mail moved by Canada Post has dropped about 11 percent (from 11 billion pieces of mail in 1996 to 9.8 billion pieces in 2002). But others pointed out that Canada Post is still important in the Canadian economy. For example:

- retailers count on Canada Post to deliver promotional flyers, credit card invoices, and products that customers order
- the Canadian Marketing Association says that it relies heavily on Canada Post in direct marketing efforts; even if a person orders something on the internet, someone has to deliver it
- the Canadian Federation of Independent Businesses estimated that the 1997 strike cost small businesses about $200 million a day in total
- when there is a strike at Canada Post, private-sector competitors simply don't have the capacity to fill the gap

Questions for Discussion

1. When the postal workers went on strike in 1997, many businesses and charities were hurt. Is this an argument for abolishing the right to strike for postal workers? Should postal workers have the right to strike? Defend your answer.
2. What is mediation? Why do you think mediation was not effective in the 1997 negotiations? Why were the parties able to reach an agreement in the 2003 negotiations?
3. Read newspaper accounts of the 1997 postal strike and the events leading up to it (consult papers dated November 15 through December 5, 1997). Also read newspaper accounts of the 2003 negotiations (consult papers dated June 15 through July 25, 2003). How do these accounts illustrate how the collective bargaining process works? What are the similarities in the accounts? What are the differences?
4. Will the services provided by Canada Post become less in demand by Canadians during the next decade? Defend your answer. ◆

CHAPTER 10

Motivating and Leading Employees

After reading this chapter, you should be able to:

1. Describe the nature and importance of *psychological contracts* in the workplace.
2. Discuss the importance of *job satisfaction* and *employee morale* and summarize their roles in human relations in the workplace.
3. Identify and summarize the most important *theories of employee motivation*.
4. Describe some of the strategies used by organizations to improve *job satisfaction* and *employee motivation*.
5. Discuss different managerial styles of *leadership* and their impact on human relations in the workplace.

Leadership in Modern Business

In times past, leaders of most business firms tried to keep a low public profile and concentrated on running their businesses. But during the past couple of decades, many business leaders—Paul Tellier, Frank Stronach, Jean Monty, Gerry Schwartz, Jimmy Pattison, Martha Stewart, and Izzy Asper, to name just a few—have developed very high profiles, and their activities have been widely publicized in both the business and popular press. Sometimes the reports about these leaders are positive, and sometimes they are negative, but everyone seems to agree that leaders are (1) important, and (2) very interesting people to read about.

Jean Monty, the CEO of BCE Inc. until he resigned in 2002, is illustrative. While at BCE, his strategy was to take money earned in the reliable Bell Canada part of the business and use it to acquire New Economy businesses, some of which would likely grow very fast and make a lot of money for BCE. Monty's leadership style was active and decisive; he would analyze a situation, then take action. Monty saw BCE as a growth company, not a stodgy utility, and took the lead in getting BCE into wireless, high-speed internet and electronic commerce and several other diversified activities (the famous "convergence" strategy). Unfortunately, these ventures were generally unsuccessful, and some of them generated large losses. Monty now acknowledges that his famous decisiveness may have been his downfall.

Paul Tellier is another leader who has received much publicity. In 2003, he topped the KPMG/Ipsos-Reid list of Most Respected Canadian Business Leaders, largely as a result of his success in moving Canadian National Railways from a poorly performing railway into a North American powerhouse. When he first became CEO of CN in 1993, critics argued that his lack of experience in the railroad business would reduce his chances of success. Tellier, who had been clerk of the Privy Council and secretary to the federal Cabinet, responded by saying that what CN needed was not an experienced railroad person, but a leader who would be willing to make the tough decisions that were necessary to turn CN around. Tellier proved his critics wrong and turned CN into a high-performing railroad. He was then appointed as CEO of Bombardier with the mandate to turn that company around.

One common thread tying leaders together is their ability to manage large business empires that employ many people and generate large salaries and bonuses for the top executives. Frank Stronach, the founder of Magna International, the Canadian auto parts giant, is typical. Over the years, he has developed a reputation for having strong views about leadership and corporate governance. Magna's constitution includes specific guidelines on research and development expenditures, shareholder dividends, charitable contributions, and executive compensation (a maximum of 6 percent of pre-tax profit). Stronach does not avoid controversy. At Magna's 2003 annual meeting, he told the assembled shareholders that the company would never change the way it operates. When a shareholder objected to the salaries paid to some Magna executives, Stronach responded that he could be operating a private company and wouldn't have to answer to any shareholders about salaries.

The issue of the compensation paid to leaders has become a hot topic. Critics argue that the millions of dollars paid to some executives cannot possibly be warranted from a financial perspective, particularly when executive salaries go up as company performance declines and workers are laid off. Unfortunately, it is not hard to find examples of this problem. The CEO of Royal Group Technologies, for example, received an 80 percent boost in total compensation from 2001 to 2002, in spite of the fact that the company's share price dropped nearly 50 percent. Frank Stronach, CEO of Magna, received $52 000 000 in compensation in 2002. This came during a period when the value of Magna's stock dropped 30 percent. A *Canadian Business* review of 150 companies found that more than half of the CEOs had their compensation increased, even though their stock prices and profits were under pressure. J. Richard Finlay, the chairman of the Centre for Corporate & Public Governance, says that executive compensation will have to drop significantly to restore investor confidence.

High executive compensation also has a negative emotional impact on workers when they see top man-

BCE Inc
www.bce.ca

agers making 20, 30, 50, or even 100 times what they are making. Those who defend large executive salaries point to the multi-million compensation received by professional sports figures and movie stars, and argue that surely top managers contribute as much to society as those individuals do. They also argue that high compensation is necessary to attract capable people to top management positions.

Henry Mintzberg, a world-renowned management scholar at McGill University, says that the leadership behaviour of CEOs has become very distorted over the last 15 years or so. In particular, he says that many CEOs fail to build trust and confidence, and fail to plan for the long term. Instead, they care only for the short term and the fat bonuses they will receive if they increase the market value of the company's shares. Mintzberg says that multi-million dollar salaries given to top executives send a terrible message to the average working person, especially when top managers talk about how important employees are. He feels that top managers should receive salaries in the $250 000 to $500 000 range. He also thinks that leaders should refuse bonuses and share monetary successes with their managers. ◆

PSYCHOLOGICAL CONTRACTS IN ORGANIZATIONS

psychological contract
The set of expectations held by an employee concerning what he or she will contribute to an organization (contributions) and what the organization will provide the employee (inducements) in return.

1. Describe the nature and importance of *psychological contracts* in the workplace.

Whenever we buy a car or sell a house, both buyer and seller sign a contract that specifies the terms of the agreement—who pays what to whom, when it's paid, and so forth. In some ways, a **psychological contract** resembles a legal contract. On the whole, however, it's less formal and less rigidly defined. A psychological contract is the set of expectations held by an employee concerning what he or she will contribute to an organization (referred to as *contributions*) and what the organization will provide the employee (referred to as *inducements*) in return.

If either party perceives an inequity in the contract, that party may seek a change. The employee, for example, might ask for a pay raise, promotion, or a bigger office. He or she might put forth less effort or look for a better job elsewhere. The organization can also initiate change by training workers to improve their skills, transferring them to new jobs, or terminating them.

human relations
Interactions between employers and employees and their attitudes toward one another.

All organizations face the basic challenge of managing psychological contracts. They want value from their employees, and they must give employees the right inducements. Valuable but underpaid employees may perform below their capabilities or leave for better jobs. Conversely, overpaying employees who contribute little incurs unnecessary costs. The foundation of good **human relations**—the interactions between employers and employees and their attitudes toward one another—is a satisfied and motivated workforce.[1]

The massive wave of downsizing and cutbacks that have swept the Canadian economy during the past 10 years has complicated the process of managing psychological contracts. Many organizations, for example, used to offer at least reasonable assurances of job permanence as a fundamental inducement to employees. Now, however, because job permanence is less likely, alternative inducements—such as lavish benefits packages—may be needed instead.

If psychological contracts are created, maintained, and managed effectively, the result is likely to be workers who are satisfied and motivated. On the other hand, poorly managed psychological contracts may result in dissatisfied, unmotivated workers. Although most people have a general idea of what "job satisfaction" is, both job satisfaction and high morale can be elusive in the workplace. Because they are critical to an organization's success, we now turn our attention to discussing their importance.

THE IMPORTANCE OF JOB SATISFACTION AND MORALE

Broadly speaking, **job satisfaction** is the degree of enjoyment that people derive from performing their jobs. If people enjoy their work, they are relatively satisfied; if they do not enjoy their work, they are relatively dissatisfied. In turn, satisfied employees are likely to have high **morale**—the overall attitude that employees have toward their workplace. Morale reflects the degree to which they perceive that their needs are being met by their jobs. It is determined by a variety of factors, including job satisfaction and satisfaction with such things as pay, benefits, co-workers, and promotion opportunities.[2]

job satisfaction
The pleasure and feeling of accomplishment employees derive from performing their jobs well.

morale
The generally positive or negative mental attitude of employees toward their work and workplace.

2. Discuss the importance of *job satisfaction* and *employee morale* and summarize their roles in human relations in the workplace.

Why Businesses Need Satisfied Employees

When workers are enthusiastic and happy with their jobs, the organization benefits in many ways. Because they are committed to their work and the organization, satisfied workers are more likely to work hard and try to make useful contributions to the organization. They will also have fewer grievances and are less likely to engage in negative behaviours (e.g., complaining, deliberately slowing their work pace, etc.). Satisfied workers are also more likely to come to work every day and are more likely to remain with the organization. So, by ensuring that employees are satisfied, management gains a more efficient and smooth-running company.

Just as the rewards of high worker satisfaction and morale are great, so are the costs of job dissatisfaction and poor morale. Dissatisfied workers, for example, are far more likely to be absent due to minor illnesses, personal reasons, or a general disinclination to go to work. Low morale may also result in high **turnover**—the percentage of an organization's workforce that leaves and must be replaced. Some turnover is a natural and healthy way to weed out low-performing workers in any organization. But high levels of turnover have many negative consequences, including numerous vacancies, disruption in production, decreased productivity, and high retraining costs.

turnover
The percentage of an organization's workforce that leaves and must be replaced.

Job Satisfaction and Dissatisfaction Trends

Canadian industry shows mixed results when companies try to give employees what they want and to keep them on the job. Consider the following:

- A survey of 2300 workers by the Wyatt Co. of Vancouver found that three-quarters of Canadian workers are satisfied with the content of their job, but fewer than half are happy with the way they are managed. Workers felt that management did not show genuine interest in them and did not treat them with dignity. Managers, on the other hand, felt that they did treat workers with dignity. Perhaps most disconcerting of all, fewer than one-third of those surveyed felt that promotions were based on merit. The longer they had been with a company, the more cynical they were about this issue.[3]
- Another survey of 1631 employees from 94 companies across Canada and the United States found that, while employees are optimistic and committed to their work, they also feel frustrated because they have no control over what happens in their job. Most employees feel that their abilities are not used to the fullest extent. They want direction and measurable goals.[4]
- Based on responses from 7000 private- and public-sector workers, a Conference Board of Canada survey found the following:

- One-third of employees felt that caring for children or elderly parents limited their career advancement.
- One-eighth had left an employer because of family responsibilities.
- Seventeen percent had turned down promotions.
- Twenty-five percent had turned down transfers.
- Women were four times as likely as men to report conflicts in home and work responsibilities.[5]
- A report by the Business and Economic Roundtable on Mental Health concluded that employee stress is costing Canadian industry about $60 billion each year, and more than half of that is in lost productivity. The top sources of stress for employees were identified as too much (or too little) work to do, lack of two-way communication up and down the hierarchy, being unappreciated, inconsistent performance review processes, career uncertainty, unclear company policies, and office politics.[6]

MOTIVATION IN THE WORKPLACE

3. Identify and summarize the most important *theories of employee motivation.*

motivation
The set of forces that causes people to behave in certain ways.

Although job satisfaction and morale are important, employee motivation is even more critical to a firm's success. As we saw in Chapter 5, motivation is one part of the managerial function of directing. Broadly defined, **motivation** is the set of forces that cause people to behave in certain ways. For example, while one worker may be motivated to work hard to produce as much as possible, another may be motivated to do just enough to get by. Managers must understand these differences in behaviour and the reasons for them.

Over the years, many theories have been proposed to address the issues of motivation. In this section, we will focus on three major approaches to motivation in the workplace that reflect a chronology of thinking in the area: *classical theory and scientific management, behaviour theory,* and *contemporary motivation theories*.

Classical Theory and Scientific Management

classical theory of motivation
A theory of motivation that presumes that workers are motivated almost solely by money.

According to the so-called **classical theory of motivation**, workers are motivated solely by money. In his book *The Principles of Scientific Management* (1911), industrial engineer Frederick Taylor proposed a way for both companies and workers to benefit from this widely accepted view of life in the workplace.[7] If workers are motivated by money, Taylor reasoned, then paying them more would prompt them to produce more. Meanwhile, the firm that analyzed jobs and found better ways to perform them would be able to produce goods more cheaply, make higher profits, and thus pay—and motivate—workers better than its competitors.

Taylor's approach is known as *scientific management*. His ideas captured the imagination of many managers in the early twentieth century. Soon, plants across Canada and the United States were hiring experts to perform *time-and-motion studies*. Industrial-engineering techniques were applied to each facet of a job to determine how to perform it most efficiently. These studies were the first "scientific" attempts to break down jobs into easily repeated components and to devise more efficient tools and machines for performing them.

Behaviour Theory: The Hawthorne Studies

The ideas of Frederick Taylor, the founder of scientific management, had a profound impact on the way manufacturing activities were carried out in the early twentieth century. His basic ideas are still used today.

One of the first challenges to the classical theory of human relations management came about by accident. In 1925, a group of Harvard researchers began a study at the Hawthorne Works of Western Electric. Their intent was to examine the relationship between changes in the physical environment and worker output, with an eye to increasing productivity.

The results of the experiment at first confused, then amazed, the scientists. Increasing lighting levels improved productivity, but so did lowering lighting levels. And against all expectations, raising the pay of workers failed to increase their productivity. Gradually they pieced together the puzzle. The explanation for the lighting phenomenon lay in workers' response to attention. In essence, they determined that almost any action on the part of management that made workers believe they were receiving special attention caused worker productivity to rise. This result, known as the **Hawthorne effect**, had a major influence on human relations management, convincing many businesses that paying attention to employees is indeed good for business.

Hawthorne effect
The tendency for workers' productivity to increase when they feel they are receiving special attention from management.

Contemporary Motivation Theories

Following the Hawthorne studies, managers and researchers alike focused more attention on the importance of good human relations in motivating employee performance. Stressing the factors that cause, focus, and sustain workers' behaviour, most motivation theorists are concerned with the ways in which management thinks about and treats employees. The major moti-

The Hawthorne studies were an important step in developing an appreciation for the human factor at work. These women worked under different lighting conditions as researchers monitored their productivity. The researchers were amazed to find that productivity increased regardless of whether lighting levels increased or decreased.

vation theories include the *human-resources model, the hierarchy of needs model, two-factory theory, expectancy theory, equity theory,* and *goal-setting theory*.

The Human-Resources Model: Theories X and Y

In an important study, behavioural scientist Douglas McGregor concluded that managers had radically different beliefs about how best to use the human resources at a firm's disposal. He classified these beliefs into sets of assumptions that he labelled "Theory X" and "Theory Y."[8] The basic differences between these two theories are highlighted in Table 10.1.

Theory X

A management approach based on the belief that people must be forced to be productive because they are naturally lazy, irresponsible, and uncooperative.

Theory Y

A management approach based on the belief that people want to be productive because they are naturally energetic, responsible, and cooperative.

Managers who subscribe to **Theory X** tend to believe that people are naturally lazy and uncooperative and must therefore be either punished or rewarded to be made productive. Managers who incline to **Theory Y** tend to believe that people are naturally energetic, growth-oriented, self-motivated, and interested in being productive.

McGregor generally favoured Theory Y beliefs. Thus he argued that Theory Y managers are more likely to have satisfied, motivated employees. Of course, Theory X and Y distinctions are somewhat simplistic and offer little concrete basis for action. Their value lies primarily in their ability to highlight and analyze the behaviour of managers in light of their attitudes toward employees.

Maslow's Hierarchy of Needs Model

hierarchy of human needs model

Theory of motivation describing five levels of human needs and arguing that basic needs must be fulfilled before people work to satisfy higher-level needs.

Psychologist Abraham Maslow's **hierarchy of human needs model** proposed that people have a number of different needs that they attempt to satisfy in their work. He classified these needs into five basic types and suggested that they are arranged in the hierarchy of importance shown in Figure 10.1. According to Maslow, needs are hierarchical because lower-level needs must be met before a person will try to satisfy those on a higher level.[9]

Abraham Maslow
www.ship.edu/~cgboeree/maslow.html

- *Physiological needs* are necessary for survival; they include food, water, shelter, and sleep. Businesses address these needs by providing both comfortable working environments and salaries sufficient to buy food and shelter.
- *Security needs* include the needs for stability and protection from the unknown. Many employers thus offer pension plans and job security.
- *Social needs* include the needs for friendship and companionship. Making friends at work can help to satisfy social needs, as can the feeling that you "belong" in a company.

Table 10.1 Beliefs About People at Work

Theory X and Theory Y convey very different assumptions about people at work.

Theory X	Theory Y
1. People are lazy.	1. People are energetic.
2. People lack ambition and dislike responsibility.	2. People are ambitious and seek responsibility.
3. People are self-centred.	3. People can be selfless.
4. People resist change.	4. People want to contribute to business growth and change.
5. People are gullible and not very bright.	5. People are intelligent.

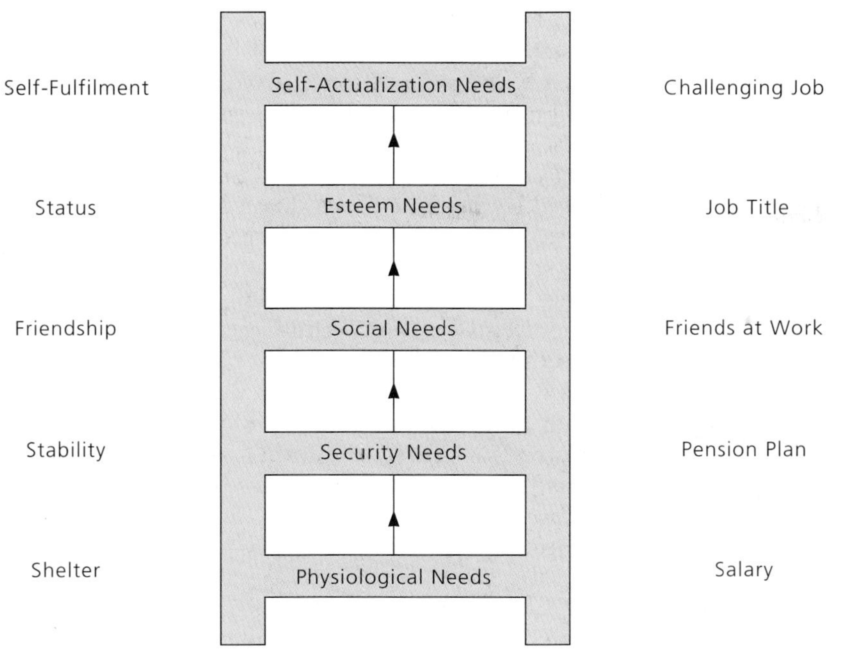

Figure 10.1
Maslow's hierarchy of human needs provides a useful categorization of the different needs people have.

- *Esteem needs* include the need for status and recognition as well as the need for self-respect. Respected job titles and large offices are among the things that businesses can provide to address these needs.
- Finally, *self-actualization needs* are needs for self-fulfilment. They include the needs to grow and develop one's capabilities and to achieve new and meaningful goals. Challenging job assignments can help satisfy these needs.

According to Maslow, once one set of needs has been satisfied, it ceases to motivate behaviour. This is the sense in which the hierarchical nature of lower- and higher-level needs affects employee motivation and satisfaction. For example, if you feel secure in your job, a new pension plan will probably be less important to you than the chance to make new friends and join an informal network among your co-workers. If, however, a lower-level need suddenly becomes unfulfilled, most people immediately refocus on that lower level. Suppose, for example, that you are seeking to meet your esteem needs by working as a divisional manager at a major company. If you learn that your division—and consequently your job—may be eliminated, you might very well find the promise of job security at a new firm as motivating as a promotion once would have been at your old company.

Maslow's theory recognizes that because different people have different needs, different things motivate them. Unfortunately, research has found that the hierarchy varies widely, not only for different people but also across different cultures.

Two-Factor Theory

After studying a group of accountants and engineers, psychologist Frederick Herzberg concluded that job satisfaction and dissatisfaction depend on two factors: *hygiene factors*, such as working conditions, and *motivating factors*,

two-factor theory
A theory of human relations developed by Frederick Herzberg that identifies factors that must be present for employees to be satisfied with their jobs and factors that, if increased, lead employees to work harder.

such as recognition for a job well done.[10] According to **two-factor theory**, hygiene factors affect motivation and satisfaction only if they are *absent* or *fail* to meet expectations. For example, workers will be dissatisfied if they believe that they have poor working conditions. If working conditions are improved, however, they will not necessarily become *satisfied*; they will simply be *not dissatisfied*. On the other hand, if workers receive no recognition for successful work, they may be neither dissatisfied nor satisfied. If recognition is provided, they will likely become more satisfied.

Figure 10.2 illustrates two-factor theory. Note that motivation factors lie along a continuum from satisfaction to no satisfaction. Hygiene factors, on the other hand, are likely to produce feelings that lie on a continuum from dissatisfaction to no dissatisfaction. While motivation factors are directly related to the work that employees actually perform, hygiene factors refer to the environment in which they perform it.

This theory thus suggests that managers should follow a two-step approach to enhancing motivation. First, they must ensure that hygiene factors—working conditions, clearly stated policies—are acceptable. This practice will result in an absence of dissatisfaction. Then they must offer motivating factors—recognition, added responsibility—to improve satisfaction and motivation.

Research suggests that two-factor theory works in some professional settings, but it is not as effective in clerical and manufacturing settings. (Herzberg's research was limited to professionals—accountants and engineers—only.) In addition, one person's hygiene factor may be another person's motivating factor. For example, if money represents nothing more than pay for time worked, it may be a hygiene factor for one person. For another person, however, money may be a motivating factor because it represents recognition and achievement.

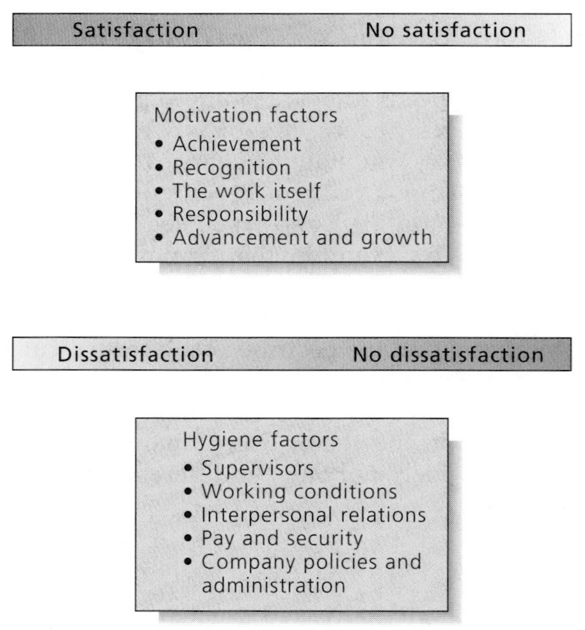

Figure 10.2
According to two-factor theory, job satisfaction depends on two factors.

Expectancy Theory

Expectancy theory suggests that people are motivated to work toward rewards that they want and that they believe they have a reasonable chance—or expectancy—of obtaining.[11] A reward that seems out of reach, for example, is not likely to be motivating even if it is intrinsically positive.

expectancy theory
The theory that people are motivated to work toward rewards that they want and that they believe they have a reasonable chance of obtaining.

Figure 10.3 illustrates expectancy theory in terms of issues that are likely to be considered by an individual employee. Consider the case of an assistant department manager who learns that her firm needs to replace a retiring division manager two levels above her in the organization. Even though she wants the job, she does not apply because she doubts that she will be selected. In this case, she raises the *performance–reward issue*: for some reason, she believes that her performance will not get her the position. Note that she may think that her performance merits the new job but that performance alone will not be enough; perhaps she expects the reward to go to someone with more seniority.

Assume that our employee also learns that the firm is looking for a production manager on a later shift. She thinks that she could get this job, but does not apply because she does not want to change shifts. In this instance, she raises the *rewards–personal goals issue*. Finally, she learns of an opening one level higher—department manager—in her own division. She may well apply for this job because she both wants it and thinks that she has a good chance of getting it. In this case, her consideration of all the issues has led to an expectancy that she can reach a given goal.

Expectancy theory helps explain why some people do not work as hard as they can when their salaries are based purely on seniority. Paying employees the same whether they work very hard or just hard enough to get by removes the financial incentive for them to work harder. In other words, they ask themselves, "If I work harder, will I get a pay raise?" and conclude that the answer is no. Similarly, if hard work will result in one or more *undesirable* outcomes—say, a transfer to another location or a promotion to a job that requires unpleasant travel—employees will not be motivated to work hard.

Equity Theory

Equity theory focuses on social comparisons—people evaluating their treatment by the organization relative to the treatment of others. This approach says that people begin by analyzing *inputs* (what they contribute to their jobs in terms of time, effort, education, experience, and so forth) relative to *outputs* (what they receive in return in terms of salary, benefits, recognition, security, etc.). The result is a ratio of contribution to return. Then they compare their own ratios with those of other employees: They ask whether their ratios are *equal to, greater than,* or *less than* those of the people with whom they are comparing themselves. Depending on the out-

equity theory
The theory that people compare (1) what they contribute to their job with what they get in return, and (2) their input/output ratio with that of other employees.

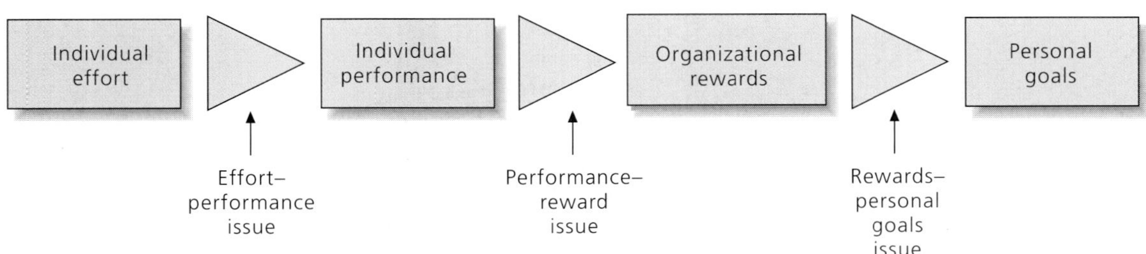

Figure 10.3
Expectancy theory model.

come of their assessments, they experience feelings of equity or inequity. Figure 10.4 illustrates the three possible results of such an assessment.

For example, suppose that a new graduate gets a starting job at a large manufacturing firm. His starting salary is $25 000 per year, he gets a compact company car, and he shares an office with another new employee. If he later learns that another new employee has received the same salary, car, and office arrangement, he will feel equitably treated. If the other newcomer, however, has received $30 000, a full-size company car, and a private office, he may experience feelings of inequity.

Note, however, that the two ratios do not have to be the *same*—they need be only *fair*. Let's assume, for instance, that our new employee has a bachelor's degree and two years of work experience. Perhaps he learns subsequently that the other new employee has an advanced degree and 10 years of work experience. After first feeling inequity, our new employee may now conclude that his comparison person is actually contributing more to the organization. The other employee is equitably entitled, therefore, to receive more in return.

When people feel that they are being inequitably treated, they may do various things to restore fairness. For example, they may ask for raises, reduce their effort, work shorter hours, or just complain to their bosses. They may also rationalize their situation ("management succumbed to pressure to promote a woman"), find different people with whom to compare themselves, or leave their jobs altogether.

Good examples of equity theory at work can be found in professional sports. Each year, for example, rookies are signed to lucrative contracts. No sooner is the ink dry than veteran players start grumbling about raises or revised contracts.

Goal-Setting Theory

goal-setting theory
The theory that people perform better when they set specific, quantified, time-framed goals.

Goal-setting theory describes the kinds of goals that better motivate employees. In general, effective goals tend to have two basic characteristics.

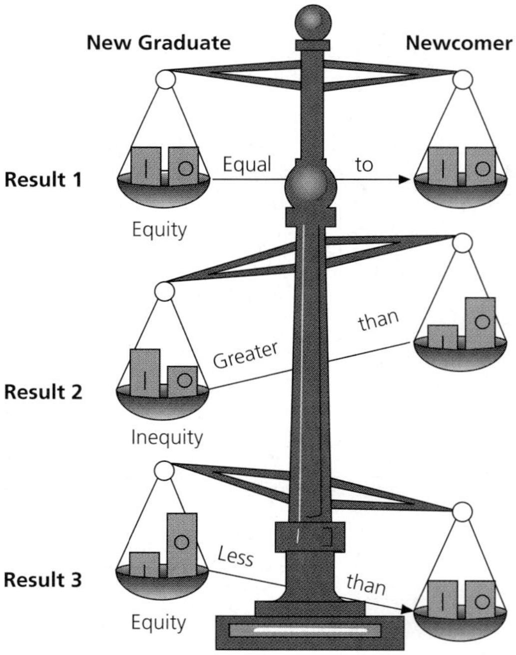

Figure 10.4
Equity theory: possible assessments.

First, they are moderately difficult: While a goal that is too easy does little to enhance effort and motivation, a goal that is too difficult also fails to motivate people. Second, they are specific. A goal of "do your best," for instance, does not motivate people nearly as much as a goal such as "increase profits by 10 percent." The specificity and clarity of this goal serve to focus attention and energy on exactly what needs to be done.[12]

An important aspect of goal setting is the employee's participation in the goal-setting process. When people help select the goals they are to work toward, they tend to accept them more readily and are more committed to achieving them. On the other hand, when goals are merely assigned to people with little or no input on their part, they are less likely to adopt them.

STRATEGIES FOR ENHANCING JOB SATISFACTION AND MORALE

4. Describe some of the strategies used by organizations to improve *job satisfaction* and *employee motivation.*

Deciding what motivates workers and provides job satisfaction is only part of the manager's battle. The other part is to apply that knowledge. Experts have suggested—and many companies have instituted—a wide range of programs designed to make jobs more interesting and rewarding and the work environment more pleasant. In this section, we will consider five of the most common types of programs: *reinforcement/behaviour modification theory, management by objectives, participative management, job enrichment and job redesign,* and *modified work schedules*.

Reinforcement/Behaviour Modification Theory

Many companies try to control, and even alter or modify, workers' behaviour through systematic rewards and punishments for specific behaviours. In other words, they first try to define the specific behaviours they want their employees to exhibit (working hard, being courteous to customers, stressing quality) and the specific behaviours they want to eliminate (wasting time, being rude to customers, ignoring quality). Then they try to shape employee behaviour by linking reinforcement with desired behaviours and punishment with undesired behaviours.

Reinforcement is used, for example, when a company pays *piecework* rewards—when workers are paid for each piece or product completed. In reinforcement strategies, rewards refer to all the positive things people receive for working (pay, praise, promotions, job security, and so forth). When rewards are tied directly to performance, they serve as *positive reinforcement*. For example, paying large cash bonuses to salespeople who exceed quotas prompts them to work even harder during the next selling period. John Deere has recently adopted a new reward system based on positive reinforcement. The firm now gives pay increases when its workers complete college or university courses and demonstrate mastery of new job skills. As well, incentive reward systems at B.C. Tel, Drexis Inc., and Toronto's SkyDome all rely on positive reinforcement.

reinforcement
Controlling and modifying employee behaviour through the use of systematic rewards and punishments for specific behaviours.

Punishment is designed to change behaviour by presenting people with unpleasant consequences if they fail to change in desirable ways. Employees who are repeatedly late for work, for example, may be suspended or have their pay docked. When the National Hockey League or Major League Baseball fines or suspends players found guilty of substance abuse, the organization is seeking to change players' behaviour.

Extensive rewards work best when people are learning new behaviours, new skills, or new jobs. As workers become more adept, rewards can be

Rewards and recognition are an important determinant of employee motivation. Here, a sales representative for a major home appliance manufacturer receives their Top Sales of the Year award from his manager.

used less frequently. Because such actions contribute to positive employer–employee relationships, managers generally prefer giving rewards and placing positive value on performance. Conversely, most managers dislike punishing employees, partly because workers may respond with anger, resentment, hostility, or even retaliation. To reduce this risk, many managers couple punishment with rewards for good behaviour. Other possible concerns about reinforcement theory are discussed in the Exercising Your Ethics box.

Management by Objectives

management by objectives (MBO) *A system of collaborative goal setting that extends from the top of an organization to its bottom.*

Management by objectives (MBO) is a system of collaborative goal-setting that extends from the top of an organization to its bottom. As a technique for managing the planning process, MBO is concerned mainly with helping managers implement and carry out their plans. As you can see in Figure 10.5, MBO involves managers and subordinates in setting goals and evaluating progress. Once the program is set up, the first step is establishing overall organizational goals. It is also these goals that will ultimately be evaluated to determine the success of the program. At the same time, however, collaborative activity—communicating, meeting, counselling, and so forth—is the key to MBO. Therefore, in addition to acting as a planning tool, MBO

EXERCISING YOUR ETHICS

Practising Controlled Behaviour

The Situation

As we noted in the text, some companies try to control—and even alter—workers' behaviour through systematic rewards and punishments for specific behaviours. Then they try to shape employee behaviour by linking reinforcement to desired behaviours and punishment to undesired behaviours.

The Dilemma

Assume that you are the new human resources manager in a medium-size organization. Your boss has just ordered you to implement a behaviour-modification program by creating an intricate network of rewards and punishments to be linked to specific desired and undesired behaviours. You, however, are uncomfortable with this approach. You regard behaviour-modification policies to be too much like experiments on laboratory rats. Instead, you would prefer to use rewards in a way that is consistent with expectancy theory—that is, by letting employees know in advance how they can most effectively reach the rewards they most want. You have tried to change your boss's mind, but to no avail. She says to proceed with behaviour modification with no further discussion.

Questions for Discussion

1. What are the ethical issues in this case?
2. What do you think most managers would do in this situation?
3. What would you do?

can serve as a program for improving satisfaction and motivation. (Note, too, that MBO represents an effort to apply throughout an entire organization the goal-setting theory of motivation that we discussed earlier.)

Indeed, according to many experts, motivational impact is the biggest advantage of MBO. When employees sit down with managers to set goals, they learn more about company-wide objectives, feel that they are an important part of a team, and see how they can improve company-wide performance by achieving their own goals. If an MBO system is used properly, employees should leave meetings not only with an understanding of the value of their contributions, but also with fair rewards for their performances. They should also accept and be committed to the moderately difficult and specific goals they have helped set for themselves.

Investors Group Financial Services has used MBO for many years to motivate its sales force in selling financial services. The MBO process begins when the vice-president of sales develops general goals for the entire sales force. This sets the stage for Planning Week, which is held annually in 73 regional centres across Canada. Sales reps review their financial accomplishments and think through their personal and financial goals for the coming year. During Planning Week, sales reps meet with their division managers and reach a consensus about the specific goals the sales reps will pursue during the next year. Each division manager then forwards the proposed objectives for his or her division to the appropriate regional manager. This process continues all the way up to the vice-president of sales, who gives final approval to the overall sales objectives of the company for the coming year.[13]

Participative Management

In **participative management** and empowerment, employees are given a voice in how they do their jobs and in how the company is managed—they become *empowered* to take greater responsibility for their own performance. Participation and empowerment generally make employees feel more committed to organizational goals because they have helped to shape them.

participative management
A method of increasing employees' job satisfaction by giving them a voice in how they do their jobs and how the company is managed.

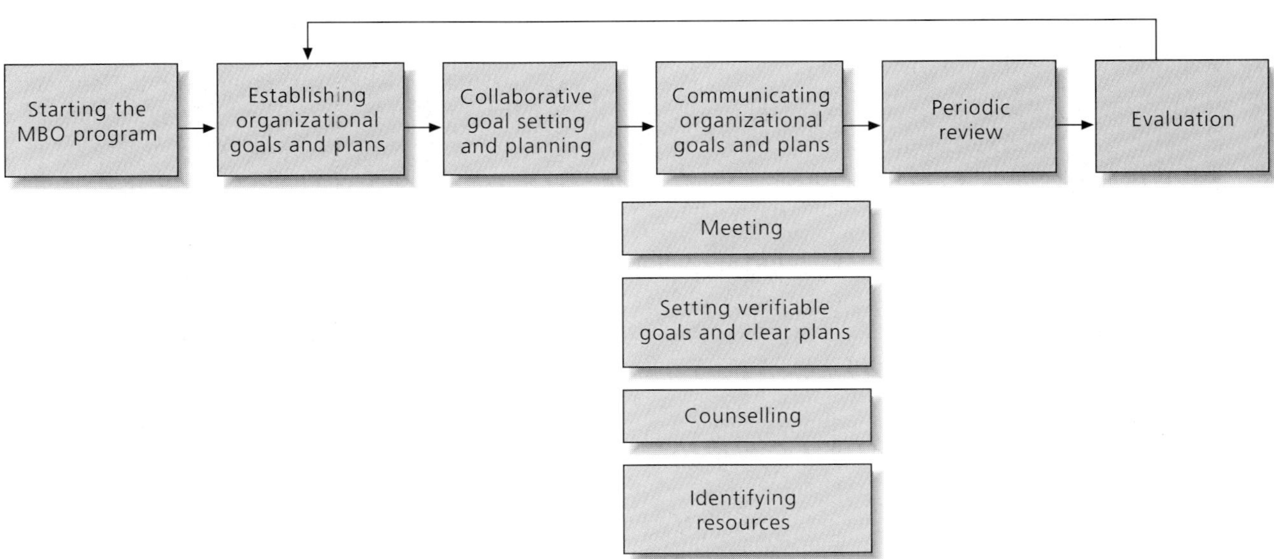

Figure 10.5
Management by objectives.

However, problems occasionally do arise, as described in the Business Today box.

Japanese companies like Honda have been especially effective at practising participative management. And participative management has become more popular in recent years in Canada, partly from imitating the Japanese and partly as businesses and labour unions have become increasingly co-operative. At CP Express and Transport, for example, truck drivers were allowed to decide how to spend $8 million on new equipment.[14]

BUSINESS TODAY

What About Employee Empowerment and Participation?

The empowerment movement involves tapping into workers' knowledge about the job, encouraging them to make suggestions for improvements, encouraging them to be self-motivated, and giving them more responsibility so that they feel they are a real part of the company's success. The South Bend, Indiana, manufacturing plant of the Eaton Corporation illustrates empowerment in practice. At this plant, the traditional factory hierarchy is avoided, and everyone wears the same blue uniforms. There are no time clocks, and workers report their hours on an honour basis. Production statistics for each work team are posted where everyone can see them. Each work team is responsible for keeping its own members productive and motivated. Empowerment has meant more authority for workers, but also more responsibility.

Workers have varying opinions about empowerment. In some cases these opinions are negative, particularly if the participation or empowerment process requires workers to share their job knowledge with other workers or with management:

- One employee who cut metal shafts for industrial pumps at Blackmer/Dover Resources Inc. in Grand Rapids, Michigan, had a reputation for being both fast and accurate in his work. He refused to share his knowledge with management (or his fellow workers) because he feared that management would use the knowledge to speed up the workflow. He is not alone. Many workers have developed extra-fast ways of doing their work, but are reluctant to share those ideas with management. Since managers are always under pressure to improve productivity, the refusal of these workers to share information is frustrating.
- One long-time employee at a small Canadian manufacturing plant taught a younger replacement worker how to run a very complicated machine. Shortly thereafter, the older worker became ill and was off work for a few weeks. When he returned, he found that the younger worker had taken over his job. The older worker had this to say: "To pass on your experience or your knowledge to others, or to pass on to your fellow workers your secrets, how you assemble it faster, better, or more efficiently for the company, be careful; tomorrow you might have lost your job."

The main reason workers conceal knowledge seems to be related to job security. Workers fear that if they share their knowledge, management will use that knowledge to increase output. The increased output will mean that management can get by with fewer workers, so some people will lose their jobs.

In some companies, workers don't share their knowledge because they have become convinced that management doesn't think they have anything to contribute. At the Blackmer/Dover plant, for example, a new plant manager was trying to resolve some production problems that had developed under his predecessor. He asked for worker participation so that he could understand what was wrong in the plant and how things might be improved. Workers were surprised they were asked for their ideas, because previous management had not solicited worker input. But in this case the workers agreed to help, and the story eventually had a happy ending.

Some employees prefer a democratic, or supportive, leader who allows them to participate in decisions that affect them. A survey at B.C. Telecom, for example, showed that people with a supportive boss missed less work, were less tense, felt more secure, and were more confident about their ability to get ahead in the company. Supervisors who received negative ratings usually were inflexible, supervised their workers too closely, and didn't communicate useful information to them.

Participative management gets employees involved in analyzing problems and suggesting solutions. This increases employee satisfaction with, and commitment to, decisions that are made. Here, employees at a company brainstorm a problem with several managers.

Managers must accept the fact that participation and empowerment are not for everyone. Some employees will be frustrated by responsibilities they are not equipped to handle. Moreover, participative programs may actually result in dissatisfied employees if workers see the invitation to participate as more symbolic than substantive. A good approach is to invite participation only to the extent that employees want to have input, and only if participation will have real value for an organization.

Participation and empowerment can be used in large firms or small firms, and with managers and operating employees. For example, managers at General Electric who once needed higher-level approval for any expenditure over $5000 now have the autonomy to make their own expense decisions up to as much as $50 000. At Adam Hat Co., a small firm that makes men's dress, military, and cowboy hats, workers who previously had to report all product defects to supervisors now have the freedom to correct problems themselves or even return products to the workers who are responsible for them.

Team Management

At one level, employees may be given decision-making responsibility for certain narrow activities, such as when to take lunch breaks or how to divide assignments with co-workers. On a broader level, employees are also being consulted on such decisions as production scheduling, work procedures and schedules, and the hiring of new employees.

Like participation and empowerment, teams are not for everyone. Levi Strauss, for example, encountered major problems when it tried to use teams. Individual workers previously performed repetitive, highly specialized tasks, such as sewing zippers into jeans, and were paid according to the number of jobs they completed each day. In an attempt to boost productivity, company management reorganized everyone into teams of 10 to 35 workers and assigned tasks to the entire group. Each team member's pay was determined by the team's level of productivity. In practice, however, faster workers became resentful of slower workers because they reduced the group's total output. Slower workers, meanwhile, resented the pressure put on them by faster-working co-workers. As a result, motivation, satisfaction, and morale all dropped, and Levi's eventually abandoned the teamwork plan altogether.[15]

By and large, however, participation and empowerment in general, and team management in particular, continue to be widely used to enhance employee motivation and company performance. Although teams are often less effective in traditional and rigidly structured bureaucratic organizations, they do help smaller, more flexible organizations make decisions more quickly and effectively, enhance company-wide communication, and encourage organizational members to feel more like a part of an organization. In turn, these attitudes usually lead to higher levels of both employee motivation and job satisfaction.[16]

Job Enrichment and Job Redesign

While MBO programs and participative management can work in a variety of settings, *job enrichment* and *job redesign* programs are generally used to increase satisfaction in jobs significantly lacking in motivating factors.[17]

Job Enrichment Programs

job enrichment

A method of increasing employees' job satisfaction by extending or adding motivating factors such as responsibility or growth.

Job enrichment is designed to add one or more motivating factors to job activities. At Continental Airlines, for example, flight attendants now have more control over their own scheduling. The jobs of flight service managers were enriched when they were given more responsibility and authority for assigning tasks to the flight crew.

Job Redesign Programs

job redesign

A method of increasing employees' job satisfaction by improving the worker–job fit through combining tasks, creating natural work groups, and/or establishing client relationships.

Job redesign acknowledges that different people want different things from their jobs. By restructuring work to achieve a more satisfactory fit between workers and their jobs, **job redesign** can motivate individuals with strong needs for career growth or achievement. Job redesign is usually implemented in one of three ways: through *combining tasks, forming natural work groups,* or *establishing client relationships*.

Combining Tasks. The job of combining tasks involves enlarging jobs and increasing their variety to make employees feel that their work is more meaningful. In turn, employees become more motivated. For example, the job done by a programmer who maintains computer systems might be redesigned to include some system design and system development work. While developing additional skills, then, the programmer also becomes involved in the overall system package.

Forming Natural Work Groups. People who do different jobs on the same projects are candidates for natural work groups. These groups are formed to help employees see the place and importance of their jobs in the total structure of the firm. They are valuable to management because the people working on a project are usually the most knowledgeable about it, and thus the most capable problem solvers.

Establishing Client Relationships. Establishing client relationships means allowing employees to interact with customers. This approach increases job variety. It gives workers both a greater sense of control and more feedback about performance than they get when their jobs are not highly interactive.

For example, software writers at Microsoft watch test users work with programs and discuss problems with them directly rather than receive feedback from third-party researchers. In Fargo, North Dakota, Great Plains Software has employee turnover of less than 7 percent, compared with an industry average of 15 to 20 percent. The company recruits and rewards in large part according to candidates' customer service skills and their experience with customer needs and complaints.

Modified Work Schedules

As another way of increasing job satisfaction, many companies are trying out different approaches to working hours and the workweek. Several types of modified work schedules have been tried, including *flextime, the compressed workweek, telecommuting,* and *workshare programs*.

Flextime

Some modifications involve adjusting a standard daily work schedule. **Flextime** allows people to pick their working hours. Figure 10.6 illustrates how a flextime system might be arranged and how different people might use it. The office is open from 6 a.m. until 7 p.m. Each employee works for eight hours each day. Core time is 9 a.m. until 11 a.m. and 1 p.m. until 3 p.m. Joe, being an early riser, comes in at 6 a.m., takes an hour lunch between 11 and 12, and finishes his day by 3 p.m. Sue, on the other hand, prefers a later day. She comes in at 9 a.m., takes a long lunch from 11 a.m. to 1 p.m., and then works until 7 p.m. Pat works a more traditional day from 8 a.m. until 5 p.m.

flextime
A method of increasing employees' job satisfaction by allowing them some choice in the hours they work.

A 2003 survey of 206 companies conducted by Mercer Human Resource Consulting found that 60 percent of Canadian companies offer some form

IT'S A WIRED WORLD

Motivation and the Machine

There was a time when blue-collar manufacturing jobs were ideal for people with no interest in high technology. Years ago, some people chose production work because they didn't care to earn a college degree. Says David Erb, a technician at Techneglas Inc., "When I finished high school, I said, 'Enough.'" But those days are long gone. Today, advances in high-tech manufacturing have made factory-floor occupations among the most technology intensive in the business world. Not surprisingly, while some workers welcome the change, others are less enthused.

At first glance, the Columbus, Ohio, plant of Techneglas seems to be a throwback—it makes the glass funnels for television picture tubes. (Right now, the demand for TVs is robust, but flat-screen TVs—which don't need conventional picture tubes—are beginning to find their way into homes.) On the plant floor, however, a technology revolution has taken place. New equipment includes electronic quality monitoring machines and computers.

All employees are under constant pressure to learn new skills, and some older workers have taken early retirement rather than upgrade computer and math skills. The plant has a learning centre, but Heidi LoRash-Neuenschwander, who runs it, reports that "older workers often demand to know exactly what they're going to get out of learning new skills, while younger workers just want to learn." As a rule, younger workers already have better technology skills; after all, most of them used PCs in high school. Erb sees another difference, too. "Younger employees," he says, "often want the latest and greatest technology, even when the upgrade confers no real benefit."

One explanation for this generational technology divide is the difference in motivating factors for older workers and younger workers. Older workers, often nervous about retirement, tend to look for job stability and security. They say that younger workers look for labour-saving devices because they're "lazy." Younger workers claim that learning technology is fun and motivating in itself. Perhaps the difference can be explained by motivation theory. Older workers want to be motivated first, and then they will achieve high performance. For younger employees, achievement may occur first, leading to higher motivation.

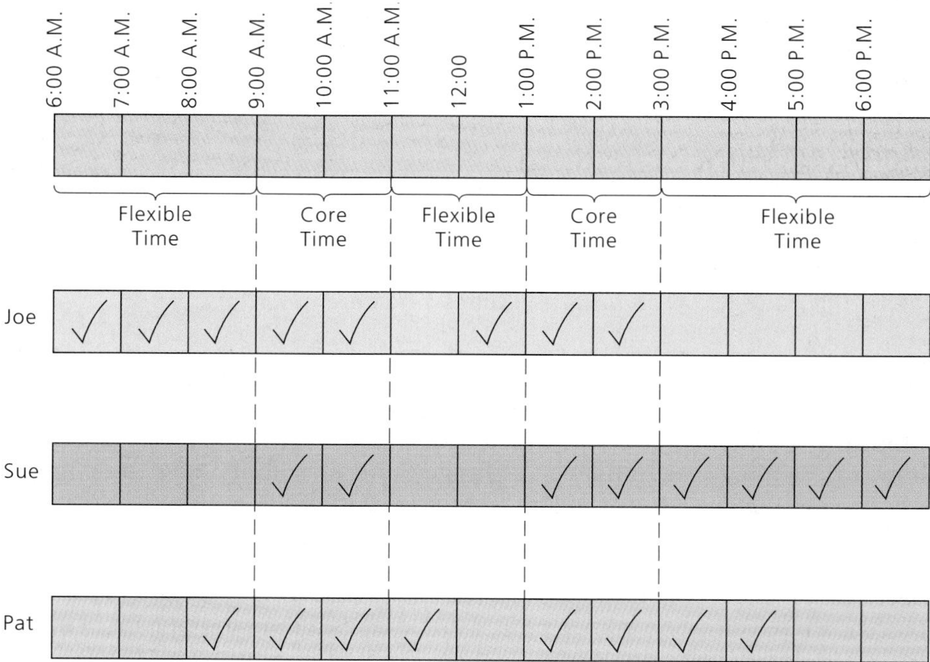

Figure 10.6
Flextime schedules include core time, when everyone must be at work, and flexible time, during which employees can set their own working hours.

of flextime option to their employees.[18] Flextime programs give employees more freedom in their professional and personal lives. Such programs allow workers to plan around the work schedules of spouses and the school schedules of young children, for example. The increased feeling of freedom and control over their work life also reduces individuals' levels of stress.

Companies can also benefit from flextime programs. In large urban areas, flextime programs reduce traffic congestion that contributes to lost work time. Companies benefit from the higher levels of commitment and job satisfaction among workers in such programs.

The Compressed Workweek

compressed workweek
Employees work fewer days per week, but more hours on the days they do work.

In the **compressed workweek**, employees work fewer days per week, but more hours on the days they do work. The most popular compressed workweek is 4 days, 10 hours per day, but some companies have also experimented with 3 days, 12 hours per day. The "weekend worker" program at 3M Canada in London, Ontario, offers workers 12-hour shifts on Saturdays and Sundays only, and pays them the same wage as if they had worked normal hours Monday through Friday. There is a long waiting list to transfer to weekend work.[19]

Tellers at the Bank of Montreal in Oakville Place work long days (up to 14 hours), but enjoy a short workweek. Some tellers work 7 a.m. to 9 p.m. Thursdays and Fridays, and 7:30 a.m. to 5:30 p.m. Saturdays. Others work Mondays to Wednesdays for 14 hours each day. Employees like the system because it allows them to do personal errands during the day on the weekdays they do not have to be at work.[20]

Telecommuting

telecommuting
Allowing employees to do all or some of their work away from the office.

A third variation in work design is **telecommuting**, which allows people to do some or all of their work away from their office. The availability of networked computers, fax machines, cellular telephones, and overnight delivery services makes it possible for many independent professionals to work at home or while travelling. Statistics Canada estimates that 1.3 million Canadians were telecommuting in 2001.[21] As an extreme example, David Longstaff, a software developer, "commutes" from Waterloo, Ontario, to Leeds, England, each day to provide support for computer programs he has written for the company.[22]

While employees like telecommuting because it saves them time and money, the federal government is concerned that holes may be developing in the health and safety net because employers may not extend workplace health and safety coverage to telecommuters who work at home. That is not the only problem with telecommuting. Workers often report feeling isolated and lonely. To avoid this problem, B.C. Tel and Bentall Development Inc. jointly developed a satellite telecommuting office in Langley, British Columbia. It allows workers who used to commute to Burnaby or Vancouver to reduce their travel time considerably and still be able to interact with other workers.[23]

But telecommuting may not be for everyone. Would-be telecommuters must ask themselves several important questions: Can I meet deadlines even when I'm not being closely supervised? What will it be like to be away from the social context of the office five days a week? Can I renegotiate family rules, so my spouse doesn't come home expecting to see dinner on the table just because I've been home all day?

Another obstacle to establishing a telecommuting program is convincing management that it will be beneficial for everyone involved. Telecommuters may have to fight the perception—from both bosses and co-workers—that if they are not being supervised, they are not working. Managers are often very suspicious about telecommuting, asking "How can I tell if someone is working when I can't see them?"

Workshare Programs

A fourth type of modified work schedule, **worksharing** (also called **job sharing**), benefits both employee and employer. This approach allows two people to share one full-time job. For example, Kim Sarjeant and Loraine Champion, who are staff lawyers at NOVA Corp. in Calgary, share a position advising the human resources department. Sarjeant works Mondays

worksharing (job sharing)
A method of increasing employee job satisfaction by allowing two people to share one job.

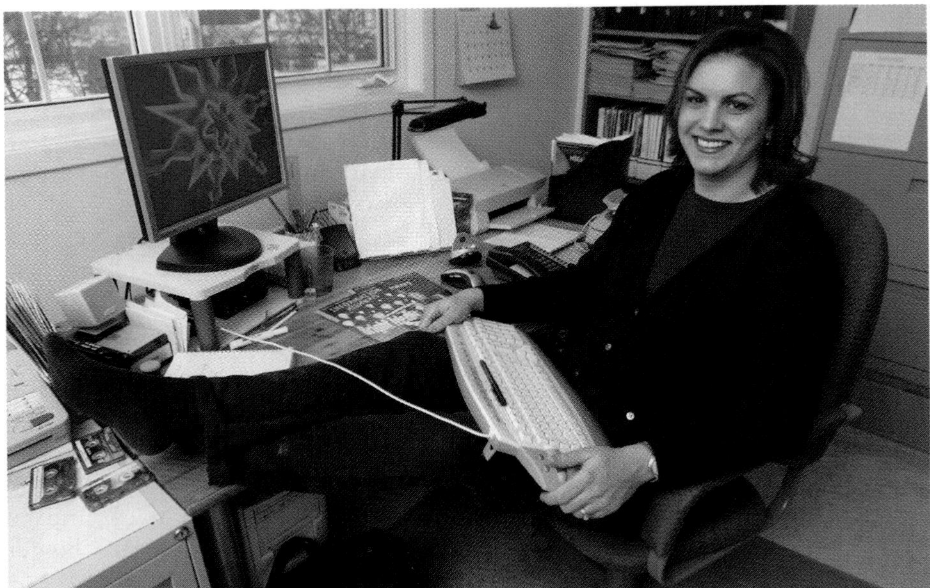

The advent of computers and fax machines has made telecommuting an increasingly popular job strategy. This marketing manager in southern Ontario is one of many people in Canada who telecommute.

through Wednesdays, and Champion works Wednesdays through Fridays.[24] A Statistics Canada survey showed that 8 percent of all part-time workers in Canada share a job with someone. People who share jobs are more likely to be women, to be university educated, and to have professional occupations such as teaching and nursing. In addition, job sharers earned more than regular part-time workers.[25]

Short-run worksharing programs can help ease experienced workers into retirement while training their replacements. Worksharing can also allow students in university co-op programs to combine academic learning with practical experience.

Long-run worksharing programs have proven a good solution for people who want only part-time work. For example, five people might decide to share one reservationist's job at Air Canada with each working one day a week. Each person earns some money, remains in the job market, and enjoys limited travel benefits.

MANAGERIAL STYLES AND LEADERSHIP

leadership
The process of motivating others to work to meet specific objectives.

5. Discuss different managerial styles of *leadership* and their impact on human relations in the workplace.

In trying to enhance morale, job satisfaction, and motivation, managers can use many different styles of leadership. **Leadership** is the process of motivating others to work to meet specific objectives. As we saw in the opening case, leading is also one of the key aspects of a manager's job and an important component of the directing function.

Joe Liemandt started a software company in Austin, Texas, in 1989. As part of his strategy, he was determined to develop and maintain a workforce of creative people who worked well in teams, adapted to rapid change, and felt comfortable taking risks. A decade later, people with these qualities—now numbering nearly 1000—have helped build Liemandt's company, Trilogy Software Inc., into a rapidly growing maker of industry-leading software for managing product pricing, sales plans, and commissions.

When Trilogy hires a new group of employees, Liemandt himself oversees their training. He sees himself as the firm's leader and believes that, as such, it is his responsibility to ensure that every employee shares his vision and understands his way of doing business. Training takes several weeks, starting with a series of classes devoted to the technical aspects of Trilogy's products and methods of software development. Then recruits move into areas in which Liemandt truly believes they make a real difference—developing risk-taking skills and the ability to recognize new opportunities.

Recruits are formed into teams, and each team is given three weeks to complete various projects, ranging from creating new products to developing marketing campaigns for existing products. Teams actually compete with one another and are scored on such criteria as risk and innovation, goal setting, and goal accomplishment. Evaluations are completed by Liemandt, other Trilogy managers, and some of the firm's venture capital backers. Winners receive free trips to Las Vegas. Losers go straight to work.

Liemandt's leadership doesn't stop there, even with regard to those employees who go to Las Vegas, where Liemandt challenges everyone to place a $2000 bet at the roulette wheel. He argues that $2000 is a meaningful sum, and one that can cause real pain, but not so much pain that it will cause financial disaster for anyone. Actually, Liemandt puts up the money, which losers pay back through payroll deductions of $400 over five months. Not everyone, of course, decides to take the chance, but enough do to make the message clear: Liemandt aims to succeed by taking chances, and he expects employees to share the risks. Those who do stand to earn bigger returns on more intrepid investments.[26]

Managerial Styles

Early theories of leadership tried to identify specific traits associated with strong leaders. For example, physical appearance, intelligence, and public speaking skills were once thought to be "leadership traits." Indeed, it was once believed that taller people made better leaders than shorter people. The trait approach, however, proved to be a poor predictor of leadership potential. Ultimately, attention shifted from managers' traits to their behaviours, or **managerial styles**—patterns of behaviour that a manager exhibits in dealing with subordinates. Managerial styles run the gamut from autocratic to democratic to free rein. These three major styles involve very different kinds of responses to human relations problems. Any given style or combination of styles may prove appropriate, depending on the situation.

managerial styles
Patterns of behaviour that a manager exhibits in dealing with subordinates.

- Managers who adopt an **autocratic style** generally issue orders and expect them to be obeyed without question. The military commander prefers and usually needs the autocratic style on the battlefield. Because no one else is consulted, the autocratic style allows for rapid decision making. It therefore may be useful in situations that test a firm's effectiveness as a time-based competitor.

autocratic style
A managerial style in which managers generally issue orders and expect them to be obeyed without question.

- Managers who adopt a **democratic style** generally request input from subordinates before making decisions but retain final decision-making power. For example, the manager of a technical group may ask other group members to interview and offer opinions about job applicants. The manager, however, will ultimately make the hiring decision.

democratic style
A managerial style in which managers generally request input from subordinates before making decisions but retain final decision-making power.

- Managers who adopt a **free-rein style** typically serve as advisers to subordinates who are allowed to make decisions. The chairperson of a volunteer committee to raise funds for a new library may find a free-rein style most effective.

free-rein style
A managerial style in which managers typically serve as advisers to subordinates who are allowed to make decisions.

According to many observers, the free-rein style of leadership is currently giving rise to an approach that emphasizes broad-based employee input into decision making and to the fostering of workplace environments in which employees increasingly determine what needs to be done and how.

Regardless of theories about the ways in which leaders should lead, the relative effectiveness of any leadership style depends largely on the desire of subordinates to share input or exercise creativity. Whereas autocratic managers frustrate some people, others prefer them because they do not want to participate in making decisions. The democratic approach, meanwhile, can be disconcerting both to people who want decision-making responsibility and to those who do not. A free-rein style lends itself to employee creativity, and thus to creative solutions to pressing problems. This style also appeals to employees who prefer to plan their own work. Not all subordinates, however, have the necessary background or skills to make creative decisions. Others are not sufficiently self-motivated to work without supervision.

Canadian Versus American Management Styles

The management style of Canadian managers might look a lot like that of Americans, but there are several notable differences. Most fundamentally, Canadian managers are more subtle and subdued than are American managers. Canadian managers also seem more committed to their companies, less willing to mindlessly follow the latest management fad, and more open to different cultures because of the multicultural nature of Canada. All these characteristics may be advantageous for Canadian companies that will increasingly be competing in global markets.[27]

William M. Mercer Inc.
www.mercer.com

In 2000, Manitoba-born Don McCaw was named CEO of William M. Mercer Inc. in the United States. Mercer is a leading human resource consulting firm, with 5000 employees and 130 offices around the world. McCaw previously had been the CEO of Mercer's Canadian operation. He is described as loyal, pleasant, and able to collaborate with others. He built a strong team in Canada because of his management style, and the U.S. operation wants him to do the same thing there. The collaborative skills of Canadian managers are legendary in the eyes of many U.S. managers.

McCaw recognizes that being able to delegate authority and to work with a diverse workforce is an increasingly valued skill in the so-called New Economy. Managers simply cannot order people around any more. McCaw isn't alone in being successful in team building. In July 2000, Tom O'Neill was appointed CEO of the U.S. operation of PricewaterhouseCoopers. He had been the CEO of the Canadian operations before that. O'Neill credits his rise to his appreciation of the contributions that teams make to corporate success.[28]

Each year a "most respected corporate leader" study is sponsored by KPMG and conducted by Ipsos-Reid. In 2002, 314 leaders were asked to list the corporate leaders they most respected (other than themselves). Paul Tellier, the newly appointed CEO of Bombardier, topped the list. Other CEOs that ranked highly were Jean Coutu (Jean Coutu Group PJC Inc.), Paul Desmarais Sr. (Power Corp. of Canada), and Gwyn Morgan (EnCana Corp.).[29]

The Contingency Approach to Leadership

Because each managerial style has both strengths and weaknesses, most managers vary their responses to different situations. Flexibility, however, has not always characterized managerial style or responsiveness. For most of the twentieth century, in fact, managers tended to believe that all problems yielded to preconceived, pre-tested solutions. If raising pay reduced turnover in one plant, for example, it followed that the same tactic would work equally well in another.

contingency approach
An approach to managerial style holding that the appropriate behaviour in any situation is dependent (contingent) on the elements unique to that situation.

More recently, however, managers have begun to adopt a **contingency approach** to managerial style. They have started to view appropriate managerial behaviour in any situation as dependent, or contingent, on the elements unique to that situation. This change in outlook has resulted largely from an increasing appreciation of the complexity of managerial problems and solutions. For example, pay raises may reduce turnover when workers have been badly underpaid. The contingency approach, however, recognizes that raises will have little effect when workers feel adequately paid but ill treated by management. This approach also recommends that training managers in human relations skills may be crucial to solving the latter problem.[30]

The contingency approach also acknowledges that people in different cultures behave differently and expect different things from their managers. A certain managerial style, therefore, is more likely to be successful in some countries than in others. Japanese workers, for example, generally expect managers to be highly participative and to allow them input in decision making. In contrast, many South American workers actually balk at participation and want take-charge leaders. The basic idea, then, is that managers will be more effective when they adapt their styles to the contingencies of the situations they face.[31]

Motivation and Leadership in the Twenty-First Century

Motivation and leadership remain critically important areas of organizational behaviour. As times change, however, so do the ways in which managers motivate and lead their employees.

Changing Patterns of Motivation

From the motivational side, today's employees want rewards that are often quite different from those valued by earlier generations. Money, for example, is no longer the prime motivator for most people. In addition, because businesses today cannot offer the degree of job security that many workers want, motivating employees to strive toward higher levels of performance requires skilful attention from managers.

One survey asked workers to identify the things they most wanted at work. Among the things noted were flexible working hours (67 percent), casual dress (56 percent), unlimited internet access (51 percent), opportunities to telecommute (43 percent), nap time (28 percent), massages (25 percent), daycare (24 percent), espresso machines (23 percent), and the opportunity to bring pets to work (11 percent).[32] In another study focusing on fathers, many men also said they wanted more flexible working hours in order to spend more time with their families.[33] Managers, then, must recognize that today's workers have a complex set of needs and must be motivated in increasingly complicated ways.

Canadian businesses are starting to respond to these employee preferences. A Conference Board of Canada survey of 312 companies showed the following:

- flexible working hours are offered by 75 percent
- leave for family-related reasons are provided by 74 percent
- childcare assistance or programs are offered by 54 percent
- telecommuting is offered by 49 percent
- eldercare is offered by 48 percent
- unpaid sabbaticals are provided by 43 percent[34]

As we saw in Chapter 8, the diversity inherent in today's workforce also makes motivating behaviour more complex. The reasons why people work reflect more varying goals than ever before, and the varying lifestyles of diverse workers mean that managers must first pay closer attention to what their employees expect to receive for their efforts and then try to link rewards with job performance.

Changing Patterns of Leadership

Leadership, too, is taking different directions as we head into the twenty-first century. For one thing, today's leaders are finding it necessary to change their own behaviour. As organizations become flatter and workers become more empowered, managers naturally find it less acceptable to use the autocratic approach to leadership. Instead, many are becoming more democratic—functioning more as "coaches" than as "bosses." Just as an athletic coach teaches athletes how to play and then steps back to let them take the field, many leaders now try to provide workers with the skills and resources to perform at their best before backing off to let them do their work with less supervision.

Diversity, too, is affecting leadership processes. In earlier times, most leaders were white males who were somewhat older than the people they supervised—people who were themselves relatively similar to one another. But as organizations become more and more diverse, leaders are also becoming increasingly diverse. They are also increasingly likely to be younger than some of the people they are leading. Leaders, therefore, must have greater sensitivity to the values, needs, and motives of a diverse group of people as they examine their own behaviour in relation to other people.

Finally, leaders must also adopt a "network" mentality rather than a "hierarchical" one. When people worked in the same place at the same time, the organizational hierarchy had a clear vertical chain of command and lines of communication. But now people work in different places and at different times. New forms of organization design may call for a person to be the leader on one project and a team member on another. Thus, people need to become comfortable with leadership based more on expertise than on organizational position and with interaction patterns that are not tied to specific places or times. The leader of tomorrow, then, will need a different set of skills and a different point of view than did the leader of yesterday.

SUMMARY OF LEARNING OBJECTIVES

1. **Describe the nature and importance of *psychological contracts* in the workplace.** A *psychological contract* is the set of expectations held by an employee concerning what he or she will contribute to an organization (referred to as *contributions*) and what the organization will provide in return to the employee (referred to as *inducements*). Until the last decade or so, businesses generally offered their employees high levels of job security and employees were very loyal to their employers. More recently, however, new psychological contracts have been created in many sectors. Now, organizations offer less security but more benefits. In turn, employees are often willing to work longer hours but also more willing to leave an employer for a better opportunity elsewhere.
2. **Discuss the importance of *job satisfaction* and *employee morale* and summarize their roles in human relations in the workplace.** Good *human relations*—the interactions between employers and employees and their attitudes toward one another—are important to business because they lead to high levels of *job satisfaction* (the degree of enjoyment that workers derive from their jobs) and *morale* (workers' overall attitudes toward their workplaces). Satisfied employees generally exhibit lower levels of absenteeism and turnover. They also have fewer grievances and engage in fewer negative behaviours.
3. **Identify and summarize the most important *theories of employee motivation*.** Views of employee motivation have changed dramatically over the years. The *classical theory* holds that people are motivated solely by money. *Scientific management* tried to analyze jobs and increase production by finding better ways to perform tasks. The *Hawthorne studies* were the first to demonstrate the importance of making workers feel that their needs were being considered. The *human resources model* identifies two kinds of managers—*Theory X managers*, who believe that people are inherently uncooperative and must be constantly punished or rewarded, and *Theory Y managers*, who believe that people are naturally responsible and self-motivated to be productive.

   Maslow's *hierarchy of needs model* proposes that people have several different needs (ranging from physiological to self-actualization), which they attempt to satisfy in their work. People must fulfill lower-level needs before seeking to fulfill higher-level needs. *Two-factor theory* suggests that if basic hygiene factors are not met, workers will be dissatisfied. Only by increasing more complex motivation factors can companies increase employees' performance.

Expectancy theory holds that people will work hard if they believe that their efforts will lead to desired rewards. *Equity theory* says that motivation depends on the way employees evaluate their treatment by an organization relative to its treatment of other workers.

4. **Describe some of the strategies used by organizations to improve *job satisfaction* and *employee motivation*.** Managers can use several strategies to increase employee satisfaction and motivation. The principle of *reinforcement*, or *behaviour modification theory*, holds that rewards and punishment can control behaviour. *Rewards*, for example, are positive reinforcement when they are tied directly to desired or improved performance. *Punishment* (using unpleasant consequences to change undesirable behaviour) is generally less effective.

   Management by objectives (a system of collaborative goal setting) and *participative management* (techniques for giving employees a voice in management decisions) can improve human relations by making an employee feel like part of a team. *Job enrichment, job redesign,* and *modified work schedules* (including *workshare programs, flextime, compressed workweeks,* and *telecommuting*) can enhance job satisfaction by adding motivation factors to jobs in which they are normally lacking.

5. **Discuss different managerial styles of *leadership* and their impact on human relations in the workplace.** Effective *leadership*—the process of motivating others to meet specific objectives—is an important determinant of employee satisfaction and motivation. Generally speaking, managers practise one of three basic managerial styles. *Autocratic managers* generally issue orders that they expect to be obeyed. *Democratic managers* generally seek subordinates' input into decisions. *Free-rein managers* are more likely to advise than to make decisions. The *contingency approach* to leadership views appropriate managerial behaviour in any situation as dependent on the elements of that situation. Managers thus need to assess situations carefully, especially to determine the desire of subordinates to share input or exercise creativity. They must also be aware of the changing nature of both motivation and leadership as we enter the twenty-first century.

KEY TERMS

autocratic style, 347
classical theory of motivation, 330
compressed workweek, 344
contingency approach, 348
democratic style, 347
equity theory, 335
expectancy theory, 335
flextime, 343
free-rein style, 347
goal setting theory 336
Hawthorne effect, 331
hierarchy of human needs model, 332
human relations, 328
job enrichment, 342
job redesign, 342
job satisfaction, 329
leadership, 346
management by objectives (MBO), 338
managerial style, 347
morale, 329
motivation, 330
participative management, 339
psychological contract, 328
reinforcement, 337
telecommuting, 344
Theory X, 332
Theory Y, 332
turnover, 329
two-factor theory, 334
worksharing (job sharing), 345

QUESTIONS AND EXERCISES

Questions for Review

1. Describe the psychological contract you currently have or have had in the past with an employer. If you have never worked, describe the psychological contract that you have with the instructor in this class.
2. Do you think that most people are relatively satisfied or dissatisfied with their work? Why are they mainly satisfied or dissatisfied?
3. Compare and contrast Maslow's hierarchy of needs with the two-factor theory of motivation.
4. How can participative management programs enhance employee satisfaction and motivation?

Questions for Analysis

5. Some evidence suggests that recent college graduates show high levels of job satisfaction. Levels then drop dramatically as they reach their late twenties, only to increase gradually once they get older. What might account for this pattern?
6. As a manager, under what sort of circumstances might you apply each of the theories of motivation discussed in this chapter? Which would be easiest to use? Which would be hardest? Why?
7. Suppose you realize one day that you are dissatisfied with your job. Short of quitting, what might you do to improve your situation?
8. List three Canadian and two U.S. managers who you think would also qualify as great leaders.

Application Exercises

9. At the library, research the manager or owner of a company in the early twentieth century and the manager or owner of a company in the 1990s. Compare and contrast the two in terms of their times, leadership styles, and views of employee motivation.
10. Interview the manager of a local manufacturing company. Identify as many different strategies for enhancing job satisfaction at that company as you can.

BUILDING YOUR BUSINESS SKILLS

Too Much of a Good Thing

Goal

To encourage students to apply different motivational theories to a workplace problem involving poor productivity.

Situation

Consider a small company that makes its employees feel as if they were members of a large family. Unfortunately, this company is going broke because too few members are working hard enough to make money for it. They are happy, comfortable, complacent—and lazy. With sales dropping, the company brings in management consultants to analyze the situation and make recommendations. The outsiders quickly identify a motivational problem affecting the sales force: sales reps are paid a handsome salary and receive automatic year-end bonuses regardless of performance. They are also treated to bagels every Friday and regular group birthday lunches that cost as much as $200 each. Employees feel satisfied, but have little incentive to work very hard. Eager to return to profitability, the company's owners wait to hear your recommendations.

Method

Step 1

In groups of four, step into the role of management consultants. Start by analyzing your client's workforce motivation problems from the following perspectives (the questions focus on key motivational issues):

Job satisfaction and morale. As part of a long-standing family-owned business, employees are happy and loyal, in part because they are treated so well. Can high morale have a downside? How can it breed stagnation, and what can managers do to prevent stagnation from taking hold?

Theory X versus Theory Y. Although the behaviour of these workers seems to make a case for Theory X, why is it difficult to draw this conclusion about a company that focuses more on satisfaction than on sales and profits?

Two-factor theory. Analyze the various ways in which improving such motivational factors as recognition, added responsibility, advancement, and growth might reduce the importance of hygiene factors, including pay and security.

Expectancy theory. Analyze the effect on productivity of redesigning the company's sales force compensation structure: namely, by paying lower base salaries while offering greater earnings potential through a sales-based incentive system. How would linking performance with increased pay that is achievable through hard work motivate employees? How would the threat of job loss motivate greater effort?

Step 2

Write a short report based on your analysis, and make recommendations to the company's owners. The goal of your report is to change the working environment in ways that will motivate greater effort and generate greater productivity.

Follow-Up Questions

1. What is your group's most important recommendation? Why do you think it is likely to succeed?
2. Changing the corporate culture to make it less paternalistic may reduce employees' sense of belonging to a family. If you were an employee, would you consider a greater focus on profits to be an improvement or a problem? How would it affect your motivation and productivity?
3. What steps would you take to improve the attitude and productivity of long-time employees who resist change?

MASTERING BUSINESS ESSENTIALS

Episode 5 In this episode, the CanGo management team must motivate employees to take on a set of new and challenging tasks. *This episode puts motivational theories, such as hierarchy of needs and Theories X and Y, into a real-world context.*

Episode 6 The CEO of CanGo faces a specific leadership challenge: how to lead two decidedly different groups—a group of experienced senior managers and a group of younger employees—toward a common goal. *This episode illustrates the reasons why so many leadership situations are contingent upon unique and variable factors.*

CRAFTING YOUR BUSINESS PLAN

Making Reservations and Other Plans

The Purpose of the Assignment

1. To familiarize students with the ways in which employee considerations (morale, motivation, and job satisfaction) enter into the development of a sample business plan, using the planning framework of the Business PlanPro (BPP) software package.
2. To stimulate students' thinking about the application of textbook information on employee morale, motivation, job satisfaction, and leadership to the preparation of a BPP business plan.

Assignment

After reading Chapter 9 in the textbook, open the BPP software and look around for information about the plans being made by a sample firm, Puddle Jumpers Airlines Inc. To find Puddle Jumpers, do the following:

Open the Business PlanPro. If it asks if you want to "create a new business plan" or "open an existing plan," select "create a new business plan" (even though you are not going to create a plan at this time). You will then be taken to the Business PlanPro EasyPlan Wizard. On the screen, click on the option entitled **Research It**. You will then be presented with a new list of options, including Sample Plan Browser. After clicking on the **Sample Plan Browser**, go down the alphabetical list of sample plans and double-click on **Airline—Regional**, which is the location for Puddle Jumpers Airlines Inc. The screen that you are looking at is the introduction page of the business plan for Puddle Jumpers. Next, scroll down until you reach the **Table of Contents** for the company's business plan. Familiarize yourself with this firm by clicking on **1.0 Executive Summary**.

Now respond to the following items:

1. Consider Puddle Jumpers' plans to lower costs by using its flight crews more effectively than its competition does. If implemented, how might these plans affect employee morale? Job satisfaction? [Sites to see in BPP for this item: On the **Table of Contents** page, click on each of the following in turn: **1.2 Mission** and **1.3 Keys to Success**. After returning to the **Table of Contents** page, click on **3.2 Competitive Comparison**. Finally, return to the **Table of Contents** page, and explore any listed categories in which you would expect to find information about employee motivation and job satisfaction.]
2. Consider both Puddle Jumpers plans for dealing with the high turnover among airline reservationists and its plans for training reservationists. Do you think the planned redesign will enrich the reservationist's job? Will it affect job satisfaction? Explain. [Sites to see in BPP for this item: On the **Table of Contents** page, click on each of the following in turn: **3.2 Competitive Comparison** and **3.5 Technology**. After returning to the **Table of Contents** page, click on **5.0 Strategy and Implementation Summary**.]
3. Consider the qualifications of Judy Land, director of reservations. Based on her background, would you say that she is qualified to lead and motivate employees under the new reservations system? Explain. [Sites to see in BPP: From the **Table of Contents** page, click on **6.2 Management Team**.]

VIDEO EXERCISE

Computing Family Values: Kingston Technology

Learning Objectives

The purpose of this video is to help you

1. Understand the importance of motivating employees.
2. Consider ways in which financial and non-financial rewards can motivate employees.
3. Explain how high morale can positively affect organizational performance.

Synopsis

Kingston Technology is the world's largest independent manufacturer of computer memory products. Founded by John Tu and David Sun, Kingston employs more than 1500 people but tries to make each employee feel like part of a family. Besides returning 10 percent of its profits to employees every year through a profit-sharing program, the company fosters mutual trust and respect between employees and management. Senior managers stay in touch with employees at all levels and conduct surveys to obtain employee feedback. For their part, employees report high job satisfaction and develop both personal and professional connections with their colleagues, thus boosting morale and motivation.

Discussion Questions

1. *For analysis*: After Kingston's sale to Softbank, employees learned from news reports that Kingston's $100 million profit-sharing distribution was one of the largest in U.S. history. What was the likely effect of this publicity on employee morale?
2. *For analysis*: Are Kingston's managers applying Theory X or Theory Y in their relations with employees? How do you know?
3. *For application*: What kinds of survey questions should Kingston ask to gauge satisfaction and morale?
4. *For application*: What might Kingston management do to help employees satisfy higher level needs such as self-actualization?
5. *For debate*: Do you agree with Kingston's policy of giving new employees profit-sharing bonuses even when they join the company just one week before profits are distributed? Support your position.

Online Exploration

Visit Kingston Technology's website at **www.kingston.com** and follow the links to company information about its awards. From the company information page, follow the links to learn about the organization's values. How do these values support the founders' intention to create a family feeling within the company? How do they support employee satisfaction of higher level needs? Why would Kingston post a list of corporate milestones (including the company's founding and the honours bestowed on it) on its website?

EXPLORING THE NET

All About Teleworking

This chapter discusses what we know about motivating employees in terms of both theories and the strategies designed to put those theories into practice. These strategies include participative management, teams, job enrichment, and modified work schedules that allow employees to share jobs, stagger hours, and work full time or part time from home through telecommuting.

Let's find out more about telecommuting by visiting the website of the International Telework Association and Council (ITAC) at www.telecommute.org.

Select **Public Sector** in the left column of buttons and link to the **Canadian Telework Association**. Once there, select **Cdn Telework Assoc** under **About** on the left-hand column.

1. What are the objectives of the CTA?

   Next, click on **About Telework**.

2. How does the CTA define telework?
3. Why isn't teleworking for everyone?

   Next, click on **Social Impacts**. Read the Introduction and some of the articles posted in the Related Articles section.

4. What are the health and social impacts of telework?

   Next, click on **Broader Impacts**.

5. What are some of the environmental impacts of telework?

Concluding Case 10-1

The Manager as Brainwasher

The Fortune 500 list contains the biggest and most important companies in the world. Wal-Mart made history when it topped that list in April 2002. The feat was historically significant because the discount giant was the first service company ever to reach the top. When *Fortune* began publishing its list in 1955 (before Wal-Mart was founded), the largest firm was General Motors. Almost ever since, General Motors and Exxon (now ExxonMobil) have dominated the number one and number two spots.

By virtually any measure, Wal-Mart's growth has been phenomenal. The firm was started by Sam Walton in 1960 and pursued a strategy of opening discount stores in rural communities across the southern United States. Walton stressed two policies—everyday low prices and reasonable service. In 1979, annual sales first topped $1 billion, and by 1993, the company was averaging $1 billion in sales every week. In 2001, Wal-Mart averaged $1 billion every day.

Throughout the 1990s, the chain sustained an 8- to 9 percent annual increase in sales and a 23 to 25 percent increase in profits. In 2001, however, Wal-Mart sales growth dipped under 6 percent, and profits grew just 9 percent. That was still much higher than the rates of its major competitors, but Wal-Mart's reduced growth was disappointing to senior managers.

The good news is that Wal-Mart has long enjoyed an unusually harmonious relationship with its employees. Although the firm pays less than many of its competitors, its corporate culture gives workers a sense that the company cares about them and their families. Indeed, Wal-Mart's psychological contract with its employees is a product of founder Sam Walton's values. "If you're good to people, and fair with them," said Walton, "they will eventually decide that you're on their side."

During Walton's tenure as CEO, Wal-Mart employees enjoyed numerous family-friendly policies and a wide array of benefits. Starting pay was always above minimum wage, and everyone got time-and-a-half pay for working on Sunday. There was a liberal internal promotion policy (70 percent of store managers were once hourly associates) and even low-wage workers had an opportunity to own stock and receive retirement benefits.

Unfortunately, the constant pressure to reduce expenses, large store sizes, and 24-hour store openings have made it hard for Wal-Mart managers to maintain the personal touch that Sam Walton employed so well. Today, many Wal-Mart employees and managers have come to believe that their contract with workers isn't being honoured or just isn't working. Says former manager Stan Fortune, "My job was brainwashing. My job was to take you from your job across town and make you want to work for me, regardless of the pay. I'm almost embarrassed to say it, but that's what I did."

Wal-Mart is changing the way it relates to its workers. But as it turns out, some of those workers aren't living up to their end of the bargain either. With little personal contact with managers, some workers miss work frequently or quit unexpectedly. Sam Walton himself noted that as more stores were built in urban areas, "We have had more trouble coming up with educated people who want to work in our industry, or with people of the right moral character and integrity."

Unhappy employees are less optimistic. Once, every Wal-Mart employee wore a blue apron that said, "Our people make the difference." Today, that slogan has been changed to "How may I help you?" For Wal-Mart workers, that change signals a shift in focus away from the worker and toward the customer. To ensure its success, Wal-Mart must find a way to provide what employees need, motivating them to continue providing quality customer service. Meanwhile, while the firm is still almost exclusively non-unionized, there have been a few union victories in recent years. A unionized workforce would clearly change the entire character of Wal-Mart's business.

There are some signs that the retailing giant may be returning to more profitable times. Wal-Mart's stock price has increased 41 percent since September 2001. That compares with a 33 percent improvement for all retail operations. The company's growth over the next five years will rely on markets outside the United States, and according to stock analyst Jeff Klinefelter, "I have no doubt they can [become the dominant retailer] globally. But it's going to change the profile of the company."

Questions for Discussion

1. Discuss the role of psychological contracts at Wal-Mart.
2. How important are job satisfaction and morale to a large retailer such as Wal-Mart?
3. Show how various theories of motivation apply to Wal-Mart.
4. What strategies might Wal-Mart use to revive employee satisfaction?
5. What role do you think leadership may have played in events at Wal-Mart? ◆

Concluding Case 10-2

Satisfying Employees' Needs

More and more companies are offering perks to both current and prospective employees because they recognize the importance of retaining productive current employees and hiring promising new employees. Emphasizing a richer mix of employee perks makes it necessary for managers to adopt the view that employees can be trusted to do what is beneficial for the company and don't have to be watched all the time to ensure they're doing the right things. Companies are doing a variety of things to make employees' work experiences more positive. For example:

- Labatt Brewing Co. Ltd. employs a full-time fitness coordinator who schedules nutritionists and massage therapists for employees. She organizes fund-raising runs, bike rides, and yoga classes, and conducts fitness classes in the company's on-site gym, which is open every day from 6 a.m. to 10 p.m.
- Kraft Ltd. also offers on-site fitness facilities as well as flexible working arrangements, an on-site dry cleaner, noon-hour seminars on diverse topics like landscaping, and a store that provides frozen meals for employees who don't have time to buy groceries.
- Trimark Investment Management Inc. wanted to make sure it kept valued employees who liked being close to big-city amenities when the company moved from downtown Toronto to the suburbs. So it built the Energy Zone, an on-site facility that offers aerobics, self-defence, and yoga classes. It also includes a weight room, massage room, pool tables,

a big-screen TV, and an internet café. The Energy Zone gives employees some diversions from work, but it also acts as a place where they can meet and interact with people from other departments. Trimark also has a Recovery Room for employees who feel under the weather while at work.

A study done for *Report on Business Magazine* found that many of the traditional things that managers have assumed are important to employees—for example, fair pay, financial incentives such as share ownership plans, and the opportunity for further training and education—are, in fact, important. However, employees also want to work for a company where the culture values people, where their opinions count, and where their judgment is trusted. Surveys also show that it is important for today's employees to be able to balance work and life activities. Employers are increasingly willing to accommodate these wishes because employee commitment and retention rise when a company recognizes that employees have a life outside work. If a company does nothing to help employees balance work and life concerns, and if it simply assumes that people are going to be totally devoted to the company, the bottom line is negatively affected because of the stress employees will experience.

A Canada @Work™ study done by Aon Consulting found that when employers recognize employee needs outside the workplace, the company's employees are more likely to stay with the company, and are more likely to recommend the company as a good place to work. Overall, companies need to have a "people-first" attitude about their employees. Flexible work arrangements such as job sharing, flextime, compressed workweeks, and work-at-home opportunities are examples of "people-first" attitudes. Consider the case of Nicole Black, who returned to her job at the Royal Bank three months after having her first child. She quickly found that she didn't have as much time with her new baby as she wanted. As a result, the bank arranged for a compressed workweek so she could work four days per week. When she became pregnant a second time, she reduced her work hours even further and started job sharing with another employee. She now works only on Mondays and Tuesdays.

A study by Hewitt Associates showed that companies that are recognized on lists such as "The 100 Best Companies to Work For" have almost twice the number of job applications and half the annual turnover as non-ranked companies. A study by the Gallup Organization showed that there was a strong correlation between employee satisfaction and company profitability.

Questions for Discussion

1. What is the difference between job satisfaction and morale? How do employee perks affect each of these concepts?
2. What do the various motivation factors discussed in this chapter say about the impact on employee satisfaction and motivation of things such as job sharing, compressed workweek, and flextime?
3. What are the various managerial styles that managers can use? What do the employee perks mentioned above imply about the most effective managerial style?
4. What strategies are available to managers to enhance employee job satisfaction? How are strategies such as compressed workweeks, job sharing, and flextime different from participative management and job enrichment?
5. Are there any potential problems with a company implementing the perks mentioned above? If so, what are they? ◆

Video Case 2-1 CBC

Stress at Work

It seems that more and more people are having trouble balancing the demands of home and job. Linda Duxbury, an HRM consultant, asked 33 000 Canadians to complete a questionnaire about their work. Among other things she found that:

- more and more people are working 50 hours or more per week
- absenteeism costs the Canadian economy $3 billion per year
- 60 percent of workers report high levels of stress
- one-third of workers report depression

Employers need to help employees find a balance between work and home life. While lots of corporations (particularly the large ones) have worker-friendly *policies*, they often don't encourage workers to use them. There's a gap between talk and action, with many organizations paying only lip service to their policies. Managers who are supportive of the idea of balancing work and home life say that businesses must do what's right for the long-term health of the workforce. They also recognize, however, that it may be difficult to achieve the ideal. But some progress is being made. Canadian workers are, for example, jumping at the chance for extended maternity leave, and compassionate leave is increasingly being offered to people who are caring for family members who are ill.

The real challenge is getting both managers and workers to understand that it's *productivity* that is important, not just putting in "face time" at work. Pressure to be at work for long hours can increase stress, and stress negatively affects productivity because stressed people make mistakes. Sometimes employees must make difficult choices (e.g., work long hours or get fired). But sometimes workers do it voluntarily. Donna Morrison is a self-confessed workaholic. Work was always on her mind, and all she talked about was her work. She was seen by co-workers as a "fireball" who knew how to motivate other people. She thought she thrived on her work, but she eventually came to see that her view was distorted. So, she got a "life trainer" who helped her identify what was really important to her. She has discovered that work isn't the only thing that can give her satisfaction, and she now makes presentations to young people in schools and tells them how to avoid stress.

The Blair government in the U.K. launched a program called Opportunity 2000 after it realized that the long hours worked by the British labour force hadn't yielded much (the U.K. is the least productive nation in the EU). The government also has a "Challenge Fund" to help employers make the workplace a happier place.

One way to achieve a better balance between work and home life is to offer employees flexible working hours (including allowing them to work at home for part of each week). A recent U.K. study found that two out of three workers would rather have flexible work hours than win the lottery. Changing the culture of organizations will be necessary to deal with the new reality of high-stress workplaces, and this will take time. New legislation in the U.K. gives parents with children under six the right to request flexible working hours.

The road to workforce utopia is a long one, but perhaps the march has started.

Questions for Discussion

1. What are the basic functions of management? Which of these functions is most important in terms of the issues raised in this case? Explain.
2. What is the difference between job satisfaction and morale? How are these two concepts relevant for the issue of balancing work and home life?
3. If managers hope to have employees who are productive and happy, they must carry out several human resource management tasks. Briefly describe each of these tasks, and then indicate how effective management of them will reduce employee stress and increase employee productivity.
4. Chapter 10 describes several strategies that managers can use to enhance job satisfaction and morale. Which of these strategies are useful in dealing with the issue of balancing work and home life?

Source: CBC *Venture*, "Work–Life Balance" (Special Edition), January 19, 2003.

Video Case 2-2 CBC

Carpenters' Investment

Carpenters work long, hard hours in a risky occupation that is notorious for injuries. Many workers have to take early retirement, so they rely heavily on their union pension plan, which has $3 billion invested in Canadian securities. But the shady nature of accounting lately has the union fighting to protect its retirement investments.

Representatives from the carpenters union are going to meet with some Bay Street types, but before they do so, they have to hit the books. Dan McCarthy is training a group of carpenters to attend annual meetings, make presentations, and (if necessary) challenge CEOs. Carpenters have to learn how a company's annual general meeting (AGM) works.

Paul Dailey is one of the carpenters being trained. The big issue this year is stock options. Options are expenses, but are often buried in accounting footnotes. If stock options aren't properly accounted for, profits may look better than they actually are. Paul learns that companies want nice tidy meetings, not meetings where contentious issues like stock options are raised. Nevertheless, at the AGM of Fairmont Hotels and Resorts, the union presents evidence that stock options should be clearly reported as an expense. The chair is asked to commit to a policy of expensing stock options. The chair refuses, and says that he can't commit to that at the moment. At the AGM of Inco, another union member, Carlos Pimental, also raises the issue of expensing stock options, even though Inco has already agreed to do that. The carpenters union wants to make sure there is actual performance before executives are given stock options. Paul Dailey also raises the issue at Imperial Oil's AGM. The CEO refuses to consider the request and brushes him off. After the meeting, Paul is frustrated. He says the union has money with Imperial and wants to have it treated carefully.

Chris Crompton is another carpenter who is worried about appearing in the white-collar world. But union members have investments, and they need to be heard just like other investors. So, Chris and a few others get dressed up in suits and go the Royal York Hotel for Celestica's AGM (the union owns 145 000 shares of Celestica). Chris congratulates the company on ensuring that its auditors are independent. Chris and his friends meet with Gerry Schwartz, CEO of Onex Corp. and a Celestica board member. Schwartz likes what they are doing. Chris leaves feeling pretty good.

At Suncor, union member Ted Ash presents the stock option proposal to the shareholders for an open vote. The board is against this idea. The vote is held and a stunning result occurs: 77 percent of the votes are in favour of the resolution. It's a huge victory. This is the first vote the carpenters have won in Canada, and it gives them instant status with the business press. If Suncor had expensed its stock options for 2002, the company's real profit would have been $32 million less than the company claimed in its annual report.

These experiences have changed the carpenters. They have learned the issues and become more professional. They have another 20 meetings to attend. As long as they're shareholders, they're going to be corporate watchdogs.

Questions for Discussion

1. What are the pros and cons of organizations like a union pension fund trying to influence management decisions in companies in which the union holds shares of stock?
2. What motivates union members to try to influence the management decisions of companies in which their pension fund holds shares of stock?
3. Read the material in the Business Today box on p. 687. Why are members of the carpenters union so concerned about stock options? What are the pros and cons of expensing stock options?

Source: CBC *Venture*, "Carpenters' Investment," May 11, 2003.

PART THREE

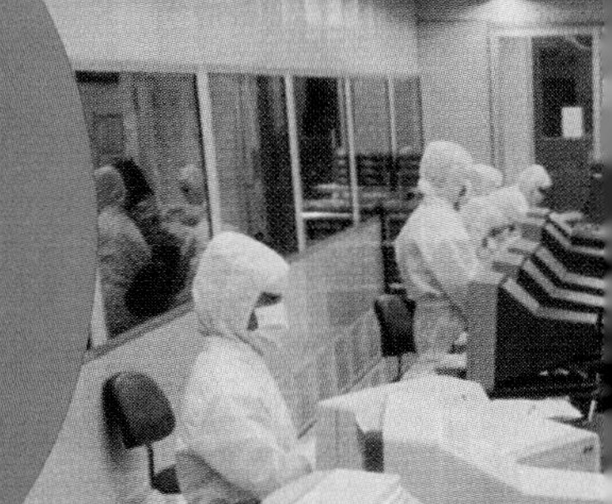

Managing Operations and Information

To be effective, Canadian business firms must produce high-quality goods and services. They must also have good information on which to base business decisions. The opening cases in the chapters in this section show how business firms have focused on more effectively managing their operations and information functions.

Part Three, Managing Operations and Information, provides an overview of four aspects of business that are important to a firm's survival: the efficient production of goods and services, increasing productivity and quality, managing information systems, and understanding principles of accounting.

- We begin in **Chapter 11, Producing Goods and Services**, by examining how firms manage the production of goods and services, and how they control both the cost and the quality of their output.
- Then, in **Chapter 12, Increasing Productivity and Quality**, we consider the various approaches companies take to improve the productivity and the quality of their output, and thus their competitive position.
- Next, in **Chapter 13, Managing Information Systems and Communication Technology**, we describe the concept of management information systems, and how modern electronic technologies have revolutionized the work of managers. Included in this discussion is an analysis of the key elements of the information system, the concept of databases and application programs, and the importance of telecommunications and networks in the effective management of information.
- Finally, in **Chapter 14, Understanding Accounting Issues**, we examine the role of accountants in gathering, assembling, and presenting financial information about a firm. We also look at the tools accountants use and the statements they prepare to report a firm's financial standing.

CHAPTER 11

Producing Goods and Services

After reading this chapter, you should be able to:

1. Explain the meaning of the terms *production* and *operations*.
2. Describe the four kinds of *utility* provided by production and explain the two classifications of *operations processes*.
3. Identify the characteristics that distinguish *service operations* from *goods production* and explain the main differences in the *service focus*.
4. Describe the factors involved in *operations planning*.
5. Explain some factors in *operations scheduling* and describe some activities involved in *operations control*, including *materials management* and the use of certain *operations control tools*.

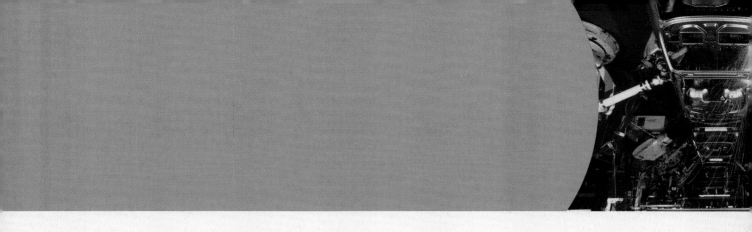

Goin' South?

In 2002, the General Motors manufacturing plant in Boisebriand, Quebec, closed after 37 years of producing various GM cars, most recently "muscle" cars like the Camaro and Firebird. The closing occurred even though the plant was rated as one of the most efficient in North America. This was the only remaining light vehicle assembly plant in Canada outside Ontario. GM closed the plant because demand for the cars produced there was not sufficient to keep the plant open. Other auto plants in Canada that closed in 2003 are the DaimlerChrysler van plant in Windsor, Ontario, and Navistar's heavy truck assembly plant in Chatham. More than 4000 high-paying jobs were lost.

Where is this production going? It's going to several southern U.S. states because carmakers like Nissan, Mercedes, Honda, and Hyundai are building new plants there. These companies have been gradually increasing market share at the expense of the so-called "Big Three" (GM, Ford, and DaimlerChrysler). General Motors, for example, had about 50 percent of the North American market in 1970, but is now down to about a 28 percent share.

But why are these non–Big Three carmakers moving to the southern U.S.? There are two key reasons. First, the companies are receiving large financial incentives to move. South Carolina shelled out $135 million in incentives to attract BMW, Mississippi gave incentives of $295 million to Nissan, and Alabama gave $253 million to Mercedes to locate there. These incentives include free land, infrastructure improvements, income tax deferrals, and money for training workers.

Some Canadian automobile executives say that Canadian provinces are being left behind because they won't give the kinds of incentives that are necessary to attract carmakers. Buzz Hargrove, the Canadian Auto Workers president, is upset that DaimlerChrysler decided to cancel plans for a new assembly plant in Windsor, which would have created 2500 jobs. He blamed the federal and Ontario governments for failing to provide monetary incentives that would have convinced DaimlerChrysler to build the new plant in Canada. In February 2003, the province of Ontario did set aside $625 million to help win investments in the province from DaimlerChrysler and Ford.

Second, automakers want to reduce their overall costs. Since wage rates are a big consideration in overall costs, automakers have been looking for places where wages are lower. One of the places they have found is the southern U.S. Almost all of these states also happen to have "right-to-work" laws. This means that no worker can be forced to join a union or pay union dues. And automakers are happy when they don't have to deal with the United Auto Workers union.

The state of Alabama has been one of the big winners in attracting new auto plants. As recently as 1996, no cars were produced in Alabama, but the state may produce as many as 600 000 cars annually by 2007. This is a major change, since the state had something of an image problem until recently. Steve Sewall, the vice-president of marketing for the Economic Development Partnership of Alabama, noted that an image study showed that companies thought Alabama was a backwoods hillbilly state with poorly educated people and a history of racial problems. That image had to be changed to attract carmakers to the state. Three new car plants have opened in Alabama: Honda, Mercedes, and Hyundai.

But the movement to the southern U.S. isn't the only move south that is evident. Automakers have also set up assembly plants in South Africa, Brazil, and Thailand. The cars produced in these plants will supply markets in Japan, Europe, and North America. Until now, automakers thought that cars produced in these areas would not be well received by consumers in industrialized countries, but that is changing. BMW, for example, has poured hundreds of millions of dollars into its South African production facility. It says the cost of land, electricity, and labour is much lower there than in industrialized countries. The decline in the value of the South African currency has also helped make wages even lower. Dealers in the United States say it doesn't seem to matter to customers where the cars are produced. A survey by J.D. Power & Associates found that the quality of cars produced at BMW's South African plant beat the quality of their cars produced in Germany and the United States.

Honda has begun making cars in Thailand and will ship them to its home market in Japan. Honda is also planning to build a new plant in China that will export much of its output. GM also builds a car in Thailand for export to Europe. Ford has built a plant in northeastern Brazil that will export mini-sport utility vehicles to the United States. All of these new plants have the latest technology and quality control systems. So far, the number of cars exported from these new plants is only a small proportion of total world car production, but that will likely increase steadily during the next decade.

Because the wages paid to workers in these overseas locations can be as little as one-tenth that paid to North American workers, the automakers have a strong incentive to move their operations. The low wages more than make up for the cost of shipping parts to these plants and then shipping the finished cars back to North America, Japan, or Europe.

Unions in North America and Europe are increasingly concerned that this trend will mean fewer high-paying jobs for their members. Buzz Hargrove, the president of the Canadian Auto Workers union, is angry that Ford is planning to import the Fusion from Brazil when it is also planning to close a pickup truck plant in Canada. Ford says the numbers are so small that they won't reduce the number of union jobs. But Ford also notes that its plant in Brazil is its lowest-cost plant, and its quality is high; that could mean much higher production and export of vehicles in the future. Ford also noted that it will produce two new SUVs at a plant in Oakville, Ontario, beginning in 2006. These vehicles were originally scheduled to be produced in Atlanta, Georgia.

The automobile industry is not the only one where high-paying manufacturing jobs are moving out of Canada. The Canadian appliance industry has been experiencing the same trends. In 1964, there were 37 companies that manufactured washing machines, stoves, and refrigerators with famous old brand names like Inglis, Kenmore, Beaumark, and Moffat. In 2003, there were only four manufacturers left. Employment in the industry in 1964 totalled 10 000, but now it is only 2500. ◆

Everywhere you go today, you encounter business activities that provide goods and services to their customers. You wake up in the morning, for example, to the sound of your favourite radio station. You stop at the corner newsstand for a newspaper on your way to the bus stop, where you catch the bus to work or school. Your instructors, the bus driver, the clerk at the 7-Eleven store, and the morning radio announcer are all examples of people who work in **service operations**. They provide you with tangible and intangible service products, such as entertainment, transportation, education, and food preparation. Firms that make tangible products—radios, newspapers, buses, and textbooks—are engaged in **goods production**.

service operations
Production activities that yield tangible and intangible service products.

goods production
Production activities that yield tangible products.

WHAT DOES "PRODUCTION" MEAN TODAY?

1. Explain the meaning of the terms *production* and *operations*.

Although the term *production* has historically referred to companies engaged in goods production (like the automobile companies in the opening case), the concept as we now use it also means services. Many of the things that we need or want, from health care to fast food, are produced by service operations. As a rule, service-sector managers focus less on equipment and technology than on the human element in operations. Why? Because success or failure may depend on provider–customer contact. Employees who deal directly with customers affect customer feelings about the service, and as we will see, a key difference between production and service operations is the customer's involvement in the latter.

Today, however, customers are increasingly involved in all kinds of production because electronic communications are key components in winning and keeping customers in a huge range of competitive industries. Orders are placed faster, schedules are accelerated, and delivery times are shrinking. Internet buyers can be linked to the production floor itself, where their orders for products ranging from cellphones to automobiles are launched and filled in real time. B2B customers also expect real-time response and online delivery.

The Growth of Global Operations

Global competition has made production a faster-paced, more complex activity. Although the factory remains the centrepiece in manufacturing, it bears little resemblance to its counterpart of a decade ago. Smoke and grease and the clang of steel on steel have been replaced by computers and other high-tech machines in contaminant-free, climate-controlled "clean rooms." Production systems have also become more environmentally friendly (see the Business Today box).

Today's firm may no longer face the pressures of continuous mass production, but it does face constant change. New technologies make machines that run cleaner, faster, and safer and that operate on a global scale. For online manufacturing, machines can log on to the internet, adjust their own settings, and make minor decisions without human help. They can communicate with other machines in the company (via an intranet) and with other companies' machines (via the internet). With the internet, producers of both services and goods can integrate their production activities with those of far-off suppliers and customers.

CREATING VALUE THROUGH PRODUCTION

2. Describe the four kinds of *utility* provided by production and explain the two classifications of *operations processes.*

To understand the production processes of a firm, you need to understand the importance of products—both goods and services. Products provide businesses with both economic results (profits, wages, goods purchased from other companies) and non-economic results (new technology, innovations, pollution). And they provide consumers with what economists call **utility**—the power of a product to satisfy a human want.

utility
The power of a product to satisfy a human want; something of value.

Four basic kinds of utility would not be possible without production. By making a product available at a time when consumers want it, production creates **time utility**, as when a company turns out ornaments in time for

time utility
That quality of a product satisfying a human want because of the time at which it is made available.

Quanta Computer Inc. of Taiwan supplies Dell Computer with 55 percent of its notebook PCs. The world's number one notebook maker does just about everything for Dell's notebook unit and pretty much does it by matching Dell's renowned skill at just-in-time manufacturing. Quanta can assemble the hardware, install the software, test the final product, and ship it to Dell in just 48 hours. The key is the internet, which allows Dell and other customers much greater freedom in placing customized orders around the clock.

BUSINESS TODAY

A New Kind of Production

Interface Inc.'s Belleville, Ontario, plant is a popular destination for government officials, academics, and corporate executives who want to find out how this carpet manufacturing plant manages to be so efficient and at the same time so environmentally friendly. While they are at the plant, the visitors learn about some fascinating new developments in the production of goods and services.

In the old days, Interface's Belleville plant produced not only carpets, but also 500 000 litres of dirty waste water every month. Solving that problem—by eliminating a printing process that used a lot of water—saved the company $15 000 a month. Interface then examined other waste, such as the 474 tonnes of carpet remnants it had to dispose of each year. After making some design changes, that remnant waste was reduced to only 39 tonnes per year. Environmentally friendly substitutes were also found to replace the toxic goo that had formerly been used to make carpets fireproof. Several other innovations, such as smaller motors, were used to reduce the company's utility bills by 70 percent. All of these actions made the plant so efficient that it now exports 60 percent of its output to the United States. In the process, sales have more than tripled.

Interface's actions are not isolated exceptions. More and more Canadian companies are pursuing something called "natural capitalism" or "eco-efficiency." Unlike the traditional production methods used in the Industrial Revolution (which polluted earth and sky), natural capitalism is dedicated to improving the bottom line by respecting Mother Nature. The key tenet of natural capitalism is doing more with fewer resources.

Many companies are jumping on the natural capitalism bandwagon. Kuntz Electroplating in Kitchener, Ontario, started recycling chrome-plating solution more than 30 years ago to save money. Now the company also ships 32 tonnes of nickel-bearing sludge to Inco Ltd. each week instead of sending it to a landfill. This nickel recycling has saved the company more than $2 million in disposal costs. Energy costs and water consumption have also been reduced by 50 percent. Employees get awards for cost or environmental improvements.

Canfor Corp. of Vancouver became interested in natural capitalism partly out of exasperation with incessant pressure from environmental groups like Greenpeace. The company studied all the environmental costs associated with making a newspaper, from the forest to the consumer's doorstep. It found that the "hot spots" in newspaper production were heavy energy use and heavy metals. The report motivated the company to do research on how to eliminate heavy metals from the process. Canfor is also pushing energy-saving strategies at its pulp mills.

The case for natural capitalism has gradually become stronger as environmental regulations have become stricter, and as banks and insurance companies have paid increasing attention to environmental liabilities. Companies that ignore these trends simply cannot remain competitive. Noranda, for example, is practising what it preaches. It "mines" magnesium from asbestos tailings at its Magnola site in Quebec. Noranda now produces 15 percent of the world's supply of magnesium and is the industry's lowest cost producer.

Getting natural capitalism to be widely used will still require a lot of effort. Much of that effort will have to go into changing the mindset of workers and managers who are used to the old ways. Interface is doing its part by not only training employees in continuous improvement initiatives, but also actively rewarding those who develop waste-fighting practices. When Interface's Belleville plant started its energy-saving incentive in the late 1990s, it encouraged employees to get involved in energy audits so they could see how they were doing. In the first few years of the program, the company saved $3 million.

place utility
That quality of a product satisfying a human want because of where it is made available.

ownership (possession) utility
That quality of a product satisfying a human want during its consumption or use.

form utility
That quality of a product satisfying a human want because of its form; requires raw materials to be transformed into a finished product.

Christmas. By making a product available in a place convenient for consumers, production creates **place utility**, as when a local department store creates a "Trim-A-Tree" section. By making a product that consumers can take pleasure in owning, production creates **ownership (possession) utility**, as when you take a box of ornaments home and decorate your tree. But above all, production makes products available in the first place. By turning raw materials into finished goods, production creates **form utility**, as when an ornament maker combines glass, plastic, and other materials to create tree decorations.

Because the term *production* has historically been associated with manufacturing, it has been replaced in recent years by *operations*, a term that reflects both services and goods production. **Operations** (or **production**) **management** is the systematic direction and control of the processes that transform resources into finished goods and services. Thus production managers are ultimately responsible for creating utility for customers.

operations (production) management
The systematic direction and control of the processes that transform resources into finished goods.

As Figure 11.1 shows, **production managers** must bring raw materials, equipment, and labour together under a production plan that effectively uses all the resources available in the production facility. As demand for a good increases, they must schedule and control work to produce the amount required. Meanwhile, they must control costs, quality levels, inventory, and plant and equipment.

production managers
Managers responsible for ensuring that operations processes create value and provide benefits.

Not all production managers work in factories. Farmers are also production managers. They create form utility by converting soil, seeds, sweat, gas, and other inputs into beef cattle, tobacco, wheat, milk, cash, and other outputs. As production managers, farmers have the option of employing many workers to plant and harvest their crops. Or they may decide to use automated machinery or some combination of workers and machinery. These decisions affect farmers' costs, the buildings and equipment they own, and the quality and quantity of goods they produce. Table 11.1 shows examples of different types of production management.

Operations Processes

An **operations process** is a set of methods and technologies used in the production of a good or a service. We classify various types of production according to differences in their operations processes. In other words, we can describe goods according to the kind of *transformation technology* they require, or according to whether their operations process combines resources or breaks them into component parts. We can describe services according to the *extent of customer contact* required.

operations process
A set of methods and technologies used in the production of a good or a service.

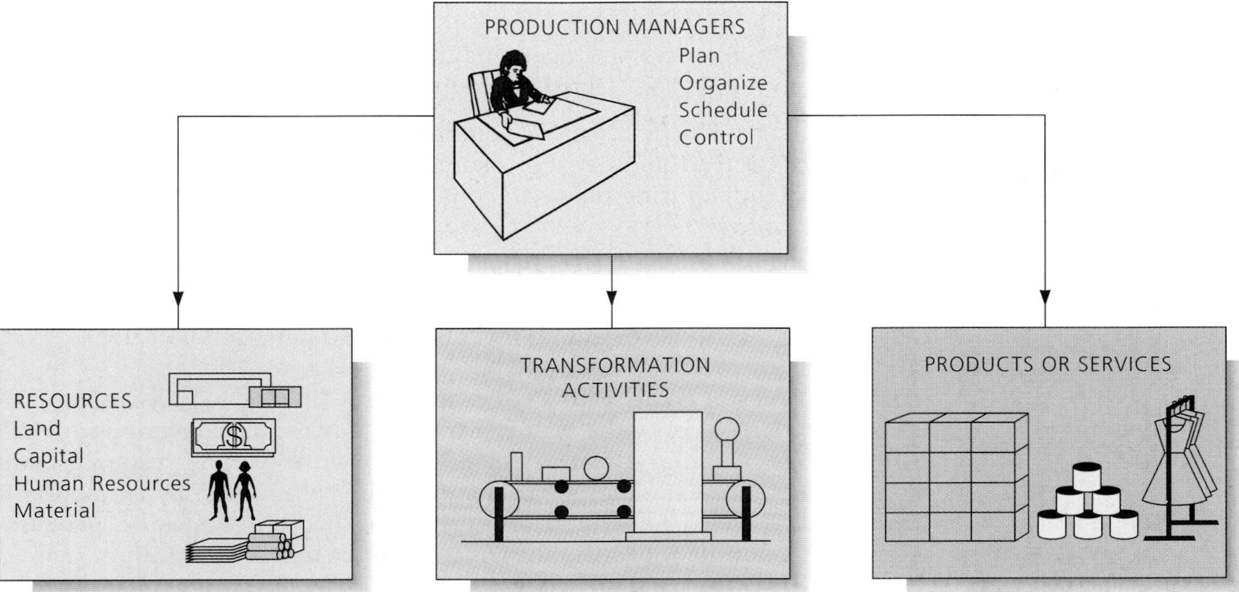

Figure 11.1
The transformation system.

Table 11.1 Inputs, Transformation, and Outputs in Production Systems

Production System	Inputs	Transformation	Outputs
Farm	Land, tractors and equipment, labour, buildings, fertilizer, farmer's management skills	Cultivation of plants and livestock	Food products, profit for owner, jobs for farmer's family
Jewellery store	Fashion-conscious customers, merchandise, sales clerks, showroom, fixtures, and equipment	Exchange of merchandise between buyer and seller	Satisfied jewellery customers
Tire producer	Rubber and chemical compounds, blending equipment, tire moulds, factory, and human skills	Chemical reactions of raw materials	Tires for autos, airplanes, trucks, trailers, and other vehicles
Furniture manufacturer	Woodworking equipment fabrics, wood, nails and screws, factory, woodworking skills	Fabrication and assembly of materials	Furniture for homes and offices

Goods-Producing Processes

All goods-manufacturing processes can be classified in two different ways: by the *type of transformation technology* that transforms raw materials into finished goods and by the *analytic or synthetic nature of the transformation process*.

Types of Transformation Technology. Manufacturers use the following types of transformation processes to turn raw materials into finished goods:

- In *chemical processes*, raw materials are chemically altered. Such techniques are common in the aluminum, steel, fertilizer, petroleum, and paint industries.
- *Fabrication processes* mechanically alter the basic shape or form of a product. Fabrication occurs in the metal forming, woodworking, and textile industries.
- *Assembly processes* put together various components. These techniques are common in the electronics, appliance, and automotive industries.
- In *transport processes*, goods acquire place utility by being moved from one location to another. For example, trucks routinely move bicycles from manufacturing plants to consumers through warehouses and discount stores.
- *Clerical processes* transform information. Combining data on employee absences and machine breakdowns into a productivity report is a clerical process. So is compiling inventory reports at a retail outlet.

analytic process
Any production process in which resources are broken down.

synthetic process
Any production process in which resources are combined.

Analytic Versus Synthetic Processes. A second way of classifying production processes is by the way in which resources are converted into finished goods. An **analytic process** breaks down the basic resources into components. For example, Alcan manufactures aluminum by extracting it from an ore called bauxite. The reverse approach, a **synthetic process**, combines a number of raw materials to produce a finished product such as fertilizer or paint.

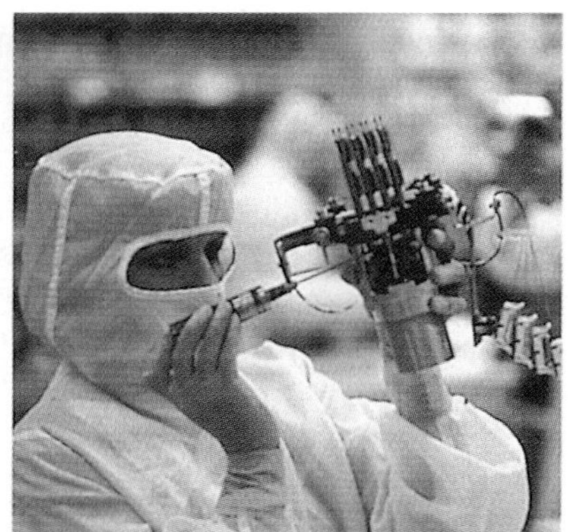

As these photos show, various industries use different transformation techniques: (from left, top) chemical, fabrication, and assembly; (bottom) transport and clerical.

Service-Producing Processes

One way of classifying services is to ask whether a given service can be provided without the customer being part of the production system. In answering this question, services are classified according to the extent of *customer contact*.

High-Contact Processes. Think for a moment about the service provided by your local public transit system. When you purchase transportation, you must board a bus or train, so public transit is a **high-contact system**. For this reason, transit managers must worry about the cleanliness of the trains and buses and the appearance of the stations. This is usually not the case in low-contact systems. Large industrial concerns that ship coal in freight trains, for example, are generally not concerned with the appearance inside those trains.

high-contact system
A system in which the service cannot be provided without the customer being physically in the system (e.g., transit systems).

Low-Contact Processes. Consider the cheque-processing operations at your bank. Workers sort the cheques that have been cashed that day and dispatch them to the banks on which they were drawn. This operation is a **low-contact system** because customers are not in contact with the bank while the service is performed. They receive the service—their funds are transferred to cover their cheques—without ever setting foot in the cheque-processing centre. Gas and electric utilities, auto repair shops, and lawn care services are also low-contact systems.

low-contact system
A system in which the service can be provided without the customer being physically in the system (e.g., lawn care services).

Differences Between Service and Manufacturing Operations

3. Identify the characteristics that distinguish *service operations* from *goods production* and explain the main differences in the *service focus*.

Service and manufacturing operations both transform raw materials into finished products. In service production, however, the raw materials, or inputs, are not glass or steel. Rather, they are people who choose among sellers because they have either unsatisfied needs or possessions for which they require some form of care or alteration. In service operations, then, "finished products" or "outputs" are people with needs met and possessions serviced. There are several key areas where service operations differ from production operations.

Focus on Performance

Wal-Mart
www.walmart.com

One very obvious difference exists between service and manufacturing operations: Whereas goods are produced, services are performed. Therefore, customer-oriented performance is a key factor in measuring the effectiveness of a service company. Wal-Mart, for example, sells to millions of people from California to China to Canada to Argentina. Its superstar status stems from an obsession with speedy product delivery that it measures not in days or even in hours, but in minutes and seconds. Wal-Mart's keen customer focus emphasizes avoiding unnecessary inventories, getting fast responses from suppliers, streamlining transaction processes, and knowing accurately the sales and restocking requirements for keeping the right merchandise moving from warehouses to store shelves. To implement this strategy, Wal-Mart has made technology—namely, its vaunted computer and telecommunications system—a core competency.[1]

In many ways, the focus of service operations is more complex than that of goods production. First, service operations feature a unique link between production and consumption—between process and outcome. Second, services are more intangible and more customized and less storable than most products. Finally, quality considerations must be defined, and managed, differently in the service sector than in manufacturing operations.

Focus on Process and Outcome

As we saw earlier, manufacturing operations focus on the outcome of the production process. The products offered by most service operations, however, are actually combinations of goods and services. Services, therefore, must focus on both the transformation process and its outcome—both on making a pizza and on delivering it to the buyer. Service operations thus require different skills from manufacturing operations. For example, local gas company employees may need the interpersonal skills necessary to calm and reassure frightened customers who have reported gas leaks. The job, therefore, can mean more than just repairing defective pipes. Factory workers who install gas pipes while assembling mobile homes are far less likely to need such skills.

Focus on Service Characteristics

Service companies' transactions always reflect the fact that service products are characterized by three key qualities: *intangibility, customization,* and *unstorability*.

Intangibility. Often services cannot be touched, tasted, smelled, or seen. An important value, therefore, is the *intangible* value that the customer experiences in the form of pleasure, satisfaction, or a feeling of safety. For example, when you hire an attorney to resolve a problem, you purchase not only the intangible quality of legal expertise but also the equally intangible reassurance that help is at hand. Although all services have some degree of intangibility, some provide tangible elements as well. Your attorney, for example, can draw up the living will that you want to keep in your safe deposit box.

Customization. When you visit a physician, you expect to be examined for your symptoms. Likewise, when you purchase insurance, have your pet groomed, or have your hair cut, you expect these services to be designed for your needs. Typically, therefore, services are *customized*.

Unstorability. Services such as rubbish collection, transportation, childcare, and house cleaning cannot be produced ahead of time and then stored. If a service is not used when it is available, it is usually wasted. Services, then, are typically characterized by a high degree of *unstorability*.

Focus on the Customer-Service Link

Because they transform customers or their possessions, service operations often acknowledge the customer as part of the operations process itself. For example, to purchase a haircut you must usually go to the barbershop or beauty salon. As physical participants in the operations process, service consumers have a unique ability to affect that process. In other words, as the customer, you expect the salon to be conveniently located, to be open for business at convenient times, to offer needed services at reasonable prices, and to extend prompt service. Accordingly, the manager adopts hours of operation, available services, and an appropriate number of employees to meet the requirements of the customer.

Ecommerce: The "Virtual Presence" of the Customer. The growth of ecommerce has introduced a "virtual presence," as opposed to a physical presence, of customers in the service system. Consumers interact electronically, in real time, with sellers, collecting information about product features, delivery availability, and after-sales service. They have around-the-

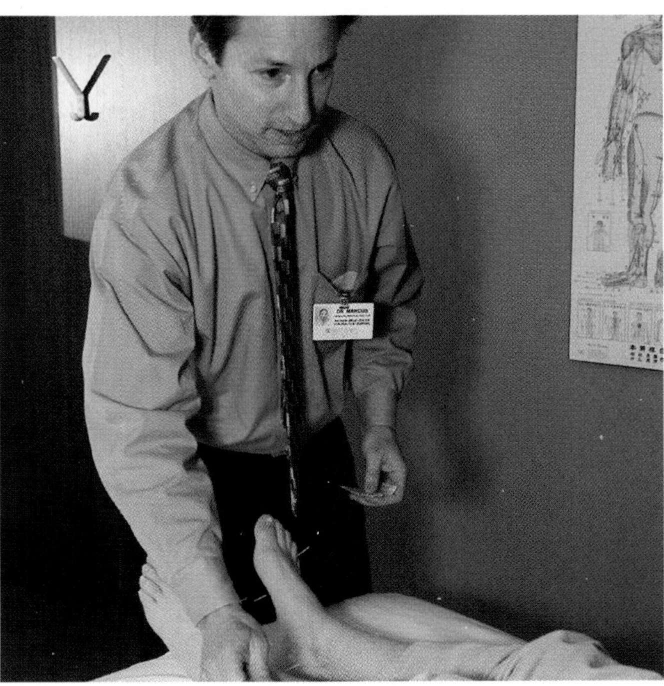

Alternative forms of medicine such as acupuncture, chiropractic, homeopathy, and herbal medicine are all high-contact services. They are tailored to meet the needs of a specific patient who must schedule a visit to a specialized service centre.

clock access to information via automated call centres, and those who want human interaction can talk with live respondents or enter chat rooms. Many companies have invited "the virtual customer" into their service systems by building customer-communications relationships. The online travel agency Expedia.ca responds to your personalized profile with a welcome email letter, presents you with a tailor-made webpage the next time you sign on, offers chat rooms in which you can compare notes with other customers, and notifies you of upcoming special travel opportunities.

Internet technology also enables firms to build relationships with industrial customers. Electronic Data Systems (EDS), for example, helps client firms develop networks among their many desktop computers. In managing more than 700 000 desktops for clients throughout the world, EDS has created a special service called Renascence® that links clients, suppliers, and employees in a private 500 000-computer electronic marketplace. Some 2000 software products can be viewed, purchased, tracked, and delivered if you are a member of the network.[2]

Focus on Service Quality Considerations

Consumers use different criteria to judge services and goods. Service managers must understand that quality of work and quality of service are not necessarily synonymous. For example, although your car may have been flawlessly repaired, you might feel dissatisfied with the service if you were forced to pick it up a day later than promised.

OPERATIONS PLANNING

4. Describe the factors involved in *operations planning.*

Now that we've contrasted goods and services we can return to a more general consideration of production that encompasses both goods and services. Like all good managers, we start with planning. Managers from many departments contribute to the firm's decisions about operations management. As Figure 11.2 shows, however, no matter how many decision makers are involved, the process can be described as a series of logical steps. The success of any firm depends on the final result of this logical sequence of decisions.

The business plan and forecasts developed by top managers guide operations planning. The business plan outlines goals and objectives, including the specific goods and services that the firm will offer. Managers also develop a long-range production plan through **forecasts** of future demand for both new and existing products. Covering a two- to five-year period, the production plan specifies the number of plants or service facilities and the amount of labour, equipment, transportation, and storage that will be needed to meet demand. It also specifies how resources will be obtained.

forecast
Estimates of future demand for both new and existing products.

In the following section, we survey the main elements of operations planning, discussing the planning activities that fall into one of five categories: *capacity, location, layout, quality,* and *methods planning.*

Capacity Planning

The amount of a product that a company can produce under normal working conditions is its **capacity**. The capacity of a goods or service firm depends on how many people it employs and the number and size of its facilities. Long-range planning must take into account both current and future capacity.

capacity
The amount of a good that a firm can produce under normal working conditions.

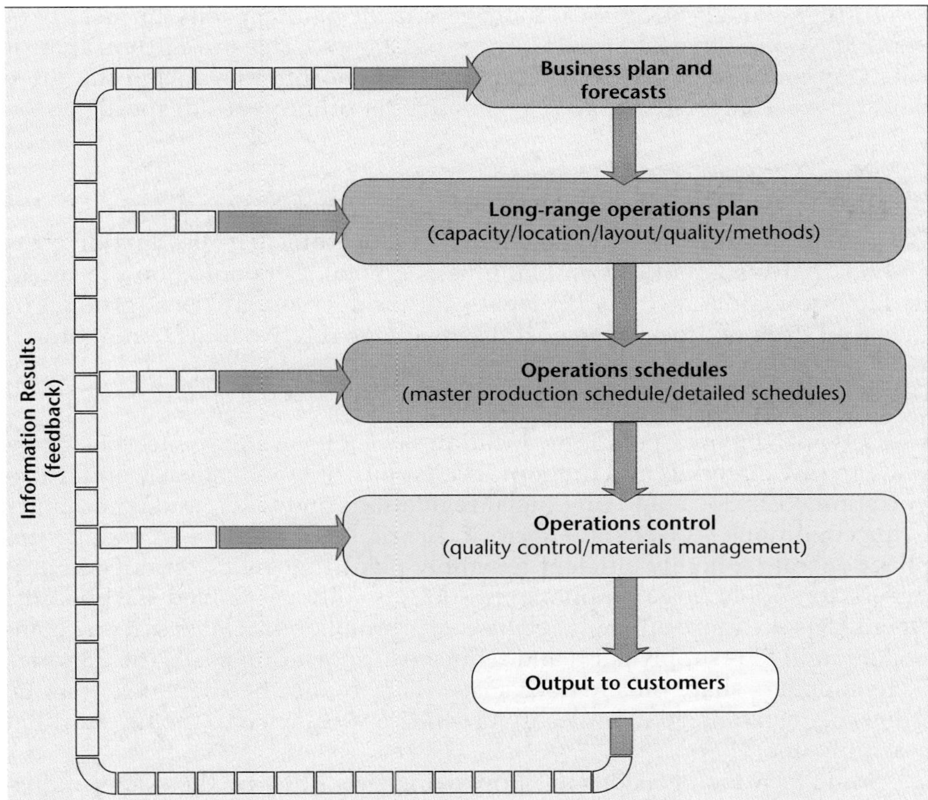

Figure 11.2
Operations planning and control.

Capacity Planning for Producing Goods

Capacity planning for goods means ensuring that a manufacturing firm's capacity slightly exceeds the normal demand for its product. To see why this policy is best, consider the alternatives. If capacity is too small to meet demand, the company must turn away customers—a situation that not only cuts into profits but also alienates both customers and salespeople. If capacity greatly exceeds demand, the firm is wasting money by maintaining a plant that is too large, by keeping excess machinery online, or by employing too many workers.

The stakes are high in the company's capacity decisions. While expanding fast enough to meet future demand and to protect market share from competitors, it must also weigh the increased costs of expanding. One reason that Intel Corp. enjoys more than 70 percent market share in the worldwide semiconductor business is the $11 billion it invested in capacity expansion in the 1990s. Will demand for semiconductors continue to grow even further? With so much invested thus far, Intel must decide whether the risks of additional capacity are worth the potential gains.[3]

Intel Corp.
www.intel.com

Capacity Planning for Producing Services

In low-contact processes, maintaining inventory allows managers to set capacity at the level of *average demand*. For example, a catalogue sales warehouse may hire enough order fillers to handle 1000 orders per day. When daily orders exceed this average demand, some orders are placed in inventory—set aside in a "to-be-done" file—to be processed on a day when fewer than 1000 orders are received.

In high-contact processes, managers must plan capacity to meet *peak demand*. A supermarket, for instance, has far more cash registers than it needs on an average day; but on a Saturday morning or during the three days before Thanksgiving, all registers will be running at full speed.

Location Planning

Because the location of a factory, office, or store affects its production costs and flexibility, sound location planning is crucial. Depending on the site of its facility, a company may be capable of producing a low-cost product or may find itself at an extreme cost disadvantage relative to its competitors.

Location Planning for Producing Goods

In goods-producing operations, location decisions are influenced by proximity to raw materials and markets, availability of labour, energy and transportation costs, local and provincial regulations and taxes, and community living conditions. At General Motors in Brazil, for example, GM and its suppliers operate a highly efficient assembly plant that relies on outside producers to supply large components such as fully assembled dashboards. Operations are more efficient because each supplier specializes in one component, and to resupply parts and reduce transportation costs, the factories of 16 suppliers share on-site floor space. They reduce needless inventory by delivering customized modules in just-in-time sequence to the nearby final assembly line.[4]

Some location decisions are now being simplified by the rise of industrial parks. Created by cities interested in attracting new industry, these planned sites come with the necessary zoning, land, shipping facilities, utilities, and waste disposal outlets already in place. Such sites offer flexibility, often allowing firms to open new facilities before competitors can get started in the same area. The ready-made site also provides faster construction start-ups because it entails no lead time in preparing the chosen site.

Location Planning for Producing Services

In planning low-contact services, companies have some options. Services can be located near resource supplies, labour, customers, or transportation outlets. For example, the typical Wal-Mart distribution centre is located near the hundreds of Wal-Mart stores it supplies, not near the companies that supply the distribution centre. Distribution managers regard Wal-Mart stores as their customers. To better serve them, distribution centres are located so that truckloads of merchandise flow quickly to the stores.

On the other hand, high-contact services are more restricted. They must locate near the customers who are a part of the system. Accordingly, fast-food restaurants such as Taco Bell, McDonald's, and Burger King have begun moving into non-traditional locations with high traffic—dormitories, hospital cafeterias, museums, and shopping malls.

Layout Planning

Once a site has been selected, managers must decide on plant layout. Layout of machinery, equipment, and supplies determines whether a company can respond quickly and efficiently to customer requests for more and different products or finds itself unable to match competitors' production speed or convenience of service.

Layout Planning for Producing Goods

In facilities that produce goods, layout must be planned for three different types of space:

- *Productive facilities:* workstations and equipment for transforming raw materials, for example
- *Non-productive facilities:* storage and maintenance areas
- *Support facilities:* offices, restrooms, parking lots, cafeterias, and so forth

In this section, we focus on productive facilities. Alternatives for layout planning include *process, cellular,* and *product layouts*.

Process Layouts. In a **process layout**, which is well suited to job shops specializing in custom work, equipment and people are grouped according to function. In a woodworking shop, for example, machines cut the wood in an area devoted to sawing, sanding occurs in a dedicated area, and jobs that need painting are taken to a dust-free area where all the painting equipment is located. The various tasks are each performed in specialized locations.

process layout

A way of organizing production activities such that equipment and people are grouped together according to their function.

The job shop produces many one-of-a-kind products, and each product, as you can see in Figure 11.3(a), requires different kinds of work. Whereas Product X needs only three production steps prior to packaging, Product Y needs four. When there is a large variety of products, there will be many flow paths through the shop and potentially much congestion. Machine shops, custom bakeries, and dry cleaning shops often feature process layouts.

Cellular Layouts. Another workplace arrangement for some applications is called the **cellular layout**. Cellular layouts are used when a family of products (a group of similar products) follows a fixed flow path. A clothing manufacturer, for example, may establish a cell, or designated area, dedicated to making a family of pockets—for example, pockets for shirts, coats, blouses, trousers, and slacks. Although each type of pocket is unique in shape, size, and style, all go through the same production steps. Within the cell, therefore, various types of equipment (for cutting, trimming, and sewing) are arranged close together in the appropriate sequence. All pockets pass stage by stage through the cell from beginning to end, in a nearly continuous flow.

cellular layout

Used to produce goods when families of products can follow similar flow paths.

In plants that produce a variety of products, there may be one or two high-volume products that justify separate manufacturing cells. Figure 11.3(b) shows two production cells, one each for Products X and Y, while all other smaller-volume products are produced elsewhere in the plant.

Cellular layouts have several advantages. Because similar products require less machine adjustment, equipment set-up time in the cell is reduced, as compared with set-up times in process layouts. Because flow distances are usually shorter, there is less material handling and transit time. Finally, inventories of goods in progress are lower and paperwork is simpler because material flows are more orderly. A disadvantage of cells is the duplication of equipment. Note, for example, in Figure 11.3(b) that two saws are needed (one in each cell) as well as two paint areas, but only one of each is needed in the process layout (see Figure 11.3(a)).

Product Layouts. In a **product layout**, equipment and people are set up to produce one type of product in a fixed sequence of steps and are arranged according to its production requirements. Product layouts are efficient for producing large volumes of product quickly and often use **assembly lines**. A partially finished product moves step by step through the plant on conveyor belts or other equipment, often in a straight line, until the product is completed. Figure 11.3(c), for example, shows the sequence

product layout

A way of organizing production activities such that equipment and people are set up to produce only one type of good.

assembly line

A type of product layout in which a partially finished product moves through a plant on a conveyor belt or other equipment.

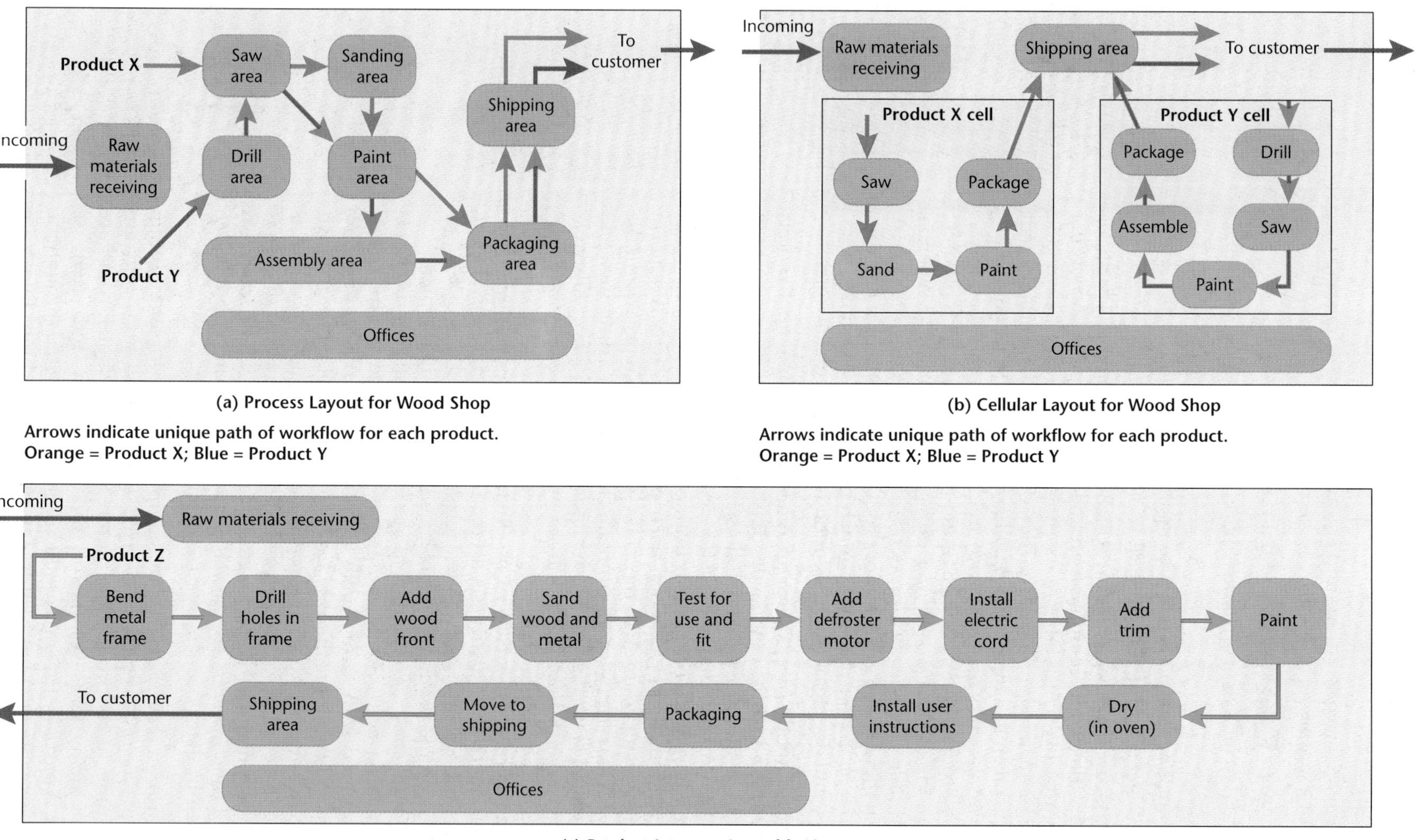

Figure 11.3
Layouts for producing goods.

of production steps performed identically, from start to finish, on all units of Product Z as they move through the line. Automobile, food processing, and television assembly plants use product layouts.

Product layouts are efficient because the work skill is built into the equipment; simplified work tasks can then use unskilled labour. However, product layouts tend to be inflexible because, traditionally, they have required heavy investment in specialized equipment that is hard to rearrange for new applications. In addition, workers are subject to boredom, and when someone is absent or overworked, those farther down the line cannot help out.

Other Developments in Layout Flexibility. In addition to variations on product layouts, there have been experiments in ways to make standard production lines more flexible. Some firms have adopted **U-shaped production lines**: Rather than stretching out in a straight line, machines are placed in a narrow *U* shape, with workers working from within the *U*. Because machines are close together, one worker in slow periods can complete all the tasks needed to make a product by moving from one side of the *U* to the other. In busier times, workers can be added until there is one per machine.

U-shaped production line
Production layout in which machines are placed in a narrow U shape rather than a straight line.

Another development is the **flexible manufacturing system (FMS)**. Using computer-controlled instructions, one factory can make a wide variety of products. By integrating sales information with factory production activities, a manufacturer can adapt both automation and human resources to meet changes in customer demand. At Toshiba, for example, workers can make 9 different desktop computers and 20 different laptop computers on adjacent assembly lines. At each post, a computer screen displays a drawing and gives instructions for the appropriate product. The goal is to produce sufficient numbers of products that are in high demand, while avoiding overproduction of products that are not in as high demand.

flexible manufacturing system (FMS)
A production system that allows a single factory to produce small batches of different goods on the same production line.

Because many companies find large FMS operations to be too complex and prone to breakdowns, some have experimented with so-called *soft manufacturing*—reducing huge FMS operations to smaller, more manageable groups of machines. Automation is less likely to fail when relegated to jobs it does best, while human workers perform the assembly-line jobs that require dexterity and decision making. Both are supported by networks of computers programmed to assist in all sorts of tasks.

In Cologne, Germany, the igus inc. plant takes flexibility as far as possible. Everything—from assembly lines to furniture and employees—is adaptable and can be rearranged at a moment's notice. In a large open space about the size of three football fields, the igus factory makes 28 000 different industrial components for sale to other companies. While workers ride from task to task on motor scooters, modular furniture and movable machines allow the plant to be reshaped and entire departments relocated 24 hours a day, seven days a week.

"The beauty of the building," says igus President Frank Blasé, "is that it allows us to see where the business is growing and to react." Because customer needs are unpredictable, the firm has to react quickly. Up to 90 percent of all orders require customization. Rapid product innovation is also a way of life at igus, which develops about 2500 new products and model variations each year. The strategy of being fast and agile has paid off. Annual revenue has increased tenfold to $100 million in the past seven years, and its workforce has more than tripled.[5]

Layout Planning for Producing Services

Service firms use some of the same layouts as goods-producing firms. In a low-contact system, for instance, the facility should be arranged to enhance the production of the service. A mail-processing facility at UPS or Federal

Express, therefore, looks very much like a product layout in a factory: machines and people are arranged in the order in which they are used in the mass processing of mail. In contrast, Kinko's copy centres use process layouts for different custom jobs: specific functions such as photocopying, computing, binding, photography, and laminating are performed in specialized areas of the store.

High-contact systems should be arranged to meet customer needs and expectations. For example, Piccadilly Cafeterias focuses both layout and services on the groups that constitute its primary market: families and elderly people. As you can see in Figure 11.4, families enter to find an array of highchairs and rolling baby beds that make it convenient to wheel children through the lineup. Servers are willing to carry trays for elderly people and for those pushing strollers. Note, too, that customers must pass by the entire serving line before making selections. Not only does this layout help them make up their minds; it also tempts them to select more.

Quality Planning

In planning production systems and facilities, managers must keep in mind the firm's quality goals.[6] Thus any complete production plan includes systems for ensuring that goods are produced to meet the firm's quality standards. The issue of quality is discussed in detail in Chapter 12.

Methods Planning

In designing operations systems, managers must clearly identify every production step and the specific methods for performing them. They can then work to reduce waste, inefficiency, and poor performance by examining procedures on a step-by-step basis—an approach sometimes called *methods improvement*.

Methods Improvement in Goods

Improvement of production for goods begins when a manager documents the current method. A detailed description, often using a diagram called the *process flow chart*, is usually helpful for organizing and recording all information. The process flow chart identifies the sequence of production activities, movements of materials, and work performed at each stage as the product flows through production. The flow can then be analyzed to identify wasteful activities, sources of delay in production flows, and other inefficiencies. The final step is implementing improvements.

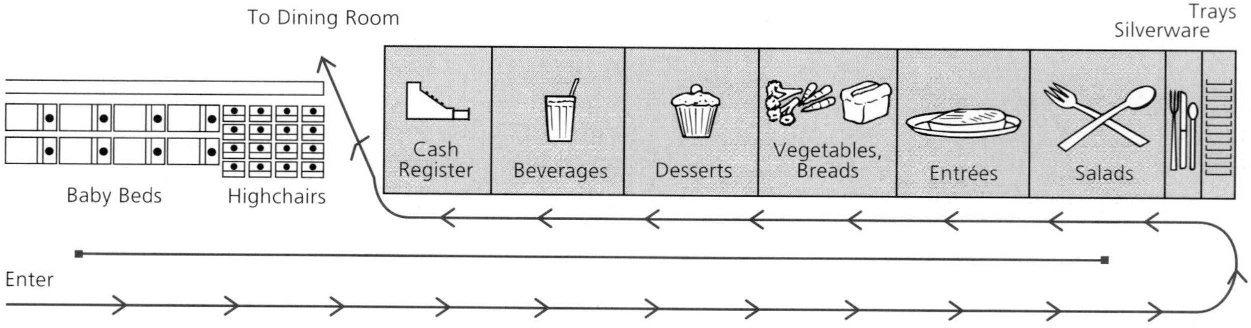

Figure 11.4
Layout of a typical Piccadilly cafeteria.

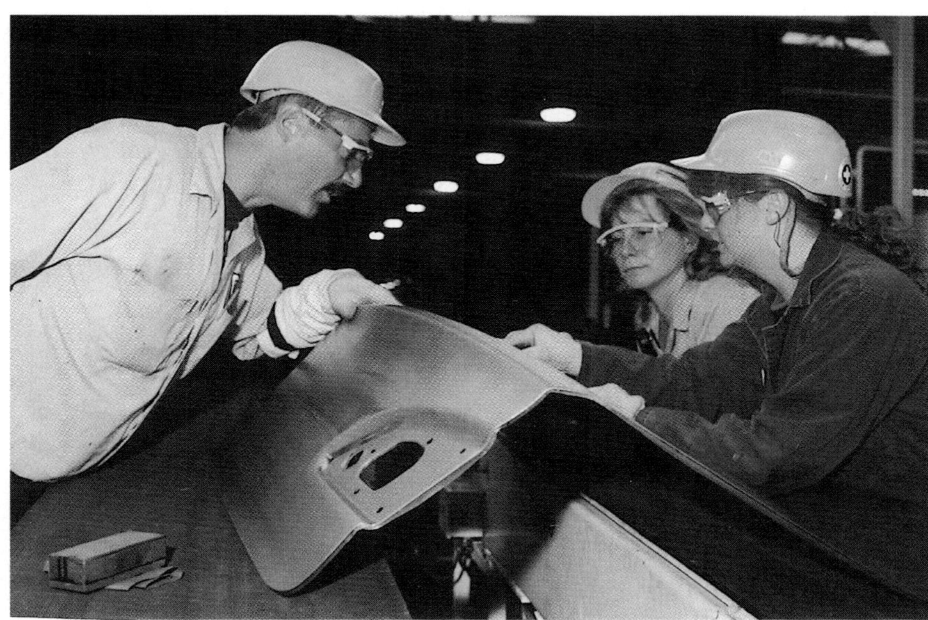

Employees at the Toyota manufacturing plant in Cambridge, Ontario, discuss a production problem. At this plant, employees are responsible not only for making automobiles, but also for monitoring quality control and for maintaining a clean work area.

Mercury Marine, for example, used methods improvement to streamline the production of stern-drive units for powerboats. Examination of the process flow from raw materials to assembly (the final production step) revealed numerous instances of waste and inefficiency. Each product passed through 122 steps, travelled nearly 7 kilometres in the factory, and was handled by 106 people. Analysis revealed that only 27 steps actually added value to the product (for example, drilling, painting). Work methods were revised to eliminate non-productive activities. Mercury ultimately identified potential savings in labour, inventory, paperwork, and space requirements. Because production lead time was also reduced, customer orders were filled more quickly.

Mercury Marine
www.mercurymarine.com

Methods Improvement in Services

In a low-contact process, managers can use methods improvements to speed services ranging from mowing lawns to filling prescriptions and

This control room operates a steel mill in Luxembourg that employs 1000 people to produce as much steel as a nearby traditional mill that needed 5000 people (and which is now out of business). Minimills like those run by Luxembourg's Arcelor melt down scrap iron. Every operation in the facility is automated. From the control room, for example, computers move raw materials through electric-arc furnaces, pour liquid steel into copper moulds, and cut strips of moulded steel into desired lengths. The workforce is really a skeleton crew of technicians.

drawing up legal documents. Dell Computer, for example, sells its computers online and over the phone, mostly to medium and large companies. Methods analysis eliminates unnecessary steps so that orders can be processed quickly for production and delivery. Dell's emphasis on efficient selling by means of electronic technology speeds its response time to provide customers with a specific value—extremely fast delivery service.

service flow analysis
An analysis that shows the process flows that are necessary to provide a service to customers; it allows managers to determine which processes are necessary.

Service-Flow Analysis. By showing the flow of processes that make up a given service, **service flow analysis** helps managers decide whether all those processes are necessary. Moreover, because each process is a potential contributor to good or bad service, analysis also helps identify and isolate potential problems (known as fail points). In Figure 11.5, for instance, the manager of a photo-finishing shop has determined that the standard execution time for developing a roll of film is 48.5 minutes. She has also found that the "develop film" stage is the one most likely to delay service because it is the most complex. Thus, she has marked it as a potential fail point, as a reminder to give special attention to this stage of operations.

Designing to Control Employee Discretion in Services. Thus far, we have stressed the importance of the human factor in service activities—that is, the direct contact of server and customer. In some cases, however, the purpose of service design is to limit the range of activities of both employees and customers. By careful planning—and sometimes even by automating to control human discretion—managers can make services more customer-oriented because they can ensure product consistency.

McDonald's, for example, has done an outstanding job of designing the fast-food business as a mass-production system. By automating processes that would otherwise rely on judgment, McDonald's has been able to provide consistent service from a staff with little specialized training. At a central supply house, for instance, hamburger patties are automatically measured and packed. Specially designed scoops measure the same amount of french fries and other items into standard-sized containers. In addition, all drawers, shelves, and bins are designed to hold the ingredients for McDonald's standard product mixes only.

Design for Customer Contact in Services. In a high-contact service, the demands on system designs are somewhat different. Here, managers must develop procedures that clearly spell out the ways in which workers interact with customers. These procedures must cover such activities as exchanging information or money, delivering and receiving materials, and even making physical contact. The next time you visit your dentist's office,

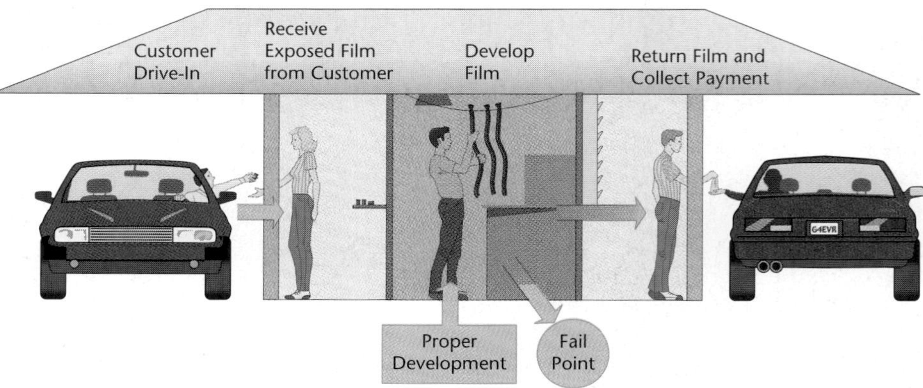

Figure 11.5
Service flow analysis.

for instance, notice the way dental hygienists scrub up and wear disposable gloves. They also scrub after patient contact, even if they intend to work on equipment or do paperwork, and they rescrub before working on the next patient. The high-contact system in a dental office consists of very strict procedures designed to avoid contact that can transmit disease.

OPERATIONS SCHEDULING

5. Explain some factors in *operations scheduling* and describe some activities involved in *operations control*, including *materials management* and the use of certain *operations control tools*.

Once plans identify needed resources and how they will be used to reach a firm's goals, managers must develop timetables for acquiring resources for production. This aspect of operations is called *scheduling*.

Scheduling Goods Operations

Scheduling of goods production occurs on different levels within the firm. First, a top-level or **master production schedule** shows which products will be produced, when production will occur, and what resources will be used during specified time periods.

master production schedule
Schedule showing which products will be produced, when production will take place, and what resources will be used.

Consider the case of Logan Aluminum Inc. Logan produces coils of aluminum that its main customers, Atlantic Richfield and Alcan Aluminum, use to produce aluminum cans. Logan's master schedule extends out to 60 weeks and shows how many coils will be made during each week. For various types of coils, the master schedule specifies how many of each will be produced. "We need this planning and scheduling system," says material manager Candy McKenzie, "to determine how much of what product we can produce each and every month."

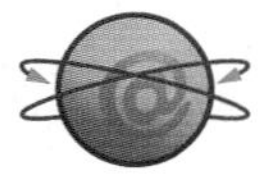

Logan Aluminum
www.logan-aluminum.com

This information, however, is not complete. For example, manufacturing personnel must also know the location of all coils on the plant floor and their various stages of production. Start and stop times must be assigned, and employees must be given scheduled work assignments. Short-term detailed schedules fill in these blanks on a daily basis. These schedules use incoming customer orders and information about current machine conditions to update the sizes and variety of coils to make each day. A classic dilemma in production scheduling is described in the Exercising Your Ethics box.

Scheduling Service Operations

Service scheduling may involve both work and workers. In a low-contact service, work scheduling may be based either on desired completion dates or on the time of order arrivals. For example, several cars may be scheduled for repairs at a local garage. Thus, if your car is not scheduled for work until 3:30 p.m., it may sit idle for several hours even if it was the first to be dropped off. In such businesses, reservations and appointments systems can help smooth ups and downs in demand.

In contrast, if a hospital emergency room is overloaded, patients cannot be asked to make appointments and come back later. As we have seen, in high-contact services, the customer is part of the system and must be accommodated. Thus, precise scheduling of services may not be possible in high-contact systems.

In scheduling workers, managers must also consider efficiency and costs. McDonald's, for example, guarantees workers that they will be scheduled for at least four hours at a time. To accomplish this goal without having workers be idle, McDonald's uses overlapping shifts—the ending hours for some employees overlap the beginning hours for others. The overlap provides max-

EXERCISING YOUR ETHICS

Promises, Promises

The Situation

Unfortunately, false promises are not uncommon when managers feel pressure to pump up profits. Many operations managers no doubt recall times when excited marketing managers asked for unrealistic commitments from production to get a new customer contract. This exercise will introduce you to some ethical considerations pertaining to such promises and commitments.

The Dilemma

You are the operations manager for a factory that makes replacement car mufflers and tailpipes. Your plant produces these items for all makes and models and sells them throughout Canada to muffler-repair shops that install them on used vehicles. After several years of modest but steady growth, your company has recently suffered a downturn and must shut down 5 percent of the factory's production capacity. Two supervisors and 70 production workers have been laid off. All of the company's stakeholders—employees, managers, the union, suppliers, and owners—are concerned about prospects for the immediate future.

After returning from lunch, you receive a phone call from the general manager of one of the nation's top three muffler-repair chains. He says the following: "I suppose you know that we're about to sign a contract under which your firm will supply us with replacement parts in large volumes, beginning two months from now. Your sales manager has assured me that you can reliably meet my needs, and I just want to confirm that promise with you before I sign the contract."

This is the first you've heard about this contract. While your potential customer is talking, you realize that meeting his needs will involve a 20 percent increase in your current production capacity. Two months, however, isn't enough time to add more equipment, acquire tools, hire and train workers, and contract for supplies. In fact, an increase this large might even require a bigger building (which would, of course, take considerably more than two months to arrange). On the other hand, you also know how much your firm needs the business. Your thoughts are interrupted when the caller says, "So what's your production situation insofar as meeting our needs?" The caller waits in silence while you gather your thoughts.

Questions for Discussion

1. What are the underlying ethical issues in this situation?
2. From an ethical standpoint, what is an appropriate response to the customer's question? What steps should you take in responding to it? Explain.
3. What would you say on the phone at this time to this customer?

imum coverage during peak periods. McDonald's also trains employees to put off minor tasks, such as refilling napkin dispensers, until slow periods.

A 24-hour-a-day service operation, such as a hospital, can be an even greater scheduling challenge. Nurses, for example, must be on duty around the clock, seven days a week. Few nurses, however, want to work on weekends or during the early hours of the morning. Similarly, although enough nurses must be scheduled to meet emergencies, most hospitals are on tight budgets and cannot afford to have too many on-duty nurses. Thus, incentives are often used to entice nurses to work at times they might not otherwise choose. For example, would you choose to work 12 hours per day, 7 days a week? Probably not, but what if you were entitled to have every other week off in exchange for working such a schedule? A number of hospitals use just such a plan to attract nurses.

Tools for Scheduling

Special projects, such as plant renovations or relocations, often require close coordination and precise timing. In these cases, special tools, such as *Gantt* and *PERT charts*, facilitate scheduling.

Gantt Charts. A **Gantt chart** diagrams steps to be performed and specifies the time required to complete each step. The manager lists all activities needed to complete the work, estimates the time required for each step, and checks the progress of the project against the chart. If it's ahead of schedule, some workers may be shifted to another project. If it's behind schedule, workers may be added or completion delayed.[7]

Gantt chart
Production schedule diagramming the steps in a project and specifying the time required for each.

Figure 11.6 shows a Gantt chart for the renovation of a college classroom. It shows progress to date and schedules for the remaining work. The current date is 5/11. Note that workers are about one-half week behind in removing old floor tiles and reworking tables and chairs.

PERT Charts. *PERT*—short for *Program Evaluation and Review Technique*—is useful for customized projects in which numerous activities must be coordinated. Like Gantt charts, **PERT charts** break down large projects into steps and specify the time required to perform each one. Unlike Gantt charts, however, PERT not only shows the necessary sequence of activities but identifies the critical path for meeting project goals.[8]

PERT chart
Production schedule specifying the sequence and critical path for performing the steps in a project.

Figure 11.7 shows a PERT chart for the classroom renovation that we visited above. The critical path consists of activities A, B, D, G, H, and I. It's critical because any delay in completing any activity will cause workers to miss the completion deadline (nine and one-half weeks after start-up). No activity along the critical path can be started until all preceding activities are done. Chairs and tables can't be returned to the classroom (H) until after they've been reworked (G) and after new tiles are installed (F). The chart also identifies activities that will cause delays unless special action is taken at the right time. By reassigning workers and equipment, managers can speed up potentially late activities and keep on schedule.

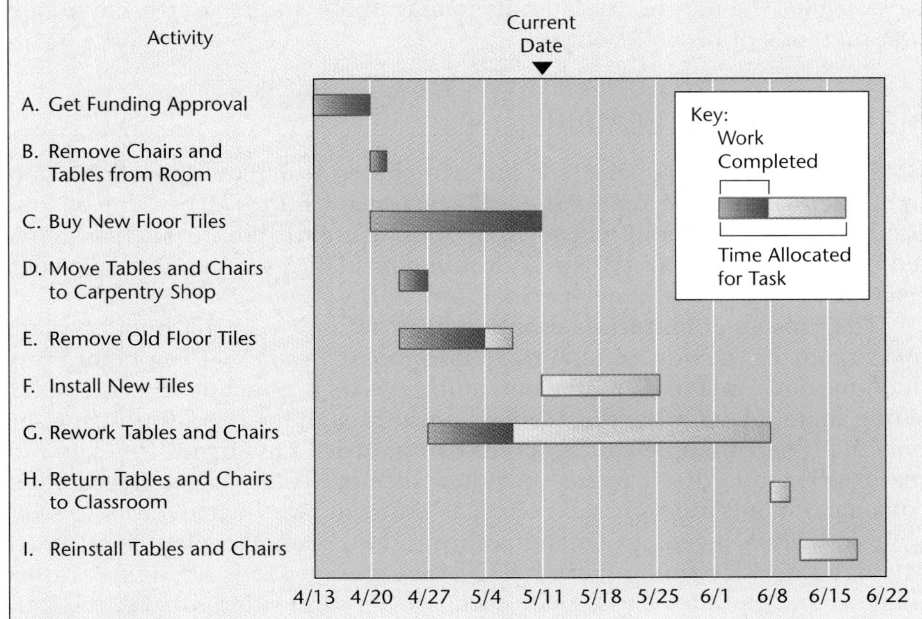

Figure 11.6
Gantt chart.

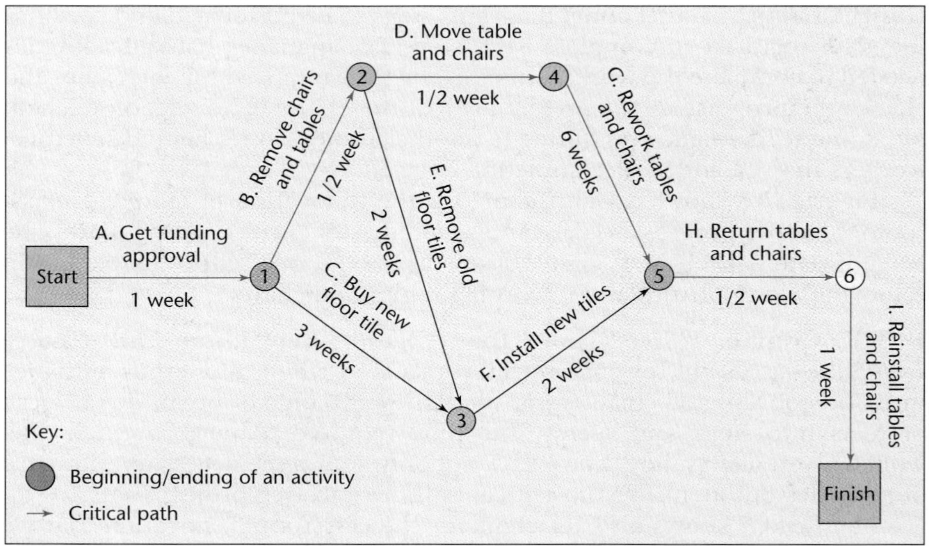

Figure 11.7
PERT chart.

OPERATIONS CONTROL

Once long-range plans have been put into action and schedules have been drawn up, **operations control** requires production managers to monitor production performance by comparing results with detailed plans and schedules. If schedules or quality standards are not met, these managers must take corrective action. **Follow-up**—checking to ensure that production decisions are being implemented—is an essential and ongoing facet of operations control.

operations control
Managers monitor production performance by comparing results with plans and schedules.

follow-up
Checking to ensure that production decisions are being implemented.

Operations control features *materials management* and *production process control*. Both activities ensure that schedules are met and that production goals are fulfilled, both in quantity and in quality. In this section, we consider the nature of materials management and look at some important methods of process control.

Materials Management

Both goods-producing and service companies use materials. For many manufacturing firms, material costs account for 50 to 75 percent of total product costs. For goods whose production uses little labour, such as petroleum refining, this percentage is even higher. Thus, companies have good reasons to emphasize materials management.

materials management
Planning, organizing, and controlling the flow of materials from purchase through distribution of finished goods.

standardization
Using standard and uniform components in the production process.

The process of **materials management** not only controls but also plans and organizes the flow of materials (also called *logistics*). Even before production starts, materials management focuses on product design by emphasizing materials **standardization**—the use of standard and uniform components rather than new or different components. Law firms, for example, maintain standardized forms and data files for estate wills, living wills, trust agreements, and various contracts that can be adjusted easily to meet your individual needs. In manufacturing, Ford's engine plant in Romeo, Michigan, uses common parts for several different kinds of engines rather than unique parts for each. Once components were standardized, the total number of different parts was reduced by 25 percent. Standardization also simplifies paperwork, reduces storage requirements, and eliminates unnecessary material flows.

Once the product has been designed, materials managers purchase the necessary materials and monitor the production process through the distribution of finished goods. There are four major areas in materials management:

- **Transportation** includes the means of transporting resources to the company and finished goods to buyers.
- **Warehousing** is the storage of both incoming materials for production and finished goods for physical distribution to customers.
- **Inventory control** includes the receiving, storing, handling, and counting of all raw materials, partly finished goods, and finished goods. It ensures that enough materials inventories are available to meet production schedules.
- **Purchasing** is the acquisition of all the raw materials and services that a company needs to produce its products; most large firms have purchasing departments to buy proper materials in the amounts needed. Because purchasing is responsible for managing large transactions to acquire material resources, we will explain its activities in more detail.

transportation
The means of transporting resources to the company and finished goods to buyers.

warehousing
The storage of both incoming materials for production and finished goods for physical distribution to customers.

inventory control
In materials management, receiving, storing, handling, and counting of all raw materials, partly finished goods, and finished goods.

purchasing
The acquisition of all the raw materials and services that a company needs to produce its products.

Purchasing Processes

Purchasing is the acquisition of all the raw materials and services needed to make products and to conduct daily operations. Most companies have purchasing departments to buy, at reasonable prices and at the right time, proper materials in required amounts. For many years, purchasing departments practised *forward buying*. They routinely bought quantities of materials large enough to fill long-term needs. The practice was popular because it allowed a firm to buy materials at quantity discounts.

But purchasing agents must balance the need for adequate inventory with the need to avoid excess supplies, which drive up **holding costs**—the costs of keeping inventory on hand.[9] These include the real costs of storage, handling, and insurance as well as *opportunity costs*—additional earnings that the company must pass up because funds are tied up in inventory.

holding costs
Costs of keeping extra supplies or inventory on hand.

Today, many purchasing departments have opted for the so-called *hand-to-mouth pattern*—placing small orders frequently. It requires fast delivery **lead times**—the gaps between the customer's order placement and the seller's shipment and delivery reliability. A radio maker who uses thousands of standard components may significantly reduce holding costs by ordering only what it needs for a coming day or week.

lead times
In purchasing control, the gap between the customer's placement of an order and the seller's shipment of merchandise.

Supplier Selection. Purchasing departments also handle **supplier selection**—deciding which suppliers to buy from. The process typically has four stages:

supplier selection
Finding and determining suppliers to buy from.

1. Investigating possible suppliers
2. Evaluating and isolating the best candidates
3. Negotiating terms of service with a final choice
4. Maintaining a positive buyer–seller relationship.

Maintaining multiple supplier relationships is expensive. It takes time to survey, contact, and evaluate potential suppliers and build good relationships. In addition, fewer suppliers mean stronger, mutually dependent purchaser–supplier relationships. Today, therefore, most purchasers try to reduce their number of suppliers. In the first year of a supplier-reduction program, one 3M factory trimmed its supplier list from 2800 to 600—and then reduced it to 300 the following year. Dana Corp., one of the world's largest suppliers of automobile components, is dropping half of its 86 000 suppliers.[10]

Finally, think about the cost-cutting possibilities for industrial buyers who band together on the internet. By forming online buying groups, they can purchase materials in huge quantities at big discounts. Online brokerage sites, such as PurchasingCenter.com, also unite buyers and sellers in a single internet marketplace, where it is easier for companies to negotiate.[11] The Wired World box describes the experiences of several companies that have experimented with online purchasing.

IT'S A WIRED WORLD

Who's Buying into Eprocurement?

Online purchasing, or *eprocurement*, has gained in popularity by promising savings over traditional purchasing and payment processes. Eprocurement reached a staggering $3 trillion in 2003, using both public and private exchanges as well as so-called *reverse auctions*, in which purchasers use websites to invite potential suppliers to submit price bids.

One source reports that, on average, companies can cut purchased-goods costs by 15 to 20 percent via eprocurement. Testimonials abound: Owens Corning, the maker of glass products and building materials, claims savings of 10 percent on annual purchases of $3.4 billion. Lucent Technologies also relies on eprocurement as a means of cost reduction. "Every dollar we can save through epurchasing is like receiving $5 to $7 of revenue," says Robert Piconi, general manager of Lucent's supply-chain strategy. Hewlett-Packard has cut both materials and energy costs. Eprocurement slashed HP's San Diego–area electrical bill from $2.2 to $1.3 million annually.

Various electronic tools are available to assist buyers and supply-chain strategists. Dutch Railways NS uses Spend Management Suite, software from Ariba Inc., to automate the spending of nearly $1.5 billion on parts, fuel, and equipment. It helps company purchasers find suppliers and negotiate contracts, and it also analyzes the firm's overall purchasing process to find ways to save money with both new and existing suppliers. Savings, of course, come from lower prices on purchased materials, but transactions are also a big savings area. Streamlining eliminates duplicated activities, and automating the process cuts costs.

Some firms, however, have had less satisfactory experiences with eprocurement. A report from the National Association of Purchasing Management and Forrester Research Inc. notes that online collaboration with suppliers among large-volume-buying organizations recently decreased by 10 percent. Why such a falloff? Forrester's Bruce Tomkin says that high technology is both a boon and a bane to internet purchasing. Buyers, he explains, "realize that eprocurement takes more than surfing on supplier websites. That's why we're seeing a growing number of organizations...running into difficulties integrating their purchasing systems." Buyers and suppliers must thoroughly integrate their electronic systems, and doing so is time-consuming and expensive. Thus, although 84 percent of survey respondents report that they plan to use internet purchasing, 47 percent admit that they're only at the earliest stages of introducing such systems.

Then there's the problem of inflated hopes. Many early adopters saw eprocurement as a way to downsize. It was thought that one person with a mouse could do the job of an army of purchasers. But ironically, because of the internet, supplier networks grew. Suddenly able to contact a vast pool of online suppliers, buyers began accumulating vendors, often duplicating and complicating services. Labour savings were offset by the costs of managing vendor relationships. In the health-care industry, unrealistic expectations have dampened the initial excitement over internet purchasing.

Are there any solutions? IBM—itself an eprocurement pioneer and promoter—recommends that firms start with a strategy and end with a technology. Translation: Think first about your procurement strategy and don't worry yet about the technology. Clarify the relationship of your company to your suppliers and customers. Then you can identify the most important elements in your buying process. Until you've taken these steps, say IBM experts, it's too early to think about the technology.

Tools for Operations Process Control

Numerous tools assist managers in controlling operations. Chief among these are *worker training, just-in-time production systems, material requirements planning,* and *quality control.*

Worker Training

Customer satisfaction is closely linked to the employees who provide the service. Effective customer relationships do not come about by accident: Service workers can be trained and motivated in customer-oriented attitudes and behaviour. In service-product design, it is important to remember that people deliver most services; that is, service system employees are both the producers of the product and the salespeople. Thus, human relations skills are vital in anyone who has contact with the public. More and more human resource experts now realize that in businesses such as airlines, employment agencies, and hotels, employees without training in relationship skills can lose customers to better-prepared competitors.

Managers realize how easily service employees with a poor attitude can reduce sales. Conversely, the right attitude is a powerful sales tool. The Walt Disney Co. has long recognized the vital link between its employees and its business success. Its methods for employee development are widely recognized by other firms who send managers to the Disney Institute to learn "The Disney Approach to People Management." Disney does an excellent job of remembering that no matter what their jobs, service employees are links to the public. Of the 35 000 employees at Disney World Resort in Buena Vista, Florida, 20 000 have direct contact with guests. For example, Disney World has a team of sweepers constantly at work picking up bits of trash as soon as they fall to the ground. When visitors have questions about directions or time, they often ask one of the sweepers. Because their responses affect visitors' overall impressions of Disney World, sweepers are trained to respond in appropriate ways. Their work is evaluated and rewarded based on strict performance appraisal standards. A pleased customer is more likely to return.[12]

Just-in-Time Production Systems

To minimize manufacturing inventory costs, some managers use **just-in-time (JIT) production systems**. JIT brings together all the needed materials and parts at the precise moment they are required for each production stage, not before. All resources are continuously flowing, from their arrival as raw materials to subassembly, final completion, and shipment of finished products. JIT reduces to practically nothing the number of goods in process (that is, goods not yet finished) and saves money by replacing stop-and-go production with smooth movement. Once smooth movements become the norm, disruptions become more visible and thus are resolved more quickly. Finding and eliminating disruptions by continuous improvement of production is a major objective of JIT. Here are just two examples:

just-in-time (JIT) production systems
A method of inventory control in which materials are acquired and put into production just as they are needed.

- Mount Sinai Hospital uses JIT. Individual suppliers no longer go to Mount Sinai to deliver the items they have sold to the hospital. Rather, all suppliers deliver their products to Livingston Healthcare Services Inc. Livingston stores these items and fills Mount Sinai's order once each day; therefore, Mount Sinai no longer keeps any inventory. Once the goods are delivered, they are sent directly to the various departments in the hospital; the former centralized storeroom at the hospital no longer exists. In the first year using the new system, the hospital saved about $200 000.[13]

- At Toyota's Cambridge, Ontario, plant, delivery trucks constantly pull in to unload tires, batteries, steering wheels, seats, and many other items needed in the JIT production system.[14] And when General Motors of Canada's Oshawa assembly plant needs seats for cars, it sends the order electronically to a local supplier. The supplier has four hours to make the seats and ship them to the plant. The supplier loads the truck in reverse order so that the last seat loaded is the first one that will be used on the assembly line. The supplier knows, for example, that the plant will be making a certain number of one model and then a certain number of another model of car.[15]

JIT can cause some unexpected problems. As more and more companies adopt the philosophy that they will carry only minimal inventories, the ordering of supplies has become much more last-minute and frantic. By definition, this makes supply systems more volatile, and it has been one of the reasons why economic indicators like capital goods orders have been swinging so wildly. This, in turn, makes it hard to know what shape the overall economy is in. The more uncertainty there is about the economy, the less investor enthusiasm there is.[16]

Material Requirements Planning

material requirements planning (MRP)

A method of inventory control in which a computerized bill of materials is used to estimate production needs so that resources are acquired and put into production only as needed.

bill of materials

Production control tool that specifies the necessary ingredients of a product, the order in which they should be combined, and how many of each are needed to make one batch.

manufacturing resource planning (MRP II)

An advanced version of MRP that ties together all parts of the organization into the company's production activities.

Like JIT, **material requirements planning (MRP)** seeks to deliver the right amount of materials at the right place and the right time for goods production. MRP uses a **bill of materials** that is basically a recipe for the finished product. It specifies the necessary ingredients (raw materials and components), the order in which they should be combined, and the quantity of each ingredient needed to make one batch of the product (say, 2000 finished telephones). The recipe is fed into a computer that controls inventory and schedules each stage of production. The result is fewer early arrivals, less frequent stock shortages, and lower storage costs. MRP is most popular among companies whose products require complicated assembly and fabrication activities, such as automobile manufacturers, appliance makers, and furniture companies.

Manufacturing resource planning (MRP II) is an advanced version of MRP that ties all parts of the organization into the company's production activities. For example, MRP inventory and production schedules are

This Delphi Automotive Systems plant makes plastic housings for electrical connectors in cars and telecom equipment. Quality checkers are important members of the production team. Their defect rate is only 14 parts per million. Delphi has spent millions of dollars on new production equipment, computers, software, and an emanufacturing network that is so efficient that the plant superintendent can work at home from his own PC.

translated into cost requirements for the financial management department and into personnel requirements for the human resources department; information about available capacity for new orders goes to the marketing department.

Quality Control

Another operation control tool is **quality control**—the management of the production process to manufacture goods or supply services that meet specific quality standards. United Parcel Service Inc. (UPS), for instance, delivers 13 million packages every day, and all of them are promised to arrive on strict delivery schedules, mostly for business clients. Quality control is essential because delivery reliability—namely, avoiding late deliveries—is critical for customer satisfaction. UPS tracks the locations, time schedules, and on-time performance for some 500 aircraft and 150 000 vehicles as they carry packages through the delivery system. Our discussion of quality control continues in Chapter 12.

quality control
The management of the production process so as to manufacture goods or supply services that meet specific quality standards.

SUMMARY OF LEARNING OBJECTIVES

1. **Explain the meaning of the terms *production* or *operations*.** *Service operations* provide intangible and tangible services products, such as entertainment, transportation, education, and food preparation. Firms that make tangible products—radios, newspapers, buses, and textbooks—are engaged in *goods production*. Because the term *production* is associated just with manufacturing, we now use *operations* to refer to both service and goods production. *Operations (or production) management* is the systematic direction and control of the processes that transform resources into finished services and goods that create value for and provide benefits to customers. In overseeing production, inventory, and quality control, *operations (or production) managers* are responsible for ensuring that operations processes create value and provide benefits.

2. **Describe the four kinds of *utility* provided by production and explain the two classifications of *operations processes*.** Products provide businesses with economic results: profits, wages, and goods purchased from other companies. They also provide consumers with *utility*—the ability of a product to satisfy a human want. There are four kinds of production-based utility: (1) *Time utility*: Production makes products available when consumers want them. (2) *Place utility*: Production makes products available where they are convenient for consumers. (3) *Ownership (or possession) utility*: Production makes products available for consumers to own and use. (4) *Form utility*: By turning raw materials into finished goods, production makes products available in the first place. An *operations process* is a set of methods and technologies used in the production of a good or a service. There are two types of operations processes for goods: (1) An *analytic process* breaks down resources into components. (2) A *synthetic process* combines raw materials to produce a finished product. Services are classified according to the *extent of customer contact*: (1) *High-contact processes*: To receive the service in a high-contact system, the customer must be a part of the system. (2) *Low-contact processes*: In a low-contact system, customers are not in contact with the provider while the service is performed.

3. **Identify the characteristics that distinguish *service operations* from *goods production* and explain the main differences in the *service focus*.** Both service and manufacturing operations transform raw materials into finished products. In service production, the raw materials are people who have either unsatisfied needs or possessions needing some form of care or alteration. "Finished products" are, thus, people with needs met and possessions serviced. The focus of service operations differs from that of goods production in five ways: (1) *Focus on performance*: Because goods are *produced* and services *performed*, customer-oriented performance is crucial to a service company. (2) *Focus on process and outcome*: Because most service products are combinations of goods and services, services focus on both the transformation *process* and its *outcome*. (3) *Focus on service characteristics*: Service transactions reflect the three key qualities of service products: (i) *Intangibility*: Because services usually can't be touched, tasted, smelled, or seen, they provide intangible value experienced as pleasure, satisfaction, or a feeling of safety. (ii) *Customization*: Each customer expects a service to be designed (customized) for his or her specific needs. (iii) *Unstorability*: Because many services can't be produced ahead of time and then stored, they have a high degree of unstorability. (4) *Focus on the customer-service link*: Because service operations often acknowledge the customer as part of the process, consumers can directly affect that process. (5) *Focus on service quality considerations*: Service providers know that quality of work and quality of service are not necessarily the same thing (a properly repaired car is one thing, but getting it back when you need it is another).

4. **Describe the factors involved in *operations planning*.** The operations-management process is as a series of logical steps. Whereas the business plan outlines goals and objectives, managers also develop long-range production plans through *forecasts* of future demand for both new and existing products. Operations planning then focuses on five major categories: (1) *Capacity planning*: The amount of a product that a company can produce under normal working conditions is its *capacity*. The capacity of a goods or service firm depends on how many people it employs and the number and size of its facilities. (2) *Location planning*: In location planning, managers in goods-producing operations consider such factors as proximity to raw materials and markets; availability of labour; energy and transportation costs; regulations and taxes; and community living conditions. (3) *Layout planning*: Layout of machinery, equipment, and supplies determines how quickly a company can respond to customer demand for more and different products. In a *process layout*, which is well suited to job shops specializing in custom work, equipment and people are grouped according to function. *Cellular layouts* take groups of similar products through fixed flow paths. Equipment set-up is easier, flow distances are shorter, and material handling and transit time are reduced. In a *product layout*, equipment and people are set up to produce one type of product in a fixed sequence. (4) *Quality planning*: Products must meet standards of quality. Such standards may include reasonable price and consistent performance. (5) *Methods planning*: When managers reduce waste and inefficiency by identifying every production stage and the specific methods for performing it, they are practising *methods improvement*. A *process flowchart* can identify the sequence of production activities, movements of materials, and work performed at each stage. The flow can then be analyzed to identify wasteful activities, sources of delay, and other inefficiencies. *Service flow analysis* helps managers decide

which processes in a service are necessary. It also helps isolate potential problems known as *fail points*.

5. **Explain some factors in *operations scheduling* and describe some activities involved in *operations control*, including *materials management* and the use of certain *operations control tools*.** A *master production schedule* shows which products will be produced, when production will take place, and what resources will be used during specified periods. For scheduling special projects, two tools—*Gantt charts* and *PERT charts*—assist managers in maintaining close coordination and timing. *Operations control* requires managers to monitor performance by comparing results with detailed plans and schedules. If schedules or quality standards are not met, managers take corrective action. *Follow-up*—checking to ensure that decisions are being implemented—is an essential facet of operations control. There are four areas in materials management: (1) *Transportation* includes the means of transporting resources to the company and finished goods to buyers. (2) *Warehousing* is the storage of incoming materials and finished goods for distribution to customers. (3) *Inventory* control includes the receiving, storing, handling, and counting of all raw materials, partly finished goods, and finished goods. It ensures that enough materials inventories are available to meet production schedules. (4) *Purchasing* is the acquisition of all the raw materials and services that a company needs for production.

KEY TERMS

analytic process, 368
assembly line, 375
bill of materials, 388
capacity, 372
cellular layout, 375
flexible manufacturing system (FMS), 377
follow-up, 384
forecast, 372
form utility, 366
Gantt chart, 383
goods production, 364
high-contact system, 369
holding costs, 385
inventory control, 385
just-in-time (JIT) production, 387
lead times, 385
low-contact system, 369
manufacturing resource planning (MRP II), 388
master production schedule, 381
material requirements planning (MRP), 388
materials management, 384
operations (or production) management, 367
operations control, 384
operations process, 367
ownership (or possession) utility, 366
PERT chart, 383
place utility, 366
process layout, 375
product layout, 375
production managers, 367
purchasing, 385
quality control, 389
service flow analysis, 380
service operations, 364
standardization, 384
supplier selection, 385
synthetic process, 368
time utility, 365
transportation, 385
U-shaped production line, 377
utility, 365
warehousing, 385

QUESTIONS AND EXERCISES

Questions for Review

1. What are the four different kinds of production-based utility?
2. What are the major differences between goods-production operations and service operations?
3. What are the major differences between high-contact and low-contact service systems?
4. What are the five major categories of operations planning?

Questions for Analysis

5. What are the resources and finished products in the following services?

   Real estate firm
   Child-care facility
   Bank
   City water and electric department

6. Analyze the location of a local firm where you do business (perhaps a restaurant, a supermarket, or a

manufacturing firm). What problems do you see with this location? What recommendations would you make to management?

7. Find good examples of a synthetic production process and an analytic process. Explain your choices.

8. Develop a service flow analysis for some service that you use frequently, such as buying lunch at a cafeteria, having your hair cut, or riding a bus. Identify areas of potential quality or productivity failures in the process.

Application Exercises

9. Interview the manager of a local service business, such as a laundry or dry-cleaning shop. Identify the major decisions involved in planning its service operations. Prepare a class report suggesting areas for improvement.

10. Select a high-contact industry. Write an advertisement seeking workers for a company in this industry. Draw up a plan for motivating workers to produce high-quality services.

BUILDING YOUR BUSINESS SKILLS

The One-on-One Entrepreneur

Goal

To encourage students to apply the concept of customization to an entrepreneurial idea

Situation

You are an entrepreneur who wants to start your own service business. You are intrigued with the idea of creating some kind of customized one-on-one service that would appeal to baby boomers, who traditionally have been pampered, and working women, who have little time to get things done.

Method

Step 1

Get together with three or four other students to brainstorm ideas for services that would appeal to harried working people. Here are just a few:

- A concierge service in office buildings that would handle such personal and business services as arranging children's birthday parties and booking guest speakers for business luncheons.
- A personal-image consultation service aimed at helping clients improve appearance, etiquette, and presentation style.
- A mobile pet-care network through which vets and groomers make house calls.

Step 2

Choose one of these ideas or one that your team thinks of. Then write a memo explaining why you think your idea will succeed. Research may be necessary as you target any of the following:

- A specific demographic group or groups (Who are your customers, and why would they buy your service?)
- The features that make your service attractive to this group
- The social factors in your local community that would contribute to success

Follow-Up Questions

1. Why is the customization of and easy access to personal services so desirable in the twenty-first century?
2. As services are personalized, do you think quality will become more or less important? Why?
3. Why does the trend toward personalized, one-on-one service present unique opportunities for entrepreneurs?
4. In a personal one-on-one business, how important are the human relations skills of those delivering the service? Can you make an argument that they are more important than the service itself?

MASTERING BUSINESS ESSENTIALS

Episode 11 stresses the reasons for comparing this year's performance with last year's. It also deals with the kinds of changes needed to improve performance. Also covered is the fit between an organization's overall strategy and its approach to operations. *This episode deals with the issues of capacity planning, quality planning, materials management, and operations control.*

CRAFTING YOUR BUSINESS PLAN

Sporting a Friendlier Atmosphere

The Purpose of the Assignment

1. To acquaint students with production and operations issues that a sample firm addresses in developing its business plan, in the framework of the Business PlanPro (BPP) software package.
2. To demonstrate how choices of goods and services, characteristics of the transformation process, facilities and equipment, and product quality considerations can be integrated as components in the BPP planning environment.

Assignment

After reading Chapter 11 in the textbook, open the BPP software and look around for information about plans for operations processes as they apply to a sample firm, a sports bar: Take Five Sports Bar & Grill. To find Take Five, do the following:

Open Business PlanPro. If you are asked whether you want to "create a new business plan" or to "open an existing plan," select "create a new business plan" (even though you are not going to create a plan at this time). You will then be taken to the Business PlanPro EasyPlan Wizard. On the screen, click on the option entitled **Research It**. You will then be presented a new list of options, including Sample Plan Browser. After clicking on the **Sample Plan Browser**, go down its alphabetical list of sample plans and double-click on **Bar—Sports**, which is the location for Take Five Sports Bar & Grill. The screen you are looking at is the introduction page for the business plan of Take Five. On this page, scroll down until you reach the **Table of Contents** for the Take Five business plan.

Now respond to the following items:

1. What type of product—physical good or service—is Take Five Sports Bar & Grill creating in its operations process? Explain. [Sites to see in BPP for this item: On the **Table of Contents** page, click on **1.0 Executive Summary**. Then click on each of the following in turn: **1.2 Mission**, **2.3 Company Locations and Facilities**.]
2. Describe the characteristics of the transformation (operations) process that results in this company's products. Be sure to include in your description some comments on the level of customer contact and its implications for the transformation process. [Sites to see in BPP: On the **Table of Contents** page, click on **4.0 Strategy and Implementation Summary**. After returning to the **Table of Contents** page, click on each of the following in turn: **4.1.2 Promotion Strategy** and **5.1 Organizational Structure**.]
3. Describe the equipment and facilities needed by a typical Take Five unit. [Sites to see in BPP: From the **Table of Contents** page, scan any headings that you expect will contain information on equipment and facilities specifications.]
4. How many Take Five stores are planned for the future? What steps can be taken in the interest of quality—that is, to ensure that the same consistent services are provided regardless of store location? [Sites to see in BPP: On the **Table of Contents** page, click on **1.1 Objectives**. After returning to the **Table of Contents** page, click on each of the following in turn: **2.3 Company Locations and Facilities**, **4.3 Milestones**, and **5.3 Management Team Gaps**.]

VIDEO EXERCISE

Managing Global Production: Body Glove

Learning Objectives

The purpose of this video is to help you

1. Recognize some of the operations challenges faced by a growing company.
2. Understand the importance of quality in operations processes.
3. Discuss how and why a company may shift production operations to other countries and other companies.

Synopsis

Riding the wave of public interest in water sports, Body Glove began manufacturing wetsuits in the 1950s. The founders, dedicated surfers and divers, came up with the idea of making the wetsuits from neoprene, which offered more comfortable insulation than the rubber wetsuits of the time. The high costs of both neoprene and labour were major considerations in Body Glove's eventual decision to do its manufacturing in Thailand. The company's constant drive for higher quality was also a factor. Now company management can focus on building Body Glove's image as a California-lifestyle brand without worrying about inventory and other production issues. In licensing its brand for a wide range of goods and services—from cellphone cases and footwear to flotation devices and vacation resorts—Body Glove has also created a network of partners around the world.

Discussion Questions

1. *For analysis*: Even though Body Glove makes its products in Thailand, why must managers continually research the ways in which North American customers use them?
2. *For analysis*: With which aspects of product quality are wetsuit buyers most likely to be concerned?
3. *For application*: When deciding whether to license its name for a new product, what production issues might Body Glove managers research in advance?
4. *For application*: How might Body Glove's Thailand facility use forecasts of seasonal demand to plan production?
5. *For debate*: Should the products that Body Glove does not manufacture be labelled to alert buyers that they are produced under licence? Support your position.

Online Exploration

Visit the Body Glove website at **www.bodyglove.com,** read the Body Glove story, and look over the variety of products, including electronics products, sold under the Body Glove brand. Then browse the licensees listing to find out which companies have licensed the Body Glove brand. How do various licensed products fit with the Body Glove brand image? What challenges might Body Glove face in coordinating its operations with so many different companies and licensed products?

EXPLORING THE NET

Copying a Formula for Success

In many firms, operations provide a combination of goods and services. Of course, basic production issues are always involved: What must production do to provide utility for customers? What are some considerations for deciding where to locate a production facility? What resource inputs are required for the production process? What role does the customer play, if any, in the operations process? Let's address such questions by exploring the website of a rags-to-riches success story that began in 1970, when Paul Orfalea, just out of college, borrowed money to open a tiny photocopy shop which he called "Kinko's."

Today, Kinko's has more than 1100 branches in Canada, the United States, and seven other countries in the Middle East, Asia, and Europe. Let's look at Kinko's website at **www.kinkos.com**. First, browse the home page. Click on **Business Solutions** and **Personal Solutions** and examine Kinko's service products. Then respond to the following items:

1. Who are Kinko's customers? Are they mostly individual consumers or other businesses? Explain.

2. Is Kinko's product line primarily goods or services? Explain using examples.
3. Consider the four kinds of utility—time, place, possession (ownership), and form—through which all operations systems provide benefits to customers. Identify a Kinko's product that provides form utility. Explain using an example. Do the same for time, place, and possession (ownership) utility.

Click on **Small Business Solutions** on the **Business Solutions** page and examine each of the categories.

4. Think about location planning for Kinko's stores. Identify the main factors that must be considered.

On the **Small Business Solutions** page, go into **Online Printing**.

5. Identify the resource inputs that Kinko's uses to make online printing services available to customers. What is the customer's role in the production process?

Concluding Case 11-1 CJ

Lockheed Martin Aeronautics

We saw in Chapter 7 that Lockheed Martin was bidding against Boeing and Northrop Grumman for a large defence contract in the United States. When the battle ended on October 26, 2001, Lockheed was given the green light to launch one of the biggest production projects in history. Cheers erupted at Lockheed's Fort Worth, Texas, conference centre as U.S. Air Force Secretary James Roche announced that Lockheed had won the $200 billion Joint Strike Fighter (JSF) contract. Capping a five-year, winner-take-all competition with rival Boeing, Lockheed had captured the largest defence contract in history—one that could be worth more than $320 billion over the next 20–30 years.

Intended to meet the needs not only of the U.S. Navy, Air Force, and Marines, but also the needs of Britain's Royal Air Force and Royal Navy and the armed forces of several other nations, Lockheed's design for the next generation of supersonic, radar-evading combat jet was just the beginning. The contract was awarded on the basis of experimental versions of the aircraft. Now the real work—detailed planning for production and then production itself—begins.

Many observers think that the next phase—System Development & Demonstration (SDD)—will be the most difficult. Says Michael Burkett, a Boston technology consultant, "Lockheed Martin and its partners have to firm up the design, detail all components, [and] put in the manufacturing process and the supply chain to support it." SDD calls for building and demonstrating 22 aircraft (known in the United States as the F-35) to be delivered by 2005. The next phase—gearing up to full production—begins in 2008, with plans calling for the production of 3000 planes—each worth from $28 million to $38 million—by 2040. During each phase, the U.S. Defense Department will insist that aircraft perform reliably, that deliveries be on time, and that costs be met.

To get started, Lockheed's JSF team needs about 4500 more personnel (up from 500) during the first 18 months. But organizing the project goes far beyond Lockheed's walls because Lockheed, as prime contractor, is collaborating with Northrop Grumman Corp. and Britain's BAE Systems PLC. More than 70 U.S. and 18 international subcontractors at some 187 locations are involved in the SDD phase. Pratt & Whitney, for example, is developing the engines. All told, more than 1500 firms will supply everything from radar systems to bolts. Not surprisingly, the program for production planning will be as futuristic as the airplane itself. Teamwork and technology will be key elements in tracking hundreds of thousands of components, and by 2005, specialists sitting at some 40 000 remote computers will be collaborating on the project.

Of course, the JSF aircraft is more than just hardware. Computers provide onboard brainpower for the advanced-performance capabilities of this electronic weapons platform. Such features as short takeoff and helicopter-like vertical-landing capabilities rely as much on software as on pilot performance. So, too, do real-time views of the battlefield (a major advance for combat pilots). The system depends on software-driven integration of various radar and sensor inputs. Electro-optic and infrared sensor inputs will track targets, and other electronic systems include communications-navigation-and-identification (CNI), targeting, and electronic warfare. Combining huge arrays of electronic and software systems is the name of the game for JSF. For example, the software-intensive CNI system, built by TRW Inc., must be integrated with other modules, such as electronic countermeasures, which will be built by Britain's BAE.

Lockheed Martin is responsible for final integration, and although the technical hurdles are enormous, managerial logistics is also an area of concern. Reflecting on the number of people that his team must hire, Lockheed program manager Tom Burbage admits, "We've got a big scaling up to do. The challenge will be trying to keep an organization intact, not lose momentum through confusion and inexperience, integrate various demands from outside parties, and keep the huge customer set engaged, onboard, and excited about the airplane."

Satisfying multiple customers won't be easy. The three U.S. armed services want different versions of the fighter, as do customers from Canada, Britain, Italy, Denmark, and Norway—all of whom want their own defence industries to share in the program. About 80 percent of all parts will be common to each model, but the rest will vary. The JSF production system, therefore, will have to be flexible enough to produce multiple models on schedule and within budget. Such requirements call for suppliers who can provide reliable components and subsystems—and the right ones for each model—to ensure a final assembly that meets delivery commitments.

Linking all of JSF's companies, customers, and suppliers in real time would be impossible without web-design and project-management tools. Keeping projects on schedule and holding down costs depend on both. Located all around the globe, thousands of design engineers, equipment engineers, logistics specialists, production planners, suppliers, and customers must move hundreds of thousands of components and share product designs, production schedules, and workflows.

With so many participants, information exchanges are essential to avoid lost time and duplicated effort. To save alliance members both time and money, Lockheed hosts a web collaboration network/product data management system. For instance, because all engineers working on a particular component are automatically notified when anyone makes a change, no one wastes time working on an outdated design. The system is also accessible to the Department of Defense for tracking progress in real time.

As the cornerstone of this project, Lockheed's internet-based system does more than help to design the aircraft. It also makes it simple for Lockheed and its suppliers to link inventory and production systems. "The scale of this program is unprecedented," says Mike Brown, senior vice-president of PTC, a project software supplier. Project managers can quickly check on inventory status and production schedules as well as determine whether suppliers will have trouble meeting delivery deadlines. In addition to keeping materials flowing throughout the supply chain, the system features shop-floor-management tools to help identify delays, quality problems, and areas for process improvement.

The system also supports the 3D-solid-modelling program that underlies both design and production. Digital definition of the aircraft provides instantaneous information needed for making production tools and for assembling parts and components. Initial plans call for building one airplane every five months, but that time span will be reduced as the team gains experience with new materials and processes.

"We're using a lot of neat stuff," says Martin McLaughlin, Northrop Grumman's chief executive for the JSF product team. "Our use of 3D-solid modelling has revolutionized the machining of parts: [L]asers in the factory ceiling can read the 3D-solid-model data and project directly onto a machine tool an outline of exactly where the mechanic should place the next ply of composite material." Laser imaging cuts production time in half, guarantees precise control over composite materials, and trims inspection time by a whopping 90 percent. Laser technology also rigs assembly fixtures digitally (rather than manually), reduces the number of required parts by 50 percent, and eliminates 90 percent of the tools that would once have been needed to build the JSF. The team expects that manufacturing flow time will eventually be reduced by half.

Finally, the task of coordinating members and activities also falls on the project's net-collaboration systems. Although separated by oceans, partners must communicate as if they were in the same room, and this intensive level of communication must be maintained for years to come. The sharing of real-time data is essential for more than just cost control. As the project progresses, the collaboration system will build stronger customer relationships and promote deeper political ties among members.

Questions for Discussion

1. How would you describe the time utility and form utility that customers will receive from the Joint Strike Fighter? List examples of each kind of utility.
2. How might scheduling tools, such as Gantt and PERT charts, be useful for the JSF project? Using examples from the JSF case description, show how Gantt and PERT charts might be used.
3. Suppose you are responsible for planning a full-scale production process slated to begin in 2008. You are concerned about the number of parts and systems suppliers who are scattered around the globe. What are some major production-planning problems posed by your supply chain and its geographic dispersion?
4. How would you describe the kinds of production or operations that will take place in the next phase of the JSF project, which will be System Development & Demonstration? Are the main products mostly services or mostly physical goods? Explain.
5. Because Lockheed is responsible for overall project coordination, it must maintain sufficient capacity to fulfill its contract with the U.S. Defense Department. How would you describe the kinds of production capacity that will be needed for the next phase of the project, SDD? What kinds of capacity will be needed for the full-scale production phase? ◆

Concluding Case 11-2

Toyota's Production System: Still the Standard

Why do executives from Ford, Chrysler, and GM want to take plant tours of Toyota manufacturing facilities? To try to figure out how Toyota is able to make cars so efficiently, that's why. Toyota doesn't charge its competitors for these tours, and it doesn't keep anything secret from them. This seems odd; would Coke let Pepsi see its secret formula? But Toyota doesn't seem worried that competitors will see its operations up close, because it knows that those competitors have been trying (unsuccessfully) for years to match its productivity.

Actually, it's not just Toyota that is a model of efficiency. All the Japanese carmakers score well on this important measure. The annual report released by Harbour and Associates showed that Nissan required the fewest hours to build the average vehicle (16.83) followed by Mitsubishi (21.33 hours), Toyota (21.83 hours), and Honda (22.27 hours). By comparison, DaimlerChrysler took 28.04 hours to build a vehicle.

The Toyota Production System (TPS) is designed to mobilize all human and capital resources in such a way that peak efficiency, productivity, and quality will be achieved in the assembly of automobiles. Mercedes-Benz may have sophisticated engineering, Honda great engine technology, and Chrysler great styling, but Toyota has the most efficient production system.

The Big 3 domestic automobile manufacturers have all adopted parts of TPS, but none of them has been able to match the efficiency produced by the total TPS system. The system looks simple enough: maximize flow, eliminate waste, and respect people. But the implementation requires huge amounts of effort and insight. For example, lots of manufacturing plants have adopted the idea that any worker who sees something wrong can pull a cord and stop the production line. But Toyota is the only company that has actually been able to drive the right philosophies about quality down to the worker level.

A key aspect of TPS is consistent, smooth production. In many manufacturing plants, workers work hard during the first few hours on the job to meet their quota, and then relax later in the day. This leads to uneven production. At Toyota, overproduction at any time is considered bad practice. Workflows are designed to move from process to process with no ups or downs. Another example: In the typical automobile plant, visitors will see stacks of half-finished parts and idle workers standing along assembly lines that are temporarily shut down for one reason or another. But at Toyota plants, workers are constantly in motion and almost look like dancers in a choreographed production.

TPS requires that experienced managers work with a highly motivated and well-trained workforce. The TPS system also involves dependence on outside suppliers who must run their own operations completely in sync with Toyota's. Because Toyota produces just 30 percent of the parts it needs (GM produces almost two-thirds of its own parts), suppliers are an integral part of Toyota's production system and often have an ownership stake in the company.

Toyota is famous for pioneering the just-in-time parts delivery system. Suppliers deliver parts up to eight times daily to Toyota factories, allowing the company to maintain inventory levels that are only one-quarter those at GM. Toyota's suppliers are also physically much closer to Toyota production plants than GM's suppliers are to its plants—an average of 100 kilometres for Toyota versus 700 kilometres for GM.

Suppliers are involved in every aspect of Toyota's production so that they can be an effective part of the team that produces cars. If the supplier has problems, Toyota helps it to improve. Two Toyota engineers once spent seven months at a supplier improving its operations so it could meet Toyota's standards. All this took place while the supplier was under contract to a Toyota competitor.

The TPS system is not restricted to just the production line. It also works in important areas like new product development. With TPS, Toyota can develop a new car model in 18 months, a much shorter time than is typical in this industry. With all of this good news, are there any problems on the horizon for Toyota? Yes. The company will have to find more foreign markets for its cars because of limited demand within Japan. Unfortunately, Toyota has not been able to completely export its TPS system to its manufacturing facilities outside Japan. Its North American plants, for example, still require 30 to 50 percent more time to build a car than its Japanese plants do. These difficulties have arisen because of a lack of middle managers with TPS experience, and because so much time has to be spent bringing supplies up to Toyota's standards.

Questions for Discussion

1. What is utility? What are the various kinds of utility? What kind of utility is Toyota providing with its automobiles?
2. What are the different kinds of transformation technologies that are used to turn raw materials into finished goods? Which one(s) does Toyota use? Explain.
3. Explain the just-in-time (JIT) inventory system. How does JIT help Toyota in its pursuit of productivity and quality?
4. Why has Toyota had difficulties exporting its TPS system to its North American production plants? What can it do to overcome these problems? ◆

CHAPTER 12

Increasing Productivity and Quality

After reading this chapter, you should be able to:

1. Describe the connection between *productivity* and *quality*.
2. Understand the importance of increasing productivity.
3. Identify the activities involved in *total quality management* and describe six tools that companies can use to achieve it.
4. Identify three trends in productivity and quality management, including *supply chain management*.
5. Discuss four strategies that companies use to improve productivity and quality.

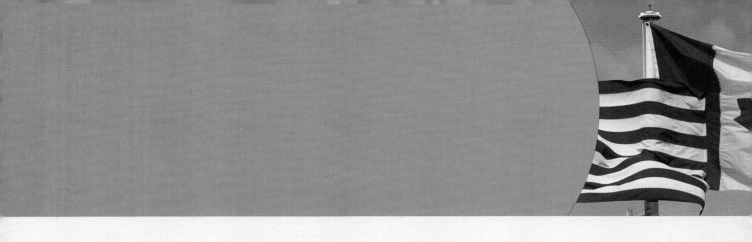

Productivity and the Standard of Living

Compared with the United States, Canada's standard of living has been slipping for the last two decades. A Conference Board of Canada study found that in 1980, Canada's standard of living was 90 percent of the U.S. level. By 2000, it had slipped to 81 percent, and it is projected to drop to 77 percent by 2010. Charles Baillie, former CEO of the Toronto-Dominion Bank, warned that unless we raise our standard of living, Canadians will experience a decline in the quality of health care, social programs, and overall quality of life.

What can we do to raise our standard of living? We must increase our productivity growth rate, which has been lagging behind the United States. For example, output per hour in Canadian manufacturing was about 14 percent below the United States for the period 1977–1994. Since 1994, the situation has actually worsened—output per hour in Canada was 29 percent lower than the United States in 2000 and 32 percent lower in 2001. Put another way, labour productivity growth was 3.8 *percentage points* higher in the United States than in Canada during the period 1994–2000. Another interesting statistic: The average weekly hours worked per week in Canada in 2001 was 34.4 hours, compared with 37.6 hours in the United States.

If we hope to catch up to the United States, Canada will have to exceed the rate of productivity growth in the United States each year by about one percentage point for the next 15 years. One percentage point doesn't sound like much, but it would require Canadian industry to achieve an annual productivity growth rate of over 3 percent. That rate of productivity growth has been achieved only twice in Canada in the last 25 years.

Another way to assess productivity is to look at trends in labour costs per unit of output. In Canada, the amount of money paid to labour for each unit of output increased by just 2 percent between 1991 and 2001. This looks quite good in terms of productivity improvements, but other countries are doing much better. For example, labour costs per unit of output *declined* by 4 percent in the United States, and by 33 percent in Sweden during the same period. Canada was able to remain competitive during the period partly because the decline in the value of the Canadian dollar made our exports cheaper and increased demand for Canadian products. But a country can't keep depreciating its currency indefinitely, and the recent increase in the Canadian dollar has hurt exporters. It is not just a comparison with the United States that is unfavourable; Canada had the second lowest productivity growth rate in output per hour for all OECD (industrialized) countries.

Why is the overall productivity of Canadian firms lower than the productivity of firms based in the United States (and other countries)? Five reasons are typically given:

1. The scale of manufacturing firms in Canada is smaller than in the United States, and small plants are less productive than large ones.
2. Important industries like machinery and electronics have lower productivity in Canadian companies.
3. Subsidiaries of foreign companies operating in Canada are more productive than Canadian-owned firms.
4. The decline of the Canadian dollar between 1995 and 2001 meant that manufacturers had little incentive to increase productivity (because they could sell their goods easily in the United States).
5. Canadian business firms conduct less research and development (R&D) than U.S. companies do (R&D expenditures in the United States are about 2.7 percent of GDP, but in Canada the figure is just 1.7 percent).

Several surveys have been conducted during the last few years asking Canadians what they think about the issues of standard of living and productivity. Below are some illustrative questions that were asked:

- "How do you think the average personal income for a Canadian worker compares with that for a U.S. worker?" (half of the respondents said it was lower, one-fifth said it was higher, and one-fifth said it was the same).
- "How do you think Canada compares with the U.S. in terms of quality of life?" (70 percent said it was higher and 18 percent said it was the same).

- "How do you think Canada compares with the U.S. in terms of standard of living?" (37 percent said it is higher in Canada, 34 percent thought it was the same, and 28 percent said it was lower).
- "How do you think Canada's level of productivity compares with that of the U.S.?" (50 percent felt it was worse, 25 percent felt it was the same, and 20 percent felt it was better).

When asked if they agreed or disagreed with the statement "Increasing productivity is essential to improving our standard of living," 82 percent agreed. When asked if they agreed or disagreed with the statement "If we don't improve our productivity our quality of life will suffer," 70 percent agreed.

What needs to be done to improve Canadian productivity? The following suggestions have been made:

- Put more money into post-secondary education
- Develop more partnerships between business and academic institutions
- Invest in upgrading workforce skills, and increase the availability of vocational, technical, and apprenticeship programs for students who don't attend university
- Create greater incentives to rejoin the workforce for those on welfare
- Levy training costs on businesses like some European countries do
- Stop subsidizing uncompetitive industries like shipbuilding
- Give tax breaks to companies who invest in new technology ◆

It is no secret that productivity and quality are watchwords in today's business. Companies are not only measuring productivity and insisting on improvements, but also insisting on quality so they can bring to market products that satisfy customers, improve sales, and boost profits. By focusing on the learning objectives of this chapter, you will better understand the increasingly important concepts of productivity and quality.

THE PRODUCTIVITY–QUALITY CONNECTION

1. Describe the connection between *productivity* and *quality*.

Productivity is a measure of economic performance. It measures how much is produced relative to the resources used to produce it. The more we are able to produce the right things while using fewer resources, the more productivity grows and everyone—the economy, businesses, and workers—benefits.

Productivity considers both the amounts and the quality of what is produced. By using resources more efficiently, the quantity of output will be greater. But unless the resulting goods and services are of satisfactory quality (the "right things"), consumers will not want them. **Quality**, then, means fitness for use—offering features that consumers want.

productivity
A measure of efficiency that compares how much is produced with the resources used to produce it.

quality
A product's fitness for use in terms of offering the features that consumers want.

Responding to the Productivity Challenge

As the opening case clearly shows, productivity has both international and domestic ramifications. Obviously, when one country is more productive than another, it will accumulate more wealth. Similarly, a nation whose productivity fails to increase as rapidly as that of competitor nations will see its standard of living fall.

It is important to understand the true meaning of *productivity* and to devise ways to measure it. Since *quality* must be defined in terms of value to the customer, companies must design their marketing efforts to cultivate a more customer-oriented focus. As quality-improvement practices are implemented, more and more firms will receive payoffs from these efforts. Four factors interact in this process: *customers, quality, productivity,* and *profits*.

Measuring Productivity

How do we know how productive a country is? Most countries use **labour productivity** to measure their level of productivity:

labour productivity
Partial productivity ratio calculated by dividing gross domestic product by total number of workers.

$$\text{labor productivity of a country} = \frac{\text{gross domestic product}}{\text{total number of workers}}$$

This equation reflects the general idea of productivity. It compares a country's total annual output of goods and services with the resources used to produce that output. The focus on labour, rather than on other resources (such as capital or energy), is preferred because most countries keep accurate records on employment and hours worked. Canada's labour productivity in 2003 was 0.4 percent lower than it was in 2002, and it continues to grow at a much slower rate than labour productivity in the United States.[1]

Productivity Among Global Competitors

A study by the Organization for Economic Cooperation and Development (OECD) reports productivity levels in 23 participating countries. Figure 12.1 compares productivity among several OECD countries. As you can see, economic output per hour worked in Belgium is about 28 percent higher than the average for OECD members. At 31 percent below average, output in New Zealand is lowest among the nations listed in Figure 12.1.

Why such differences from nation to nation? The answer lies in many factors: technologies, human skills, economic policies, natural resources—and even in traditions. Consider, for example, just one industrial sector—food production. In Japan, the food-production industry employs more workers than the automotive, computer, consumer electronics, and machine-tool industries combined. It is a fragmented, highly protected

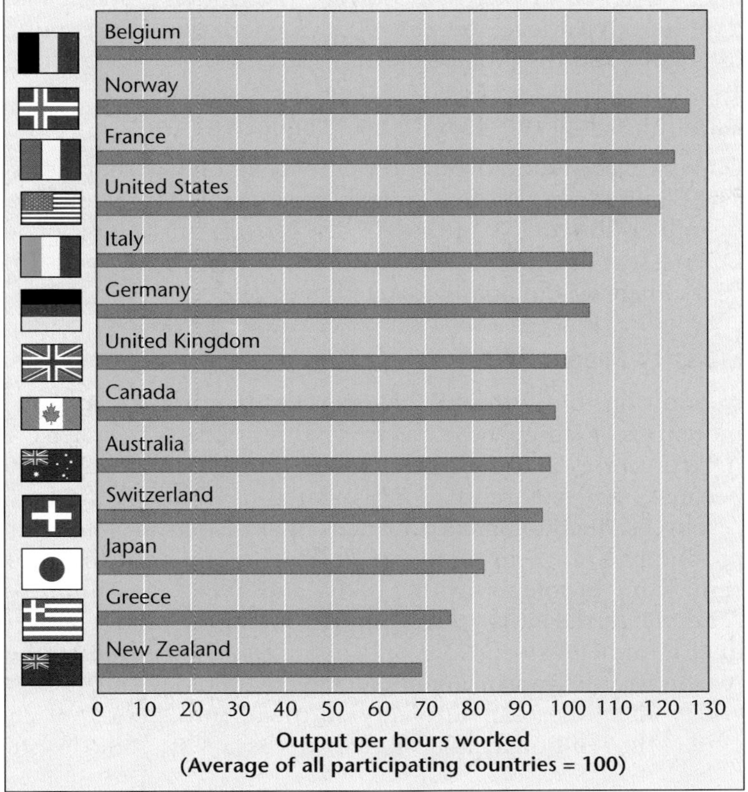

Figure 12.1
International productivity comparisons.

industry—and, compared with U.S. food production, it is extremely inefficient. The average U.S. worker produces 3.5 times as much food as his or her Japanese counterpart. Overall, data show that in the time it takes a U.S. worker to produce $100 worth of goods, Japanese workers produce about $68 worth. Belgian workers, on the other hand, produce $107 worth.[2]

According to Michael Porter, a Harvard University expert on international competitiveness, Canada's competitiveness is a concern because we have been living off our rich diet of natural resources. In Porter's view, Canada will have to start emphasizing innovation and develop a more sophisticated mix of products if it hopes to be successful in international markets. Porter criticizes Canadian business, government, and labour for failing to abandon outdated ways of thinking regarding productivity and innovation.[3]

Domestic Productivity

Nations must be concerned about domestic productivity regardless of their global standing. A country that improves its ability to make something out of its existing resources can increase the wealth of all its inhabitants. Conversely, a decline in productivity shrinks a nation's total wealth. When that happens, an increase in one person's wealth comes only at the expense of others with whom he or she shares a social-economic system.

For example, additional wealth from higher productivity can be shared among workers (as higher wages), investors (as higher profits), and customers (as stable prices). When productivity drops, however, wages can be increased only by reducing profits (penalizing investors) or by increasing prices (penalizing customers). It is understandable, then, that investors, suppliers, managers, and workers are all concerned about the productivity of specific industries and companies.

National Productivity Trends

level of productivity
The dollar value of goods and services produced by each worker.

The **level of productivity** refers to the value of goods and services produced by each worker in a country. The United States leads the world, with a productivity level of $65 900. Second place is occupied by Belgium ($64 200) and third place by Italy ($61 700).[4]

Manufacturing Versus Service Productivity

Currently, manufacturing productivity is higher than service productivity. Thus, manufacturing is primarily responsible for recent rises in the nation's overall productivity. With services growing as a proportion of Canadian businesses, productivity must increase more rapidly in that sector in the years ahead if Canada is to keep its edge.

Industry Productivity

2. Understand the importance of increasing productivity.

In addition to differences between the manufacturing and service sectors, industries within these sectors differ vastly in terms of productivity. Agriculture is more productive in Canada than in many other nations because we use more sophisticated technology and superior natural resources. Technological advances have also given the computer industry a productivity edge in many areas. Steel manufacturing, which experienced significant problems in the 1970s and 1980s, has improved recently. For example, in the early 1980s, about 10 hours of labour were required to produce a tonne of steel. Now, only about four hours of labour are needed. One reason for the improvement is a new technology called continuous casting. Today, machines can turn molten metal into slabs that can be processed while still red-hot. It is no longer necessary to cool the steel, strip off the moulding, and then reheat it for processing. This new process has meant immense savings in both labour and energy.[5]

In an effort to increase productivity, Canfor Corp. developed a system called Genus, which it is using to manage its forestry operations. Genus, a computerized database containing geographic information and other essential data about Canfor's vast lumber and pulp operations in British Columbia and Alberta, will be used as a strategic planning tool to determine how the company should adjust its logging plans to reflect both market demand and logging regulations laid down by the Forest Practices Code of British Columbia Act.[6]

Canfor Corp.
www.canfor.com

The productivity of specific industries concerns many people for different reasons. Labour unions need to take it into account in negotiating contracts, since highly productive industries can give raises more easily than can less productive industries. Investors and suppliers consider industry productivity when making loans, buying securities, and planning their own future production.

Company Productivity

High productivity gives a company a competitive edge because its costs are lower. As a result, it can offer its product at a lower price (and gain more customers), or it can make a greater profit on each item sold. Increased productivity also allows companies to pay workers higher wages without raising prices.

The productivity of individual companies is also important to investors, workers, and managers. Comparing the productivity of several companies in the same industry helps investors in buying and selling stocks. Employee profit-sharing plans are often based on the company's productivity improvements each year. And managers use information about productivity trends to plan for new products, factories, and funds to stay competitive in the years ahead.

On the left, workers assemble a truck the old way, manually lowering and bolting frames onto axles. On the right, the process is highly automated (and safer), with robotic grippers to flip and align the bulky frames.

TOTAL QUALITY MANAGEMENT

It is no longer enough for businesses to simply measure productivity in terms of the numbers of items produced. They must also take quality into account. But Canadian business has not always recognized the importance of quality. In the decades after the Second World War, business consultant W. Edwards Deming tried to persuade firms in North America that they needed to improve quality at least as much as quantity. He wasn't very successful, but his arguments won over the Japanese. Through years of meticulous hard work, Japan's manufacturers have changed "Made in Japan" from a synonym for cheap, shoddy merchandise into a hallmark of reliability. A current example of an attempt to convey quality to consumers is described in the Business Today box.

Juran Institute
www.juran.com

Quality advocates such as Joseph Juran and Kaoru Ishikawa introduced methods and tools for implementing quality. Juran's "Quality Trilogy"—quality planning, quality control, and quality improvement—was the first structured process for managing quality. It identifies management steps for ensuring quality. In addition to management actions, Juran, like Deming and

BUSINESS TODAY

Rating the Quality of Diamonds

How do you rate the quality of diamonds? Historically, diamond quality has been assessed by reference to 4 C's: *cut, colour, clarity,* and *carat*. But perhaps a fifth C is emerging, and that is "country of origin." Better yet, the fifth C may also stand for "Canada."

Until just a few years ago, Canada was not even a player in the international diamond business. But in 1991, a promising diamond field was located in the Northwest Territories and the race was on to exploit the possibilities. Skeptics said that even if diamonds were found in commercial quantities in Canada, the diamonds would have to be sold to DeBeers, the company that controlled the world diamond trade. But once diamond wholesalers were shown the first Canadian diamonds, they realized that the quality was as high as that from the best diamond mines in the world, and they eagerly bought them. The myth of DeBeers control soon evaporated.

The first Canadian diamond mine was opened in the Northwest Territories in 1998, and by 2003 it was already producing 6 percent of the total world's supply of rough diamonds. A second mine opened in 2003, and another is scheduled for 2006. By that time, Canada will produce 12 percent of the world's diamonds.

In recent years, there has been much negative press about so-called "blood diamonds," that is, diamonds that were mined by armed workers in war-torn African countries like Botswana. These diamonds were then exported, and the money used to support further military campaigns. The developing Canadian diamond industry has no such image problems. Diamonds in Canada are mined under very ethical and environmentally strict conditions. And there's one added advantage: the quality of Canadian diamonds is very high. Canadian rough diamonds average $170 per carat in value, far above the $100 level at which diamonds are considered precious.

But is country of origin important enough to influence consumers when they purchase a diamond? In the minds of many consumers, the quality of certain products *is* associated with the product's country of origin. Think, for example, of Swiss watches, Italian leather, and French wines. Oren Sofer, CEO of diamond wholesaler Beny Sofer & Sons LLC, says that if you can brand water, you certainly should be able to brand diamonds. He wants consumers to eventually recognize "Canadian diamonds" as an important brand name.

This is not an impossible goal. The move is already underway to establish a high quality reputation for Canadian diamonds. Sirius Diamond Inc., a Vancouver diamond wholesaler, engraves a tiny polar bear on the Canadian diamonds it sells, and Birks & Sons Inc. engraves a maple leaf on its diamonds. The government of the Northwest Territories provides a certificate for each diamond that has come from its mines. This ensures that diamonds from other countries cannot be passed off as Canadian stones.

Ishikawa, championed the idea of company-wide employee participation. These theorists also developed quality tools for day-to-day work activities because they knew that without employee participation, real quality improvement would never happen. Ishikawa, for example, developed so-called "fishbone diagrams," also known as "cause-and-effect diagrams" or "Ishikawa diagrams," that help teams of employees investigate and track down causes of quality problems in their work areas. The diagram in Figure 12.2, for instance, was designed to help an airport manager find out why his facility had so many delayed departures. Focusing on five major categories of possible causes, he then noted several potential causes of the problem in each. (It turns out that there weren't enough tow trucks to handle baggage transfers.)[7]

Managing for Quality

Total quality management (TQM) (sometimes called *quality assurance*) includes all the activities necessary for getting high-quality goods and services into the marketplace. It must consider all parts of the business, including customers, suppliers, and employees. TQM emphasizes that no defects are tolerable, and that employees are responsible for maintaining quality standards. At Toyota's Cambridge, Ontario, plant, for example, workers can push a button or pull a rope to stop the production line when something is not up to standard.[8]

total quality management (TQM)
A concept that emphasizes that no defects are tolerable and that all employees are responsible for maintaining quality standards.

3. Identify the activities involved in *total quality management* and describe six tools that companies can use to achieve it.

The strategic approach to TQM begins with leadership and the desire for TQM. This approach involves getting people's attention, getting them to think in an entirely new way about what they do, and then getting them to improve both processes and products.[9]

Customer focus is the starting point. Companies must develop methods for determining what customers want, and then direct all their resources toward fulfilment of those needs to gain greater customer satisfaction. Total participation is mandatory. Unless all employees are working toward improved quality, the firm is wasting potential contributions from its

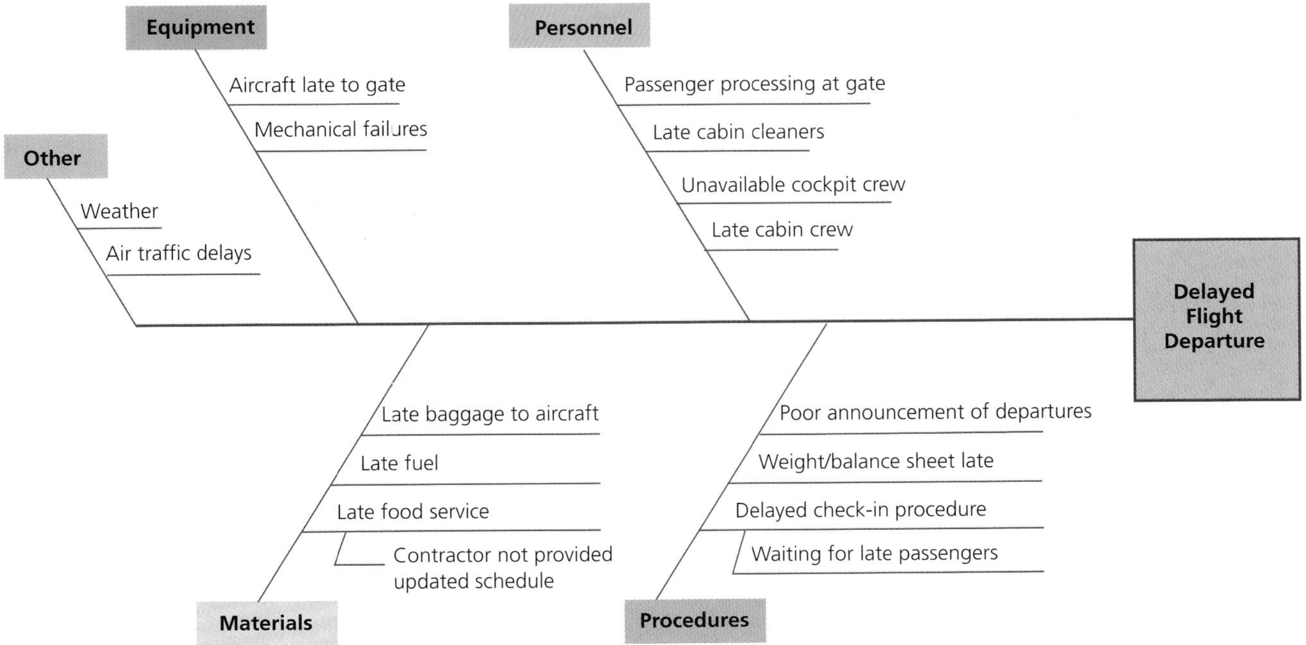

Figure 12.2
"Fishbone" or cause-and-effect diagram.

human resources, and is missing a chance to become a stronger competitor in the marketplace. TQM in today's competitive markets demands unending and continuous improvement of products, after-sales services, and all of the company's internal processes, such as accounting, delivery, billing, and information flow.

Says John Kay, director of Oxford University's School of Management: "You can't run a successful company if you don't care about customers and employees, or if you are systematically unpleasant to suppliers."[10] To bring the interests of all these stakeholders together, TQM involves planning, organizing, directing, and controlling.

Successful use of TQM requires a high level of commitment from all members of the organization. Consider the case of Standard Aero in Winnipeg, which is in the business of aircraft overhaul. When the company instituted TQM, the process began with the formation of a "change council" consisting of the CEO and five senior managers. This council ensured that the TQM initiative received the money, equipment, and support it needed for success. Next, a nine-person task force was formed that consisted of employees who had done the full range of jobs on one of Standard's major overhaul contracts. Its first job was to find out what the customer wanted. It did this by designing a questionnaire and visiting customer plants around the world to gather information. The task force also worked within Standard Aero to determine exactly how the company did its aircraft overhaul work. After weeks of analysis, the task force was able to significantly reduce the time required for overhaul work. For example, the number of times a certain gearbox was handled as it moved through the repair process was reduced by 84 percent.[11]

Planning for Quality

Planning for quality should begin before products are designed or redesigned. Managers need to set goals for both quality levels and quality reliability in the beginning. **Performance quality** refers to the features of a product and how well it performs. For example, Maytag gets a price premium because its washers and dryers offer a high level of performance quality. Customers perceive Maytags as having more advanced features and being more durable than other brands. (Everyone knows that the Maytag repairman is a lonely and idle person.)

performance quality
The overall degree of quality; how well the features of a product meet consumers' needs and how well the product performs.

Performance quality may or may not be related to quality reliability in a product. **Quality reliability** refers to the consistency or repeatability of performance. Toyota's small cars may not equal the overall quality level or have the luxury features of Rolls Royce; consequently, Toyota's prices are much lower. But Toyotas have high quality reliability. The firm has a reputation for producing very few "lemons."

quality reliability
The consistency of quality from unit to unit of a product.

Organizing for Quality

Perhaps most important to the quality concept is the belief that producing quality goods and services requires an effort from all parts of the organization. The old idea of a separate "quality control" department is no longer enough. Everyone—from the chairperson of the board to the part-time clerk-purchasers, engineers, janitors, marketers, machinists, and other personnel—must work to ensure quality. In Germany's Messerschmitt-Boelkow-Blohm aerospace company, for example, all employees are responsible for inspecting their own work. The overall goal is to reduce eventual problems to a minimum by making the product correctly from the beginning. The same principle extends to teamwork practice at Heinz Co., where teams of workers are assigned to inspect virtually every activity in the company. Heinz has realized substantial cost savings by eliminating waste and rework.

At Motorola, the concept of teamwork as a key to organizational quality has resulted in an international event called the Total Customer Satisfaction Team Competition. Teams are composed of Motorola employees and also include customers and outside suppliers. Teams are judged on their success not only in promoting productivity but also in sharing innovative ideas with people both inside and outside the company.

Although everyone in a company contributes to product quality, responsibility for specific aspects of total quality management is often assigned to specific departments and jobs. In fact, many companies have quality assurance, or quality control, departments staffed by quality experts. These people may be called in to help solve quality-related problems in any of the firm's other departments. They keep other departments informed of the latest developments in equipment and methods for maintaining quality. In addition, they monitor all quality control activities to identify areas for improvement.

Leading for Quality

Too often, firms fail to take the initiative to make quality happen. Leading for quality means that managers must inspire and motivate employees throughout the company to achieve quality goals. They need to help employees see how they affect quality and how quality affects their jobs and their company. Leaders must continually find ways to foster a quality orientation by training employees, encouraging their involvement, and tying wages to quality of work. If managers succeed, employees will ultimately accept **quality ownership**—the idea that quality belongs to each person who creates or destroys it while performing a job.

quality ownership
The concept that quality belongs to each employee who creates or destroys it in producing a good or service; the idea that all workers must take responsibility for producing a quality product.

General Electric Co. embarked on a strong quality control initiative a few years ago. Top management commitment to the program was ensured by tying executive bonuses to actual implementation of the quality control program. The program involves training managers to be "Black Belts" in quality improvement. These Black Belts then spent their time in GE plants setting up quality improvement projects. Young managers were told that they wouldn't have much of a future at GE unless they became Black Belts.

Controlling for Quality

By monitoring its products and services, a company can detect mistakes and make corrections. To do so, however, managers must first establish specific quality standards and measurements. Consider the following control system for a bank's teller services. Observant supervisors periodically evaluate transactions against a checklist. Specific aspects of each teller's work—appearance, courtesy, efficiency, and so on—are recorded. The results, reviewed with employees, either confirm proper performance or indicate changes that are needed to bring performance up to standards.

TOOLS FOR TOTAL QUALITY MANAGEMENT

In managing for quality, many leading companies rely on assistance from proven tools. Often, ideas for improving both the product and the production process come from **competitive product analysis**. For example, Toshiba will take apart a Xerox photocopier and test each component. Test results help Toshiba's managers decide which Toshiba product features are satisfactory (in comparison to the competition), which product features need to be upgraded, or whether Toshiba's production processes need improvement.

competitive product analysis
Process by which a company analyzes a competitor's products to identify desirable improvements.

There are many specific tools that can be used to achieve TQM. Here, we briefly describe the following: *value-added analysis, statistical process control, quality/cost studies, quality improvement teams, benchmarking, getting closer to the customer, ISO 9000, re-engineering,* and *adding value through supply chains*.

Value-Added Analysis

value-added analysis
The evaluation of all work activities, material flows, and paperwork to determine the value they add for customers.

Value-added analysis refers to the evaluation of all work activities, material flows, and paperwork to determine the value that they add for customers. Value-added analysis often reveals wasteful or unnecessary activities that can be eliminated without harming (and even improving) customer service. When Hewlett-Packard, for example, simplified its contracts and reduced them from 20 pages to as few as 2 pages for all customers, computer sales rose by more than 18 percent.

Statistical Process Control

statistical process control (SPC)
Statistical analysis techniques that allow managers to analyze variations in production data and to detect when adjustments are needed to create products with high quality reliability.

Although every company would like complete uniformity in its outputs, all firms experience unit-to-unit variations in their products. Companies can gain better control, however, by understanding the sources of variation. **Statistical process control (SPC)** methods—especially process variation studies and control charts—allow managers to analyze variations in production data.

Process Variation

Variations in a firm's products may arise from the inputs in its production process. As people, materials, work methods, and equipment change, so do production outputs. While some amount of **process variation** is acceptable, too much can result in poor quality and excessive operating costs. Consider the box-filling operation for Honey Nuggets cereal. Each automated machine fills two 400-gram boxes per second. Even under proper conditions, slight variations in cereal weight from box to box are normal. Equipment and tools wear out, the cereal may be overly moist, and machinists make occasional adjustments. But how much variation is occurring? How much is acceptable?

process variation

Any change in employees, materials, work methods, or equipment that affects output quality.

Information about variation in a process can be obtained from a *process capability study*. Boxes are taken from the filling machines and weighed. The results are plotted, as in Figure 12.3, and compared with the upper and lower specification limits (quality limits) for weight. These limits define good and bad quality for box filling. Boxes with more than 410 grams are a wasteful "giveaway." Underfilling has a cost because it is unlawful.

The chart in Figure 12.3 reveals that Machine A's output is acceptable because none of its boxes violate the quality limits. Machine A, then, is fully capable of meeting the company's quality standards. Machines B and C, however, have problems. In their present condition, they are not "capable" because they cannot reliably meet Honey Nuggets' quality standards. The company must take special—and costly—actions to sort the good from the bad boxes before releasing the cereal for shipment. Unless machines B and C are renovated, substandard production quality will plague Honey Nuggets.

Control Charts

Knowing that a process is capable of meeting quality standards is not enough. Managers must still monitor the process to prevent its drifting

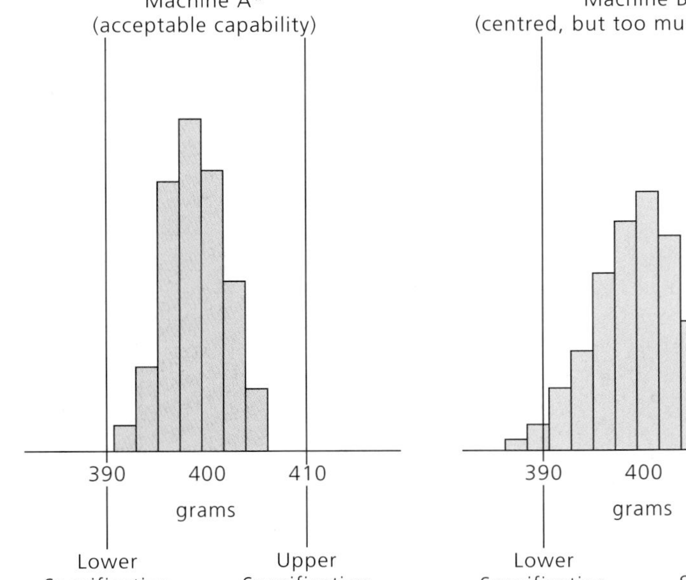

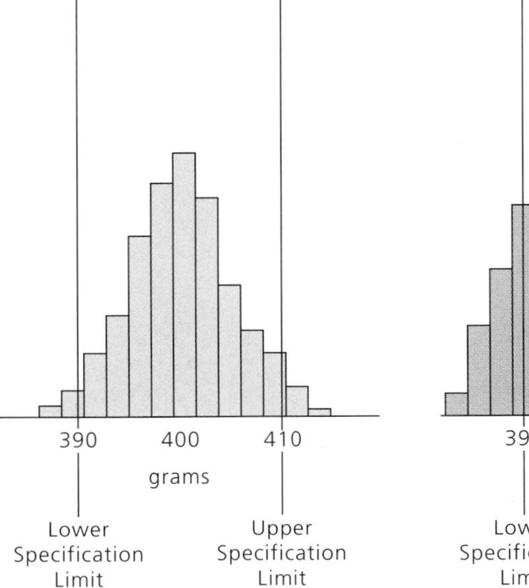

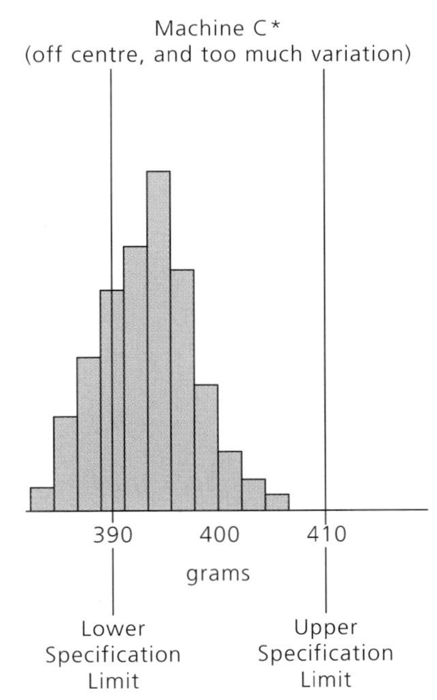

*Distribution of weights for 500 boxes from each machine

Figure 12.3
Process variation in box filling for Honey Nuggets cereal.

astray during production. To detect the beginning of bad conditions, managers can check production periodically and plot the results on a **control chart**. For example, several times a day a machine operator at Honey Nuggets might weigh several boxes of cereal together to ascertain the average weight.

control chart

A statistical process control method in which results of test sampling of a product are plotted on a diagram that reveals when the process is beginning to depart from normal operating conditions.

Figure 12.4 shows the control chart for machine A, in which the first five points are randomly scattered around the centre line, indicating that the machine was operating well. However, the points for samples 5 through 8 are all above the centre line, indicating that something was causing the boxes to overfill. The last point falls outside the upper *control limit*, confirming that the process is out of control.

At this point, the machine must be shut down so that a manager and/or the operator can investigate what is causing the problem—equipment, people, materials, or work methods. Control is completed by correcting the problem and restoring the process to normal.

Quality/Cost Studies

Statistical process controls help keep operations up to existing capabilities. But in today's competitive environment, firms must consistently raise quality capabilities. Any improvement in products or production processes means additional costs, however, whether for new facilities, equipment, training, or other changes. Managers thus face the challenge of identifying those improvements that offer the greatest promise. **Quality/cost studies** are useful because they not only identify a firm's current costs but also reveal areas with the largest cost-savings potential.[12]

quality/cost study

A method of improving product quality by assessing a firm's current quality-related costs and identifying areas with the greatest cost-saving potential.

Quality costs are associated with making, finding, repairing, or preventing defective goods and services. All of these costs should be analyzed in a quality/cost study. For example, Honey Nuggets must determine its costs for **internal failures**. These are expenses—including the costs of overfilling boxes and the costs of sorting out bad boxes—incurred during production and before bad products leave the plant. Studies indicate that many manufacturers incur very high costs for internal failures—up to 50 percent of total costs.

internal failures

Expenses incurred during production and before bad product leaves the plant.

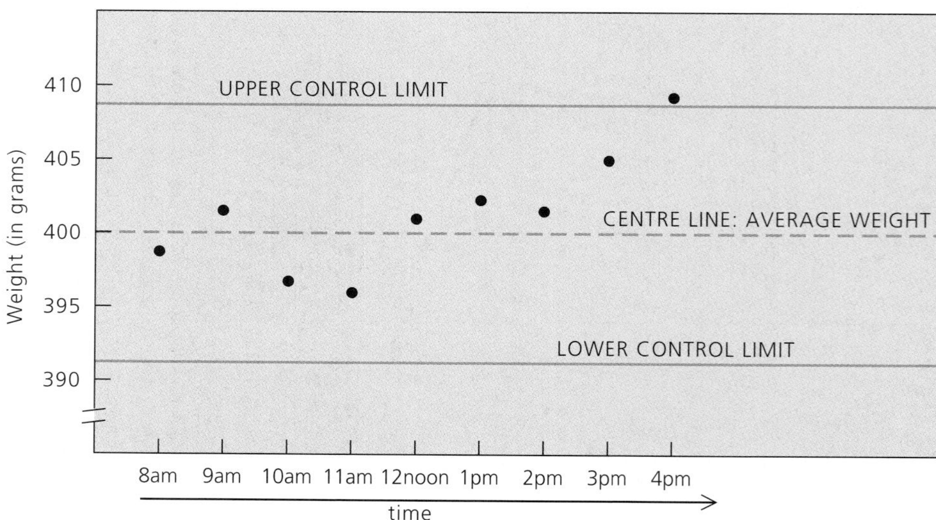

Figure 12.4
Honey Nuggets cereal process control chart for machine A.

Despite quality control procedures, however, some bad boxes may get out of the factory, reach the customer, and generate complaints from grocers and cereal eaters. These are **external failures** that occur outside the factory. The costs of correcting them—refunds to customers, transportation costs to return bad boxes to the factory, possible lawsuits, factory recalls—should also be tabulated in the quality/cost study.

external failures
Allowing defective products to leave the factory and get into consumers' hands.

Quality Improvement Teams

Quality improvement (QI) teams are groups of employees from various work areas who meet regularly to define, analyze, and solve common production problems. Their goal is to improve both their own work methods and the products they make.[13] Many QI teams organize their own work, select leaders, and address problems in the workplace. Motorola sponsors company-wide team competitions to emphasize the value of the team approach, to recognize outstanding team performance, and to reaffirm the team's role in the company's continuous-improvement culture. Teams get higher marks for dealing with projects closely tied to Motorola's key initiatives. Over the years, competing teams have increased cellular phone production by 50 percent and cut electronic-circuit defects by 85 percent (for a one-year savings of $1.8 million).[14]

quality improvement (QI) team
TQM tool in which groups of employees work together to improve quality.

Benchmarking

A powerful TQM tool that has been effective for some firms is called **benchmarking**. To improve its own products or its business procedures, a company compares its current performance against its own past performance, or one company finds and implements the best practices of others. With *internal benchmarking*, a firm tracks its own performance over time to evaluate its progress and to set goals for further improvement. As an example, the percentage of customer phone calls with more than two minutes of response time may be 15 percent this month. Compared with past months, this percentage may be high or low. In short, past performance is the benchmark for evaluating recent results.

benchmarking
Comparing the quality of the firm's output with the quality of the output of the industry's leaders.

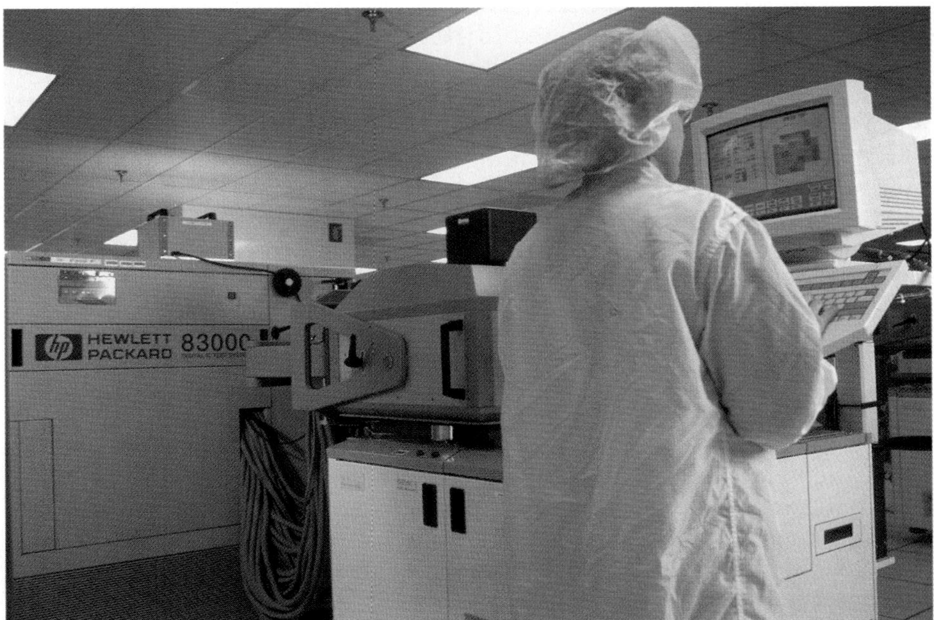

At Hewlett-Packard, testing machines use tiny probes to ensure that the electronic characteristics of every semiconductor are correct. Such systems are designed to check primarily for so-called "class defects"—problems that can affect a whole range of products on the assembly line. One bad wafer at the end of the line can represent a waste of $10 000 in costs, and its commercial value is zero.

External benchmarking begins with a critical review of competitors (or even companies in other lines of business) to determine which goods or services perform the best; these activities and products are called *best practices*. For example, Toronto Hospital gathered performance data on 26 indicators from various Canadian hospitals so that it could determine how well it was performing compared with other organizations in the health care industry.[15] Executives from Ford, DaimlerChrysler, and General Motors frequently tour Toyota manufacturing facilities as they try to figure out how Toyota makes cars so efficiently.

Getting Closer to the Customer

As one advocate of quality improvement has put it, "Customers are an economic asset. They're not on the balance sheet, but they should be." One of the themes of this chapter has been that struggling companies have often lost sight of customers as the driving force for all business activity. Perhaps they waste resources designing products that customers do not want. Sometimes they ignore customer reactions to existing products or fail to keep up with changing consumer tastes. By contrast, the most successful businesses keep close to their customers and know what they want in the products they consume.

Greyhound Lines of Canada
www.greyhound.ca

At Greyhound Lines of Canada, the marketing and operations vice-president wanted to drive home the point to managers that clean restrooms are important to customers. He warned regional managers that he would visit bus depots on one-hour's notice to see if the restrooms were clean enough to eat dinner in. Within weeks, photos of regional managers having dinner in spotless restrooms began pouring in to the vice-president's office.[16]

MBNA, a credit-card company, has learned that speed of service is vital for serving 4300 groups with custom Visa and MasterCards. These premium customers want good service, and they want it now. MBNA was one of the first in the industry to make service representatives available 24 hours per day. Furthermore, MBNA continually monitors its own performance using 15 measures, many of them relating to speed of service. The phone must be picked up within two rings, incoming calls at the switchboard must be transferred within 21 seconds to the correct party, and customer address changes must be processed in one day. The company-wide goal on the 15 standards is 98.5 percent. That means, for example, that responses to credit-line inquiries will be answered in 30 minutes 98.5 percent of the time, and the phone will be answered within two rings 98.5 percent of the time. Results are posted daily on 60 scoreboards throughout the company. By placing the customer at the head of its organizational culture, MBNA is able to retain a remarkable 98 percent of its profitable customers, and its common stock price has increased 600 percent in five years.

Getting close to the customer is important, but some difficult questions must be asked along the way, as the Exercising Your Ethics box shows.

TRENDS IN PRODUCTIVITY AND QUALITY MANAGEMENT

4. Identify three trends in productivity and quality management, including *supply chain management*.

Intensified competition has stimulated new ideas regarding quality management. Among them are the international quality standards and the radical redesign of business processes to improve products. A third trend emphasizes gains in productivity and service quality through supply chain management.

EXERCISING YOUR ETHICS

Calculating the Cost of Conscience

The Situation

Product quality and cost affect every firm's reputation and profitability as well as the satisfaction of customers. This exercise will expose you to some ethical considerations that pertain to certain cost and service decisions that must be made by operations managers.

The Dilemma

As director of quality for a major appliance manufacturer, Ruth was reporting to the executive committee on the results of a recent program for correcting problems with a newly redesigned rotary compressor that the company had recently begun putting in its refrigerators. After receiving several customer complaints, the quality lab and the engineering department had determined that some of the new compressor units ran more loudly than expected. Some remedial action was needed. One option was simply waiting until customers complained and responding to each complaint if and when it occurred. Ruth, however, had decided that this approach was inconsistent with the company's policy of offering the highest quality in the industry. Deciding that the firm's reputation called for a proactive, "pro-quality" approach, Ruth had initiated a program for contacting all customers who had purchased refrigerators containing the new compressor.

Unfortunately, her "quality-and-customers-first" policy was expensive. Local service representatives had to phone every customer in each area of the country, make appointments for home visits, and replace original compressors with a newer model. But because replacement time was only one-half hour, customers were hardly inconvenienced, and food stayed refrigerated without interruption. Customer response to the replacement program was overwhelmingly favourable.

Near the end of Ruth's report, an executive vice president was overheard to comment, "Ruth's program has cost this company $400 million in service expenses." Two weeks later, Ruth was fired.

Questions for Discussion

1. What are the underlying ethical issues in this situation?
2. What are the respective roles of profits, obligations to customers, and employee considerations for the firm in this situation?
3. Suppose you were an employee who realized that your company was selling defective appliances. Suppose that the cost of correction might put the firm out of business. What would you do?

ISO 9000:2000 and ISO 14000

After the terrorist attacks in the U.S. in 2001, the U.S. Transportation Security Administration embarked on a mission to prevent terrorist attacks on U.S transportation systems. A unit known as AAR-500 was given responsibility for bolstering security at American airports. AAR-500 recognized a major quality problem: the need to train and certify individual employees to perform specific tasks in a revamped screening system. To train 28 000 new airport security personnel, AAR-500 turned to international quality standards that had been applied successfully in private service businesses. To instill public confidence in the new screening system, AAR-500 also adopted the principle of independent third-party certification of the system.[17]

Both the training and certification systems were based on the world-class standards of **ISO 9000**—a certification program attesting to the fact that a factory, a laboratory, or an office has met the rigorous quality management requirements set by the International Organization for Standardization. ISO 9000 (pronounced *ICE-o nine thousand*) originated in Europe to standardize materials received from suppliers in such high-technology industries as electronics, chemicals, and aviation. Today, more than 140 countries have adopted ISO 9000 as a national standard. More than 400 000 certificates have been issued in 160 countries.[18]

ISO 9000
Program certifying that a factory, laboratory, or office has met the quality management standards of the International Organization for Standardization.

The latest version, *ISO 9000:2000*, indicates that it was revised in 2000. Revised standards allow firms to show that they follow documented procedures for testing products, training workers, keeping records, and fixing defects. To become certified, companies must document the procedures followed by workers during every stage of production. The purpose is to ensure that a manufacturer's product is exactly the same today as it was yesterday and as it will be tomorrow. Ideally, standardized processes would ensure that goods are produced at the same level of quality even if all employees were replaced by a new set of workers.

ISO 14000
Certification program attesting to the fact that a factory, laboratory, or office has improved environmental performance.

The **ISO 14000** program certifies improvements in *environmental* performance. Extending the ISO approach into the arena of environmental protection and hazardous waste management, ISO 14000 requires a firm to develop an *environmental management system (EMS)*: a plan documenting how the company has acted to improve its performance in using resources (such as raw materials) and in managing pollution. A company must not only identify hazardous wastes that it expects to create, but it must also stipulate plans for treatment and disposal. ISO 14000 covers practices in environmental labelling—the use of such terms as *energy efficient* and *recyclable*—and assesses the total environmental impact of the firm's products, not just from manufacturing, but also from use and disposal.

Process Re-engineering

Every business consists of *processes*—activities that it performs regularly and routinely in conducting business. Examples abound: receiving and storing materials from suppliers, billing patients for medical treatment, filing insurance claims for auto accidents, inspecting property for termites, opening chequing accounts for new customers, filling customer orders from internet sales. Any business process can add value and customer satisfaction by performing processes well. By the same token, any business can disappoint customers and irritate business partners by managing them poorly.

business process re-engineering
Redesigning of business processes to improve performance, quality, and productivity.

Business process re-engineering focuses on improving both the productivity and quality of business processes—rethinking each step of an organization's operations by starting from scratch. *Re-engineering* is the fundamental rethinking and radical redesign of business processes to achieve dramatic improvements in measures of performance, such as cost, quality, service, and speed.[19] The calling-services company GTE, for example, found that its over-the-phone service was not user-friendly for customers wanting to correct service or billing problems. To provide fast, accurate one-stop service, GTE re-engineered the whole service process by improving equipment, retraining employees, and connecting software to formerly inaccessible corporate databases.

GTE (Verizon)
www.gte.com

The Re-engineering Process

Figure 12.5 shows the six steps involved in the re-engineering process. It starts with a statement of the benefits envisioned for customers and the company and then flows logically through the next five steps:

1. Identify the business activity that will be changed.
2. Evaluate information and human resources to see if they can meet the requirements for change.
3. Diagnose the current process to identify its strengths and weaknesses.
4. Create the new process design.
5. Implement the new design.

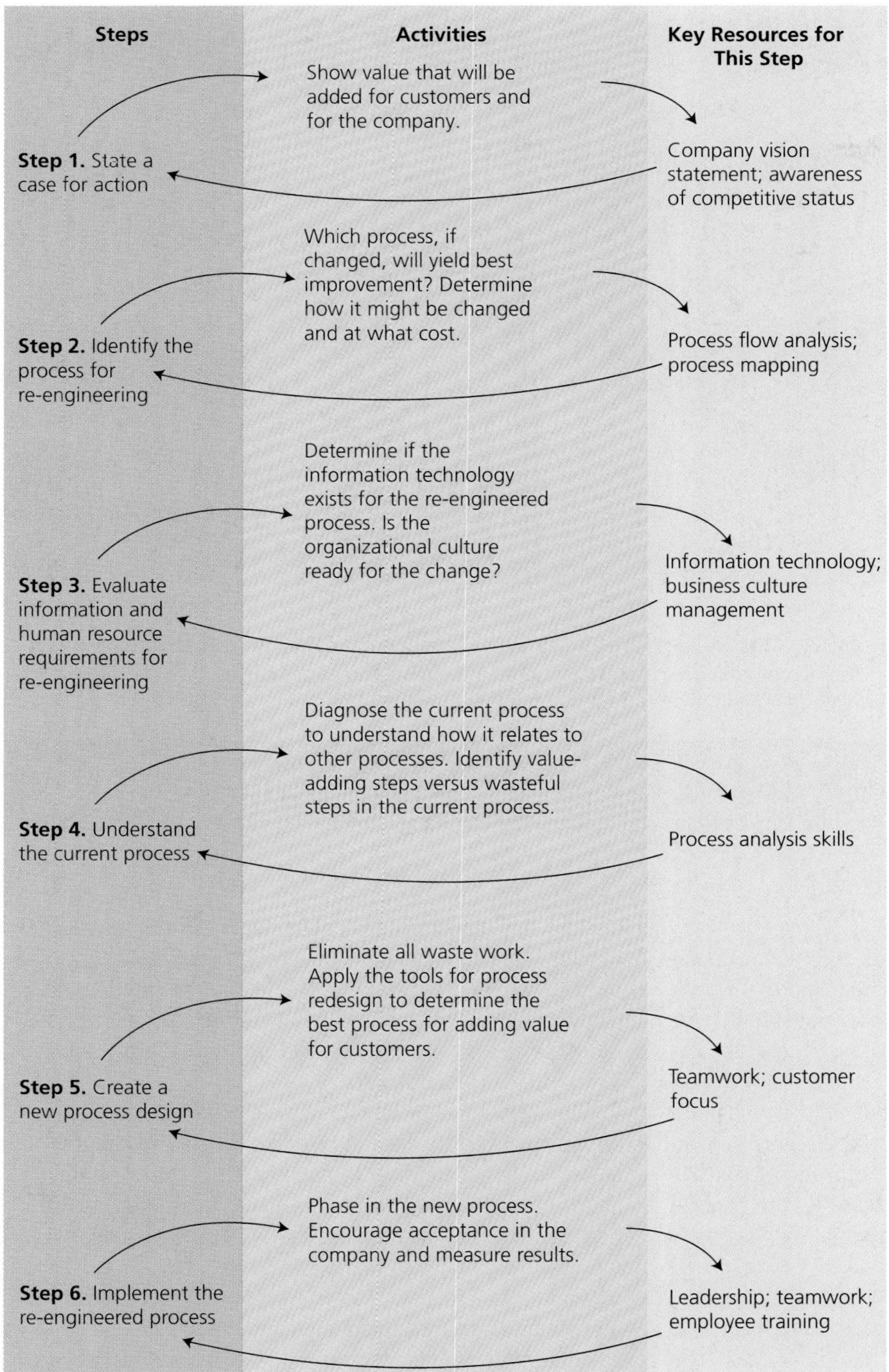

Figure 12.5
Re-engineering process.

As you can see, re-engineering is a broad undertaking that requires know-how in technical matters, depends on leadership and management skills, and calls upon knowledge about customer needs and how well they are being met by the company and its competition. The bottom line in every re-engineering process is adopting a company-wide customer-first philosophy. Redesign is guided by a desire to improve operations so that goods and services are produced at the lowest possible cost and at the highest value for the customer.

Seagate Technology, a maker of computer hard drives, used to build everything itself—disks, motors for spinning disks, and tracking mechanisms for reading and writing on disks. But it needed factories in Malaysia, Ireland, and the U.S., each with its own supplies of inventory. Seagate wasn't flexible enough to respond to changes required by customers until it teamed up with a consulting firm called DesignShop and figured out how to reorganize itself. Now, company-wide operations are run by a computer-based planning system, the supplier list has been slashed, and even important components are being outsourced.

But as the Wired World box shows, a company may have difficulty convincing employees to work in ways that give the highest value to the customer.

IT'S A WIRED WORLD

Selling the Idea of a Culture Shift

When a firm decides to trade in its traditional operations for high-tech processes, there's more involved than just financial and technical considerations. Consider, for example, a company with successful sales procedures established long before today's electronic-sales processes were available. What problems does it face in moving from its established (and highly personalized) sales process into the realm of internet sales?

That's the issue at Mercury Marine, the market leader in recreational boat engines. With various choices of engine types, horsepower ratings, and "salt water" versus "blue water" options, Mercury sells about 400 different outboard engines and enjoys a substantial market share in both the Canadian and the U.S. markets. Sales are even better for inboard engines and stern drives, where Mercury's market share is over 70 percent. Needless to say, Mercury's $1.4 billion annual sales are vital to its parent company, Brunswick Corp.

Mercury's markets consist of two kinds of customers:

1. Outboard motors are sold mainly to distributors and boat dealers, who resell them
2. Inboard engines and stern drives are sold to boat builders

In addition to its current person-to-person selling process, Mercury wants to sell motors to outboard dealers and boat builders over the internet. In other words, Mercury wants to use technology as a competitive weapon by making it easier for customers to do business with Mercury. Internet access can increase sales productivity and promote better service quality for customers.

So what's the problem? Resistance from the sales department. With person-to-person sales, Mercury's salespeople get to know the customers, and up-selling and cross-selling are important sales tools that would be threatened by the changeover. Currently, salespeople can explain to customers the advantages of upgrading to a more expensive motor (up-selling), thus increasing Mercury's sales revenues. They can also talk customers into buying some of Mercury's complementary products (cross-selling), such as propellers, inflatable boats, and other accessories, which increases sales revenues. Admits Geof Storm, Mercury's chief information officer: "There are a lot of culture changes involved when tightening the supply chain." Although the sales department still prefers the more personal touch, some of its resistance is being overcome—Mercury has decided to proceed with internet sales of inboard engines to boat builders. However, until the climate changes further, the decision to sell outboards on the internet is likely to remain on hold.

Adding Value Through Supply Chains

Managers sometimes forget that a company belongs to a network of firms that must coordinate their activities. The term *supply chain* refers to the group of companies and stream of activities that work together to create a product. A **supply chain** for any product is the flow of information, materials, and services that starts with raw-materials suppliers and continues through other stages in the operations process until the product reaches the end customer.[20]

supply chain
Flow of information, materials, and services that starts with raw-materials suppliers and continues through other stages in the operations process until the product reaches the end customer.

Figure 12.6 shows the supply chain activities involved in supplying baked goods to consumers. Each stage adds value for the final customer. Although a typical beginning stage is product design, our bakery example begins with raw materials (grain harvested from the farm). It also includes additional storage and transportation activities, factory operations for baking and wrapping, and distribution to retailers. Each stage depends on the others for success in getting fresh-baked goods to consumers.

The Supply Chain Strategy

Traditional strategies assume that companies are managed as individual firms rather than as members of a coordinated supply system. Supply chain strategy is based on the idea that members of the chain, working as a coordinated unit, will gain competitive advantage. Although each company looks out for its own interests, it works closely with suppliers and customers throughout the chain. Everyone focuses on the entire chain of relationships rather than on just the next stage in the chain.[21]

A traditionally managed bakery, for example, would focus simply on getting production inputs from flour millers and paper suppliers and supplying baked goods to distributors. Unfortunately, this approach limits the chain's performance and doesn't allow for possible improvements when activities are more carefully coordinated. Supply chain management can improve performance and, as a result, provide higher quality at lower prices.

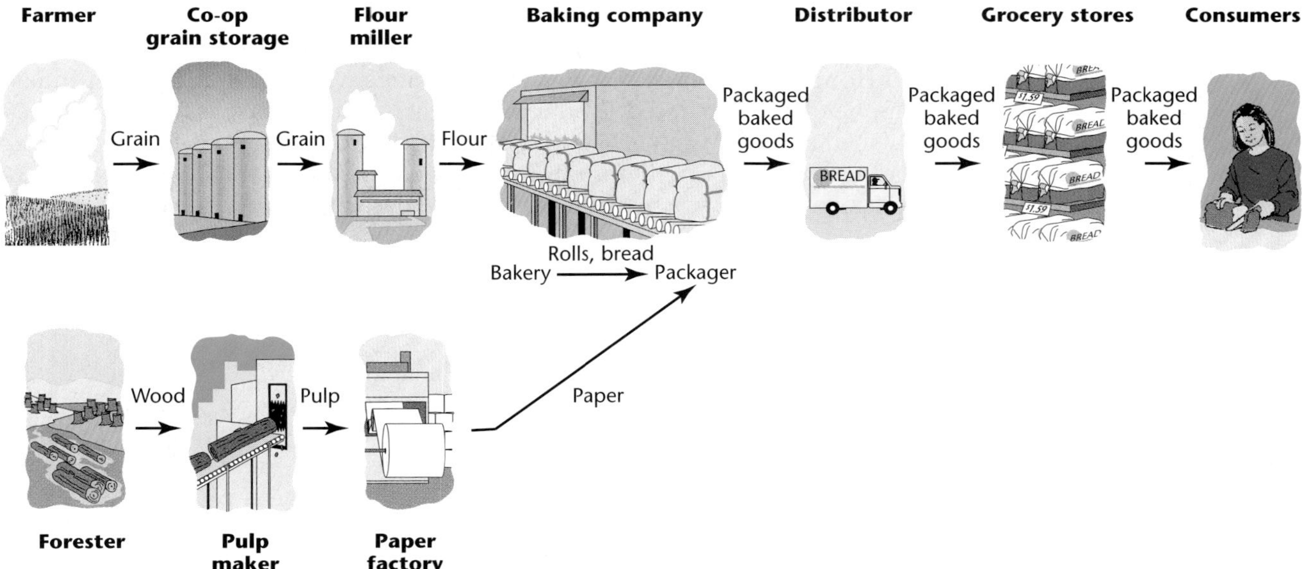

Figure 12.6
Supply chain for baked goods.

Supply Chain Management

supply chain management (SCM)
Principle of looking at the chain as a whole to improve the overall flow through the system.

Supply chain management (SCM) looks at the chain as a whole to improve the overall flow through a system composed of companies working together. Because customers ultimately get better value, SCM gains competitive advantage for each supply-chain member.[22] Dell Computer's supply chain, for example, improves performance by allowing people to share information. Dell shares long-term production plans and up-to-the-minute sales data with suppliers via the internet. The process starts when customer orders are automatically translated into updated production schedules on the factory floor. These schedules are used not only by operations managers at Dell but also by such parts suppliers as Sony, which adjust their own production and shipping activities to better meet Dell's production needs. In turn, parts suppliers' updated schedules are transmitted to their materials suppliers, and so on. As Dell's requirements change, suppliers synchronize their schedules to produce the right materials and parts efficiently.

Because the smooth flow of accurate information along the chain reduces unwanted inventories, avoids delays, and cuts supply times, materials move faster to business customers and individual consumers. For both, the efficiency of SCM means faster deliveries and lower costs than customers could get if each member acted only according to its own operations requirements.

Re-engineering Supply Chains for Better Results

By lowering costs, speeding up service, or coordinating flows of information and materials, process improvements and re-engineering often improve supply chains. Consider, for example, the supply chain for transistor radios. For a long time, Li & Fung, the largest export trading company in Hong Kong, imported radio components made in both the United States and Asia. After supplying these components to a Hong Kong assembly factory, Li & Fung shipped finished radios to U.S. and European distributors. Gradually, however, rising wage rates in Hong Kong became a threat to Li & Fung. Increases in assembly costs would cut into its profits and market share. The company thus re-engineered its supply chain. First, it added a new stage. It created little kits—plastic bags filled with all the components needed to make a radio. Second, one supply-chain link was replaced. The kits were shipped to a new assembler in southern China instead of to the old Hong Kong factory. Finally, another stage was added. After the Chinese supplier had completed the labour-intensive, low-wage assembly process, finished radios were shipped back to Hong Kong for final inspection and testing by Li & Fung before being shipped to customers. The result: lower prices and increased business for companies throughout the chain.

PRODUCTIVITY AND QUALITY AS COMPETITIVE TOOLS

5. Discuss four strategies that companies used to improve productivity and quality.

A company's ability to compete by improving productivity and quality depends on participation by all parts of the firm. And total firm involvement stems from having company-wide strategies that we consider in this section: the company's willingness to invest in innovation, its long-run perspective on its goals, its concern for the quality of work life, and the improving of its service operations.

Invest in Innovation and Technology

Many firms that have continued to invest in innovative technology have enjoyed rising productivity and rising incomes. For example, while Steinway & Sons' piano factory is just as concerned as ever about maintaining the highest quality in its products, it's using newer technology to help the woodworkers do their jobs more efficiently and precisely. "It still takes us a year to craft one of these things," says Steinway president Bruce Stevens, "but technology is assisting us in making more precise parts that our people can assemble. It's helping us create a better instrument."[23]

Steinway & Sons
www.steinway.com

Adopt a Long-Run Perspective

Instead of emphasizing short-run results, many quality-oriented firms are committed to a long-run perspective for **continuous improvement**—the ongoing commitment to improving products and processes, step by step, in pursuit of ever-increasing customer satisfaction. Motorola is a good example (see Concluding Case 12-1 on p. 428). Its Six Sigma program originally set a target of 3.4 defects per million parts. By 1996, Motorola was thinking in terms of errors per *billion* rather than errors per million quality levels. As of 2000, the company's production-monitoring software (called Manufacturing Intellitrak) had helped to reduce errors in some applications to two defects per billion parts.[24]

continuous improvement
The ongoing commitment to improve products and processes, step by step, in pursuit of ever-increasing customer satisfaction.

Emphasize Quality of Work Life

The products and services of businesses represent such a large part of total national output that the well-being and participation of their workers is central to improving national productivity. How can firms make their employees' jobs more challenging and interesting? Many companies are enhancing workers' physical and mental health through recreational facilities, counselling services, and other programs. In addition, more and more firms have started programs to empower and train employees.

Operators at Dofasco monitor the production of steel products with the latest in high-tech monitoring equipment.

Employee Empowerment

Many firms are replacing the environments of yesterday, based on the principle of management-directed mass production, with worker-oriented environments that foster loyalty, teamwork, and commitment. Trident Precision Manufacturing has a program for full employee involvement. Over 95 percent of employee recommendations for process improvements have been accepted since the program started. As a result, employee turnover has fallen from 41 percent to less than 5 percent. Sales per employee have more than doubled.

employee empowerment

Principle that all employees are valuable contributors to a firm's business and should be entrusted with decisions regarding their work.

Firms using this approach have found success in the concept of **employee empowerment**—the principle that all employees are valuable contributors to a business and should be entrusted with certain decisions regarding their work. The Hampton Inns motel chain, for example, initiated a program of refunds to customers who were dissatisfied with their stays for any reason. Managers were pleased, and the refund policy created far more additional business than it cost. A surprise bonus was the increased morale when employees—everyone from front-desk personnel to maids—were empowered to grant refunds. With greater participation and job satisfaction, employee turnover was reduced to less than one-half its previous level. Such confidence in employee involvement contrasts sharply with the traditional belief that managers are the primary source of decision making and problem solving.

Employee Training

Employee involvement is effective when it is implemented with preparation and intelligence. *Training* is a key method of preparing employees for productivity-improvement programs. In fact, a recent American Management Association survey found a direct relationship between training and greater productivity profitability: Firms that increased training activities were 66 percent more likely to report improved productivity and three times more likely to report increased profits. Moreover, after training, waste diminishes and quality increases. Finally, team training not only teaches employees to work in groups, but it also acquaints them more fully with the company's markets and operations.[25]

Improve the Service Sector

As important as employee attitudes are to goods production, they are even more crucial to service production, since employees often *are* the service. The service sector has grown rapidly, but this growth has often come at a cost of high inefficiency. Many newly created service jobs have not been streamlined. Some companies operate effectively, but many others are very inefficient, dragging down overall productivity. As new companies enter these markets, however, the increased need to compete should eventually force service producers to operate more productively.

Quality begins with listening to customers to determine what services they want. Companies in the temporary-services industry, for example, have long emphasized the needs of clients for clerical and light-industrial employees. More recently, however, temp services have realized the need for highly skilled, specialized temps such as nurses, accountants, and scientists.

In trying to offer more satisfactory services, many providers have discovered five criteria that customers use to judge service quality:[26]

- *Reliability:* Perform the service as promised, both accurately and on time.
- *Responsiveness:* Be willing to help customers promptly.

- *Assurance:* Maintain knowledgeable and courteous employees who will earn the trust and confidence of customers.
- *Empathy:* Provide caring, individualized attention to customers.
- *Tangibles:* Maintain a pleasing appearance of personnel, materials, and facilities.

SUMMARY OF LEARNING OBJECTIVES

1. **Describe the connection between *productivity* and *quality*.** *Productivity* is a measure of economic performance; it compares how much is produced with the resources used to produce it. *Quality* is a product's fitness for use. However, an emphasis solely on productivity or solely on quality is not enough. Profitable competition in today's business world demands high levels of both productivity and quality.

2. **Understand the importance of increasing productivity.** It is important that Canadian business firms increase their rate of productivity growth so that they can be competitive in world markets. As the productivity of Canadian business firms increases, they will be able to produce a greater quantity of goods without using more resources.

3. **Identify the activities involved in *total quality management*, and describe six tools that companies can use to achieve it.** *Total quality management (TQM)* (sometimes called *quality assurance*) includes all the activities necessary for getting high-quality goods and services into the marketplace. The strategic approach to TQM begins with customer focus. It includes methods for determining what customers want and then directing all the company's resources toward satisfying those wants and needs. Total participation is mandatory, and TQM is more than part-time. It demands continuous improvement of products, services, and improvement in all of the company's internal processes, such as accounting, delivery, billing, and information flows. Six tools that are used to achieve TQM include (1) *Value-added analysis* (the evaluation of all work activities, material flows, and paperwork to determine the value that they add for customers); (2) *Statistical process control (SPC)* (methods by which employees can gather data and analyze variations in production activities to determine when adjustments are needed); (3) *Quality/cost studies* (identify a firm's current costs but also reveal areas with the largest cost-savings potential); (4) *quality improvement (QI)* teams (groups of employees from various work areas who meet regularly to define, analyze, and solve common production problems); (5) *benchmarking* (improving business products or procedures by comparing them to either the firm's own past performance or the best practices of others); and (6) *getting closer to the customer* (know what customers want in the products they consume).

4. **Identify three trends in productivity and quality management, including *supply chain management*.** (1) *ISO 9000* is a certification program attesting to the fact that a factory, a laboratory, or an office has met the rigorous quality-management requirements set by the International Organization for Standardization. It allows firms to show that they follow documented procedures for testing products, training workers, keeping records, and fixing product defects. *ISO 14000* certifies improvements in *environmental* performance. (2) *Business process*

re-engineering focuses on improving both the productivity and quality of business processes—rethinking each step of an organization's operations by starting from scratch. *Re-engineering* is the fundamental rethinking and redesign of processes to achieve dramatic improvements in measures of performance. (3) The *supply chain* refers to the group of companies and stream of activities that operate together to create a product. Traditional strategies assume that companies are managed as individual firms rather than as members of a coordinated supply chain. *Supply chain management (SCM)* looks at the chain as a whole to improve the overall flow through a system composed of companies working together. Because customers ultimately get better value, SCM gives chain members a competitive advantage.

5. **Discuss four strategies that companies use to improve productivity and quality.** (1) *Invest in innovation and technology:* Many firms that have continued to invest in innovative technology have enjoyed rising productivity and rising incomes. Increasingly, investments in the internet and information technology are rising, with new applications in every major industry. (2) *Adopt a long-run perspective:* Many quality-oriented firms are committed to long-term efforts at continuous improvement: the ongoing commitment to improving products and processes, step by step, in pursuit of ever-increasing customer satisfaction. (3) *Emphasize quality of work life:* Business products and services represent such a large part of total national output that the well-being and participation of workers is crucial to improving national productivity. (4) *Improve the service sector:* As important as employee attitude is to goods production, it is even more crucial to service production, where employees often are the service. In trying to offer more satisfactory services, many companies have discovered five criteria that customers use to judge service quality: *reliability, responsiveness, assurance, empathy,* and *tangibles.*

KEY TERMS

benchmarking, 413
business process reengineering, 416
competitive product analysis, 409
continuous improvement, 421
control chart, 412
employee empowerment, 422
external failures, 413
internal failures, 412
ISO 14000, 416
ISO 9000, 415
labour productivity, 403
level of productivity, 404
performance quality, 408
process variation, 411
productivity, 402
quality improvement (QI) team, 413
quality ownership, 409
quality reliability, 408
quality, 402
quality/cost study, 412
statistical process control (SPC), 410
supply chain management (SCM), 420
supply chain, 419
total quality management (TQM), 407
value-added analysis, 410

QUESTIONS AND EXERCISES

Questions for Review

1. What is the relationship between productivity and quality?

2. Why do labour unions care about the productivity of an industry?

3. What part do inputs and outputs play in the basic equation for measuring labour productivity?

4. What activities are involved in total quality management?

5. What are the essential steps in process engineering?

Questions for Analysis

6. How would you suggest that benchmarking be used to increase productivity in the service sector?

7. Why is employee empowerment essential to successful quality improvement teams?

8. Why is high productivity in the service sector so difficult to achieve?

Application Exercises

9. Using a local company as an example, show how you would conduct a quality/cost study. Identify the cost categories and give some examples of the costs in each category. Which categories do you expect to have the highest and lowest costs? Why?

10. Select a company of interest to you and consider the suggestions for competing that are detailed in this chapter. Which of these suggestions apply to this company? What additional suggestions would you make to help this company improve its overall quality and productivity?

BUILDING YOUR BUSINESS SKILLS

Making Your Benchmark in the Business World

Goal

To encourage students to understand ways in which benchmarking can improve quality and productivity

Situation

As the director of maintenance for a regional airline, you are disturbed to learn that the cost of maintaining your 100-plane fleet is skyrocketing. A major factor is repair time; when maintenance or repairs are required, work often proceeds slowly. As a result, additional aircraft must be pressed into service to meet the schedule. To address the problem, you decide to use a powerful total quality management tool called benchmarking: You will approach your problem by studying ways in which other companies have successfully managed similar problems. Your goal is to apply the best practices to your own maintenance and repair operation.

Method

Step 1

Working with three or four other students, choose your benchmarking target from among the following choices:

The maintenance and repair operations of a competing airline

The pit crew operations of an Indianapolis 500 race car team

The maintenance and repair operations of a nationwide trucking company

Write a memo explaining the reasons for your choice.

Step 2

Write a list of benchmarking questions that will help you learn the best practices of your targeted company. Your goal is to ask questions that will help you improve your own operation. These questions will be asked during on-site visits.

Step 3

As part of a benchmarking project, you will be dealing with your counterparts in other companies. You have a responsibility to prepare for these encounters, and you must remember that what you learn during the exchange process is privileged information. Given these requirements, describe the steps that you would take before your first on-site visit, and outline your benchmarking code of ethics.

Follow-Up Questions

1. Why is benchmarking an important method for improving quality?
2. Why did you make your benchmarking choice? Explain why the company you selected holds more promise than other companies in helping you solve your internal maintenance problems.
3. What kind of information would help you improve the efficiency of your operations? Are you interested in management information, technical information, or both?
4. In an age of heightened competition, why do you think companies are willing to benchmark with each other?

CRAFTING YOUR BUSINESS PLAN

Ensuring Structural Integrity

The Purpose of the Assignment

1. To acquaint students, within the framework of Business PlanPro (BPP) software package, with some of the quality considerations that a sample firm addresses in developing its business plan.
2. To demonstrate how customers' expectations of service quality, the role of quality in a firm's business strategy, the dimensions of service quality, and methods for ensuring quality can be integrated as components of the BPP planning environment.

Assignment

After reading Chapter 12 in the textbook, open the BPP software and look for information about plans for service quality as they apply to a sample firm called StructureAll Ltd., a consulting firm that specializes in structural engineering services. To find StructureAll, do the following:

Open the Business PlanPro. If it asks if you want to "create a new business plan" or to "open an existing plan," select "create a new business plan" (even though you are not going to create a plan at this time). You will then be taken to the Business PlanPro EasyPlan Wizard. On the screen, click on the option entitled **Research It**. You will then be presented with a new list of options, including **Sample Plan Browser**. After clicking on the **Sample Plan Browser**, go down the alphabetical list of sample plans, and double-click on **Engineering—Consulting**, which is the location for StructureAll Ltd. The screen at which you are now looking is the introduction page to the StructureAll business plan. Next, scroll down this page until you reach the **Table of Contents** for the StructureAll business plan.

Now respond to the following items:

1. Who are StructureAll's customers? What do you suppose they expect from the quality of services received from StructureAll? What aspects of quality are important to them? [Sites to see in BPP for this item: On the **Table of Contents** page, click on **1.0 Executive Summary.** Then click on each of the following in turn: **1.2 Mission, 1.3 Keys to Success, 3.1 Service Description, 3.2 Competitive Comparison, 4.0 Market Analysis Summary,** and **4.1 Market Segmentation.**]
2. What role does quality play in StructureAll's business strategy? [Sites to see in BPP: On the **Table of Contents** page, click on each of the following in turn: **1.2 Mission, 1.3 Keys to Success,** and **3.2 Competitive Comparison.**]
3. What are some specific dimensions of quality in the services offered by StructureAll? [Sites to see in BPP: From the **Table of Contents page**, click on **1.0 Executive Summary**. Then click on each of the following in turn: **3.1 Service Description** and **3.2 Competitive Comparison.**]
4. What are some of the procedures, methods, and policies by which StructureAll ensures quality? [Sites to see in BPP: On the **Table of Contents** page, click on **3.1 Service Description**. After returning to the **Table of Contents** page, click on each of the following in turn: **3.4 Fulfillment, 3.5 Technology, 3.6 Future Services,** and **5.1 Competitive Edge.**]

VIDEO EXERCISE

Glowing with Quality: Liquid Lab

Learning Objectives

The purpose of this video is to help you:

1. Consider the quality decisions made by a manufacturing firm.
2. Understand how quality and productivity affect a company's global competitiveness.
3. Discuss the ways in which a company can use quality assurance to produce high-quality goods that satisfy customers.

Synopsis

The CEO of Liquid Lab invented and patented the process for making the glowing multi-chambered neon necklaces that you can buy at sporting events, amusement parks, and concerts. As the patents expired, however, Liquid Lab faced an onslaught of competition from global rivals selling cheaper versions, especially manufacturers in China, where lower labour costs make production less expensive. Through years of experience, Liquid Lab has found ways to boost productivity while maintaining high quality. To compete on the basis of quality, the company rigorously tests materials and accommodates the few customers who want to return necklaces.

Discussion Questions

1. *For analysis:* Why must Liquid Lab pay close attention to performance quality as well as to quality reliability?
2. *For analysis:* If Liquid Lab never sells directly to consumers, how can it determine what they want in terms of product quality?
3. *For application:* How might Liquid Lab use external benchmarking to identify ideas for reducing returns due to breakage in transit?
4. *For application:* Which total quality management tools might Liquid Lab use to find opportunities for cost-cutting while maintaining high quality?
5. *For debate:* Given the increase in competition, should Liquid Lab seek ISO 9000 certification to showcase its emphasis on quality? Support your position.

Online Exploration

Use your favourite search engine (such as **www.ixquick.com**) to search for sites promoting "Made in America" products. What kinds of quality claims do these sites make about their products? How do they back up those claims? Do any sites explain their quality-assurance techniques or compare their American-made products to those of foreign competitors? What kind of information would persuade you, as a consumer, to buy from a U.S.-based company if competing foreign-made products cost much less?

EXPLORING THE NET

In Pursuit of Quality

Throughout this chapter we have examined both the elements and tools used in total quality management. For an organization to be quality focused, all of its members, and especially its managers, must be quality focused. Such a focus requires a manager to constantly update her/his skills. The Manitoba Quality Network (QNET) (**www.qnet.mb.ca**) is an organization that can provide some assistance. QNET is an organization that offers resources, services, and activities designed to assist individuals (and organizations) in their pursuit of quality and organizational effectiveness.

1. One of the quality and excellence frameworks used by QNET is The Canadian Quality Criteria Framework for Business Excellence. For which type of organization(s) should this framework be used? What areas of an organization does this framework encompass?
2. What is "lean thinking"? Which company is responsible for starting off the lean thinking trend?
3. What is workplace wellness? How does workplace wellness tie into total quality management?

Concluding Case 12-1

Marshalling the Arts of Quality

If it's been around since the 1980s, it's too old-fashioned to be much good, right? Not necessarily. With companies seeking better products, happier customers, greater productivity, and higher profits, the Six Sigma concept of quality is just hitting its stride. Introduced at Motorola Inc. in 1987, Six Sigma works continuously to capture, measure, and eliminate defects in every company-wide process—from financial transactions and accounting practices, to R&D and production processes, to marketing and human resources activities. It strives for excellence in every facet of the business. Materials from suppliers, for example, must contain no defects; press releases should contain purely valid information; and, of course, customers should get error-free products and get them on time.

Is error-free performance really possible? Before Six Sigma came along, most companies could only dream about it. But Motorola and other leading Six Sigma firms have made the dream an organizational reality. Today, the gates of higher quality are defended by so-called Six Sigma Black Belts—trained experts who implement quality-improvement programs, project by project and company by company. Before Black Belts, companies thought about quality in terms of percentages of defective-free parts or defective parts per hundred. In approaching perfection, Motorola's Six Sigma target of 99.99966 percent, or 3.4 defects per *million*, renders previous measures virtually meaningless.

What does such a target mean in practical terms? Consider the fact that a company deals with customers, both internally and externally, through thousands of activities and transactions. There are thus thousands of opportunities to make mistakes (which Motorola calls *defectives*). Six Sigma strives to reduce defectives to 3.4 *per million opportunities*. In fact, Motorola plans to reach the point at which it makes sense only to count defectives per *billion*.

Naturally, Six Sigma has caught the eye of other quality-conscious companies. 3M, for instance, has made Six Sigma its top priority. "Our other initiatives," says 3M director of marketing David Powell, "are shorter-term, tied to our three-year strategic plan, but Six Sigma is forever. It's the umbrella." The International Society of Six Sigma Professionals has grown to more than 8000 members from over 600 companies. In addition to Fortune 500 firms, hundreds of other organizations are in various stages of instituting Six Sigma. Why? It is a proven fact that as quality goes up, other benefits soon follow—not the least of which are lower costs and higher productivity.

Getting started, however, can mean major organizational changes. The driving force behind Six Sigma is a customer focus aimed ultimately at bottom-line results. Motorola, explains Senior VP Dennis Sester, "views quality from a customer perspective, meaning we have only one opportunity per each product we deliver to favourably impact a customer. If the product doesn't meet expectations, we run the risk of losing that customer. It isn't enough to simply meet industry averages—every single product that reaches a customer should exhibit a uniform standard of quality."

Other major proponents of Six Sigma include former General Electric CEO Jack Welch and CEO Lawrence Bossidy of Honeywell (formerly Allied-Signal). Early adopters were primarily manufacturing firms, such as Ford, DuPont, and Dow Chemical. But as more and more Black Belts arrived on the scene, Six Sigma methods began spreading to service firms such as CitiGroup, McKesson HBOC, American Express, and GE Capital Services. In fact, it's gaining strength precisely at a time when service-sector firms need a boost in quality and productivity.

First Data Resources of Omaha, Nebraska, is a recent convert to Six Sigma. The firm ships six million credit cards a month from its warehouse for such customers as MasterCard and Visa. Workers personalize each card, attach a label with an activation phone number, and prepare envelopes and paper inserts for mailing. Finally, they ensure that each card is mailed to the right person. One misplaced card can cost hundreds of thousands of dollars. Warehouse accuracy, then, is crucial.

Back in 1999, First Data had no system for tracking quality, and warehousing activities were in disarray. The possibility of expensive mistakes was high. "With the volumes we handle and the amount of material we put out, we could say we are at 99.99 percent," says materials manager Cliff Radcliff, "but the banks are saying that's not good enough."

Aiming for zero tolerance for errors, the warehouse inventory team implemented Six Sigma and improved quality by 40 percent in 2000, followed by another 30 to 40 percent in 2001. Warehouse accuracy is now 99.9969 percent, and although the figure is not quite Six Sigma quality, Radcliff was *Warehousing Management's* 2001 Peak Performer. "By going to Six Sigma," explains Radcliff, "we can't rest on our laurels at 99.99, and it makes it easier to focus in on where we need to go to get to near perfection."

How can Radcliff earn a Six-Sigma Black Belt? As in the disciplined self-defence system, candidates begin as novices and work their way through the ranks. They earn promotions by demonstrating skills, passing proficiency tests, and getting on-the-job results. Some companies have their own training and testing programs, but industry-wide acceptance usually goes to certification programs sponsored by professional associations, most notably the American Society for Quality (ASQ). The ASQ eLearning Center offers a series of web-based Six Sigma courses, beginning with "Introduction to Six Sigma" (an overview of method, concepts, and language) and culminating in "Black Belt Certification Review" (a preparatory course for the certification exam). Interactive courses emphasize practice exercises and online assessments.

Many firms insist that Six Sigma deliver certain financial benefits. In 2002, for example, the financial-services firm Conseco Services LLC expects to see $100 million in first-year savings by improving customer-service and internal operations. Spearheaded by a team of 170 Six Sigma professionals, Conseco's program started with 230 projects designed to reduce customer dissatisfaction and ineffective processes. Project teams are led by 145 Black Belts in sales, finance, information technology, and customer service. Twenty-three Master Black Belts spend four weeks training other Black Belts and then oversee projects and coach the project leaders. After two weeks of training, 18 Green Belts serve as project leaders.

Of course, having a title means being responsible for results: Each Black Belt has an annual cost-saving goal of $500 000 and is required to prove that project savings are real by submitting results to the Finance Department. "We don't want just the Black Belts saying a project will save a million dollars," says Ruth Fattori, executive VP for process and productivity. "We want Finance saying it....We don't want Black Belts giving us the theoretical savings; we want Finance to tell us what in fact we have saved."

Questions for Discussion

1. Of what significance is leadership for a Six Sigma program? Give some examples of ways that leadership might affect such a program.
2. List some of the main elements in training for a Six Sigma Black Belt. What skills does such training teach?
3. Consider the kinds of improvements made by companies cited in this case. Did improvements relate merely to quality, merely to productivity, or to both? Explain.
4. Do you believe that Six Sigma programs have a better chance of success in manufacturing or service firms? Explain.
5. Suppose you want to start a Six Sigma program for a company. Identify the managerial skills that will be most important for a successful program. Explain why you chose those particular skills over certain others. ◆

Concluding Case 12-2 CC

Where the Rubber Hits the Road

In the summer of 2000, Bridgestone/Firestone Inc. announced that it was recalling 6.5 million Wilderness AT and Firestone ATX tires. Most of these had been installed as original equipment on Ford Explorer SUVs. Hints that there were problems with Firestone tires began cropping up in the early 1990s. There was often a pattern: the tread of a rear tire on a heavily loaded Explorer travelling at high speed separated, and the vehicle swerved out of control and flipped over. These reports generally came from warmer parts of the United States (California, Arizona, Texas, and Florida), and from Venezuela and the Persian Gulf. The investigation revealed that about 100 people had been killed in these kinds of accidents in the United States, and about 50 people had been killed overseas.

Transport Canada launched a probe to determine if there were similar problems in Canada, but no hard evidence of tire defects was found, even though as many as 500 000 of these tires are on vehicles in Canada. One million Firestone tires were eventually recalled in Canada.

Both Ford and Firestone tested the suspect tires, but no particular problems were found. In public, the two companies portrayed themselves as working together to solve the mystery, but there was tension behind the scenes. Ford noted that it didn't have any problem with blown tires or rollovers with any of its vehicles except Explorers, and those vehicles had the suspect Firestone tires on them. Firestone, on the other hand, accused Ford of contributing to the problem by recommending tire pressures of only 26 pounds when Firestone recommended 30 pounds of pressure. (Lower tire pressure improves the ride of a vehicle, but under-inflation leads to heat build-up and an increased chance of tire failure.) Firestone also claimed that Ford had made design changes in the Explorer that increased the chance that rear tires would fail. Firestone noted that the suspect tires were on other types of vehicles and that the tires on those vehicles had not failed.

What was the problem? Experts thought there were several possibilities: (1) the quality of the material that was used to make the glue that holds the tire's steel belts together wasn't up to standard; (2) the raw materials that were used to make the glue weren't sufficiently well mixed; (3) the steel wires that form the belts may have rusted due to high humidity during manufacturing; (4) the tire wasn't properly cured (vulcanized); (5) too much adhesive was used to bond the steel belts to the rubber, and this actually made the treads more likely to separate.

After a four-month investigation, Bridgestone/Firestone finally concluded that there were quality problems at its plant in Decatur, Illinois. Apparently, that plant did not properly process the rubber that was used to make the tires. However, Firestone also put some of the blame on the Ford Explorer, arguing that higher load limits and lower inflation pressures were part of the problem.

Firestone spent $450 million recalling the problem tires. In the aftermath of the crisis, Firestone's sales plummeted 40 percent, and its stock lost half its value. What is Bridgestone/Firestone doing now to recover its public image? Several steps have been taken. A new senior vice-president was appointed and given a mandate to impose strict production standards and fix operating problems at the company's U.S. unit.

In May 2001, Bridgestone/Firestone abruptly ended its 100-year relationship as a tire supplier to Ford, business that had been worth about $350 million a year to Firestone. But Firestone was not taking all the blame. It accused Ford of refusing to acknowledge safety concerns about the Ford Explorer, and provided evidence showing that Ford Explorers were 10 times more likely to roll over after a tread separation than were Ford Rangers, even though both vehicles were equipped with the same Firestone tires. Ford countered by saying that the Ford Explorer has been near the top of the vehicle safety rankings for years, and that Ford Explorers equipped with Goodyear tires haven't had any tread separation problems.

The loss of business with Ford meant that Firestone would have to rebuild the market share it had lost. To do so, it launched an aggressive advertising campaign that emphasized the Bridgestone name. In spite of all the bad publicity it had received, by early 2003, Firestone had lost only two percentage points of its market share. Part of the reason for this was the failure of Goodyear Tire to capitalize on Firestone's public relations problems.

A new method of examining product performance data was introduced to address the criticism that the company was unaware it had quality problems with its tires. U.S. factories were brought more into line with the higher standards of Bridgestone's Japanese operation. Quality assurance controls were introduced that will make it easier for information about tire failures to be shared throughout the company.

Questions for Discussion

1. What is total quality management? To what extent was total quality management pursued at Bridgestone/Firestone? At Ford?
2. What are the various tools for quality assurance that are available? Which ones are appropriate for helping to resolve this problem?
3. The plant where the faulty tires were made was ISO-certified. How could problems like these arise at such a plant?
4. How is quality a competitive tool?
5. Can Firestone gets its quality image back? How? ◆

CHAPTER 13 Managing Information Systems and Communication Technology

After reading this chapter, you should be able to:

1. Explain why businesses must manage *information* and show how computer systems and communication technologies have revolutionized *information management.*
2. Identify and briefly describe three elements of *data communication networks*—the internet, the World Wide Web, and intranets.
3. Describe five *new options for organizational design* that have emerged from the rapid growth of information technologies.
4. Discuss different information-systems *applications* that are available for users at various organizational levels.
5. Identify and briefly describe the *main elements of an information system.*

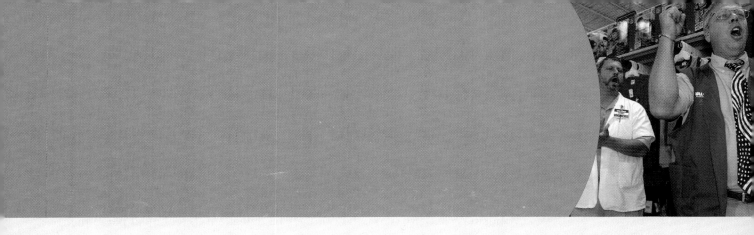

It's All About Information

With sales of $220 billion annually, Wal-Mart has taken the retail world by storm. How has Wal-Mart accomplished this feat? One reason is Wal-Mart's policy of everyday low prices. Of course, if you simply lower prices without also lowering costs, you will go broke. So Wal-Mart offers low prices, but is also obsessive about lowering its costs. Wal-Mart's policy of having everyday low prices (and no sales) means that it doesn't have to cope with big swings in demand for products that other stores do when they put on big promotions. That makes it easier for Wal-Mart to ensure that a given product is always available to customers.

A second reason is product availability. When consumers go to a store to buy something, they can become very unhappy if the product is not available. Wal-Mart is a master at providing products that are virtually always in stock. Its customers are therefore more confident that they can find what they want at Wal-Mart.

But exactly how has Wal-Mart been able to provide these two critical things to customers? The answer is a space-age information system that keeps track of every single item sold in every Wal-Mart store around the world. The system puts into practice founder Sam Walton's belief that to be successful in retailing, you have to keep an eye on what is selling at each retail store, and why it is selling.

The information system works like this. When a customer in a Wal-Mart store buys a certain item, its Uniform Product Code (UPC) is scanned. The information is first beamed to Wal-Mart's own satellite, and then to Wal-Mart's Computer Data Processing Center in Bentonville, Arkansas. All sales are recorded and put into the database that allows Wal-Mart to track the shopping and spending patterns of its customers. In each retail store, Wal-Mart employees can get the same information by reading the UPC bar code with their Telxon wireless device.

Next, orders are sent to suppliers when restocking of an item is needed. These suppliers respond by shipping the required products to the appropriate Wal-Mart distribution centre. Supplier trucks pull up on one side of the building to unload, and Wal-Mart trucks load up on the other side. Each Wal-Mart store that the distribution centre serves has its own loading door. Once loaded, the trucks race off to the local Wal-Mart to deliver the goods to re-supply the shelves.

The distribution centre in Bentonville, Arkansas, is typical. The centre employs 900 people who move 100 000 different items from unloading to loading dock in just a few hours. It contains 20 miles of conveyor belts that snake around the 28-acre building. The centre serves 116 of Wal-Mart's 3000 stores (other distribution centres serve between 85 and 120 stores each).

Wal-Mart's information system not only keeps the shelves of Wal-Mart stores stocked, it also helps to cut costs because products are not sent to individual stores until they are actually needed. It is really just-in-time retailing. The information system also provides an added benefit: it allows Wal-Mart's suppliers to better plan their production schedules because they know almost instantaneously what is going on at the retail level. ◆

INFORMATION MANAGEMENT: AN OVERVIEW

1. Explain why businesses must manage *information* and show how computer systems and communication technologies have revolutionized *information management*.

As the opening case shows, today's businesses rely on information management in ways that we could not foresee as recently as just a decade ago. Managers now turn to digital technology as an integral part of organizational resources and as a means of conducting everyday business. Every major firm's business activities—designing services, ensuring product delivery and cash flow, evaluating personnel, creating advertising—is linked to information systems. Thus the management of information systems is a core business activity that can no longer be delegated to technical personnel.

information manager
The manager responsible for the activities needed to generate, analyze, and disseminate information that a company needs to make good decisions.

information management
An internal operation that arranges the firm's information resources to support business performance and outcomes.

Most businesses regard their information as a private resource—an asset that they plan, develop, and protect. It is not surprising, then, that companies have **information managers**, just as they have production, marketing, and finance managers. **Information management** is an internal operation that arranges the firm's information resources to support business performance and outcomes.

To find the information they need to make critical decisions, managers must often sift through a virtual avalanche of reports, memos, magazines, and phone calls. Thus the question that faces so many businesses today is how to get useful information to the right people at the right time. In this section, we will explore the ways in which companies manage information with computers and related information technologies.

Data Versus Information

data
Raw facts and figures.

information
A meaningful, useful interpretation of data.

Although business people often complain that they receive too much information, they usually mean that they get too much **data**—raw facts and figures. **Information** is usefully interpreted data (see Figure 13.1).

Consider the following data:

- fifty million tubes of toothpaste were sold last year

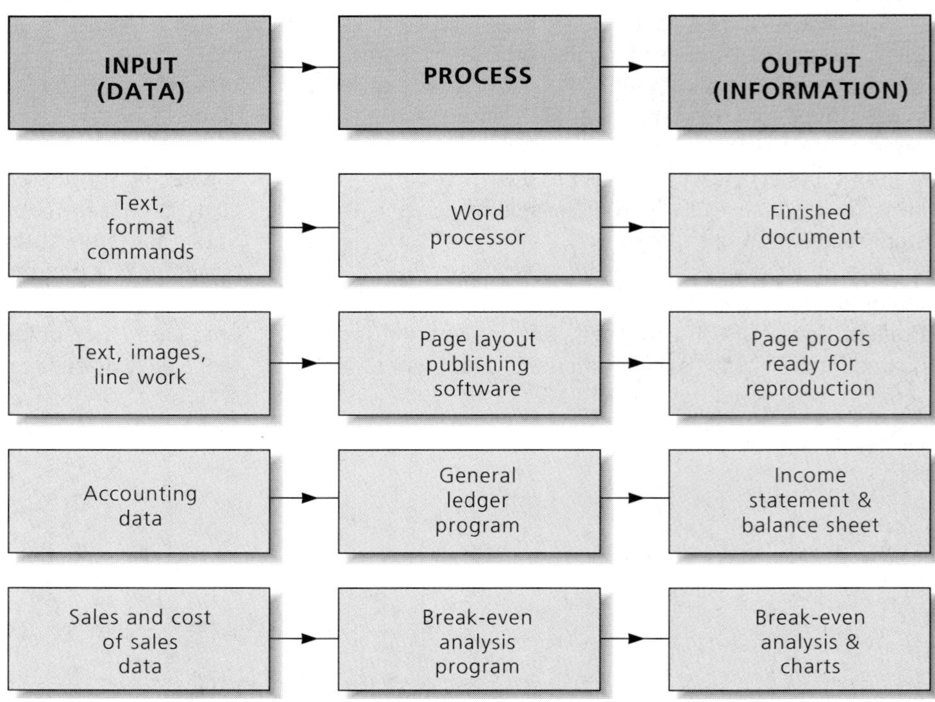

Figure 13.1
From data to information and knowledge.

- the birth rate is rising slowly
- forty-four million tubes of toothpaste were sold the year before last
- advertising for toothpaste increased 23 percent last year
- a major dentists' group recently came out in favour of brushing three times a day.

If all these data can be put together in a meaningful way, they may produce information about what sells toothpaste and whether manufacturers should build new plants. The challenge for businesses is to turn a flood of data into information and to manage that information to their best advantage.

Information Systems

One response to this challenge has been the growth of the **information system (IS)**—a system for transforming raw data into information and transmitting it for use in decision making. IS managers must first determine what information is needed. Then they must gather the data and apply the technology to convert data into information. They must also control the flow of information so that it goes only to those people who need it.[1]

information systems (IS)
An organized method of transforming data into information that can be used for decision making.

Supplied information varies according to such factors as the functional areas in which people work (say, accounting or marketing) and their management levels. At all levels, informational quality depends on an organization's technological resources and on the people who manage them. In the following section, we discuss the evolution of information-processing technology and then describe the information requirements of today's organization.

NEW BUSINESS TECHNOLOGIES IN THE INFORMATION AGE

Employees at every level in the organization, ranging from operational specialists to the top executive, use information systems to improve perform-

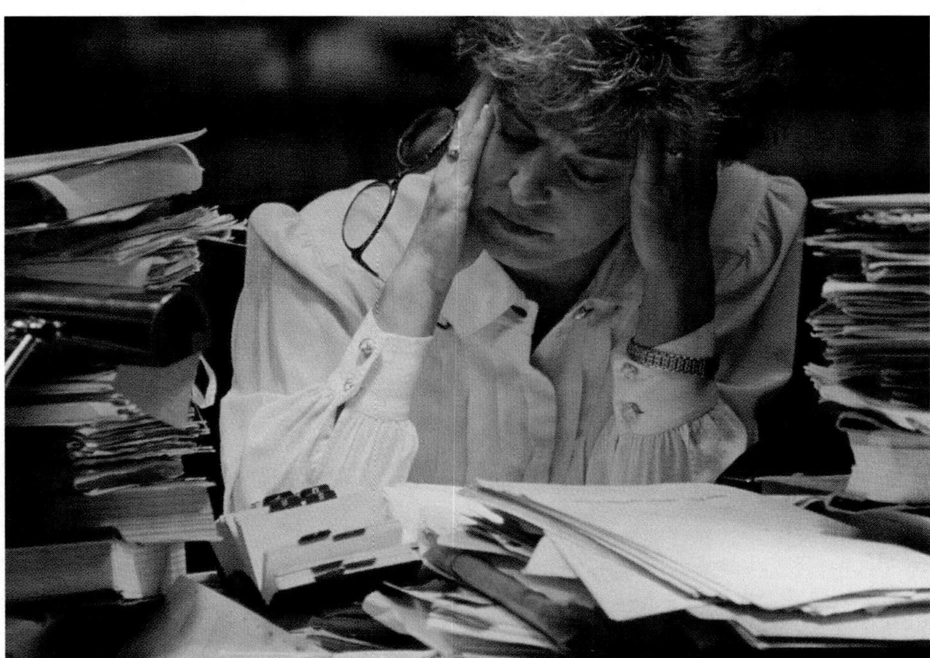

Information systems are becoming increasingly important as managers try to cope with the flood of data they are confronted with each day.

ance. Information systems assist in scheduling day-to-day vehicle trips, evaluating prospective employees, and formulating the firm's business strategy. The widening role of IS results from rapid developments in electronic technologies that allow faster and broader flows of information and communications. As we shall see, however, the networked enterprise is more than a firm equipped with the latest technology. Technology has inspired new organizational designs, innovative relationships with other organizations, and new management processes for improved competitiveness.

The top 10 information technology companies in Canada are listed in Table 13.1.

The Expanding Scope of Information Systems

The relationship between information systems and organizations is among the fastest-changing aspects of business today. At one time, IS applications were narrow in scope and technically focused—processing payroll data, simulating new engineering designs, compiling advertising expenditures. But as you can see in Figure 13.2, managers soon began using IS systems not merely to solve technical problems, but to analyze management problems, especially for control purposes—applying quality-control standards to production, comparing costs against budgeted amounts, keeping records on employee absences and turnover.

Today, information systems are also crucial in planning. Managers routinely use IS to decide on a firm's products and markets for the next 5 to 10 years. The same database that helps marketing analyze demographics for millions of customers is also used for such higher-level applications as financial planning, managing materials flows, and setting up electronic funds transfers with suppliers and customers.

Another basic change in organizations is an increased interdependence between a company's business strategy and its IS. Today, the choice of a business strategy—say, to be the low-cost provider or the most flexible provider or the high-quality provider—requires an information system that can support that strategy. As Figure 13.3 shows, a given strategy will fail if a system's software, hardware, and other components are not integrated to support it.

Electronic Business and Communications Technologies

The pressures to maintain better communications and information systems are increasing as competition intensifies and as organizations expand into global and ebusiness operations. Firms like Ralston Purina Co., for

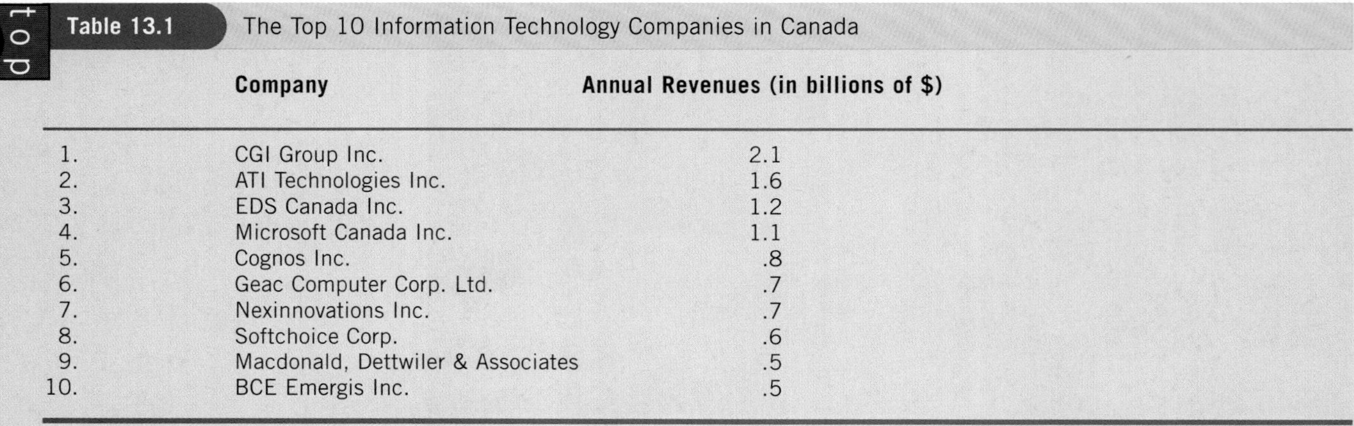

Table 13.1 The Top 10 Information Technology Companies in Canada

	Company	Annual Revenues (in billions of $)
1.	CGI Group Inc.	2.1
2.	ATI Technologies Inc.	1.6
3.	EDS Canada Inc.	1.2
4.	Microsoft Canada Inc.	1.1
5.	Cognos Inc.	.8
6.	Geac Computer Corp. Ltd.	.7
7.	Nexinnovations Inc.	.7
8.	Softchoice Corp.	.6
9.	Macdonald, Dettwiler & Associates	.5
10.	BCE Emergis Inc.	.5

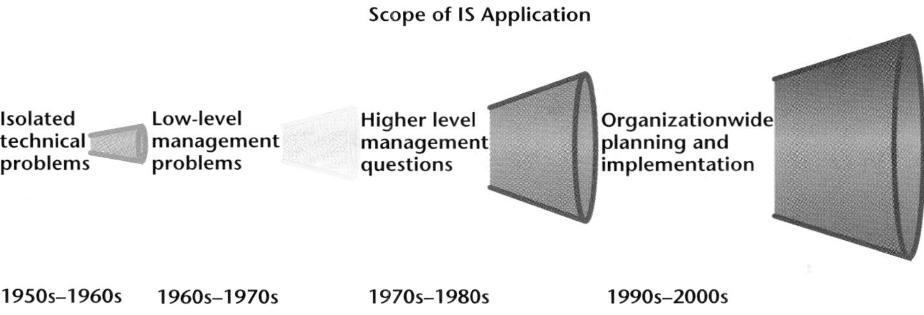

Figure 13.2
Evolution of IS scope.

instance, need instantaneous communications among managers in those countries in which they either sell products or buy raw materials, including Canada, China, Columbia, Brazil, and the United States. New electronic information technologies and more advanced data communication networks are meeting the needs of such companies.

Electronic Information Technologies

Electronic information technologies (EIT) are IS applications based on telecommunications technologies. EITs use networks of appliances or devices (such as cellphones and computers) to communicate information by electronic means. EITs enhance the performance and productivity of general business activities by performing two functions:

electronic information technologies (EIT)
IS applications based on telecommunications technologies.

1. Providing coordination and communication within the firm
2. Speeding up transactions with other firms

Six of the most widely used innovations in today's digital business systems are as follows:

- The **fax machine** (short for *facsimile machine*) can transmit and receive digitized images of text documents, drawings, and photographs over telephone lines in a matter of seconds, thus permitting written communication over long distances. Fax machines are popular with both large and small firms because of speed and low cost.

fax machine
A machine that can quickly transmit a copy of documents or graphics over telephone lines.

- **Voice mail** refers to a computer-based system for receiving and delivering incoming telephone calls. Incoming calls are never missed because a voice responds to the caller, invites a message, and stores it for later retrieval. A company with voice mail networks each employee's phone for receiving, storing, and forwarding calls.

voice mail
A computer-based system for receiving and delivering incoming telephone calls.

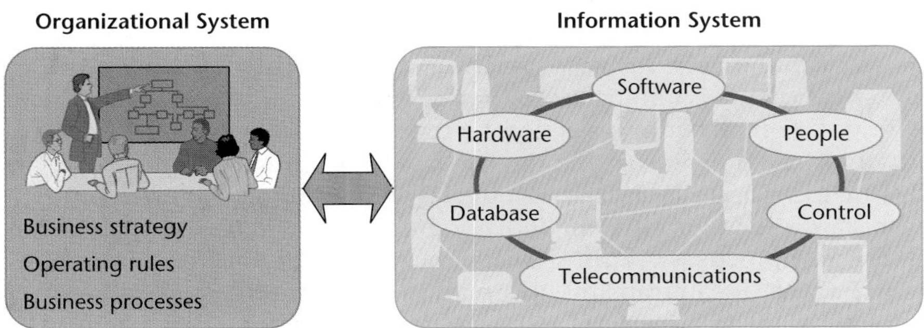

Figure 13.3
Aligning business strategy and the IS.

electronic mail (email) system
Electronic transmission of letters, reports, and other information between computers.

- An **electronic mail** (or **email**) **system** electronically transmits letters, reports, and other information between computers, whether in the same building or in another country. It is also used for voice transmission and for sending graphics and videos from one computer to another. Email thus substitutes for the flood of paper and telephone calls that threatens to engulf many offices.

electronic conferencing
Allows people to communicate simultaneously from different locations via telephone, video, or mail group software.

- **Electronic conferencing** is becoming increasingly popular because it eliminates travel and thus saves money. It is also increasingly accessible and speeds up information flows. Teleconferencing allows people to communicate simultaneously from various locations via email group software or via telephone. One form of electronic conferencing, *data conferencing*, allows people in remote locations to work simultaneously on the same document. Working as a team, they can modify part of a database, revise a marketing plan, or draft a press release. Another form of electronic conferencing, *videoconferencing*, allows participants to see one another on a video screen while the teleconference is in progress.

groupware
A system that allows two or more individuals to communicate electronically between desktop PCs.

- Collaborative work by teams and other groups is facilitated by **groupware**—software that connects members of the group for email distribution, electronic meetings, message storing, appointments and schedules, and group writing. Linked by groupware, members can work together on their own desktop computers even if they are remotely located. Groupware is especially useful when members work together regularly and rely on intensive information sharing. Groupware products include Lotus Development Corp.'s Lotus Notes, Netscape Communicator, and Microsoft's Office 2000 software suite, which uses web technology.
- Information from outside a company can be linked to its electronic network and the information can be made available at every workstation. Commercial *digital information services* provide online information for both special-purpose and general topics. Lexis, for example, is specifically a source for legal-research information. In contrast, America Online offers a variety of business information as well as general-interest information.

Data Communication Networks

2. Identify and briefly describe three elements of *data communication networks*—the internet, the World Wide Web, and intranets.

Data communication networks carry streams of digital data (electronic messages, documents, and other forms of video and sound) back and forth quickly and economically on telecommunication systems. The most prominent network, the internet, and its companion system, the World Wide Web, have emerged as powerful communication technologies. Let's look a little more closely at each of these networks.

data communication networks
Global networks that permit users to send electronic messages quickly and economically.

internet
A gigantic network of networks that serves millions of computers, offers information on business, science, and government, and provides communication flows among more than 170 000 separate networks around the world.

The Internet. The **internet**—the largest public data communications network—is a gigantic network of networks that serves millions of computers, offers information on business, science, and government, and provides communication flows among more than 170 000 separate networks around the world. Originally commissioned by the U.S. military as a communication tool for use during war, the internet allows personal computers in virtually any location to be linked together. The internet has gained in popularity because it is an efficient tool for information retrieval that makes available an immense wealth of academic, technical, and business information. Because it can transmit information quickly and at low cost—lower than long-distance phone service, postal delivery, and overnight delivery—the internet has also become the most important email system in the world. For thousands of businesses, therefore, the internet has joined—and is even

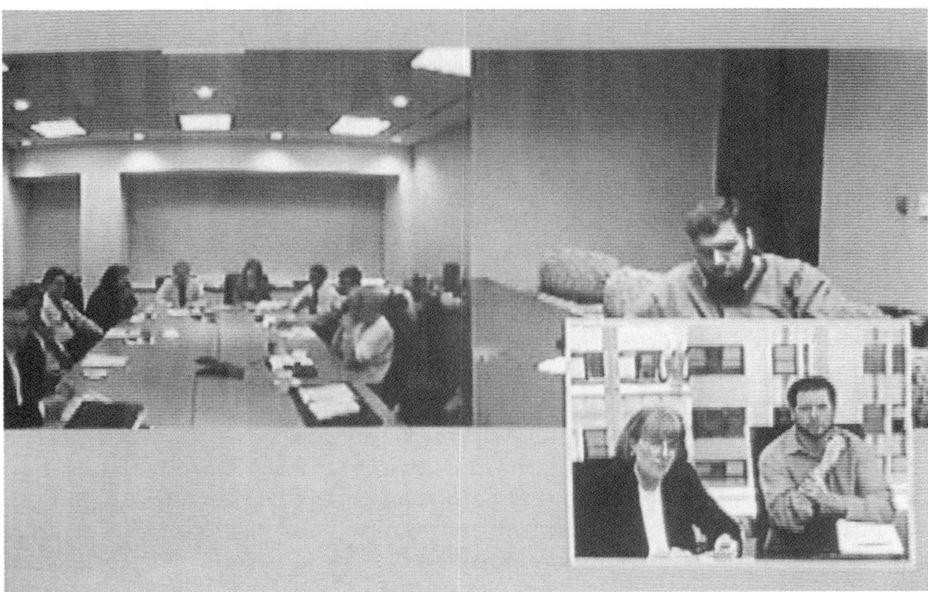

A sluggish economy and a reluctance to fly are hampering business travel. More and more companies are turning to videoconferencing as a means of holding meetings among people located in distant places. The technology allows people to analyze each other's body language in addition to what they are saying. This helps create richer communication.

replacing—the telephone, fax machine, and express mail as a standard means of communication.

Although individuals cannot connect directly to the internet, for small monthly usage fees they can subscribe to the internet via an **internet service provider (ISP)**, such as Prodigy, America Online, or Earthlink. An ISP is a commercial firm that maintains a permanent connection to the internet and sells temporary connections to subscribers.[2] By 2002, more than 700 million net users were active in more than 180 countries. In North America, more than 95 million users over the age of 16 were on the net every day. Its power to change the way business is conducted has been amply demonstrated in both large and small firms.

internet service provider (ISP)

A commercial firm that maintains a permanent connection to the internet and sells temporary connections to subscribers.

The World Wide Web. Thanks to the **World Wide Web** (or simply "the web"), the internet is easy to use and allows users around the world to communicate electronically with little effort. The World Wide Web is a system with universally accepted standards for storing, retrieving, formatting, and

World Wide Web

A system with universally accepted standards for storing, retrieving, formatting, and displaying information on the internet.

displaying information.[3] It provides the "common language" that enables us to "surf" the internet and makes the internet available to a general audience, rather than merely to technical users such as computer programmers. To access a website, for example, the user must specify the *Uniform Resource Locator (URL)* that points to the resource's unique address on the Web. For example, Air Canada's URL is **www.aircanada.ca**—a designation that specifies the storage location of Air Canada's webpages.

Each website opens with a *home page*—a screen display that welcomes the visitor with a greeting that may include graphics, sound, and visual enhancements introducing the user to the site. Additional *pages* provide details on the sponsor's products and explain how to contact help in using the site. Often, sites furnish URLs for related websites that the user can link to by simply pointing and clicking. The person responsible for maintaining an organization's website is usually called a *webmaster*. Large websites use dedicated work stations—large computers—known as **web servers** that are customized for managing, maintaining, and supporting websites.

web servers
Dedicated work stations—large computers—that are customized for managing, maintaining, and supporting websites.

With hundreds of thousands of new webpages appearing each day, cyberspace is now serving up billions of pages of publicly accessible information. Sorting through this maze would be frustrating and inefficient without access to a web **browser**—software that enables the user to access information on the web. A browser runs on the user's PC and supports the graphics and linking capabilities needed to navigate the web. Netscape Navigator has enjoyed as much as an 80 percent market share, although its dominance is now being challenged by other browsers, including its own Netscape Communicator and Microsoft's Internet Explorer.

browser
Software that enables a user to access information on the web.

The web browser offers additional tools—website directories and search engines—for navigating the web. Among the most successful cyberspace enterprises are companies such as Yahoo! that maintain free-to-use **directories** of web content. When Yahoo! is notified about new websites, it classifies them in its directory. The user enters one or two key words (for example, "compact disc") and the directory responds by retrieving a list of websites with titles containing those words.

directories
Features that help people find the content they want on the web. The user types in key words and the directory retrieves a list of web sites with titles containing those words.

In contrast to a directory, a **search engine** will search cyberspace's millions of webpages without pre-classifying them into a directory. It searches for webpages that contain the same words as the user's search terms. Then it displays addresses for those that come closest to matching, those that are the next closest, and so on. A search engine, such as AltaVista or Lycos, may respond to more than 10 million inquiries per day. It is thus no surprise that both directories and search engines are packed with paid ads.

search engine
Software for searching webpages that does not pre-classify them into a directory.

Intranets. The success of the internet has led some companies to extend its technology internally, so that employees can browse internal websites containing information. These private networks, or **intranets**, are accessible only to employees via entry through electronic firewalls. **Firewalls** are hardware and software security systems that are not accessible to outsiders.[4] Compaq Computer Corp.'s intranet allows employees to shuffle their retirement savings among various investment funds. Ford Motor Co.'s intranet connects 120 000 workstations in Asia, Europe, and the United States to thousands of Ford websites containing private information on Ford activities in production, engineering, distribution, and marketing. Sharing such information has helped reduce the lead time for getting new models into production from 36 to 24 months. The savings to Ford, of course, will be billions of dollars in inventory and fixed costs.[5]

intranet
A company's private network that is accessible only to employees via entry through electronic firewalls.

firewall
Hardware and software security systems that are not accessible to outsiders.

Extranets. Sometimes firms allow outsiders access to their intranets. These so-called **extranets** allow outsiders limited access to a firm's internal information system. The most common application allows buyers to enter the seller's system to see which products are available for sale and delivery,

extranet
A network that allows outsiders limited access to a firm's internal information system.

thus providing product-availability information quickly to outside buyers. Industrial suppliers, too, are often linked to their customers' intranets so that they can see planned production schedules and ready supplies as needed for customers' upcoming operations.

New Options for Organizational Design: The Networked Enterprise

3. Describe five *new options for organizational design* that have emerged from the rapid growth of information technologies.

The rapid growth of information technologies has changed the very structure of business organizations. We begin this section with a discussion of changes wrought by technology in the workforce and organizational structures of many organizations. We then examine ways in which electronic networks are contributing to greater flexibility in dealing with customers. After discussing the growing importance of collaboration in the workplace, we look at the ways in which information networks can help make the workplace independent of a company's physical location. Finally, we describe new management processes inspired by the availability of electronic networks.

Leaner Organizations

Information networks are leading to leaner companies with fewer employees and simpler organizational structures. Because today's networked firm can maintain information linkages among both employees and customers, more work can be accomplished with fewer people. As a bank customer, for example, you can dial into a 24-hour information system and find out your current balance from a digital voice. You no longer need bank tellers or phone operators. In the industrial sector, assembly workers at an IBM plant used to receive instructions from supervisors or special staff. Now instructions are delivered electronically to their workstations.

Widespread reductions in middle-management positions and the shrinkage of layers in organizational structure are possible because information networks now provide direct communications between the top managers and workers at lower levels. Electronic information networks are replacing the operating managers who formerly communicated company policies, procedures, or work instructions to lower-level employees.

More Flexible Operations

Electronic networks allow businesses to offer customers greater variety and faster delivery cycles. Products such as cellular phones, PCs, and audio systems can be custom-ordered, too, with your choice of features and options and next-day delivery. The principle is called **mass-customization**: although companies produce in large volumes, each unit features the unique variations and options that the customer prefers. As you can see in Figure 13.4, flexible production and fast delivery depend on an integrated network to coordinate all the transactions, activities, and process flows necessary to make quick adjustments in the production process. The ability to organize and store massive volumes of information is crucial, as are the electronic linkages between customers, manufacturers, materials suppliers, and shippers.

mass-customization
Producing large volumes of products or services, but giving customers the choice of features and options they want.

Increased Collaboration

Collaboration, not only among internal units but with outside firms as well, is on the rise because networked systems make it cheaper and easier to contact everyone, whether other employees or outside organizations. Aided by intranets, more companies are learning that complex problems can be

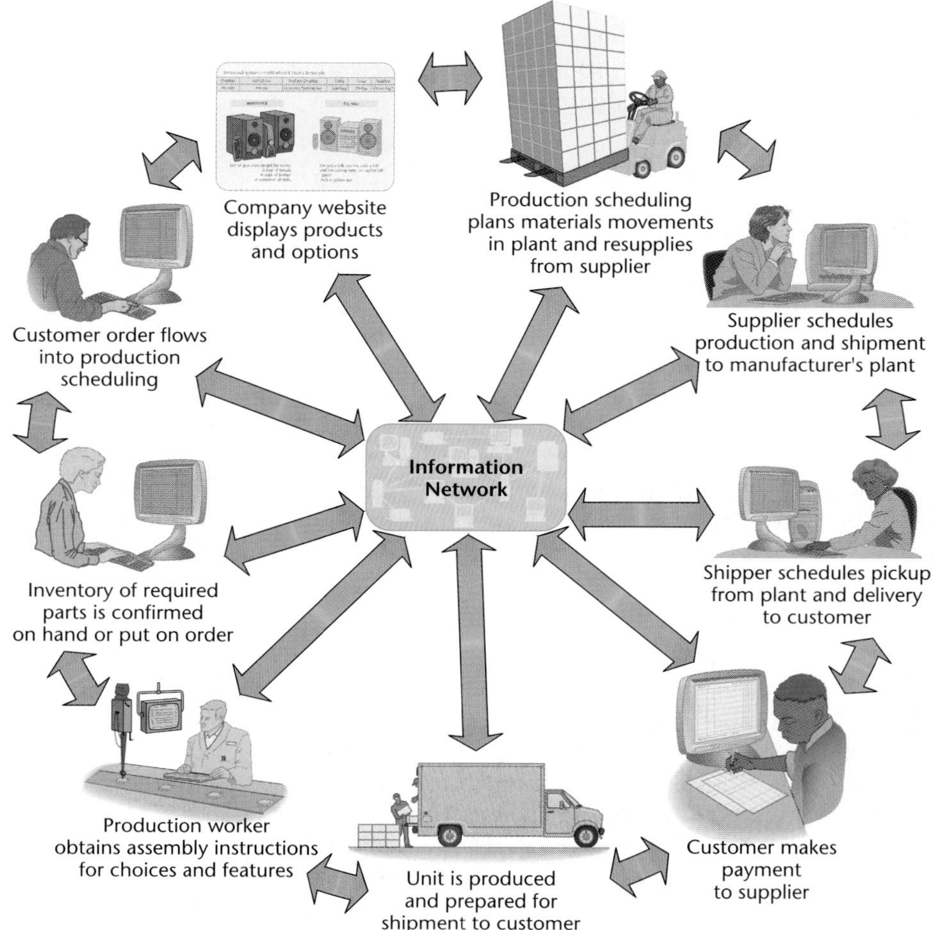

Figure 13.4
Networking for mass-customization.

solved better by means of collaboration, either in formal teams or through spontaneous interaction. In the new networked organization, decisions that were once the domain of individuals are now shared as both people and departments have become more interdependent. The design of new products, for example, was once an engineering responsibility. Now, in contrast, it can be a shared responsibility because so much information is accessible for evaluation from various perspectives. Marketing, finance, production, engineering, and purchasing can share their different stores of information and determine a best overall design.

Networking and the Virtual Company. Networked systems can also improve collaboration between organizations through the so-called *virtual company*. This can be a temporary team assembled by a single organization, but a virtual company can also be created by several allied firms.[6] Each contributes different skills and resources that collectively result in a competitive business that wouldn't be feasible for any one of them working alone. A company with marketing and promotional skills, for example, may team up with firms with expertise in warehousing and distribution, engineering, and production. Networking lets collaborators exchange ideas, plan strategy, share customer information, and otherwise coordinate efforts, even if their respective facilities are far apart.

Greater Independence of Company and Workplace

Geographic separation of the workplace from the company headquarters is more common than ever because of networked organizations. Employees no longer work only at the office or the factory, nor are all of a company's operations performed at one location. The sales manager for an advertising agency may visit the company office in Toronto once every two weeks, preferring instead to work over the firm's electronic network from her home office in Montreal. A medical researcher for the Calgary Clinic may work at a home office networked into the clinic's system.

A company's activities may also be geographically scattered but highly coordinated, thanks to a networked system. Many ebusinesses, for example, do not conduct any activities at one centralized location. When you order products from an internet storefront—say, a chair, a sofa, a table, and two lamps—the chair may come from a cooperating warehouse in Windsor and the lamps from a manufacturer in Toronto, while the sofa and table may be direct-shipped from two manufacturers in North Carolina. All of these activities are launched instantaneously by the customer's order and coordinated through the network, just as if all of them were being processed at one location.

Improved Management Processes

Networked systems have changed the very nature of the management process. The activities, methods, and procedures of today's manager differ significantly from those that were common just a few years ago. Once, for example, upper-level managers did not concern themselves with all the detailed information that filtered upward in the workplace. Why? Because it was expensive to gather and slow in coming and quickly became out of date. Workplace management was delegated to middle and first-line managers.

With networked systems, however, instantaneous information is accessible in a convenient and usable format. Consequently, more and more upper managers use it routinely for planning, leading, directing, and controlling operations. Today, a top manager can find out the current status of any customer order, inspect productivity statistics for each workstation, and analyze the delivery performance of any driver and vehicle. More importantly, managers can better coordinate company-wide performance. They can identify departments that are working well together and those that are creating bottlenecks.

Enterprise Resource Planning. One type of networked system is **enterprise resource planning (ERP)**—a large information system for integrating the activities of all of a company's units.[7] It is supported by one large database through which everyone shares the same information when any transaction occurs. The biggest supplier of commercial ERP packages is Germany's SAP AG, followed by Oracle. Hershey Foods uses the SAP system. It identifies the status of any order and traces its progress from order entry through customer delivery and receipt of payment. Progress and delays at intermediate stages—materials ordering, inventory availability, production scheduling, packaging, warehousing, distribution—can be checked continuously to determine which operations should be more closely coordinated with others to improve overall performance.

enterprise resource planning (ERP) *Large information systems for integrating all the activities of a company's business units.*

TYPES OF INFORMATION SYSTEMS

In a sense, the phrase *information system* may be a misnomer. It suggests that there is one system when, in fact, a firm's employees will have differ-

4. Discuss different information-systems *applications* that are available for users at various organizational levels.

ent interests, job responsibilities, and decision-making requirements. One information system cannot accommodate such a variety of information requirements. Instead, "the information system" is a complex of several information systems that share information while serving different levels of the organization, different departments, or different operations.

User Groups and System Requirements

knowledge workers
Employees whose jobs involve the use of information and knowledge as the raw materials of their work.

Four user groups, each with different system requirements, are identified in Figure 13.5, which also indicates the kinds of systems best suited to each user level. Among users we include **knowledge workers**—employees whose jobs involve the use of information and knowledge as the raw materials of their work. Knowledge workers are specialists, usually professionally trained and certified—engineers, scientists, information technology specialists, psychologists—who rely on information technology to design new products or create new business processes.

Managers at Different Levels

Because they work on different kinds of problems, top managers, middle managers, knowledge workers, and first-line managers have different information needs. First-line (or operational) managers, for example, need information to oversee the day-to-day details of their departments or projects. Knowledge workers need special information for conducting technical projects. Meanwhile, middle managers need summaries and analyses for setting intermediate and long-range goals for the departments or projects under their supervision. Finally, top management analyzes broader trends in the economy, the business environment, and overall company performance to conduct long-range planning for the entire organization.

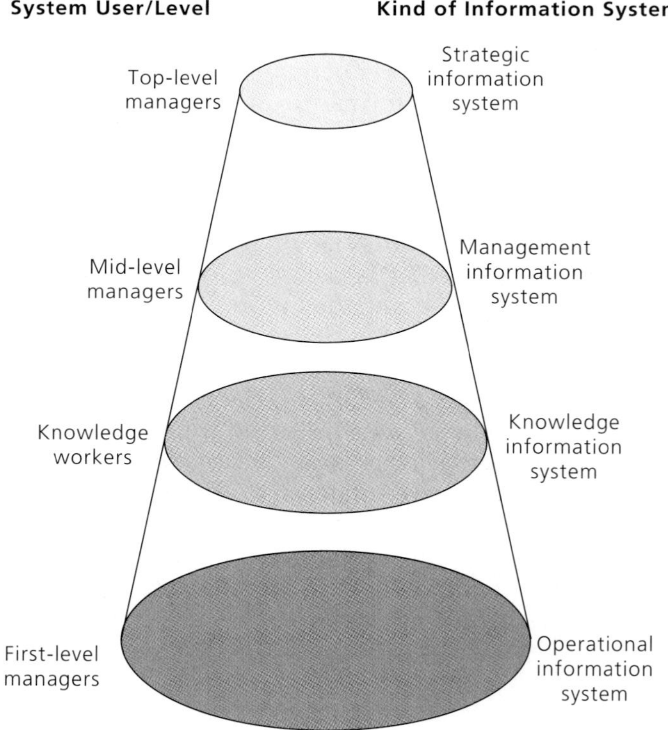

Figure 13.5
Matching users and systems.

Consider the various information needs of a flooring manufacturer. Sales managers (first-level managers) supervise salespeople, assign territories to the sales force, and handle customer service and delivery problems. They need current information on the sales and delivery of products: lists of incoming customer orders and daily delivery schedules to customers in their territories. Regional managers (middle managers) set sales quotas for each sales manager, prepare budgets, and plan staffing needs for the upcoming year. They need information on monthly sales by product and region. Knowledge workers developing new flooring materials need information on the chemical properties of adhesives and compression strengths for floor structures. Finally, top managers need both external and internal information. Internally, they use sales data summarized by product, customer type, and geographic region, along with comparisons to previous years. Equally important is external information on consumer behaviour patterns, the competition's performance, and economic forecasts.

Functional Areas and Business Processes

Each business *function*—marketing, human resources, accounting, production, and finance—has its own information needs. In addition, in businesses organized according to business processes, process groups need special information. Each user group and department is represented by an IS. Now add to these systems the four systems needed by the four levels of users that we just discussed: The total number of systems and applications increases significantly.

Each cell on the left side of Figure 13.6 represents a potential IS associated with a given functional group. Top-level finance managers, for instance, plan long-range spending for facilities and equipment, and they determine sources of capital. The arrows on the right side of Figure 13.6 show that a business-process group will include users, both managers and employees, drawn from all organizational levels. The supply chain management group, for instance, may need to cut the number of suppliers. The IS supporting this project would contain information cutting across different functions and management levels. The group will need information on and expertise in marketing, warehousing and distribution, production, communications technology, purchasing, and finance. It will also need

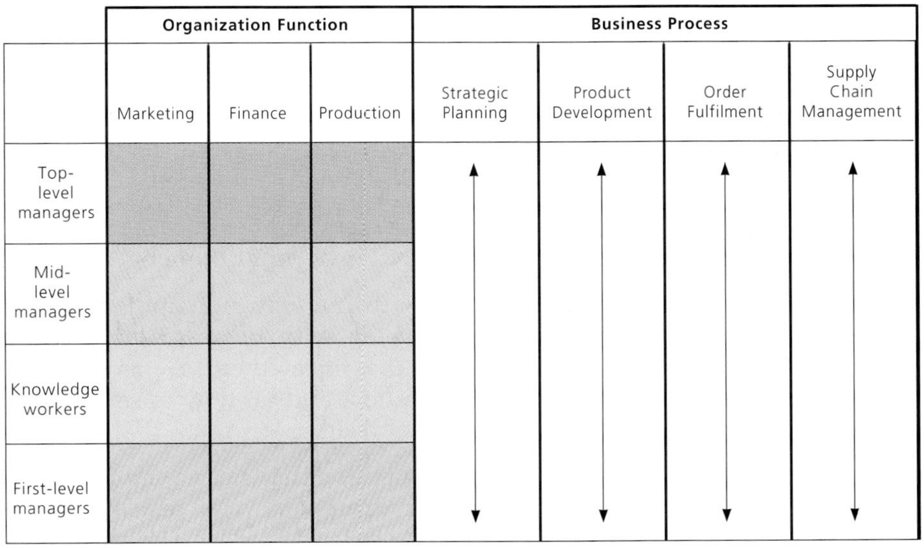

	Organization Function			Business Process			
	Marketing	Finance	Production	Strategic Planning	Product Development	Order Fulfilment	Supply Chain Management
Top-level managers							
Mid-level managers							
Knowledge workers							
First-level managers							

Figure 13.6
Matching user levels with functional areas and business processes.

input on operational, technical, and managerial issues—say, technical requirements for new suppliers and future financial requirements.

Major Systems by Level

In this section, we discuss different kinds of systems that provide applications at some organizational levels but not at others. For any routine, repetitive, highly structured decision, a specialized application will suffice. System requirements for knowledge workers, however, will probably vary because knowledge workers often face a variety of specialized problems. Applications of information systems for middle or top-level management decisions must also be flexible, though for different reasons. In particular, they will use a broader range of information collected from both external and internal sources.

Transaction Processing Systems

transaction processing systems (TPS)
Applications of information processing for basic day-to-day business transactions.

Transaction processing systems (TPS) are applications of information processing for basic day-to-day business transactions. Customer order-taking by online retailers, approval of claims at insurance companies, receiving and confirming reservations by airlines, payroll processing and bill payment at almost every company—all are routine business processes. Typically, the TPS for first-level (operational) activities is well defined, with predetermined data requirements, and follows the same steps to complete all transactions in the system.

A diagram representing the TPS for a customer-billing process is shown in Figure 13.7. The process begins when finished products for a customer's order are packed and ready for shipment. Using data stored in the company's master files, billing staffers match the customer's identification number (from the billing master file) with code numbers for products (from the products master file). The system instantly tallies the payment amount due (including the bill of the current shipment plus any past-due payments), creates the billing document (invoice), and provides status reports to first-level managers and other system users with online access. Information from the billing and products master files flows electronically to the accounting system for updating accounts receivables and inventory accounts.

Systems for Knowledge Workers and Office Applications

Systems for knowledge workers and office applications support the activities of both knowledge workers and employees in clerical positions. They provide assistance for data processing and other office activities, including the creation of communications documents. Like other departments, the IS department includes both knowledge workers and data workers.

IS Knowledge Workers. IS knowledge workers include both systems analysts (and designers) and application (or systems) programmers:

- *Systems analysts and designers* deal with the entire computer system. They represent the IS group in working with users to learn users' requirements and to design systems that meet them. Generally, they decide on the types and sizes of computers and on how to set up links among computers to form a network of users.
- *Programmers* write the software instructions that tell computers what to do. Application programmers, for example, write instructions to address particular problems. Systems programmers ensure that a system can handle the requests made by various application programs.

Operations Personnel (Data Workers). People who run the company's computer equipment are called **system operations personnel**. They ensure that the right programs are run in the correct sequence and monitor equipment to ensure that it is operating properly. Many organizations also have personnel for entering data into the system for processing.

system operations personnel
People who run a company's computer equipment.

Knowledge-Level and Office Systems

New support systems—word processing, document imaging, desktop publishing, computer-aided design, simulation modelling—have increased the productivity of both office and knowledge workers. We will discuss word processing—systems for formatting, editing, and storing documents—later

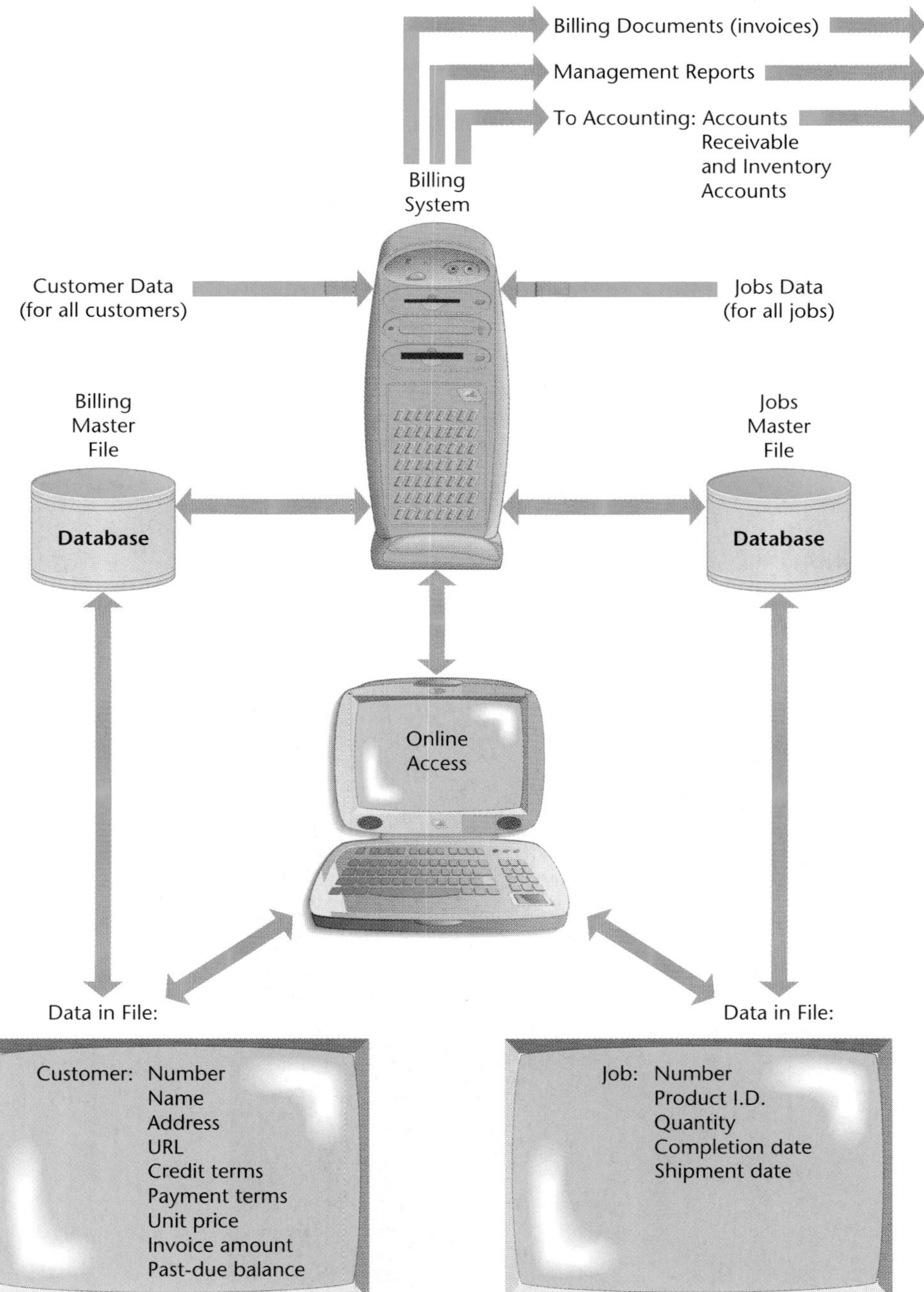

Figure 13.7
Flow diagram for customer-billing TPS.

in this chapter. Desktop publishing, also discussed later, combines graphics and word-processing text to publish professional-quality print and web documents. Document imaging systems can scan paper documents and images, convert them into digital form for storage on disks, retrieve them, and transmit them electronically to workstations throughout the network.

World-class firms are using system applications for knowledge workers to reduce product-design times, reduce production-cycle times, and make faster deliveries to customers.

computer-aided design (CAD)
Computer analysis and graphics programs that are used to create new products.

- **Computer-aided design (CAD)** assists in designing products by simulating the real product and displaying it in three- dimensional graphics. Immersion's MicroScribe-3D software, for example, uses a pen-like tool to scan the surface of any three-dimensional object, such as a football helmet, and electronically transforms it into a 3D graphic. The helmet designer can then try different shapes and surfaces in the computer and analyze the new designs on a video monitor.[8] Products ranging from cellphones to auto parts are created using CAD because it creates faster designs at lower cost than manual modelling methods. The older method—making handcrafted prototypes (trial models) from wood, plastic, or clay—is replaced with *rapid prototyping (RP):* the CAD system electronically transfers instructions to a computer-controlled machine that then automatically builds the prototype.[9]

computer-aided manufacturing (CAM)
Computer systems used to design and control all the equipment and tools for producing goods.

- **Computer-aided manufacturing (CAM)** is used to design the manufacturing equipment, facilities, and plant layouts for better product flows and productivity. *Computer operations control* refers to any system for managing the day-to-day production activities for either goods or service production. Hospitals, for instance, use computer-based scheduling for preparing patients' meals, just as manufacturers do for making cars, clocks, and paper products.

management information systems (MIS)
Systems that support an organization's managers by providing daily reports, schedules, plans, and budgets.

Management Information Systems

Management information systems (MIS) support an organization's managers by providing daily reports, schedules, plans, and budgets. Each manager's information activities vary according to his or her functional area

As late as the 1980s, computers hadn't had much impact on industrial automation, largely because there were no good software programs for computer-operated manufacturing. Myron Zimmerman recognized a need, and he founded VenturCom, which develops programs for controlling industrial production equipment like this metal cutting machine.

(say, accounting or marketing) and management level. Whereas mid-level managers focus mostly on internal activities and information, higher-level managers are also engaged in external activities. Middle managers, the largest MIS user group, need networked information to plan such upcoming activities as personnel training, materials movements, and cash flows. They also need to know the current status of the jobs and projects being carried out in their departments: What stage is it at now? When will it be finished? Is there an opening so the next job can be started? Many of a firm's management information systems—cash flow, sales, production scheduling, and shipping—are indispensable for helping managers find answers to such questions.

Decision Support Systems (DSS)

Middle- and top-level managers receive decision-making assistance from a **decision support system (DSS)**—an interactive system that locates and presents information needed to support the decision-making process. Whereas some DSSs are devoted to specific problems, others serve more general purposes, allowing managers to analyze different types of problems. Thus a firm that often faces decisions on plant capacity, for example, may have a *Capacity DSS* in which the manager inputs data on anticipated levels of sales, working capital, and customer-delivery requirements. Then the system's built-in transaction processors manipulate the data and make recommendations on the best levels of plant capacity for each future time period.

decision support system (DSS)
Computer systems used to help managers consider alternatives when making decisions on complicated problems.

Executive Support Systems

An **executive support system (ESS)** is a quick-reference, easy-access application of information systems specially designed for upper-level managers. ESSs are designed to assist with executive-level decisions and problems, ranging from "What lines of business should we be in five years from now?" to "Based on forecasted developments in electronic technologies, to what extent should our firm be globalized in five years? In 10 years?" An ESS also uses a wide range of both internal information and external sources, such as industry reports, global economic forecasts, and reports on competitors.

executive support system (ESS)
A quick-reference, easy-access application of information systems specially designed for upper-level managers.

Robotics is a category of artificial intelligence. Robots can "learn" repetitive tasks and "remember" the causes of past mistakes.

BUSINESS TODAY

The Automated Factory: Just a Dream?

For many years, production managers have dreamed of the automated factory, a place where industrial robots and computer-assisted machines would tirelessly crank out products without any human involvement in the process. When industrial robots were developed in the 1970s, many people thought that they would quickly be adopted and would revolutionize the workplace. But progress was slowed because robots were high-priced. And the initial purchase price was just part of the problem. Exhaustive studies also had to be performed by company personnel to determine the precise task that could be accomplished by a robot. Workers had to be trained to operate and work with robots, and computer scientists were needed to program and reprogram the robots. It was also discovered that robots simply weren't good enough to keep making high quality parts for hours on end without any human attention. So the dream of the automated factory faded for a while.

As the years passed, however, the dream slowly moved closer to reality. The increased reliability of industrial robots and computerized machines, and the intensification of international competition, have motivated more and more companies to look at automation to increase their productivity. The use of industrial robots—often called "lights-out manufacturing" because there is no need to light the factory where the work is done—is now making steady progress in industry.

A 1999 report by a United Nations economic commission found that orders for industrial robots soared 60 percent over one year earlier. The increase points to a continuing drive toward automation of manufacturing facilities. The UN report says that we have seen only the first phase of industrial robots, and that they will increasingly be used in manufacturing and other industries. A sharp drop in the price of robots is one of the reasons for their increased adoption. The price of robots at the end of the 1990s was as much as 40 percent less than it was at the beginning of the decade. This drop in prices, coupled with increasing human labour costs, has motivated more and more companies to consider the purchase of an industrial robot.

It is not difficult to find examples of the use of industrial robots:

- at Honda Canada's minivan plant in Alliston, Ontario, a giant robot with huge arms grasps an automobile chassis and welds the floor, roof, and sides in one motion
- Harber Manufacturing of Fort Erie, Ontario, uses five arc-welding robot systems to make wood-burning stoves
- Canadian National Railways runs a fully computerized robotic paint shop for railroad cars in Winnipeg, Manitoba
- Evans Findings Co. in East Providence, Rhode Island, uses metal stamping machines to make parts like the tiny cutting devices on dental floss packages; the machines run one shift each day without any workers in attendance
- submersible robots are replacing divers in offshore oil and gas operations, and they toil for hours in areas of nuclear power plants where humans once worked in very short relays to minimize their exposure to radiation.

While progress is evident, two factors are still inhibiting rapid movement toward automation. First, consumers are increasingly demanding higher-quality products. In order to meet these demands, machines must be increasingly sophisticated. Higher levels of investment are required to improve the capability of robots even further. But the uncertain state of the world economy in the first few years of the twenty-first century means that companies are reluctant to invest in robotic technology, particularly if it isn't certain what benefits they will gain. Companies are also concerned that workers would raise a fuss because it is obvious that the installation of robots means fewer jobs.

Second, human beings are superior to robots in a great many ways, especially in tasks requiring sensory input and adaptation. For example, the most sophisticated robots can recognize about 20 slightly different shapes as airplanes, but humans can identify thousands of slightly different shapes as planes. As one researcher notes, the human eye has about 100 million vision cells and four layers of neurons, all capable doing about 10 billion calculations a second. In other words, it would take 100 000 supercomputers to imitate the visual calculations of a one-eyed human being.

What does the future hold? The use of robots will continue to increase in Canadian industry. But the truly automated factory still seems a long way off.

Artificial Intelligence and Expert Systems

Artificial intelligence (AI) is the construction of computer systems to imitate human behaviour—in other words, systems that perform physical tasks, use thought processes, and learn. In developing AI systems, business specialists, modellers, and information-technology experts try to design computer-based systems capable of reasoning so that computers, instead of people, can perform certain activities. A credit-evaluation system may decide which loan applicants are creditworthy and which too risky, and it may then compose acceptance and rejection letters accordingly.[10]

artificial intelligence (AI)
The construction and/or programming of computers to imitate human thought processes.

Robotics—the combination of computers with industrial robots—is a category of AI. With certain "reasoning" capabilities, robots can "learn" repetitive tasks such as painting, assembling components, and inserting screws. They also avoid repeating mistakes by "remembering" the causes of past mistakes and, when those causes reappear, adjusting or stopping until adjustments are made. The Business Today box describes how robotics is affecting how some factories are operated.

robotics
The use of computer-controlled machines that perform production tasks.

There are also AI systems that possess sensory capabilities, such as lasers that "see," "hear," and "feel." In addition, as machines become more sophisticated in processing natural languages, humans can give instructions and ask questions merely by speaking to a computer. AND Corporation of Toronto has developed a software program—called HNeT—that can learn to recognize faces. This may seem like a simple thing, but millions of dollars had been spent on this problem without success until AND Corporation developed the software. The system can be used to improve airport security and to track terrorists.[11]

Expert Systems. A special form of AI program, the **expert system**, is designed to imitate the thought processes of human experts in a particular field.[12] Expert systems incorporate the rules that an expert applies to specific types of problems, such as the judgments a physician makes when diagnosing illnesses. In effect, expert systems supply everyday users with "instant expertise."

expert system
A form of artificial intelligence in which a program draws on the rules an expert in a given field has laid out to arrive at a solution for a problem.

Nortel Networks uses an expert system called Engineering Change Manager, which simplifies and speeds up product design changes by suggesting redesigns to meet product requirements. Campbell Soup developed an expert system to mimic complex decision processes and save the expert knowledge that was going to be lost when a long-time expert soup maker announced his intention to retire.[13]

ELEMENTS OF THE INFORMATION SYSTEM

5. Identify and briefly describe the *main elements of an information system.*

We now know that an *information system* is a group of interconnected devices at several different locations that can exchange information. We also know that *networking*—connecting these devices—allows otherwise decentralized computers to exchange data quickly and easily. Obviously, a key component of the information system is its **computer network**—all of the computer and information technology devices that, working together, drive the flow of digital information throughout the system.

computer network
A form of computer system architecture in which computers at different locations can function independently but are also interconnected and able to exchange information with one another.

The computer is a powerful machine, but it is only one part of the information system. Every system has six components:

Hardware
Software
Control
Database
People
Telecommunications

In this section, we will describe each of the first four components in detail. We have already described the fifth element, the people at various levels who use and prepare the system. We will reserve our discussion of telecommunications for the next section. Remember that all six of these components must be present and properly coordinated for a networked information system to function effectively.

Hardware

hardware
The physical components of a computer system.

input device
Hardware that gets data into the computer in a form the computer can understand.

central processing unit (CPU)
Hardware in which the actual transforming of data into information takes place; contains the primary storage unit, the control unit, and the arithmetic logic unit.

main memory
The part of a computer's CPU that stores those programs that it needs to operate.

program
Any sequence of instructions to a computer.

output device
That part of a computer's hardware that presents results to users; common forms include printers and video monitors.

Figure 13.8 shows the various systems and components that make up IS **hardware**—the physical components of a computer system. The functioning of a computer's hardware is not as complicated as it looks. To get a bird's-eye view of how the system works, suppose that you are a very simple piece of data (say, the number 3).

- To get into the computer, data must be entered by an **input device**. Optical scanners, voice pickups, CD drives, and computer mice are all input devices, but let's assume that you are entered by a friend using the most common input device, a keyboard. When your friend presses the number 3 on the keyboard, an electronic signal is sent to the computer's **central processing unit (CPU)**, where the actual processing of data takes place.
- You are now inside the CPU in a form that the computer can understand. What happens now? As a piece of data, you must go first to **main memory**—the part of the computer's CPU that stores those programs that it needs to operate.
- Now the CPU searches through its memory for instructions—**programs**—on what to do with you. Using the appropriate instructions, it then performs the calculations (addition, subtraction, multiplication, and division) and comparisons as directed by the program. Then, the CPU sends the results to one or more **output devices**: a video monitor, a printer, or a voice output.

Software

software
Programs that instruct the computer in what to do and how to do it.

system program
A program that tells a computer what resources to use and how to use them.

application program
A program that actually processes data according to a particular user's specific needs.

Although hardware is a vital component, it needs programs—**software**—to function. There are two types of software programs:

- **System programs** tell the computer what resources to use and how. For example, an operating system program tells the computer how and when to transfer data from secondary to primary storage and return information to the user.
- Most computer users do not write programs but rather use **application programs**—software packages written by others. Each different type of application (such as financial analysis, word processing, or web browsing) uses a program that meets that need. Thus, a computer system usually has many application programs available, such as Lotus 1-2-3, Quicken, and WordPerfect. We review some of these later in this chapter.

Graphical User Interface

graphical user interface (GUI)
The user-friendly display that helps users select from among the many possible applications of the computer.

icons
Small images on a computer screen that represent various applications.

An important software development is the **graphical user interface (GUI)**—the user-friendly visual display that helps users select from among the computer applications. The screen displays numerous **icons** (small images) representing such choices as word processing, graphics, fax, printing, CD, or games. The user tells the computer what to do by moving a

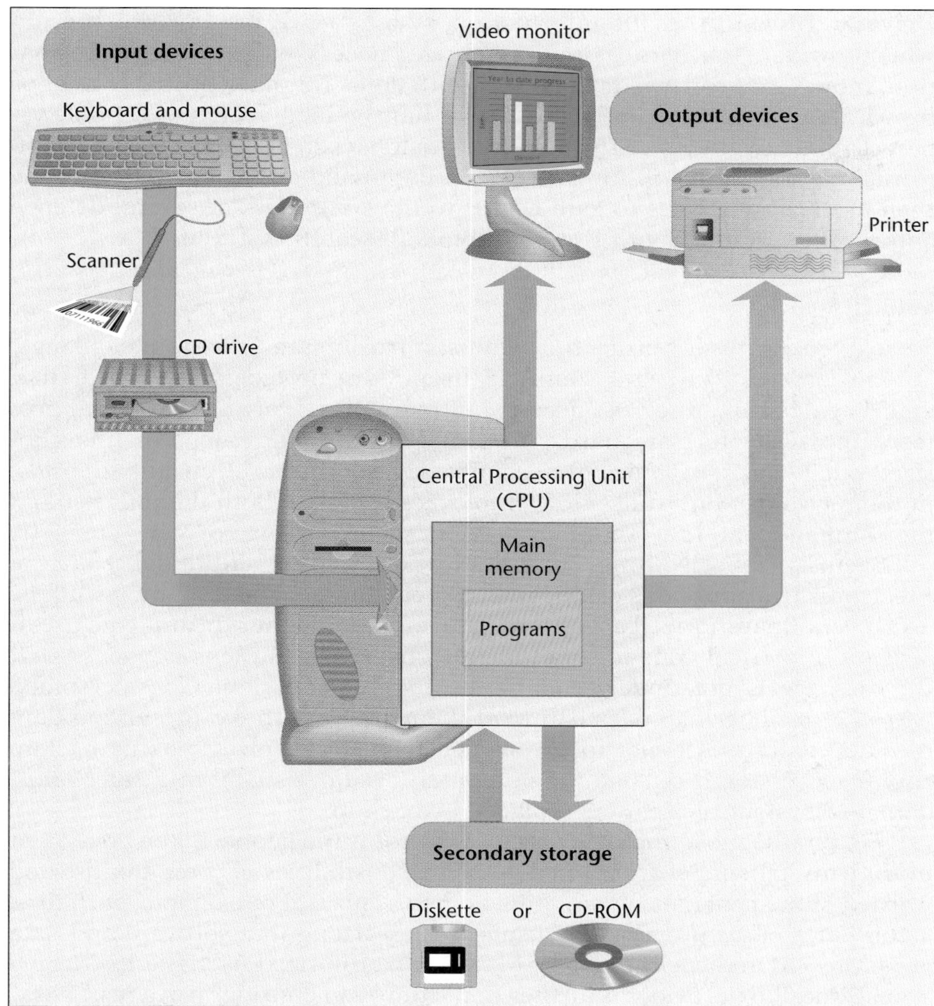

Figure 13.8
Hardware components of an IS.

pointing device (usually an arrow) around the screen to activate the desired icon. Simple printed instructions explain activated features.

Control

Control ensures that the system is operating according to specific procedures and within specific guidelines. These procedures include guidelines for operating the system, responsibilities of the personnel involved with it, and plans for dealing with system failure. For example, a key aspect of information management is controlling two groups of people—those who have access to input or change the system's data and those who receive output from it. For example, most firms limit access to salary information. Another aspect of control is management surveillance of employees as they work.

Problems of Privacy and Security

"Breaking and entering" no longer refers merely to physical intrusions into one's home or business. Today, it applies to IS intrusions as well. In this section, we will describe one of the most common forms of intrusion: *privacy invasion*. We will also discuss some of the methods that companies use to provide *security* for their information systems.[14]

Privacy Invasion. With information systems, privacy invasion occurs when intruders (hackers) gain unauthorized access, either to steal information, money, or property or to tamper with data. You have probably read or heard about computer enthusiasts who have gained access to school systems to change grades. A 16-year-old British hacker, for example, made 150 intrusions into the U.S. Air Force's top command-and-control facility. He then used those entries to gain access to the computers of several defence contractors and the South Korean Atomic Research Institute.

Security

Security measures for protection against intrusion are a constant challenge. To gain entry into most systems, IS users have protected passwords that guard against unauthorized access, but many firms rely on additional protective software for safeguards. To protect against intrusions by unauthorized outsiders, companies use security devices, called electronic *firewalls*, in their systems. Firewalls allow employees access to both the internet and the company's internal computer network while barring entry by outsiders.

Security for electronic communications is an additional concern. Electronic transmissions can be intercepted, altered, and read by intruders. To prevent unauthorized access, many firms rely on **encryption**—the use of a secret numerical code to scramble the characters in the message, so that the message is not understandable during transmission. Only personnel with the deciphering codes can read them. Protection for preserving data files and databases is not foolproof and typically involves making backup copies to be stored outside the computer system, usually in a safe. Thus, damaged system files can be replaced by backup.

encryption
The use of a secret numerical code to scramble characters in a message, so that the message is not understandable during transmission.

Finally, the most important security factor is the people in the system. At most firms, personnel are trained in the responsibilities of computer use and warned of the penalties for violating system security. For example, each time a computer boots up, a notice displays the warning that software and data are protected and spells out penalties for unauthorized use. The Exercising Your Ethics box provides a further opportunity to consider privacy issues.

Databases and Application Programs

All computer processing is the processing of data. It is carried out by programs—instructions that tell the system to perform specified functions. In

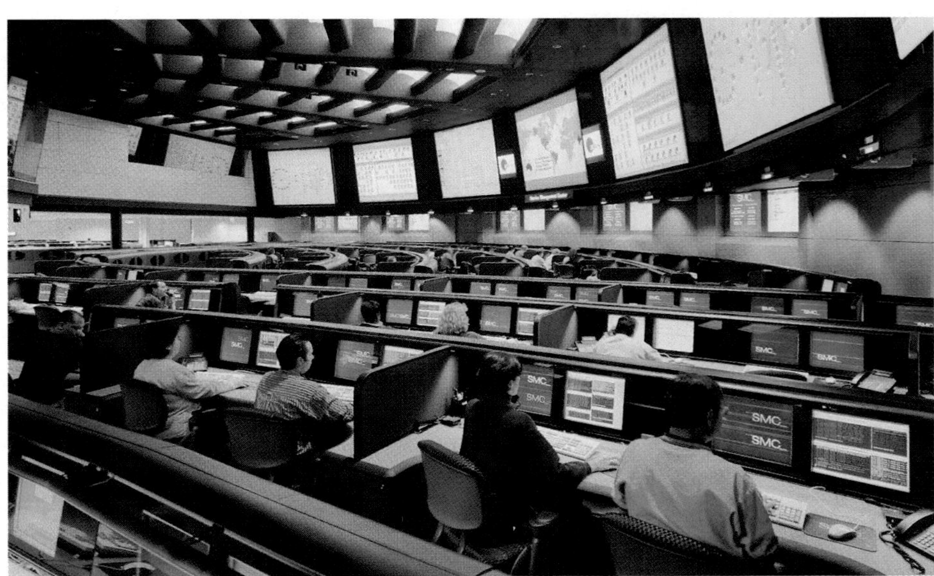

Network security is a serious matter at Electronic Data Systems (EDS). The company not only provides security services for 2500 clients, but must also secure its own information systems. That's why it keeps data centres small, spreads operations across geographic areas, and continually tests its networks. EDS partners with EMC Corp. to run networks that instantaneously "mirror" databases to back up crucial information in case of network failure or cyber terrorism.

EXERCISING YOUR ETHICS

Supplying the Right Answers

The Situation

Networked systems facilitate information sharing among companies and often involve sensitive customer data. This exercise asks you to consider ethical issues that might arise when firms are developing information technologies for use in networked systems.

The Dilemma

Home Sweet Home-e (HSH-e) was an ebusiness start-up that sold virtually everything in home furnishings—from linens and towels to cleaning supplies and furniture. From home computers, HSH-e members could shop in virtual storefronts, chat online with other shoppers, talk live with virtual store clerks, and pay electronically at a one-stop website. In reality, HSH-e was a virtual store: a network of numerous suppliers located around the country, each specializing in a particular line of goods. The network was connected by a centrally controlled information technology that HSH-e developed, owned, and operated. Once a customer's order was placed, suppliers instantaneously received information on what to ship, where to ship it, and how much to charge.

HSH-e chose only suppliers who guaranteed fast, reliable deliveries and promised to supply HSH-e exclusively. The linen supplier, for example, could not supply products to other home-furnishings ebusinesses. In return, the supplier was guaranteed all HSH-e orders for linen products. As HSH-e grew, suppliers stood to gain more business and prosper in an expanding etail industry. As it turns out, some prospective suppliers refused to join the network and others in the network were discontinued by HSH-e for failing to expand fast enough to keep up with demand.

Questions for Discussion

1. For a potential HSH-e supplier of a specialized product line, what are the ethical issues in this situation?
2. Consider past suppliers who have been discontinued or have withdrawn from the HSH-e network. Do they face any ethical issues involving HSH-e customers? Involving HSH-e operations? Involving other HSH-e suppliers?
3. Suppose you work at HSH-e and discover a non-network supplier that is more attractive than one of the company's existing suppliers. What ethical considerations do you face in deciding whether or not to replace an existing supplier?

this section we begin by briefly describing the nature of computer data and databases. We then discuss a few of the specialized applications programs designed for business use.

Data and Databases

Computers convert data into information by organizing them in some meaningful manner. Within a computer system, chunks of data—numbers, words, and sentences—are stored in a series of related collections called *fields, records,* and *files*. Taken together, all of these data files constitute a **database**—a centralized, organized collection of related data.

database
A centralized, organized collection of related data.

Application Programs

Most computer users don't write programs. Programs are available for a huge range of business-related tasks. Some address such common, longstanding needs as accounting and inventory control, while others have been developed for an endless variety of specialized needs. Most business programs fall into one of four categories: *word processing, spreadsheets, database management,* and *graphics.* Of all PC software applications, 70 percent are designed for the first three types of programs.[15]

Word Processing. Popular **word-processing programs**, such as Microsoft Word for Windows and Lotus's Word Pro, allow computer users to store, edit, display, and print documents. Sentences and paragraphs can

word-processing programs
Application programs that allow the computer to act as a sophisticated typewriter to store, edit, and print letters and numbers.

be added or deleted without retyping or restructuring an entire document, and mistakes are easily corrected.

electronic spreadsheets
Application programs that allow the user to enter categories of data and determine the effect of changes in one category (e.g., sales) on other categories (e.g., profits).

Spreadsheets. Electronic spreadsheets spread data across and down the page in rows and columns. Users enter data, including formulas, at row and column intersections, and the computer automatically performs the necessary calculations. Payroll records, sales projections, and a host of other financial reports can be prepared in this manner.

Spreadsheets are good planning tools because they let managers see how making a change in one item affects related items. For example, you can insert operating-cost percentages, tax rates, or sales revenues into the spreadsheet. The computer will automatically recalculate all the other figures and determine net profit. Popular spreadsheet packages include Lotus 1-2-3, Quattro Pro, and Microsoft Excel for Windows.[16]

database management systems
Application programs that keep track of and manipulate the relevant data of a business.

Database Management. Another popular type of personal-productivity software is a **database management program**. Such programs as Microsoft Access for Windows and Borland's InterBase are popular for desktop applications. Oracle9i is a popular database for internet computing. These systems can create, store, sort, and search through data and integrate a single piece into several different files.

Figure 13.9 shows how a database management program might be used at a company called Artists' Frame Service. In this case, the program is integrating the file for customer orders with the company's inventory file. When sales to Jones and Smith are entered into the customer orders file, the database system automatically adjusts the frame inventory file; the quantities of materials B5 and A3 are reduced because those materials were used to make the frames for Jones and Smith.

computer graphics programs
Application programs that convert numerical and character data into pictorial forms.

Graphics. Computer graphics programs convert numeric and character data into pictorial information, such as charts and graphs. They make computerized information easier to use and understand in two ways. First, graphs and charts summarize data and allow managers to detect problems, opportunities, and relationships more easily. Second, graphics contribute to clearer and more persuasive reports and presentations.

Two of the most common graphics displays are the pie chart and the bar graph. As Figure 13.10 shows, both types of graphics can convey different kinds of information—in this case, the types of materials that should be ordered by a framing shop like Artists' Frame Service. Both types of graphs are more likely to help a manager make decisions than the raw numbers on which they are based.

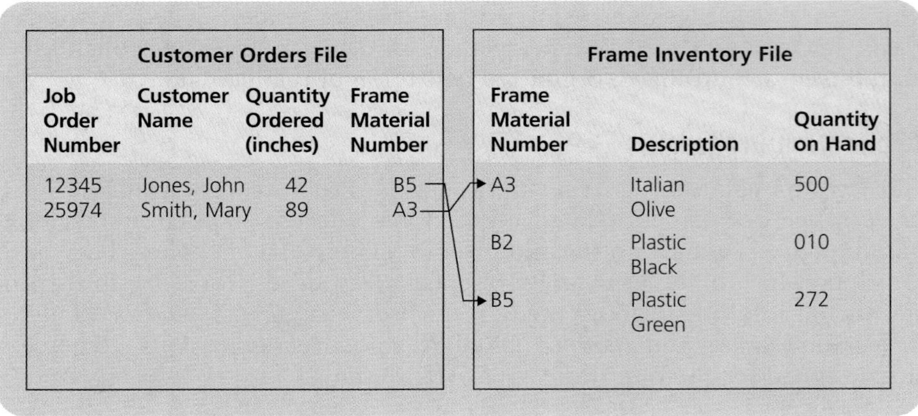

Customer Orders File
Job Order Number
Customer Name
Quantity Ordered (inches)
Frame Material Number
12345 Jones, John 42 B5
25974 Smith, Mary 89 A3
Frame Inventory File
Frame Material Number
Description
Quantity on Hand
A3 Italian Olive 500
B2 Plastic Black 010
B5 Plastic Green 272

Figure 13.9
Artists' Frame Service.

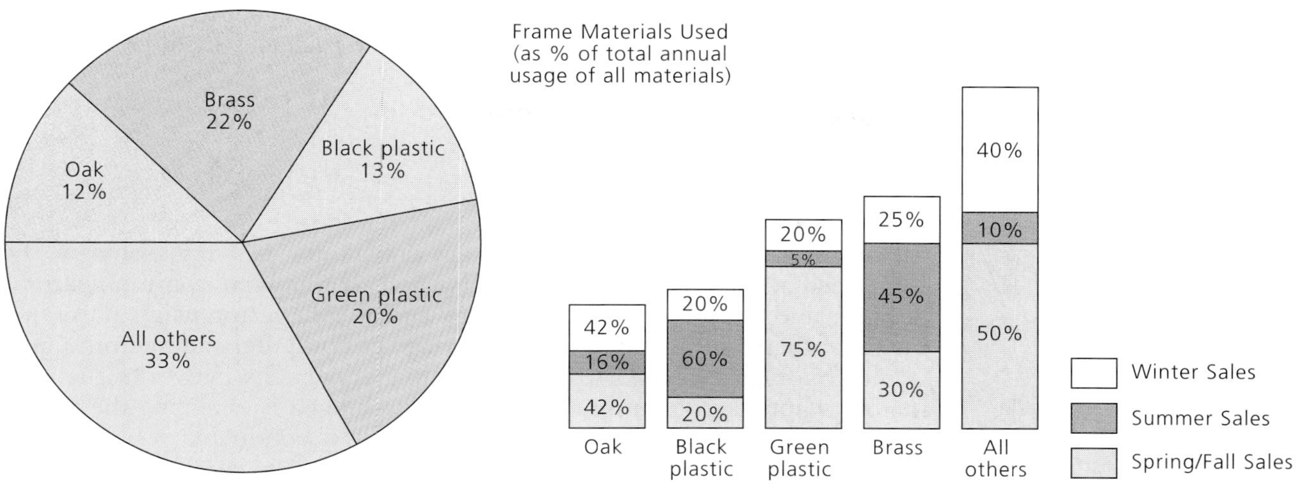

Figure 13.10
Both the pie chart and the bar graph show that four frame materials are the most used, but the bar graph also shows that brass and oak are most popular in winter.

Presentation graphics software, such as CorelDRAW, Microsoft PowerPoint for Windows, and Microsoft Visio 2002, lets users assemble graphics for visual displays, slides, video, and even sound splices for professional presentations. Varying colour and size and using pictures and charts with three-dimensional effects and shading with animation and sound make for far more visually interesting presentations.

presentation graphics software
Application programs that offer choices for assembling graphics for visual displays, slides, video, and even sound splices for professional presentations.

Computer graphics capabilities go beyond data presentation. They also include stand-alone programs for artists, designers, and special effects engineers. Everything from simple drawings to motion picture special effects are now created by computer graphics software. The sinking ship in *Titanic*, the aliens in *Men in Black II*, and the dog in *Scooby-Doo* were all created with computer graphics.

Some software allows firms to publish sales brochures, in-house magazines, and annual reports. The latest **desktop publishing** packages for the PC combine word-processing and graphics to produce typeset-quality text with stimulating visual effects. They also eliminate printing costs for reports and proposals. QuarkXPress, which can manipulate text, tables of

desktop publishing
Combines word processing and graphics capability in producing typeset-quality text from personal computers.

The realism of the space creatures and alien environments in *Star Wars* is due to special effects created with computer graphics.

numbers, graphics, and full-colour photographs, is used by ad agencies such as J. Walter Thompson because its computer-generated designs offer greater control over colour and format. Other packages include Microsoft Publisher and Adobe Systems PageMaker.

TELECOMMUNICATIONS AND NETWORKS

Although communications systems are constantly evolving, some of the fundamental elements are well established: computers, communications devices, and networking. The most powerful vehicle for using these elements to their full potential is the marriage of computers and communication technologies. Thanks to lower-cost, higher-capacity networks, the joining of computers, communication, and mass media is changing the nature of information and the ways in which business is conducted.

A *network* is a means of organizing telecommunications components into an effective system. When a company decides how to organize its equipment and facilities, it also determines how its information resources will be shared, controlled, and applied for users in its network. In this section, we will first discuss *multimedia communications technologies* and the devices found in today's systems. We will then describe different ways of organizing information resources into effective systems.

Multimedia Communication Systems

multimedia communication systems
Connected networks of communication appliances such as faxes, televisions, sound equipment, cellphones, printers, and photocopiers that may also be linked by satellite with other remote networks.

Today's information systems include not only computers but also **multimedia communication systems**. These systems are connected networks of communication appliances such as faxes, televisions, sound equipment, cellphones, printers, and photocopiers that may also be linked by satellite with other remote networks. Not surprisingly, the integration of these elements is changing the ways in which we live our lives and manage our businesses.

A good example is the modern grocery store. The checkout scanner reads the bar code on the product you buy. Data are then transmitted to the store's inventory-control system, which updates the number of available units. If inventory falls below a given level, more product is ordered electronically. Meanwhile, the correct price is added to your bill and checkout coupons are printed automatically according to the specific product you bought. Your debit card transfers funds, sales reports are generated for the store's management, and all the while, satellite transmissions are dispatching a remote truck to begin loading replacement supplies for the store.

Communication Devices

Today's technology lets people conduct business across large distances and from places where communications were once unavailable. *Global positioning systems (GPSs),* for example, use satellite transmissions to track the geographic locations of targets, such as boats or even people. When you're linked to a GPS network, your firm can know your whereabouts at all times. *Personal digital assistants (PDAs)* are tiny hand-held computers with wireless telecommunications capabilities. Many can access the internet, even receiving and sending email messages from the most primitive locations. *Paging systems* and *cellular telephones* connect us instantly with distant networks.

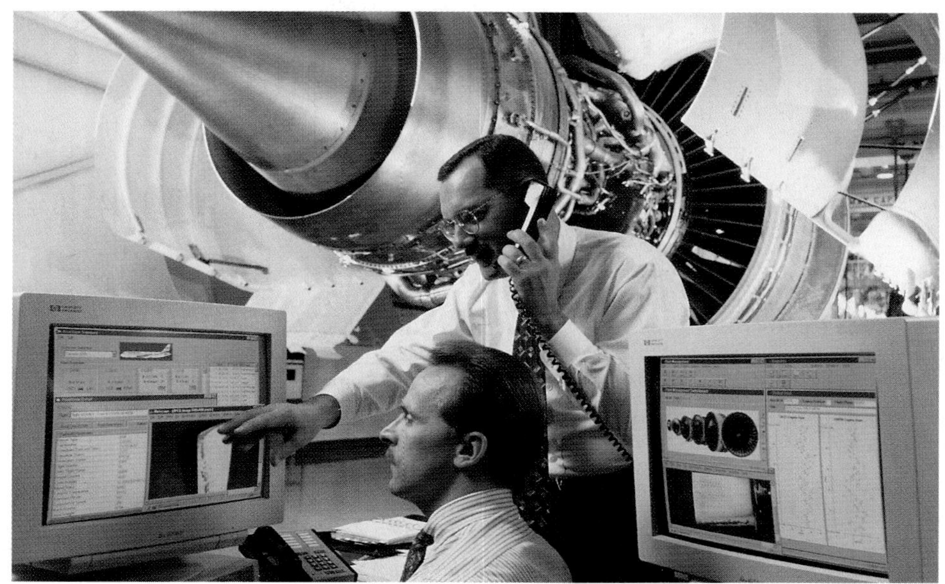

Demonstrating how computers have changed communications, these engineers at GE's corporate research and development centre can monitor engines in flight from the ground via satellite. The new system can diagnose potential engine problems, plan for maintenance or overhaul, and resolve problems more quickly than ever.

Communication Channels

Communication channels, including wired and wireless transmission, are the media that make all these transmissions possible.[17]Most of us use communication channels when we use wired telephone systems, but today most telephone transmissions are data, not conversations. Fax data account for 90 percent of all telephone signals between the United States and Japan.

Meanwhile, microwave systems transmit wireless radio signals between transmission stations. Satellite communications have also gained popularity with the growth in demand for wireless transmission. Accessible through satellite networks built by McCaw, Hughes, Motorola, AT&T, and Loral, the net is available in remote areas where underground cable isn't feasible.

System Architecture

There are several ways to organize the components in computer and communications networks. One way to classify networks is according to *geographic scope*. Another is according to the *pattern of connections* among the system's devices.

Local and Wide Area Networks

Networked systems classified according to geographic scope may be either local or wide area networks. Computers may be linked province-wide or even nationwide through telephone lines, microwave, or satellite communications, as in a **wide area network (WAN)**. Firms can lease lines from communications vendors or maintain private WANs. Wal-Mart, for example, depends heavily on a private satellite network that links more than 2000 retail stores to its Bentonville, Arkansas, headquarters.

wide area network (WAN)
A system to link computers across the country through telephone wires or satellites.

Internal networks covering limited distances may link all of a firm's nearby computers, as in a **local area network (LAN)**. Computers within a building, for example, can be linked by cabling (fibre optic, coaxial, or twisted wire) or by wireless technology. Internally networked computers share processing duties, software, storage areas, and data. On the Home Shopping Network, hundreds of operators seated at monitors in a large room are united by a LAN to enter call-in orders from customers. This arrangement allows the use of a single computer system with one database and software system.

local area network (LAN)
A system to link computers in one building or in a small geographical area by cabling or wireless technology.

IT'S A WIRED WORLD

Going to School in Networking

Ninety percent of freshmen arriving at the University of Michigan are PC owners. More than 41 percent have already created at least one website, and 39 percent say they're on the cellphone 250 hours a month. At nearby drinking spots, students are just as apt to pull out laptops as they are to order up brews. They love hi-tech gadgets, especially when they're networked. Josh Michaels, a senior at the University of Illinois, keeps a laptop on his nightstand. "I want to be able to control every device in this apartment without getting out of my bed," he explains. Those devices include two lamps, a TiVo, a coffee grinder and espresso machine, an Xbox, a DVD player, and a homemade security camera, all of which are wired into a private network.

Michaels's devotion to gadgetry may be extreme, but communications technology is as much a part of campus life today as classes, coffee breaks, and the library. Many campuses guarantee fast network access, and some, like Pittsburgh's Carnegie Mellon, have already gone wireless. For keeping in touch with friends and classmates, instant messaging (IM) is replacing email and phone calls. Because it's real-time and instant, IM tells you who else is connected at a given moment. Allowing the immediate exchange of messages and documents among networked "others," IM is a great means of staying connected with family and friends. As for entertainment, file sharing is still alive and well. Sites like Morpheus and Kazaa post loads of fun stuff—TV hits, software, movies, and music—for downloading at home or school. Both video games for solitary play—such as Snood, a puzzle game—and fantasy games played with others have become a popular activity at so-called LAN (for local area network) parties.

Living quarters are also showing the effects of networking. On many campuses, dorms are enjoying renewed attention because they're usually wired (thereby forcing off-campus houses to remodel and get wired if they want to compete for tech-savvy students). "I considered moving off campus," says a University of Chicago junior, "but then I realized I'd lose my internet access. So I dropped that idea!"

What about overloading a school's information system, especially with an upsurge of non-academic applications? You might be surprised. Administrators at the University of California at San Diego actually encourage students to network in full force. In fact, they're handing out wireless PDAs in the hope that students will use them to IM one another, check email, and surf the web. What's in it for the school? University officials want to see how students learn to use technology so that they can design classes to attract technology-savvy students.

Wireless Networks. Wireless technologies use airborne electronic signals for linking network appliances. In addition to mobile phones, wireless technology extends to laptops, hand-held computers, and applications in cars (including internet access and music players, map terminals, and game machines). Businesses benefit by avoiding webs of wires crisscrossing facilities. Ford, for example, uses an innovative industrial information system—WhereNet—for tracking inventory by means of identification tags that transmit radio waves. Antennas mounted on the factory ceiling receive transmissions and send information to a central computer that locates tags in the plant. The system saves time and money by coordinating the delivery of hundreds of parts to assembly lines.[18]

client–server network
A network composed of both clients (users) and servers that allows the clients to access various services without costly and unnecessary duplication.

client
A point of entry in a client–server network.

server
A computer that provides the services shared by network users.

Client–Server Systems. An obvious advantage of networks is the sharing of resources—thus avoiding costly and unnecessary duplication. In a **client–server network**, **clients** are the users of services. They are the points of entry, usually laptop computers, workstations, or desktop computers. The **server** provides the services shared by network users. The powerful *minicomputer* at the network hub, for example, which is larger and more sophisticated than your PC or *microcomputer*, may be the server for the surrounding client PCs in an office network.

More specifically, the server may act as a file server, a print server, and a fax server. As a *file server*, the minicomputer has a large-capacity disk for storing the programs and data shared by all the PCs in the network. It contains customer files plus the database, word-processing, graphics, and spreadsheet programs that may be used by clients. As a *print server*, the minicomputer controls the printer, stores printing requests from client PCs, and routes jobs to the printer as it becomes available. As the *fax server*, the minicomputer receives, sends, and otherwise controls the system's fax activities. Only one disk drive, one printer, and one fax, therefore, are needed for an entire system of users. Internet computing uses the client–server arrangement.

SUMMARY OF LEARNING OBJECTIVES

1. **Explain why businesses must manage *information* and show how computer systems and communication technologies have revolutionized *information management*.** Because businesses are faced with an overwhelming amount of *data* and *information* about customers, competitors, and their own operations, the ability to manage this input can mean the difference between success and failure. The management of its information system is a core activity because all of a firm's business activities are linked to it. New digital technologies have taken an integral place among an organization's resources for conducting everyday business.

2. **Identify and briefly describe three elements of *data communication networks*—the internet, the World Wide Web, and intranets.** *Data communication networks*, both public and private, carry streams of digital data (electronic messages) back and forth quickly and economically via *telecommunication systems*. The largest public communications network, the *internet*, is a gigantic network of networks linking millions of computers and offering information on business around the world. The internet is the most important email system in the world. Individuals can subscribe to the internet via an *internet service provider (ISP)*. The *World Wide Web* is a system with universally accepted standards for storing, formatting, retrieving, and displaying information. It provides the common language that enables users around the world to "surf" the internet using a common format. *Intranets* are private networks that any company can develop to extend internet technology internally—that is, for transmitting information throughout the firm. Intranets are accessible only to employees, with access to outsiders prevented by hardware and software security systems called *firewalls*.

3. **Describe five *new options for organizational design* that have emerged from the rapid growth of information technologies.** Information networks are leading to *leaner* organizations—businesses with fewer employees and simpler organizational structures—because networked firms can maintain electronic, rather than human, information links among employees and customers. Operations are *more flexible* because electronic networks allow businesses to offer greater product variety and faster delivery cycles. Aided by intranets and the internet, *greater collaboration* is possible, both among internal units and with outside firms. *Geographic separation* of the workplace and company headquarters is more common because electronic links are replacing the need for physical proximity between the company and its workstations. *Improved management processes* are feasible because managers have rapid access to more information about the current status of company activities and easier access to electronic tools for planning and decision making.

4. **Discuss different information-systems *applications* that are available for users at various organizational levels.** *Transaction processing systems (TPS)* are applications for basic day-to-day business transactions. They are useful for routine transactions, such as taking reservations and meeting payrolls, that follow predetermined steps. Systems for knowledge workers and office applications include *personal productivity tools* such as word processing, document imaging, desktop publishing, computer-aided design (CAD), and simulation modelling. *Management information systems (MIS)* support an organization's managers by providing daily reports, schedules, plans, and budgets. Middle managers, the largest MIS user group, need networked information to plan upcoming activities and track current activities. *Decision support systems (DSS)* are interactive applications that assist the decision-making processes of middle and top-level managers. *Executive support systems (ESS)* are quick-reference, easy-access programs to assist upper-level managers. *Artificial intelligence (AI)* and *expert systems* are designed to imitate human behaviour and provide computer-based assistance in performing certain business activities.

5. **Identify and briefly describe the *main elements of an information system.*** *Hardware* is the physical devices and components, including the computer, in the *information system (IS)*. It consists of an input device (such as a keyboard), a central processing unit (CPU), a main memory, disks for data storage, and output devices (such as video monitors and printers). *Software* includes the computer's operating system, application programs (such as word processing, spreadsheets, and web browsers), and a graphical user interface (GUI) that helps users select among the computer's many possible applications.

   Control is important to ensure not only that the system operates correctly but also that data and information are transmitted through secure channels to people who really need them. Control is aided by the use of electronic security measures, such as firewalls, that bar entry to the system by unauthorized outsiders. The *database* is the organized collection of all the data files in the system. *People* are also part of the information system. IS *knowledge workers* include systems analysts who design the systems and programmers who write software instructions that tell computers what to do. System users, too, are integral to the system. *Telecommunications* components include multimedia technology that incorporates sound, animation, video, and photography along with ordinary graphics and text. Electronic discussion groups, videoconferencing, and other forms of interactive dialogue are possible with communication devices (such as global positioning systems and personal digital assistants) and communication channels (such as satellite communications).

KEY TERMS

application program, 452
artificial intelligence (AI), 451
browser, 440
central processing unit (CPU), 452
client, 460
client-server network, 460
computer graphics program, 456
computer network, 451
computer-aided design (CAD), 448
computer-aided manufacturing (CAM), 448
data communication network, 438
data, 434
database, 455
database management program, 456
database management system, 456
decision support system (DSS), 449
desktop publishing, 457
directories, 440
electronic conferencing, 438
electronic information technologies (EIT), 437

electronic mail (email), 438
electronic spreadsheet, 456
encryption, 454
enterprise resource planning (ERP), 443
executive support system (ESS), 449
expert system, 451
extranet, 440
fax machine, 437
firewall, 440
graphical user interface (GUI), 452
groupware, 438
hardware, 452
icon, 452
information management, 434
information manager, 434
information system (IS), 435
information, 434
input device, 452
internet service provider (ISP), 439
internet, 438
intranet, 440
knowledge worker, 444
local area network (LAN), 459
main memory, 452
management information systems (MIS), 448
mass-customization, 440
multimedia communication system, 458
output device, 452
presentation graphics software, 457
program, 452
robotics, 451
search engine, 440
server, 460
software, 452
system operations personnel, 447
system program, 452
transaction processing system (TPS), 446
voice mail, 437
web server, 440
wide area network (WAN), 459
word-processing program, 455
World Wide Web, 439

QUESTIONS AND EXERCISES

Questions for Review

1. Why must a business manage information as a resource?
2. How can an electronic conferencing system increase productivity and efficiency?
3. Why do the four levels of user groups in an organization need different kinds of information from the IS?
4. In what ways are local area networks (LANs) different from or similar to wide area networks (WANs)?
5. What are the main types of electronic information technologies being applied in business information systems?

Questions for Analysis

6. Give two examples (other than those in this chapter) for each of the major types of business application programs.
7. Describe three or four activities in which you regularly engage that might be made easier by multimedia technology.
8. Give three examples (other than those in this chapter) of how a company can become leaner by adopting a networked IS.

Application Exercises

9. Describe the IS at your school. Identify its components and architecture. What features either promote or inhibit collaboration?
10. Visit a small business in your community to investigate the ways it's using communication technologies and the ways it plans to use them in the future. Prepare a report for class presentation.

BUILDING YOUR BUSINESS SKILLS

The Art and Science of Point-and-Click Research

Goal

To introduce students to World Wide Web search sites.

Background

In a recent survey of nearly 2000 web users, two-thirds said they used the web to obtain work-related information. With an estimated 320 million pages of information on the web, the challenge for business users is fairly obvious: how to find what they're looking for.

Method

You'll need a computer and access to the World Wide Web to complete this exercise.

Step 1
Get together with three classmates and decide on a business-related research topic. Choose a topic that interests you—for example, "Business Implications of the Most Recent Census," "Labour Disputes in

Professional Sports," or "Marketing Music Lessons and Instruments to Parents of Young Children."

Step 2

Search the following sites for information on your topic (dividing them among group members to speed the process):

Alta Vista **www.altavista.com**
Ask Jeeves **www.askjeeves.com**
Dogpile **www.dogpile.com**
Excite **www.excite.com**
Google **www.google.ca**
Hotbot **www.hotbot.lycos.com**
Infoseek **infoseek.go.com**
Lycos **www.lycos.com**
Metacrawler **www.metacrawler.com**
Northern Light **www.northernlight.com**
Yahoo! **www.yahoo.com**

Take notes as you search so that you can explain your findings to other group members.

Step 3

Working as a group, answer the following questions about your collective search:

1. Which sites were the easiest to use?
2. Which sites offered the most helpful results? What specific factors made these sites better than the others?
3. Which sites offered the least helpful results? What were the problems?
4. Why is it important to learn the special code words or symbols, called operators, that target a search? (Operators are words like AND, OR, and NOT that narrow search queries. For example, using AND in a search tells the system that all words must appear in the results—for example, American AND Management AND Association.)

Follow-Up Questions

1. Research the differences between search engines and search directories. Then place the sites listed in Step 2 in the proper category. Did you find search engines or directories more helpful in this exercise?
2. Why is it important to learn how to use the search-site "Help" function?
3. Based on your personal career goals, how do you think that mastering web-research techniques might help you in the future?
4. How has the web changed the nature of business research?

CRAFTING YOUR BUSINESS PLAN

Getting Wired into Better Information

The Purpose of the Assignment

1. To acquaint students with issues involving information systems that a sample firm faces in developing its business plan, in the framework of Business PlanPro (BPP) software package.
2. To demonstrate how communications technologies, the internet, and database considerations can be integrated as components in the BPP planning environment.

Assignment

After reading Chapter 13 in the textbook, open the BPP software and look around for information about plans for computer and communications technologies as they apply to a sample firm, a travel agency called Adventure Travel International (ATI). To find Adventure Travel, do the following:

Open the Business PlanPro. If it asks if you want to "create a new business plan" or "open an existing plan," select "create a new business plan" (even though you are not going to create a plan at this time). You will then be taken to the Business PlanPro EasyPlan Wizard. Click on the option entitled **Research It.** You will then be presented with a new list of options, including Sample Plan Browser. After clicking on **Sample Plan Browser**, go down the alphabetical list of sample plans and double-click on **Travel Agency—Adventure**, which is the location for ATI. The screen that you are looking at is the introduction page for the ATI business plan. Next, scroll down from this page until you reach the **Table of Contents** for the ATI business plan.

Now respond to the following items:

1. How have the internet and related communications technologies changed the travel agency industry? [Sites to see in BPP for this question: On the **Table of Contents** page, click in turn on each of the following: **3.2 Competitive Comparison** and **4.3.1 Business Participants.**]
2. How might databases be used to advantage at ATI? [Sites to see in BPP: On the **Table of Contents** page, click in turn on each of the following: **3.3 Sales Literature, 3.5 Technology, 4.1 Market Segmentation, 5.0 Strategy and Implementation Summary,** and **5.3.5 Marketing Programs.**]
3. What are the advantages in ATI's Computerized Reservation System? [Sites to see in BPP: From the **Table of Contents** page, click in turn on each of the following: **3.5 Technology** and **4.3.2 Distributing a Service.**]
4. How can ATI's distribution system benefit from the web? After exploring the ATI plan, what suggestions would you make about using the web? [Sites to see in BPP: In the **Table of Contents** page, click on **5.3.4 Distribution Strategy** and **5.5 Strategic Alliances.**]

VIDEO EXERCISE

Space Age Information Systems: Boeing Satellite Systems

Learning Objectives

The purpose of this video is to help you:

1. Understand why a business must manage information.
2. Consider the role of information systems in an organization.
3. Understand how information systems and communications technology contribute to efficiency and performance.

Synopsis

The world's leading manufacturer of commercial communications satellites, Boeing Satellite Systems is a wholly owned subsidiary of Boeing and serves customers in 14 countries. Boeing's information system collects and analyzes data from all departments and then disseminates the results to help management make decisions for boosting performance, productivity, and competitiveness. The chief information officer also oversees security precautions, disaster recovery plans, and procedures for safeguarding valuable data. In addition, each of the company's more than 8000 employees is equipped with a personal computer or laptop that can also serve as a television to receive broadcasts about company activities.

Discussion Questions

1. *For analysis:* What role do information systems play at Boeing Satellite Systems?
2. *For analysis:* What are some of the ways in which IT can improve productivity and performance at Boeing Satellite Systems?
3. *For application:* What potential problems might Boeing Satellite Systems have encountered when introducing computer kiosks into factory operations?
4. *For application:* In addition to scenes of Boeing-made satellite launches, what else should the company broadcast over employee computers? Why?
5. *For debate:* Should Boeing Satellite Systems try to prevent potential abuses by using software for monitoring employee use of PCs and laptops? Support your position.

Online Exploration

Visit the Boeing Satellite Systems website at **www.boeing.com/satellite** and search for more information about the firm's state-of-the-art integration and test facility. Also browse the site to see what the company says about its use of information systems and communication technology. Why would the company discuss technology in detail on a public website? What specific benefits of IS does Boeing Satellite Systems highlight? Why are these benefits important to customers who buy satellites?

EXPLORING THE NET

On the Cutting Edge with Experts

What are a company's information needs? How might the information system help employees increase productivity? Is the firm's information system consistent with its basic orientation? Are communications links adequate for networking among the departments and branches of the business? What kinds of equipment does the firm's information system need?

Let's look at these questions by exploring the website of Cisco Systems Inc., the worldwide leader in networking. Cisco's product line includes just about everything needed for networking, and by examining Cisco's products—hardware, software, and services—we can learn more about the needs of internet users and some of the leading-edge information-technology solutions available to them. To find out more about Cisco, its products, and its customers, go the firm's website at www.cisco.com.

First, to get an idea of the variety of Cisco products and services, browse the home page, including the various subject gates located around the page. Then go to the subject gate entitled **Networking Solutions**, and from the sub-listings, select the category **Large Enterprise.** Then select **Wireless/Mobility Solutions.** After exploring the various pages that result from the search, respond to the following item:

1. "Greater Independence of Company and Workplace" is a topic discussed in the first part of this chapter. What does its website say about products and services that Cisco offers for the geographic separation of the workplace from company headquarters?

Beginning again from the home page, return to the subject gate entitled **Networking Solutions,** and from the sub-listings, select the category **Small & Medium Business.** From here, select **Business Solutions.** Select **E-Commerce.** Choose **Implementation Roadmap** and respond to the following question:

2. Of what value is the information on this page to Cisco's potential customers? What is the purpose of this page?

Return to the **Small & Medium Business** page. On the left-side panel, select **Technology Solutions.** Select **Mobility** and click on **On the Road: Mobile Professional.** After reading this page, respond to the following questions:

3. What is a mobile professional and what information requirements does he or she have?
4. How does this webpage information relate to this chapter's textbook discussion?

Go back to the drop-down menu entitled **Technology Solution,** and click on and read the page entitled **Security.** After reading these pages, respond to the following question:

5. What kinds of internet access and security assistance does Cisco offer?

Concluding Case 13-1

More Productive Than a Speeding Locomotive

Locomotive manufacturing: Is it a twilight industry? Yes and no. At GE Transportation Systems, a unit of General Electric Co., the core business of making locomotives is in a severe downturn. Sales of locomotives have dropped by two-thirds in the last five years. So why is CEO John Krenicki Jr. so upbeat about the future? One reason is an industry-wide shift toward improving railroad services rather than just buying more trains.

Railroads want to raise productivity, improve on-time delivery, and cut costs—and GE is in a position to help with its remote monitoring diagnostics. Developed at GE's corporate R&D centre, the technology has been used in GE Medical Systems products and aircraft engines. Now it's being customized for the locomotive business. For 2002, revenues from Transportation Systems services, including remote diagnostics applications, were $1.5 billion—triple the 1996 total. New technologies, reports Krenicki, are changing the industry. "We're also digitizing all of our workflows—not just in our own factories but in customers' service shops." Krenicki wants to run service shops like a racing car pit crew. If shops run smoothly, freight rolls on time and at lower cost.

What do remote diagnostics do? They're designed to anticipate breakdowns before they happen. An unexpected breakdown can cost hundreds of thousands of dollars in lost operations, rescheduling, and unhappy customers. Remote sensing transmits signals from equipment to a satellite and then to the internet, where specialists anywhere can view data, perform tests, predict maintenance needs, and troubleshoot equipment operating in out-of-the-way places. Monitoring key components can catch failures ahead of time so that they can be repaired less expensively, with less disruption to schedules, and with shorter downtimes. The ideal is just-in-time maintenance: performing work when it's needed, not before or too late. "There are two kinds of mistakes," says Gerald Hahn, retired founder of GE's Applied Statistics Program. "Replacing too soon and replacing too late. We want to minimize both."

Remote monitoring is possible because of two advances in technology. First is the miniaturization of sensors—the devices that attach to components and detect system characteristics (temperature, pressure, and so forth). New devices are easier to install, take up little room, and don't interfere with normal operation. Second, advanced computing power makes it easier to process data for diagnosis. Today's 6000-horsepower locomotive engine is controlled by two dozen microprocessors that monitor such variables as speed, horsepower output, and voltage. Sensor data are relayed from a satellite to GE's service centre in Erie, Pennsylvania, where technicians monitor 300 locomotives around the country.

Let's say that GE's diagnostics team detects a clogged fuel filter, which can cut horsepower by 30 percent. Even the engineer wouldn't detect the loss if the train were pulling a light load, but it would slow down a heavily loaded train on an uphill grade, and the effect would soon be felt throughout the entire rail system. Other trains would fall behind, and the rescheduling would be expensive. With remote monitoring, technicians can check real-time data on hundreds of variables and detect problems that would otherwise go unsuspected. Much of the rail industry's increase in effectiveness, therefore, is due not to bigger or even better equipment, but rather to advanced technology and better information.

Consider another example: As an Airbus 340 flies from Tokyo to San Francisco, the jet engines are monitored and readings are collected by onboard computers transmitted to a GE monitoring station in Cincinnati, Ohio. By detecting impending component failures, airlines can avoid not only expensive repairs, but also flight diversions and delays. An aircraft engine costs U.S.$5 million to U.S.$10 million, and remote monitoring also helps with maintenance scheduling. Each engine needs an overhaul—costing between U.S.$500 000 and U.S.$2 million—every three to five years. Using software that runs statistical tests on monitored data, GE's Engine Services team can predict when engines will deteriorate to the point at which servicing is justified. By forecasting how many engines will need repair, service teams can anticipate how many spare engines and parts will be needed, thereby avoiding delays from shortages and the costs of storing too many expensive extras. In factories, too, remote monitoring tools are used for advanced maintenance programs on pumps, motors, machining centres, assembly lines, and automated painting systems.

The goal of remote monitoring is early detection. In the trucking industry, wireless communications combine data from onboard sensors with real-time data gathered from global positioning systems (GPSs). Detecting low pressure in tire number seven of a fleet truck in Montana, a dispatcher in Chicago may signal the driver that a repair station is located 15 miles ahead, thus avoiding tire failure and lost road time. Diagnostics also monitor other potential breakdowns—low coolant, alternator failure, engine oil or lube depletion, and electrical system deterioration.

There will soon be similar applications for consumer products, not only for household appliances—washers, dryers, refrigerators, and air conditioners—but also for cars and home alarm systems. Studded with computing chips, tiny sensors, and communications ports, your refrigeration compressor will detect and report potential failures before breakdown spoils a week's worth of food. GE, Whirlpool, Samsung, IBM, and several carmakers are working on systems that will detect and report maintenance problems over the internet.

Whatever the application, the key is the diagnostics centre, including data inflow and the software needed to extract useful information from it. Specialists must create the diagnostics software that receives data, discovers and stores correlations among variables, interprets the data, and reports findings in a format that's useful to maintenance personnel. As applications expand, don't be surprised if signals from your new car, television set, or refrigerator are being monitored at some diagnostics centre far, far away.

Questions for Discussion

1. What role, if any, does human judgment play in GE's remote monitoring diagnostics system?
2. What are the financial risks, if any, in subscribing to the GE system? What are risks of not subscribing?
3. Consider the kinds of software that might be useful in remote monitoring and diagnosis. What kinds of software might be needed, and what functions would it have to perform? ◆

Concluding Case 13-2 CC

Buying Drugs on the Internet

There is an international drug war going on. No, not the one against heroin and cocaine. This drug war pits internet pharmacies against drug companies. Here's the story.

For many years, Americans who live in border cities have been coming to Canada to purchase prescription drugs because these drugs are cheaper in Canada. Drugs are cheaper because the Canadian dollar is not worth nearly as much as the U.S. dollar, but also because the prices of drugs are regulated in Canada. When only a relatively small number of Americans came across the border to buy drugs, not much of a fuss was made. But the rise of the internet has suddenly made it possible for Americans living anywhere in the United States to purchase Canadian drugs without even coming to Canada. Instead, they can simply go online and order the drugs (they must provide a U.S. doctor's prescription).

Consider the case of Marlene Bodner, a Chicago-area senior who has arthritis. She orders her Celebrex from a Manitoba-based internet pharmacy that fills her prescription. She orders from Manitoba because it costs her a lot less money than if she purchased the drug in the United States. One hundred capsules of Celebrex, for example, costs Ms. Bodner about U.S.$180 if purchased in Canada, but well over U.S.$300 if she purchased them in the United States. Actos (a diabetes drug) costs about U.S.$350 for 90 tablets if purchased in Canada, but over U.S.$550 if purchased in the United States. No wonder U.S. seniors are ordering lots of prescription drugs from Canadian internet pharmacies.

All this demand for Canadian drugs has created a group of Canadian entrepreneurs who want to satisfy it (and, of course, make a profit doing so). One of the largest internet pharmacies is MediPlan Pharmacy of Minnedosa, Manitoba. It employs 230 people, and recently announced that it was building a new facility in Niverville, Manitoba. The internet drug industry in Manitoba employs over 1000 people and generates about $400 million annually in sales. There are currently about 150 internet pharmacies in Canada.

Both the big drug companies and the Canadian Pharmacists Association (CPhA) oppose internet pharmacies. Depending on who you talk to, their reasons are either selfish (they fear loss of profit) or because they are concerned about others. GlaxoSmithKline (GSK), for example, refused to sell internet pharmacies any of their products, and the Canadian Competition Bureau concluded that no laws were violated by this decision. GSK said that several problems existed with respect to internet pharmacies:

- the safety of drugs is compromised when they are sold over the internet because the internet pharmacist doesn't know if the patient is taking other drugs that might interfere with the patient's prescription request
- the internet system can't easily verify that the person wanting the prescription filled hasn't already had it filled from some other internet pharmacy as well
- the internet system can't verify whether the prescription is authentic
- when drugs are shipped, they can be exposed to various hazards that might reduce their effectiveness

The Canadian Pharmacists Association (CPhA) opposes internet pharmacies for these same reasons, but they are also concerned about another issue: disruptions in the market for pharmacy graduates. The demand for pharmacists has skyrocketed since internet pharmacies opened up, and this has pushed up the starting salaries for pharmacy grads. This means that the traditional pharmacy in a retail store like a Shoppers Drug Mart may have trouble recruiting new grads. (Traditional pharmacists start at about $40/hour, but internet pharmacists are being paid about $60/hour.) The CPhA fears that the number of traditional pharmacies in retail outlets is going to decline, and that Canadians are going to have difficulty getting their prescriptions filled at a convenient location.

The internet pharmacies respond to these claims with several arguments:

- the drug companies won't sell to Canadian-based internet pharmacies because the drug companies will make lower profit margins than if they sold to U.S. pharmacies
- internet pharmacies are providing patients with more affordable prescription drugs; without these drugs, the quality of life of these patients would be much lower
- traditional pharmacists oppose internet pharmacies simply because they are resisting new ways of doing things

The fight has become very political. While it is technically illegal for U.S. citizens to buy prescription drugs from Canada, the U.S. Food and Drug Administration essentially allows some prescription drugs to come in as long as they are for personal use, and as long as they are not for a period of more than 90 days. The FDA is, however, cracking down on U.S. storefront operations for Canadian internet pharmacies. Rx Depot, which has several storefronts in Arkansas, received a warning from the FDA that what it was doing is illegal. Rx Depot responded by threatening court action if the FDA tried to shut them down. In Canada, Quebec has moved to shut down internet pharmacies in that province, but in Manitoba and Alberta, the provinces have been supportive of these pharmacies.

U.S. seniors are an important voting group in the United States, and they were upset by GSK's decision to stop selling to Canadian-based internet pharmacies. Attempts are now being made to organize a boycott of GSK's products. For their part, the internet pharmacies are trying to get around GSK's refusal to sell drugs to them. MediPlan, for example, tried to get some local pharmacists in Manitoba to increase their orders to GSK and then give them the surplus. The CPhA condemned this move, claiming it was unethical and possibly illegal.

A deal was reached between the Manitoba Pharmaceutical Association (MPhA) and the Manitoba internet pharmacies that allows Manitoba pharmacists to fill prescriptions written by U.S. doctors. It also says that if there are shortages of drugs, the needs of Manitobans must be satisfied first.

In July 2003, the U.S. House of Representatives approved a bill that allowed Americans to import drugs from 25 different nations (including Canada). This gave a big boost to Canadian internet pharmacies.

Questions for Discussion

1. Explain how the internet has facilitated the growth of internet pharmacies.
2. Should internet pharmacies be allowed to operate? What regulations, if any, should the Canadian government put on internet pharmacies?
3. Would you buy prescription drugs from an internet pharmacy? Why or why not?
4. Critique each of the arguments that are being made by the drug companies and the Canadian Pharmacists Association. Then do the same for each of the arguments being made by the internet pharmacies. Which arguments do you think are the most compelling? Explain. ◆

CHAPTER 14 Understanding Accounting Issues

After reading this chapter, you should be able to:

1. Explain the role of accountants and distinguish between the kinds of work done by *public* and *private accountants.*

2. Explain how the *accounting equation* and *double-entry accounting* are used in record keeping.

3. Describe the three basic *financial statements* and show how they reflect the activity and financial condition of a business.

4. Explain the key standards and principles for reporting financial statements.

5. Show how computing key *financial ratios* can help in analyzing the financial strengths of a business.

6. Explain some of the special issues facing accountants at firms that do international business.

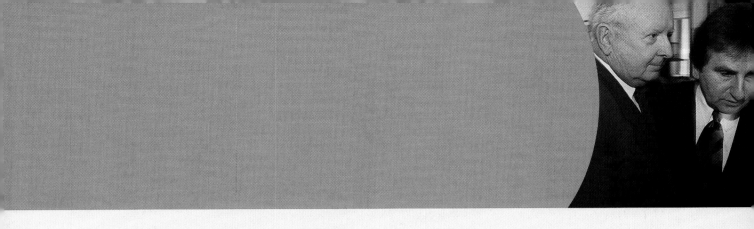

Accountants Under Fire

The large amount of negative publicity that has been given to firms like Enron and WorldCom during the last few years makes very interesting reading, but it is making accountants very nervous. More and more people seem to be asking, "How much confidence can I really have when a company is audited and I'm told that they are financially sound?"

In 2001, Enron was one of the largest companies in the world, and Arthur Andersen (its auditor) was one of the world's "big five" accounting firms. One year later, Enron was in bankruptcy, and Andersen was fighting to stay alive after the firm was found guilty of shredding documents dealing with Enron. In violation of its own ethical policies, Enron allowed some executives to set up special "off the books" partnerships that were then used by Enron to hide costs and artificially inflate revenues (for more details about this practice, see Concluding Case 14-1).

The Enron case is just one of the many problems that popped up during the stock market excesses of the late 1990s. The economic boom, and the ever-increasing expectations that went with it, caused many managers to be under intense pressure to show impressive gains in corporate revenues and profits. This led some companies to engage in unethical practices as they tried to artificially inflate financial gains. In 2002, for example, Xerox announced that it had overstated revenues by billions of dollars. It was fined $10 million by the U.S. Securities and Exchange Commission. Other companies—including Tyco and WorldCom—also succumbed to the temptation to inflate revenue and profit numbers.

How did all these things happen when the companies' financial statements were audited by accounting firms that are supposed to give an independent opinion about the appropriateness of a company's accounting statements? The answer is that accounting firms sometimes looked the other way when carrying out their auditing activities. But why would accounting firms not point out questionable accounting practices when they found them? One reason is that many accounting firms also do management consulting for the firms they are auditing. Management consulting fees are lucrative, often exceeding the auditing fees the accounting firm receives. Managers in these accounting firms fear that clients will be upset if they question certain accounting practices, and if the clients get upset enough, they may not give the accounting firm any management consulting contracts. If that happens, the accounting firm loses revenue.

The obvious solution to this problem is to prohibit accounting firms from doing both auditing and management consulting for a given client. The accounting profession resisted this solution for many years, but the magnitude of the Enron debacle has suddenly made this idea more palatable. In 2002, for example, the Canadian Imperial Bank of Commerce (CIBC) announced that it would no longer allow its auditors to do any management consulting for CIBC. Other Canadian companies are also scrambling to reassure their investors that everything is in order. In 2001, TransAlta Corp. made it clear that its auditors did not provide any consulting services to TransAlta.

The issue of consulting is not the only controversy facing the accounting industry. The following criticisms have also been made:

- there is sometimes a "chummy" relationship between auditors and their clients; this makes it more difficult for auditors to be completely objective
- there is considerable "elasticity" in the application of generally accepted accounting principles; thus, companies have a lot of leeway in their accounting practices
- if a person from an accounting firm takes a management position with a firm that is a client, future audits may be too "cozy" and fail to be objective
- self-regulation by the accounting industry doesn't work
- there has been much fruitless debate in accounting firms about how to deal with stock options that are given to executives (if these are shown as expenses, they depress corporation earnings and lower the stock price)

- the decline of the stock market and the drop in interest rates has meant that the pension funds of many companies are now underfunded, yet many companies don't record pension liabilities on their balance sheets (for more information about this issue, see Concluding Case 14-2)
- the accounting profession has moved away from establishing broad accounting principles and instead spent much of its time drafting detailed rules; even if these detailed rules are followed, the financial statements that are produced can present a distorted picture of a company's financial condition

What should be done to resolve these problems? A few of the more commonly heard solutions are as follows:

- auditors should clarify their language so that readers of financial statements will have a better idea of how a company is doing before they invest in it
- auditors should give more consideration to the users of financial statements, perhaps emphasizing different data for different user groups
- auditors should be charged with detecting fraud and reporting when they find it
- firms should be required to change their auditors on a regular basis (for example, once every five years) to prevent "chummy" relationships from developing
- auditors should not be allowed to take jobs with former clients until after a specified time period has passed (say, 3–5 years)
- a truly independent monitoring group should be formed that would assess the extent to which companies are meeting standards in their financial reporting
- stock options should be shown as expenses
- when earnings forecasts are made, there must be a clear statement of how the forecasted numbers were arrived at
- companies should be required to show how much they paid for auditing services, and how much they paid for management consulting from the same auditor
- auditors should be required to rank a company's accounting practices in terms of how "aggressive" they are, rather than just saying the books are okay or not okay

There are some hopeful developments. Canada's accounting profession issued new rules in 2002 that limit the use of off-balance-sheet entities like the kind that Enron used, and this should also help to reduce Enron-type problems. The new standards will force companies to include the financial impact of special purpose entities (SPEs) on the parent company's balance sheet. Canadian companies that were keeping SPEs off the balance sheet will now be forced to change that practice.

Another major development: Canada's six largest accounting firms will now be supervised, inspected, and disciplined by a new Canadian Public Accountability Board (CPAB). The accounting firms will have to get CPAB clearance before their clients' financial statements are accepted. In short, the auditors are going to be audited. ◆

WHAT IS ACCOUNTING AND WHO USES IT?

accounting
A comprehensive system for collecting, analyzing, and communicating financial information.

bookkeeping
Recording accounting transactions.

Accounting is a comprehensive information system for collecting, analyzing, and communicating financial information. As such, it is a system for measuring business performance and translating those measures into information for management decisions. **Bookkeeping** is just one phase of accounting—the recording of accounting transactions. Clearly, accounting is much more comprehensive than bookkeeping because accounting involves more than just the recording of information.

Accounting also uses performance measures to prepare performance reports for owners, the public, and regulatory agencies. To meet these objectives, accountants keep records of such transactions as taxes paid, income received, and expenses incurred, and they analyze the effects of these transactions on particular business activities. By sorting, analyzing, and recording thousands of transactions, accountants can determine how well a business is being managed and how financially strong it is. As the opening case shows, the accounting system can produce distorted results that, in turn, can create huge problems for both owners and managers.

Because businesses engage in many thousands of transactions, ensuring consistent, dependable financial information is mandatory. This is the job of the **accounting information system (AIS)**: an organized procedure for identifying, measuring, recording, and retaining financial information so that it can be used in accounting statements and management reports. The system includes all the people, reports, computers, procedures, and resources for compiling financial transactions.[1]

accounting information system (AIS)
An organized procedure for identifying, measuring, recording, and retaining financial information so that it can be used in accounting statements and management reports.

Noranda Inc., Canada's biggest natural resource company, faced an accounting challenge when it announced plans to refocus on the mining and metals side of its activities by selling its forest products and oil and natural gas interests. In preparation for the announcement, corporate officers relied on accounting to provide information for everyone who might be interested in the firm's activities. A statement was issued to shareholders and the public to show clearly how much each of the three segments contributed to Noranda's overall sales, expenses, and earnings. Current and potential stockholders also had to be told how the new stock shares would be distributed.[2] Upon receiving accounting answers to questions such as these, different information users (owners, employees, regulatory agencies, lenders, and the public) are better prepared to make decisions for themselves and for their organizations.

As the Noranda story illustrates, there are numerous users of accounting information:

- *Business managers* use accounting information to set goals, develop plans, set budgets, and evaluate future prospects.
- *Employees and unions* use accounting information to get paid and to plan for and receive such benefits as health care, insurance, vacation time, and retirement pay.
- *Investors and creditors* use accounting information to estimate returns to stockholders, to determine a company's growth prospects, and to decide if it is a good credit risk before investing or lending.
- *Taxing authorities* use accounting information to plan for tax inflows, to determine the tax liabilities of individuals and businesses, and to ensure that correct amounts are paid in a timely fashion.
- *Government regulatory agencies* rely on accounting information to fulfill their duties; the provincial securities commissions, for example, require firms to file financial disclosures so that potential investors have valid information about a company's financial status.

WHO ARE ACCOUNTANTS AND WHAT DO THEY DO?

1. Explain the role of accountants and distinguish between the kinds of work done by *public* and *private accountants.*

At the head of the AIS is the **controller**, who manages all the firm's accounting activities. As chief accounting officer, the controller ensures that the accounting system provides the reports and statements needed for planning, controlling, and decision-making activities. This broad range of activities requires different types of accounting specialists. In this section, we will begin by distinguishing between the two main fields of accounting, *financial* and *managerial.* Then we will discuss the different functions and activities of the three professional accounting groups in Canada.

controller
The individual who manages all the firm's accounting activities.

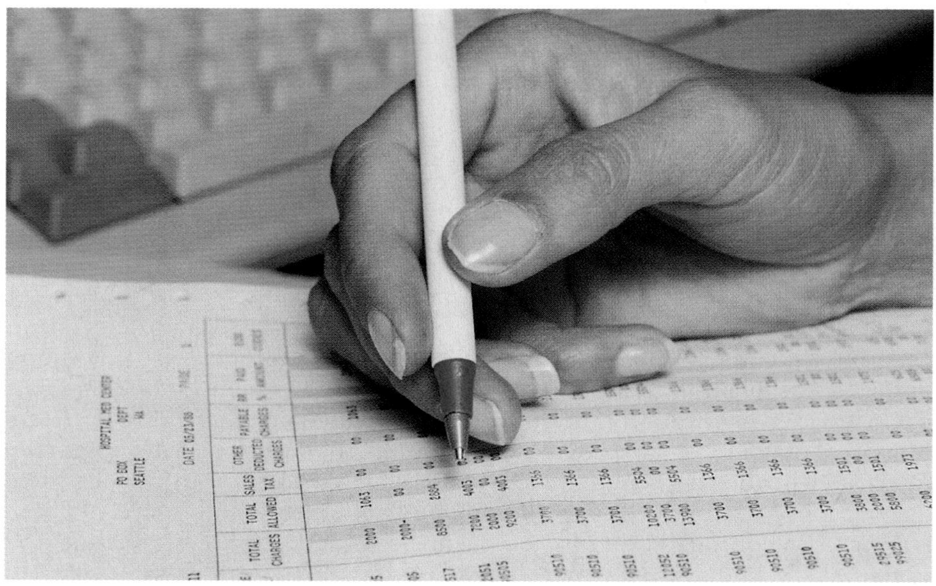

A financial report is an integral component of the financial accounting system.

Financial and Managerial Accounting

In any company, two fields of accounting—financial and managerial—can be distinguished by the different users they serve. As we have just seen, it is both convenient and accurate to classify users of accounting information as users outside the company and users inside the company. This same distinction allows us to categorize accounting systems as either *financial* or *managerial.*

Financial Accounting

financial accounting system
The process whereby interested groups are kept informed about the financial condition of a firm.

A firm's **financial accounting system** is concerned with external users of information—consumer groups, unions, shareholders, and government agencies. It prepares and publishes income statements and balance sheets at regular intervals. All of these documents focus on the activities of *the company as a whole,* rather than on individual departments or divisions.

In reporting data, financial accountants must conform to standard reporting formats and procedures imposed by both the accounting profession and government regulatory agencies. This requirement helps ensure that users can clearly compare information, whether from many different companies or from the same company at different times. The information in such reports is mostly *historical*: That is, it summarizes financial transactions that have occurred during past accounting periods.

Managerial Accounting

managerial (management) accounting
Internal procedures that alert managers to problems and aid them in planning and decision making.

In contrast, **managerial** (or **management**) **accounting** serves internal users. Managers at all levels need information to make decisions for their departments, to monitor current projects, and to plan for future activities. Other employees, too, need accounting information. Engineers, for instance, want to know costs for materials and production so they can make product or operations improvements. To set performance goals, salespeople need data on past sales by geographic region. Purchasing agents use information on materials costs to negotiate terms with suppliers.

Reports to these users serve *the company's individual units,* whether departments, projects, plants, or divisions. Internal reports may be designed in any form that will assist internal users in planning, decision making, and controlling. Furthermore, as *projections* and *forecasts* of both financial data and business activities, internal reports are an extremely important part of the management accounting system: They are forward-looking rather than historical in nature.

In spite of the problems with accounting that have been publicized during the last few years, the field is highly developed in Canada and the United States. As the Business Today box demonstrates, this is not true in some other countries.

BUSINESS TODAY

The Arcane Art of Accounting in Russia

In Russia, the word *profit* does not mean the same thing it does in the West. Some companies in Russia—major oil companies, the natural gas monopoly, and some large corporations—have been producing Western-style financial statements for a few years now. But many enterprises still stick to the old ways. For example, the chief accountant at the Moscow Electrode Factory, Nadezhda Belobrovkina, learned her trade many years ago. She has never heard of generally accepted accounting principles (GAAP), and she still keeps records by hand in a big white ledger. The factory has trouble paying its staff, has fallen heavily into debt, and is way behind in paying its energy bills. But according to Belobrovkina's calculations, the factory still makes money.

The accounting software department at 1C, a Russian computer company, designs software to help other companies convert their raw financial data into two different sets of accounts, one Russian and one Western. Even though the Soviet era is long gone, the Russian accounting system has not been reformed. It was never designed to account for things like profit. The Russian Finance Ministry would like to see a change, as would the International Monetary Fund.

Russia's Chart of Accounts is the framework for corporate bookkeeping. But it is designed to help the state's central planners (and more recently the tax police) prevent people from stealing by keeping close tabs on inventories. It is not designed to help managers develop their businesses. Under the old system, accountants focused on production and tracking of inputs and outputs. They could not say whether value had been added, or whether profit had been made.

Another problem: Accountants were not allowed to set realistic depreciation rates. Rather, the state's published guidelines, which stipulated the lifespan of everything from chairs to machine tools, discouraged replacement of obsolete equipment and buildings. Western accountants, for example, usually set the useful life of a building at 30 years; in Russia they are decreed to last up to 100 years.

The problems with the Russian accounting system are illustrated at Bratsk Aluminum, Russia's largest aluminum producer. In one recent year, the company claimed it made $37 million in profit, but when Arthur Andersen Company audited the books it reported that the company had actually lost more than $7 million. Profit is not the only area of disagreement. Andersen estimated depreciation at Bratsk at about $56 million, while the company put the figure at only $19 million.

The Russian accounting system creates other problems, too. The old Soviet system never accounted for advertising or for employee travel and training costs. But these costs are an important part of doing business in the modern world. Russian authorities seem to view these activities as simply another possibility for tax fraud and therefore put strict limits on deductions.

But changes are in the air, and in the long run an emerging new breed of accountants will help Russia make the transition to a market economy. The head of the Russian Finance Ministry's Department of Accounting Methodology, Alexander Bakaev, is also pushing for more Western-style accounting. He has drafted various reform guidelines and says that Russia must adopt International Accounting Standards. However, he faces an uphill battle. Companies try to avoid value-added tax by shunning accrual accounting in favour of cash accounting. This means that they record transactions not when goods are delivered, but when they receive payment. However, in the Russian system bad debts are endemic, which means that some transactions are never recorded because they are never paid.

Russia's outdated accounting system will also change as eager new Russian entrepreneurs try to attract foreign capital. They realize that they cannot be successful unless they have reasonable accounting records.

Professional Accountants

Users of financial statements want to be confident that the accountants who have prepared them have a high level of expertise and credibility. Three professional accounting organizations have developed in Canada to certify accounting expertise.

Chartered Accountants

chartered accountant (CA)
An individual who has met certain experience and education requirements and has passed a licensing examination; acts as an outside accountant for other firms.

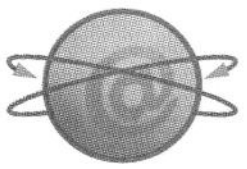

Canadian Institute of Chartered Accountants (CICA)
www.cica.ca

The Canadian Institute of Chartered Accountants (CICA) grants the **chartered accountant (CA)** designation. To achieve this designation, a person must earn a university degree, then complete an educational program and pass a national exam. About half of all CAs work in CA firms that offer accounting services to the public; the other half work in government or industry. CA firms typically provide audit, tax, and management services (see Table 14.1 for a list of the 10 largest CA firms in Canada). CAs focus on external financial reporting, that is, certifying for various interested parties (shareholders, lenders, Canada Customs and Revenue Agency, etc.) that the financial records of a company accurately reflect the true financial condition of the firm.

Certified General Accountants

certified general accountant (CGA)
An individual who has completed an education program and passed a national exam; works in private industry or a CGA firm.

The Certified General Accountants Association of Canada grants the **certified general accountant (CGA)** designation. To become a CGA, a person must complete an education program and pass a national exam. To be eligible, a person must have an accounting job with a company. Formerly, CGAs were not allowed to audit the financial statements of publicly held companies, but this is rapidly changing, and now CGAs can audit corporate financial statements in most provinces. Most CGAs work in private companies, but there are a few CGA firms. Some CGAs also work in CA firms. CGAs also focus on external financial reporting, and emphasize the use of the computer as a management accounting tool.

Certified Management Accountants

certified management accountant (CMA)
An individual who has completed a university degree, passed a national examination, and completed a strategic leadership program; works in industry and focuses on internal management accounting.

The Society of Management Accountants of Canada grants the **certified management accountant (CMA)** designation. To achieve the designation, a person must a have university degree, pass a two-part national entrance examination, and complete a strategic leadership program while gaining practical experience in a management accounting environment. CMAs work in organizations of all sizes, and focus on applying best management

Table 14.1 The Top 10 Accounting Firms in Canada

	Company	Annual Revenues (in millions of $)
1.	Deloitte & Touche LLP	892
2.	KPMG LLP	745
3.	PricewaterhouseCoopers LLP	676
4.	Ernst & Young LLP	534
5.	Grant Thornton	301
6.	BDO Dunwoody LLP	222
7.	Meyers Norris Penny LLP	86
8.	Collins Barrow/Mintz & Partners	84
9.	Richter, Usher & Vineberg	83
10.	HLB/Schwartz Levitsky Feldman	42

practices in all the operations of a business. CMAs bring a strong market focus to strategic management and resource deployment, synthesizing and analyzing financial and non-financial information to help organizations maintain a competitive advantage. CMAs emphasize the role of accountants in the planning and overall strategy of the firm in which they work.

The Society of Management Accountants of Canada
www.cma-canada.org

Accounting Services

CAs and CGAs usually perform several accounting services for their clients. The most common of these are auditing, tax services, and management services.

Auditing

In an **audit**, the accountant examines a company's AIS to determine whether the company's financial reports fairly present its financial operations. Companies normally must provide audited financial reports when applying for loans or when selling stock. The audit will determine if the firm has controls to prevent errors or fraud from going undetected. Auditors also examine receipts such as shipping documents, cancelled cheques, payroll records, and cash receipts records. In some cases, an auditor may physically check inventories, equipment, or other assets, even if it means descending 200 metres underground in a lead mine.

audit
An accountant's examination of a company's financial records to determine if it used proper procedures to prepare its financial reports.

When audits are being conducted, **forensic accountants** may be used to track down hidden funds in business firms. Because white-collar crime is on the increase, the number of forensic accountants has increased in recent years. Forensic accountants were used to examine Swiss bank accounts for assets deposited by victims of Nazi persecution during the Second World War.[3] Al Rosen, who writes articles about accounting practices, is a well-known Canadian forensic accountant.

forensic accountant
An accountant who tracks down hidden funds in business firms, usually as part of a criminal investigation.

One of the auditor's responsibilities is to ensure that the client's accounting system adheres to generally accepted accounting principles. **Generally accepted accounting principles (GAAP)** are a body of theory and procedure developed and monitored by the CICA. At the end of an audit, the auditor will certify whether the client's financial reports comply with GAAP. Recently, some non-profit organizations such as churches and universities have said that they felt pressured by their auditors to use GAAP. They argue, however, that GAAP principles are designed for profit-seeking business firms, not non-profit organizations. Non-profits should be judged on how well they meet their goals—for example, helping people—rather than on a financial criterion like profit.[4]

generally accepted accounting principles (GAAP)
Standard rules and methods used by accountants in preparing financial reports.

Tax Services

Tax services include helping clients not only with preparing their tax returns but also in their tax planning. Tax laws are complex. A CA's advice can help a business structure (or restructure) its operations and investments and save millions of dollars in taxes. To serve their clients best, of course, accountants must stay abreast of changes in tax laws—no simple matter.

Management Consulting Services

Management consulting services range from personal financial planning to the planning of corporate mergers. Other services include plant layout and design, marketing studies, production scheduling, computer feasibility studies, and design and implementation of accounting systems. Some accounting firms even assist in executive recruitment. Small wonder that

management consulting services
Specialized accounting services to help managers resolve a variety of problems in finance, production scheduling, and other areas.

Employees at telecommunications giant WorldCom were surprised to hear about the company's U.S.$3.8 billion restatement of 2002 earnings, and they were shocked when they were laid off a few months later. The bankruptcy put 17 000 people out of work. Many of them blamed WorldCom's auditor, Arthur Andersen, for failing to uncover WorldCom's financial problems. Financial analysts questioned whether Andersen could maintain any objectivity as an auditor while collecting millions of dollars in consulting fees from the same client.

the staffs of accounting firms may include engineers, architects, mathematicians, and even psychologists.

The Wired World box describes another interesting dilemma for accounting firms that wish to provide auditing and management consulting services to new dot-com firms.

Private Accountants

private accountant
An accountant hired as a salaried employee to deal with a company's day-to-day accounting needs.

To ensure the fairness of their reports, CAs and CGAs must be independent of the firms they audit. They are employees of accounting firms and provide services for many clients. But businesses also hire their own **private accountants** as salaried employees to deal with the company's day-to-day accounting needs.

Private accountants perform a variety of accounting jobs. An internal auditor at Petro-Canada, for example, might fly to the Hibernia site to confirm the accuracy of oil-flow meters on the offshore drilling platform. But a supervisor responsible for $200 million in monthly accounts payable to vendors and employees may travel no further than the executive suite. The nature of the accounting job thus depends on the specific business and the activities needed to make that business a success. Large businesses employ specialized accountants in such areas as budgets, financial planning, internal auditing, payroll, and taxation. Each accounting area has its own challenges and excitement. In small businesses, a single individual may handle all accounting tasks. The Exercising Your Ethics box on page 480 presents an ethical dilemma for an accountant who is considering changing jobs.

The CPA Vision Project

Accounting scandals like Enron have caused both Canadian and U.S. accounting groups to take a hard look at their practices. In the United States, the CPA Vision Project was established to assess the future of accounting.[5] In recognizing a rapidly changing business world, the project focuses on certain desired goals for the profession and identifies the changes that will be needed to accomplish them. The Vision Project explains how six classes of global forces (see Figure 14.1 on page 481) are driving the profession's reorientation.

IT'S A WIRED WORLD

A Roundabout Look at Conflicting Interests

With all the new dot-com companies popping up, things are looking up for accounting firms. Because all those ebusinesses need accounting services—setting up accounting systems, preparing taxes and financial reports, conducting audits—prospects are good for an upsurge of new clients. Or are they? Two factors are getting in the way, one having to do with the lean purses of the dot-com companies, and the other having to do with the structure of today's large accounting firms. As a result, accounting firms are running into roadblocks in trying to pursue dot-com clients.

Many dot-coms are short on cash; most of them are operating in the red even though prospects may be bright for future earnings. Some of today's financially strapped dot-coms will prosper and become tomorrow's ecommerce giants. Naturally, public accounting firms would like them to become giant clients in need of accounting services for years to come. PricewaterhouseCoopers, for example, expects that about half of its consulting revenues will eventually come from ebusinesses. Unfortunately, would-be e-giants need accounting services now, including management advisory services to help formulate focused strategies, target desirable markets, and improve operations now, while they're getting started, instead of later. The problem is that they can't pay now.

The solution? Increasingly, accounting firms are accepting equity positions instead of cash payment. In return for its services, the accounting firm becomes part owner of the dot-com company. Generally speaking, it's a good arrangement. While the accounting firm gets a new client (and stands to gain future revenues from its ownership position), the dot-com gets timely professional management help without laying out badly needed cash.

But there's a problem. What the accounting firm gains in a present consulting client it may lose in a future auditing client. Accounting firms are not allowed to make the kind of ownership-investment arrangement described above and provide auditing (or other financial accounting) services for the same client because there is a potential conflict of interest. Rules require that auditors have no investment stake in the companies they audit. In fact, it stands to reason that allowing an accounting firm to audit a company in which it has an ownership interest is an invitation to financial mischief. It would be like asking a bank to audit itself rather than hiring an independent auditor.

Nor do the problems stop there. As part owner, the accounting firm must steer away from other part owners in the company. Suppose, for example, that a number of other firms, such as a shipping company, an investment firm, a wholesaler, and a computer supplier, also have ownership interests in the same dot-com. The accounting firm must also decline to audit those firms. Again, there is a potential conflict of interest: The accounting firm could make the dot-com's financial position look good to improve the appearance of its fellow part-owners' financial positions.

At present, therefore, it appears that the dot-com explosion that looks like such a terrific opportunity for accounting firms may turn out to be much more limited. Currently, an accountant is forced to make a choice: to take on the dot-com as a client for auditing services or as a client for management advisory services. Accountants can't have it both ways. And whatever choice the accountant makes, the accounting firm also has to ensure that its auditors and management consultants know what its accountants are doing.

Recommendations for Change

The Vision Project indicates that accounting educators and accounting professionals must make changes in the functioning of the profession. Among the top recommendations for change:

- The profession should adopt a broader focus beyond "numbers" that includes "strategic thinking."
- The profession should provide more value to society by expanding knowledge, education, and experience.
- CPA education must be revitalized to meet the demands of the future.

EXERCISING YOUR ETHICS

Confidentially Yours

The Situation

Accountants are often entrusted with private, sensitive information that should be used confidentially. In this exercise, you're encouraged to think about ethical considerations that might arise when an accountant's career choices come up against a professional obligation to maintain confidentiality.

The Dilemma

Assume that you're the head accountant in a large electronics firm. Your responsibilities include preparing income statements and balance sheets for financial reporting to stockholders. In addition, you regularly prepare confidential budgets for internal use by managers responsible for planning departmental activities, including future investments in new assets. You've also worked with auditors and supplied sensitive information to consultants from a CA firm that assesses financial problems and suggests solutions.

Now let's suppose that you're approached by another company—one of the electronics industry's most successful firms—and offered a higher-level position. If you accept, your new job will include developing financial plans and serving on the strategic planning committee. Thus, you'd be involved not only in developing strategy but also in evaluating the competition. You'll undoubtedly be called upon to use your knowledge of your previous firm's competitive strengths and weaknesses. You realize that your insider knowledge could be useful in your new job.

Questions for Discussion

1. What are the roles of financial accounting, managerial accounting, and accounting services in this scenario?
2. What are the chief ethical issues in this situation?
3. As the central figure in this scenario, how would you handle this situation?

- To attract qualified members, the profession must increase opportunities for advancement, rewards, and lifestyle preferences.

TOOLS OF THE ACCOUNTING TRADE

2. Explain how the *accounting equation* and *double-entry accounting* are used in record keeping.

All accountants, whether public or private, rely on record keeping. Private accountants use journals and ledgers to enter and keep track of business transactions for their company. Underlying these records are the two key concepts of accounting: the *accounting equation* and *double-entry bookkeeping.*

The Accounting Equation

At various points in the year, accountants use the following equation to balance the data pertaining to financial transactions:

$$\text{Assets} = \text{Liabilities} + \text{Owners' equity}$$

To understand the importance of this equation, we must first understand the terms *assets, liabilities,* and *owners' equity.*[6]

Assets and Liabilities

asset
Anything of economic value owned by a firm or individual.

liability
Any debt owed by a firm or individual to others.

An **asset** is any economic resource that is expected to benefit a firm or an individual who owns it. Assets include land, buildings, equipment, inventory, and payments due the company (accounts receivable). A **liability** is a debt that the firm owes to an outside party.

Economic forces
- globalization of capital markets
- electronic movement of capital
- interdependent worldwide system of trade, finance, management

Political forces
- spread of democracy
- democratized management styles
- public interest groups
- globalization of politics

Technical forces
- displacement of human activity by expert systems and automation
- advent of digital technology, new ways of working, different points of decision, and more complicated decision tasks

Social forces
- new educational methods
- new global standards for conducting business
- changing worldwide demographics
- colliding and merging of ethnic groups

The new CPA profession

Human resource forces
- fragmentation of traditional employer–employee relationships
- growth in outsourcing, permanent temporaries, and just-in-time employment
- advent of multiple jobs and multiple careers
- premium pay for knowledge workers and digital-tech employees

Regulatory forces
- influence of globalized corporations, public interest groups, and professional organizations
- collaboration of organizations and groups to shape reform for the future
- collaboration of organizations and companies to force viewpoints onto political agendas

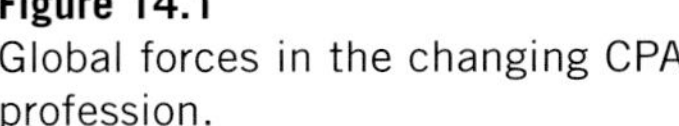

Figure 14.1
Global forces in the changing CPA profession.

The inventory at this car dealership is part of the company's assets. The cars constitute an economic resource because the firm will benefit financially as it sells them. When they are sold, at the end of the company's accounting period, the dealership will convert the cost of the cars as expenses and show them as costs of goods sold.

Owners' Equity

owners' equity
Any positive difference between a firm's assets and its liabilities; what would remain for a firm's owners if the company were liquidated, all its assets were sold, and all its debts were paid.

You may have heard of the equity that a homeowner has in a house—that is, the amount of money that could be made by selling the house and paying off the mortgage. Similarly, **owners' equity** is the amount of money that owners would receive if they sold all of a company's assets and paid all of its liabilities. We can rewrite the accounting equation to highlight this definition:

Assets – Liabilities = Owners' equity

If a company's assets exceed its liabilities, owners' equity is *positive*; if the company goes out of business, the owners will receive some cash (a gain) after selling assets and paying off liabilities. If liabilities outweigh assets, owners' equity is *negative*; assets are insufficient to pay off all debts. If the company goes out of business, the owners will get no cash and some creditors won't be paid. Owners' equity is meaningful for both investors and lenders. Before lending money to owners, for example, lenders want to know the amount of owners' equity in a business. Owners' equity consists of two sources of capital:

1. The amount that the owners originally invested
2. Profits earned by and reinvested in the company

When a company operates profitably, its assets increase faster than its liabilities. Owners' equity, therefore, will increase if profits are retained in the business instead of paid out as dividends to stockholders. Owners' equity also increases if owners invest more of their own money to increase assets. However, owners' equity can shrink if the company operates at a loss or if owners withdraw assets.

Double-Entry Accounting

double-entry accounting system
A bookkeeping system, developed in the fifteenth century and still in use, that requires every transaction to be entered in two ways—how it affects assets and how it affects liabilities and owners' equity—so that the accounting equation is always in balance.

If your business buys inventory with cash, you decrease your cash and increase your inventory. Similarly, if you buy supplies on credit, you increase your supplies and increase your accounts payable. If you invest more money in your business, you increase the company's cash and increase your owners' equity. In other words, *every transaction affects two accounts*. Accountants thus use a **double-entry accounting system** to record the dual effects of transactions.[7] This practice ensures that the accounting equation always balances.

FINANCIAL STATEMENTS

3. Describe the three basic *financial statements* and show how they reflect the activity and financial condition of a business.

financial statement
Any of several types of broad reports regarding a company's financial status; most often used in reference to balance sheets, income statements, and/or statements of cash flows.

As we noted earlier, the job of accounting is to summarize the results of a firm's transactions and to issue reports to help managers make informed decisions. Among the most important reports are **financial statements,** which fall into three broad categories—*balance sheets, income statements,* and *statements of cash flows*.[8] In this section, we will discuss these three types of financial statements, as well as the function of the budget as an internal financial statement. We'll conclude by explaining the most important reporting practices and the standards that guide accountants in drawing up financial statements.

Balance Sheets

Balance sheets supply detailed information about the accounting equation factors: assets, liabilities, and owners' equity. Because they also show a firm's financial condition at one point in time, balance sheets are sometimes called *statements of financial position*. Figure 14.2 shows the balance sheet for Perfect Posters.

balance sheet
A type of financial statement that summarizes a firm's financial position on a particular date in terms of its assets, liabilities, and owners' equity.

Assets

As we have seen, an asset is any economic resource that a company owns and from which it can expect to derive some future benefit. From an accounting standpoint, most companies have three types of assets: *current, fixed,* and *intangible.*

Current Assets. Current assets include cash and assets that can be converted into cash within a year. They are normally listed in order of **liquidity**—the ease with which they can be converted into cash. Business debts, for example, can usually be satisfied only through payments of cash. A company that needs but cannot generate cash (in other words, a company that is not liquid) may thus be forced to sell assets at sacrifice prices or even go out of business.

current assets
Cash and other assets that can be converted into cash within a year.

liquidity
The ease and speed with which an asset can be converted to cash; cash is said to be perfectly liquid.

By definition, cash is completely liquid. *Marketable securities* purchased as short-term investments are slightly less liquid but can be sold quickly if

Perfect Posters, Inc.
555 Riverview, Toronto, Ontario

Perfect Posters, Inc.
Balance Sheet
As of December 31, 2003

Assets			
Current Assets:			
Cash		$7,050	
Marketable securities		2,300	
Accounts receivable	$26,210		
Less: Allowance of doubtful accounts	(650)	25,560	
Merchandise inventory		21,250	
Prepaid expenses		1,050	
Total current assets			**$57,210**
Fixed Assets:			
Land		18,000	
Building	65,000		
Less: Accumulated depreciation	(22,500)	42,500	
Equipment	72,195		
Less: Accumulated depreciation	(24,815)	47,380	
Total fixed assets			107,880
Intangible Assets:			
Patents	7,100		
Trademarks	900		
Total intangible assets			8,000
Total assets			**$173,090**

Liabilities and Owners' Equity			
Current liabilities:			
Accounts payable	$16,315		
Wages payable	3,700		
Taxes payable	1,920		
Total current liabilities			**$21,935**
Long-term liabilities:			
Notes payable, 8% due 2001	10,000		
Bonds payable, 9% due 2003	30,000		
Total long-term liabilities			**40,000**
Total liabilities			**$61,935**
Owners' Equity			
Common stock, $5 par		40,000	
Additional paid-in capital		15,000	
Retained earnings		56,155	
Total owners' equity			**111,155**
Total liabilities and owners' equity			**$173,090**

Figure 14.2
Perfect Posters' balance sheet shows clearly that the firm's total assets equal its total liabilities and owners' equity.

necessary. Marketable securities include stocks or bonds of other companies, government securities, and money market certificates. There are three other important non-liquid assets held by many companies: *accounts receivable, merchandise inventory,* and *prepaid expenses.*

accounts receivable
Amounts due to the firm from customers who have purchased goods or services on credit; a form of current asset.

Accounts receivable are amounts due from customers who have purchased goods on credit. Most businesses expect to receive payment within 30 days of a sale. In our hypothetical example, the entry labelled *Less: Allowance of doubtful accounts* in Figure 14.2 indicates $650 in receivables that Perfect Posters does not expect to collect. Total accounts receivable assets are decreased accordingly.

merchandise inventory
The cost of merchandise that has been acquired for sale to customers but is still on hand.

Following accounts receivable on the Perfect Posters balance sheet is **merchandise inventory**—the cost of merchandise that has been acquired for sale to customers and is still on hand. Accounting for the value of inventories on the balance sheet is difficult because inventories are flowing in and out throughout the year. Therefore, assumptions must be made about which ones were sold and which ones remain in storage.

prepaid expense
Includes supplies on hand and rent paid for the period to come.

Prepaid expenses include supplies on hand and rent paid for the period to come. They are assets because they have been paid for and are available to the company. In all, Perfect Posters' current assets as of December 31, 2003, totalled $57 210.

fixed assets
Assets that have long-term use or value to the firm such as land, buildings, and machinery.

depreciation
Distributing the cost of a major asset over the years in which it produces revenues; calculated by each year subtracting the asset's original value divided by the number of years in its productive life.

Fixed Assets. Fixed assets (for example, land, buildings, and equipment) have long-term use or value. But as buildings and equipment wear out or become obsolete, their value decreases. To reflect decreasing value, accountants use **depreciation** to spread the cost of an asset over the years of its useful life. Depreciation means calculating an asset's useful life in years, dividing its worth by that many years, and subtracting the resulting amount each year. Each year, therefore, the asset's remaining value decreases on the books. In Figure 14.2, Perfect Posters shows fixed assets of $107 880 after depreciation.

intangible assets
Non-physical assets, such as patents, trademarks, copyrights, and franchise fees, that have economic value but whose precise value is difficult to calculate.

goodwill
The amount paid for an existing business beyond the value of its other assets.

Intangible Assets. Although their worth is hard to set, intangible assets have monetary value. **Intangible assets** usually include the cost of obtaining rights or privileges such as patents, trademarks, copyrights, and franchise fees. **Goodwill** is the amount paid for an existing business beyond the value of its other assets. Perfect Posters has no goodwill assets; however, it does own trademarks and patents for specialized storage equipment. These are intangible assets worth $8000. Larger companies, of course, have intangible assets that are worth much more.

Liabilities

current liabilities
Any debts owed by the firm that must be paid within one year.

accounts payable
Amounts due from the firm to its suppliers for goods and/or services purchased on credit; a form of current liability.

Like assets, liabilities are often separated into different categories. **Current liabilities** are debts that must be paid within one year. These include **accounts payable**—unpaid bills to suppliers for materials as well as wages and taxes that must be paid in the coming year. Perfect Posters has current liabilities of $21 935.

long-term liabilities
Any debts owed by the firm that are not due for at least one year.

Long-term liabilities are debts that are not due for at least one year. These normally represent borrowed funds on which the company must pay interest. Perfect Posters' long-term liabilities are $40 000.

Owners' Equity

The final section of the balance sheet in Figure 14.2 shows owners' equity broken down into *common stock, paid-in capital,* and *retained earnings.* When Perfect Posters was formed, the declared legal value of its common stock was $5 per share. By law, this $40 000 ($5 × 8000 shares) cannot be distributed as dividends. **Paid-in capital** is additional money invested in the firm by its owners. Perfect Posters has $15 000 in paid-in capital.

paid-in capital
Any additional money invested in the firm by the owners.

Retained earnings are net profits minus dividend payments to stockholders. Retained earnings accumulate when profits, which could have been distributed to stockholders, are kept instead for use by the company. At the close of 2003, Perfect Posters had retained earnings of $56 155.

retained earnings

A company's net profits less any dividend payments to shareholders.

Income Statements

The **income statement** is sometimes called a **profit-and-loss statement**, because its description of revenues and expenses results in a figure showing the firm's annual profit or loss. In other words,

Revenues – Expenses = Profit (or loss)

income (profit-and-loss) statement

A type of financial statement that describes a firm's revenues and expenses and indicates whether the firm has earned a profit or suffered a loss during a given period.

Popularly known as "the bottom line," profit or loss is probably the most important figure in any business enterprise. Figure 14.3 shows the 2003 income statement for Perfect Posters, whose bottom line that year was $12 585. The income statement is divided into three major categories: *revenues, cost of goods sold,* and *operating expenses.*

Revenues

When a law firm receives $250 for preparing a will or when a supermarket collects $65 from a customer buying groceries, both are receiving

Perfect Posters, Inc.
555 Riverview, Toronto, Ontario

Perfect Posters, Inc.
Income Statement
Year ended December 31, 2003

Revenues (gross sales)			**$256,425**
Costs of goods sold:			
Merchandise inventory, January 1, 2003	$22,380		
Merchandise purchases during year	103,635		
Goods available for sale		$126,015	
Less: Merchandise inventory, December 31, 2003		21,250	
Cost of goods sold			**104,765**
Gross profit			**151,660**
Operating expenses:			
Selling and repackaging expenses:			
Salaries and wages	49,750		
Advertising	6,380		
Depreciation—wahouse and repackaging equipment	3,350		
Total selling and repackaging expenses		59,480	
Administrative expenses:			
Salaries and wages	55,100		
Supplies	4,150		
Utilities	3,800		
Depreciation—office equipment	3,420		
Interest expense	2,900		
Miscellaneous expenses	1,835		
Total administration expenses		71,205	
Total operating expenses			**130,685**
Operating income (income before taxes)			20,975
Income taxes			8,390
Net income			**$12,585**

Figure 14.3
Perfect Posters' income statement. The final entry on the income statement, the bottom line, reports the firm's profit or loss.

revenues

Any monies received by a firm as a result of selling a good or service or from other sources such as interest, rent, and licensing fees.

revenues—the funds that flow into a business from the sale of goods or services. In 2003, Perfect Posters reported revenues of $256 425 from the sale of art prints and other posters.

Cost of Goods Sold

cost of goods sold

Any expenses directly involved in producing or selling a good or service during a given time period.

In Perfect Posters' income statement, the **cost of goods sold** category shows the costs of obtaining materials to make the products sold during the year. Perfect Posters began 2003 with posters valued at $22 380. Over the year, it spent $103 635 to purchase posters. During 2003, then, the company had $126 015 worth of merchandise available to sell. By the end of the year, it had sold all but $21 250 of those posters, which remained as merchandise inventory. The cost of obtaining the goods sold by the firm was thus $104 765.

gross profit (gross margin)

A firm's revenues (gross sales) less its cost of goods sold.

Gross Profit (or Gross Margin). To calculate **gross profit** (or **gross margin**), subtract cost of goods sold from revenues obtained from goods sold. Perfect Posters' gross profit in 2003 was $151 660 ($256 425 – $104 765). Expressed as a percentage of sales, gross profit is 59.1 percent ($151 660 ÷ $256 425).

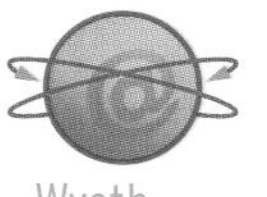

Wyeth
www.wyeth.com

Gross profit percentages vary widely across industries. In retailing, Home Depot reports 30 percent. In manufacturing, Harley-Davidson reports 34 percent; and in pharmaceuticals, Wyeth reports 75 percent. For companies with low gross margins, product costs are a big expense. If a company has a high gross margin, it probably has low cost-of-goods-sold but high selling and administrative expenses.

Operating Expenses

operating expenses

Costs incurred by a firm other than those included in cost of goods sold.

In addition to costs directly related to acquiring goods, every company has general expenses ranging from erasers to the president's salary. Like cost of goods sold, **operating expenses** are resources that must flow out of a company for it to earn revenues. As you can see in Figure 14.3, Perfect Posters had operating expenses of $130 685 in 2003. This figure consists of $59 480 in selling and repackaging expenses and $71 205 in administrative expenses.

Selling expenses result from activities related to selling the firm's goods or services. These may include salaries for the sales force, delivery costs, and advertising expenses. General and administrative expenses, such as

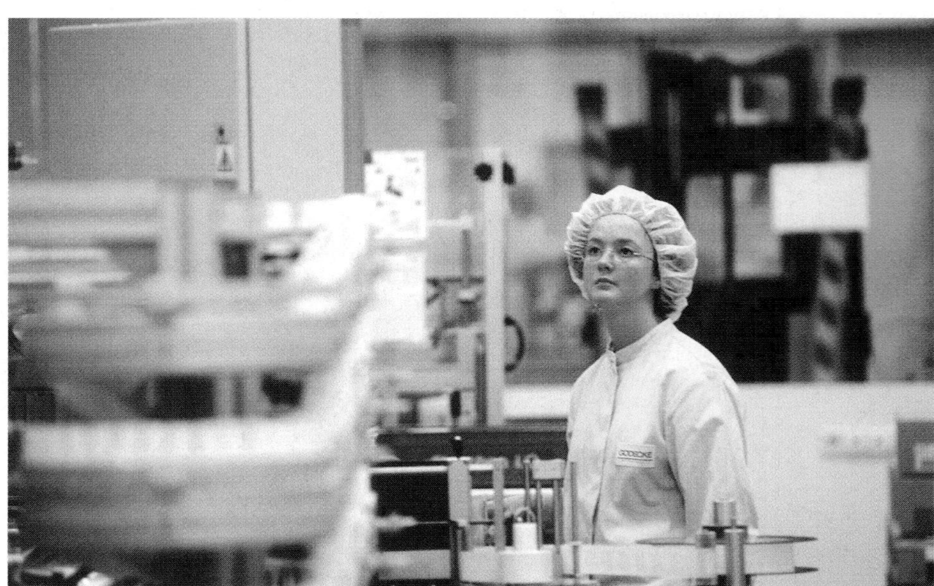

At the end of its accounting period, this pharmaceuticals company will subtract the cost of making the goods that it sold from the revenues received from sales. The difference will be its gross profit (or gross margin). Cost of goods sold does not include the firm's operating expenses, including such selling expenses as advertising and sales commissions. In part, gross margins in the pharmaceuticals industry are high because they do not account for high selling expenses.

management salaries, insurance expenses, and maintenance costs, are expenses related to the general management of the company.

Operating Income and Net Income. Sometimes managers must determine **operating income**, which compares the gross profit from business operations against operating expenses. This calculation for Perfect Posters ($151 660 – $130 685) reveals an operating income, or income before taxes, of $20 975. Subtracting income taxes from operating income ($20 975 – $8390) reveals net income (also called net profit or net earnings). In 2003, Perfect Posters' net income was $12 585.

operating income
Compares the gross profit from business operations against operating expenses.

net income (net profit or net earnings)
A firm's gross profit less its operating expenses and income taxes.

Statement of Cash Flows

Some companies prepare only balance sheets and income statements. However, many firms also report a **statement of cash flows.** This statement describes a company's yearly cash receipts and cash payments. It shows the effects on cash of three business activities:

statement of cash flows
A financial statement that describes a firm's generation and use of cash during a given period.

- *Cash flows from operations.* This part of the statement is concerned with the firm's main operating activities: the cash transactions involved in buying and selling goods and services. It reveals how much of the year's profits result from the firm's main line of business (for example, Jaguar's sales of automobiles) rather than from secondary activities (for example, licensing fees a clothing firm paid to Jaguar for using the Jaguar logo on shirts).
- *Cash flows from investing.* This section reports net cash used in or provided by investing. It includes cash receipts and payments from buying and selling stocks, bonds, property, equipment, and other productive assets.
- *Cash flows from financing.* The final section reports net cash from all financing activities. It includes cash inflows from borrowing or issuing stock as well as outflows for payment of dividends and repayment of borrowed money.

The overall change in cash from these three sources provides information to lenders and investors. When creditors and stockholders know how firms obtained and used their funds during the course of a year, it is easier for them to interpret the year-to-year changes in the firm's balance sheet and income statement.

This concession stand at SkyDome is operated by the Toronto Blue Jays. It sells products manufactured mostly by members of the Sporting Goods Manufacturers Association (SGMA), which makes apparel, footwear, and equipment. Much of this merchandise is licensed from Major League Baseball Properties Inc., which distributes licensing revenues to the sport's 30 franchises. MLB teams (who own logos and uniform designs) and MLB Properties treat sales of licensed products as cash flows from operations.

The Budget: An Internal Financial Statement

budget
A detailed financial plan for estimated receipts and expenditures for a period of time in the future, usually one year.

For planning, controlling, and decision making, the most internal financial statement is the **budget**—a detailed statement of estimated receipts and expenditures for a period of time in the future. Although that period is usually one year, some companies also prepare budgets for three- or five-year periods, especially when considering major capital expenditures.

Budgets are also useful for keeping track of weekly or monthly performance. Procter & Gamble, for example, evaluates all of its business units monthly by comparing actual financial results with monthly budgeted amounts. Discrepancies in "actual versus budget" totals signal potential problems and initiate action to get financial performance back on track.

Although the accounting staff coordinates the budget process, it requires input from many people in the company regarding proposed activities, needed resources, and input sources.[9] Figure 14.4, for example, is a sample sales budget. In preparing such a budget, the accounting department must obtain from the sales group both its projections for units to be sold and expected expenses for each quarter of the coming year. Accountants then draw up the final budget, and throughout the year, the accounting department compares the budget with actual expenditures and revenues.

Reporting Standards and Practices

4. Explain the key standards and principles for reporting financial statements.

Accountants follow numerous standard reporting practices and principles when they prepare external reports, including financial statements. The common language dictated by standard practices is designed to give external users confidence in the accuracy and meaning of the information in any financial statement. Spelled out in great detail in GAAP, these principles cover a wide range of issues, such as when to recognize revenues from oper-

Perfect Posters, Inc.
555 Riverview, Toronto, Ontario

Perfect Posters, Inc.
Sales Budget
First Quarter, 2004

	January	February	March	Quarter
Budgeted sales (units)	7,500	6,000	6,500	20,000
Budgeted selling price per unit	$3.50	$3.50	$3.50	$3.50
Budgeted sales revenue	**$26,250**	**$21,000**	**$22,750**	**$70,000**
Expected cash receipts:				
From December sales	$26,210[a]			$26,210
From January sales	$17,500[b]	$8,750		26,250
From February sales		14,000	$7,000	21,000
From March sales			15,200	15,200
Total cash receipts:	**$43,710**	**$22,750**	**$22,200**	**$88,660**

[a] This cash from December sales represents a collection of the Account Receivable appearing on the December 31, 2003, Balance Sheet.
[b] The company estimates that two-thirds of each month's sales revenues will result in cash receipts during the same month. The remaining one-third is collected during the following month.

Figure 14.4
Perfect Posters, Inc. sales budget, First Quarter 2004.

ations, the so-called "matching" of revenues and expenses, and full public disclosure of financial information to the public. Without agreed-upon practices in these and many other accounting categories, users of financial statements would be unable to compare financial information from different companies and thus misunderstand—or be led to misconstrue—a given company's true financial status.

Revenue Recognition

As we noted earlier, revenues are funds that flow into a business as a result of its operating activities during the accounting period. *Revenue recognition* is the formal recording and reporting of revenues in the financial statements. Although any firm earns revenues continuously as it makes sales, earnings are not reported until the earnings cycle is completed. This cycle is complete under two conditions:

1. The sale is complete and the product has been delivered
2. The sale price to the customer has been collected or is collectable (accounts receivable)

The completion of the earning cycle, then, determines the timing for revenue recognition in the firm's financial statements. Revenues are recorded for the accounting period in which sales are completed and collectable (or collected). This practice assures the reader that the statement gives a fair comparison of what was gained for the resources that were given up.

Matching

Net income is calculated by subtracting expenses from revenues. The *matching principle* states that expenses will be matched with revenues to determine net income for an accounting period.[10] Why is this principle important? It permits the user of the statement to see how much net gain resulted from the assets that had to be given up in order to generate revenues during the period covered in the statement. Consequently, when we match revenue recognition with expense recognition, we get net income for the period.

Consider the hypothetical case of Little Red Wagon Co. Let's see what happens when the books are kept in two different ways:

1. Correct Method: Revenue recognition is matched with expense recognition to determine net income when the earnings cycle is *completed*.
2. Incorrect Method: Revenue recognition occurs *before* the earnings cycle is completed.

Suppose that 500 red wagons are produced and delivered to customers at a sales price of $20 each during 2002. In 2003, 600 red wagons are produced and delivered. In part (A) of Table 14.2, the correct matching method has been used: Revenues are recorded for the accounting period in which sales are completed and collectable from customers, as are the expenses of producing and delivering them. The revenues from sales are matched against the expenses of completing them. By using the matching principle, we see clearly how much better off the company is at the end of each accounting period as a result of that period's operations: It earned $2000 net income for 2002 and $3000 for 2003.

In part (B) of Table 14.2, revenue recognition and the matching principle have been violated. Certain activities of the two accounting periods are disguised and mixed together rather than separated for each period. The result is a distorted performance report that incorrectly shows that 2002 was a better year than 2003. Here's what Red Wagons' accountants did

Table 14.2 Revenue Recognition and the Matching Principle

(A) The correct method reveals each accounting period's activities and results

	Year ended December 31, 2002	Year ended December 31, 2003
Revenues	$10,000	$12,000
Expenses	8,000	9,000
Net income	2,000	3,000

(B) The incorrect method disguises each accounting period's activities and results

	Year ended December 31, 2002	Year ended December 31, 2003
Revenues	$14,000	$8,000
Expenses	8,000	9,000
Net income	6,000	(1,000)

wrong: The sales department sold 200 red wagons (with revenues of $4000) to a customer late in 2002. Those *revenues* are included in the $14 000 for 2002. But because the 200 wagons were produced and delivered to the customer in 2003, the *expenses* are recorded, as in (A), for 2003. The result is a distorted picture of operations. It looks as if expenses for 2003 are out of line for such a low sales level, and it looks as if expenses (as compared with revenues) were kept under better control during 2002. The firm's accountants violated the matching principle by ignoring *the period during which the earnings cycle was completed.* Although $4000 in sales of wagons occurred in 2002, the earnings cycle for those wagons was not completed until they were produced and delivered, which occurred in 2003. Accordingly, both the revenues and expenses for those 200 wagons should have been reported in the same period—namely, in 2003, as was reported in part (A). There, we can see clearly what was gained and what was lost on activities that were completed *in an accounting period.* By requiring this practice, the matching principle provides consistency in reporting and avoids financial distortions.

Full Disclosure

Full disclosure means that financial statements should include not just numbers, but also interpretations and explanations by management so that external users can better understand information contained in the statements. Because they know more about inside events than outsiders, management prepares additional useful information that explains certain events or transactions or discloses the circumstances underlying certain financial results.

ANALYZING FINANCIAL STATEMENTS

5. Show how computing key *financial ratios* can help in analyzing the financial strengths of a business.

Financial statements present a great deal of information, but what does it all mean? How, for example, can statements help investors decide what stock to buy or help managers decide whether to extend credit? Statements provide data, which in turn can be applied to various ratios (comparative numbers). These ratios can then be used to analyze the financial health of one or more companies. They can also be used to check a firm's progress by comparing current and past statements.

Ratios are normally grouped into three major classifications:

- **Solvency ratios,** both short-term and long-term, estimate risk.
- **Profitability ratios** measure potential earnings.
- **Activity ratios** reflect management's use of assets.

Depending on the decisions to be made, a user may apply none, some, or all the ratios in a particular classification.

solvency ratios
Ratios that estimate the financial risk that is evident in a company.

profitability ratios
Measures of a firm's overall financial performance in terms of its likely profits; used by investors to assess their probable returns.

activity ratios
Measures of how efficiently a firm uses its resources; used by investors to assess their probable returns.

Short-Term Solvency Ratios

In the short run, a company's survival depends on its ability to pay its immediate debts. Such payments require cash. Short-term solvency ratios measure a company's relative liquidity and thus its ability to pay immediate debts. The higher a firm's **liquidity ratios**, then, the lower the risk involved for investors.

liquidity ratios
Measures of a firm's ability to meet its immediate debts; used to analyze the risks of investing in the firm.

Current Ratio

The current ratio has been called the "banker's ratio" because it focuses on a firm's creditworthiness. The **current ratio** measures a company's ability to meet current obligations out of current assets. It thus reflects a firm's ability to generate cash to meet obligations through the normal, orderly process of selling inventories and collecting accounts receivable. It is calculated by dividing current assets by current liabilities.

current ratio
A form of liquidity ratio calculated as current assets divided by current liabilities.

As a rule, a current ratio is satisfactory if it is 2:1 or higher—that is, if current assets are more than double current liabilities. A smaller ratio may indicate that a company will have difficulty paying its bills. Note, however, that a larger ratio may imply that assets are not being used productively and should be invested elsewhere.

How does Perfect Posters measure up? Look again at the balance sheet in Figure 14.2 (see page 483). Judging from its current assets and current liabilities at the end of 2003, we see that

$$\frac{\text{Current assets}}{\text{Current liabilities}} = \frac{\$57\ 210}{\$21\ 935} = 2.61$$

How does Perfect Posters' ratio compare with those of other companies? It's lower than O'Reilly Automotive's ratio (2.94) and higher than those of Gillette (1.56), Cisco Systems (2.14), and Starwood Hotels & Resorts Worldwide (0.23). Although Perfect Posters may be holding too much uninvested cash, it looks like a good credit risk.

Working Capital. A related measure is **working capital**—the difference between the firm's current assets and its current liabilities. Working capital indicates the firm's ability to pay off short-term debts (liabilities) that it owes to outsiders. At the end of 2003, Perfect Posters' working capital was $35 275 ($57 210 – $21 935). Because current liabilities must be paid off within one year, current assets are more than enough to meet current obligations.

working capital
The difference between a firm's current assets and current liabilities.

Long-Term Solvency Ratios

To survive in the long run, a company must be able to meet both its short-term (current) debts and its long-term liabilities. These latter debts usually involve interest payments. A firm that cannot meet them is in danger of collapse or takeover—a risk that makes creditors and investors quite cautious.

debt ratios
Measures of a firm's ability to meet its long-term debts; used to analyze the risks of investing in the firm.

debt-to-owners'-equity ratio
A form of debt ratio calculated as total liabilities divided by owner's equity.

debt
A company's total liabilities.

Debt-to-Owners'-Equity Ratio

To measure the risk that a company may encounter this problem, analysts use long-term solvency ratios called **debt ratios**. The most commonly used debt ratio is the **debt-to-owners'-equity ratio** (or debt-to-equity ratio), which describes the extent to which a firm is financed through borrowed money. It is calculated by dividing **debt**—total liabilities—by owners' equity. Companies with debt-to-equity ratios above 1.0 are probably relying too much on debt. Such firms may find themselves owing so much that they lack the income needed to meet interest payments or to repay borrowed money.

In the case of Perfect Posters, we can see from the balance sheet in Figure 14.2 that the debt-to-equity ratio calculates as follows:

$$\frac{\text{Debt}}{\text{Owners' equity}} = \frac{\$61\ 935}{0.56} = \$111\ 155$$

leverage
Using borrowed funds to make purchases, thus increasing the user's purchasing power, potential rate of return, and risk of loss.

Leverage. Note that a fairly high debt-to-equity ratio may sometimes be not only acceptable but desirable. Borrowing funds provides **leverage**—the ability to make otherwise unaffordable purchases. In leveraged buyouts (LBOs), firms have willingly taken on huge debt to buy out other companies. When the purchased company allows the buying company to earn profits above the cost of the borrowed funds, leveraging makes sound financial sense, even if it raises the buyer's debt-to-equity ratio. Unfortunately, many buyouts have led to financial trouble when actual profits fell short of anticipated levels or when rising rates increased interest payments on the debt acquired by the buyer.

Profitability Ratios

Although it is important to know that a company is solvent in both the long term and the short term, safety or risk alone is not an adequate basis for investment decisions. Investors also want some measure of the returns they can expect. *Return on equity* and *earnings per share* are two commonly used profitability ratios.

Return on Equity

return on equity
A form of profitability ratio calculated as net income divided by total owners' equity.

Owners are interested in the net income earned by a business for each dollar invested. **Return on equity** measures this performance by dividing net income (recorded in the income statement, Figure 14.3) by total owners' equity (recorded in the balance sheet, Figure 14.2).[11] For Perfect Posters, the return-on-equity ratio in 2003 can be calculated as follows:

$$\frac{\text{Net income}}{\text{Total owners' equity}} = \frac{\$12\ 585}{\$111\ 155} = 11.3\%$$

Is this figure good or bad? There is no set answer. If Perfect Posters' ratio for 2003 is higher than in previous years, owners and investors should be encouraged. But if 11.3 percent is lower than the ratios of other companies in the same industry, they should be concerned.

Earnings per Share

earnings per share
A form of profitability ratio calculated as net income divided by the number of common shares outstanding.

Defined as net income divided by the number of shares of common stock outstanding, **earnings per share** determines the size of the dividend a company can pay to its shareholders. Investors use this ratio to decide whether to buy or sell a company's stock. As the ratio gets higher, the stock value increases, because investors know that the firm can better afford to pay dividends. Naturally, stock will lose market value if the latest financial statements report a decline in earnings per share. For Perfect Posters, we can use the net income total from the income statement in Figure 14.3 to calculate earnings per share as follows:

$$\frac{\text{Net income}}{\text{Number of common shares outstanding}} = \frac{\$12\ 585}{8000} = \$1.57 \text{ per share}$$

As a baseline for comparison, note that Gucci's recent earnings were $3.31 per share, while Phillips Petroleum earned $7.26.

Activity Ratios

The efficiency with which a firm uses resources is linked to profitability. As a potential investor, then, you want to know which company gets more mileage from its resources. Activity ratios measure this efficiency. For example, suppose that two firms use the same amount of resources or assets. If Firm A generates greater profits or sales, it is more efficient and thus has a better activity ratio.

Inventory Turnover Ratio

Certain specific measures can be used to explain how one firm earns greater profits than another. One of the most important measures is the **inventory turnover ratio**, which calculates the average number of times that inventory is sold and restocked during the year—that is, how quickly inventory is produced and sold.[12] First, a company needs to know its average inventory: the typical amount of inventory on hand during the year. Average inventory can be calculated by adding end-of-year inventory to beginning-of-year inventory and dividing by two. The company can then calculate the inventory turnover ratio, which is expressed as the cost of goods sold divided by average inventory:

inventory turnover ratio

An activity ratio that measures the average number of times inventory is sold and restocked during the year.

$$\frac{\text{Cost of goods sold}}{\text{Average inventory}} = \frac{\text{Cost of goods sold}}{(\text{Beginning inventory} + \text{Ending inventory}) \div 2}$$

High inventory turnover ratio means efficient operations. Because a smaller amount of investment is tied up in inventory, the company's funds can be put to work elsewhere to earn greater returns. However, inventory turnover must be compared with both prior years and industry averages. An inventory turnover rate of 5, for example, might be excellent for an auto supply store, but it would be disastrous for a supermarket, where a rate of about 15 is common. Rates can also vary within a company that markets a variety of products. To calculate Perfect Posters' inventory turnover ratio for 2003, we take the merchandise inventory figures for the income statement in Figure 14.3. The ratio can be expressed as follows:

$$\frac{\$104\ 765}{(\$22\ 380 + \text{S}21\ 250) \div 2} = 4.8 \text{ times}$$

In other words, new merchandise replaces old merchandise every 76 days (365 days divided by 4.8). The 4.8 ratio is below the average of 7.0 for comparable wholesaling operations, indicating that the business is slightly inefficient.

Inventory turnover ratio measures the average number of times that a store sells and restocks its inventory in one year. The higher the ratio, the more products that get sold and the more revenue that comes in. Supermarkets must have a higher turnover ratio than, say, auto supply or toy stores. In almost all retail stores, products with the highest ratios get the shelf spaces that generate the most customer traffic and sales.

INTERNATIONAL ACCOUNTING

6. Explain some of the special issues facing accountants at firms that do international business.

As we saw in Chapter 4, companies such as McCain Foods, Sabian Cymbals, and MacMillan-Bloedel receive large portions of their operating revenues from foreign sales. Many Canadian companies also purchase components from foreign countries. Retailers such as The Bay and Sears buy merchandise from other countries for sale in Canada. In addition, more and more companies own subsidiaries in foreign countries. With all this international activity, there is obviously a need to keep track of foreign transactions. One of the most basic accounting needs is translating the values of the currencies of different countries.

Sabian Cymbals
www.sabian.com

Foreign Currency Exchange

A unique consideration in international accounting is the value of currencies and their exchange rates. As we saw in Chapter 4, the value of any country's currency is subject to occasional change. Political and economic conditions, for instance, affect the stability of a nation's currency and its value relative to the currencies of other countries.

As it's traded around the world, market forces determine a currency's value—what buyers are willing to pay for it. The resulting values are called **foreign currency exchange rates**. When a currency becomes unstable—that is, when its value changes frequently—it is regarded as a *weak currency*. The value of the Brazilian real, for example, fluctuated between 0.416 and 0.957—a variation of 130 percent in U.S. dollars—during the period from 1997 to 2002. On the other hand, a *strong currency* historically rises or holds steady in comparison to other currencies.

foreign currency exchange rate
What buyers are willing to pay for a given currency.

As changes in exchange rates occur, they must be considered by accountants when recording international transactions. They will affect, perhaps profoundly, the amount that a firm pays for foreign purchases and the amount it gains from sales to foreign buyers.

"It's up to you now, Miller. The only thing that can save us is an accounting breakthrough."

International Transactions

International purchases, credit sales, and accounting for foreign subsidiaries all involve transactions affected by exchange rates. When a Canadian company imports Bordeaux wine from the French company Pierre Bourgeois, the Canadian company's accountant must be sure that the company's books reflect its true costs. The amount owed to Pierre Bourgeois changes daily along with the exchange rate between euros and Canadian dollars. Thus, the accountant must identify the actual rate *on the day that payment in euros is made* so that the correct Canadian-dollar cost of the purchase is recorded.

International Accounting Standards

Professional accounting groups from about 80 countries are members of the International Accounting Standards Board (IASB), which is trying to eliminate national differences in financial reporting procedures.[13] Bankers, investors, and managers want procedures that are comparable from country to country and applicable to all firms regardless of home nation. Standardization is occurring in some areas but is far from universal. IASB financial statements include an income statement, balance sheet, and statement of cash flows similar to those issued by Canadian and U.S. accountants. International standards, however, do not require a uniform format, and variety abounds.

SUMMARY OF LEARNING OBJECTIVES

1. **Explain the role of accountants and distinguish between the kinds of work done by *public* and *private accountants*.** *Accounting* is a comprehensive system for collecting, analyzing, and communicating financial information. It measures business performance and translates the results into information for management decisions. It also prepares performance reports for owners, the public, and regulatory agencies. To meet these objectives, accountants keep records of income, expenses, and taxes, and they analyze the effects of these transactions on particular business activities. *Bookkeeping* (just one phase of accounting) is the recording of transactions. Ensuring consistent, dependable financial information is the job of the *accounting information system (AIS)*—an organized procedure for identifying, measuring, recording, and retaining financial information so that it can be used in accounting statements and management reports. Users of such information include: (1) business managers, (2) employees and unions, (3) investors and creditors, (4) tax authorities, and (5) government regulatory agencies.

   There are two main fields in accounting: (1) A *financial accounting system* deals with external information users (consumer groups, unions, stockholders, and government agencies). It regularly prepares income statements, balance sheets, and other financial reports published for shareholders and the public. (2) *Managerial (or management) accounting* serves internal users, such as managers at all levels.

2. **Explain how the *accounting equation* and *double-entry accounting* are used in record keeping.**

   Accountants use the *accounting equation* to balance the data pertaining to financial transactions:

   Assets = Liabilities + Owners' equity

   (1) An *asset* is any economic resource that is expected to benefit its owner (such as buildings, equipment, inventory, and payments due the company). (2) A *liability* is a debt that the firm owes to an outside party. (3) *Owners' equity* is the amount of money that owners would receive if they sold all of a company's assets and paid all of its liabilities.

   Because every transaction affects two accounts, accountants use a *double-entry accounting* system to record the dual effects. Because the double-entry system requires at least two bookkeeping entries for each transaction, it keeps the accounting equation in balance.

3. **Describe the three basic *financial statements* and show how they reflect the activity and financial condition of a business.** Accounting summarizes the results of a firm's transactions and issues reports to help managers make informed decisions. The class of reports known as *financial statements* are divided into three categories—balance sheets, income statements, and statements of cash flows. *Balance sheets* (sometimes called statements of financial position) supply detailed information about the accounting-equation factors: assets, liabilities, and owners' equity. The *income statement* (sometimes called a profit-and-loss statement) describes revenues and expenses to show a firm's annual profit or loss. The *statement of cash flow* reports cash receipts and payments from operating, investing, and financing activities.

4. **Explain the key standards and principles for reporting financial statements.** Accountants follow standard reporting practices and prin-

ciples when they prepare financial statements. Otherwise, users wouldn't be able to compare information from different companies, and they might misunderstand—or be led to misconstrue—a company's true financial status. The following are three of the most important standard reporting practices and principles: (1) *Revenue recognition* is the formal recording and reporting of revenues in the financial statements. All firms earn revenues continuously as they make sales, but earnings are not reported until the earnings cycle is completed; (2) The *matching principle* states that expenses will be matched with revenues to determine net income. It permits users to see how much net gain resulted from the assets that had to be given up in order to generate revenues; (3) Because they have inside knowledge, management prepares additional information that explains certain events or transactions or discloses the circumstances behind certain results. *Full disclosure* means that financial statements include management interpretations and explanations to help external users understand information contained in statements.

5. **Show how computing key *financial ratios* can help in analyzing the financial strengths of a business.** Financial statements provide data that can be applied to *ratios* (comparative numbers). Ratios can then be used to analyze the financial health of one or more companies. They can also be used to check a firm's progress by comparing current with past statements. Ratios are grouped into three major classifications:

   (1) *Solvency ratios* estimate risk. *Short-term solvency ratios* measure relative liquidity and thus a company's ability to pay immediate debts. The higher a firm's liquidity ratios, the lower the risk for investors. The most common liquidity ratio is the current ratio, which measures ability to meet current obligations out of current assets. It thus reflects a firm's ability to generate cash to meet obligations through the normal process of selling inventories and collecting accounts receivable. Working capital is the difference between current assets and current liabilities. It indicates ability to pay off short-term debts (liabilities) owed to outsiders. *Long-term solvency ratios* measure ability to meet long-term liabilities consisting of interest payments. Debt ratios are long-term solvency ratios. The most common debt ratio is the debt-to-owners' equity ratio (or debt-to-equity ratio), which describes the extent to which a firm is financed through borrowed money. A fairly high debt-to-equity ratio may sometimes be desirable because borrowing funds provides leverage—the ability to make otherwise unaffordable purchases.

   (2) *Profitability ratios* measure potential earnings. Return on equity measures income earned for each dollar invested. Earnings per share determines the size of the dividend that a company can pay shareholders. Investors use it when deciding whether to buy or sell a company's stock. As it gets higher, stock value increases, because investors know that the firm can better afford to pay dividends.

   (3) *Activity ratios* reflect management's use of assets by measuring the efficiency with which a firm uses its resources. The inventory turnover ratio measures the average number of times that inventory is sold and restocked annually—that is, how quickly it is produced and sold. A high inventory turnover ratio means efficient operations: Because a smaller amount of investment is tied up in inventory, the firm's funds can be put to work elsewhere to earn greater returns.

6. **Explain some of the special issues facing accountants at firms that do international business.** Accounting for foreign transactions

involves special procedures, such as translating the values of different countries' currencies and accounting for the effects of exchange rates. Moreover, currencies are subject to change: As they're traded each day around the world, their values are determined by market forces—what buyers are willing to pay for them. The resulting values are *foreign currency exchange rates*, which can be fairly volatile. When a currency becomes unstable—when its value changes frequently—it is called a weak currency. The value of a strong currency historically rises or holds steady in comparison with the U.S. dollar.

International purchases, sales on credit, and accounting for foreign subsidiaries all involve transactions affected by exchange rates. When a U.S. company imports a French product, its accountant must be sure that its books reflect its true costs. The amount owed to the French seller changes daily along with the exchange rate between euros and dollars. The American accountant must therefore identify the actual rate on the day that payment in euros is made so that the correct U.S.-dollar cost of the product is recorded.

With accounting groups from 80 countries, the International Accounting Standards Board (IASB) is trying to eliminate national differences in financial reporting. Bankers, investors, and managers want financial reporting that is comparable from country to country and across all firms regardless of home nation. Standardization governs some areas but is far from universal.

KEY TERMS

account receivable, 484
accounting information system (AIS), 473
accounting, 472
accounts payable, 484
activity ratio, 491
asset, 481
audit, 477
balance sheet, 483
bookkeeping, 472
budget, 488
certified general accountant (CGA), 476
certified management accountant (CMA), 476
chartered accountant (CA), 476
controller, 473
cost of goods sold, 486
current asset, 483
current liability, 484
current ratio, 491
debt, 492
debt ratios, 492
debt-to-owners'-equity ratio, 492
depreciation, 484
double-entry accounting system, 482
earnings per share, 492
financial accounting system, 474
financial statement, 482
fixed asset, 484
foreign currency exchange rate, 494
forensic accountant, 477
generally accepted accounting principles (GAAP), 477
goodwill, 484
gross profit (or gross margin), 486
income statement (or profit-and-loss statement), 485
intangible asset, 484
inventory turnover ratio, 493
leverage, 492
liability, 482
liquidity ratio, 491
liquidity, 483
long-term liability, 484
management consulting services, 477
managerial (or management) accounting, 474
merchandise inventory, 484
net income (or net profit or net earnings), 487
operating expenses, 486
operating income, 487
owners' equity, 482
paid-in capital, 484
prepaid expense, 484
private accountant, 478
profitability ratio, 491
retained earnings, 485
return on equity, 492
revenues, 486
solvency ratio, 491
statement of cash flows, 487
working capital, 491

QUESTIONS AND EXERCISES

Questions for Review

1. Identify the three types of services that CAs and CGAs perform.

2. How does the double-entry system reduce the chances of mistakes or fraud in accounting?

3. What are the three basic financial statements and what major types of information does each contain?

4. Identify the four major classifications of financial statement ratios and give an example of one ratio in each category.

5. Explain how financial ratios allow managers to monitor their own efficiency and effectiveness.

Questions for Analysis

6. Suppose that Inflatables Inc., makers of air mattresses for swimming pools, has the following transactions in one week:

- sale of three deluxe mattresses to Al Wett (paid cash—$75) on 7/16
- received cheque from Ima Flote in payment for mattresses bought on credit ($90) on 7/13
- received new shipment of 200 mattresses from Airheads Mfg. (total cost $2000) on 7/17

Construct a journal for Inflatables Inc.

7. If you were planning to invest in a company, which of the three types of financial statements would you most want to see? Why?

8. Dasar Company reports the following data in its September 30, 2003, financial statements:

Gross sales $225 000
Current assets 40 000
Long-term assets 100 000
Current liabilities 16 000
Long-term liabilities 44 000
Owners' equity 80 000
Net income 7 200

a. Compute the current ratio.

b. Compute the debt-to-equity ratio.

c. Compute the return on sales.

d. Compute the return on owners' equity.

Application Exercises

9. Interview an accountant at a local manufacturing firm. Trace the process by which budgets are developed in that company. How does the firm use budgets? How does budgeting help its managers plan business activities? How does budgeting help them control business activities? Give examples.

10. Interview the manager of a local retail or wholesale business about taking inventory. What is the firm's primary purpose in taking inventory? How often is it done?

BUILDING YOUR BUSINESS SKILLS

Putting the Buzz in Billing

Goal

To encourage students to think about the advantages and disadvantages of using an electronic system for handling accounts receivable and accounts payable.

Method

Step 1

Study Figure 14.5. The outside cycle depicts the seven steps involved in issuing paper bills to customers, payment of these bills by customers, and handling by banks of debits and credits for the two accounts. The inside cycle shows the same bill issuance and payment process handled electronically.

Step 2

As the chief financial officer of a provincial hydroelectric utility, you are analyzing the feasibility of switching from a paper to an electronic system of billing and bill payment. You decide to discuss the ramifications of the choice with three business associates (choose three classmates to take on these roles). Your discussion requires that you research electronic payment systems now being developed. Specifically, using online and library research, you must find out as much as you can about the electronic bill-paying systems being developed by Visa International, Intuit, IBM, and the Checkfree Corp. After you have researched this information, brainstorm the advantages and disadvantages of using an electronic bill-paying system in your company.

Follow-Up Questions

1. What cost savings are inherent in the electronic system for both your company and its customers? In your answer, consider such costs as handling, postage, and paper.
2. What consequences would your decision to adopt an electronic system have on others with whom you do business, including manufacturers of cheque-sorting equipment, Canada Post, and banks?
3. Switching to an electronic bill-paying system would require a large capital expenditure for new computers and computer software. How could analyzing the company's income statement help you justify this expenditure?
4. How are consumers likely to respond to paying bills electronically? Are you likely to get a different response from individuals than you get from business customers?

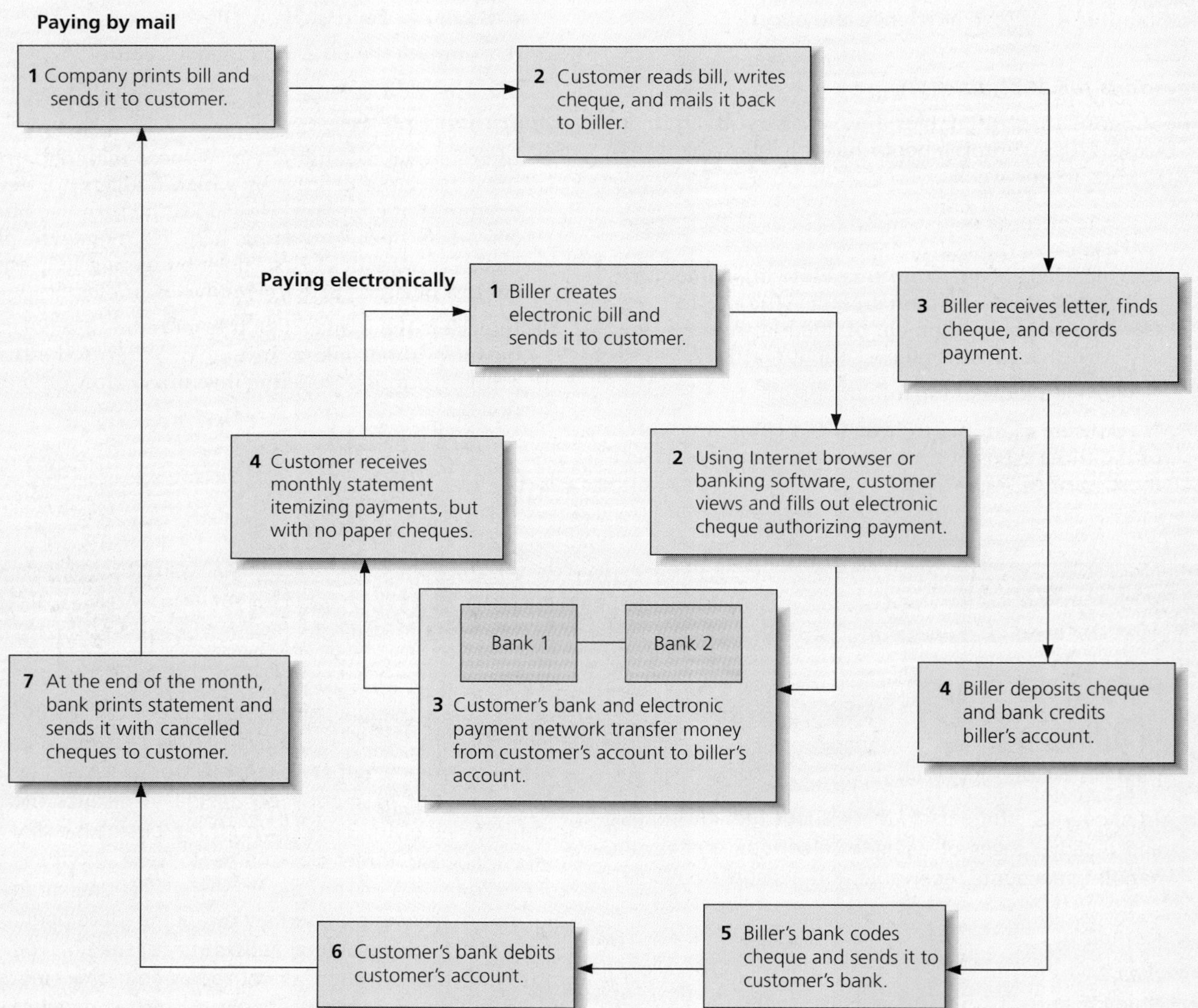

Figure 14.5
Managing operations and information.

CRAFTING YOUR BUSINESS PLAN

The Profitability of Planning

The Purpose of the Assignment

1. To acquaint students with accounting issues faced by a sample firm in developing its business plan, in the framework of Business PlanPro (BPP) software package.
2. To demonstrate how three chapter topics—accounting skills, financial data reports, and the profit-and-loss statement—can be integrated as components in the BPP planning environment.

Assignment

After reading Chapter 14 in the textbook, open the BPP software and search for information about plans for accounting as it applies to a sample firm: AMT Computer Store (American Management Technology). To find AMT Computer Store, do the following:

Open Business PlanPro. If it asks if you want to "create a new business plan" or "open an existing plan," select "create a new business plan" (even though you are not going to create a plan at this time). You will then be taken to the Business PlanPro EasyPlan Wizard. On the screen, click on the option entitled **Research It**. You will then be presented with a new list of options, including Sample Plan Browser. After clicking on the **Sample Plan Browser**, go down the alphabetical list of sample plans and double-click on **Computer Hardware—Reseller**, which is the location for AMT Computer Store. The screen that you're now looking at is the introduction page for the AMT Computer Store business plan. Next, scroll down until you reach the **Table of Contents** for AMT's business plan.

Now respond to the following items:

1. What is your assessment of the accounting skills possessed by AMT's management team? What do you recommend? [Sites to see in BPP for this item: On the **Table of Contents** page, click on each of the following, in turn: **6.1 Organizational Structure, 6.2 Management Team,** and **6.3 Management Team Gaps.**]
2. Use BPP's computer graphics to explore AMT's financial data reports. Describe the kinds of accounting information you find in the charts. [Sites to see in BPP: Beginning on the **Table of Contents** page, go to the outline section entitled **7.2 Key Financial Indicators,** including **Benchmark Comparison Chart.**]
3. At the time of this plan, AMT Computer Store was expecting large changes in annual net profits during the next three years. Based on the company's planned profit-and-loss statement, identify the key factors—changes in revenues and expenses—that account for changes in expected net profits from year to year. [Sites to see in BPP: From the **Table of Contents** page, click on **7.4 Projected Profit and Loss,** including **Table: Profit and Loss (Planned).**]

VIDEO EXERCISE

Accounting for Billions of Burgers: McDonald's

Learning Objectives

The purpose of this video is to help you:

1. Understand the challenges that a company may face in managing financial information from operations in multiple countries.
2. Consider ways in which managers and investors use financial information reported by a public company.
3. Understand how different laws and monetary systems can affect the accounting activities of a global corporation.

Synopsis

Collecting, analyzing, and reporting financial data from 30 000 restaurants in 119 countries is no easy task, as the accounting experts at McDonald's are well aware. Every month, individual restaurants send their sales figures to be consolidated with data from other restaurants at the local or country level. From there, the figures are sent to country-group offices and then to one of three major regional offices before going to their final destination at McDonald's headquarters in Oak Brook, Illinois. In the past, financial information arrived in Illinois in bits and pieces, sent by courier, mail, or fax. Today, local and regional offices enter month-end figures into a special secure website, enabling the corporate controller to produce financial statements and projections for internal and external use.

Discussion Questions

1. *For analysis:* Why does McDonald's use "constant currency" comparisons when reporting its financial results?
2. *For analysis:* What types of assets might McDonald's list under depreciation in its financial statements?
3. *For application:* What effect do corporate income tax rates in the countries where it operates have on the income statements prepared at McDonald's local offices?
4. *For application:* What problems might arise if individual restaurants were required to enter sales data directly on the company's centralized accounting website instead of following the current procedure of sending it through country and regional channels?
5. *For debate:* To help investors and analysts better assess the company's worldwide financial health, should McDonald's be required to disclose detailed financial results for every country and region? Support your position.

Online Exploration

Visit the McDonald's corporate website at **www.mcdonalds.com/corporate**. Locate the most recent financial report (quarterly or annual) and examine both overall and regional results. What aspects of its results does McDonald's highlight in this report? Which regions are doing particularly well? Which are lagging? How does management explain any differences in performance? What does McDonald's say about its use of constant currency reporting?

EXPLORING THE NET

Getting to Know the Accounting Profession

Professional accountants such as those with CA, CMA, and CGA designations often work in public practice for an accounting firm. This chapter outlines a number of areas normally covered by public practising accountants such as auditing, forensic accounting, tax, and management consulting services. Deloitte Touche Tohmatsu is one of the larger international accounting firms. Let's examine their website at **http://www.deloitte.com**.

1. Under the career section of this website you will find a section called "Where Do You Fit. "What exactly does an individual in the Assurance & Advisory area do?
2. Taxation is another area that this firm specializes in. Look under the service section of this website. How does Deloitte describe the Canadian tax system?
3. Using the country locator at the top of the screen, select Canada. In the career section under building your skills, what exactly does a person need to do to become a CA?
4. Compare the types of service described in this chapter with Deloitte's offerings. What other services does Deloitte offer beyond those mentioned in this chapter?

Concluding Case 14-1

Humpty-Dumpty Time at Arthur Andersen

Rarely does a single event shake a whole industry as dramatically as Arthur Andersen's failed attempts to cover up the role of accounting in the dubious activities of oil-trading giant Enron. With employee and stockholder losses totalling tens of billions of dollars, the Enron breakdown certainly caused monumental damage to the business psyche of the United States. But in many ways, it's really small stuff compared with the widespread failure of confidence that Andersen has spawned.

As Enron's auditors, Andersen's accountants were supposed to assess Enron's financial status, evaluate its financial statements, and report on its adherence to generally accepted accounting practices. Had it done what it was supposed to, how could Andersen have failed to see through the bookkeeping sleight of hand that soon led to Enron's mammoth collapse? And what if Andersen did foresee the collapse? What if its accountants had actually helped Enron hide its financial shortfalls and ethical shortcomings?

In March 2002, the U.S. Department of Justice (DOJ) filed obstruction-of-justice charges against Andersen, accusing the firm of shredding tons of Enron documents that should have been preserved as legal records. Andersen executives denied that any crimes had been committed. Prosecutors argued that months before Enron's collapse, Andersen knew that its second-biggest client was in an accounting mess. To implement damage control, Chicago-based Andersen executives moved to Houston, but it was too late. "It was Humpty Dumpty time for Arthur Andersen," says U.S. Prosecutor Samuel Buell. "They brought all the king's horses and all the king's men, and they couldn't put Humpty together again. Enron's accounting was made up of eggshells."

Meanwhile, a pall of cynicism has fallen over the accounting industry: If it can happen at Andersen, what's to keep it from happening to anyone else in the accounting industry? Such questions lead, at best, to a profound skepticism about the profession's methods and mores, and, at worst, to further questions of possible corruption. As of mid-2002, suspicious investors were questioning the accounting practices of thousands of firms, and people are still extremely skeptical about the honesty of independent auditors who are supposed to keep clients honest. Without unbiased audits, how much can investors know about a company's financial health and trust its financial reports? Long among the world's most trusted professionals, accountants have been regarded as providers of valid information on corporate performance and as watchdogs of the public interest. Almost single-handedly, Andersen has changed all that. The public is suspicious. If a firm with Andersen's reputation can't be trusted, how much confidence can be placed in the paperwork spewing from anywhere else?

Loss of confidence—on the part of investors, employees, retirees, unions, and government—has contributed to a plunging stock market, with losses in the hundreds of billions since Enron's demise. Corporate mischief and the willingness of accountants to cover it up have done untold damage to public trust. "We all too often forget," says one securities analyst, "that markets depend on trust to operate. Enron and the...corporate scandals that followed have all but destroyed that trust."

Although Andersen executives claimed that no one had committed any crimes, that story turned to fiction when a former partner pleaded guilty to obstruction charges. As a witness for the government, David Duncan admitted that he'd broken the law by destroying documents. Even more damning for Andersen was news that the Enron affair wasn't its first brush with charges of shady auditing. Four years earlier, the firm's Fort Lauderdale office had destroyed sensitive documents when the Securities and Exchange Commission (SEC) came to look into Andersen's restatement of Sunbeam's earnings following a barrage of lawsuits by Sunbeam stockholders. According to another Andersen partner, employees were ordered to destroy anything that didn't agree with the firm's final statement of Sunbeam's earnings.

In a case involving another client—Waste Management—Andersen agreed in 2001 to pay $7 million to settle federal charges of filing false auditing reports dating back to before the Sunbeam case. In assessing the largest civil penalty ever levied against a major accounting firm, the SEC claimed that Andersen had filed false audits of its client's books from 1992 to 1996. Andersen claimed that all financial statements were prepared according to GAAP, but income was, in fact, overstated by more than $1 billion.

In an even larger action—one of the largest non-profit frauds in history—Andersen agreed in 2002 to a $217 million settlement involving the Baptist Foundation of Arizona. The Foundation, with Andersen as its auditor, allegedly swindled elderly people out of $590 million. The suit accused Andersen of ignoring danger signs, falsifying documents, and destroying records.

In June 2002, Andersen was convicted of obstructing justice in the Enron case by destroying files while on notice of a federal investigation. Both accountants and clients began leaving Andersen once its entanglement with Enron came to light. Hundreds of accountants, many of them partners in the firm, have jumped to other major firms, and many others have started their own consulting or accounting firms. Even before the conviction in June, more than 500 clients, including the 15 biggest publicly traded firms that Andersen had audited the year before, had found new auditors.

Enron wasn't the only problem. Tyco, WorldCom, Rite Aid, Adelphia Communications, Dynegy, and ImClone Systems all were involved in a wide range of practices that should have been noticed by vigilant auditors. The auditors' failures to notice these practices spooked investors and strained public trust to the breaking point. By early 2003, stock markets in both the United States and Canada had lost more than 20 percent of their value—amounting to hundreds of billions in losses for retirees and other investors.

We need auditors to monitor auditors. And unfortunately, we don't yet have an answer to the next obvious question: How many layers of monitors monitoring monitors will be needed to restore public trust in the accounting profession?

Questions for Discussion

1. Why do you suppose Andersen auditors were reluctant to disclose deficiencies in clients' financial statements and accounting practices?
2. Do you think that Arizona authorities were overly harsh with the penalties they imposed on Andersen? Why or why not?
3. Consider the obligations of accountants employed by Arthur Andersen. Is the accountant's first obligation to Andersen or to the accounting profession? Explain your reasoning.
4. Suppose that you're a CA at a major accounting firm, and you suspect that a client isn't abiding by GAAP. You also get the impression that your boss would prefer you to keep your suspicions under wraps. How would you handle this situation?
5. What changes, if any, do you recommend be made by the accounting profession or by regulatory agencies to restore public confidence in the business of financial reporting? ◆

Concluding Case 14-2 CC

The Winds of Change Are Blowing Through the Accounting Profession

The corporate accounting and insider trading scandals in the United States were one of the motivating factors behind a 2003 Canadian Senate Banking Committee report, which focused on ways to restore investor confidence and trust in the financial data that is presented on the balance sheets and income statements of business firms. The chair of the committee, Senator Leo Kolber, said that Canadian companies must demonstrate integrity and honesty before investor confidence can be restored. The Committee made several recommendations, including:

- forcing CEOs to vouch for the truthfulness of their financial statements
- passing new legislation governing the conflicts of interest faced by investment analysts
- requiring companies to have only independent directors on their audit committees

The report was released just a week after Justice Minister Martin Cauchon had introduced legislation that would make more money available to prosecute white-collar crime and would impose stronger penalties for corporate fraud. The new regulations would mean a maximum sentence of 10 years for insider trading, and the creation of new law enforcement teams to find and catch corporate criminals. David Brown, the chair of the Ontario Securities Commission (OSC), noted that several of the recommendations in the Senate Banking Committee Report were going to be introduced by the OSC and would likely be adopted by most provinces.

Most of the really dramatic cases of corporate fraud have occurred in the United States, but Canada has the dubious distinction of having one of its own in the limelight. Canadian-born Bernard Ebbers, CEO of WorldCom Inc., was the focus of two reports that were released in 2003. They allege that much of the blame for WorldCom's collapse rests on Ebbers, noting that he and other senior executives were involved in a massive accounting fraud that caused the company to pile up $41 billion in debts while at the same time paying Ebbers and others large amounts of money. The WorldCom collapse was the largest in U.S. history. The Bank of Nova Scotia was part of a consortium of banks that lent a total of $2.65 billion to WorldCom (Scotiabank's share was $100 million). Ebbers was forced to step down as CEO in 2002, but the board of directors agreed to pay him $1.5 million a year for life. They also didn't require him to repay $408 million in loans that he had been given, accepting instead a promissory note. To date, Ebbers has not been charged with any crime.

In addition to outright accounting fraud, there has also been increasing concern about the difficulty investors have in understanding what accounting statements really mean. In recent years, two issues have become prominent: overstating sales revenue and understating pension plan liabilities.

Overstating Sales Revenue

During the stock market boom of the late 1990s, many companies used "creative accounting" to inflate sales revenue, which yielded a distorted picture of how much product or service a company was actually selling. This was done so that the company would not disappoint the expectations of the stock market and then see their stock price drop. There are different ways that sales revenue can be overstated. For example, some software makers sell a lot of product at the end of a quarter and then count all those sales as revenue without taking into account the future costs the firm will incur to support the software or to provide the free upgrades they promised. Or, a company that acts as a sales agent for an airline might include the ticket price, plus the commission it earns, as revenue. When the airline firm is paid, the cost goes on the expense line. This approach vastly overstates revenue (but not profit). The company should have included only its sales commissions as revenue.

High-tech firms in particular are seen as too liberal in recording revenues on their financial statements. The OSC asked 70 of these companies to explain in detail what policies they follow in reporting revenue. The OSC is also shifting its emphasis from examining prospectuses to analyzing the way companies report income. It has set up a continuous disclosure team to review the financial reports of corporations in a systematic manner. To get a better understanding of the revenue problem, the OSC is also asking companies how they account for revenue from things like service contracts, and whether they benchmark their accounting practices against those used by other firms in their industry. Forensic accountant Al Rosen considers the OSC's move as desirable because companies have discovered that it's pretty easy to fool around with revenue figures. Rosen says that the OSC should issue its own guidelines about how revenue should be reported and should not wait for the professional accounting groups to do so.

Understating Pension Liabilities

Under current accounting rules, companies can delay recognizing changes in the value of their pension plans. Using a practice called "smoothing," companies can spread the reporting of changes over several years. When stock markets were booming, no one scrutinized pension plans much because their value was obviously going up. But when stock markets started dropping, large liabilities began building up (but companies kept that information off their balance sheets). For companies with defined benefit pension plans (that is, pensions which guarantee employees a certain pension based on their earnings and years of service), liabilities have sharply increased. One study of the 100 largest defined benefit pension plans in Canada showed that 77 percent of them had a surplus in 2000, but that only about 20 percent of them had a surplus in 2003. These 100 plans were actually underfunded by a total of $1.8 billion, yet the balance sheets of these companies showed assets totalling $6.7 billion. Thus, about $8.5 billion in debt was not shown on the balance sheets of these 100 companies.

Canadian and international accounting regulators are working on changes to accounting rules that will bring more realism to pension reporting. The most obvious change involves ending the practice of smoothing and reporting pension fund returns as they actually take place. This means that income from the pension fund would be reported as investment income and the costs of running the pension fund would be reported as expenses. Regulators recognize that a change like this will increase the volatility in the earnings that corporations report, but they point out that investors will be able to more clearly see what is happening (good or bad) in a company's pension fund.

Questions for Discussion

1. Who are the various users of accounting information? How will each of these users be influenced if sales revenues are overstated and pension liabilities are understated?
2. What are the three basic financial statements that accountants generate for business firms? What does each one show? How will overstating sales revenue and understating pension liabilities affect each of these statements?
3. Read the sections in the chapter on revenue recognition and matching. How is the material in those sections helpful in dealing with the "overstating of sales revenue" problem noted in the case?
4. Consider the following statement: "Since sales revenues and pension returns are measured in dollars, and since dollars are easy to quantify, it should be very clear what sales revenues and investment income a firm had in a given period. It is therefore unnecessary to have policies about how sales revenues and pension returns should be reported." Do you agree or disagree? Explain. ◆

Video Case 3-1 CBC

Alabama Auto Jobs

It's a Tuesday night in Toronto, and the Canadian Auto Workers (CAW) union is bargaining with DaimlerChrysler in an attempt to reach a new collective agreement. What happens next will determine whether there will be a strike at the company. The talks have turned nasty as the deadline for reaching agreement looms, and the negotiators don't know if they can get an agreement. DaimlerChrysler has just announced that it's cancelling production at a Canadian auto plant that formerly provided 1200 jobs. They're arguing over the contract language that will contain DaimlerChrysler's promise that the company will build a new auto manufacturing plant in Ontario sometime in the future.

Eventually agreement is reached, and a strike is averted. But there's a loophole in the agreement allowing DaimlerChrysler to scale back its operations in Canada if it doesn't get government incentives to support its plans. The same deal was made with Ford earlier. So, while bargaining is ostensibly between labour and management, government is involved as well.

To see how important incentives are, go south to the state of Alabama. It's a poor state, but it has already given more than $1 billion in investment incentives to automobile manufacturing companies. In fact, Alabama has been so successful at attracting car companies that it's now called "Detroit south." Mercedes, Honda, and Hyundai all have plants here. There are also lots of plants that make automotive parts.

Just a few years ago, no automobiles were made in Alabama, but now 600 000 cars are built each year. Mercedes, for example, received $250 000 000 in incentives (such as allowances for employee training and tax breaks) when they agreed to build their North American headquarters in Alabama. They also got their own exit ramp off the interstate. Companies are attracted by the low-wage, non-union environment in many southern U.S. states. The incentives are so large that it will take a long time before the number of new jobs created by these plants will equal the incentive dollars that were given. But many people are moving to Alabama, and home construction is booming.

Billy Joe Camp earns his money shopping around for the best incentive deals for automobile companies that are planning to build new plants. When he was in Ontario, he told people that incentives like training allowances are needed in order to attract new automobile manufacturing plants. The pressure is on for Canada to join the incentives game, but in Canada the view is that incentives are already built in (like the Canadian health care system). But are these incentives enough to attract automobile manufacturers? Carlos Gomes, an economist at Scotiabank, says failure to give incentives will limit the growth of the automobile industry in Canada. Recently, DaimlerChrysler announced that it was building a new plant in Georgia. Windsor wanted the plant, but didn't get it. If the Canadian government keeps saying it doesn't do incentives, there will likely be a decline in the automobile business here. But giving tax dollars to private-sector companies is also a hard sell in Canada, so it's a real dilemma.

Questions for Discussion

1. What are the different kinds of utility that production creates? Which of these types of utility is most obvious in the production of automobiles?
2. Describe the different types of transformation technology that business firms use. Which type is evident in the production of automobiles?
3. The following statement is made on p. 376 of the text: "Depending on the site of its facility, a company may be capable of producing a low-cost product or may find itself at an extreme cost disadvantage relative to its competitors." Explain the relevance of this statement to this case.
4. What are the pros and cons of the Canadian government giving financial incentives to automobile companies?

Source: CBC *Venture*, "Alabama Auto Jobs," October 20, 2002.

Video Case 3-2 CBC

African Accountants

In Canada's business jungle, all tracks lead to Bay Street, where lions of modern industry reign. Accountants keep Bay Street's books, but the heat is on to keep better books. Accountants don't like people who bring in shoeboxes full of receipts and then ask the accountant to organize them. Instead, accountants want the material organized before they try to do any calculations. But all this organizing costs money, and small- and mid-sized businesses don't usually have the money to pay for it.

For George Wall, of Wall & Associates, finding enough casual workers to do data organization and entry was a big challenge. He had to pay them up to $20 an hour, and that service was way too pricey for many of his clients. But what if Wall could find workers who would do this work for one-tenth the hourly wage he had to pay people in Toronto? He found the solution by adopting global outsourcing. It works like this: when that shoebox arrives, each piece of paper is first fed into a high-speed scanner, then stored on a server, and then sent to the internet. While Bay Street sleeps, the material is sent to Kampala, Uganda, where the data are keyed in by African accountants who are paid only about $1 a day.

In a freshly painted office in Kampala, a dozen computers have just been taken out of their boxes, and a dozen workers have just been hired. Their boss is 20-something Abu Luaga, a Ugandan with a commerce degree who has the contract to do accounting work for Wall & Associates. He teaches the new hires what to do. His start-up funds came from his family, and he got involved with Wall & Associates through his connections with a Canadian business consultant.

There is much competition from other developing countries to get this kind of business. But his workers are keen, and they're already trained as bookkeepers. They're eager to see what the developed world has to offer, but many have never had a computer before and need training so that they can recognize various financial documents and learn Canadian accounting jargon. They're also being trained to think the way Canadian businesses do. As well, Luaga reminds them about deadlines and privacy. Because these workers are dealing with sensitive information, no cellphones are allowed in the office and the copying or saving of files or images is prohibited.

What are the implications of all this information flowing from the first world to the third world and back again? It may be just the kind of miracle Uganda needs. The telecommunications industry has been a bright spot in the Ugandan economy, but Ugandans still make only about $1 a day. The country still relies on money earned by exporting coffee, and the government is dependent on foreign donors for part of its budget. Officials admit that the technical skills of workers aren't as good as those of people in some Asian countries, but this system allows educated Ugandans to work in their home country.

Luaga's workers say the work has already changed their career prospects. But not all Canadian clients have jumped at the chance to zip their documents to Africa. George Wall is convinced they will eventually be comfortable with the idea, and Luaga is banking on it. He's leasing bigger and better office space because he thinks that a new office and clients in Canada will impress other potential clients in Africa.

Questions for Discussion

1. What is the difference between financial and managerial accounting? Is the work that the African accountants are doing financial or managerial accounting? Explain.
2. Why might Canadian clients be reluctant to have Wall & Associates send their data to Africa for organizing? What can George Wall do to respond to their concerns?
3. Suppose that you read a newspaper editorial condemning the practice of sending documents to Africa on the grounds that this was yet another example of exporting Canadian jobs overseas to low-wage countries. How would you respond?

Source: CBC *Venture,* "African Accountants," February 16, 2003.

PART FOUR

Managing Marketing

What is the first thing you think of when you hear the names Coffee Crisp, Post-It, Crest, and Eno? If you grew up in Canada, you probably didn't hesitate at all before picturing candy, little slips of paper with one sticky edge, toothpaste, and something to calm your stomach. Your rapid association of company names and the goods or services they provide is a tribute to the effectiveness of the marketing managers of the firms that produce these goods. These and many other names have become household words because companies have developed the right products to meet customers' needs, have priced those products appropriately, have made prospective customers aware of the products' existence and qualities, and have made the products readily available.

Part Four, Managing Marketing, provides an overview of the many elements of marketing, including developing, pricing, promoting, and distributing various types of goods and services.

- We begin in **Chapter 15, Understanding Marketing Processes and Consumer Behaviour**, by examining the ways in which companies distinguish their products, determine customer needs, and otherwise address consumer buying preferences.
- Then, in **Chapter 16, Developing and Promoting Goods and Services**, we explore the development of different types of products, the effect of brand names and packaging, how promotion strategies help a firm meet its objectives, and the advantages and disadvantages of several promotional tools.
- Finally, in **Chapter 17, Pricing and Distributing Goods and Services**, we look at the strategies firms use to price their products. We also consider the various outlets business firms use to distribute their products, and we discuss the problems of storing goods and transporting them to distributors.

CHAPTER 15

Understanding Marketing Processes and Consumer Behaviour

After reading this chapter, you should be able to:

1. Explain the concept of *marketing* and describe the five forces that constitute the *external marketing environment*.
2. Explain the purpose of a *marketing plan* and identify the four components of the *marketing mix*.
3. Explain *market segmentation* and show how it is used in *target marketing*.
4. Explain the purpose and value of *marketing research*.
5. Describe the key factors that influence the *consumer buying process*.
6. Discuss the three categories of *organizational markets* and explain how *organizational buying behaviour* differs from consumer buying behaviour.
7. Describe the *international* and *small business marketing mixes*.

What Happened to the Youth Culture?

Different countries have different age distributions in their populations. Some have a high proportion of old people (the so-called "old" countries), while others have a high proportion of young people ("young" countries). In old countries, the median age is high and rising, and difficulties are already being experienced with rising health care costs and the funding of pension plans. In "young" countries, the median age is low and is rising only slowly, and fewer difficulties of this type will be experienced because a large proportion of the population will still be of working age for many decades yet.

For many years, population experts predicted that the world's population would increase to unsustainable levels in the future. Most of this increase would be generated in the young countries. But the world's birthrate is actually falling, and fears of overpopulation may be unfounded. In fact, some experts are predicting that the world's population could stabilize or even start declining in the next 100 years.

Population and demographic changes will have a big impact on the marketing strategies of companies that are trying to sell everything from diapers to arthritis medicine. To understand why, remember that companies have typically focused on the youth market. That strategy still looks pretty good in young countries like Mexico, Brazil, and Vietnam, but not so good in old countries like Japan, Germany, and France. Many companies still believe that there is a big market for young people in Asia, but the youth market there is projected to shrink by 10 percent during the next decade. During the same period, the number of people in the 40–59 age bracket is projected to increase by 30 percent.

While most companies continue to be fixated on marketing to youth, some companies are starting to get the idea that marketing products to older (and more affluent) people will pay off. Procter & Gamble has targeted older women with two new products—"Rejuvenating Effects" toothpaste, and Olay Anti-Aging Cream. It has also developed Actonel, an osteoporosis drug, which is likely to do well in Japan, Italy, and France because of the aging populations there. Motorola has introduced a new phone that should be of interest to older consumers because its zoom function allows the user to increase the font size so that it's more readable. The phone also has speakers that can be connected to a hearing aid. In Japan, Meiji Dairies Corp. has started making a yogourt brand for people over 40. Japanese automakers haven't opened an assembly plant in Japan since the early 1990s; instead, they are expanding in North America where the population will continue to grow.

In North America, the importance of demographics in marketing can be seen in a variety of situations. Consider the following:

- Many marketers have discovered that university and community college students are an important market segment. Students across Canada have discretionary income totalling $4 to $5 billion. Ford Motor of Canada has marketed to students since the mid-1980s, and gives graduates a $750 rebate on their first-time purchase of a car.
- Binney & Smith Canada Ltd., the makers of Crayola crayons, discovered that the number of children aged 3 to 7—the top users of crayons—was declining. They also noticed that the size of the age group 8 to 12 was increasing. This latter group, called "tweens" by demographers because they are between the ages of children and teenagers, is much more sophisticated and brand conscious than younger children. They have very distinct preferences, and don't like crayons much, viewing them as "babyish." Tweens prefer coloured pencils, so Binney & Smith introduced a new line of coloured pencils called "Crayola IQ" aimed at the tweens group. They abandoned the famous yellow-and-green Crayola package and replaced it with a new all-green package. Sales jumped 44 percent.
- In January 2003, the *Toronto Star* started a youth-oriented newspaper aimed at kids 9 to 14. This complements the existing Starship feature (aimed at kids 6 to 12) and the boom! feature (aimed at teenagers).
- Mattel Inc., the maker of the Barbie doll, formerly targeted girls from ages 2 to 8 for this product. But

7- and 8-year-old girls are now less and less interested in Barbie dolls and see them as something that "little kids" play with. However, these dolls can be marketed to girls aged 7 to 10 as collectibles.

- The over-50 age group is becoming increasingly important in Canada. Francine Tremblay recognized this trend some years ago and launched *Le Bel Age*, a French-language magazine for "mature" Canadians. Soon after, she began producing *Good Times*, an English-language magazine aimed at the same age group.
- Major League Baseball Enterprises (MLB) tracks demographic trends to set marketing goals for its $6 billion-a-year business. Two decades ago, for instance, the typical fan was a child, but today's average fan is about 37 years old. With teens more interested in basketball and football, many baseball executives are worried about the aging of the game's core fan base. ◆

WHAT IS MARKETING?

1. Explain the concept of *marketing* and describe the five forces that constitute the *external marketing environment.*

Because we are all consumers and because we all buy goods and services, we are influenced by the marketing activities of companies that want us to buy their products rather than those of competitors. But as consumers, we are in fact *the* essential ingredients in the marketing process. Every day, we express *needs* for such essentials as food, clothing, and shelter and *wants* for such nonessentials as entertainment and leisure activities. Our needs and wants are the forces that drive marketing. Most of us think of marketing as advertisements for detergents and soft drinks. Marketing, however, encompasses a much wider range of activities. The American Marketing Association, an international body of academics and professional marketers, defines **marketing** as the "the process of planning and executing the conception, pricing, promotion, and distribution of ideas, goods, and services to create exchanges that satisfy individual and organizational goals."[1]

marketing
Planning and executing the development, pricing, promotion, and distribution of ideas, goods, and services to create exchanges that satisfy both buyers' and sellers' objectives.

We begin our study of marketing by looking at how marketing focuses on providing value and utility for consumers. We then explore the marketing environment and the development of marketing strategy. Finally, we focus on the four activities that comprise the marketing mix: *developing, pricing, promoting,* and *placing products*.

Providing Value and Satisfaction

What attracts buyers to one product instead of another? While our desires for the many goods and services available to us may be unbounded, limited financial resources force most of us to be selective. Accordingly, consumers buy products that offer the best value when it comes to meeting their needs and wants.

Value and Benefits

value
Relative comparison of a product's benefits versus its costs.

Value compares a product's benefits with its costs. The benefits of a *high-value* product are much greater than its costs. *Benefits* include not only the functions of the product, but also the emotional satisfactions associated with owning, experiencing, or possessing it. Every product has costs, including sales price, the expenditure of the buyer's time, and the emotional costs of making a purchase decision. The satisfied buyer perceives the benefits derived from the purchase to be greater than its costs. Thus the simple but important ratio for value:

$$\text{Value} = \frac{\text{Benefits}}{\text{Costs}}$$

Marketing strategies focus on increasing value for customers. Marketing resources are deployed to add value to products to satisfy customers' needs and wants. Satisfying customers may mean developing an entirely new product that performs better (provides greater benefits) than existing products. Or it may mean keeping a store open extra hours during a busy season (adding the benefit of greater shopping convenience). Some companies simply offer price reductions (the benefit of lower cost). Customers may also gain benefits from an informational promotion that explains how a product can be used in new ways.

Value and Utility

To understand how marketing creates value for customers, we need to know the kind of benefits that buyers get from a firm's goods or services. Products provide consumers with **utility**—the ability of a product to satisfy a human want or need.

utility
Ability of a product to satisfy a human want or need.

Marketing strives to provide four kinds of utility:

- When a company turns out ornaments in time for Christmas, it creates *time utility*: It makes products available when consumers want them.
- When a department store opens its annual Christmas department, it creates *place utility*: It makes products available where customers can conveniently purchase them.
- When the store sells ornaments, it provides *ownership utility* by conveniently transferring ownership from store to customer.
- By making products available in the first place—by turning raw materials into finished ornaments—the ornament maker creates *form utility*.

Marketing plays a role in all four areas—determining the timing, place, terms of sale, and product features that provide utility and add value for customers. Marketers, therefore, must begin with an understanding of customers' wants and needs. Their methods for creating utility are described in this and the following two chapters.

Goods, Services, and Ideas

The marketing of tangible goods is obvious in everyday life. You walk into a department store and are given a free scented paper strip as an initial product sample of a new perfume. A pharmaceutical company proclaims the virtues of its new cold medicine. Your local auto dealer offers to sell you an automobile with no interest charges for four years. These products—the perfume, the cold medicine, and the car—are all **consumer goods**: products that you, the consumer, buy for personal use. Firms that sell products to consumers for personal consumption are engaged in *consumer marketing*.

consumer goods
Products purchased by individuals for their personal use.

Marketing is also important for **industrial goods**, which are products used by companies to produce other products. Surgical instruments and earthmovers are industrial goods, as are such components and raw materials as integrated circuits, steel, and unformed plastic. Firms that sell products to other manufacturers are engaged in *industrial marketing*.

industrial goods
Products purchased by companies to use directly or indirectly to produce other products.

Marketing is also relevant for **services**—intangible products such as time, expertise, or some activity that you can purchase. *Service marketing* has become a major growth area in Canada. Insurance companies, airlines, investment counsellors, health clinics, and accountants all engage in *service marketing*, both to individuals and to other companies.

services
Intangible products, such as time, expertise, or an activity that can be purchased.

Finally, marketers also promote *ideas*. Television ads, for example, can remind us that teaching is an honourable profession and that teachers are "heroes." Other ads stress the importance of driving only when sober and the advantages of not smoking.

Relationship Marketing

relationship marketing
A type of marketing that emphasizes lasting relationships with customers and suppliers.

Although marketing often focuses on single transactions for products, services, or ideas, marketers also take a longer-term perspective. Thus, **relationship marketing** emphasizes lasting relationships with customers and suppliers. Stronger relationships—including stronger economic and social ties—can result in greater long-term satisfaction and customer loyalty.[2]

Banks, for example, offer *economic* incentives to encourage longer-lasting relationships. Customers who purchase more of the bank's products (for example, chequing accounts, savings accounts, and loans) accumulate credits toward free or reduced-price services, such as free traveller's cheques. As another example, motorcycle manufacturer Harley-Davidson offers social incentives through the Harley Owners Group (H.O.G.). H.O.G. gives motorcyclists the opportunity to bond with other riders and to develop long-term friendships.

The Marketing Environment

Coca-Cola
www.coca-cola.com

external environment
Outside factors that influence marketing programs by posing opportunities or threats.

Marketing plans, decisions, and strategies are not determined unilaterally by any business—not even by marketers as experienced and influential as Coca-Cola and Procter & Gamble. Rather, they are strongly influenced by powerful outside forces. As you can see in Figure 15.1, any marketing program must recognize the outside factors that comprise a company's **external environment**. In this section, we will describe five of these environmental factors: *the political/legal, social/cultural, technological, economic,* and *competitive environments*.

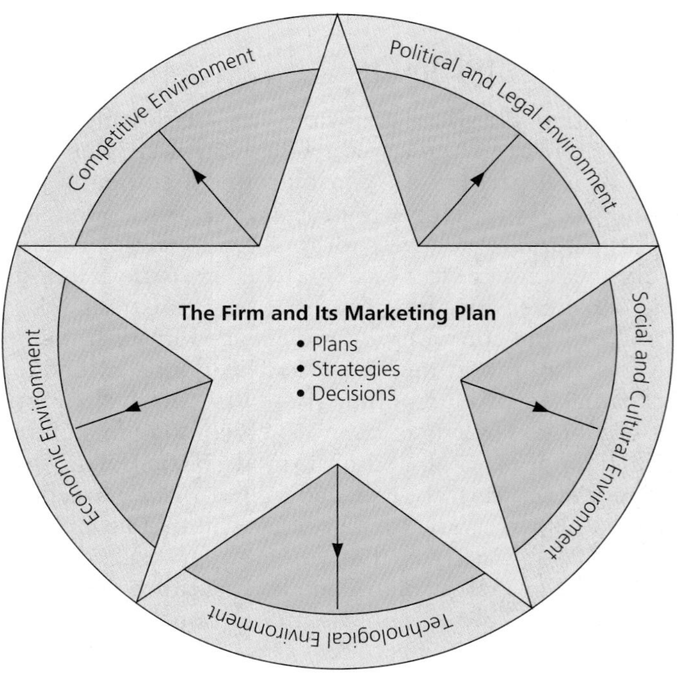

Figure 15.1
The external marketing environment.

Political and Legal Environment

Political activities, both foreign and domestic, have profound effects on business (refer back to Chapter 1 for a discussion of how government influences business). Legislation on the use of cellphones in cars and pollution legislation can determine the destinies of entire industries. Marketing managers therefore try to maintain favourable political/legal environments in several ways. For example, to gain public support for their products and activities, marketing uses advertising campaigns for public awareness on issues of local, regional, or national importance. They also lobby and contribute to political candidates (although there are legal restrictions on how much they can contribute). Such activities sometimes result in favourable laws and regulations and may even open new international business opportunities.

Social and Cultural Environment

More people are working at home, more women are entering the workforce, the number of single-parent families is increasing, food preferences and physical activities reflect the growing concern for healthful lifestyles, and the growing recognition of cultural diversity continues. These and other issues reflect the values, beliefs, and ideas that form the fabric of Canadian society today. Obviously, these broad attitudes toward issues have direct effects on business. Today, for example, as we continue to insist on a "greener" Canada, we have seen the demise of freon in air conditioners and increased reliance on recycling materials in the goods that we consume.

Changing social values force companies to develop and promote new products for both individual consumers and industrial customers. For example, although most of us value privacy, web surfers are discovering that a loss of privacy is often a price for the convenience of internet shopping. Dot-com sites regularly collect personal information that they use for marketing purposes and which they often sell to other firms. Responding to the growing demand for better privacy protection, firms like iNetPrivacy offer such products as Anonymity 4 Proxy software, which allows you to surf the Net anonymously.

iNetPrivacy
www.inetprivacy.com

Technological Environment

New technologies affect marketing in several ways. Obviously, they create new goods (say, the satellite dish) and services (home television shopping). New products make some existing products obsolete (for example, compact discs are replacing audiotapes), and many of them change our values and lifestyles. In turn, they often stimulate new goods and services not directly related to the new technology itself. Cellular phones, for example, not only facilitate business communication, but also free up time for recreation and leisure.

Consider the phenomenon of DNA "fingerprinting." The O.J. Simpson trial (United States), the Guy Paul Morin case (Canada), and the television show *CSI: Crime Scene Investigation* have made just about everyone aware of its availability to law-enforcement officials. Bear in mind, however, that it is also the focal point of a new industry—one that involves biological science and laboratory analysis and instrumentation as well as criminology. DNA fingerprinting, then, is a product. Along with its technical developments, therefore, it involves marketing decisions—such as pricing and promotion. This has been the case with literally thousands of technological breakthroughs in such fields as genetics, electronics, aeronautics, medicine, information sciences, communications systems, transportation, the internet (which we discussed in Chapter 13), and emarketing (which we discuss in Chapter 17).

Each of these advertisements provides information about a specific product, service, or idea. Mott's Fruitsations, for example, is a tangible consumer product. The advertisement for the National Gallery of Canada promotes a service that can be enjoyed. Weight Watchers promotes the idea of healthy behaviour.

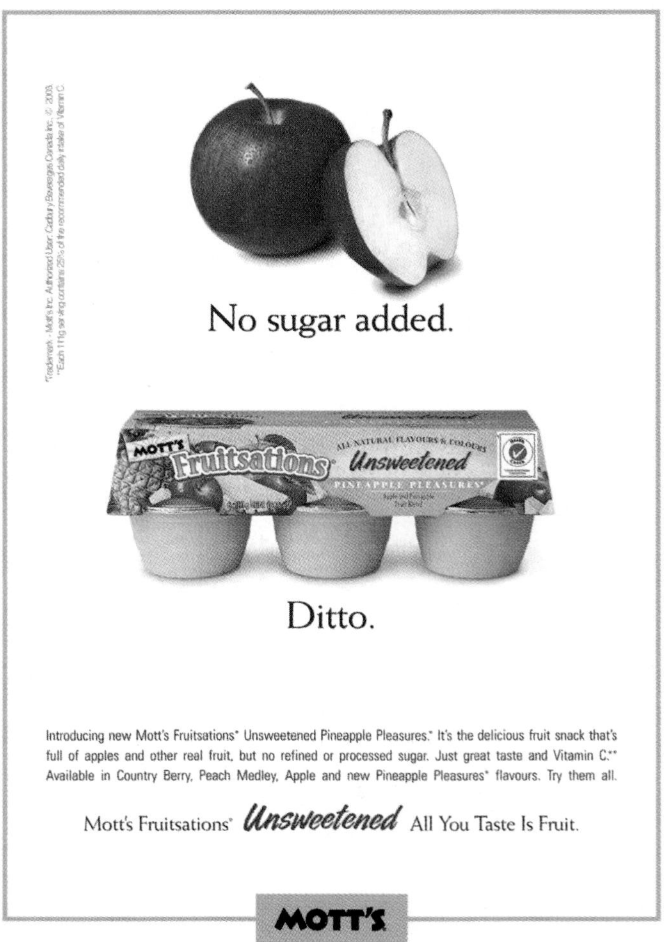

Economic Environment

Economic conditions determine spending patterns by consumers, businesses, and governments. Thus they influence every marketer's plans for product offerings, pricing, and promotional strategies. Among the more significant economic variables, marketers are concerned with inflation, interest rates, recession, and recovery. In other words, they must monitor the general business cycle, which typically features a pattern of transition from periods of prosperity to recession to recovery (return to prosperity). Not surprisingly, consumer spending increases as "consumer confidence" in economic conditions grows during periods of prosperity. Conversely it decreases during low-growth periods, when unemployment rises and purchasing power declines.

Traditionally, analysis of economic conditions focused on the national economy and the government's policies for controlling or moderating it. Increasingly, however, as nations form more and more economic connections, the "global economy" is becoming more prominent in the thinking of marketers everywhere. With pacts like the 1993 North American Free Trade Agreement and the 1994 General Agreement on Tariffs and Trade now in place, global economic conditions—indeed, conditions from nation to nation—will directly influence the economic fortunes of all trading partners (see Chapter 4). Certainly, marketers must now consider this new and unpredictable economic variable in developing both domestic and foreign marketing strategies.

Competitive Environment

In a competitive environment, marketers must convince buyers that they should purchase their products rather than those of some other seller. In a broad sense, because both consumers and commercial buyers have limited resources to spend, every dollar spent to buy one product is no longer available for other purchases. Each marketing program, therefore, seeks to make its product the most attractive; theoretically, a failed program loses the buyer's dollar forever (or at least until it is time for the next purchase decision).

Increased competition and the growth of consumer discretionary income have given added impetus to an idea that had its beginnings early in the twentieth century. This idea or philosophy, known as the **marketing concept**, means that the whole firm is coordinated to achieve one goal—to serve its present and potential customers and to do so at a profit. This concept means that a firm must get to know what customers really want and follow closely the changes in tastes that occur. The various departments of the firm—marketing, production, finance, and human resources—must operate as a system, well coordinated and unified in the pursuit of a common goal—customer satisfaction.

marketing concept
The idea that the whole firm is directed toward serving present and potential customers at a profit.

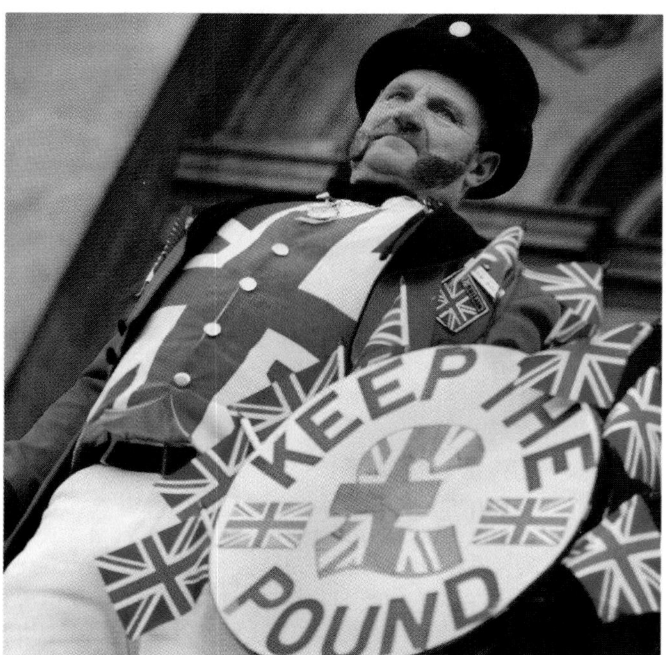

The euro, the common currency of the European Union, is a variable in Great Britain's economic environment. On the one hand, it eliminates exchange-rate risk for companies of member nations that are doing international business within the Union. That's why multinationals and banks in England—a non-euro country—favour adopting the euro. On the other hand, protestors fear that Britain would have to enact labour and other regulations like those of the EU countries to keep the British economy in line with those of euro nations.

By studying the competition, marketers determine how best to position their own products for three specific types of competition:

substitute product
A product that is dissimilar from those of competitors but that can fulfill the same need.

brand competition
Competitive marketing that appeals to consumer perceptions of similar products.

international competition
Competitive marketing of domestic against foreign products.

- **Substitute products** are dissimilar from those of competitors but can fulfill the same need. For example, your cholesterol level may be controlled with either a physical-fitness program or a drug regimen; the fitness program and the drugs compete as substitute products.
- **Brand competition** occurs between similar products, such as the auditing services provided by large accounting firms like Ernst & Young and KPMG Peat Marwick. The competition is based on buyers' perceptions of the benefits of products offered by particular companies.
- **International competition** matches the products of domestic marketers against those of foreign competitors—say, a flight on Swissair versus Air Canada. The intensity of international competition has been heightened by the formation of alliances such as the European Union and NAFTA.

Strategy: The Marketing Mix

2. Explain the purpose of a *marketing plan* and identify the four components of the *marketing mix*.

As a business activity, marketing requires management. Although many individuals also contribute to the marketing of a product, a company's **marketing managers** are typically responsible for planning and implementing all the marketing-mix activities that result in the transfer of goods or services to its customers. These activities culminate in the **marketing plan**: a detailed and focused strategy for gearing marketing activities to meet consumer needs and wants. Marketing, therefore, begins when a company identifies a consumer need and develops a product to meet it.

marketing managers
Managers responsible for planning and implementing all the marketing-mix activities that result in the transfer of goods or services to customers.

marketing plan
A detailed strategy for gearing the marketing mix to meet consumer needs and wants.

marketing mix
The combination of product, pricing, promotion, and distribution strategies used in marketing a product.

product
A good, service, or idea that satisfies buyers' needs and demands.

product differentiation
The creation of a product or product image that differs enough from existing products to attract consumers.

In planning and implementing strategies, marketing managers develop the four basic components (often called the "Four Ps") of the **marketing mix**. In this section, we describe each of those components: *product, pricing, place,* and *promotion*.

Product

Marketing begins with a **product**—a good, a service, or an idea designed to fill a consumer need or want. Conceiving and developing new products is a constant challenge for marketers, who must always consider the factor of change—changing technology, changing consumer wants and needs, and changing economic conditions. Meeting consumer needs, then, often means changing existing products to keep pace with emerging markets and competitors.

Producers often promote particular features of products to distinguish them in the marketplace. **Product differentiation** is the creation of a feature or image that makes a product differ enough from existing products to attract consumers. For example, Volvo automobiles provide newer, better safety features to set them apart from competitors. Customers of E*Trade™, the online investment service, gain value from after-hours trading not offered by conventional investment-service firms.

Price

price
That part of the marketing mix concerned with choosing the appropriate price for a product to meet the firm's profit objectives and buyers' purchasing objectives.

Determining the best **price** at which to sell a product is often a balancing act. On the one hand, prices must support a variety of costs—operating, administrative, and research costs as well as marketing costs. On the other hand, prices can't be so high that consumers turn to competitors. Successful pricing means finding a profitable middle ground between these two requirements.

Jann Wenner started *Rolling Stone* magazine in 1967, and it's been the cash cow of Wenner Media ever since. In 1985, Wenner bought *Us* magazine and set out to compete with *People*, perhaps the most successful magazine ever published. Wenner's latest strategy calls for greater differentiation between the two products. *People* is news driven, reporting on ordinary people as well as celebrities, and Wenner intends to punch up *Us* with more coverage of celebrity sex and glitter. So far, he hasn't been successful. *People* reaches 3.7 million readers, *Us* about 900 000.

Both low- and high-price strategies can be effective in different situations. Low prices, for example, generally lead to larger sales volumes. High prices usually limit market size but increase profits per unit. High prices may also attract customers by implying that a product is of high quality. We discuss pricing in more detail in Chapter 17.

Place (Distribution)

In the marketing mix, *place* refers to **distribution**. Placing a product in the proper outlet—say, a retail store—requires decisions about several activities, all of which are concerned with getting the product from the producer to the consumer. Decisions about warehousing and inventory control are distribution decisions, as are decisions about transportation options.

distribution
That part of the marketing mix concerned with getting products from the producer to the buyer, including physical transportation and choice of sales outlets.

Firms must also make decisions about the *channels* through which they distribute products. Many manufacturers, for instance, sell goods to other companies that, in turn, distribute them to retailers. Others sell directly to major retailers such as Sears, Wal-Mart, or Safeway. Still others sell directly to final consumers. We explain distribution decisions further in Chapter 17.

Promotion

The most highly visible component of the marketing mix is *promotion*, which refers to techniques for communicating information about products. The most important promotional tools include advertising, personal selling, sales promotions, and public relations. We describe promotional activities more fully in Chapter 16.

Product, price, place, and promotion focus on the seller's perspective. From the buyer's perspective, each of the 4 Ps provides a certain benefit. In effect, the seller's 4 Ps are a mirror image of the buyer's 4 Cs: customer solution (product), customer cost (price), customer convenience (place), and customer communication (promotion).[3]

By providing both distribution and advertising for Grand & Toy, this truck plays a dual role in the company's marketing.

TARGET MARKETING AND MARKET SEGMENTATION

3. *Explain market segmentation and show how it is used in target marketing.*

Marketing managers long ago recognized that they cannot be "all things to all people." People have different tastes, different interests, different goals, different lifestyles, and so on. The marketing concept's recognition of consumers' various needs and wants led marketing managers to think in terms of target marketing. **Target markets** are groups of people with similar wants and needs.

target market
Any group of people who have similar wants and needs and may be expected to show interest in the same product(s).

market segmentation
Dividing a market into categories according to traits customers have in common.

Target marketing clearly requires **market segmentation**, dividing a market into categories of customer types or "segments." For example, Mr. Big-and-Tall sells to men who are taller and heavier than average. Certain special interest magazines are oriented toward people with specific interests (see Table 15.1). Once they have identified market segments, companies may adopt a variety of product strategies. Some firms decide to provide a range of products to the market in an attempt to market their products to more than one segment. For example, General Motors of Canada offers compact cars, vans, trucks, luxury cars, and sports cars with various features and prices. Its strategy is to provide an automobile for nearly every segment of the market.

In contrast, some businesses restrict production to one market segment. Rolls-Royce understands that only a relatively small number of people are willing to pay $310 000 for exclusive touring limousines. Rolls, therefore, makes no attempt to cover the entire range of possible products; instead, it markets only to a very small segment of the total automobile buyers market.

Table 15.2 shows how a marketer of home-electronic equipment might segment the radio market. Note that segmentation is a strategy for analyzing consumers, not products. The analysis in Table 15.2, for example, identifies consumer-users—joggers, commuters, and travellers. Only *indirectly*, then, does it focus on the uses of the product itself. In marketing, the process of fixing, adapting, and communicating the nature of the product itself is called *positioning*.

Identifying Market Segments

By definition, the members of a market segment must share some common traits or behaviours that will affect their purchasing decisions. In identify-

Table 15.1 Magazines with Specific Target Audiences

Accounting	**Fishing/Hunting**
CAmagazine	*Canadian Fly Fisher*
CGA Magazine	*Outdoor Canada*
CMA Management	*B.C. Outdoors Sport Fishing*
Agriculture	**Automotive**
Agro-Nouvelles	*Aftermarket Canada*
Meat & Poultry Magazine	*Bodyshop*
Country Life in B.C.	*World of Wheels*
Sports	**Boating**
Cycle Canada	*Boating Business*
Chalk and Cue	*Canadian Boating*
Athletics Canada	*Porthole Magazine*
Gardening	**Music**
Canadian Gardening	*CHART Magazine*
The Gardener for the Prairies	*CODA Magazine*
Gardening Life	*Opus*

ing market segments, researchers look at geographic, demographic, psychographic, and product-use variables.

Geographic Variables

In some cases, where people live affects their buying decisions. The heavy rainfall in British Columbia prompts its inhabitants to purchase more umbrellas than does Arizona's desert. Urban residents have less demand for pickup trucks than do their rural counterparts. Sailboats sell better along both coasts than they do in the prairie provinces. **Geographic variables** are the geographical units, from countries to neighbourhoods, that may be considered in a segmentation strategy.

geographic variables
Geographical units that may be considered in a segmentation strategy.

These patterns affect marketing decisions about what products to offer, at what price to sell them, how to promote them, and how to distribute them. For example, consider marketing down parkas in rural Saskatchewan. Demand will be high, price competition may be limited, local newspaper advertising may be very effective, and the best location may be one easily reached from several small towns.

Although the marketability of some products is geographically sensitive, others enjoy nearly universal acceptance. Coke, for example, gets more than 70 percent of its sales from markets outside the United States. It is the market leader in Great Britain, China, Germany, Japan, Brazil, and Spain. By contrast, Pepsi earns 78 percent of its income from the United States. Coke's chief competitor in most countries is not Pepsi, but some local soft drink.

Demographic Variables

Demographic variables describe populations by identifying characteristics such as age, income, gender, ethnic background, marital status, race, religion, and social class. Table 15.3 lists some demographic market seg-

demographic variables
Characteristics of populations that may be considered in developing a segmentation strategy.

Table 15.2 Possible Segmentation of the Radio Market

Segmentation	Product/Target Market
Age	Inexpensive, unbreakable, portable models for young children
	Inexpensive equipment—possibly portable—for teens
	Moderate-to-expensive equipment for adults
Consumer attitude	Sophisticated components for audio buffs
	All-in-one units in furniture cabinets for those concerned with room appearance
Product use	Miniature models for joggers and commuters
	"Boom box" portables for taking outdoors
	Car stereo systems for travelling
	Components and all-in-one units for home use
Location	Battery-powered models for use where electricity is unavailable
	AC current for North American users
	DC current for other users

ments. Note that these are objective criteria that cannot be altered. Marketers must work with or around them. We saw in the opening case how important one demographic variable—the age distribution of a country's population—is to marketing managers.

Psychographic Variables

psychographic variables
Psychological traits that a group has in common, including motives, attitudes, activities, interests, and opinions.

Members of a market can also be segmented according to such **psychographic variables** as lifestyle, opinions, interests, and attitudes. One company that is using psychographic variables to revive its brand is Burberry, whose plaid-lined gabardine raincoats have been a symbol of British tradition since 1856. After a recent downturn in sales, Burberry is repositioning itself as a global luxury brand, like Gucci and Louis Vuitton. The strategy calls for luring top-of-the-line, fashion-conscious customers. Burberry pictures today's luxury-product shopper as a world traveller who identifies with prestige fashion brands and monitors social and fashion trends in *Harper's Bazaar*.[4]

Psychographics are particularly important to marketers because, unlike demographics and geographics, they can sometimes be changed by marketing efforts. For example, many companies have succeeded in changing at least some consumers' opinions by running ads highlighting products that have been improved directly in response to consumer desires. Many companies in Poland have succeeded in overcoming consumer resistance to buying on credit by promoting the safety and desirability of using credit rather than depending solely on cash for family purchases. One product of such changing attitudes is a booming economy and the emergence of a growing and robust middle class. The increasing number of Polish households that own televisions, appliances, automobiles, and houses is fuelling the status of Poland's middle class as the most stable in the former Soviet bloc.[5]

Behavioural Variables

behavioural variables
Consumer characteristics based on the use of a product, benefits expected from it, reasons for purchasing it, and loyalty to it.

The term **behavioural variables** refers to the ways in which consumers use a product, the benefits they expect from it, their reasons for purchasing it,

Table 15.3 Demographic Market Segmentation

Age	Under 5; 5–11; 12–19; 20–34; 35–49; 50–64; 65+
Education	Grade school or less; some high school; graduated high school; some college or university; college diploma or university degree; advanced degree
Family life cycle	Young single; young married without children; young married with children; older married with children under 18; older married without children under 18; older single; other
Family size	1, 2–3, 4–5, 6+
Income	Under $9000; $9000–$14 999; $15 000–$25 000; over $25 000
Nationality	Including but not limited to African, Asian, British, Eastern European, French, German, Irish, Italian, Latin American, Middle Eastern, and Scandinavian
Race	Including but not limited to Inuit, Asian, black, and white
Religion	Including but not limited to Buddhist, Catholic, Hindu, Jewish, Muslim, and Protestant
Sex	Male, female
Language	Including but not limited to English, French, Inuktitut, Italian, Ukrainian, and German

and their loyalty to it.[6] A women's shoemaker might identify three segments—wearers of athletic, casual, and dress shoes. Each segment is looking for different benefits in a shoe. A woman buying an athletic shoe may not care about its appearance but may care a great deal about arch support and traction in the sole. A woman buying a casual shoe will want it to look good and feel comfortable. A woman buying a dress shoe may require a specific colour or style and may even accept some discomfort. Consumers who always buy one brand are classified as *hard-core loyalists,* whereas *switchers* buy various brands.

The Wired World box describes how automobile companies use demographics and consumer variables to identify target markets for new technology applications.

Although Nike leads the $15.5 billion athletic footwear industry, it still has a serious problem: Women's footwear accounts for 33 percent of industry sales but generates only 20 percent of Nike's. Nike is going after this demographic segment with a marketing campaign that focuses on differences between the way men and women think about sports and the way they shop for clothing. According to Nike marketers, for example, women are more interested in image trends and active lifestyles than in athletic competition and sports celebrities.

IT'S A WIRED WORLD

High-Tech Hits the Highway

Nicole Gunther's four-year-old daughter is happy in the back seat of the family's Honda minivan. There are no more whining cries of "When are we going to get there?" With the rear-seat DVD player delivering Disney films, Nicole is absorbed in entertainment that lets Mom concentrate on after-school traffic. Other services, such as a satellite-controlled navigation system, keep drivers from getting lost and alert them to road or traffic conditions. Competitors are also getting in on the act. Cadillac's OnStar navigation service offers satellite radio services in more than 30 GM car and truck models, and satellite feeds are linked into dozens of Ford, GM, and DaimlerChrysler models.

Telematics, automobile versions of the electronic entertainment systems that have become staples in many homes, were packaged in about 2 percent of new vehicles sold in 2002, but the industry is on the verge of a boom: Wireless communications for the highway had total sales of $1.6 billion in 2001 but will reach $20 billion annually in 2006.

Industry demographics are changing, too. Currently, buyers consist mostly of middle- to upper-class drivers who can afford pricey upscale vehicles—DVD players and navigation systems cost up to $2000—and, especially, families with younger children. Electronic services are a welcome stress reliever for today's busy suburban lifestyles in which many parents find themselves staffing dawn-to-dusk transportation services.

Launched in Cadillacs during the 1999 to 2001 model years, the first in-car communications systems offered on-road monitoring of performance and location and traffic-guidance advisories for high-income drivers. But that target audience, say industry experts, will change by 2007, when 80 percent of all new cars will contain factory-installed telematics. For model years 2002–2004, the target is active families in midrange- and higher-income groups who have young children and who use in-car technology for safety and entertainment. Even midrange, lower-priced cars will be equipped with a variety of wireless appliances—hands-free cellphones, monitoring systems for roadside assistance, and satellite radios. Satellite subscription fees, currently ranging from $200 to $400 per year for GM's OnStar, will permit technology-oriented drivers to receive music and movies from home and elsewhere.

Still another target group for 2003–2006 is high-income professionals who use in-car communications technologies for business and personal transactions. Business-minded drivers will have at their fingertips palm-held computers, web-connected PCs, voice-activated email, and satellite-transmitted stock market reports.

Market Segmentation: A Caution

Segmentation must be done carefully. A group of people may share an age category, income level, or some other segmentation variable, but their spending habits may be quite different. Look at your friends in school. You may all be approximately the same age, but you have different needs and wants. Some of you may wear cashmere sweaters while others wear sweatshirts. The same holds true for income. University professors and truck drivers frequently earn about the same level of income. However, their spending patterns, tastes, and wants are generally quite different.

In Canada, the two dominant cultures—English and French—show significant differences in consumer attitudes and behaviour. Researchers have found, for example, that compared with English Canadians, French Canadians are more involved with home and family, attend ballet more often, travel less, eat more chocolate, and are less interested in convenience food. Obviously, prudent marketers should take these differences into account when developing marketing plans. This is, however, easier said than done.

It is one thing to know that consumers in Quebec buy large quantities of certain products; it is quite another to capitalize on these differences. One problem is that differences may not continue over time. Change is continually occurring in consumption patterns across Canada, and data may quickly become outdated. Another problem is that consumption patterns differ from region to region in Canada even where culture is not the main cause. The buying behaviour of Quebec and Ontario consumers may be more similar than the behaviour of British Columbia and Newfoundland consumers.

MARKET RESEARCH

4. Explain the purpose and value of *marketing research.*

Market research, the study of what buyers need and how best to meet those needs, can address any element in the marketing mix. Business firms spend millions of dollars each year as they try to figure out their customers' habits and preferences. Market research can greatly improve the accuracy and effectiveness of market segmentation.[7]

market research
The systematic study of what buyers need and how best to meet those needs.

The relationship of marketing research in the overall marketing process is shown in Figure 15.2. Ultimately, its role is to increase the firm's competitiveness by understanding the relationship among the firm's customers, its marketing variables, and its marketing decisions. Marketing researchers use a variety of methods to obtain, interpret, and use information about customers. They determine the kinds of information that are needed for decisions on marketing strategy, goal setting, and target-market selection. In doing so, they may conduct studies on how customers will respond to proposed changes in the current marketing mix. One researcher, for example, might study consumer response to an experimental paint formula (new product). Another might explore the response to a price reduction (new price) on calculators. A third might check response to a proposed advertising campaign (new promotion). Marketers can also try to learn whether

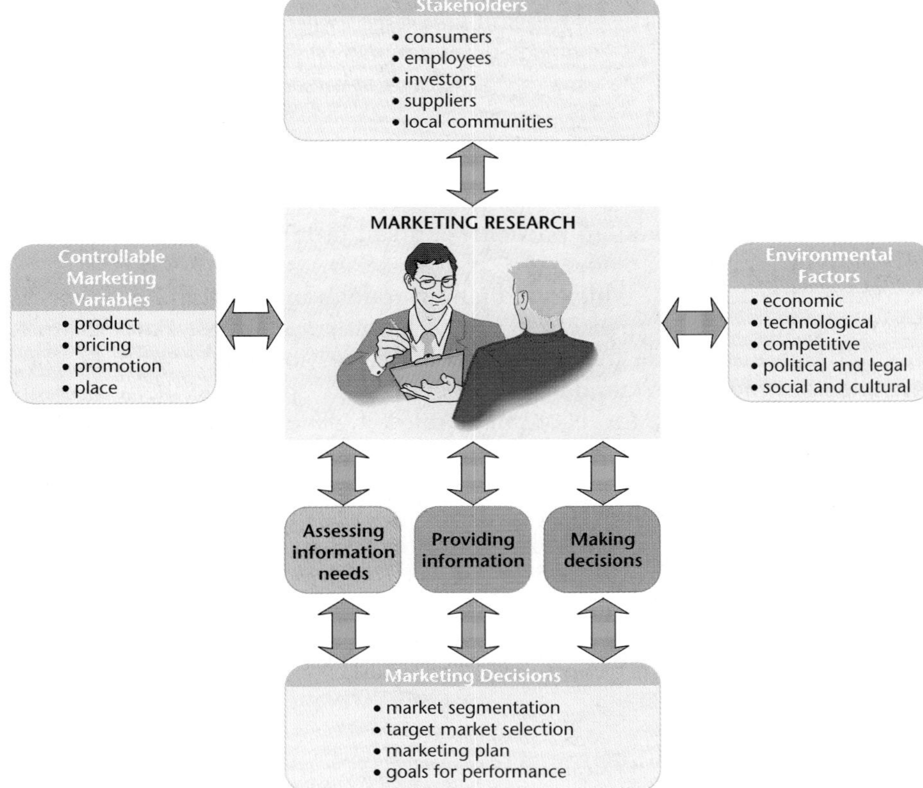

Figure 15.2
Market research and the marketing process.

BUSINESS TODAY

Is There an International Market?

For many years, marketers debated whether the same basic products and services could be sold in many different countries, or whether differences in culture, values, and attitudes meant that different products had to be developed for different countries. In the early 1980s, companies like McDonald's and Parker Pen tried international product launches and a single promotion campaign worldwide. But they didn't work too well, and it seemed that differences were still significant enough that products and services had to be tailored to specific countries or regions.

But in the last few years, the idea of international products has gained momentum. Mattel, the maker of Barbie dolls, is just one company that is learning some interesting lessons about the international market. Until recently, the company's strategy was to see which products sold well in the United States, and then launch the product internationally. But when it conducted focus groups with kids in dozens of countries, it found that worldwide demand existed for many of the same products. Mattel discovered, in essence, that children have similar tastes no matter where they live.

Mattel's experience with its famous Barbie doll is illustrative. The dolls sold in Japan, for example, had always had black hair and Asian features, not the blonde, blue-eyed appearance of Barbie dolls sold in North America. This seemed to make intuitive sense, but now Mattel is finding that the original Barbie doll is selling just as well in Asia as in North America. A new product, Rapunzel Barbie (with ankle-length blonde hair), was released in 59 countries on the same day in 2002. The new doll made the top 10 bestseller list in North America, Europe, and Asia.

Mattel's experience is not unique. Various other companies that sell products to international consumers have found the same phenomenon:

- The Harry Potter book series already had a global following when the first Harry Potter movie was released. The movie was released internationally on the same day, which was a departure from the usual Hollywood practice of opening a movie in the United States first and then later releasing it overseas. The sale of Harry Potter products like video games, trading cards, and Hogwarts Castle was coordinated with release of the movie.
- The Disney movie *Lizzie McGuire* was released internationally in 2003, and Disney plans to promote identical books, pillows, and clothing that are tied to the TV comedy of the same name.
- Harlequin Enterprises, which sells millions of romance novels in many different countries, uses the same book covers around the world. The pictures of Caucasians on the book covers

customers are more likely to purchase a given product in a specialty shop or on the internet (new place).

The importance of selling products in today's international markets is expanding the role of marketing research into new areas. For example, when companies decide to sell goods or services in other countries, they must decide whether to standardize products or to specialize them by offering different versions for each new market. The Business Today box describes how globalization is affecting this process.

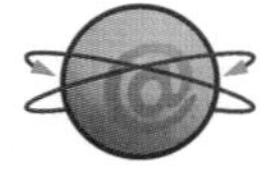

Mattel
www.mattel.com

Harry Potter
www.harrypotter.com

MTV
www.mtvcanada.com

Most companies will benefit from market research, but they need not do the research themselves. O-Pee-Chee Co. Ltd. of London, Ontario (the bubble gum and candy manufacturer) does no market research and no product testing, yet it continues to be successful in a market where products change at a dizzying pace. By signing a licensing agreement with two U.S. giants, O-Pee-Chee simply looks at what's hot in the United States and then starts manufacturing those lines in Canada.[8]

The Research Process

Market research can occur at almost any point in a product's existence. Most commonly, however, it is used when a new or altered product is being do not seem to deter customers in other countries from buying Harlequin romance novels.

- MTV is causing a revolution in worldwide marketing. At present, it is difficult to sell the same products to 35-year-olds in different countries because they never were exposed to anything but products from the country in which they were raised. Not so for the upcoming generation of teenagers. They see (and buy) products from various countries and will probably continue to do so as they get older. Teen fashion fads are also spreading around the world. Hip-hop, first popularized by African Americans, emphasizes loose-fitting urban street wear, baggy jeans, sweatshirts, hiking boots, athletic shoes, and baseball caps (worn backwards). Within this fashion category, certain brands have become very popular. Levi jeans, Nike or Reebok athletic shoes, and Timberland boots are some of the brands that have profited.
- Sports is another universal language. Basketball stars like Michael Jordan and Shaquille O'Neal have high name recognition overseas. In a poll of Chinese students in rural Shaanxi province, Michael Jordan tied with former Chinese premier Zhou En-lai for the title "World's Greatest Man." Not surprisingly, testimonial advertisements by big-name sports stars have a big impact on potential buyers. It is not uncommon for students to own multiple pairs of Nike Air Jordans.
- Tastes in consumer electronics are also similar across countries. Kodak is developing an advertising campaign directed specifically at teenagers in the hope that when they have their own children they will use Kodak products to take pictures of them. Teens are also more comfortable with personal computers than their parents are. So, even if the parents are buying the machine, the teen determines what brand is purchased.

Two trends are making world markets more homogeneous (especially for products bought by consumers under 20 years of age). The first is electronic media like cable and satellite TV channels, movies, and the internet. These expose people around the world to popular icons, and influence people to buy certain products. The second is the tremendous worldwide power of retailers like Wal-Mart, Toys 'R' Us, and Carrefour SA. These mass retailers sign exclusive agreements with consumer product companies and then sell them around the world using large promotional campaigns.

But marketers know that there are still differences between countries, and these cannot be ignored. For example, German children aren't attracted to action toys the way Canadian and U.S. children are. There are also differences even within basic product lines; U.S. kids want Nascar toy cars, while European children want Formula One models. When promoting products in international markets, companies must obviously take into account factors like language, cultural receptiveness, and brand image (see Chapter 16). But it seems likely that more and more companies will be able to sell basic products and services to customers in many different countries.

considered. These are the five steps in performing market research:[9]

1. *Study of the current situation.* What is the need and what is being done to meet it at this point?
2. *Select a research method.* In choosing a method, marketers must bear in mind the effectiveness and costs of different methods.
3. *Collect data.* **Secondary data** is information already available as a result of previous research by the firm or other agencies. For example, Statistics Canada publishes a great deal of data that is useful for business firms. Using secondary data can save time, effort, and money. But in some cases secondary data are unavailable or inadequate, so **primary data**—new research by the firm or its agents—must be obtained. Hostess Frito-Lay, the maker of Doritos, spent a year studying how to best reach its target market—teenagers. The researchers hung around shopping malls, schools, and fast-food outlets to watch the teens.[10]

secondary data
Information already available to market researchers as a result of previous research by the firm or other agencies.

primary data
Information developed through new research by the firm or its agents.

4. *Analyze the data.* Data are not useful until they have been organized into information.
5. *Prepare a report.* This report should include a summary of the study's methodology and findings. It should also identify alternative solutions

(where appropriate) and make recommendations for the appropriate course of action.

Research Methods

The four basic types of methods used by market researchers are *observation, surveys, focus groups,* and *experimentation.*

Observation

observation

A market research technique involving viewing or otherwise monitoring consumer buying patterns.

Probably the oldest form of market research is simple **observation** of what is happening. A store owner notices that customers are buying red children's wagons, not green ones. The owner reorders more red wagons, the manufacturer's records show high sales of red wagons, and marketing concludes that customers want red wagons. Today, computerized systems allow marketers to "observe" consumers' preferences rapidly and with tremendous accuracy. For example, electronic scanners in supermarkets enable store owners to see what is and is not selling without having to check the shelves. Observation is also a popular research method because it is relatively low in cost, often drawing on data that must be collected for some other reason, such as reordering.

Surveys

survey

A market research technique based on questioning a representative sample of consumers about purchasing attitudes and practices.

Sometimes marketers need to ask questions about new marketing ideas or about how well the firm is doing its marketing tasks. One way to get answers is by conducting a **survey**. The heart of any survey is a questionnaire. Traditionally, surveys have been mailed to individuals for their completion, but recently online surveys are being increasingly used because the company gets immediate results, and because the process is a less intrusive way of gathering data. Surveys can be expensive to carry out and may vary widely in their accuracy. Because no firm can afford to survey everyone, marketers must be careful to get a representative group of respondents. They must also construct their questions so that they get honest answers that address the specific issue being researched.

UPS

www.ups.ca

When United Parcel Service (UPS) surveyed customers to find out how it could improve service, it found that clients wanted more interaction with drivers because they can offer practical advice on shipping. UPS thus added extra drivers, freeing up some time for drivers to get out of their trucks and spend time with customers.[11]

Companies like Media Metrix and Nielsen Media Research help companies determine how consumers are responding to their efforts. Companies that want to know how popular their website is can ask Media Metrix to gather data on how many "hits" their site is experiencing. Companies that want to know how many people are watching a certain TV program can consult the Nielsen ratings.

Focus Groups

focus group

A market research technique involving a small group of people brought together and allowed to discuss selected issues in depth.

Many firms also use **focus groups**, where 6 to 15 people are brought together to talk about a product or service. A moderator leads the group's discussion, and employees from the sponsoring company may observe the proceedings from behind a one-way mirror. The people in the focus group are not usually told which company is sponsoring the research. The comments of people in the focus group are taped, and then researchers go through the data looking for common themes.

This market research technique allows selected issues to be discussed in depth. At farm implement manufacturer John Deere, focus groups have suggested many improvements in farm tractors, including different ways to change the oil filter and making the steps to the tractor cab wider.[12] But the focus group approach is no guarantee of success. When Sears Canada bought some of Eaton's best stores after Eaton's went bankrupt, Sears reopened these stores but retained the Eaton's name. Before doing that, Sears conducted focus groups using former Eaton's customers to determine if the new ideas it had for the revamped Eaton's stores would be viewed favourably.[13] In spite of all this market research, Sears eventually closed all the Eaton's stores.

Experimentation

The last major form of market research, experimentation, also tries to get answers to questions that surveys cannot address. As in science, **experimentation** in market research attempts to compare the responses of the same or similar individuals under different circumstances. For example, a firm trying to decide whether to include walnuts in a new candy bar probably would not learn much by asking people what they thought of the idea. But if it made some bars with nuts and some without and then asked people to try both, the responses could be very helpful.[14]

experimentation
A market research technique in which the reactions of similar people are compared under different circumstances.

Data Warehousing and Data Mining

Almost everything you do leaves a trail of information about you. Your preferences in movie rentals, television viewing, internet sites, and groceries; the destinations of your phone calls, your credit-card charges, your financial status; personal information about age, gender, marital status, and even health—these are just some of the items in a huge cache of data that are stored about each of us. The collection, storage, and retrieval of such data in electronic files is called **data warehousing**. For marketing researchers, the data warehouse is a gold mine of clues about consumer behaviour.[15]

data warehousing
Process of collecting, storing, and retrieving data in electronic form.

The Uses of Data Mining. After collecting information, marketers use **data mining**—the application of electronic technologies for searching, sifting, and reorganizing pools of data—to uncover useful marketing information and to plan for new products that will appeal to target segments in the marketplace.[16] Using data mining, for example, the insurance company

data mining
Application of electronic technologies for searching, sifting, and reorganizing data to collect marketing information and target products in the marketplace.

When consumers are brought together in a focus group, the sponsoring company hopes to get valuable insights into consumer attitudes and values that will impact the sales of the company's products. This market research technique allows selected issues to be discussed in depth.

Farmers Group
www.farmersinsurance.com

Farmers Group discovered that a sports car is not an exceptionally high insurance risk if it's not the only family car. The company thus issued more liberal policies on Corvettes and Porsches and so generated more revenue without significantly increasing payout claims. Among retailers, Wal-Mart has long been a data-mining pioneer, maintaining perhaps the world's largest privately held data warehouse. Data include demographics, markdowns, returns, inventory, and other data for forecasting sales and the effects of marketing promotions.[17]

UNDERSTANDING CONSUMER BEHAVIOUR

Market research in its many forms can be of great help to marketing managers in understanding how the common traits of a market segment affect consumers' purchasing decisions. Why do people buy DVDs? What desire are they fulfilling? Is there a psychological or sociological explanation for why consumers purchase one product and not another? These questions and many others are addressed in the area of marketing known as consumer behaviour. **Consumer behaviour** focuses on the decision process by which customers come to purchase and consume a product or service.

consumer behaviour
The study of the process by which customers come to purchase and consume a product or service.

Influences on Consumer Behaviour

To understand consumer behaviour, marketers draw heavily on the fields of psychology and sociology. The result is a focus on four major influences on consumer behaviour: psychological, personal, social, and cultural. By identifying the four influences that are most active, marketers try to explain consumer choices and predict future purchasing behaviour:

- *psychological influences* include an individual's motivations, perceptions, ability to learn, and attitudes
- *personal influences* include lifestyle, personality, economic status, and life-cycle stage
- *social influences* include family, opinion leaders (people whose opinions are sought by others), and reference groups such as friends, co-workers, and professional associates
- *cultural influences* include culture (the "way of living" that distinguishes one large group from another), subculture (smaller groups, such as ethnic groups, with shared values), and social class (the cultural ranking of groups according to criteria such as background, occupation, and income)

Although these factors can have a strong impact on a consumer's choices, their effect on actual purchases is sometimes weak or negligible. Some consumers, for example, exhibit high **brand loyalty**—they regularly purchase products because they are satisfied with their performance. Such people (for example, users of Craftsman tools) are less subject to influence and stick with preferred brands. On the other hand, the clothes you wear and the food you eat often reflect social and psychological influences on your consuming behaviour.

brand loyalty
Pattern of regular consumer purchasing based on satisfaction with a product.

5. Describe the key factors that influence the *consumer buying process.*

The Consumer Buying Process

Researchers who have studied consumer behaviour have constructed models that help marketing managers understand how consumers come to purchase products. Figure 15.3 presents one such model. At the heart of this

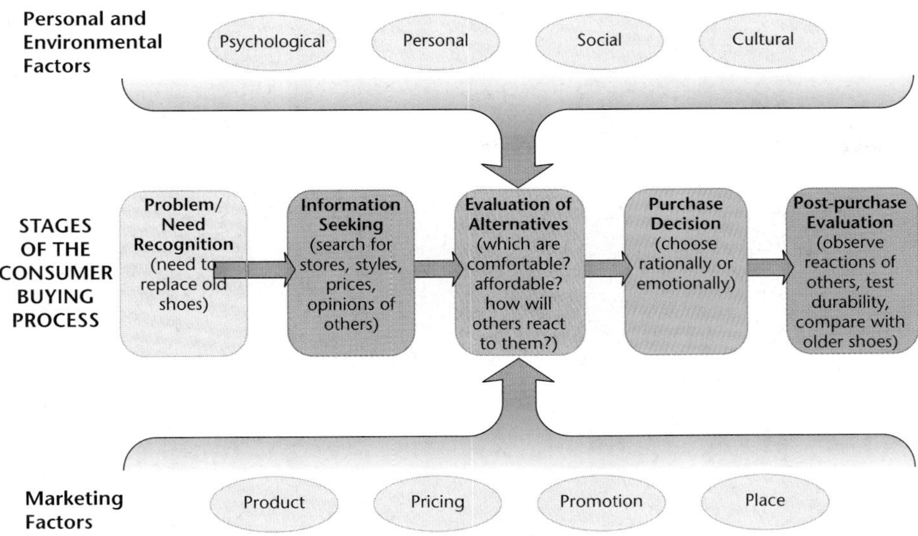

Figure 15.3
Consumer buying process.

and similar models is an awareness of the psychosocial influences that lead to consumption. Ultimately, marketing managers use this information to develop marketing plans.

Problem/Need Recognition. The buying process begins when a consumer becomes aware of a problem or need. After strenuous exercise, you may recognize that you are thirsty and need refreshment. After the birth of twins, you may find your one-bedroom apartment too small for comfort. After standing in the rain to buy movie tickets, you may decide to buy an umbrella. Need recognition also occurs when you have a chance to change your purchasing habits. For example, the income from your first job after graduation will allow you to purchase items that were too expensive when you were a student. You may also discover a need for professional clothing, apartment furnishings, and cars. Visa and The Bay recognize this shift and market their credit cards to graduates.

Information Seeking. Having recognized a need, consumers seek information. This search is not always extensive. If you are thirsty, you may ask where the pop machine is, but that may be the extent of your information search. Other times you simply rely on your memory for information. Before making major purchases, most people seek information from personal sources, marketing sources, public sources, and experience. For example, if you move to a new town, you will want to find out who is the best local dentist, physician, hair stylist, butcher, or pizza maker. To get this information, you may check with personal sources such as acquaintances, co-workers, and relatives. Before buying an exercise bike, you may go to the library and read the latest *Consumer Reports*—a public source of consumer ratings—on such equipment. You may also ask market sources such as the salesclerk or rely on direct experience. For example, you might test ride the bike to learn more before you buy. The internet has become an important source of information; one-third of consumers rely on the internet to gather information.[18]

Evaluation of Alternatives. If you are in the market for a set of golf clubs, you probably have some idea of who produces clubs and how they differ. You may have accumulated some of this knowledge during the information-seeking stage and combined it with what you knew before. Based on prod-

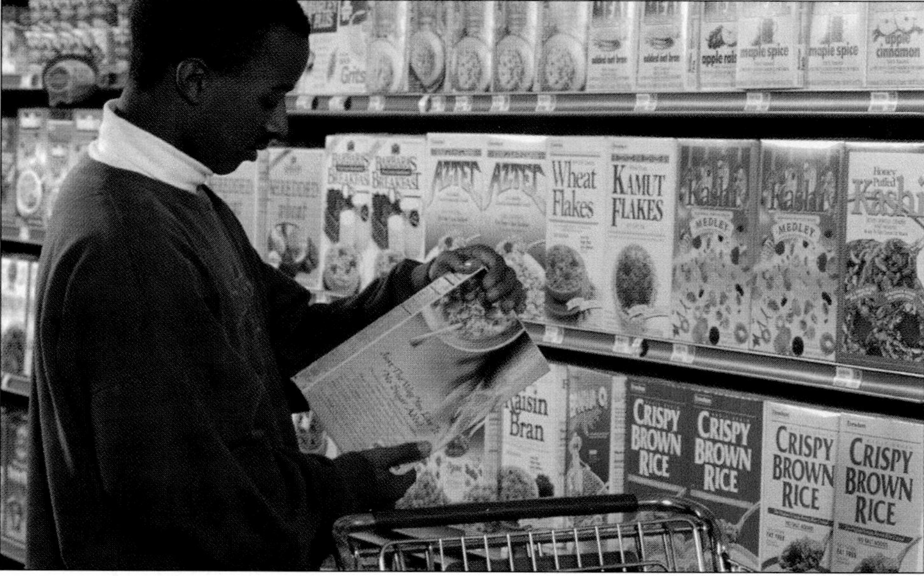

What information is this shopper looking for to decide on his (her) purchase? Marketers would like to know how and why consumers buy the products they buy. A better understanding of the customer buying process allows sellers to tailor their products to meet customer needs.

uct attributes such as colour, taste, price, prestige, quality, and service record, you will decide which product best meets your needs.

rational motives

Those reasons for purchasing a product that involve a logical evaluation of product attributes such as cost, quality, and usefulness.

emotional motives

Those reasons for purchasing a product that involve non-objective factors.

Purchase Decisions. Ultimately, you make a purchase decision. You may decide to defer the purchase until a later time or you may decide to buy now. "Buy" decisions are based on rational and emotional motives. **Rational motives** involve a logical evaluation of product attributes: cost, quality, and usefulness. **Emotional motives** can lead to irrational decisions. Many spur-of-the-moment decisions are emotionally driven, though not all irrational decisions are sudden. Emotional motives include fear, sociability, imitation of others, and aesthetics. You might buy mouthwash to avoid ostracism. You might buy the same brand of jeans as your friends. And you might buy a chocolate milkshake because you like the taste.

Post-Purchase Evaluations. Marketing does not stop with the sale of a product or service, but includes the process of consumption. What happens *after* the sale is very important. A marketer wants consumers to be happy after the consumption of the product so that they will buy the product again. In fact, since consumers do not want to go through a complex decision process for every purchase, they often choose a product they have used and liked. Not all consumers are satisfied with their purchases, of course. Dissatisfied consumers may complain, file a lawsuit, or publicly criticize the product and the company. They are unlikely to purchase the product again. In addition, dissatisfied customers are much more likely to speak about their experience with a product than are satisfied customers. For example, people can complain about products or services at **www.complaints.com**. Dissatisfied customers can have a very negative impact on a company's marketing effort. *Word of mouth* marketing (also known as "buzz marketing") is therefore a very influential marketing tool. Krispy Kreme, for example, has benefited from buzz marketing. It can, however, also be the most devastating, since businesses cannot control it.[19]

The Exercising Your Ethics box describes a situation where the customer's buying process did not fit with the marketing methods being used by the company. The result was an unhappy customer.

EXERCISING YOUR ETHICS

Driving a Legitimate Bargain

The Situation

This exercise illustrates how ethical issues can become entwined with personal selling activities, product pricing, and customer relations.

The Dilemma

In buying his first-ever new car, Matt visited showrooms and websites for every make of SUV. After weeks of reading and test-driving, he settled on a well-known Japanese-made vehicle with a manufacturer's suggested retail price of $34 500 for the 2003 model. The price included accessories and options that Matt considered essential. Because he planned to own the car for at least five years, he was willing to wait for just the right package rather than accept a lesser-equipped car already on the lot. Negotiations with Gary, the sales representative, continued for two weeks. Finally, a sales contract was signed for $32 600, with delivery due no more than two or three months later if the vehicle had to be special-ordered from the factory, earlier if Gary found the exact car when he searched other dealers around the country. On April 30, to close the deal, Matt had to write a cheque for $1000.

Matt received a call on June 14 from Angela, Gary's sales manager: "We cannot get your car before October," she reported, "so it will have to be a 2004 model. You will have to pay the 2004 price." Matt replied that the agreement called for a stated price and delivery deadline for 2003, pointing out that money had exchanged hands for the contract. When asked what the 2004 price would be, Angela responded that it had not yet been announced. Angrily, Matt replied that he would be foolish to agree now on some unknown future price. Moreover, he didn't like the way the dealership was treating him. He told Angela to send back to him everything he had signed; the deal was off.

Questions for Discussion

1. Given the factors involved in the consumer buying process, how would you characterize the particular ethical issues in this situation?
2. From an ethical standpoint, what are the obligations of the sales rep and the sales manager regarding the pricing of the product in this situation?
3. If you were responsible for maintaining good customer relations at the dealership, how would you handle this matter?

ORGANIZATIONAL MARKETING AND BUYING BEHAVIOUR

6. Discuss the three categories of *organizational markets* and explain how *organizational buying behaviour* differs from consumer buying behaviour.

Buying behaviour is observable daily in the consumer market, where marketing activities, including buying–selling transactions, are visible to the public. Equally important, however, but far less visible, are *organizational* (or *commercial*) *markets*—organizations that buy goods and services to be used in creating and delivering consumer products. Marketing to these buyers involves different kinds of organizational markets and buying behaviours that are quite different from those found in consumer markets.

Organizational Markets

Organizational or commercial markets fall into three categories: *industrial, reseller,* and *government/institutional markets*.

Industrial Market

industrial market
Businesses that buy goods to be converted into other products that will be sold to ultimate consumers.

The **industrial market** includes businesses that buy goods falling into one of two categories: goods to be converted into other products and goods that are used up during production. This market includes farmers, manufacturers, and some retailers. For example, Seth Thomas purchases electronics, metal components, and glass to make clocks for the consumer market. The company also buys office supplies, tools, and factory equipment—items never seen by clock buyers—to be used during production.

Reseller Market

reseller market
Intermediaries like wholesalers and retailers who buy finished products and resell them.

Before products reach consumers, they pass through a **reseller market** consisting of intermediaries, including wholesalers and retailers, who buy the finished goods and resell them (wholesalers and retailers are discussed in Chapter 17). Retailers like department stores, drugstores, and supermarkets buy clothing, appliances, foods, medicines, and other merchandise for resale to the consumer market. Retailers also buy such services as maintenance, housekeeping, and communications.

Government and Institutional Market

institutional market
Nongovernment organizations such as hospitals, churches, and schools.

Federal, provincial, and municipal governments purchase millions of dollars worth of computer equipment, buildings, paper clips, and other items. The **institutional market** consists of nongovernmental organizations, such as hospitals, churches, museums, and charitable organizations, which also comprise a substantial market for goods and services. Like organizations in other commercial markets, these institutions use supplies and equipment, as well as legal, accounting, and transportation services.

Organizational Buying Behaviour

In some respects, industrial buying behaviour bears little resemblance to consumer buying practices. Differences include the buyers' purchasing skills and an emphasis on buyer–seller relationships.

Differences in Buyers

Unlike most consumers, organizational buyers are professional, specialized, and expert (or at least well informed).

- As *professionals*, organizational buyers are trained in methods for negotiating purchase terms. Once buyer–seller agreements have been reached, they also arrange for formal contracts.
- As a rule, industrial buyers are company *specialists* in a line of items. As one of several buyers for a large bakery, for example, you may specialize in food ingredients. Another buyer may specialize in baking equipment (industrial ovens and mixers), while a third may buy office equipment and supplies.
- Industrial buyers are often *experts* about the products they buy. On a regular basis, organizational buyers study competing products and alternative suppliers by attending trade shows, by reading trade magazines, and by conducting technical discussions with sellers' representatives.

Differences in the Buyer–Seller Relationship

Consumer–seller relationships are often impersonal, short-lived, one-time interactions. In contrast, industrial situations often involve frequent and enduring buyer–seller relationships. The development of a long-term relationship provides each party with access to the technical strengths of the other as well as the security of knowing what future business to expect. Thus, a buyer and a supplier may form a design team to create products of benefit to both. Accordingly, industrial sellers emphasize personal selling by trained representatives who understand the needs of each customer.

THE INTERNATIONAL MARKETING MIX

7. Describe the *international* and *small business marketing mixes*.

Marketing products internationally means mounting a strategy to support global business operations. Obviously, this is no easy task. Foreign customers, for example, differ from domestic buyers in language, customs, business practices, and consumer behaviour. When they decide to go global, marketers must reconsider each element of the marketing mix: product, pricing, promotion, and place.

International Products

Some products, of course, can be sold abroad with virtually no changes. Budweiser, Coca-Cola, and Marlboros are exactly the same in Toronto, Tokyo, and Timbuktu. In other cases, firms have been obliged to create products with built-in flexibility—for example, electric shavers that adapt to either 115- or 230-volt outlets.

Sometimes only a redesigned—or completely different—product will meet the needs of foreign buyers, however. To sell the Macintosh in Japan, for example, Apple had to develop a Japanese-language operating system. Whether they are standard domestic products or custom-made products for foreign markets, however, the most globally competitive products are usually reliable, low-priced products with advanced features.

Apple
www.apple.ca

International Pricing

When pricing for international markets, marketers must handle all the considerations of domestic pricing while also considering the higher costs of transporting and selling products abroad. Some products cost more overseas than in Canada because of the added costs of delivery. Due to the higher costs of buildings, rent, equipment, and imported meat, a McDonald's Big Mac that sells for $2.99 in Canada has a price tag of over $10 in Japan. In contrast, products like jet airplanes are priced the same worldwide because delivery costs are incidental; the huge development and production costs are the major considerations regardless of customer location.

Feathercraft is a small British Columbia manufacturer that has been successful selling kayaks in the Japanese market.

International Promotion

Some standard Canadian promotional techniques do not always succeed in other countries. In fact, many Europeans believe that a product must be inherently shoddy if a company does any hard-sell advertising. International marketers must also be aware that cultural differences can cause negative reactions to products that are advertised improperly. Some Europeans, for example, are offended by television commercials that show weapons or violence. Advertising practices are regulated accordingly. Consequently, Dutch commercials for toys do not feature the guns and combat scenes that are commonplace on Saturday morning television in North America. Meanwhile, liquor and cigarette commercials that are banned from Canadian and U.S. television are thriving in many Asian and European markets.

Symbolism, too, is a sometimes-surprising consideration. In France, for instance, yellow flowers suggest infidelity. In Mexico, they are signs of death—an association made in Brazil by the colour purple. Clearly, product promotions must be carefully matched to the customs and cultural values of each country.

International Distribution

In some industries, delays in starting new distribution networks can be costly. Therefore, companies with existing distribution systems often enjoy an advantage over new businesses. Several companies have gained advantages in time-based competition by buying existing businesses. Procter & Gamble, for example, saved three years of start-up time by buying Revlon's Max Factor and Betrix cosmetics, both of which are well established in foreign markets. P&G can thus immediately use these companies' distribution and marketing networks for selling its own brands in the United Kingdom, Germany, and Japan.

Other companies contract with foreign firms or individuals to distribute and sell their products abroad. Foreign agents may perform personal selling and advertising, provide information about local markets, or serve as exporters' representatives. But having to manage interactions with foreign personnel complicates a marketing manager's responsibilities. In addition, packaging practices in Canada must sometimes be adapted to withstand the rigours of transport to foreign ports and storage under conditions that differ radically from domestic conditions.

SMALL BUSINESS AND THE MARKETING MIX

As we noted in Chapter 3, far more small businesses fail than succeed. Yet many of today's largest firms were yesterday's small businesses. McDonald's began with one restaurant, a concept, and one individual (Ray Kroc) who had tremendous foresight. Behind the success of many small firms lies a skilful application of the marketing concept and careful consideration of each element in the marketing mix.

Small Business Products

Some new products—and firms—are doomed at the start simply because few consumers want or need what they have to offer. Too often, enthusiastic entrepreneurs introduce products that they and their friends like, but they fail to estimate realistic market potential. Other small businesses offer new products before they have clear pictures of their target segments and how to reach them. They try to be everything to everyone, and they end up serving no one well. In contrast, sound product planning has paid off for many small firms. "Keep it simple" is a familiar key to success—that is, fulfil a specific need and do it efficiently.

Small Business Pricing

Haphazard pricing that is often little more than guesswork can sink even a firm with a good product. Most often, small business pricing errors result from a failure to project operating expenses accurately. Owners of failing businesses have often been heard to utter statements like "I didn't realize how much it costs to run the business!" and "If I price the product high enough to cover my expenses, no one will buy it!" But when small businesses set prices by carefully assessing costs, many earn very satisfactory profits—sometimes enough to expand or diversify.

Small Business Promotion

Successful small businesses plan for promotional expenses as part of start-up costs. Some hold down costs by taking advantage of less expensive promotional methods. Local newspapers, for example, are sources of publicity when they publish articles about new or unique businesses. Other small businesses have succeeded by identifying themselves and their products with associated groups, organizations, and events. Thus a custom-crafts gallery might join with a local art league and local artists to organize public showings of their combined products.

Small Business Distribution

Problems in arranging distribution can make or break small businesses. Perhaps the most critical aspect of distribution is facility location, especially for new service businesses. The ability of many small businesses—retailers, veterinary clinics, and gourmet coffee shops—to attract and retain customers depends partly on the choice of location.

In distribution, as in other aspects of the marketing mix, however, smaller companies may have advantages over larger competitors, even in highly complex industries. They may be quicker, for example, in applying service technologies. Everex Systems Inc. sells personal computers to wholesalers and dealers through a system the company calls "Zero Response Time." Phone orders are reviewed every two hours so that the factory can adjust assembly to match demand.

SUMMARY OF LEARNING OBJECTIVES

1. **Explain the concept of *marketing* and describe the five forces that constitute the *external marketing environment*.** Marketing is "the process of planning and executing the conception, pricing, promotion, and distribution of ideas, goods, and services to create exchanges that satisfy individual and organizational goals." Products provide consumers with *utility*—the ability of a product to satisfy a human want or need. Marketing can be used to promote consumer and industrial goods and services, as well as ideas. The *external environment* consists of the

outside forces that influence marketing strategy and decision making. The *political/legal environment* includes laws and regulations, both domestic and foreign, that may define or constrain business activities. The *social and cultural environment* is the context within which people's values, beliefs, and ideas affect marketing decisions. The *technological environment* includes the technological developments that affect existing and new products. The *economic environment* consists of the conditions, such as inflation, recession, and interest rates, that influence both consumer and organizational spending patterns. Finally, the *competitive environment* is the environment in which marketers must persuade buyers to purchase their products rather than their competitors'.

2. **Explain the purpose of a *marketing plan* and identify the four components of the *marketing mix*.** *Marketing managers* plan and implement all the marketing activities that result in the transfer of products to customers. These activities culminate in the *marketing plan*—a detailed strategy for focusing the effort to meet consumer needs and wants. Marketing managers rely on the "Four Ps" of marketing, or the *marketing mix*. (1) *Product*: Marketing begins with a product, a good, a service, or an idea designed to fill a consumer need or want. *Product differentiation* is the creation of a feature or image that makes a product differ from competitors. (2) *Pricing*: Pricing is the strategy of selecting the most appropriate price at which to sell a product. (3) *Place* (Distribution): All distribution activities are concerned with getting a product from the producer to the consumer. (4) *Promotion*: Promotion refers to techniques for communicating information about products and includes advertising.

3. **Explain *market segmentation* and show how it is used in *target marketing*.** Marketers think in terms of *target markets*—groups of people who have similar wants and needs and who can be expected to show interest in the same products. Target marketing requires *market segmentation*—dividing a market into customer types or "segments." Four of the most important influences are: (1) *geographic variables* (the geographical units that may be considered in developing a segmentation strategy); (2) *demographic variables* (describe populations by identifying such traits as age, income, gender, ethnic background, marital status, race, religion, and social class); (3) *psychographic variables* (such as lifestyles, interests, and attitudes); and (4) *behavioural variables* (the ways in which consumers use a product, the benefits they expect from it, their reasons for purchasing it, and their loyalty to it).

4. **Explain the purpose and value of *marketing research*.** *Market research* is the study of what buyers need and of the best ways to meet those needs. This process involves a study of the current situation, the selection of a research method, the collection of data, the analysis of data, and the preparation of a report that may include recommendations for action. The four most common research methods are *observation, surveys, focus groups,* and *experimentation*.

5. **Describe the key factors that influence the *consumer buying process*.** *Consumer behaviour* is the study of the process by which customers decide to purchase products. The result is a focus on four major influences on consumer behaviour: (1) *Psychological influences* include motivations, perceptions, ability to learn, and attitudes. (2) *Personal influences* include lifestyle, personality, and economic status. (3) *Social influences* include family, opinion leaders, and such reference groups as friends, co-workers, and professional associates. (4) *Cultural influences*

include culture, subculture, and social class. By identifying which influences are most active in certain circumstances, marketers try to explain consumer choices and predict future purchasing behaviour.

6. **Discuss the three categories of *organizational markets* and explain how *organizational buying behaviour* differs from consumer buying behaviour.** *Organizational* (or *commercial*) *markets*, in which organizations buy goods and services to be used in creating and delivering consumer products, fall into three categories. (1) The *industrial market* consists of businesses that buy goods to be converted into other products or goods that are used during production. (2) Before products reach consumers, they pass through a *reseller market* consisting of intermediaries that buy finished goods and resell them. (3) *Government and institutional market*: Federal, provincial, and local governments buy durable and nondurable products. The institutional market consists of non-governmental buyers such as hospitals, churches, museums, and charities. Organizational buying behaviour differs from consumer buyer behaviour in two major ways: (1) *Differences in buyers*: Organizational buyers are professionals trained in arranging buyer–seller relationships and negotiating purchase terms. They are usually specialists in a line of items and are often experts about the products they are buying. (2) *Differences in the buyer–seller relationship*: Whereas consumer–seller relationships are often fleeting, one-time interactions, industrial situations often involve frequent, enduring buyer–seller relationships.

7. **Describe the *international* and *small business marketing mixes*.** When they decide to go global, marketers must reconsider each element of the marketing mix. (1) *International products*: Whereas some products can be sold abroad with virtually no changes, sometimes only a redesigned product will meet the needs of foreign buyers. (2) *International pricing*: When pricing for international markets, marketers must consider the higher costs of transporting and selling products abroad. (3) *International distribution*: In some industries, companies have gained advantages by buying businesses already established in foreign markets. (4) *International promotion*: Occasionally, a good ad campaign can be transported to another country virtually intact. Quite often, however, standard Canadian promotional tactics do not succeed in other countries.

   Behind the success of many small firms lies an understanding of each element in the marketing mix. (1) *Small-business products*: Understanding of what customers need and want has paid off for many small firms. (2) *Small-business pricing*: Haphazard pricing can sink even a firm with a good product. Small-business pricing errors usually result from failure to project operating expenses accurately. But when small businesses set prices by carefully assessing costs, many earn satisfactory profits. (3) *Small-business distribution*: Perhaps the most critical aspect of distribution is facility location: The ability of many small businesses to attract and retain customers depends partly on the choice of location. (4) *Small-business promotion*: Successful small businesses plan for promotional expenses as part of start-up costs. Some take advantage of less expensive promotional methods.

KEY TERMS

behavioural variables, 522
brand competition, 518
brand loyalty, 530
consumer behaviour, 530
consumer goods, 513
data mining, 529
data warehousing, 529
demographic variables, 521
distribution, 519
emotional motives, 532
experimentation, 529
external environment, 514
focus group, 528
geographic variables, 521
industrial goods, 513
industrial market, 533
institutional market, 534
international competition, 518
market segmentation, 520
marketing, 512
marketing concept, 517
marketing manager, 518
marketing mix, 518
marketing plan, 518
marketing research, 525
observation, 528
price, 518
primary data, 527
product differentiation, 518
product, 518
psychographic variables, 522
rational motives, 532
relationship marketing, 514
reseller market, 534
secondary data, 527
services, 513
substitute product, 518
survey, 528
target market, 520
utility, 513
value, 512

QUESTIONS AND EXERCISES

Questions for Review

1. What are the key similarities and differences between consumer buying behaviour and organizational buying behaviour?
2. Why and how is market segmentation used in target marketing?
3. How do the needs of organizations differ as a result of the various organizational markets of which they are members?
4. How are data mining and data warehousing useful in finding new information for marketing research?

Questions for Analysis

5. Select an everyday product (books, CDs, skateboards, dog food, or shoes, for example). Show how different versions of your product are aimed toward different market segments. Explain how the marketing mix differs for each segment.
6. Select a second everyday product and describe the consumer buying process that typically goes into its purchase.
7. Consider a service product, such as transportation, entertainment, or health care. What are some ways that more customer value might be added to this product? Why would your improvements add value for the buyer?
8. If you were starting your own small business (say, marketing a consumer good that you already know something about), which of the forces in the external marketing environment do you think would have the greatest impact on your success?

Application Exercises

9. Interview the marketing manager of a local business. Identify the degree to which this person's job is focused on each element in the marketing mix.
10. Select a product made by a foreign company and sold in Canada. What is the product's target market? What is the basis on which the target market is segmented? Do you think that this basis is appropriate? How might another approach, if any, be beneficial? Why?

BUILDING YOUR BUSINESS SKILLS

Dealing in Segments and Variables

Goal

To encourage students to analyze the ways in which various market segmentation variables affect business success.

Situation

You and four partners are thinking of purchasing a heating and air conditioning (H/AC) dealership that specializes in residential applications priced between $2000 and $40 000. You are now in the process of deciding where that dealership should be. You are considering four locations: Miami, Florida; Toronto, Ontario; Vancouver, B.C.; and Dallas, Texas.

Method

Step 1

Working with four classmates (your partnership group), do library research to learn how H/AC makers market their residential products. Check for articles in *The Globe and Mail, Canadian Business, The Wall Street Journal*, and other business publications.

Step 2

Continue your research. This time, focus on the specific marketing variables that define each prospective location. Check Statistics Canada data at your library and on the internet and contact local chambers of commerce (by phone and via the internet) to learn about the following factors for each location:

- geography
- demography (especially age, income, gender, family status, and social class)
- psychographic variables (lifestyles, interests, and attitudes)

Step 3

Meet with group members to analyze which location holds the greatest promise as a dealership site. Base your decision on your analysis of market segment variables and their effects on H/AC sales.

Follow-Up Questions

1. Which location did you choose? Describe the market segmentation factors that influenced your decision.
2. Identify the two most important variables you believe will have the greatest impact on the dealership's success. Why are these factors so important?
3. Which factors were least important in your decision? Why?
4. When equipment manufacturers advertise residential H/AC products, they often show them in different climate situations (in winter, summer, or high-humidity conditions). Which market segments are these ads targeting? Describe these segments in terms of demographic and psychographic characteristics.

MASTERING BUSINESS ESSENTIALS

Episode 9 stresses the importance of developing a marketing strategy that identifies and makes the best use of a company's competitive advantage: A firm must not only develop one or more capabilities that are superior to those of competitors, but must also turn its advantage into an effective marketing strategy and growth plan. *This episode illustrates and enhances the chapter discussion of marketing strategy.*

Episode 10 reminds us that the consumer buying process is complex and unpredictable. *This episode builds on the chapter discussion of personal, psychological, social, and cultural influences on consumer behaviour.*

CRAFTING YOUR BUSINESS PLAN

Picking and Packaging the Right Products

The Purpose of the Assignment

1. To familiarize students with the various marketing issues that a sample firm faces in developing its business plan, in the framework of Business PlanPro (BPP) 2002 software package.
2. To demonstrate how four chapter topics—consumer versus organizational marketing, relationship marketing, market segmentation, and product differentiation—can be integrated as components of the BPP planning environment.

Assignment

After reading Chapter 10 in the textbook, open the BPP software and look for information about the marketing plan for a sample firm, a promotional products manufacturer called Elsewares Promotional Products & Packaging. To find Elsewares, do the following:

Open Business PlanPro 2002. If you are asked if you want to "create a new business plan" or to "open an existing plan," select "create a new business plan" (even though you are not going to create a plan at this time). You will then be taken to the Business PlanPro EasyPlan Wizard. On the screen, click on the option entitled **Research It**. You will then be presented with a new list of options, including Sample Plan Browser. After clicking on **Sample Plan Browser**, scan its alphabetical list of sample plans and double-click on **Promotional Products Manufacturer**, which is the location for Elsewares Promotional Products & Packaging. The screen you are looking at is the introduction page for the Elsewares business plan. Next, scroll down this page until you reach the Table of Contents for the Elsewares business plan.

Now respond to the following items:

1. Is Elsewares involved in consumer marketing or organizational marketing? [Sites to see in BPP (for this item): On the **Table of Contents** page, click on and read **1.0 Executive Summary**. After returning to the **Table of Contents** page, click on and read each of the following: **1.1 Objectives, 1.2 Mission,** and **1.3 Keys to Success**.]
2. Identify Elsewares' strategy and methods for building relationships with its customers. [Sites to see in BPP: On the **Table of Contents** page, click on and read **5.0 Strategy and Implementation Summary**. Also visit **5.1.4 Service and Support**. Then read **1.0 Executive Summary** and **1.3 Keys to Success**.]
3. What basis—geographic, demographic, psychographic, or behavioural—does Elsewares plan to use for its market segmentation strategy? [Sites to see in BPP: On the **Table of Contents** page, click on and read each of the following in turn: **4.0 Market Analysis Summary** and **4.1 Market Segmentation**.]
4. Describe Elsewares' plans for differentiating its product. Is the plan clear enough on this matter? Why or why not? [Sites to see in BPP: On the **Table of Contents** page, click on and read **4.0 Market Analysis Summary**. Then go to **4.2 Industry Analysis**, and explore the information in that section.]

VIDEO EXERCISE

In Consumers' Shoes

Learning Objectives

The purpose of this video is to help you:

1. Describe the role of the "Four Ps" in a company's marketing mix.
2. Explain how a company shapes its market research to fit its marketing goals.
3. Discuss the effectiveness of target marketing and segmentation in analyzing consumers.

Background Information

Skechers USA (**www.skechers.com**) enjoys a reputation for producing footwear that combines comfort with innovative design. It has built its product line into a globally recognized brand distributed in more than 110 countries. From its corporate headquarters in Manhattan Beach, California, Skechers has engineered steady growth in market share while competing against some powerful players in the high-ticket, branded athletic shoe industry.

Since its start in 1992, Skechers has enhanced its image as a maker of hip footwear through a savvy marketing strategy that calls for catering to a closely targeted consumer base. Maintaining brand integrity and its reputation for innovation is a crucial goal in all of Skechers' product development and marketing activities.

The Video

Director of public relations Kelly O'Connor discusses her work and the marketing activities that are critical to maintaining Skechers' edge in the highly competitive footwear marketplace. She describes the company's goal of creating a megabrand with an image, personality, and "feel" that can be translated and marketed globally. Skechers has been successful in brand building by means of an "Ask, Don't Tell" approach to product development and marketing: It aims to find out what the market wants and then appeal to customers' wants rather than trying to influence the market with the products that it makes available.

Discussion Questions

1. Which of the "Four Ps" of the marketing mix seems to govern Skechers' marketing strategy? Why? How do you suppose Skechers alters elements of its American marketing mix to attract consumers in international markets?
2. Skechers collects a lot of primary data in its market research. What kinds of primary data does the company prefer to gather? Why does this kind of data suit its marketing goals? How does it suit the firm's consumer base? Given Skechers' fairly limited consumer base, are there other types of research data that you would recommend?
3. Describe Skechers' target market and explain how company marketers segment it. How effective is this strategy in analyzing customers? How successful are Skechers' marketing efforts among 12- to 24-year-olds (and consumers wishing they were in that demographic segment)?
4. Discuss the impact of brand loyalty on the sale of Skechers products. Building brand loyalty is a major effort that presents both opportunities and challenges to marketers and product developers. What are some of the opportunities and challenges encountered by Skechers marketing managers?

Online Exploration

Go online to find out about the product lines and target markets of such companies as Nike (**www.nike.com**), Reebok (**www.reebok.com**), Lady Foot Locker (**www.ladyfootlocker.com**), and FUBU (**www1.fubu.com**). How does the approach to segmentation at these companies compare with that of Skechers? How do you think Skechers might expand its current product lines? What other new products might Skechers research, such as clothing or accessories? How could the company go about investigating the market potential for such products?

EXPLORING THE NET

Welcome to Marriott

In the first part of this chapter, we discussed the concept of marketing products to meet the needs and wants of customers in both consumer and industrial markets. We also saw how relationship marketing promotes customer loyalty and found that a sound marketing strategy involves the entire marketing mix—product, pricing, place (distribution), and promotion. Let's look further into these marketing practices by exploring the website of a successful international company—Marriott International Inc., at **www.marriott.com**. The home page has five sections that we will use for exploring the marketing function at Marriott:

Our Family of Brands
Explore & Plan
Marriott Rewards
Events & Meetings
Vacation Ownership

Begin by clicking on each of the following—Our Family of Brands, Events & Meetings, and Explore & Plan—and examine their contents.

1. What types of products does Marriott offer in its marketing mix?

On the home page, go to Our Family of Brands and select Marriott Hotels & Resorts. Then drop down to the bottom of the page and click on Specials & Packages and examine the information on that page:

2. Which type of customer—consumer or industrial—is the target for information on this page?

At the home page, go to Our Family of Brands and select ExecuStay. On the Marriott ExecuStay screen, go to the left side and click on About ExecuStay. Examine the information on that page.

3. What product features on this page indicate the type of customer—consumer or industrial—that Marriott is targeting for this product?

On the home page, click on Marriott Rewards. After examining the contents of this page, go to the left side of the screen, click on Elite Membership, and read its contents.

4. Is the Marriott Rewards program an example of relationship marketing? Give examples of incentives that Marriott uses to build relationships with its clients.

Briefly review the material at the webpages entitled Marriott Resorts and ExecuStay.

5. Which segmentation variables—demographic, geographic, psychographic, or behavioural—has Marriott used for differentiating its Marriott Resorts and ExecuStay products?

Concluding Case 15-1

Xbox Marks the Spot

Once the domain of teenage boys, interactive games now lure a much broader audience, including younger kids and adults. It's easy to become addicted: With cinematically realistic graphics and challenging action sequences, games require split-second timing and rapid-fire reactions. Today's communications technology allows real-time interaction among gaming enthusiasts, either in side-by-side competition or among opponents anywhere in the world.

Consider one such enthusiast, Josh Bell, a Grammy Award–winning violinist and one of *People* magazine's "50 Most Beautiful People" for 2001. Bell spends 20 hours a week gaming, sometimes at the expense of violin practice. He uses a wireless keyboard hooked into a 50-inch plasma wall TV. Six speakers provide surround sound for total immersion in such virtual games as Quake III and Defense, an internet game. To justify time away from the violin, admits Bell, "I used to tell my mother it would improve my hand–eye coordination." At 32, Bell is at the older end of the gaming-enthusiast spectrum. The mainstream is in its mid-20s, late and early teens, and, at the youngest end of the demographic spectrum, 10 years old.

Computer- and video-game sales have grown 15 percent a year for four years. By 2001, they had caught up with sales of DVDs and videotapes. Sales of game hardware and software in the three biggest markets—the United States, Europe, and Japan—reached $16.5 billion in 2001 and will top $20 billion by 2003. It's no surprise that the prospect of such a vast market has attracted the attention of Microsoft.

Before its launch in November 2001, Xbox—Microsoft's entry into console gaming—was one of the industry's most anticipated products. Its $500 million marketing budget included a pre-launch website (**www.xbox.com**) to tantalize players with the most advanced hardware and hottest graphics in the industry. Microsoft intends for the site to become the gathering place for players and to promote enthusiasm among gamers everywhere. Thus far, Xbox.com has succeeded both in establishing relationships among gamers and in forming new bonds between gamers and the Xbox brand. Microsoft wants gamers to become loyal members of an Xbox community.

But industry experts know that it takes more than relationship building and nifty hardware to succeed in this market. Success depends on a steady flow of exciting software—games that capture players' imaginations. Xbox hardware, reports Phaedra Boinodiris, head of Womengamers.com, "far outweighs the competition for speed and memory," but she adds that "there's a serious problem with the lineup [of games] so far." The initial launch featured 12 to 20 games, most of them action and sports oriented. By early 2002, the list had grown to 56 but included only two—Shrek and Rise of Parethi—that cater to the market for adventure and strategy games.

Nevertheless, Microsoft's start-up marketing has already had an impact: By December 2001, more than 1.4 million Xbox units had been sold, many of them even before reaching store shelves. Microsoft's marketing strategy differs from that of competitors, especially Nintendo, which targets the younger end of the market. Xbox, says product-team leader Robbie Rash, targets a different audience. "Let's face it," he says, "Nintendo's system is for kids. We're for sophisticated gamers. I don't know any 30-year-olds who want a GameCube [by Nintendo]." Both Xbox and PlayStation 2 (by Sony) are aimed at the 16- to 26-year-old audience. Nintendo, however, wants to shed its "kids only" image and attract more players in the 20s age group, too. Both Xbox and GameCube would like to bump Sony's PlayStation 2 (PS2) from the top spot in the console market.

With its current selling price of $199, the revenue from each Xbox doesn't begin to cover the cost of making it. In fact, Microsoft will lose about $125 on every box it sells. Because the consoles cost so much to make, the profits for console makers—Sony and Nintendo as well as Microsoft—depend on software sales. Thus, the console maker that fails to supply a constant stream of new titles is doomed. For international appeal, Sega's participation also gives Xbox an important boost: Many Japanese gamers doubted Xbox's credibility until they learned of Microsoft's alliance with Sega's respected game publishers.

The Xbox product itself is also different from competing products. Sony's PS2 plays music CDs and DVD movies right out of the box. Xbox can also play music and movies—in fact, it delivers theatre-quality 3D sound—but if you want DVD, you need a separate remote controller. Nintendo plays games only—no movies or CDs. Xbox also offers broadband multiplayer gaming and lets players take advantage of high-speed networks by playing online. By uniting gamers on the Internet via the Xbox, Microsoft is laying the groundwork for a future home-networking strategy that will use the Xbox console as a hub.

Questions for Discussion

1. What social and technological factors have influenced the growth of the interactive entertainment market?
2. What demographics would you use to define the Xbox target market? How about the target market for Nintendo's GameCube?
3. Do you agree or disagree with Microsoft's strategy of featuring hardware, sound, and graphics rather than immediately offering lots of game titles?
4. Which is more important to Xbox's success—the product itself or Microsoft's marketing program for it? Explain your reasoning.
5. Why do you suppose Sega's participation was so meaningful for Japanese customers? ◆

Concluding Case 15-2

JNCO Jeans

Adults don't know how to pronounce "JNCO" jeans, and, more importantly, they have no idea why teenagers like to wear them. With billowing 100-centimetre bottoms and cavernous 45-centimetre-deep pockets, JNCO has made wide legs fashionable, albeit no easier to wear. Ever try climbing stairs with pants that wide? And what about the dirt and chewing gum that collects at the cuff?

Nevertheless, boys aged 12 to 15 recently rated JNCO the sixth-"coolest" brand, right behind Tommy Hilfiger and Adidas. Strength in this market translates into millions of consumer dollars. According to *Tactical Retail Monitor*, the market for wide-leg jeans has recently grown five times as fast as the entire men's jeans category. That's why Revatex, the Los Angeles firm that manufactures JNCO, pays serious attention to marketing research that tells them what teenagers want and how they are likely to spend their consumer dollars.

Conscious of the independent, rebellious spirit of their target audience, Revatex marketers take a stealth approach to cultivating JNCO's cool image. They don't buy billboards or place GAP-style ads in popular magazines. Instead, Revatex supplies free clothes to trendsetting DJs and band members who play at all-night dance parties. It advertises in such magazines as *Electric Ink* and *Thrasher*, which target skateboarders and extreme rollerbladers. Recording artist J-Smooth will be wearing JNCO clothes in targeted ads in *Spin, Vibe, Blaze*, and *Urb*.

With wholesale revenues somewhere between U.S.$100 and $200 million, Revatex is hitting Levi Strauss and other mainstream jeans makers where it hurts—in the wallet. Nicholas Lynch, who owns 11 pairs of JNCOs, says he'll never own a pair of Levi's: "Levi's came out with wide jeans," he admits, "but it just isn't the same because of who wears them." Translation: Baby boomers (also known as losers) wear Levi's, but those on the cutting edge wear JNCOs.

Revatex continues to be proactive in its search for market share. It is expanding its young men's offerings with sportswear, sleepwear, and underwear, which were rolled out in the spring of 2003. They clearly remain one of the bigger names in the jeans market, although they are no longer the current hot ticket.

Finding and defining the cutting edge in teen taste is the work of marketing researchers who specialize in the teen market. Companies pay a high price for this research to attract a share of the roughly U.S.$4 billion that teens spend every year on clothes, cosmetics, CDs, and other personal and fashion items. According to Teen-Age Research Unlimited, one of the most respected marketing research firms in this segment, understanding teen buying behaviour means identifying and targeting teen decision makers known as influencers. A dream-come-true category for marketers, influencers spend money on fashion trends before they are popular and then influence conformers to follow suit. Conformers, explains one researcher, "make up the bulk of the teenage population. They're looking for brands and badges to...get them to the next level."

As a group, teenagers have more money and more control over spending than any teen generation before it. With both parents working and their spending habits learned from self-gratifying baby-boomer parents, today's teens are worth studying. However, teenagers aren't the only youths with discretionary cash. To the delight of marketers, 4- to 12-year-olds now spend millions (of their parents' money) on food and drink, clothes, movies, games, and toys. Both this surge in children's spending power and their maturing tastes are linked to the ways in which dual-career parents raise their kids. "The style of child rearing today," suggests one child psychologist, "is to empower very young children and give them choices about everything. When you give small children power, they act like adolescents."

With newfound maturity and anchored buying decisions, children are now viewed as a prime marketing target. It's no coincidence that retail stores for sophisticated children are opening in malls throughout the country. The Limited Too, Abercrombie & Fitch, Gap Kids, and Gymboree are stocking clothes and gear for 6- to 12-year-olds and doing land-office business.

Even when parents make the final buying decision, marketers now realize the influence exerted by children. That's why Ford's Lincoln Mercury division launched its new Mercury Villager minivan to coincide with the 1998 premiere of the first Rugrats movie. Some marketers are thriving because of the maturity shift, but others are being forced to rethink long-standing strategies. Mattel Inc., manufacturer of the Barbie doll, can no longer count on 7- to 8-year-old buyers. "We're losing them sooner," laments Mattel president Bruce Stein, whose core Barbie market has been trimmed to 2- to 6-year-olds. "They're in sensory overload.... There are too many things competing for their interests."

Other marketers have decided to cater to the special needs of the youngest sophisticates. When the Limited Too opened in 1991, it targeted girls aged 2 to 16. Six years later, it narrowed its focus to 6- to 14-year-olds, because it recognized preteens as a special market segment. The preteen girl, explains the chain's vice-president of marketing, is "moving out of the fantasy play world. She's kind of caught between Barbie and a driver's licence."

Questions for Discussion

1. What social and cultural factors have influenced the growth of the teen and preteen markets?
2. How would you define the teenage target market? Why is it growing in importance?
3. What characteristics would you include in a psychographic profile of teenagers and preteenagers?
4. Do you agree or disagree with Revatex's stealth marketing tactics to reach teenage influencers? How do influencers affect consumer buying behaviour?
5. If you worked in Mattel's marketing department, how would you re-attract 7- to 8-year-old buyers? What spin-off Barbie products might interest this market segment? ◆

CHAPTER 16

Developing and Promoting Goods and Services

After reading this chapter, you should be able to:

1. Identify a *product*, distinguish between *consumer* and *industrial products*, and explain the *product mix*.
2. Describe the *new product development process* and trace the stages of the *product life cycle*.
3. Explain the importance of *branding, packaging,* and *labelling*.
4. Identify the important objectives of *promotion* and discuss the considerations in selecting a *promotional mix*.
5. Discuss the most important *advertising strategies* and describe the key *advertising media*.
6. Outline the tasks involved in *personal selling* and list the steps in the *personal selling process*.
7. Describe the various types of *sales promotions*.

How Sweet It Is!

In the world of candy, four international firms—Nestlé, Hershey, Cadbury's, and M&M/Mars—dominate the world market. But two Canadian companies are carving out a market for their products in this highly competitive business. One is a recent start-up from Winnipeg, and the other is a 130-year-old firm from the Maritimes. Here are their stories.

Krave Candy Co.

Winnipeg entrepreneurs Chris Emery and Larry Finnson started Krave Candy Co. in 1995. Their company's main product—Clodhoppers—is a popcorn-sized cluster of cashew nuts, white chocolate, and graham wafers. In just a few short years, Emery and Finnson have turned Clodhoppers into a hot new product that produced sales revenue in excess of $10 million in 2003.

In the company's first year, Clodhoppers were packaged in plastic peanut butter jars and sold locally in Winnipeg. The market segment that was being targeted was boxed chocolates, but the jar and the packaging didn't stand out next to competitors' products. Since the candy was visible in the jar, retailers often mistakenly placed it in the snack section instead of with other boxed chocolates. The solution was to put the jar in a box. In 1998, the packaging was revamped and the product was put in a foil pouch in a classy-looking black carton with gold embossed lettering and a coating that kept the packaging looking shiny.

Those changes helped Clodhoppers get a contract with Wal-Mart. During the 1999 Christmas season, Wal-Mart sold out its supply of Clodhoppers and ordered more for Easter and Mother's Day. The Wal-Mart contract gave Krave's credibility and other orders followed from Shoppers Drug Mart and Zellers. Krave was also given a big boost when it was featured on a segment of the CBC's *Venture*.

In May 2003, the company signed a deal to have their product sold in 274 Rogers Video stores and 400 Blockbuster video outlets across Canada. The successes mean that Clodhoppers will likely become one of the top 10 candy brand names in Canada, alongside such well-known brand names as Hershey's Bites, M&M's Skittles, and Werther's Original Sweets & Toffees.

Krave's promotion strategy has been to forgo television advertising and instead put money into a national sampling blitz that hits stores around the holiday season. This gives shoppers a chance to actually taste the product. Krave also launched its second product—milk chocolate Clodhoppers—in March 2000. It also tested a Clodhopper Blizzard at Dairy Queens in Manitoba, Saskatchewan, and British Columbia in August 2000. In the spring of 2001, Krave Candy became the first Canadian candy company to own a Blizzard flavour at Dairy Queen Canada. The product is available at all 538 Dairy Queen locations across Canada. Getting equal billing with other Blizzard flavours such as Oreo Cookies, Reese's Pieces, and Crispy Crunch gives Clodhoppers instant credibility.

Ganong Bros. Ltd.

Ganong Bros. Ltd. was started in St. Stephens, New Brunswick, in 1873. Arthur Ganong, one of the founders, is generally credited as being the inventor of the chocolate bar. For many years, the company operated in a relatively secure environment behind Canada's protectionist tariffs. But when free trade came along in the 1990s, Ganong had to start thinking about how it was going to compete with foreign candy companies.

One of its strategies was to upgrade its production facilities to achieve lower costs. It replaced its old buildings, increased plant capacity, and installed new production and packaging machinery. Skilled workers focus on creating specialty products by hand, while machines do the more simplified work. The result is a modern production line that still allows for a custom-made touch.

In spite of all these improvements, Ganong knows it cannot knock heads with the multinational giants like Hershey, Cadbury, or Nestlé in products like standardized candy bars. These products are sold in very high volumes, and to compete in that market a company must be able to achieve very low unit costs. Ganong's strategy has therefore been to grow by carefully choosing specialty product lines where it can compete. Ganong's niche focuses on four products: boxed chocolates, fruit snacks, bagged candies, and bulk candy products. These specialized products are well suited to a small company like Ganong because they require a lot of hand labour. They also allow the company to retain its down-home, high quality image.

The international market is important to Ganong, which hopes to generate 50 percent of its revenue from U.S. sales within a few years (the current level is 31 percent). To achieve this goal, Ganong will have to build brand awareness for products such as Delecto chocolates and Sunkist fruit snacks. Ganong currently ranks number two in Canada in assorted chocolate boxes, and its Fruitfull brand controls 43 percent of fruit jelly sales. David's daughter Bryana is the product development manager. She heads up the effort to increase customer recognition of the Ganong brand. ◆

In Chapter 15, we introduced the four components of the marketing mix: product, price, promotion, and place (distribution). In this chapter, we look in more detail at products and how they are priced. New product development—like that at Krave Candy Co.—is a critically important activity for companies because all products—including once-popular TV shows like *Seinfeld*, *L.A. Law*, and *M.A.S.H.*—eventually reach the end of their life cycles and expire. There is a basic rule of thumb for developing new products in any industry: Begin by identifying the changing demands of your target audience and then develop new products to meet those demands.

Let's begin this chapter by looking at the products that have been developed by Oracle Corp., IBM, and Microsoft Corp. These companies are all major players in database-software products—computer programs that other companies use for storing and manipulating massive volumes of internal data. Oracle holds the top position, with a near 34 percent share of the market; IBM is next, with more than 30 percent, and Microsoft is a distant third, with about 15 percent. While all are successful, surveys show that they rely on quite different strategies. Oracle is the hands-down winner in terms of product innovation, specializing in cutting-edge features that substantially improve performance. Microsoft products rate lower in both reliability and performance, but they are priced below Oracle software and cost less to operate. IBM gets high marks for satisfaction with technical and customer support. So whose product is best? Says one industry analyst, "It's hard to say who is the technological leader in this market, since it depends on what you value and how you want it delivered."[1]

In making their strategic decisions, Oracle, IBM, and Microsoft face a basic fact of business: It is virtually impossible to focus on just one element of the marketing mix (for example, product design) without having to deal with the other marketing variables (price, promotion, and distribution). It is important that you keep this fact in mind as you read Chapters 16 and 17.

WHAT IS A PRODUCT?

1. Identify a *product*, distinguish between *consumer* and *industrial products*, and explain the *product mix*.

In developing the marketing mix for any products—whether ideas, goods, or services—marketers must consider what consumers really buy when they purchase products. Only then can they plan their strategies effectively. We will begin this section where product strategy begins—with an understanding of product *features* and *benefits*. Next, we will describe the major *classifications of products*, both consumer and industrial. Finally, we will discuss the most important component in the offerings of any business—its *product mix*.

The Value Package

Whether it is a physical good, a service, or some combination of the two, customers get value from the various benefits, features, and even intangible rewards associated with a product. Product **features** are the qualities, tangible and intangible, that a company builds into its products, such as a 12-horsepower motor on a lawn mower. But to attract buyers, features also must provide *benefits*: The mower must produce an attractive lawn. The owner's pleasure in knowing that the mower is nearby when needed is an intangible reward.

features

The qualities, both tangible and intangible, that a company builds into its products.

Today's consumer regards a product as a bundle of attributes which, taken together, marketers call the **value package**. Increasingly, buyers expect to receive products with greater *value*—with more benefits at reasonable costs. Consider, for example, the possible attributes in a personal computer value package:

value package

Product marketed as a bundle of value-adding attributes, including reasonable cost.

- easy access to understandable pre-purchase information
- choices in keyboards, monitors, and processing capacities
- choices of colour
- attractive software packages
- attractive prices
- fast, simple ordering via the internet
- protection for credit card purchasing
- assurance of speedy delivery
- warranties
- easy access to around-the-clock post-purchase technical support
- internet chat room capability
- prestige of owning a state-of-the art system

Although the computer includes physical *features*—processing devices and other hardware—most items in the value package are services or intangibles that, collectively, add value by providing *benefits* that increase the customer's satisfaction. Reliable data processing is certainly a benefit, but so too are pride of ownership, access to technical support, and a feeling of security. Today, more and more firms compete on the basis of enhanced value packages. They find that the addition of a simple new service often pleases customers far beyond the cost of providing it. Just making the purchase transaction more convenient, for example, adds value by sparing customers long waits and cumbersome paperwork.[2]

Look carefully at the ad in Figure 16.1 for SAS Institute (**www.sas.com**), a major designer of statistical software. In this ad SAS does not emphasize the technical features of its products, nor even the criteria that companies use in selecting software—efficiency, compatibility, support. Rather, the ad focuses on the customer-oriented benefits that a buyer of SAS software can expect from using the firm's products: "Only SAS provides you with a complete view of your customers." These benefits are being marketed as part of a complete value package.

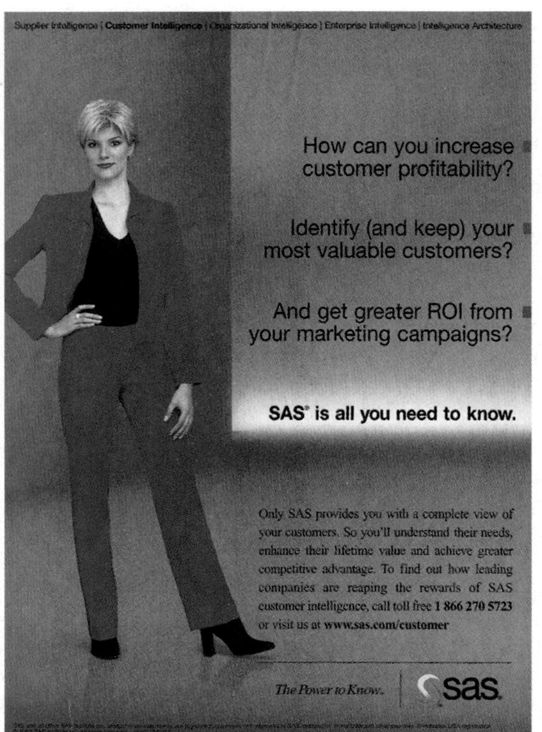

Figure 16.1
SAS ad.

Classifying Goods and Services

One way to classify a product is according to expected buyers. Buyers fall into two groups: buyers of *consumer* products and buyers of *industrial* products. As we saw in Chapter 15, the consumer and industrial buying processes differ significantly. Not surprisingly, then, marketing products to consumers is vastly different from marketing them to other companies.

Classifying Consumer Products

Consumer products are commonly divided into three categories that reflect buyers' behaviour: convenience, shopping, and specialty products.

- **Convenience goods** (such as milk and newspapers) and **convenience services** (such as those offered by fast-food restaurants) are consumed rapidly and regularly. They are relatively inexpensive and are purchased frequently and with little expenditure of time and effort.
- **Shopping goods** (such as stereos and tires) and **shopping services** (such as insurance) are more expensive and are purchased less frequently than convenience goods and services. Consumers often compare brands, sometimes in different stores. They may also evaluate alternatives in terms of style, performance, colour, price, and other criteria.
- **Specialty goods** (such as wedding gowns) and **specialty services** (such as catering for wedding receptions) are extremely important and expensive purchases. Consumers usually decide on precisely what they want and will accept no substitutes. They will often go from store to store, sometimes spending a great deal of money and time to get a specific product.

convenience goods/services
Relatively inexpensive consumer goods or services that are bought and used rapidly and regularly, causing consumers to spend little time looking for them or comparing their prices.

shopping goods/services
Moderately expensive consumer goods or services that are purchased infrequently, causing consumers to spend some time comparing their prices.

specialty goods/services
Very expensive consumer goods or services that are purchased rarely, causing consumers to spend a great deal of time locating the exact item desired.

Classifying Industrial Products

Depending on how much they cost and how they will be used, industrial products can be divided into two categories:

- **Expense items** are any materials and services that are consumed within a year by firms producing other goods or supplying services. The most obvious expense items are industrial goods used directly in the production process, for example, bulk loads of tea processed into tea bags.
- **Capital items** are permanent—that is, expensive and long lasting—goods and services. All these items have expected lives of more than a year—typically up to several years. Expensive buildings (offices, factories), fixed equipment (water towers, baking ovens), and accessory equipment (computers, airplanes) are capital goods. Capital services are those for which long-term commitments are made. These may include purchases for employee food services, building and equipment maintenance, or legal services. Because capital items are expensive and purchased infrequently, they often involve decisions by high-level managers.

expense items
Relatively inexpensive industrial goods that are consumed rapidly and regularly.

capital items
Expensive, long-lasting industrial goods that are used in producing other goods or services and have a long life.

The Product Mix

The group of products a company has available for sale, be it consumer or industrial, is known as the firm's **product mix**. Black & Decker, for example, makes toasters, vacuum cleaners, electric drills, and a variety of other appliances and tools. 3M makes everything from Post-it Notes to laser optics.

product mix
The group of products a company has available for sale.

Product Lines

Most companies begin with a single product. Over time, successful companies may find that the initial product does not suit all consumers shopping for the product type. So they often introduce similar products designed to reach other consumers. Apple Computer introduced the first successful personal computer. Shortly thereafter, Apple produced a range of personal computers for various applications—for example, the Apple 2C, 2E, 2GS, Macintosh Plus, and Macintosh SE. A group of similar products intended for a similar group of buyers who will use them in similar fashions is known as a **product line**.

product line
A group of similar products intended for a similar group of buyers who will use them in a similar fashion.

Companies may also extend their horizons and identify opportunities outside of their existing product line. The result—multiple (or diversified) product lines—is evident in firms like Procter & Gamble, which began by making soap, but which now also produces paper products, foods, coffee, and baby products. Multiple product lines allow a company to grow more rapidly and minimize the consequences of slow sales in any one product line.

DEVELOPING NEW PRODUCTS

To expand or diversify product lines—indeed, just to survive—firms must develop and successfully introduce streams of new products. Faced with competition and shifting consumer preferences, no firm can count on a single successful product to carry it forever. Even basic products that have been widely purchased for decades require nearly constant renewal. Consider the unassuming facial tissue. The white tissue in the rectangular box has been joined (if not replaced) by tissues of many different colours and patterns. Some tissues are extra-soft, some contain menthol, and some are extra-large. They arrive in boxes shaped and decorated for nearly every room in the house, and they are made to be placed or carried not only in the bathroom but also in the purse, the briefcase, and the car.

Research and Development (R&D) refers to those activities that are necessary to provide new products, services, and processes. It usually requires a large investment in laboratories, equipment, and scientific talent. Technology plays an important role in R&D. **Technology** is the application of science that enables people to do entirely new things or to perform established tasks in new and better ways. Consider the following examples:

technology
The application of science that enables people to do entirely new things or to perform established tasks in a new and better way.

- After studying the movement of the human foot in minute detail, Canstar Sports Inc. developed the Micron Mega skate, which is now worn by 70 percent of NHL players.
- Alcan developed a ceramic and aluminum composite called Duralcan. A mountain bike built with Duralcan weighs half as much as a bike built with a standard steel frame.
- Toyota Motor Corp. has demonstrated an experimental car that monitors driver alertness with a pulse sensor worn on the wrist. The car sounds a chime to wake up a drowsy driver.

Business firms must embrace technology so that their products and product features will not become obsolete. If a firm is aggressive, it will be the first to introduce a new and cheaper way to make its Product X. It might also introduce Product X-Mark II with features that make a competitor's Product Y obsolete. But R&D does not automatically guarantee success, because it may be difficult to find a market for a new product that has been developed. Inuktun Services Ltd. developed small, submersible, remotely operated vehicles (ROVs) equipped with lights and a video camera. The idea was that boat owners could guide these devices down into the water and view the bottom of their boat on a TV monitor. Boat owners weren't interested, but the nuclear industry was. Now Inuktun's ROVs travel up and down stairs, around corners, over obstacles, in water up to 30 metres deep, and through ducts and pipes as little as 15 centimetres in diameter.[3]

The New Product Development Process

2. Describe the *new product development process* and trace the stages of the *product life cycle.*

Companies often face multi-year time horizons and high risks when developing new products. In 1989, discussions about the possibility of manufacturing a new long-range executive jet began at Bombardier Inc. of Montreal. Over the next few years, the company spent millions of dollars developing the product, which finally became available in 1998.

High-definition television (HDTV) is an example of a new product that has taken much longer than expected to develop. Because HDTV gives much-improved picture quality, it was originally assumed that consumers would quickly accept it. But HDTV has been plagued by a classic chicken-and-egg problem: broadcasters haven't decided to offer high-definition programs (because they require special transmitters and cameras) and manufacturers of HDTVs have been holding back because they don't know whether broadcasters are going to produce high-definition programs for consumers to watch. Another product that has taken a long time to develop—the hydrogen fuel cell—is described in the Business Today box.

Product Mortality Rates

Typically, new products move through a series of stages, beginning with the search for ideas and culminating in introduction to consumers. At each stage of this process, potential products fall from further consideration as the company pursues more attractive alternatives. In fact, it is estimated that it takes 50 new product ideas to generate one product that finally reaches the marketplace. Even then, of course, only a few of those survivors become *successful* products. Many seemingly great *ideas* have failed as *products*. Indeed, creating a successful new product has become more and more difficult.

Pharmaceutical companies spend large amounts of money on research and development, yet bring relatively few products to market.

Speed to Market

The more rapidly a product moves from the laboratory to the marketplace, the more likely it is to survive. By introducing new products ahead of competitors, companies establish market leadership. They become entrenched in the market before being challenged by newer

BUSINESS TODAY

Will the Hydrogen Fuel Cell Ever Be Perfected?

Automobile manufacturers face a long time horizon as they try to develop a new engine to replace the internal combustion engine that has powered automobiles for over a century. Over the years, a succession of new product ideas—the steam powered car, the electric car, the rotary engine—were all touted as solutions, but none of them were ever widely adopted. In 1993, Vancouver-based Ballard Power Systems Inc. said it had developed a new technology—the hydrogen fuel cell—that would revolutionize power generation and solve the problems of the internal combustion engine. The fuel cell combines hydrogen (one of earth's most common elements) with oxygen to produce electricity. The only exhaust is warm water. The electricity generated by the fuel cell can be used to power anything that runs on electricity, including cars.

Initially, enthusiasm for the hydrogen fuel cell was high. DaimlerChrysler invested $450 million in the company, and Ford Motor Co. put in another $600 million to pursue the development of fuel cells. A DaimlerChrysler executive said the company expected to sell 100 000 cars powered by fuel cells by 2004. The CEO of Ballard said that the fuel cell would replace the internal combustion engine. Ballard stock soared from its initial public offering price of $8 per share to $210 per share. Ballard sold prototypes to several automobile companies for testing, the Chicago Transit Authority put three fuel cell-powered buses into service, and the B.C. government purchased three buses.

But then the problems began. In 1997, Geoffrey Ballard resigned as chairman of the company. Other companies like General Motors, United Technologies, and Mitsubishi also began development work on fuel cells. Sales revenues at Ballard weren't keeping up with development costs. The revolution, which was always just around the corner, seemed to stay tantalizingly in the future. In 2003, Ballard estimated that it wouldn't become profitable until 2007. Geoffrey Ballard now says that the company's plan to manufacture the fuel cell is ill advised. He says they should have licensed the technology to someone else and collected royalties. That way they could have continued to focus on the development of the technology.

Critics argue that fuel cells will not become a mainstream power source for many years. They give four reasons for their pessimism. First, to get the hydrogen in the first place requires that it be extracted from the substances that contain it (e.g., natural gas). But stripping the hydrogen from natural gas creates carbon dioxide, which is precisely what the standard internal combustion car engines emit.

Second, there are fears about the flammability of hydrogen. When you mention the word hydrogen, many people immediately think of the spectacular explosion and fire that destroyed the Hindenburg dirigible. That accident effectively ended transatlantic passenger service on dirigibles. In the modern experimental facilities that are testing the hydrogen fuel cell, sensors have been installed which detect hydrogen leaks (it is an odourless and colourless gas). And at experimental hydrogen fuelling stations, technicians wear anti-static coats to prevent sparks from igniting the hydrogen.

Third, there are concerns that not enough hydrogen-dispensing gas stations will be built. If that is the case, consumer demand will never be high enough to encourage mass production of cars that are powered by fuel cells. The state of California has several hydrogen-generating stations in operation, and many more are planned. But for hydrogen fuel cells to be of interest to consumers, there have to be enough gas stations to make it convenient for consumers who want to fill their tanks. It is likely to be a long time before there will be enough such stations.

Fourth, the hydrogen fuel cell is likely to be very expensive. The most environmentally sound way to make hydrogen is to extract it from water using electricity made from solar or wind power. This is exactly what Honda Motors is doing at an experimental site in California. Honda has discovered that this method is not cheap, and large areas of land are required for enough solar panels to produce the required electricity.

Given all these problems, why has so much time and money been invested in the development of hydrogen fuel cells? The answer is both environmental (less air pollution) and political (less reliance on foreign oil). This new product may eventually be commercially viable, but there is still a long way to go. General Motors, which has invested $1 billion in fuel cell research, is still optimistic: It thinks that by 2015 it will have one million cars on the road that are powered by fuel cells.

speed to market
Strategy of introducing new products to respond quickly to customer and/or market changes.

competitors. How important is **speed to market**—that is, a firm's success in responding to customer demand or market changes? A product that is only three months late to market (three months behind the leader) loses 12 percent of its lifetime profit potential. At six months, it will lose 33 percent.

The Seven-Step Development Process

To increase their chances of developing a successful new product, many firms adopt some variation on a basic seven-step process (see Figure 16.2).

1. **Product ideas.** Product development begins with a search for ideas for new products. Product ideas can come from consumers, the sales force, research and development people, or engineering personnel. The key is to actively seek out ideas and to reward those whose ideas become successful products.
2. **Screening.** This second stage is an attempt to eliminate all product ideas that do not mesh with the firm's abilities, expertise, or objectives. Representatives from marketing, engineering, and production must have input at this stage.
3. **Concept testing.** Once ideas have been culled, companies use market research to solicit consumers' input. In this way, firms can identify benefits that the product must provide as well as an appropriate price level for the product.
4. **Business analysis.** This stage involves developing an early comparison of costs versus benefits for the proposed product. Preliminary sales projections are compared with cost projections from finance and production. The aim is not to determine precisely how much money the product will make but to see whether the product can meet minimum profitability goals.
5. **Prototype development.** At this stage, product ideas begin to take shape. Using input from the concept-testing phase, engineering and/or research and development produce a preliminary version of the prod-

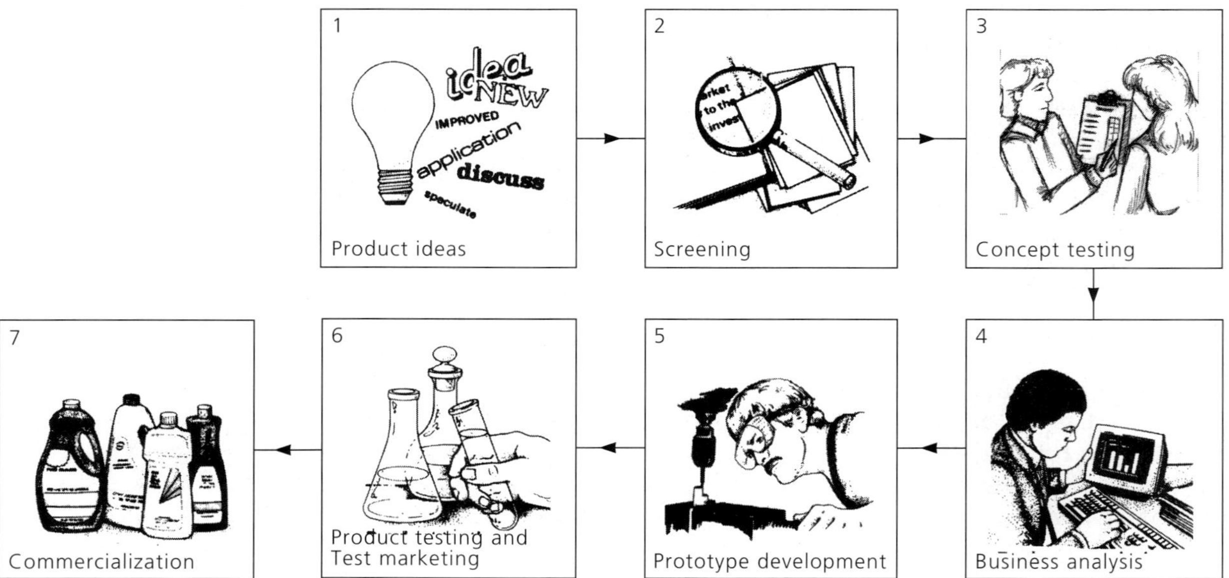

Figure 16.2
The new product development process.

uct. Prototypes can be extremely expensive, often requiring extensive hand crafting, tooling, and development of components. But this phase can help identify potential production problems.

6. **Product testing and test marketing.** Using what it learned from the prototype, the company begins limited production of the item. The product is then tested internally to see if it meets performance requirements. If it does, it is made available for sale in limited areas. This stage is very costly, since promotional campaigns and distribution channels must be established for test markets. But test marketing gives a company its first information on how consumers will respond to a product under real market conditions.
7. **Commercialization.** If test-marketing results are positive, the company will begin full-scale production and marketing of the product. Gradual commercialization, with the firm providing the product to more and more areas over time, prevents undue strain on the firm's initial production capabilities. But extensive delays in commercialization may give competitors a chance to bring out their own version.

Variations in the Process for Services

The development of services (both for consumers and industrial buyers) involves many of the same stages as goods development. Basically, Steps 2, 3, 4, 6, and 7 are the same. There are, however, some important differences in Steps 1 and 5:

1. **Service Ideas.** The search for service ideas includes a task called defining the **service package**, which involves identification of the tangible and intangible features that define the service (see Chapter 11) and stating service specifications. For example, a firm that wants to offer year-end cleaning services to office buildings might commit itself to the following specifications: "The building interior will be cleaned by midnight, January 5, including floor polishing of all aisles, carpets swept free of all dust and debris, polished washbowls and lavatory equipment, with no interruption or interference to customer."

service package
Identification of the tangible and intangible features that define the service.

5. **Service Process Design.** Instead of prototype development, services require a **service process design**. This step involves selecting the process, identifying worker requirements, and determining facilities requirements so that the service can be provided as promised in the service specifications. *Process selection* identifies each step in the service, including the sequence and the timing. *Worker requirements* specify employee behaviours, skills, capabilities, and interactions with customers during the service encounter. *Facilities requirements* designate all of the equipment that supports delivery of the service.

service process design
Selecting the process, identifying worker requirements, and determining facilities requirements so that the service can be effectively provided.

THE PRODUCT LIFE CYCLE

Products that reach the commercialization stage begin a new series of stages known as the product life cycle. **Product life cycle (PLC)** is the concept that products have a limited profit-producing life for a company. This life may be a matter of months, years, or decades, depending on the ability of the product to attract customers over time. Strong products such as Kellogg's Corn Flakes, Coca-Cola, Ivory soap, Argo cornstarch, and Caramilk candy bars have had extremely long productive lives.

product life cycle (PLC)
The concept that the profit-producing life of any product goes through a cycle of introduction, growth, maturity (levelling off), and decline.

Stages in the Product Life Cycle

The life cycle for both goods and services is a natural process in which products are born, grow in stature, mature, and finally decline and die.[4] Look at the two graphics in Figure 16.3. In Figure 16.3(a), the four phases of the PLC are applied to several products with which you are familiar.

1. *Introduction*. The introduction stage begins when the product reaches the marketplace. During this stage, marketers focus on making potential consumers aware of the product and its benefits. Because of extensive promotional and development costs, profits are nonexistent.
2. *Growth*. If the new product attracts and satisfies enough consumers, sales begin to climb rapidly. During this stage, the product begins to show a profit. Other firms in the industry move rapidly to introduce their own versions.
3. *Maturity*. Sales growth begins to slow. Although the product earns its highest profit level early in this stage, increased competition eventually leads to price cutting and lower profits. Toward the end of the stage, sales start to fall.
4. *Decline*. During this final stage, sales and profits continue to fall. New products in the introduction stage take away sales. Companies remove or reduce promotional support (ads and salespeople) but may let the product linger to provide some profits.

(a)

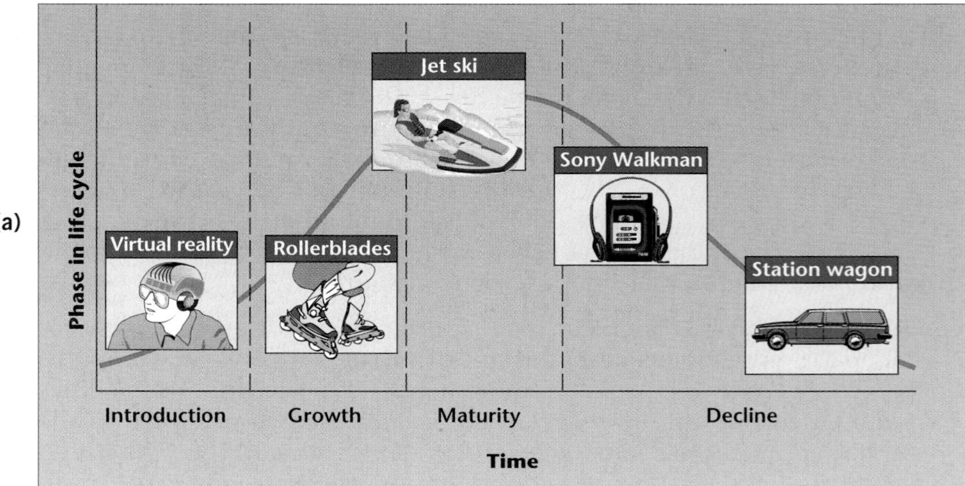

(b)

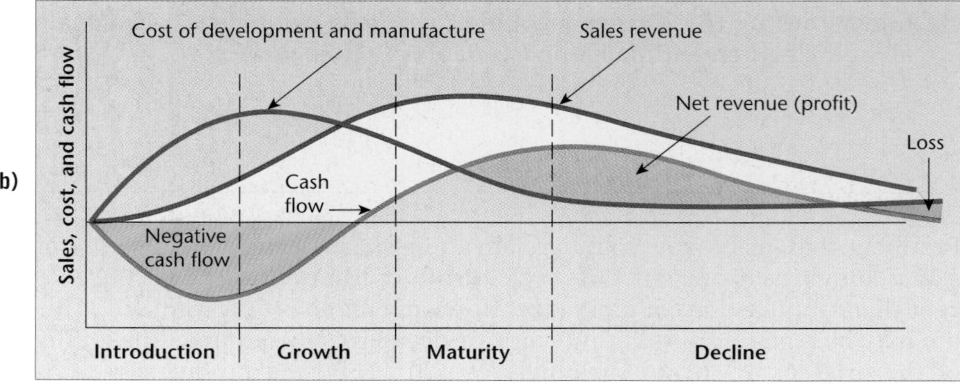

Figure 16.3
The product life cycle: stages, sales, cost, and profit.

Figure 16.3(b) plots the relationship of the PLC to a product's typical sales, costs, and profits. Although the early stages of the PLC often show negative cash flows, successful products usually recover those losses and, in fact, continue to generate profits until the decline stage. For most products, profitable life spans are short—thus, the importance placed by so many firms on the constant replenishment of product lines.

Extending Product Life: An Alternative to New Products

Companies try to keep products in the maturity stage as long as they can. Sales of TV sets, for example, have been revitalized by such feature changes as colour, portability, miniaturization, and stereo capability. In fact, companies can extend product life through a number of creative means. Foreign markets, for example, offer three approaches to longer life cycles:

1. In **product extension**, an existing product is marketed globally instead of just domestically. Coca-Cola and Levi's 501 jeans are prime examples of international product extensions.
2. With **product adaptation**, the product is modified for greater appeal in different countries. In Germany, a McDonald's meal includes beer, and Ford puts the steering wheel on the right side for exports to Japan. Because it involves product changes, this approach is usually more costly than product extension.
3. **Reintroduction** means reviving, for new markets, products that are becoming obsolete in older ones. NCR, for instance, has reintroduced manually operated cash registers in Latin America.

product extension
Existing, unmodified product that is marketed globally.

product adaptation
Product modified to have greater appeal in foreign markets.

reintroduction
Process of reviving for new markets products that are obsolete in older ones.

Thus, the beginning of a sales downturn in the maturity stage is not necessarily the time to start abandoning a product. Often, it is a time to realize that the old approach is starting to fade and to search for a new approach.

IDENTIFYING PRODUCTS

As we noted earlier, developing a product's features is only part of a marketer's job. Marketers must also identify products so that consumers recognize them. Three important tools for this task are *branding*, *packaging*, and *labelling*.

3. Explain the importance of *branding, packaging,* and *labelling.*

Branding Products

Coca-Cola is the best-known brand in the world. Indeed, some Coke executives claim that if all the company's other assets were obliterated, they could go to the bank and borrow $100 billion on the strength of the brand name alone. Brand names such as Coca-Cola and emblems such as the McDonald's golden arches are symbols that characterize products and distinguish them from one another. **Branding** is a process of using symbols to communicate the qualities of a particular product made by a particular producer. Brands are designed to signal uniform quality: Customers who try and like a product can return to it by remembering its name.

branding
Process of using symbols to communicate the qualities of a product made by a particular producer.

Adding Value Through Brand Equity

Many companies that once measured assets in terms of cash, buildings, equipment, and inventories now realize that a strong brand is an equally important asset. Widely known and admired brands are valuable because of their power to attract customers. Those with higher **brand equity** have greater brand awareness and loyalty on the part of consumers and larger

brand equity
Degree of consumers' loyalty to and awareness of a brand and its resultant market share.

It's pronounced a little differently—STAH-buks-zu—but the brand means pretty much the same: large cups of gourmet coffee served in comfortable surroundings to the sound of hip-hop and reggae music. In Japan, Starbucks has opened 300 stores since 1996 and plans another 180 over the next three years. In a recession-ridden country of traditional tea drinkers, volume per store is twice that of North American outlets. The brand has become so popular that Starbucks earned U.S.$242 million in 2002, even though it doesn't advertise in Japan.

market shares than competing brands (and are perceived to have greater quality). Because a brand adds value to a product, marketers manage brands to increase that value. In other words, they build equity in a brand by maintaining or improving brand awareness and perceived quality in much the same manner that you build up ownership equity in your house by maintaining or improving its condition and features.[5] The Irving family of New Brunswick recently embarked on a plan to increase the brand equity of Royale, a once-popular brand of tissue. The goal is to make Royale a major brand in Canada.[6]

Table 16.1 shows the rankings of the top global brands according to estimates of each brand's dollar value. It reflects the *earnings boost* that each brand delivers—that is, an index of a brand's power to increase sales and earnings, both present and the future—and shows how much those future earnings are worth today. Only *global brands*—those with sales of at least 20 percent outside the home country—are included.[7]

brand awareness
Extent to which a brand name comes to mind when the consumer considers a particular product category.

Several factors are involved in brand equity, including *brand loyalty* (which we discussed in Chapter 15) and **brand awareness**—the brand name that first comes to mind when you consider a particular product category. What company, for example, comes to mind when you need to send a document a long way on short notice? For many people, FedEx has the associated brand awareness.

Table 16. 1 The World's 10 Most Valuable Brands

	Brand	2003 Brand Value (in billions of U.S. dollars)
1.	Coca-Cola	$70.4
2.	Microsoft	65.1
3.	IBM	51.7
4.	GE	42.3
5.	Intel	31.1
6.	Nokia	29.4
7.	Disney	28.0
8.	McDonald's	24.6
9.	Marlboro	22.1
10.	Mercedes	21.3

Ebusiness Branding

Cisco Systems Inc.
www.cisco.com

It takes a long time to establish national or global brand recognition.[8] After years of work, Cisco Systems Inc., the network-equipment manufacturer, reached new heights in branding for business-to-business, or B2B, ecommerce. The company's "Cisco Internet Generation" promotional campaign for 2001 stressed reliability and innovation, and in analyzing the campaign, Cisco found that its brand awareness increased by 80 percent (boosting it past rivals Lucent Technologies and Nortel Networks). The campaign also lifted Cisco's reputation as an internet expert above that of Microsoft, IBM, and Lucent.[9]

The expensive, sometimes fierce struggle for brand recognition is perhaps nowhere more evident than in the current branding battles among dot-com firms. Collectively, the top internet brands—America Online, Yahoo!, and Amazon.com—spend billions a year even though they have just barely cracked the ranks of top-60 global brands. Even with 210 million visitors each month, Yahoo! still faces formidable competitors in AOL Time Warner and Microsoft. Moreover, the costs of branding promotions are hitting all dot-coms at a time when they are trying to survive the near collapse of the industry.[10] The mounting costs of brand identity mean that many more would-be ebusinesses will probably fail.[11]

It's not just ebusinesses that are trying to catch the attention of consumers. Even traditional retailers are choosing attention-getting names such as Gadzooks, Wet Seal, Noodle Kidoodle, Koo Koo Roo, and Ugly Duckling.[12]

Firms that sell products internationally face an issue of growing importance in branding strategy. They must consider how product names will translate in various languages. In Spanish, for example, the name of Chevrolet's now-defunct Nova simply became *no va*—"it does not go." Sales were particularly poor in South America. Similarly, Rolls Royce was once going to name a new touring car "Silver Mist." Rolls changed the name to "Silver Shadow" when it discovered that mist is German for "manure."[13] Naturally, foreign companies hoping to sell in Canada must be equally careful.

Types of Brand Names

Virtually every product has a brand name of some form. However, different types of brand names tell the alert consumer something about the product's origin.

National Brands. Brand name products that are produced and distributed by the manufacturer are called **national brands**. These brands, such as Scotch tape, are often widely recognized by consumers because of large national advertising campaigns. The costs of developing a positive image for a national brand are high, so some companies use their national brand on several related products. Procter & Gamble now markets Ivory shampoo, capitalizing on the widely recognized name of its soaps.

national brands
Products distributed by and carrying a name associated with the manufacturer.

Licensed Brands. More and more nationally recognized companies and personalities have sold other companies the right to place their names on products, which are **licensed brands**. Licensing has become big business. Franklin the Turtle, the subject of 26 books and an animated television series produced by Nelvana, is a Canadian product that is also popular in the United States. Nelvana and U.S.-based Sears Roebuck & Co. signed a licensing agreement allowing Sears to set up Franklin boutiques at its more than 850 stores. These boutiques market Franklin clothing and accessories that are available exclusively at Sears.[14]

licensed brands
Selling the right to use a brand name, a celebrity's name, or some other well-known identification mark to another company to use on a product.

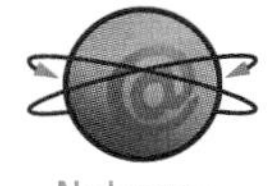

Nelvana
www.nelvana.com

Private Brands. When a wholesaler or retailer develops a brand and has the manufacturer place that brand name on the product, the resulting prod-

private brands
Products promoted by and carrying a name associated with the retailer or wholesaler, not the manufacturer.

uct name is a **private brand**. One of the best-known purveyors of private brands is Sears, with its Craftsman tools and Kenmore appliances.

J. Sainsbury PLC, the largest supermarket chain in Britain, introduced its own private brand of cola in a can that looks strikingly like the one used by Coke. The two products are stocked side by side on store shelves, and Sainsbury's offering is noticeably cheaper than Coke. The product is made by Cott Corp. of Toronto. The story is much the same in North America. Under the Sam's "American Choice" label, Cott sells a billion cans of soft drinks each year at Wal-Mart.

Holt Renfrew
www.holtrenfrew.com

Loblaw Cos. Ltd., owned by George Weston, has created a line of upscale products under the private brand "President's Choice." Clever advertising, fancy labels, and exotic product names differentiate the line and draw consumer attention to items such as peanut butter and cookies. Another Weston-owned company, Holt Renfrew, emphasizes its private brand. A stylish Prada suit sells for \$2000 to \$4000, but the Holt Renfrew equivalent is priced at only \$300 to \$700.[15]

Trademarks, Patents, and Copyrights. Because brand development is very expensive, a company does not want another company using its name and confusing consumers into buying a substitute product. Many companies apply to the Canadian government and receive a **trademark**, the exclusive legal right to use a brand name. Trademarks are granted for 15 years and may be renewed for further periods of 15 years, but only if the company continues to protect its brand name.

trademark
The exclusive legal right to use a brand name.

Just what can be trademarked is not always clear, however. If the company allows the name to lapse into common usage, the courts may take away protection. Common usage occurs when the company fails to use the ® symbol for its brand. It also occurs if the company fails to correct those who do not acknowledge the brand as a trademark. Windsurfer (a popular brand of sailboards by WSI Inc.) lost its trademark. Like the trampoline, yo-yo, and thermos, the brand name has become the common term for the product and can now be used by any sailboard company. But companies like Xerox, Coke, Jello, and Scotch tape have successfully defended their brand names.

Companies want to be sure that both product brands and new product ideas are protected. A **patent** protects an invention or idea for a period of 20 years. The cost is \$1000 to \$1500; it takes nine months to three years to secure a patent from the Canadian Patent Office.[16]

patent
Protects an invention or idea for a period of 20 years.

The Toronto Raptors benefit both from the licensing fees they receive as well as from the free advertising they get whenever these products are used.

Copyrights give exclusive ownership rights to the creators of books, articles, designs, illustrations, photos, films, and music. Computer programs and even semiconductor chips are also protected. Copyrights extend to creators for their entire lives and to their estates for 50 years thereafter in Canada. Copyright protection differs from country to country. For example, in the United States, copyright extends to creators' estates for 70 years. Copyrights apply to the tangible expressions of an idea, not to the idea itself. For example, the idea of cloning dinosaurs from fossil DNA cannot be copyrighted, but Michael Crichton, the author of *Jurassic Park*, could copyright his novel because it is the tangible result of the basic idea.

copyright

Exclusive ownership rights granted to creators for the tangible expression of an idea.

Brand Loyalty

Companies that spend the large amount of money it takes to develop a brand are looking for one thing from consumers: **brand loyalty**. That is, they want to develop customers who, when they need a particular item, will go back to the same brand and buy the company's products.

brand loyalty

Customers' recognition of, preference for, and insistence on buying a product with a certain brand name.

Brand loyalty is measured in three stages. First, the company wants *brand recognition*. By putting the brand in front of consumers many times and associating it with a type of product, the producer hopes that consumers will become aware of its existence. Recognition is not enough, however. The owner of the brand wants consumers to start showing *brand preference* when they make a purchase. Brand preference requires not only awareness that the brand exists but also a favourable attitude toward the ability of the brand to provide benefits. Finally, because a brand may be unavailable in a store from time to time, companies seek *brand insistence*. Brand insistence is highly valued by brand owners, but it is very difficult to achieve.

A survey sponsored by Reader's Digest Canada found that Canadians have less trust in product brands than they did 20 years ago. However, some well-known brands like Becel Margarine, Robin Hood flour, Wal-Mart, and Black & Decker are still viewed postively.[17]

Packaging Products

With a few exceptions, including fresh fruits and vegetables, structural steel, and some other industrial products, products need some form of **packaging** in which to be carried to the market. Packaging serves the following functions:

packaging

The physical container in which a product is sold, including the label.

- it serves as an in-store advertisement that makes the product attractive
- it clearly displays the brand, and identifies product features and benefits
- it is the marketer's last chance to say "buy it" to the consumer
- it reduces the risk of damage, breakage, or spoilage

Labelling Products

Every product has a **label** on its package. Like packaging, labelling can help market the product. First, it *identifies* the product or the brand, as do the names Campbell on a can or Chiquita on a banana. Labels also *promote* products by getting consumers' attention; attractive colours and graphics provide visual cues to products that otherwise might be overlooked on the shelf. Finally, the label *describes* the product: It provides information about nutritional content, directions for use, proper disposal, and safety.

label

That part of a product's packaging that identifies the product's name and contents and sometimes its benefits.

The federal government regulates the information on package labels. The **Consumer Packaging and Labelling Act** has two main purposes: the

Consumer Packaging and Labelling Act

A federal law that provides comprehensive rules for packaging and labelling of consumer products.

first is to provide a comprehensive set of rules for packaging and labelling of consumer products, and the second is to ensure that the manufacturer provides full and factual information on labels. All pre-packaged products must state in French and English the quantity enclosed in metric and imperial units. The name and description of the product must also appear on the label in both French and English.

PROMOTING PRODUCTS AND SERVICES

4. Identify the important objectives of *promotion* and discuss the considerations in selecting a *promotional mix*.

promotion
Any technique designed to sell a product.

As we noted in Chapter 15, **promotion** is any technique designed to sell a product. It is part of the *communication mix* : the total message a company sends to consumers about its product. Promotional techniques, especially advertising, must communicate the uses, features, and benefits of products. Sales promotions also include various programs that add value beyond the benefits inherent in the product. For example, it is nice to get a high-quality product at a reasonable price but even better when the seller offers a rebate or a bonus pack with "20 percent more *free*."

In this section, we will look at the different objectives of and approaches to promotion. We will show when and why companies use particular strategies and tools and then describe the special promotional problems faced by both international and small businesses. First, however, we will explain the two general values to be gained from any promotional activity, regardless of the particular strategy or tools involved: *communicating information* and *creating satisfying exchanges*.

Information and Exchange Values

In free-market systems, a business uses promotional methods to communicate information about itself and its products to consumers and industrial buyers. The purpose, of course, is to influence purchase decisions. From an information standpoint, promotions seek to accomplish four things with potential customers:

- make them aware of products
- make them knowledgeable about products
- persuade them to like products
- persuade them to purchase products

The buyer gains from the exchange (a more attractive product), as does the seller (more unit sales or higher prices). Successful promotions provide communication about the product and create exchanges that satisfy both the customer's and the organization's objectives. However, because promotions are expensive, choosing the best promotional mix becomes critical. The promotional program, then, whether at the introduction stage (promoting for new product awareness) or the maturity stage (promoting brand benefits and customer loyalty), can determine the success or failure of any business or product.

Promotional Objectives

The ultimate objective of any promotion is to increase sales. However, marketers also use promotion to communicate information, position products, add value, and control sales volume.[18]

Communicating Information

Consumers cannot buy a product unless they have been informed about it. Information can advise customers about the availability of a product, educate them on the latest technological advances, or announce the candidacy of someone running for a government office. Information may be communicated in writing (newspapers and magazines), verbally (in person or over the telephone), or visually (television, a matchbook cover, or a billboard). Today, the communication of information regarding a company's products or services is so important that marketers try to place it wherever consumers may be. If you are an average consumer, you come in contact with approximately 1500 bits of promotional communication per day.

Positioning Products

Another objective of promotion, **product positioning**, is to establish an easily identifiable image of a product in the minds of consumers. For example, by selling only in department stores, Estée Lauder products have positioned themselves as more upscale than cosmetics sold in drugstores. With product positioning, the company is trying to appeal to a specific segment of the market rather than to the market as a whole.

product positioning
The establishment of an easily identifiable image of a product in the minds of consumers.

Adding Value

Today's value-conscious customers gain benefits when the promotional mix is shifted so that it communicates value—added benefits in its products. Burger King, for instance, shifted its promotional mix by cutting back on advertising dollars and using those funds for customer discounts. Receiving the same food at a lower price is "value-added" for Burger King's customers.

Controlling Sales Volume

Many companies, such as Hallmark Cards, experience seasonal sales patterns. By increasing promotional activities in slow periods, these firms can achieve more stable sales volume throughout the year. They can thus keep production and distribution systems running evenly. Promotions can even turn slow seasons into peak sales periods. For example, greeting card companies and florists together have done much to create Grandparents' Day. The result has been increased consumer demand for cards and flowers in the middle of what was once a slow season for both industries.

Promotional Strategies

Once a firm's promotional objectives are clear, it must develop a promotional strategy to achieve these objectives. Promotional strategies may be of the push or pull variety. A company with a **push strategy** will aggressively "push" its product through wholesalers and retailers, who persuade customers to buy it. In contrast, a company with a **pull strategy** appeals directly to customers, who demand the product from retailers, who in turn demand the product from wholesalers. Advertising "pulls" while personal selling "pushes." In rare cases, a company may purposely do very little promotion of its products. For example, Langlitz Leathers makes leather jackets that cost as much as $800. They are worn by rebels like Hell's Angels, rockers like Bruce Springsteen, and actors like Sylvester Stallone. Even though the company does virtually no advertising, customers who want a Langlitz have to wait seven months to get one after they place their order.[19]

push strategy
A promotional strategy in which a company aggressively pushes its product through wholesalers and retailers, which persuade customers to buy it.

pull strategy
A promotional strategy in which a company appeals directly to customers, who demand the product from retailers, which demand the product from wholesalers.

Makers of industrial products most often use a push strategy, and makers of consumer products most often use a pull strategy. Many large firms use a combination of the two strategies. For example, General Foods uses advertising to create consumer demand (pull) for its cereals. It also pushes wholesalers and retailers to stock these products.

The Promotional Mix

As we noted in Chapter 15, there are four types of promotional tools: *advertising, personal selling, sales promotions,* and *publicity and public relations*. The best combination of these tools—the best **promotional mix**—depends on many factors. The most important is the target audience.

promotional mix
That portion of marketing concerned with choosing the best combination of advertising, personal selling, sales promotions, and publicity to sell a product.

The Target Audience: Promotion and the Buyer Decision Process

In establishing a promotional mix, marketers match promotional tools with the five stages in the buyer decision process:

1. Buyers must first recognize the need to make a purchase. At this stage, marketers must make sure that buyers are aware of their products. Advertising and publicity, which can reach many people quickly, are important.
2. Buyers also want to learn more about available products. Advertising and personal selling are important because both can be used to educate consumers.
3. Buyers compare competing products. Personal selling can be vital. Sales representatives can demonstrate product quality and performance in comparison with competitors' products.
4. Buyers choose products and purchase them. Sales promotion is effective because it can give consumers an incentive to buy. Personal selling can help by bringing products to convenient purchase locations.
5. Buyers evaluate products after purchase. Advertising, or even personal selling, is sometimes used to remind consumers that they made wise purchases.[20]

Figure 16.4 summarizes the effective promotional tools for each stage of the consumer buying process.

ADVERTISING PROMOTIONS

5. Discuss the most important *advertising strategies* and describe the key *advertising media.*

What candy bar is "a nice light snack"? What soap is "99 and 44/100% pure"? What is the store where "the lowest price is the law"? What product is "only available in Canada? Pity"? If you are like most Canadians, you can

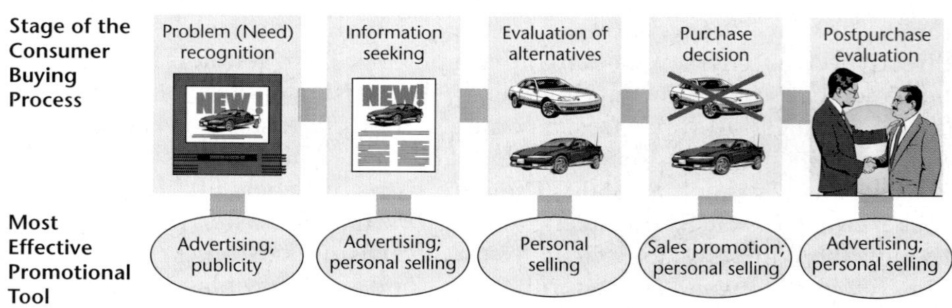

Figure 16.4
The consumer buying process and the promotional mix.

answer these questions because of **advertising**. (The answers are Coffee Crisp, Ivory Soap, Zellers, and Red Rose Tea.)

advertising
Promotional tool consisting of paid, non-personal communication used by an identified sponsor to inform an audience about a product.

Consumers remember brand names more easily if the company has a catchy advertising slogan. Buckley's Mixture, a well-known product in Canada, is trying to crack the U.S. market. In one advertisement on U.S. television, the announcer intones "Buckley's Mixture, the famous Canadian cough remedy, is now available here. It tastes awful, and it works."[21]

As important and high profile as advertising is, it has limits. Both Eaton's and Canadian Airlines were enthusiastic advertisers, but this didn't keep them in business. Advertising can convince customers to try a company's product or service, but it is the customer's experience with the product or service that determines whether they will make repeat purchases.

Advertising Strategies

Advertising strategies most often depend on which stage of the product life cycle their product is in. During the introduction stage, **informative advertising** can help develop an awareness of the company and its product among buyers and can establish a primary demand for the product. For example, before a new textbook is published, instructors receive direct-mail advertisements notifying them of the book's contents and availability.

informative advertising
An advertising strategy, appropriate to the introduction stage of the product life cycle, in which the goal is to make potential customers aware that a product exists.

As products become established, advertising strategies must change. During the growth stage, **persuasive advertising** can influence consumers to buy the company's products rather than those of its rivals. Persuasive advertising is also important during the maturity stage to maintain the product's level of sales. **Comparative advertising** involves comparing the sponsoring company's brand name with a competitor's brand name in such a way that the competitor's brand looks inferior. For example, Procter & Gamble aired advertisements claiming that its Bounty brand had more absorbency than Scott Paper's competing product. Scott retaliated by producing an advertisement that said that Scott Clean Ultra was 60 percent more absorbent than P&G's Bounty.[22] In many countries (for example, Japan), advertisements that knock a competitor's product are frowned on. But this is not so in Canada or the United States. In the European Union comparative advertising became legal in 1993, but advertisers must meet several limiting conditions.[23]

persuasive advertising
An advertising strategy, appropriate to the growth stage of the product life cycle, in which the goal is to influence the customer to buy the firm's product rather than the similar product of a competitor.

comparative advertising
An advertising strategy, appropriate to the growth stage of the product life cycle, in which the goal is to influence the customer to switch from a competitor's similar product to the firm's product by directly comparing the two products.

During the latter part of the maturity stage and all of the decline stage, **reminder advertising** keeps the product's name in front of the consumer. Atari, a pioneer in video games, continues to advertise, even though market attention has shifted to competitors like Nintendo and Saga Genesis.

reminder advertising
An advertising strategy, appropriate to the latter part of the maturity stage of the product life cycle, in which the goal is to keep the product's name in the minds of customers.

Advertising Media

Consumers tend to ignore the bulk of advertising messages that bombard them. Marketers must therefore find out who their customers are, which media they pay attention to, what messages appeal to them, and how to get their attention. Thus, marketers use several different **advertising media**—specific communication devices for carrying a seller's message to potential customers. IBM uses television ads to keep its name fresh in the minds of consumers, newspaper and magazine ads to educate them about product features, and trade publications to introduce new software.

advertising medium
The specific communication device—television, radio, newspapers, direct mail, magazines, billboards—used to carry a firm's advertising message to potential customers.

An advertiser selects media with a number of factors in mind. The marketer must first ask: Which medium will reach the people I want to reach? If a firm is selling hog breeding equipment, it might choose a business magazine read mostly by hog farmers. If it is selling silverware, it might choose a magazine for brides. If it is selling toothpaste, the choice might be a general audience television program or a general audience magazine such as *Reader's Digest* (or *Sélection du Reader's Digest*, for exposure to a similar audience of francophones).

The following are the most common advertising media. Each medium has advantages and disadvantages.

Newspapers

Newspapers remain the most widely used advertising medium. They offer excellent coverage, since each local market has at least one daily newspaper, and many people read the paper every day. This medium offers flexible, rapid coverage, since ads can change from day to day. It also offers believable coverage, since ads are presented side by side with news. However, newspapers are generally thrown out after one day, often do not print in colour, and have poor reproduction quality. Moreover, newspapers do not usually allow advertisers to target their audience well.

Television

Television allows advertisers to combine sight, sound, and motion, thus appealing to almost all of the viewer's senses. Information on viewer demographics for a particular program allows advertisers to promote to their target audiences. National advertising is done on television because it reaches more people than any other medium.

One disadvantage of television is that too many commercials cause viewers to confuse products. Most people, for example, can't recall whether a tire commercial was sponsored by Firestone, Goodyear, or B.F. Goodrich. In addition, VCR viewers often fast-forward past the ads of TV shows they have recorded. Moreover, because "commercial spots" last only a short time (usually 30 seconds), the impact of the commercial is lost if the viewer is not paying attention. The brevity of TV ads also makes television a poor medium in which to educate viewers about complex products. Finally, television is the most expensive medium in which to advertise. A 30-second commercial during the NFL Super Bowl costs more than U.S.$2 million. Ads during prime-time evening hours are lower, but still expensive, at upwards of U.S.$190 000 for a 30-second commercial.

Direct Mail

direct mail
Printed advertisements, such as flyers, mailed directly to consumers' homes or places of business.

Canada Post
www.canadapost.com

Direct mail involves fliers or other types of printed advertisements mailed directly to consumers' homes or places of business. Direct mail allows the company to select its audience and personalize its message. Although many people discard "junk mail," targeted recipients with stronger-than-average interest are more likely to buy. Although direct mail involves the largest advance costs of any advertising technique, it does appear to have the highest cost effectiveness. Particularly effective have been "fax attacks," in which advertisers send their "mail" messages electronically via fax machines and get higher response rates than they would if they used Canada Post.

Radio

A tremendous number of people listen to the radio each day, and radio ads are inexpensive. In addition, since most radio is programmed locally, this medium gives advertisers a high degree of customer selectivity. For example, radio stations are already segmented into listening categories such as rock and roll, country and western, jazz, talk shows, news, and religious programming. Like television, however, radio ads are over quickly. And radio permits only an audio presentation. As well, people tend to use the radio as "background" while they are doing other things, paying little attention to advertisements.

Magazines

The many different magazines on the market provide a high level of consumer selectivity. The person who reads *Popular Photography* is more likely to be interested in the latest specialized lenses from Canon than is a *Gourmet* magazine subscriber. Magazine advertising allows for excellent reproduction of photographs and artwork that not only grab buyers' attention but also may convince them of the product's value. And magazines allow advertisers plenty of space for detailed product information. Magazines have a long life and tend to be passed from person to person, thus doubling and tripling the number of exposures. The latest gimmick in print advertising is to catch the reader's eye by having the top half of an advertisement printed right side up and the bottom half printed upside down.[24]

Outdoor Advertising

Outdoor advertising—billboards, signs, and advertisements on buses, taxis, and subways—is relatively inexpensive, faces little competition for customers' attention, and is subject to high repeat exposure. Unfortunately, companies have little control over who will see their advertisements. Because roadside billboards are prohibited on some major Ontario arteries, Moving Impressions Inc. introduced "rolling billboards"—advertisements attached to the sides of large freight trucks. The truck companies get a piece of the action.[25]

Word of Mouth

Consumers form very strong opinions about products as a result of conversations with friends and acquaintances. If **word of mouth** says that a product is good, higher product sales are very likely. Of course, word of mouth will also spread bad news about a product. Some companies rely heavily on word-of-mouth advertising. Big Rock Brewery does no advertising, but relies on word of mouth to expand its market share. It already has a 7 percent share of Alberta's draft beer market, and its exports to the United States are increasing rapidly.[26]

word of mouth
Opinions about the value of products passed among consumers in informal discussions.

Big Rock Brewery
www.bigrockbeer.com

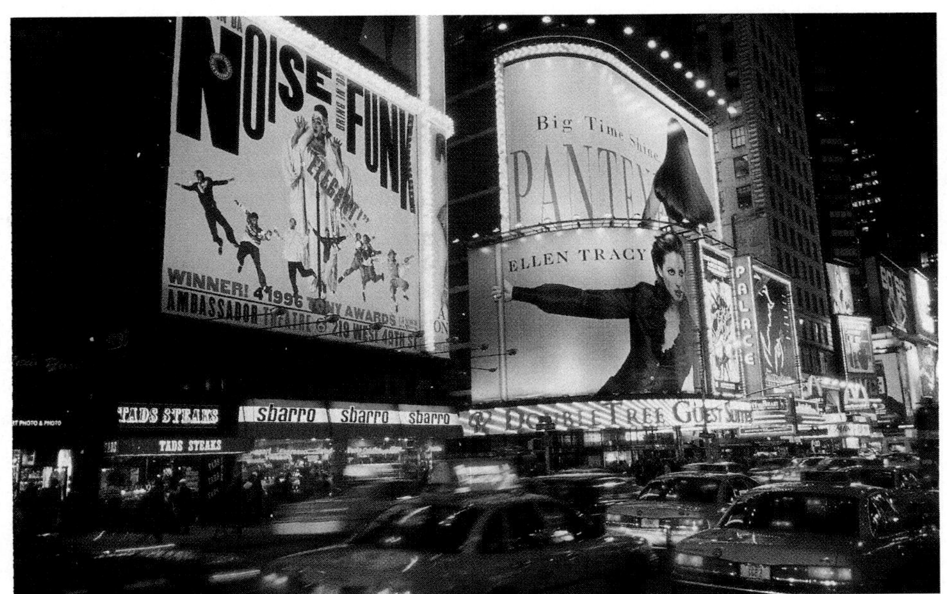

Speed and creativity have given billboards like these a new prominence in the world of advertising media. Instead of relying on highly skilled human artists, outdoor ad sellers can now commission digital creations that not only turn heads but also still cost less than most other media. Whereas it used to take a month to launch a billboard-based campaign, it now takes just days.

The Internet

The most recent advertising medium to arise is the internet, where thousands of well known and lesser-known firms have all placed ads. Although internet advertising is still in its infancy and offers high potential, most marketers recognize that it also has limitations. In particular, consumers don't want to wade through electronic pages looking at details about hundreds of products. One expert offers the disappointing opinion that most of the commercial advertisements on the internet may never be read by anyone.

Targeted advertising, however, is appealing because internet advertisers can measure the success of messages: They count how many people see each ad and track the number of click-throughs to the advertiser's own website. Electronic tracking devices relay such information as which ads generate more purchases, what sales margins result from each sale, and which ads attract the most attention from target audiences. DoubleClick, a global internet advertising firm, was one of the first companies to help other advertisers take advantage of the web's unique capacity for tailoring ad messages and tracking user behaviour online. DoubleClick also sells ad space that allows advertisers to reach as many as 80 million users worldwide on thousands of websites, such as Nasdaq.com, Zagat.com, TravelWeb, Macromedia, and Hollywood.com.[27]

Although still an immature marketing medium, the internet's potential for reaching customers continues to lure more advertisers. The Wired World box tells the story of one company that hired an emarketing specialist to help it devise and implement an internet marketing strategy.

IT'S A WIRED WORLD

The Sound Approach to Internet Marketing

You may not recognize the name Altec Lansing Technologies Inc., but you've probably listened to its products. Altec designs, manufactures, and markets high-quality sound systems for personal computers and home-entertainment systems. Its customers are mostly other companies—Compaq, Dell Computer, IBM, and Fujitsu—that use Altec industrial products to make consumer products. Altec has built strategic partnerships with such leading companies as Intel Corp., Dolby® Labs, and Microsoft, but Altec managers decided they could use some outside help getting into internet marketing. They selected Agency.Com Ltd., experts in ebusiness marketing, to determine how to best promote the company to competitive advantage on the net.

Step 1 called for an overall internet strategy: Altec and Agency.Com had to identify the firm's basic goal in net marketing and then devise a way to implement the best strategy for achieving that goal. One consideration was Altec's intention to maintain long-lasting relationships with business customers. Another consideration was changing industry trends. At the time, the markets for home computing, office computing, and home entertainment were converging, and the technology was changing from analog to digital. To address these considerations, Altec and Agency.Com proposed a strategy featuring five elements. Altec would:

1. Go online and stress relationship marketing to ensure ongoing relationships with customers
2. Position its products on quality—to provide the best audio experience possible
3. Secure current customers and encourage further sales
4. Seek new customers
5. Strive for greater brand recognition

The company's website, **www.alteclansing.com**, is now the focal point for all of its online activity. It is a commerce centre featuring information pages, and, along with email, it provides an online communication channel for building and maintaining customer relationships. Customers can access product listings, assess system requirements and performance specs, download speaker-system software, link directly to Altec distributors, and make online purchases. The site includes pages devoted to customer support and a feature called System Builders, which provides special services to companies that buy Altec systems for computers and sound systems. Altec also purchases space on third-party sites and uses co-marketing to bring new customers to the website.

Data Mining. The internet allows efficient targeting because volumes of data can be gathered electronically from internet users. User behaviour patterns can be traced by analyzing files of information, gathered over time, from millions of users. Called *data mining*, this efficient searching, sifting, and reorganizing of vast pools of data on user purchase behaviour reveals who has bought which products; how many, when, and over what website; how they paid; and so on. By analyzing what customers actually do, the emarketer can determine what subsequent purchases they are likely to make and then send them tailor-made ads.

To reach its full potential, ecommerce is going to have to improve its image. An Angus Reid/*Globe and Mail* poll of 1500 Canadians found that their main concern about ecommerce was security. People who had made at least one purchase on the internet were more likely to list security as their top concern than were those who had never purchased anything on the internet. People were concerned that their credit card number might end up in the wrong hands, and that their privacy would be invaded if they purchased on the internet.[28]

Virtual Advertising

An even newer method of advertising, called *virtual advertising*, uses digital implants of brands or products onto live or taped programming, giving the illusion that the product is part of the show. With this technique, an advertiser's product can appear as part of the television show, when viewers are paying more attention, instead of during commercial breaks. In a televised basketball game, for example, the digital image of a brand—for example, the round face of a Rolex watch or an Acura hubcap—can be electronically enlarged and superimposed on centre court without physically changing the playing floor. The image will be seen for the duration of the game. For videotaped movies, digital images can be inserted easily. A K-Mart shopping bag can be digitally added to the table in a kitchen scene, a Philips Flat TV can be superimposed on the wall for display during a dramatic scene in the den, and your favourite stars can be digitally dressed to display Polo and other brands on their shirts and sweaters.[29]

Other Advertising Channels

A combination of many additional media, including catalogues, sidewalk handouts, *Yellow Pages*, skywriting, telephone calls, special events, and door-to-door communications, make up the remaining advertisements to which Canadians are exposed. The combination of media through which a company chooses to advertise its products is called its **media mix**. Although different industries use different mixes, most depend on multiple media to advertise their products and services.

media mix
The combination of media through which a company chooses to advertise its products.

Types of Advertising

Regardless of the media used, advertisements fall into one of several categories. **Brand advertising** promotes a specific brand, such as Kodak 126 film, Air Canada, or Nike Air Jordan basketball shoes. A variation on brand advertising, **product advertising** promotes a general type of product or service such as dental services and milk. The "Got Milk?" advertisements are an example of product advertising. **Advocacy advertising** promotes a particular candidate or viewpoint, as in ads for political candidates at election time and anti-drug commercials. **Institutional advertising** promotes a firm's long-term image rather than a specific product.

brand advertising
Advertising that promotes a specific brand-name product.

product advertising
A variation on brand advertising that promotes a general type of product or service.

advocacy advertising
Advertising that promotes a particular viewpoint or candidate.

institutional advertising
Advertising that promotes a firm's long-term image, not a specific product.

retail advertising
Advertising by retailers designed to reach end-users of a consumer product.

co-operative advertising
Advertising in which a manufacturer together with a retailer or a wholesaler advertise to reach customers.

trade advertising
Advertising by manufacturers designed to reach potential wholesalers and retailers.

industrial advertising
Advertising by manufacturers designed to reach other manufacturers' professional purchasing agents and managers of firms buying raw materials or components.

In consumer markets, local stores usually sponsor **retail advertising** to encourage consumers to visit the store and buy its products and services. Larger retailers, such as Kmart and The Bay, use retail advertising both locally and nationally. Often retail advertising is actually **co-operative advertising**, with the cost of the advertising shared by the retailer and the manufacturer.

In industrial markets, to communicate with companies that distribute its products, some firms use **trade advertising** publications. For example, a firm that makes plumbing fixtures might advertise in *Hardware Retailer* to persuade large hardware stores to carry its products. And to reach the professional purchasing agent and managers at firms buying raw materials or components, companies use **industrial advertising**.

Preparing the Campaign with an Advertising Agency

advertising campaign
The arrangement of ads in selected media to reach target audiences.

An **advertising campaign** is the arrangement of ads in selected media to reach target audiences. It includes several activities that, taken together, constitute a program for meeting a marketing objective, such as introducing a new product or changing a company's image in the public mind. A campaign typically includes six steps:

1. Identifying the target audience
2. Establishing the advertising budget
3. Defining the objectives of the advertising messages
4. Creating the advertising messages
5. Selecting the appropriate media
6. Evaluating advertising effectiveness

advertising agency
A firm that specializes in creating and placing advertisements in the media for clients.

Advertising agencies—independent companies that provide some or all of their clients' advertising needs—help in the development of advertising campaigns by providing specialized services. The agency works together with the client company to determine the campaign's central message, create detailed message content, identify advertising media, and negotiate media purchases.[30]

A company hires an advertising agency to identify the target audience for its product and to ensure that the whole range of its advertising is aimed at that market. The agency is also responsible for planning the campaign and selecting the appropriate media. In this campaign for Stihl Power Tools, the Howard, Merrell & Partners advertising agency uses television as the best medium for putting the product in the most effective context. That context, in turn, is determined by the agency's understanding of the product and the crucial message that the company wants to get across. For Stihl, the message is the importance of buying the best possible equipment.

MUSIC UP AND UNDER THROUGHOUT
BROOKS V/O: I learned from...

my father and my grandfather,

don't think about trying to buy

but concentrate on buying the best.

You work hard for your money.

You've got to put it where you know it's gonna do the best.

That have held their quality.

But for my money,

I would go out and buy a Stihl chainsaw.

The advantage offered by agencies is expertise in developing advertising themes, message content, and artwork, as well as in coordinating advertising production and advising on relevant legal matters. Today, even more specialized agencies have emerged to cater to clients with very specific goals in specific industries or market segments. Some agencies, for example, specialize in the marketing of pharmaceuticals.

As payment for its services, the agency usually receives a percentage, traditionally 15 percent of the media purchase cost. For example, if an agency purchases a $1 million television commitment for a client's campaign, it would receive $150 000 for its services. (See Table 16.2 for a list of the top 10 advertising agencies in Canada.)

The globalization of business has affected advertising agencies, both in Canada and elsewhere. Increasingly, large U.S. companies are using one single agency (often headquartered somewhere other than Canada). The Association of Quebec Advertising Agencies says that big U.S. companies often bypass Montreal-based advertising agencies when they are developing advertising campaigns for Quebec. The group says that it is pointless to try to simply translate into French a campaign that is developed by a New York or Toronto agency for the rest of Canada. As an example of the right way to do it, consider advertisements for Pepsi. In the rest of English-speaking North America, big name singers and movie stars were used to promote the product, but in Quebec, successful commercials featured popular local comedian Claude Meunier to make Pepsi the number one soft drink in the province.[31]

Association of Quebec Advertising Agencies
www.aapq.qc.ca

PERSONAL SELLING

6. Outline the tasks involved in *personal selling* and list the steps in the *personal selling process*.

Virtually everyone has done some personal selling. Perhaps you had a lemonade stand or sold candy for the drama club. Or you may have gone on a job interview, selling your abilities and service as an employee to the interviewer's company. In personal selling, a salesperson communicates one-to-one with a potential customer to identify the customer's need and match that need with the seller's product.

Personal selling—the oldest form of selling—provides the personal link between seller and buyer. It adds to a firm's credibility because it provides buyers with someone to interact with and to answer their questions. Because it involves personal interaction, personal selling requires a level of trust between the buyer and the seller. When a buyer feels cheated by the seller, that trust has been broken and a negative attitude toward salespeople in general can develop.

personal selling
Promotional tool in which a salesperson communicates one-on-one with potential customers.

top

Table 16.2 The Top 10 Advertising Agencies in Canada

	Company	Annual Revenues (in millions of $)
1.	Maxxcom Inc.	$559.5
2.	Cossette Communication Group Inc.	157.6
3.	MacLaren McCann Canada Inc.	102.5
4.	BBDO Canada Inc.	74.2
5.	Envoy Communications Group Inc.	59.1
6.	Publicis Canada Inc.	51.0
7.	Palmer Jarvis DDB	35.4
8.	Leo Burnett Co. Ltd.	31.9
9.	Marketel	20.5
10.	CP Ltd.	10.4

Personal selling is the most expensive form of promotion per contact because presentations are generally made to one or two individuals at a time. Personal selling expenses include salespeople's compensation and their overhead, usually travel, food, and lodging. The average cost of an industrial sales call has been estimated at nearly $300.[32]

Telemarketing and Personal Sales

Costs have prompted many companies to turn to *telemarketing*: using telephone solicitations to conduct the personal selling process. Telemarketing is useful in handling any stage of this process and in arranging appointments for salespeople. For example, it cuts the cost of personal sales visits to industrial customers, each of whom requires about four visits to complete a sale. Such savings are stimulating the growth of telemarketing, which places billions of phone calls each year and is responsible for billions of dollars of sales in North America. It averages more than a $7 return for every dollar invested.[33]

Sales Force Management

sales force management

Setting goals at top levels of an organization; setting practical objectives for salespeople; organizing a sales force to meet those objectives; implementing and evaluating the success of a sales plan.

Sales force management means setting goals at top levels of the organization, setting practical objectives for salespeople, organizing a sales force that can meet those objectives, and implementing and evaluating the success of the overall sales plan. Obviously, then, sales management is an important factor in meeting the marketing objectives of any large company. In this section, we first describe the basic types of *personal selling situations*. Then we discuss the *personal selling tasks* for which managers set objectives and the *personal selling process* whose success managers judge.

Personal Selling Situations

Managers of both telemarketers and traditional salespeople must consider the ways in which personal sales activities are affected by the differences between consumer and industrial products:

retail selling

Selling a consumer product for the buyer's own personal or household use.

industrial selling

Selling products to other businesses, either for manufacturing other products or for resale.

- **Retail selling** is selling a consumer product for the buyer's personal or household use.
- **Industrial selling** is selling products to other businesses, either for the purpose of manufacturing other products or for resale.

Levi's, for instance, sells jeans to the retail clothing chain Gap Inc. (industrial selling). In turn, consumers purchase Levi's jeans at one of The Gap's stores (retail selling). Each of these situations has distinct characteristics. In retail selling, the buyer usually comes to the seller, whereas the industrial salesperson typically calls on the prospective buyer. An industrial decision may take longer than a retail decision because it involves more money, decision makers, and weighing of alternatives. As we saw in Chapter 15, industrial buyers are professional purchasing agents accustomed to dealing with salespeople. Consumers in retail stores, on the other hand, are not professionals and may actually be intimidated by salespeople. The Exercising Your Ethics box provides an interesting personal selling dilemma.

Personal Selling Tasks

Improving sales efficiency requires marketers to consider salespeople's tasks. Three basic tasks are generally associated with selling: *order processing, creative selling,* and *missionary selling*. Sales jobs usually require salespeople to perform all three tasks to some degree, depending on the product and the company.

EXERCISING YOUR ETHICS

Cleaning Up in Sales

The Situation

Selling a product—whether a good or a service—requires the salesperson to believe in it, to be confident of his or her own sales skills, and to keep commitments made to clients. Because so many people and resources are involved in making and delivering a product, numerous uncertainties and problems arise that can raise ethical issues. This exercise encourages you to examine some of the ethical issues that can surface in the personal selling process for industrial products.

The Dilemma

Along with 16 other newly hired graduates, Ethel Skilsel has just completed the sales training program for a new line of high-tech machinery that ABC Technologies manufactures for industrial cleaners. As an aspiring salesperson, Ethel is eager to get on the road and meet potential clients, all of whom are professional buyers for companies—such as laundries and dry cleaners, carpet cleaners, and military cleaners—that use ABC products or those of ABC's competitors. Ethel is especially enthusiastic about several facts that she learned during training: ABC's equipment is the most technically advanced in the industry, carries a 10-year performance guarantee, and is safe—both functionally and environmentally.

The first month was difficult but successful: In visits to seven firms, Ethel successfully closed three sales, earning handsome commissions (her pay is based on sales results) as well as praise from her sales manager. Moreover, after listening to her presentations, two more potential buyers had given verbal commitments and were about to sign for much bigger orders than any Ethel had closed to date. But as she was catching her flight to close those sales, Ethel received two calls—one from a client and one from a competitor. The client was just getting started with ABC equipment and was having some trouble: Employees stationed nearby were getting sick when the equipment was running. The competitor told Ethel that he thought ABC's new technology was environmentally unsafe because of noxious emissions.

Questions for Discussion

1. As a sales professional, does Ethel have any ethical obligations to ABC Technologies?
2. From an ethical standpoint, what should Ethel say to the two client firms she is scheduled to visit? What would you say to those clients?
3. Are there any ethical issues involved when an employee of one company calls a competitor's employee, as in this case of an ABC competitor calling Ethel? Explain.

Order Processing. At selling's most basic level, **order processing**, a salesperson receives an order and oversees the handling and delivery of that order. Route salespeople are often order processors. They call on regular customers to check the customer's supply of bread, milk, snack foods, or soft drinks. Then, with the customer's consent, they determine the size of the reorder, fill the order from their trucks, and stack the customer's shelves.

order processing
In personal sales, the receiving and follow-through on handling and delivery of an order by a salesperson.

Creative Selling. When the benefits of a product are not clear, **creative selling** may persuade buyers. Most industrial products involve creative selling because the buyer has not used the product before or may not be familiar with the features and uses of a specific brand. Personal selling is also crucial for high-priced consumer products, such as homes, where buyers comparison shop. Any new product can benefit from creative selling that differentiates it from other products. Finally, creative selling can help to create a need.

creative selling
In personal sales, the use of techniques designed to persuade a customer to buy a product when the benefits of the product are not readily apparent or the item is very expensive.

Missionary Selling. A company may also use **missionary selling** to promote itself and its products. Drug company representatives promote their companies' drugs to doctors who, in turn, prescribe them to their patients. The sale is actually made at the drugstore. In this case, the goal of missionary selling is to promote the company's long-term image rather than to make a quick sale.

missionary selling
In personal sales, the indirect promotion of a product by offering technical assistance and/or promoting the company's image.

The Personal Selling Process

Although all three sales tasks are important to an organization using personal selling, perhaps the most complicated is creative selling. It is the creative salesperson who is responsible for most of the steps in the personal selling process described here.

prospecting
In personal sales, the process of identifying potential customers.

qualifying
In personal sales, the process of determining whether potential customers have the authority to buy and the ability to pay for a product.

Prospecting and Qualifying. To sell, a salesperson must first have a potential customer or *prospect*. **Prospecting** is the process of identifying potential customers. Salespeople find prospects through past company records, customers, friends, relatives, company personnel, and business associates. Prospects must then be **qualified** to determine whether they have the authority to buy and the ability to pay.

Approaching. The approach refers to the first few minutes that a salesperson has contact with a qualified prospect. The success of later stages depends on the prospect's first impression of the salesperson, since this impression affects the salesperson's credibility. Salespeople need to present a neat, professional appearance and to greet prospects in a strong, confident manner.

Presenting and Demonstrating. Next, the salesperson must *present* the promotional message to the prospect. A presentation is a full explanation of the product, its features, and its uses. It links the product's benefits to the prospect's needs. A presentation may or may not include a demonstration of the product. But it is wise to demonstrate a product whenever possible, since most people have trouble visualizing what they have been told.

Handling Objections. No matter what the product, prospects will have some *objections*. At the very least, prospects will object to a product's price, hoping to get a discount. Objections show the salesperson that the buyer is interested in the presentation and which parts of the presentation the buyer is unsure of or has a problem with. They tell the salesperson what customers feel is important and, essentially, how to sell to them.

closing
In personal sales, the process of asking the customer to buy the product.

Closing. The most critical part of the selling process is the **closing**, in which the salesperson asks the prospective customer to buy the product. Successful salespeople recognize the signs that a customer is ready to buy. For example, prospects who start to figure out monthly payments for the product are clearly indicating that they are ready to buy. The salesperson should then attempt to close the sale. Salespeople can ask directly for the sale or they can indirectly imply a close. Questions such as "Could you take delivery Tuesday?" and "Why don't we start you off with an initial order of 10 cases?" are implied closes. Such indirect closes place the burden of rejecting the sale on the prospect, who will often find it hard to say no.

Following Up. The sales process does not end with the close of the sale. Most companies want customers to come back again. Sales *follow-up* activities include fast processing of the customer's order and on-time delivery. Training in the proper care and use of the product and speedy service if repairs are needed may also be part of the follow-up.

7. Describe the various types of *sales promotions*.

SALES PROMOTIONS

sales promotion
Short-term promotional activities designed to stimulate consumer buying or co-operation from distributors and other members of the trade.

Sales promotions are short-term promotional activities designed to stimulate consumer buying or co-operation from distributors, sales agents, or other members of the trade. They are important because they increase the likelihood that buyers will try products. They also enhance product recognition and can increase purchase size and amount. For example, soap may be bound into packages of four with the promotion, "Buy three and get one free."

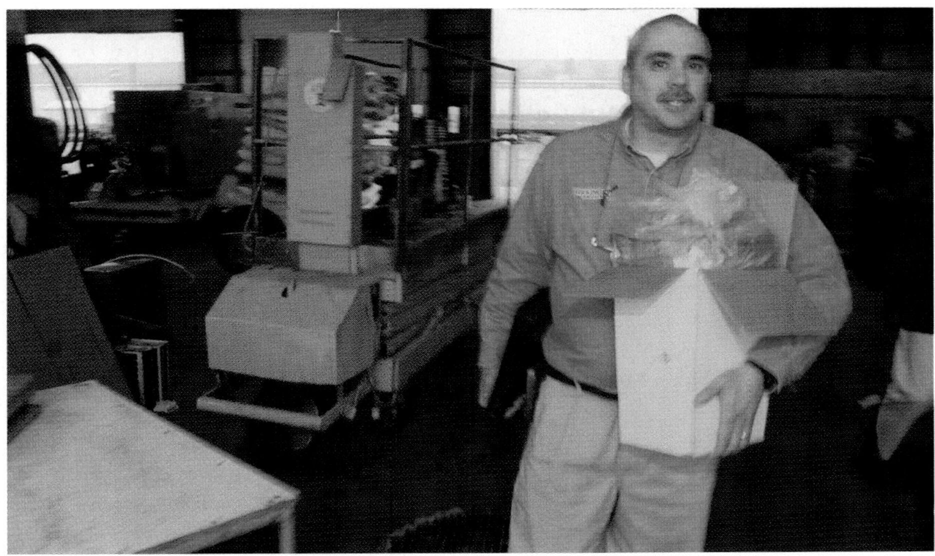

Tom Giorgio sells tools and other industrial supplies for W.W. Grainger Inc. After 9/11, the business of his best clients started to slump, so Giorgio made some changes in his selling strategies. He used to spend 80 percent of his time with 20 percent of his customers—the ones who bought big-ticket items, such as hydraulic coolers and belt-driven generators. Now, his presentations feature more modest products from the Grainger catalogue, such as light fixtures and janitorial supplies, and he calls more often on the prospects that are likely to buy them.

To be successful, sales promotions must be convenient and accessible when the decision to purchase occurs. If Harley-Davidson has a one-week motorcycle promotion and you have no local dealer, the promotion is neither convenient nor accessible to you, and you will not buy. But if The Bay offers a 20 percent-off coupon that you can save for use later, the promotion is convenient and accessible.

Types of Sales Promotions

The best known sales promotions are coupons, point-of-purchase displays, purchasing incentives (such as free samples, trading stamps, and premiums), trade shows, and contests and sweepstakes.

- Certificates entitling the bearer to stated savings off a product's regular price are **coupons**. Coupons may be used to encourage customers to try new products, to attract customers away from competitors, or to induce current customers to buy more of a product. They appear in newspapers and magazines and are often sent through direct mail.

coupon
A method of sales promotion featuring a certificate that entitles the bearer to stated savings off a product's regular price.

- To grab customers' attention as they walk through a store, some companies use **point-of-purchase (POP) displays**. Displays located at the end of the aisles or near the checkout in supermarkets are POP displays. POP displays often coincide with a sale on the item(s) being displayed. They make it easier for customers to find a product and easier for manufacturers to eliminate competitors from consideration. The cost of shelf and display space, however, is becoming more and more expensive.

point-of-purchase (POP) display
A method of sales promotion in which a product display is so located in a retail store as to encourage consumers to buy the product.

- Free samples and premiums are *purchasing incentives*. Free samples allow customers to try a product for a few days without any risk. They may be given out at local retail outlets or sent by manufacturers to consumers via direct mail. **Premiums** are free or reduced-price items, such as pens, pencils, calendars, and coffee mugs, given to consumers in return for buying a specified product. For example, Molson Canadian includes a free T-shirt with certain packages of its beer.[34] Premiums may not work as well as originally hoped, since customers may switch to a competitor's brand to get the premiums that company is offering.

premium
A method of sales promotion in which some item is offered free or at a bargain price to customers in return for buying a specified product.

- Periodically, industries sponsor **trade shows** for their members and customers. Trade shows allow companies to rent booths to display and

trade shows
A method of sales promotion in which members of a particular industry gather for displays and product demonstrations designed to sell products to customers.

demonstrate their products to customers who have a special interest in the products or who are ready to buy. Trade shows are relatively inexpensive and are very effective, since the buyer comes to the seller already interested in a given type of product. International trade shows are becoming more important.

- Customers, distributors, and sales representatives may all be persuaded to increase sales of a product through the use of *contests*. Distributors and sales agents may win a trip to Hawaii for selling the most pillows in the month of February.

PUBLICITY AND PUBLIC RELATIONS

publicity
Information about a company that is made available to consumers by the news media; it is not controlled by the company, but it does not cost the company any money.

Much to the delight of marketing managers with tight budgets, **publicity** is free. Moreover, because it is presented in a news format, consumers see publicity as objective and highly believable. Thus, it is an important part of the promotional mix. However, marketers often have little control over publicity.

For example, in the mid-1990s, Canadian Silken Laumann and her rowing teammates were stripped of their gold medals at an international competition because Laumann had inadvertently used a little-known product called Benadryl that contained a banned substance. The maker of Benadryl, Warner Wellcome, suddenly saw its product mentioned prominently on national newscasts, and it didn't have to pay a cent for the advertising. However, the company was not happy that its product was associated with an unfortunate incident.

The Miss Canada International organization also received negative publicity when the 1996 beauty contest winner was stripped of her title after being involved in a fight with a woman in a Newfoundland bar. Then, the

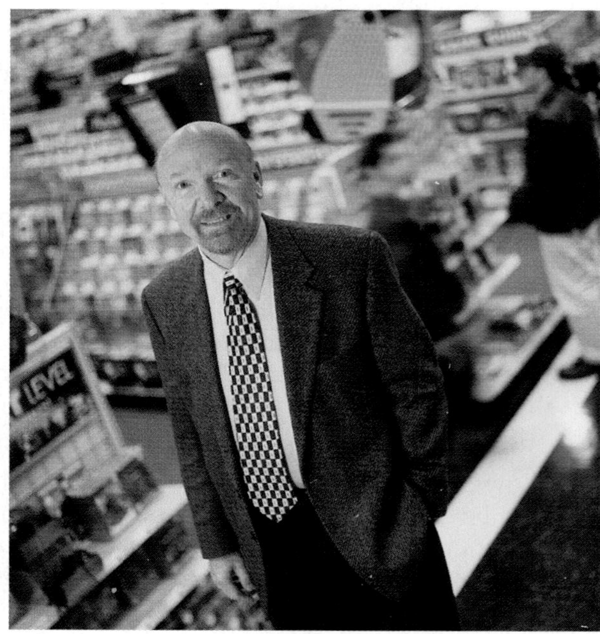

Best Buy, a 1900-store chain once known for consumer electronics and appliances, has added software and entertainment to its inventory and is now a major retailer of CDs and DVDs. To promote its entertainment products, Best Buy uses promotional tie-ins, such as deals to become the exclusive retailer of U2's latest DVD. In return, Best Buy spent $10 million to put U2 in newspaper circulars and on the sides of buses. Meanwhile, CEO Richard Schultze (right) pursues his strategy of putting electronics and entertainment under one roof.

first runner-up was denied the title because the pageant's organizer claimed she was not performing her duties. The first runner-up disputed these claims and accused the pageant's organizer of lying about her. All of this negative publicity was widely reported in newspapers across Canada.[35]

In contrast to publicity, **public relations** is company-influenced publicity. It attempts to establish a sense of goodwill between the company and its customers through public-service announcements that enhance the company's image. For example, a bank may announce that senior citizens' groups can have free use of a meeting room for their social activities. Corporate sponsorships of athletic events also help promote a company's image. At the 2000 Summer Olympics, Roots provided red-and-white hats to athletes, who wore them throughout the games. Roots has also been successful in getting other high-profile individuals to wear its products. And, in spite of doping and bribery scandals at the Olympic Games, big-name sponsors such as McDonald's, Coca-Cola, and UPS have continued to sponsor Olympic athletes. Most of them even extended their agreements for the Olympic Games in 2002 and 2004.

public relations
Public-service announcements by the company designed to enhance the company's image.

INTERNATIONAL PROMOTIONAL STRATEGIES

As we saw in Chapter 4, recent decades have witnessed a profound shift from "home-country" marketing to "multi-country" marketing and now to "global" marketing. Nowhere is this rapidly growing global orientation more evident than in marketing promotions, especially advertising.

Emergence of the Global Perspective

Every company that markets products in several countries faces a basic choice: use a *decentralized approach*, maintaining separate marketing management for each country, or adopt a *global perspective*, directing a coordinated marketing program at one worldwide audience. Thus, the **global perspective** is a philosophy that directs marketing toward a worldwide rather than toward local or regional markets.

global perspective
Company's approach to directing its marketing toward worldwide rather than local or regional markets.

The Movement Toward Global Advertising

A truly global perspective means designing products for multinational appeal—that is, genuinely global products.[36] A few brands, such as Coca-Cola, McDonald's, Mercedes Benz, Rolex, and Xerox, enjoy global recognition and have become truly global brands. Not surprisingly, globalization is affecting the promotional activities of such firms. In effect, they have already posed the question, "Is it possible to develop global advertising?"

Certainly, one universal advertising program would be more efficient and cost-effective than developing different programs for each of many countries. For several reasons, however, global advertising is not feasible for many companies. Four factors make global advertising a challenging proposition:

- *Product variations.* Even if a product has universal appeal, some variations, or slightly different products, are usually preferred in different cultures. In the magazine business, Hearst Corp. has expanded to 33 editions of *Cosmopolitan* magazine, including one for Central America; English and Spanish editions for the United States; and local editions for Italy, Turkey, Russia, Hong Kong, and Japan. *Reader's Digest* has 48 editions in 19 languages.

Marlboro is the number one cigarette in the world and one of the world's most successful brands. Why does the Marlboro Man succeed in selling cigarettes in Hanoi, the capital of Vietnam? Marlboro's maker, Philip Morris, has known for a long time that the image of the cowboy, coupled with an appeal to the urge for independence, is a universally attractive image.

- *Language differences.* Compared with those in other languages, ads in English require less print space and airtime because English is a more efficient and precise language than most others. Moreover, translations are often inexact and confusing: When Coke first went to China, the direct translation of "Coca-Cola" came out "Bite the wax tadpole." Advertising agencies have set up worldwide agency networks that can coordinate a campaign's central theme while allowing regional variations.
- *Cultural receptiveness.* There is a lot of difference across nations regarding the mass advertising of sensitive products (such as birth control or personal hygiene products), not to mention those for which advertising may be legally restricted (alcohol, cigarettes). A Canadian in Paris may be surprised to see nudity in billboard ads and even more surprised to find that France is the only country in the European Union (EU) that bans advertising or selling wine on the internet. In the EU and through much of Asia, comparative advertising is considered distasteful or even illegal.
- *Image differences.* Any company's image can vary from nation to nation, regardless of any advertising appeals for universal recognition. American Express, IBM, and Nestlé have better images in the United States than in the United Kingdom, where Heinz, Coca-Cola, and Ford have better images.

Universal Messages and Regional Advertising Skills

Although universal advertising themes are cost-effective and promote brand awareness, major companies have found that without a local or national identity, universal ads don't cause consumers to buy. Coca-Cola's "think global, act local" strategy and Nestlé's approach to small-scale local advertising call for ads tailored to different areas. Such ads are designed to toy with variations on a universal theme while appealing to local emotions, ideas, and values.

PROMOTIONAL PRACTICES IN SMALL BUSINESS

From our discussion so far, you might think that only large companies can afford to promote their goods and services. Although small businesses generally have fewer resources, cost-effective promotions can improve sales and enable small firms to compete with much larger firms.

Small-Business Advertising

Has any other development in modern history provided more advertising opportunities than the internet? Cheaper access to computing equipment, to online services, and to website expertise puts cyberspace within the grasp of nearly every firm. Still, owners must decide which audiences to target and what messages to send. And even though the web can instantaneously reach distant customers, other methods depend on the market that the small business is trying to reach: local, national, or international.

Non-prime-time ads on local or cable TV have good impact at costs within the reach of many small firms. More often, however, they use newspaper, radio, and, increasingly, direct mail to reach local markets. For year-round advertising, the *Yellow Pages* are popular for both industrial and consumer products. However, many small businesses, especially those selling to consumer markets, rely more on seasonal advertising.

Many businesses have grown by using direct mail, particularly catalogues. By purchasing mailing lists from other companies, small firms can cut costs with targeted mailings. The ability to target an audience also makes specialized magazines attractive to small businesses. When it comes to international markets, television, radio, and newspapers are too expensive for small businesses. Most small firms find direct mail and carefully targeted magazine ads the most effective tools.

The Role of Personal Selling in Small Business

As with advertising, small-business personal-selling strategies depend on intended markets. Some small firms maintain sales forces, especially in local markets, where clients can be quickly visited. But most small companies cannot afford to establish international offices (though some entrepreneurs, such as Art de Fehr of Winnipeg-based Palliser Furniture, do visit prospective customers in other countries). For most small businesses, even sending sales representatives overseas is too expensive. Others contract with *sales agencies*—companies that act on behalf of several clients. Because the costs of a national sales force are high, small companies prefer sales agencies and such methods as telemarketing. By combining telemarketing with catalogues or other print media, small businesses can sometimes compete with larger companies on a national scale. Syncsort Inc. combined a telemarketing staff with eight national sales reps to become the number-one developer of computer software for sorting data into convenient formats. Number two is IBM.

Small-Business Promotions

Small companies use the same sales promotion incentives as larger companies. Large firms tend to rely on coupons, POP displays, and sales contests, but because these tools are expensive and difficult to manage, small firms prefer premiums and special sales.[37] An automobile dealership, for example, might offer you a fishing reel if you come in to road-test a new four-wheel-drive vehicle. Service companies ranging from martial arts centres to dry cleaners frequently feature special sale prices.

SUMMARY OF LEARNING OBJECTIVES

1. **Identify a *product*, distinguish between *consumer* and *industrial products*, and explain the *product mix*.** A *product* is a good, service, or idea that is marketed to fill consumer needs and wants. A successful product is a *value package* that provides the right features and offers the right benefits. *Features* are the qualities, tangible and intangible, that a company builds into its products.

   Consumer products are divided into three categories that reflect buyer behaviour: (1) *Convenience goods* and *convenience services* are inexpensive and purchased often and with little expenditure of time and effort. (2) *Shopping goods* and *shopping services* are more expensive; consumers often compare brands and evaluate alternatives. (3) *Specialty goods* and *specialty services* are important and expensive purchases; consumers usually decide on precisely what they want and accept no substitutes.

   Industrial products can be divided into two categories: (1) *Expense items* are goods and services consumed within a year by firms producing other goods or services. (2) *Capital items* are permanent (expensive and long-lasting) goods and services. Capital services are those for which long-term commitments are made.

   The group of products that a company makes available for sale, whether consumer, industrial, or both, is its *product mix*. A group of similar products intended for similar but not identical buyers who will use them in similar ways is a *product line*. When companies expand beyond existing product lines, the result is multiple (or diversified) product lines, which allow a company to grow rapidly and can help to offset the consequences of slow sales in any one product line.

2. **Describe the new *product development process*, and trace the stages of the *product life cycle*.** To expand or diversify product lines, firms must develop and introduce new products. *Speed to market* is often key to a product's survival. To increase their chances of developing successful new products, many firms adopt some version of a basic seven-step process: (1) *Product ideas:* Searching for ideas for new products. (2) *Screening:* Eliminating all product ideas that do not mesh with the firm's abilities or objectives. (3) *Concept testing:* Using market research to get consumers' input about product benefits and prices. (4) *Business analysis:* Comparing manufacturing costs and benefits to see whether a product meets minimum profitability goals. (5) *Prototype development:* Producing a preliminary version of a product. (6) *Product testing and test marketing:* Going into limited production, testing the product to see if it meets performance requirements, and, if so, selling it on a limited basis. (7) *Commercialization:* Beginning full-scale production and marketing.

   In the development of services, there are two important differences in the seven-step model: (1) *Service ideas:* The search for service ideas means defining the service package: identifying the tangible and intangible features that characterize the service and stating service specifications. (2) *Service process design:* Instead of prototype development, services require a three-part service process design. Process selection identifies each step in the service, including the sequence and the timing, as well as worker requirements and facility requirements.

The *product life cycle (PLC)* is a series of four stages or phases characterizing a product's profit-producing life: (1) *Introduction:* Marketers focus on making potential consumers aware of the product and its benefits. (2) *Growth:* Sales begin to climb and the product begins to show a profit. (3) *Maturity:* Although the product earns its highest profit level, increased competition eventually leads to price cutting and lower profits; sales start to fall. (4) *Decline:* Sales and profits are further lost to new products in the introduction stage.

Foreign markets offer three approaches to longer life cycles: (1) In *product extension,* an existing product is marketed globally instead of just domestically. (2) With *product adaptation,* the basic product is modified to give it greater appeal in different countries. (3) *Reintroduction* means reviving for new markets products that are becoming obsolete in older ones.

3. **Explain the importance of *branding, packaging,* and *labelling.*** *Branding* is a process of using symbols to communicate the qualities of a particular product made by a particular producer. There are three types of brand names: (1) National brands, (2) Licensed brands, and (3) Private brand (or private label).

   With a few exceptions, a product needs some form of *packaging*—a physical container in which it is sold, advertised, or protected. A package makes the product attractive, displays the brand name, and identifies features and benefits. It also reduces the risk of damage, breakage, or spoilage, and it lessens the likelihood of theft. Every product has a *label* on its package that identifies its name, manufacturer, and contents; like packaging, labelling can help market a product.

4. **Identify the important objectives of *promotion* and discuss the considerations in selecting a *promotional mix.*** *Promotion* is any technique designed to sell a product. It is part of the *communication mix*: the total message any company sends to consumers about its products. Promotional techniques must communicate the uses, features, and benefits of products. There are two general values to be gained from any promotional activity: (1) *Communicating information,* and (2) *Creating more satisfying exchanges.*

   Besides the ultimate objective of increasing sales, marketers may use promotion to accomplish any of the following four goals: (1) *Communicating information,* (2) *Positioning products,* (3) *Adding value,* and (4) *Controlling sales volume.*

   Once its larger marketing objectives are clear, a firm must develop a *promotional strategy* to achieve them. Two strategies are available: (1) A *pull strategy* appeals directly to consumers who will demand the product from retailers who, in turn, will demand it from wholesalers. (2) A *push strategy* aggressively markets a product to wholesalers and retailers who then persuade consumers to buy it. Many large firms use a combination of pull and push strategies.

   There are four types of *promotional tools*: advertising, personal selling, sales promotions, and publicity and public relations. The best combination of these tools—the best *promotional mix*—depends on several factors, the most important of which is the target audience and buyer decision process: Marketers try to match promotional tools with stages in the buyer decision process.

5. **Discuss the most important *advertising strategies* and describe the key *advertising media*.** Advertising is paid, non-personal communication used by an identified sponsor to inform an audience about a product. The advertising strategies used for a product most often depend on the stage of the product life cycle the product is in. As products become established and competition increases, advertisers may choose one of three strategies: (1) *Persuasive advertising*, (2) *Comparative advertising*, and (3) *Reminder advertising*.

   Marketers use several different advertising media-specific communication devices for carrying a seller's message to potential customers: (1) *Television*, (2) *Newspapers*, (3) *Direct mail*, (4) *Radio*, (5) *Magazines*, (6) *Outdoor advertising*, (7) *Internet advertising*, and (8) *Virtual advertising*.

   Other advertising channels include catalogues, sidewalk handouts, *Yellow Pages*, skywriting, telephone calls, special events, and door-to-door communication. The combination of media through which a company advertises is its media mix. Different industries use different mixes, and most depend on a variety of media rather than on just one to reach target audiences.

   An *advertising campaign* is the arrangement of ads in selected media to reach target audiences. *Advertising agencies*—independent companies that provide some or all of a client's advertising needs—provide specialized services to help develop campaigns.

6. **Outline the tasks involved in *personal selling* and list the steps in the *personal selling process*.** In *personal selling*, a salesperson communicates one to one with potential customers to identify their needs and align them with a seller's products. It adds to a firm's credibility because it allows buyers to interact with and ask questions of the seller. Unfortunately, expenses are high, and high costs have turned many companies to *telemarketing*—the use of telephone solicitations to conduct the personal selling process.

   Sales force management means setting goals at the top levels of the organization, setting practical objectives for salespeople, organizing a sales force that can meet those objectives, and implementing and evaluating the success of the overall plan. Managers of both telemarketers and traditional salespeople must always consider the ways in which personal sales are affected by the differences between consumer and industrial products: (1) *Retail selling* promotes a consumer product for the buyer's own personal or household use. (2) *Industrial selling* promotes products to other businesses, either for the purpose of manufacturing other products or for resale.

   There are three basic tasks in personal selling: (1) *Order processing*, (2) *Creative selling*, and (3) *Missionary selling*.

   The creative salesperson goes through most of the following six steps in the personal selling process. (1) *Prospecting and qualifying*: Prospecting identifies potential customers, who are then qualified to determine whether they have the authority to buy and ability to pay. (2) *Approaching*: The first few minutes of a contact with a qualified prospect make up the approach. (3) *Presenting and demonstrating*: After the approach, the salesperson makes a presentation. (4) *Handling objections*: Objections pinpoint the parts of the presentation with which the buyer has a problem and which the salesperson must overcome. (5) *Closing*: In the closing, the salesperson asks the prospective customer to buy the product. (6) *Following up*: To cement lasting relationships with buyers, sellers supply additional after-sale services.

7. **Describe the various types of sales promotions.** *Sales promotions* are short-term promotional activities designed to stimulate consumer buying or co-operation from members of the trade. The following are the best-known forms of promotions: (1) Certificates entitling bearers to savings off regular prices are *coupons*. (2) To grab customers' attention as they move through stores, companies use *point-of-purchase (POP) displays*. (3) *Free samples* are purchasing incentives that allow customers to try products without risk. (4) *Premiums* are gifts to consumers in return for buying certain products. (5) Industries sponsor *trade shows*, at which companies rent booths to display and demonstrate products to customers with a special interest in them. (6) Customers, distributors, and sales reps may all be persuaded to increase sales by means of *contests*.

   Publicity is a promotional tool in which information about a company or product is created and transmitted by general mass media. It is free, and because it is presented in a news format, consumers often see it as objective and credible. However, marketers often have little control over it, and it can be as easily detrimental as beneficial. *Public relations* is company-influenced publicity that seeks to build good relations with the public and to deal with unfavourable events.

KEY TERMS

advertising agency, 572
advertising campaign, 572
advertising medium, 567
advertising, 567
advocacy advertising, 571
brand advertising, 571
brand awareness, 560
brand equity, 559
brand loyalty, 563
branding, 559
capital items, 552
closing, 576
comparative advertising, 567
Consumer Packaging and Labelling Act, 563
convenience goods/services, 552
co-operative advertising, 572
copyright, 563
coupon, 577
creative selling, 575
direct mail, 568
expense items, 552
features, 551
global perspective, 579
industrial advertising, 572
industrial selling, 574
informative advertising, 567
institutional advertising, 571
label, 563
licensed brands, 561
media mix, 571
missionary selling, 575
national brands, 561
order processing, 575
packaging, 563
patent, 562
personal selling, 573
persuasive advertising, 567
point-of-purchase (POP) display, 577
premium, 577
private brands, 562
product adaptation, 559
product advertising, 571
product extension, 559
product life cycle (PLC), 557
product line, 553
product mix, 553
product positioning, 565
promotion, 564
promotional mix, 566
prospecting, 576
public relations, 579
publicity, 578
pull strategy, 565
push strategy, 565
qualifying, 576
reintroduction, 559
reminder advertising, 567
retail advertising, 572
retail selling, 574
sales force management, 574
sales promotion, 576
service package, 557
service process design, 557
shopping goods/services, 552
specialty goods/services, 552
speed to market, 556
technology, 553
trade advertising, 572
trade shows, 577
trademark, 562
value package, 551
word of mouth, 569

QUESTIONS AND EXERCISES

Review Questions

1. What are the various classifications of consumer and industrial products? Give an example of a good and a service for each category different from the examples given in the text.

2. List the four stages in the product life cycle and discuss some of the ways in which a company can extend product life cycles.

3. Explain how brand names can be used to foster brand loyalty.

4. What are the differences between push and pull strategies? Why would a firm choose one over the other?

5. Compare the advantages and disadvantages of different advertising media.

6. What are the advantages of personal selling over other promotional tools?

7. Which promotional tools have proven most useful in mounting global advertising campaigns? Why?

8. Is publicity more or less available to small firms than to larger firms? Why?

Analysis Questions

9. How would you expect the branding, packaging, and labelling of convenience shopping and specialty goods to differ? Why? Give examples to illustrate your answers.

10. Take a look at some of the advertising conducted by businesses based in your area. Choose two campaigns—one that you think is effective and one that you think is ineffective. What differences in the campaigns make one better than the other?

11. Select a good or service that you have purchased recently. Try to retrace the relevant steps in the buyer decision process as you experienced it. Which steps were most important to you? Least important?

12. Find examples of publicity about some business, either a local firm or a national firm. Did the publicity have, or is it likely to have, positive or negative consequences for the business? Why?

Application Exercises

13. Interview the manager of a local manufacturing firm. Identify the company's different products according to their positions in the product life cycle.

14. Select a product that is sold nationally. Identify as many media used in its promotion as you can. Which medium is used most often? On the whole, do you think the campaign is effective? Why or why not?

15. Interview the owner of a local small business. Identify the company's promotional objectives and strategies, and the elements in its promotional mix. What, if any, changes would you suggest? Why?

16. Check out your college or university's website and determine how effective it is as a tool for promoting your school.

BUILDING YOUR BUSINESS SKILLS

Greeting Start-Up Decisions

Goal

To encourage students to analyze the potential usefulness of two promotional methods—personal selling and direct mail—for a start-up greeting card company.

Situation

You are the marketing adviser for a local start-up company that makes and sells specialty greeting cards in a city of 400 000. Last year's sales totalled 14 000 cards, including personalized holiday cards, birthday cards, and special-events cards for individuals. Although revenues increased last year, you see a way of further boosting sales by expanding into card shops, grocery stores, and gift shops. You see two alternatives for entering these outlets:

1. Use direct mail to reach more individual customers for specialty cards
2. Use personal selling to gain display space in retail stores

Your challenge is to convince the owner of the start-up company which alternative is the more financially sound decision.

Method

Step 1

Get together with four or five classmates to research the two kinds of product segments: *personalized cards* and *retail store cards*. Find out which of the two kinds of marketing promotions will be more effective for each of the two segments. What will be the reaction to each method from customers, retailers, and card company owners?

Step 2

Draft a proposal to the company owner. Leaving budget and production details to other staffers, list as many reasons as possible for adopting direct mail. Then list as many reasons as possible for adopting personal selling. Defend each reason. Consider the following reasons in your argument:

- *Competitive environment:* Analyze the impact of other card suppliers that offer personalized cards and cards for sale in retail stores.
- *Expectations of target markets:* Who buys personalized cards, and who buys ready-made cards from retail stores?
- *Overall cost of the promotional effort:* Which method—direct mail or personal selling—will be more costly?
- *Marketing effectiveness:* Which promotional method will result in greater consumer response?

Follow-Up Questions

1. Why do you think some buyers want personalized cards? Why do some consumers want ready-made cards from retail stores?
2. Today's computer operating systems provide easy access to software for designing and making cards on home PCs. How does the availability of this product affect your recommendation?
3. What was your most convincing argument for using direct mail? For using personal selling?
4. Can a start-up company compete in retail stores against industry giants such as Hallmark?

MASTERING BUSINESS ESSENTIALS

Episode 10 focuses on the ways that marketers communicate with consumers at each stage in the buying process. It also shows how advertisers use different strategies to inform consumers about products they may need or want. *This episode enhances the coverage of promotions, especially advertising, as a means of both informing consumers and appealing to their changing needs and wants.*

CRAFTING YOUR BUSINESS PLAN

Hitting the Sauce Customer

The Purpose of the Assignment

1. To familiarize students with promotion-related issues that a sample firm addresses in developing its business plan, within the framework of Business PlanPro (BPP) software package.
2. To demonstrate how four chapter topics—promotional strategy, product positioning, personal selling, and advertising—can be integrated as components of the BPP planning environment.

Assignment

After reading Chapter 16 in the textbook, open the BPP software and look for information on plans for promotion as it applies to a sample firm, a salsa manufacturer: Salvadore's Sauces (Salvadore's, Inc.). To find Salvadore's, do the following:

Open Business PlanPro. If you are asked whether you want to "create a new business plan" or to "open an existing plan," select "create a new business plan" (even though you are not going to create a plan at this time). You will then be taken to the Business PlanPro EasyPlan Wizard. On the screen, click on the option entitled **Research It**. You will then be presented with a new list of options, including Sample Plan Browser. After clicking on the **Sample Plan Browser**, go down its alphabetical list of sample plans and double-click on **Salsa Manufacturer**, which is the location for Salvadore's Sauces. The screen you are looking at is the introduction page for the business plan of Salvadore's Sauces. On this page, scroll down until you reach the Table of Contents for Salvadore's Sauces business plan.

Now respond to the following items:

1. As we saw in Chapter 16, product positioning is an important promotional objective. What are Salvadore's Sauces' plans for positioning its products? [Sites to see in BPP (for this item): On the **Table of Contents** page, click on **4.1 Market Segmentation** and read its contents. After returning to the **Table of Contents** page, click on each of the following in turn: **4.3.1 Industry Participants, 4.3.2 Distribution Patterns, 4.3.3 Competition and Buying Patterns,** and **4.3.4 Main Competitors**.]
2. Describe Salvadore's Sauces' promotional strategy. [Sites to see in BPP: On the **Table of Contents** page, click on and read **5.1.2 Promotion Strategy**. After returning to the **Table of Contents** page, click on **5.1.1 Pricing Strategy**.]
3. What kinds of advertising does Salvadore's Sauces plan to use? Do you agree or disagree with the firm's advertising plans? Explain. [Sites to see in BPP: On the **Table of Contents** page, click on each of the following in turn: **4.0 Market Analysis Summary** and **5.0 Strategy and Implementation Summary**.]
4. What role does personal selling play in the promotional plans at Salvadore's? Who will do the personal selling? Are these individuals qualified for the job? [Sites to see in BPP (for this assignment): On the **Table of Contents** page, click on **5.2 Sales Strategy** and **5.2.2 Sales Programs**. After returning to the **Table of Contents** page, click on each of the following: **6.0 Management Summary** and **6.2 Management Team**.]

VIDEO EXERCISE

Revving Up Promotion: BMW Motorcycles

Learning Objectives

The purpose of this video is to help you:

1. Describe the purpose of product promotion.
2. Understand how and why a company must coordinate the elements in its promotional mix.
3. Explain how message and media work together in an effective advertising campaign.

Synopsis

Although car buyers are quite familiar with the BMW brand, it enjoys much lower awareness among motorcycle buyers. This low profile is a major challenge for BMW Motorcycles, which has been producing high-end motorcycles for more than 80 years. The company's main promotional goal is to attract serious riders who are looking for an exceptional riding experience. To meet this objective, marketers carefully coordinate every promotional detail to convey a unified brand message positioning the BMW as "the ultimate riding machine." Using print and television advertising, personal selling by dealers, sales promotion, and a virtual showroom on the web, BMW is driving its brand message home to motorcycle enthusiasts.

Discussion Questions

1. *For analysis:* What are the advantages of using more personal advertising copy and encouraging customers to become missionaries for BMW motorcycles?
2. *For analysis:* Why would BMW use its website as a virtual showroom rather than as a site for selling directly to consumers?
3. *For application:* What are some ways that BMW might use public relations to build brand awareness?
4. *For application:* How might BMW use direct mail to bring potential buyers into dealerships?
5. *For debate:* Should BMW develop and promote a new brand to differentiate its motorcycles not only from competing brands but from BMW cars as well? Support your position.

Online Exploration

Visit the BMW Motorcycle site at **www.bmwmotorcycle.com** and observe the links on the home page. Go to the pages promoting new models and pre-owned motorcycles. Finally, follow the link to the contact page. Which elements of the promotional mix are evident on this site? How does the site support the company's message about the "ultimate riding machine"? How does the site make it easy for customers to obtain more information and ask questions about BMW motorcycles and dealer services?

EXPLORING THE NET

Marketing Help Is Just a Click Away

In the first part of this chapter, we discussed advertising promotions, including advertising strategies and media. The choice of media, or the media mix, includes both direct mail and internet advertising for reaching specific markets. We saw also that firms sometimes call upon outside specialists to help formulate effective advertising campaigns. In what ways can such outside specialists help a company plan its advertising? What services do they offer, and what value do those services provide? What kinds of results might a client firm expect from such specialists?

Let's look further into these questions by exploring the website of a successful internet company—DoubleClick Inc.—at **www.doubleclick.com**. At the top of the home page are several links, including those labelled Advertisers, Direct Marketers, and Web Publishers.

Begin at the top of the home page by clicking **About DoubleClick** and read that page.

1. What is DoubleClick's main line of business?

Now return to the top of the home page and click on Direct Marketers. In the drop-down menu, select Direct Marketing. Scan the categories of available services:

2. Of what value is Abacus for developing an advertising campaign?
3. In what ways might DoubleClick's direct mail services be of value to an advertiser?

Select **Products** and scan the list of available services:

4. In what ways might a client expect to benefit from the DoubleClick Brand Network?

Return to the homepage and click on **Customer Solutions**. Examine the contents of this page.

5. What kinds of advertising services are available?

Concluding Case 16-1

Who Wants to Be a Survivor?

It's more often famine than feast in the struggle for survival in the network-TV jungle. Consider both the weight that ABC was able to throw around because of Regis Philbin's *Who Wants to Be a Millionaire*? and, more recently, the show's anemic performance in the ratings. The game show that propelled ABC into the network ratings lead just a year earlier suffered a whopping 50 percent ratings drop at the end of the 2001 viewing season. The network's most reliable sitcoms—*The Drew Carey Show* and *Dharma & Greg*—have also tumbled in the ratings that measure program viewership.

Like other products, it seems, even the very best programs go through life cycles, and for TV shows, the end comes when viewers stop watching. The relationship between viewers and programs is simply a matter of demand and supply. Tastes change and, eventually, even producers of the top shows can only watch helplessly as viewers channel surf for more interesting or exciting programs. The financial aspect of this phenomenon is fairly simple: Without enough viewers, networks lose money. Viewers lost interest in ABC network's lineup, and with no new hit shows to boost ratings, ABC plummeted from a U.S.$150-million profit in 2001 to a projected U.S.$300-million loss in 2002—a reversal in fortunes of nearly half a billion dollars. The network's ill-fated attempt to replace Ted Koppel and *Nightline* with David Letterman and *The Late Show* from CBS was an effort to attract a larger audience—especially younger viewers—during the evening hours. ABC also opted to refurbish another old warhorse, *Monday Night Football*, by bringing in John Madden, the popular football commentator from Fox.

Unfortunately, a TV network's lifeblood is new programming. To turn things around, ABC needs a viewer-friendly mix of new shows, upgrades of existing programs, and successful properties purchased from competitors. ABC's last in-house megahit was 1999's *Who Wants to Be a Millionaire?*, which, according to some critics, the network mishandled in two ways. First, *Millionaire* probably suffered from overexposure when ABC began airing four episodes a week during the 2000 season. Especially among younger viewers, familiarity quickly bred contempt. "Just over a year ago," lamented ABC co-chairman Lloyd Braun, "we were No. 1..." and had four shows in the top 10. Of course, "...all four shows were *Millionaire*." ABC further compounded the problem, not only by putting too many eggs in its *Millionaire* basket, but also by failing to look to the future with other programs to help carry the ratings load. Seduced by *Millionaire's* initial blockbuster ratings and envisioning it as a hit for years to come, network executives cut investment in new shows. "They rode it like the Pony Express," says one industry analyst, "and then had no horse to jump to" when they had ridden *Millionaire* into the ground.

Now, ABC's prime-time audience is down 23 percent, far behind NBC and CBS and only slightly ahead of Fox. The network has no shows in the Top 10, and its only Top 30 shows—*NYPD Blue* and *The Practice*—are on the downside of their life cycles. Translated into bottom-line terms, the ratings hemorrhage means that for every available minute of prime-time advertising, the network is generating U.S.$100 000 less than it was a year ago.

As one of television's all-time most profitable shows—earning more than half a billion dollars in profits for ABC—does *Millionaire*'s demise spell doomsday or just a bump in the road for ABC? CEO Michael Eisner of ABC's parent company, Disney, says that the problem can be solved. And after all, concedes Goldman Sachs analyst Richard Greenfield, "It only takes one or two hit shows to jump-start a network." But coming up with a new show is doubtful when spending has been cut on program development. It's going to take time for ABC to rebuild its entertainment lineup. As ABC's Braun admits, "This won't be fixed overnight."

As it struggles for higher Nielson ratings, ABC, rather than seeking the widest possible audience, is looking for programs that appeal to younger viewers. Why? Because the 18–49 age group generates more lucrative ad revenue than do older audiences. Sponsors who pay for advertising are the driving force in programming for younger audiences. They want to reach consumers who are hard to reach by other methods, and they are willing to pay premium fees for ads that do the trick. In March 2002, an episode of Fox's *That 70s Show*, a comedy about teenagers, drew just 9.9 million viewers, while CBS's *JAG*, a drama with a military background, boasted 17.1 million. But fewer than 2 million *JAG* viewers were 18-to-34-year-olds, whereas 3.5 million *That 70s Show* viewers fell into the coveted age group. To reach those profitable 18-to-34-year-olds, sponsors will pay more to advertise on *That 70s Show* even though more people watch *JAG*.

When it comes to television programming, it is difficult to separate the design of the programming from the methods that will be used to advertise products to viewers. Marketing researchers know which shows various demographic groups watch, which products they prefer, and which advertising methods will reach them. The challenge, therefore, is to develop new programs that will appeal to the target audience. In the United States and Canada, the 18-to-49 group represents nearly 50 percent of the population above the age of one. Moreover, they're willing to change brands, and they tend to buy more of the kinds of products that are advertised on television: beer, SUVs, fast food, computers, movies, and soft drinks.

Older viewers, although they typically have more money to spend than their younger counterparts, are more limited in the scope of their purchasing, usually buying such products as travel, retirement plans, and cars. Not surprisingly, they don't watch the same TV shows as 18- to 49-year-olds.

Questions for Discussion

1. How would you describe the pattern of life cycles among TV programs? What social factors affect program life cycles?
2. What methods for new product development are most common in this industry? Cite some examples.
3. Some people might argue that the age and spending considerations in this case seem illogical. ABC, for example, seems intent on attracting younger viewers even though older people have more money. Does that make good business sense? Explain.
4. From a cost-and-profit standpoint, which strategy makes more sense: developing new television programs starting from scratch or buying successful programs from other networks?
5. If you were a network executive, what factors would you consider in pricing programs for various sponsors? ◆

Concluding Case 16-2

Brand Name Prescription Drugs

There was a time when patients didn't care about the name of the drug that the doctor prescribed—so long as it cured the ailment. Not so in today's consumer-empowered environment. If you watch television, you know the names of such medicines as Vioxx, Prilosec, Zocor, Viagra, Celebrex, and Allegra whether you need them or not. What's more, a lot of people want to know more about them. It's all part of a revolutionary marketing movement known as direct-to-consumer (DTC) marketing.

DTC is a form of "pull" marketing in which ads tell consumers about a prescription drug and encourage them to ask their doctors about it. Some ads, for example, target allergy sufferers. "Congested? Stuffed Up? Watery Eyes? Talk to your doctor about Allegra-D, send in for your rebate, and start enjoying real relief today."

In using DTC, drug makers are appealing to end users—today's informed health-care consumers—who, instead of passively entrusting themselves to a doctor's care, not only expect educational information about available treatments, but also often engage in self-diagnosis. The concept behind DTC is to motivate the consumer, rather than the MD, to initiate the consumption of a specific drug. Ads are designed to increase consumer awareness, thereby stimulating more inquiries to MDs who, in turn, will prescribe the advertised drug more often than its competitors.

Generating a flurry of spiralling ad expenditures and skyrocketing drug prices, DTC advertising is the most prominent and expensive—and controversial—promotional method in the history of pharmaceuticals. Drug companies argue that DTC encourages patients to see their doctors and informs them about the latest health news. Critics counter that DTC drives up prices and stimulates excessive spending on drugs. They also charge that ads often contain incomplete or misleading information that could lead to misuse.

And how do physicians feel about such changes in promotional conditions? In many cases, they are less than enthusiastic when a patient comes into their office and demands a drug they saw advertised on television. Doctors also complain that ads are biased, circulate incomplete information, and have already degenerated into a competition to see who can sell the most antihistamines or nasal sprays. The patient, says Dr. Angelo Agro, "is at best incompletely informed and at worst...deluded." Agro also argues that DTC ads undermine the MD's credibility, especially if the doctor disagrees with the patient's choice among advertised drugs.

The pharmaceuticals business is risky because it involves expensive research and development (R&D) for new drugs. Sales revenues must recover not only the costs of developing successful drugs, but also the costs of unsuccessful research. To stimulate sales, drug companies have historically relied on various methods for persuading doctors to prescribe products, such as sponsoring educational events, providing promotional gifts, and funding medical research. But the shift to DTC promotions is an expensive multimedia thrust that embraces TV (national and cable), radio, telephone (for instance, 1-800-for-Nexium), internet (**www.purplepill.com**), magazines, newspapers, Sunday supplements, and outdoor advertising. Both advertising costs and drug prices are skyrocketing, while product information—sometimes informative, sometimes misleading—is at an all-time high.

In 2002, the National Health Council (NHC), a nonprofit group of 118 U.S. health-related organizations, concluded that, on balance, DTC marketing is more beneficial than detrimental to most patients and doctors. Says the NHC report, "The Council recognizes that DTC advertising provides important information to consumers and patients, which often is beneficial to their health." It adds, however, that while some ads are merely unclear about the conditions that drugs are supposed to treat, others fail to report product risks. Some even make drugs seem more effective than they are. The NHC also reports that one-third of MDs are concerned about the negative effects of DTC advertising on physician–patient relationships.

Aside from questions of consumer motivation and patient–doctor relationships, controversy rages over how to curb the rising prices of prescription drugs. A 2002 study of health-care managers reported that DTC advertising—the fastest-growing expense in the industry's promotional budget—is the number-one factor in the explosion of drug costs. It is greater even than the cost of developing new drugs. The study overwhelmingly singles out pharmaceutical companies—rather than consumers, government, or health-care organizations—as being responsible for high drug costs.

At the same time, it advises caution in dealing with the problem. Most respondents dislike the idea of government management of prices, arguing that bureaucrats aren't qualified to set prices and would just make matters worse. Let the free market, say these experts, correct itself. A dissenting minority, however, noted that runaway costs must be kept down—and that the only way to do this is to regulate the industry. DTC advertising, they contend, should be banned, and price controls should be put in place.

How do matters look to observers outside the United States? Foreign observers are wary about the U.S. experience and the danger posed by DTC to health-care inside their own borders. Here in Canada, for example, DTC ads are banned (but, of course, viewers can see them on U.S.-based cable TV). Officials in the European Union have also banned DTC ads, but they are experimenting with a pilot plan to "ensure the availability of better, clear, and reliable information" on authorized drugs. The EU allows drug makers to supply limited information, but only when patients request it. While protecting the public from misleading information is a prime goal, officials also worry that U.S.-style DTC advertising could spur both higher prescription costs and the use of unsafe and unnecessary drugs. Gradually, the ban on DTC broadcast ads may be softened, because health-conscious Europeans and Canadians are already getting doses of medical information from other sources, especially from the internet.

So is DTC advertising good, bad, or a little of both?

Questions for Discussion

1. Why do you suppose TV is the industry's medium of choice for DTC promotions?
2. In addition to prescription drugs, can you think of any other industry that uses a DTC promotional strategy? What elements must be present in the marketing environment for such a strategy to be successful?
3. Why are physicians in the United States concerned about the effect of DTC advertising on doctor–patient relationships? List some ways in which those relationships might be changed. Are the changes you listed good or bad?
4. List at least four measures that drug companies might take to hold down consumer prices. What are the disadvantages and advantages of each measure?
5. What might the U.S. government do to prevent the rise of prescription drug prices? Outline the pros and cons for each action you identify. Which action(s) do you recommend?
6. Has the emergence of DTC advertising created any ethical or social-responsibility issues for physicians? Explain why or why not. ◆

CHAPTER 17 Pricing and Distributing Goods and Services

After reading this chapter, you should be able to:

1. Identify the various *pricing objectives* that govern pricing decisions and describe the price-setting tools used in making these decisions.
2. Discuss *pricing strategies* and tactics for existing and new products.
3. Explain the distribution mix, the different *channels of distribution*, and different *distribution strategies*.
4. Explain the differences between *merchant wholesalers* and *agents/brokers*, and describe the activities of e-intermediaries.
5. Identify the different types of *retailing* and *retail stores*.
6. Define *physical distribution* and describe the major activities in *warehousing* operations.
7. Compare the five basic forms of *transportation* and explain how distribution can be used as a marketing strategy.

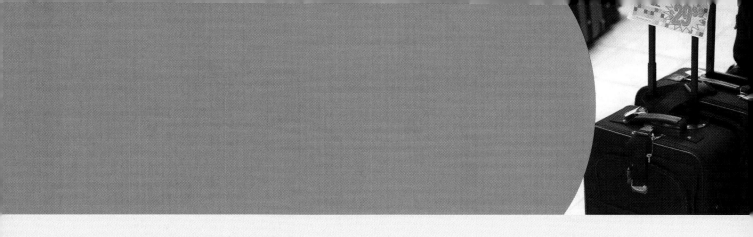

What's the Price?

In this era of intense global competition, customers are carefully looking for the lowest prices, and companies are constantly looking for ways to increase the prices they charge. The success of Wal-Mart and the pricing revolution that is occurring in the commercial airline industry (see the Business Today box in this chapter) are just two examples of the importance of price in the marketing activity of business firms. Pricing is important for both consumer and industrial products.

Consumer Products

Some companies use the strategy of raising prices without *appearing* to have done so. In 2002, Kimberly-Clark Corp. cut the price of its diapers, but cut the quantity in the package even more. This was, in effect, a 5 percent price increase. In 2003, General Motors started charging extra for antilock brakes instead of including them at no charge as it used to do. This also constituted a price increase. At Goodyear Tire & Rubber Co., large tire distributors had routinely been given big discounts on the tires they purchased. But the company discovered that the discounts were so deep that the distributors were ordering large quantities of tires and selling them outside their normal business area. This reduced the sales of smaller distributors in other areas that Goodyear also sold tires to, and had the overall effect of reducing the price of Goodyear tires in the marketplace. In 2003, Goodyear reduced the discounts it had been giving to its biggest distributors, and found that revenue per tire went up.

The pricing of cigarettes is another interesting case. The North American cigarette market is an oligopoly that is dominated by a few very large tobacco companies like Imperial Tobacco, R.J. Reynolds, Philip Morris, Brown & Williamson, and Lorillard Tobacco. The pricing strategy that has historically been used by these companies is to increase prices to maintain (or increase) profits. This strategy has worked for decades because customers have been very loyal to their favourite brand.

But the cigarette business has become much more difficult for the major cigarette companies in the last few years—they must put explicit warnings on their products indicating that cigarettes are dangerous, cigarettes are highly taxed by the government, and class action lawsuits have resulted in some billion dollar judgments against the major companies. To make matters worse, some new cigarette manufacturing companies have started up and are pricing their cigarettes as much as 50 percent lower than the majors. The majors are responding with incentives like 2-for-1 deals, but that has reduced their profits by 50 percent or more. The major cigarette companies are likely to have less control over the market than they used to, and they are going to have much more difficulty simply raising prices in the future.

Industrial Products

Companies that sell to industrial customers typically set prices by figuring out how much it costs to make a product and then adding a markup to that number. Now, some companies are figuring out what their industrial customers are willing to pay and charging accordingly. St. Louis-based Emerson Electric Co., for example, developed a new sensor that measures the flow of fluids in various factory operations. If they had applied the traditional cost-plus pricing formula, they would have charged about U.S.$2650 for each sensor. But after asking industrial customers what price they would be willing to pay for the sensor, they ended up charging U.S.$3150.

Other companies are dealing with the pricing issue by advertising a lower-quality product at a very low price and then convincing their industrial customers to "buy-up" to a higher quality, higher-priced product. When Wildeck, Inc., a manufacturer of storage rack protectors for factories, was faced with a threat from a lower-priced product made by a competitor, it introduced its own cheaper version to initially attract customers. During the product demonstration, Wildeck's salespeople also presented the company's higher-priced (and higher quality) alternative, which customers often ended up buying.

Transportation companies have responded to the pricing issue by introducing new services that command a premium price because they promise the customer faster delivery. Another approach is to institute minimum prices that are higher than the least profitable customers have been paying. If these customers get upset and stop doing business with the transportation company, it really hasn't lost any serious source of revenue and profit. In fact, it frees up capacity for other industrial customers that are more profitable. ◆

In this chapter, we continue with our analysis of the 4 Ps of marketing by looking at "price" and "place" (channels of distribution). Price is an important element of the marketing mix because it influences both consumer demand for a product and company profitability. Consumers want products that satisfy their needs, and they want them to be available in the right places, but they also look aggressively for the lowest prices possible. As the opening case shows, this element of the marketing mix has become intensely competitive during the last few years.

PRICING OBJECTIVES AND TOOLS

1. Identify the various *pricing objectives* that govern pricing decisions and describe the price-setting tools used in making these decisions.

pricing
Deciding what the company will receive in exchange for its product.

pricing objectives
Goals that producers hope to attain in pricing products for sale.

In **pricing**, managers decide what the company will receive in exchange for its products. In this section, we first discuss the objectives that influence a firm's pricing decisions. Then we describe the major tools that companies use to meet those objectives.

Pricing to Meet Business Objectives

Companies often price products to maximize profits. But sellers hope to attain other **pricing objectives** when selling products. Some firms want to dominate the market or secure high market share. Pricing decisions are also influenced by the need to survive in the marketplace, by social and ethical concerns, and even by corporate image.

Profit-Maximizing Objectives

Pricing to maximize profits is tricky. If prices are set too low, the company will probably sell many units of its product. But it may miss the opportunity to make additional profit on each unit—and may indeed lose money on each exchange. Conversely, if prices are set too high, the company will make a large profit on each item but will sell fewer units. Again, the firm loses money. In addition, it may be left with excess inventory and may have to reduce or even close production operations. To avoid these problems, companies try to set prices to sell the number of units that will generate the highest possible total profits.

Coca-Cola tested an innovative way to avoid some of the traditional problems of what the price of a product should be. It looked at two possibilities: a vending machine that automatically raises the price of a Coke as the temperature climbs, and setting prices at different vending machines at different levels depending on how many customers use the machine.[1] In professional baseball, the New York Mets charged fans twice as much for tickets when they were playing their cross-town rivals the New York Yankees, and when home run king Barry Bonds played with the visiting San Francisco Giants. The Ottawa Senators increased prices 20 percent for games against the Toronto Maple Leafs and the champion Detroit Red Wings.[2]

In calculating profits, managers weigh receipts against costs for materials and labour to create the product. But they also consider the capital resources (plant and equipment) that the company must tie up to generate that level of profit. The costs of marketing (such as maintaining a large sales staff) can also be substantial. Concern over the efficient use of these resources has led many firms to set prices so as to achieve a targeted level of return on sales or capital investment.[3]

Pricing for Ebusiness Objectives. Marketers pricing for sales on the internet must consider different kinds of costs and different forms of consumer awareness than those pricing products to be sold conventionally. Many ebusinesses are lowering both costs and prices because of the internet's unique marketing capabilities. Because the web, for example, typically provides a more direct link between producer and ultimate consumer, buyers avoid the costs entailed by wholesalers and retailers.

Another factor in lower internet prices is the ease of comparison shopping. Obviously, point-and-click shopping is much more efficient than driving from store to store in search of the best price. In addition, both consumers and businesses can force lower prices by joining together in the interest of greater purchasing power. Numerous small businesses, for instance, are joining forces on the internet to negotiate lower prices for employee health care.

Market Share Objectives

In the long run, a business must make a profit to survive. Nevertheless, many companies initially set low prices for new products. They are willing to accept minimal profits—even losses—to get buyers to try products. In other words, they use pricing to establish **market share**: a company's percentage of the total market sales for a specific product. Even with established products, market share may outweigh profits as a pricing objective. For a product like Philadelphia Brand Cream Cheese, dominating a market means that consumers are more likely to buy it because they are familiar with a well-known, highly visible product.

market share
A company's percentage of the total market sales for a specific product.

Other Pricing Objectives

In some instances, neither profit maximizing nor market share is the best objective. During difficult economic times, for instance, loss containment and survival may become a company's main objectives. Thus in the mid-1980s, John Deere priced agricultural equipment low enough to ensure the company's survival in a severely depressed farm economy.

Price-Setting Tools

Whatever a company's objectives, managers must measure the potential impact before deciding on final prices. Two basic tools are often used for this purpose: *cost-oriented pricing* and *break-even analysis*. As a rule, these tools are combined to identify prices that will allow the company to reach its objectives.

Cost-Oriented Pricing

Cost-oriented pricing considers the firm's desire to make a profit and takes into account the need to cover production costs. A music store manager, for instance, would begin to price CDs by calculating the cost of making them available to shoppers. Included in this figure would be store rent, employee wages, utilities, product displays, insurance, and, of course, the cost of buying CDs from the manufacturer.

Let's assume that the cost from the manufacturer is \$8 per CD. If the store sells CDs for this price, it will not make any profit. Nor will it make a profit if it sells CDs for \$8.50 each or even for \$10 or \$11. The manager must account for product and other costs and set a figure for profit. Together, these figures constitute markup. In this case, a reasonable markup of $7 over costs would result in a $15 selling price. Markup is usually stated as a percentage of selling price. Markup percentage is thus calculated as follows:

$$\text{Markup percentage} = \frac{\text{Markup}}{\text{Sales price}}$$

In the case of our CD retailer, the markup percentage is 46.7:

$$\text{Markup percentage} = \frac{\$7}{\$15} = 46.7\%$$

In other words, out of every dollar taken in, 46.7 cents will be gross profit for the store. From this profit the store must still pay rent, utilities, insurance, and all other costs. Markup can also be expressed as a percentage of cost: The $7 markup is 87.5 percent of the $8 cost of a CD ($7÷$8).

In some industries, cost-oriented pricing doesn't seem to be very important. When you go to a first-run movie theatre, for example, you pay the same price for each film you see. But it may cost as little as $2 million or as much as $200 million to make a film. Shouldn't the admission price be based on how much the film cost to make? After all, you pay a lot more for a Lincoln Continental than you do for a Ford because the Lincoln costs more to make. Shouldn't the same pricing system apply to Hollywood? Apparently not.

Break-even Analysis: Cost-Volume-Profit Relationships

variable costs
Those costs that change with the number of goods or services produced or sold.

fixed costs
Those costs unaffected by the number of goods or services produced or sold.

break-even analysis
An assessment of how many units must be sold at a given price before the company begins to make a profit.

Using cost-oriented pricing, a firm will cover its **variable costs**—costs that change with the number of goods or services produced or sold. It will also make some money toward paying its **fixed costs**—costs that are unaffected by the number of goods or services produced or sold. But how many units must the company sell before all of its fixed costs are covered and it begins to make a profit? To determine this figure, it needs a **break-even analysis**.[4]

To continue our music store example, suppose again that the variable cost for each CD (in this case, the cost of buying the CD from the producer) is $8. This means that the store's annual variable costs depend on how many CDs are sold—the number of CDs sold multiplied by $8 cost per CD. Say that fixed costs for keeping the store open for one year are $100 000. These costs

Some homeowners have the opportunity to take out fixed-price fuel oil contracts to lock in the heating oil prices they'll pay during the winter. In some years, it's a good bet. If a homeowner locks in at $1.15 per gallon and prices go up to $1.80 per gallon, the homeowner obviously benefits. But if prices decline to $0.85 per gallon, the homeowner loses. "It's like buying insurance," says one analyst. "When you buy a fixed-price deal, you're saying you want the peace of mind."

are unaffected by the number of CDs sold; costs for lighting, rent, insurance, and salaries are steady however many CDs the store sells. Therefore, how many CDs must be sold to cover both fixed and variable costs and to start to generate some profit? The answer is the **break-even point**, which is 14 286 CDs. We arrive at this number through the following equation:

break-even point
The number of units that must be sold at a given price before the company covers all of its variable and fixed costs.

$$\text{Break-even point (in units)} = \frac{\text{Total fixed costs}}{\text{Price} - \text{Variable cost}}$$

$$= \frac{\$100\ 000}{\$15 - \$8} = 14\ 286 \text{ CDs}$$

Figure 17.1 shows the break-even point graphically. If the store sells fewer than 14 286 CDs, it loses money for the year. If sales exceed 14 286 CDs, profits grow by $7 for each CD sold. If the store sells exactly 14 286 CDs, it will cover all of its costs but will earn zero profit.

PRICING STRATEGIES AND TACTICS

2. Discuss *pricing strategies* and tactics for existing and new products.

The pricing tools discussed in the previous section provide a valuable guide for managers trying to set prices on specific goods. But they do not provide general direction for managers trying to set a pricing philosophy for their company. In this section, we discuss *pricing strategy*—that is, pricing as a planning activity that affects the marketing mix. We then describe some basic *pricing tactics*—ways in which managers implement a firm's pricing strategies.

Pricing Strategies

Let's begin this section by asking two questions. First: Can a manager really identify a single "best" price for a product? The answer is: probably not. For example, a study of prices for popular non-aspirin pain relievers (such as Tylenol and Advil) found variations of 100 percent.[5] In this market, in other words, some products sold for *twice* the price of other products with similar properties.

Granted, such differences may reflect some differences in product costs. The issue, however, is a little more complex. Such wide price differ-

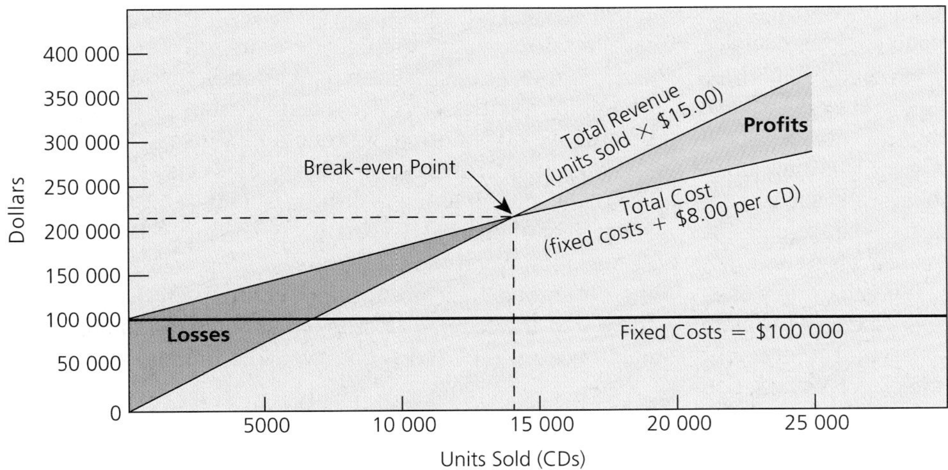

Figure 17.1
Break-even analysis.

BUSINESS TODAY

Wal-Mart in the Sky

Passenger traffic at North America's largest airlines is falling, but it is increasing at the discount airlines. How could this happen in the same industry? The answer is that the discount airlines (WestJet, Southwest, JetBlue, Jetsgo, and others) are doing a better job of giving customers what they want, namely low airfares. The discount airlines are essentially "Wal-Marting" the airline business. It seems that both business and pleasure travellers want low fares.

Not too long ago, major airlines like Air Canada and United Airlines dominated the industry. The business model involved expensive "hub-and-spoke" systems that funnelled travellers in from various regional areas to major centres. From there they transferred to other, longer-haul destinations that were more lucrative for the airlines. This was an expensive system, because the airlines had to lease many gates to accommodate all the transferring passengers. But until recently the hub generated enough revenue to cover the extra operating costs.

The major airlines also provided many frills such as in-flight meals, movies, and special business class seats with more legroom. They also developed a fare structure that featured relatively low-priced "restricted" tickets (that included a penalty if customers wanted to change their schedule at the last minute) and high-priced "unrestricted" tickets (which allowed last minute changes with no penalty). The restricted tickets were typically purchased by pleasure travellers, and the unrestricted tickets by business travellers.

The new discount airlines use a completely different strategy that involves no hub-and-spoke system, selling all tickets at bargain prices (many of them on the internet), offering good customer service (but no meals), and flying mostly short-haul trips between carefully chosen markets. They also have newer planes (which require far less maintenance) and workers who are not unionized. This new business model has suddenly become very successful, and the discount airlines are causing big, big trouble for the established airlines. Business travellers are now far less willing to pay higher fares than they used to be, largely because of the increased uncertainty about the economy and the drive to cut costs (it seems that even business travellers get satisfaction from having purchased a very low-priced ticket). Because of these changes, the market share held by the established airlines is steadily declining, and the market share of the discount airlines is increasing.

The differences between the old and new business model can be clearly seen when comparing the cost differences at United Airlines and JetBlue on the route from Dulles International Airport in Washington, D.C., to Oakland International Airport in Oakland, California. Both companies use the same plane (the Airbus 320), but the similarity ends there. United's ticket prices for the flight vary from about U.S.$129 to nearly U.S.$2000, depending on what type of ticket the customer purchases. JetBlue's ticket prices range from U.S.$129 to U.S.$307.50. JetBlue serves no meals, flies its planes more hours per day, and sells more than 50 percent of its tickets on the internet. United does serve meals, flies its planes fewer hours per day, and sells a much lower percentage of its tickets on the internet. An analysis of costs and revenues for the two airlines for this route that was carried out by an industry expert showed that JetBlue's cost for the trip was about U.S.$9000 less than United's. The result of all this is simple: JetBlue makes a profit on the flight and United doesn't.

In Canada, the situation is similar. Consider one telling statistic in comparing WestJet and Air Canada: WestJet operates with fewer than 60 people per aircraft, while rival Air Canada uses more than 140. Obviously WestJet has higher productivity. Air Canada's financial situation became untenable in 2003, and CEO Robert Milton announced that the company needed to cut labour costs by $650 million a year to return to profitability. He also said that the world has changed in the airline business, and the days of guaranteeing no layoffs are gone. Predictably, union leaders said they would resist wage cuts and layoffs. Buzz Hargrove, president of the Canadian Auto Workers, blamed the federal government for deregulating the airline industry and creating destructive competition between air carriers.

WestJet's CEO Clive Beddoe doesn't have much sympathy for Air Canada. He says that Air Canada spent a lot of energy trying to run new competitors out of business, when they should have been concentrating on getting their costs under control. He doesn't think that the federal government should step in and help because Air Canada got itself into trouble.

ences reflect differing brand images that attract different types of customers. In turn, these images reflect vastly different pricing philosophies and strategies.

Our second question is this: Just how important is pricing as an element in the marketing mix? As we have already seen, it is a mistake to try to isolate any element in the marketing mix from the others. Nevertheless, because pricing has a direct and visible impact on revenues, it is extremely important to overall marketing plans. The Business Today box illustrates the critical importance of pricing as part of the marketing mix.

In this section, we will focus on the ways in which pricing strategies for both new and existing products can result in widely differing prices for very similar products. Whatever price strategy a company is using, it must be communicated to buyers. Wal-Mart clearly communicates a low price strategy to consumers, but Eaton's strategy was not clear. For many years, Eaton's had a high-price strategy, coupled with a generous return policy. In 1991, Eaton's switched to an "everyday low price" strategy, but then slowly drifted back to a high-price strategy with occasional sales. Industry experts think that consumers were confused by the changes in strategy, and that this contributed to Eaton's demise.

Pricing Existing Products

A firm has three options available in pricing its existing products:

- pricing above prevailing market prices for similar products
- pricing below market prices
- pricing at or near market prices

Companies pricing above the market play on customers' beliefs that higher price means higher quality. Curtis Mathes, a maker of televisions, VCRs, and stereos, promotes itself as the most expensive television set, "but worth it." Companies such as Godiva chocolates and Rolls Royce have also succeeded with this pricing philosophy.

Godiva Chocolates
www.godiva.com

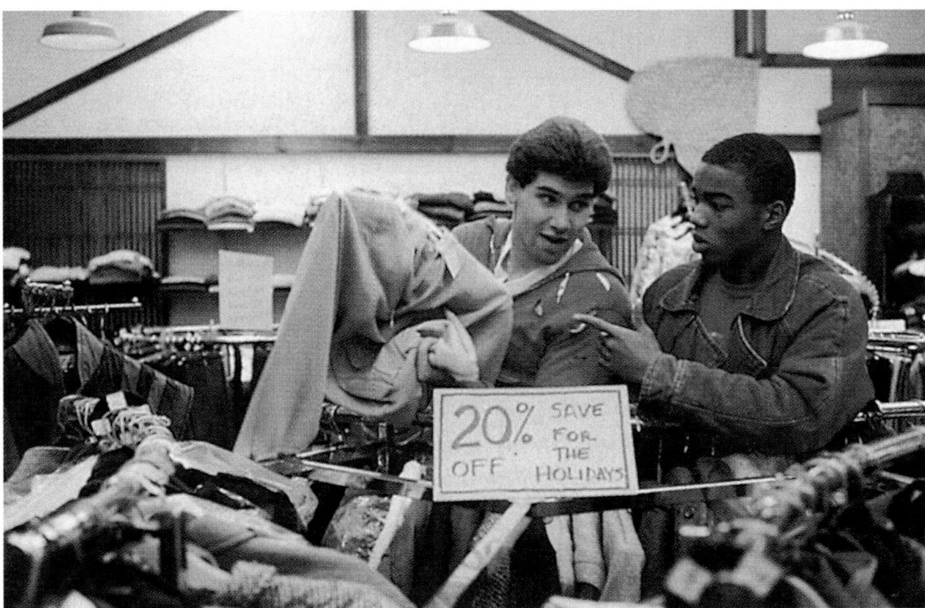

These teens are as concerned with the price tags as they are with the style of the clothing they might buy.

In contrast, both Budget and Dollar car rental companies promote themselves as low-priced alternatives to Hertz and Avis. Pricing below the prevailing market price can succeed if the firm can offer a product of acceptable quality while keeping costs below those of higher-priced options.

price leadership
The dominant firm in the industry establishes product prices and other companies follow suit.

In some industries, a dominant firm establishes product prices and other companies follow along. This is called **price leadership**. (Don't confuse this approach with *price fixing*, the illegal process of producers agreeing among themselves what prices will be charged.) Price leadership is often evident in products such as structural steel, gasoline, and many processed foods. These products differ little in quality from one firm to another. Companies compete through advertising campaigns, personal selling, and service, not price.

Pricing New Products

price-skimming strategy
The decision to price a new product as high as possible to earn the maximum profit on each unit sold.

penetration-pricing strategy
The decision to price a new product very low to sell the most units possible and to build customer loyalty.

Companies introducing new products into the market have to consider two contrasting pricing policy options: coming in with either a very high price or a very low one. **Price skimming**—setting an initially high price to cover costs and generate a profit—may generate a large profit on each item sold. The revenue is often needed to cover development and introduction costs. Skimming works only if marketers can convince consumers that a product is truly different from those already on the market. Today's expensive high-definition television (HDTV) is an example. Like HDTVs, microwave ovens, calculators, video games, and video cameras were all introduced at high skim prices. In contrast, **penetration pricing**—setting an initially low price to establish a new product in the market—seeks to create consumer interest and stimulate trial purchases.

Fixed Versus Dynamic Pricing for Ebusiness

The electronic marketplace has introduced a highly variable pricing system as an alternative to more conventional—and more stable—pricing structures for both consumer and B2B products. *Dynamic pricing* works because information flow on the web notifies millions of buyers of instantaneous changes in product availability. To attract sales that might be lost under traditional fixed-price structures, sellers can alter prices privately, on a one-to-one, customer-to-customer basis.[6]

At present, fixed pricing is still the most common option for cybershoppers. Etail giant Amazon.com has maintained the practice as the pricing strategy for its 16 million retail items. That situation, however, is beginning to change as dynamic-price challengers, such as eBay (the online, person-to-person auction website) and Priceline.com (the online clearinghouse for person-to-business price negotiation), grow in popularity.

NexTag.com Inc. takes an even more novel approach. Instead of asking buyers to bid up prices against each other, NexTag asks customers to state the prices that they are willing to pay for products. Merchants then compete for the sales. Unlike Priceline customers, NexTag customers do not commit in advance to sale prices: They wait to see how low the price goes. NexTag gathers offers from merchants, each of whom decides how low to price a product. The customer then chooses the lowest price. According to one expert, NexTag's dynamic pricing may be the trend of the future. "Fixed prices," she points out, "are only a 100-year-old phenomenon. I think they will disappear online, simply because it is possible—cheap and easy—to vary prices online."[7]

The Wired World box discusses the methods of online pricing used by FreeMarkets, an internet auction firm.

Pricing Tactics

Regardless of its pricing strategy, a company may adopt one or more *pricing tactics*, such as *price lining* or *psychological pricing*. Managers must also decide whether to use *discounting* tactics.

Price Lining

Companies selling multiple items in a product category often use **price lining**—offering all items in certain categories at a limited number of prices. A department store, for example, carries thousands of products. Setting separate prices for each brand and style of suit, glassware, or couch would take far too much time. With price lining, a store predetermines three or four *price points* at which a particular product will be sold. If price points for men's suits are $175, $250, and $400, all men's suits will be priced at one

price lining
The practice of offering all items in certain categories at a limited number of predetermined price points.

IT'S A WIRED WORLD

The World of Cyberprice Bidding

Sometimes, a company is better off outsourcing some activities to an ebusiness rather than doing them all itself. Consider the experience of United Technologies Corp. (UTC) **www.utc.com**. The Connecticut-based conglomerate needed to renew contracts with the eight suppliers from whom it bought the printed circuit boards for UTC elevators, air conditioners, and other products. Before accepting supplier estimates, UTC hoped to cut overall prices by 4 percent and, based on the going rate, expected to pay out U.S.$74 million. It also decided to outsource the entire bidding process to FreeMarkets Inc., an internet auction company. The results were stunning. FreeMarkets received bids from 29 circuit-board suppliers in the United States, Europe, and Asia. Winning suppliers ultimately signed contracts for U.S.$42 million—some 43 percent below UTC's projections.

As an auction marketplace for industrial goods, the net has changed the rules for price setting by firms selling to industrial customers. Conventional price-setting methods generally follow established patterns:

- incumbent suppliers have the inside edge for the new contracts
- closed bids prohibit suppliers from knowing competitors' prices
- only a few suppliers are invited to submit bids
- if a firm's bid is rejected, it has no opportunity to revise it

FreeMarkets is changing these patterns and, in so doing, saving client companies an average of 15 percent on the costs of purchases. By 2002, FreeMarkets had helped customers outsource the purchase of more than U.S.$30 billion in products, with savings of U.S.$6.4 billion. H.J. Heinz expects savings of more than U.S.$50 million, and the savings potential in the $5 trillion industrial-parts market is obvious. That's why FreeMarkets is now attracting customers such as Raytheon, Quaker Oats, Emerson Electric, and Owens Corning.

To get suppliers on board, FreeMarkets does not charge sellers for placing bids. Instead, large industrial buyers pay fixed subscription fees of up to $4 million a year. The auction package includes the software and computer technology necessary to conduct the bidding and standardizes all technical requirements. Delivery quantities and schedules, inventory quantities, and quality standards are all clarified before bidding starts. In a recent auction, the client set the most recent price for the parts it needed, U.S.$745 000, as a starting point. Twenty-five suppliers instantly saw each bid as it was received and posted at FreeMarkets' communications headquarters, and then an official 20-minute deadline for submitting better prices was set. The low bid dropped to U.S.$612 000 after 10 minutes and then to U.S.$585 000 with 30 seconds left. When a bid is received in the last minute of regulation time, the auction kicks into a series of 60-second overtime periods. After 13 minutes of overtime bidding, the final price came in at U.S.$518 000—31 percent below the client's expectations. In this environment, the fixed-price approach to selling industrial goods is quickly becoming a thing of the past.

of these three levels. The store's buyers, therefore, must select suits that can be purchased and sold profitably at one of these three prices.

Psychological Pricing

psychological pricing
The practice of setting prices to take advantage of the nonlogical reactions of consumers to certain types of prices.

odd-even psychological pricing
A form of psychological pricing in which prices are not stated in even dollar amounts.

Psychological pricing takes advantage of the fact that customers are not completely rational when making buying decisions. One type of psychological pricing, **odd-even pricing**, is based on the theory that customers prefer prices that are not stated in even dollar amounts. Thus customers regard prices of $1000, $100, $50, and $10 as significantly higher than $999.95, $99.95, $49.95, and $9.95, respectively.

Discounting

discount
Any price reduction offered by the seller to persuade customers to purchase a product.

cash discount
A form of discount in which customers paying cash, rather than buying on credit, pay lower prices.

seasonal discount
A form of discount in which lower prices are offered to customers making a purchase at a time of year when sales are traditionally slow.

trade discount
A discount given to firms involved in a product's distribution.

quantity discount
A form of discount in which customers buying large amounts of a product pay lower prices.

The price that is eventually set for a product is not always the price at which all items are sold. Many times a company has to offer a price reduction—a **discount**—to stimulate sales. Cash, seasonal, trade, and quantity discounts are the most common forms.

In recent years, **cash discounts** have become popular, even at retail stores. Stores may offer **seasonal discounts** to stimulate the sales of products during times of the year when most customers do not normally buy the product. Travellers can find low prices on summer trips to tropical islands and July shoppers can get sale prices on winter coats thanks to seasonal discounts. **Trade discounts** are available only to those companies or individuals involved in a product's distribution. Thus, wholesalers, retailers, and interior designers pay less for fabric than the typical consumer does. Related to trade discounts are **quantity discounts**—lower prices for purchases in large quantities. Case price discounts for motor oil or soft drinks at retail stores are examples of quantity discounts.

International Pricing

When Procter & Gamble reviewed its prospects for marketing products in new overseas markets, it encountered an unsettling fact: Because it typically priced products to cover hefty R&D costs, profitably priced items were out of reach for too many foreign consumers. The solution was, in effect, to reverse the process. Now P&G conducts research to find out what foreign

If the manufacturer (say, JVC or Sony) says a product should retail for $349.00, why do most retailers sell it for, say, $229.00? Such discrepancies between a manufacturer's suggested retail price and the actual retail price are the norm in the electronics industry, and consumers have come to expect discounted prices. It is no surprise that retailers advertise these lower prices. They want consumers to know that they are willing to take a lower margin on the product to get the customer's business. But this raises an interesting question: If no one charges suggested retail prices, is anyone really getting a discount?

buyers can afford and then develops products that they can buy. P&G penetrates markets with lower-priced items and encourages customers to trade up as they become able to afford higher-quality products.

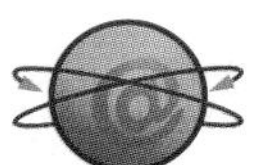

Procter & Gamble
www.pg.com

As P&G's experience shows, pricing products for other countries is complicated because additional factors are involved. Income and spending trends must be analyzed. In addition, the number of intermediaries varies from country to country, as does their effect on a product's cost. Exchange rates change daily, there may be shipping costs, import tariffs must be considered (Chapter 4), and different types of pricing agreements may be permitted.

Another strategy calls for increasing foreign market share by pricing products below cost. As a result, a given product is priced lower in a foreign market than in its home market. As we saw in Chapter 4, this practice is called *dumping*, which is illegal.

THE DISTRIBUTION MIX

3. Explain the distribution mix, the different *channels of distribution*, and different *distribution strategies*.

We have already seen that a company needs an appropriate *product mix*. But the success of any product also depends in part on its **distribution mix**: the combination of distribution channels a firm selects to get a product to end-users. In this section, we will consider some of the many factors that enter into the distribution mix. First, we will explain the need for *intermediaries*. We will then discuss the basic *distribution strategies*. Finally, we will consider some special issues in channel relationships—namely, conflict and leadership.

distribution mix
The combination of distribution channels a firm selects to get a product to end-users.

As you are reading the material on the next few pages, keep in mind one key point: intermediaries must provide added value to customers to stay in business. Over the next decade, traditional intermediaries may become smaller or disappear altogether as the internet increasingly provides more and more products and services to customers in a more efficient way.[8]

Intermediaries and Distribution Channels

Once called *middlemen*, **intermediaries** are the individuals and firms who help distribute a producer's goods. They are generally classified as wholesalers or retailers. **Wholesalers** sell products to other businesses, which resell them to final consumers. **Retailers** sell products directly to consumers. While some firms rely on independent intermediaries, others employ their own distribution networks and sales forces.

intermediary
Any individual or firm other than the producer who participates in a product's distribution.

wholesalers
Intermediaries who sell products to other businesses, which in turn resell them to the end-users.

retailers
Intermediaries who sell products to end-users.

Distribution of Consumer Products

A **distribution channel** is the path that a product follows from producer to end user. Figure 17.2 shows how eight primary distribution channels can be identified according to the kinds of channel members involved in getting products to buyers. Note that all channels must begin with a producer and end with a consumer or an industrial user. Channels 1 through 4 are most often used for the distribution of consumer goods and services.

distribution channel
The path a product follows from the producer to the end-user.

Channel 1: Direct Distribution of Consumer Products. In a **direct channel**, the product travels from the producer to the consumer without intermediaries. Using their own sales forces, companies such as Avon, Fuller Brush, and Tupperware use this channel.

direct channel
A distribution channel in which the product travels from the producer to the consumer without passing through any intermediary.

This direct channel is also prominent on the internet for thousands of products ranging from books and automobiles to insurance and vacation packages sold directly by producers to consumers. The Gateway 2000 internet storefront, for example, handles annual sales of more than U.S.$6 bil-

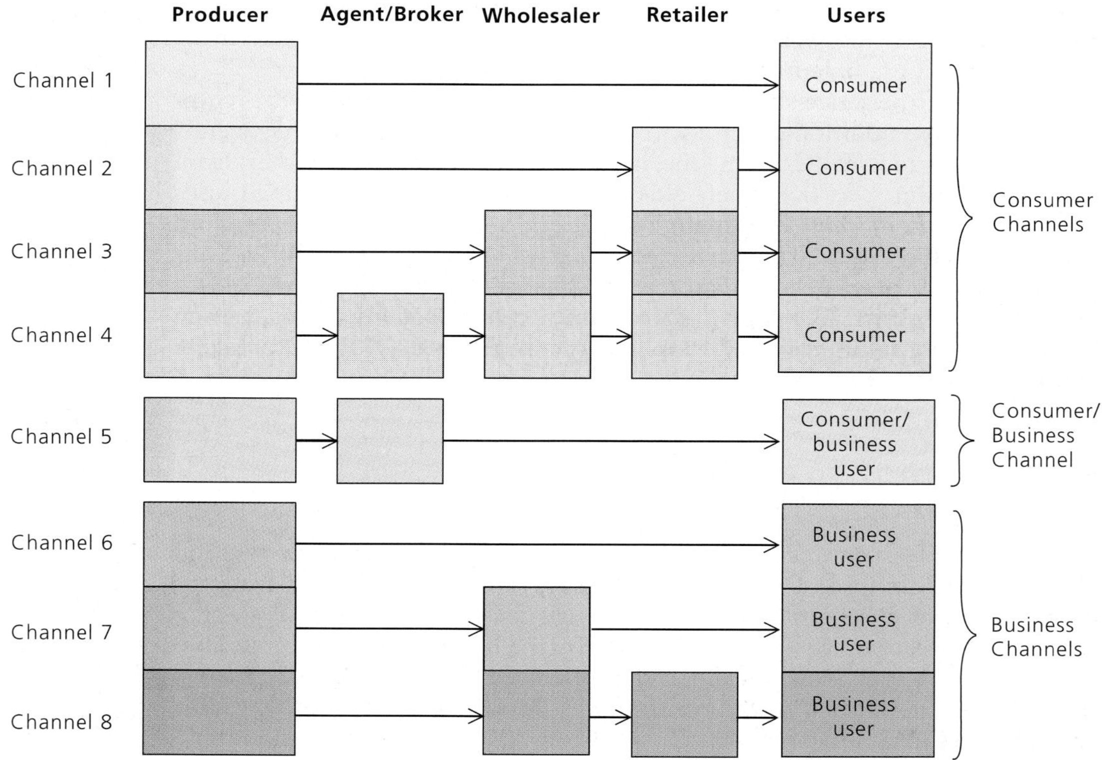

Figure 17.2
Channels of distribution: How the product travels from producer to consumer or user.

Gateway Computers
www.gateway.com

lion in computers and related products for home and workplace. Likewise, you can purchase airline reservations directly from internet sites.

Channel 2: Retail Distribution of Consumer Products. In Channel 2, producers distribute products through retailers. Goodyear, for example, maintains its own system of retail outlets. Levi's has its own outlets but also produces jeans for other retailers such as Gap Inc. Many retailers offer internet sales. Grocery shoppers, for example, can browse the electronic aisles of Grocery Gateway.

Channel 3: Wholesale Distribution of Consumer Products. Once the most widely used method of non-direct distribution, Channel 2 requires a large amount of floor space, both for storing merchandise and for displaying it in stores. Faced with the rising cost of store space, many retailers found that they could not afford both retail and storage space. Thus, wholesalers entered the distribution network to take over more of the storage function. The combination convenience store/gas station is an example of Channel 3. With approximately 90 percent of the space used to display merchandise, only 10 percent is left for storage and office facilities. Wholesalers store merchandise and restock it frequently.

Wholesalers are prominent in ecommerce because internet stores give customers access to information and product displays 24 hours a day. Buyers can also place orders electronically and confirm delivery almost instantaneously. In the diamond industry, retail companies can access wholesalers such as Diasqua Group, visually examine diamonds, place orders, and receive delivery dates, all over the internet.

Channel 4: Distribution Through Sales Agents or Brokers. Channel 4 uses **sales agents**, or **brokers**, who represent producers and sell to wholesalers, retailers, or both. They receive commissions based on the prices of the goods they sell. Lafferty and Co. Food Brokers Inc. represents several prominent food manufacturers—Pillsbury, Old El Paso, and Sunkist—in the Midwestern United States. To relieve manufacturers of sales activities, Lafferty arranges sales of their products to other companies, allowing manufacturers to do what they do best—process food products—rather than divert resources to sales and distribution.

sales agent (or broker)
An independent business person who represents a business and receives a commission in return, but never takes legal possession of the product.

Agents generally deal in the related product lines of a few producers and work on a long-term basis. Travel agents, for example, represent airlines, car-rental companies, and hotels. In contrast, brokers match sellers and buyers as needed. The real estate industry relies on brokers to match buyers and sellers of property.

The Pros and Cons of Non-Direct Distribution

Each link in the distribution chain makes a profit by charging a markup or commission. Thus, non-direct distribution means higher prices: The more members in the channel—the more intermediaries—the higher the final price. Calculated as a percentage of cost, *markups* are applied each time a product is sold. They may range from 10 to 40 percent for manufacturers, from 2 to 25 percent for wholesalers, and from 5 to 100 percent for retailers. *E-intermediaries*—wholesalers and agents who use internet channels—also charge markups. In general, markup levels depend on competitive conditions and practices in a particular industry.

Creating Added Value. Intermediaries, however, can provide *added value* by saving consumers both time and money. Moreover, the value accumulates with each link in the supply chain. Intermediaries provide time-saving information and make the right quantities of products available where and when you need them. Consider Figure 17.3, which illustrates the problem of making chili without benefit of a common intermediary—the supermarket. As a consumer/buyer, you would obviously spend a lot more time, money, and energy if you tried to gather all the ingredients from one retailer at a time. In any case, even if we did away with intermediaries, you would not eliminate either their tasks or the costs entailed by performing those tasks. They exist because they do necessary jobs in cost-efficient ways.

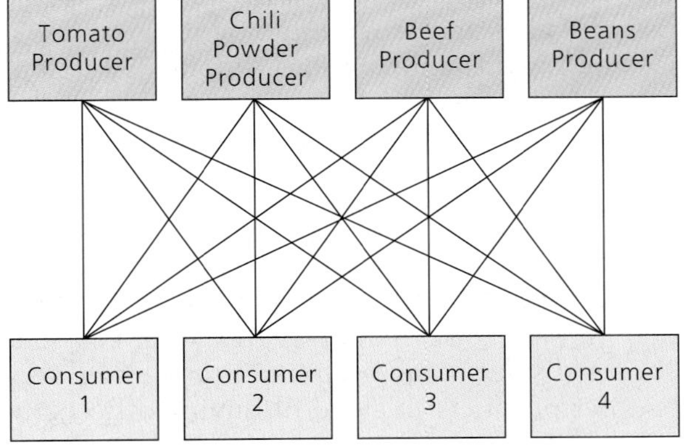

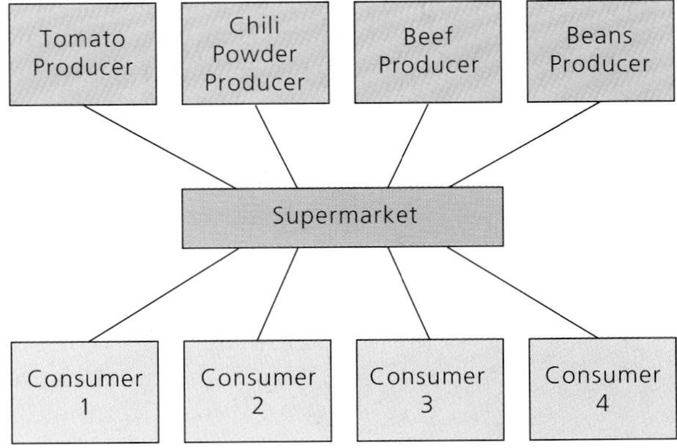

Figure 17.3
Advantages of intermediaries.

Uniglobe
www.uniglobe.com

Channel 5: Distribution by Agents to Consumers and Businesses. Channel 5 differs from previous channels in two ways: (1) An agent functions as the sole intermediary and (2) the agent distributes to both consumers and business customers. Consider Vancouver-based Uniglobe Travel International, a travel agent representing airlines, car-rental companies, and hotels. Uniglobe books flight reservations and arranges complete recreational-travel services for consumers. The firm also services companies whose employees need lodging and transportation for business travel.

Ecommerce works well in this channel because it directly informs more people about products. At Uniglobe, for instance, a new online subsidiary combines a high-tech website with an old-fashioned human touch in a specialty market—booking cruises. Customers can scan for destinations, cruise lines, restaurants, and cabin locations for any of 70 ships. Using Uniglobe's online chat function, travellers can simply open a window to speak in real time with one of 75 cruise specialists. The strategy has paid off: Uniglobe.com leads the market in online cruise bookings.[9]

Distribution of Business Products

industrial (business) distribution
The network of channel members involved in the flow of manufactured goods to industrial customers.

Industrial channels are important because every company is also a customer that buys other companies' products. The Kellogg Co., for example, buys grain to make breakfast cereals, and Imperial Tobacco buys tobacco to make cigarettes. **Industrial (business) distribution** is the network of channel members involved in the flow of manufactured goods to business customers. Unlike consumer products, business products are traditionally distributed through Channels 6, 7, and 8 (refer back to Figure 17.2).

sales offices
Offices maintained by sellers of industrial goods to provide points of contact with their customers.

Channel 6: Direct Distribution of Business Products. Most business goods are sold directly by the manufacturer to the industrial buyer. Lawless Container Corp., for instance, produces packaging containers for direct sale to Fisher-Price (toys), Dirt Devil (vacuum cleaners), Peak antifreeze, and Mr. Coffee (coffeemakers). Many manufacturers maintain **sales offices** as contact points with customers and headquarters for salespeople.

Intermediaries are often unnecessary because goods distributed through Channel 6 are usually purchased in large quantities. In some cases, however, brokers or agents may enter the chain between manufacturers and buyers. Finally, ecommerce technologies have also popularized Channel 6. Dell Computer Corp., a pioneer in direct internet sales, now gets about two-thirds of its U.S.$32 billion in sales from other businesses, governments, and schools.[10]

Channel 7: Wholesale Distribution of Industrial Products. Wholesalers function in only a few industrial channels. Brokers and agents are even rarer. Channel 7 mostly handles accessory equipment (computers, fax machines, and other office equipment) and supplies (floppy disks, pencils, copier paper). Manufacturers produce these items in large quantities, but companies buy them in small quantities. For example, few companies order truckloads of paper clips. Intermediaries, then, help end users by breaking down large quantities into smaller sales units. Thus, the traditional office-supply store wholesales a variety of goods to other businesses.

Channel 8: Wholesale Distribution to Business Retailers. In some industries, the roles of channel members are changing. In the office-products industry, Channel 7 is being displaced by a channel that looks very much like Channel 3 for consumer products: Instead of buying office supplies from wholesalers (Channel 7), many businesses are now shopping at office discount stores such as Staples, Office Depot, and Office Max. Before selling to large companies, these warehouse-like superstores originally targeted retail consumers and small businesses that bought supplies at retail stores (and at retail prices). Today, however, small-business buyers shop at discount stores designed for industrial users, selecting from 7000 items at prices 20 to 75 percent lower than retail.

Ecommerce is fuelling the rapid growth in the office-superstore industry. In Japan, customers of the largest office supplier, Askul, can shop the internet in real time and receive orders within 24 hours. Askul can charge low prices because it locates high-tech distribution warehouses on cheap land and uses electronic transactions to reduce the workforce needed for face-to-face selling.

Distribution Strategies

Choosing a distribution network is a vital consideration for a company. It can make the firm succeed or fail. The choice of distribution strategy determines the amount of market exposure the product gets and the cost of that exposure. The appropriate strategy depends on the product class. The goal is to make a product accessible in just enough locations to satisfy customers' needs. Milk can be purchased at many retail outlets (high exposure). But there is only one distributor for Rolls Royce in a given city.

Three strategies—*intensive, exclusive,* and *selective distribution*—provide different degrees of market coverage. **Intensive distribution** means distributing a product through as many channels and channel members (using both wholesalers and retailers) as possible. For example, as Figure 17.4 shows, Caramilk bars flood the market through all suitable outlets. Intensive distribution is normally used for low-cost consumer goods such as candy and magazines.

intensive distribution

A distribution strategy in which a product is distributed in nearly every possible outlet, using many channels and channel members.

In contrast, **exclusive distribution** occurs when a manufacturer grants the exclusive right to distribute or sell a product to one wholesaler or retailer in a given geographic area. Exclusive distribution agreements are most

exclusive distribution

A distribution strategy in which a product's distribution is limited to only one wholesaler or retailer in a given geographic area.

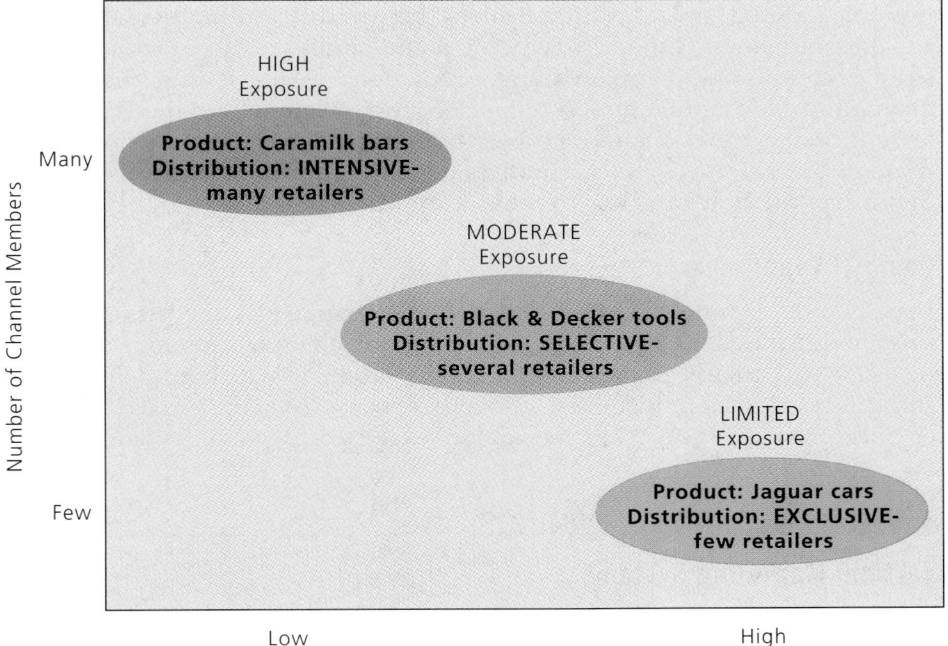

Figure 17.4
Amounts of market exposure from the three kinds of distribution.

common for high-cost, prestige products. For example, only a single dealer servicing a large metropolitan area sells Jaguar automobiles.

selective distribution
A distribution strategy that falls between intensive and exclusive distribution, calling for the use of a limited number of outlets for a product.

Selective distribution falls between intensive and exclusive distribution. A company that uses this strategy carefully selects only wholesalers and retailers who will give special attention to the product in terms of sales efforts, display position, etc. Selective distribution policies have been applied to virtually every type of consumer product. It is usually embraced by companies like Black & Decker, whose product lines do not require intense market exposure to increase sales.

Para Paints uses an interesting selective distribution policy. It keeps its high-end paint products out of the "big-box" stores such as Canadian Tire and Home Depot. Doing so has increased Para's margins (because big-box stores demand steep discounts), and has also increased sales by 15 to 20 percent because the independent stores that sell Para paint have remained loyal to Para. The company repeatedly turns down requests from big-box stores to carry its paints because it doesn't want to harm its good relations with independent dealers.[11]

Channel Conflict and Channel Leadership

Manufacturers can choose to distribute through more than one channel or wholesaler. They can also choose to make new uses of existing channels. Similarly, most retailers are free to strike agreements with as many producers as capacity permits. In such cases, *channel conflict* may arise. Conflicts are resolved when members' efforts are better coordinated. A key factor in coordinating the activities of independent organizations is *channel leadership*. Another strategy for improving coordination is known as the *vertical marketing system*.

Channel Conflict

channel conflict
Conflict arising when the members of a distribution channel disagree over the roles they should play or the rewards they should receive.

Channel conflict occurs when members of the channel disagree over the roles they should play or the rewards they should receive. John Deere, for example, would object if its dealers began distributing Russian and Japanese tractors. Similarly, when a manufacturer-owned factory outlet store discounts the company's apparel or housewares, it runs the risk of alienating the manufacturer's retail accounts. Channel conflict may also arise if one member has more power than others or is viewed as receiving preferential treatment. Such conflicts defeat the purpose of the system by disrupting the flow of goods to their destinations.

Channel Leadership

channel captain
The channel member that is the most powerful in determining the roles and rewards of organizations involved in a given channel of distribution.

Usually, one channel member—the **channel captain**—can determine the roles and rewards of other members. Often, the channel captain is a manufacturer, particularly if the manufacturer's product is in high demand. In some industries, an influential wholesaler or a large retailer such as Wal-Mart or Sears may emerge as channel captain because of large sales volumes.

Vertical Marketing Systems

Vertical Marketing Systems

vertical marketing system (VMS)
A system in which there is a high degree of coordination among all the units in the distribution channel so that a product moves efficiently from manufacturer to consumer.

To overcome problems posed by channel conflict and issues of channel leadership, the **vertical marketing system (VMS)** has emerged. In a VMS, separate businesses join to form a unified distribution channel, with one member coordinating the activities of the whole channel. There are three types of VMS arrangements:

The dresses being shipped from this Kahn-Lucas factory are bound for department-store retail shelves. If they don't arrive when promised, there may be conflict in the distribution channel. In fact, the buyer could charge Kahn-Lucas 5 percent on every item in the shipment. Such penalties are called charge backs, and retailers can charge suppliers for putting bar codes in the wrong place, attaching labels improperly, and unloading boxes out of order.

- In a *corporate* VMS, all stages in the channel are under single ownership. The Limited, for example, owns both the production facilities that manufacture its apparel and the retail stores that sell it.
- In a *contractual* VMS, channel members sign contracts agreeing to specific duties and rewards. The Independent Grocers' Alliance (IGA), for example, consists of independent retail grocers joined with a wholesaler who contractually leads—but does not own—the VMS. Most franchises are contractual VMSs.
- In an *administered* VMS, channel members are less formally coordinated than in a corporate or contractual VMS. Instead, one or more of the members emerge as leader(s) and maintain control as a result of power and influence. Although the administered VMS is more fragile than the corporate and contractual forms, it is more unified than channels relying on independent members.

Independent Grocers' Alliance
www.iga.com

WHOLESALING

4. Explain the differences between *merchant wholesalers* and *agents/brokers*, and describe the activities of e-intermediaries.

Now that you know something about distribution channels, we can consider the broader role played by intermediaries. Wholesalers provide a variety of functions for their customers, who are buying products for resale or for business use. In addition to storing products and providing an assortment of products for their customers, wholesalers offer delivery, credit, and information about products. Not all wholesalers provide all of these functions. The specific services they offer depend on the type of intermediary involved: *merchant wholesaler, agents/broker,* or *e-intermediary*.

Merchant Wholesalers

merchant wholesaler
An independent wholesaler that buys and takes legal possession of goods before selling them to customers.

Most wholesalers are independent operators who derive their income from sales of goods produced by a variety of manufacturers. All **merchant wholesalers** take title to merchandise. That is, merchant wholesalers buy and own the goods they resell to other businesses. They usually provide storage and a means of delivery.

full-service merchant wholesaler
A merchant wholesaler that provides storage and delivery in addition to wholesaling services.

limited-function merchant wholesaler
An independent wholesaler that provides only wholesaling—not warehousing or transportation—services.

drop shipper
A type of wholesaler that does not carry inventory or handle the product.

rack jobber
A full-function merchant wholesaler specializing in non-food merchandise that sets up and maintains display racks of some products in retail stores.

A **full-service merchant wholesaler** provides credit, marketing, and merchandising services. Approximately 80 percent of all merchant wholesalers are full-service wholesalers. **Limited-function merchant wholesalers** provide only a few services, sometimes merely storage. Their customers are normally small operations that pay cash and pick up their own goods. One such wholesaler, the **drop shipper**, does not even carry inventory or handle the product. Drop shippers receive orders from customers, negotiate with producers to supply goods, take title to them, and arrange for shipment to customers. The drop shipper bears the risks of the transaction until the customer takes title to the goods.

Other limited-function wholesalers, known as **rack jobbers**, market consumer goods—mostly non-food items—directly to retail stores.[12] Procter & Gamble, for example, uses rack jobbers to distribute products like Pampers diapers. After marking prices, setting up display racks, and displaying diapers in one store, the rack jobber moves on to another outlet to check inventories and shelve products.

Agents and Brokers

Agents and brokers, including internet e-agents, serve as sales forces for various manufacturers. They are independent representatives of many companies' products. They work on commissions, usually about 4 to 5 percent of net sales. Unlike merchant wholesalers, they do not take title to—that is, they do not own—the merchandise they sell. Rather, they serve as the sales and merchandising arms of manufacturers that do not have their own sales forces.

Consider, for instance, the role of On Air Digital Audio as an *e-agent* (or *shopping agent*). Corporate clients need the right kind of voices for radio ads; likewise, voice talents are looking for jobs. As the intermediary between clients and artists, On Air Digital transmits ad scripts and artists' readings electronically and, in doing so, saves clients time. Samples from On Air's voice bank are transmitted digitally to clients who scan and select the best voices. On Air then arranges for the artist to record the message, receives it electronically, and sends it electronically to the client, thus avoiding the cost entailed in mailing CDs and tapes back and forth.[13]

The value of agents and brokers lies primarily in their knowledge of markets and their merchandising expertise. They also provide a wide range of services, including shelf and display merchandising and advertising layout. Finally, they maintain product saleability by removing open, torn, or dirty packages, arranging products neatly, and generally keeping them attractively displayed. Many supermarket products are handled through brokers.

The Advent of the E-Intermediary

e-intermediaries
Internet-based distribution-channel members that collect information about sellers and present it in convenient form to consumers and/or help deliver internet products to consumers.

The ability of ecommerce to bring together millions of widely dispersed consumers and businesses continues to change the types and roles of intermediaries in distribution channels. **E-intermediaries** are internet-based distribution-channel members that perform one or both of two functions: (1) they collect information about sellers and present it in convenient form to consumers, or (2) they help deliver internet products to consumers. Internet intermediaries such as Chapters.com and Amazon.com account for sales to millions of consumers who otherwise might walk into traditional retail outlets instead of shopping online. We will examine three types of emerging e-intermediaries: *syndicated sellers, shopping agents,* and *business-to-business brokers*.

Syndicated Sellers

Syndicated selling occurs when one website offers another a commission for referring customers. Here's how it works. With 9.2 million users each month, Expedia.com is a heavily visited travel-services website. Expedia has given Dollar Rent A Car a special banner on its webpage. When Expedia customers click on the banner for a car rental, they are transferred from the Expedia site to the Dollar site. Dollar pays Expedia a fee for each booking that comes through this channel. Although the new intermediary increases the cost of Dollar's supply chain, it adds value for customers. Travellers avoid unnecessary cyberspace searches and are efficiently guided to a car-rental agency.[14]

syndicated selling
Occurs when a website offers other websites a commission for referring customers.

Shopping Agents

Shopping agents (or **e-agents**) help internet consumers by gathering and sorting information. Although they don't take possession of products, they know which websites and stores to visit, give accurate comparison prices, identify product features, and help consumers complete transactions by presenting information in a usable format—all in a matter of seconds. PriceScan is a well-known shopping agent for computer products. For CDs and tapes, evenbetter.com searches for vendors, does price comparisons, lists prices from low to high, and then transfers you to the websites of 50 different estores.

shopping agent (e-agent)
A type of intermediary that helps internet consumers by gathering and sorting information they need to make purchases.

Business-to-Business Brokers

Ecommerce intermediaries have also emerged for business customers. One such company is ecMarkets, which uses ecommerce technology to combine the purchasing requirements of multiple buyers. The buyers save money because ecMarkets purchases in such large volumes that it acquires goods for lower prices. ecMarkets does not take possession of products. In 2003, ecMarkets launched a group procurement initiative with the National Grocers Association (NGA) in the United States. Members of the NGA get the benefits of ecMarkets' sourcing professionals, who find qualified suppliers and manage specification requirements for the purchasers.

RETAILING

5. Identify the different types of *retailing* and *retail stores*.

You probably have had little contact with merchant wholesalers, merchandise brokers, or manufacturers. If you are like most Canadians, you buy nearly all the goods and services you consume from retailers. Most retailers are small operations, often consisting of just the owners and part-time help. But there are a few very large retailers, and these account for billions of dollars of sales each year (see Table 17.1 for a list of retailers in Canada).

In the past few years, U.S. retailers have become very aggressive in expanding into Canada. American Eagle Outfitters Inc. bought the Braemar Women's Wear chain in 2000. It converted 35 Braemar stores to American Eagle stores, which sell mid-priced basics to the 16 to 34 age group. It also purchased Dylex's 115 Thrifty's outlets and changed their name to Bluenotes.[15] Old Navy, the discount division of California-based Gap Inc., also set up shop in Canada in 2001.

Types of Retail Outlets

Retail operations in Canada vary as widely by type as they do by size. They can be classified in various ways: by pricing strategies, location, range of

Table 17.1 The Top 10 Retailers in Canada

	Company	Annual Revenues (in billions of $)
1.	Hudson's Bay Co.	7.3
2.	Costco Wholesale Canada Ltd.	7.3
3.	Sears Canada Inc.	6.5
4.	Canadian Tire Corp. Ltd.	5.9
5.	Liquor Control Board of Ontario	2.9
6.	RONA Inc.	2.2
7.	B.C. Liquor Distribution Branch	1.7
8.	Société des alcools du Québec	1.6
9.	The Forzani Group Ltd.	.9
10.	The Brick Warehouse Corp.	.8

Note: Wal-Mart is the largest retailer in Canada (with estimated sales of nearly $9 billion), but it has no Canadian subsidiary.

services, or range of product lines. Choosing the right types of retail outlets is a crucial aspect of every seller's distribution strategy. In this section, we describe retail stores by using two classifications: *product line retailers* and *bargain retailers*.

Product Line Retailers

department stores
Large retail stores that offer a wide variety of high-quality items divided into specialized departments.

supermarkets
Large retail stores that offer a variety of food and food-related items divided into specialized departments.

specialty stores
Small retail stores that carry one line of related products.

Retailers that feature broad product lines include **department stores**, which are organized into specialized departments such as shoes, furniture, women's clothing, and so forth. Stores are usually large and handle a wide range of goods. In addition, they usually offer a variety of services, such as generous return policies, credit plans, and delivery. Similarly, **supermarkets** are divided into departments of related products: food products, household products, and so forth. The emphasis is on low prices, self-service, and wide selection.

In contrast, **specialty stores** are small stores that carry one line of related products. They serve specific market segments with full product lines in narrow product fields and often feature knowledgeable sales per-

It took a few years after the fall of communism before entrepreneurs braved the uncertain economic climate of Russia and opened supermarkets and other retail chains. Ikea, the Swedish home-furnishings seller, has been successful in Moscow, as has Kopeika, a home-owned discount chain that models itself after Wal-Mart. Russian shoppers (who used to go to drab stores called "Food" and "Furniture") are enthusiastic, and more companies are opening outlets in Moscow, which has more people than all of Belgium.

sonnel. Sunglass Hut International, for instance, has 1600 outlets in Canada, the United States, Europe, and Australia that carry a deep selection of competitively priced sunglasses. Retailers who carry an extremely deep selection of goods in a relatively narrow product line and hire technical experts to give customers advice are called **category killers**. Home Depot and Staples are examples of category killers.

category killers
Retailers who carry a deep selection of goods in a narrow product line.

Bargain Retailers.

Bargain retailers carry wide ranges of products and come in many forms. The first **discount houses** sold large numbers of items (such as televisions and other appliances) at substantial price reductions to certain customers. As name-brand items became more common, they offered better product assortments while still transacting cash-only sales in low-rent facilities. As they became firmly entrenched, they began moving to better locations, improving decor, and selling better-quality merchandise at higher prices. They also began offering a few department store services, such as credit plans and non-cash sales. Wal-Mart and Zellers are bargain retailers.

Catalogue showrooms mail catalogues to attract customers into showrooms to view display samples, place orders, and wait briefly while clerks retrieve orders from attached warehouses. **Factory outlets** are manufacturer-owned stores that avoid wholesalers and retailers by selling merchandise directly from factory to consumer. The **warehouse club** (or **wholesale club**) offers large discounts on a wide range of brand-name merchandise to customers who pay annual membership fees. Neighbourhood food retailers such as 7-Eleven and Circle K stores are **convenience store** chains, which offer ease of purchase: They stress easily accessible locations, extended store hours, and speedy service. They differ from most bargain retailers in that they do not feature low prices. Like bargain retailers, they control prices by keeping in-store service to a minimum.

The Exercising Your Ethics box presents one of many dilemmas that can arise when customers deal with retail outlets.

bargain retailers
Retail outlets that emphasize low prices as a means of attracting consumers.

discount houses
Bargain retail stores that offer major items such as televisions and large appliances at discount prices.

catalogue showroom
A bargain retail store in which customers place orders for items described in a catalogue and pick up those items from an on-premises warehouse.

factory outlets
Bargain retail stores that are owned by the manufacturers whose products they sell.

warehouse club (wholesale club)
Huge, membership-only, combined retail-wholesale operations that sell brand-name merchandise.

convenience stores
Retail stores that offer high accessibility, extended hours, and fast service on selected items.

Non-Store and Electronic Retailing

Not all goods and services are sold in stores. In fact, some of the nation's largest retailers sell all or most of their products without bricks-and-mortar

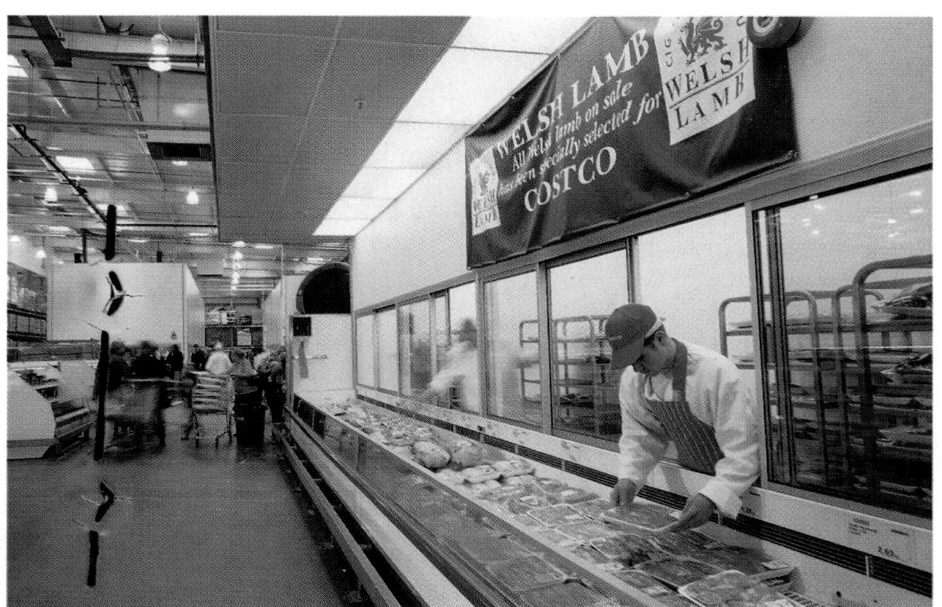

In the mid-1990s, top management at Costco warehouse clubs began to worry that its markets in the United States were becoming saturated. So, it decided to expand into other countries. The Costco concept—low prices on high-quality merchandise available to members only—travels well. This store in the London suburb of Watford, England, is one of the chain's most successful outlets anywhere.

EXERCISING YOUR ETHICS

The Chain of Responsibility

The Situation

Because several stages are involved when distribution chains move products from supply sources to end consumers, the process offers ample opportunity for ethical issues to arise. This exercise encourages you to examine some of the ethical issues that can emerge during transactions among suppliers and customers.

The Dilemma

A customer bought an expensive wedding gift at a local store and asked that it be shipped to the bride in another province. Several weeks after the wedding, the customer contacted the bride because she had sent no word confirming the arrival of the gift. In fact, it hadn't arrived. Charging that the merchandise had not been delivered, the customer requested a refund. The store manager uncovered the following facts:

- A well-known national delivery firm handles all shipments from the store.
- The delivery firm verified that the package had been delivered to the designated address two days after the sale.
- Normally, the delivery firm does not obtain recipient signatures; deliveries are made to the address of record, regardless of the name on the package.

The gift giver argued that even though the package had been delivered to the right address, it had not been delivered to the named recipient. It turns out that, unbeknownst to the gift giver, the bride had moved. It stood to reason, then, that the gift was in the hands of the new occupant of the bride's former address. The manager informed the gift giver that the store had fulfilled its obligation. The cause of the problem, she explained, was the incorrect address given by the customer. She refused to refund the customer's money and suggested that the customer might want to recover the gift by contacting the stranger who received it at the bride's old address.

Questions for Discussion

1. What are the responsibilities of each party—the customer, the store, the delivery firm—in this situation?
2. From an ethical standpoint, in what ways is the store manager's action right? In what ways is it wrong?
3. If you were appointed to settle this matter, what actions would you take?

stores. For example, certain types of consumer goods—soft drinks, candy, and cigarettes—lend themselves to distribution in vending machines. However, vending machine sales still represent only a small proportion of all retail sales. And so-called "etailing" sales are expected to increase sharply during the next few years as people shop online with their personal computers.

direct-response retailing *A type of retailing in which firms make direct contact with customers both to inform them about products and to receive sales orders.*

direct selling *Form of non-store retailing typified by door-to-door sales.*

mail order (catalogue marketing) *A form of non-store retailing in which customers place orders for merchandise shown in catalogues and receive their orders via mail.*

telemarketing *Use of the telephone to sell directly to consumers.*

Non-store retailing also includes **direct-response retailing**, in which firms contact customers directly to inform them about products and to receive sales orders. The oldest form of retailing, **direct selling,** is still used by companies that sell door-to-door or through home-selling parties. Most of us have talked with salespeople from World Book, Avon, or Fuller Brush as they make door-to-door sales calls.

The Fuller Brush Company was started in 1906 by Arthur Fuller, a self-described "country bumpkin" from Nova Scotia. The company used to be well known in door-to-door selling, but sweeping changes in North American society—women leaving the home to work, mass retailing, and the globalization of business—caused the company to fall on hard times. Two of its most famous salesmen were the Reverend Billy Graham and disc jockey Dick Clark. The company has continued to be successful in Mexico and Argentina, where direct selling still works well.

Mail order (or **catalogue marketing**), such as that practised by Eddie Bauer, is a form of direct-response retailing. So is **telemarketing**—the use of the telephone to sell directly. Telemarketing is growing rapidly in the

United States, Canada, and Great Britain, and experts estimate that U.S. sales alone could top U.S.$800 billion in 2004.[16]

The Boom in Electronic Retailing

Electronic retailing is made possible by communications networks that let sellers post product information on consumers' PCs. With over 3.6 million subscribers, Prodigy Communications Corp. is among the largest home networks.

electronic retailing
Non-store retailing in which information about the seller's products and services is connected to consumers' computers, allowing consumers to receive the information and purchase the products in the home.

Internet-Based Stores. Use of the internet to interact with customers—to inform, sell to, and distribute to them—is growing steadily, but still constitutes only a very small proportion of total retail sales. A study by Statistics Canada showed that Canadians spent nearly $2 billion shopping the net in 2001. This was just three-tenths of one percent of total retail sales of $621 billion in Canada.[17] Ecommerce is still in its infancy; there is a lot of room for growth.

Electronic Catalogues. Ecatalogues use the internet to display products for both retail and business customers. By sending electronic versions (instead of traditional mail catalogues), firms give millions of users instant access to pages of product information. The seller avoids mail-distribution and printing costs, and once an online catalogue is in place, there is little cost in maintaining and accessing it. Recognizing these advantages, about 85 percent of all cataloguers are now on the internet, with sales via websites accounting for 10 percent of all catalogue sales. The top 10 consumer ecatalogues include JCPenney (number 1), Fingerhut (number 3), L.L. Bean (number 7), and Victoria's Secret (number 8). Top B2B ecatalogues include Dell Computer (number 1) and Office Depot (number 5).[18]

ecatalogues
Non-store retailing that uses the internet to display products and services for both retail shoppers and business customers.

Electronic Storefronts and Cybermalls. Today, a seller's website is an **electronic storefront** (or *virtual storefront*) from which consumers collect information about products and buying opportunities, place orders, and pay for purchases. Producers of large product lines, such as Dell Computer, dedicate storefronts to their own product lines. Other sites are category sellers whose storefronts feature products from many manufacturers.

electronic storefront
A seller's website in which consumers collect information about products and buying opportunities, place sales orders, and pay for their purchases.

Search engines like Yahoo! serve as **cybermalls**—collections of virtual storefronts representing diverse products. After entering a cybermall, shoppers can navigate by choosing from a list of stores (for example, Eddie Bauer), product listings (Pokémon or MP3 players), or departments (apparel or bath/beauty). When your virtual shopping cart is full, you check out and pay your bill. The value-added properties of cybermalls are obvious: speed, convenience, 24-hour access, and, most important, efficient searching that avoids the "click-'til-you-drop" syndrome—the endless wandering through cyberspace experienced by early internet users.[19]

cybermalls
Collections of virtual storefronts representing diverse products.

From Door-to-Door to Esales? Not surprisingly, cyberspace is encroaching on door-to-door distribution. Amway is famous for a **multilevel marketing** channel in which self-employed distributors get commissions for recruiting new customers and new Amway reps. Now Amway is expanding this system to the internet with a spinoff called Quixstar. With help from Quixstar, you can start your own at-home internet business. You will be paid for directing new customers to the Quixstar site and for encouraging others to become Quixstar reps. The internet's huge at-home sales potential is also luring other famous door-to-door names—Tupperware, Avon, and Mary Kay. Such firms are racing to board the internet train even though they are courting potential channel conflict. Thousands of loyal door-to-door sales reps stand to lose customers to their own companies' internet outlets.[20]

multilevel marketing
A system in which a salesperson earns a commission on their own sales and on the sales of any other salespeople they recruit.

Interactive and Video Marketing. Today, both retail and B2B customers interact with multimedia websites using voice, graphics, animation, film clips, and access to live human advice. One good example of **interactive marketing** is LivePerson, a leading provider of real-time sales and customer service for over 450 websites. When customers log on to the sites of e-Loan, Playboy, or IgoGolf—all of which are LivePerson clients—they enter a live chat room where a service operator initiates a secure one-on-one text chat. Questions and answers go back and forth to help customers with answers to specific questions that must be answered before they decide on a product. Another form of interaction is the so-called *banner ad* that changes as the user's mouse moves about the page, revealing new drop-down, check, and search boxes.[21]

interactive marketing
Selling products and services by allowing customers to interact with multimedia websites using voice, graphics, animation, film clips, and access to live human advice.

Video marketing, a long-established form of interactive marketing, lets viewers shop at home from TV screens. Most cable systems offer video marketing through home-shopping channels that display and demonstrate products and allow viewers to phone in or email orders. One network, QVC, operates in the United Kingdom, Germany, Mexico, and South America and has also launched iQVC as an interactive website.

video marketing
Selling to consumers by showing products on television that consumers can buy by telephone or mail.

PHYSICAL DISTRIBUTION

6. Define *physical distribution* and describe the major activities in *warehousing* operations.

Physical distribution refers to the activities needed to move products efficiently from manufacturer to consumer. The goals of physical distribution are to keep customers satisfied, to make goods available when and where consumers want them, and to keep costs low. Thus physical distribution includes *warehousing* and *transportation operations*, as well as *distribution for ecustomers*.

physical distribution
Those activities needed to move a product from the manufacturer to the end consumer.

Warehousing Operations

Storing, or **warehousing**, is a major part of distribution management. In selecting a strategy, managers must keep in mind both the different characteristics and costs of warehousing operations.

warehousing
That part of the distribution process concerned with storing goods.

Types of Warehouses

There are two basic types of warehouses: *private* and *public*. Facilities can be further divided according to use as *storage warehouses* or *distribution centres*.

Public and Private Warehouses. Private warehouses are owned by a single manufacturer, wholesaler, or retailer. Most are run by large firms that deal in mass quantities and need regular storage. **Public warehouses** are independently owned and operated. Because companies rent only the space they need, they are popular with firms needing storage only during peak periods. Manufacturers who need multiple storage locations to get products to multiple markets also use them.

private warehouse
A warehouse owned and used by just one company.

public warehouse
An independently owned and operated warehouse that stores the goods of many firms.

Storage Warehouses and Distribution Centres. Storage warehouses provide storage for extended periods. Producers of seasonal items, such as agricultural crops, use this type of warehouse. **Distribution centres** provide short-term storage of products whose demand is both constant and high. Retail chains, wholesalers, and manufacturers who need to break down large quantities of merchandise into the smaller quantities that stores or customers demand use them.

storage warehouse
A warehouse used to provide storage of goods for extended periods of time.

distribution centre
A warehouse used to provide storage of goods for only short periods before they are shipped to retail stores.

Distribution centres are common in the grocery and food industry. Kellogg's, for example, stores virtually no products at its plants. Instead, it ships cereals from factories to regional distribution centres. As wholesalers place orders for combinations of products, warehouses fill and ship them. Because warehouses are regional, wholesalers receive orders quickly.

Warehousing Costs

Typical warehouse costs include such obvious expenses as storage-space rental or mortgage payments (usually computed on a square-foot basis), insurance, and wages. They also include the costs of *inventory control* and *materials handling*.

Inventory Control. Inventory control means more than keeping track of what is on hand at any time. It often involves the tricky balancing act of ensuring that although an adequate supply of a product is in stock at all times, excessive supplies are avoided.

inventory control
The part of warehouse operations that keeps track of what is on hand and ensures adequate supplies of products in stock at all times.

Materials Handling. Most warehouse personnel are involved in **materials handling**: the transportation, arrangement, and orderly retrieval of inventoried goods. Holding down materials-handling costs means developing a strategy that takes into account product placement within the warehouse. Other considerations include packaging decisions (whether to store products as individual units, in multiple packages, or in sealed containers).

materials handling
The transportation and arrangement of goods within a warehouse and orderly retrieval of goods from inventory.

The strategy known as *unitization* calls for standardizing the weight and form of materials. A GE warehouse in Kentucky, for instance, receives apartment-size refrigerators from Europe in containers of 56 refrigerators each. Dealing with the huge containers rather than individual boxes not only makes handling easier but also reduces theft and damage. It also optimizes shipping space and makes restocking easier.

Transportation Operations

7. Compare the five basic forms of *transportation* and explain how distribution can be used as a marketing strategy.

Cost is a major factor when a company chooses a transportation method. But cost is not the only consideration. A company must also consider the nature of its products, the distance the product must travel, timeliness, and customers' needs and wants. A company shipping orchids or other perishable goods will probably use air transport, while a company shipping sand or coal will use rail or water transport.

Transportation Modes

The major transportation modes are trucks, railroads, planes, water carriers, and pipelines. Differences in cost are most directly related to delivery speed.

Trucks. The advantages of trucks include flexibility, fast service, and dependability. Nearly all sections of Canada, except the far north, can be reached by truck. Trucks are a particularly good choice for short-distance distribution and more expensive products. Large furniture and appliance retailers in major cities, for example, use trucks to shuttle merchandise between their stores and to make deliveries to customers. Trucks can, however, be delayed by bad weather. They also are limited in the volume they can carry in a single load.

Planes. Air is the fastest available transportation mode. In Canada's far north, it may be the only available transportation. Other advantages include greatly reduced costs in packing, handling, unpacking, and final preparations necessary for sale to the consumer. Also, eliminating the need to store certain commodities can reduce inventory-carrying costs. Fresh fish, for example, can be flown to restaurants each day, avoiding the risk of spoilage that comes with packaging and storing. However, air freight is the most expensive form of transportation. In recent years a whole new industry has evolved to meet the customer's need to receive important business papers and supplies "overnight."

Railroads. Railroads have been the backbone of our transportation system since the late 1800s. Until the 1960s, when trucking firms lowered their rates and attracted many customers, railroads were fairly profitable. They are now used primarily to transport heavy, bulky items such as cars, steel, and coal.

Water Carriers. Of all the transportation modes, water transportation is the least expensive. Unfortunately, water transportation is also the slowest way to ship. Boats and barges are mainly used for extremely heavy, bulky materials and products (like sand, gravel, oil, and steel) for which transit times are unimportant. Manufacturers are beginning to use water carriers more often because many ships are now specially constructed to load and store large standardized containers. The St. Lawrence Seaway is a vital link in Canada's water transportation system. Water transportation is also important in Canada's far north, where barges deliver commodities such as fuel oil to various isolated hamlets along the western edge of Hudson's Bay during the summer months.

Pipelines. Like water transportation, pipelines are slow in terms of overall delivery time. They are also completely inflexible, but they do provide a constant flow of the product and are unaffected by weather conditions. Traditionally, this delivery system has transported liquids and gases. Lack of adaptability to other products and limited routes make pipelines a relatively unimportant transportation method for most industries.

Changes in Transportation Operations

For many years, transport companies specialized in one mode or another. With deregulation, however, this pattern has changed. New developments in cost-efficiency and competitiveness include *intermodal transportation, containerization,* and *order fulfillment through ecommerce channels*.

intermodal transportation
The combined use of different modes of transportation.

Intermodal Transportation. Intermodal transportation—the combined use of different modes of transportation—has come into widespread use. For example, shipping by a combination of truck and rail (piggyback),

A container train crosses the Salmon River bridge in New Brunswick.

water and rail ("fishyback"), or air and rail ("birdyback") has improved flexibility and reduced costs.

Containerization. To make intermodal transport more efficient, **containerization** uses standardized heavy-duty containers in which many items are sealed at points of shipment and opened at final destinations. Containers may be stowed on ships for ocean transit, transferred to trucks, loaded onto railcars (piggyback service), and delivered to final destinations by other trucks. Unloaded containers are then returned for future use.

containerization
The use of standardized heavy-duty containers in which many items are sealed at the point of shipment and opened only at the final destination.

Physical Distribution and Ecustomer Satisfaction. New ecommerce companies often focus on sales, only to discover that delays in after-sale distribution cause customer dissatisfaction. Any delay in physical distribution is a breakdown in fulfillment. **Order fulfillment** begins when the sale is made: It involves getting the product to each customer in good condition and on time. But the volume of a firm's transactions can be huge—web retailers shipped 300 million packages in 2001—and fulfillment performance has been disappointing for many ebusinesses.

order fulfillment
All activities involved in completing a sales transaction, beginning with making the sale and ending with on-time delivery to the customer.

To improve on-time deliveries, many businesses, such as Amazon.com, maintain distribution centres and ship from their own warehouses. Other etailers, however, entrust order-filling to distribution specialists such as the giant UPS e-Logistics and the much smaller Atomic Box. Atomic Box clients range from manufacturers to dot-coms such as BODUM Inc. (an etailer of coffee and tea appliances), Decora Inc. (an etailer of window dressings), and Innovon LLC (an etailer of specially designed bags and storage devices). The company maintains 325 000 square feet of warehousing through which it annually delivers products worth more than $200 million. It handles the flow of goods and information in both B2B and business-to-consumer transactions.

Bodum
www.bodum.com

Both Atomic Box and UPS e-Logistics process customer orders, ship goods, provide information about product availability, inform customers about the real-time status of orders, and handle returns. To perform these tasks, the client's computer system must be integrated with that of the distribution specialist. In deciding whether to build their own distribution centres or to use third-party distributors, clients must consider fixed costs as well as the need for shipping expertise. Because the capital investment required for a one-million-square-foot distribution centre is $60 to $80 million, only high-volume companies can afford it. The alternative is paying a third-party distributor about 10 percent of each sale to fulfill orders.[22]

Companies Specializing in Transportation

The major modes of transportation are available from one or more of four types of transporting companies: common carriers, freight forwarders, contract carriers, and private carriers. Table 17.2 shows the top 10 transportation companies in Canada.

The nation's **common carriers** transport merchandise for any shipper—manufacturers, wholesalers, retailers, and even individual consumers. They maintain regular schedules and charge competitive prices. The best examples of common carriers are truck lines and railroads.

common carriers
Transportation companies that transport goods for any firm or individual wishing to make a shipment.

In 1897, the Crow's Nest Pass Agreement established the rate that railways could charge for hauling grain. This agreement was essentially a freight subsidy that helped prairie farmers pay some of their transportation costs to distant ports. But in 1995, the Liberal government abolished the Crow subsidy. Freight rates increased for prairie farmers, which caused them to reduce their emphasis on growing wheat and increase their emphasis on raising livestock.[23] Since the Crow rate was eliminated, livestock production and agricultural processing have increased on the prairies.

Table 17.2 The Top 10 Transportation Companies in Canada

	Company	Annual Revenues (billions of $)
1.	Air Canada	9.8
2.	Laidlaw Inc.	6.9
3.	Canadian National Railway Co.	6.1
4.	Canada Post Corp.	5.9
5.	CP Ships Ltd.	4.2
6.	Canadian Pacific Railway Ltd.	3.6
7.	Transat A.T. Inc.	2.0
8.	NAV CANADA	.9
9.	WestJet Airlines Ltd.	.6
10.	Toronto Transit Commission	.6

freight forwarders
Common carriers that lease bulk space from other carriers and resell that space to firms making small shipments.

Not all transportation companies own their own vehicles. A **freight forwarder** is a common carrier that leases bulk space from other carriers, such as railroads or airlines. It then resells parts of that space to smaller shippers. Once it has enough contracts to fill the bulk space, the freight forwarder picks up whatever merchandise is to be shipped. It then transports the goods to the bulk carrier, which makes delivery to an agreed-on destination and handles billing and any inquiries concerning the shipment.

contract carriers
Independent transporters who contract to serve as transporters for industrial customers only.

Some transportation companies will transport products for any firm for a contracted amount and time period. These **contract carriers** are usually self-employed operators who own the vehicle that transports the products. When they have delivered a contracted load to its destination, they generally try to locate another contract shipment (often with a different manufacturer) for the return trip.

private carriers
Transportation systems owned by the shipper.

A few manufacturers and retailers maintain their own transportation systems (usually a fleet of trucks) to carry their own products. The use of such **private carriers** is generally limited to very large manufacturers such as Kraft Foods and Canada Safeway.

Distribution as a Marketing Strategy

Distribution is an increasingly important way of competing for sales. Instead of just offering advantages in product features and quality, price, and promotion, many firms have turned to distribution as a cornerstone of their business strategies. This approach means assessing and improving the entire stream of activities—wholesaling, warehousing, and transportation—involved in getting products to customers.

The Use of Hubs

hub
Central distribution outlet that controls all or most of a firm's distribution activities.

One approach to streamlining is the use of **hubs**: central distribution outlets that control all or most of a firm's distribution activities. Two contrasting strategies have emerged from this approach: *supply-side and "pre-staging" hubs* on the one hand and *distribution-side hubs* on the other.

Supply-Side and "Pre-Staging" Hubs. *Supply-side hubs* are located at the same site where production activities take place. They make sense when large shipments flow regularly to a single industrial user, such as an automobile manufacturer. But these incoming shipments can create a lot of congestion, so some firms use *pre-staging hubs*, which are located near the factory. For example, Saturn maintains a pre-staging hub—managed by Ryder

System—where all incoming material is organized to ensure that Saturn's production schedule at the factory is not disrupted. At the hub, long-haul tractors are disconnected from trailers and sent on return trips to any of 339 suppliers in 39 states. Responding to Saturn's up-to-the-minute needs, hub headquarters arranges transport for presorted and pre-inspected materials to the factory by loading them onto specially designed tractors.

The chief job of the hub, then, is to coordinate the customer's materials needs with supply-chain transportation. If the hub is successful, factory inventories are virtually eliminated, storage-space requirements reduced, and long-haul trucks kept moving instead of queued up at the unloading dock. By outsourcing distribution activities to its hub, Saturn can focus on what it does best: manufacturing. Meanwhile, Ryder, the nation's largest logistics-management firm, is paid for its specialty: handling transportation flows.

Distribution-Side Hubs. Whereas supply-side hubs are located near industrial customers, *distribution-side hubs* may be located much farther away, especially if customers are geographically dispersed. National Semiconductor, one of the world's largest chip makers, is an example. Finished silicon microchips are produced in plants around the world and shipped to customers such as IBM, Toshiba, Siemens, Ford, and Compaq, which also run factories around the globe. Chips originally sat waiting at one location after another—on factory floors, at customs, in distributors' facilities, and in customers' warehouses. Typically, they travelled 20 000 different routes on as many as 12 airlines and spent time in 10 warehouses before reaching customers. National has streamlined the system by shutting down six warehouses and now airfreights chips worldwide from a single centre in Singapore. Every activity—storage, sorting, and shipping—is run by Federal Express. As a result, distribution costs have fallen, delivery times have been reduced by half, and sales have increased.

SUMMARY OF LEARNING OBJECTIVES

1. **Identify the various *pricing objectives* that govern pricing decisions and describe the price-setting tools used in making these decisions.** In *pricing*, managers decide what the company will get in exchange for its products. *Pricing objectives* refer to the goals that producers hope to attain as a result of pricing decisions. These objectives can be divided into two major categories: (1) pricing to maximize profits (pricing to sell the number of units that will generate the highest possible total profits), and (2) market share objectives (ensuring continuous sales by maintaining a strong percentage of the total sales for a specific product type). Sometimes, neither profit maximizing nor market share is the best objective. During difficult economic times, loss containment and survival may be the main objectives.

   Managers must measure the potential impact before deciding on final prices. For this purpose, they use two basic tools (which are often combined): (1) *cost-oriented pricing* (managers price products by calculating the cost of making them available to shoppers, including rent, wages, and manufacturer's cost), and (2) *break-even analysis* (using cost-oriented pricing, a firm will cover its variable costs and will also make some money to pay fixed costs). Break-even analysis assesses total costs versus revenues for various sales volumes. It shows, at any particular sales price, the financial result—the amount of loss or profit—for each possible sales volume.

2. **Discuss *pricing strategies* and tactics for both existing and new products.** Pricing strategy is important because pricing has a direct impact on revenues and is very flexible. There are three options for pricing existing products: (1) *Pricing above the market* takes advantage of the common assumption that higher price means higher quality. (2) *Pricing below the market* works if a firm can offer a product of acceptable quality while keeping costs below those of higher priced competitors. (3) *Pricing at or near market prices* is often another option.

   Companies pricing new products must often choose between two pricing policy options: (1) *Price skimming*—setting an initially high price to cover costs and generate a profit—may allow a firm to earn a large profit on each item sold; marketers must convince consumers that a product is truly different from existing products. (2) *Penetration pricing*—setting an initially low price to establish a new product in the market—seeks to generate consumer interest and stimulate trial purchase.

   Regardless of its pricing strategy, a company may adopt various pricing tactics. (1) Companies selling multiple items in a product category often use *price lining*, offering all items in certain categories at a limited number of prices. (2) *Psychological pricing* takes advantage of the fact that customers are not completely rational when making buying decisions. *Odd-even pricing* is based on the theory that customers prefer prices not stated in even-dollar amounts. (3) Often a seller must offer *price reductions*—discounts—to stimulate sales.

3. **Explain the distribution mix, the different *channels of distribution* and different *distribution strategies*.** In selecting a distribution mix, a firm may use all or any of eight distribution channels. The first four are aimed at getting products to consumers, the fifth is for consumers or business customers, and the last three are aimed at getting products to business customers. Channel 1 involves direct sales to consumers. Channel 2 includes a *retailer*. Channel 3 involves both a retailer and a *wholesaler*, and Channel 4 includes an *agent* or *broker* who enters the system before the wholesaler and retailer. Channel 5 includes only an agent between the producer and the customer. Channel 6, which is used extensively for ecommerce, involves a direct sale to an industrial user. Channel 7, which is used infrequently, entails selling to business users through wholesalers. Channel 8 includes retail superstores that get products from producers or wholesalers (or both) for re-selling to business customers. *Distribution strategies* include intensive, exclusive, and selective distribution, which differ in the number of products and channel members involved and in the amount of service performed in the channel.

4. **Explain the differences between *merchant wholesalers* and *agents/brokers*, and describe the activities of e-intermediaries.** Services offered by wholesalers to buyers of products for resale depend on the type of intermediary involved: (1) *Merchant wholesalers* buy products from manufacturers and sell them to other businesses, usually providing storage and delivery. A *full-service merchant wholesaler* also provides credit, marketing, and merchandising. *Limited-function merchant wholesalers* provide only a few services, sometimes merely storage. (2) *Agents and brokers* are independent representatives of many companies and work on commissions. They serve as sales and merchandising arms of producers that don't have sales forces.

   E-intermediaries are internet-based channel members who perform one or both of two functions: (1) They collect information about sellers and present it to consumers; (2) they help deliver internet products. There are three types of e-intermediaries: (1) *Syndicated selling* occurs when a website offers other websites a commission for referring customers. (2) *Shopping agents* (or *e-agents*) help internet consumers by gathering and sorting information (such as comparison prices and product features) for making purchases. (3) *Business-to-business brokers* are ecommerce intermediaries for business customers. They may provide up-to-date market information and price and product data.

5. **Identify the different types of *retailing* and *retail stores*.**

Retail operations fall under two classifications: (1) *Product line retailers*, which feature broad product lines. Types of stores include department stores and supermarkets, which are divided into departments of related products. Small specialty stores serve clearly defined market segments by offering full product lines in narrow product fields. (2) *Bargain retailers* carry wide ranges of products and come in many forms, such as discount houses, catalogue showrooms, factory outlets, the warehouse club (or wholesale club), and convenience stores.

Important forms of *non-store retailing* include direct-response retailing, in which firms make direct contact with customers to inform them about products and take sales orders. *Mail order* (or *catalogue marketing*) is a form of direct-response retailing, as is *telemarketing*—using the telephone to sell directly to consumers. *Direct selling* is still used by companies that sell door-to-door or through home-selling parties.

Electronic retailing uses communications networks that allow sellers to connect to consumers' computers. Sellers provide members with internet access to product displays. Buyers can examine detailed descriptions, compare brands, send for free information, or purchase by credit card. *Ecatalogues* use the internet to display products for both retail and business customers. Today, a seller's website is an electronic storefront in which consumers collect information about products, place orders, and pay for purchases. Search engines such as Yahoo! serve as *cybermalls*: collections of virtual storefronts representing diverse products and offering such added value as speed, convenience, and efficient searching.

Cyberspace is encroaching on door-to-door distribution channels. In a *multilevel marketing channel*, self-employed distributors get commissions for recruiting new customers and reps. Both retail and B2B customers participate in *interactive marketing*: They interact with multimedia websites featuring voice, graphics, animation, film clips, and access to live human advice. The so-called banner ad, for example, changes as the user's mouse moves about the page. *Video marketing* lets viewers shop at home from television screens.

6. **Define *physical distribution*, and describe the major activities in *warehousing* operations.** *Physical distribution* refers to the activities needed to move products from manufacturer to consumer. These activities make goods available when and where consumers want them, keep costs low, and provide customer services. They include *warehousing*, or the storage of goods. There are two types of warehouses: *Private warehouses* are owned and used by a single manufacturer, wholesaler, or retailer. *Public warehouses* are independently owned and operated and permit companies to rent only the space they need. Facilities can be further divided according to their uses: *Storage warehouses* provide storage for extended periods. *Distribution centres* store products whose market

demand is constant and high. Retail chains, wholesalers, and manufacturers use them to break down large quantities of merchandise into the smaller quantities that stores or customers demand.

Typical warehouse operations include two important costs: In addition to keeping track of what is on hand at any time, *inventory control* involves the balancing act of ensuring that although an adequate supply of a product is in stock at all times, excessive supplies are avoided. *Materials handling* refers to the transportation, arrangement, and orderly retrieval of inventoried goods.

7. **Compare the five basic forms of *transportation*, and explain how distribution can be used as a marketing strategy.** The highest cost faced by many companies is the cost of physically moving a product. But firms must consider other factors: the nature of the product, the distance it must travel, the speed with which it must be received, and customer wants and needs. There are five different modes of transportation. (1) *Trucks*: The advantages of trucks include flexibility, fast service, and dependability. (2) *Railroads*: Railroads are now used primarily to transport heavy, bulky items such as cars and steel. Railroad services now include faster delivery and piggyback service, in which truck trailers are placed on railcars. (3) *Planes*: Air is the fastest available mode of transportation and also boasts lower costs in handling and packing and unpacking. However, air freight is the most expensive form of transportation. (4) *Water carriers*: Water is the least expensive and the slowest. (5) *Pipelines*: Used to transport liquids and gases, pipelines are slow and inflexible but do provide a constant flow of products and are unaffected by weather.

   Important developments in cost-efficiency and competitiveness include *intermodal transportation*—combining different modes of transportation. *Containerization* uses standardized heavy-duty containers in which goods are sealed at points of shipment and opened at final destinations. To improve *order fulfillment*—all activities involved in sales transactions—many ebusinesses maintain distribution centres and ship their own products from warehouses near major shipping hubs. Others entrust order filling to distribution specialists.

   Many firms regard distribution as a cornerstone of business strategy. One approach to streamlining distribution is the use of *hubs*. Two contrasting strategies have emerged from this approach: (1) *Supply-side hubs* make the most sense when large shipments flow regularly to a single industrial user. To clear congestion, some firms operate *prestaging hubs* at which all incoming supplies are managed to meet production schedules. (2) Whereas supply-side hubs are located near industrial customers, *distribution-side hubs* may be located much farther away, especially if customers are geographically dispersed. From these facilities, finished products, which may be produced in plants throughout the world, can be shipped to customer locations around the globe.

KEY TERMS

bargain retailers, 615
break-even analysis, 598
break-even point, 599
cash discount, 606
catalogue showroom, 615
category killers, 615
channel captain, 610
channel conflict, 610
common carriers, 621
containerization, 621
contract carriers, 622
convenience stores, 615
cybermalls, 617
department stores, 614
direct channel, 605
direct selling, 616
direct-response retailing, 616
discount, 604
discount houses, 615
distribution centre, 618
distribution channel, 605
distribution mix, 605
drop shipper, 612
ecatalogues, 617
e-intermediaries, 612
electronic retailing, 617
electronic storefront, 617
exclusive distribution, 609
factory outlets, 615
fixed costs, 598
freight forwarders, 622
full-service merchant wholesaler, 612
hub, 622
industrial (business) distribution, 608
intensive distribution, 609
interactive marketing, 618
intermediary, 605
intermodal transportation, 620
inventory control, 619
limited-function merchant wholesaler, 612
mail order (catalogue marketing), 616
market share, 597
materials handling, 619
merchant wholesaler, 611
multilevel marketing, 617
odd-even psychological pricing, 604
order fulfillment, 621
penetration-pricing strategy, 602
physical distribution, 618
price leadership, 602
price lining, 603
price-skimming strategy, 602
pricing objectives, 596
pricing, 596
private carriers, 622
private warehouse, 618
psychological pricing, 604
public warehouse, 618
quantity discount, 604
rack jobber, 612
retailers, 605
sales agent (or broker), 607
sales offices, 608
seasonal discount, 604
selective distribution, 610
shopping agent (e-agent), 613
specialty stores, 614
storage warehouse, 618
supermarket, 614
syndicated selling, 613
telemarketing, 616
trade discount, 604
variable costs, 598
vertical marketing system (VMS), 610
video marketing, 618
warehouse club (wholesale club), 615
warehousing, 618
wholesalers, 605

QUESTIONS AND EXERCISES

Questions for Review

1. How do cost-oriented pricing and break-even analysis help managers measure the potential impact of prices?
2. Identify four types of discounting and give an example for each that is different from the examples in the text.
3. What is the overall goal of price skimming? Of penetration pricing?
4. From the manufacturer's point of view, what are the advantages and disadvantages of using intermediaries to distribute products? From the end-user's point of view?
5. Identify the eight channels of distribution. In what key ways do the four channels used only for consumer products differ from the channels used only for industrial products?
6. Identify and explain the differences between the three distribution strategies.
7. Explain the different roles played by merchant wholesalers and agents/brokers.
8. Explain how the activities of e-agents (internet shopping agents) or brokers differ from those of traditional agents/brokers.
9. Identify the five modes of transportation used in product distribution. What factors lead companies to choose one mode over the others to deliver products to end-users?

Questions for Analysis

10. Suppose that a small publisher selling to book distributors has fixed operating costs of $600 000 each year and variable costs of $3 per book. How many books must the firm sell to break even if the selling price is $6? If the company expects to sell 50 000 books next year and decides on a 40 percent markup, what will the selling price be?
11. Suppose that your company produces industrial products for other firms. How would you go about determining the prices of your products? Describe the method you would use to arrive at a pricing decision.

12. Give three examples (other than those provided in the chapter) of products that use intensive distribution. Do the same for products that use exclusive distribution and selective distribution. For which category was it easiest to find examples? Why?

13. Consider the various kinds of non-store retailing. Give examples of two products that typify the products sold to at-home shoppers through each form of non-store retailing. Explain why different products are best suited to each form of non-store retailing.

14. If you could own a firm that transports products, would you prefer to operate an intermodal transportation business or one that specializes in a single mode of transportation (say, truck or air)? Explain your choice.

Application Exercises

15. Select a product with which you are familiar and analyze various possible pricing objectives for it. What information would you want to have if you were to adopt a profit-maximizing objective? A market share objective? An image objective?

16. Interview the manager of a local manufacturing firm. Identify the firm's distribution strategy and the channels of distribution that it uses. Where applicable, describe the types of wholesalers or retail stores used to distribute the firm's products.

17. Choose any consumer item at your local supermarket and trace the chain of physical distribution activities that brought it to the store shelf.

BUILDING YOUR BUSINESS SKILLS

Are You Sold on the Net?

Goal

To encourage students to consider the value of online retailing as an element in a company's distribution system.

Situation

As the distribution manager of a privately owned clothing manufacturer specializing in camping gear and outdoor clothing, you are convinced that your product line is perfect for online distribution. However, the owner of the company is reluctant to expand distribution from a successful network of retail stores and a catalogue operation. Your challenge is to convince the boss that retailing via the internet can boost sales.

Method

Step 1

Join together with four or five classmates to research the advantages and disadvantages of an online distribution system for your company. Among the factors to consider are the following:

- The likelihood that target consumers are internet shoppers. Young, affluent consumers who are comfortable with the web generally purchase camping gear.
- The industry trend to online distribution. Are similar companies doing it? Have they been successful?
- The opportunity to expand inventory without increasing the cost of retail space or catalogue production and mailing charges.
- The opportunity to have a store that never closes.
- The lack of trust many people have about doing business on the web. Many consumers are reluctant to provide credit card data over the web.
- The difficulty that electronic shoppers have in finding a website when they do not know the store's name.
- The frustration and waiting time involved in web searches.
- The certainty that the site will not reach consumers who do not use computers or who are uncomfortable with the web.

Step 2

Based on your findings, write a persuasive memo to the company's owner stating your position about expanding to an online distribution system. Include information that will counter expected objections.

Follow-Up Questions

1. What place does online distribution have in the distribution network of this company?
2. In your view, is online distribution the wave of the future? Is it likely to increase in importance as a distribution system for apparel companies? Why or why not?

CRAFTING YOUR BUSINESS PLAN

Getting the Caffeine into Your Cup

The Purpose of the Assignment

1. To acquaint students with product distribution issues that a sample firm addresses in developing its business plan, in the framework of the Business PlanPro (BPP) 2002 software package.
2. To demonstrate how channels of distribution, supply chains, and warehousing can be integrated as components in the BPP planning environment.

Assignment

After reading Chapter 17 in the textbook, open the BPP software and look for information about plans for supply chains and channels of distribution as they apply to a sample firm, a coffee exporter: Silvera & Sons Ltd. To find Silvera, do the following:

Open the Business PlanPro. If it asks if you want to "create a new business plan" or to "open an existing plan," select "create a new business plan" (even though you are not going to create a plan at this time). You will then be taken to the Business PlanPro EasyPlan Wizard. On the screen, click on the option entitled **Research It**. You will then be presented a new list of options, including Sample Plan Browser. After clicking on the **Sample Plan Browser**, scan its alphabetical list of sample plans and double-click on **Export—Coffee**, which is the location for Silvera & Sons Ltd. The screen you are looking at is the introduction page for the Silvera business plan. Next, scroll down from this page until you reach the Table of Contents for the Silvera business plan.

Now respond to the following items:

1. Describe Silvera's products and customers. Then identify the steps in the supply chain, beginning from raw materials to the final consumer. [Sites to see in BPP for this item: In the **Table of Contents** page, click on **1.0 Executive Summary**. Then click on each of the following in turn: **1.1 Objectives, 2.0 Company Summary, 2.2 Company History,** and **3.0 Products**.]
2. Where is Silvera's main warehouse located? What are its activities? [Sites to see in BPP: In the **Table of Contents** page, click on **2.3 Company Locations and Facilities**. After returning to the **Table of Contents** page, click on **3.0 Products**.]
3. Describe the equipment and warehousing activities that are needed to prepare coffee beans for shipment. [Sites to see in BPP: From the **Table of Contents** page, click on each of the following in turn: **3.1 Competitive Comparison** and **3.4 Technology**.]
4. What steps are involved in getting the product from Silvera's plant in Ouro Fino to Miami? Who is responsible for paying the distribution charges? [Sites to see in BPP: In the **Table of Contents** page, click on **4.2.2 Distribution Patterns**. After returning to the **Table of Contents** page, click on **5.3.4 Distribution Strategy**.]

VIDEO EXERCISE

Through the Grapevine: Clos du Bois Winery

Learning Objectives

The purpose of this video is to help you:

1. Understand how a company works with wholesalers and retailers to make its products available to consumers.
2. Discuss the factors that affect a company's distribution strategy.
3. Consider the goals and challenges of physical distribution.

Synopsis

Riding a tidal wave of consumer interest in California wines, Clos du Bois Winery sells its wines from coast to coast. The company now ships more than one million cases of wine every year, although less than 20 percent is sold in California. The winery works through a network of state-wide and regional distributors that sell to retailers and restaurants which, in turn, serve the wine to consumers. For efficient order fulfillment and inventory management, Clos du Bois ships from a central warehouse to more than 300 wholesaler warehouses around the United States. To ensure that quality is not compromised by temperature extremes, the company also pays close attention to the details of physical distribution. Now it is tapping the infrastructure of parent company Allied Domecq to arrange for wider distribution in Europe.

Discussion Questions

1. *For analysis:* Why does Clos du Bois sell through wholesalers rather than selling directly to retailers and restaurants?
2. *For analysis:* How does the U.S. pattern of table wine consumption affect the winery's domestic distribution strategy?
3. *For application:* What might Clos du Bois do if its supply of a certain vintage runs low?
4. *For application:* What effect does the cost of storing and shipping Clos du Bois wine have on the prices paid by retailers and, ultimately, consumers?
5. *For debate:* Given its long-term relationships with established wholesalers, should Clos du Bois lobby against direct sales of wine to U.S. consumers through internet channels? Support your position.

Online Exploration

Visit the website of the Clos du Bois Winery at **www.closdubois.com/home.html** and (if you are of legal drinking age) enter and read what the company says about its wines, winery, and wine club. Also follow the link to explore the trade site and find out where Clos du Bois wines are sold. Considering the winery's dependence on distributors, why would it invest so heavily in a consumer-oriented website? What channel conflict might be caused by this site? If you cannot legally enter the winery's website, use your favourite search engine (such as Google.com) to see whether other online retailers are selling this wine. If so, why would Clos du Bois make its wine available through these intermediaries?

EXPLORING THE NET

A New Chapter in Retailing

This particular chapter examines a variety of retail operations ranging from department stores to electronic retailing. Chapters is one example of a popular retailer in Canada. Examine their website at **www.chapters.indigo.ca**.

1. Based on the types of retail operations described in this chapter, what retail classification would you place Chapters in? Does Chapters operate in more than one classification?
2. After examining this website, how would you describe Chapters' product mix?
3. Are there any categories listed on the Chapters' website that are targeted toward organizations rather than individual consumers?
4. What tools are used by Chapters to ensure that their ecustomers are satisfied?
5. How does Chapters get the products ordered from the website to their customers? Specifically describe what forms of physical distribution are used.

Concluding Case 17-1

Ice.Com

Mayer, Schmuel, and Pinny Gniwisch and their brother-in-law Moshe Krasnanski are Montreal rabbis who started an online company called Ice.com. The company sells mid- and low-priced jewellery over the internet, and (surprise!) it's profitable. Company sales were U.S.$10 million in 2002, and should hit U.S.$20 million in 2003. Almost all of the company's customers are in the United States. In the December 2002 issue of *Internet Retailer*, Ice.com was named as one of the top 50 etailers.

The four men have discovered that they can make a profit selling jewellery online because margins are higher than they are for books or electronics. It also helps that jewellery fits well in the ecommerce environment because it is high in value but small in size. This makes it easy to ship products to customers. Although there are only a few instantly recognizable brand names in this business (e.g., Cartier and Tiffany), there are opportunities for companies who are able to convince customers that unbranded products are good deals. Ice.com has been able to do that.

Before they started Ice.com, the Gniwisch brothers knew a lot about the jewellery business, but they didn't know anything about the internet. They did have one big advantage: their mother owned a company called Delmar International, which supplies mid-priced jewellery products to stores like Wal-Mart, The Bay, and Sears. The brothers knew that they would have a steady source of products to sell, and they also knew they wouldn't have to bear the cost of inventory. The savings they achieved could be passed on to consumers in the form of lower prices, which would make Ice.com attractive to buyers.

Ice.com keeps its costs low by using four other strategies. First, everyone in the company does whatever needs to be done to make the company profitable. For example, although Pinny is the CEO, he often talks on the phone with customers because that is where the action is. Second, Ice.com also keeps wage costs low by being in Montreal, where labour costs are half what they would be if the company was located in California. Third, the company's 4000 square foot warehouse is in the low-rent district, and this further reduces costs. Finally, all the jewellery that is sold is privately labelled and designed by independent contractors.

From the beginning, the Gniwisch brothers identified their target market as consumers in the low- to mid-price range. Most of the items that Ice.com sells cost between $50 and $750. Pinny thinks that internet surfers may buy products at the lower end of this price range on impulse, and that of course increases sales revenue. More than two-thirds of the Ice.com shoppers are female. The busiest time of day is around noon, when professional women are surfing the web on their lunch hour.

A big problem for many etailers is that their sites are not easy for customers to navigate. The Ice.com site has a search function that shoppers can use to find items in various ways. They can, for example, look for items on the basis of price, or by type of jewellery, or by what is selling well. Ice.com has also introduced a multi-payment plan that makes jewellery more affordable. A by-product of this strategy is that consumer trust in Ice.com has increased because they know that the company is willing to send them merchandise before they've fully paid for it.

Unlike a lot of razzle-dazzle dot.coms that went bankrupt, Ice.com has adopted a more conservative "slow and steady" strategy. The Gniwisch brothers have also kept their father's advice in mind: Buy for a dollar and sell for two.

Questions for Discussion

1. Which of the channels of distribution depicted in Figure 17.2 is being used by Ice.com? Explain your answer.
2. Which of the pricing strategies discussed in this chapter is Ice.com using? Explain.
3. Is Ice.com a retail or wholesale business? Explain.
4. How does Ice.com get the products they sell into the hands of consumers? (You may have to do a little research to answer this question.) ◆

Concluding Case 17-2

What's the Latest in File-Sharing?

Everyone knows that the internet is changing the way we get our musical entertainment—from when we buy, to whom we get it from, to what we pay, to how it gets from sellers to consumers. Just a few years ago, record stores were the standard sites for finding CDs and audiotapes. You could save some money by going from store to store and comparing prices. In fact, browsing display stands for artists and labels was a way of life for many music buyers.

Then came internet stores, many of them offering discount prices. You go to a site like **www.cdhitlist.com**, which offers thousands of titles among CDs, cassettes, and VHS/DVD movies. You search the lists, place orders electronically or over the phone, and then receive your music or movie by mail.

Then came an online music service called Napster, where you could exchange music with other Napster users, sending your albums to others on the internet and receiving albums from them. The music itself was not actually traded on Napster's website. Instead, you went to the website to obtain the Napster software, which you could download (again, for free) onto your computer. The software found albums that you had stored (in MP3 format) on your hard disk and published that information on Napster's website, along with similar lists from millions of other users. Then you could start trading with anyone else who was live on the internet at the same time. For free. Napster was accessible 24 hours per day, and you didn't have to wait for the mail because albums were transmitted digitally and downloaded onto your computer in just a few minutes. At its peak, Napster had 60 million users.

The record industry was not impressed with Napster's channel of distribution. It argued that file-sharing denied music artists the right to earn their living from royalties on the sales of their albums, and it pointed to declines in record sales as proof that file-sharing was a big problem. In Canada, for example, record sales declined from 64.1 million albums in 1999 to only 51.9 million in 2002. Illegal downloading may have caused much of that decline.

Each time a file-swapping user gets a free album instead of buying it from a legitimate vendor, the recording artist is denied royalties. Without paying for an album, how can the costs of production be recovered? And at a market price of zero dollars for an album, how can record stores hope to stay in business when, obviously, they cannot lower their prices to zero?

The threat from Napster was seen as so great that a recording industry trade organization, the Recording Industry Association of America (RIAA), decided to prosecute. Napster proclaimed its innocence, arguing that it did nothing more than supply software. It neither took possession of albums nor did it buy or sell them. The trading of albums occurred solely among individuals on the open market. The courts didn't buy this argument, and Napster was shut down for copyright infringement. To the recording industry's dismay, the victory was short-lived, as other file-sharing services like Morpheus, Kazaa, and Grokster popped up.

In response, the RIAA announced that it would start filing charges against individuals who used file-sharing services. File-sharing networks were searched and individuals who were heavy users were identified. By mid-2003, several university students in the United States had been successfully sued by record companies. As part of the settlement, they agreed to pay between U.S.$12 000 and U.S.$17 500 apiece as the penalty for file-swapping. They also were required to disable the websites that helped users at their schools to do the same. The RIAA also announced that it would soon be bringing charges against hundreds of other users of file-swapping services. To date, the Canadian Recording Industry Association (CRIA) has launched legal action against online distributors, but has not yet targeted individual users of the services. It has also produced commercials that are designed to make people feel guilty for downloading free music.

As part of their overall strategy to combat illegal downloading, the recording industry has launched two online music services—MusicNet and Pressplay. If you use MusicNet, you pay $9.95 a month and get 100 downloads (but you can't copy them and the deal expires at the end of the month). If you use Pressplay, you get 100 downloads for $24.95 per month (and the right to burn 20 tracks to a CD).

In early 2003, a new threat to the recording industry appeared. Plans were announced to start a new internet peer-to-peer service in the city of Arnhem in the Netherlands. The company would provide software and legal advice to anyone who wanted to start the next Morpheus or Kazaa. The companies would be started in the Netherlands, where (at the moment anyway) there is legal protection for companies that do this.

Where will all this lead? Will this aggressive action by record companies alienate their customers? Will customers be willing to start paying for the right to download, especially if they might be arrested if they don't? Will the record industry succeed in its attempts to stop file-sharing? Shawn Fanning, the person who started Napster, doesn't think the recording industry will be able to stop music piracy by taking people to court. He says that the nature of the internet is such that when one service shuts down, another one will pop up.

Time will tell.

Questions for Discussion

1. Consider the traditional channels of distribution for music albums. Which channel elements are most affected by the presence of services like Napster, Morpheus, and Kazaa? Explain how those elements are affected.
2. Why is the music industry so concerned about internet distribution? Are there any opportunities for the recording industry in internet distribution?
3. Develop arguments opposing the legality of services offered by Morpheus and Kazaa. Then take the reverse position and develop an argument in favour of these services.
4. Does file-sharing raise any ethical issues or social responsibility concerns?
5. What other products, besides music albums, are the most likely candidates for distribution on the internet, now and in the future? ◆

Video Case 4-1 CBC

Clodhoppers

You probably remember Larry Finnson and Chris Emery and their ever-expanding Krave Candy empire (see the opening case in Chapter 16). They've had triumphs, tragedies, and growing pains, but they've managed to turn a family recipe into a multi-million dollar candy business. And they've expanded into ice cream, with their Clodhoppers Blizzard being sold at Dairy Queen.

Larry and Chris recently attended a Dairy Queen conference, and they wanted to make themselves known to the worldwide Dairy Queen operation. They were nobodies at the conference; that is, until they were the successful bidders at a conference auction. What they bought was a day's work from Chuck Moody, the president of Dairy Queen International. Moody will be coming to Winnipeg for one day to work for them. He'll know who they are after that.

Larry and Chris want to pitch the Clodhopper Blizzard to Moody when he's in Winnipeg. The product has sold well at Canadian Dairy Queens so far, and Larry and Chris would like to expand sales to U.S. Dairy Queen stores. This would be a big step up, since there are only 534 Dairy Queens in Canada but 5700 in the U.S.

Larry and Chris also want to establish a relationship with Moody because he reports to Warren Buffett, the legendary fund manager and a major shareholder in Dairy Queen. Hopefully Moody's appearance in Winnipeg will be more than just a photo opportunity. Does Moody have any idea of what he's in for?

Larry and Chris meet him at the hotel and tell him what they're going to do for the day. They give him a brief tour of Winnipeg and then take him to the Clodhoppers plant. He puts on a hairnet, does some production work, and learns how to package Clodhoppers candy. He also tastes the product, and then autographs a box for posterity. He's given a 30-minute lunch break at a local Dairy Queen, where he has a Clodhopper Blizzard.

Larry and Chris meet with Chuck after lunch. They want to raise awareness for the Children's Miracle Network. They also make known their wish to have the Clodhopper Blizzard sold in U.S. Dairy Queens. Chuck says the product is good, but unknown, and he thinks DQ could make it better. He's receptive to a trial, and wants Larry and Chris to come down and develop a taste profile. He also wants to assess how much consumer interest there is in the product.

Chuck then heads back to Minneapolis. He knew he would be given a sales pitch when he decided to come to Winnipeg. He's glad the two guys are enthusiastic. Warren Buffett would see two energetic individuals with a passion for the business. Maybe Clodhoppers Blizzard will turn into an international treat.

Questions for Discussion

1. Briefly describe the factors in Krave Candy's external marketing environment. Which of these factors are particularly important in the development of the Clodhopper Blizzard?
2. What are the four basic types of research methods used by market researchers? Which of these methods do you think would be most useful in determining consumer interest in the Clodhopper Blizzard? Explain.
3. What are the steps in the new product development process? Explain the difficulties that might be encountered in moving the Clodhopper Blizzard through the various stages in the new product development process.

Source: CBC *Venture*, "Clodhoppers," September 15, 2002.

Video Case 4-2 CBC

Hydrogen Fuel Cell

There are 600 million automobiles in the world, and almost all of them are powered by the internal combustion engine. Developed in the late nineteenth century, the engine is now well-entrenched because it's powerful, reliable, convenient, and efficient. Unfortunately, it also pollutes the air, so there's a great deal of interest in finding an alternative source of power for automobiles. In recent years, the hydrogen fuel cell has been touted as the wave of the future. The fuel cell creates electric power while producing virtually no pollution, just water vapour.

But North American drivers are unlikely to change to the fuel cell unless it can be shown that it is better than the internal combustion engine. It will also take many years to displace the internal combustion engine because changing the entire automobile industry is a massive undertaking. A group called The California Fuel Cell Partnership is plotting a campaign to accomplish the change. It brings together executives from oil companies and car makers along with scientists and government officials.

Honda is one car maker that's interested; it leases an experimental fuel cell car to the city of Los Angeles. Everyone agrees that the fuel cell is an impressive technological achievement, but it's nowhere near ready for the mass market. There are two key problems. First, fuel cell cars can only go about 160 miles before they need refuelling. Developers think that they'll have to achieve at least 300 miles before the general public is interested. Second, there are virtually no hydrogen refuelling stations in existence that would make it convenient for customers to fuel up. There is a reluctance to build hydrogen refuelling stations until the fuel cell has been perfected for use in cars.

Two Canadian companies are working on solving these two major problems. Stuart Energy is the world leader in building hydrogen refuelling stations. Jon Slangerup, CEO of Stuart, says the company currently has nine such stations and is building more. He admits that changing the world is going to take a long time, but his company is making a start. Ballard Power Systems is the second company. It received a great deal of publicity in the 1990s about its hydrogen fuel cell development efforts. However, its star has fallen because results have been slow to come and the investment community has become disillusioned. Fuel cell testing continues, but the optimistic predictions of just a few years ago have been abandoned.

Experts think that the fuel cell will eventually displace the internal combustion engine as the power source for automobiles, but that it will likely take several decades. There's also a feeling that once the fuel cell is perfected, fuelling stations will quickly become common, just as gas stations did in the early twentieth century once the internal combustion engine was perfected.

Frustrated proponents of the fuel cell claim that car companies have been holding back on R&D spending on fuel cells because they're too focused on making profits out of the existing internal combustion technology. They say that many billions of dollars must be invested in R&D before the fuel cell will come into wide use. In 2002, the U.S. government announced that it was allocating $1.2 billion for research on fuel cells. This may cause some businesses to get more interested. Allan Lloyd, chair of the California Fuel Cell Partnership, says the government's action may motivate some of the car companies to focus more on fuel cells because they may fear getting left behind if they don't. DaimlerChrysler, meanwhile, is the first car company to get serious about hydrogen fuel cells.

The world may want hydrogen fuel cells, but the internal combustion engine still rules as king of the road.

Questions for Discussion

1. Briefly describe the factors in a company's external marketing environment. Which of these factors are particularly important in the development of the hydrogen fuel cell for use in automobiles?
2. What are the four basic types of research methods used by market researchers? Which of these methods do you think would be most useful in determining consumer interest in a fuel cell–powered automobile? Explain.
3. How is the concept of the product life cycle relevant to the hydrogen fuel cell?
4. What are the steps in the new product development process? Using the information in this case and in the Business Today box on p. 557 of the text, explain the difficulties that might be encountered in moving the fuel cell through the various stages in the new product development process.

Source: CBC *Venture*, "Powering the Future," March 2, 2003.

PART FIVE

TSX
S&P/TSX Indices
Dow Jones
TSX % Losers
S&P/TSX Venture
TSX Venture Most Actives
Money Markets
Asia/Pacific Indices
Canadian Dollar
REUTERS
S&P TSX 60 IDX (XIU)
100 @ 43.11 0.08
WESTJET AIRLINE (WJA)
300 @ 25.00 0.70
MITEC TELECOM (MTM)
500 @ 0.54
CDN NTL RAILWY
500 @ 74.64
CDN NTL RAILWY (CNR)
500 @ 74.64 0.01

Managing Financial Issues

Management of the financial transactions of a business firm is absolutely critical to its survival. Whether it involves raising money to start a new firm, assessing the riskiness of the firm's investments, managing the firm's cash, or monitoring the firm's activities in securities markets, financial management is a key business activity. The opening cases of the chapters in this section describe the importance of financial management to companies such as the Royal Bank of Canada, the Bank of Montreal, RT Capital Management, and Eaton's.

Part Five, Managing Financial Issues, provides an overview of business finance, including how firms raise and manage money, how they define and manage risk, and how they use Canadian and international securities markets to meet their financial needs.

- We begin in **Chapter 18, Understanding Money and Banking**, by exploring the nature of money, its creation through the banking system, and the role of the Bank of Canada in the nation's financial system. We also describe other important financial services organizations.
- Next, in **Chapter 19, Understanding Securities and Investments**, we consider the markets in which firms raise long-term funds by examining how these markets operate and how they are regulated.
- Finally, in **Chapter 20, Financial Decisions and Risk Management**, we look at three reasons businesses need funds and how financial managers raise both long- and short-term funds. We also examine the kinds of risks businesses encounter and the ways in which they deal with such risks.

CHAPTER 18 Understanding Money and Banking

After reading this chapter, you should be able to:

1. Define *money* and identify the different forms it takes in the nation's money supply.
2. Describe the different kinds of *financial institutions* that make up the Canadian financial system and explain the services they offer.
3. Explain how banks create money and identify the means by which they are regulated.
4. Explain the functions of the *Bank of Canada* and describe the tools it uses to control the money supply.
5. Identify ways in which the banking industry is changing.
6. Understand some of the key activities in *international banking and finance*.

What's Happening to the Canadian Dollar?

During the period 1999–2003, the Canadian dollar was worth about U.S.$0.65. During the spring of 2003, however, the value of the Canadian dollar suddenly rose sharply to U.S.$0.74. Many people felt relieved that the Canadian dollar had moved up from its formerly low value, but some other Canadians weren't so happy. They were the ones who owned and operated manufacturing and natural resource firms.

Here's why: a low Canadian dollar means that goods we export to the United States are relatively cheap for U.S. buyers. The low price therefore increases demand for Canadian products and improves our ability to export a lot of manufactured goods and natural resources like timber and oil. But when the loonie rose in value in early 2003, the price of Canadian exports rose and that was likely to decrease demand. Since the Canadian economy is so dependent on exports to other countries (particularly the United States), the rising value of the loonie is problematic. Consider the experience of the following companies:

- Oakville, Ontario-based GSW Inc. manufactures building products, 80 percent of which are sold in the United States. The company reported a $1.5 million foreign exchange loss in the first quarter of 2003 because of the increase in the value of the Canadian dollar. This occurred because the profits generated from the company's U.S. operations were worth much less in Canadian dollars than previously because the Canadian dollar had risen so much in value.
- Toronto-based Sun Life Financial Services also has extensive U.S. operations. The rise in the value of the Canadian dollar reduced its profit for the first quarter of 2003 by about $4 million.
- Lunenberg, Nova Scotia-based High Liner Foods Inc. sells more than 50 percent of its output in the United States. Its revenue was reduced by $2.4 million in the first quarter of 2003 because of the increase in the value of the Canadian dollar.
- Potash Corporation of Saskatchewan, which reports its earnings in U.S. dollars, gained about half a million dollars on foreign exchange operations in the first quarter of 2002, but lost nearly $17 million in the first quarter of 2003.
- Montreal-based Peerless Clothing ships large numbers of men's suits to the United States. The increase in the Canadian dollar meant that Peerless could either accept less revenue (if it kept its U.S. prices the same) or it could raise prices in the United States to avoid a decline in revenue. The trouble is, Peerless will sell fewer suits in the United States if it raises prices.

Are there any benefits to a rising dollar? Yes. A Canadian company that has debts payable in U.S. dollars is obviously better off when the Canadian dollar rises. It can buy more U.S. dollars for a given number of Canadian dollars now than it could when the Canadian dollar was lower, and this reduces the total payout it has to make. There is also an emotional factor: Canadians probably feel better if those in other countries view our currency favourably. This idea was summed up by Jim Buckee, the CEO of Talisman Energy Inc., who said that a country can't depreciate its way to greatness. He meant that continuously depreciating a country's currency might mean more export sales in the short run, but problems for the country in the long run.

In very general terms, there are winners and losers when the Canadian dollar goes up in value. Winners include:

- Canadian consumers (giant retailers like Wal-Mart plan to cut prices because they benefit when the value of the Canadian dollar increases)
- Canadian professional sports teams (they usually pay their players in U.S. funds, so when the Canadian dollar goes up, it costs them less money)
- Canadians travelling to the United States (the Canadian dollar is worth more, so it costs less to travel in the United States)
- Canadian firms with U.S. dollar debt (their debt declines as the value of the Canadian dollar increases)

Losers include:

- Canadian railroads (they take in much of their revenue in U.S. dollars, so when the Canadian dollar increases in value, they get less money than they did when the Canadian dollar was low)

- Canadian exporters (their goods cost more in the United States when the Canadian dollar rises)
- Canadian film production (the costs of Canadian film production rise for U.S. companies, so they are less likely to come to Canada)
- Canadians who invest in U.S. stocks (while stocks have increased in value, the increase in the Canadian dollar has been even greater, so Canadian investors' mutual funds may be worth less than when the dollar was low)
- Canadians who keep U.S. dollars savings accounts (the value of the U.S. dollar has declined relative to the Canadian dollar) ◆

WHAT IS MONEY?

1. Define *money* and identify the different forms it takes in the nation's money supply.

When someone asks you how much money you have, what do you say? Do you count the bills and coins in your pockets? Do you mention the funds in your chequing and savings accounts? What about stocks, bonds, or your car? Taken together, the value of everything you own is your personal *wealth*. Not all of it, however, is *money*. In this section, we will consider what money is and what it does. As the opening case shows, the value of money can fluctuate, and this can have a big effect on a country and the people living in it.

The Characteristics of Money

Modern money usually takes the form of stamped metal or printed paper—Canadian dollars, U.S. dollars, British pounds, Japanese yen—that is issued by governments. But over the centuries, items as diverse as stone wheels, salt, wool, livestock, shells, and spices have been used as money. As early as 1100 BCE, the Chinese were using metal money that represented the objects they were exchanging (for example, bronze spades and knives). Coins probably came into use sometime around 600 BCE and paper money around 1200 CE. Just about any object can serve as **money** if it is portable, divisible, durable, and stable. To understand why these qualities are important, imagine using as money something valuable that lacks these features—a 35-kilogram salmon, for example.

money
Any object generally accepted by people as payment for goods and services.

- *Portability*. If you wanted to use the salmon to buy goods and services, you would have to lug a 35-kilogram fish from shop to shop. Modern currency, by contrast, is lightweight and easy to handle.
- *Divisibility*. Suppose you wanted to buy a hat, a book, and some milk from three different stores—all using the salmon as money. How would you divide the fish? First, out comes a cleaver at each store. Then, you would have to determine whether a kilogram of its head is worth as much as a kilogram from its middle. Modern currency is easily divisible into smaller parts with fixed values for each unit. In Canada, for example, a dollar can be exchanged for 4 quarters, 10 dimes, 20 nickels, 100 pennies, or any combination of these coins. It is easy to match units of money with the value of all goods.
- *Durability*. Fish seriously fail the durability test. Each day, whether or not you "spend" it, the salmon will be losing value (and gaining scents). Modern currency, on the other hand, does not spoil, it does not die, and, if it wears out, it can be replaced with new coins and paper money.

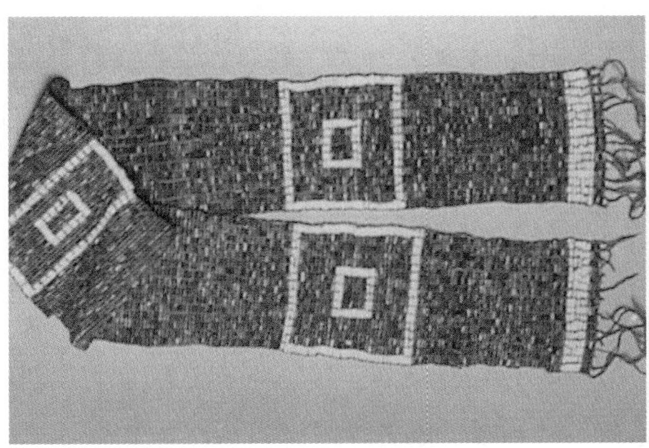

Throughout the ages, people have used many monetary devices. Two interesting ones that were in common circulation are the Iroquois wampum belt (early nineteenth century from eastern North America) and this ancient Greek coin (circa 375 BCE).

- *Stability.* If salmon were in short supply, you might be able to make quite a deal for yourself. But in the middle of a salmon run, the market would be flooded with fish. Since sellers would have many opportunities to exchange their wares for salmon, they would soon have enough fish and refuse to trade for salmon. While the value of the paper money we use today has fluctuated over the years, it is considerably more stable than salmon.

The Functions of Money

Imagine a successful fisherman who needs a new sail for his boat. In a *barter economy*—one in which goods are exchanged directly for one another—he would have to find someone who not only needs fish but who is willing to exchange a sail for it. If no sailmaker wants fish, the fisherman must find someone else—say, a shoemaker—who wants fish and will trade for it. Then the fisherman must hope that the sailmaker will trade for his new shoes. In a *money economy*, the fisherman would sell his catch, receive money, and exchange the money for such goods as a new sail. The barter economy is quite inefficient, but it is still used in various places around the world. It is active in Russia, where major problems have arisen as the country tries to move toward a market-based system and away from the command economy that existed under communism. In the late 1990s, barter accounted for more than half of the business transactions in Russia.[1]

Money serves three functions:

- *Medium of exchange.* Like the fisherman "trading" money for a new sail, we use money as a way of buying and selling things. Without money, we would be bogged down in a system of barter.
- *Store of value.* Pity the fisherman who catches a fish on Monday and wants to buy a few bars of candy on, say, the following Saturday. By then, the fish would have spoiled and be of no value. In the form of currency, however, money can be used for future purchases and therefore "stores" value.
- *Unit of account.* Money lets us measure the relative values of goods and services. It acts as a unit of account because all products can be valued and accounted for in terms of money. For example, the concepts of "$1000-worth of clothes" or "$500 in labour costs" have universal meaning because everyone deals with money every day.

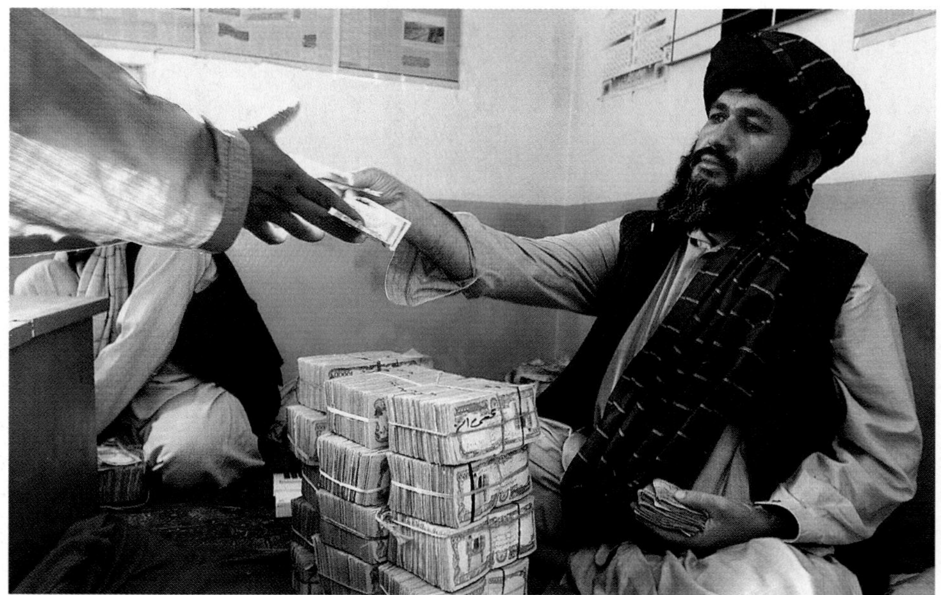

In the modern world, we've become used to highly structured monetary systems. But in some places, centuries-old systems still survive. In Quetta, Pakistan, for example, traders like Mohammad Essa transfer funds through handshakes and code words. The system is called *hawala*, which means "trust" in Arabic. The worldwide *hawala* system, though illegal in most countries, moves billions of dollars past regulators annually and is alleged to be the system of choice for terrorists because it leaves no paper trail.

The Spendable Money Supply: M-1

For money to serve as a medium of exchange, a store of value, or a unit of account, buyers and sellers must agree on its value. The value of money, in turn, depends in part on its supply, that is, how much money is in circulation. When the money supply is high, the value of money drops. When the money supply is low, the value of money increases.

Unfortunately, it is not easy to measure the supply of money, nor is there complete agreement on exactly how it should be measured. The "narrow" definition of the money supply is called M-1. **M-1** counts only the most liquid forms of money: currency and demand deposits (chequing accounts) in banks. As of March 2003, M1 totalled $135.9 billion.[2]

M-1
Only the most liquid forms of money (currency and demand deposits).

currency
Paper money and coins issued by the government.

cheque
An order instructing the bank to pay a given sum to a specified person or firm.

demand deposit
Money in chequing accounts; counted as M-1 because such funds may be withdrawn at any time without notice.

Currency is paper money and coins issued by the Canadian government. It is widely used to pay small bills. Canadian currency states clearly: "This note is legal tender." Legal tender is money the law requires a creditor to accept in payment of a debt.

The majority of Canadian households have chequing accounts against which millions of cheques are written each year. A **cheque** is an order instructing the bank to pay a given sum to a specified person or firm. Although not all sellers accept cheques in payment for goods and services, many do. Cheques enable buyers to make large purchases without having to carry large amounts of cash. Sellers gain a measure of safety because the cheques they receive are valuable only to them and can later be exchanged for cash. Money in chequing accounts, known as **demand deposits**, is counted in M-1 because such funds may be withdrawn at any time without notice.

M1 Plus the Convertible Money Supply: M-2

M-2
Everything in M-1 plus savings deposits, time deposits, and money market mutual funds.

M-2 includes everything in M-1 plus items that cannot be spent directly but that are easily converted to spendable forms: *time deposits, money market mutual funds,* and *savings deposits*. M-2 accounts for nearly all of the nation's money supply. It thus measures the store of monetary value that is available for financial transactions. As this overall level of money increases, more is available for consumer purchases and business investment. When the supply is tightened, less money is available; financial transactions, spending, and business activity thus slow down. As of March 2003, M-2 totalled $566.1 billion.[3]

Unlike demand deposits, **time deposits** require prior notice of withdrawal and cannot be transferred by cheque. On the other hand, time deposits pay higher interest rates. The supply of money in time deposits—such as *certificates of deposit (CDs)* and *savings certificates*—grew rapidly in the 1970s and 1980s as interest rates rose to 15 percent. But when interest rates dropped in the late 1990s, consumers began putting more of their money in mutual funds.

time deposit
A deposit that requires prior notice to make a withdrawal; cannot be transferred to others by cheque.

Money market mutual funds are operated by investment companies that bring together pools of assets from many investors. The fund buys a collection of short-term, low-risk financial securities. Ownership of and profits (or losses) from the sale of these securities are shared among the fund's investors. These funds attracted many investors in the 1980s and 1990s because of high payoffs. But the sharp decline in the stock market in the past few years has meant reduced consumer interest in mutual funds.

money market mutual funds
Funds operated by investment companies that bring together pools of assets from many investors.

Credit Cards: Plastic Money?

Although not included in M-1 or M-2, credit—especially credit cards—has become a major factor in the purchase of consumer goods in Canada. The use of MasterCard, Visa, American Express, Discover, and credit cards issued by individual businesses has become so widespread that many people refer to credit cards as "plastic money." Nevertheless, credit cards do not qualify as money. Rather, they are a *money substitute*; they serve as a temporary medium of exchange but are not a store of value.

Credit cards are big business for two reasons. First, they are quite convenient. Second, credit cards are extremely profitable for issuing companies. Profits derive from two sources:

1. Some cards charge annual fees to holders. All charge interest on unpaid balances. Depending on the issuer, cardholders pay interest rates ranging from 11 to 20 percent.
2. Merchants who accept credit cards pay fees to card issuers. Depending on the merchant's agreement with the issuer, 2 to 5 percent of total credit-sales dollars goes to card issuers.

Credit cards are used to purchase very diverse products. They are profitable for the companies that issue them, and they are convenient for consumers.

THE CANADIAN FINANCIAL SYSTEM

2. Describe the different kinds of *financial institutions* that make up the Canadian financial system and explain the services they offer.

Many forms of money, especially demand deposits and time deposits, depend on the existence of financial institutions to provide a broad spectrum of services to both individuals and businesses. Just how important are reliable financial institutions to both businesses and individuals? Try asking financial consumers in a country in which banking can be an adventure.

In Russia, for example, there is almost no banking regulation and no way to distinguish qualified from unscrupulous bankers in the thousands of different financial institutions, large and small, that exist. Businesses need stable financial institutions to underwrite modernization and expansion, and individuals need them to handle currency. The Moscow City Bank has no deposit insurance, and only recently added a customer service desk, loan officers, and a cash machine. Imagine, then, just before these new steps toward modernization, the disappointment of Vladimir Shcherbakov, who needed to withdraw U.S.$500 from his account to buy a car but was turned away by a sign announcing that no withdrawals would be allowed for 10 days. "I'm resigned to losing my money," sighed Shcherbakov. "But if I do get it back, I'll change my rubles into dollars and hold on to it myself."

Moscow City Bank
www.mcbank.ru

In the sections that follow, we describe the major types of financial institutions, explain how they work, and survey some of the special services they offer. We also explain their role as creators of money and discuss the regulation of the Canadian banking system.

Financial Institutions

The main function of financial institutions is to ease the flow of money from sectors with surpluses to those with deficits. They do this by issuing claims against themselves and using the proceeds to buy the assets of—and thus invest in—other organizations. A bank, for instance, can issue financial claims against itself by making available funds for chequing and savings accounts. In turn, its assets will be mostly loans invested in individuals and businesses and perhaps in government securities.

There are a variety of financial intermediaries in Canada. They vary in size, in importance, in the types of sources they appeal to, in the form of the claim they give to sources of funds, in the users they supply credit to, and in the type of claim they make against the users of funds.

For many years, the financial community in Canada was divided rather clearly into four distinct legal areas. Often called the "four financial pillars," they were: (1) chartered banks; (2) alternate banks, such as trust companies and *caisses populaires* or credit unions; (3) life insurance companies and other specialized lending and saving intermediaries, such as factors, finance companies, venture capital firms, mutual funds, and pension funds; and (4) investment dealers. We will discuss the role of these four financial divisions in a moment, but it is important to understand that so many changes have taken place in the financial services industry that the differences across the four divisions are now very blurred.

Bank Act
laws.justice.gc.ca/en/B-1.01

The crumbling of the four financial pillars began in 1980 when several changes were made to the Bank Act. The process accelerated when additional changes were made in 1987 and 1992. Canadian banks, for example, are now permitted to own securities dealers (in 1996, Royal Bank purchased investment dealer Richardson Greenshields); they are also permitted to sell commercial paper and to own insurance companies (although they are not allowed to sell insurance in their own bank branches). Banks have also established subsidiaries to sell mutual funds.

The changes to the Bank Act have also allowed subsidiaries of U.S. banks to set up business in Canada, and over 40 of them have done so. In 1997, legislation was changed again to allow branches of U.S. banks to conduct business in Canada.

Trust companies have declined in importance during the last few years, and many trust companies have been bought by banks or insurance companies. Insurance companies are facing increased challenges since banks can now sell insurance. The mutual fund business is booming and has created many new jobs during the last decade.

All of these significant changes must be kept in mind as we now turn to a discussion of the four financial pillars of the Canadian economy.

FINANCIAL PILLAR #1—CHARTERED BANKS

A **chartered bank** is a privately owned, profit-seeking firm that serves individuals, non-business organizations, and businesses as a financial intermediary. Chartered banks offer chequing and savings accounts, make loans, and provide many other services to their customers. They are the main source of short-term loans for business firms.

chartered bank
A privately owned, profit-seeking firm that serves individuals, non-business organizations, and businesses as a financial intermediary.

Chartered banks are the largest and most important financial institution in Canada. They offer a unique service. Their liability instruments (the claims against their assets) are generally accepted by the public and by business as money or as legal tender. Initially, these liability instruments took the form of bank notes issued by individual banks. The Bank Act amendments of 1944 removed the right to issue bank notes.

Canada has a branch banking system. Unlike the United States, where there are hundreds of banks, each with a few branches, in Canada there are only a few banks, each with hundreds of branches. The largest chartered banks in Canada are shown in Table 18.1.

The 1980 Bank Act requires Schedule A banks to be Canadian-owned and have no more than 10 percent of voting shares controlled by a single interest. It also permits Schedule B banks, which may be domestically owned banks that do not meet the 10 percent limit or may be foreign controlled. Schedule B banks are initially limited to one main office and one branch. Since the passing of the Act, several foreign banks have set up Schedule B subsidiaries. The Act limits foreign-controlled banks to deposits that do not exceed 8 percent of the total domestic assets of all banks in Canada.

The five largest Schedule A banks account for about 90 percent of total bank assets. Some of them also have branches in other countries. There are thousands of branch bank offices in Canada, about one for every 3300 people.

Table 18.1 The Top 10 Banks in Canada

	Company	Annual Revenues (in billions of $)
1.	Royal Bank of Canada	23.2
2.	The Bank of Nova Scotia	18.3
3.	Canadian Imperial Bank of Commerce	17.0
4.	The Toronto-Dominion Bank	16.6
5.	The Bank of Montreal	13.0
6.	National Bank of Canada	4.1
7.	HSBC Bank Canada	1.8
8.	Laurentian Bank of Canada	1.2
9.	Alberta Treasury Branches	.8
10.	Amex Bank of Canada Inc.	.6

Services Offered by Banks

The banking business today is a highly competitive industry. No longer is it enough for banks to accept deposits and make loans. Most, for example, now offer bank-issued credit cards and safe-deposit boxes. In addition, many offer pension, trust, international, and financial advice, and electronic money transfer.

Pension Services

Most banks help customers establish savings plans for retirement. Banks serve as financial intermediaries by receiving funds and investing them as directed by customers. They also provide customers with information on investment possibilities.

Trust Services

Many banks offer trust services—the management of funds left "in the bank's trust." In return for a fee, the trust department will perform such tasks as making your monthly bill payments and managing your investment portfolio. Trust departments also manage the estates of deceased persons.

International Services

The three main international services offered by banks are *currency exchange, letters of credit,* and *banker's acceptances*. Suppose, for example, that a Canadian company wants to buy a product from a French supplier. For a fee, it can use one or more of three services offered by its bank:

1. It can exchange Canadian dollars for French francs at a Canadian bank and then pay the French supplier in francs.
2. It can pay its bank to issue a **letter of credit**—a promise by the bank to pay the French firm a certain amount if specified conditions are met.
3. It can pay its bank to draw up a **banker's acceptance**, which promises that the bank will pay some specified amount at a future date.

letter of credit
A promise by a bank to pay money to a business firm if certain conditions are met.

banker's acceptance
A promise that the bank will pay a specified amount of money at a future date.

A banker's acceptance requires payment by a particular date; letters of credit are payable only after certain conditions are met. The French supplier, for example, may not be paid until shipping documents prove that the merchandise has been shipped from France.

Financial Advice

Many banks, both large and small, help their customers manage their money. Depending on the customer's situation, the bank may recommend different investment opportunities. The recommended mix might include guaranteed investment certificates, mutual funds, stocks, and bonds. Today, bank advertisements often stress the role of banks as financial advisers.

Automated Teller Machines

Electronic automated teller machines (ATMs) allow customers to withdraw money and make deposits 24 hours a day, seven days a week. They also allow transfers of funds between accounts and provide information on account status. Some banks offer cards that can be used in affiliated nationwide systems. Machines are now located at bank buildings, grocery stores, airports, shopping malls, and other locations around the world. Among the world's nearly one million ATMs, 32 percent are located in Asia, 31 percent are located in North America, 25 percent in western Europe, and 8 percent

Citibank now has consumer banking outlets in 41 countries, where it strives to make once specialized products universal. One of the key functions of overseas ATMs is to attract customers to the bank's retail branches, and the strategy has been particularly successful in Japan. Since 1986, Citibank Japan has offered Japanese customers such services as free ATM and telephone banking and multicurrency accounts.

in Latin America. Many banks now offer international ATM services. Citicorp, for example, installed Shanghai's first 24-hour ATM and is the first foreign bank to receive approval from the People's Bank of China to issue local currency through ATMs. The Exercising Your Ethics box provides an interesting dilemma with regard to ATMs.

People's Bank of China
www.pbc.gov.cn/english

Figure 18.1 summarizes the services that chartered banks offer. Banks are chartered by the federal government and are closely regulated when they provide these services.

EXERCISING YOUR ETHICS

Telling the Ethical from the Strictly Legal

The Situation

When upgrading services for convenience to customers, chartered banks are concerned about setting prices that cover all costs so that, ultimately, they make a profit. This exercise challenges you to evaluate one banking service—ATM transactions—to determine if there are also ethical issues that should be considered in a bank's pricing decisions.

The Dilemma

Assume that a bank has more than 300 ATMs serving the nearly 400 000 chequing and savings accounts of its customers. Customers are not charged a fee for their 30 million ATM transactions each year, so long as they use their bank's ATMs. For issuing cash to non-customers, however, the bank charges a $2 ATM fee. The bank's officers are re-examining their policies on ATM surcharges because of public protests.

In considering its current policies, the bank's vice president for community relations is concerned about more than mere legalities. She wants to ensure that her company is "being a good citizen and doing the right thing." Any decision on ATM fees will ultimately affect the bank's customers, its image in the community and industry, and its profitability for its owners.

Questions for Discussion

1. From the standpoint of a chartered bank, can you find any economic justification for ATM access fees?
2. Based on the scenario described for our bank, do you find any ethical issues in this situation? Or do you find the main issues legal and economic rather than ethical?
3. As an officer for this bank, how would you handle this situation?

Figure 18.1
Examples of services by many chartered banks and trust companies.

Bank Deposits

Chartered banks provide a financial intermediary service by accepting deposits and making loans with this money. Banks make various types of loans to businesses. When applying for a business loan, it is wise for the manager to remember that the banker is interested in making money for the bank through the loan. The banker is also interested in how the loan will be repaid and how it will be secured. A brief written statement accompanied by a cash-flow analysis is a useful approach when applying for a loan.

chequable deposit
A chequing account.

One type of deposit a customer can make in a bank is a chequable, or demand, deposit. A **chequable deposit** is a chequing account. Customers who deposit coins, paper currency, or other cheques in their chequing accounts can write cheques against the balance in their accounts. Their banks must honour these cheques immediately; this is why chequing accounts are also called demand deposits.

term deposit
Money that remains with the bank for a period of time with interest paid to the depositor.

The other type of deposit a customer can make in a chartered bank is a term deposit. A **term deposit** is one that remains with the bank for a period of time. Interest is paid to depositors for the use of their funds. There are two types of term deposits. The most popular is the regular passbook savings account. Although banks can require notice before withdrawals can be made, they seldom do. These accounts are intended primarily for small individual savers and non-profit organizations.

Another type of term deposit is the guaranteed investment certificate. This deposit is made for a specified period of time ranging from 28 days to several years. These certificates are available to all savers. The interest rate paid on a guaranteed investment certificate is higher than that paid on a regular savings account, but many GICs cannot be cashed in before their maturity dates, so they are less flexible than a savings account.

Bank Loans

Banks are the major source of short-term loans for business. Although banks make long-term loans to some firms, they prefer to specialize in providing short-term funds to finance inventories and accounts receivable.

A *secured* loan is backed by collateral such as accounts receivable or a life insurance policy. If the borrower cannot repay the loan, the bank sells the collateral. An *unsecured* loan is backed only by the borrower's promise to repay it. Only the most creditworthy borrowers can get unsecured loans.

Borrowers pay interest on their loans. Large firms with excellent credit records pay the prime rate of interest. The **prime rate of interest** is the lowest rate charged to borrowers. This rate changes constantly owing to changes in the demand for and supply of loanable funds as well as to policies of the Bank of Canada. The so-called "Big Six" Canadian banks (Royal Bank, CIBC, Bank of Montreal, Bank of Nova Scotia, Toronto-Dominion, and National Bank of Canada) typically act in concert with respect to the prime rate.

prime rate of interest
The lowest rate charged to borrowers.

Banks as Creators of Money

3. Explain how banks create money and identify the means by which they are regulated.

In the course of their activities, financial institutions provide a special service to the economy—they create money. This is not to say that they mint bills and coins. Rather, by taking in deposits and making loans, they expand the money supply. We will first look at how this expansion process works, assuming that banks have a **reserve requirement**, that is, that they must keep a portion of their chequable deposits in vault cash or as deposits with the Bank of Canada. (This reserve requirement was dropped in 1991).

reserve requirement
The requirement (until 1991) that banks keep a portion of their chequable deposits in vault cash or as deposits with the Bank of Canada.

Suppose that you saved $100, took it to a bank, and opened a chequing account. Some portion of your $100 is likely to stay in your account, so your bank can earn interest by lending some of it to other borrowers. Let's assume that there is a reserve requirement, and that it is 10 percent. Your bank must therefore keep $10 of your $100 deposit in reserve, so it has only $90 to lend.

Now suppose that a person named Jennifer Leclerc borrows $90 from your bank. She now has $90 added to her chequing account. Assume that she writes a cheque for $90 payable to Canadian Tire. Canadian Tire's bank ends up with a $90 deposit, and that bank is also required to keep $9 in reserve. It therefore has $81 to lend out to someone else.

This process of deposit expansion can continue as shown in Figure 18.2. As you can see, your original deposit of $100 could result in an increase of $1000 in new deposits for all banks in the system. However, what happens if there is no reserve requirement? At the extreme, it means that banks could (theoretically) create infinite amounts of money because they don't have to keep any in reserve. But banks will not do this because it is risky. So, in practice, the dropping of the reserve requirement simply means that banks will be able to create more money than they did when there was a reserve requirement.

Other Changes in Banking

5. Identify ways in which the banking industry is changing.

Fundamental changes in addition to those already described are taking place in banking. These include deregulation, changing consumer demands, the impact of electronic technologies, and changes in international banking.

Deregulation

Deregulation has caused banks to shift away from their historical role as intermediaries between depositors and borrowers. Canada's banks are diversifying to provide a wider array of financial products to their clients. Training bankers to be effective in this environment is necessary. For example, over 100 executives at Toronto-Dominion Bank attended a Harvard University course that taught them to think like investment bankers. The Bank of Montreal conducted a similar course for over 400 executives.

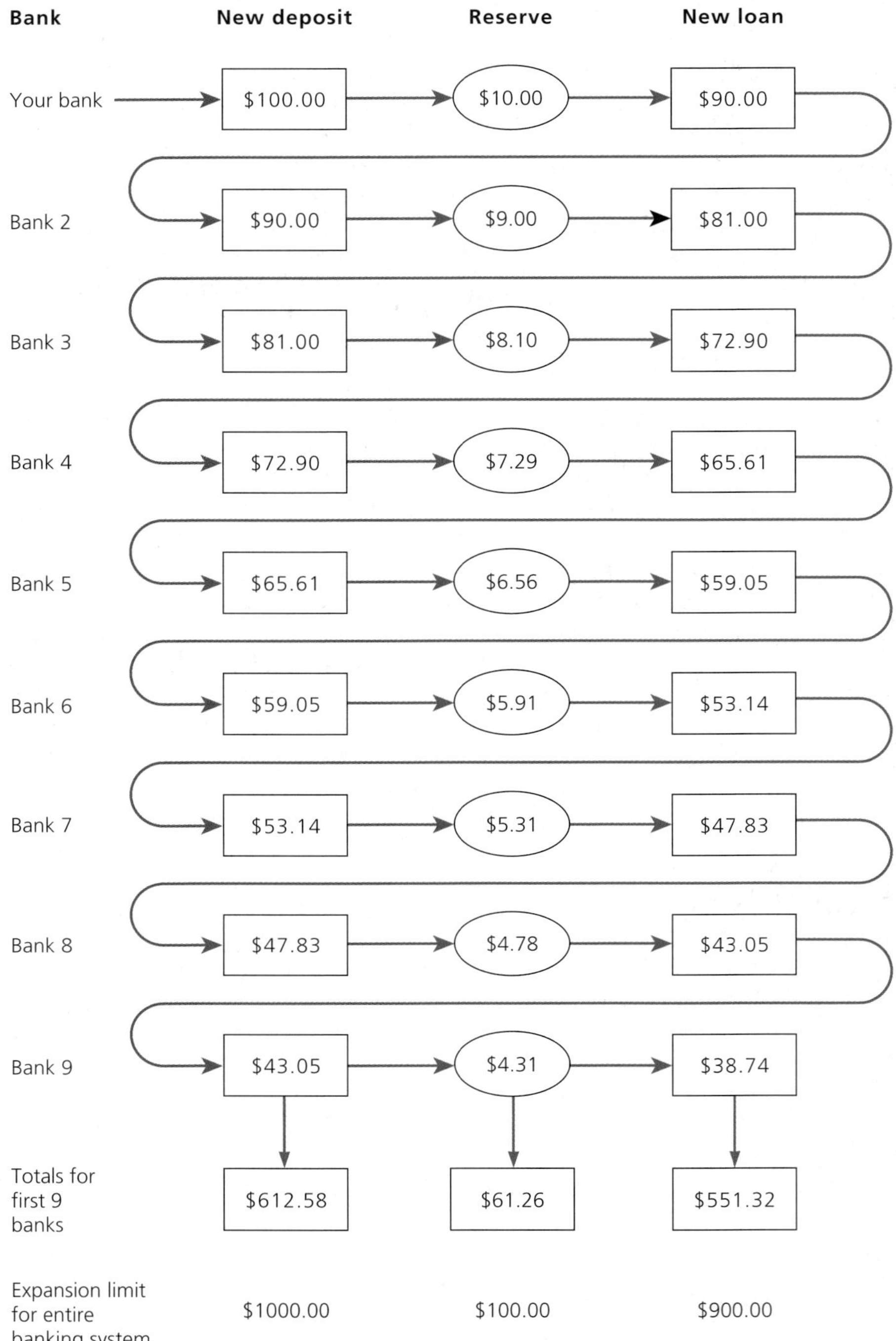

Figure 18.2
How the chartered banking system creates money.

In the last few years, large companies have reduced their use of bank loans. To compensate for this loss, banks are setting up money market operations. For example, until deregulation, only securities firms were allowed to sell commercial paper, but banks expect to dominate in this area before too long. (Commercial paper is usually issued by blue-chip companies that pay a fee to investment dealers or banks to sell the security. See Chapter 20 for more information about commercial paper.) Banks have been allowed to sell commercial paper since June 1987, when deregulation opened up this possibility. The Bank of Montreal and the Toronto-Dominion Bank have been the most active in this market. In Canada, about 200 companies have a credit rating good enough for commercial paper. Banks want to use commercial paper more because they do not have to keep capital reserves on hand for commercial paper as they do for acceptances.

Changing Consumer Demands

Changes are also taking place in banking because consumers are no longer content to simply keep money in a bank when they can get more for it elsewhere. They are increasingly turning to non-traditional, electronic banks like ING Direct and President's Choice Financial that have very few tellers or branches. As well, retailers like Sears and Canadian Tire are opening their own branches.[4] Traditional banks are responding by selling a growing array of corporate and government securities through their branches. All of this activity is transforming the profit base of banks. In the past, they made most of their money from the spread between interest rates paid to depositors and the rates charged on loans. Investment banking, on the other hand, is fee-based. Banks are making a larger proportion of their profits from fees, and this is blurring the traditional boundary between banks and securities firms.

President's Choice Financial
www.preschoicefinancial.com

The Impact of Electronic Technologies

Like so many other businesses, banks are increasingly investing in technology as a way to improve efficiency and customer service levels. Many banks offer ATMs and EFT systems. Some offer TV banking, in which customers use television sets and terminals—or home computers—to make transactions. The age of electronic money has arrived. Digital money is replacing cash in stores, taxicabs, subway systems, and vending machines. The following are examples:

Debit Cards. One of the electronic offerings from the financial industry that has gained popularity is the debit card. Unlike credit cards, **debit cards** allow only the transfer of money between accounts. They do not increase the funds at an individual's disposal. They can, however, be used to make retail purchases. In stores with **point-of-sale (POS) terminals**, customers insert cards that transmit to terminals information relevant to their purchases. The terminal relays the information directly to the bank's computer system. The bank automatically transfers funds from the customer's account to the store's account.

debit card
A type of plastic money that immediately on use reduces the balance in the user's bank account and transfers it to the store's account.

point-of-sale (POS) terminals
Electronic device that allows customers to pay for retail purchases with debit cards.

Smart Cards. The so-called **smart card** is a credit-card-size plastic card with an embedded computer chip that can be programmed with "electronic money." Also known as electronic purses or stored-value cards, smart cards have existed for more than a decade. Phone callers and shoppers in Europe and Asia are the most avid users, holding the majority of the nearly two billion cards in circulation in 2001. Although small by European standards, card usage in North America grew by more than 40 percent since 2000, reaching more than 50 million cards in 2002. They are most popular in financial services, followed by prepaid long distance or wireless phone cards.[5]

smart card
A credit card-sized computer that can be programmed with "electronic money."

Why are smart cards increasing in popularity today? For one thing, the cost of producing them has fallen dramatically, from as much as \$10 to as little as \$1. Convenience is equally important, notes Donald J. Gleason, president of Smart Card Enterprise, a division of Electronic Payment Services. "What consumers want," Gleason contends, "is convenience, and if you look at cash, it's really quite inconvenient."

Smart cards can be loaded with money at ATM machines or with special telephone hookups, even at home. After using your card to purchase an item, you can then check an electronic display to see how much money your card has left. Analysts predict that in the near future, smart cards will function as much more than electronic purses. For example, travel industry experts predict that people will soon book travel plans at home on personal computers and then transfer their reservations onto their smart cards. The cards will then serve as airline tickets and boarding passes. As an added benefit, they will allow travellers to avoid waiting in lines at car rental agencies and hotel front desks.

ecash
Money that moves among consumers and businesses via digital electronic transmissions.

Mondex
www.mondexusa.com

Ecash. A new, revolutionary world of electronic money has begun to emerge with the rapid growth of the internet. Electronic money, known as **ecash**, is money that moves along multiple channels of consumers and businesses via digital electronic transmissions. Ecash moves outside of the established network of banks, cheques, and paper currency. Companies as varied as new start-up Mondex and giant Citicorp are developing their own forms of electronic money that allow consumers and businesses to spend money more conveniently, quickly, and cheaply than they can through the banking system. In fact, some observers predict that by the year 2005, as much as 20 percent of all household expenditures will take place on the internet.

How does ecash work? Traditional currency is used to buy electronic funds, which are downloaded over phone lines into a PC or a portable "elec-

IT'S A WIRED WORLD

Why Aren't We Cashing in on Ecash?

Whatever became of the ecash craze that advocates just a few years ago were predicting would replace paper money? Cybercash still has a ways to go before it catches up with old-fashioned coin and paper currency. Contrary to predictions, the demand for hard currency seems to be increasing rather than decreasing. Consider the following data: U.S. currency held by the public is more than U.S.$620 billion, or about U.S.$2200 for every woman, man, and child in the United States. Sixty-five percent of it was held in $100 bills, and yet a Federal Reserve survey reports that the typical family doesn't hold even a single $100 bill. And most people don't have U.S.$2200 in cash on hand.

So where's the money? Experts estimate that most of it—up to 75 percent—is probably held abroad by foreigners who want the security of U.S. dollars, while the rest is stashed away by U.S. businesses and citizens. The Japanese people are even greater currency lovers, with per capita cash (in yen) of more than U.S.$4000 per person. Unlike the U.S. dollar, holdings of the yen outside Japan are relatively small. Europeans, in contrast, have somewhat smaller currency holdings, with Austrians and Germans holding over U.S.$1800 per person, while on the lower end of cash keepers, the average four-person French family held the equivalent of just U.S.$3000.

Unregulated ecash is regarded as somewhat risky. Some would-be customers are frightened away by the prospect of emoney getting drained away and lost forever in cyberspace. Others fear internet intrusions into personal privacy, and still others are concerned with possibilities for electronic counterfeiting, fraud, and money laundering. While some regulatory efforts are underway to require uniform reporting and record keeping among money services businesses (MSBs), further assurances will be required to brighten emoney's image sufficiently to keep pace with hard currency's popularity. Unlike brick-and-mortar banks and financial institutions, MSBs do not accept deposits. They do, however, offer consumers alternative methods to make payments and to obtain cash through stored value cards and through internet-based payments, money transfers, and foreign currency exchange.

Regardless of assurances from cryptography, ecash creators have yet to devise guarantees of transaction anonymity. Banks, for example, can electronically identify the person who originally withdraws money from the bank, and they can then track some of the electronic money as it moves through the economy. Many consumers and businesses don't want outsiders knowing what they do with private money. Instead, they prefer to hold cash because it can move through the system without leaving trails, electronic or otherwise. And, paper currency has a "feel-good" quality that's hard to duplicate electronically.

tronic wallet" that can store and transmit ecash. Ecash is purchased from any company that issues (sells) it. When shopping online—for example, to purchase jewellery—a shopper sends digital money to the merchant instead of using traditional cash, cheques, or credit cards. Businesses can purchase supplies and services electronically from any merchant that accepts ecash. It flows from the buyer's into the seller's ecash funds, which are instantaneously updated and stored on a microchip. One system, operated by CyberCash, tallies all ecash transactions in the customer's account and, at the end of the day, converts the ecash balance back into dollars in the customer's conventional banking account. The Wired World box describes some problems with the ecash idea.

Changes in International Banking

Another change concerns international banking. Because U.S. and other foreign banks are now allowed to do business in Canada, Canada's "Big Six" banks are going to experience increased competition. They are responding to this threat with a variety of tactics, including co-operating to spread their fixed costs. Syncor Services, for example, is a joint venture between three of the "Big Six" banks that provides cheque-clearing services across Canada.[6] The Business Today box describes some key differences between Canadian and U.S. banks.

BUSINESS TODAY

Consumer Satisfaction with Banks: Canada Versus the U.S.

How satisfied are you with the Canadian banking system? Bank bashing is the second most popular sport in Canada after politician bashing. Consumers feel that even while banks are making multibillion-dollar profits, they provide poor service and do a poor job of listening to customer concerns. But bank customers are even less happy in the United States.

A survey by the Gallup Organization and *American Banker* magazine found that:

- only slightly more than half the respondents were satisfied with their bank
- the banks' most desirable customers—young, university-educated people with above-average incomes—are the most unhappy
- the larger the bank, the less satisfied the customers

Why would this be so? One reason is competition. Even though there are far more banks in the United States than in Canada, there is typically less competition in a given U.S. market than there is in Canada. Each of the "Big Six" banks in Canada competes in virtually every market, but in the United States a given market may have only two or three banks. This means, in effect, that service fees are higher in the United States because there is less competition there. The service fees charged for ATMs are illustrative.

Consumer groups in the United States are on the warpath over rapidly rising ATM fees. Access to ATMs had been free until 1997, but now most banks—particularly the large ones—are charging users on both ends of the transaction. Customers pay about $1.25 to their own bank every time they use another institution's ATM, but they also pay up to $2.50 to the machine's owner. That is three or four times higher than what a Canadian customer would pay for a similar transaction.

Other differences exist between the U.S. and Canadian banking systems. For example, Canadians expect that if they write or cash a cheque, it will clear overnight, but in the United States it may take a week to clear. And other services that Canadians take for granted—currency exchange or the ability to pay bills at ATMs—may not even be available at a given bank in the United States.

All of these specific issues are reasons why U.S. customers are unhappy with their banks. But perhaps the most fundamental advantage of the Canadian banking system is its stability. Since the early 1980s, there have been only two bank failures in Canada, while there have been 1600 bank failures in the United States.

4. Explain the functions of the *Bank of Canada* and describe the tools it uses to control the money supply.

Bank of Canada
Canada's central bank; formed in 1935.

The Bank of Canada

The **Bank of Canada**, formed in 1935, is Canada's central bank. It has a crucial role to play in managing the Canadian economy and in regulating certain aspects of chartered bank operations. The Bank of Canada is managed by a board of governors composed of a governor, a deputy governor, and 12 directors appointed from different regions of Canada. The directors, with cabinet approval, appoint the governor and deputy governor. The deputy minister of finance is also a non-voting member of the board. Between meetings of the board, normally held eight times per year, an executive committee acts for the board. This committee is composed of the governor, the deputy governor, two directors, and the deputy minister of finance. The executive committee meets at least once a week.

Operation of the Bank of Canada

The Bank of Canada plays an important role in managing the money supply in Canada. (See Figure 18.3.) If the Bank of Canada wants to increase the money supply, it can buy government securities. The people selling these bonds deposit the proceeds in their banks. These deposits increase banks' reserves and their willingness to make loans. The Bank of Canada can also lower the bank rate; this action will cause increased demand for loans from businesses and households because these customers borrow more money when interest rates drop.

If the Bank of Canada wants to decrease the money supply, it can sell government securities. People spend money to buy bonds, and these withdrawals bring down banks' reserves and reduce their ability to make loans. The Bank of Canada can also raise the bank rate; this action will cause decreased demand for loans from businesses and households because these customers borrow less money when interest rates rise.

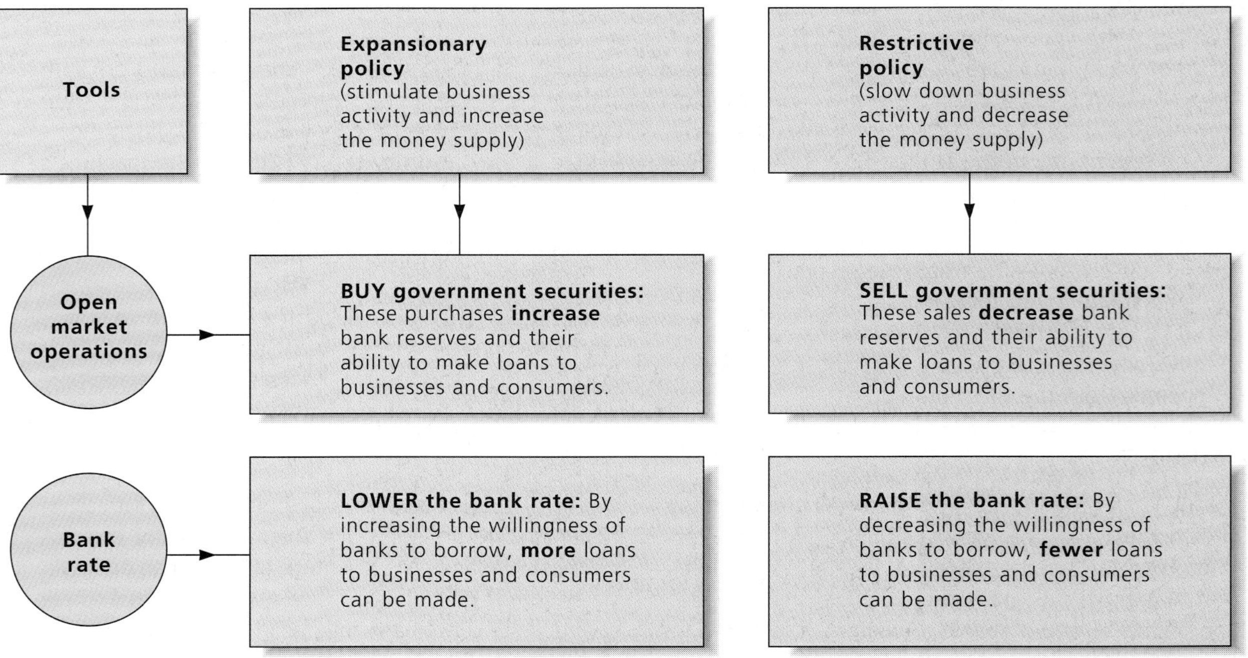

Figure 18.3
Bank of Canada monetary policy actions.

Member Bank Borrowing from the Bank of Canada

The Bank of Canada is the lender of last resort for chartered banks. The rate at which chartered banks can borrow from the Bank of Canada is called the bank, or rediscount, rate. It serves as the basis for establishing the chartered banks' prime interest rates. By raising the bank rate, the Bank of Canada depresses the demand for money; by lowering it, the demand for money increases. In practice, chartered banks seldom have to borrow from the Bank of Canada. However, the bank rate is an important instrument of monetary policy as a determinant of interest rates.

FINANCIAL PILLAR #2—ALTERNATE BANKS

Trust Companies

Another financial intermediary that serves individuals and businesses is the alternate, or near, bank: the trust company. A **trust company** safeguards property—funds and estates—entrusted to it; it may also serve as trustee, transfer agent, and registrar for corporations and provide other services.

trust company
Safeguards funds and estates entrusted to it; may also serve as trustee, transfer agent, and registrar for corporations.

A corporation selling bonds to many investors appoints a trustee, usually a trust company, to protect the bondholders' interests. A trust company can also serve as a transfer agent and registrar for corporations. A transfer agent records changes in ownership of a corporation's shares of stock. A registrar certifies to the investing public that stock issues are correctly stated and comply with the corporate charter. Other services include preparing and issuing dividend cheques to shareholders and serving as trustee for employee profit-sharing funds. Trust companies also accept deposits and pay interest on them.

Credit Unions/Caisses Populaires

Credit unions (called *caisses populaires* in Quebec) are also alternate banks. They are important to business because they lend money to consumers to buy durable goods such as cars and furniture. They also lend money to businesses. **Credit unions** and *caisses populaires* are co-operative savings and lending associations formed by a group with common interests. Members (owners) can add to their savings accounts by authorizing deductions from their paycheques or by making direct deposits. They can borrow short-term, long-term, or mortgage funds from the credit union. Credit unions also invest substantial amounts of money in corporate and government securities. The largest credit unions in Canada are listed in Table 18.2.

credit union
Co-operative savings and lending association formed by a group with common interests.

top

Table 18.2 The Top 10 Credit Unions in Canada

	Company	Annual Revenues (in millions of $)
1.	Le Mouvement des caisses Desjardins	6937
2.	Vancouver City Savings Credit Union	498
3.	Caisse centrale Desjardins	378
4.	Coast Capital Savings Credit Union	319
5.	Credit Union Central of Saskatchewan	297
6.	Credit Union Central of B.C.	172
7.	Envision Credit Union	132
8.	Capital City Savings & Credit Union Ltd.	109
9.	Credit Union Central Alberta Ltd.	96
10.	Community Credit Union Ltd.	91

Credit unions (*caisses populaires*) are co-operative saving and lending organizations that loan money to both consumers and businesses.

FINANCIAL PILLAR #3—SPECIALIZED LENDING AND SAVINGS INTERMEDIARIES

Life Insurance Companies

life insurance company
A mutual or stock company that shares risk with its policyholders for payment of premiums.

An important source of funds for individuals, non-business organizations, and businesses is the life insurance company. A **life insurance company** is a mutual or stock company that shares risk with its policyholders in return for payment of a premium. It lends some of the money it collects from premiums to borrowers. Life insurance companies are substantial investors in real estate mortgages and in corporate and government bonds. Next to chartered banks, they are the largest financial intermediaries in Canada. We discuss insurance companies in more detail in Chapter 20.

Factoring Companies

factoring company
Buys accounts receivable from a firm for less than their face value, and then collects the face value of the receivables.

An important source of short-term funds for many firms is factoring companies. A **factoring company** (or factor) buys accounts receivable (amounts due from credit customers) from a firm. It pays less than the face value of the accounts but collects the face value of the accounts. The difference, minus the cost of doing business, is the factor's profit.

A firm that sells its accounts receivable to a factor without recourse shifts the risk of credit loss to the factor. If an account turns out to be uncollectable, the factor suffers the loss. However, a factor is a specialist in credit and collection activities. Using a factor may enable a business firm to expand sales beyond what would be practical without the factor. The firm trades accounts receivable for cash. The factor then notifies the firm's customers to make their overdue payments to the factor.

Financial Corporations

sales finance company
Specializes in financing instalment purchases made by individuals or firms.

There are two types of financial corporations: sales finance companies and consumer finance companies. A **sales finance company** specializes in financing instalment purchases made by individuals and firms. When you buy durable goods from a retailer on an instalment plan with a sales finance company, the loan is made directly to you. The item itself serves as security for the loan. Sales finance companies enable many firms to sell on credit, even though the firms could not afford to finance credit sales on their own. General Motors Acceptance Corporation (GMAC) is a sales finance company. It is a captive company because it exists to finance instalment contracts resulting from sales made by General Motors. Industrial Acceptance Corporation is a large Canadian sales finance company. Sales finance companies also finance instalment sales to business firms.

A **consumer finance company** makes personal loans to consumers. Often the borrower pledges no security (collateral) for the loan. For larger loans, collateral may be required, such as a car or furniture.

consumer finance company
Makes personal loans to consumers.

Venture Capital or Development Firms

A **venture capital firm**, or development firm, will provide funds for new or expanding firms thought to have significant potential. Venture capital firms obtain their funds from initial capital subscriptions, from loans from other financial intermediaries, and from retained earnings.

venture capital firm
Provides funds for new or expanding firms thought to have significant potential.

Venture capital firms may provide either equity or debt funds to firms. Financing new, untested businesses is risky, so venture capital firms want to earn a higher-than-normal return on their investment. The ideal situation is an equity investment in a company that becomes very successful and experiences substantial increases in its stock value.

Pension Funds

A **pension fund** accumulates money that will be paid out to plan subscribers at some time in the future. The money collected is invested in corporate stocks and bonds, government bonds, or mortgages until it is to be paid out. Pension funds are discussed in more detail in Chapter 19.

pension fund
Accumulates money that will be paid out to plan subscribers in the future.

FINANCIAL PILLAR #4—INVESTMENT DEALERS

Investment dealers (called stockbrokers or underwriters) perform two important financial functions. First, they are the primary distributors of new stock and bond issues (underwriting). Second, they facilitate secondary trading of stocks and bonds, both on stock exchanges and on over-the-counter stock and bond markets (the brokerage function). These functions are discussed in more detail in Chapter 19.

INTERNATIONAL BANKING AND FINANCE

6. Understand some of the key activities in *international banking and finance.*

Along with international banking networks, electronic technologies now permit nearly instantaneous financial transactions around the globe. The economic importance of international finance is evident from both the presence of foreign banks in the Canadian market and the sizes of certain banks around the world. In addition, each nation tries to influence its currency exchange rates for economic advantage in international trade. The subsequent country-to-country transactions result in an *international payments process* that moves money between buyers and sellers on different continents.

Exchange Rates and International Trade

As we saw in Chapter 4, every country's currency exchange rate affects its ability to buy and sell on the global market. The value of a given currency (say, the Canadian dollar) reflects the overall supply and demand for Canadian dollars both at home and abroad. This value changes with economic conditions. Around the world, therefore, firms will watch those trends, and decisions about doing business in Canada will be affected by more or less favourable exchange rates. In 2003, for example, the Canadian dollar was valued at U.S.$0.74, whereas in the 1960s U.S. and Canadian dollars were about equal. Thus, with the Canadian dollar trading for so much less than the U.S. dollar, American companies have become more interested in buying Canadian companies.

The Law of One Price

How do firms determine when exchange rates are favourable? When a country's currency becomes overvalued, its exchange rate is higher than warranted by its economic conditions. Its high costs make it less competitive. Because its products are too expensive to make and buy, fewer are purchased by other countries. The likely result is a trade deficit (see Chapter 4). In contrast, an undervalued currency means low costs and low prices. It attracts purchases by other countries, usually leading to a trade surplus.

law of one price
The principle that identical products should sell for the same price in all countries.

How do we know whether a currency is overvalued or undervalued? One method involves a simple concept called the **law of one price**: the principle that identical products should sell for the same price in all countries. In other words, if the different prices of a Rolex watch in different countries were converted into a common currency, the price should be the same everywhere.

But what if prices are not equal? In theory, the pursuit of profits should equalize them. Sellers in high-priced countries will have to reduce prices if they are to compete successfully and make profits. As prices adjust, so should the exchange rates between different currencies until the Rolex can be purchased for the same price everywhere.

A simple example that illustrates over- and undervalued currencies is the Big Mac Currencies, an index published annually in the British magazine *The Economist*. The identical product here is always McDonald's Big Mac, which is made locally in many countries. The first two columns in Table 18.3 list several countries and Big Mac prices in terms of local currencies. Each country's price is then converted into U.S. dollars (based on recent exchange rates). As you can see, the Israel price is most expensive, and the Chinese price is the cheapest.

According to the Big Mac index as shown in Table 18.3, the Swiss franc is the most overvalued currency (against the U.S. dollar), and the Chinese yuan is the most undervalued currency. In theory, this means that you could buy Big Macs in China (using yuan) and resell them in Switzerland (for francs) at a handsome profit. In China, therefore, the demand for burgers would increase, driving up the price toward the higher prices in the other countries. In other words, the law of one price would set in. The index also indicates that the exchange rate of South Korea is neither overvalued nor undervalued, and that the Canadian dollar is undervalued against the U.S. dollar. While this index is easy to understand, governments and businesses use far more sophisticated methods to measure the purchasing power of different currencies in making much more complex transactions.

Table 18.3 Big Mac Currency Index

Country	Big Mac Prices in Local Currency	Big Mac Prices in Equivalent U.S. Dollars	Local Currency Overvaluation (+) Undervaluation (–)
Switzerland	6.30 francs	4.50	+69
Denmark	27.75 krone	4.10	+51
Britain	1.99 pounds	3.14	+16
S. Korea	3000 won	2.71	–
United States	2.71	2.71	–
Canada	3.20 Cdn. dollars	2.21	–18
New Zealand	3.95 NZ dollars	2.21	–18
Japan	262 yen	2.19	–19
Mexico	23.00 pesos	2.18	–19
Argentina	4.10 pesos	1.43	–47
Russia	41.00 rubles	1.32	–51
China	9.90 yuan	1.20	–56

Government Influence on Exchange Rates

What happens when a currency becomes overvalued or undervalued? A nation's economic authorities may take action to correct its balance-of-payments conditions. Typically, they will devalue or revalue the nation's currency. The purpose of *devaluing* is to cause a decrease in the home country's exchange value. It will then be less expensive for other countries to buy the home country's products. As more of its products are purchased, the home country's payment deficit goes down. The purpose of *revaluation*, of course, is the reverse: to increase the exchange value and reduce the home country's payment surplus.

In 2001, for instance, the exchange rate was 1.0 Argentine peso per U.S. dollar throughout the year. Then, in January 2002, the Argentine government devalued the peso to 1.4 pesos per dollar. By July 2002, the rate had gone to 3.57 on the world market, meaning that each peso was worth just $0.28. Argentine officials sought the more favourable exchange rate to encourage other countries to buy more Argentine products, thereby reducing Argentina's payments deficit.

The International Payments Process

Now we know why a nation tries to control its balance of payments and what, at least in part, it can do about an unfavourable balance. Exactly how are payments made? Transactions among buyers and sellers in different countries are simplified through the services provided by their banks. For example, payments from buyers flow through a local bank that converts them from the local currency into the foreign currency of the seller. Likewise, the local bank receives and converts incoming money from the banks of foreign buyers. The payments process is shown in Figure 18.4.[7]

Step 1. A Canadian olive importer withdraws $1000 from its chequing account to buy olives from a Greek exporter. The local Canadian bank converts those dollars into Greek drachmas at the current exchange rate (230 drachmas per dollar).

Step 2. The Canadian bank sends the cheque for 230 000 drachmas (230×1000) to the exporter in Greece.

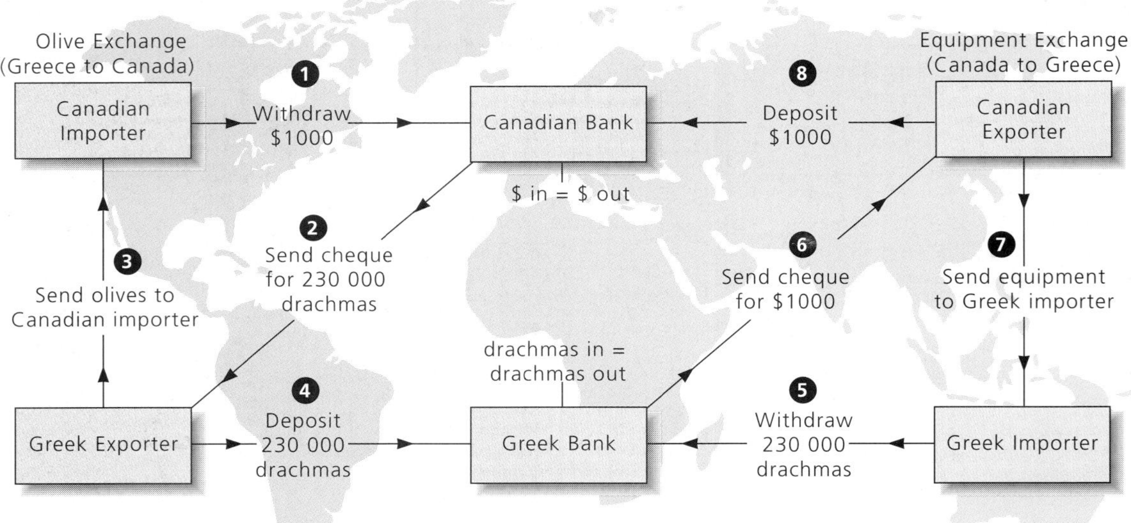

Figure 18.4
The international payments process.

Steps 3 and 4. The exporter sends olives to its Canadian customer and deposits the cheque in its local Greek bank. While the exporter now has drachmas that can be spent in Greece, the importer has olives to sell in Canada.

At the same time, a separate transaction is being made between a Canadian machine exporter and a Greek olive oil producer. This time, the importer/exporter roles are reversed between the two countries: The Greek firm needs to import a $1000 olive oil press from Canada.

Steps 5 and 6. Drachmas (230 000) withdrawn from a local Greek bank account are converted into $1000 Canadian and sent via cheque to the Canadian exporter.

Steps 7 and 8. The olive oil press is sent to the Greek importer, and the importer's cheque is deposited in the Canadian exporter's local bank account.

In this example, trade between the two countries is *in balance*: Money inflows and outflows are equal for both countries. When such a balance occurs, *money does not actually have to flow between the two countries*. Within each bank, the dollars spent by local importers offset the dollars received by local exporters. In effect, therefore, the dollars have simply flowed from Canadian importers to Canadian exporters. Likewise, the drachmas have moved from Greek exporters to Greek importers.

The International Bank Structure

There is no worldwide banking system that is comparable, in terms of policy making and regulatory power, to the system of any single industrialized nation. Rather, worldwide banking stability relies on a loose structure of agreements among individual countries or groups of countries.

The World Bank and the IMF

Two United Nations agencies, the World Bank and the International Monetary Fund (IMF), help to finance international trade. Unlike true banks, the **World Bank** (technically the International Bank for Reconstruction and Development) actually provides only a very limited scope of services. For instance, it funds national improvements by making loans to build roads, schools, power plants, and hospitals. The resulting improvements eventually enable borrowing countries to increase productive capacity and international trade.

World Bank
A United Nations agency that provides a limited scope of financial services, such as funding national improvements in undeveloped countries.

The **International Monetary Fund** is a group of some 150 nations that have combined their resources for the following purposes:

International Monetary Fund (IMF)
A United Nations agency consisting of about 150 nations that have combined resources to promote stable exchange rates, provide temporary short-term loans, and serve other purposes.

- to promote the stability of exchange rates
- to provide temporary, short-term loans to member countries
- to encourage members to co-operate on international monetary issues
- to encourage development of a system for international payments

The IMF makes loans to nations suffering from temporary negative trade balances. By making it possible for these countries to continue buying products from other countries, the IMF facilitates international trade. However, some nations have declined IMF funds rather than accept the economic changes that the IMF demands. For example, some developing countries reject the IMF's requirement that they cut back social programs and spending to bring inflation under control.

World Bank
www.worldbank.org

International Monetary Fund (IMF)
www.imf.org

SUMMARY OF LEARNING OBJECTIVES

1. **Define *money* and identify the different forms it takes in the nation's money supply.** Any item that is portable, divisible, durable, and stable satisfies the four basic characteristics of *money*. Money also serves three functions: it is a medium of exchange, a store of value, and a unit of account. The nation's money supply is often determined by two measures: *M-1* includes liquid (or spendable) forms of money: currency (bills and coins), demand deposits, and other "chequable" deposits (such as chequing accounts and ATM withdrawals). *M-2* includes M-1 plus items that cannot be directly spent but which can be easily converted to spendable forms: time deposits, money market funds, and savings deposits. Credit must also be considered as a factor in the money supply.
2. **Describe the different kinds of *financial institutions* that make up the Canadian financial system and explain the services they offer.** The financial intermediaries that form the "four financial pillars" in Canada are chartered banks, alternate banks, specialized lending and savings intermediaries, and investment dealers. The chartered banks, which are at the heart of our financial system, are the most important source of short-term funds for business firms. The chartered banking system creates money in the form of expanding demand deposits. The four kinds of financial institutions offer services like financial advice and brokerage services, electronic funds transfer, pension and trust services, and lending of money.
3. **Explain how banks create money and identify the means by which they are regulated.** By taking in deposits and making loans, banks create money, or more accurately, they expand the money supply. The Bank of Canada controls the overall supply of money.

4. **Explain the functions of the *Bank of Canada* and describe the tools it uses to control the money supply.** The Bank of Canada manages the Canadian economy, controls the money supply, and regulates certain aspects of chartered banking operations. If the Bank of Canada wants to increase the money supply, it can buy government securities or lower the bank rate. If it wants to decrease the money supply, it can sell government securities or increase the bank rate.

5. **Identify ways in which the financial industry is changing.** The clear divisions between the activities of the "four financial pillars" are becoming less obvious. For example, deregulation has allowed banks to begin selling commercial paper. Other financial intermediaries are also beginning to get involved in new financial activities. For example, life insurance companies are starting to take over trust companies so they can get a foothold in the trust business. *Electronic technologies* offer a variety of new financial conveniences to customers. *Debit cards* are plastic cards that permit users to transfer money between bank accounts. *Smart cards* are credit card-sized computers that can be loaded with "electronic money" at ATMs or over special telephone hookups. *Ecash* is money that can be moved among consumers and businesses via digital electronic transmissions.

6. **Understand some of the key activities in *international banking and finance*.** Electronic technologies now permit speedy global financial transactions to support the growing importance of international finance. Country-to-country transactions are conducted according to an *international payment process* that moves money among buyers and sellers in different nations. Each nation tries to influence its currency exchange rates to gain advantage in international trade. For example, if its currency is overvalued, a higher exchange rate usually results in a trade deficit. Conversely, undervalued currencies can attract buyers and create trade surpluses. Governments may act to influence exchange rates by *devaluing* or *revaluing* their national currencies (that is, by decreasing or increasing them). Devalued currencies make it less expensive for other countries to buy the home country's products.

KEY TERMS

Bank of Canada, 654
banker's acceptance, 646
chartered bank, 645
chequable deposit, 648
cheque, 642
consumer finance company, 657
credit union, 655
currency, 642
debit card, 651
demand deposit, 642
ecash, 652
factoring company, 656
International Monetary Fund (IMF), 661
law of one price, 658
letter of credit, 646
life insurance company, 656
M-1, 642
M-2, 642
money market mutual fund, 643
money, 640
pension fund, 657
point-of-sale (POS) terminal, 651
prime rate of interest, 649
reserve requirement, 649
sales finance company, 656
smart card, 651
term deposit, 648
time deposit, 643
trust company, 655
venture capital firm, 657
World Bank, 661

QUESTIONS AND EXERCISES

Questions for Review

1. What is money? What are its ideal characteristics?
2. What are the components of M-1? Of M-2?
3. Describe the structure and operation of the Bank of Canada.
4. List and describe the sources of short-term funds for business firms.

Questions for Analysis

5. What kinds of changes in banking are shifting banks away from their historical role?
6. Do we really need all the different types of financial institutions we have in Canada? Could we make do with just chartered banks? Why or why not?
7. Should credit cards be counted in the money supply? Why or why not?
8. Should chartered banks be regulated or should market forces be allowed to set the money supply? Defend your answer.

Application Exercises

9. Interview several consumers to determine which of the new banking services and products they use (debit cards, ATMs, smart cards, etc.). If interviewees are using these services, determine the reasons. If they are not, find out why not.
10. Interview the manager of a local chartered bank. Identify the ways in which the Bank of Canada helps the bank and the ways in which it limits the bank.

BUILDING YOUR BUSINESS SKILLS

The Risks and Rewards of Credit Cards

Goal

To help students evaluate the risks and rewards associated with excessive credit card use.

Situation

Suppose that you've been out of school for a year and are now working in your first job. Your annual $30 000 salary is enough to support your apartment, car, and the basic necessities of life, but the luxuries are still out of reach. You pay cash for everything until one day you get a pre-approved credit card solicitation in the mail, which offers you a $1500 line of credit. You decide to take the offer and begin charging purchases. Within a year, five other credit card companies have contacted you, and you accumulate a total credit card debt of $12 000.

Method

Step 1
Working with three or four classmates, evaluate the advantages and dangers inherent in this situation, both to the consumer and to credit card issuers. To address this issue, research the current percentage of credit card delinquencies and rate of personal bankruptcies. Find out, for example, how these rates compare with those in previous years. In addition, research the profitability of the credit card business.

Step 2
Evaluate the different methods that credit card companies use to attract new customers. Specifically, look at the following practices:

- sending unsolicited, pre-approved credit card applications to consumers with questionable and even poor credit
- offering large credit lines to consumers who pay only monthly minimums
- lowering interest rates on accounts as a way of encouraging revolving payments
- charging penalties on accounts that are paid in full at the end of every billing cycle (research the GE Rewards MasterCard)
- sending cardholders catalogues of discounted gifts that can be purchased with their charge cards
- linking credit card use to a program of rewards—say, frequent flier miles linked to amounts charged

Step 3
Compile your findings in the form of a set of guidelines designed for consumers receiving unsolicited credit card offers. Your guidelines should analyze the advantages and disadvantages of excessive credit card use.

Follow-Up Questions

1. If you were the person in our hypothetical example, how would you handle your credit situation?

2. Why do you think credit card companies continue to offer cards to people who are financially overextended?
3. What criteria can you suggest to evaluate different credit card offers?
4. How do you know when you have enough credit?

MASTERING BUSINESS ESSENTIALS

Episode 10 reveals that CanGo enjoys an extremely large Japanese customer base and intends to expand further into global markets. *This episode explains some practical reasons why a small company may need to understand international banking and finance.*

CRAFTING YOUR BUSINESS PLAN

How to Bank on Your Money

The Purpose of the Assignment

1. To familiarize students with banking issues that a sample firm faces in developing its business plan, in the framework of the Business PlanPro (BPP) software package.
2. To demonstrate how two chapter topics—bank services and interest rates—can be integrated as components in the BPP planning environment.

Assignment

After reading Chapter 18 in the textbook, open the BPP software and search for information about the financial plans of a sample firm: Fantastic Florals Inc. To find Fantastic Florals, do the following:

Open the Business PlanPro. If it asks if you want to "create a new business plan" or "open an existing plan," select "create a new business plan" (even though you are not going to create a plan at this time). You will then be taken to the Business PlanPro EasyPlan Wizard. Click on the option entitled **Research It**. You will then be presented a new list of options, including Sample Plan Browser. After clicking on the **Sample Plan Browser**, go down the alphabetical list of sample plans and double-click on **Import—Artificial Flowers**, which is the location for Fantastic Florals Inc. (FFI). The screen you are looking at is the introduction page for the Fantastic Florals business plan. Now scroll down until you reach the Table of Contents for the Fantastic Florals business plan.

Now respond to the following items:

1. Consider interest rates that are assumed in the business plan. Are the short-term and long-term rates reasonable in today's economy? Explain. [Sites to see in BPP for this item: On the **Table of Contents** page, click on **7.1 Important Assumptions**.]
2. Identify some international banking services that would benefit FFI in its daily operations. [Sites to see in BPP: On the **Table of Contents page**, click on **1.0 Executive Summary**. Return to the **Table of Contents** page, and click on each of the following in turn: **3.4 Sourcing** and **3.6 Future Products**.]
3. From FFI's financial plan, can you see any need for bank credit? When, during the planning horizon, might the firm need a line of credit, and how much might it need? [Sites to see in BPP: From the **Table of Contents** page, click on each of the following in turn: **7.0 Financial Plan** and **7.5 Projected Cash Flow**.]
4. Does FFI plan to have excess cash that can be deposited in the bank to earn interest? When, during the planning horizon, might the firm accumulate excess cash, and how much might it have? [Sites to see in BPP: On the **Table of Contents** page, click on **5.2.1 Sales Forecast**. Return to the **Table of Contents** page, and click on **7.5 Projected Cash Flow**. Observe the cash balance at the bottom of the table.]

VIDEO EXERCISE

Funding the Business World: Coast Business Credit

Learning Objectives

The purpose of this video is to help you to:

1. Recognize how and why banks use customer deposits as the basis of loans.
2. Understand the role of banks and financial services firms in providing funding for business expansion, operations, and acquisitions.
3. Identify the risks that financial services firms take when loaning money to businesses.

Synopsis

Coast Business Credit, a division of Southern Pacific Bank, provides money for business. When evaluating the risk that a loan will not be repaid, Coast carefully considers the borrower's collateral, cash flow, and management. Business customers may apply for a short-term line of credit, a long-term loan, or other types of financing for a variety of purposes. One company may need operating capital; another may need money to make a major acquisition or to expand. Coast analyzes each lending opportunity in terms of potential risk, potential profit, and—in some cases—the ability to create or save jobs and thus benefit the community at large.

Discussion Questions

1. *For analysis*: How might the amount of time deposits gathered by parent company Southern Pacific Bank affect the loans made by Coast Business Services?
2. *For analysis*: If the Federal Reserve lowers the discount rate by a significant amount, what would be the likely effect on business loan rates?
3. *For application*: What type of collateral might Coast Business Credit prefer when considering a loan application?
4. *For application*: In addition to collateral, Coast Business Credit looks at cash flow and management when considering a loan application. Why is management such an important element?
5. *For debate*: Should Coast Business Credit establish a separate lending department specifically for financing internet start-ups? Support your chosen position.

Online Exploration

In February 2003, the California Division of Financial Institutions closed Southern Pacific Bank and Beal Bank of Texas assumed their insured deposits. Visit the Beal Bank website at **www.bealbank.com**. After browsing the home page, follow the links to learn more about this wholesale bank. What type of loans does Beal Bank specialize in? What services does it provide to the general public? Why does Beal Bank use their website to promote commercial properties for sale? How has the bank utilized its corporate website for promotional purposes? To what does Beal Bank attribute its top ranking for return on equity? How does Beal Bank make it easy for businesses and individuals to make contact?

EXPLORING THE NET

What Do You Know About the Bank of Canada?

As highlighted in this chapter, the Bank of Canada plays an instrumental role in ensuring both the economic and financial welfare of Canada. In order to focus on these roles, the Bank of Canada has set distinct priorities. These priorities include focusing on monetary policy, currency rates/levels, financial stability, and funds management. Visit their website at **www.bank-banque-canada.ca**.

1. Describe how the Bank of Canada promotes both the economic and financial welfare of Canada.
2. According to this website there are over $204 million dollars in unclaimed bank balances. What exactly is an unclaimed bank balance? How do you go about claiming such a balance?
3. What is the overnight target rate? What is the purpose of this rate? Is this rate different from the prime rate?

Concluding Case 18-1

Argentines No Longer Bank on the Peso

They get in line before dawn. Peaceful at first, they become unruly when they have to protect their places in line. No, they're not jockeying for seats at a rock concert or a World Cup soccer game. These frenzied people are customers at one of the largest banks in Buenos Aires, a bank that, like every other bank in the country's depleted system, has to say "No" to angry account holders. Denied access to their life savings, many will return tomorrow (and be rejected again). In one day, panicked depositors had yanked U.S.$2 billion, and to stop the bleeding, the government has temporarily limited withdrawals to U.S.$250 a week regardless of the size of the account. Transfers abroad are limited to U.S.$1000 a month, and even the accounts of the wealthiest patrons are frozen. The result? Not surprisingly, a serious shortage of money. "As long as I live, I shall never again put a peso in a bank in Argentina," says Buenos Aires real estate agent Pablo Pechague. "I'm going to put everything in Uruguay where there is a much more serious banking system."

Argentina's currency—the peso—was long known as the most stable in Latin America. The country's free-market economy, South America's second largest (after Brazil), was the darling of emerging markets with its fast-paced economic growth during the 1990s. Billions of investment dollars flowed in from abroad as Argentina undertook the privatization of state industries by selling off hundreds of inefficient businesses.

A healthy 9 percent growth rate and low unemployment meant economic prosperity—until a turnaround started in the late 1990s, with a recession that worsened in 2002. With unemployment reaching 18 percent, investors from Canada, the United States, and Europe feared that Argentina would devalue the peso to help the economy and, by doing so, would slash investors' profits and, perhaps, even cause the government to protect local industry by reverting back to old policies that are less market friendly than the recent privatization movement.

As the recession lingered, the peso, long considered the foundation of Argentina's steady economy, gradually came to be viewed as overvalued, making the country's exports too expensive and uncompetitive in foreign markets. In late 2001, worried investors and savers started a run on the banks in hopes of reclaiming their money rather than risking financial loss if the economy failed. By year-end 2001, Argentines had withdrawn 17 percent of all bank deposits, or U.S.$14.5 billion, causing a sharp decline in the central bank reserves. In early 2002, Economy Minister Jorge Remes Lenicov broke the news: "We are devaluing; we are in collapse. Argentina is bankrupt."

The currency devaluation could cause further job cuts and inflation for Argentina's citizens. As the threat of further instability continued, fears mounted that a steep drop in the peso's value could trigger huge losses for foreign companies in telecommunications, oil, banks, and utilities. And those fears were justified: By mid-2002, foreign creditors, too, were taking a financial beating. Citigroup, for example, the New York-based financial giant, reported losses of $470 million in one calendar quarter from economic problems in Argentina. J.P. Morgan Chase & Co. was hurt even worse, and FleetBoston Financial Corp. took the rare step of postponing its regularly scheduled earnings report until it could sort out the full financial impact of its Argentine losses. Meanwhile, frustrated Argentines, starved for cash, have to rely on bank debit cards, credit cards, and cheques to pay for day-to-day purchases.

As the run on Argentina's banks continued into 2002, unpopular banking restrictions were tightened even further, triggering widespread street protests. The government froze bank accounts. All chequing accounts with money over U.S.$10 000 were switched into fixed-term deposits, meaning the money was not available to depositors for at least a year. The same was true for savings accounts of $3000 or more. "We want our money and we want it now," shouted Rubin Orlando, a 46-year-old doctor, as he slammed two trash can lids together. Angry vandals set fires in downtown Buenos Aires, shattered windows, and destroyed ATMs. The economic and social chaos led to a government turnover that included five presidents in two weeks. So intense and violent was public unrest that Roque Maccarone, the head of Argentina's central bank, resigned.

As economist Raul Buonuome of SBS Brokerage noted, however, "Simply changing the head of the bank would not be enough by itself to bolster confidence of Argentines in the banking system." Overall, he says, the government has two main tasks: revamping Argentina's financial system and restructuring debt. President Eduardo Duhalde's government has taken two steps to rescue the country: First, devaluing the currency should help increase Argentina's exports, and second, temporarily halting debt payments should help stabilize the domestic economy.

In a move to assist in the crisis, the IMF granted Argentina a one-year extension for repaying a nearly U.S.$1 billion loan due early in 2002, hoping the reprieve will help restart the economy and calm social unrest. Meanwhile, Horst Koehler, Managing Director of IMF, is offering more than just short-term assistance for getting Argentina's economy back on track: "We have been in close contact with the government of President Duhalde from the beginning. We have sent technical experts for the banking sector there, for the debt operation and for fiscal measures, so everything is offered to Argentina if [it wants] to get our technical assistance to work on a comprehensive strategy."

In addition to the government defaulting on its U.S.$132 billion debt, companies, too, are joining in non-payment on obligations. In the country's biggest corporate default to date, Telecom Argentina, the nation's No. 2 phone carrier, announced it would suspend principal payments on its U.S.$3.2 billion in debt. Most of the debt is in the form of bonds and bank loans. Telecom Argentine issued most of its debt in dollars during the past decade, while the peso was stable. When the Argentine government devalued the peso by 30 percent to 1.4 pesos per dollar in January 2002, it continued to fall on the world markets and quickly lost 65 percent of its value as the recession deepened, so there are not enough funds to pay what is owed. It is paying interest—U.S.$200 million in interest is due in 2002—but it will not be paying the U.S.$900 million in principal that is due. And the firm cannot raise prices to cover its debt because the government froze prices—in pesos—that utility companies can charge customers.

As the downslide continues, additional defaults include U.S.$1 billion by Argentina's wireless unit of Verizon, U.S.$1 billion by CTI Holdings, and U.S.$425 million by Metrogas SA, a giant natural gas company.

Questions for Discussion

1. Assume for a moment that you're a consumer of retail goods in Argentina. Can you identify any problems you might expect to encounter during your country's transition to the devalued peso?
2. Suppose you are manager of an Argentine retail store that sells imported clothing. What preparations would you make to ensure that your business is ready for the transition to the devalued peso?
3. Identify the advantages to be gained—for both individuals and companies—by the payment of all debt by the Argentine government and businesses, instead of both sectors defaulting on debt payments. What are the disadvantages?
4. Consider the actions taken by the government to stop the run on cash from the Argentine banking system. Do you think the actions were effective? Can you propose alternative actions that might have been better than those that were implemented?
5. Consider the risks that foreign banks and businesses took by investing in Argentina. In consideration of their financial losses and other economic and political factors, do you expect those businesses will invest again in Argentine-based ventures? Explain why or why not. ◆

Concluding Case 18-2 CC

The Urge to Merge

At a press conference on June 23, 2003, Finance Minister John Manley announced that mergers between Canadian banks would not be allowed until the fall of 2004 at the earliest. The issue of bank mergers was a complex one, he said, and the government needed more time to study the issue. One of the documents that needed study was a report by a parliamentary committee that made 11 recommendations regarding bank mergers. Among other things, the report recommended that banks that merged should be required to maintain their level of customer service without raising prices, maintain loan access for small- and medium-sized businesses, and guarantee that rural areas would not be denied services.

Manley's announcement dashed the hopes of Canadian bankers, who had been hoping for approval of bank mergers. Canadian banks have been trying to merge for some time now. In 1998, for example, two mega-mergers were proposed by Canadian banks: Royal Bank wanted to merge with the Bank of Montreal, and the Toronto-Dominion Bank wanted to merge with the Canadian Imperial Bank of Commerce. These banks wanted to merge so they could become larger and more competitive in international markets. The Competition Bureau came to the conclusion that bank mergers would result in branch closings, higher service charges to customers, and substantially less competition. The federal government blocked both mergers on the following grounds:

- there would be too much power in the hands of too few financial institutions
- the mergers would reduce competition in the banking sector

- services available to consumers might decline and the prices charged for services might increase
- the Canadian government would have less flexibility to deal with future banking concerns

Canadian banks want to merge because they know that Canadian banks are slipping in the world rankings. Consider some dramatic statistics: In 1975, Canada's largest bank—Royal Bank—was the twenty-third largest bank in the world, as measured by assets. By 2002, it had slipped to fifty-third place. The other "Big Six" Canadian banks have also lost ground in the rankings. In 1984, all of Canada's "Big Six" banks were ranked in the top 40. Now, none of them are in the top 40.

The absolute difference in size between Canadian banks and foreign banks is large. For example, Citigroup (United States) has about $1 trillion dollars in assets, Deutsche Bank (Germany) has about $808 billion, and UBS (Switzerland) has about $750 billion. The Royal Bank has only $220 billion in assets. Bankers say that if Canadian banks fail to merge it will be like the corner hardware store simply waiting to be put out of business by Home Depot.

Why have Canadian banks slipped so badly in the world rankings? There are three reasons:

- the Canadian dollar began dropping in value in the early 1980s, and no recovery was evident until 2003
- Canadian banks have, until recently, focused more on increasing profits than they have on increasing size
- Canadian banks have not been allowed to merge as banks in other countries have

The Canadian Bankers Association says that the international stature of Canada's banks has fallen sharply during the last 20 years. The Association also argues that Canadian consumers benefit from the international activity of Canadian banks, noting that while banks earn 40 percent of their profit outside of Canada, they pay 80 percent of their taxes in Canada, and keep 90 percent of their staff here. But a spokeswoman for the Consumers Association of Canada says that it doesn't make sense that a country like Canada, with its small population, would have banks that are among the world's largest. She says that the banks should stop worrying about how big they are and start improving the way they operate within Canada.

The extremely large profits that Canadian banks have made in the last few years also do not help their public relations with consumers. Canadian banks may be having problems on the size front, but they are doing fine in terms of profits, even compared with their international competitors. A *Globe and Mail* ranking of 11 banks in North America, Europe, and Japan showed that the "Big Six" Canadian banks ranked fifth in terms of average return on equity. British banks ranked first, and Japanese banks ranked last.

But Canadian bankers have not given up hope. In mid-2003, it was widely believed that Paul Martin would look favourably on bank mergers if he became the next prime minister.

Questions for Discussion

1. What arguments have been made by those who support the idea of bank mergers? Assess the validity of each of these arguments.
2. What arguments have been made by those who oppose the idea of bank mergers? Assess the validity of each of these arguments.
3. Opponents of bank mergers argue that consumer services will decline and the price of services will increase if banks are allowed to merge. What is the logic behind this argument? Do you think the logic is correct? Defend your answer.
4. To what extent does the trend toward electronic banking impact the arguments for and against the merger of Canadian banks? Explain. ◆

CHAPTER 19 Understanding Securities and Investments

After reading this chapter, you should be able to:

1. Explain the difference between *primary* and *secondary securities markets*.
2. Discuss the value of *common stock* and *preferred stock* to shareholders and describe the secondary market for each type of security.
3. Distinguish among various types of *bonds* in terms of their issuers, safety, and retirement.
4. Describe the investment opportunities offered by *mutual funds* and *commodities*.
5. Explain the process by which securities are bought and sold.
6. Explain how securities markets are regulated.

Stock Market Manipulations

Some people seem unable to resist the temptation to make money by manipulating stock prices. Bre-X became famous in the 1990s for being involved in a "mine-salting" incident (meaning gold was planted in an area and then "discovered"). In 1993, Bre-X did some test drilling at a site in Indonesia called Busang. Soon, word leaked out that Bre-X had discovered gold there. Bre-X stock naturally went up (to about $2 per share). By 1994, Bre-X was claiming that the find was even bigger than originally supposed. When this was announced the stock went up to $15 per share. By 1996, the estimates had increased even more and Bre-X stock had risen to $150 per share. Then, in 1997, rumours began circulating that the drilling samples had been "salted" to make it look like gold had been discovered. As these rumours spread, the price of the stock dropped back to $3 per share. Eventually, an independent study of Busang revealed that there was actually no gold there. In the panic that ensued, the stock price dropped from $3 per share to 8 cents in one day. Investors lost millions.

Unfortunately, the Bre-X case is not unusual. In 1997, Delgratia Mining Corp. said that promising core samples from a Nevada property that it owned were salted. In 1996, Timbuktu Gold Corp. stock was trading for $30 per share (up from 30 cents a share the year before) when it was discovered that core samples had also been salted.

Salting mines is only one way to manipulate stock prices. Some other manoeuvres are more sophisticated. The activities at Yorkton Securities, RT Capital Management, and Visa Gold Explorations are illustrative.

Yorkton Securities

In December 2001, the Ontario Securities Commission endorsed a negotiated settlement that saw Yorkton Securities pay $1.25 million for violating Toronto Stock Exchange rules. Yorkton's CEO, G. Scott Paterson, agreed that some of his actions were contrary to the public interest, but he denied that he had broken any specific securities rules. He was fined $1 million, banned from trading for six months, and fired as president of Yorkton. Many people in the investment community thought the fine was far too light.

What Paterson (and several other executives) did was to buy stock in various companies for pennies a share, then convert them to high-tech companies, then tout them to its clients. When these companies were taken public, the Yorkton executives made large profits because the stock price had risen a great deal. The OSC concluded that Paterson consistently put his own interests ahead of those of Yorkton's clients.

RT Capital Management

In the summer of 2000, several employees at RT Capital Management Inc., the investment arm of the Royal Bank of Canada, were charged with illegal trading in an attempt to manipulate stock prices. The Ontario Securities Commission (OSC) and the Toronto Stock Exchange (TSE) concluded that the stock prices of many different Canadian companies were being manipulated using a practice called "juicing" or "high-closing." The practice works like this: Just before the stock exchange closes, a trader buys enough shares of a given stock so that the price of that stock rises above the price of the previous trade. This makes it look as if the stock has upward momentum. The motivation to high-close a stock can be strong for money managers, because they are under intense pressure to increase the value of their portfolios so they can demonstrate high performance and attract more clients. The temptation is particularly strong at year-end because money managers' annual bonuses are tied to their performance.

A software program that had been specifically designed by the TSE to catch artificially pumped-up stock prices detected high-closing activities. A surveillance team analyzed computer output to determine whether any stock prices looked suspicious. When they identified several such stocks, the surveillance team requested verification from brokerage houses about who the trader was. Once the surveillance team had received copies of stock orders from various brokers identifying the traders and customers behind each purchase, it became clear that one customer, a prominent pension fund manager, had ordered most of the trades.

RT Capital admitted that it had manipulated the closing price of 26 stocks over 8 days in late 1998 and early 1999. The employees who were involved included a senior vice-president and two traders, all of whom were suspended, and the company was fined $3 million. Twelve traders at 11 different brokerage firms who were also charged were fined and suspended for their illegal actions.

The case may have been just the tip of the iceberg. A study by the *Globe and Mail* covering the years 1997, 1998, and 1999 found many examples of unexplained upward jumps in stock prices on the last trading day of a year. These jumps were followed by steep declines early in the new year. The study found that in one year 80 percent of the stocks that had gained 5 percent or more on December 31 (and reached their daily high at the end of the day) also fell early in the new year.

Visa Gold Exploration

This company hunts for treasure found in sunken ships off the coast of Cuba. Officials at the Toronto-Dominion Bank alerted government regulators to suspicious trading patterns in the company's stock in November 2000. The alleged manipulation involved "wash trading," which occurs when the people who want to manipulate the price of a stock use several different brokerage accounts to establish an artificial price for a stock. This makes it look like there is a lot of interest in the stock by the general public, and that may cause its price to go up. Those individuals who already own the stock benefit because of the increased price. In reality, very few buyers were involved in purchasing the stock of Visa Gold Exploration. The price of Visa Gold's stock declined from $1.15 per share in November 2000 to 5 cents a share by the end of 2001. Trading in the stock was suspended in December 2002. ◆

SECURITIES MARKETS

1. Explain the difference between *primary* and *secondary* securities markets.

Stocks and bonds are known as **securities** because they represent *secured*, or *asset-based*, claims on the part of investors. In other words, holders of stocks and bonds have a stake in the business that issued them. As we saw in Chapter 3, stockholders have claims on some of a corporation's assets (and a say in how the company is run) because each share of stock represents part ownership. In contrast, *bonds* represent strictly financial claims for money owed to holders by a company. Companies sell bonds to raise long-term funds. The markets in which stocks and bonds are sold are called *securities markets*.

securities
Stocks and bonds (which represent a secured-asset-based claim on the part of investors) that can be bought and sold.

Primary and Secondary Markets for Securities

Primary securities markets handle the buying and selling of new stocks and bonds by firms or governments. New securities are sometimes sold to one buyer or a small group of buyers. These so-called *private placements* allow the businesses that use them to keep their plans confidential.

primary securities market
The sale and purchase of newly issued stocks and bonds by firms or governments.

Investment Banking

Most new stocks and some bonds are sold to the wider public market. To bring a new security to market, the issuing corporation must obtain approval from a provincial securities commission. It also needs the services of an investment banker. **Investment bankers** serve as financial specialists in issuing new securities. Such well-known firms as RBC Dominion Securities and TD Securities provide three types of investment banking services:

investment banker
Any financial institution engaged in purchasing and reselling new stocks and bonds.

1. They advise the company on the timing and financial terms for the new issue

2. By *underwriting* (buying) the new securities, investment bankers bear some of the risk of issuing the new security.
3. They create the distribution network that moves the new securities through groups of other banks and brokers into the hands of individual investors

New securities represent only a small portion of securities traded, however. The market for existing stocks and bonds, the **secondary securities market**, is handled by organizations such as the Toronto Stock Exchange. We will consider the activities of these markets later in this chapter.

secondary securities market
The sale and purchase of previously issued stocks and bonds.

STOCKS

2. Discuss the value of *common stock* and *preferred stock* to shareholders and describe the secondary market for each type of security.

Each year, financial managers, along with millions of individual investors, buy and sell the stocks of thousands of companies. This widespread ownership has become possible because of the availability of different types of stocks and because markets have been established for conveniently buying and selling them. In this section, we will focus on the value of *common* and *preferred stock* as securities. We will also describe the *stock exchanges* where they are bought and sold.

Common Stock

Individuals and other companies buy a firm's common stock in the hope that the stock will increase in value, affording them a capital gain, and/or will provide dividend income. But what is the value of a common stock? Stock values are expressed in three different ways: as par value, as market value, and as book value.

Par Value

The face value of a share of stock, its **par value**, is set by the issuing company's board of directors. Each company must preserve the par value money in its retained earnings, and it cannot be distributed as dividends.

par value
The arbitrary value of a stock set by the issuing company's board of directors and stated on stock certificates; used by accountants but of little significance to investors.

Market Value

A stock's real value is its **market value**—the current price of a share on the stock market. Market value reflects buyers' willingness to invest in a company. The market price of a stock can be influenced by both objective factors (e.g., a company's profits) and by subjective factors. Subjective factors include *rumours* (unverified information such as a claim that a company has made a big gold strike), *investor relations* (playing up the positive aspects of a company's financial condition to financial analysts and financial institutions), and *stockbroker recommendations* (a recommendation to buy a stock may increase demand for the stock and cause its price to increase, while a recommendation to sell can decrease demand and cause the price to fall). None of these actions are illegal, but others, like the ones described in the opening case, are.

market value
The current price of one share of a stock in the secondary securities market; the real value of a stock.

Book Value

Recall from Chapter 14 our definition of *stockholders' equity*—the sum of a company's common stock par value, retained earnings, and additional paid-in capital. The **book value** of common stock represents stockholders' equity divided by the number of shares. Book value is used as a comparison

book value
Value of a common stock expressed as total stockholders' equity divided by the number of shares of stock.

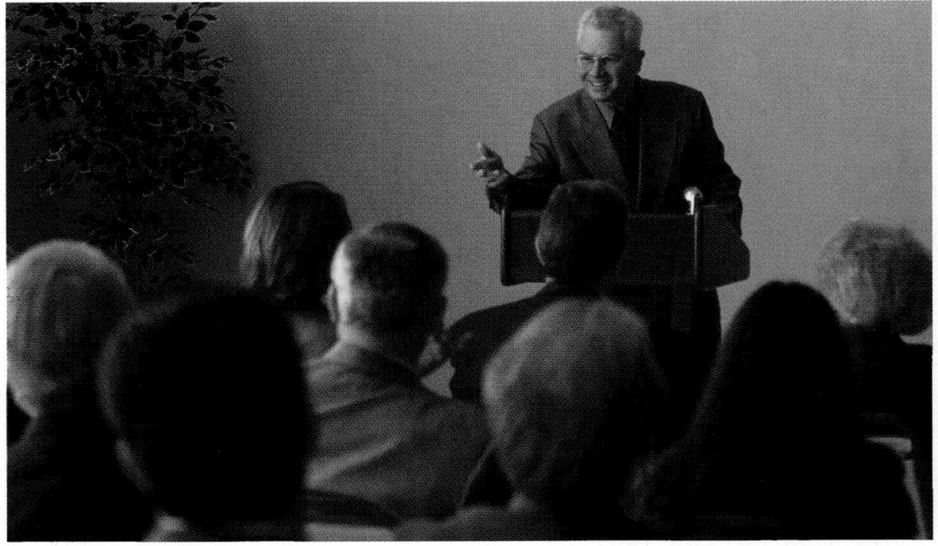

Managers are very interested in publicizing positive news about their company because it will have an effect on the price of the company's stock. Here, a company representative extols the virtue of the company's stock to a group of stockbrokers and financial analysts.

indicator because, for successful companies, the market value is usually greater than its book value. Thus, when market price falls to near book value, some investors buy the stock on the principle that it is underpriced and will increase in the future.

Investment Traits of Common Stock

Common stocks are among the riskiest of all securities. Uncertainties about the stock market itself, for instance, can quickly change a given stock's value. Furthermore, when companies have unprofitable years, they often cannot pay dividends. Shareholder income—and perhaps share price—may both drop. At the same time, however, common stocks offer high growth potential. Naturally the prospects for growth in various industries change from time to time, but the blue-chip stocks of well-established, financially sound firms such as IBM and Imperial Oil have historically provided investors with steady income through consistent dividend payouts.

What Is a Blue-Chip Stock?

Because the very nature of the stock market is continuously changing, the future performance of any stock is often unpredictable. With the proliferation of internet and start-up dot-coms, experts realize that many of the old rules for judging the market prospects of stocks are changing. Conventional methods don't seem to apply to the surprising surges in "new economy" stock prices. Old performance yardsticks—a company's history of dividend payouts, steady growth in earnings per share, and a low price-earnings ratio (current stock price divided by annual earnings per share)—do not seem to measure the value of new economy stocks. In some cases, market prices are soaring for start-ups that have yet to earn a profit.

blue-chip stocks
Stocks of well-established, financially sound firms.

While some of the newcomers—America Online, Amazon, eBay, Yahoo!—are regarded by many on Wall Street as Internet Blue Chips, their financial performance is quite different from that of traditional **blue-chip stocks**, which are well-established, financially sound firms.[1] Let's compare Yahoo! and Wal-Mart. If you had invested $10 000 in Wal-Mart stock in July 1997, the market value of this blue chip would have increased to more than $35 000 in just five years (see Figure 19.1). The same investment in Yahoo! would have also grown to about $35 000. At peak value during the five-year period, however, the Yahoo! investment surged to nearly $600 000 versus Wal-Mart's nearly $40 000.

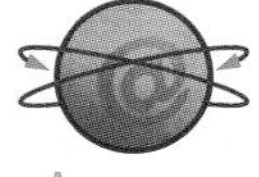

Amazon
www.amazon.ca

Could this huge difference be predicted from indicators traditionally used by market experts? Hardly. The initial public offering (IPO) of Yahoo! stock in 1996 was priced at $13 per share. It quickly jumped to $43, then settled down to close the day at $33 even though the company had not yet turned a profit. Subsequently, because Yahoo! was the leading internet portal brand name, investors were betting that it would become a profitable business in the future—a bet that many traditionalists would view as extremely risky.

Consider the fact that Wal-Mart's book value is more than double that of Yahoo!. Even more glaring is the fact that entering 2002, Yahoo! has had zero or negative earnings per share for the last six years, whereas Wal-Mart's net earnings have grown steadily during the previous 10 years. The comparison is similar for dividends: Whereas Wal-Mart has a steady history of payouts to stockholders, Yahoo! has never paid a cash dividend. Overall, then, the traditional performance yardsticks favour Wal-Mart heavily. Nevertheless, investors are betting the future on Yahoo!. In July 2000, the original $10 000 investment had accumulated in three years to a market value more than 10 times that of the same investment in Wal-Mart.[2]

The drastic change in the price of Yahoo! was illustrative of the sharp drop that occurred in high-tech stocks as 2000 drew to a close. Two Calgary-based high-tech stocks—Cell-Loc and Wi-Lan—also dropped dramatically during 2000. By December 2000, Cell-Loc had dropped 84 percent from its March high, and Wi-Lan had dropped 88 percent.

Market Capitalization. The market value of a company's stock is known as its **market capitalization**. It is computed by multiplying the number of a company's outstanding shares times the value of each share. Table 19.1 compares the Top 10 Canadian companies in 2000 and 2003. In the stock market boom of the late 1990s, telecom and dot-com companies had very high market capitalizations, but when the stock market declined, the market value of these companies dropped dramatically. The market capitalization of Nortel Networks, for example, was $221.9 billion in 2000, but the company didn't even make the Top 10 list in 2003.

market capitalization
The dollar value (market value) of stocks listed on a stock exchange.

Preferred Stock

Preferred stock is usually issued with a stated par value, such as $100. Dividends paid on preferred stock are usually expressed as a percentage of the par value. For example, if a preferred stock with a $100 par value pays

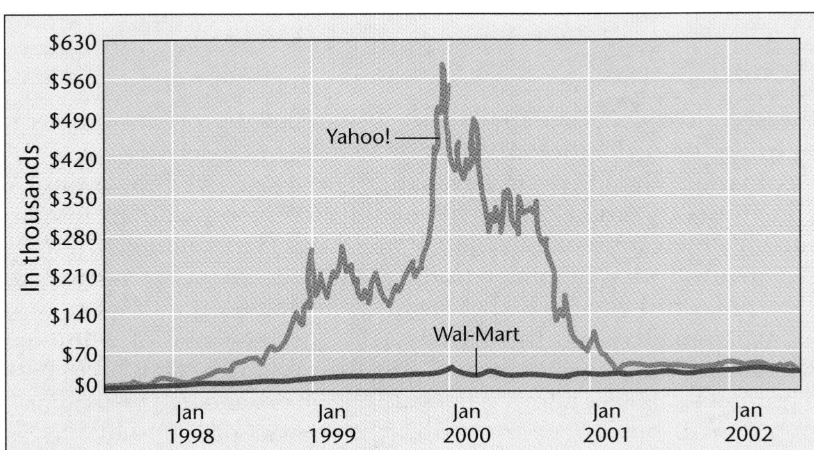

Figure 19.1
Market value growth: Wal-Mart versus Yahoo!.

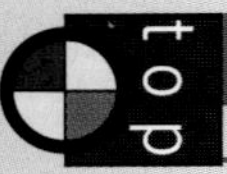

Table 19.1 The Top 10 Canadian Companies (in Terms of Market Capitalization)

	Company	Market Capitalization (in billions) 2003	2000
1.	Royal Bank of Canada	38.7	18.8
2.	The Bank of Nova Scotia	26.5	13.7
3.	The Thomson Corp.	26.0	32.2
4.	BCE Inc.	25.4	101.6
5.	EnCana Corp.	23.1	–
6.	The Toronto-Dominion Bank	21.5	22.7
7.	Bank of Montreal	20.7	11.7
8.	Imperial Oil Ltd.	17.9	11.6
9.	CIBC	17.2	14.4
10.	Sun Life Financial	16.9	–

a 6 percent dividend, shareholders would receive an annual dividend of $6 on each share.

Some preferred stock is *callable*. The issuing firm can require the preferred shareholders to surrender their shares in exchange for a cash payment. The amount of this cash payment, known as the *call price*, is specified in the agreement between the preferred shareholders and the firm.

Investment Traits of Preferred Stock

cumulative preferred stock

Preferred stock on which dividends not paid in the past must first be paid up before the firm may pay dividends to common shareholders.

Because of its preference on dividends, preferred stock's income is less risky than the common stock of the same company. Moreover, most preferred stock is cumulative. With **cumulative preferred stock**, any dividend payments the firm misses must be paid later, as soon as the firm is able. Typically, the firm cannot pay any dividends to its common shareholders until it has made up all late payments to preferred shareholders. If a firm with preferred stock having a $100 par value and paying a 6 percent dividend fails to pay that dividend for two years, it must make up the arrears of $12 per share before it can pay dividends to common shareholders.

Even the income from cumulative preferred stock is not as certain as the corporate bonds of the same company. The company cannot pay dividends if it does not make a profit. The purchase price of the preferred stock can also fluctuate, leading to a capital gain or loss for the shareholder. And the growth potential of preferred stock is limited due to its fixed dividend.

Stock Exchanges

stock exchange

A voluntary organization of individuals formed to provide an institutional setting where members can buy and sell stock for themselves and their clients in accordance with the exchange's rules.

Most of the secondary market for stocks is handled by organized stock exchanges. In addition to stock markets, a so-called "dealer," or the over-the-counter market, handles the exchange of some stocks. A **stock exchange** is an organization of individuals formed to provide an institutional setting in which stock can be bought and sold. The exchange enforces certain rules to govern its members' trading activities. Most exchanges are non-profit corporations established to serve their members.

To become a member, an individual must purchase one of a limited number of memberships—called "seats"—on the exchange. Only members (or their representatives) are allowed to trade on the exchange. In this sense, because all orders to buy or sell must flow through members, they have a legal monopoly. Memberships can be bought and sold like other assets.

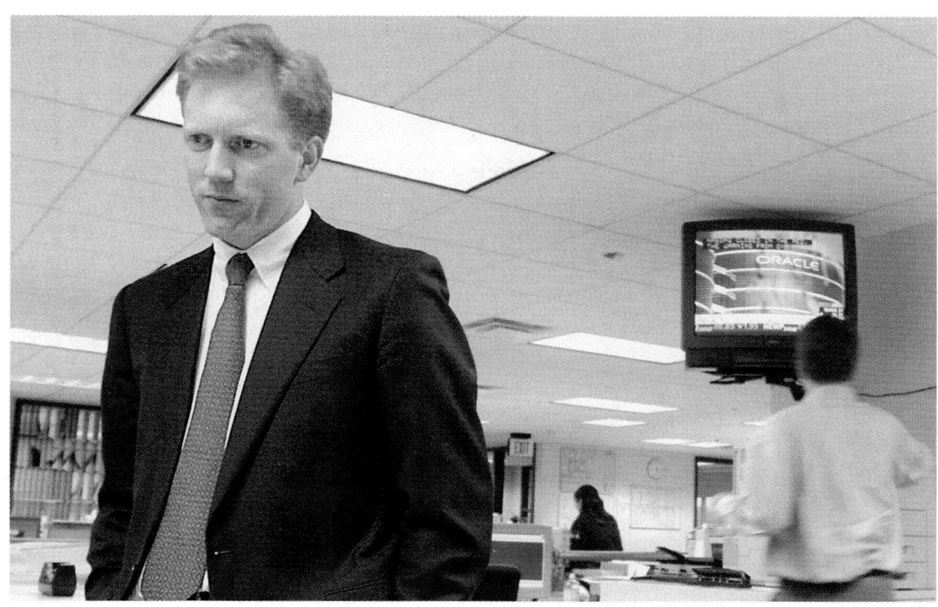

In 1998, when Henry Blodget, an analyst with Merrill Lynch, predicted (correctly) that the price of Amazon.com would climb from $240 to $400 per share, Merrill's leading internet analyst at the time just laughed. But the value of Amazon—and that of hundreds of dot-coms—soared until early 2000. Then came the dot-com crash. By March 2001, Amazon.com had dropped to $9.56 per share. It has since risen some, but is nowhere near its former high. Blodget maintains that he and Merrill Lynch rode but did not fuel the internet euphoria of the late 1990s.

The Trading Floor

Each exchange regulates the places and times at which trading may occur. Trading is allowed only at an actual physical location called the *trading floor*. The floor is equipped with a vast array of electronic communications equipment for conveying buy and sell orders or confirming completed trades. A variety of news services furnish important up-to-the-minute information about world events as well as business developments. Any change in these factors, then, may be swiftly reflected in share prices.

On April 23, 1997, the Toronto Stock Exchange trading floor closed after 145 years of operation. Buy and sell orders are now placed through computers. At its heyday in the 1980s, over 400 traders worked on the floor.[3]

Brokers

Some of the people working on the trading floor are employed by the exchange; others trade stocks for themselves. A large number of those working on the trading floor are brokers. A **broker** receives buy and sell orders from those who are not members of the exchange and executes the orders. In return, the broker earns a commission from the order placer.

broker
An individual licensed to buy and sell securities for customers in the secondary market; may also provide other financial services.

Discount Brokers. Like many products, brokerage assistance can be purchased at either discount or at full-service prices. Buying 200 shares of a $20 stock in 2002 cost the investor anywhere from $8 to $20 at discount brokers like E*Trade, and more than $100 at a full-service brokerage firm. Price differences are obvious even among the discount brokers, but the highest discount price is well below the price of the full-service broker.[4] Discount brokers offer well-informed individual investors a fast, low-cost way to participate in the market. Discount brokerage services are low cost because sales personnel receive fees or salaries, not commissions. Unlike many full-service brokers, they do not offer investment advice or person-to-person sales consultations. They do, however, offer automated online services, such as stock research, industry analysis, and screening for specific types of stocks.

E*Trade
www.etrade.com

Online Trading. The popularity of online trading stems from convenient access to the internet, fast no-nonsense transactions, and the opportunity for self-directed investors to manage their own portfolios while paying low fees for trading. Only 14 percent of all equity trades were executed online in 1998, but the number was growing rapidly until the market decline started in 2000. It remains to be seen what will happen to online trading. One thing that has happened: the competition among brokers has driven commission fees sharply downward.[5]

UBS Financial Services
financialservicesinc.ubs.com/Home

Full-Service Brokers. Despite the growth in online investing, there remains an important market for full-service brokerages, both for new, uninformed investors and for experienced investors who don't have time to keep up with all the latest developments. When you deal with busy people who want to invest successfully, says Joseph Grano of UBS Financial Services, "you can't do it through a telephone response system. In a world that's growing more and more complicated, the advice and counsel of a broker will be more important, not less important."

With full lines of financial services, firms such as Merrill Lynch can offer clients consulting advice in personal financial planning, estate planning, and tax strategies, along with a wider range of investment products. IPOs of stock, for example, are generally not available to the public through online retail brokers. Rather, a full-service broker, who is also the investment banker that sells the IPO shares, can sell IPO shares to its clients. Financial advisers also do more than deliver information. They offer interpretations of and suggestions on investments that clients might overlook when trying to sift through an avalanche of online financial data.

Canadian Stock Exchanges

TSX Group
www.tse.com

There are two major Canadian stock exchanges. The *Toronto Stock Exchange (TSE)* is the largest stock exchange in Canada. It is made up of about 100 individual members who hold seats. The securities of most major corporations are listed here. A company must pay a fee before it can list its security on the exchange. Formerly, there were also stock exchanges in Calgary, Vancouver, and Montreal, but in 1999 an agreement was reached that (1) created the new Canadian Venture Exchange (CDNX) from the Vancouver and Alberta stock markets, (2) shifted all derivative trading to the Montreal stock exchange, and (3) consolidated all senior equity trading at the TSE.[6] The CDNX now focuses on junior companies.

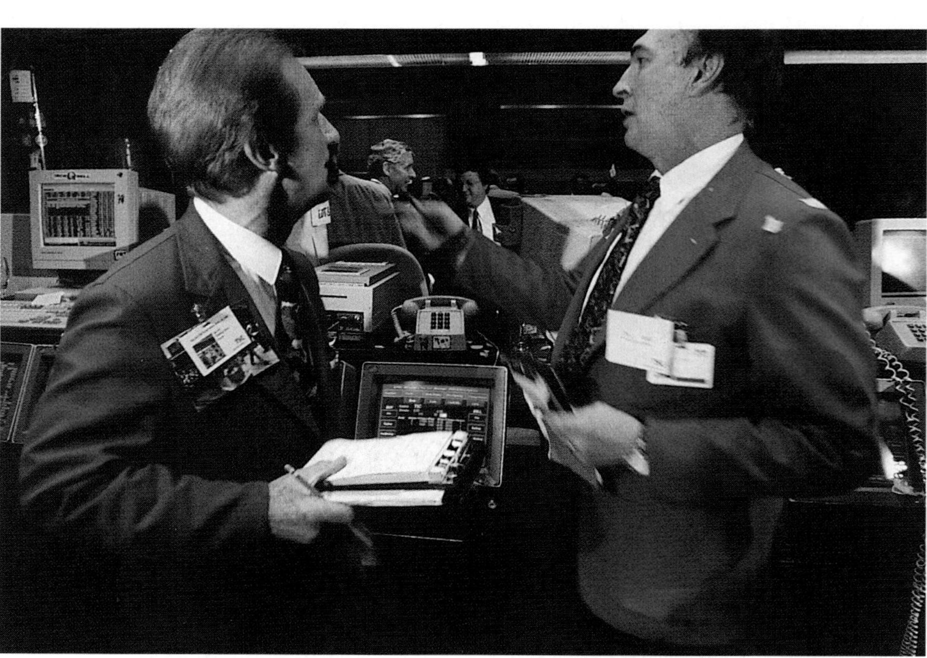

The Toronto Stock Exchange is one of several in Canada where shares of stock in Canadian companies are bought and sold.

Foreign Stock Exchanges

Many foreign countries also have active stock exchanges. In fact, several foreign stock exchanges—most notably those in the United States and England—trade far more shares each day than the TSE does.

The New York Stock Exchange. For many people, "the stock market" means the *New York Stock Exchange (NYSE)*. Founded in 1792 and located at the corner of Wall and Broad Streets in New York City, the largest of all U.S. exchanges is the model for exchanges worldwide. An average of 1.24 billion shares valued at U.S.$42.3 billion change hands each day. About 41 percent of all shares traded on U.S. exchanges are traded here. Only firms meeting certain minimum requirements—earning power, total value of outstanding stock, and number of shareholders—are eligible for listing on the NYSE.[7]

The New York Stock Exchange has recently begun to face stiff competition from both the electronic market in the United States and large foreign exchanges, especially in London and Tokyo. The most important differences between exchanges and the electronic market are (1) the activity of *dealers* and (2) the geographic location of the market. On the trading floor of an exchange, one dealer, called a *specialist*, is appointed by the exchange to control trading for each stock. The specialist not only buys and sells that stock for his or her own inventory but also acts as exclusive auctioneer for it.[8] The electronic market, on the other hand, conducts trades electronically among thousands of dealers in remote locations around the world.

The American Stock Exchange. The second-largest floor-based U.S. exchange, the *American Stock Exchange (AMEX)*, is also located in New York City. It accounts for about 2 percent of all shares traded on U.S. exchanges and, like the NYSE, has minimum requirements for listings. They are, however, less stringent. The minimum number of publicly held shares, for example, is 500 000 versus 1.1 million for the NYSE.

Regional stock exchanges were established long before the advent of modern communications. They were organized to serve investors in places other than New York. The largest regional exchanges are the Chicago (formerly the Midwest) Stock Exchange and the Pacific Stock Exchange in Los Angeles and San Francisco. Other exchanges are located in Philadelphia, Boston, Cincinnati, and Spokane, Washington. Many corporations list their stocks both regionally and on either the NYSE or the AMEX.

Other Foreign Stock Exchanges. As recently as 1980, the U.S. market accounted for more than half the value of the world market in traded stocks. Indeed, as late as 1975, the equity of IBM alone was greater than the national market equities of all but four countries. Market activities, however, have shifted as the value of shares listed on foreign exchanges continues to grow. The annual dollar value of trades on exchanges in London, Tokyo, and other cities is in the trillions. In fact, the London exchange exceeds even the NYSE in number of stocks listed. In market value, however, transactions on U.S. exchanges remain larger than those on exchanges in other countries. Relatively new exchanges are also flourishing in cities from Shanghai to Warsaw.

The Over-the-Counter Market. The **over-the-counter (OTC) market** is so called because its original traders were somewhat like retailers. They kept supplies of shares on hand and, as opportunities arose, sold them over the office counter to interested buyers. Even today, the OTC market has no trading floor. Rather, it consists of many people in different locations who hold an inventory of securities that are not listed on any of the major exchanges. The over-the-counter market consists of independent dealers who own the securities that they buy and sell at their own risk. Although

over-the-counter (OTC) market
Organization of securities dealers formed to trade stock outside the formal institutional setting of the organized stock exchanges.

OTC activities are of interest from a historical perspective, trading volume is small in comparison with other markets.[9]

Nasdaq and NASD. In the 1960s, a study by the U.S.-based Securities and Exchange Commission recommended automation of the OTC, calling for a new system to be implemented by the National Association of Securities Dealers Inc. (NASD). The resulting automated OTC system, launched in 1971, is known as the **National Association of Securities Dealers Automated Quotation**—or **Nasdaq—system**, the world's first electronic stock market.[10] In 2001, NASD became a separate organization from the Nasdaq system so that NASD could focus solely on securities regulation.

National Association of Securities Dealers Automated Quotation (NASDAQ)

A stock market implemented by NASD that operates by broadcasting trading information on an intranet to more than 350 000 terminals worldwide.

With more than 5500 member firms, NASD is the largest private-sector securities-regulation organization in the world. Every broker/dealer in the United States who conducts securities business with the public is required by law to be a member of the NASD.[11] NASD includes dealers (not just brokers) who must pass qualification exams and meet certain standards for financial soundness. The privilege of trading in the market is granted by federal regulators and by NASD.

Meanwhile, the Nasdaq telecommunications system operates the Nasdaq Stock Market by broadcasting trading information on an intranet to over 350 000 terminals worldwide. Whereas orders at the NYSE are paired on the trading floor, Nasdaq orders are paired and executed on a computer network. Currently, Nasdaq is working with officials in an increasing number of countries who want to replace the trading floors of traditional exchanges with electronic networks like Nasdaq.

Nasdaq trades the stocks of nearly 4100 companies. Newer firms are often listed here when their stocks first become available in the secondary market. Current listings include Starbucks and such well-known technology stocks as Intel, Dell Computer, Oracle Technology, and Microsoft.

In early 2001, Nasdaq set a record volume of over three billion shares traded in one day. Its 2001 volume of 471 billion shares traded was the industry leader, and it is the leading U.S. market for non-U.S. listings, with a total of 461 non-U.S. companies. Although the volume of shares traded surpasses that of the New York Stock Exchange, the total market value of Nasdaq's U.S. stocks is only about one-half of that of the NYSE.

Steps Toward a Global Stock Market. With its electronic telecommunication system, Nasdaq possesses an infrastructure that could eventually lead to a truly global stock market—one that would allow buyers and sellers

In the battle for premier companies, both the New York Stock Exchange and Nasdaq have taken to marketing themselves much more aggressively. Each, for example, has expanded operations at its broadcast centre and permitted more and more TV stations to air real-time stock prices. A virtual high-tech market site, the Nasdaq centre features 100 video monitors and provides a showplace to impress new or prospective companies.

to interact from any point in the world. Currently, Nasdaq provides equal access to both the market and market information via simultaneous broadcasts of quotes from more than 1000 participating firms. Nasdaq communication networks enter customer orders and then display new quotes reflecting those orders.

In laying the groundwork for a system that would connect listed companies and investors for worldwide 24-hour-a-day trading, Nasdaq is taking the following steps:

- The Nasdaq Japan Market was launched in 2000 in partnership with the Osaka Securities Exchange. In 2001, it captured nearly 30 percent of Japan's new public stock offerings. This electronic securities market uses a technology that can eventually link Europe and the United States as well.
- Nasdaq—Europe, an internet-accessible stock market patterned after Nasdaq, was opened in June 2001. It offers European traders access to the stocks of listed U.S. and Asian companies.
- In 2001, Nasdaq opened offices in Shanghai, China, primarily for educational purposes, and in Bangladore, India.
- It has agreed to a deal with the government of Quebec to launch Nasdaq Canada.
- An agreement with the Hong Kong Stock Exchange allows some of Nasdaq's shares to trade in Hong Kong and some of Hong Kong's shares to trade in the United States.
- News reports indicate that Nasdaq has established relationships with Sydney, Australia's, stock market and that negotiations are underway with South Korea's stock market.[12]

BONDS

3. Distinguish among various types of *bonds* in terms of their issuers, safety, and retirement.

A **bond** is an IOU—a written promise that the borrower will pay the lender, at some stated future date, a sum of money (the principal) and a stated rate of interest. Bondholders have a claim on a corporation's assets and earnings that comes before the claims of common and preferred shareholders. Bonds differ from one another in terms of maturity, tax status, and level of risk versus potential yield (the interest rate). Potential investors must take these factors into consideration to evaluate which particular bond to buy.

bond
A written promise that the borrower will pay the lender, at a stated future date, the principal plus a stated rate of interest.

To help bond investors make assessments, several services rate the quality of bonds from different issuers. Table 19.2 shows ratings by three principal rating services: Standard & Poor's, Moody's, and the Canadian Bond Rating Service. The rating measures the bond's default risk—the chance that one or more promised payments will be deferred or missed altogether.

Although all corporations issue common stock, not all issue bonds. Shareholders provide equity (ownership) capital, while bondholders are lenders (although they are also considered "investors" as far as the securities market is concerned). Stock certificates represent ownership, while bond certificates represent indebtedness. Federal, provincial, and city governments as well as non-profit organizations also issue bonds.

Table 19.2 Bond Ratings

	High Grade	Medium Grade (Investment Grade)	Speculative	Poor Grade
Moody's	Aaa Aa	A Baa	Ba B	Caa to C
Standard & Poor's	AAA AA	A BBB	BB B	CCC to D
Canadian Bond Rating Service	A++	B++	C	B

Government Bonds

government bond
Bond issued by the federal government.

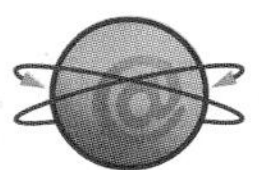

Canada Savings Bonds
www.csb.gc.ca/eng/default.asp

municipal bonds
Bonds issued by provincial or local government.

Government bonds—for example, Canada Savings Bonds—are among the safest investments available. However, securities with longer maturities are somewhat riskier than short-term issues because their longer lives expose them to more political, social, and economic changes. The Canadian government, however, backs all federal bonds. Government securities are sold in large blocks to institutional investors who buy them to ensure desired levels of safety in portfolios. As their needs change, they may buy or sell government securities to other investors.

Provincial and local governments also issue bonds (called **municipal bonds**) to finance school and transportation systems and a variety of other projects. Banks invest in bonds nearing maturity because they are relatively safe, liquid investments. Pension funds, insurance companies, and private citizens also make longer-term investments in municipal bonds.

Corporate Bonds

corporate bond
Bond issued by a company as a source of long-term funding.

Corporate bonds are a major source of long-term financing for Canadian corporations. They have traditionally been issued with maturities ranging from 20 to 30 years, but in the past few years, 10-year maturities have come into wider use. As with government bonds, longer-term corporate bonds are somewhat riskier than shorter-term bonds. Bond ratings of new and proposed corporate issues are published to keep investors informed of the latest risk evaluations on many bonds. Negative ratings do not preclude a bond's success, but they do raise the interest rate that issuers must offer. Corporate bonds may be categorized in one of two ways: (1) according to methods of interest payment, and (2) according to whether they are *secured* or *unsecured*.

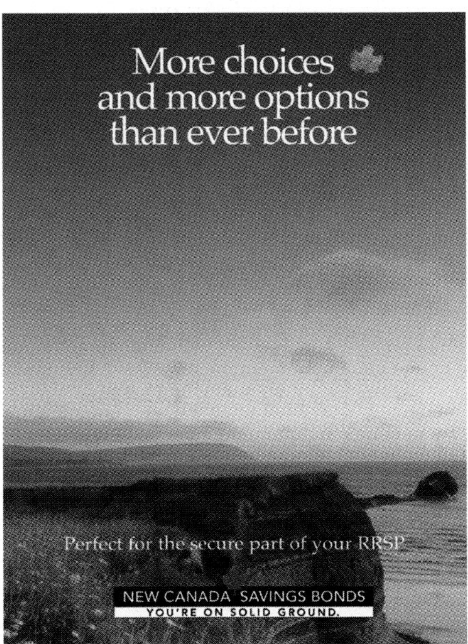

More choices and more options than ever before
Perfect for the secure part of your RRSP
NEW CANADA SAVINGS BONDS
YOU'RE ON SOLID GROUND.

Private corporations are not the only organizations that issue bonds. The government of Canada issues Canada Savings Bonds to finance its debt.

Interest Payment: Registered and Bearer Bonds

registered bond
The names of holders are registered with the company.

Registered bonds register the names of holders with the company, which simply mails out cheques to the bondholders. Certificates are of value only to registered holders. **Bearer** (or **coupon**) **bonds** require bondholders to clip coupons from certificates and send them to the issuer to receive payment. Coupons can be redeemed by anyone, regardless of ownership.

bearer (coupon) bond
Require bondholders to clip coupons from certificates and send them to the issuer to receive interest payments.

Secured Bonds

With **secured bonds**, borrowers can reduce the risk of their bonds by pledging assets to bondholders in the event of default. First mortgages, other mortgages, or other specific assets can back secured bonds. If the corporation does not pay interest when it is due, the firm's assets can be sold and the proceeds used to pay the bondholders.

secured bonds
Bonds issued by borrowers who pledge assets as collateral in the event of non-payment.

Unsecured Bonds

Unsecured bonds are called **debentures**. No specific property is pledged as security for these bonds. Holders of unsecured bonds generally have claims against property not otherwise pledged in the company's other bonds. Accordingly, debentures have inferior claims on the corporation's assets. Financially strong corporations often use debentures.

debentures
Unsecured bonds.

The Retirement of Bonds

Maturity dates on bonds of all kinds may be very long. Of course, all bonds must be paid off, or retired, at some point. With regard to maturity dates, there are three types of bonds: *callable, serial,* and *convertible*.

Callable Bonds

The issuer of **callable bonds** may call them in and pay them off at a price stipulated in the indenture, or contract, before the maturity date. Usually, the issuer cannot call the bond for a certain period of time after issue, often within the first five years.

callable bond
A bond that may be paid off by the issuer before the maturity date.

Issuers usually call in existing bonds when prevailing interest rates are lower than the rate being paid on the bond. The issuer must still pay a *call price* to call in the bond. The call price usually gives a premium to the bondholder. The premium is merely the difference between the face value and call price. For example, a bond that bears a $100 face value might be callable by the firm for $108.67 any time during the first year after issue. The call price (and therefore the premium) decreases annually as bonds approach maturity.

Sinking Funds

Callable bonds are often retired by the use of **sinking fund provisions**. The issuing company is required annually to put a certain amount of money into a special bank account. At the end of a certain number of years, the money (including interest) will be sufficient to redeem the bonds. Failure to meet the sinking fund provision places the issue in default. Obviously, such bonds are generally regarded as safer investments than many other bonds.

sinking fund provision
A clause in the bond indenture (contract) that requires the issuing company to put enough money into a special bank account each year to cover the retirement of the bond issue on schedule.

Serial and Convertible Bonds

Some corporations issue serial or convertible bonds. With a **serial bond**, the firm retires portions of the bond issue in a series of different preset dates. For example, a company with a $100 million issue maturing in 20 years may retire $5 million each year. Serial bonds are most popular among local and state governments.

serial bond
A bond issue in which redemption dates are staggered so that a firm pays off portions of the issue at different predetermined dates.

convertible bond

Any bond that offers bondholders the option of accepting common stock instead of cash in repayment.

Corporations can issue **convertible bonds**. These bonds can be converted into the common stock of the issuing company. At the option of the holder, payment is made in stock instead of in cash. When holders are given such flexibility and because of the potential benefits of converting bonds into stock, firms can offer lower interest rates when the bonds are issued. However, because holders cannot be forced to accept stock instead of cash, conversion works only when the bond buyer also regards the issuing corporation as a good investment.

Suppose that in 1999, Canadian Arctic Explorations sold a $100 million issue of 4.5 percent convertible bonds. The bonds were issued in $1000 denominations; they mature in 2009. At any time before maturity, each debenture of $1000 is convertible into 19.125 shares of the company's common stock. Between October 1999 and March 2003, the stock price ranged from a low of $28 to a high of $67. In that time, then, 19.125 common shares had a market value ranging from $535 to $1281. The bondholder could have exchanged the $1000 bond in return for stock to be kept or sold at a possible profit (or loss).

Secondary Markets for Bonds

Nearly all secondary trading in bonds occurs in the OTC market rather than on organized exchanges. Thus, precise statistics about annual trading volumes are not recorded. As with stocks, however, market values and prices change daily. The direction of bond prices and interest rates move in opposite directions. As interest rates move up, bond prices tend to go down. The prices of riskier bonds fluctuate more widely than those of higher grade bonds.

OTHER INVESTMENTS

4. Describe the investment opportunities offered by *mutual funds* and *commodities.*

Although stocks and bonds are very important, they are not the only marketable securities for businesses. Financial managers are also concerned with investment opportunities in *mutual funds, commodities,* and *options*. In striking the right balance for risk among investment alternatives, financial managers use *diversification* and *asset allocation*.

Mutual Funds

mutual fund

Any company that pools the resources of many investors and uses those funds to purchase various types of financial securities, depending on the fund's financial goals.

no-load fund

A mutual fund in which investors are not charged a sales commission when they buy into or sell out of the fund.

load fund

A mutual fund in which investors are charged a sales commission when they buy into or sell out of the fund.

Companies called **mutual funds** pool investments from individuals and other firms to purchase a portfolio of stocks, bonds, and short-term securities. Investors are part owners of this portfolio. For example, if you invest $1000 in a mutual fund that has a portfolio worth $100 000, you own 1 percent of the portfolio. Mutual funds usually have portfolios worth many millions of dollars. Investors in **no-load funds** are not charged a sales commission when they buy into or sell out of the mutual fund. **Load funds** carry a charge of between 2 and 8 percent of the invested funds.

Mutual funds vary by the investment goals they stress. Some stress safety. The portfolios of these mutual funds include treasury bills and other safe issues that offer immediate income (liquidity). Short-term municipal bond funds emphasize immediate income. Other funds seek higher current income and are willing to sacrifice some safety. Long-term municipal bond mutual funds, corporate bond mutual funds, and income mutual funds (which invest in common stocks with good dividend-paying records) all fall into this category.

Still other funds stress growth. Examples include balanced mutual funds, which hold a mixture of bonds, preferred stocks, and common stocks. Growth mutual funds stress common stocks of established firms. Aggressive growth mutual funds seek maximum capital appreciation. To get it, these funds sacrifice current income and safety. They invest in stocks of new companies, troubled companies, and other high-risk securities.

Mutual funds give small investors access to professional financial management. Their managers have up-to-date information about market conditions and the best large-scale investment opportunities. But there are no guarantees of good returns, and in the difficult market conditions that prevailed in 2001–2003, many people pulled their money out of mutual funds. Table 19.3 lists the top 10 mutual funds in Canada.

Commodities

Individuals and businesses can buy and sell commodities as investments. *Commodities* are products ranging from coffee beans and hogs to propane and platinum. **Futures contracts**—agreements to purchase specified amounts of commodities at given prices on set dates—can be bought and sold in the **commodities market**. These contracts are available not only for commodities but also for stocks. Because selling prices reflect traders' *estimates* of future events and values, futures prices are quite volatile, and trading is risky.

futures contract

Agreement to purchase specified amounts of a commodity (or stock) at a given price on a set future date.

commodities market

Market in which futures contracts are traded.

To clarify the workings of the commodities market, let us look at an example. On December 12, 2001, the price of gold on the open market was $274 per ounce. Futures contracts for July 2002 gold were selling for $275 per ounce. This price reflected investors' judgment that gold prices would be higher the following July. Now suppose that you purchased a 100-ounce gold futures contract in December for $27 500 ($275 × 100). If in February 2002, the July gold futures sold for $299 (which they really did), you could sell your contract for $29 900. Your profit after the two months would be $2400.

Margins

Usually, buyers of futures contracts need not put up the full purchase amount. Rather, the buyer posts a smaller amount—the **margin**—that may be as little as $3000 for contracts up to $100 000. Let us look again at our gold futures example. If you had posted a $3000 margin for your July gold contract, you would have earned a $2400 profit on that investment of $3000 in only two months.

margin

The percentage of the total sales price that a buyer must put up to place an order for stock or a futures contract.

However, you also took a big risk involving two big *ifs*: If you had held onto your contract until July *and* if gold had dropped, say to $240, you would have lost $3500 ($27 500 – $24 000). If you had posted a $3000 mar-

top

Table 19.3 The Top 10 Mutual Funds in Canada

	Company	Assets (in billions of $)
1.	Investors Group	36.1
2.	RBC Funds Inc.	33.4
3.	CIBC Asset Management	32.6
4.	AIM Trimark Investments	32.0
5.	Mackenzie Financial Corp.	28.9
6.	TD Asset Management Inc.	28.4
7.	C.I. Mutual Funds Inc.	26.5
8.	Fidelity Investments Canada Ltd.	26.3
9.	AGF Management Ltd.	20.9
10.	Franklin Templeton Investments	14.6

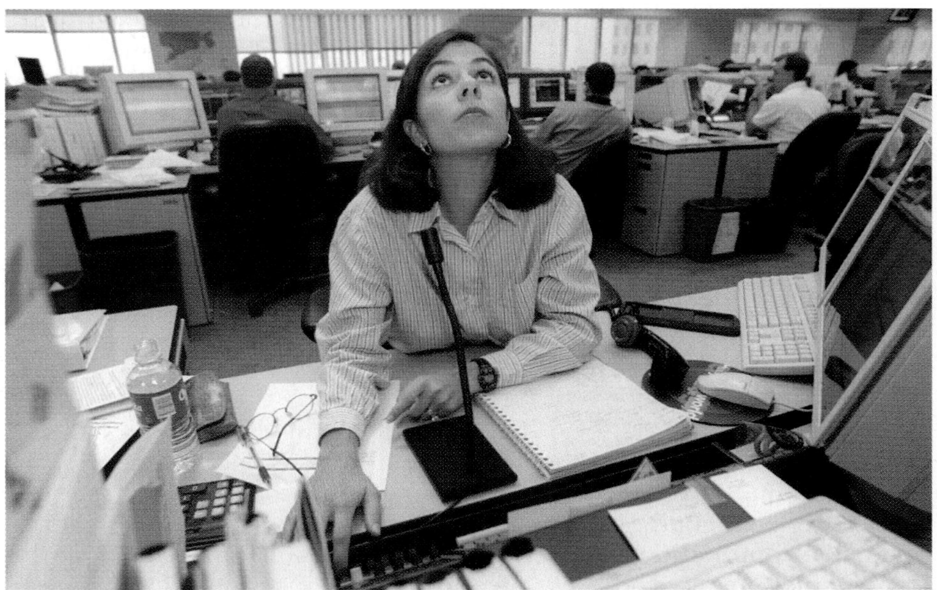

Back when Terri Clynes was trading commodities for Enron, the company's trading portfolio boasted thousands of contracts for commodities ranging from paper and metals to crude oil and power. At one time, Enron assessed the value of its commodities holdings at more than $12 billion. Within two months of its bankruptcy filing in December 2001, that figure had fallen to a mere $1.3 billion. Why the dramatic drop in value? In part because of ups and downs in the market, and in part because of the collapse of Enron's strategy of overestimating the value of its contracts to inflate profits.

gin to buy the contract, you would have lost all of that margin and would owe an additional $500. As it turns out, July gold prices increased to $315, so your investment of $27 500 would have gained $4000 in July. In fact, however, between 75 and 90 percent of all small-time investors lose money in the futures market. For one thing, the action is fast and furious, with small investors trying to keep up with professionals ensconced in seats on the major exchanges. Although the profit potential is exciting, experts recommend that most novices retreat to safer stock markets. Of course, as one veteran financial planner puts it, commodities are tempting. "After trading commodities," he reports, "trading stocks is like watching the grass grow."

Silver is one of the many commodities for which futures contracts can be bought.

More than 400 "commodity exchanges" have opened up in the former Soviet Union. These exchanges bring together buyers and sellers of many different types of goods. Although they call themselves commodity exchanges, they are in fact far more primitive than commodity exchanges in Canada and the United States. One trader says they are more like flea markets than commodity exchanges.[13]

Stock Options

stock option *The purchased right to buy or sell a stock.*

call option *The purchased right to buy a particular stock at a certain price until a specified date.*

Trading in stock options has become a popular investment activity. A **stock option** is the right to buy or sell a stock. A **call option** gives its owner the right to buy a particular stock at a certain price, with that right lasting until a particular date. A **put option** gives its owner the right to sell a particular stock at a specified price, with that right lasting until a particular date. These options are traded on several stock exchanges.

put option
The purchased right to sell a particular stock at a certain price until a specified date.

Suppose that you thought the price of Alcan (which sold for $49.10 per share on August 15, 2000) was going to go up. You might buy a call option giving you the right to buy 100 shares of Alcan any time in the next two months at a so-called strike price of $65. If the stock rose to $75 before

BUSINESS TODAY

Are Stock Options a Good Idea?

At one time in the not-too-distant past, stock options were touted as a great thing. They seemed like a great tool to motivate managers to work hard for the company. Both executives and shareholders would benefit (or so the argument went) because the price of the stock would go up. But the flaws in options were revealed in the stock market boom and bust of the last few years. Greed was one of those flaws.

Suppose you were a manager in a company and you were given 100 000 options to buy the company's shares at $20 per share (the current market price is $15). You know that if the market price rises above the option price, you will make a profit. If the market price rises to, say, $40 per share, you could exercise your options and buy 100 000 shares at $20 per share and then turn around and sell the shares for $40 per share. You would therefore make a $2 million profit (100 000 × $20). Would this be enough to motivate you to work hard to increase the market price of the company's shares? Would it be enough to cause you to do something unethical or illegal (such as recording sales revenues before they actually occurred)?

Ironically, when options first became common in the 1980s, it was thought that they would be good because managers would see the world like shareholders saw it. The soaring stock market of the late 1990s caused a fundamental human characteristic—greed—to emerge. Managers soon started thinking: "How fast can I get my money out?" Many executives became obsessed with the price of the company's stock and took short-term actions that were designed to increase it, because that's the way you make money with options. The motivation was overwhelming to do almost anything to make sure the options were valuable. In some companies, executives were paid a very low salary, but were attracted on the basis that they could make a lot of money on stock options. It is not surprising that these executives would become obsessed with the price of the company's stock.

Some managers made stunning amounts of money from stock options. At the end of 2002, the *Wall Street Journal* published a "Top 10" list of managers who made the most money from exercising stock options. Number 1 on the list was Lawrence Ellison, CEO of Oracle ($706 million), followed by Michael Eisner, CEO of Disney ($569 million), and Michael Dell, CEO of Dell Computer ($233 million). Even the number 10 person on the list (Howard Solomon, CEO of Forest Laboratories) made $147 million. The average person cannot really comprehend the magnitude of these payments.

There has been a great deal of negative publicity in the business press about stock options during the last few years. Shareholders have also complained loudly as the value of their stock tumbled during the stock market decline of 2001–2002. Regular investors are not impressed when already-rich executives get richer while shareholders see their investments decline in value. Shareholders also don't like the fact that options have the effect of diluting the company's stock (because more shares are issued to honour stock options given to executives). In many companies, the price of the shares dropped shortly after top executives exercised their options. The executives made large profits, and the common shareholders watched as the value of their stock declined.

Recently, companies have begun to change the way they deal with stock options. Here are some examples:

- Royal Bank of Canada has eliminated options for members of its board of directors and reduced their availability to executives; as well, executives are now required to keep the shares they gain from exercising options
- Nortel Networks now expenses the cost of its stock options
- Bank of Montreal has also reduced the use of stock options and introduced performance hurdles that must be met before the options can be exercised

October, you would exercise your call option. Your profit would be $10 per share ($75 – $65) less the price you paid to buy the option. However, if the stock price fell instead of rising, you would not exercise your call option because Alcan would be available on the open market for less than $65 per share. (Your stock option would be "under water," that is, it would be worthless.) You would lose whatever you paid for the option.

In contrast, if you thought the price of Alcan would fall below $49.10 sometime during the two months after August 15, 2000, you might buy a put option. Assume that this option gave you the right to sell 100 shares for $54.10 per share any time before October 2000. If the stock price fell to $44.10, your profit would be $10 per share ($54.10 – $44.10), less whatever you paid for the option. Assume that the price of a put option was $3.00 per share at that time. If the stock price increased, you would not exercise your option to sell, and you would lose what you paid for the put option. The daily prices of put and call options are listed in the financial press.

In recent years, there has been much publicity about stock options that are given to executives. The Business Today box describes this controversy.

Making Choices for Diversification, Asset Allocation, and Risk Reduction

Investors seldom take an extreme approach—total risk or total risk avoidance—in selecting their investments. Extreme positions attract extreme results, and most investors have a preference toward either risk or risk avoidance, but they are not totally immersed at either end of the risk spectrum. Instead, they select a mixture, or *portfolio*, of investments—some riskier and some more conservative—that, collectively, provides the level of risk and financial stability at which they are comfortable. They do this in two ways: through *diversification* and *asset allocation*.

Diversification

diversification
Purchase of several different kinds of investments rather than just one.

Diversification means buying several different kinds of investments rather than just one. Diversification as applied to common stocks means, for example, that you invest in stocks of several different companies, such as Inco, IBM, Cisco Systems, and Bombardier, rather than put all your money into just one of them. The risk of loss is reduced by spreading the total investment across more stocks because, while any one stock may tumble, there is less chance that all of them will fall, especially if the companies are from different industries. Even more diversification is gained when funds are spread across more kinds of investment alternatives—stocks, bonds, mutual funds, real estate, and so on. Among the tragedies resulting from the scandals at Enron and WorldCom are the lifelong employees who did not diversify their retirement investments and, instead, had all their retirement funds invested in their firm's stock. This was an extremely risky position, as they sorrowfully learned. When their firm's stock took a free-fall to near zero, their retirement funds disappeared. The Exercising Your Ethics box presents a decision-making dilemma that illustrates the idea of risk.

Asset Allocation

asset allocation
The relative amount of funds invested in (or allocated to) each of several investment alternatives.

Asset allocation is the proportion—the relative amounts—of funds invested in (or allocated to) each of the investment alternatives. You may decide for example, to allocate $20 000 to common stocks, $10 000 to a money market mutual fund, and $10 000 to a Canada Savings Bond. Ten years later, you may decide on a less risky asset allocation of $10 000, $15 000, and $15 000 in the same investment categories, respectively. As your investment objec-

EXERCISING YOUR ETHICS

Are You Endowed with Good Judgment?

The Situation

Every organization faces decisions about whether to make conservative or risky investments. Let's assume that you have been asked to evaluate the advantages and drawbacks of conservative versus risky investments, including all relevant ethical considerations, by Youth Dreams Charities (YDC), a local organization that assists low-income families in gaining access to educational opportunities. YDC is a not-for-profit firm that employs a full-time professional manager to run daily operations. Overall governance and policy making reside with a board of directors—10 part-time community-minded volunteers who are entrusted with carrying out YDC's mission.

For the current year, 23 students receive tuition totalling $92 000 paid by YDC. Tuition comes from annual fund-raising activities (a white-tie dance and a seafood carnival) and from financial returns from YDC's $2.1 million endowment. The endowment has been amassed from charitable donations during the past 12 years, and this year, it has yielded some $84 000 for tuitions. The board's goal is to increase the endowment to $4 million in five years to provide $200 000 in tuition annually.

The Dilemma

Based on the Finance Committee's suggestions, the board is considering a change in YDC's investment policies. The current, rather conservative approach invests the endowment in GICs and other low-risk instruments that have consistently yielded a 6 percent annual return. This practice has allowed the endowment to grow modestly (at about 2 percent per year). The remaining investment proceeds (4 percent) flow out for tuitions. The proposed plan would invest one-half of the endowment in conservative instruments and the other half in blue-chip stocks. Finance Committee members believe that with market growth, the endowment has a good chance of reaching the $4 million goal within five years. While some board members like the prospects of faster growth, others think the proposal is too risky. What happens if, instead of increasing, the stock market collapses and the endowment shrinks? What will happen to YDC's programs then?

Questions for Discussion

1. Why might a conservative versus risky choice be different at a not-for-profit organization than at a for-profit organization?
2. What are the main ethical issues in this situation?
3. What action should the board take?

tives change (in this example from moderate risk to lower risk for capital preservation), your asset allocation must be changed accordingly.

BUYING AND SELLING SECURITIES

5. Explain the process by which securities are bought and sold.

The process of buying and selling stocks, bonds, and other financial instruments is complex. To start, you need to find out about possible investments and match them to your investment objectives. Then you must decide whether you want to use a broker to buy and sell stocks, or whether you want to do it yourself.

Using Financial Information Services

Have you ever looked at the financial section of your daily newspaper and found yourself wondering what all those tables and numbers mean? If you cannot read stock and bond quotations, you probably should not invest in these issues. Fortunately, this skill is easily mastered.

Stock Quotations

Figure 19.2 shows the type of information newspapers provide about daily market transactions of individual stocks. The corporation's name is shown along with the number of shares sold, the high and low prices of the stock for that trading day, the closing price of the stock, and the change from the closing price on the previous day.

Bond Quotations

Bond prices also change from day to day. These changes form the *coupon rate*, which provides information for firms about the cost of borrowing funds. Prices of domestic corporation bonds, Canadian government bonds, and foreign bonds are reported separately. Bond prices are expressed in terms of 100, even though most have a face value of $1000. Thus, a quote of 85 means that the bond's price is 85 percent of its face value, or $850.

A corporation bond selling at 155 1/4 would cost a buyer $1552.50 ($1000 face value × 1.5525), plus commission. The interest rate on bonds is also quoted as a percentage of par, or face, value. Thus "6 1/2s" pay 6.5 percent of par value per year. Typically, interest is paid semi-annually at half of the stated interest or coupon rate.

The market value (selling price) of a bond at any given time depends on its stated interest rate, the "going rate" of interest in the market, and its redemption or maturity date. A bond with a higher stated interest rate than the going rate on similar quality bonds will probably sell at a premium above its face value—its selling price will be above its redemption price. A bond with a lower stated interest rate than the going rate on similar quality bonds will probably sell at a discount—its selling price will be below its

- *Stock*
  Inco (Name of Company)
- *Sales*
  376 030
  Total number of shares traded on this date. There were 376 030 shares sold.
- *High* *Low*
  29.150 28.500
  During the trading day, the highest price was $29.15 and the lowest price was $28.50.
- *Close*
  28.600
  At the close of trading on this date, the last price paid per share was $28.60.
- *Net Change*
  -0.400
  Difference between today's closing price and previous day's closing price. Price decreased by $0.40.

Company	Sales	High	Low	Close	Change
H Bay Co	347 106	34.500	32.000	32.250	-2.500
Humbird	196 310	50.250	47.250	48.850	-2.900
Hy Zels	1 500	4.700	4.700	4.700	-0.100
IBEX T	3 500	5.600	5.250	5.400	-0.200
IITC A	7 000	1.000	1.000	1.000	0.000
IPL eng	38 329	53.000	52.000	52.650	+0.150
ISG Tech	6 583	4.050	3.900	3.950	-0.150
Imasco L	439 447	44.800	44.000	44.250	-0.500
Imax	46 058	35.000	34.000	35.000	+0.500
Imp Metal	22 879	1.630	1.530	1.590	-0.020
Imperial Oil	311 141	87.700	84.750	87.100	+1.100
Inco	**376 030**	**29.150**	**28.500**	**28.600**	**-0.400**
Indochin o	6 100	5.700	5.500	5.500	-0.100
Inex Ph o	8 800	5.250	5.000	5.250	-0.100
Infocorp o	24 400	0.750	0.660	0.740	-0.010
Innova T o	15 000	0.870	0.870	0.870	-0.030
Insulpro	12 000	1.180	1.080	1.130	+0.020

Figure 19.2
How to read a stock quotation.

redemption price. How much the premium or discount is depends largely on how far in the future the maturity date is. The maturity date is shown after the interest rate. Figure 19.3 shows the type of information daily newspapers provide about bond transactions.

Bond Yield

Suppose you bought a $1000 par-value bond in 1983 for $650. Its stated interest rate is 6 percent, and its maturity or redemption date is 2003. You therefore receive $60 per year in interest. Based on your actual investment of $650, your yield is 9.2 percent. If you hold it to maturity, you get $1000 for a bond that originally cost you only $650. This extra $350 increases your true, or effective, yield.

Market Indexes

Although they do not indicate how particular securities are doing, **market indexes** provide a useful summary of trends in specific industries and the stock market as a whole. Market indexes reveal bull and bear market trends. **Bull markets** are periods of upward-moving stock prices. The years 1981–1990 and 1993–1999 featured strong bull markets. Periods of falling stock prices are called **bear markets**. The years 1972–1974, 1991–1992, and 2000–2002 were bear markets. During the latter period, financial failures closed many dot-com firms, and the terrorist attacks on the U.S. occurred.

The Dow Jones Industrial Average. The most widely cited market index is the **Dow Jones Industrial Average (DJIA)**. The Dow is the sum of market prices for 30 of the largest industrial firms listed on the NYSE. By tra-

market index
A measure of the market value of stocks; provides a summary of price trends in a specific industry or of the stock market as a whole.

bull market
A period of rising stock prices; a period in which investors act on a belief that stock prices will rise.

bear market
A period of falling stock prices; a period in which investors act on a belief that stock prices will fall.

Dow Jones Industrial Average (DJIA)
Market index based on the prices of 30 of the largest firms listed on NYSE and Nasdaq.

- *BC Tel*
  Company name is British Columbia Telephone.
- *Coupon*
  The annual rate of interest at face value is 9.65 percent.
- *Maturity*
  The maturity date is April 8, 2022.
- *Price*
  On this date, $138.48 was the price of the last transaction.
- *Yield*
  This is computed by dividing the annual interest paid by the current market price.
- *Change*
  The closing price on this day was up $1.11 from the closing price on the previous day.

Issuer	Coupon	Maturity	Price	Yield	Change
GOVERNMENT OF CANADA					
Canada	4.00	Mar 15-99	100.175	3.865	+0.158
Canada	7.75	Sep 1-99	105.627	4.514	+0.124
Canada	5.50	Feb 1-00	101.897	4.600	+0.155
Canada	8.50	Mar 1-00	108.417	4.648	+0.164
Canada	7.50	Sep 1-00	107.122	4.780	+0.199
PROVINCIALS AND GUARANTEED					
Alta	8.00	Mar 1-00	107.242	4.673	+0.130
BC	9.00	Jan 9-02	114.729	5.046	+0.250
Hy Que	7.00	Jun 1-04	108.100	5.514	+0.460
Man	7.75	Sep 14-00	107.604	4.868	+0.172
Ont Hy	7.75	Nov 3-05	114.086	5.546	+0.493
PEI	8.50	Oct 27-15	123.663	6.285	+0.845
CORPORATE					
Bell	8.80	Aug 24-04	119.790	5.491	+0.490
BC Tel	**9.65**	**Apr 8-22**	**138.489**	**6.488**	**+1.118**
Cdn Util	8.43	Jun 1-05	117.385	5.583	+0.475
Nova Gas	8.30	Jul 15-03	113.508	5.503	+0.386
Royal Bk	5.40	Sep 7-02	100.461	5.289	+0.297
Suncor	6.10	Aug 7-07	100.959	5.967	+0.515

Figure 19.3
How to read a bond quotation.

dition, the Dow is an indicator of blue-chip stock price movements. Because of the small number of firms it considers, however, it is a limited gauge of the overall stock market. The Dow increased sharply in the late 1990s. It reached 11 000 early in 2000, but dropped to below 8000 in 2002. By mid-2003, it had risen to 9200.

Over the decades, the firms included in the Dow have been changed to reflect the changing composition of U.S. companies and industries. In November 1999, for example, four companies were added—Home Depot, Intel, Microsoft, and SBC Communications—and four companies were dropped—Chevron, Goodyear, Sears, and Union Carbide. These changes not only reflect the increasing importance of technology stocks, but also include for the first time two stocks from the Nasdaq market rather than only companies listed on the NYSE.

Standard & Poor's Composite Index (S&P 500)
Market index based on the performance of 400 industrial firms, 40 utilities, 40 financial institutions, and 20 transportation companies.

The S&P 500. Because it considers very few firms, the Dow is a limited gauge of the overall U.S. stock market. **Standard & Poor's Composite Index (S&P 500)** is a broader report. It consists of 500 stocks, including 400 industrial firms, 40 utilities, 40 financial institutions, and 20 transportation companies. Because the index average is weighted according to market capitalization of each stock, the more highly valued companies exercise a greater influence on the index.

S&P/TSX index
An average computed from 225 different large Canadian stocks from various industry groups.

The S&P/TSX Average. The **S&P/TSX index** is an average computed from 225 different large Canadian stocks from various industry groups.[14] The index (formerly called the TSE 300) has been very volatile during the last few years. It moved sharply upwards during the bull market of the late 1990s, and topped 11 000 in the summer of 2000. It then dropped to 6500 by the end of 2000. By late 2003, the TSE had risen to 7800.

Nasdaq Composite Index
Value-weighted market index that includes all Nasdaq-listed companies, both domestic and foreign.

The Nasdaq Composite. Because it considers more stocks, some Wall Street observers regard the **Nasdaq Composite Index** as the most important of all market indexes. Unlike the Dow and the S&P 500, all Nasdaq-listed companies, not just a selected few, are included in the index, for a total of over 4000 firms (both domestic and foreign)—more than most other indexes.

The popularity of the Nasdaq Index goes hand-in-hand with investors' interest in technology and small-company stocks. Compared with other markets, the Nasdaq market has enjoyed a remarkable level of activity. By 1998, so many shares were being traded on Nasdaq that its share-of-market surpassed that of the NYSE. Figure 19.4 shows the steady growth in the dollar volume of Nasdaq trades, which continue to capture market share. In a further display of Nasdaq's emerging role in the stock market, it has also overtaken the NYSE in terms of investor awareness. NYSE's historical dominance as the market's flagship brand is being challenged by the newer Nasdaq, which, according to one study, even enjoys greater name recognition among U.S. investors. The index has, however, been very volatile. In early 2000, it reached 5000, but by 2001 had dropped to just 1300.

Buying and Selling Stocks

market order
An order to a broker to buy or sell a certain security at the current market price.

limit buy order
An order to a broker to buy a certain security only if its price is less than or equal to a given limit.

limit sell order
An order to a broker to sell a certain security only if its price is equal to or greater than a given limit.

Based on your own investigations and/or recommendations from your broker, you can place many types of orders. A **market order** authorizes the broker to buy or sell a certain stock at the prevailing market price. A **limit buy order** authorizes the broker to purchase a stock if its price is less than or equal to a given limit. For example, a limit buy order at $80 per share means that the broker is to buy it if and only if the stock price is $80 or less. A **limit sell order** authorizes the sale of a stock when its price is equal to or greater than a given limit. For example, a limit sell order at $80 per share means that the broker is to sell it if and only if the stock price is $80 or

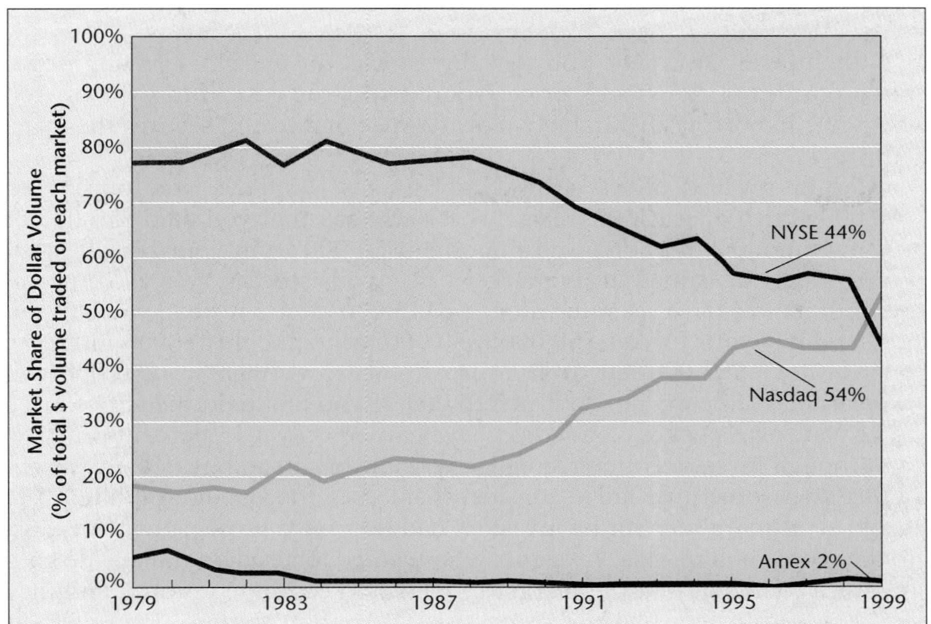

Figure 19.4
The U.S. stock markets: Comparative dollar volume of trades.

more. A **stop order** instructs the broker to sell a stock if its price falls to a certain level. For example, a stop order of $80 on a particular stock means that the broker is to sell it if and only if its price falls to $80 or below.

stop order
An order to a broker to sell a certain security if its price falls to a certain level or below.

You can also place orders of different sizes. A **round lot** order requests 100 shares or some multiple thereof. Fractions of a round lot are called **odd lots**. Trading odd lots is usually more expensive than trading round lots, because an intermediary called an odd-lot broker is often involved, which increases brokerage fees.

round lot
The purchase or sale of stock in units of 100 shares.

odd lots
The purchase or sale of stock in units other than 100 shares.

The business of buying and selling stocks is changing rapidly. Formerly, a person had to have a broker to buy and sell stocks. However, major changes have occurred in this industry in the last few years. More and more individuals are buying and selling stocks on the internet, and traditional brokers are worried that before long customers will avoid using their services altogether. To make matters worse for brokers, it will soon be possible for Canadians to purchase shares of stock directly from the companies that issue them instead of having to go through a broker or the internet. The fees that customers will have to pay for these direct purchases will be even lower than the fees currently charged by discount brokers. Thus, customers will be able to "cut out the middleman."[15]

Financing Securities Purchases

When you place a buy order of any kind, you must tell your broker how you will pay for the purchase. You might maintain a cash account with your broker. Then, as stocks are bought and sold, proceeds are added into the account and the broker withdraws commissions and costs of purchases. In addition, as with almost every good in today's economy, you can buy shares on credit.

Margin Trading

As with futures contracts, you can buy stocks on margin—putting down only a portion of the stock's price. You borrow the rest from your broker, who, in turn, borrows from the banks at a special rate and secures the loans with stock.

Margin trading offers several advantages. Suppose you purchased \$100 000 worth of stock in WestJet. Let's also say that you paid \$50 000 of your own money and borrowed the other \$50 000 from your broker at 10 percent interest. Valued at its market price, your stock serves as your collateral. If shares have risen in value to \$115 000 after one year, you can sell them and pay your broker \$55 000 (\$50 000 principal plus \$5000 interest). You will have \$60 000 left over. Your original investment of \$50 000 will have earned a 20 percent profit of \$10 000. If you had paid the entire price out of your own pocket, you would have earned only a 15 percent return.

Although investors often recognize possible profits to be made in margin trading, they sometimes fail to consider that losses, too, can be amplified. The rising use of margin credit by investors had become a growing concern during the recent bull market. Investors who seemed focused on the upside benefits were confident that the market trend would continue upward, and they were less sensitive to the downside risks of margin trading. Especially at online brokerages, inexperienced traders were borrowing at an alarming rate, and some were using the borrowed funds for risky and speculative day trading. So-called *day traders* visited websites online to buy and sell a stock in the same day (so-called *intraday trades*), seeking quick in-and-out fractional gains on large volumes (many shares) of each stock. While some day traders were successful, most ended up financial losers. With more investors buying on debt, more of them were headed for a serious accelerated crash. Bradley Skolnick, president of the North American Securities Administrators Association, voices the opinion held by many investment experts: "A lot of people are purchasing rather speculative, high-risk stocks with borrowed money, and that's a source of concern for me. In a volatile market, trading on margin can find you in a whole lot of hurt very quickly."[16] More information on day trading is provided in the Wired World box.

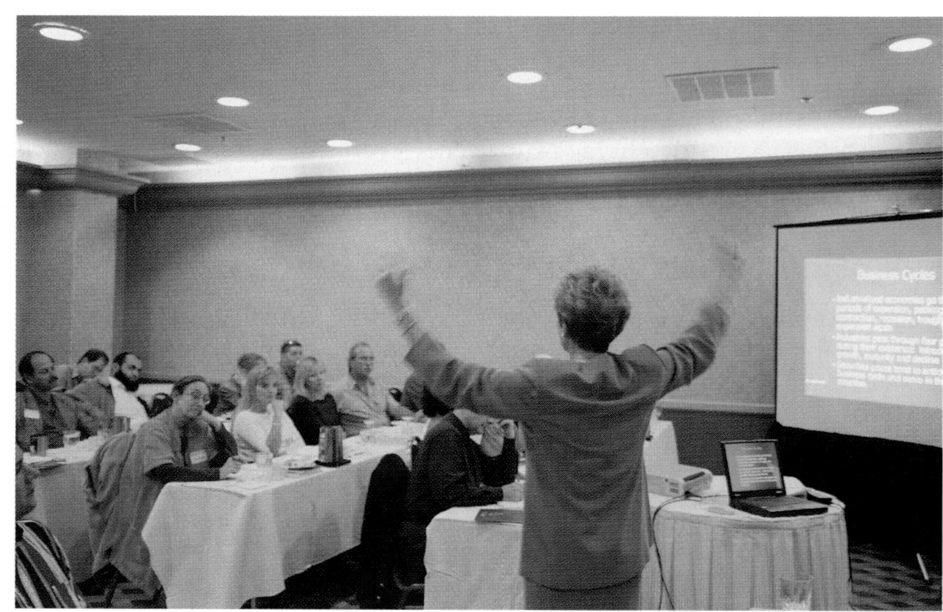

These people have paid \$595 each for a one-day class with Toni Turner. What special message makes Turner worth that much? She teaches a type of day trading called "swing trading." This system discourages buying and selling stocks in a matter of minutes (the strategy of the typical day trader) and explains when and why it's better to study price and patterns over the course of days. If you're interested in day trading, there are several websites that can tell you about the perils and perks. See www.daytradingworld.com as a start.

Short Sales

In addition to money, brokerages also lend securities to buyers. A short sale begins when you borrow a security from your broker and sell it (one of the few times it is legal to sell what you do not own). At a given time in the future, you must restore an equal number of shares of that issue to the brokerage, along with a fee.

For example, suppose that in June you believe the price of Alcan stock will soon fall. You order your broker to sell short 100 shares at the market price of $38 per share. Your broker will make the sale and credit $3800 to your account. If Alcan's price falls to $32 per share in July, you can buy 100 shares for $3200 and give them to your broker, leaving you with a $600 profit (before commissions). The risk is that Alcan's price will not fall but will hold steady or rise, leaving you with a loss.

SECURITIES REGULATION

The buying and selling of securities is regulated in both Canada and the United States. We describe the regulatory environment in the two countries

IT'S A WIRED WORLD

The Daily Grind of Keystroking

Want some excitement? Try day trading. Especially if you enjoy the thrill of risking your money, have the courage to trust your own judgment, and like to make split-second decisions. You'll also need a computer that's wired for real-time stock market transactions. These are some of the difference between day traders and other investors. Investors buy or sell securities with longer-term price changes in mind. Day traders count price volatility—on within-day price changes—as opportunities for buying and selling within a single day. Each day is an adventure. In fact, there's an adventure to be had hundreds or even thousands of times during a fatiguing six-hour trading period, as day traders scour computer monitors for second-to-second changes in market prices for soybeans, index funds, common stocks, or even foreign currencies. And when they find something, they buy and sell in rapid-fire transactions, some lasting only a matter of seconds.

Because daily price variations of 10 percent or more are commonplace for most stocks and commodities, day traders thrive on within-day changes. You'll find them focused on monitors, scrolling numbers, watching TV financial news, and browsing chat rooms. News flashes about companies, economic events, and even the weather might signal momentary price swings that quickly disappear. Judging the timing, direction, and size of those changes is what day trading is all about.

It's all made possible by lightening-fast computer networks and real-time information. If traders expect a stock to rise, they buy and resell shares in a matter of seconds. The strategy for falling prices is buying short, then immediately reselling. At Swift Trade Securities in Toronto, for example, short selling lets some day-trading clients walk home with $20 000 in a single day. Of course, when prices move in the wrong direction, traders lose money, and for every day trader, wrong movements are a daily fact of life. The final tally—pluses versus minuses—at day's end is all that matters. Although the popularity of day trading has slackened in recent years, avid traders still regard it as capitalism's last bastion of fast and vast riches.

If you'd like to see the range of within-day price swings for your favourite stock or commodity, visit a popular securities market website (for example, **www.cnnfn.com**). Among other data for each stock, an intra-day bar chart shows the time-phased pattern of prices that are so alluring to the day trader. Interested in trying it? All you need to do to enter the world of day trading is to establish a computer connection to real-time market data, set up an account of about $20 000, learn a little about particular stocks and commodities, muster the courage to buy and sell at breath-taking speeds, and then use rapid keystroking to move your money around. At day's end, you can go home, relax, and, if you survived, get ready for tomorrow's action.

below. There are both similarities and differences in the way the two countries regulate securities.

U.S. Securities Regulation

6. Explain how securities markets are regulated.

In addition to regulation by government agencies, both the NASD and the NYSE exercise self-regulation to maintain the public trust and to ensure professionalism in the financial industry. A visible example is the NYSE's actions in establishing so-called *circuit breakers*—trading rules for reducing excessive market volatility and promoting investor confidence—that suspend trading for a preset length of time. For example, if the DJIA drops more than 1050 points before 2 p.m., trading is halted for an hour. The interruption provides a "cooling off" period that slows trading activity, gives investors time to reconsider their trading positions, and allows computer programs to be revised or shut down.[17] Bigger drops lead to longer "cooling off" periods.

program trading
Large purchase or sale of a group of stocks, often triggered by computerized trading programs that can be launched without human supervision or control.

One oft-cited cause of sudden market fluctuations is **program trading**—the portfolio trading strategy involving the sale or purchase of a group of stocks valued at $1 million or more, often triggered by computerized trading programs that can be launched without human supervision or control. It works in the following way. As market values change and economic events transpire during the course of a day, computer programs are busy recalculating the future values of stocks. Once a calculated value reaches a critical point, the program automatically signals a buy or sell order. Because electronic trading could cause the market to spiral out of control, it has contributed to the establishment of circuit breakers.

The Securities and Exchange Commission (SEC)

To protect the investing public and to maintain smoothly functioning markets, the SEC oversees many phases of the process through which securities are issued. The SEC regulates the public offering of new securities by requiring that all companies file prospectuses before proposed offerings commence. To protect investors from fraudulent issues, a **prospectus** contains pertinent information about both the offered security and the issuing company. False statements are subject to criminal penalties.

prospectus
A detailed registration statement about a new stock filed with a provincial securities exchange; must include any data helpful to a potential buyer.

insider trading
The use of special knowledge about a firm to make a profit on the stock market.

Insider Trading. The SEC also enforces laws against **insider trading**—the use of special knowledge about a firm for profit or gain. The most famous recent case occurred in June 2002, when the SEC filed suit in federal court in New York against Samuel Waksal, the former CEO of ImClone Systems, Inc. on charges of using insider information to gain illegal profits. The suit charged that Waksal received disappointing news in late December 2001 that the U.S. Food and Drug Administration (FDA) would soon reject ImClone's application to market its cancer treatment drug, Erbitux. The next day, before the FDA was scheduled to notify ImClone of its rejection, Waksal's family members sold more than $9 million in ImClone stock. For two days, Waksal himself tried to sell his shares, which were worth nearly $5 million, but two brokerage firms refused to execute the orders. The following day, after the stock market had closed, ImClone publicly announced the FDA decision. The next trading day, ImClone's stock price dropped 16 percent—from $55.25 to $46.46. By mid-2002, ImClone's stock had plummeted to $8 per share.[18]

Family members, the suit alleges, avoided millions in losses by illegally using the insider information. In June, 2003, Martha Stewart, the home decor entrepreneur and a friend of Waksal, was indicted on charges that she also profited from selling 3900 shares at $58 each the day before ImClone made its public announcement. Stewart denied any wrongdoing. At the time this is written, she is scheduled to go on trial in January 2004.

Canadian Securities Regulations

Canada, unlike the United States, does not have comprehensive federal securities legislation or a federal regulatory body. Government regulation is primarily provincial and emphasizes self-regulation through the various provincial securities exchanges. A 2003 report by a government-appointed committee that studied Canada's system of securities regulation concluded that it is in dire need of reform. The committee noted that Canada is the only country in the industrialized world with a patchwork of provincial regulations. It recommended a single regulator for Canada. The main complaints the committee noted were lack of meaningful enforcement of securities laws, and unnecessary costs and time delays that make Canada's capital markets uncompetitive internationally.

Ontario is generally regarded as having the most progressive securities legislation in Canada. The Ontario Securities Act contains disclosure provisions for new and existing issues, prevention of fraud, regulation of the Toronto Stock Exchange, and takeover bids. It also prohibits insider trading. The Toronto Stock Exchange provides an example of self-regulation by the industry. The TSE has regulations concerning listing and delisting of securities, disclosure requirements, and issuing of prospectuses for new securities.

In 1912, the Manitoba government pioneered in Canada laws applying mainly to the sale of new securities. Under these "**blue-sky laws**," corporations issuing securities must back them up with something more than the blue sky. Similar laws were passed in other provinces. Provincial laws also generally require that stockbrokers be licensed and securities be registered before they can be sold. In each province, issuers of proposed new securities must file a prospectus with the provincial securities exchange. The prospectus must be made available to prospective investors.

blue-sky laws
Laws regulating how corporations must back up securities.

With the decline in the stock markets of both the United States and Canada during 2000–2001, there has been a public outcry for more regulation of securities. Both countries are in the process of developing much tougher legislation in the hope of restoring public trust in the stock market.

SUMMARY OF LEARNING OBJECTIVES

1. **Explain the difference between *primary* and *secondary securities markets*.** *Primary securities markets* involve the buying and selling of new securities, either in public offerings or through *private placements* (sales to single buyers or small groups of buyers). *Investment bankers* specialize in trading securities in primary markets. *Secondary markets* involve the trading of existing stocks and bonds through such familiar bodies as the New York Stock Exchange and Toronto Stock Exchange.

2. **Discuss the value of *common stock* and *preferred stock* to shareholders and describe the secondary market for each type of security.** *Common stock* affords investors the prospect of capital gains, dividend income, or both. Common stock values are expressed in three ways: as *par value* (the face value of a share when it is issued), *market value* (the current market price of a share), and *book value* (the value of shareholders' equity compared with that of other stocks). Market value is the most important value to investors. *Preferred stock* is less risky than common stock; for example, cumulative preferred stock entitles holders to receive missed dividends when the company is financially capable of paying. It also offers the prospect of steadier income than common stock. Shareholders of preferred stock must be paid dividends before shareholders of common stock.

Both common and preferred stock are traded on *stock exchanges* (institutions formed to conduct the trading of existing securities) and in *over-the-counter (OTC) markets* (dealer organizations formed to trade securities outside stock exchange settings). "Members" who hold seats on exchanges act as *brokers*—agents who execute buy-and-sell orders—for non-members. Exchanges include the New York Stock Exchange, the Toronto Stock Exchange, and regional and foreign exchanges. In the OTC market, licensed traders serve functions similar to those of exchange members.

3. **Distinguish among various types of *bonds* in terms of their issuers, safety, and retirement.** The safety of bonds issued by various borrowers is rated by such services as Moody's and the Canadian Bond Rating service. *Government bonds* are the safest investment because the federal government backs them. *Municipal bonds*, which are offered by provincial and local governments to finance a variety of projects, are also usually safe. *Corporate bonds* are issued by businesses to gain long-term funding. They may be *secured* (backed by pledges of the issuer's assets) or *unsecured* (debentures) and offer varying degrees of safety. *Serial bonds* are retired as portions are redeemed at preset dates; *convertible bonds* may be retired by conversion into the issuer's common stock or by cash. Some government and corporate bonds are callable; that is, they can be paid off by the issuer prior to their maturity dates.

4. **Describe the investment opportunities offered by *mutual funds* and *commodities*.** Like stocks and bonds, *mutual funds*—companies that pool investments to purchase portfolios of financial instruments—offer investors different levels of risk and growth potential. *Load funds* require investors to pay commissions of 2 to 8 percent; *no-load funds* do not charge commissions when investors buy in or out. *Futures contracts*—agreements to buy specified amounts of commodities at given prices on preset dates—are traded in the *commodities market*. Commodities traders often buy on *margins*, percentages of total sales prices that must be put up to order futures contracts.

5. **Explain the process by which securities are bought and sold.** Investors generally use such financial information services as newspaper and online stock, bond, and OTC quotations to learn about possible investments. *Market indexes* such as the S&P/TSX index, the Dow Jones Industrial Average, the Standard & Poor's Composite Index, and the NASDAQ Composite provide useful summaries of trends, both in specific industries and in the market as a whole. Investors can then place different types of orders. *Market orders* are orders to buy or sell at current prevailing prices. Because investors do not know exactly what prices will be when market orders are executed, they may issue *limit* or *stop orders* that are to be executed only if prices rise to or fall below specified levels. *Round lots* are purchased in multiples of 100 shares. *Odd lots* are purchased in fractions of round lots. Securities can be bought on margin or as part of *short sales*—sales in which investors sell securities that are borrowed from brokers and returned at a later date.

6. **Explain how securities markets are regulated.** To protect investors, provincial securities commissions regulate the public offering of new securities and enforce laws against such practices as *insider trading* (using special knowledge about a firm for profit or gain). Many provincial governments prosecute the sale of fraudulent securities and enforce *blue-sky laws* that require dealers to be licensed and registered where they conduct business.

KEY TERMS

asset allocation, 688
bear market, 691
bearer (or coupon) bond, 683
blue-chip stock, 674
blue-sky laws, 697
bond, 681
book value, 673
broker, 677
bull market, 691
call option, 686
callable bond, 683
commodities market, 685
convertible bond, 684
corporate bond, 682
cumulative preferred stock, 676
debenture, 683
diversification, 688
Dow Jones Industrial Average (DJIA), 691
futures contract, 685
government bond, 682
insider trading, 696
investment banker, 672
limit order, 692
load fund, 684
margin, 685
market capitalization, 675
market index, 691
market order, 692
market value, 673
municipal bond, 682
mutual fund, 684
Nasdaq Composite Index, 692
National Association of Securities Dealers Automated Quotation (Nasdaq) system, 680
no-load fund, 684
odd lot, 693
over-the-counter (OTC) market, 679
par value, 673
primary securities market, 672
program trading, 696
prospectus, 696
put option, 687
registered bond, 682
round lot, 693
S&P/TSX index, 692
secondary securities market, 673
secured bond, 683
securities, 672
serial bond, 683
sinking fund provision, 683
Standard & Poor's Composite Index, 692
stock exchange, 676
stock option, 686
stop order, 693

QUESTIONS AND EXERCISES

Questions for Review

1. What are the purposes of the primary and secondary markets for securities?

2. Which of the three measures of common stock value is most important? Why?

3. What is the difference between callable and convertible bonds?

4. How might an investor lose money in a commodities trade?

5. How do the provincial securities commissions regulate securities markets?

Questions for Analysis

6. Which type of stock or bond would be most appropriate for your investment purposes at this time? Why?

7. Which type of mutual fund would be most appropriate for your investment purposes at this time? Why?

8. Choose from a newspaper an example listing of a recent day's transactions for each of the following: a stock on the NYSE; a stock on the TSE; an OTC stock; a bond on the NYSE. Explain what each element in the listing means.

Application Exercises

9. Interview the financial manager of a local business or your school. What are the investment goals of this organization? What mix of securities does it use? What advantages and disadvantages do you see in its portfolio?

10. Contact a broker for information about setting up a personal account for trading securities. Prepare a report on the broker's requirements for placing buy/sell orders, credit terms, cash account requirements, services available to investors, and commissions/fees schedules.

BUILDING YOUR BUSINESS SKILLS

Market Ups and Downs

Goal

To encourage students to understand the forces that cause fluctuations in stock prices.

Background

Investing in stocks requires an understanding of the various factors that affect stock prices. These factors may be intrinsic to the company itself or part of the external environment.

- Internal factors relate to the company itself, such as an announcement of poor or favourable earnings, earnings that are more or less than expected, major layoffs, labour problems, management issues, and mergers.
- External factors relate to world or national events, such as a threatened war in the Persian Gulf, the SARS epidemic, weather conditions that affect sales, the Bank of Canada's adjustment of interest rates, and employment figures that were higher or lower than expected. By analyzing these factors, you will often learn a lot about why a stock did well or why it did poorly. Being aware of these influences will help you anticipate future stock movements.

Method

Step 1
Working alone, choose a common stock that has experienced considerable price fluctuations in the past few years. Here are several examples (but there are many others): Nortel Networks, IBM, Amazon.com, and Apple Computer. Find the symbol for the stock and the exchange on which it is traded.

Step 2
At your library, find the *Daily Stock Price Record*, a publication that provides a historical picture of daily stock closings. There are separate copies for the various stock exchanges. Find your stock, and study its trading pattern.

Step 3
Find four or five days over a period of several months or even a year when there have been major price fluctuations in the stock. (A two- or three-point price change from one day to the next is considered major.) Then research what happened on that day that might have contributed to the fluctuation. The best place to begin is with the *Globe and Mail* or the *Wall Street Journal*.

Step 4
Write a short analysis that links changes in stock price to internal and external factors. As you analyze the data, be aware that it is sometimes difficult to know why a stock price fluctuates.

Step 5
Get together with three other students who studied different stocks. As a group, discuss your findings, looking for fluctuation patterns.

Follow-Up Questions

1. Do you see any similarities in the movement of the various stocks during the same period? For example, did the stocks move up or down at about the same time? If so, do you think the stocks were affected by the same factors? Explain your thinking.
2. Based on your analysis, did internal or external factors have the greater impact on stock price? Which factors had the more long-lasting effect? Which factors had the shorter effect?
3. Why do you think it is so hard to predict changes in stock price on a day-to-day basis?

MASTERING BUSINESS ESSENTIALS

Episode 4 reveals that Can Go has enjoyed rapid growth and expects to continue growing. The question, of course, is how to finance this growth, and the management team examines the company's options. *This episode provides a context for the study of stock issues, including initial public offerings.*

CRAFTING YOUR BUSINESS PLAN

A Capital Idea

The Purpose of the Assignment

1. To familiarize students with securities and investment issues that a sample firm may face in developing its business plan, in the framework of Business PlanPro (BPP) software package.
2. To demonstrate how three chapter topics—issuing stock, issuing bonds, and making securities-market transactions—can be integrated as components in the BPP planning environment.

Assignment

After reading Chapter 19 in the textbook, open the BPP software, and search for information about financial plans, equity financing (stocks), and debt financing via bonds as they apply to a sample firm: Sample Software Company (Sample Software Inc.). To find Sample Software, do the following:

Open the Business PlanPro. If it asks if you want to "create a new business plan" or "open an existing plan," select "create a new business plan" (even though you are not going to create a plan at this time). You will then be taken to the Business PlanPro EasyPlan Wizard. Click on the option entitled **Research It**. You will then be presented with a new list of options, including Sample Plan Browser. After clicking on the **Sample Plan Browser**, go down the alphabetical list of sample plans, and double-click on **Software Publishing—Printing and...**, which is the location for Sample Software Company. The screen you are looking at is the introduction page for the Sample Software business plan. Scroll down until you reach the Table of Contents for the company's business plan.

Now respond to the following items:

1. Evaluate Sample Software's plans for financing its operations. Does the company have any outstanding stock? Does it plan to issue stock or bonds in the future? [Sites to see in BPP for this question: On the **Table of Contents** page, click on **7.0 Financial Plan**.]
2. What sources of capital have been used to meet Sample Software's financial requirements? What equity (stock) sources are available for meeting the firm's financial needs? What debt sources are available? [Sites to see in BPP: On the **Table of Contents** page, click on **1.0 Executive Summary**. Return to the **Table of Contents** page, and click on each of the following in turn: **2.1 Company Ownership, 2.2 Company History,** and **7.1 Important Assumptions.**]
3. Based on the company's net profit projections, at what points in time will Sample Software be able to pay dividends or repay its debt obligations? How much financing will be needed according to this plan, and at what points in time? [Sites to see in BPP: From the **Table of Contents** page, click on **7.4 Projected Profit and Loss**.]

VIDEO EXERCISE

Information Pays Off: Motley Fool

Learning Objectives

The purpose of this video is to help you to:

1. Identify the wide variety of investments available to individuals.
2. Describe the process by which securities are bought and sold.
3. Recognize the risks involved in commodities and other investments.

Synopsis

Despite news reports about lottery winners and other overnight millionaires, individuals have a better chance of getting rich if they learn to select investments that are appropriate for their long-term financial goals. Experts advise looking for investments that will beat inflation and keep up with or—ideally—beat general market returns. You can invest in preferred or common stock, newly issued stock from IPOs, managed or index mutual funds, bonds, or commodities. These investments, however, are far from risk-free. Commodities and IPOs can be particularly risky. Thus, if you're planning to invest, you might want to educate yourself about securities and investment strategies by surfing websites such as the Motley Fool (**www.fool.com**).

Discussion Questions

1. *For analysis:* Why is the SEC concerned about stock rumours that circulate on the internet?
2. *For application:* What should you consider when deciding whether to buy and sell stock through a broker, through a web-based brokerage, or directly through the company issuing the stock?
3. *For application:* If you were about to retire, why might you invest in preferred stock rather than common stock?
4. *For debate:* Should stock rumours that circulate on the internet be covered by the individual's constitutional right to freedom of speech rather than be regulated by the SEC? Support your chosen position.

Online Exploration

Mutual funds that seek out environmentally and socially conscious firms in which to invest are becoming more popular because they offer investors a way to earn returns that don't offend their principles. Investigate the following websites: **www.efund.com**, **www.ethicalfunds.com**, and **www.domini.com**. What types of firms does each fund avoid? What type does each prefer? Would you choose one of these funds if you wanted to invest in a mutual fund? Explain your answer.

EXPLORING THE NET

The Tough Job of Securities Regulation

In this chapter we have examined the basics of investing in stocks and bonds. For these instruments to work, there must be some legislation in place to aid in protecting the investor. The Ontario Securities Commission (OSC) is an organization challenged with the role of administering and enforcing securities legislation in the province of Ontario. According to this organization's website, their mandate is threefold: to protect investors from unfair, improper, and fraudulent practices; to foster fair and efficient capital markets; and to maintain public and investor confidence in the integrity of those markets. Let's further explore this organization's website, **www.osc.gov.on.ca**.

1. What are the challenges that the OSC has outlined for the coming year?
2. Examine the "fast answers" section of the website. What guidelines can you use to select a broker? If you experience difficulties with your broker, what process do you need to go through to file a complaint?
3. If you have an old stock certificate, how do you find out its worth?
4. How do you find out information about a publicly traded corporation and how much does this information cost?

Concluding Case 19-1

And the Markets Came Tumbling Down

In the late 1990s, thousands of Canadian and U.S. investors became "paper millionaires" in a booming economy spurred by a vibrant stock market. Annual returns of 15 to 25 percent were commonplace as investors pumped money into the market at a record pace. Major market indexes—the Toronto Stock Exchange, the Dow Jones Industrials, and the Nasdaq Composite—climbed to record highs. Dot-coms and other beneficiaries of the new economy led a parade toward record levels of wealth and prosperity. Government revenues grew so fast that legislators struggled to figure out how to spend the nation's newfound wealth. As investor assets accumulated, older workers began planning for early retirement. Young parents felt confident that their kids' education would be paid for.

Then something happened: A slowdown that had first surfaced in late 1999 gradually gained momentum and began to dampen stock prices in 2000. Soon the slowdown became an unmistakable retreat. Unprofitable dot-coms started failing, unemployment started to climb, and the stock market was hit by further economic downturns that continued throughout 2001, even before the September 11 terrorist attacks. To further depress an already downcast market, more setbacks came in a series of corporate scandals involving well-known firms—RT Capital Management, Global Crossings, Enron, Arthur Andersen, ImClone, WorldCom, and a host of others—that struck both fear and anger in retirees, employees, and investors. As more reports rolled in, the public's trust dwindled until, by fall 2002, the market had tumbled to its lowest level in years as wary investors pulled money out of stocks and went looking for safer investments.

In the wake of the precipitous fall of the Toronto and New York stock markets, many erstwhile millionaires began assessing the damage. How bad was it? One prominent publication pointed out that if you owned 500 shares of JDS Uniphase Corp., a producer of components for fibre-optic networks, in March 2000, you could have bought a new Porsche 911 Carrera. By July 2002, those same shares would have bought you a 1990 Dodge Omni Hatchback with 100 000 miles and no air conditioning. Aside from millionaires, blue-collar investors were also hit hard. Some would-be early retirees began planning to delay retirement. Others were left with no retirement funds at all. Young parents started saving all over again for their children's education.

Many investors, having experienced only bull market years during the 1970s to 1999, were unprepared for the bear market that greeted them in the 2000–2002 period. By mid-July 2002, dazed traders and market analysts were using words like "crash" and "panic," and the numbers bore them out: The Toronto Stock Exchange index fell from more than 11 000 in 2000 to below 7000 by the summer of 2002. The Nasdaq Composite fell from a record high of 5100 in 2000 to just above 1300 in mid-July 2002, losing 74 percent of its value. In that same period, the Dow fell 32 percent. Individual companies fared no better. Nortel Networks fell from $124 per share in 2000 to less than $1 per share in 2002.

So, what will it take for the market to recover? By the middle of 2003, markets had recovered somewhat, but the public's faith in corporations and the market was still low. There were some positive economic signs—increases in sales and industrial production, low inflation, strong consumer spending—but investors continue to retreat to safer ground as new reports surfaced about conniving CEOs cooking corporate books.

Individual investors still have their own problems. After more than two years of losses, those still brave enough to remain in the market face the possibility of sinking even farther or pulling out. Should they hang in or get out? Should they put their money in money market mutual funds? Should they gamble on further downfalls by selling short? How about buying more stock because current prices are so low? Although the answers to these and other questions are by no means clear, there is general agreement that an important lesson has been learned. Because it's volatile and unpredictable, the market is a very disturbing place for those who can't deal with economic uncertainty.

Questions for Discussion

1. In a volatile stock market, why is it important for investors to assess their reactions to financial risk and to put together short-term and long-term financial plans?
2. What do you think about the media's role in stock market volatility?
3. As the market was falling during the 2000–2002 period, why do you suppose that some market indexes experienced larger changes than others?
4. What factors will be most significant—economic, social, political, or psychological—for reversing the market crash?
5. Suppose your retirement account had reached $500 000 in 2000 and was invested half-and-half in a bond mutual fund and a stock mutual fund. By mid-July 2003, the stock market fund had fallen to $150 000 in market value, while the bond fund was worth $280 000. At mid-July 2003, what would be your investment strategy? Why? ◆

Concluding Case 19-2 CC

Ups and Downs at Marvel Comics

When you say "Marvel Comics," most people think of comic book characters like X-Men, the Incredible Hulk, and Spiderman. And indeed, Marvel comic books were a staple for young readers for many years. But Marvel Enterprises discovered that comic books alone couldn't save it from bankruptcy. Here is the story.

Marvel Comics started up in the 1930s. For the next 40 years, it produced mainly comic books and comic strips in newspapers. In the 1970s, the comic book collectors market started to heat up, and this drove comic books to new highs in sales volume. One X-Men comic book, for example, sold 7 million copies in 1991. But then the collector market collapsed, sales revenues declined, and debts began to pile up.

In 1991, Marvel Comics sold 4.2 million shares of stock at $16.50 per share and raised $69.3 million. It used the cash to retire the debt it had accumulated. For a time, things were looking up again. By 1992, the price of the company's stock had risen to $65 per share. But then *Barron's* magazine ran an article that was critical of Marvel. The article noted that a large proportion of Marvel's total revenue came from comic books, and comic book sales were levelling off. After the article appeared, Marvel's stock price began to fall. The concerns expressed in the *Barron's* article turned out to be true, and Marvel's stock price declined steadily over the next four years. In 1996, Marvel filed for bankruptcy protection. The stock closed at $2.38 per share that day. Industry experts concluded that Marvel went bankrupt because collector interest in comic books had declined and competition in the market had increased.

Marvel emerged from bankruptcy in 1998 with new managers, a new focus, and a new owner (toy maker Ike Perlmutter) who wasn't content to just print comic books and collector cards. He reduced the number of comic book titles and eliminated expensive exclusive deals with authors. He also recognized the potential of movies containing Marvel's superheroes, and was able to sign several lucrative licensing arrangements with film studios. These licensing deals have since yielded movies like *Spider-Man*, *X-Men, X-Men II*, *The Hulk*, and *Daredevil*. Marvel also plans to leverage the licensing deals into spin-off toy products and TV shows. In April 2002, just before the release of the *Spider-Man* movie, Marvel shares were trading at just over $9 per share.

Marvel now gets most of its revenues from two sources: licensing agreements on comic book characters, and a percentage of movie theatre receipts. This means that Marvel makes money on any movie that contains its characters, whether or not the movie itself makes any money. Marvel has a continuing cast of characters that have appeared in big-screen movies. During 2003, for example, both *The Hulk* and *X-Men II* were released. By mid-2003, Marvel shares were trading at nearly $20 each.

In 2003, for the first time in its history, Marvel generated more money from licensing deals than from the sale of comic books, where it controls about 40 percent of the market. Stock analyst Robert Routh noted that the licensing business is great if you have something marketable that you can license. Marvel certainly has that. In May 2003, *X-Men II* opened at the No. 1 box office position, raking in $85.6 million in ticket sales. That was the sixth consecutive movie with Marvel characters that had opened at number one.

The future now looks much brighter for this old-line comic book company.

Questions for Discussion

1. What causes the price of a company's stock to go up or down? Are these factors objective or subjective? Explain.
2. What kind of investors do you think buy Marvel stock? Why?
3. What is the difference between common stock and bonds? What would motivate a company like Marvel to sell stock instead of borrowing money to finance its operations?
4. Check the current price of Marvel stock on the New York Stock Exchange. Is it higher or lower than it was in mid-2003? What might be some of the reasons the price movement occurred? ◆

CHAPTER 20

Financial Decisions and Risk Management

After reading this chapter, you should be able to:

1. Describe the responsibilities of a *financial manager.*
2. Distinguish between *short-term (operating)* and *long-term (capital)* expenditures.
3. Identify four sources of short-term financing for businesses.
4. Distinguish among the various sources of *long-term financing* and explain the risks involved in each.
5. Discuss some key issues in financial management for small businesses.
6. Explain how *risk* affects business operations and identify the five steps in the *risk-management process.*
7. Explain the distinction between *insurable* and *uninsurable risks*, and distinguish among the different *types of insurance* purchased by businesses.

Three Sad Tales of Failed Risk Management

In October 2002, John Rusnak, a currency trader at Allfirst Financial, the U.S. subsidiary of Allied Irish Banks PLC (AIB), was sentenced to seven-and-a-half years in prison after he admitted that he defrauded the company of $691 million by creating phony currency trades. During 1997–2001, Rusnak ran up currency trading losses while trading Japanese yen. But he devised a scheme to evade detection that involved providing false information showing that his trading activity had actually been profitable. He did this by creating fictitious trades showing large profits that seemingly covered his actual trading losses. Rusnak's manipulation of Allfirst's computer tracking system led to the conclusion that the bank had made profits during 1997–2001, when it had actually incurred large losses. Rusnak earned bonuses of more than $650 000 as a result of these apparent profits.

Eugene Ludwig, former comptroller of the currency for the U.S. government, carried out an investigation into how this could have happened. His report showed that AIB had done a questionable job of monitoring its U.S. subsidiary, especially since there were clues that something was not right. For example, when AIB's CEO talked to one of Allfirst's auditors about unusually heavy trading being done at Allfirst, he was told that everything was normal, in spite of the fact that trading volume was more than 20 times normal. The AIB CEO took the auditor's report at face value and did not pursue the matter further. As a result of Ludwig's investigation, seven key executives at Allfirst Financial were either dismissed or retired.

Rusnak is not the only rogue trader that has circumvented his company's financial control system. Two other traders—Stephen Humphries and Nicholas Leeson—also made big splashes in the news during the last decade.

The Stephen Humphries Case

In 1999, Stephen Humphries, age 25, was working as a trader at Sussex Futures Ltd. in England. One August afternoon he engaged in so much fraudulent trading activity that he destroyed the company he worked for. Humphries bet that U.S. unemployment figures were going to go up, but when data were published showing no change in the unemployment rate, this made U.S. interest rates more likely to rise, which in turn reduced the value of fixed-interest investments such as government bonds. Humphries continued to buy bonds in the hope that things would somehow turn around, but in the end he lost U.S.$1.1 million in just 90 minutes. Sussex Futures ceased operations a few months later, and 70 people lost their jobs. Ironically, Humphries had lost his job at another trading firm because a rogue trader had bankrupted that firm.

The Nicholas Leeson Case

Nicholas Leeson, age 28, worked for Barings PLC, a British merchant bank. Leeson's job involved buying and selling futures contracts, particularly investments known as derivatives. Over a three-week period, Leeson managed to incur trading losses of nearly $1 billion by wagering that the sluggish Japanese Nikkei stock index would go up. If the Nikkei rose as he predicted, Leeson would cash in and profit because the contract price on which he had originally agreed would be lower than the actual level of the index when the contract came due. He would profit by the amount of the difference. But the Nikkei fell below Leeson's contract price, and Barings was obligated to pay the difference. Leeson convinced Barings officials in London to advance him the cash by claiming that he was trading on behalf of a client who would soon be depositing funds with the bank. But it was not enough, and when losses spiralled out of control, Leeson fled, and Barings had to declare bankruptcy. After his arrest in Germany, he was kept in jail while awaiting extradition to Singapore. Leeson was eventually sentenced to six-and-a-half years in prison.

How could traders like Rusnak, Humphries, and Leeson rack up such huge losses without being detected? The problem, experts agreed, is a lack of internal risk management controls. In some very vague and general sense, the activities of these three traders were subject to control by risk-management officials at their companies. But in each case, the companies' financial control systems had loopholes that a clever person could exploit. In each situation, there were also company-specific factors at work. In Rusnak's case, the company's commitment to decentralization of authority was partly to blame. When Allied Irish Banks bought U.S.-based Allfirst Financial, its top executives felt that foreign financial services companies had not been as successful as they might have been in the United States because they didn't give their U.S. subsidiaries enough independence. So AIB gave Allfirst personnel a lot of freedom. One of the employees who took advantage of that was John Rusnak.

In Leeson's case, there were internal rivalries and turf battles pitting Barings' London-based banking operations against the company's trading divisions worldwide. Following Leeson's arrest, accusations flew regarding which Barings executive should have been responsible for preventing the fiasco. ◆

THE ROLE OF THE FINANCIAL MANAGER

1. Describe the responsibilities of a *financial manager.*

We have seen that production managers are responsible for planning and controlling the output of goods and services. We have noted that marketing managers must plan and control the development and marketing of products. Similarly, **financial managers** plan and control the acquisition and dispersal of the company's financial assets. The business activity known as **finance** (or corporate finance) typically involves four responsibilities:

financial managers
Those managers responsible for planning and overseeing the financial resources of a firm.

finance
The business function involving decisions about a firm's long-term investments and obtaining the funds to pay for those investments.

- determining a firm's long-term investments
- obtaining funds to pay for those investments
- conducting the firm's everyday financial activities
- helping to manage the risks that the firm takes

Objectives of the Financial Manager

Financial managers collect funds, pay debts, establish trade credit, obtain loans, control cash balances, and plan for future financial needs. But a financial manager's overall objective is to increase a firm's value—and thus stockholders' wealth. Whereas accountants create data to reflect a firm's financial status, financial managers make decisions for improving that status. Financial managers, then, must ensure that a company's earnings exceed its costs—in other words, that it earns a profit. In sole proprietorships and partnerships, profits translate directly into increases in owners' wealth. In corporations, profits translate into an increase in the value of common stock.

Responsibilities of the Financial Manager

The various responsibilities of the financial manager in increasing a firm's wealth fall into three general categories: *cash flow management, financial control,* and *financial planning.*

Cash Flow Management

To increase a firm's value, financial managers must ensure that it always has enough funds on hand to purchase the materials and human resources that it needs to produce goods and services. At the same time, of course, there may be funds that are not needed immediately. These must be invested to earn more money for a firm. This activity—**cash flow management**—requires careful planning. If excess cash balances are allowed to sit idle instead of being invested, a firm loses the cash returns it could have earned.

cash flow management
Managing the pattern in which cash flows into the firm in the form of revenues and out of the firm in the form of debt payments.

How important to a business is the management of its idle cash? One study has revealed that companies averaging $2 million in annual sales typically hold $40 000 in non-interest-bearing accounts. Larger companies hold even larger sums. More and more companies, however, are learning to put their idle funds to work. By locating idle cash and putting it to work, firms not only gain additional income, but also can avoid having to borrow from outside sources. The savings on interest payments can be substantial.

Financial Control

Because things never go exactly as planned, financial managers must be prepared to make adjustments for actual financial changes that occur each day. **Financial control** is the process of checking actual performance against plans to ensure that the desired financial status occurs. For example, planned revenues based on forecasts usually turn out to be higher or lower than actual revenues. Why? Simply because sales are unpredictable. Control involves monitoring revenue inflows and making appropriate financial adjustments. Excessively high revenues, for instance, may be deposited in short-term interest-bearing accounts. Or they may be used to pay off short-term debt. Otherwise earmarked resources can be saved or put to better use. In contrast, lower-than-expected revenues may necessitate short-term borrowing to meet current debt obligations.

financial control
The process of checking actual performance against plans to ensure that the desired financial status is achieved.

Budgets (as we saw in Chapter 14) are often the backbone of financial control. The budget provides the "measuring stick" against which performance is evaluated. The cash flows, debts, and assets not only of the whole company but also of each department are compared at regular intervals against budgeted amounts. Discrepancies indicate the need for financial adjustments so that resources are used to the best advantage.

Financial Planning

The cornerstone of effective financial management is the development of a **financial plan**. A financial plan describes a firm's strategies for reaching some future financial position. In constructing the plan, a financial manager must ask several questions:

financial plan
A description of how a business will reach some financial position it seeks for the future; includes projections for sources and uses of funds.

- What amount of funds does the company need to meet immediate plans?

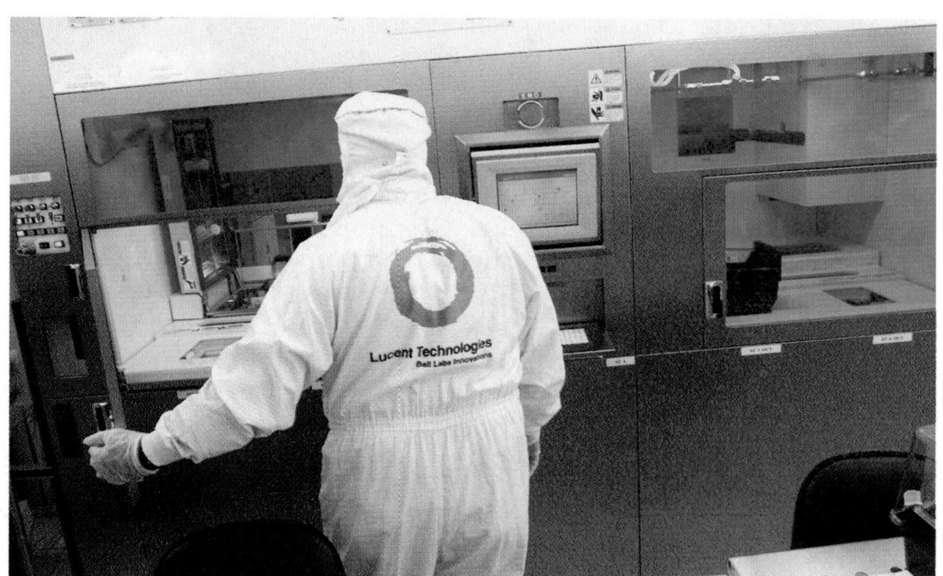

There's always room for creative cash-flow management. Analysts report, for example, that Lucent Technologies has added employee compensation that's paid out in stock options (instead of cash) into its operating cash flow. Technically, that category should include only money that's earned from operating activities such as manufacturing microchips. But when operating cash flow is inflated in this manner (which is perfectly legal), unwary investors may be led to believe that the company's earnings are higher than they really are.

- When will it need more funds?
- Where can it get the funds to meet both its short-term and its long-term needs?

To answer these questions, a financial manager must develop a clear picture of *why* a firm needs funds. Managers must also assess the relative costs and benefits of potential funding sources. In the sections that follow, we will examine the main reasons for which companies generate funds and describe the main sources of business funding, for both the short term and the long term.

WHY DO BUSINESSES NEED FUNDS?

2. Distinguish between *short-term (operating)* and *long-term (capital)* expenditures.

Every company needs money to survive. Failure to make a contractually obligated payment can lead to bankruptcy and the dissolution of the firm. However, the successful financial manager must distinguish between two different kinds of financial outlays: *short-term (operating) expenditures* and *long-term (capital) expenditures*.

Short-Term (Operating) Expenditures

A firm incurs short-term expenditures regularly in its everyday business activities. To handle these expenditures, financial managers must pay attention to *accounts payable, accounts receivable,* and to *inventories*. We also describe the measures used by some firms in managing the funds known as *working capital*.

Accounts Payable

In Chapter 14, we defined *accounts payable* as unpaid bills owed to suppliers plus wages and taxes due within the upcoming year. For most companies, this is the largest single category of short-term debt. To plan for funding flows, financial managers want to know *in advance* the amounts of new accounts payable as well as when they must be repaid. For information about such obligations and needs—say, the quantity of supplies required by a certain department in an upcoming period—financial managers must rely on other managers. The Exercising Your Ethics box presents an interesting dilemma regarding accounts payable.

Accounts Receivable

As we also saw in Chapter 14, *accounts receivable* consist of funds due from customers who have bought on credit. A sound financial plan requires financial managers to project accurately both how much credit is advanced to buyers and when they will make payments on their accounts. For example, managers at Kraft Foods must know how many dollars' worth of cheddar cheese Safeway supermarkets will order each month; they must also know Safeway's payment schedule. Because accounts receivable represent an investment in products for which a firm has not yet received payment, they temporarily tie up its funds. Clearly, the seller wants to receive payment as quickly as possible.

credit policy
Rules governing a firm's extension of credit to customers.

Credit Policies. Predicting payment schedules is a function of **credit policy**: the rules governing a firm's extension of credit to customers. This policy sets standards as to which buyers are eligible for what type of credit. Typically, credit is extended to customers who have the ability to pay and who honour their obligations. Credit is denied to firms with poor payment histories.

EXERCISING YOUR ETHICS

Doing Your Duty When Payables Come Due

The Situation

Assume you work as a manager for one of the world's best-known conglomerates. As the end of the fiscal year approaches, you are attending an Executive Committee meeting at which the CEO, the firm's dominant leader, expresses concern that the firm's year-end cash position will be less favourable than projected. The firm has exceeded analysts' performance expectations in each of his eight years at the helm and he is determined that stockholders will never be disappointed as long as he is CEO. The purpose of the meeting is to find solutions to the cash problem and decide on a course of action.

The Dilemma

To open the meeting, the CEO announces, "We have just two weeks either to reduce expenses or to increase revenues; we need a $400 million swing to get us where market analysts predicted we'd be on cash flows for the year. Any suggestions?"

Discussion reveals that the firm has outstanding payables, amounting to hundreds of millions of dollars, owed to hundreds of firms that supply manufacturing components and operating supplies. The payables are due before year-end. According to the financial officer, "Our cash outflows for the year will be lower if we delay paying suppliers, which will help the bottom line. And, it's like getting a free loan." The procurement director is concerned, however. "Our agreements with suppliers call for faithful payments at designated times, and many of the smaller firms depend on receiving that cash to meet their obligations. Also, we've worked hard for two years at improving relationships with all suppliers, and that effort could go down the drain if we don't meet our financial commitments as promised."

As the meeting drew to a close, the CEO announced, "Keep me posted on any unexpected developments, but if nothing helpful comes up in the next few days, let's go ahead and withhold supplier payments for three weeks."

Questions for Discussion

1. What are the ethical issues in this case?
2. What are the basic arguments for and against the CEO's position on withholding payments?
3. What do you think most managers would do in this situation? What would you do?

Credit policy also sets payment terms. For example, credit terms of "2/10, net 30" mean that the selling company offers a 2 percent discount if the customer pays within 10 days. The customer has 30 days to pay the regular price. Under these terms, the buyer would have to pay only $980 on a $1000 invoice on days 1 to 10, but all $1000 on days 11 to 30. The higher the discount, the more incentive buyers have to pay early. Sellers can thus adjust credit terms to influence when customers pay their bills.

Inventories

Between the time a firm buys raw materials and the time it sells finished products, it ties up funds in **inventory**—materials and goods that it will sell within the year. Failure to manage inventory can have grave financial consequences. Too little inventory of any kind can cost a firm sales. Too much inventory means tied-up funds that cannot be used elsewhere. In extreme cases, a company may have to sell excess inventory at low profits simply to raise cash.

There are three basic types of inventories: raw materials, work-in-process, and finished goods. The basic supplies a firm buys to use in its production process are its **raw materials inventory**. Levi Strauss's raw materials inventory includes huge rolls of denim. **Work-in-process inventory** consists of goods partway through the production process. Cut-out but not-yet-sewn jeans are part of the work-in-process inventory at Levi's. Finally,

inventory
Materials and goods currently held by the company that will be sold within the year.

raw materials inventory
That portion of a firm's inventory consisting of basic supplies used to manufacture products for sale.

work-in-process inventory
That portion of a firm's inventory consisting of goods partway through the production process.

finished goods inventory
That portion of a firm's inventory consisting of completed goods ready for sale.

the **finished goods inventory** is those items ready for sale. Completed blue jeans ready for shipment to dealers are finished goods inventory.

Working Capital

As we saw in Chapter 14, working capital is the difference between a firm's current assets and current liabilities. It is a liquid asset out of which current debts can be paid. A company calculates its working capital by adding up the following:

- inventories—that is, raw materials, work-in-process, and finished goods on hand
- accounts receivable (minus accounts payable)

How much money is tied up in working capital? Large companies typically devote 20 cents of every sales dollar to working capital. What are the benefits of reducing these sums? There are two very important pluses:

1. Every dollar that is not tied up in working capital becomes a dollar of more useful cash flow.
2. Reduction of working capital raises earnings permanently.

The second advantage results from the fact that money costs money (in interest payments and the like). Reducing working capital, therefore, means saving money.

Long-Term (Capital) Expenditures

Companies need funds to cover long-term expenditures for fixed assets. As noted in Chapter 14, *fixed assets* are items that have a lasting use or value, such as land, buildings, and machinery. The Hudson Bay Oil and Gas plant in Flin Flon, Manitoba, is a fixed asset.

Long-term expenditures are usually more carefully planned than short-term outlays because they pose special problems. They differ from short-term outlays in the following ways, all of which influence the ways that long-term outlays are funded:

- unlike inventories and other short-term assets, they are not normally sold or converted into cash
- their acquisition requires a very large investment
- they represent a binding commitment of company funds that continues long into the future

SOURCES OF SHORT-TERM FUNDS

3. Identify four sources of short-term financing for businesses.

Firms can call on many sources for the funds they need to finance day-to-day operations and to implement short-term plans. These sources include *trade credit, secured and unsecured loans,* and *factoring accounts receivable.*

Trade Credit

trade credit
The granting of credit by a selling firm to a buying firm.

Accounts payable are not merely an expenditure. They are also a source of funds to the company, which has the use of both the product purchased and the price of the product until the time it pays its bill. **Trade credit**, the granting of credit by one firm to another, is effectively a short-term loan.

Trade credit can take several forms.

- The most common form, **open-book credit**, is essentially a "gentlemen's agreement." Buyers receive merchandise along with invoices stating credit terms. Sellers ship products on faith that payment will be forthcoming.
- When sellers want more reassurance, they may insist that buyers sign legally binding **promissory notes** before merchandise is shipped. The agreement states when and how much money will be paid to the seller.
- The **trade draft** is attached to the merchandise shipment by the seller and states the promised date and amount of payment due. To take possession of the merchandise, the buyer must sign the draft. Once signed by the buyer, the document becomes a **trade acceptance**. Trade drafts and trade acceptances are useful forms of credit in international transactions.

open-book credit
Form of trade credit in which sellers ship merchandise on faith that payment will be forthcoming.

promissory note
Form of trade credit in which buyers sign promise-to-pay agreements before merchandise is shipped.

trade draft
Form of trade credit in which buyers must sign statements of payment terms attached to merchandise by sellers.

trade acceptance
Trade draft that has been signed by the buyer.

Secured Short-Term Loans

For most firms, bank loans are a vital source of short-term funding. Such loans almost always involve a promissory note in which the borrower promises to repay the loan plus interest. In **secured loans**, banks also require the borrower to put up **collateral**—to give the bank the right to seize certain assets if payments are not made as promised. Inventories, accounts receivable, and other assets may serve as collateral for a secured loan.

secured loan
A short-term loan in which the borrower is required to put up collateral.

collateral
Any asset that a lender has the right to seize if a borrower does not repay a loan.

Secured loans allow borrowers to get funds when they might not qualify for unsecured credit. Moreover, they generally carry lower interest rates than unsecured loans. Collateral may be in the form of inventories or accounts receivable, and most businesses have other types of assets that can be pledged. Some, for instance, own marketable securities, such as stocks or bonds of other companies (see Chapter 19). Many more own fixed assets, such as land, buildings, or equipment. Fixed assets, however, are generally used to secure long-term rather than short-term loans. Most short-term business borrowing is secured by inventories and accounts receivable.

Inventory Loans

When a loan is made with inventory as a collateral asset, the lender loans the borrower some portion of the stated value of the inventory. Inventory is more attractive as collateral when it provides the lender with real security for the loan amount: For example, if the inventory can be readily converted into cash, it is relatively more valuable as collateral. Other inventory—say, boxes full of expensive, partially completed lenses for eyeglasses—is of little value on the open market. Meanwhile, a thousand crates of boxed, safely stored canned tomatoes might well be convertible into cash.

Accounts Receivable as Collateral

When accounts receivable are used as collateral, the process is called **pledging accounts receivable**. In the event of non-payment, the lender may seize the receivables—that is, funds owed the borrower by its customers. If these assets are not enough to cover the loan, the borrower must make up the difference. This option is especially important to service companies such as accounting firms and law offices. Because they do not maintain inventories, accounts receivable are their main source of collateral. Typically, lenders who will accept accounts receivable as collateral are financial institutions with credit departments capable of evaluating the quality of the receivables.

pledging accounts receivable
Using accounts receivable as collateral for a loan.

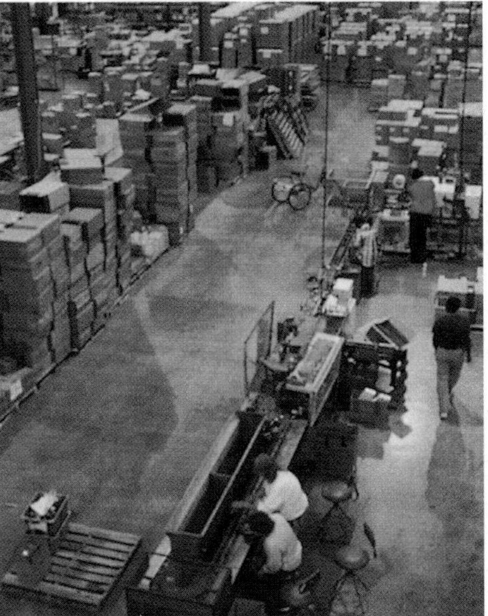
The inventory in this auto parts warehouse is good collateral because it is neatly stored, accessible, can be readily evaluated, and is quickly disposable.

Factoring Accounts Receivable

A firm can raise funds rapidly by *factoring*: selling the firm's accounts receivable. In this process, the purchaser of the receivables, usually a financial institution, is known as the factor. The factor pays some percentage of the full amount of receivables due to the selling firm. The seller gets this money immediately.[1] For example, a factor might buy \$40 000 worth of receivables for 60 percent of that sum (\$24 000). The factor profits to the extent that the money it eventually collects exceeds the amount it paid. This profit depends on the quality of the receivables, the cost of collecting them, and interest rates.

Unsecured Short-Term Loans

unsecured loan
A short-term loan in which the borrower is not required to put up collateral.

With an **unsecured loan**, the borrower does not have to put up collateral. In many cases, however, the bank requires the borrower to maintain a *compensating balance*: The borrower must keep a portion of the loan amount on deposit with the bank in a non-interest-bearing account.

The terms of the loan—amount, duration, interest rate, and payment schedule—are negotiated between the bank and the borrower. To receive an unsecured loan, then, a firm must ordinarily have a good banking relationship with the lender. Once an agreement is made, a promissory note will be executed and the funds transferred to the borrower. Although some unsecured loans are one-time-only arrangements, many take the form of *lines of credit, revolving credit agreements,* or *commercial paper*.

Lines of Credit

line of credit
A standing agreement between a bank and a firm in which the bank specifies the maximum amount it will make available to the borrower for a short-term unsecured loan; the borrower can then draw on those funds, when available.

A standing agreement with a bank to lend a firm a maximum amount of funds on request is called a line of credit. With a **line of credit**, the firm knows the maximum amount it will be allowed to borrow if the bank has sufficient funds. The bank does not guarantee that the funds will be available when requested, however.

For example, suppose that the Toronto-Dominion Bank gives Sunshine Tanning Inc. a \$100 000 line of credit for the coming year. By signing promissory notes, Sunshine's borrowings can total up to \$100 000 at any time. Sunshine benefits from the arrangement by knowing in advance that the bank regards the firm as creditworthy and will loan funds to it on short notice.

Revolving Credit Agreements

revolving credit agreement
A guaranteed line of credit for which the firm pays the bank interest on funds borrowed as well as a fee for extending the line of credit.

Revolving credit agreements are similar to bank credit cards for consumers. Under a revolving credit agreement, a lender agrees to make some amount of funds available on demand to a firm for continuing short-term loans. The lending institution guarantees that funds will be available when sought by the borrower. In return, the bank charges a *commitment fee*—a charge for holding open a line of credit for a customer even if the customer does not borrow any funds. The commitment fee is often expressed as a percentage of the loan amount, usually 0.5 to 1 percent of the committed amount.

For example, suppose that the Toronto-Dominion Bank agrees to lend Sunshine Tanning up to $100 000 under a revolving credit agreement. If Sunshine borrows $80 000, it still has access to $20 000. If it pays off $50 000 of the debt, reducing its debt to $30 000, then it has $70 000 available to it. Sunshine pays interest on the borrowed funds and also pays a fee on the unused funds in the line of credit.

Commercial Paper

Some firms can raise funds in the short run by issuing **commercial paper**. Since commercial paper is backed solely by the issuing firm's promise to pay, it is an option for only the largest and most creditworthy firms. Here's how it works. Corporations issue commercial paper with a face value. Companies that buy commercial paper pay less than that value. At the end of a specified period (usually 30 to 90 days but legally up to 270 days), the issuing company buys back the paper—*at the face value*. The difference between the price the buying company paid and the face value is the buyer's profit.

commercial paper
A method of short-run fundraising in which a firm sells unsecured notes for less than the face value and then repurchases them at the face value within 270 days; buyers' profits are the difference between the original price paid and the face value.

For example, if Noranda needs to borrow $10 million for 90 days it might issue commercial paper with a face value of $10.2 million. Insurance companies with $10 million excess cash will buy the paper. After 90 days, Noranda would pay $10.2 million to the insurance companies.

SOURCES OF LONG-TERM FUNDS

4. Distinguish among the various sources of *long-term financing* and explain the risks involved in each.

Firms need long-term funding to finance expenditures on fixed assets—the buildings and equipment necessary for conducting their business. They may seek long-term funds through *debt financing* (that is, from outside the firm) or through *equity financing* (by drawing on internal sources). We will discuss both options in this section, as well as a middle ground called *hybrid financing*. We will also analyze some of the options that enter into decisions about long-term financing, as well as the role of the *risk-return relationship* in attracting investors to a firm.

Debt Financing

Long-term borrowing from outside the company—**debt financing**—is a major component of most firms' long-term financial planning. The two primary sources of such funding are *long-term loans* and the sale of *corporate bonds*.

debt financing
Raising money to meet long-term expenditures by borrowing from outside the company; usually takes the form of long-term loans or the sale of corporate bonds.

Long-Term Loans

Most corporations get their long-term loans from a chartered bank, usually one with which the firm has developed a long-standing relationship. Credit companies (like Household Finance Corp.), insurance companies, and pension funds also grant long-term business loans. Long-term loans are attractive to borrowers for several reasons:

- Because the number of parties involved is limited, loans can often be arranged very quickly.
- The firm need not make public disclosure of its business plans or the purpose for which it is acquiring the loan. (In contrast, the issuance of corporate bonds requires such disclosure.)

- The duration of the loan can easily be matched to the borrower's needs.
- If the firm's needs change, loans usually contain clauses making it possible to change terms.

Long-term loans also have some disadvantages. Large borrowers may have trouble finding lenders to supply enough funds. Long-term borrowers may also have restrictions placed on them as conditions of the loan. They may have to pledge long-term assets as collateral. And they may have to agree not to take on any more debt until the borrowed funds are repaid.

Interest Rates. Interest rates are negotiated between borrower and lender. Although some bank loans have fixed rates, others have floating rates tied to the prime rate that the bank charges its most creditworthy customers (see Chapter 18). A loan at 1 percent above prime, then, is payable at one percentage point higher than the prime rate. This rate may fluctuate, or float, because the prime rate itself goes up and down as market conditions change.

Corporate Bonds

Like commercial paper, a corporate bond is a contract—a promise by the issuing company or organization to pay the holder a certain amount of money on a specified date. Unlike commercial paper, however, bond issuers do not pay off quickly. In many cases, bonds may not be redeemed for 30 years from the time of issue. In addition, unlike commercial paper, most bonds pay the bondholder a stipulated sum of interest semi-annually or annually. If it fails to make a bond payment, the company is in default.

Corporate bonds are the major source of long-term debt financing for most corporations. Bonds are attractive when companies need large amounts of funds for long periods of time. The issuing company gets access to large numbers of lenders through nationwide bond markets and stock exchanges. But bonds involve expensive administrative and selling costs. They also may require very high interest payments if the issuing company has a poor credit rating.

Bond Indenture. The terms of a bond, including the amount to be paid, the interest rate, and the maturity (payoff) date, differ from company to company and from issue to issue. They are spelled out in the bond contract,

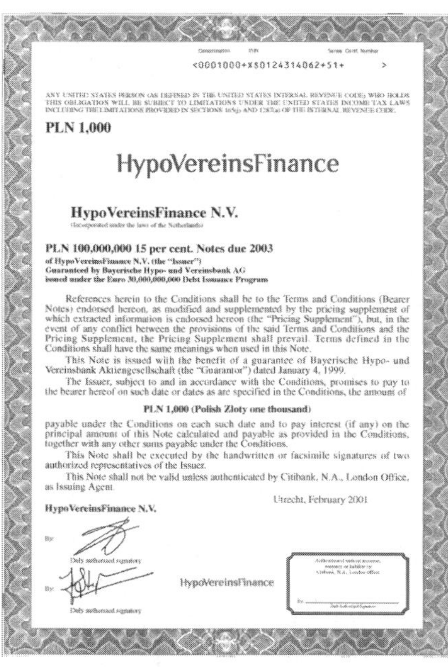

<0001000+XS0124314062+51+ >

ANY UNITED STATES PERSON (AS DEFINED IN THE UNITED STATES INTERNAL REVENUE CODE) WHO HOLDS THIS OBLIGATION WILL BE SUBJECT TO LIMITATIONS UNDER THE UNITED STATES INCOME TAX LAWS INCLUDING THE LIMITATIONS PROVIDED IN SECTIONS 165(j) AND 1287(a) OF THE INTERNAL REVENUE CODE.

PLN 1,000

HypoVereinsFinance

HypoVereinsFinance N.V.
(Incorporated under the laws of the Netherlands)

PLN 100,000,000 15 per cent. Notes due 2003
of HypoVereinsFinance N.V. (the "Issuer")
Guaranteed by Bayerische Hypo- und Vereinsbank AG
issued under the Euro 30,000,000,000 Debt Issuance Program

References herein to the Conditions shall be to the Terms and Conditions (Bearer Notes) endorsed hereon, as modified and supplemented by the pricing supplement of which extracted information is endorsed hereon (the "Pricing Supplement"), but, in the event of any conflict between the provisions of the said Terms and Conditions and the Pricing Supplement, the Pricing Supplement shall prevail. Terms defined in the Conditions shall have the same meanings when used in this Note.

This Note is issued with the benefit of a guarantee of Bayerische Hypo- und Vereinsbank Aktiengesellschaft (the "Guarantor") dated January 4, 1999.

The Issuer, subject to and in accordance with the Conditions, promises to pay to the bearer hereof on such date or dates as are specified in the Conditions, the amount of

PLN 1,000 (Polish Zloty one thousand)

payable under the Conditions on each such date and to pay interest (if any) on the principal amount of this Note calculated and payable as provided in the Conditions, together with any other sums payable under the Conditions.

This Note shall be executed by the handwritten or facsimile signatures of two authorized representatives of the Issuer.

This Note shall not be valid unless authenticated by Citibank, N.A., London Office, as Issuing Agent.

Utrecht, February 2001

HypoVereinsFinance N.V.

By: Duly authorized signatory

By: Duly authorized signatory

HypoVereinsFinance

A eurobond is a corporate bond that is usually issued by an international corporation. A corporation issuing eurobonds can determine the currency and the country in which to issue their bond. An example would be a eurodollar bond, denominated in U.S. dollars and issued in France by a Canadian company. The Canadian company is permitted to issue the eurodollar bond in any country other than Canada.

or **bond indenture**. The indenture also identifies which of the firm's assets, if any, are pledged as collateral for the bonds.

bond indenture
Statement of the terms of a corporate bond.

Equity Financing

Although debt financing has strong appeal in some cases, looking inside the company for long-term funding is preferable under other circumstances. In small companies, the founders may increase their personal investment in the firm. In most cases, however, **equity financing** takes the form of issuing common stock or of retaining the firm's earnings. As you will see, both options involve putting the owners' capital to work.

equity financing
Raising money to meet long-term expenditures by issuing common stock or by retaining earnings.

Common Stock

When shareholders purchase common stock, they seek profits in the form of both dividends and appreciation. Overall, shareholders hope for an increase in the market value of their stock because the firm has profited and grown. By selling shares of stock, the company gets the funds it needs for buying land, buildings, and equipment.

Suppose that Sunshine Tanning's founders invested $10 000 by buying the original 500 shares of common stock (at $20 per share) in 1997. If the company used these funds to buy equipment and succeeded financially, by 2003 it might need funds for expansion. A pattern of profitable operations and regularly paid dividends might allow Sunshine to raise $50 000 by selling 500 new shares of stock for $100 per share. This additional paid-in capital would increase the total shareholders' equity to $60 000, as shown in Table 20.1.

The use of equity financing via common stock can be expensive because paying dividends is more expensive than paying bond interest. Why? Interest paid to bondholders is a business expense and, hence, a tax deduction for the firm. Stock dividends are not tax-deductible.

Retained Earnings

Another approach to equity financing is to use retained earnings. As we saw in Chapter 14, these earnings represent profits not paid out in dividends. Using retained earnings means that the firm will not have to borrow money and pay interest on loans or bonds. A firm that has a history of eventually reaping much higher profits by successfully reinvesting retained earnings may be attractive to some investors. But the smaller dividends that can be paid to shareholders as a result of retained earnings may decrease demand for—and thus the price of—the company's stock.

Table 20.1 Stockholders' Equity for Sunshine Tanning

Common Stockholders' Equity, 1997	
Initial common stock (500 shares issued @ $20 per share, 1997)	$10,000
Total stockholders' equity	$10,000
Common Stockholders' Equity, 2003	
Initial common stock (500 shares issued @ $20 per share, 1997)	$10,000
Additional paid-in capital (500 shares issued @ $100 per share, 2003)	50,000
Total stockholders' equity	$60,000

For example, if Sunshine Tanning had net earnings of $50 000 in 2003, it could pay a $50-per-share dividend on its 1000 shares of common stock. But if it plans to remodel at a cost of $30 000 and retains $30 000 of earnings to finance the project, only $20 000 is left to distribute for stock dividends ($20 per share).

Financial Burden on the Firm

If equity funding can be so expensive, why don't firms rely instead on debt capital? Because long-term loans and bonds carry fixed interest rates and represent a fixed promise to pay, regardless of economic changes. If the firm defaults on its obligations, it may lose its assets and even go into bankruptcy.

During the 2001–2002 Argentine financial crisis, banks around the world suffered when borrowers (large companies and government borrowers) could not repay outstanding debt. Some borrower companies went bankrupt, defaulting on obligations to foreign investors. Faced with a struggling economy, Argentina's government could not meet payments on its $132 billion debt. Argentine President Fernando de la Rua proposed a rescue plan that would require holders of the debt to swap their bonds for ones paying lower interest, leaving lenders no choice but to take losses on their original agreements. FleetBoston Financial Corp., the Boston-based banking company, attributed much of its $386 million second-quarter losses for 2002 to investments in Argentina. Spanish banks like Santander Central Hispano and Banco Bilbao Vizcaya Argentaria have written off losses in Argentina. Credit Lyonnais and SocGen, two French banks, set aside more than 500 million francs to cover bad loans, while Lloyds of London lost more than 100 million pounds as a result of bad loans. Even as it defaults on current obligations, however, the Argentine government is seeking additional instalments of new credit from the International Monetary Fund (IMF) to help make payments on existing debt.[2]

Because of the risk of default, debt financing appeals most strongly to companies in industries that have predictable profits and cash flow patterns. For example, demand for electric power is quite steady from year to year and predictable from month to month. Thus, provincial hydroelectric utility companies enjoy steady streams of income and can carry substantial amounts of debt.

Hybrid Financing: Preferred Stock

Falling somewhere between debt and equity financing is the *preferred stock* (see Chapter 19). Preferred stock is a hybrid because it has some of the features of corporate bonds and some features of common stocks. As with bonds, payments on preferred stock are for fixed amounts, such as $6 per share per year. Unlike bonds, however, preferred stock never matures. It can be held indefinitely, like common stock. And dividends need not be paid if the company makes no profit. If dividends are paid, preferred shareholders receive them first in preference to dividends on common stock.

A major advantage of preferred stock to the issuing corporation is its flexibility. It secures funds for the firm without relinquishing control, since preferred shareholders have no voting rights. It does not require repayment of principal or the payment of dividends in lean times.

Choosing Between Debt and Equity Financing

Part of financial planning involves striking a balance between debt and equity financing to meet the firm's long-term need for funds. Because the mix of debt versus equity provides the firm's financial base, it is called the **capital structure** of the firm. Financial plans contain targets for the capital structure, such as 40 percent debt and 60 percent equity. But choosing a target is not easy. A wide range of debt-versus-equity mixes is possible.

capital structure
Relative mix of a firm's debt and equity financing.

The most conservative strategy would be to use all equity financing and no debt. Under this strategy, a company has no formal obligations for financial payouts. But equity is a very expensive source of capital. The most risk-filled strategy would be to use all debt financing. While less expensive than equity funding, indebtedness increases the risk that a firm will be unable to meet its obligations and will go bankrupt. Magna International, for example, has had a high debt-to-equity ratio in the past. Industry analysts believe that increased demand for automobiles will allow the firm to make large profits and pay off much of the debt, causing its debt-to-equity ratio to fall.[3] Somewhere between the two extremes, financial planners try to find a mix that will maximize shareholders' wealth. Figure 20.1 summarizes the factors management must take into account when deciding between debt and equity financing.

Indexes of Financial Risk

To help understand and measure the amount of financial risk they face, financial managers often rely on published indexes for various investments. *Financial World*, for example, publishes independent appraisals of mutual funds (see Chapter 19), using risk-reward ratings of A (very good) to E (poor) to indicate each fund's riskiness in comparison with its anticipated financial returns. An A-rated fund is judged to offer very good returns relative to the amount of risk involved. An E-rated fund carries the greatest risk with smaller returns. Similarly, Standard & Poor's publishes various indexes for numerous funds and for stocks that are available for purchase by financial managers.

By using such indexes, financial managers can determine how a particular investment compares with other opportunities in terms of its stability. A bond, for example, is considered to be investment grade if it qualifies for one of the top four ratings of either S&P or Moody's. Bonds below investment grade are called junk bonds because they have unusually high default rates. Nonetheless, junk bonds appeal to many investors because they promise uncommonly high yields.

If bond rating agencies like Moody's and Standard & Poor's downgrade a company's ratings to low enough levels, its bonds become junk bonds. That's what happened to The Gap in early 2002, after sales at virtually every store in the chain fell every single month for nearly two years. The reasons for the steep and rapid decline are complex, but now that it's been relegated to junk status, The Gap is finding it harder to raise money. Banks that were once willing to extend lines of credit now want collateral, such as inventory.

Debt financing	Equity financing
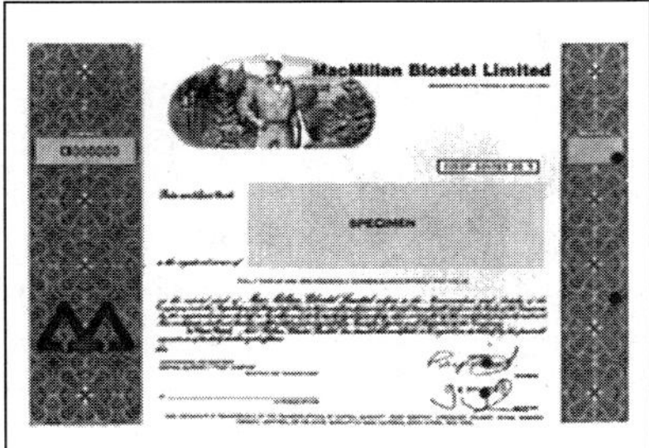	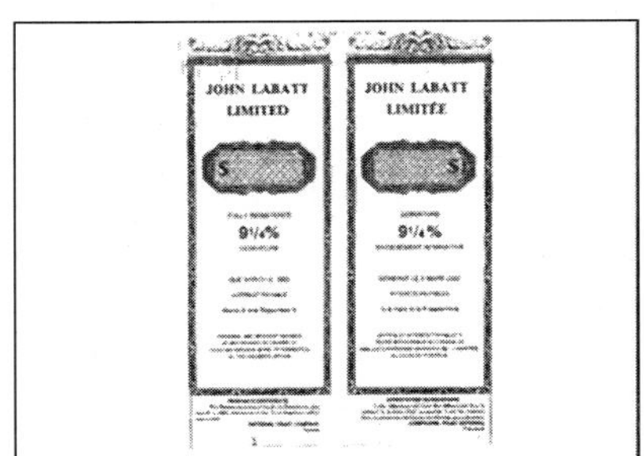
When must it be repaid?	
Fixed deadline	No limit
Will it make claims on income?	
Yes, regular and fixed	Only residual claim
Will it have claims on assets?	
In liquidation, creditors come first	In liquidation, shareholders must wait until creditors are paid and preferred equity precedes common equity
Will it affect management control?	
No	May cause challenge for corporation control
How are taxes affected?	
Bond interest is deductible	Dividends are not deductible
Will it affect management flexibility?	
Yes, many constraints	No, few constraints

Figure 20.1
Comparing debt and equity financing.

The Risk-Return Relationship

While developing plans for raising capital, financial managers must be aware of the different motivations of individual investors. Why, for example, do some individuals and firms invest in stocks while others invest only in bonds? Investor motivations, of course, determine who is willing to buy a given company's stocks or bonds. Everyone who invests money is expressing a personal preference for safety versus risk. Investors give money to firms and, in return, anticipate receiving future cash flows.

Some cash flows are more certain than others. Investors generally expect to receive higher payments for higher uncertainty. They generally do not expect large returns for secure investments such as government-insured bonds. Each type of investment, then, has a risk-return relationship. Figure

20.2 shows the general **risk–return relationship** for various financial instruments. High-grade corporate bonds, for example, rate low in terms of risk on future returns but also low on size of expected returns. The reverse is true of junk bonds, those with a higher risk of default.

risk–return relationship
Shows the amount of risk and the likely rate of return on various financial instruments.

Risk-return differences are recognized by financial planners, who try to gain access to the greatest funding at the lowest possible cost. By gauging investors' perceptions of their riskiness, a firm's managers can estimate how much it must pay to attract funds to their offerings. Over time, a company can reposition itself on the risk continuum by improving its record on dividends, interest payments, and debt repayment.

FINANCIAL MANAGEMENT FOR SMALL BUSINESSES

5. Discuss some key issues in financial management for small businesses.

Most new businesses have inadequate funding. An Ontario government study found that the average investment needed to start a new enterprise was about $58 000, but that more than half of all new companies had less than $15 000 invested.[4] Another study of nearly 3000 new companies revealed a survival rate of 84 percent for new businesses with initial investments of at least $50 000. Those with less funding had a much lower survival rate.[5]

Why are so many start-ups underfunded? For one thing, entrepreneurs often underestimate the value of establishing *bank credit* as a source of funds and use *trade credit* ineffectively. In addition, they often fail to consider *venture capital* as a source of funding, and they are notorious for not *planning cash-flow needs* properly.

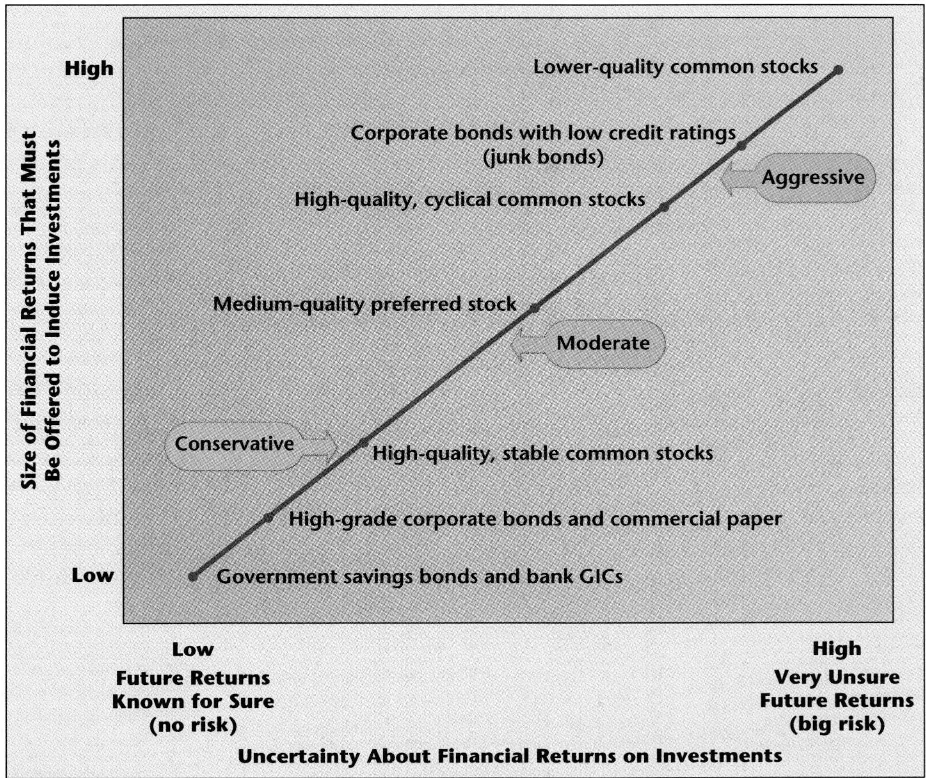

Figure 20.2
The risk–return relationship.

Establishing Bank Credit and Trade Credit

Some banks have liberal credit policies and offer financial analysis, cash flow planning, and suggestions based on experiences with other local firms. Some provide loans to small businesses in bad times and work to keep them going. Some, of course, do not. Obtaining credit, therefore, begins with finding a bank that can—and will—support a small firm's financial needs. Once a *line of credit* is obtained, the small business can seek more liberal credit policies from other businesses. Sometimes, for instance, suppliers give customers longer credit periods—say, 45 or 60 days rather than 30 days. Liberal trade credit terms with their suppliers let firms increase short-term funds and avoid additional borrowing from banks.

The Business Plan as a Tool for Credit

Start-up firms without proven financial success usually must present a business plan to demonstrate that the firm is a good credit risk.[6] The business plan is a document that tells potential lenders why the money is needed, the amount, how the money will be used to improve the company, and when it will be paid back (see Chapter 3).

Photographer David Cupp, for example, needed $50 000 in funding for his new firm, Photos Online Inc., which displays and sells photos over the internet. His business plan had to be rewritten many times until it became understandable, in financial terms, to potential lenders. The plan eventually reached 35 pages and contained information on the competition as well as cash flow projections. After four failed attempts, Cupp found a fifth bank that approved a $26 000 term loan and granted a $24 000 line of credit, to be used for computers, software, and living expenses to get the business started.[7]

Venture Capital

venture capital
Outside equity financing provided in return for part ownership of the borrowing firm.

Many newer businesses—especially those undergoing rapid growth—cannot get the funds they need through borrowing alone. They may, therefore, turn to **venture capital**: outside equity funding provided in return for part ownership of the borrowing firm. As we saw in Chapter 3, venture capital firms actively seek chances to invest in new firms with rapid growth potential. Because failure rates are high, they typically demand high returns, which are now often 20 to 30 percent.

Planning for Cash-Flow Requirements

Although all businesses should plan for their cash flows, it is especially important for small businesses to do so. Success or failure may hinge on anticipating times when cash will be short and when excess cash is expected.

Figure 20.3 shows possible cash inflows, cash outflows, and net cash position (inflows minus outflows), month by month, for Slippery Fish Bait Supply. In this highly seasonal business, bait stores buy heavily from Slippery during the spring and summer months. Revenues outpace expenses, leaving surplus funds that can be invested. During the fall and winter, expenses exceed revenues. Slippery must borrow funds to keep going until sales revenues pick up again in the spring. Comparing predicted cash inflows from sales with outflows for expenses shows the firm's monthly cash-flow position.

By anticipating shortfalls, a financial manager can seek funds in advance and minimize their cost. By anticipating excess cash, a manager can plan to put the funds to work in short-term, interest-earning investments.

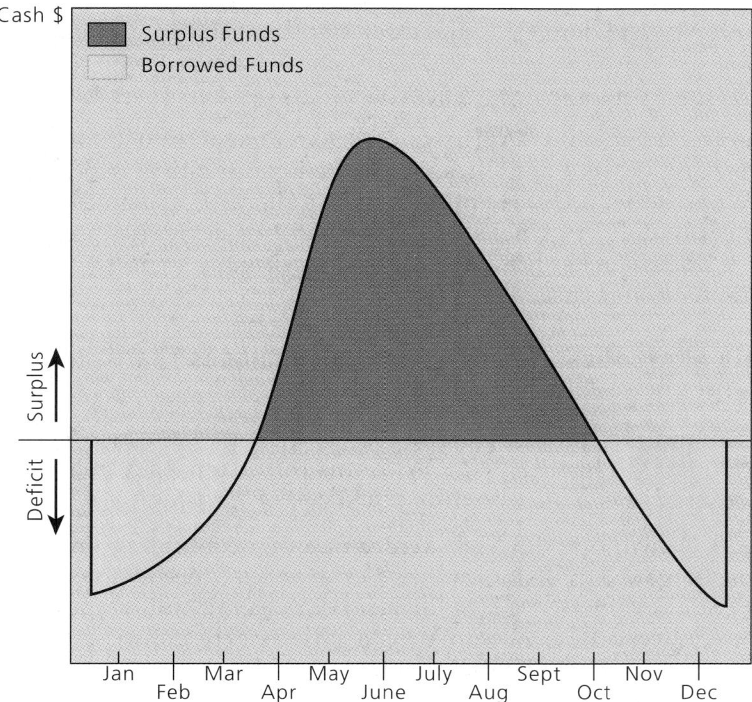

Figure 20.3
Cash flow for Slippery Fish Bait Supply Company.

RISK MANAGEMENT

6. Explain how *risk* affects business operations and identify the five steps in the *risk-management process.*

Risk is a factor in every manager's job, and because nearly every managerial action involves risk—that is, the possibility of either desirable outcomes or negative results—risk management is essential.[8] Not surprisingly, then, firms devote considerable resources not only to recognizing potential risks but also to positioning themselves to make the most advantageous decisions.

Coping with Risk

Businesses constantly face two basic types of **risk**—that is, uncertainty about future events. **Speculative risks**, such as financial investments, involve the possibility of gain or loss. **Pure risks** involve only the possibility of loss or no loss. Designing and distributing a new product, for example, is a speculative risk: the product may fail or it may succeed and earn high profits. The chance of a warehouse fire is a pure risk.

For a company to survive and prosper, it must manage both types of risk in a cost-effective manner. We can thus define the process of **risk management** as "conserving the firm's earning power and assets by reducing the threat of losses due to uncontrollable events."[9] The opening case for this chapter describes several situations where risk management activities were not properly carried out. In every company, each manager must be alert for risks to the firm and their impact on profits. The risk-management process usually involves the five steps outlined in Figure 20.4.

risk
Uncertainty about future events.

speculative risk
An event that offers the chance for either a gain or a loss.

pure risk
An event that offers no possibility of gain; it offers only the chance of a loss.

risk management
Conserving a firm's (or an individual's) financial power or assets by minimizing the financial effect of accidental losses.

Step 1: Identify Risks and Potential Losses

Managers analyze a firm's risks to identify potential losses. For example, a firm with a fleet of delivery trucks can expect that one of them will eventually be involved in an accident. The accident may cause bodily injury to the driver or others, may cause physical damage to the truck or other vehicles, or both.

Step 2: Measure the Frequency and Severity of Losses and Their Impact

To measure the frequency and severity of losses, managers must consider both past history and current activities. How often can the firm expect the loss to occur? What is the likely size of the loss in dollars? For example, our firm with the fleet of delivery trucks may have had two accidents per year in the past. If it adds trucks, however, it may reasonably expect the frequency of accidents to increase.

Step 3: Evaluate Alternatives and Choose the Techniques That Will Best Handle the Losses

Having identified and measured potential losses, managers are in a better position to decide how to handle them. With this third step, they generally have four choices: *risk avoidance, control, retention,* or *transfer*.

risk avoidance
Stopping participation in or refusing to participate in ventures that carry any risk.

Risk Avoidance. A firm opts for **risk avoidance** by declining to enter or by ceasing to participate in a risky activity. For example, the firm with the delivery trucks could avoid any risk of physical damage or bodily injury by closing down its delivery service. Similarly, a pharmaceutical maker may withdraw a new drug for fear of liability suits.

risk control
Techniques to prevent, minimize, or reduce losses or the consequences of losses.

Risk Control. When avoidance is not practical or desirable, firms can practise **risk control**—say, the use of loss-prevention techniques to minimize the frequency of losses. A delivery service, for instance, can prevent losses by training its drivers in defensive-driving techniques, mapping out safe routes, and conscientiously maintaining its trucks.

Risk Retention. When losses cannot be avoided or controlled, firms must cope with the consequences. When such losses are manageable and pre-

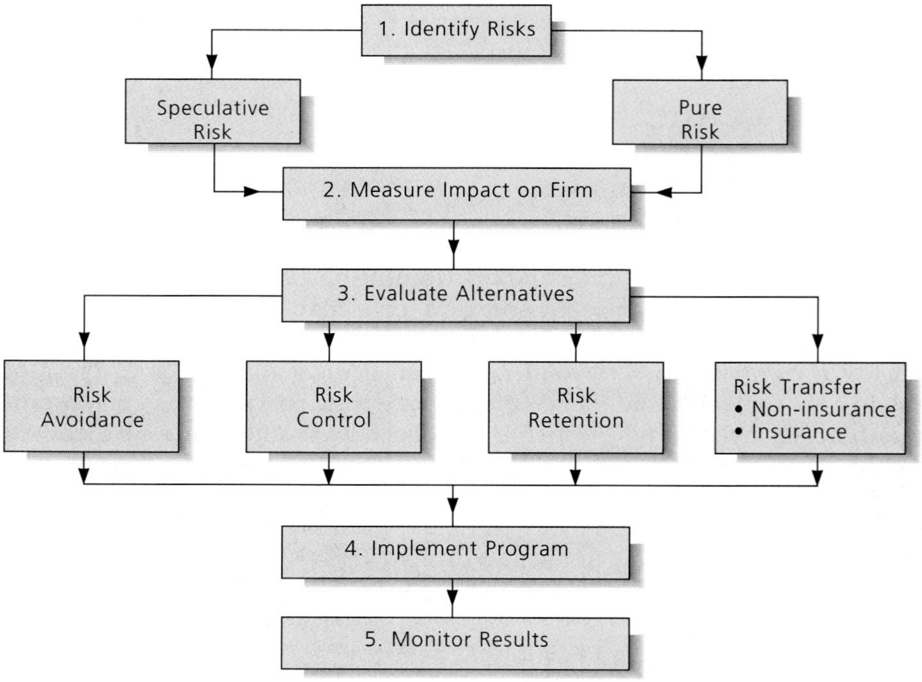

Figure 20.4
The risk-management process.

dictable, they may decide to cover them out of company funds. The firm is thus said to "assume" or "retain" the financial consequences of the loss: hence the practice known as **risk retention**. For example, the firm with the fleet of trucks may find that vehicles suffer vandalism totalling $100 to $500 per year. Depending on its coverage, the company may find it cheaper to pay for repairs out of pocket rather than to submit claims to its insurance company.

risk retention
The covering of a firm's unavoidable losses with its own funds.

Risk Transfer. When the potential for large risks cannot be avoided or controlled, managers often opt for **risk transfer**. They transfer the risk to another firm—namely, an insurance company. In transferring risk to an insurance company, a firm pays a sum called a *premium*. In return, the insurance company issues an *insurance policy*—a formal agreement to pay the policyholder a specified amount in the event of certain losses. In some cases, the insured party must also pay a *deductible*—an agreed-upon amount of the loss that the insured must absorb prior to reimbursement. Thus, our hypothetical company may buy insurance to protect itself against theft, physical damage to trucks, and bodily injury to drivers and others involved in an accident. Table 20.2 lists the top 10 life insurance companies in Canada.

risk transfer
The transfer of risk to another individual or firm, often by contract.

Step 4: Implement the Risk-Management Program

The means of implementing risk-management decisions depends on both the technique chosen and the activity being managed. For example, risk avoidance for certain activities can be implemented by purchasing those activities from outside providers, such as hiring delivery services instead of operating delivery vehicles. Risk control might be implemented by training employees and designing new work methods and equipment for on-the-job safety. For situations in which risk retention is preferred, reserve funds can be set aside out of revenues. When risk transfer is needed, implementation means selecting an insurance company and buying the right policies.

Step 5: Monitor Results

Because risk management is an ongoing activity, follow-up is always essential. New types of risks, for example, emerge with changes in customers, facilities, employees, and products. Insurance regulations change, and new types of insurance become available. Consequently, managers must continually monitor a company's risks, re-evaluate the methods used for handling them, and revise them as necessary.

top

Table 20.2 The Top 10 Life Insurance Companies in Canada

	Company	Annual Revenues (in billions of $)
1.	Sun Life Financial Services	23.1
2.	Great-West Lifeco Inc.	16.6
3.	Manulife Financial Corp.	16.5
4.	Canada Life Financial Corp.	8.5
5.	Industrial-Alliance Life Insurance Co.	2.8
6.	The Maritime Life Assurance Co.	2.4
7.	SSQ, Société d'assurance-vie Inc.	.7
8.	The Independent Order of Foresters	.7
9.	Transamerica Life Canada	.6
10.	UnumProvident Corp.	.5

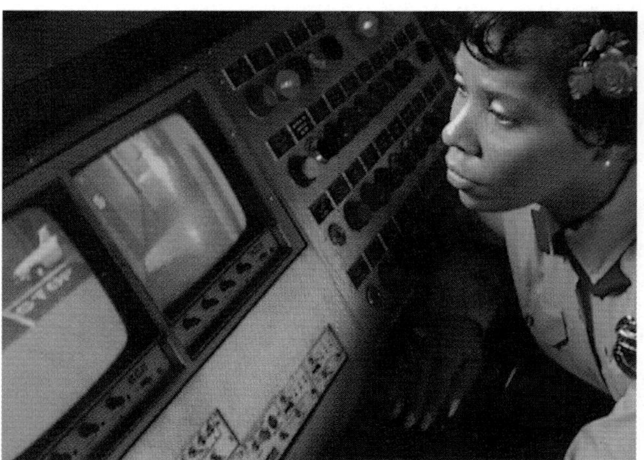

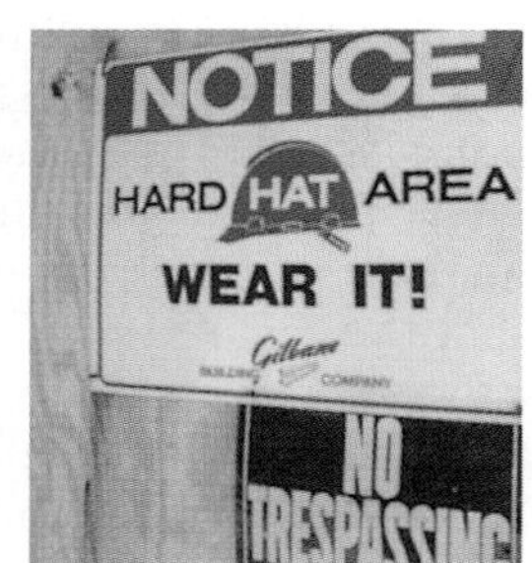

Losses are reduced or prevented when this security specialist uses electronic surveillance (left), when valuables are stored under lock and key (top right), and when workers are reminded to wear safety gear at this construction site (bottom right).

The Contemporary Risk-Management Program

Virtually all business decisions involve risks having financial consequences. As a result, the company's chief financial officer (CFO), along with managers in other areas, usually has a major voice in applying the risk management process. In some industries, most notably insurance, the companies' main line of business revolves around risk-taking and risk management for themselves and their clients.

Today, many firms are taking a systematic approach to risk management. The key to that approach is developing a program that is both comprehensive and companywide. In the past, risk management was often conducted by different departments or by narrowly focused financial officers. Now, however, more and more firms have not only created high-level risk-management positions, but they are also stressing the need for middle managers to practise risk management on a daily basis. Advises one global risk-management expert, "The breadth of products offered, the complexity of those products, and the global nature of markets, all make top-down, centralized risk management a necessity."

Insurance as Risk Management

To deal with some risks, both businesses and individuals may choose to purchase one or more of the products offered by insurance companies. Buyers find insurance appealing for a very basic reason: In return for a relatively small sum of money, they are protected against certain losses, some of them potentially devastating. In this sense, buying insurance is a function of risk management. To define it as a management activity dealing with insurance, we can thus amplify our definition of *risk management* to say that it is the logical development and implementation of a plan to deal with chance losses.

With insurance, then, individuals and businesses share risks by contributing to a fund out of which those who suffer losses are paid. But why are insurance companies willing to accept these risks for other companies? Insurance companies make profits by taking in more **premiums** than they pay out to cover policyholders' losses. Quite simply, although many policyholders are paying for protection against the same type of loss, by no means will all of them suffer such a loss.

premiums
Money paid to an insurance company by customers in return for being covered for certain types of losses should they occur.

Insurable Versus Uninsurable Risks

Like every business, insurance companies must avoid certain risks. Insurers thus divide potential sources of loss into *insurable* and *uninsurable risks*.[10] Obviously, they issue policies only for insurable risks. Although there are some exceptions, an insurable risk must satisfy the four criteria described below. As the Business Today box illustrates, some insurable risks are very interesting.

7. Explain the distinction between *insurable* and *uninsurable risks*, and distinguish among the different *types of insurance* purchased by businesses.

Predictability. The insurer must be able to use statistical tools to forecast the likelihood of a loss. For example, an auto insurer needs information about the number of car accidents in the past year to estimate the expected number of accidents for the following year. With this knowledge, the insurer can translate expected numbers and types of accidents into expected dol-

BUSINESS TODAY

Some Interesting Insurance Situations

Some people may think that the insurance business is not very interesting, what with all the mathematical calculations and actuarial tables that are required. But insurance is not only practical and important; it can also be very interesting. Consider the following situations:

Insurance for Boards of Directors

Canadian companies routinely buy liability insurance for members of the board of directors to shield them from lawsuits that allege negligence or failure to carry out their duty to shareholders. For many years, this was a "sleepy" line of business characterized by very modest year-to-year increases in premiums. But in the late 1990s, lawyers for disgruntled shareholders started suing boards of directors for failing to protect shareholders. Some big wins for shareholders meant that insurance companies had to pay out large sums of money. After this became a trend, insurance companies started sharply raising their rates. Canadian companies have not escaped these rate increases. Here are some examples:

- Sierra Wireless Inc. of Richmond, B.C., saw its directors and officers insurance premium triple from 2001 to 2002
- Royal Bank of Canada saw its premiums increase fivefold to $4.2 million
- ATI Technologies Inc. (which was investigated by securities regulators) saw its premiums increase tenfold

Insurance experts predict that premiums will continue their sharp rise as insurance companies are forced to pay out large sums as a result of shareholder lawsuits against various business firms. Insurance companies are also examining companies more carefully before they sell them insurance, and they are selling insurance for a shorter term. The biggest increases in premiums have come in the financial services and technology sectors.

Insurance for Broadway Musicals

Producers of the Broadway show *Titanic* paid about U.S.$400 000 for insurance to cover things such as a member of the audience being hit by a flying deck chair, or a cast member being injured during the performance. Interestingly, Chubb Corp., the company that covered the real *Titanic* (the one that sank on April 15, 1912, claiming 1523 lives), also covered the Broadway show. That real *Titanic* disaster cost the insurance company U.S.$100 000, but the Broadway show was insured for U.S.$14 million.

Chubb's man on the scene was Jim Titterton, who has a degree in fire science and experience as a fire inspector. His first experience with theatre insurance came when he was asked to do a loss-control inspection for the Stephen Sondheim musical *Into the Woods*. When Titterton does an inspection, he looks for anything that might cause injury to the actors or the audience. In the *Titanic* production, for example, powerful motors beneath the stage raise sections of the ship high above the stage, and in the most dramatic moment of the production, these motors tilt the ship just like the real *Titanic* tilted moments before it sank. It is at this point that the actors are in the greatest danger of injury. Titterton's work is not just an idle exercise. A few years ago, a worker on the set of *Phantom of the Opera* was injured when he was knocked into the orchestra pit by a swinging light fixture. That settlement cost Chubb Corp. well into six figures to settle.

Another show business example comes from the musical *Victor/Victoria*. Here, an insurance policy was purchased on Julie Andrews. The policy premium—U.S.$157 985—insured the producers of the show for up to U.S.$2 million if Andrews missed some performances, and up to U.S.$8.5 million if she had to leave the show. Producers routinely buy this kind of insurance because if a star is unable to perform on a given night, many patrons who have bought tickets want their money back. As it happened, Andrews missed many performances because of various illnesses, and an unusually large number of patrons requested refunds. Total losses to the producers exceeded U.S.$1 million. But when the producers tried to collect their money, the insurance companies refused to pay, arguing that Andrews had given false answers to questions about her medical history.

Insurance for Rap Concerts

Well-known rap artists such as Snoop Doggy Dogg can earn more than U.S.$50 000 per night on a multi-city concert tour. But national tours by rap artists have been virtually nonexistent for over a decade because stabbings and gunfire were becoming all too common at these shows. Remember when rappers like Biggie Smalls and Tupac Shakur were killed in a gangland-style hits? Even when occasional live shows were staged, violence often erupted. Most rap artists have therefore had to rely on videos and radio-station promotions to sell their records and keep their names prominently before their fans.

Reliance National Insurance is one of the largest underwriters of music events. It also insures many concerts by crooners and rappers. When musicians perform live, insurance costs are usually shared by the performer, the concert promoter, and the arena where the event is being held. Music companies also take out "key man" insurance on musicians. Insuring an all-rapper concert, particularly a "gangsta rap" concert, is seen by industry experts as being very difficult, given the violence that has occurred in the past. Some rap bands like the Fugees are seen as more insurable because they perform "feel-good rap."

lar losses. The same forecast, of course, also helps insurers determine premiums charged to policyholders.

Casualty. A loss must result from an accident, not from an intentional act by the policyholder. Obviously, insurers do not have to cover damages if a policyholder deliberately sets fire to corporate headquarters. To avoid paying in cases of fraud, insurers may refuse to cover losses when they cannot determine whether policyholders' actions contributed to them.

Unconnectedness. Potential losses must be random and must occur independently of other losses. No insurer can afford to write insurance when a large percentage of those who are exposed to a particular kind of loss are likely to suffer such a loss. One insurance company, for instance, would not want all the hail coverage in Saskatchewan or all the earthquake coverage in Vancouver. By carefully choosing the risks it will insure, an insurance company can reduce its chances of a large loss or even insolvency.

Verifiability. Finally, insured losses must be verifiable as to cause, time, place, and amount. Did an employee develop emphysema because of a chemical to which she was exposed or because she smoked 40 cigarettes per day for 30 years? Did the policyholder pay the renewal premium before the fire destroyed his factory? Were the goods stolen from company offices or from the president's home? What was the insurable value of the destroyed inventory? When all these points have been verified, payment by the insurer goes more smoothly.

The Insurance Product

The types of insurance coverage they offer often distinguish insurance companies. Whereas some insurers offer only one area of coverage—life insurance, for example—others offer a broad range. In this section, we briefly describe three major categories of business insurance: *liability, property,* and *life*. (A more detailed description of insurance products is presented in Appendix B.)

Liability Insurance. As we will see in Appendix B, *liability* means responsibility for damages in case of accidental or deliberate harm to individuals or property. **Liability insurance** covers losses resulting from damage to people or property when the insured party is judged liable.

liability insurance
Covers losses resulting from damage to people or property when the insured party is judged liable.

A business is liable for any injury to an employee when the injury arises from activities related to occupation. When workers are permanently or temporarily disabled by job-related accidents or disease, employers are required by law to provide **workers' compensation coverage** for medical expenses, loss of wages, and rehabilitation services.

workers' compensation coverage
Compensation for medical expenses, loss of wages, and rehabilitation services for injuries arising from activities related to occupation.

There is growing concern about fraudulent claims submitted by people who buy liability insurance. One popular scam is the "staged accident." The swindler purposely (but carefully) runs into a telephone pole, and then everyone in the car claims that they are suffering from whiplash. After the accident is reported, the insurance company contacts the car occupants and sends them accident benefit packages. Sometimes people who aren't even insured are paid benefits because they use counterfeit "proof of insurance" cards.[11]

The insurance industry estimates that between $10 and $15 of every $100 dollars you pay in premiums goes to cover fraud losses. The Canadian Coalition Against Insurance Fraud (CCAIF) estimates that insurance fraud costs insurers in Canada more than $1 billion each year. Across Canada, the CCAIF is working with Crime Stoppers; it offers a reward to tipsters who provide information leading to the discovery of fraud.

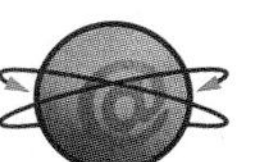

Canadian Coalition Against Insurance Fraud
www.ibc.ca/ccaif_about.asp

Property Insurance. Firms purchase **property insurance** to cover injuries to themselves resulting from physical damage to or loss of real estate or personal property. Property losses may result from fire, lightning, wind, hail, explosion, theft, vandalism, or other destructive forces. In some cases, loss to property is minimal in comparison with loss of income. A manufacturer, for example, may have to close down for an extended time while repairs to fire damage are being completed. During that time, of course, the company is not generating income. Even so, however, certain expenses—such as taxes, insurance premiums, and salaries for key person-

property insurance
Covers injuries to firms resulting from physical damage to or loss of real estate or personal property.

Catastrophic losses like those caused by fire are avoided when a business buys property insurance. The insurance company will pay the cost of the rebuilding. But interruption of the firm's normal operations will also be harmful, so many businesses buy business interruption insurance as well.

nel—may continue. To cover such losses, a firm may buy business interruption insurance (see Appendix B).

life insurance
Insurance that pays benefits to survivors of a policyholder.

Life Insurance. Insurance can also protect a company's human assets. As part of their benefits packages, many businesses purchase **life insurance** for employees. Life insurance companies accept premiums in return for the promise to pay beneficiaries after the death of insured parties. As with other types of insurance, a portion of the premium is used to cover the insurer's own expenses.

group life insurance
Life insurance underwritten for a group as a whole rather than for each individual member.

Most companies buy **group life insurance**, which is underwritten for groups as a whole rather than for each individual member. The insurer's assessment of potential losses and its pricing of premiums are based on the characteristics of the entire group.

IT'S A WIRED WORLD

A Healthy Approach to Risk Response

An internet-based system for health assessment called Network Health Systems (NHS) **www.nhsinfo.com** uses demographics and lifestyle data to evaluate the chances that any particular individual will experience various kinds of diseases or ailments. That same system also serves as an online resource for managing employee health programs. Many companies use it to assess the risk they run from poor employee health, the costs that they can expect to incur from those risks, and actions that they can take to counter those risks. Employee health is a pure risk for employers. Poor health results in the disruption of business and potentially high costs. Although risk transfer—usually in the form of health insurance for medical services—offsets part of the risk, there still remain health-related consequences (such as absenteeism) that insurance alone does not cover. To overcome these additional consequences, firms can turn to some form of risk control, usually an effective health-promotion program. Although such programs cannot guarantee against additional losses, they permit firms to minimize their harm by allowing them to respond with planned actions.

Armed with health profiles for all client-company employees, the NHS has created a system that collates them into a summary profile—a kind of "company health profile." NHS provides two kinds of organizational reports that are useful in the management of health risks:

1. The Organizational Assessment uses personal data collected from employees' responses to an NHS questionnaire to provide a breakdown of the specific risks from unhealthy behaviours. It also itemizes predicted costs of care in terms of hospitalization, medical care, lost time, and replacement of employees. The client company is given detailed reports on 44 different risk factors (such as weight, age at first pregnancy) and their impact on a possible 52 different diseases or conditions (nerve disorders, suicide). Finally, it lists potential problem areas applicable to this specific group of employees. The demographic information then breaks down the group by work type, gender, and specific health risks. The reports also provide information on various resources that the client company can adopt—intervention programs, education materials, benefit plans, and incentive systems—to influence lifestyle changes that will improve employee health.
2. The Cost Analysis evaluates the costs that the organization will incur over an upcoming 12-month period as a result of risk factors present and specifies the portion of those costs likely to be entailed by employee lifestyle. Further, it identifies which costs are non-reversible versus those that can be reversed through various wellness actions. It also cites the costs of implementing those actions. Using this data, the organization targets those areas of risk that offer savings justifying the program expense. The report makes specific recommendations on those areas that are most likely to realize the greatest savings.

In essence, therefore, health-profile reports provide a cost/benefit analysis in the area of health promotion, which, until now, has been either neglected, or, at best, an area of subjective decision making. In addition to helping to structure a company's benefit and insurance offerings, these reports form the basis for the planning of case management, employee-assistance programs, health promotion, and wellness programs, as well as structuring the company's benefit and insurance offerings.

Special Forms of Business Insurance

Many forms of insurance are attractive to both businesses and individuals. For example, homeowners are as concerned about insuring property from fire and theft as are businesses. Businesses, however, have some special insurable concerns. In this section, we will discuss two forms of insurance that apply to the departure or death of key employees or owners.

Key Person Insurance. Many businesses choose to protect themselves against loss of the talents and skills of key employees. For example, if a salesperson who annually rings up $2.5 million dies or takes a new job, the firm will suffer loss. It will also incur recruitment costs to find a replacement and training expenses once a replacement is hired. **Key person insurance** is designed to offset both lost income and additional expenses.[12]

key person insurance
Insurance that protects a company against loss of the talents and skills of key employees.

Business Continuation Agreements. Who takes control of a business when a partner or an associate dies? Surviving partners are often faced with the possibility of having to accept an inexperienced heir as a management partner. This contingency can be handled in **business continuation agreements**, whereby owners make plans to buy the ownership interest of a deceased associate from his or her heirs. The value of the ownership interest is determined when the agreement is made. Special policies can also provide survivors with the funds needed to make the purchase.

business continuation agreement
An agreement in which owners of a business make plans to buy the ownership interest of a deceased associate from his or her heirs.

SUMMARY OF LEARNING OBJECTIVES

1. **Describe the responsibilities of a *financial manager*.** *Finance* (or corporate finance) entails four responsibilities: (1) determining long-term investments; (2) obtaining funds to pay for those investments; (3) conducting everyday financial activities; and (4) helping to manage risks. *Financial managers* plan and control the acquisition and dispersal of financial resources. But a financial manager's overall objective is to increase a firm's value and stockholders' wealth.

   The responsibilities of the financial manager fall into two general categories: (1) *cash-flow management*: Financial managers must ensure that the company has enough funds on hand to purchase the resources that it needs to produce products. Funds not needed immediately must be invested to earn money, and (2) *financial control:* the process of checking actual performance against plans to ensure that desired financial results occur.

2. **Distinguish between *short-term (operating)* and *long-term (capital)* expenditures.** *Short-term (operating) expenditures* are incurred in a firm's everyday business activities. Managers must pay special attention to three areas of financial activity: (1) *accounts payable,* (2) *accounts receivable:* Predicting payment schedules is a function of *credit policy*—the rules governing a firm's extension of credit to customers, and (3) *inventories*: Between the time a firm buys raw materials and the time it sells finished products, it ties up funds in inventory—materials and goods that it will sell within the year. Too little inventory can cost sales; too much inventory means tied-up funds. *Working capital* is the difference between a firm's current assets and current liabilities. It is a liquid asset from which current debts can be paid. We calculate working capital by adding up (i) inventories (raw materials, work-in-process, and finished goods on hand) and (ii) accounts receivable (minus accounts payable).

3. **Identify four sources of short-term financing for businesses.** (1) *Trade credit* is really a short-term loan from one firm to another. (2) *Secured short-term loans*: Bank loans usually involve promissory notes in which the borrower promises to repay the loan plus interest. In secured loans, banks also require collateral: a legal interest in assets that can be seized if payments are not made as promised. (3) *Factoring accounts receivable*: A firm can raise funds rapidly by factoring—selling the firm's accounts receivable. (4) *Unsecured short-term loans*: With an unsecured loan, the borrower does not have to put up collateral. The bank may, however, require the borrower to maintain a *compensating balance*—a portion of the loan amount kept on deposit with the bank.

4. **Distinguish among the various sources of *long-term financing* and explain the risks entailed by each type.** Firms may seek long-term funds to pay for fixed assets through two channels. (1) Long-term borrowing from sources outside the company is called *debt financing*. There are two primary sources of such funding: (i) Many corporations get *long-term loans* from chartered banks. (ii) A *corporate bond* is a promise by the issuer to pay the holder a certain amount of money on a specified date. Bonds are attractive when firms need large amounts for long periods of time.

   (2) Looking inside the company for long-term funding is sometimes preferable to debt financing. *Equity financing* usually means issuing common stock or retaining earnings. (i) *Common stock*: Equity financing by means of common stock can be expensive because paying dividends is more expensive than paying bond interest. (ii) *Retained earnings*: Retained earnings are profits retained for the firm's use rather than paid out in dividends.

   A middle ground between debt financing and equity financing is the use of *preferred stock*. As with bonds, payments on preferred stock are fixed amounts. But like common stock, preferred stock can be held indefinitely. A key aspect of financial planning is striking a balance between debt and equity financing. A firm relies on a mix of debt and equity to raise the cash needed for capital outlays; that mix is called its *capital structure*. A range of mixes is possible, and strategies range from conservative to risky. The most conservative strategy is all-equity financing and no debt; the riskiest strategy is all-debt financing.

5. **Discuss some key issues in financial management for small business.** Obtaining credit begins with finding a bank that will support a small firm's financial needs. Once a line of credit is obtained, the small business can seek more liberal credit policies from other businesses. Obtaining long-term loans is more difficult for new businesses than for established companies, and start-ups pay higher interest rates than older firms. To demonstrate that it's a good credit risk, a start-up must usually present a business plan—a document explaining why the money is needed, the amount, how it will be used to improve the company, and when it will be paid back.

   Many newer businesses can't get needed funds through borrowing alone. They may turn to *venture capital*: outside equity funding provided in return for part ownership. But with high failure rates, such investors demand high returns. Planning for cash flows is especially important for small businesses. Success or failure may hinge on anticipating those times when either cash will be short or excess cash can be expected.

6. **Explain how *risk* affects business operations and identify the five steps in the *risk management process*.** Businesses face two basic types of *risk*. (1) *Speculative risks*, such as financial investments, involve the possibility of gain or loss. (2) *Pure risks* (such as the chance of a warehouse fire) involve only the possibility of loss or no loss. *Risk management* entails conserving earning power and assets by reducing the threat of losses due to uncontrollable events. The process has five steps: (1) Step 1: Identify risks and potential losses: Analyze risks to identify potential losses. (2) Step 2: Measure the frequency and severity of losses and their impact: To measure the frequency and severity of losses, consider past history and current activities. (How often can the firm expect a loss to occur?) (3) Step 3: Evaluate alternatives, and choose the techniques that will best handle the losses: Decide how to handle risks from among four choices: (i) A firm opts for *risk avoidance* by declining to enter or by ceasing to participate in a risky activity. (ii) Firms can practise *risk control* when they use loss-prevention techniques to minimize the frequency of losses. (iii) When unavoidable losses are manageable and predictable, firms may cover them out of company funds. Thus, they assume or retain the financial consequences through *risk retention*. (iv) When the potential for large risks can't be avoided or controlled, firms may opt for *risk transfer*: They transfer the risk to another firm—namely, an *insurance company*. (4) Step 4: Implement the risk-management program: The means of implementing risk-management decisions depend on both the technique chosen and the activity being managed. (5) Step 5: Monitor results: Managers must monitor risks, re-evaluate methods for handling them, and revise them as necessary.

7. **Explain the distinction between *insurable* and *uninsurable risks* and distinguish among the different *types of insurance* purchased by businesses.** In return for a relatively small sum of money, insurance buyers are protected against certain losses. Thus, buying *insurance* is a function of risk management, which is the implementation of a plan to deal with chance losses. Insurance companies make profits by taking in more *premiums* than they pay out to cover policyholders' losses. Insurers divide potential losses into *insurable* and *uninsurable risks*, and an insurable risk must meet four criteria: (1) *Predictability*: The insurer must be able to use statistical tools to forecast the likelihood of a loss. (2) *Casualty*: A loss must result from an accident, not from an intentional act. (3) *Unconnectedness*: Potential losses must be random and occur independently of other losses. (4) *Verifiability*: Insured losses must be verifiable as to cause, time, place, and amount.

   There are three major categories of business insurance: (1) *Liability insurance*: Liability means responsibility for damages in case of accidental or deliberate harm, and liability insurance covers losses resulting from damage to people or property when the insured party is held liable. The law requires most employers to provide employees injured on the job with *workers' compensation coverage* for medical expenses, loss of wages, and rehabilitation services. (2) *Property insurance*: Firms purchase property insurance to cover injuries to themselves resulting from damage to or loss of real estate or personal property. A firm may buy *business interruption insurance* to cover expenses incurred when it is closed down and generating no income. (3) *Life insurance*: Life insurance policies promise to pay beneficiaries after the death of insured parties. Most companies buy *group life insurance*, which is underwritten for groups as a whole rather than for each individual member.

   Two forms of business insurance apply to the loss of key employees or owners: (1) Many businesses protect themselves against loss of the talents and skills of key employees by buying *key-person insurance*. (2) Certain contingencies are handled in *business continuation agreements*, in which owners make plans to transfer the ownership interest of a deceased associate.

KEY TERMS

bond indenture, 717
business continuation agreement, 731
capital structure, 719
cash flow management, 708
collateral, 713
commercial paper, 715
credit policy, 710
debt financing, 715
equity financing, 717
finance, 708
financial control, 709
financial managers, 708
financial plan, 709
finished goods inventory, 712
group life insurance, 730
inventory, 711
key person insurance, 731
liability insurance, 729
life insurance, 730
line of credit, 714
open-book credit, 713
pledging accounts receivable, 713
premiums, 726
promissory note, 713
property insurance, 729
pure risk, 723
raw materials inventory, 711
revolving credit agreement, 714
risk, 723
risk avoidance, 724
risk control, 724
risk management, 723
risk retention, 725
risk transfer, 725
risk–return relationship, 721
secured loan, 713
speculative risk, 723
trade acceptance, 713
trade credit, 712
trade draft, 713
unsecured loan, 714
venture capital, 722
workers' compensation coverage, 729
work-in-process inventory, 711

QUESTIONS AND EXERCISES

Questions for Review

1. What are four short-term sources of funds for financing day-to-day business operations? Identify the advantages and disadvantages of each.
2. In what ways do the two sources of debt financing differ from each other? How do they differ from the two sources of equity financing?
3. Describe the relationship between investment risk and return. In what ways might the risk–return relationship affect a company's financial planning?
4. Give two examples of risks that are uninsurable. Why are they uninsurable?
5. Describe the risk-management process. What are the major roles of a company's risk manager?

Questions for Analysis

6. How would you decide on the best mix of debt, equity, and preferred stock for a company?
7. Why is liability insurance important to business firms?
8. As a risk manager of a large firm, what risks do you think your firm faces? For a small firm? What accounts for the most important differences?

Application Exercises

9. Interview the owner of a small local business. Identify the types of short-term and long-term funding that this firm typically uses. Why has the company made the financial management decisions that it has?
10. Interview the owner of a small local business. Ask this person to describe the risk management process that he or she follows. What role, for example, is played by risk transfer? Why has the company made the risk-management decisions that it has?

BUILDING YOUR BUSINESS SKILLS

Understanding Risk Management Issues

Goal

To encourage students to gain a better understanding of the major financial and risk-management issues that face large companies.

Method

During the last few years, all the following companies reported financial problems relating to risk management:

Air Canada
Bombardier
EarthLink Inc.
Levi Strauss & Co.
Nortel Networks

Step 1
Working alone, research one of the companies listed above to learn more about the financial risks that were reported in the news.

Step 2
Write a short explanation of the risks and financial-management issues that were faced by the firm you researched.

Step 3
Join in teams with students who researched other companies and compare your findings.

Follow-Up Questions

1. Were there common themes in the "big stories" in financial management?
2. What have the various companies done to minimize future risks and losses?

CRAFTING YOUR BUSINESS PLAN

Picking Up Speed on the Fast Track

The Purpose of the Assignment

1. To familiarize students with financial and risk management issues that a sample firm may face in developing its business plan, in the framework of Business PlanPro (BPP) software package.
2. To demonstrate how three chapter topics—start-up financing, risk management, and pure risks—can be integrated as components in the BPP planning environment.

Assignment

After reading Chapter 20 in the textbook, open the BPP software and search for information about both financial risks for a start-up company and risk management as they apply to a sample firm: Southeast Racing Parts. To find Southeast Racing, do the following:

Open the Business PlanPro 2002. If it asks if you want to "create a new business plan" or "open an existing plan," select "create a new business plan" (even though you are not going to create a plan at this time). You will then be taken to the Business PlanPro EasyPlan Wizard. Click the option entitled **Research It**. You will then be presented with a new list of options, including Sample Plan Browser. After clicking on the **Sample Plan Browser**, go down the alphabetical list of sample plans, and double-click on **Automotive—Parts Mfr.**, which is the location for Southeast Racing Parts. The screen you are looking at is the introductory page for the Southeast Racing business plan. Next, scroll down from this page until you reach the Table of Contents for the company's business plan.

Now respond to the following items:

1. Based on its business plan, would you loan Southeast Racing the $60 625 start-up capital? What are your reasons? What payback terms would you require? Explain. [Sites to see in BPP (for this item): On the **Table of Contents** page, click on each of the following in turn: **1.1 Objectives, 2.1 Company Ownership, 2.2 Startup Summary, 6.1 Management Team,** and **7.0 Financial Plan**.]
2. Consider Southeast Racing's facility needs—specifically, 3000 square feet in the office build-

ing. If you were the building manager, would you see any risks in leasing to Southeast Racing? If so, identify them. [Sites to see in BPP: On the **Table of Contents** page, click on each of the following in turn: **2.4 Company Facility** and **7.4 Projected Profit and Loss**.]

3. Chapter 20 discusses pure risks and ways to cope with them. Identify some pure risks and potential losses that Southeast Racing faces in its day-to-day operations. What techniques do you recommend for handling Southeast's potential losses? [Sites to see in BPP: From the **Table of Contents** page, click on each of the following in turn: **3.0 Products and Services, 3.1 Product and Service Description, 3.6 Future Products and Services, 4.2.2 Market Trends,** and **5.1.3 Distribution Strategy**.]

VIDEO EXERCISE

Nailing Down Financial Management: Seche International

Learning Objectives

The purpose of this video is to help you to:

1. Understand the financial consequences of protecting intellectual property such as patented product formulations and trademarks.
2. Identify some of the ways a small company can manage its funding requirements.
3. Discuss the role of the chief financial officer in a growing business.

Synopsis

Seche International makes innovative nail-care products used in salons around the world. But just two years after introducing its first product, the company learned that some rivals were copying the formula and others selling counterfeit versions of the product. To fight back, Seche management embarked on a legal battle to remove fakes from the market and to protect the company's patents. Unfortunately, the aftermath of the lengthy and expensive legal struggle found the firm faced with the daunting task of rebuilding its financial position. Through responsible and conscientious financial management, Seche emerged more secure and ready for the challenge of implementing an aggressive growth strategy.

Discussion Questions

1. *For analysis:* Why would Seche have a negative cash flow at the beginning of its production cycle?
2. *For analysis:* Why would venture capital firms be reluctant to invest in Seche during its legal battles?
3. *For application:* Which sources of short-term funds should Seche's CFO pursue now that the company's financial position is stronger?
4. *For application:* Which short-term expenditures would most likely increase as Seche implements an aggressive growth strategy?
5. *For debate:* Seche's management made a deliberate decision to take legal action against competitors who infringed on its patents and trademarks. Considering the huge financial burden that these legal battles placed on the company, do you agree with management's decision? Support your chosen position.

Online Exploration

Visit the Seche International site at **www.seche.com**. Browse various links to read about the company, its products, its global distributors, and its trademarks. Also read the question-and-answer section. Why would Seche post trademark details on its site? Why would Seche alert customers to ways of detecting counterfeit products? As a consumer, what concerns might you have about using a nail-care product that appeared to be made by Seche but turned out to be counterfeit?

EXPLORING THE NET

Taking Finances Personally

Many of the issues in organizational finance are also issues in personal finance. In managing your own finances and pursuing your personal financial goals, you must consider cash management, financial planning and control, investment alternatives, and risk management. Questions, of course, will arise on your prospects for making or losing money with alternative investments. How about diversification? Can it provide some protection from financial risk? What kinds of diversification are available to individual investors from prominent financial services companies?

Let's explore some of these questions of personal financial management by visiting the website of one of the world's leading financial services firms, The Vanguard Group, at **www.vanguard.com**. The opening page offers two choices—Personal Investors and Institutional Investors. Select **Personal Investors**. Look around the Personal Investors home page to learn about the company and the kinds of services it offers for personal investing.

Five major sections across the top of the page include Home, My Portfolios, Research Funds & Stocks, Planning & Advice, and Buy & Sell.

Let's start by clicking on **Planning & Advice**. The screen then displays a page with several selections, including Get a Financial Start. After selecting **Get a Financial Start**, you will be shown a webpage with a section entitled Frequently Asked Questions (located near the bottom of the page). Select the question: **How do mutual fund investors make money?** Based on the information from that page, respond to the following questions:

1. What are the three ways in which an investor can make money from stock and bond mutual funds?
2. Is there any risk that an investor might lose money from stock and bond mutual funds?

Now return to the page entitled **Get a Financial Start**. In the section entitled Frequently Asked Questions (located near the bottom of the page), select this question: **Is it risky to have most or all of my investments with one mutual fund company?** Based on the information that you find on this page, respond to the following questions:

3. What role does diversification play in Vanguard's response to the issue of risk when investing with one company?
4. What is Vanguard's response to the question of risk associated with placing all investments with one company?
5. What is your evaluation of Vanguard's response?

Concluding Case 20-1

Getting a Kick Out of the Soccer Business

The challenge of World Cup soccer isn't just for sports fans. Just as challenging as playing the games themselves is planning, financing, and scheduling all the activities that go into mounting the world's premier sporting event. While fans are concerned about the strengths of the next opponent and the health of key players, organizers worry about insurance coverage and other precautions against financial loss from weather, terrorism, hooliganism, and other risks to the success of the tournament.

Financial and risk management, as well as a host of other business decisions in preparing for the tournament, are prominent concerns for the Federation Internationale de Football Associations (FIFA), soccer's world governing body. In addition to television rights, FIFA sells the rights to its brand name to consumer-products companies around the world that want to enhance their products—soft drinks, transportation, clothing, sporting goods, shoes, soap—with World Cup symbols and the FIFA logo. These rights alone are worth more than $300 million, money that FIFA uses to help cover its costs for the competition that it holds once every four years.

To improve cash flow and avoid excessive borrowing, FIFA changed its strategy for 2002. It sold the rights to its brand to International Sports and Leisure (ISL), a Swiss marketing firm. The deal called for ISL to make all the arrangements for worldwide marketing, collect the revenues, make payments to FIFA, and pocket a residual fee for its services. In addition to stabilizing FIFA's cash inflows, the deal with ISL was cheaper than borrowing from banks, FIFA's traditional means of financing the World Cup.

With fans from around the world supporting teams from 32 nations, the 2002 event held in Japan and South Korea ultimately generated about $475 million. Before the games began, however, organizers bought insurance to protect against interruptions to the income flow from the tournament. Individual businesses, too, upped insurance protection—especially against hooliganism—for the revenues they expected from fans and tourists.

Past World Cup hosts, including France in 1998, had suffered considerable damage from rampaging hooligans both before and after Cup games, and Japan's culture was especially unprepared for the rowdiness typical of some European fans. Japanese venues were not geared for increased security demands. According to Kazuyuki Hoshi of the World Cup Preparation Office in Sendai, "Although this is the world's biggest sporting event, we not only have to construct new stadiums but prepare access and security strategies that Europe and South America, for example, have been developing for decades. The Japanese do not think in terms of security measures, like fencing and separate access for supporters." But he also noted that for the World Cup, Japan knew what to expect. "When it comes to crisis management, to think that hooligans won't travel to Japan is being too optimistic."

In setting up security measures, the Japanese started from scratch. Restaurants and retail shops bought protection against the hooliganism that rowdy fans traditionally ignited before and after their teams took the field. Seoul-based Hyundai Fire & Marine Insurance sold more than 1000 policies to local business for protection of up to U.S.$40 000 from damages related to vandalism. While hoping they wouldn't have to collect on their various policies, businesses in the host countries placed their trust in the old adage: Better safe than sorry.

Hooliganism wasn't the only threat to the World Cup Championships. Weather, too, posed financial risks. FIFA and the host cities had to be prepared for Southeast Asia's rainy season, which coincided with the month-long tournament in June 2002. In addition to cities where the games were played, 22 other towns hosted training camps that would generate revenues for local businesses. All of this money could be lost if matches were rescheduled or cancelled due to bad weather. Thus businesses located near stadiums paid U.S.$8000 for coverage from Tokyo-based Mitsui Sumitomo Insurance Co., which would pay out U.S.$12 000 for each day that rain reached 0.4 inches (up to a limit of U.S.$120 000).

Aside from weather, the two host countries posed different kinds of risks. Earthquakes can hit in Japan, and political unrest poses a threat in South Korea. Earthquake insurance covered all 10 Japanese stadiums, with coverage applying to any quake measuring between 6.8 and 7.9 on the Richter scale. The cost for such insurance is high, but so are the potential losses from shutting down the World Cup games. As for the possibility of political unrest and terrorism, FIFA purchased event cancellation coverage, with payouts of up to U.S.$870 million for a shutdown due to terrorism, from a consortium of insurance firms led by Paris-based insurer AXA S.A. Citing "the current uncertain international climate," AXA terminated the coverage in October 2001, following the September 11 terrorist attacks in the United States, but FIFA was able to secure new coverage with U.S.-based National Indemnity Co.

Even with all of this insurance, FIFA took additional risk-management steps on several fronts. To reduce vandalism and hooliganism, French security strategies were studied; 5500 riot police officers in Japan were trained to handle violent fans; and plans were developed with other nations to keep known hooligans away from the games. Above all, however, stadium location was a major factor in risk reduction. Many of the stadiums were located in rural venues, and railways and roads were built to take fans directly to and from hotels and stadiums without stopovers and crowd interference. "One of the main reasons for outbreaks of violence," explained a FIFA spokesman, "is the geographic layout of the city. In Europe, for example, the town centre is within reachable distance of the stadium. It's easy for fans to get drunk, go to the stadium, and cause havoc."

Another way to protect against stadium shutdowns is to arrange for backup stadiums. Although the tournament could be played in seven stadiums, 20 were made available—10 in each host country. If an earthquake hit in one location, matches could be moved to replacement sites in the other so that the tournament would not have to be cancelled.

It turns out that terrorism and political unrest did not materialize during the 2002 championships. Hooliganism, too, was minimal. The rains came but caused little disruption and, overall, the games—won by Brazil—were successful from both a sporting and financial standpoint. But the game isn't over for Switzerland-based FIFA. It is now preparing for the 2006 competition, to be held in Germany, which will present its own set of risks.

Questions for Discussion

1. Give an example of the use of risk control and an example of risk transfer in the 2002 World Cup Championships.
2. What are some additional risks, other than those discussed in the case, that FIFA officials faced in choosing Japan and Korea as host countries for 2002?
3. From a financial-management standpoint, why was it a good idea for FIFA to hire a single firm to manage the marketing of worldwide branding rights?

4. Why might an insurance company prefer to participate in a consortium of insurers, rather than alone, in providing earthquake or terrorism coverage for the World Cup Championships?

5. In what ways might the risks for the 2002 venues in Japan and Korea differ from those for the 2006 World Cup in Germany? ◆

Concluding Case 20-2 CC

What Next for Brascan?

Toronto-based Brascan is one of Canada's few remaining conglomerates, i.e., a company that owns a diverse group of other companies. Brascan owns Noranda Inc. (mining), Nexfor Inc. (paperboard), Brookfield Properties Corp. (real estate), Great Lakes Power, Inc. (hydroelectric generation), Trilon Financial Corp. (financial services), and two Brazilian cattle ranches that it bought very cheaply when the Brazilian currency collapsed.

In the 1980s, the conglomerate model was very popular, but it is now out of favour because markets like so-called "pure-play" companies that focus on a single industry. Investors have been unhappy with Brascan's reluctance to give up the conglomerate strategy, and have essentially attached a "holding company discount" to its stock price. This has occurred in spite of the fact that Brascan has regularly been profitable.

Jack Cockwell, the CEO of Brascan until 2002, was a legendary bargain hunter whose strategy was to buy undervalued companies. In the early 1990s, he took $20 million of Seagram Co. Ltd. stock owned by Peter and Edward Bronfman and parlayed it into Canada's most powerful and controversial conglomerate—Edper Group. But when real estate prices dropped, Edper faced bankruptcy because it was unable to pay its debts. The company sold assets to stay alive and by the mid-1990s had sold nearly $5 billion in assets and had raised $6.6 billion in new financing. The company was renamed Brascan in 2000.

In the mid-1990s, Cockwell became convinced that the overpriced high-tech stock market would experience a big decline, so during 1997 and 1998 Brascan sold assets, reduced its debt, and stockpiled cash. The decline of dot-com stocks during 2000 was exactly what he had predicted, and Cockwell thought that once the market correction is over, investors would be much more interested in companies like Brascan. If he is wrong, he will be remembered as the last of a dying breed of conglomerate moguls who once ruled the Canadian business scene. However, if he is right, he will be remembered as the first of a new breed of successful managers in the post-dot-com era.

Brascan's strategy of continuing to emphasize "old economy" businesses has been criticized by industry observers as out-of-date and ineffective. Brascan's stock price performance has lagged behind that of the TSE 300 index since 1998, leading various business commentators to suggest that Brascan be split up into separate companies because in total they would be worth more than Brascan is worth now. But Cockwell remained committed to the conglomerate strategy and rejected many break-up proposals.

In 2002, Cockwell was succeeded by Bruce Flatt, who says that he will do whatever it takes to deliver value for shareholders. After being appointed CEO, Flatt said that his strategy calls for Brascan to focus on just three core businesses: real estate, hydroelectricity, and financial services. He said that he would not sell resource companies like Noranda or Nexfor during a time of cyclical downturn, but he did not rule out selling them at a later date.

Flatt says that assets must meet a threshold return or they won't be kept. He wants to achieve a 15 percent annual growth in sustainable cash flow and a 20 percent cash return on equity. These goals may be achievable in real estate, financial services, and power generation, but not in highly cyclical businesses like mining and paperboard. This may mean that Noranda and Nexfor may be sold. In fact, Brascan has already sharply reduced its emphasis on resource-based assets (which accounted for 60 percent of Brascan's assets in 1997, but less than 10 percent in 2002).

Questions for Discussion

1. Why might a profitable company like Brascan be out of favour with investment analysts? What can a company do to regain favour?
2. What are the advantages and disadvantages of debt and equity financing? How did these advantages and disadvantages manifest themselves in the Brascan/Edper case?
3. What are the two basic sources of long-term funds? Explain Brascan/Edper's strategy with regard to long-term funding.
4. Discuss the risk-return relationship as it applies to Brascan.
5. How is Bruce Flatt's view of the organization different from that of former CEO Jack Cockwell? ◆

Video Case 5-1 CBC

Is Anyone Interested in Oat Processing?

Dan Bouchard manages the seed cleaning co-operative in Falher, Alberta (population about 1000). Dan has developed an idea for an oat processing plant that will use some empty grain elevators that he's planning to buy and convert for oat processing. Dan is trying to raise $2 million to make his dream come true (he needs 400 people to invest $5000 each). He's planning to hold a meeting at the town hall, where he'll pitch his idea and ask his friends to invest their money to help him build the processing plant. Dan has put thousands of dollars of his own money and his reputation on the line to make the oat processing plant a reality.

Dan has brought in a consultant to help him with his business plan. He needs to make some tough decisions, such as deciding where costs are going to be cut. Dan is willing to build the oat processing plant in stages to make the deal work. He may have to consider second-hand equipment instead of new equipment. After three hours of work with the consultant, he's figured out how to cut $120 000, but that's still not enough. What Dan needs is a big crowd at the town hall meeting, and big investor commitment.

In the days before the big meeting, Dan promotes his idea at several different places. The Smoky River Agricultural Trade Show is underway, and it's a good place to start. Dan is not a high-pressure salesman, but he must convince half the people in town to invest in his idea. His trade-show strategy is to attract the attention of potential investors with a raffle (free T-shirts). But people are cautious; equipment costs are twice what was originally expected (when Dan thought he needed to convince only 200 people to invest).

He also goes to his old elementary school to pitch his idea to the teachers there. They don't look very excited, and they don't ask any questions (not a good sign). Dan knows his sales pitch needs some polishing. Next, he goes to his old high school and explains his idea; the teachers there ask him some tough questions, but Dan gives them some encouraging statistics. By the end of the meeting, the teachers are talking about buying shares.

On the day of the big investor meeting, Dan is making last-minute preparations. At the local truck stop, he encourages people to come to the meeting that evening. They don't seem overly receptive, but then a radio station calls him on his cellphone and offers to give him some air time to publicize the meeting.

By evening, the hall is pretty full (lots of people were listening to the radio). Just before the meeting begins, Dan gets some pre-pitch encouragement from his wife. But then there's a last-minutes glitch with the material that goes in the share-purchase package. That's quickly cleared up and Dan begins his presentation. He explains the basic business plan, talks about earnings predictions, and indicates that he'll be the general manager of the plant. He asks people to make their intentions known as soon as possible. He's happy the turnout is so good. After the presentation, 150 people take investor information packages.

Dan feels that he's made a good start, but in the days following the big meeting he is disappointed to learn that only about 30 shares are sold.

Questions for Discussion

1. What are the various sources of short-term funds for businesses? Which of these sources is most likely to be used by a person like Dan Bouchard?
2. What are the sources of long-term funds for businesses? Which of these sources is most likely to be used by a person like Dan Bouchard?
3. What are the main reasons why small businesses fail? How might these reasons be of concern to Dan Bouchard? (Review the material in Chapter 3 before answering this question.)
4. Why are so many start-up businesses underfunded? Are any of these typical reasons applicable to Dan Bouchard's situation?

Source: CBC *Venture*, "Falher, Alberta," May 4, 2003.

Video Case 5-2 CBC

The Million Dollar Man

Doug Hall is a consultant who gives entrepreneurs and small business owners advice on how their business can be run more effectively. He's in Prince Edward Island to visit a few high-tech businesses that need help. On this trip, Doug isn't charging anyone for his advice. He gives each company a half-day session where he listens to their problems and then makes suggestions on how to solve them.

Arc Biomedical is his first stop. This company configures microwave ovens for special purposes. Their product seems as though it should be a winner, but sales have been far below what was expected. The company is using an outside sales team in the U.S., but the salespeople have been ineffective. The manager of Arc Biomedical wants to borrow money to finance sales trips. But Doug says that a small company should try to finance initiatives internally, and that the CEO has to be personally involved in selling the product. He recommends that Arc do all its production in one season, and then the CEO should spend the rest of the time on selling trips.

Doug's next visit is to a business that teaches people how to read better. This company isn't making any money, either. Doug thinks the company has two big problems: they have a poor name (SpellRead P.A.T.), and the managers in the company have a difficult time clearly explaining how their product works. This company has just raised a lot of money, so financing isn't their problem. They need to increase sales. To do this, they need to spend time working on their marketing strategy. Doug says the company is "promising the world" (i.e., they claim they're going to teach people how to read), and that they're claiming they have a "miracle cure" that's different from what other companies are offering. Doug is critical of their marketing material because it doesn't clearly explain how their product differs from other similar products. Doug recommends that the company adopt a strategy promising that their product will "turbo-charge people's brains." Doug's proposed advertising copy is designed to be easily understandable by potential customers. At the end of the session he again recommends that they change the name of their company, but the managers resist. Doug says he can't understand why they're resisting, given that they don't have much of a business with their current name.

Doug's last stop is at a company called Hockey Line. The owner, Ray McPherson, has a high-tech product that he thought would make him a million dollars, but so far he's had trouble getting any buyers interested. The product is a computer unit that collects hockey game statistics as they happen and sends these statistics from the rink to the internet. Doug asks who would care about this feature, and Ray explains that parents, family members, and players all want to see results like these. Ray says that the real money in hockey is in the media that provide results, so Doug recommends that Ray create a phone-to-webcast system so that parents in the stands can give a play-by-play of a game. Doug says that Ray shouldn't just upload a few statistics to a webpage. Rather, he should start an internet radio broadcast and do it on a big scale. Doug points out that Ray's company needs sales revenue quick, and that Ray's optimism and energy will eventually run out unless he gets some revenue for his company. Doug says that Ray needs to operate his business on a bigger scale to make these new ideas work. The advertising theme, he says, should be this: How do we turn every child into a hero?

Questions for Discussion

1. Briefly review the material in Chapter 3. What is the difference between a small business person and an entrepreneur? Are the three companies described above examples of entrepreneurship or small business? Explain.
2. What are the advantages and disadvantages of debt versus equity financing? How are these advantages and disadvantages relevant for the three companies described in this case?
3. What are the sources of short-term funds for businesses? Which of those sources are most likely to be used by each of the businesses that Doug Hall visited?

Source: CBC *Venture*, "Doug Hall," January 12, 2003.

Appendix A

BUSINESS LAW

THE ROLE OF LAW IN CANADIAN SOCIETY

law
The set of rules and standards that a society agrees upon to govern the behaviour of its citizens.

Law is the set of rules and standards that a society agrees upon to govern the behaviour of its citizens. Both the British and the French influenced the development of law in Canada. In 1867, the British North America (BNA) Act created the nation of Canada. The BNA Act was "patriated" to Canada in 1982 and is known as the Constitution Act. This act divides legislative powers in Canada between the federal and provincial governments.

Sources of Law

The law in Canada has evolved and changed in response to our norms and values. Our laws have arisen from three sources: (1) customs and judicial precedents (the source of common law), (2) the actions of provincial and federal legislatures (the source of statutory law), and (3) rulings by administrative bodies (the source of administrative law).

common law
The unwritten law of England, derived from precedent and legal judgments.

Common law is the unwritten law of England, derived from ancient precedents and judges' previous legal opinions. Common law is based on the principle of equity, the provision to every person of a just and fair remedy. Canadian legal customs and traditions derive from British common law. All provinces except Quebec, which uses the French Civil Code, have laws based on British common law, and court decisions are often based on precedents from common law. That is, decisions made in earlier cases that involved the same legal point will guide the court.

statutory law
Written law developed by city councils, provincial legislatures, and parliament.

Statutory law is written law developed by city councils, provincial legislatures, and parliament. Most law in Canada today is statutory law.

administrative law
Rules and regulations that government agencies develop based on their interpretations of statutory law.

Administrative law is the rules and regulations that government agencies and commissions develop based on their interpretations of statutory laws. For example, Consumer and Corporate Affairs Canada develops regulations on false advertising using federal legislation.

The Court System

In Canada, the judiciary branch of government has the responsibility of settling disputes among organizations or individuals by applying existing laws. Both provincial and federal courts exist to hear both criminal and civil cases. The Supreme Court of Canada is the highest court in Canada. It decides whether to hear appeals from lower courts.

BUSINESS LAW

business law
Laws that specifically affect how businesses are managed.

Business firms, like all other organizations, are affected by the laws of the country. **Business law** refers to laws that specifically affect how business firms are managed. Some laws affect all businesses, regardless of size, industry, or location. For example, the Income Tax Act requires businesses to pay income tax. Other laws may have a greater impact on one industry than on others. For example, pollution regulations are of much greater concern to Inco than they are to Carlson Wagonlit Travel.

Business managers must have at least a basic understanding of eight important concepts in business law:

- contracts
- agency
- bailment
- property
- warranty
- torts
- negotiable instruments
- bankruptcy

Contracts

Agreements about transactions are common in a business's day-to-day activity. A **contract** is an agreement between two parties to act in a specified way or to perform certain acts. A contract might, for example, apply to a customer buying a product from a retail establishment or to two manufacturers agreeing to buy products or services from each other. A valid contract includes several elements:

contract
An agreement between two parties to act in a specified way or to perform certain acts.

- *an agreement*—All parties must consciously agree about the contract.
- *consideration*—The parties must exchange something of value (e.g., time, products, services, money, etc.).
- *competence*—All parties to the contract must be legally able to enter into an agreement. Individuals who are below a certain age or who are legally insane, for example, cannot enter into legal agreements.
- *legal purpose*—What the parties agree to do for or with each other must be legal. An agreement between two manufacturers to fix prices is not legal.

The courts will enforce a contract if it meets the criteria described above. Most parties honour their contracts, but occasionally one party does not do what it was supposed to do. **Breach of contract** occurs when one party to an agreement fails, without legal reason, to live up to the agreement's provisions. The party who has not breached the contract has three alternatives under the law in Canada: (1) discharge, (2) sue for damages, or (3) require specific performance.

breach of contract
When one party to an agreement fails, without legal reason, to live up to the agreement's provisions.

An example will demonstrate these three alternatives. Suppose that Barrington Farms Inc. agrees to deliver 100 dozen long-stemmed roses to the Blue Violet Flower Shop the week before Mother's Day. One week before the agreed-upon date, Barrington informs Blue Violet that it cannot make the delivery until after Mother's Day. Under the law, the owner of Blue Violet can choose among any of the following:

Discharge

Blue Violet can also ignore its obligations in the contract. That is, it can contract with another supplier.

Sue for Damages

Blue Violet can legally demand payment for losses caused by Barrington's failure to deliver the promised goods. Losses might include any increased price Blue Violet would have to pay for the roses or court costs incurred in the damage suit.

Require Specific Performance

If monetary damages are not sufficient to reimburse Blue Violet, the court can force Barrington's to live up to its original contract.

Agency

agency–principal relationship
When one party (the agent) is authorized to act on behalf of another party (the principal).

In many business situations, one person acts as an agent for another person. Well-known examples include actors and athletes represented by agents who negotiate contracts for them. An **agency–principal relationship** is established when one party (the agent) is authorized to act on behalf of another party (the principal).

The agent is under the control of the principal and must act on behalf of the principal and in the principal's best interests. The principal remains liable for the acts of the agent as long as the agent is acting within the scope of authority granted by the principal. A salesperson for IBM, for example, is an agent for IBM, the principal.

Bailment

bailor–bailee relationship
When a bailor, a property owner, gives possession of the property to a bailee, a custodian, but retains ownership of the property.

Many business transactions are not covered by the agency–principal relationship. For example, suppose that you take your car to a mechanic to have it repaired. Because the repair shop has temporary possession of something you own, it is responsible for your car. This is a **bailor–bailee relationship**. In a bailor–bailee relationship, the bailor (the car owner) gives possession of his or her property to the bailee (the repair shop) but retains ownership of the item. A business firm that stores inventory in a public warehouse is in a bailor–bailee relationship. The business firm is the bailor and the warehouse is the bailee. The warehouse is responsible for storing the goods safely and making them available to the manufacturer upon request.

The Law of Property

property
Anything of tangible or intangible value that the owner has the right to possess and own.

real property
Land and any permanent buildings attached to that land.

personal property
Tangible or intangible assets other than real property.

Property includes anything of tangible or intangible value that the owner has the right to possess and use. **Real property** is land and any permanent buildings attached to that land. **Personal property** is tangible or intangible assets other than real property. Personal property includes cars, clothing, furniture, money in bank accounts, stock certificates, and copyrights.

Transferring Property

deed
A document that shows ownership of real property.

lease
A document that grants the use of an asset for a specified period of time in return for payment.

title
A document that shows legal possession of personal property.

From time to time, businesses and individuals need to transfer property to another person or business. A **deed** is a document that shows ownership of real property. It allows the transfer of title of real property.

A **lease** grants the use of an asset for a specified period of time in return for payment. The business or individual granting the lease is the lessor and the tenant is the lessee. For example, a business (the lessee) may rent space in a mall for one year from a real estate development firm (the lessor).

A **title** shows legal possession of personal property. It allows the transfer of title of personal property. When you buy a snowmobile, for example, the former owner signs the title over to you.

Warranty

When you buy a product or service, you want some assurance that it will perform satisfactorily and meet your needs. A **warranty** is a promise that the product or service will perform as the seller has promised it will.

There are two kinds of warranties—express and implied. An **express warranty** is a specific claim that the manufacturer makes about a product. For example, a warranty that a screwdriver blade is made of case-hardened steel is an express warranty. An **implied warranty** suggests that a product will perform as the manufacturer claims it will. Suppose that you buy an outboard motor for your boat and the engine burns out in one week. Because the manufacturer implies by selling the motor that it will work for a reasonable period of time, you can return it and get your money back.

Because opinions vary on what is a "reasonable" time, most manufacturers now give limited time warranties on their products. For example, they will guarantee their products against defects in materials or manufacture for six months or one year.

warranty
A promise that the product or service will perform as the seller has promised it will.

express warranty
A specific claim that a manufacturer makes about a product.

implied warranty
An assumption that a product will perform as the manufacturer claims it will.

Torts

A **tort** is a wrongful civil act that one party inflicts on another and that results in injury to the person, to the person's property, or to the person's good name. An **intentional tort** is a wrongful act intentionally committed. If a security guard in a department store suspects someone of shoplifting and uses excessive force to prevent him or her from leaving the store, the guard might be guilty of an intentional tort. Other examples are libel, embezzlement, and patent infringement.

Negligence is a wrongful act that inadvertently causes injury to another person. For example, if a maintenance crew in a store mops the floors without placing warning signs in the area, a customer who slips and falls might bring a negligence suit against the store.

In recent years, the most publicized area of negligence has been product liability. **Product liability** means that businesses are liable for injuries caused to product users because of negligence in design or manufacturing. **Strict product liability** means that a business is liable for injuries caused by their products even if there is no evidence of negligence in the design or manufacture of the product.

tort
A wrongful civil act that one party inflicts on another.

intentional tort
A wrongful act intentionally committed.

negligence
A wrongful act that inadvertently causes injury to another person.

product liability
The liability of businesses for injuries caused to product users because of negligence in design or manufacture.

strict product liability
The liability of businesses for injuries caused by their products even if no evidence of negligence in the product's design or manufacture exists.

Negotiable Instruments

Negotiable instruments are types of commercial paper that can be transferred among individuals and business firms. Cheques, bank drafts, and certificates of deposit are examples of negotiable instruments.

The Bills of Exchange Act specifies that a negotiable instrument must

- be written
- be signed by the person who puts it into circulation (the maker or drawer)
- contain an unconditional promise to pay a certain amount of money
- be payable on demand
- be payable to a specific person (or to the bearer of the instrument)

Negotiable instruments are transferred from one party to another through an endorsement. An **endorsement** means signing your name to a negotiable instrument; this makes it transferable to another person or organization. If you sign only your name on the back of a cheque, you are

negotiable instrument
Types of commercial paper that can be transferred among individuals and business firms.

endorsement
Signing your name to a negotiable instrument, making it transferable to another person or organization.

making a *blank* endorsement. If you state that the instrument is being transferred to a specific person, you are making a *special* endorsement. A *qualified* endorsement limits your liability if the instrument is not backed up by sufficient funds. For example, if you get a cheque from a friend and want to use it to buy a new stereo, you can write "without recourse" above your name. If your friend's cheque bounces, you have no liability. A *restrictive* endorsement limits the negotiability of the instrument. For example, if you write "for deposit only" on the back of a cheque and it is later stolen, no one else can cash it.

Bankruptcy

bankruptcy

Permission granted by the courts to individuals and organizations not to pay some or all of their debts.

At one time, individuals who could not pay their debts were jailed. Today, however, both organizations and individuals can seek relief by filing for **bankruptcy**, which is the court-granted permission to not pay some or all of their debts.

Thousands of individuals and businesses file for bankruptcy each year. They do so for various reasons, including cash flow problems, reduced demand for their products, or some other problem that makes it difficult or impossible for them to resolve their financial problems. In recent years, large businesses like Eaton's, Olympia & York, and Enron have sought the protection of bankruptcy laws. Three main factors account for the increase in bankruptcy filings:

1. The increased availability of credit
2. The "fresh-start" provisions in current bankruptcy laws
3. The growing acceptance of bankruptcy as a financial tactic

insolvent person (or company)

One who cannot pay current obligations to creditors as they come due, or whose debts exceed their assets.

bankrupt person (or company)

One who has either made a voluntary application to start bankruptcy proceedings (voluntary bankruptcy) or has been forced by creditors into bankruptcy (involuntary bankruptcy) by a process referred to as a receiving order.

In Canada, jurisdiction over bankruptcy is provided by the Bankruptcy and Insolvency Act. An **insolvent person (or company)** is defined as one who cannot pay current obligations to creditors as they come due, or whose debts exceed their assets. A **bankrupt person (or company)** is one who has either made a voluntary application to start bankruptcy proceedings (voluntary bankruptcy) or has been forced by creditors into bankruptcy (involuntary bankruptcy) by a process referred to as a *receiving order*. A person who is insolvent may or may not be bankrupt, and a person who is bankrupt may or may not be insolvent, as there are other bases for bankruptcy under the Act. Another procedure under the Act is referred to as a *proposal*, which can delay or avoid liquidation by providing the debtor with time to reorganize affairs and/or propose a payment schedule to creditors.

On a practical basis, business bankruptcy under the Act may be resolved or avoided by one of three methods:

- Under a *liquidation plan*, the business ceases to exist. Its assets are sold and the proceeds are used to pay creditors.
- Under a *repayment plan*, the bankrupt company works out a new payment schedule to meet its obligations. The time frame is usually extended, and payments are collected and distributed by a court-appointed trustee.
- *Reorganization* is the most complex form of business bankruptcy. The company must explain the sources of its financial difficulties and propose a new plan for remaining in business. Reorganization may include a new slate of managers and a new financial strategy. A judge may also reduce the firm's debts to ensure its survival. Although creditors naturally dislike debt reduction, they may agree to the proposal, since getting, say, 50 percent of what you are owed is better than getting nothing at all.

Appendix B

INSURANCE

WHY INSURANCE COMPANIES EXIST—AND THRIVE

The reason why companies often find insurance appealing is clear—in return for a sum of money, they are protected against certain potentially devastating losses. But why are insurance companies willing to accept these risks for other companies?

Like all firms, insurance companies are in business to make a profit. They do so by taking in more premiums than they pay out to cover policyholder losses. They profit because they have many policyholders paying them for protection against the same type of loss, yet not all policyholders will experience a loss.

The Statistical Basis of Insurance

For example, consider a town with 5000 insured houses. Based on past history, insurers know that about 50 of these will be involved in a fire each year and that damages will average $40 000 per house involved. That is, insurance companies can expect to pay $2 million ($40 000 × 50) to cover their policyholders. By charging each household in the town $500 per year for fire insurance the company effectively spreads out the risk. It also earns a gross profit of $500 000 ($2.5 million in premiums versus $2 million in damages). This is the insurer's gain for providing risk-spreading services.

To earn a profit, insurance companies must know the likelihood of a particular loss. The more they know, the better their predictions and the fairer the rates they set will be. Insurance companies also benefit from a statistical principle called the **law of large numbers**. As the number of people who seek insurance rises, so does the chance that the actual loss rate will be the same as the statistically calculated rate.

law of large numbers
The statistical principle that the larger the number of cases involved, the more closely the actual rate will match the statistically calculated rate.

To help them properly price insurance policies, insurers use a system of classification that rates possible losses based on certain characteristics. The frequency of loss from an automobile accident varies with the number of kilometres driven per year, whether the driving is done in a rural or urban area, and with the driver's experience. An individual driving under 5000 kilometres per year on uncongested roads with many years of experience will probably have fewer accidents than someone in the opposite situation. Therefore, individuals with a lower probability of accidents as determined by these classification characteristics should pay a relatively lower premium. If insurance companies did not try to make rates equitable, so few customers might buy policies that the insurance company could not cover its costs.

The ultimate purpose of insurance is to *indemnify* policyholders. That is, policyholders should be brought back to their financial position before the loss. No policyholder should gain financially from insurance. To remain financially viable, an insurance company must be sure never to pay for losses not covered by the policy nor to pay too much for each loss.

Types of Insurance Companies

Insurance firms can be either private or public (government).

Private Insurance Companies

stock insurance company

Any insurance company whose stock is held by members of the public, who may or may not be policyholders of the company.

mutual insurance company

Any insurance company that is owned by its policyholders, who share in its profits.

Private insurers may be shareholder-owned or mutually owned. **Stock insurance companies**, as the former are known, are like any other corporation. They sell stock to the public, which hopes to earn a profit on its investment. Shareholders can be, but do not have to be, policyholders of the insurance company.

Mutual insurance companies are owned by their policyholders, for whom they seek to provide insurance at lower rates. As co-operative operations, they divide profits among policyholders, either by issuing dividends or by reducing premiums. In other words, the company's profits are generated for the direct benefit of policyholders rather than for outside shareholders. As non-profit operations, they divide any profit among policyholders at the end of the year.

underwriting

Determining which applications for insurance to accept and deciding what rates the insurer will charge.

Two of the most important activities of private insurers are the underwriting and marketing of insurance offerings. **Underwriting** involves two basic tasks:

1. determining which applications for insurance to accept and which ones to reject
2. deciding what rates the insurer will charge

These decisions are made by *underwriters*—experts who gather information and tabulate data, assess loss probabilities, and decide which applications will be accepted. The purpose of all these functions, of course, is to maximize the insurer's profits.

insurance agent

A person who markets insurance and is paid a commission by the insurance company.

insurance broker

A freelance agent who represents insurance buyers rather than insurance sellers.

Agents and brokers are the people who market insurance. An **insurance agent** represents and is paid a commission by an insurance company. The agent, then, represents the insurance seller. An **insurance broker**, on the other hand, is a freelance agent who represents insurance buyers rather than sellers. Brokers work for clients by seeking the best coverage for them. The insurers that they recommend to their clients then pay them commissions. Some brokers also offer risk-management advice for clients.

Public Insurers

Most insurance that businesses buy is written by private insurance companies. But some—and a great deal of individual insurance—is issued by government agencies.

Provincial governments administer workers' compensation insurance and the federal government administers the employment insurance program. Employers, employees, and the government share the cost of these programs. The federal government also operates the Social Insurance program. It has become an important part of our economic life and is a major means of protecting older, disabled, and poor citizens from economic hardship.

INSURANCE PRODUCTS TO MEET DIVERSE NEEDS

Insurance companies are often distinguished by the types of insurance coverage they offer. While some insurers offer only one area of coverage—life insurance, for example—others offer a broad range. In this section, we describe three major categories of business insurance: *liability, property*, and *life*. Each of these broad categories includes a wide variety of coverage plans and options.

Liability Insurance

Liability means responsibility for damages in case of accidental or deliberate harm to individuals or property. Who, for example, might be financially responsible—liable—for the medical expenses, lost wages, and pain and suffering incurred by an individual temporarily or permanently disabled because of another's actions? **Liability insurance** covers losses resulting from damage to people or property when the insured party is judged liable.

liability insurance
Insurance covering losses resulting from damage to persons or property of other people or firms.

General Liability

General liability policies protect business policyholders in cases involving four types of problems:

- **Personal liability** coverage would protect a firm if one of its truck drivers runs over a customer's foot.
- **Professional liability** coverage would protect a surgeon who leaves a pair of scissors inside a patient.
- **Product liability** coverage would protect the maker of a new hair conditioner that causes users' hair to fall out.
- **Premises liability** coverage would protect a firm if a customer slips on a wet floor and suffers a severe concussion.

personal liability
For a business, responsibility for certain actions of those who work for the business.

professional liability
For a business or a business person, responsibility for an individual's actions in working at the business or profession.

product liability
For a business, responsibility for the actions of its products.

premises liability
For a business, responsibility for occurrences on its premises.

Selected Types of Liability Coverage

Businesses often choose to purchase comprehensive general liability policies, which provide coverage for all these problems and more. In this section, we will focus on three types of such coverage: *umbrella policies, automobile policies*, and *workers' compensation*.

Umbrella Policies. Because the dollar value of a liability loss can be huge, many insurers will write coverage only up to a certain limit. Moreover, many liability contracts exclude certain types of losses. To cover financial consequences that exceed the coverage of standard policies, some businesses buy **umbrella insurance**: insurance intended to cover losses in addition to or excluded by an underlying policy.

umbrella insurance
Insurance that covers losses over and above those covered by a standard policy as well as losses excluded by a standard policy.

For example, suppose that a business has an automobile policy with the following coverage:

- a limit of $500 000 for bodily injury and property damage
- a premises liability policy with a limit of $500 000
- a product liability policy with a limit of $750 000

Figure B.1 shows how an umbrella policy might double the coverage in each area. Another umbrella policy might extend product liability coverage to items not covered by the firm's existing policy.

Automobile Policies. A firm that owns and maintains automobiles for business use needs a *business automobile policy*. This policy will protect it against liability for bodily injury and property damage inflicted by its vehicles. Typically, such policies provide the following types of coverage:

- *Bodily injury and property damage*. Coverage that pays the firm if it is held legally liable for bodily injury or property damage.
- *Medical*. Coverage that pays for medical expenses incurred by persons in an insured vehicle.

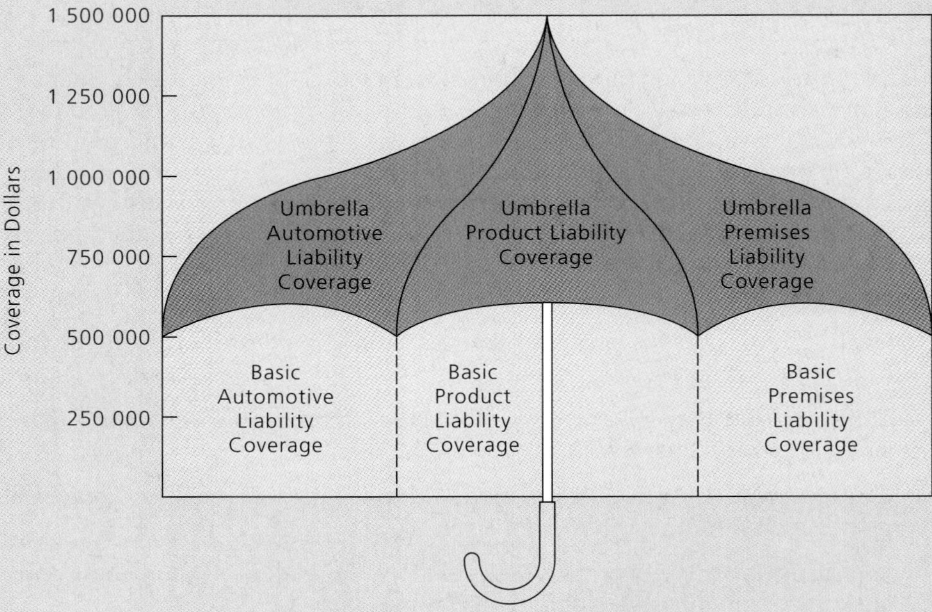

Figure B.1
Umbrella insurance coverage.

- *Uninsured motorists*. Coverage that pays bodily-injury expenses when injury to an insured driver is caused by an uninsured motorist, a hit-and-run driver, or a driver whose employer is insolvent.

Workers' Compensation. A business is liable for any injury to an employee when the injury arises from activities related to occupation. When workers are permanently or temporarily disabled by job-related accidents or disease, employers are required by law to provide **workers' compensation** coverage for medical expenses, loss of wages, and rehabilitation services.

workers' compensation
A business's liability for injury to its employee(s) resulting from any activities related to the occupation.

Property Insurance

property insurance
Insurance covering losses resulting from physical damage to real estate or personal property.

Firms purchase **property insurance** to cover injuries resulting from physical damage to or loss of real personal property. Property losses might result from fire, lightning, wind, hail, explosion, theft, vandalism, or other destructive forces. Many different forms of property insurance exist to cover the many types of property losses.

Fire and Allied Lines

The typical fire insurance policy covers damage to specified property caused by fire, lightning, or theft. Coverage can be extended to cover other perils such as windstorm, hail, riot, smoke, aircraft, vehicles, explosion, vandalism, malicious mischief, and sonic boom. Some policies also include special provisions insuring the firm's property against sprinkler leakage, earthquake, or flood.

Marine Insurance

marine insurance
A form of transportation insurance covering both the act of transportation (by water, land, or air) and the transported goods.

Another area of property insurance is **marine insurance**, a form of transportation insurance. Marine insurance includes two distinct areas: ocean marine and inland marine. *Ocean marine insurance* has been around for more than 500 years. Medieval shippers used a system of insurance to protect their cargoes from loss. As commerce grew, so did the need for specialized services to guarantee financial solvency in the face of navigation disasters.[1] Today's ocean marine insurance covers the liability and loss of or damage to ships and their cargo.

Waterborne commerce was the most important method of transporting goods for centuries. As industry moved inland, land transportation of cargo became important and the inland marine policies were created. Although *inland marine insurance* sounds like a contradiction in terms, it is truly an extension of the ocean marine form, since it covers transportation (whether by truck, rail, or plane) and transported property. There are four main categories of inland marine insurance: property in transit (such as parcel post), bailee liability (such as dry cleaners), instrumentalities of transportation (such as bridges), and mobile property (such as farm animals).

Title Insurance

When real property is purchased, it is customary to research the *title* (ownership) of that property to determine whether it is free of defects such as tax liens. The easiest way for a purchaser to verify that the seller has a clear legal right to convey the property is through the purchase of **title insurance**. A title insurance company will search a variety of sources and guarantee that the seller is the proper owner and that there are no unknown debts or liens against the property. For instance, if the person selling the property owned it with a former spouse, a title search would verify whether the seller has the legal right to sell the property. If the title insurance company erroneously indicates that the title is free of defects and the policyholder subsequently suffers a loss, then the insurance company must reimburse the insured to an amount specified in the policy.

title insurance
Insurance that guarantees a seller has clear title to a property.

Business Interruption Insurance

In some cases the loss to property may be minimal in comparison with the loss of income suffered as a result of the property damage. A manufacturer may be required to close down for an extended period of time while repairs are being completed. During that time the company is not generating income. However, certain expenses—taxes, insurance premiums, and salaries for key personnel—may continue to accrue. The company may also need to keep running advertisements to make customers aware that repairs are progressing so that they don't take their business elsewhere permanently. To cover these potential losses a firm may buy **business interruption insurance**.

business interruption insurance
Insurance to cover potential losses incurred during times when a company is unable to conduct its business.

Credit Insurance

In addition to protecting its physical assets, a firm may also purchase **credit insurance** to protect its financial assets. If a customer does not pay its bills to the business, the selling company loses the value of the goods or services that it sold to the customer on credit. Linda Lingerie Inc. (LLI) bought credit insurance when it heard rumours that Eaton's was in financial trouble. The premium was high—$200 000—but LLI's president, Carolyn Farha, says it gave her peace of mind knowing that her firm would not lose money if Eaton's went bankrupt and was unable to pay its bills to suppliers.[2]

credit insurance
Insurance to protect against customers' failure to pay their bills.

Coinsurance

Because a total loss of property is not likely, property owners have traditionally bought less than the total value in coverage. This practice results in coverage of losses on all parts of the property, but the insurer receives a premium for only a fraction of the property's value. To counter this problem, policies include a coinsurance provision requiring policyholders to insure to a certain minimum percentage of the total value of the property. If the policyholder fails to insure to the required percentage, the insurance company's payment will not cover the entire loss. Instead, insurance pays a smaller amount, as determined by the following formula:

$$\frac{\text{Amount of insurance owned}}{\text{Amount of insurance}} \times \text{Amount of property loss}$$

$$= \text{Insurance company's payment}$$

If, for example, a building has a replacement value of $80 000 and the insurance policy has an 80 percent coinsurance requirement, the required amount of insurance coverage is $64 000 ($80 000 × 0.8). If the owner carries $64 000 worth of insurance coverage, then a $25 000 loss will be paid in full, as will any other loss up to $64 000. However, if the owner carries only $50 000 of insurance coverage, the insurance company will pay only $19 531.25 of the $25 000 loss, as the following calculation shows:

$$\frac{\$50\ 000}{\$64\ 000} \times \$25\ 000 = \$19\ 531.25$$

The policyholder bears the remainder of the loss ($25 000 – $19 531.25 = $5468.75), in effect, a penalty for underinsuring the property.

Multi-Line Policies

Because companies have many risks, they may need many kinds of insurance. Rather than purchasing many separate policies, firms may elect to buy one of the *multi-line package policies* now offered. These policies combine coverage for property losses with coverage for liability losses. Examples of multi-line policies include the Special Multi-Peril Policy (SMP) for owners of large businesses and the Business Owners Policy (BOP) designed for small to medium-sized retail stores, office buildings, apartment buildings, and similar firms.

Life Insurance

life insurance
Insurance that pays benefits to survivors of a policyholder.

beneficiary
The person to whom benefits of a life insurance policy are paid.

Insurance can protect not only a company's physical and capital assets but its labour assets as well. As part of their benefits packages, many businesses buy **life insurance** for their employees. Life insurance companies accept premiums from policyholders in return for the promise to pay a **beneficiary** after the death of the policyholder. A portion of the premium is used for current losses and expenses. The remainder is invested in various types of financial instruments such as corporate bonds and stocks. A portion of the investment income generated offsets the premium paid by the policyholder. Therefore, an insurance company with a high investment return theoretically should charge less than one with a lower investment return, assuming that both companies have similar loss experience and expenses.

Life insurance is a profitable business in Canada. In 2002, the top 10 insurance companies received over $48.4 billion in premiums from policyholders; net profit for the top 10 firms combined was almost $4.1 billion.[3] Among the many products life insurance companies offer are whole life, term insurance, endowment, and universal life policies.

Whole Life Insurance

In **whole life insurance**, a business or individual pays a sum that is sufficient to keep the policy in force for the whole of the person's life. This sum can be paid every year for life or for a stated period of years (such as 20 years). For example, Evita Guard may pay $115 each year and be assured that her beneficiary, her husband, will receive the stated face value upon her death. Alternatively, she could pay $198 each year for 20 years and receive the same benefit. In both cases, the policy is said to be paid up.

whole life insurance
Insurance coverage in force for the whole of a person's life, with a build-up of cash value.

Whole life policies have an internal build-up called a *cash value*. This value can never be forfeited even if the policyholder chooses to stop paying the premium. In some cases, the policyholder can borrow against this value. Or a policyholder can surrender (discontinue) the insurance policy and receive its cash value from the insurance company. Cash value makes whole life policies attractive to some insurance purchasers.

Term Insurance

As its name suggests, **term insurance** provides coverage for a term (a temporary time period) stated in the policy. The term can be for 1, 5, 10, or 20 years. Term insurance has no cash value and is less expensive than any of the other forms discussed in this section. A policyholder receives maximum death protection for the premium paid. An individual who has a limited insurance budget but a significant need for death protection should consider term insurance. Term insurance is also the form of life insurance companies supply most often to their employees.

term insurance
Insurance coverage for a fixed period of time, often 1, 5, 10, or 20 years.

Endowments

A type of policy called an **endowment** pays the face value of the policy whether the policyholder is dead or alive. The purpose of an endowment is to allow accumulation of a fund. For example, a father might buy a $20 000, 10-year endowment in order to accumulate $20 000 within a 10-year period for his daughter's university education. If he dies before the 10 years are up, the insurance company will pay his beneficiary (his daughter). However, if the father lives to the tenth year, the company turns the accumulated $20 000 over to him. Table B.1 compares these three types of policies with regard to premiums, benefits, and use.

endowment
Insurance that pays face value after a fixed period of time whether the policyholder is alive or dead.

Universal Life Insurance

The life insurance industry was very profitable for many years selling only the three policies described above. Whole life was the backbone of the industry. But as interest rates spiralled in the 1960s and 1970s, many policyholders became disillusioned with the very low rate of interest they earned in whole life and endowment policies. Policyholders began surrendering their policies and investing their funds in higher-yielding instruments such as guaranteed investment certificates. This withdrawal of funds, coupled with the difficulty of selling new policies, caused serious problems for life insurance companies. They responded by developing a new product to lure policyholders back to buying insurance: **universal life policies**.

universal life policy
A term insurance policy with a savings component.

Universal life policies combine a term insurance product with a savings component. Although this product may require a high initial premium, premium payments are flexible and interest earned on the savings component is competitive with other money market instruments.

Variable Life Insurance

variable life insurance (VLI)
A modified form of life insurance where the policyholder chooses the minimum face value of the policy.

Another new form of life insurance is a modified form of whole life insurance. **Variable life insurance (VLI)** allows flexibility regarding the minimum face value of the policy, the types of investments supporting it, and even the amount and timing of the premiums.

How does VLI work? Instead of buying a whole life policy with a fixed face value of $100 000, a policyholder may choose a variable life policy with a $100 000 *minimum* face value. The actual face value can exceed the minimum, depending on the market performance of the VLI investment portfolio. VLI policyholders can stipulate the portfolio mix, choosing among a variety of investment instruments such as common stocks, short-term bonds, and high-yield money market securities. The increase in the policy's face value depends on the success of the underlying investments. VLIs are a growing segment of the insurance market because they offer more flexibility than traditional policies.

Group Life Insurance

group life insurance
Life insurance written for a group of people rather than an individual.

Most companies buy **group life insurance**, which is underwritten for groups as a whole rather than for each individual member. The insurer's assessment of potential losses and its pricing of premiums are based on the

Table B.1 Comparison of Basic and Common Life Insurance Contracts

Basic type	Protection period	When benefits are payable	Approximate costs for $10 000 at age 20*	How long premiums are paid	Uses
1. Whole Life	Permanent	At death, any time	—	—	Combination of moderate savings and protection
a. Straight or ordinary life	"	"	$115	Throughout life	"
b. 20-payment life	"	"	$198	For 20 years	Paying up premiums during working life
c. Life paid up at 65	"	"	$127	To age 65	
2. Term	Temporary	At death, only during term	—	—	Protection only
a. Yearly renewable term	"	"	$25 increasing each year	Varies—can be to age 60–70	Maximum protection
b. Five-year level term (renewable and convertible)	"	"	$53	5 years	Very high protection for limited period
3. Endowment	Temporary or long term	At death, or if living, at end of endowment period	—	—	Combination of higher savings and protection
a. 20-year endowment	"	"	$426	20 years	"
b. Retirement income at 65	"	"	$177	To age 65	"

*Costs are necessarily approximate for such general comparisons. Participating policies would be slightly higher, with net costs reduced by annual dividends. Nonparticipating policies would be somewhat lower. Smaller policies under $10 000 will be slightly higher; those over this amount may have a lower rate per $1000. Those insuring women will also be somewhat lower in cost. Extra policy features, such as waiver of premium, accidental death benefits, and so on, would increase these estimates.

characteristics of the whole group. Johnson & Johnson's benefit plan, for example, includes group life coverage with a standard program of protection and benefits—a master policy purchased by J&J—that applies equally to all employees.

Key Insurance

Many businesses choose to protect themselves against the loss of the talents and skills of key employees. If a salesperson who brings in $2.5 million in sales every year dies or takes a new job elsewhere, the firm will suffer loss. Moreover, the firm will incur recruitment costs to find a replacement and training expenses once a replacement is hired. *Key person insurance* can offset the lost income and the additional expenses.

A related matter is who takes control of a business when a partner or associate dies. At issue is whether the surviving business partners are willing to accept an inexperienced heir as a management partner in the business. Business continuation agreements are traditionally used to plan for this situation. The business owners can plan to buy the ownership interest of the deceased associate from his or her heirs. The value of the ownership interest is determined when the agreement is made. Special business insurance policies can provide the funds needed to make the purchase.

NOTES, SOURCES, AND CREDITS

Reference Notes

Chapter 1

1. "Largest Profits," *National Post Business* (June, 2003): 48.

2. See Robert A. Collinge and Ronald M. Ayers, *Economics by Design: Principles and Issues*, 2nd ed. (Upper Saddle River, NJ: Prentice Hall, 2000), 41–42; Michael J. Mandel, "The New Economy," *Business Week* (January 31, 2000): 73–77.

3. Karl E. Case and Ray C. Fair, *Principles of Economics*, 6th ed. (Upper Saddle River, NJ: Prentice Hall, 2003), 224–225.

4. Howard W. French, "On the Street, Cubans Fondly Embrace Capitalism," *The New York Times*, February 3, 1994, A4.

5. James Kynge, "Private Firms' Growth in China Striking: Report," *National Post*, May 11, 2000, C14.

6. Richard I. Kirkland, Jr., "The Death of Socialism," *Fortune* (January 4, 1988): 64–72.

7. See Karl E. Case and Ray C. Fair, *Principles of Economics*, 5th ed. (Upper Saddle River, NJ: Prentice Hall, 1999), 69–74; Robert A. Collinge and Ronald M. Ayers, *Economics by Design: Principles and Issues*, 2nd ed. (Upper Saddle River, NJ: Prentice Hall, 2000), 51–52.

8. Deborah Orr, "The Post Office with a Ticker," *Forbes* (November 29, 1999): 77–78; Matthew L. Wald, "Canada's Private Control Towers," *The New York Times*, October 23, 1999, C1. See also National Center for Policy Analysis, "Privatization," http://www.public-policy.org/~ncpa/pd/private/privat.html, March 8, 2000.

9. Keith McArthur, "Air Canada Accused of Predatory Pricing," *The Globe and Mail*, September 8, 2000, B3.

10. Janet McFarland, "Power Failure: Ontario's Aborted Plan," *The Globe and Mail*, November 16, 2002, B1, B5.

11. Barrie McKenna, "Hyundai Gorged on Federal Funds," *The Globe and Mail*, March 25, 1994, B3.

12. Peter Burrows, "Personal Computers: Are the Glory Days Over?" *Business Week* (February 14, 2000): 50.

13. See Karl E. Case and Ray C. Fair, *Principles of Economics*, 5th ed. (Upper Saddle River, NJ: Prentice Hall, 1999), 70–90; Robert A. Collinge and Ronald M. Ayers, *Economics by Design: Principles and Issues*, 2nd ed. (Upper Saddle River, NJ: Prentice Hall, 2000), 74–77.

14. See Paul Heyne, Peter J. Boettke, and David L. Prychitko, *The Economic Way of Thinking*, 10th ed. (Upper Saddle River, NJ: Prentice Hall, 2003), 190, 358–59.

15. See Gina M. Larson, "bebe Bridges Style Gap," www.office.com/global/0,2724,509-10386_1,FF.html, July 10, 2001; Natural Fibers Information Center, "Ranking of Top U.S. Public Apparel Companies," www.utexas.edu/depts/bbr/natfiber, June 2001; "bebe.com Finishes #1," *Fashion Windows.com*, www.fashion windows. com/beauty/2002/bebe.asp, January 14, 2002.

16. Karl E. Case and Ray C. Fair, *Principles of Economics*, 6th ed., updated (Upper Saddle River, NJ: Prentice Hall, 2003), 300–309.

17. *Hoover's Handbook of World Business 2002* (Austin, TX: Hoover's Business Press, 2002), 74–75.

18. John Partridge and Lawrence Surtees, "Rogers Faces Assault from Telcos," *The Globe and Mail*, March 28, 1994, B1–B2.

19. Madelaine Drohan, "Ottawa Targets Interprovincial Barriers," *The Globe and Mail*, May 14, 1991, B5.

Chapter 2

1. See Jay B. Barney and William G. Ouchi (Eds.), *Organizational Economics* (San Francisco: Jossey-Bass, 1986), for a detailed analysis of linkages between economics and organizations.

2. Karl E. Case and Ray C. Fair, *Principles of Economics*, 6th ed., updated (Upper Saddle River, NJ: Prentice Hall, 2003), 432–433.

3. Karl E. Case and Ray C. Fair, *Principles of Economics*, 6th ed., updated (Upper Saddle River, NJ: Prentice Hall, 2003), 15.

4. Karl E. Case and Ray C. Fair, *Principles of Economics*, 6th ed., updated (Upper Saddle River, NJ: Prentice Hall, 2003), 15.

5. Table H1, *Bank of Canada Review* (May 2003): S-94.

6. Barry Marquardson, "GDP Fails as a Measurement," *The Globe and Mail*, July 16, 1998, B2.

7. Olivier Blanchard, *Macroeconomics*, 3rd ed. (Upper Saddle River, NJ: Prentice Hall, 2003), 24–26.

8. Jay Heizer and Barry Render, *Operations Management*, 6th ed. (Upper Saddle River, NJ: Prentice Hall, 2001), 15–16.

9. Table J1, *Bank of Canada Review* (May 2003): S-109.

10. Table G1, *Bank of Canada Review* (May 2003): S-83.

11. This section is based on Paul Heyne, Peter J. Boettke, and David L. Prychitko, *The Economic Way of Thinking*, 10th ed. (Upper Saddle River, NJ: Prentice Hall, 2003), 491–493.

12. See Warren J. Keegan, *Global Marketing Management*, 7th ed. (Upper Saddle River, NJ: Prentice Hall, 2002), 39–42.

13. G. Thomas Sims, "Already Stumbling, Germany Now Faces Threat of Deflation," *The Wall Street Journal*, June 23, 2003, A1, A7.

14. Paul Heyne, Peter J. Boettke, and David L. Prychitko, *The Economic Way of Thinking*, 10th ed. (Upper Saddle River, NJ: Prentice Hall, 2003), 403–409, 503–504.

15. Robert A. Collinge and Ronald M. Ayers, *Economics by Design: Principles and Issues*, 2nd ed. (Upper Saddle River, NJ: Prentice Hall, 2000), 362–365.

16. Karl E. Case and Ray C. Fair, *Principles of Economics*, 6th ed., updated (Upper Saddle River, NJ: Prentice Hall, 2003), 416.

17. Ram Charan and Geoffrey Colvin, "Managing for the Slowdown," *Fortune* (February 5, 2001): 78–88.

18. See "Rethinking the Internet," *Business Week* (March 26, 2001): 116–136.

19. Michael J. Mandel et al., "The 21st Century Economy," *Business Week* (August 31, 1998): 58–67. See also David Fairlamb and Gail Edmondson, "Work in Progress—Signs Abound of a Nascent New Economy," *Business Week* (January 31, 2000): 80–87.

20. See also Brian Bremner and Moon Ihlwan, "Edging Toward the Information Age," *Business Week* (January 31, 2000): 90–91.

21. Ram Charan and Geoffrey Colvin, "Managing for the Slowdown," *Fortune* (February 5, 2001): 78–88.

22. Brian Bremner and Moon Ihlwan, "Edging Toward the Information Age," *Business Week* (January 31, 2000): 91.

23. Statistics Canada, *Statistics Canada Service Bulletin, Science Statistics* (July, 2003).

24. Statistics Canada, *Industrial Research and Development, 2002 Intentions* (2002): 16.

25. Statistics Canada, *Industrial Research and Development, 2002 Intentions* (2002): 18.

26. Statistics Canada, *Industrial Research and Development, 2002 Intentions* (2002): 19.

27. Statistics Canada, *Industrial Research and Development, 2002 Intentions* (2002): 11.

28. Statistics Canada, *A Comparison of International R&D Performance: An Analysis of Countries That Have Significantly Increased their GERD/GDP Ratios During the Period 1989–1999* (February, 2003): 7.

29. Thomas Wheelen and J. David Hunger, *Strategic Management and Business Policy* (Upper Saddle River, NJ: Pearson, 2004), 280.

30. L.G. Franko, "Global Corporate Competition: Who's Winning, Who's Losing, and the R&D Factor as One Reason Why," *Strategic Management Journal* (September–October, 1989): 449–474.

31. Roberta S. Russell and Bernard W. Taylor III, *Operations Management*, 4th ed. (Upper Saddle River, NJ: Prentice Hall, 2003), Chapter 12.

32. Brian Laghi, "U.S. Backlash Seen Growing," *The Globe and Mail*, March 27, 2003, B1, B10.

33. Karen Howlett, Sinclair Stewart, and Paul Waldie, "CIBC 'Aided' Enron Fraud: Report," *The Globe and Mail*, July 29, 2003, A1, A6; Paul Waldie, Karen Howlett, and Sinclair Stewart, "Skeptical CIBC Still Did Enron Deals," *The Globe and Mail*, July 30, 2003, B1, B4.

34. Paul Waldie and Sinclair Stewart, "TD's Transactions Larger Than Thought," *The Globe and Mail*, July 30, 2003, B1, B4.

35. "Andersen Ends Role As Public Auditor," *USATODAY.com*, www.usatoday.com, September 4, 2002.

36. Michael Porter. *Competitive Strategy: Techniques for Analyzing Industries and Competitors* (New York: The Free Press, 1980).

37. Lee J. Krajewski and Larry P. Ritzman, *Operations Management: Strategy and Analysis*, 6th ed. (Upper Saddle River, NJ: Prentice Hall, 2002), 102–106.

38. Virginia Galt, "Take Our Business, Take Our People: BMO," *The Globe and Mail*, May 19, 2003, B1, B4.

39. Anne T. Coughlin et al., *Marketing Channels*, 6th ed. (Upper Saddle River, NJ: Prentice Hall, 2001), 168–172.

40. Judy Strauss and Raymond Frost, *E-Marketing* (Upper Saddle River, NJ: Prentice Hall, 2001), 245–246.

41. Lee J. Krajewski and Larry P. Ritzman, *Operations Management: Strategy and Analysis*, 6th ed. (Upper Saddle River, NJ: Prentice Hall, 2002), 3–4.

42. Lee J. Krajewski and Larry P. Ritzman, *Operations Management: Strategy and Analysis*, 6th ed. (Upper Saddle River, NJ: Prentice Hall, 2002), Chapter 3.

Chapter 3

1. Strategis, Industry Canada, http://strategis.ic.gc.ca.

2. Thomas W. Zimmerer and Norman M. Scarborough, *Essentials of Entrepreneurship and Small Business*, 3rd ed. (Upper Saddle River, NJ: Prentice Hall, 2002), 4–6.

3. The Heritage Foundation, 214 Massachusetts Ave. NE, Washington, D.C. 20002-4999, at http://www.heritage.org.

4. Natalie Southworth, "Canada Gets Top-Tier Ranking," *The Globe and Mail*, November 14, 2000, B9.

5. Simon Tuck, "Canada Will be No. 1 Spot for business, Study Says," *The Globe and Mail*, July 17, 2003, B3.

6. Paulette Thomas, "A New Generation Re-Writes the Rules," *Wall Street Journal*, May 22, 2002, R4.

7. Gayle MacDonald, "War Stories from the World's Top Female Owners," *The Globe and Mail*, May 2, 1997, B9; Murray McNeill, "Women Step Out on Their Own," *The Winnipeg Free Press*, December 8, 1994, C10.

8. Laura Ramsay, "A League of Their Own," *The Globe and Mail*, November 29, 2002, B11.

9. Alan M. Cohen, "Entrepreneur and Entrepreneurship: The Definition Dilemma," Working Paper Series No. NC89-08, National Centre for Management Research and Development, The University of Western Ontario, London, February 1989.

10. Thomas W. Zimmerer and Norman M. Scarborough, *Essentials of Entrepreneurship and Small Business*, 3rd ed. (Upper Saddle River, NJ: Prentice Hall, 2002), Chapter 10.

11. Thomas W. Zimmerer and Norman M. Scarborough, *Essentials of Entrepreneurship and Small Business*, 3rd ed. (Upper Saddle River, NJ: Prentice Hall, 2002), Chapter 8. See also Charles T. Horngren, Srikant M. Datar, and George Foster, *Cost Accounting: A Managerial Emphasis*, 11th ed. (Upper Saddle River, NJ: Prentice Hall, 2003), 195–199.

12. Thomas W. Zimmerer and Norman M. Scarborough, *Essentials of Entrepreneurship and Small Business*, 3rd ed. (Upper Saddle River, NJ: Prentice Hall, 2002), Chapter 5.

13. Mary Agnes Welch, "When Name Is Everything," *The Winnipeg Free Press*, May 12, 2002, B1, B2.

14. The statistics in this section are from *Small Business in Canada: Growing to Meet Tomorrow* (Ottawa: Supply and Services Canada), Cat. No. C28-12 1989E; D.P. Moore and E.H. Buttner, *Women Entrepreneurs: Moving Beyond the Glass Ceiling* (Thousand Oaks, CA: Sage Publishing, 1997); *The State of Small Business 1989, Annual Report on Small Business in Ontario* (Toronto: Ministry of Industry, Trade and Technology, 1990).

15. http://www.jimpattison.com/home.htm, October 4, 2003.

16. Catherine Mulroney, "Incorporating Has Its Benefits," *The Globe and Mail*, April 14, 2003, B16.

17. Quoted in Lowell B. Howard, *Business Law* (Woodbury, NY: Barron's Woodbury Press, 1965), 332.

18. Julie Demers, "In the Public Eye," *CGA Magazine* (May 2000): 25–28.

19. Lawrence Surtees, "Takeover Concern Prompts BCE Poison Pill Plan," *The Globe and Mail*, February 25, 2000, B5.

20. Margot Gibb-Clark, "Share Plans Can Benefit More Than Employees," *The Globe and Mail*, February 14, 2000, B6.

21. "Nunavut Diamond Find Sends Shares Soaring," *The Winnipeg Free Press*, February 4, 2003, B10.

22. "Inco, LionOre Mining Form Strategic Alliance," *The Winnipeg Free Press*, March 14, 2003, B6.

Chapter 4

1. See Ricky W. Griffin and Michael W. Pustay, *International Business: A Managerial Perspective*, 2nd ed. (Reading, MA: Addison-Wesley, 1999), pp. 431–433; John J. Wild, Kenneth L. Wild, and Jerry C.Y. Han, *International Business: An Integrated Approach* (Upper Saddle River, NJ: Prentice Hall, 2000), pp. 456–458.

2. "New Global Trade Regulator Starts Operations Tomorrow," *The Winnipeg Free Press*, December 31, 1994, A5.

3. Helene Cooper and Bhushan Bahree, "World's Best Hope for Global Trade Topples Few Barriers," *The Wall Street Journal*, December 3, 1996, A1, A8.

4. Heather Scoffield and Greg Keenan, "Canada Told to Scrap Auto Pact," *The Globe and Mail*, October 14, 1999, A1, A2.

5. Barrie McKenna, "NAFTA Dealt Blow by WTO Ruling," *The Globe and Mail*, July 12, 2003, B1, B5.

6. Michelle MacAfee, "Trade Protest Turns Violent," *The Winnipeg Free Press*, July 29, 2003, A9.

7. Andrew Purvis, "Super Exporter," *Time* (April 28, 1997): 36.

8. Peter Cook, "Free Trade Free-for-All Causes Confusion," *The Globe and Mail*, December 5, 1994, B7.

9. Ricky W. Griffin and Michael W. Pustay, *International Business: A Managerial Perspective*, 2nd ed. (Reading, MA: Addison-Wesley, 1999), pp. 44–45. See also Warren J. Keegan, *Global Marketing Management*, 6th ed. (Upper Saddle River, NJ: Prentice Hall, 1999), pp. 42–45.

10. Trade Partners UK, "Automotive Industries Market in Mexico," http://www.tradepartners.gov.uk/automotive/mexico/profile/characteristics.shtml, July 10, 2001; NAFTA Works, "Mexico Auto Sector Sees $15 Billion Investment in 5 Years," www.naftaworks.org/papers/2000/automex.htm, July 10, 2001.

11. David Fairlamb and Gail Edmondson, "Work in Progress," *Business Week* (January 31, 2000): 80–81+.

12. David Fairlamb and Gail Edmondson, "Work in Progress," *Business Week* (January 31, 2000): 80–81+.

13. See Edmund L. Andrews, "The Metamorphosis of Germany Inc.," *The New York Times*, March 12, 2000, section 3, pp. 1, 12.

14. See Mark Landler, "Mapping Out Silicon Valley East," *The New York Times*, April 5, 1999, C1, C10; Bruce Einhorn with Cathy Yang, "Portal Combat," *Business Week* (January 17, 2000): 96–97.

15. John Wild, Kenneth Wild, and Jerry Han, *International Business*, 2nd ed. (Upper Saddle River, NJ: Prentice Hall, 2003), 239.

16. See Ricky W. Griffin and Michael W. Pustay, *International Business: A Managerial Perspective*, 2nd ed. (Reading, MA: Addison-Wesley, 1999), Chapter 3. Dominick Salvatore, *International Economics*, 6th ed. (Upper Saddle River, NJ: Prentice Hall, 1998), 27–33; Karl E. Case and Ray C. Fair, *Principles of Economics*, 5th ed. (Upper Saddle River, NJ: Prentice Hall, 1999), 813–17.

17. This section is based on Michael Porter, *The Competitive Advantage of Nations* (Boston: Harvard Business School Press, 1990), Chapters 3 and 4. Warren J. Keegan, *Global Marketing Management*, 6th ed. (Upper Saddle River, NJ: Prentice Hall, 1999), 312–321; John J. Wild, Kenneth L. Wild, and Jerry C.Y. Han, *International Business: An Integrated Approach* (Upper Saddle River, NJ: Prentice Hall, 2000), 175–178.

18. Madelaine Drohan, "Dependency on U.S. Leaves Canada 'Vulnerable': WTO," *The Globe and Mail*, November 20, 1996.

19. Table J2, *Bank of Canada Review* (May, 2003): S-110.

20. See Karl E. Case and Ray C. Fair, *Principles of Economics*, 5th ed. (Upper Saddle River, NJ: Prentice Hall, 1999), 818–821.

21. Robyn Meredith, "Dollar Makes Canada a Land of the Spree," *The New York Times*, August 1, 1999, sec. 3, pp. 1, 11.

22. Heather Scoffield, "Move Toward Common Currency Speeds Up," *The Globe and Mail*, April 22, 2000, B1, B5.

23. Marian Stinson, "Keep Canadian Dollar: Economist," *The Globe and Mail*, April 14, 2000, B3.

24. "Exports, Eh?" *Canadian Business* (January 1997): 21.

25. Peggy Berkowitz, "You Say Potato, They Say McCain," *Canadian Business* (December 1991): 44–48.

26. Daniel Stoffman, "Cross-Border Selling," *Report on Business Magazine* (November 1991): 61–68.

27. Ray August, *International Business Law: Text, Cases, and Readings*, 3rd ed. (Upper Saddle River, NJ: Prentice Hall, 2000), 192–197.

28. Paola Hjelt, "The Fortune Global 500," *Fortune* (July 22, 2002): 144–147.

29. Warren J. Keegan, *Global Marketing Management*, 6th ed. (Upper Saddle River, NJ: Prentice Hall, 1999), 290–292; Ricky W. Griffin and Michael W. Pustay, *International Business: A Managerial Perspective*, 2nd ed. (Reading, MA: Addison-Wesley, 1999), 427–431; John J. Wild, Kenneth L. Wild, and Jerry C.Y. Han, *International Business: An Integrated Approach* (Upper Saddle River, NJ: Prentice Hall, 2000), 454–456.

30. Ricky W. Griffin and Michael W. Pustay, *International Business: A Managerial Perspective*, 2nd ed. (Reading, MA: Addison-Wesley, 1999), 431–433; John J. Wild, Kenneth L. Wild, and Jerry C.Y. Han, *International Business: An Integrated Approach* (Upper Saddle River, NJ: Prentice Hall, 2000), 456–458.

31. Warren J. Keegan, *Global Marketing Management*, 6th ed. (Upper Saddle River, NJ: Prentice Hall, 1999), 292–294; John J. Wild, Kenneth L. Wild, and Jerry C.Y. Han, *International Business: An Integrated Approach* (Upper Saddle River, NJ: Prentice Hall, 2000), 461–466.

32. John J. Wild, Kenneth L. Wild, and Jerry C.Y. Han, *International Business: An Integrated Approach* (Upper Saddle River, NJ: Prentice Hall, 2000), Chapter 7; Ricky W. Griffin and Michael W. Pustay, *International Business: A Managerial Perspective*, 2nd ed. (Reading, MA: Addison-Wesley, 1999), 436–439.

33. Eric Reguly, "The Devouring of Corporate Canada," *The Globe and Mail*, September 4, 1999, B1, B4.

34. Eric Reguly, "The Devouring of Corporate Canada," *The Globe and Mail*, September 4, 1999, B1, B4.

35. Shawn McCarthy, "Business Sounds Alarm on Vulnerability," *The Globe and Mail*, May 8, 2000, B1, B3.

36. Roger Thurow and Scott Kilman, "In U.S., Cotton Farmers Thrive; In Africa, They Fight to Survive," *The Wall Street Journal*, June 26, 2002, A1, A4.

37. Keith McArthur, "Canada Hit with WTO Sanctions," *The Globe and Mail*, December 24, 2002, B2.

38. Roger Thurow and Geoff Winestock, "How an Addiction to Sugar Subsidies Hurts Development," *The Wall Street Journal*, September 16, 2002, A1, A10.

39. Anthony DePalma, "Chiquita Sues Europeans, Citing Banana Quota Losses," *New York Times*, January 26, 2001, C5; Brian Lavery, "Trade Feud on Bananas Not as Clear as it Looks," *New York Times*, February 7, 2001, W1; David E. Sanger, "Miffed at Europe, U.S. Raises Tariffs for Luxury Goods," *New York Times*, March 4, 1999, A1, A5.

40. Konrad Yakabuski, "Quebec Courts Margarine War," *The Globe and Mail*, October 14, 1997, B1, B4.

41. Bertrand Marotte, "Ontario Calls for Dispute Panel in Quebec Margarine Battle, " *The Globe and Mail*, March 26, 2002, B10.

42. Neville Nankivell, "Spilled Milk Over Provincial Trade," *The National Post*, April 24, 2000, C9.

43. Dawn Walton, "Builders Most Likely to Bribe, Report Finds," *The Globe and Mail*, January 21, 2000, B5.

44. Transparency International, "Corruptions Perception Index, 2002," www.transparency.org.

45. Nicholas Bray, "OECD Ministers Agree to Ban Bribery as Means for Companies to Win Business," *The Wall Street Journal*, May 27, 1997, A2.

46. Barrie McKenna, "Aluminum Producers Whispering Dirty Word," *The Globe and Mail*, March 5, 1994, B1, B5.

47. Jalil Hamid, "Coffee Rally Reignited," *The Globe and Mail*, May 22, 1997, B9.

48. Oliver Bertin, "Coffee Cartel Moves Fast on Price," *Globe and Mail*, May 20, 2000, B3.

49. "Ottawa Confirms Dumping," *The Globe and Mail*, July 4, 2000, B15.

Chapter 5

1. Constance L. Hays, "Aide Was Reportedly Ordered to Warn Stewart on Stock Sales," *The New York Times*, August 6, 2002, C1, C2.

2. Thomas Donaldson and Thomas W. Dunfee, "Toward a Unified Conception of Business Ethics: An Integrative Social Contracts Theory," *Academy of Management Review* 19, no. 2 (1994): 252–284.

3. "Drug Companies Face Assault on Prices," *The Wall Street Journal*, May 11, 2000, B1, B4.

4. Jeremy Kahn, "Presto Chango! Sales are Huge," Fortune (March 20, 2000): 90–96; "More Firms Falsify Revenue to Boost Stocks," *USA Today* (March 29, 2000), 1B.

5. This section follows the logic of Gerald F. Cavanaugh, *American Business Values with International Perspectives*, 4th ed. (Upper Saddle River, NJ: Prentice Hall, 1998), Chapter 3.

6. See "Are Your Work Ethics in Line?" CNN.com, www.cnn.com/TECH/computing/9906/22/ethics.ent.idg/, July 11, 2001.

7. Patricia Sellers, "Crunch Time for Coke," *Fortune* (July 19, 1999): 72–74+.

8. Mark Schwartz, "Heat's on to Get an Effective Code," *The Globe and Mail*, November 27, 1997, B2.

9. Jeffrey S. Harrison and R. Edward Freeman, "Stakeholders, Social Responsibility, and Performance: Empirical Evidence and Theoretical Perspectives," *Academy of Management Journal* 42, no. 5, pp. 479–485. See also David P. Baron, *Business and Its Environment*, 3rd ed. (Upper Saddle River, NJ: Prentice-Hall, 2000), Chapter 17.

10. James R. Healey, "Ford to Reveal Plans for Think Brand," *USA Today*, January 10, 2000, p. 1B; Gwen Kinkead, "In the Future, People Like Me Will Go to Jail," *Fortune* (May 24, 1999): 190–200.

11. David P. Baron, *Business and Its Environment*, 4th ed. (Upper Saddle River, NJ: Prentice Hall, 2003), Chapter 11.

12. Jeremy Main, "Here Comes the Big New Cleanup," *Fortune* (November 21, 1988): 102–118.

13. Steven Chase, "PM Hails Approval of Kyoto," *The Globe and Mail*, December 11, 2002, A1, A9.

14. Andrew C. Revkin, "Who Cares About a Few Degrees?" *The New York Times*, December 12, 1997, F4.

15. Catherine Collins, "The Race for Zero," *Canadian Business* (March 1991): 52–56.

16. Allan Robinson and Allan Freeman, "Mining's Dam Problem," *The Globe and Mail*, May 16, 1998, B1–B2.

17. Geoffrey Scotton, "Cleanups Can Hurt, Companies Warned," *The Financial Post*, June 25, 1991, p. 4.

18. Marc Huber, "A Double-Edged Endorsement," *Canadian Business* (January 1990): 69–71.

19. Charles Davies, "Strategy Session 1990," *Canadian Business* (January 1990): 48.

20. "Room Service and the Recyclable Rubber Chicken," *Canadian Business* (May 1991): 19.

21. Casey Mahood, "Bell Zeros in on Waste," *The Globe and Mail*, May 4, 1992, B1.

22. Daniel Machalaba, "As Old Pallets Pile Up, Critics Hammer Them as New Eco-Menace," *The Wall Street Journal*, April 1, 1998, A1.

23. "Hot Spots," *Canadian Business* (March 17, 2003): 30–31.

24. Richard B. Schmitt and Robert Langreth, "American Home Products Agrees to Pay Up to $3.75 Billion in Diet-Drug Lawsuits," WSJ Interactive Edition, www.productslaw.com/diet21.html, July 11, 2001. See also Nancy Shute, "Pills Don't Come with a Seal of Approval," U.S. News Online, www.usnews.com/usnews/issue/970929/29fen.htm, July 11, 2001.

25. John Saunders, "Polar Plastic Plot Flops," *The Globe and Mail*, June 10, 1994, B1.

26. Department of Justice, "F. Hoffmann-La Roche and BASF Agree to Pay Record Criminal Fines for Participating in International Vitamin Cartel," www.usdoj.gov/atr/public/press_releases/1999/2450.htm, July 11, 2001; Alain L. Sanders, "The 'C' in Vitamin C No Longer Stands for Cartel," Time.com, www.time.com/time/nation/article/0,8599,25068,00.html, July 11, 2001.

27. Michael McCarthy and Lorrie Grant, "Sears Drops Benetton After Controversial Death Row Ads," *USA Today*, February 18, 2000, p. 2B.

28. Shona McKay, "Willing and Able," *Report on Business Magazine* (October 1991): 58–63.

29. "Why Business Is Hiring the Mentally Abled," *Canadian Business* (May 1991): 19.

30. J. Southerst, "In Pursuit of Drugs," *Canadian Transportation* (November 1989): 58–65.

31. G. Bylinsky, "How Companies Spy on Employees," *Fortune* (November 4, 1991): 131–140.

32. Greg Farrell, "Enron Law Firm Called Accounting Practices 'Creative'," *USA Today*, January 16, 2002, 1B.

33. Jerald Greenberg and Robert A. Baron, *Behavior in Organizations: Understanding and Managing the Human Side of Work*, 7th ed. (Upper Saddle River, NJ: Prentice Hall, 2000), 374–375.

34. Rick Lyman, "A Tobacco Whistle-Blower's Life Is Transformed," *The New York Times*, October 15, 1999, A24.

35. Cora Daniels, "'It's a Living Hell,'" *Fortune* (April 15, 2002): 367–368.

36. Andy Pasztor and Peter Landers, "Toshiba to Pay $2B Settlement on Laptops," ZD Net News www.zdnet.com/zdnn/stories/news/0,4586,2385037,00.html, July 12, 2001.

37. Richard Blackwell, "OSC Scores Trading Conviction," *The Globe and Mail*, July 22, 2000, B1–B2; "CEO Jailed for Insider Trading," *Winnipeg Free Press*, September 19, 2000, B8.

38. Greg Farrell, "Enron Law Firm Called Accounting Practices 'Creative'," *USA Today*, January 16, 2002, 1B.

39. Daniel Stoffman, "Good Behavior and the Bottom Line," *Canadian Business* (May 1991): 28–32.

40. Tom Kierans, "Charity Begins at Work," *Report on Business Magazine* (June 1990): 23.

41. Theresa Ebden and Dawn Walton, "Walkerton Recipient of New-Style Corporate Giving," *The Globe and Mail*, June 3, 2000, B1, B6.

42. Theresa Ebden and Dawn Walton, "Walkerton Recipient of New-Style Corporate Giving," *The Globe and Mail*, June 3, 2000, B1, B6.

43. David Dias, Phil Froats, and John Guise, "Who Gives: Canada's Top Philanthropists," *Canadian Business* (December, 2002): 87.

44. Sandra Waddock and Neil Smith, "Corporate Responsibility Audits: Doing Well by Doing Good," *Sloan Management Review* (Winter 2000), 75–85.

Chapter 6

1. Janet Guyon, "Getting the Bugs Out at VW," *Fortune* (March 29, 1999): 96–102.

2. Stephen P. Robbins and Mary Coulter, *Management*, 7th ed. (Upper Saddle River, NJ: Prentice Hall, 2002), 202–204; and Thomas L. Wheelan and J. David Hunger, *Strategic Management and Business Policy*, 7th ed. (Upper Saddle River, NJ: Prentice Hall, 2000), 107.

3. Melanie Wells, "Red Baron," *Forbes* (July 3, 2000): 150–160; Andrew Ross Sorkin, "Taking Virgin's Brand into Internet Territory," *The New York Times*, February 14, 2000, C1, C17.

4. Michael Porter, *Competitive Strategy: Techniques for Analyzing Industries and Competitors* (New York: The Free Press, 1980).

5. "Cruise-Ship Delays Leave Guests High and Dry," *The Wall Street Journal*, October 24, 1997, B1, B10; *Hoover's Handbook of American Business 2000* (Austin, TX: Hoover's Business Press, 2000), 1512–1513.

6. Peter Burrows, "The Hottest Property in the Valley?" *Business Week* (August 30, 1999): 69–74.

7. Alex Taylor III, "How a Top Boss Manages His Day," *Fortune* (June 19, 1989): 95–100.

8. Frank Rose, "Vivendi's High Wireless Act," *Wired*, www.wired.com/wired/archive/8.12/vivendi.html, July 18, 2001; Mike Trigg, "Vivendi Grabs Houghton Mifflin," *The Motley Fool*,

www.fool.com/news/2001/v010601.htm, July 18, 2001.

9. Kamal Fatehi, *International Management: A Cross-Cultural and Functional Perspective* (Upper Saddle River, NJ: Prentice Hall, 1996), 5–8, 153–64.

10. Ric Dolphin, "Magna Force," *Canadian Business* (May 1988).

11. Isadore Sharp, "Quality for All Seasons," *Canadian Business Review* (Spring 1990): 21–23.

12. Bruce McDougall, "The Thinking Man's Assembly Line," *Canadian Business* (November 1991): 40–44.

13. Peter Verburg, "Prepare for Takeoff," *Canadian Business* (December 25, 2000): 95–99.

14. Doug Nairne, "Mounties Riding the Vision Thing," *Winnipeg Free Press*, September 16, 1996, A5.

15. Gabriella Stern, "How a Young Manager Shook Up the Culture at Old Chrysler Plant," *The Wall Street Journal*, April 21, 1997, A1, A6.

16. "Rallying the Troops at P&G," *The Wall Street Journal*, August 31, 2000, B1, B4.

Chapter 7

1. Robert L. Simison, "Ford Rolls Out New Model of Corporate Culture," *The Wall Street Journal*, January 13, 1999, B1, B4.

2. Joann Muller, "Ford: Why It's Worse Than You Think," *Business Week* (June 25, 2001): 80–84.

3. John A. Wagner and John R. Hollenbeck, *Management of Organizational Behavior* (Englewood Cliffs, NJ: Prentice Hall, 1992), 563–565.

4. Jay Diamond and Gerald Pintel, *Retailing*, 6th ed. (Upper Saddle River, NJ: Prentice Hall, 1996), 83–84.

5. Jacquie McNish, "A Chairman with Worries Lots of Others Would Like," *The Globe and Mail*, April 14, 1990, B6.

6. Michael E. Raynor and Joseph L. Bower, "Lead From the Center," *Harvard Business Review* (May 2001), 93–102.

7. Bruce Horovitz, "Restoring the Golden-Arch Shine," *USA Today*, June 16, 1999, 3B

8. Joann Muller, "Thinking Out of the Cereal Box," *Business Week* (January 15, 2001): 54–55.

9. Peter Larson, "Winning Strategies," *Canadian Business Review* (Summer 1989): 41.

10. Ian Allaby, "The Search for Quality," *Canadian Business* (May 1990): 31–42.

11. Donna Fenn, "Redesign Work," *Inc.* (June 1999): 75–83.

12. Gary Yukl, *Leadership in Organizations*, 5th ed. (Upper Saddle River, NJ: Prentice Hall, 2002), 35–36.

13. "Multi-Tasking: Cost-Reduction Strategy at Case Corp.," *Machinery Systems Inc.*, www.machinerysystems.com/RavingFan/CaseCorp.html, July 20, 2001.

14. Donna Fenn, "The Buyers," *Inc.* (June 1996): 46–48+.

15. Nelson Wyatt, "Bell Canada Plan Creates 3 Divisions," *Winnipeg Free Press*, May 8, 2003, B7.

16. Robert Berner and Kevin Helliker, "Heinz's Worry: 4,000 Products, Only One Star," *The Wall Street Journal*, September 17, 1999, B1, B4.

17. J. Galbraith, "Matrix Organization Designs: How to Combine Functional and Project Forms," *Business Horizons* (1971): 29–40; H.F. Kolodny, "Evolution to a Matrix Organization," *Academy of Management Review* 4 (1979): 543–553.

18. Interview with Tom Ward, operations manager for Genstar Shipyards.

19. Lawton R. Burns, "Matrix Management in Hospitals: Testing Theories of Matrix Structure and Development," *Administrative Science Quarterly* 34 (1989): 48–50.

20. Diane Brady, "Martha Inc.," *Business Week* (January 17, 2000): 62–66.

21. Gail Edmondson, "Danone Hits Its Stride," *Business Week* (February 1, 1999): 52–53.

22. Thomas A. Stewart, "See Jack. See Jack Run," *Fortune* (September 27, 1999): 124–127+.

23. Jerald Greenberg and Robert A. Baron, *Behavior in Organizations: Understanding and Managing the Human Side of Work*, 7th ed. (Upper Saddle River, NJ: Prentice Hall, 2000), 308–09.

24. Tyler Hamilton, "Welcome to the World Wide Grapevine," *The Globe and Mail*, May 6, 2000, B1, B6.

Chapter 8

1. See Angelo S. DeNisi and Ricky W. Griffin, *Human Resource Management* (Boston: Houghton Mifflin, 2001) for a complete overview.

2. Elizabeth Church, "Store Owners Struggle with Staffing," *The Globe and Mail*, November 25, 1996, B6.

3. Caroline Alphonso, "Job Fairs Draw a Crowd," *The Globe and Mail*, August 25, 2000, B7.

4. Malcolm MacKillop, "An Employer's Guide to Drug Testing," *The Globe and Mail*, April 9, 1998, B13.

5. Margot Gibb-Clark, "Ruling Narrows Options for Drug Testing," *The Globe and Mail*, July 28, 1998, B11.

6. Charles Davies, "Strategy Session 1990," *Canadian Business* (January 1990): 50.

7. Scott Feschuk, "Phi Beta Cuppa," *The Globe and Mail*, March 6, 1993, B1, B4.

8. Abby Ellin, "Training Programs Often Miss the Point on the Job," *The New York Times*, March 29, 2000, C12.

9. Janet McFarland, "Executives Saw Bonuses Slide," *The Globe and Mail*, May 1, 2003, B1, B12.

10. Elizabeth Church, "Nortel Workers Pick Tailor-Made Perks," *The Globe and Mail*, December 8, 2000, B11.

11. David Roberts, "A Long Way from Cambodia," *The Globe and Mail*, July 5, 1994, B18.

12. Ken Kilpatrick and Dawn Walton, "What a Joy to Work for Dofasco," *The Globe and Mail*, February 23, 2000, B1, B8.

13. Peter Verburg, "The Man of Steel's Fed Up," *Canadian Business* (June 26/July 10, 1998): 69.

14. Virginia Galt, "Medicare Cut Seen Raising Labour Costs," *The Globe and Mail*, February 12, 2002, B10.

15. Elizabeth Church, "Pension Plans Face $225 Billion Shortfall," *The Globe and Mail*, May 24, 2003, B1, B4.

16. Bruce McDougall, "The Thinking Man's Assembly Line," *Canadian Business* (November 1991): 40.

17. John Partridge, "B of M Lauded for Promoting Women's Careers," *The Globe and Mail*, January 7, 1994, B3.

18. Vivian Smith, "Breaking Down the Barriers," *The Globe and Mail*, November 17, 1992, B24.

19. Bob Cox, "Women Gaining on Men's Wages," *The Globe and Mail*, January 18, 1994, B4.

20. Gordon Pitts, "Equal Pay Issue: Business Uneasy," *The Financial Post*, August 31, 1985, 1–2.

21. Bruce Little, "Male Earning Power Wanes," *The Globe and Mail*, September 18, 1997, B1, B4.

22. Ted Kennedy, "Beware of Health and Safety Law: It Could Bite You," *Canadian Business* (December 1990): 19.

23. Virginia Galt and Caroline Alphonso, "Mandatory Retirement Review Launched," *The Globe and Mail*, July 28, 2000, B1–B2.

24. "Canadians Are Retiring Earlier," *Winnipeg Free Press*, June 12, 1997, B12.

25. Michael Moss, "For Older Employees, On-the-Job Injuries Are More Often Deadly," *The Wall Street Journal*, June 17, 1997, A1, A10.

26. Max Boisot, *Knowledge Assets* (Oxford: Oxford University Press, 1998).

27. Thomas Stewart, "In Search of Elusive Tech Workers," *Fortune* (February 16, 1998): 171–172.

28. Matt Richtel, "Need for Computer Experts Is Making Recruiters Frantic," *The New York Times*, December 18, 1999, C1.

29. Aaron Bernstein, "When Is a Temp Not a Temp?" *Business Week* (December 7, 1998): 90–92.

Chapter 9

1. David Lipsky and Clifford Donn, *Collective Bargaining in American Industry* (Lexington, MA: Lexington Books, 1981).

2. Statistics Canada, "Perspectives in Labour and Income," Autumn 2003, 15, 3, p. 50.

3. Statistics Canada, "Perspectives in Labour and Income," Autumn 2003, 15, 3, p. 51.

4. Susan Bourette, "Organized Labour Lures Growing Number of Youth," *The Globe and Mail*, July 4, 1997, B1, B4; Susan Bourette, "Women Make Strides in Union Movement," *The Globe and Mail*, August 29, 1997, B1–B2.

5. Greg Keenan, "CAW Targets Honda, Toyota," *The Globe and Mail*, June 15, 1999, B1, B8.

6. Sarah Binder, "McDonald's Store Closes, Union Wails," *The Globe and Mail*, February 14, 1998, B23.

7. Steven Erwin, "Inco Reaches Tentative Deal with Union," *Winnipeg Free Press*, August 27, 2003, B7.

8. Andrew Nikiforuk, "Why Safeway Struck Out," *Canadian Business* (September 1997): 27.

9. Margot Gibb-Clark, "Wounds Left by Strike Require Healing," *The Globe and Mail*, September 30, 1991, B4.

10. Jeffrey Ball, Glenn Burkins, and Gregory White, "Why Labor Unions Have Grown Reluctant to Use the S-word," *The Wall Street Journal*, December 16, 1999, A1, A8.

11. Phil Taylor, "To the Victor Belongs the Spoils," *Sports Illustrated* (January 18, 1999): 48–52.

12. Peter Verburg, "The Man of Steel's Fed Up," *Canadian Business* (June 26/July 10, 1998): 68.

13. Paul McKie, "Goldcorp Workers Accept Offer, Dismantle Union," *Winnipeg Free Press*, April 22, 2000, A6.

Chapter 10

1. Michael Stern, "Empowerment Empowers Employees," *The Globe and Mail*, December 9, 1991, B4.

2. For a detailed treatment of this entire subject area, see Gregory Moorhead and Ricky W. Griffin, *Organizational Behavior*, 6th ed. (Boston: Houghton Mifflin, 2001).

3. Margot Gibb-Clark, "Canadian Workers Need Some Respect," *The Globe and Mail*, September 4, 1991, B1, B6.

4. Margot Gibb-Clark, "Frustrated Workers Seek Goals," *The Globe and Mail*, May 2, 1991, B7.

5. Margot Gibb-Clark, "Family Ties Limit Workers," *The Globe and Mail*, January 22, 1991, B1–B2.

6. Virginia Galt, "Worker Stress Costing Economy Billions, Panel Warns," *The Globe and Mail*, July 21, 2000, B9.

7. Frederick W. Taylor, *Principles of Scientific Management* (New York: Harper and Brothers, 1911).

8. Douglas McGregor, *The Human Side of Enterprise* (New York: McGraw-Hill, 1960).

9. Abraham Maslow, "A Theory of Human Motivation," *Psychological Review* (July 1943): 370–96.

10. Frederick Herzberg, Bernard Mausner, and Barbara Bloch Snydeman, *The Motivation to Work* (New York: Wiley, 1959).

11. Victor Vroom, *Work and Motivation* (New York: Wiley, 1964); Craig Pinder, *Work Motivation* (Glenview, IL: Scott, Foresman, 1984).

12. Edwin Locke, "Toward a Theory of Task Performance and Incentives," *Organizational Behavior and Human Performance*, 3 (1968), 157–189.

13. Interviews with Sterling McLeod and Wayne Walker, senior vice-presidents of sales for Investors Group Financial Services.

14. Wilfred List, "On the Road to Profit," *The Globe and Mail*, July 10, 1991, B1, B3.

15. Gregory Moorhead and Ricky W. Griffin, *Organizational Behavior*, 6th ed. (Boston: Houghton Mifflin, 2001), Chapter 7.

16. Gregory Moorhead and Ricky W. Griffin, *Organizational Behavior*, 6th ed. (Boston: Houghton Mifflin, 2001), Chapter 7.

17. Gregory Moorhead and Ricky W. Griffin, *Organizational Behavior*, 6th ed. (Boston: Houghton Mifflin, 2001), Chapter 7.

18. Virginia Galt, "Flex-Time Helps to Attract, Keep Best Workers," *Winnipeg Free Press*, August 12, 2003, D7.

19. Robert White, "Changing Needs of Work and Family: A Union Response," *Canadian Business Review* (Autumn 1989): 31–33.

20. Margot Gibb-Clark, "Banks' Short Work Week Improves Service," *The Globe and Mail*, September 23, 1991, B4.

21. "Telecommuting Causing Work Condition Worries," *The Globe and Mail*, January 7, 2000, B8.

22. Margot Gibb-Clark, "What Shaped the Workplace in 1998," *The Globe and Mail*, December 29, 1998, B6.

23. Margot Gibb-Clark, "Satellite Office a Hit with Staff," *The Globe and Mail*, November 18, 1991, B4.

24. "Slaves of the New Economy," *Canadian Business* (April 1996): 86–92.

25. Dawn Walton, "Survey Focuses on Job Sharing," *The Globe and Mail*, June 10, 1997, B4.

26. "Insanity, Inc.," *Fast Company* (January 1999): 100–108.

27. Madelaine Drohan, "What Makes a Canadian Manager?" *The Globe and Mail*, February 25, 1997, B18.

28. Natalie Southworth, "Canadian Team Builders Turn U.S. Heads," *The Globe and Mail*, August 28, 2000, B8.

29. Bertrand Marotte, "Tellier Rises to Top in Annual Poll of Peers," *The Globe and Mail*, January 21, 2003, B1, B7.

30. Gregory Moorhead and Ricky W. Griffin, *Organizational Behavior*, 6th ed. (Boston: Houghton Mifflin, 2001), Chapters 13 and 14.

31. Gregory Moorhead and Ricky W. Griffin, *Organizational Behavior*, 6th ed. (Boston: Houghton Mifflin, 2001), Chapters 13 and 14.

32. "A Better Workplace," *Time* (April 17, 2000): 87.

33. Stephanie Armour, "More Dads Tap into Family Benefits at Work," *USA Today*, June 16, 2000, 1B.

34. Employee-Friendly Workplaces Raises Issues for Unions," *The Globe and Mail*, December 27, 2000, B1, B4.

Chapter 11

1. Eryn Brown, "America's Most Admired Companies," *Fortune* (March 1, 1999): 68, 70–73; www.walmartstores.com, accessed April 24, 2000.

2. Judy Strauss and Raymond Frost, *Marketing on the Internet* (Upper Saddle River, NJ: Prentice Hall, 1999), 266–71.

3. "Digital and Intel Complete Sale of Digital Semi-Conductor Manufacturing Operations," Intel press release, May 18, 1998.

4. Barbara McClellan, "Brazilian Revolution," *Ward's Auto World* (September 2000): 69–74. See also "E-GM Expands Its Online Sales Model," ITWorld.com, www.itworld.com/Tech/2397/IW001206hnehm, December 6, 2000.

5. Chuck Salter, "This Is One Fast Company," *Fast Company* (August 2001): 32–33.

6. Don Marshall, "Time for Just in Time," *P&IM Review* (June 1991): 20–22. See also Gregg Stocker, "Quality Function Deployment: Listening to the Voice of the Customer," *APICS: The Performance Advantage* (September 1991): 44–48.

7. Lee J. Krajewski and Larry P. Ritzman, *Operations Management: Strategy and Analysis*, 6th ed. (Upper Saddle River, NJ: Prentice Hall, 2002), 153–154, 828–829; and Robert S. Russell and Bernard W. Taylor III, *Operations Management*, 4th ed. (Upper Saddle River, NJ: Prentice Hall, 2003), 221–222, 593–595.

8. Robert S. Russell and Bernard W. Taylor III, *Operations Management*, 4th ed. (Upper Saddle River, NJ: Prentice Hall, 2003), 222–224.

9. Lee J. Krajewski and Larry P. Ritzman, *Operations Management: Strategy and Analysis*, 6th ed. (Upper Saddle River, NJ: Prentice Hall, 2002), 595.

10. Tom Murphy, "E Cyber Squeeze: The Pressure Is On," *Ward's Auto World* (December 2000), 44–47.

11. Kevin Ferguson, "Purchasing in Packs," *Business Week Online*, www.businessweek.com/1999/99_44/b3653024.htm, November 1, 1999; and Bob Wallace, "Wireless Buying Service Targets Workers in the Field," *InformationWeek Online*, www.informationweek.com/792/wireless.htm, June 26, 2000; and Jim Romeo, "U.S. B2B to Reach $2.8 Trillion by 2003," *E-Commerce Times*, www.ecommercetimes.com/perl/story/2191.html, January 12, 2000.

12. "The Disney Institute," http://www.disney.go.com/DisneyWorld/DisneyInstitute/ProfessionalPrograms/DisneyDifference/index.html, April 25, 2000.

13. Bruce Little, "Stock Answers," *The Globe and Mail*, June 6, 1995, B12.

14. Bruce McDougall, "The Thinking Man's Assembly Line," *Canadian Business* (November 1991): 40.

15. Alan Freeman, "Why Firms Avoid Taking Inventory," *The Globe and Mail*, December 12, 1994, B1, B4.

16. Clare Ansberry, "A New Hazard for Recovery: Last-Minute Pace of Orders," *The Wall Street Journal*, June 25, 2002, A1, A12.

Chapter 12

1. Marian Stinson, "Labour Productivity Continues to Fall," *The Globe and Mail*, June 13, 2003, B3.

2. Bart VanArk and Robert McGuckin, "International Comparisons of Labor Productivity and Per Capita Income," *Monthly Labor Review* (Washington, DC: U.S. Department of Labor, July 1999), 33–41.

3. Harvey Enchin, "Canada Urged to Stop Living Off Fat of the Land," *The Globe and Mail*, October 25, 1991, B1, B6.

4. U.S. Department of Labor, "Comparative Real Gross Domestic Product per Capita and per Employed Person: Fourteen Countries, 1960–1998," (Washington, DC: Bureau of Labor Statistics, March 30, 2000).

5. John Sheridan, "More Steel Productivity Gains Ahead?" *Industry Week* (September 15, 1997): 86–96.

6. Peter Kennedy, "Canfor Goes High Teach to Cut Costs," *The Globe and Mail*, July 29, 2000, 3.

7. Lee J. Krajewski and Larry P. Ritzman, *Operations Management: Strategy and Analysis*, 5th ed. (Reading, MA: Addison-Wesley, 1999), 229–230.

8. Bruce McDougall, "The Thinking Man's Assembly Line," *Canadian Business* (November 1991): 40.

9. Thomas Foster Jr., *Managing Quality: An Integrative Approach* (Upper Saddle River, NJ: Prentice Hall, 2001), 22–23.

10. Joel Kurtzman, "Is Your Company Off Course? Now You Can Find Out Why," *Fortune* (February 17, 1997): 133.

11. Ted Wakefield, "No Pain, No Gain," *Canadian Business* (January 1993): 50–54.

12. Thomas Foster Jr., *Managing Quality: An Integrative Approach* (Upper Saddle River, NJ: Prentice Hall, 2001), 325–339.

13. Thomas Foster Jr., *Managing Quality: An Integrative Approach* (Upper Saddle River, NJ: Prentice Hall, 2001), 325–329.

14. James Evans and James Dean Jr., *Total Quality: Management, Organization, and Strategy*, 2nd ed. (Cincinnati, OH: South-Western, 2000), 230.

15. Margot Gibb-Clark, "Hospital Managers Gain Tool to Compare Notes," *The Globe and Mail*, September 9, 1996, B9

16. "Customer Service You Can Taste," *Canadian Business* (July 1991): 19–20.

17. See "ISO 9001 Registration Helps Improve Airport Security," *Quality Digest*, www.qualitydigest.com/currentmag/html/news.html, June 9, 2002; and "A Call for Consistency in the Quality of Airline Security Screening Services," *American Society for Quality*, www.asq.org/news/interest/airportsecurity.html, December 18, 2002.

18. Roberta S. Russell and Bernard W. Taylor III, *Operations Management*, 4th ed. (Upper Saddle River, NJ: Prentice Hall, 2003), 658–662; and Thomas Foster Jr., *Managing Quality: An Integrative Approach* (Upper Saddle River, NJ: Prentice Hall, 2001), 85–86.

19. Roberta S. Russell and Bernard W. Taylor III, *Operations Management*, 4th ed. (Upper Saddle River, NJ: Prentice Hall, 2003), 137–140.

20. Sunil Chopra and Peter Meindl, *Supply Chain Management: Strategy, Planning, and Operation*, 6th ed. (Upper Saddle River, NJ: Prentice Hall, 2001), 3–6; Lee J. Krajewski and Larry P. Ritzman, *Operations Management: Strategy and Analysis*, 5th ed. (Reading, MA: Addison-Wesley, 1999), Chapter 11; Roberta S. Russell and Bernard W. Taylor III, *Operations Management*, 4th ed. (Upper Saddle River, NJ: Prentice Hall, 2003), Chapter 7; and Thomas Foster Jr., *Managing Quality: An Integrative Approach* (Upper Saddle River, NJ: Prentice Hall, 2001), Chapter 9.

21. Sunil Chopra and Peter Meindl, *Supply Chain Management: Strategy, Planning, and Operation*, 6th ed. (Upper Saddle River, NJ: Prentice Hall, 2001), Chapter 20.

22. Sunil Chopra and Peter Meindl, *Supply Chain Management: Strategy, Planning, and Operation*, 6th ed. (Upper Saddle River, NJ: Prentice Hall, 2001), 348–349.

23. Catherine Greenman, "An Old Craft Learns New Tricks," *The New York Times*, June 10, 1999, G1, G7.

24. "Motorola," *Online.Internet*, www.motorola.com, May 24, 2000.

25. Evaluate the Value of Training," *Quality* (April 2002): 48.

26. Leonard L. Berry, A. Parasuraman, and Valarie A. Zeithaml, "Improving Service Quality in America: Lessons Learned," *Academy of Management Executive* 8, no. 2 (1994): 32–45.

Chapter 13

1. Kenneth C. Laudon and Jane P. Laudon, *Management Information Systems: Managing the Digital Firm*, 7th ed. (Upper Saddle River, NJ: Prentice Hall, 2002), 7–11.

2. Kenneth C. Laudon and Jane P. Laudon, *Essentials of Management Information Systems*, 3rd ed. (Upper Saddle River, NJ: Prentice Hall, 1999), 267.

3. Kenneth C. Laudon and Jane P. Laudon, *Essentials of Management Information Systems*, 3rd ed. (Upper Saddle River, NJ: Prentice Hall, 1999), 270.

4. Kenneth C. Laudon and Jane P. Laudon, *Essentials of Management Information Systems*, 3rd ed. (Upper Saddle River, NJ: Prentice Hall, 1999), 273.

5. Mary J. Cronin, "Ford's Intranet Success," *Fortune* (March 30, 1998): 158.

6. Lee J. Krajewski and Larry P. Ritzman, *Operations Management: Strategy and Analysis*, 6th ed. (Upper Saddle River, NJ: Prentice Hall, 2002), 106.

7. Lee J. Krajewski and Larry P. Ritzman, *Operations Management: Strategy and Analysis*, 6th ed. (Upper Saddle River, NJ: Prentice Hall, 2002), 232–233.

8. Joshua Macht, "The Ultimate Head Trip," *Inc. Technology* 3 (1997): 77.

9. Gene Bylinsky, "Industry's Amazing Instant Prototypes," *Fortune* (January 12, 1998): 120(B–D).

10. Kenneth C. Laudon and Jane P. Laudon, *Essentials of Management Information Systems*, 3rd ed. (Upper Saddle River, NJ: Prentice Hall, 1999), 383–391.

11. Geoffrey Rowan, "Unique Software Thinks Like a Human," *The Globe and Mail*, December 31, 1996, B1, B4.

12. Kenneth C. Laudon and Jane P. Laudon, *Essentials of Management Information Systems*, 3rd ed. (Upper Saddle River, NJ: Prentice Hall, 1999),

383–388. E. Wainwright Martin et al., *Managing Information Technology: What Managers Need to Know*, 3rd ed. (Upper Saddle River, NJ: Prentice Hall, 1999), 225–227.

13. Emily Smith, "Turning an Expert's Skills into Computer Software," *Business Week* (October 7, 1985): 104–107.

14. Heather Green et al., "It's Time for Rules in Wonderland," *Business Week* (February 21, 2000): 82–88+; Ira Sager et al., "Cyber Crime," *Business Week* (February 21, 2000): 36–42; Ira Sager, Neil Gross, and John Carey, "Locking Out the Hackers," *Business Week* (February 28, 2000): 32–34.

15. Larry Long and Nancy Long, *Computers: Information Technology in Perspective*, 9th ed. (Upper Saddle River, NJ: Prentice Hall, 2002), 52–54.

16. Larry Long and Nancy Long, *Computers: Information Technology in Perspective*, 9th ed. (Upper Saddle River, NJ: Prentice Hall, 2002), 101–106.

17. Kenneth C. Laudon and Jane P. Laudon, *Management Information Systems: Managing the Digital Firm*, 7th ed. (Upper Saddle River, NJ: Prentice Hall, 2002), 237–244.

18. Nathalie Raffray, "Portal Power," *Communications International* (August 2001), 30–35; and David Maloney, "The Newest Better Idea at Ford," *Modern Materials Handling* (June 2000), 34–39. Kenneth C. Laudon and Jane P. Laudon, *Management Information Systems: Managing the Digital Firm*, 7th ed. (Upper Saddle River, NJ: Prentice Hall, 2002), 239–244.

Chapter 14

1. Ronald Hilton, *Managerial Accounting*, 2nd ed. (New York: McGraw-Hill, 1994), 7.

2. Mark Heinzl, "Noranda to Shed Interests in Forestry and Energy, Refocusing on Mining," *The Wall Street Journal*, November 19, 1997, A3, A6.

3. Elizabeth MacDonald, "Accounting Sleuths Ferret Hidden Assets," *The Wall Street Journal*, December 18, 1996, B1–B2.

4. Philip Mathias, "Non-Profits Fight Move to GAAP Accounting," *The Financial Post*, March 5, 1994, 15.

5. This section is based on material from the following sources: AICPA, "CPA Vision Project," www.aicpa.org/vision/index.htm, August 12, 2002; and AICPA, "CPA Vision Project: 2011 and Beyond," www.cpavision.org, August 12, 2002.

6. Charles T. Horngren, Walter T. Harrison Jr., and Linda Smith Bamber, *Accounting*, 5th ed. (Upper Saddle River, NJ: Prentice Hall, 2002), 11–12, 39–41.

7. Charles T. Horngren, Walter T. Harrison Jr., and Linda Smith Bamber, *Accounting*, 5th ed. (Upper Saddle River, NJ: Prentice Hall, 2002), 41–56.

8. Charles T. Horngren, Walter T. Harrison Jr., and Linda Smith Bamber, *Accounting*, 5th ed. (Upper Saddle River, NJ: Prentice Hall, 2002), 17–20.

9. Ronald Hilton, *Managerial Accounting*, 2nd ed. (New York: McGraw-Hill, 1994), 402–403.

10. Billie Cunningham, Loren Nikolai, and John Bazley, *Accounting: Information for Business Decisions* (Fort Worth, TX: Dryden, 2000), 133–134.

11. Charles T. Horngren, Walter T. Harrison, Jr., and Linda Smith Bamber, *Accounting*, 4th ed. (Upper Saddle River, NJ: Prentice Hall, 1999), 562–563; Arthur J. Keown et al., *The Foundations of Finance: The Logic and Practice of Financial Management*, 2nd ed. (Upper Saddle River, NJ: Prentice Hall, 1998), 89–95.

12. Charles T. Horngren, Walter T. Harrison, Jr., and Linda Smith Bamber, *Accounting*, 4th ed. (Upper Saddle River, NJ: Prentice Hall, 1999), 201–202.

13. Frederick D. S. Choi, Carol Ann Frost, and Gary K. Meek, *International Accounting*, 4th ed. (Upper Saddle River: Prentice Hall, 2002), 267–279.

Chapter 15

1. American Marketing Association, "Marketing Services Guide," www.ama.org/about/ama/markdef.asp, August 23, 2001.

2. Philip Kotler, *Marketing Management*, 11th ed. (Upper Saddle River, NJ: Prentice Hall, 2003), 76–78.

3. Philip Kotler and Peggy Cunningham, *Marketing Management* (Toronto: Prentice-Hall, 2004), 18.

4. Lauren Goldstein, "Dressing Up an Old Brand," *Fortune* (November 9, 1998): 154–156.

5. Jane Perlez, "Joy of Debts: Eastern Europe on Credit Fling," *The New York Times*, May 30, 1998, A3.

6. Philip Kotler, *Marketing Management*, 11th ed. (Upper Saddle River, NJ: Prentice Hall, 2003), 292–294.

7. John Morton, "How to Spot the Really Important Prospects," *Business Marketing* (January 1990): 62–67.

8. Paul Sutter, "How to Succeed in Bubble Gum Without Really Trying," *Canadian Business* (January 1992): 48–50.

9. Alvin C. Burns and Ronald F. Bush, *Marketing Research*, 3rd ed. (Upper Saddle River, NJ: Prentice Hall, 2000), 70-84.

10. Marina Strauss, "First You Have to Get Their Attention," *The Globe and Mail*, July 12, 1991, B1.

11. Alvin C. Burns and Ronald F. Bush, *Marketing Research*, 3rd ed. (Upper Saddle River, NJ: Prentice Hall, 2000), Chapter 9.

12. Oliver Bertin, "John Deere Reaps the Fruits of Its Labours," *The Globe and Mail*, September 2, 1991, B1, B3.

13. Sean Silcoff, "2nd Time Trendy," *Canadian Business* (May 29, 2000): 34–39.

14. Alvin C. Burns and Ronald F. Bush, *Marketing Research*, 3rd ed. (Upper Saddle River, NJ: Prentice Hall, 2000), 140–148.

15. Kenneth C. Laudon and Jane P. Laudon, *Management Information Systems: Managing the Digital Firm*, 7th ed. (Upper Saddle River, NJ: Prentice Hall, 2002), 221–222.

16. Kenneth C. Laudon and Jane P. Laudon, *Management Information Systems: Managing the Digital Firm*, 7th ed. (Upper Saddle River, NJ: Prentice Hall, 2002), 222–224.

17. Paul S. Foote and Malini Krishnamurthi, "Forecasting Using Data Warehousing Model: Wal-Mart's Experience," *The Journal of Business Forecasting Methods & Systems* (Fall 2001): 13–17.

18. Robyn Greenspan, "The Web as a Way of Life," www.cyberatlas.com, May 21, 2002.

19. Thomas Russell, Glenn Verrill, and W. Ronald Lane, *Kleppner's Advertising Procedure*, 11th ed. (Englewood Cliffs, NJ: Prentice-Hall, 1990); James Engel, Martin Warshaw, and Thomas Kinnear, *Promotional Strategy*, 6th ed. (Homewood, IL: Richard D. Irwin, 1987).

Chapter 16

1. Dan Verton, "Oracle Scraps Unpopular Database Pricing Model: Oracle Faces Challenges in the Marketplace," *Computerworld* (June 18, 2001): 6, 8.

2. Philip Kotler, *Marketing Management*, 11th ed. (Upper Saddle River, NJ: Prentice Hall, 2003), Chapter 3; Roger J. Best, *Market-Based Management: Strategies for Growing Customer Value and Profitability*, 2nd ed. (Upper Saddle River, NJ: Prentice Hall, 2000), 87–100.

3. Patricia Lush, "From Pipe Dream to Profit," *The Globe and Mail*, December 12, 1994, B6.

4. Philip Kotler, *Marketing Management*, 11th ed. (Upper Saddle River, NJ: Prentice Hall, 2003), 328–339.

5. Philip Kotler, *Marketing Management*, 11th ed. (Upper Saddle River, NJ: Prentice Hall, 2003), 422–424.

6. Gordon Pitts, "New Irving Generation Broadens Horizons," *The Globe and Mail*, January 18, 2003, B1, B4.

7. Gerry Khermouch, Stanley Holmes, and Moon Ihlwan, "The Best Global Brands," *Business Week* (August 6, 2001): 50–57.

8. Eloise Coupey, *Marketing and the Internet* (Upper Saddle River, NJ: Prentice Hall, 2001), 174–179.

9. John Frook, "Cisco Scores with Its Latest Generation of Empowering Tools," *B to B* (August 20, 2001): 20.

10. Marc Gunther, "The Cheering Fades for Yahoo," *Fortune* (November 12, 2001), 151–158.

11. Lori Mitchell, "Branding Equals Smart E-Business," *InfoWorld*, www.InfoWorld.com/articles/tc/xml/00/12/18/001218tcbranding.xml, December 15, 2000; Robyn Greenspan, "Brand Opening," *ECommerce-Guide*, http://ecommerce.internet.com/news/insights/ectips/article/0,,6311_557131,00.html, January 10, 2001; Kris Wadia, "Top 10 Myths of E-Branding," *Business-Minds*, www.business-minds.com/article.asp?item=68, May 17, 2001.

12. Eileen Kinsella, "Corporate Names Go Quirky," *The Globe and Mail*, May 20, 1997, B12.

13. Cyndee Miller, "Little Relief Seen for New Product Failure Rate," *Marketing News* (June 21, 1993): 1; Nancy J. Kim, "Back to the Drawing Board," *The Bergen [New Jersey] Record*, December 4, 1994, B1, B4.

14. Brian Milner, "Canada's Franklin the Turtle Heads South," *The Globe and Mail*, February 14, 2000, B1, B10.

15. Marina Strauss, "Holt Renfrew Brands a Strategy," *The Globe and Mail*, March 20, 1997, B13.

16. David Square, "Mouse Pad Gets Oodles of Nibbles," *The Winnipeg Free Press*, July 26, 1997, B10.

17. Marina Strauss, "Consumers Less Trusting of Brands," *The Globe and Mail*, February 13, 2003, B3.

18. William Pride and O.C. Ferrell, *Marketing*, 5th ed. (Boston: Houghton Mifflin, 1987).

19. Robert Berner, "The Rolls-Royce of Leather Jackets Is Hard to Come By," *The Wall Street Journal*, November 22, 1996, A1, A10.

20. Kenneth E. Clow and Donald Baack, *Integrated Advertising, Promotion, and Marketing Communications* (Upper Saddle River, NJ: Prentice Hall, 2002), Chapter 5.

21. John Heinzl, "Buckley Wants U.S. to Swallow Its Bad Taste," *The Globe and Mail*, November 11, 1999, B1, B12.

22. Marina Strauss, "Towel War Turns to Name-Naming," *The Globe and Mail*, December 5, 1995, B1, B10.

23. "Regulators Wary of Ads Rapping Rivals," *The Globe and Mail*, May 23, 1991, B4.

24. Stuart Elliot, "Topsy-turvey Becomes Darling of Print Ads," *The Globe and Mail*, February 25, 1992, B1, B6.

25. Marina Strauss, "This Billboard Wants to Pass You By," *The Globe and Mail*, February 27, 1992, B4.

26. Laurie Ward, "Big Rock Brews Strong U.S. Growth," *The Financial Post*, September 25, 1993, 7.

27. "BMCMedia Signs DART Contract with DoubleClick," *List-News.com*, http://listnews.com/articles/01may/20010508.html, May 1, 2001.

28. Simon Tuck, "Security Rated Top On-Line Fear," *The Globe and Mail*, July 5, 1999, B5.

29. Stuart Elliott, "Real or Virtual? You Call It," *The New York Times*, October 1, 1999, C1, C6.

30. William Wells, John Burnett, and Sandra Moriarty, *Advertising: Principles and Practice*, 5th ed. (Upper Saddle River, NJ: Prentice Hall, 2000), 77–83.

31. Ann Gibbon, "Ad Group Tries to Demystify Quebec," *The Globe and Mail*, November 25, 1993, B6.

32. "Regulators Wary of Ads Rapping Rivals," *The Globe and Mail*, May 23, 1991, B4.

33. Ira Teinowitz and Cara B. Dipasquale, "Direct Marketers Take Issue with Proposed FTC Rules," *Advertising Age* (January 28, 2002): 3, 29; Larry Neilson, "Look Out for Telemarketing Speed Bumps," *National Underwriter* (September 17, 2001): 12–14.

34. John Heinzl, "Beer Firms Rethink Giveaways," *The Globe and Mail*, March 3, 2003, B1, B5.

35. "Pageant Runner-Up Looks for Compensation," *The Winnipeg Free Press*, February 3, 1998, A4.

36. Warren J. Keegan, *Global Marketing Management*, 7th ed. (Upper Saddle River, NJ: Prentice Hall, 2002), Chapter 14.

37. Norman M. Scarborough and Thomas W. Zimmerer, *Effective Small Business Management: An Entrepreneurial Approach*, 6th ed. (Upper Saddle River, NJ: Prentice Hall, 2000), Chapter 11.

Chapter 17

1. Constance L. Hays, "Coke Tests Weather-Linked Pricing," *The Globe and Mail*, October 29, 1999, B11.

2. Stefan Fatsis, "The Barry Bonds Tax: Teams Raise Prices for Good Games," *The Wall Street Journal*, December 3, 2002, D1, D8.

3. Stephen Kindel, "Tortoise Gains on Hare," *Financial World* (February 23, 1988): 18–20.

4. Chet Zelasko, "Acesulfame-K," *Better Life Institute*, www.blionline.com/HDB/Acesulfame-K.htm, May 17, 2001.

5. Stewart A. Washburn, "Establishing Strategy and Determining Cost in the Pricing Decision," *Business Marketing* (July 1985): 64–78.

6. Judy Strauss and Raymond Frost, *E-Marketing*, 2nd ed. (Upper Saddle River, NJ: Prentice Hall, 2001), 166–167; Eloise Coupey, *Marketing and the Internet* (Upper Saddle River, NJ: Prentice Hall, 2001), 281–283.

7. Robert D. Hof and Linda Himelstein, "eBay vs. Amazon.com," *Business Week* (May 31, 1999): 128–321; Janet Rae-Dupree and Diane Brady, "Let the Buyer Be in Control," *Business Week* (November 8, 1999), 100.

8. Duncan Stewart, "Say Goodbye to the Middleman," *The Globe and Mail*, April 19, 2000, B14.

9. Ahmad Diba, "An Old-Line Agency Finds an Online Niche," *Fortune* (April 3, 2000): 258.

10. Dell Annual Report: *FY2001 Year in Review*, www.dell.com, April 22, 2002. Qiao Song, "Legend Outlines Role in China's Wireless Future," *ebn* (March 25, 2002): 3; Faith Hung, "Legend Looks to Defend Its Turf—WTO Entry Will Force China's Top PC Maker to Fend Off Unrestricted Rivals," *ebn* (December 17, 2001): 44; and Neel Chowdhury, "Dell Cracks China," *Fortune* (June 21, 1999): 120–124.

11. Keith McArthur, "Para Paints' Bold Stroke," *The Globe and Mail*, October 18, 1999, M1.

12. Dale M. Lewison, *Retailing*, 5th ed. (New York: Macmillan, 1994), 454; Louis Stern and Adel I. El-Ansary, *Marketing Channels*, 4th ed. (Englewood Cliffs, NJ: Prentice Hall, 1992), 129–130.

13. Leigh Buchanan, "The Best of the Small Business Web," *Inc. Tech* 4 (1999): 67, 72.

14. *Expedia.com*, www.expedia.com, July 8, 2002.

15. Marina Strauss, "American Eagle Snares Chains from Dylex," *The Globe and Mail*, August 25, 2000, B1, B2.

16. Gene Gray, "The Future of the Teleservices Industry—Are You Aware," *Telemarketing* (January 1999): 90–96.

17. "Canadians Spent $2 Billion Net Shopping," *Winnipeg Free Press*, September 20, 2002, B10.

18. "Did You Know?" *Catalog News.com*, www.catalog-news.com, April 8, 2002; Judy Strauss and Raymond Frost, *E-Marketing*, (Upper Saddle River, NJ: Prentice Hall, 2001), 140.

19. Carolyn Brackett, "Setting Up Shop in Cyberspace," *Inc.com*, www.inc.com/conducting_commerce/advice/15237.html, May 20, 2002; David Radin, "'Electronic Mall Syndrome' Gives Way to Unified Buying," *eBusiness News*, http://ebusiness.dci.com/articles/1998/05/14radin.htm, May 20, 2002; Garrett Wasny, "Free Electronic Storefronts," www.howtoconquertheworld.com/gohome111.htm, July, 2000.

20. Peter Elkind, "Shhhhh! Amway's on the Web," *Fortune* (March 6, 2000): 76.

21. "LivePerson.com™," www.liveperson.com, April 19, 2000.

22. Anne T. Coughlan et al., *Marketing Channels*, 6th ed. (Upper Saddle River, NJ: Prentice Hall, 2001), 458–462.

23. Bill Redekop, "The Crow Subsidy Is History," *Winnipeg Free Press*, February 28, 1995, 1.

Chapter 18

1. Andrew Higgins, "Lacking Money to Pay, Russian Firms Survive on Deft Barter System," *The Wall Street Journal*, August 27, 1998, pp. A1, A6.

2. Table E1, *Bank of Canada Review* (May, 2003), S-50.

3. Table E1, *Bank of Canada Review* (May, 2003), S-50.

4. Nancy Carr, "More Canadians Turning to Alternative Banks," *Winnipeg Free Press*, July 21, 2003, B7.

5. Jim Middlemiss, "Banks Get Smart About Computer Chips," *Bank Systems & Technology* (April 2002): 44; and Lisa Daigle, "Beyond Expectations," *Credit Card Management* (May 2000): 50–52.

6. Karen Horcher, "Reconstruction Zone," *CGA Magazine* (June 1997): 19.

7. Robert J. Carbaugh, *International Economics*, 5th ed. (Cincinnati: South-Western, 1995), Chapter 11.

Chapter 19

1. Joseph Nocera, "Do You Believe? How Yahoo! Became a Blue Chip," *Fortune* (June 7, 1999): 76–81.

2. Cory Johnson, "The Internet Blue Chip," *The Industry Standard*, www.thestandard.com/article/0,1902,4088,00html, August 7, 2001; and Chris Nerney "Yahoo!: Bargain or Big Trouble?" *The Internet Stock Report*, www.internetstockreport.com/column/print/0,,530021,00.html, August 7, 2001.

3. George G. Kaufman, *The U.S. Financial System: Money, Markets, and Institutions*, 6th ed. (Englewood Cliffs, NJ: Prentice Hall, 1995), 432.

4. Chilik Wollenberg, "How Does Your Broker Measure Up?" *Medical Economics* (May 28, 2001): 98–100; and Leah Nathans Spiro and Edward C. Baig, "Who Needs a Broker?" *Business Week* (February 22, 1999): 113–161.

5. Borzou Daragahi, "E-Finance Forecast," *Money* (March 2001): 129–133; and Joseph Kahn, "Schwab Lands Feet First on Net," *New York Times*, February 10, 1999, C1, C5.

6. Richard Blackwell, "TSE Sees Few Gains from Realignment," *The Globe and Mail*, May 23, 2000, 12.

7. Gordon J. Alexander, William F. Sharpe, and Jeffery V. Bailey, *Fundamentals of Investments*, 3rd ed. (Upper Saddle River, NJ: Prentice Hall, 2001), 36–39.

8. Gordon J. Alexander, William F. Sharpe, and Jeffery V. Bailey, *Fundamentals of Investments*, 3rd ed. (Upper Saddle River, NJ: Prentice Hall, 2001), 39.

9. Gordon J. Alexander, William F. Sharpe, and Jeffery V. Bailey, *Fundamentals of Investments*, 3rd ed. (Upper Saddle River, NJ: Prentice Hall, 2001), 44–46.

10. *Nasdaq*, www. nasdaq.com/about/timeline.stm, June 25, 2000.

11. *NASD*, www.nasd.com, June 25, 2000.

12. "Nasdaq 2001 Annual Report, " www.nasdaq.com/investorrelations/annualreport2001, October 31, 2002. "The World in Its Hands," *The Economist* (May 6, 2000): 77; "The Nasdaq Japan Market Launches First Day of Trading; First Step in Creating Nasdaq Global Platform Is Achieved," www.nasdaq.co.uk/reference, June 19, 2000; and "Globalization and International Reach," *Nasdaq Initiatives*, www.nasdaq.com, June 23, 2000.

13. Steven Greenhouse, "Exchanges Thrive as Russians Pursue Market Economy," *Winnipeg Free Press*, November 3, 1991, B13.

14. Richard Blackwell, "TSE 300 Shift Will Shrink Index," *The Globe and Mail*, January 31, 2002, B17.

15. Rob Carrick, "Direct Plans Cut Brokers Out," *The Globe and Mail*, August 21, 1999, B8.

16. Gretchen Morgenson, "Buying on Margin Becomes a Habit," *New York Times* (March 24, 2000), C1, C7; and David Barboza, "Wall Street after Dark," *New York Times* (February 13, 2000), BU1, BU14–BU15.

17. Gordon J. Alexander, William F. Sharpe, and Jeffery V. Bailey, *Fundamentals of Investments*, 3rd ed. (Upper Saddle River, NJ: Prentice Hall, 2001), 37–38.

18. U.S. Securities and Exchange Commission, "SEC Charges Former ImClone CEO Samuel Waksal with Illegal Insider Trading," www.sec.gov/news/press.shtml, June 12, 2002; Andrew Pollack, "ImClone's Ex-Chief in Talks with U.S. on Plea Agreement," *New York Times on the Web*, www.nytimes.com/2002/07/13/business, July 13, 2002; "Martha Scrutiny Heats Up," *CNNMoney*, www.cnnfn.com, June 14, 2002.

Chapter 20

1. David F. Scott et al., *Basic Financial Management*, 8th ed. (Upper Saddle River, NJ: Prentice Hall, 1999), 626–627.

2. "Britain's Third Biggest Bank Sees 2001 Net Profit Fall as Bad-Debt Provisions Rise," *CNNMoney* www.cnnfn.com, February 15, 2002; "SocGen, Abbey National Set Aside Money for Bad Loans, Profits Decline," *CNNMoney*, www.cnnfn.com, February 21, 2002; and James Cox, "Argentina Pins Hope On Debt-Swap proposal," *World Business*, www.usatoday.com, November 11, 2002.

3. John Heinzl, "Good Strategy Gone Awry, Top Retailer's Tale of Woe," *The Globe and Mail*, March 7, 1992, B1, B4.

4. *The State of Small Business, 1989 Annual Report on Small Business in Ontario* (Toronto: Ministry of Industry, Trade and Technology, 1990).

5. J.W. Duncan, *D&B Reports* (September–October 1991): 8.

6. Norman M. Scarborough and Thomas W. Zimmerer, *Effective Small Business Management: An Entrepreneurial Approach*, 6th ed. (Upper Saddle River: Prentice Hall, 2000), esp. pp. 298–300.

7. Susan Hodges, "One Big Step Toward a Loan," *Nation's Business* (August 1997): 34–36.

8. Richard S. Boulton, Barry D. Libert, and Steve M. Samek, "Managing Risk in an Uncertain World," *Upside* (June 2000): 268–278.

9. Thomas P. Fitch, *Dictionary of Banking Terms*, 2nd ed. (Hauppauge, NY: Barron's, 1993), 531.

10. Mark S. Dorfman, *Introduction to Risk Management and Insurance*, 6th ed. (Upper Saddle River, NJ: Prentice Hall, 2000), Chapter 1.

11. Denyse O'Leary, "The Scams That Drive Up Premiums," *The Globe and Mail*, May 2, 1995, B1; Denyse O'Leary, "Insurers United Against Fraud Face Serious Obstacles," *The Globe and Mail*, May 2, 1995, B1.

12. Mark S. Dorfman, *Introduction to Risk Management and Insurance*, 6th ed. (Upper Saddle River, NJ: Prentice Hall, 2000), 420–421.

Appendix B

1. Figure estimated from 1988-89 *Property/Casualty Fact Book*, p. 19.

2. Gayle MacDonald, "How an Eaton's Supplier Cut Risk," *The Globe and Mail*, March 17, 1997, p. B7.

3. *National Post*, June 2003, p. 140.

Source Notes

Chapter 1

The Long Road to Voisey's Bay Wendy Stueck, "Inco Shares Fall on Voisey's Overrun," *The Globe and Mail*, March 21, 2003, B13; Allan Robinson, "Inco, Province Inch Toward Deal on Voisey's Bay," *The Globe and Mail*, October 12, 2001, B3; James Stevenson, "Inco Grilled Despite Impressive Rebound," *Winnipeg Free Press*, April 20, 2000, B7; "Giant Newfoundland Nickel Project May Soon Proceed," *Winnipeg Free Press*, November 23, 1999, B8; Allan Robinson, "Inco President Willing to Compromise on Voisey's Bay," *The Globe and Mail*, April 29, 1999, B1, B4; Allan Robinson, "Inco to Halt Voisey's Bay Work," *The Globe and Mail*, July 28, 1998, B1, B6; Allan Robinson, "Inco Chairman Defends Actions," *The Globe and Mail*, April 23, 1998, B3. **It's a Wired World** James Careless, "Airlines Going On-Line with 'Virtual Marketplace'," *The Globe and Mail*, July 31, 2003, B8; Dawn Walton, "Net B2B Soaring to Lofty Heights," *The Globe and Mail*, April 28, 2000, B10; Oracle Corp., "Partner Solutions," www.oracle.com/partners/content.html, March 8, 2000; John Partridge, "Two Banks, Bell Part of Big E-commerce Venture," *The Globe and Mail*, September 27, 2000, B1, B11. **Table 1.1** *National Post Business* (June 2003): 124. **Business Today** Trevor Harrison, "Demon Rum and the Perils of Privatization," *Winnipeg Free Press*, June 19, 2003, A13; John Cotter, "Privatized Liquor Stores a Flop, Study Suggests," *Winnipeg Free Press*, June 6, 2003, A20; Bill Redekopp, "Private Wine Stores Cheesed with MLCC," *Winnipeg Free Press*, July 8, 2000, A6; David Menzies, "Sour Grapes," *Canadian Business* (February 26, 1999): 28–35; Brian Hutchinson, "Cheers!," *Canadian Business* (November 1994): 23–28. **Concluding Case 1-1** Summarized from Gregory L. White, "How Ford's Big Batch of Rare Metal Led to $1 Billion Write-Off," *The Wall Street Journal*, February 6, 2002, A1, A6. **Concluding Case 1-2** Chris Taylor, "California Scheming," *Time* (May 20, 2002): 42–44; Richard A. Oppel Jr., "How Enron Got California to Buy Power It Didn't Need," *New York Times*, May 8, 2002, C1, C6; Mark Gimein, "Who Turned the Lights Out?" *Fortune* (February 5, 2001): 110–141; Holman Jenkins Jr., "Enron for Beginners," *The Wall Street Journal*, January 23, 2002, A1, A17; Delroy Alexander, "Keener Focus on Enron Deals," *Chicago Tribune*, February 20, 2002, C1; Brock N. Meeks, "Enron Sailed into a Perfect Storm," *QwestLightspeed*, www.msnbc.com/news/692391.asp, January 23, 2002; Nelson D. Schwartz, "Is Energy Trading a Big Scam?" *Fortune* (June 10, 2002): 126–281; Neela Banerjee, "Who Will Needle Regulators Now That Enron's Muzzled?" *New York Times*, January 20, 2002, Sec. 3, 1, 12

Chapter 2

Upheaval in the Airline Industry Jacquie McNish, "Skittish Travelers Shifting Bus Tour Firm Into Reverse," *The Globe and Mail*, June 11, 2003, B1, B4; Keith McArthur, "Air Canada to Fight Hostile Motions," *The Globe and Mail*, April 21, 2003, B1, B8; Bruce Little, "SARS Infects Asian Growth," *The Globe and Mail*, April 22, 2003, B1, B2; John Saunders, "Outbreak Causes High Demand for Masks," *The Globe and Mail*, April 22, 2003, B1, B2; Paul Waldie, Brent Jang, and Dawn Walton, "Tourism Industry Braces for Slack Season," *The Globe and Mail*, April 14, 2003, B1, B7; Allan Swift, "Air Canada Fighting for Life," *Winnipeg Free Press*, April 2, 2003, A1, A5; Steve Erwin, "Nav Takes Air Canada to Court," *Winnipeg Free Press*, April 22, 2003, B7; Gordon Pitts, "War Seen Spurring Air Revamp," *The Globe and Mail*, March 20, 2003, B7; Jacquie McNish, "Bus Firm Feels Ill Effects of SARS Outbreak," *The Globe and Mail*, April 28, 2003, B1, B5. **Figure 2.3** *Bank of Canada Banking and Financial Statistics* (June 2000); Table H-8, *Bank of Canada Banking and Financial Statistics, June 2000*. *Bank of Canada Review* (May 2003): S-102. **Figure 2.4** *Bank of Canada Banking and Financial Statistics* (June 2000); Table H5, *Bank of Canada Banking and Financial Statistics*, June 2000, Table H5, p. 599; *Bank of Canada Review* (May 2003): S-99. **Figure 2.5** Michael J. Mandel, "The New Economy," *Business Week* (January 31, 2000): 75; Data from *Computer Industry Almanac*. **Figure 2.6** Michael J. Mandel, "The New Economy," *Business Week* (January 31, 2000): 77. Data from International Data Corp. **Figure 2.7** Michael J. Mandel, "The New Economy," *Business Week* (January 31, 2000): 75. Data from Standard & Poor's DRI. **Figure 2.8** Statistics Canada, *Industrial R & D Statistics* (1989, catalogue number 88-202), 15, 21, chart 1.1; Statistics Canada, *Industrial Research and Development, 2002 Intentions*, p. 14. **Figure 2.9** Adapted from Cedric X. Scalle and Mark J. Cotteleer, *Enterprise Resource Planning (ERP)*. (Boston: Harvard Business School Publishing, No. 9-699-020, 1999). **Figure 2.10** Michael E. Porter, *Competitive Strategy: Techniques for Analyzing Industries and Competitors* (New York: The Free Press, 1980). Reprinted with permission. **It's a Wired World** Jens Clausen, Jesper Hansen, Jesper Larsen, and Allan Larsen, "Disruption Management," *ORMS Today* (October 2001): 40–43. **Business Today** Peter Schroedter, "Ranchers Will Pay Price for BSE," *Winnipeg Free Press*, June 24, 2003, A13; Ted Davis, "Toronto Fights Back," *Winnipeg Free Press*, June 7, 2003, E1, E12; David Paddon, "SARS Outbreak Slows Growth in China, Nortel CEO Says," *Winnipeg Free Press*, May 29, 2003, B8; "SARS Outbreak Increases Demand for Firm's Products," *Winnipeg Free Press*, May 13, 2003, B7; Peter Kennedy, "SARS Seen Stifling Asian Growth," *The Globe and Mail*, April 29, 2003, B10; Jacquie McNish, "Bus Firm Feels Ill Effects of SARS," *The Globe and Mail*, April 28, 2003, B1, B5; Marina Strauss, "Some Companies Clean Up with SARS-Aimed Products," *The Globe and Mail*, April 25, 2003, B11; John Partridge, "Disease Cramps Manulife Sales in Asia," *The Globe and Mail*, April 25, 2003, B3; John Saunders, "Outbreak Causes High Demand for Masks," *The Globe and Mail*, April 22, 2003, B1, B2; Bruce Little, "SARS Infects Asian Growth," *The Globe and Mail*, April 22, 2003, B1, B2; Katherine Harding, "How HP Handled Urgent SARS Alert," *The Globe and Mail*, April 17, 2003, B1, B8; Paul Waldie, Brent Jang, and Dawn Walton, "Tourism Industry Braces for Slack Season," *The Globe and Mail*, April 14, 2003, B1, B7. **Concluding Case 2-1** Richard Bloom, "RBC Reclaims Top Spot in Survey," *The Globe and Mail*, January 20, 2003, B1, B5; Matthew Boyle, "The Right Stuff," *Fortune* (March 4, 2002): 85–86; Matthew Boyle, "The Shiniest Reputations in Tarnished Times," *Fortune* (March 4, 2002): 70–72; Justin Fox, "What's So Great About GE?," *Fortune* (March 4, 2002): 64–67. **Concluding Case 2-2** Summarized from Gautam Naik, Vanessa Fuhrmans, Jonathan Karp, Joel Millman, Farnaz Fassihi, and Joanna Slater, "Global Baby Bust," *The Wall Street Journal*, January 24, 2003, B1, B4.

Chapter 3

Family Feuds Gordon Pitts, "Dare Leader No Chip Off the Old Block," *The Globe and Mail*, December 5, 2002, B1, B15; Paul Waldie, "Mitchell's Feud Goes Public," *The Globe and Mail*, November 30, 2002, B3; Gordon Pitts, "The Cuddy Situation Is an Extreme Case of Family Company Dysfunctionality, *The Globe and Mail*, April 17, 2000, B9; David Berman, "Carving Up Cuddy," *Canadian Business* (March 27, 1998): 39–44. **Figure 3.1** Statistics Canada, *Quality of Work in the Service Sector*, 11-612E, No. 6, 1992. **It's a Wired World** Timothy Mullaney, "Break Out the Black Ink," *Business Week* (May 13, 2002): 74–76; Robet Hof, "How E-Biz Rose, Fell, and Will Rise Anew," *Business Week* (May 13, 2002): 64–72. **Table 3.3**, Mel Scott and Richard Bruce, "Five Stages of Growth in Small Business," *Long Range Planning* 20 (1987): 48. **Table 3.6** *National Post Business*, June 2003, p. 68. **Business Today** Jacquie McNish, "Onex Chief Ripped for Appointing Wife," *The Globe and Mail*, May 9, 2003, B1, B7; Janet McFarland, "How ROB Created the Rating System," *The Globe and Mail*, October 7, 2002, B6; Janet McFarland, Elizabeth Church, and Lily Nguyen, "Board Games," *The Globe and Mail*, October 7, 2002, B1, B8; Elizabeth Church, "How the Best Companies Do It," *The Globe and Mail*, October 7, 2002, B7. **Concluding Case 3-1** Paul Judge, "From Country Boys to Big Cheese," *Fast*

Company (December 2001): 38–40; Sue Robinson, "Saving Our Farms," BurlingtonFreePress.com, November 27, 2001. **Concluding Case 3-2** Summarized from Peter Verburg, "Prepare for Takeoff," *Canadian Business* (December 25, 2000): 95–99.

Chapter 4

Bombardier Encounters Turbulence in International Airspace Rasha Mourtada, "Tellier's Task," *Canadian Business* (April 14, 2003): 53–56; Bertrand Marotte, "Tellier Overhauls Bombardier," *The Globe and Mail*, April 4, 2003, B1, B4; also Konrad Yakabuski, "Bombardier Soars on Jet Orders, but Turbulence May Loom Ahead," *The Globe and Mail*, February 22, 1999, B1, B5; Heather Scoffield, "Bombardier-Embraer Dogfight Heats Up," *The Globe and Mail*, February 15, 1999, B1, B6; www.bombardier.com (refer to "Corporate Profile" and "Bombardier at a Glance"). **Figure 4.4** Michael E. Porter, *The Competitive Advantage of Nations* (New York: Free Press, 1990), 72. **Figure 4.5** *Bank of Canada Banking and Financial Statistics* (June 2000), Table J1, p. S106; *Bank of Canada Review* (May 2003), Table J1, p. S108 **Table 4.1** *Bank of Canada Review* (May 2003), Table J1, p. S108. **Figure 4.7** Ricky Griffin Ronald Ebert, *Business*, 4th ed. (Englewood Cliffs, NJ: Prentice Hall, 1996). **It's a Wired World** Ron Lieber, "Give Us This Day Our Global Bread," *Fast Company* (March 2001): 164–167. **Table 4.3** *National Post Business* (June 2003): 116. **Business Today** Dirk Meissner, "Industry Cheers Softwood Ruling," *The Winnipeg Free Press*, August 14, 2003, B9; Steven Chase and Peter Kennedy, "Canada, U.S. Strike Lumber Proposal," *The Globe and Mail*, July 29, 2003, B1, B8; Sandra Cordon, "Canada Wins Softwood Round," *The Winnipeg Free Press*, May 28, 2003, B7; Barrie McKenna, "Talks Aim for Softwood Deal," *The Globe and Mail*, February 1, 2003, B1, B5; Sandra Cordon, "Canada Wins Round 1," *The Winnipeg Free Press*, July 27, 2002, B1; Peter Kennedy, "Huge Setback Seen for Industry," *The Globe and Mail*, March 23, 2002, B5; Wendy Stueck, "Fallout from Softwood War Leaves B.C. Forestry Workers at Loose Ends," *The Globe and Mail*, March 23, 2002, B4; Barrie McKenna and Steven Chase, "Canada Vows to Fight Duty," *The Globe and Mail*, March 23, 2002, B1, B4; Barrie McKenna, Peter Kennedy, and Steven Chase, "Canada Quits Lumber Talks," *The Globe and Mail*, March 20, 2002, B1, B6; Barrie McKenna and Steven Chase, "Softwood Lumber Deal in Sight," *The Globe and Mail*, March 8, 2002, B1, B6; Peter Kennedy, "Lumber Duties Could Hit $1.5 Billion," *The Globe and Mail*, November 2, 2001, B1, B12. **Concluding Case 4-1** Chester Dawson et al., "The Americanization of Toyota," *Business Week* (April 15, 2002): 52–54; Todd Zaun, "Auto Makers Look for Another Edge Farther from Home," *The Wall Street Journal*, July 31, 2002, A1, A8. **Concluding Case 4-2** Geoffrey York, "Russian Accuse McDonald's of Union Bashing," *The Globe and Mail*, June 14, 1999, A17; Geoffrey York, "Beeg Maks on a Roll," *The Globe and Mail*, September 12, 1996, B1, B17; Peter Foster, "McDonald's Excellent Soviet Venture?" *Canadian Business* (May 1991): 51–64.

Chapter 5

Back on Track at CINAR Corp.? Allan Swift, "Cinar Chairman's Motives Questioned," *Winnipeg Free Press*, August 22, 2003, B6; Bertrand Marotte, "New Cinar Head Planning an Encore for Company," *The Globe and Mail*, April 10, 2003, B4; Bertrand Marotte, "Cinar Founders' Trustee Stages Coup," *The Globe and Mail*, April 30, 2002, B1, B10; Bertrand Marotte, "Cinar Settlement $2 Million," *The Globe and Mail*, March 16, 2002, B1–B2; Susanne Craig, John Partridge, and Bertrand Marotte, "Cinar Co-Founder Okayed Investment," *The Globe and Mail*, March 22, 2000, B1, B4; Susanne Craig, "Cinar Co-Founder Pushed Out," *The Globe and Mail*, March 15, 2000, B1, B9; Susanne Craig and Bertrand Marotte, "Cinar to Take Hit Following Probe," *The Globe and Mail*, February 21, 2000, B1, B3. **Business Today** Karen Howlett and Sinclair Stewart, "ATI Executives Accused of Illegal Insider Trades," *The Globe and Mail*, January 17, 2003, B1, B4; Gillian Linvingston, "Scandal Hits Canada," *The Globe and Mail*, October 23, 2002, B3; David Wessel, "Why the Bad Guys of the Boardroom Emerged en Masse," *The Wall Street Journal*, June 20, 2002, A1, A6; Barrie McKenna, "Andersen Hit with Charges," *The Globe and Mail*, March 15, 2002, B1, B4. **Figure 5.1** Based on Gerald S. Cavanaugh, *American Business Values: With International Perspectives*, 4th ed. (Upper Saddle River, NJ: Prentice Hall, 1998), 71, 84. **It's a Wired World** Daniel H. Pink, "America's Top Cybercop," *Fast Company* (February, 2002): 28–35; John Simons, "Stop Moaning About Gripe Sites and Log On," *Fortune* (February 26, 2002): 95–98; Michael Shrage, "E-Mail or E-Sting? Your Boss Knows, but He's Not Telling," *Fortune* (March 20, 2000): 240; "OTG Software Introduces Transparent Email Surveillance for Policy Enforcement," *Business Wire* (December 5, 2001): 76. **Figure 5.2** Guiding principles of Great-West Life Assurance Company, Winnipeg, Manitoba. Reproduced with permission. **Figure 5.3** David P. Baron, *Business and Its Environment*, 4th ed. (Upper Saddle River, NJ: Prentice Hall, 2003), 768. **Figure 5.5** Based on Andrew C. Revkin, "Who Cares about a Few Degrees?" *The New York Times*, December 12, 1997, F1. **Concluding Case 5-1** Erin McClam, "Stewart Indicted in Stock Scandal," *Winnipeg Free Press*, June 5, 2003, B9; Geeta Anand, Jerry Markon, and Chris Adams, "ImClone's Ex-CEO Arrested, Charged with Insider Trading," *The Wall Street Journal*, June 13, 002, A1, A8; Greg Farrell, "Waksal Indictment Unsealed," *USA Today*, August 8, 2002, 1B; Amy Barrett, "No Quick Cure," *Business Week* (May 6, 2002): 30–33; Andrew Pollack, "For ImClone Drug Entrepreneur, a Past of Celebrity and Notoriety," *The New York Times*, January 24, 2002, C1, C9. **Concluding Case 5-2** Terrence Corcoran, "Corporate Ungiving," *National Post*, April 1, 2000, D5; "Nortel's New Style Giving," *National Post*, April 1, 2000, D5.

Chapter 6

What to Do After Seagram? Allen Swift, "Bronfman Jr. Wants His Toy Again," *Winnipeg Free Press*, May 26, 2003, B7; Brian Milner, "Broken Spirits," *Report on Business Magazine* (September, 2002): 26–38; Allan Swift, "Polygram Bid Heats Up," *Winnipeg Free Press*, November 5, 1998, B12; Brian Milner, "Seagram's Top Gun Shoots for the Stars," *The Globe and Mail*, June 6, 1998, B1, B6; Brian Milner, "Seagram Snares Polygram," *The Globe and Mail*, May 22, 1998, B1, B4; Brian Milner, "The Selling of Edgar Bronfman Jr.," *The Globe and Mail*, February 15, 1999, B15. **Figure 6.1** Based on Stephen P. Robbins and Mary Coulter, *Management*, 7th ed. (Upper Saddle River, NJ: Prentice Hall, 2002), 199. **Figure 6.2** Based on Thomas L. Wheelen and J. David Hunger, *Strategic Management and Business Policy*, 7th ed. (Upper Saddle River, NJ: Prentice Hall, 2000), 13. **It's a Wired World** Chris Sandllund, "Stay Plugged In," *Fortune* (February 27, 2002): 24–26; Eyal Ravinovitch, "Life in the Fast Lane," *Fortune* (February 1, 2002): 98–104; "It Takes a Cell Phone," *The Wall Street Journal*, June 25, 1999, B1, B6. **Concluding Case 6-1** Chuck Salter, "Fresh Start 2002: On the Road Again," *Fast Company* (January, 2002): 50–58; Matthew Boyle, "America's Most Admired Companies: The Right Stuff," *Fortune* (March 4, 2002); *Yellow Corporation 2000 Annual Report*, March 2001, www.yellowcorp.com. **Concluding Case 6-2** Dave Ebner, "BCE Cutting Costs, Staff, Focusing on Bell Canada," *The Globe and Mail*, December 19, 2002, B1, B4; Jacquie McNish and Paul Waldie, "BCE Reacquiring 20% Stake in Bell Canada," *The Globe and Mail*, June 29, 2002, B1, B4; Karen Howlett and John Saunders, "Teleglobe to Abandon Huge Internet Investment, *The Globe and Mail*, May 16, 2002, B1, B11; Ian Austen, "On the Hook," *Canadian Business* (May 13, 2002): 35–39; Bertrand Marotte, "Sabia: BCE Committed to Emergis," *The Globe and Mail*, May 8, 2002, B5; Eric Reguly, "Decision Time for BCE Boss Is Now," *The Globe and Mail*, March 22, 2002, B1–B2; Gordon Pitts, "Monty Ends 28 Years with a Clean Break," *The Globe and Mail*, April 25, 2002, B3.

Chapter 7

Frantic Films Gets Organized Interviews with Jamie Brown, CEO of Frantic Films; documents provided by Frantic Films. **Business Today** Dan Morse, "A Hardware Chain Struggles to Adjust to a New Blueprint," *The Wall Street Journal*, January 27, 2003, A1, A4; Chad Terhune and Dan Morse, "Tweaking Home Depot," *The Wall Street Journal*, June 25, 2002, B1, B5; Debbie Howell, "The Super Growth Leaders—The Home Depot: Diversification Builds Bridge to the Future," *DSN Retailing Today* 40, no. 23 (December 10, 2001): 17–18. **It's a Wired World** Anne Fisher, "Virtual Teams and Long-Distance Meetings: More on Staying Grounded," *Fortune* (October 15, 2001); Faith Keenan and Spencer E. Ante, "The New Teamwork," *Business Week* (February 18, 2002); Faith Keenan, "Giants Can Be Nimble," *Business Week E. Biz* (September 18, 2000); Nadav Enbar, "Meet Yale's Admissions Director," *Business Week* (May 20, 2002); "Paul Gudonis, Chairman and CEO Genuity Inc.," *Fast Company* (May 20, 2002); Polly LaBarre, "Strategic Innovation: The Children's Hospital at Montefiore," *Fast Company* (May, 2002). **Concluding Case 7-1** Bill Breen, "High Stakes, Big Bets," *Fast Company* (April, 2002): 66–78; Michael A. Dornheim, "Boeing: Lift Fan Put LockMart Over the Top in JSF Competition," *Aviation Week & Space Technology* (March 12, 2002); Massachusetts Institute of Technology's Engineering Systems Division," Special Seminar: Lockheed Martin Aeronautics Company," www.mit.edu/headline/seminar0306.htm, April 4, 2002.

Chapter 8

Progress, but not Parity Janet McFarland, "Women Still Find Slow Rise to Power Positions," *The Globe and Mail*, March 13, 2003, B1, B7; Virginia Galt, "Top Women Still Finding Barriers," *The Globe and Mail*, September 25, 2002, B7; Elizabeth Church, "Women Still Shut Out of Many Top Posts," *The Globe and Mail*, February 10, 2000, B15; Anita Leahy, "Homegrown," *Canadian Business* (August 13, 1999): 33–35; Belle Rose Ragins, "Gender Gap in the Executive Suite: CEO's and Female Executives Report on Breaking the Glass Ceiling," *Academy of Management Executive* (February, 1998): 28–42; Greg Keenan, "Ford Canada Gets New CEO," *The Globe and Mail*, April 9, 1997, B1; Joseph White and Carol Hymowitz, "Watershed Generation of Women Executives Is Rising to the Top," *The Globe and Mail*, February 19, 1997, A1, A6; Greg Keenan and Janet McFarland, "The Boys' Club," *The Globe and Mail*, September 27, 1997, B1, B5; Greg Keenan, "Woman at the Wheel, " *The Globe and Mail*, July 8, 1995, B1, B6. **Table 8.1** *National Post Business* (June 2003): 118. **It's a Wired World** Eric Wahlgren, "Have Investors Missed the Boat on Pier 1?," *Business Week* (December 21, 2001); James C. Cooper and Kathleen Madigan, "The Surprise Economy," *Business Week* (March 18, 2002); Karen E. Klein, "Making Performance Reviews Pay Off," *Business Week* (February 6, 2002); Michelle Conlin, "The Software Says You're Just Average," *Business Week* (February 25, 2002). **Business Today** Alfie Kohn, *Punished by Rewards: The Trouble with Gold Stars, Incentive Plans, A's, Praise, and Other Bribes* (New York: Houghton-Mifflin, 1993); Oliver Bertin, "Is There Any Merit in Giving Merit Pay?," *The Globe and Mail*, January 31, 2003, C1, C7. **Concluding Case 8-1** David Leonhardt, "Did Pay Incentives Cut Both Ways?," *The New York Times*, April 7, 2002, BU1–3; Dean Foust and Michelle Conlin, "A Smarter Squeeze?," *Business Week* (December 31, 2001): 42–44; also Rick Perera, "Siemens Offers Workers 'Time-Outs' to Save Cash," *The Industry Standard* (August 31, 2001); Tischelle George, "Bye-Bye Employee Perks," *Information Week* (October 15, 2001). **Concluding Case 8-2** Interview with Ray Sherwood, Chief Financial Officer of Frantic Films, July 15, 2003; Grant Buckler, "In Tough Times, Contractors Can Fill Key Gaps," *The Globe and Mail*, May 22, 2003, B17; Mark Brender, "Free Isn't Easy," *The Globe and Mail*, August 9, 1994, B18; Merle MacIsaac, "New Broom Sweeps Schools," *The Globe and Mail*, March 22, 1994, B22; Margot Gibb-Clark, "Temps Take on New Tasks," *The Globe and Mail*, December 22, 1993, B1; Sally Ritchie, "Rent-A-Manager," *The Globe and Mail*, August 17, 1993, B22; Robert Williamson, "Tradition Gives Way to World of Freelancers," *The Globe and Mail*, January 15, 1993, B1, B4.

Chapter 9

Management and Unions Sing the Blues at Air Canada "Unions, Airline Give Nod to Deal," *Winnipeg Free Press*, May 25, 2003, A6; Cassandra Szklarski, "Air Canada Reaches Tentative Deal with Machinists," *Winnipeg Free Press*, May 28, 2003, B6, B10; "1,000 AirCan Mechanics Told to Take Summer Off," *Winnipeg Free Press*, May 16, 2003, B7; David Paddon, "Airline Charting New Territory," *Winnipeg Free Press*, April 2, 2003, B4, B5; Keith McArthur, "Air Canada to Fight Hostile Motions," *The Globe and Mail*, April 21, 2003, B1, B8; Allan Swift, "Air Canada Unions OK Cuts," *Winnipeg Free Press*, April 1, 2003, B1, B8; David Paddon, "Air Canada to Shed More Jobs," *Winnipeg Free Press*, April 23, 2003, B9. **It's a Wired World** L.M. Sixel, "Networking on the Web: Union Leaders Turn to Internet for Recruiting, Doing Research," *Houston Chronicle*, March 30, 2000, B1; Bill Leonard, "Disgruntled Employees Take Their Beefs to the World Wide Web," *HRMagazine* (November, 1999): 89–94. **Figure 9.1** Statistics Canada, "Perspectives in Labour and Income," Autumn 2003, 15, 3, p. 50. **Figure 9.2** Ricky Griffin, Ronald Ebert, *Business*, 2nd ed. (Englewood Cliffs, NJ: Prentice Hall, 1996). **Business Today** Virginia Galt, "Wal-Mart Must Give Union Access," *The Globe and Mail*, May 13, 2003, B5; "Union Is Trying to Organize Staff at Wal-Mart," *Winnipeg Free Press*, May 13, 2003, A7; Zena Olijnyk, "CAW Walks Away from Wal-Mart, *National Post*, April 20, 2000, C5; Susan Bourettte, "Wal-Mart Staff Want Out of Union," *The Globe and Mail*, April 23, 1999, B9; John Heinzl and Marina Strauss, "Wal-Mart's Cheer Fades," *The Globe and Mail*, February 15, 1997, B1, B4; Margot Gibb-Clark, "Why Wal-Mart Lost the Case," *The Globe and Mail*, February 14, 1997, B10. **Figure 9.4** Labour Canada, *Labour Organizations in Canada, 1991*, p. xxv. Used by permission of the Minister of Supply and Services Canada. **Concluding Case 9-1** Martin Cash, "Dominion Tanners Shuts Down," *Winnipeg Free Press*, July 25, 2003, B4; "Unions, Airline Give Nod to Deal," *Winnipeg Free Press*, May 25, 2003, A6; Allan Swift, "Air Canada Unions OK Cuts," *Winnipeg Free Press*, April 1, 2003, B5, B8; Keith MacArthur and Steven Chase, "Air Canada Seeks Pay Cut," *The Globe and Mail*, May 3, 2003, B1, B7; Bertrand Marotte, "Bombardier Threatens Big Layoffs," *The Globe and Mail*, May 8, 2003, B3; Steven Erwin, "Auto Workers Angry and Frustrated," *Winnipeg Free Press*, May 23, 2003, B5; Jordan Heath-Rawlings, "Imperial Tobacco to Close Plant, Cut Staff," *The Globe and Mail*, June 19, 2003, B1, B12; Peter Kennedy, "CPR Slashing More Jobs," *The Globe and Mail*, June 19, 2003, B1, B12; Greg Keenan, "GM and CAW Forge an Improved Relationship," *The Globe and Mail*, October 23, 1999, B1, B14; Greg Keenan, "CAW Face Declining Numbers in Auto Sector," *The Globe and Mail*, October 23, 1999, B14; Jeb Blount, "Behind the Lines," *Canadian Business* (January, 1990): 63; Aaron Bernstein and Wendy Zellner, "Detroit vs. the UAW: At Odds Over Teamwork," *Business Week* (August 24, 1987): 54+; Peter Downs, "Drudgery at Wentzille: The Team Concept Strikes Out," *Commonweal* (September 9, 1988): 453+; John Hoerr, "Is Teamwork," *Business Week* (July 10, 1989): 56+; John Holusha, "A New Spirit at U.S. Auto Plants," *New York Times*, December 29, 1987, D1+. **Concluding Case 9-2** "Canada Post Gets Tentative Agreement with Union," *Winnipeg Free Press*, July 28, 2003, A8; Terry Pedwell, "New Strike Deadline Set," *Winnipeg Free Press*, July 19, 2003, A13; Bruce Cheadle, "Postal Strike Sends Chill," *Winnipeg Free Press*, July 12, 2003, A10, A11; "Posties Return to Work, Vow to Sabotage Service," *Winnipeg Free Press*, December 5, 1997, B4; Paul Samyn, "Back-to-Work Legislation in the Mail," *Winnipeg Free Press*, December 2, 1997, B1; Nahiah Ayed, "Postal Workers Picket Manning's Residence," *Winnipeg Free Press*, December 1, 1997, B1; Jennifer Ditchburn, "Commons Passes Back-to-Work Law," *Winnipeg Free Press*, December 3, 1997, B3.

Chapter 10

Leadership in Modern Business Howard Book, "Following the Leader," *The Globe and Mail,* May 14, 2003, C1, C7; John Gray, "High on the Hog," *Canadian Business* (May 12, 2003): 41–44; Gordon Pitts, "Monty Quietly Returns from the Wilderness," *The Globe and Mail,* May 10, 2003, B1, B5; Greg Keenan, "Frank's Doing It His Way at Magna," *The Globe and Mail,* May 9, 2003, B1, B7; Bertrand Marotte, "Management Guru Assails Excessive CEO Salaries," *The Globe and Mail,* May 8, 2003, B7. **Figure 10.2** Ricky Griffin and Ronald Ebert, *Business*, 2nd ed. (Englewood Cliffs, NJ: Prentice Hall, 1996). **Business Today** Margot Gibb-Clark, "BC Telecom Managers Get an Overhaul," *The Globe and Mail,* July 23, 1994, B3; Frederick A. Starke, Bruno Dyck, and Michael Mauws, "Coping with the Sudden Loss of an Indispensable Worker," *Journal of Applied Behavioural Science*, forthcoming, 2003; Timothy Aeppel, "On Factory Floors, Top Workers Hide Secrets to Success," *The Wall Street Journal*, July 1, 2002, A1, A10; Timothy Aeppel, "Not All Workers Find Idea of Empowerment as Neat as it Sounds," *The Wall Street Journal*, September 8, 1997, A1, 13. **It's a Wired World** Aaron Bernstein, "Too Many Workers? Not for Long," *Business Week* (May 20, 2002); Timothy Aeppel, "Young and Old See Technology Sparking Friction on Shop Floor," *The Wall Street Journal*, April 7, 2000, A1, A10; Ed Michaels, Helen Handfield-Jones, and Beth Axelrod, *The War for Talent* (Boston, Mass.: Harvard Business School Press, 2001), excerpt reprinted in *Business Week* (December 12, 2001). **Concluding Case 10-1** Brian O'Keefe, "The High Price of Being No. 1," *Fortune* (April 15, 2002); Cait Murphy, "Now That Wal-Mart Is America's Largest Corporation, the Service Economy Wears the Crown," *Fortune* (April 15, 2002); "Fourteen Top CEOs (and One President) Gauge the Year Ahead," *Fortune* (April 15, 2002); Mark Gimein, "Sam Walton Made Us a Promise," *Fortune* (March 18, 2002): 120–130. **Concluding Case 10-2** Virginia Galt, "Statscan Studies Workplace Stress," *The Globe and Mail,* June 26, 2003, B3; Anne Howland, "There's No Place Like Work," *CGA Magazine* (July–August, 2000): 21–25.

Chapter 11

Goin' South? Greg Keenan, "Ford Plans SUV's for Oakville," *The Globe and Mail*, June 18, 2003, B1, B18; Oliver Bertin, "Appliance Makers in Canada: A Dying Breed," *The Globe and Mail*, March 31, 2003, B5; Greg Keenan, "Auto Sector's Best-Paid Jobs Vanishing," *The Globe and Mail*, March 29, 2003, B1, B2; Thomas Watson, "Car Trouble," *Canadian Business* (March 17, 2003): 69–71; Steve Erwin, "Auto Workers 'Angry and Frustrated,'" *Winnipeg Free Press*, May 23, 2003, B5; Bertrand Marotte, "Quebec GM Plant Closing the End of an Era," *The Globe and Mail*, August 24, 2002, B1, B5; Todd Zaun, Gregory White, Norihiko Shirouzu, and Scott Miller, "Auto Makers Get Even More Mileage from Third World," *The Wall Street Journal*, July 31, 2002, A1, A8; Greg Keenan, "Auto Plants Gone with the Wind," *The Globe and Mail*, June 24, 2002, B1, B4. **Business Today** Summarized from Andrew Nikiforuk, "Pure Profit," *Canadian Business* (April 3, 2000): 70–76. **It's a Wired World** Michael A. Verespej, "E-Procurement Explosion," *Industry Week* (March, 2002): 24–28; Steve Konicki, "E-Procurement: From (Shop) Rags to Riches," *Informationweek* (March 4, 2002): 26; "B2B Outlook Mixed," *Industrial Distribution* (September, 2001): 15–16; Karen Tourigny and Steve Sidorchuk, "Exploding the Myth of E-Procurement," *Semiconductor International* (November, 2001): S10–S12; Paul DeJohn, "Buyers Impatient with E-Commerce Delays," *Hospital Materials Management* (May, 2001): 2. **Concluding Case 11-1** Bill Breen, "High Stakes, Big Bets," *Fast Company* (April 2002): 66–78; William H. Miller, "Reaching New Heights," *Industry Week* (February 2002): 61–62; Norm Alster, "Managing a Mega Project," *Electronic Business* (February 2002): 47–49; Chuck Moozakis, "Web Powers Fighter Project—Linking All the Contractors in Real Time Would Have Been Impossible Without the Web, Says Northrop's Dave Torchia," *Internetweek* (November 12, 2001): 1, 49; Steve Konicki, "Collaboration Is Cornerstone of $19 Billion Defense Contract," *Informationweek* (November 12, 2001): 30; James Dao with Laura M. Holson, "Lockheed Wins $200 Billion Deal for Fighter Jet," *The New York Times*, October 21, 2001, A1, A9; Laura M. Holson, "Pursuing Limits, Finding None," *The New York Times*, November 1, 2001, C1, C6; Edward H. Phillips, "LockMart Bracing for JSF Transition Phase," *Aviation Space & Space Technology* (November 19, 2001): p. 86; Faith Keenan and Spencer E. Ante, "The New Teamwork," *Business Week Online*, Febraury 18, 2002. **Concluding Case 11-2** Greg Keenan, "Japan's Big Three Still Lead Race," *The Globe and Mail*, June 19, 2003, B6; Alex Taylor, "How Toyota Defies Gravity," *Fortune* (December 8, 1997): 100–108.

Chapter 12

Productivity and the Standard of Living "Canada's Standard of Living," *National Post Business* (June, 2003): 19–20; Jeffrey Bernstein, Richard Harris, and Andrew Sharpe, "The Widening Canada–US Manufacturing Productivity Gap," *International Productivity Monitor* (Fall, 2002): 3–22; Pierre Fortin, "Differences in Annual Work Hours per Capita Between the United States and Canada," *International Productivity Monitor* (Spring, 2003): 38–46; Frank Graves and Richard Jenkins, "Canadian Attitudes Towards Productivity: Balancing Standard of Living and Quality of Life," *The Review of Economic Performance and Social Progress* (2002), 243–258; Andrew Sharpe, "Why Are Americans More Productive Than Canadians?," *International Productivity Monitor* (Spring, 2003): 19–37; Jason Myers, "Back to Basics: Canada's Productivity Challenge," *Canadian Manufacturers and Exporters* (April, 2003): 14-18; Pierre Fortin, "Canadian Productivity: When Do We Catch Up?," *ISUMA* (Spring, 2002). **Figure 12.1** Bart Van Ark and Robert McGuckin, "International Comparisons of Labor Productivity and Per Capita Income," *Monthly Labor Review* (July 1999): 33–41. **Business Today** Joel Baglole, "Political Correctness by the Carat," *The Wall Street Journal*, April 17, 2003, B1, B3; Matthew Hart, "The Ice Storm," *Canadian Business* (November, 2002): 52–62. **Figure 12.2** Adapted from D. Daryl Wickoff, "New Tools for Achieving Service Quality." *The Cornell Hotel and Restaurant Administrative Quarterly* (November 1984): 89. *Cornell HRA Quarterly*. Used by permission. All rights reserved. **Figure 12.5** Adapted from Richard B. Chase, Nicholas J. Aquilano, and F. Robert Jacobs, *Production and Operations Management*, 8th ed. (Boston: Irwin McGraw-Hill, 1998), 771. **It's a Wired World** Philip Siekman, "Mercury Marine: Focusing on the Demand Side," *Fortune* [Industrial Management & Technology] (November 8, 1999): 272N–272O; "Mercury: the Water Calls," www.mercurymarine.com/mercury-home/merchome.cfm, May 22, 2000; Lynne M Almvig, "Robotics Milling Department," *Robotics Today* (First Quarter, 2000): 1–4. **Concluding Case 12-1** Wayne Sander, "Six Sigma Project Management: A Pocket Guide," *Quality Progress* (May, 2002): 114; "E-Learning Center Offers New Six Sigma Courses," *Quality Progress* (May, 2002): 17; "Green Belt Training Starts Feb. 4," *Quality Progress* (February, 2002): 13; Dennis Sester, "Motorola: A Tradition of Quality," *Quality* (October, 2001): 30-34; Roxanne O'Brasky, "Translating Six Sigma Methodology," *Best's Review* (November, 2001): 56–57; "Six Sigma Continues as a Hot Media Topic," *Quality Progress* (January, 2002): 25; John R. Johnson, "Giving Credit Where Credit Is Due," *Warehousing Management* (January/February, 2002): 26–32; Ron Panko, "Stealth Solution," *Best's Review* (November, 2001): 53–57; "Conseco Moves Full Speed Ahead with Six Sigma," *Best's Review* (November 2001): 58–62. **Concluding Case 12-2** Timothy Aeppel, "How Goodyear Blew Its Chance to Capitalize on Rival's Woes," *The Wall Street Journal*, February 19, 2003, A1, A10; Joseph B. White, Stephen Power, and Timothy Aeppel, "Firestone Severs Ford Ties, " *The Globe and Mail*, May 22, 2001, B1, B9; "Bridgestone Faults Self, Ford for Separations," *Winnipeg Free*

Press, December 20, 2000, B8; Todd Zaun, Kanji Ishibashi, and Timothy Aeppel, "Firestone Tire Sales Plummet," *The Globe and Mail*, November 13, 2000, B8; Timothy Aeppel, Norihiko Shirouzu, and Michael Williams, "Pit Crew," *The Wall Street Journal*, October 11, 2000, A1, A10; "Answers Still Elusive in Tire Crisis," *The Wall Street Journal*, September 15, 2000, B1, B4; Barrie McKenna, "Canada Joins Firestone Tire Fray," *The Globe and Mail*, September 8, 2000, B1, B5; Barrie McKenna, "Companies Accused of Delaying Tire Recall," *The Globe and Mail*, September 7, 2000, B1, B2; Timothy Aeppel, Clare Ansberry, Milo Geyelin, and Robert L. Simison, "Road Signs," *The Wall Street Journal*, September 6, 2000, A1, A16; Robert L. Simison, Karen Lundegaard, Norihiko Shirouzu, and Jenny Heller, "Blowout," *The Wall Street Journal*, August 10, 2000, A1, 16.

Chapter 13

It's All About Information Kevin Lubin, "The Last Retailer in Canada?" *Canadian Business* (March 18, 2002): 31–40; Casey Mahood, "Wal-Mart Claims Another Victim," *The Globe and Mail*, February 7, 1998, B1, B5; Mark Stevenson, "The Store to End All Stores," *Canadian Business* (May, 1994): 20–29. **Table 13.1** *National Post Business* (June 2003): 130. **Figure 13.3** Adapted from Kenneth C. Laudon and Jane P. Laudon, *Essentials of Management Information Systems: Managing the Digital Firm*, 5th ed. (Upper Saddle River, NJ: Prentice Hall, 2003), 16. **Figure 13.5** Kenneth C. Laudon and Jane Laudon, *Essentials of Management Information Systems*, 3rd ed. (Upper Saddle River, NJ: Prentice Hall, 1999), 39. **Figure 13.7** Adapted from Kenneth C. Laudon and Jane P. Laudon, *Essentials of Management Information Systems: Managing the Digital Firm*, 5th ed. (Upper Saddle River, NJ: Prentice Hall, 2003), 44. **Business Today** Timothy Aeppel, "Workers Not Included," *The Wall Street Journal*, November 19, 2002, B1, B11; Martin Stinson, "Assembly Line Robots Taking Workers' Jobs: UN Report," *The Globe and Mail*, February 8, 2000, B6; Wally Dennison, "Robotics Paint System Makes Splash at CN," *Winnipeg Free Press*, October 6, 1988, 30; "Robots Aren't for Burning," *Canadian Business* (September, 1984): 45. **It's a Wired World** Scott Sonneborn, "33 Days, 8 Campuses, 127 Kids, and an Infinity of Gizmos," *Fortune* (June 24, 2002): 126–132; Johna Till Johnson, "Boosting Your IM IQ Will Pay Off," *Network World* (March 11, 2002): 48; "New Palm Targets Wireless Enterprise," *Frontline Solutions* (March, 2002): 44; Scott Kirsner, "IM Is Here, RU Prepared?" *Darwin* (February, 2002): 22–24. **Concluding Case 13-1** Larry Adams, "Diagnostics from Afar," *Quality* (November, 2001): 26–28; Robert Pool, "If It Ain't Broke, Fix It," *Technology Review* (September, 2001): 64–69; Richard Baxter, "Remote M&D Leverages Expertise," *Power* (March 20, 2002): 44–52; Jim Mele, "Diagnostics on the Fly," *Fleet Owner* (September, 2001): 73–78; Chuck Moozakis, "Planes, Trains, Autos, Monitored from Afar," *Internetweek* (March 12, 2001): 1, 70; "Working on the Railroad: A Talk with John Krenicki," *Business Week* (April 29, 2002): 28b. **Concluding Case 13-2** Leonard Zehr, "Net Pharmacies Cheer New U.S. Import Bill," *The Globe and Mail*, July 26, 2003, B1, B4; Leah Janzen, "Internet Pharmacy's Drug Search Denounced," *Winnipeg Free Press*, July 5, 2003, A3; David Kuxhaus, "An Internet Pharmacy Primer," *Winnipeg Free Press*, June 22, 2003, A1, A8; Carol Sanders, "Net Druggists Pen Deal," *Winnipeg Free Press*, June 3, 2003, B1; David Kuxhaus, "U.S. Drug Agency Deals Blow to Net Pharmacy Operation," *Winnipeg Free Press*, March 27, 2003, A3; Paul Samyn, "Competition Bureau Backs Drug Giant," *Winnipeg Free Press*, March 22, 2003, B3.

Chapter 14

Accountants Under Fire Elizabeth Church, "Accounting Overhaul Coming," *The Globe and Mail*, December 23, 2002, B1, B6; Marcy Gordon, "Earnings Inflated $9 Billion; WorldCom Charges Grow," *Winnipeg Free Press*, November 6, 2002, B3; Richard Blackwell, "Auditing Firms Get Tighter Rules," *The Globe and Mail*, July 18, 2002, B1, B4; John Christoffersen, "Xerox Overstated Revenue by Billions of Dollars," *Winnipeg Free Press*, June 29, 2002, B3; John Partridge and Karen Howlett, "CIBC Restricts Its Auditors," *The Globe and Mail*, March 1, 2002, B1, B4; Lily Nguyen, "Accountants Primed for Change," *The Globe and Mail*, February 4, 2002, B9; Barrie McKenna, "Enron Disclosure Corrodes Andersen Credibility," *The Globe and Mail*, January 15, 2002, B1, B4; Richard Blackwell, "Accountants to Issue New Rules," *The Globe and Mail*, March 28, 2002, B1, B7; "Andersen Set to Name Interim Worldwide CEO," *The Globe and Mail*, March 28, 2002, B7; John Gray, "Hide and Seek," *Canadian Business* (April 1, 2002): 28–32; Steve Liesman, Jonathan Weil, and Michael Schroeder, "Accounting Debacles Spark Calls for Change: Here's the Rundown," *The Wall Street Journal*, February 6, 2002, A1, A8; Edward Clifford, "Big Accounting Firms Face Insurance Crunch," *The Globe and Mail*, November 13, 1993, B3; "Cooperants' Auditors Sued," *The Financial Post*, October 30, 1993, 8; Patricia Lush, "Gap Widens Between Views on Auditor's Role in Canada," *The Globe and Mail*, February 14, 1986, B3; Chris Robinson, "Auditor's Role Raises Tough Questions," *The Financial Post*, June 22, 1985. **Business Today** Summarized from Andrew Higgins, "At Russian Companies, Hard Numbers Often Are Hard to Come By," *The Wall Street Journal*, August 20, 1998, A1, A9. **Table 14.1** *National Post Business* (June 2003): 142. **It's a Wired World** David LeonHardt, "Consultants Are Putting a New Price on Advice," *New York Times*, January 19, 2000, C1, C10; Floyd Norris, "Accounting Firm Is Said to Violate Rules Routinely," *The New York Times*, January 7, 2000, A1, C6; Floyd Norris, "Rules That Only an Accountant Could Fail to Understand?," *The New York Times*, January 8, 2000, C1, C14. **Figure 14.1** Adapted from "CPA Vision Project: 2011 and Beyond," www.cpavision.org/final_report, September 24, 2002. **Concluding Case 14-1** John A. Byrne, "Fall from Grace," *Business Week* (August 12, 2002): 50–56; Kurt Eichenwald, "Andersen Witnesses Defend Intent of Shredding," *The New York Times*, June 1, 2002, C1, C2; Eichenwald, "Andersen Guilty in Effort to Block Inquiry on Enron," *The New York Times*, June 16, 2002, 1, 20; Eichenwald, "Andersen Trial Yields Evidence in Enron's Fall," *The New York Times*, June 17, 2002, A1, A14; Mark M. Meinaro and Parija Bhatnagar, "Andersen Loses More Partners, Key Clients," *USA Today* (May 21, 2002); Alex Berenson and Jonathan D. Glater, "A Tattered Andersen Fights for Its Future," *The New York Times*, January 13, 2002, Sec. 3, 1, 10; Greg Farrell, "Arthur Andersen Fined $7 Million by SEC for Audits," *USA Today*, www.usatoday.com, June 19, 2001; Edward Iwata, "Andersen to Pay $217M in Baptist Foundation Case," *USA Today*, www.usatoday.com, March 1, 2002. **Concluding Case 14-2** Paul Waldie and Karen Howlett, "Reports Reveal Tight Grip of Ebbers on WorldCom," *The Globe and Mail*, June 11, 2003, B1, B7; Barrie McKenna, Karen Howlett, and Paul Waldie, "Probes Cite Ebbers in 'Fraud,'" *The Globe and Mail*, June 10, 2003, B1, B16; Elizabeth Church, "Accounting Overhaul Coming," *The Globe and Mail*, December 23, 2002, B1, B6; Richard Blackwell," OSC Targets Tech Accounting," *The Globe and Mail*, September 26, 2000, B1, B6.

Chapter 15

What Happened to the Youth Culture? Andre Mayer, "Star's New Paper Woos Tween Readers," *The Globe and Mail*, March 12, 2003, B7; Gautam Naik, Leslie Chang, and Joanna Slater, "Leveraging the Age Gap," *The Wall Street Journal*, February 27, 2003, B1, B4; Cris Prystay and Sarah Ellison, "Time for Marketers to Grow Up?," *The Wall Street Journal*, February 27, 2003, B1, B4; Sebastian Moffett, "For Ailing Japan, Longevity Begins to Take Its Toll," *The Wall Street Journal*, February 11, 2003, A1, A12; John Heinzl, "Crayon Maker Draws in an Older Kid," *The Globe and Mail*, March 5, 1998; Shawna Steinberg, "Have Allowance, Will Transform Economy," *Canadian Business* (March 13, 1998): 59–71; Lisa Bannon, "Little Big Spenders," *The Wall Street Journal*, October 13, 1998, A1, A6; Sheryl

Ubelacker, "Magazines Target Over-50 Crowd," *The Winnipeg Free Press*, April 9, 2000, B3; Allen St. John, "Baseball's Billion Dollar Question: Who's On Deck?," *American Demographics* (October, 1998): 60–62, 65–69. **It's a Wired World** Associated Press, "High-Tech Hits the Road," *Columbia Daily Tribune*, February 25, 2002, 1B; *Fortune: Technology Guide* (Winter, 2001): 37–38. **Figure 15.2** Erick Schonfield, "Changes in the U.S. Population: Betting on the Boomers," *Fortune* (December 25, 1995): 78–80. Reprinted from the December 25, 1995 issue of *Fortune* by special permission; © 1995, Time Inc. **Business Today** Lisa Bannon and Carlta Vitzthum, "One-Toy-Fits-All: How Industry Learned to Love the Global Kid," *The Wall Street Journal*, April 29, 2003, A1, A12; Shawn Tully, "Teens: The Most Global Market of All," *Fortune* (May 16, 1994): 90–97; Gina Mallet, "Greatest Romance on Earth," *Canadian Business* (August, 1993): 19–23. **Figure 15.3** Adapted from Naresh K. Malhorta, *Marketing Research: An Applied Orientation*, 3rd ed. (Upper Saddle River, NJ: Prentice Hall, 1999), 10. **Concluding Case 15-1** Chris Gaither, "Microsoft Explores a New Territory: Fun," *The New York Times*, November 4, 2001, Sec. 3, 1, 7; Leslie P. Norton, "Toy Soldiers," *Barron's* (May 14, 2001): 25–30; Chris Taylor, "The Battle of Seattle," *Time* (May 21, 2001): 58–59; N'Gai Croal, "Game Wars 5.0," *Newsweek* (May 28, 2001): 651; Tobi Elkin, "The X Factor: Microsoft, Sony Prepare for E3," *Advertising Age* (April 23, 2001): 41; Bill Powell, "Gamemakers Aren't Racking Up Bonus Points," *Fortune* (April 16, 2001): 58; Danny Bradbury, "Home Free," *Communications International* (February 2001): 41; Tobi Elkin, "Gearing Up for Xbox Lunch," *Advertising Age* (November 20, 2000): 161; Arlene Weintraub, "Video Games: The Sky's the Limit," *Business Week* (January 14, 2002): 100–101. **Concluding Case 15-2** Julie McElwain, "JNCO Branches Out from Wide-Leg Jeans Roots," *Bobbin* (April, 1999): 32–38; Becky Ebenkamp and T.L. Stanley, "Lee Takes the Niche Road in Jeans: Retail Eyes Destination Departments," *Brandweek* (September 6, 1999): 12; Lisa Bannon, "As Children Become More Sophisticated, Marketers Think Older," *The Wall Street Journal*, October 13, 1998, A1; Nina Munk, "How Teens Buy," *Fortune* (April 13, 1998): 28–30; Jennifer Steinhauer, "Lulu and Her Friends Are, Therefore They Shop," *The New York Times*, April 29, 1998, 6; JNCO Jeans USA, www.jnco.com, March 20, 2000.

Chapter 16

How Sweet It Is! Gordon Pitts, "Ganong Aims for Sweet Spot," *The Globe and Mail*, March 3, 2003, B4; Geoff Kirbyson, "City Candy Firm Signs National Retail Deals," *The Winnipeg Free Press*, March 31, 2003, B4, B6; Laurie Nealin, "Growth-Focused Firms Think 'Export,'" *The Winnipeg Free Press*, October 28, 2002, B8; Geoff Kirbyson, "Candy Firm Finds U.S. Hungry for Product," *The Winnipeg Free Press*, January 25, 2000, C11; Casey Mahood, "Madeover Clodhoppers Stepping Out," *The Globe and Mail*, January 7, 2000, M1; "Sweet Love," *Ciao*, Spring 2000, p. 32; Geoff Kirbyson, "Success Sweet for Krave's," *The Winnipeg Free Press*, November 30, 2000, B7; Oliver Bertin, "In Pursuit of the Sweet Smell of Success," *The Globe and Mail*, August 6, 1991, B3. **Business Today** Peter Kennedy, "GM Aims to Finish First in Fuel Cell Race," *The Globe and Mail*, June 10, 2003, B5; Chris Nuttall-Smith, "Waiting for the Revolution," *Report on Business* (February, 2003): 44–54; Jeffrey Ball, "Hydrogen Fuel May Be Clean, But Getting It Here Looks Messy," *The Wall Street Journal*, March 7, 2003; Rebecca Blumenstein, "Auto Industry Reaches Surprising Consensus: It Needs New Engines," *The Wall Street Journal*, January 5, 1998, A1, A10. **Table 16.1** Sahm Adrangi, "World Is Oblivious to Canadian Brands," *The Globe and Mail*, July 25, 2003, B9. **It's a Wired World** Michelle Fradette and Heather Kelly, "Altec Lansing Unveils New Corporate Direction at CES 2002," Press Release, January 8, 2002, at www.alteclansing.com; Keith Shaw, "Car Tools," *Network World* (April 15, 2002): 46; Matt Beer, "Eight Extraordinary Gizmos Stand Out at the Fall Show," *San Francisco Examiner*, November 21, 1999, B5; "Agency.Com" and "Altec Lansing," April 25, 2000, at www.agency.com and www.altecmm.com. **Table 16.2** *National Post Business* (June, 2003): 142. **Concluding Case 16-1** David Lieberman, "ABC's Actions Reflect Network's Troubles," *USA Today*, March 6, 2002, 1B; Gary Levin, "Youth Served in Ratings Game," *USA Today*, March 6, 2002, 3D; Peter Johnson, "The View From Here: News Deserves Respect," *USA Today*, March 6, 2002, 3D; Joe Schlosser, "Who Wants to Program ABC?" *Broadcasting & Cable* (December 3, 2001): 57; Johnnie Roberts, "Disney's Lost Magic," *Newsweek* (December 10, 2001): 52. **Concluding Case 16-2** Paul Jung, "No Free Lunch," *Health Affairs* (March/April 2002): 226–231; Richard Haugh, "DTC Drug Advertising Soars," *Hospitals & Health Networks* (February 2002): 49; Lindsey Tanner, "U.S. Doctors Seek Ban on Prescription Drug Ads," *C-Health*, www.canoe.ca, June 18, 2001; Victoria Stagg Elliott, "Questions Swirl Around Drug Ads for Patients," *amednews.com*, www.ama-assn.org, July 9/16, 2001; *USA Weekend* (April 19–21, 2002): 9; Andra Brichacek and Sibyl Shalo, "Location, Location, Location," *Pharmaceutical Executive* (June 2001): 126; Jill Wechsler, "DDMAC Queries Docs, Patients About DTC Advertising," *Pharmaceutical Executive* (March 2002): 38; "National Health Council Backs DTC Advertising," *Medical Marketing and Media* (March 2002): 8; Sandra Levy, "Survey Says: DTC Advertising, R&D Driving Up Drug Costs," *Drug Topics* (April 1, 2002): 56; Kevin Gopal, "Consumer Communication in Europe Stalls," *Pharmaceutical Executive* (February 2002): 38; Jackie Judd, "Truth in Advertising?" ABCNews.com, abcnews.go.com, January 3, 2002; Kathleen Blankenhorn, Nancy Duckwitz, and Marjorie Sherr, "Power to the People," *Medical Marketing and Media* (August 2001): 66–70.

Chapter 17

What's the Price? Summarized from Gordon Fairclough, "Four Biggest Cigarette Makers Can't Raise Prices As They Did," *The Wall Street Journal*, October 25, 2002, A1, A8; also Timothy Aeppel, "After Cost Cutting, Companies Turn Toward Price Increases," *The Wall Street Journal*, September 18, 2002, A1, A12. **Business Today** Judy Monchak, "No Sympathy for Airline," *The Winnipeg Free Press*, February 7, 2003, B9; Allan Swift, "Air Canada Hit With $428 Million Loss," *The Winnipeg Free Press*, February 7, 2003, B1, B9; Susan Carey, "Costly Race in the Sky," *The Wall Street Journal*, September 9, 2002, B1, B3; Melanie Trottman and Scott McCartney, "The Age of 'Wal-Mart' Airlines Crunches the Biggest Carriers," *The Wall Street Journal*, June 18, 2002, A1, A8. **It's a Wired World** Shawn Tully, "The B2B Tool That Really Is Changing the World," *Fortune* (March 20, 2000): 132–341; Ken Zapinsky, "FreeMarkets Is the Easy Winner in Having the Biggest Stock Price Increase," *Post-Gazette.com*, www.post-gazette.com/businessnews/20000409stock.asp, April 9, 2000; "American Management Systems and FreeMarkets Form Strategic Alliance to eEmpower Public Sector Purchasing," *AMS News Room*, www3.amsinc.com/CMC/newsroom.nsf/prMBRY-4HQM3Z, March 9, 2000; "FreeMarkets and webPLAN Form Strategic Alliance to Deliver Web-Based B2B eMarketplace and e-Supply Chain Solutions," *TechMall*, www8.techmall.com/techdocs/TS000516-html, May 16, 2000; "The H.J. Heinz Company," *FreeMarkets*, www.freemarkets.com/benefits/case_studies/hjheinz.asp, April 3, 2002. **Table 17.1** *National Post Business* (June 2003), 130. **Table 17.2** *National Post Business* (June 2003): 132. **Concluding Case 17-1** Summarized from Zena Olijnyk, "Dot-Com Wonder Boys," *Canadian Business* (April 14, 2003): 30–36. **Concluding Case 17-2** Nick Wingfield, "The Day the Music Died," *The Wall Street Journal*, May 2, 2003, B8; "The End of File-Shares as We Know Them," *The Winnipeg Free Press*, July 4, 2003, A8; Ted Birdis, "Music Industry Escalates Net Fight," *The Winnipeg Free Press*, June 26, 2003, A12; Matthew Ingram, "Digital Music Industry Gets New Spin on Napster Judge's Decision," *The Globe and Mail*, February 26, 2002; Nick Wingfield, "Napster Boy, Interrupted," *The Wall Street Journal*, October 1, 2002, B1, B3; Anna Matthews and Charles Goldsmith, "Music Industry

Faces New Threats on Web," *The Wall Street Journal*, February 21, 2003, B1, B4.

Chapter 18

What's Happening to the Canadian Dollar? "20 Ways the Rising Loonie Is Changing Canada's Landscape," *The Globe and Mail*, July 5, 2003, B1, B4; John Saunders, "Exporters Facing Some Loonie Math," *The Globe and Mail*, May 7, 2003, B1, B4; Janet McFarland, "Rising Dollar Hurting Export, Resource Firms," *The Globe and Mail*, May 2, 2003, B1–B2. **Table 18.1** *National Post Business* (June 2003): 138. **It's a Wired World** Kenneth R. Rogoff, "The Surprising Popularity of Paper Currency," *Finance & Development* (March, 2002): 56; "Switzerland: Electronic Money," *International Financial Law Review* (April, 2001): 62–63; Lisa Cantos, Lorin Fine, and Randi Singer, "NCCUSL Proposes Uniform Act to Regulate Cybercash and Other Electronic Money," *Intellectual Property & Technology Law Journal* (October, 2000): 23. **Business Today** Summarized from Barrie McKenna, "U.S. Banking Industry Riles Consumers," *The Globe and Mail*, October 13, 1997, B1, B6. **Table 18.2** *National Post Business* (June 2003): 138. **Table 18.3** *The Economist* (April 29, 2000): 75. **Concluding Case 18-1** Associated Press, "Argentina Devalues Peso," *Columbia Daily Tribune*, January 7, 2002, 2B; Pamela Druckerman, "Telecom Argentina Plans to Suspend Debt Payments," *The Wall Street Journal*, April 3, 2002, A16; "Argentina Bank Chief Quits," *CNNMoney*, www.cnnfn.com, January 18, 2002; "Argentina Gets Reprieve," *CNNMoney*, www.cnnfn.com, January 17, 2002; "Citigroup 4Q Profit Rises," *CNNMoney*, www.cnnfn.com, January 17, 2002; "Peso Plan Encourages IMF," *CNNMoney*, www.cnnfn.com, January 15, 2002; "Argentina's Currency Test," *CNNMoney*, www.cnnfn.com, January 11, 2002; "Argentina Deepens Bank Curbs," *CNNMoney*, www.cnn fn.com, January 10, 2002; "Argentina Limits Cash Bank Withdrawals," *USA Today*, www.usatoday.com, December 3, 2001. **Figure 18.1** Data compiled from Federal Reserve Board of Governors, www.stls.frb.org/fred/data/monetary/, July 20, 2002. **Concluding Case 18-2** Sinclair Stewart, "Martin Seen As Merger Friendly," *The Globe and Mail*, June 13, 2003, B3; Simon Tuck, "Committee Report Seen Delaying Bank Mergers," *The Globe and Mail*, March 28, 2003, B1, B5; Sandra Cordon, "Bank Mergers Waiting in the Wings," *The Winnipeg Free Press*, March 21, 2003, B6; Kevin Libin, "For Business, the War Is On," *Canadian Business* (March 3, 2003): 31–33; "The World's Safest Banks," *Global Finance* (October, 2002); Mark MacKinnon, "Canadian Banks Have Fallen Many Storeys in Worldwide Ranking," *The Globe and Mail*, August 9, 1999, B1, B4; Mark MacKinnon, "Canadian Banks, If Not the Biggest, Are Among the Most Profitable," *The Globe and Mail*, August 4, 1999, B4.

Chapter 19

Stock Market Manipulations Karen Howlett, "Below The Decks of Treasure Ship Deals," *The Globe and Mail*, July 19, 2003, B1, B4; Karen Howlett, Sinclair Stewart, and Paul Waldie, "Brokers Caught Up in Police Probe," *The Globe and Mail*, June 20, 2003, B1, B20; Richard Blackwell, "Firm, Ex-CEO Pay Millions in Penalties," *The Globe and Mail*, December 20, 2001, B1, B6; Andrew Willis, "Paterson's Words Give Ugly Spin to Debacle," *The Globe and Mail*, December 20, 2001, B1, B6; David Paddon and Hollie Shaw, "Top Heads Roll at Royal After Scandal," *The Winnipeg Free Press*, July 21, 2000, B7, B12; Karen Howlett, Janet McFarland, and Dawn Walton, "Stock Rigging Appears Widespread," *The Globe and Mail*, July 1, 2000, B1, B4; Keith McArthur, "Business Seeps Away from Royal Pensions," *The Globe and Mail*, July 1, 2000, B1, B5; Richard Blackwell and Jacquie McNish," OSC prepared to Deal with RT," *The Globe and Mail*, July 1, 2000, B5; Jacquie McNish, "How the High Closing High Fliers Got Caught," *The Globe and Mail*, July 3, 2000, B1, B3. **Figure 19.1** "Yahoo Inc (YHOO)/Wal-Mart Stores Inc (WMT)," *Quicken.com*, www.quicken.com/invest ments/charts/, July 13, 2002. **Table 19.1** *National Post Business* (June, 2003): 63; *National Post Business* (June, 2000): 92. **Table 19.2** *National Post* (June 2000): 168. **Table 19.3** *National Post Business* (June 2003): 148. **Business Today** Janet McFarland, "Companies Reform Stock Option Plans," *The Globe and Mail*, February 24, 2003, B1, B5; Matt Murray, "Options Frenzy: What Went Wrong?," *The Wall Street Journal*, December 17, 2002, B1, B3; David Wessel, "Why the Bad Guys of the Boardroom Emerged En Masse," *The Wall Street Journal*, June 20, 2002, A1, A6. **Figure 19.4** Nasdaq, "Market Performance & Highlights: Section 3," *Nasdaq.com*, www.nas daq.com/about/NBW2000Sec3.pdf, June 23, 2000. **It's a Wired World** Andrew Wahl, "Swift Change Artists," *Canadian Business* (March 18, 2002): 57–59; Daniel P. Collins, "Day Trading—Not Just for the Tech-Savvy and Locals Anymore," *Futures* (June, 2002): 66–69; Mark Etzkorn, "All in a Day's Work," www.futuresmag.com, July 19, 2002. **Concluding Case 19-1** Justin Lahart, "The Crash of 2002," *CNNMoney*, www.cnnfn.com, July 19, 2002; "We All Got Burned—Now What?," *CNNMoney*, www.cnnfn.com, July 19, 2002; "Dow Plunges Below Its Post-Terrorist Attack Low," *USAToday*, at www.usatoday.com, July 19, 2002. **Concluding Case 19-2** Paul Waldie, "Licensing Deals Revive Marvel," *The Globe and Mail*, May 7, 2003, B13; Richard Bloom, "Marvel Has Analyst's Spidey Senses Tingling," *The Globe and Mail*, May 17, 2002, B14; Douglas A. Kass, "Pow! Smash! Kerplash!" *Barron's* (February 17, 1992): 14+; Floyd Norris, "Boom in Comic Books Lifts New Marvel Stock Offering," *The New York Times*, July 15, 1991, D1, D8; "Is This the End of Marvel? Or..." *The Winnipeg Free Press*, December 28, 1996, B11.

Chapter 20

Three Sad Tales of Failed Risk Management Miro Cernetig, "Accused Rogue Trader Clever Bully," *The Globe and Mail*, March 15, 2002, 1, B9; Brian Witte, "Former Currency Trader Jailed for Bank Fraud," *The Winnipeg Free Press*, October 25, 2002, B12; Miro Cernetig and Alan Freeman, "Trader Accused of Huge Fraud," *The Globe and Mail*, February 7, 2002, B1, B9; Andrew Willis, "Rusnak Report Should Be Required Reading for Banks," *The Globe and Mail*, March 15, 2002, B9; Jill Lawless, "Rogue Trader Ruins Firm in 92 Minutes," *The Globe and Mail*, October 4, 2000, B9; "Leeson's Six-and-a-Half Year Sentence Greeted with Mixed Reviews," *The Globe and Mail*, December 4, 1995, B1, B10; Sara Webb et al., "A Royal Mess: Britain's Barings PLC Bets on Derivatives—and the Cost Is Dear," *The Wall Street Journal*, February 27, 1995, A1, A6. **Figure 20.2** Carl Beidleman, *The Handbook of International Investing* (Chicago: Probus, 1987), 133. **Table 20.2** *National Post Business* (June 2003): 140. **Business Today** Jacquie McNish and Elizabeth Church, "Insurance Hikes Rock Firms," *The Globe and Mail*, February 10, 2003, B1-B2; Leslie Scism," If Disaster Strikes This 'Titanic,' Chubb Could Lose Millions," *The Wall Street Journal*, April 9, 1997, A1, A4; Leslie Scism, "Maybe Julie Andrews Could Offer Insurers a Spoonful of Sugar," *The Wall Street Journal*, April 4, 1997, A1, A4; Patrick Reilly, "Insurers Are Downbeat on Rap Concert Tours," *The Wall Street Journal*, March 26, 1997, B1, B12. **It's a Wired World** *Costpredict: Organizational Health Cost Analysis* (Columbia, Missouri: Network Health Systems, 2000); *Health & Lifestyle Assessment Handbook* (Columbia, Mo: Network Health Systems, 1999). **Concluding Case 20-1** Sarah Veysey, "World Cup Organizers Step Up Against Risks," *Business Insurance* (June 3, 2002): 15–16; Carolyn Aldred, "Insurers Scrutinize World Cup Risk," *Business Insurance* (September 3, 2001): 43; "FIFA to Innovate with ABS on World Cup Brand Rights," *Euroweek* (January 5, 2001): 35; Rob Gilhooly, "Hooligan Fears Worry 2002 World Cup Host City Officials," *Japan Times* (June 1–June 15, 1999): 17. **Concluding Case 20-2** Jacquie McNish, "Brascan Sticks with Its Vision," *The Globe and Mail*, November 13, 2000, B1, B7; Eric Reguly, "Brascan Should Follow CP's Lead," *The Globe and Mail*, February 15, 2001, B12.

Photo and Cartoon Credits

Chapter 1 Al Harvey/The Slide Farm, pages 2 and 3; Voisey's Bay Nickel Company, page 5; Thomas Sandberg, page 12; New York Times Pictures, page 19; Kathleen Bellesiles/Little Apple Studio, page 24; The Granger Collection, page 27; Tara Photography Sdn. Bhd., page 29

Chapter 2 Andre Forget/CP Photo Archive, page 39; New York Times Pictures, page 45; New York Times Pictures, page 50; Getty Images, Inc.—Liaison, page 59; Getty Images, Inc.—Liaison, page 61; CP Photo, page 68

Chapter 3 Courtesy of Cuddy Farms, page 79; S. Houston, page 81; Dick Hemingway, page 84; Dick Hemingway, page 90; First Light/D. Pollack, page 94; Dick Hemingway, page 96; Imperial Oil Limited, page 100; Al Harvey/The Slide Farm, page 103; Courtesy of BASF, page 105

Chapter 4 Bombardier Inc., page 117; Namas Bhojani, page 119; Palliser Furniture, page 122; New York Times Pictures, page 124; Stone/Paul Chesley, page 127; Timepix, page 139; Canapress/Jacques Boissinot, page 142

Chapter 5 John Mahonney/CP Photo Archive, page 155; New York Times Pictures, page 158 (left); New York Times Pictures, page 158 (right); David R. Frazier/Photo Researchers, page 168; Sipa Pres, page 170; Getty Images, Inc.—Liaison, page 171; Courtesy of Construction Association of Ontario, page 173; McDonald's Restaurant, page 178

Chapter 6 Robert Daly/Stone/Getty, pages 190 and 191; CP Picture Archive (Laurent Rebours), page 193; CP Photo, page 201; IT Stock/First Light, page 203; Frank Gunn/CP Photo, page 204; Frank Siteman/agefotostock/firstlight.ca., page 206 (top); Stuart:Pearce/agefotostock/firstlight.ca., page 206 (middle); Saxpix/agefotostock/firstlight.ca., page 206 (bottom); Kistone Photography, page 213; Courtesy of Mainframe Entertainment Inc., page 214

Chapter 7 Frantic Films, page 225; Twentieth Century Fox Films, page 229; Dick Hemingway, page 230; Vincent Prado, page 234; Telus Corporation, page 239; Bernd Auers, page 243; Bob Scott/Image Bank, page 248

Chapter 8 Tannis Toohey/CP Photo Archive, page 259; Javier Larrea/agefotostock/firstlight.ca, page 264; Hunt Personnel, page 266; Harry Sieplinga/HMS Images/Getty Images, page 269; Andre Pichette/CP Photo, page 276; The Stock Market/John Madere, page 284; Mark Richards, page 285

Chapter 9 Tom Hanson/CP Photo Archive, page 297; Prentice Hall Archieves, p. 299; Pierre Obendrauf/CP Photo Archive, p. 308; Kevin Frayer/CP Photo Archive, p. 313; Gino Donato/CP Photo Archive, p. 315

Chapter 10 Ryan Remiorz/CP Photo Archive, page 327; Corbis, page 331 (top); Courtesy Western Electric, page 331 (bottom); © Masterfile, page 338; Loren Santow/Stone/Getty Images, page 341; Grank Gunn/CP Photo Archive, page 345

Chapter 11 CP Photo, pages 360 and 361; imagestate/firstlight.ca, page 363; Lockheed Martin Aeronautics Col, page 365; Canapress Photo Service, page 369 (top two right, bottom left photos); Plus Pix/First Light, page 369 (top left photo); PhotoDisc, page 369 (bottom right photo); Diane L. Chrisman, page 371; Toyota Motor Manufacturing Canada Inc., page 379 (top); Regina Maria Anzenberger, page 379 (bottom); LTI New York, page 388

Chapter 12 © Steve Craft/Masterfile, page 401; Ted Rice, page 405 (left); Ted Rice, page 405 (right); The New Yorker Collection 2002 Aaron Bacall from cartoonbank.com. All rights reserved, page 410; Ray Ng Photography, Inc., page 413; Steven Ahlgren, page 418; Dofasco Canada, page 421

Chapter 13 © Reuters New Media Inc./CORBIS/Magmaphoto.com, page 433; Bruce Ayers/Stone, page 435; Richard B. Levine/Frances M. Roberts, page 439 (top); Richard B. Levine/Frances M. Roberts, page 439 (bottom); Jonathan Saunders, page 448; EDS Creative Services, page 454; Photofest, page 457; Brownie Harris, page 459

Chapter 14 Jeff DeBooy/CP Photo Archive, page 471; PhotoDisc, page 474; AP/Wide World Photos, page 478; AP/Wide World Photos, page 481; Contact Press Images, Inc., page 486; Kevin Frayer/CP Photo Archive, page 487; Getty Images Inc.—Hulton Archive Photos, page 494; © The New Yorker Collection 1991 Robert Weber from cartoonbank.com. All rights reserved, page 495

Chapter 15 Getty Images Inc., pages 508 and 509; Tom Grill/firstlight.ca, page 511; National Gallery of Canada, page 516 (left); Courtesy of Weight Watchers, page 516 (top right); Cadbury Beverages, Inc., page 516 (bottom right); Getty Images, Inc., page 517; New York Times Pictures, page 519; Grand & Toy, page 520; New York Times Pictures, page 523; Rachel Epstein, PhotoEdit, Inc., page 529; © Bryan F. Peterson/CORBIS/Magmaphoto.com, page 532; Feathercraft Products Ltd., page 535

Chapter 16 Courtesy of Krave Candy Company, page 549; © 2002, SAS Institute, Inc., Cary, NC, USA. All rights reserved. Reproduced with permission of SAS Institute, Inc. Cary NC, page 553; PhotoDisc, page 554; AP/Wide World Photos, page 560; Dick Hemingway, page 562; Contact Press Images, Inc., page 569; Howard, Merrel & Partners, Inc., page 572; New York Times Pictures, page 577; Agence France-Presse AFP, page 578 (left); Knutson Photography, Inc., page 578 (right); Agence France-Presse AFP, page 580

Chapter 17 Dick Hemingway, page 595; New York Times Pictures, page 598; Richard Hutchings/Photo Researchers, page 601; AP/Wide World Photos, page 604; Kalim A. Bhatti, page 611; New York Times Pictures, page 614; David Gamble, page 615; Canadian National, page 620

Chapter 18 Courtesy of TSX, pages 636 and 637; Ricardo Ordonez/firstlight.ca, page 639; The Granger Collection, page 641; New York Times Pictures, page 642; Dick Hemingway, page 643; Corbis/SABA Press Photos, Inc., page 647; Bob Carroll/Leucar, page 648; Dick Hemingway, page 656

Chapter 19 Tony Bock/CP Photo Archive, page 671; © Rob Lewine/CORBIS/Magmaphoto.com, page 674; Michael Dwyer, page 677; Toronto Star/D. Loek, page 678; Richard B. Levine/Frances M. Roberts, page 680; Reproduced with permission of the Minister of Finance, page 682; Houston Chronicle Library, page 686 (top); © J.L. de Zorzil/CORBIS/Magmaphoto.com, page 686 (bottom); Robert Wright Photography, page 694

Chapter 20 Matt Houston/CP Photo Archive, page 707; AP. Wide World Photos, page 709; David Pollack/The Stock Market, page 714; Quebecor World Financial, page 716; Aileen Tat Photography, page 719; Lawrence Migdale; Ulrich Welch; Eunice Harris/Photo Researchers, page 726; David Mah/CP Photo Archive, page 729

NAME AND ORGANIZATION INDEX

D

E

F

SUBJECT INDEX

Each key term and the page on which is defined are set in boldface type.

Q

R

"AS IS" LICENSE AGREEMENT AND LIMITED WARRANTY

READ THIS LICENSE CAREFULLY BEFORE OPENING THIS PACKAGE. BY OPENING THIS PACKAGE, YOU ARE AGREEING TO THE TERMS AND CONDITIONS OF THIS LICENSE. IF YOU DO NOT AGREE, DO NOT OPEN THE PACKAGE. PROMPTLY RETURN THE UNOPENED PACKAGE AND ALL ACCOMPANYING ITEMS TO THE PLACE YOU OBTAINED THEM. *THESE TERMS APPLY TO ALL LICENSED SOFTWARE ON THE DISK EXCEPT THAT THE TERMS FOR USE OF ANY SHAREWARE OR FREEWARE ON THE DISKETTES ARE AS SET FORTH IN THE ELECTRONIC LICENSE LOCATED ON THE DISK:*

1. GRANT OF LICENSE and OWNERSHIP: The enclosed computer programs <<and any data>> ("Software") are licensed, not sold, to you by Pearson Education Canada Inc. ("We" or the "Company") in consideration of your adoption of the accompanying Company textbooks and/or other materials, and your agreement to these terms. You own only the disk(s) but we and/or our licensors own the Software itself. This license allows instructors and students enrolled in the course using the Company textbook that accompanies this Software (the "Course") to use and display the enclosed copy of the Software for academic use only, so long as you comply with the terms of this Agreement. You may make one copy for back up only. We reserve any rights not granted to you.

2. USE RESTRICTIONS: You may not sell or license copies of the Software or the Documentation to others. You may not transfer, distribute or make available the Software or the Documentation, except to instructors and students in your school who are users of the adopted Company textbook that accompanies this Software in connection with the course for which the textbook was adopted. You may not reverse engineer, disassemble, decompile, modify, adapt, translate or create derivative works based on the Software or the Documentation. You may be held legally responsible for any copying or copyright infringement which is caused by your failure to abide by the terms of these restrictions.

3. TERMINATION: This license is effective until terminated. This license will terminate automatically without notice from the Company if you fail to comply with any provisions or limitations of this license. Upon termination, you shall destroy the Documentation and all copies of the Software. All provisions of this Agreement as to limitation and disclaimer of warranties, limitation of liability, remedies or damages, and our ownership rights shall survive termination.

4. DISCLAIMER OF WARRANTY: THE COMPANY AND ITS LICENSORS MAKE NO WARRANTIES ABOUT THE SOFTWARE, WHICH IS PROVIDED "AS-IS." IF THE DISK IS DEFECTIVE IN MATERIALS OR WORKMANSHIP, YOUR ONLY REMEDY IS TO RETURN IT TO THE COMPANY WITHIN 30 DAYS FOR REPLACEMENT UNLESS THE COMPANY DETERMINES IN GOOD FAITH THAT THE DISK HAS BEEN MISUSED OR IMPROPERLY INSTALLED, REPAIRED, ALTERED OR DAMAGED. THE COMPANY DISCLAIMS ALL WARRANTIES, EXPRESS OR IMPLIED, INCLUDING WITHOUT LIMITATION, THE IMPLIED WARRANTIES OF MERCHANTABILITY AND FITNESS FOR A PARTICULAR PURPOSE. THE COMPANY DOES NOT WARRANT, GUARANTEE OR MAKE ANY REPRESENTATION REGARDING THE ACCURACY, RELIABILITY, CURRENTNESS, USE, OR RESULTS OF USE, OF THE SOFTWARE.

5. LIMITATION OF REMEDIES AND DAMAGES: IN NO EVENT, SHALL THE COMPANY OR ITS EMPLOYEES, AGENTS, LICENSORS OR CONTRACTORS BE LIABLE FOR ANY INCIDENTAL, INDIRECT, SPECIAL OR CONSEQUENTIAL DAMAGES ARISING OUT OF OR IN CONNECTION WITH THIS LICENSE OR THE SOFTWARE, INCLUDING, WITHOUT LIMITATION, LOSS OF USE, LOSS OF DATA, LOSS OF INCOME OR PROFIT, OR OTHER LOSSES SUSTAINED AS A RESULT OF INJURY TO ANY PERSON, OR LOSS OF OR DAMAGE TO PROPERTY, OR CLAIMS OF THIRD PARTIES, EVEN IF THE COMPANY OR AN AUTHORIZED REPRESENTATIVE OF THE COMPANY HAS BEEN ADVISED OF THE POSSIBILITY OF SUCH DAMAGES. SOME JURISDICTIONS DO NOT ALLOW THE LIMITATION OF DAMAGES IN CERTAIN CIRCUMSTANCES, SO THE ABOVE LIMITATIONS MAY NOT ALWAYS APPLY.

6. GENERAL: THIS AGREEMENT SHALL BE CONSTRUED AND INTERPRETED ACCORDING TO THE LAWS OF THE PROVINCE OF ONTARIO. This Agreement is the complete and exclusive statement of the agreement between you and the Company and supersedes all proposals, prior agreements, oral or written, and any other communications between you and the company or any of its representatives relating to the subject matter.

Should you have any questions concerning this agreement or if you wish to contact the Company for any reason, please contact in writing: Editorial Manager, Pearson Education Canada, 26 Prince Andrew Place, Don Mills, Ontario, M3C 2T8.

Use of this CD-ROM is restricted to the purchasing (or acquiring) institution or to situations under the auspices of the institution. No copying, alteration, broadcast, cable distribution, digital delivery, or sale is permitted, and the video content included herein may not be transferred to any other source.